The Content Of Religious Instruction

The Content Of Religious Instruction

A SOCIAL SCIENCE APPROACH

**JAMES
MICHAEL
LEE**

RELIGIOUS EDUCATION PRESS
BIRMINGHAM, ALABAMA

Library of Congress Cataloging in Publication Data

Lee, James Michael.
   The content of religious instruction.

   Includes bibliographies and index.
   1. Christian education.   2. Sociology, Christian.
I. Title.
BV1471.2.L4418   1984   268   84-18255
ISBN 0-89135-050-0

10 9 8 7 6 5 4 3 2

Religious Education Press Inc.
1531 Wellington Road
Birmingham, Alabama 35209

Religious Education Press publishes books exclusively in religious education and in areas closely related to religious education. It is committed to enhancing and professionalizing religious education through the publication of serious, significant, and scholarly works.

PUBLISHER TO THE PROFESSION

To James Lee V,
MY SON

CONTENTS

PREFACE

"Nach durch das Morgentor des Schönen
Drangst du in der Erkenntnis Land."[1]
    —Friedrich Schiller

I began this book in 1973 and am finishing it now in 1984. The first page was written on one of those clear, slightly crisp and glowing days of very early autumn in northern Indiana, just about the time when the first few golden leaves begin to drift quietly to the waiting ground beneath. On a bright and fresh spring day eleven years later, I am writing this Preface in a place and in an atmosphere quite at the other end of the spectrum from northern Indiana.

The actual writing of this book took place in four principal locations. Chapters One, Two, Three, Four, and Six were written at the University of Notre Dame where I served for many years as the director of the graduate program in religious education. Chapter Five was written in Munich during my year there on a Senior Fulbright Research fellowship. Chapters Seven and Eight were written at the University of Alabama in Birmingham where I am currently teaching. The final chapters were completed in Rome where I am finishing my sabbatical year.

While the actual writing was done in the four places mentioned in the previous paragraph, much of the reflective time which I devoted to preparing and organizing my theoretical framework and research findings was done in a wide variety of experiential circumstances. These marvelously diverse and richly textured occasions enabled me to appreciate in a way not otherwise possible the cultural roundness, the existential fullness, and the intrinsic interrelatedness of each of the eight molar substantive contents with which I was dealing. A few of these settings still stand out in my mind, though there were many others which exerted subtle influence on the eventual contours of this book. Sitting on summer nights at Delphi where the leaves of a million olive trees reflect the shining moon above and bathe the hills and valleys with a silvery luminescence which almost seems to induce an altered state of consciousness not altogether different from that of the Oracle of old. Tramping around the ruins of Ephesus, one of the greatest of all cities in the ancient world—Ephesus, where Paul the Apostle labored and where a great council of the church was once convened. Sauntering through the bazaars in Tunisia which exhale aromas of all sorts, haggling with eager merchants, sipping strong Turkish coffee, and being drenched in all kinds of exotic sights and sounds. Walking through the veil of time into half-forgotten but eternally fresh small Romanesque churches nestled in the high country of the Auvergne in France. Relaxing with a warming cup of *Glühwein* in a cozy Tyrolian *Gasthaus* after spending the day trudging knee-deep through the January snow on the hilltops of the Austrian alps. Lifting *ein Mass,* singing *Wiesen Lieder,* and joining in the raucous good times in the enormous beer tents at Munich's Oktoberfest. Strolling down the Croisette in Cannes, my favorite town on the Côte d'Azur, and musing on how the style and sophistication all around me could somehow make its way into the field of religious instruction. Traveling over the years throughout Italy where substantive content is never seen apart from structural content, where art is recognized as a fusion of subject matter and technique. Journeying through Spain where the warm blood of the people seems to mingle with the jagged harshness of the countryside to produce sad sinuous songs and soaring sensuous mysticism.

The high crests and the low mudholes of my personal experiences during these past eleven years also impacted upon me in a significant way. One of the soaring peaks during this time consisted in being present in the delivery room during the births of my children. For me, the events were incredibly stupendous because in and through these births the transcendent God was pushing his hand through the pages of life and declaring: "It's here, it's now!" Birth is the real reality, the continuing incarnation, the primal actuality with which every person and every theory must be in constant touch. Without a doubt the lowest mudhole in my life was the heavy-handed despoliation of the Notre Dame graduate program in religious education by James Tunstead Burtchaell, the only genuinely cruel priest I have ever met. The wanton and senseless liquidation of the Notre Dame program is a graphic reminder of an enigma which has been with Christianity since its founding, namely that some of the greatest enemies of prophetic religious endeavor are to be found within the ranks of the Christian household itself.

The footnotes and citations mentioned in this book indicate to the reader the specific scholarly sources on which I drew as I wrote this book. More hidden are the life experiences which inevitably added a certain subtle flavor and human breadth to the material which I fashioned. A reader who is aware of some of these life experiences which impacted in one way or another upon the writing of any serious book is in a more favored position to appreciate that volume than a reader who is not so informed. This is the reason why I wrote the previous two paragraphs in this Preface.

Let me elaborate on the point which I have just made. As is probably true with most serious authors, any book on which I am working haunts my personal life throughout the entire time I am writing it. This fact is eminently true for this book which I am finishing at long last. Eleven years is quite a large chunk out of any person's life, and in that period of time a wide variety of diverse events occurred which exerted a certain influence on this book. In stating this important point I am not suggesting that either the book's theoretical perspective or the research data are exclusively, primarily, or even significantly a product of my personal experiences. Valid scientific theory and research, after all, must have a universal objective character, and hence cannot depend on any individual's own personal experiences. The point I am making is that the events in my life during the past eleven years helped me to fill in some of the spaces in my theoretical framework and enabled me to add new dimensions to the applicability of my research for religious instruction practice. Since religious instruction takes place in life situations, its foundational theory and research ought to incorporate relevant life experiences of the theorist and researcher in a manner entirely in consonance with the scientific canons of the theory and research. Even in the natural and "hard" sciences, the life experiences of the theorist or researcher often serve as the initial stimulus to the discovery of some new fact or law, or leads to a fresher and more fruitful interpretation of an already existing fact or law or theory. The life experiences of the theorist or researcher also serve as valuable negative checks on the construction and generalizability of his theory as well as on the usefulness of his research findings for practice.

The Content of Religious Instruction is the third volume of my trilogy on religious instruction. The purpose of the trilogy is to provide for the first time in the history of the field a truly comprehensive and systematic macrotheory which possesses the power to adequately explain, predict, and verify the religious instruction act.

This book is simultaneously independent and interrelated. It is independent because it stands on its own two feet and hence can be satisfactorily comprehended without necessarily having to read the other two volumes of the trilogy. It is interrelated because its full meaning and potency can be appreciated only when it is seen within the overall context of the trilogy as a relatively complete system.

There are two primal contents which are existentially fused into the religious instruction act. The first of these is structural content, that is, the actual pedagogical dynamic in and of itself. The second of these is substantive content, that is, subject matter.

Structural content is the theme of *The Flow of Religious Instruction,* the second volume of the trilogy. Substantive content is the theme of *The Content of Religious Instruction,* the final volume of the trilogy.

The form of substantive content falls into two classes, namely, fundamental form and specific form. By fundamental form of substantive content I mean the essential molar constituents which are present in virtually every bit of subject matter as this subject matter is taught and learned. By specific form of substantive content I mean the particularities which the subject matter assumes in a given pedagogical transaction. Product content is an example of fundamental form of substantive content; it is present in virtually every religious instruction act. Learning the Ten Commandments is an example of specific form of substantive content; this particular kind of product content is present only in those religion lessons dealing in one way or another with that topic.

The substantive content of religious instruction is religion as religion exists in the religious instruction act. Thus the substantive content of religious instruction is not theology, not philosophy, not church history, not human relations, and so forth. Theology, philosophy, church history, human relations, and the like, enter into the religious instruction act as substantive contents only to the extent to which they enhance religion and only in the mode in which they flow into religion—religion as it is in the religious instruction act.

Because this book (like the other two volumes in the trilogy) offers a macrotheoretical approach, it is vital that it deal primarily with the fundamental form of religion as religion exists in the religious instruction act. If this book were to deal chiefly with specific forms of religion as these forms exist in the religious instruction act, it would become inextricably enmeshed in this or that particularity, thereby effectively destroying its character as a macrotheoretical approach. Because I deal in a macrotheoretical way with religion as it exists in the religious instruction act, this book is eminently relevant and applicable to specific religious subject matter of every kind.

Upon careful examination of the religious instruction act, I discovered that at least nine types of fundamental molar forms of substantive content exist. These global forms are present in virtually every pedagogical transaction. The nine fundamental forms of substantive content are product content, process content, cognitive content, affective content, verbal content, nonverbal content, conscious content, unconscious content, and lifestyle content. This book contains separate chapters for each of these fundamental forms of substantive content with the exception of conscious content, though I do devote some pages to conscious content in the chapter on unconscious content.

From what I wrote in the last paragraph it is clear that the fundamental form of substantive content consists of many molar dimensions rather than just one or even several dimensions. From the substantive standpoint, the richness of a religion lesson is directly proportional to the degree to which the religious educator brings to salience all of the molar substantive contents, as appropriate.

Because it is grounded in the social-science approach to religious instruction, the trilogy involves a fundamental change in the personal self-organization and in the professional perception of many individuals in the field. Change of this sort is highly threatening and so tends to be resisted. The more deeply and the more subconsciously a religious educator has rooted his personal and professional life in the theological approach, the more vigorously and the more irrationally will he tend to resist the altogether new approach. This resistance takes on various forms. Some people react almost hysterically to the social-science approach, lashing out at it with the pent-up fury of one whose hard-won personal level of existence is in mortal peril. Other individuals in their fear simply ignore this new approach, somehow hoping that it will go away by itself, by some dramatic new development in theology, by political maneuver, or by ecclesiastical edict or censorship. Still others attempt to assuage their fear by trying to rip out selective bits and pieces from the unified framework of the social-science approach and inserting these disjointed fragments into the personally comforting but nonetheless inappropriate framework of the theological approach. This last-mentioned attempt will always be fundamentally unsuccessful because the two frameworks have essentially different bases, starting points, procedures, objectives, and goals. It seems to me that an encounter with any new reality represents a wonderful growth opportunity and not a threat. A person is threatened when he is frightened that he may be wrong. The greater the fear of error, the greater the threat and consequently the more vigorous and irrational the resistance. The religious educator who truly wishes to grow as a person and as a professional should seriously and openly ask himself this fundamental question: Which approach, theological or social-scientific, more satisfactorily enables the religious educator to explain, predict, and verify what actually happens in the religious instruction act? Once the religious educator honestly faces up to this most basic of all questions, he is already on the way to the answer. But to arrive at the answer, the religious educator must discard all preconceived notions and ceremonial slogans, using instead common sense and convincing empirical evidence to arrive at the solution.

All of the research for this book, just as for all of the books which I have ever written, was done solely by myself. But I did have valuable assistance in other ways, assistance which significantly supported my research and writing. Generous travel grants by the Graduate School and by the School of Education of the University of Alabama in Birmingham enabled me to go to research libraries in other parts of the nation. Librarians in these and other libraries over the past eleven years have been extremely helpful to me. Most notable among them include the energetic librarians at the University of Notre Dame, the extraordinarily helpful librarians at Columbia University's Teachers College, the obliging librarians at the Gregorian University in Rome, the cellar-situated but still cheerful librarians at Vanderbilt University's Divinity School, the courteous librarians at Pitts in Emory University, and the very cooperative librarians at the University of Munich and the Bavarian State Library. Of most help day in and day out during the final years of research and writing were the especially competent and highly efficient librarians at the University of Alabama in Birmingham, notably Gordon Dunkin, Virginia Jackson, Bonnie Ledbetter, and Tinker Dunbar at the Interlibrary Loan desk. Milly Cowles, Clay Sheffield, and particularly James Davidson III, my administrative superiors at the University of Alabama in Birmingham were particularly supportive of my research and writing endeavors. I also wish to express my gratitude to Kathy Hyche for typewriting portions of this manuscript and to Janet Crocker who assisted me with the proofreading. Nick and Kernie Ardillo, the consummate war eagles, seemed to be always there to lend a neighborly hand. But most of all I wish to thank Marlene, Jimmy V, Mikey, and the little one now in Mommy's tummy, for being with me.

I began to outline the first volume of the trilogy in 1969 on a yellow legal-size pad while sitting on a park bench on the banks of the Salzach river in Salzburg, with the Festung Hohensalzburg rising majestically upriver and the pilgrimage church of Maria-Plain sitting serenely downriver. Now fifteen years later I am writing the final lines of the final volume of the trilogy on a yellow legal-size pad while kneeling at the *confessio* situated under the successive spatially-separated layers of the pontifical altar, Bernini's baldacchino, and Michelangelo's dome, in the Patriarchical Basilica of St. Peter's in Rome. My research and writing has taken me here at last to St. Peter's. Just as the setting at Salzburg symbolized what I was trying to do in the first volume of the trilogy, so too St. Peter's typifies what I am attempting to accomplish in the third volume. If it is nothing else, St. Peter's Patriarchical Basilica is unabashedly multicontent—a multicontent celebration of the rich texture of Christianity. Like any other church edifice, St. Peter's has two principal functions, namely sacramental and religious instructional. In terms of religious instruction, St. Peter's shouts the fact that substantive content is not unidimensional but rather multidimensional. Product and process, cognitive and affective, verbal and nonverbal, conscious and unconscious inhabit these sacred precincts in a powerful and moving manner. But it is religious lifestyle which reigns supreme here, lifestyle into which all the other molar substantive contents pour themselves. St. Peter's Patriarchical Basilica is a lifestyle-soaked place. It exists for personal blood-and-sweat Christianity. It does not exist primarily to raise critical consciousness, to promote clear thinking, to enlarge feelings, to encounter the unconscious. St. Peter's exists primarily to deepen religious experience and to facilitate richer religious living. The statues, the mosaics, the lighting, the dome, the liturgical services, the seemingly ceaseless pilgrimages, all exist for one main purpose, namely to facilitate a deeper and more focused religious lifestyle.

The pilgrimages! My sabbatical year coincided with the special Holy Year of Our Redemption set into motion by John Paul II. Because of the Holy Year there were even more pilgrims than usual coming into St. Peter's. Pilgrims poured into this magnificent basilica from every continent and walk of life to visit, pray, sing, and especially to quicken their religious lives. Even as I write these words, there is a pilgrimage group from France on the opposite side of the *confessio* singing a hymn of praise lustily yet with a certain tender devotion. The countless pilgrimages to St. Peter's, like the very basilica which constitutes the object of their pilgrimage, represent a forceful and focused testimony to religion as the substantive content of their journey. These pilgrims from far-flung lands, these pilgrims praying and singing hymns, do not come to St. Peter's Patriarchical Basilica primarily for cultural reasons, not primarily for an emotional high, not primarily to raise their critical consciousness. These pilgrims travel here primarily for religious reasons, to praise God, to thank him, to petition him, and most especially to love him more deeply. Religion is a lifestyle which embraces many molar contents and fuses them into a pattern of life. To be a pilgrim is to walk in the valley of life, to walk The Way.

The religious instruction act is a pilgrimage. And we are all pilgrims. Pilgrims of religion. But religion is a lifestyle composed of many and diverse molar substantive contents. This is the central message of *The Content of Religious Instruction*.

I came to Rome on my sabbatical year as a scholar and as a pilgrim, but more as a scholar than as a pilgrim. Today, on the eve of my departure for the United States, I leave as a scholar and as a pilgrim, but more as a pilgrim than as a scholar. I am utterly confident that my scholarship will gain, not lose, because of this. My personal life surely is all the richer for this experience.

Vatican City State   JAMES MICHAEL LEE
May 28, 1984

NOTES

1. Friedrich Schiller, *Die Künstler*

CHAPTER ONE

PROLEGOMENON

*"Look at Fletcher! Lowell! Charles Roland! Judy Lee!
Are they also special and gifted and divine? No more
than you are, no more than I am. The only difference is
that they have begun to understand what they really are
and have begun to practice it."* [1]

—Richard Bach

THE SCOPE OF CONTENT

Of crucial importance to effective religious instruction is the careful delineation of its scope. Pedagogically speaking, scope refers to the breadth, range, variety, and types of educational experiences which are provided to learners during the teaching-learning situation(s). Scope, therefore, suggests the parameters of the content with which the learners will deal. It concerns itself with the problem, "What shall be included in the program, in the curriculum, in the lesson?" Scope represents the latitudinal axis for selecting instructional experiences. It specifies what shall be included and what shall be excluded from the curriculum or lesson. [2] (Parenthetically, I should underscore the fact that by the term "lesson" I mean an intentional set of pedagogical experiences. Thus a religion lesson is truly a lesson, regardless of whether the setting in which it is enacted is a formal or an informal one and regardless of whether the religious educator facilitating the lesson is a schoolteacher or parent or any other kind of person who is deliberatively educating religiously. The same concept of setting-free and teacher-free holds true for my use of the term "curriculum.")

By definition, the scope of the content of *religious* instruction is religion rather than simply theology. More precisely speaking, *the scope of the content of religious instruction is the religious instruction act itself,* because it is in this total concrete existential situation that the learner's religious experience occurs. Thus the scope of the religious instruction enterprise is not restricted to theological reflection but rather encompasses the entire range of the learner's present and potential religious experience as it takes place in the religion lesson. Theology is frequently a part, and often an indispensable part of the learner's present and potential religious experience — but it is only a part.

RELIGIOUS CONTENT AND THEOLOGICAL CONTENT

Because this book treats of the scope of religious instruction content, it will be helpful to briefly consider the basic difference between religious content per se and theological content per se.[3] One of the most serious shortcomings of religious instruction both in the United States and in Europe lies in the frequent failure of teachers, curriculum builders, and other kinds of religious educators to recognize the essential difference in scope between religious content and theological content. The result of this is that either theology is asked to perform a service outside its range and capabilities, or that religious experiences are inserted into a theological lesson in a manner at odds with and therefore disruptive of sound theologizing.

Religious Content

There appears to be no generally accepted definition of religion.[4] Quite possibly this is due to the fact that first and finally religion is a personal, lived experience rather than a conceptualization. Experiences can better be described or characterized than cast into the form of abstract definitions. Thus, in *The Shape of Religious Instruction*[5] I observe that highly complex, deeply existential phenomena such as religion are better framed in an operational definition than in a notional definition. After all, religion is, as Edward Schillebeeckx pithily observes, "a personal communion between God and man";[6] such a lived relationship can adequately be understood only in terms of the concrete behaviors which compromise it. Doubtless a reorientation toward an operational definition of religion which specifies concrete behaviors as opposed to a notional definition of religion which proposes abstract essences would enable both theology and religious instruction to more accurately and more effectively probe the nature and effects of the religious act. Sociologists of religion have been moving in this direction. Thus, for example, Charles Glock has identified five dimensions of religious behavior which, all together as a composite unit, comprise a person's lived religion: (1) the ideological dimension, that is, religious belief; (2) the ritualistic dimension, that is, religious practices; (3) the experiential dimension, that is, religious feeling; (4) the intellectual dimension, that is, religious knowledge; (5) the consequential dimension, that is, religious effects.[7] Religion is the person's actualizing all five dimensions in concert.

On the basis of the analysis made in the previous paragraph, my own definition of religion is as follows: Religion is that form of lifestyle which expresses and enfleshes the lived relationship a person enjoys with a transpersonal being as a consequence of the actualized fusion in his self-system of that knowledge, belief, feeling, experience, and practice that are in one way or another connected with that which the individual perceives to be divine. This definition suggests that religion is an activity of the whole person. This definition also suggests that religion is ontically different from theology.

There is an impressive number of twentieth-century scholars who assert that there is a vast difference between religion and *a* religion. For such thinkers, religion consists in a series of particularized, identifiable behaviors which may or may not occur within the context of *a* religion. From the agnostic-atheistic viewpoint, John Dewey states that religion is a societally-organized entity such as a historic religion or an existing church. In contrast to religion, the word ''religious'' is a set of attitudes a person might have ''toward every object and every proposed end or ideal.'' For Dewey, the opposition between religious and religion (in my terminology, religion and *a* religion) ought never to be bridged, and all identification between the two should be dissolved in order for individuals and society to optimally develop.[8] For several outstanding Protestant thinkers, spanning the range from conservative to liberal, religion and *a* religion are likewise distinct and often opposing entities. Karl Barth, for example, believes that the revelation of God is not only above all religions, but in its fullness and plenitude is actually destructive of *a* religion.[9] Paul Tillich is noted for his refusal to identify the Christian faith with the existing Christian religions.[10] Dietrich Bonhoeffer's thesis of a ''religionless Christianity,'' when properly understood, is yet another elaboration of this view.[11] From a Roman Catholic perspective, Hubert Halbfas suggests that religion is not necessarily expressed in the ritual observances or in the institutional arrangements of organized religions, but rather in the personal existential relationship between man and the transcendence of his own being. Of especial interest is that Halbfas, perhaps unwittingly, focuses on the centrality of religious behavior instead of on the structure in which this behavior occurs. Thus he criticizes what he understands to be Bonhoeffer's view of religionless Christianity by pointedly asking: "What did the 'form' of religion 'express' and what 'form' does that selfsame 'expression' take when religion disappears?"[12] Indeed one can find a constant theme of *super ecclesiam deus est* throughout the long history of the church.

In this book, and indeed throughout this trilogy, religious content is taken to mean either religion as it exists in itself or as it exists within the context of *a* religion. Central to the task of religious instruction is the facilitation of religious behaviors, regardless of whether or not these behaviors occur within the context of *a* religion. In the theological systems of many Christian religions, authentic religious behavior occurs only within the framework of that particular organized religion. For persons belonging to such religions, this theological hypothesis does in fact take on the force of religious behavior; it is on this ground, rather than on the ground of the underlying theological hypothesis per se, that this theological hypothesis becomes religious content in the lives of these persons.

Theological Content

Edward Schillebeeckx's brief but comprehensive chronicle shows that originally the term "theology" was used with reference to the mythical stories of the gods. Aristotle altered the term to mean the highest level of human abstract thought, namely the supreme form of philosophical reasoning. Abelard seems to have been the first scholar in the West to use the word "theology" in the modern sense. For Abelard, theology referred to a treatise about God as he is in himself. Aquinas seldom used the word "theology," and when he did it was typically in the Aristotelean sense. Indeed, what is now called "theology" was typically referred to as "sacred doctrine" until sometime after the death of Aquinas. It was then that the term "theology" became more popular; it was during this time also that theology tended to be regarded as "speculative theology." With the passing centuries, what was once the unitary science of "sacred doctrine" became divided into speculative theology, moral theology, ascetical theology, mystical theology, biblical theology, and so forth. The twentieth century has witnessed an attempt to restore the pristine unity to theological science.[13]

Throughout the centuries of usage, nonusage, and adaptation of the term "theology," one thing seems to have remained constant: theology is an intellectual endeavor. Thus Karl Rahner gives a succinct operational definition of theology when he writes that "theology is thinking."[14] Edward Schillebeeckx similarly operationalizes theology by stating that if there is Christian faith in intellectual reflection, then there is theology. "Theology is Christian faith *in* human reflection. This is really all there is to it. The law of faith becomes visible in human thought."[15] Gregory Baum says the same thing in another way when he observes that theology is a reflection on experience which is clarified in terms of a doctrinal basis.[16] Paul Tillich unequivocally states as follows: "Theology is the methodological explanation of the contents of the Christian faith. This definition is valid for all theological disciplines."[17] John Macquarrie has this to say: "Theology may be defined as the study which, through participation in and reflection upon a religious faith, seeks to express the content of this faith in the clearest, most coherent language available."[18] In a very arresting and *au point* statement, Helmut Thielicke writes: "In view of its structure, theological thinking is in some way an 'alien' medium into which statements of faith must be transposed."[19] Theology thus has the twin task of seeking and clarifying the meaning of life and life activities through the filter of faith and revelation.[20]

It would be misleading and inaccurate to maintain that because theology belongs to the area of speculative intellectual inquiry it is therefore wholly separated from life. After all, theology is a form of cognitive *life*. Further, theologizing is often done from within a context of *living* faith; this faith serves as both initiator, context, and filter for theologizing. Finally, as the theologian is speculating, as he is theologizing, he is attempting to drink some of the waters of life in which he sits in the here-and-now concrete existential situation; these waters naturally exert an influence on his theologizing, even if these waters are often removed from the hurly-burly of life as the person-in-the-street lives this life.[21] Theology deals, among other things, with what Christians *de facto* think, feel, and do, and uses the ecclesia's Spirit-filled experience as a vital tool for its investigative activity.[22]

While theology is an important component of religion, it is not of itself a religious act. Thus Edward Schillebeeckx flatly states that "theology, although based on faith, is a formal science and not a religious act."[23] Theology may be rendered a religious act by a theologian's intention or by the offering of his theological speculation to God; however, any other human activity, be it swimming or kissing can also be rendered a religious act by an individual's intention or offering. As I observe in *The Shape of Religious Instruction,* theology flows from the act of faith as context and filter and serves the life of faith — but this is far different from equating theology and faith.[24] In Edward Schillebeeckx's words, theology "may not become something devotional" and still remain theology.[25] This position is by no means new; on the contrary, it is centuries old in the Roman Church. Thomas Aquinas, for example, states that a theologian might be able to make correct theological judgments about the morality of certain acts even though he himself is immoral with regard to these very same acts. Theological competence, says Aquinas, is acquired by study rather than by leading a religious life.[26] Much the same is true in psychotherapy when it happens that the therapist suffers from the same affliction as his patient, yet due to the therapist's high-level psychological knowledge, he is able to make an accurate diagnosis of the patient's illness.

While theology per se is not a religious act, nevertheless it frequently receives considerable nourishment from the texture of the faith relationship which the theologizer[27] has with God. Karl Barth holds that "dogmatics is possible only as an act of faith."[28] It should be noted that Barth here carefully distinguishes the theological act from the religious act. Edward Schillebeeckx's position might seem contrary to that of Barth when the Dutch theologian writes that "it may not even be claimed that theology is impossible without a personally experienced religious life.[29] Yet I do not regard Barth and Schillebeeckx as basically opposed on this point. What Schillebeeckx is saying, it seems to me, is that the caliber of a particular theological proposition or interpretation is not dependent on the level of the religious life of the theologizer making the proposition or interpretation. To be sure, it has happened in the church that some of the best theology has been produced by individuals or propounded by institutions whose religious life at the time was at best morally questionable. Or again, a theologizer may have a basic faith commitment yet be quite imperfect in the operationalizing of this commitment in his daily life. There is no empirical evidence which indicates that a necessary correlation exists between the quality of a theologian's religious life and the quality of his theologizing. Nor is there any available empirical evidence which indicates that personally lived faith is necessary for theologizing. To be sure, there is a considerable ontic difference between living a religious life and theorizing about religious life and its conditions. It is possible to see a grain of truth in the old saw that it is not necessary to be a horse in order to be a horse doctor, though it helps.

Religion not only forms the very grounding of a person's existence, but it also seeps through and permeates his entire lifestyle. Religion is so basic to effective fruitful living that one internationally acclaimed social scientist is able to state unequivocally that on the basis of thirty years of psychiatric practice every one of his patients over thirty-five years of age had become psychically sick because each had lost that religious perspective toward life which has been the gift of the living religions of every age. This psychiatrist, Carl Jung, goes on to observe that every psychological problem these patients had could be ultimately reduced to the need for finding a religious outlook or attitude toward life. Jung discovered that none of his patients was ever healed until that individual came to and adopted a religious outlook on and a religious attitude toward life.[30] For Jung, the problem of mending broken souls is first and foremost a religious problem, a religious affair.[31] Throughout his books, Jung seems to strongly imply that the clue to faithful living on the part of every person, normal as well as abnormal, can be found in operationalizing the religious perspective in one's life.

The Contrast in Brief

Theology is the speculative science investigating the nature and workings of God. Religion, on the other hand, comprises a lifestyle, a total way of life engaging the whole person. Religion is often cast into institutional form, though such a form is not intrinsically necessary for its existence. As a science, theology can be put into books. As a lifestyle, religion cannot be put into books; only the history of religion or a description of religious experience can be put into books. Theology is abstract, while religion is concrete. As a general rule, theology is objective whereas religion is both subjective and objective.

THE PROPER CONTENT OF RELIGIOUS INSTRUCTION

Simply and unambiguously stated, *the proper content of religious instruction is the religious instruction act itself — nothing more, nothing less*. Since the religious instruction act is the *religious* instruction act and not the theological instruction act, priority of substantive content is necessarily accorded to religion rather than to theology. *Religion is thus the substantive content; instructional practice is the structural content. The substantive content plus the structural content as they are existentially formed and fused in the religious instruction act itself comprise the proper content of religious instruction.* This is a most crucial point and indeed is the major thesis of this volume. Just as volume II of the trilogy focuses on the structural content of religious instruction, this volume deals with the substantive content.

THE SUBSTANTIVE CONTENT OF RELIGIOUS INSTRUCTION

Delineation of the proper content of religious instruction is vitally important because all religious instruction regardless of the setting is rooted in the desired or actual outcomes acquired by the learners.[32] The substantive content, for its part, helps shape the focus and utilization of each of the six structural elements of the curriculum, namely design, scope, sequence, continuity, balance, and integration.[33] (Suffice it to say that curricular structure, while helping to shape the structure of instructional practice, is not coextensive with it.) The choice of substantive content serves as the axis around which every religion curriculum and every religion lesson necessarily revolve.[34]

In addition to the concept of religion as the substantive content, three other notions have historically been proposed and concretized into religious instruction programs. The first of these other proposals is that theology comprises the substantive content of religious instruction. This vision seems to unduly narrow and restrict the content of religious instruction. Earlier in this chapter the essential difference between religion and theology was etched. Theology cannot be legitimately equated with religion; indeed such an identification does violence to both theology and religion. Theological content is not the same as religious content. Unfortunately, all too many religious educationists and educators seem to assume that because theological content is often targeted toward religious activity, it follows that theology and religion are therefore coextensive. Yet properly speaking, theology qua theology is targeted at nothing other than theology. To be sure, theology is highly relevant to religion, and theologians often (but not always) spell out this relevance. But the fact remains that this relevancy and this application are dimensions outside of theological science properly considered. Religious content is not only distinct from theological content, but is also far wider than theological content. To regard religion as nothing more than either theological content or the outering of this content is to cramp religion. For people living in a world not characterized by a great deal of conscious theologizing, such a cramped concept of religion might at best make life dull or at worst induce crises of faith.

Theology, in short, is not coextensive with religion. Going one step further, theology does not necessarily generate acts of religion or even religious content. In Emil Brunner's words, "Dogmatics is not the Word of God. God can make his Word prevail without theology."[35] Hence, while theology is extremely helpful and in some ways indispensable to both religion and religious instruction, still theology does not in and of itself automatically give rise to religious behavior. This relates to what I observed earlier when I pointed out that theology qua theology is targeted at nothing other than theology. Strictly speaking, theology cannot be faulted because it does not automatically produce religious behavior. By the same token, religious instruction can legitimately be criticized when it fails to facilitate the desired religious outcomes.

In *The Flow of Religious Instruction* I explore in some detail the practical consequences of an instructional program which has religious content as its axis as contrasted with one which is organized around theological content.[36] Theological instruction is aimed at enabling the learner to adequately theologize; religious instruction is directed toward facilitating religious behavior in the learner. Theology is an academic subject while religion is not an academic subject in the classical sense of the term. Religious instruction is more than an academic subject and thus necessitates different variations in pedagogical practice (including different evaluation procedures) from those used in the traditional academic sciences or disciplines such as theology or physics or mathematics or literature. There is, of course, a great deal of theology which is inserted into a religion curriculum or lesson as needed; however, this theological content is introduced into the lesson, not for its own sake, but only in the manner and only to the extent that it is useful in broadening and deepening the substantive religious content comprising the curriculum or lesson.[37]

The second of the three other notions which have been historically proposed and concretized into religious instruction programs is that the religion curriculum and lesson are broad as life itself. In this view, teaching literature or teaching history or teaching science can be regarded as fundamentally the same as teaching religion. The underpinning of this notion appears to be the idea that, since everything is intrinsically religious, it follows that anything and everything per se comprises formal religious content. Advocates of this position believe that one advantage of this viewpoint is that religion can be made more alive and relevant to the learners. Gabriel Moran characterizes this position as the "disappearance act" in religious instruction — religious instruction fades into other areas of the curriculum until it finally disappears, all in the name of improving the religion program. With a deft touch of wit and irony, Moran observes that "there is something very peculiar about a field which seems to disappear as it improves."[38] (Parenthetically I might add that curricula which are based on the "disappearance act" not only make religion disappear, but seem to bring about a disappearance of religion teachers as well.) Moran goes on to ask:

> Could it be possible that it is paradoxically true that the best way to teach religion is not to teach religion at all but to teach literature, social science or art in the best way possible? Before anyone enthusiastically embraces this paradox, another consideration should be kept in mind. If religious instruction is identical without remainder to general education, can one expect the continuance of any church bodies?[39]

This position of equating direct religious instruction with all of life's activities is neither good theology nor good pedagogy.[40] Theologically speaking, this position takes a solid immanentist theology to a *reductio ad absurdum*. Pedagogically, it is devoid of sense in that it provides no parameters for content and therefore renders inoperative the previously mentioned six structural elements inherent in any curriculum. As I observe elsewhere,[41] to teach religion means to teach religion; it does not mean to teach art or history or literature or biology. Learners come to the religion lesson to learn religion; they engage in other home, church, club, or school activities to learn about other areas of life. Theologically it is unjust, and pedagogically it is unsound for a religion curriculum or a religion teacher to deprive the learner of the opportunity of learning religion.[42] My previous distinction between substantive content and structural content is illuminative in this instance. It is true, as I observe throughout *The Flow of Religious Instruction,* that the structural content of teaching and learning is essentially the same in the teaching of religion or the teaching of literature or the teaching of physics. However, it is their respective substantive contents which make religion teaching different from the teaching of literature or the teaching of physics. Since substantive content and structural content of religious instruction exist ontically nowhere else than in the concrete religious instruction act itself, the distinction between religious instruction and other forms of instruction is an actual and real one.

The research evidence clearly indicates that Christian laypersons wish the church to teach religion rather than to teach a diluted version of religion. The two nationwide studies conducted in the mid-1960's, one by Reginald Neuwien[43] and the other by Andrew Greeley and Peter Rossi [44] found that the primary reason why parents send their offspring to Catholic schools is to ensure that these children will receive religious instruction. Neuwien's study also disclosed that students in Catholic schools believed that the most important reason for their attendance at these institutions was to learn religion.[45] A two-year (1969–1971) carefully conducted research investigation of a broad cross section of fifteen Protestant denominations in North America concluded that the most important service which the layperson expected of the church was that of religion, especially in the areas of worship, religious instruction, and evangelistic activity. Of interest also is that this study discovered that while the clergy all too often tended to believe that their church's religious activities should be watered down and subsumed by other areas of life, the laity believed quite the opposite.[46] There are no data to suggest that the conclusions of the three studies mentioned in this paragraph fail to hold true in the present time.

The third of the other three notions which have been historically proposed and concretized into religious instruction programs is that religious content per se is so lofty, so elevated, and so "supernatural" that it cannot be taught by the teacher. The taproot of this position is sunk deep in the blow "theory."[47] If this position is correct, then any deliberative, organized curriculum or lesson or religious encounter is fatuous and ineffectual. On the other hand, if this position is incorrect, then it is without pedagogical merit. In either case, this position is a useless one for religious instruction.

What I have written in the preceding few paragraphs by no means implies that I believe that religion is or should be cut off from the rest of life. Rather, I underscore the distinctiveness of religion as a unique kind of human experience. Vital religion does indeed draw much sustenance from other areas of reality and is organically related to these other areas not only at its very core but at every level; nonetheless, religion remains a distinctive phenomenon. This suggests that any curriculum or lesson which is geared to facilitating religious outcomes must be at once unique in itself and intimately related to other areas of reality on its (religion's) own terms. Hence there should be three kinds of structural pedagogical relationships situated in every religion curriculum or lesson: (1) relationships between those activities which for one or more reasons constitute religious experience per se; (2) relationships between religious experience and the various academic disciplines or fields of knowledge; (3) relationships between religious experience and human activity of every sort.[48]

This threefold set of curricular or lesson interrelationships can be accomplished in religious instruction because of the deeply experiential nature and scope of its content. The content of religious instruction, it will be recalled, is the religious instruction *act*. Personal experience is the great human integrator of all substantive and structural relationships. Knowledge, affect, lifestyle, and all the other modes of religious content are fused and bonded together in the white heat of personal experienc*ing*. Thus Carl Jung can note that Saul owed his conversion not to love alone, nor to faith alone, nor to knowledge alone, nor to any other truth alone, but rather to that decisive experience on the road to Damascus which put all these elements into a new form. When all is said and done, true religious knowledge and true religious faith and true religious love — all vital religious contents — can come only from a context of personal experienc*ing*. No individual can obtain beforehand, observes Jung, that which only experience can give him.[49] Thus the task of the religion curriculum or religion lesson is to provide structured units of experience which enable the learners to interact in a living fashion with the various substantive contents of religious instruction.

THE NATURE OF RELIGIOUS INSTRUCTION CONTENT

"Content" is the name given to that which the teacher teaches and the student learns. Content, then, is a multidimensional reality. There is much oversimplification and indeed primitive reductionism of the nature of content on the part of religious educators unfamiliar with pedagogy. Content is a term which refers to many kinds of learning outcomes all of which are in various degrees acquired concomitantly by the learner. Content, then, is not a single concrete learning outcome, such as knowing that the name of the Christian hero who worked with the Apostle Paul in evangelizing Iconium was Barnabas. Rather, content is really a cluster of several interrelated learning outcomes.

The Nine Substantive Contents

The substantive content of religious instruction is religion. Constitutive of this content is a cluster of many interrelated contents. Each of these contents is as fully a content as any other of the constitutive contents. It well may be that a particular encounter or lesson or unit or even curriculum might be focused more on one of the substantive contents than on the others, yet each of the other substantive contents is as fully present in the learning experience and as fully valid for the learning experience as the one content which is being focused on. Each substantive content yields a different form or mode of learning outcome; it is the sum total of these outcomes which together with instructional practice of both content and outcome forms the overall "content" or religious instruction.

Over the years I have been empirically and speculatively analyzing the overall content of religious instruction, namely the religious instruction act itself. My analyses have consistently revealed that there are at least nine discrete and distinctive contents which, in concert, form the cluster or bundle known as the substantive content of religious instruction. (It is this substantive content which, when fused with structural content, goes to form the overall content of religious instruction.) The composition of substantive content, then, is an amalgam of nine separate substantive contents, all of which must be present and interactive for there to be a substantive content of the religious instruction act. The nine contents which go to make up substantive content are: product content, process content, cognitive content, affective content, verbal content, nonverbal content, conscious content, unconscious content, and lifestyle content.

During the course of my years of investigating the composition of substantive content, I have discovered that these nine contents fall into five distinct groupings. These groupings are: (1) product/process; (2) cognitive/affective;[50] (3) verbal/nonverbal; (4) conscious/ unconscious; (5) lifestyle. I did not devise these five groupings arbitrarily, but rather on the basis of the distinctive way in which each grouping represents a special and discrete dimension of the whole of substantive content. Each constitutive element of each grouping suggests the way in which that particular element exhibits the dimensionality of which it is a part. Thus, for example, in the verbal/nonverbal grouping, verbal content is substantive content in word form, while nonverbal content is substantive content in the form of gesture, physiological movement, and the like. The constitutive element of each grouping is antipodal to the other element situated within that same grouping. For example, product content is antipodal to process content, cognitive content is antipodal to affective content, and so forth. It is the intra-action between, interaction among, and combination of these antipodal groupings which give the whole of substantive content such richness and variety of texture.

As I have just suggested, each of the five dimensionalities of the whole of substantive content is at once intra-active and interactive. Each dimensionality is intra-active in the sense that the elements which comprise that dimensionality continually and dynamically mesh with each other, often deeply shaping and profoundly influencing one another.[51] Further, each dimensionality is constantly interactive with the other four; indeed, it is the simultaneous presence of all five of these dimensionalities interacting with each other which bestows on substantive content its very essence. The particular form and thrust which the whole of substantive content takes at any given moment is determined by how these five dimensionalities intra-act and interact with each other and with the structural content (instructional practice) to which they are fused in the religious instruction act itself.

There tends to be an inbuilt but by no means a necessary tendency for one element of the different dimensionality-pairings to be linked to particular elements of other pairings. Thus, typically, but not always, in most actual teaching situations product content, cognitive content, and verbal content tend to form one major pattern of the way the teacher treats substantive content. Process content, affective content, nonverbal content, unconscious content, and lifestyle content tend to be the second of these two major patterns.

It is regrettable that no educationist or educator in either general instruction or in religious instruction has ever made this kind of conceptualization of substantive content. This conceptualization of the nine kinds of substantive content, together with the five dimensionalities which encompass them, enables the teacher to possess the comprehensive perspective to successfully orchestrate the various modes of substantive content so that each kind of substantive content can be properly employed and deployed in the instructional act.

In this third and final volume of the trilogy I will deal only with eight of the nine kinds of substantive content. I am omitting a separate treatment of conscious content for reasons which should be obvious to any reader who is conscious.

Ramifications

This conceptualization of content as a cluster of necessary constitutive contents does away with the false dichotomy which so many religious educators have erected between so-called "content-centeredness" on the one hand, and "experience-centeredness" on the other.[52] Each of the constitutive contents is a particularly valenced and focused form of experience; furthermore, experience is not formless, but rather in the concrete assumes the form of one or other of the constitutive contents. Even John Dewey, who can hardly be counted among those who dilute the uniqueness of experience, observes that "experiencing has no existence apart from the subject matter experienced."[53] Thus, for example, a religion lesson based entirely on process content to the exclusion of product content (or vice versa) is not only existentially impossible but is also totally insufficient for the *content* of religious instruction. The various contents of the entire "content bundle" go on simultaneously, whether the religion teacher is aware of this or not. Thus the affective content an individual experiences is accompanied by some sort of cognitive reflection and awareness of that content during the very moments in which the individual is experiencing the affective content.[54] To be sure, the teacher structures the learning situation by giving special salience in the lesson to one content or another on the basis of which content enhances the probability that the desired learning outcome will indeed be attained. But this is vastly different from contending that the salience of one or more of the contents in the lesson takes place to the exclusion of the other contents. The entire nature of curriculum building and lesson planning is predicated on the synthesizing of various kinds of contents into one vital, interactive whole.[55] Religious instruction, like poetry, painting, the arts, or science, is most effectively accomplished when there is unity *in* variety and unity *from* variety.[56]

Content is not only the composite of substantive and structural forms being experienced; it is also the goal or outcome to be attained. Hence whenever the word ''content'' appears, the term ''outcome'' can usually be substituted. Pedagogically speaking, content is important in the religion lesson only to the extent that it is rendered an outcome. It is in this sense that John Dewey remarks that ''every experience is a moving force. Its value can be judged only on the ground of what it moves toward and into.''[57]

It is fairly safe to assert that the organizing principle of most Catholic and Protestant religious instruction curricula has been a combination of product content and cognitive content[58] at the expense of the other contents. Such a lopsided curricular emphasis is unfortunate for two reasons. First, it is based on a defective and stunted view of content and its rich forms. Second, it is founded on an inadequate notion of the nature of the pedagogical dynamic. As my model of the teaching-learning act[59] clearly indicates, even just that part of content we call ''substantive content'' partly originates from and is shaped by the other three interactive elements of the ongoing pedagogical dynamic, namely the teacher, the learner, and the instructional environment. Substantive content is not, as Wayne Rood suggests, simply the objective element in the religion lesson.[60] The substantive content of religious learning, as John Westerhoff aptly remarks, often grows out of the learner.[61] Teaching religion is a cooperative art-science, not an operative one.

The notion of content as a bundle of many constituent interrelated contents rather than as a single product-cognitive content is, unhappily, quite new in the field of religious instruction. In fact, it is seldom if ever treated at any length or with discrimination in the professional literature. Only a handful of American or European graduate programs in religious instruction under Catholic or Protestant auspices seem to enable their students to identify various contents or to relate those instructional behaviors most appropriate to effective learning of these kinds of content. To be sure, the conceptualization of content as a bundle of discrete contents represents a radical shift from the traditional vague objectives of "teaching subject matter," "providing relevant experiences," "educating the whole person," and "inculcating a richer faith life" toward a more careful and precise specification of the kinds of content (outcome) to be taught. Such a delineation enables the religion teacher to significantly increase his pedagogical effectiveness. This kind of specification makes it possible for the curriculum builder, the teacher, and the parent to more easily move to behavioral objectives[62] and performance-based criteria[63] in the instructional enterprise.

SOME PRACTICAL CONSEQUENCES

Numerous and beneficial are the practical consequences of the affirmation that the religious instruction act comprises the content of religious instruction. Principal among these consequences is the successful resolution of that posited series of nonexistent ontic dualities which for so long have unduly preoccupied religious educators. Indeed this preoccupation has had the damaging effect of deflecting the attention of religious educators away from that concentrated focus on the religious instruction act, a focus which is so essential for the full flowering of the enterprise.

Chief among these posited series of nonexistent dualities are the content-experience duality, the person-content duality, and the practice-content duality.

Content-Experience Duality

We have already seen a few pages previously that the conceptualization of religion as a cluster of many constitutive, interactive, substantive contents destroys the posited duality of content versus experience. Each of these contents, ranging from product content all the way through lifestyle content is, in actual existential fact, a particularly valenced and focused form of experience. Each content, then, is a description of one or other form of experience which occurs during the religious instruction act. In the pedagogical dynamic, the substantive content with which the learner is dealing is perforce an experienced content for him. Only in the realm of abstraction and speculation can these contents be separated from the here-and-now act of experiencing. Thus one can ask, "Where is substantive content to be found if it is not within the realm of the learner's experiencing during the religion lesson?" Just as each kind of substantive content represents a particular form of experience, so is the cluster of contents as a totality equivalent to all of experience.

Experience and content, understood in this way, are corelative terms. Content is the form which experience takes. Experience, for its part, is itself a content. This is not only sound pedagogy; it also lies at the philosophical basis of sound theology. Thus Karl Barth, who can scarcely be numbered among the foes of content, writes: "It is rare in life to be able to separate form and content."[64] For Barth, as for many other theologians spanning the conservative and liberal wings of Protestant and Catholic thought, the nature of divine revelation, its content, that is, cannot be torn asunder from its forms because form "is obviously always the form of a content."[65] Form can be separated from content only intellectually, for the sake of cognitive analysis. In actual experience, form cannot be separated from content.

Person-Content Duality

This presumed but erroneous dichotomy posits a radical split in the religious instruction act itself between the content or subject matter on the one hand and the person of the learner on the other.[66] Religious educationists and educators have typically assumed that a curriculum builder or religion teacher has to choose one of the two poles. Traditionally, most religious educationists and curriculum builders have opted for the first of these. Thus William Bedford Williamson's review of the pertinent Protestant literature "reveals both an attempt to preserve a hearty concern for subject matter and an overwhelming decision to organize the resulting curriculum by way of 'how to present the material,' rather than fulfilling an announced intention to present a curriculum geared to the question, How do children learn?"[67] Catholic writing on this topic is markedly similar in its approach.

The alleged radical duality between person (subject) and content (object) has serious deficiencies from the standpoint of philosophy, theology, psychology, and pedagogy. Philosophically, it is quite impossible in the here-and-now existential order to have object without subject or subject without object. As Paulo Freire puts it, "neither can exist without the other, nor can they be dichotomized."[68] The positing of object as existing ontically apart from subject in the real world is a very naive form of philosophical objectivism because it proposes a world (and a religion lesson) devoid of persons. Conversely, the denial of object results in a solipsistic stance by rejecting not only the power but the very existence of objective reality. From the philosophical standpoint, subject and object exist in a dynamic tension.[69] The degree and force to which subject and object exist together in dynamic tension has been a recurrent theme of philosophy down through the centuries. The twentieth century, particularly since World War II, has witnessed a "triumph of subjectivity" in philosophy, to use Quentin Lauer's phrase,[70] but usually not to the exclusion or denial of objectivity. Indeed the philosophical position popularly known as Existentialism totally disavows any distinction between subject and object on the ground that the person's individual subjective here-and-now experience is all that exists for him — this experience fuses any and all duality of subject and object which might be hypothesized to exist in the logical order.[71]

Theologically, the radical subject-object duality goes against the very nature of creation, of the Incarnation, and of revelation. Creation clearly suggests a God who as subject outered himself in a certain respect as object in the world. The Incarnation of the Word into flesh represents a unique example of the divine subject joining himself to object. Finally, revelation is, in one sense, an interpersonal relationship between God and man as mediated through Jesus and through the world in Jesus.[72]

Psychologically, the radical subject-object duality is an impossibility. In the act of knowing, the subject becomes the object in a certain sense, and the object takes on the coloration of the subject. *Quidquid recipitur, ad modum recipientis recipitur* is not simply a quaint Scholastic axiom; it is the touchstone of all modern psychology of learning.

Pedagogically, there is no foundation to the dilemma that the religion teacher must teach either subject-matter content on the one hand or persons on the other. Any valid theory of instruction, such as, for example, the teaching theory proposed in *The Flow of Religious Instruction*[73] takes into consideration the fact that any lesson reflects, not only the nature of substantive content itself, but also of structural contents including the nature of the learner, the way he learns, the environment in which the learning takes place, and the process by which the teacher facilitates the learning. It is in the teaching-learning dynamic itself that the presumed radical duality between subject and object, any overemphasis on one to the heavy downplaying or extinction of the other is eradicated. The affirmation that the proper content of religious instruction is the religious instruction act itself thus sounds the death knell to any presumed radical dichotomy between subject and object in the religion lesson.

Even the conceptualization of religion as the substantive content of religious instruction is sufficient by itself to deal the death blow to the alleged fundamental duality between subject and object in the religion lesson. Virtually all Protestant and Catholic theologians agree that religion is simultaneously a subjective and an objective phenomenon. Religion is a subjective phenomenon in that it is a personal, lived relationship between the believer and his God. It is an objective phenomenon in that certain objective (for him) truths form an integral part of this dynamic lived relationship. The "facts" or truths about God are indeed objective enough in themselves, but in the religious act these facts take on the texture and tint of each particular person. Thus the affirmation of religion as the substantive content of religious instruction clearly implies that while the learner is indeed at the center of the pedagogical dynamic, nonetheless critical "non-I realities" (objects, in the loose sense of this term) such as the teacher, the environment, and the subject matter (including cognitive content, affective content, and so forth) are absolutely indispensable to the lesson. The interaction during the pedagogical dynamic between these Jesus-suffused "non-I realities" and the Jesus-suffused learner serves to bond subject and object into a unified content.

Practice-Content Duality

This presumed but fallacious dichotomy posits a primal gulf in the religious instruction act itself between practice and content.[74] Popularly, this duality is often called the "how" versus the "what." The practice-content duality has assumed an almost axiomatic status in Protestant and Catholic religious instruction circles. American Protestant religious educationists like to speak of the three historical periods, namely the missionary phase, the educational (practice) phase, and after World War II, the theological (content) phase.[75] Catholic religious educationists both in America and in Europe often refer to the pre-World War II period as the methodological (practice) phase and the post-War period as the content phase. Thus in the 1950s Randolph Crump Miller[76] claimed to rediscover theological content as the "clue" to religious instruction. A decade later, Josef Goldbrunner[77] and Johannes Hofinger[78] announced that instructional practice is the "handmaid" and "servant" of theological content. This "handmaid" and "servant" status of religious instruction has been widely held by religious educators ever since. Thus, Matthew Hayes regards religious instruction simply as the practice of providing theological language, concepts, and categories for the ordinary Christian who is attempting to "theologize."[79] The apogée of the theological content phase is probably Richard McBrien's categorical assertion that a religious educator cannot teach or directly enhance faith; rather the religious educator can only "transmit" one or another theology of faith.[80]

Quite obviously, the conceptualization of the content of religious instruction as the religious instruction act itself (an amalgam of structural contents plus substantive contents) is *ipso facto* sufficient to consign the alleged practice-content duality to the pool of nonsense from whence it originated. But perhaps a few explanatory words might be in order. When religious educationists speak of content in the practice-content paradigm, they are typically referring exclusively to product content from the substantive standpoint. Yet we have seen earlier in this chapter that there are many other contents in religious instruction besides substantive product content. Instructional practice is much more than the arrangement of product content. Instructional practice is itself a content, a structural content. Because instructional practice is itself a content, the presumed practice-content duality is nonexistent. There obviously can be no such thing as a content-content duality.

A simple example will serve to illustrate the fatuousness of this alleged practice-content duality. Many religion teachers — to say nothing of religious instruction theorists — regard motivation as an entry vehicle to the lesson, a phenomenon preparatory to and outside of the real business of facilitating the so-called content. Motivation thus is envisioned as an instructional practice external to or apart from the content, the real business of religious instruction.[81] But this standpoint ignores the fact that motivation is itself a content. Not only is motivation a structural content; the way it is shaped and executed by the teacher also means that it is suffused with substantive contents such as affective content, verbal content, and so on. Viewed from this perspective, motivation is not an instructional practice external to or distinct from the lesson, but rather a vital content of the lesson.[82] I strongly suspect that religious educationists have fallen into the trap of positing a practice-content duality because all too often they adhere to a faulty or inadequate theory of the teaching act. Instead of embracing some form of the teaching theory, these educationists advocate some pseudo-theory such as, for example, the blow "theory," the proclamation "theory," or the witness "theory."[83]

What I am suggesting is that practice and content are at once essences and modalities. As both essences and modalities, they are brought into concrete existence and shaped by the ongoing *existentiel* of the here-and-now religious instruction act. Instructional practice does not exist in itself; it exists only in conjunction with another content outside itself, e.g., substantive content. Conversely, in the actual religious instruction dynamic, substantive content does not exist existentially apart from practice. It is the total religious instruction *act* itself, as this act exists in the concrete here-and-now religion lesson, which comprises the content. The sundering of practice from content represents a false dichotomy from the point of view of the *existential* religion lesson. It is from this existential vantage point that I like to interpret Gabriel Moran's contention that "the confident statement made [by most Catholic religious educationists] that the catechetical movement has passed from an early methodological phase into the really important concentration on 'content' shows the continuing failure to see the whole issue."[84] The whole issue is, I believe, the dynamic interpenetration and interrelationship between instructional practice and all of the substantive contents which take place at every moment in the here-and-now existential teaching-learning act. It is the concrete, here-and-now religious instruction act which brings both practice (structural content) and substantive content into existence. Thus both structural content and substantive content condition or determine each other both at the deepest ontological level as well as throughout every moment of the teaching-learning dynamic. John Westerhoff suggests this when he asks, "Do the 'how' and 'where' we learn help determine 'what' we learn?"[85] From a philosophical-theological perspective, Paul Tillich observes that practice and content "determine each other." Practice, continues Tillich, "is not an 'indifferent net in which reality [content] is caught, but the practice is an element of the reality[content] itself."[86]

I believe that the basic reason why religious educationists and educators have for so long proposed a nonexistent content-method duality is that most of these people have been locked into the theological approach to religious instruction. From a social-science perspective, such a dichotomy between practice and content is patently absurd. As more and more religious educationists adopt the social-science approach, we can look forward to the jettisoning of this erroneous duality on the one hand and a deeper exploration of practice-as-content, content-as-practice unity on the other. From such an exploration there will be born many significant, fruitful advances in the doing of religious instruction.

THEOLOGY AND SOCIAL SCIENCE—TWO FUNDAMENTAL APPROACHES

The conceptualization of content as set forth in this chapter illumines from yet another perspective the basic difference between the social-science approach to religious instruction and the theological approach. Because I devote the whole of Volume I of this trilogy (*The Shape of Religious Instruction*) to an elaboration of this position, and all of Volume II (*The Flow of Religious Instruction*) to a consideration of how the social-science approach is pedagogically implemented in the religious instruction act, it is unnecessary here to do more than briefly recapitulate the fundamental differences between the theological approach and the social-science approach. The theological approach claims that religious instruction is a mode of theology; the social-science approach contends that religious instruction is a mode of social-science. The thesis of the theological approach is that religious instruction draws its norms and practices from theology; the thesis of the social-science approach is that religious instruction draws its norms and its activities from the analysis and enactment of the teaching process itself. The theological approach holds that the lesson should unfold basically according to the way theological science itself unfolds; the social-science approach holds that in the religious instruction act, theology, like any other relevant kind of content, is interwoven in the lesson according to the way in which the learner learns most effectively. The theological approach asserts that the key to religious instruction is to search for the deepest and most authentic theology and then "impart" this to the learners in as pure and pristine a form as possible; the social.science approach asserts that the key to religious instruction is to examine and to implement the manner in which religious behavior is most effectively facilitated in each individual learner. The theological approach is value-laden in that in the religious instruction act itself it takes the form of one specific kind of theological thought while excluding part or all of others, e.g., Methodist theology and Catholic theology, immanentist theology and transcendentist theology, process theology and product theology, Arminian theology and Calvinist theology, Christian theology and Hindu theology. The social-science approach, in contrast, is value-free in the sense that in the religious instruction act itself the relatively neutral facilitation dynamic can and does take on the coloration of any one or other of theological systems of thought.

Immediate Relevance to Religious Instruction

Religion is the substantive content of religious instruction. But religion, it will be recalled, is not only an objective set of truths and realities; it is also a subjective set of personal behaviors on the part of the religionist.[87] Yet religion, like all other human phenomena, exists in a situational context. Hence in the religion lesson, the content is religion as it exists in the shape of the learner's religious behaviors in the situational context of the teaching-learning dynamic. Thus from still another vantage point we can appreciate why the content of religious instruction is the entire religious instruction act itself, that is, religion as it exists in the concrete teaching-learning dynamic for each and every learner here-and-now.

From this analysis we can now more clearly see why the real content of religious instruction is the existential fusion of both religion and instructional practice. Put another way, the content of religious instruction is the sum of all nine contents presented earlier in this chapter, as these contents are all bonded together in and through the pedagogical act. Instructional practice, then, far from being opposed to or outside of content, actually is both one (or more) of these constituent contents, *plus* the actual existential fus*ing* together of these nine contents into the concrete, existential, here-and-now religious instruction act.

This fuller conceptualization of the content of religious instruction as set forth in the two preceding paragraphs indicates once again why religious instruction is properly a mode of social science and not a form of theological science.

At this juncture it might be helpful to examine how this integrative, subsumptional conceptualization of the content of religious instruction is intimately related to and indeed is an aspect of the all-important mediation stage of religious instruction.[88] The mediation stage, it will be recalled from Volume II of this trilogy, realizes that religious instruction is a *fundamentally new entity* composed of both substantive contents (such as theology) and structural contents (such as the pedagogical dynamic itself) *in a radically new ontic reality*. It is the religious instruction act itself which is the mediator. This new reality of mediator is of such a nature that it not only unites its components (substantive contents and structural contents) but unites them in such a fashion that the components are no longer separate entities but rather are subsumed into a new reality, the reality called religious instruction. This new reality simultaneously (1) incorporates and retains the essential features of its original components, and (2) puts the essential features of the original components into a new fused relationship with each other so that they are no longer separate but become inextricably combined in the new reality — so inextricably combined, in fact, that in this new reality the components are no longer separate and distinct ontic entities but exist only in their united state. Mediatorship means that substantive content and structural content are so united in religious instruction that religion no longer exists as religion *in se* but now exists under the form of religious instruction, and that instruction does not exist as instruction *in se* but now exists under the form of religious instruction.[89]

The mediation stage, it seems to me, represents a more adequate and more accurate understanding of the religious instruction act than does either the messenger-boy stage or the translation stage. The messenger-boy stage regards religious instruction as a sort of errand boy through whom the wisdom and understanding acquired in theological science can be delivered by the teacher to the learner. The all-too-familiar consequence of the messenger-boy notion is that religious instruction was reduced to the level of servant or handmaiden to theology.[90] Advocates of the messenger-boy stage such as James Smart,[91] Roger Lincoln Shinn,[92] Johannes Hofinger,[93] and Josef Goldbrunner[94] all share the belief in the dictation of religious instruction by theological decision. The translation stage conceives of religious instruction as a translation of theology back into the truth from which it arose and which it represents, where it can be learned in life and in relationships.[95] Like the messenger-boy stage, the translation stage regards religious instruction as a mode of theology. Hence the task of religious instruction is to continually receive global and often specific instructions from theology on curricular scope, pedagogical practice, and so forth. Pedagogical practice evolves from theology, and it is on this basis that there is presumed to be an organic relation between content and practice.[96] Despite the fact that the translation stage retains the theological imperialism of the messenger-boy stage, it nonetheless is more sophisticated in that it regards the relationship of theology to religious instruction as a two-way street in contrast to the one-way street posited by the messenger-boy approach. In the translation stage, both theological science and life experience insert their dimensionalities into religious instruction according to the distinct modes of theology and life experience, all within the general outlook, thrust, and watchful eye of theological science. What the translation stage does is to elevate religious instruction from the level of second-class messenger to the level of first-class messenger.

Beginning in the late 1960s and continuing into the present, a few religious educationists seem to have been moving cautiously toward adopting the conceptualization stage of religious instruction as mediator, though none seems to have articulated it or systematized it. Didier-Jacques Piveteau in France, Hans van der Ven in The Netherlands, Herman Lombaerts in Belgium, and Hubert Halbfas in Germany have recognized that religious instruction must start from the principles of effective education. But even here, Halbfas repeatedly slips back into a basic theological approach to religious instruction.[97] Piveteau, van der Ven, and Lombaerts do not seem to be so enmeshed in the web of theological imperialism as does Halbfas. On this side of the Atlantic, the later Gabriel Moran[98] appears to have moved toward mediationism to a greater or lesser degree. Newer scholars such as Donald Bossart,[99] Bailey Gillespie,[100] Lucie Barber,[101] and John Peatling[102] seem to wholeheartedly embrace one or another view of mediationism. With a more sophisticated analysis of the nature of religious instruction content, with a deeper probing into the form and ramifications of the mediation stage, and with a thoroughgoing adoption at the affective as well as the cognitive level of the social-science approach, there should emerge a new era in religious instruction as a field of study and a field of work.[103]

NOTES

1. Richard Bach, *Jonathan Livingston Seagull* (New York: Macmillan, 1970), p. 83.

2. James Michael Lee, *Principles and Methods of Secondary Education* (New York: McGraw-Hill, 1963), pp. 208–209; Hilda Taba, *Curriculum Development* (New York: Harcourt Brace Jovanovich, 1962), pp. 186–188; Daniel Tanner and Laurel N. Tanner, *Curriculum Development*, 2d edition (New York: Macmillan, 1980), pp. 100–190.

3. In Volume I of this trilogy, I spend considerable time exploring the relationship of theology to the religious instruction enterprise in general and to the social-science approach to religious instruction in particular. In Volume II, I devote an entire chapter to examining the basic differences between religious instruction and theological instruction. It is against that backdrop that I am presenting this brief analysis of the distinction between religious content and theological content.

4. See Merton P. Strommen, "Introduction," in Merton P. Strommen, editor, *Research on Religious Development* (New York: Hawthorn, 1971), pp. xvi–xvii; also E. Magnin, "Religion," in A. Vacant, E. Mangenot, and E. Amann, editors, *Dictionnaire de Théologie Catholique*, tome XIII, pt. 2 (Paris: Letouzey et Ané, 1937), columns 2182–2187; L. B. Brown and J. P. Forgas, "The Structure of Religion: A Multi-Dimensional Scaling of Informal Elements," in *Journal for the Scientific Study of Religion* XIX (December, 1980), pp. 423–431.

5. James Michael Lee, *The Shape of Religious Instruction* (Birmingham, Ala.: Religious Education Press, 1971), pp. 72–73.

6. E. Schillebeeckx, *Revelation and Theology*, volume 1, translated by N. D. Smith (New York: Sheed and Ward, 1967), p. 93.

7. Charles Y. Glock, "On the Study of Religious Commitment," in *Religious Education*, research supplement, LVII (July-August, 1962), pp. s-98—s-100.

8. John Dewey, "The Religious in Experience," in Joseph Ratner, editor, *Intelligence in the Modern World* (New York: Random House Modern Library, 1939), pp. 1010, 1037.

9. Karl Barth, *Church Dogmatics*, volume 1, pt. 2, translated by G. T. Thomson and Harold Knight (Edinburgh: Clark, 1956), pp. 280–361.

10. Paul Tillich, *Systematic Theology*, volume 3 (Chicago: University of Chicago Press, 1963).

11. Dietrich Bonhoeffer, *Letters and Papers from Prison*, 3d edition, edited by Eberhard Bethge (London: SCM, 1967), pp. 152–155.

12. Hubert Halbfas, *Theory of Catechetics* (New York: Herder and Herder, 1971), p. 15.

13. E. Schillebeeckx, *Revelation and Theology*, volume 1, pp. 87–95; Leonard Swidler editor, *Consensus in Theology?* (Philadelphia, Westminster, 1980).

14. Karl Rahner, *Theological Investigations*, volume 1, 2d edition, translated by Cornelius Ernst (Baltimore, Md.: Helicon, 1965), p. 14.

15. E. Schillebeeckx, *Revelation and Theology*, volume 1, p. 100.

16. Gregory Baum, *Man Becoming* (New York: Herder and Herder, 1970), p. 32. Baum observes that once Catholic theologians make this clarification, then "eventually the hierarchy tests the development that has taken place and ap-

proves it [or I might add, disapproves it] in an authoritative statement." As I note in *The Shape of Religious Instruction* (pp. 104–105), the role of the official magisterium is central in the work of Roman Catholic theology, especially in terms of the verification process.

17. Paul Tillich, *Systematic Theology*, volume 1 (Chicago: University of Chicago Press, 1951), p. 28.

18. John Macquarrie, *Principles of Christian Theology* (New York: Scribner's, 1966), p. 1.

19. Helmut Thielicke, *The Evangelical Faith*, volume 2, translated and edited by Geoffrey W. Bromily (Grand Rapids, Mich.: Eerdmans, 1977), p. 3.

20. Bernard Lonergan proposes eight functional specialities or tasks of theology, the last of which is to communicate itself to others, namely "to lead another to share in one's cognitive, constitutive, effective meaning" (p. 362). It should be emphasized, however, that Lonergan does not suggest that religious instruction comprises or is included in the communicative task of theology. Lonergan clearly indicates that his eighth functional speciality of theology is to communicate theology, namely the cognitive, constitutive, and effective fruits of theologizing. This point seems suitably lost on Berard Marthaler who regards catechesis (a term denoting the officially approved Roman Catholic form of religious instruction) as falling within the eighth functional speciality. It is quite possible, furthermore, to question whether the positing of communication as a major task of theology is warranted. In this connection two major points must be raised. First, the work of theology (seeking and clarifying meaning) seems to be significantly distinct from what the theologian later chooses to do with the fruits of this theologizing — it is quite possible to theologize and not communicate the efforts of this work to others. Second, the nature and structure of communication (e.g., teaching, counseling, etc.) are ontically different from that of theologizing — this fact explains why there is no necessary correlation between the quality of a theologian's theology and the effectiveness by which he communicates this theology. Bernard J. F. Lonergan, *Method in Theology* (New York: Herder and Herder, 1972); Wayne Rood, *The Art of Teaching Christian Doctrine* (Nashville, Tenn.: Abingdon, 1968); Berard L. Marthaler, "Catechesis and Theology," in *Proceedings of the Catholic Theological Society of America* XXVIII (June, 1973), pp. 263–267.

21. One wonders whether Mary Boys is really serious when she seems to imply that theologians are truly immersed in the hurly-burly of life. Theologians are not generally employed as coal miners, religious social workers dealing with the indigent, or religious educators teaching the dying and youth groups, and so on. See Mary C. Boys, *Biblical Interpretation in Religious Education* (Birmingham, Ala.: Religious Education Press), 1980, p. 335.

22. Gregory Baum, *Man Becoming*, p. 249; John Macquarrie, *Principles of Christian Theology*, pp. 4–17; Bernard E. Meland, *Fallible Forms and Symbols* (Philadelphia: Fortress, 1976), pp. 150–171.

23. E. Schillebeeckx, *Revelation and Theology*, volume 1, p. 101.

24. James Michael Lee, *The Shape of Religious Instruction*, pp. 111–112.

25. E. Schillebeeckx, *Revelation and Theology*, volume 1, p. 101.

26. Thomas Aquinas, *Summa Theologica*, I, q.1, a.1, ad.3.

27. I am employing the term "theologizer" here to suggest that theologizing is not done exclusively by professional theologians.

28. Karl Barth, *Church Dogmatics: The Doctrine of the Word of God*, volume I, part 1, translated by G. T. Thomson (Edinburgh: T & T Clark, 1936), p. 25.
29. E. Schillebeeckx, *Revelation and Theology*, volume 1, pp. 101–102.
30. C. G. Jung, *Zur Psychologie westlicher und östlicher Religion*, Band XI in *Gesammelte Werke* (Zürich: Rascher, 1963), p. 362, (#509).
31. *Ibid.*, p. 369, (#523).
32. At the outset of *The Flow of Religious Instruction* I specifically state that religious instruction is of its very essence setting-free. To be sure, the very concept of instruction necessitates the inescapable conclusion that teaching is validly and authentically and fully carried on in all kinds of formal and informal settings. Some religious educationists do not seem to grasp this point. See Jack L. Seymour, "Contemporary Approaches to Christian Education," in *Chicago Theological Seminary Register* LXIX (Spring, 1979), pp. 1–10.
33. For a short summary of the nature and function of these six elements, see James Michael Lee, *Principles and Methods of Secondary Education*, pp. 190–213.
34. David Hunter, *Christian Education as Engagement* (New York: Seabury, 1963), p. 37.
35. Emil Brunner, *The Christian Doctrine of God: Dogmatics*, volume 1, translated by Olive Wyon (Philadelphia: Westminster, 1950), p. v.
36. James Michael Lee, *The Flow of Religious Instruction* (Birmingham, Ala.: Religious Education Press, 1973), pp. 24–26.
37. Mary K. Cove and Mary Louise Mueller, *Regarding Religious Education* (Birmingham, Ala.: Religious Education Press, 1977), pp. 81–98.
38. Gabriel Moran, *Design for Religion* (New York: Herder and Herder, 1970), p. 15.
39. *Ibid.*, p. 16. I have substituted the word "instruction" for the word "education" in the Moran text. These words are equivalent in the Moran text.
40. Nonintentional education, as distinct from intentional education and intentional instruction, is of course as wide as all of life. However, my triology expressly deals with intentional religious instruction, not with nonintentional religious education. Charles Melchert seems not to have grasped this elemental point. See Charles F. Melchert, "Does the Church Really Want Religious Education?" in John H. Westerhoff III, *Who are We: The Quest for a Religious Education* (Birmingham, Ala.: Religious Education Press, 1978), p. 251.
41. James Michael Lee, "How to Be a Better Religion Teacher," Thomas More Association Meditape Cassette Series, M118.
42. Evangelical Protestants are generally very insistent on this point. See, for example, Joseph Bayly, "Evangelical Curriculum Development," in *Religious Education* LXXV (September-October, 1980), pp. 539–545.
43. Reginald A. Neuwien, editor, *Catholic Schools in Action: A Report* (Notre Dame, Ind.: University of Notre Dame Press, 1966), pp. 261–273.
44. Andrew M. Greeley and Peter H. Rossi, *The Education of Catholic Americans* (Chicago: Aldine, 1966), p. 206.
45. Reginald A. Neuwien, editor, *Catholic Schools in Action: A Report*, pp. 228–234. See also Dean R. Hoge et al., "Desired Outcomes of Religious Education and Youth Ministry," in *Living Light* XVIII (Spring, 1981), pp. 18–35.
46. Douglas W. Johnson and George W. Cornell, *Punctured Preconceptions* (New York: Friendship, 1972), pp. 12–13. Further, the Protestant laypeople surveyed were more supportive of interdenominational cooperation than the clergy who

were almost twice as likely to oppose ecumenical activity as laypeople (p. 12). A constant finding throughout this study was the divergence of conceptions and attitudes of the laity on the one hand and the clergy on the other.

47. In *The Flow of Religious Instruction* (pp. 174–180) I discuss the blow "theory" at some length.

48. See Arno A. Bellack, "Knowledge Structure and the Curriculum," in Stanley Elam, editor, *Education and the Structure of Knowledge* (New York: Rand McNally, 1964), pp. 263–267; M. Frances Klein and Kenneth A. Tye, "The Domains of Curriculum and Their Study," in John I. Goodlad et al., editors, *Curriculum Inquiry* (New York: McGraw-Hill, 1979), pp. 43–76.

49. C. G. Jung, *Zur Psychologie westlicher und östilicher Religion,* p. 360, (#s 502–503).

50. Some educationists and psychologists would add conative or volitional content to these two. While there are many strong grounds to support the inclusion of conative or volitional content, there are also some persuasive grounds which militate against its inclusion as a distinct content within the substantive-content bundle. The basic reason for my exclusion of conative or volitional content is the relative lack of enough hard or comprehensive empirical research data and theories derived from these data on the whole area of conation. I myself entertain the hypothesis that conation or volition is a discrete content and belongs alongside cognition and affect. My hypothesis awaits confirmation (or rejection) from conclusive data which I hope social scientists will produce before the twentieth century is history.

51. This, of course, does not hold true for lifestyle which, admitting of no reciprocal element, is its own grouping.

52. Fortunately there is an awareness beginning to grow among perceptive religious educationists that experience itself is an authentic content in its own right. See, for example, Helen DeLaurentis, "Experience as Subject Matter in Religious Education," in *Living Light* XIII (Fall, 1976), pp. 442–443. Not surprisingly, DeLaurentis appears to embrace a form of the mediation stage discussed later in this chapter. Furthermore, as DeLaurentis observes, "without the criteria afforded by an adequate philosophy of education, there is no independent source for critiquing goals and methods" of religious instruction (p. 442).

53. John Dewey, *Philosophy and Civilization* (New York: Putnam, 1931), p. 261.

54. See Brian S. Crittenden, "Introduction" (to Discussion) in C. M. Beck, B. S. Crittenden, and E. V. Sullivan, editors, *Moral Education: Interdisciplinary Approaches* (Toronto: University of Toronto Press, 1971), p. 287; also Philip W. Jackson, *Life in Classrooms* (New York: Holt, 1968), pp. 33–34.

55. See, for example, John I. Goodlad, *School Curriculum Reform in the United States* (New York: Fund for the Advancement of Education, 1964); Robert S. Gilchrist et al., *Curriculum Development: A Humanized Systems Approach* (Belmont, Caif.: Fearon, 1974), pp. 19–48.

56. See J. Bronowski, *Science and Human Values,* revised edition (New York: Harper & Row Torchbooks, 1965), pp. 16–19.

57. John Dewey, *Experience and Education* (New York: Macmillan, 1959), p. 31.

58. The mid-1960's saw a broadening of this principle to include more of process content; notwithstanding, I believe my original assertion holds true. See Mary C. Boys, "Curriculum Thinking From a Roman Catholic Perspective," in *Religious Education* LXXV (September-October, 1980), pp. 516–527; Mary Jo Osterman, "The Two Hundred Year Struggle for Protestant Religious Education

Curriculum Theory,'' in *ibid.*, pp. 528–538; D. Campbell Wyckoff, "Curriculum Theory and Practice,'' in Marvin J. Taylor, *Foundations for Christian Education in an Era of Change* (Nashville, Tenn.: Abingdon, 1976), pp. 127–137.

59. For a treatment of this Lee model, together with a diagram, see James Michael Lee, *The Flow of Religious Instruction*, pp. 233–240.

60. Wayne R. Rood, *The Art of Teaching Christianity*, p. 58. Rood gets himself into this difficulty because he appears to equate all of content with product content only. Indeed, Rood's conceptualization of content as the objective element is somewhat at variance with much of his other speculations, which might suggest that the West Coast religious educationist has not thought through his position with that degree of care and analytical depth which is characteristic of high-level scholarship.

61. John H.Westerhoff III, *Values for Tomorrow's Children* (Philadelphia: Pilgrim, 1970), p. 90.

62. To assert, as Richard McBrien does, that behavioral objectives "accord little value to the mystical, the playful, the celebrative, and the artistic dimensions of religious existence and of religious consciousness'' is as nonsensical as it is unhistorical, as McBrien himself would readily realize if he would more carefully examine how artists work, how people play, and what mystics have written. See, for example, Leonardo DaVinci, "Extract From Notebooks," in Robert Goldwater and Marco Treves, compilers and translators, *Artists on Art* (New York: Pantheon, 1945), pp. 49–54; Germain Bazain, *The Loom of Art,* translated by Jonathan Griffin (New York: Simon and Schuster, 1962), pp. 124–158; Jean Piaget, *The Moral Judgment of the Child,* translated by Marjorie Gabain (New York: Free Press, 1965), pp. 13–50; Annie L. Butler, Edward Earl Gotts, and Nancy L. Quisenberry, editors, *Play as Development* (Columbus, Ohio: Merrill, 1978), pp. 17–43; Jan van Ruysbroeck, *The Adornment of the Spiritual Marriage, Etc.,* translated by C. A. Wynschenk (New York: Dutton, 1916), pp. 80–81; John of the Cross, *Dark Night of the Soul,* translated by E. Allison Peers (New York: Doubleday, 1959), pp. 167–175; Pierre Teilhard de Chardin, *Hymn of the Universe* (New York: Harper & Row, 1965). I suspect that McBrien has made a categorical statement about an area of education (behavioral objectives) about which he seems to know little, heard little, and observed little. See Richard P. McBrien, "Toward An American Catechesis,'' in *Living Light* XIII (Summer, 1976), pp. 175.

63. Howard Benoist and Robert Gibbons, "The Competence Movement and the Liberal Arts Tradition: Enemies or Allies?'', in *Journal of Higher Education LI* (November-December, 1980), pp. 683–692; Alvah H. Kilgore, "PBTE: A Follow-Up Study,'' in *Journal of Teacher Education XXXI* (January-February, 1980), pp. 55–60; Barak Rosenshine and Norma Furst, "Research on Teacher Performance Criteria,'' in B. Othanel Smith, editor, *Research in Teacher Education: A Symposium* (Englewood Cliffs, N.J.: Prentice-Hall, 1971), pp. 37–66.

64. Karl Barth, *Dogmatics in Outline,* translated by G. T. Thompson [sic] (New York: Harper & Row, 1959), p. 96.

65. Karl Barth, *Church Dogmatics: The Doctrine of the Word of God,* volume 1, pt. 1, p. 149.

66. For a brief historical overview of this duality, see Marcel van Caster, *The Structure of Catechetics,* translated by Edward J. Dirkswager, Jr., Olga Guedetarian, and Nicolas Smith (New York: Herder and Herder, 1965), pp. 7–9;

see also Harold William Burgess, *An Invitation to Religious Education* (Birmingham, Ala.: Religious Education Press, 1975).

67. William Bedford Williamson, *Language and Concepts in Christian Education* (Philadelphia: Westminster, 1970), p. 134.

68. Paulo Freire, *Pedagogy of the Oppressed,* translated by Myra Bergman Ramos (New York: Herder and Herder, 1970), p. 35.

69. For a significant exploration of this point from the perspective of a neo-Marxist stance, see Thomas H. Groome, *Christian Religious Education* (San Francisco: Harper & Row, 1980).

70. Quentin Lauer, *The Triumph of Subjectivity* (New York: Fordham University Press, 1958).

71. For some helpful treatments on the implications of Existentialism for the educational enterprise, see George F. Kneller, *Existentialism and Education* (New York: Wiley, 1958); Van Cleve Morris, *Existentialism in Education* (New York: Harper & Row, 1966); David E. Denton, editor, *Existentialism and Phenomenology in Education* (New York: Teachers College Press, 1974).

72. Karl Rahner, *Foundations of Christian Faith,* translated by William V. Dych (New York: Seabury, 1978), pp. 71–89; Edward Schillebeeckx, *Jesus: An Experiment in Christology,* translated by Hubert Hoskins (New York: Seabury, 1979), pp. 626–636.

73. James Michael Lee, *The Flow of Religious Instruction,* pp. 196–204, 233–240.

74. Typically this is referred to in the literature as the "method-content duality." However, as indicated in *The Flow of Religious Instruction* (pp. 31–35), I use the word method as a technical term indicating one of the levels in the taxonomy of instructional practice.

75. See, for example, D. Campbell Wyckoff, *Theory and Design in Christian Education Curriculum* (Philadelphia: Westminster, 1961), p. 50.

76. Randolph Crump Miller, *The Clue to Christian Education* (New York: Scribner's, 1950).

77. Josef Goldbrunner, "Cathechetical Method as Handmaid of Kerygma" in Johannes Hofinger, editor, *Teaching All Nations,* revised and partly translated by Clifford Howell (New York: Herder and Herder, 1961), pp. 108–121.

78. Johannes Hofinger, *The Art of Teaching Christian Doctrine,* 2d edition (Notre Dame, Ind.: University of Notre Dame Press, 1962) p. 49.

79. Matthew J. Hayes, "How Much Theology Should Coordinators and DRE's Know?" in *Living Light* XIV (Fall, 1977), p. 365.

80. Richard P. McBrien, "Faith, Theology and Belief," in *Commonweal* CI (November 15, 1974), p. 135.

81. David Hunter has likewise decried this duality, albeit on somewhat different grounds. See David Hunter, *Christian Education as Engagement,* pp. 42–43.

82. See James Michael Lee, *Principles and Methods of Secondary Education,* pp. 403–430.

83. For an overview of these "theories," see *The Flow of Religious Instruction,* pp. 149–205.

84. Gabriel Moran, *Catechesis of Revelation* (New York: Herder and Herder, 1966), p. 38.

85. John H. Westerhoff III, *Values for Tomorrow's Children,* p. 25.

86. Paul Tillich, *Systematic Theology,* volume 1 (Chicago: University of Chicago Press, 1951), p. 60. I have substituted the word "practice" for the word "method" in the Tillich text. These words are equivalent in the Tillich text.

87. See, for example, Antoine Vergote, "The Dynamics of the Family and Its Significance for Moral and Religious Development," in Christiane Brusselmans, convenor, *Toward Moral and Religious Maturity* (Morristown, N.J.: Silver Burdett, 1980), pp. 90–114; John H. Westerhoff, *Tomorrow's Church* (Waco, Tex.: Word, 1976), pp. 105–130.

88. A fuller treatment of the mediation stage, together with the messenger-boy stage and the translation stage, is found in James Michael Lee, *The Flow of Religious Instruction*, pp. 17–19; also James Michael Lee, "The Authentic Source of Religious Instruction," in Norma H. Thompson, editor, *Religious Education and Theology* (Birmingham, Ala.: Religious Education Press, 1982), pp.156–172.

89. James Michael Lee, *The Shape of Religious Instruction*, p. 229.

90. See William Bean Kennedy, "The Genesis and Development of the *Christian Faith and Life Series,*" unpublished doctoral dissertation, Yale University, 1957, pp. 557–558.

91. James Smart, *The Teaching Ministry of the Church* (Philadelphia: Westminster, 1954), pp. 24–45.

92. Roger Lincoln Shinn, *The Educational Mission of our Church* (Boston: United Church Press, 1962), p. 52. "Method . . . must flow from faith and purpose."

93. Johannes Hofinger, *The Art of Teaching Christian Doctrine*, p.62.

94. Josef Goldbrunner, "Catechetical Method as Handmaid of Kerygma," pp. 108–121.

95. See Randolph Crump Miller, *The Clue to Christian Education*, p. 8; Randolph Crump Miller, *The Theory of Christian Education Practice* (Birmingham, Ala.: Religious Education Press, 1980), pp. 153–162.

96. Randolph Crump Miller, *Education for Christian Living*, 2d edition (Englewood Cliffs, N.J.: Prentice-Hall, 1963), p. 174. There appears to be a contradiction between this basic thesis of Miller's and his conceptualization of method on p. 168.

97. Hubert Halbfas, *Theory of Catechetics*.

98. I write "the later Gabriel Moran" because in 1966 (*The Theology of Revelation*, and *The Catechesis of Revelation*) Moran was clearly in the camp of the messenger-boy stage as Gerard Sloyan duly observes in his general editor's introduction (n.p.) of the first-mentioned of these two books; however, in his 1970 *Design for Religion* (see especially the opening sentence of p. 121), in his 1971 "Foreword" to Hubert Halbfas's *Theory of Catechetics* (pp. 9–10), and in his 1979 *Education Toward Adulthood* (pp. 56–58) Moran seems to have shifted decidedly in the direction of the mediation stage. Molar shifts and radical switches in position are not uncommon in Moran's writings, as he himself noted in a 1977 paper presented at a religious education symposium held at Boston College. Like Moran, Iris Cully also seems to have shifted her position from an ardent messenger-boy conceptualization (see Iris V. Cully, *The Dynamics of Christian Education*, Philadelphia: Westminster, 1958) to a position somewhat aligned with the mediation stage (see Iris V. Cully, *Change, Conflict, and Self-Determination* Philadelphia: Westminster, 1972, pp. 163–165; also Iris V. Cully, "The Problem and the Clue," in Iris V. Cully and Kendig Brubaker Cully, editors, *Process and Relationship*, Birmingham, Ala.: Religious Education Press, 1978, pp. 1–6).

99. Donald E. Bossart, *Creative Conflict in Religious Education and Church Administration* (Birmingham, Ala.: Religious Education Press, 1980).

100. V. Bailey Gillespie, *Religious Conversion and Personal Identity* (Birmingham, Ala.: Religious Education Press, 1979).
101. Lucie W. Barber, *The Religious Education of Preschool Children* (Birmingham, Ala.: Religious Education Press, 1981).
102. John H. Peatling, *Religious Education in a Psychological Key* (Birmingham, Ala.: Religious Education Press, 1981).
103. See James Michael Lee, "Religious Education's Future," in *National Catholic Reporter* IX (October 27, 1972), pp. 10–11.

CHAPTER TWO

PRODUCT CONTENT

*"Yet when each of us in his own heart looks,
He finds the God there, far unlike his Books."* [1]

—Fulke Grenville, Lord Brooke

THE NATURE OF PRODUCT CONTENT

Product content refers to a particularized, static, and usually "tangible" kind of content. "Tangible" here does not necessarily mean concrete; rather it denotes a specified content which can be pinpointed. To illustrate: in the arithmetic example "two times two equal four" the product content is four.[2] Product, then, is the consequence of something. Product content is typically regarded as the outcome of a cognitive operation, but as I have pointed out elsewhere[3] it can also be the result of an affective activity.

A more precise understanding of the nature of product content emerges when it is contrasted to process content. (At this juncture I shall treat of process content only insofar as it more clearly illumines the character of product content, since I devote the next chapter exclusively to a consideration of process content.) Product content is the end result of the process; it is the consequence of the processing interaction of a particular set of conditions. Product content, then, is something which *has been* performed in the sense of a completed process; process content is something which *is being* performed. Gilbert Ryle conceptualizes product and process contents in terms of task achievement. Product content is something which has been achieved, while process content denotes the performance involved in getting this achievement. In Ryle's view, the statement "Jack is *winning* the race" makes no sense, because the word "winning" is an achievement word (product content), specifying in this instance, the person who first hits the tape at the finish line. It is more accurate to state "Jack is *running* (performance or process content) with sufficient speed to *win* (achievement or product content) the race. It is only after the running (process content) is completed that the winning (product content) can occur.[4]

To draw an analogy from computer technology, product content is the datum or bit, while process content is, among other things, the organizing of many data or bits. Ryle asserts that product content is "knowing *that*" and process content is "knowing *how.*" Put another way, Ryle etches the distinction between "wondering *whether*" (product content) and "wondering *how*" (process content).[5]

Product content and process content are difficult to tease apart satisfactorily because in and of themselves they are conceptual entities and not existential, independent ontic realities. There is no real, concrete, here-and-now act which is wholly composed of either pure product content or pure process content; indeed, any existential act, be it a religious instruction act or any other kind of act, is a compound of product content and process content. In any form of terrestrial existence, product and process exist as constituent complementaries. For example, experiencing is process content. Yet, as I note in Chapter One, there is no such thing in the real order as pure, naked experiencing. A person always experiences something (product content). Conversely, there is not anything (product content) that is not had in experience (process content). Process content in the real order, then, is always joined to some particular form of product content, and vice versa. It is important to note in this connection that the fusing together of product content and process content in any reality is not done according to the mode of the product content[6] but rather according to the *existentiel* of the act into which they are subsumed. (This fundamental principle is of supreme importance in accurately understanding the whole issue of the relationship of theology to religious instruction.)[7]

Let us look from another perspective at why it is so difficult to satisfactorily rip apart product content and process content even for conceptual analysis, to say nothing of *hic-et-nunc* existence. Earlier I observed that one way of conceptualizing product content is "knowing that," and one way of conceptualizing process content is "knowing how." Yet in here-and-now actuality, there is never a "that" without a "how," just as there is never a "how" without a "that." To employ another example: operations can be regarded as process contents, whereas the truths or results of these operations can be thought of as product contents. Yet again, in the real world, it is impossible to existentially separate operations from their outcomes; only in conceptual analysis is this possible, and even here there are major difficulties. Let me give one final illustration. Learning is typically regarded as a process content, and that which is learned is usually considered a product content. Nevertheless, learning itself often takes on many of the characteristics of product content in the sense that it is not just the sum total of the operations but indeed the fruit of these operations, as for example, when the religion teacher intends that his students learn how to learn, i.e., that they learn the processes of learning.

It seems to me that one way out of the dilemma of teasing apart product and process contents in the existential order is to regard all content as outcome. By so doing it is indeed possible to have a product content that is, to some degree at least, existentially distinct from process content. But even here the distinction is not that total, especially in the real order.

The delineation and distinction between product and process contents are more tacitly assumed than formally discussed in the religious instruction literature.[8] When content is examined from the product-process perspective, it often is not treated from a sophisticated point of view. Thus, even George Coe, while he must be credited with discussing product and process contents specifically, nonetheless does so in a rather muddy and jumbled way.[9] The upshot is that Coe's conceptualizations on this matter are often not readily usable by the religion teacher or curriculum builder.

When the religion teacher speaks specifically of "content," he typically refers not only to product content almost exclusively, but also to the cognitive variety of product content. These teachers not only fail to see the indispensability and richness of process as a content in its own right, but even deprive product content of any affective or unconscious components. As I observe elsewhere[10] "it is important to note that content is not identical with product. Indeed, the identification of product with content is a mistake into which many religion teachers seem to fall. The same is true of religious instruction writers who identify product with message. In reality both product and process are contents and messages—different kinds of contents and messages, but contents and messages indeed.''

The Importance of Product Content

What I say in the foregoing paragraph in no way denigrates the great importance of product content; rather, the preceding paragraph places the role and function of product content in a balanced perspective. To be sure, one of the most effective ways of minimizing the importance and significance of product content is to unduly exaggerate its scope and potency—an all-too-common failing among some religious educationists and educators.

In itself, product content is of inestimable value in the religious instruction act. Of the many contents which comprise the overall substantive content of the religious instruction act, product content certainly occupies a vitally important (though not the preeminent) position. Religion, the substantive content of the religious instruction act, would be existentially impossible without the constant suffusion of product contents of every sort. Religious conduct, that supreme outcome of the religious instruction act, is laced through and through with product content. To be sure, the consequences of all religious behaving are product contents. One highly significant and indeed requisite product content inhering in religious conduct is religious knowledge: an adequate grasp of religious thought, of religious phenomena, of the psychology of religion, of the bible, and so forth. Another key product content contained within the parameters of religious conduct is religious experience: adequate experience of God as he encounters the individual in worship, in Christian fellowship, in nature, in prayer, and in all of life.

Product content is significant, not only in itself, but also because it enriches process content and each of the other substantive contents involved in the religous instruction act. In the existential order there could be no process content, no cognitive content, no affective content, no unconscious content, and so forth, without there being in each of these a strong suffusing of product content. Every religious educator is familiar with the learner who complains that the lesson is just "empty experiencing" or "empty thinking" or "empty feeling." What these learners are saying is that experiencing without product content is empty, that thinking without product content is empty, that feeling without product content is empty. Their point is well worth remembering because in the last half of the twentieth century so much emphasis has been placed on process and experiencing that some religion teachers overlook the fact that there is product in every process and that "to experience" is a transitive verb.

THE FORM OF PRODUCT CONTENT

Basic Principles

The form which a specific product content takes is determined at the first level by its dynamic relationship with the substantive content of which it is a constituent, and at the second level by the way in which this substantive content is fused with the structural content in that new mediational entity called religious instruction.[11] Applying this basic principle to religious instruction, we can say that at first level, the product contents of religious instruction such as religious knowledge, religious phenomena, biblics, psychology of religion, history of religion, religious feelings, religious experience, and so forth, are utilized in such a way that they contribute to the creation and enhancement of the substantive content, namely religion. At the second level, this substantive content (religion) with its component contents takes on the form given to it by virtue of its dynamic fusion with structural content (instructional practice) as they are subsumed into that new entity we call the religious instruction act.

It is basically the first level around which I will focus my attention for the remainder of this chapter.

Religion as a Field

The substantive content of religious instruction is religion. Religion is a reality which contains many product contents, such as religious knowledge, biblics, psychology of religion, religious feelings, religious experience, and so on. Therefore, religion per se is not a discipline, because by definition a discipline is the smallest integral, irreducible body of knowledge composed of systematized facts, laws, and theories. Nor is religion a science because a science by definition is that combination of interrelated disciplines which are bundled together in a single, broadly distinctive, common set of systematized interactive facts, laws, and theories.[12] Indeed, both a discipline and a science are exclusively fields of knowledge. Religion, by way of contrast, not only contains knowledge components, but also contains affective and lifestyle components. To be sure, religion is the integration of cognitive, affective, and overt behaviors into a pattern of living, into a lifestyle. Hence religion is far broader than either a discipline or a science. *Religion is a field of personal and/or communal activity.*[13] Religion as a field of activity is brought into being through a mediational subsumption of the dynamic interaction between the product contents which make up religion and the religious experiences of the person and/or community.

As a sidenote, it is well worth recalling that a science or a discipline per se is not committed to any practical end. A science or discipline is committed only to a deeper cognitive exploration and understanding of that sector of reality within its purview. A field of activity, on the other hand, is essentially geared to the attainment of a practical end. Thus, for example, practical theology (a discipline within theological science) is not coextensive with religious practice (a field of activity). Practical theology is the cognitive study of religious practice from the vantage point of theological science. As a field of activity, religion is by its very nature oriented toward a most practical end, namely the forming and deepening of the dynamic, existential synapse between God and man which is called religious living.

Regrettably, many Catholic and Protestant religious educationists have failed to recognize that there are many and varied product contents which are part and parcel of the field of religion. These persons have assumed somewhat uncritically that there is only one product content in religion, namely theology; or what is even worse, some of them have even adopted the theologically imperialistic posture that religion is nothing more than the outering of theology.[14] To be sure, theology frequently, but not always, holds pride of place among all the other cognitive product contents in religion and in religious instruction; but this is far different from the simplistic assertion that theology is all there is to the cognitive product content of religion or religious instruction.[15] In a particular instructional circumstance, it well might be that psychological[16] and sociological[17] data on the causes and manifestations of religious behavior patterns of modern adolescents could prove a far more important cognitive product content in the religion lesson than theological information about the operations of grace in the life of an individual.

By its nature, product content tends to be more closely linked to cognitive content than to either affective content or to lifestyle content. However, it is important to note that both affective content and lifestyle content do contain many important and necessary product contents.

The affective domain contains product contents which are indispensable in religious instruction endeavor. An attitude, for example, is one of the most axial and influential of all affective contents. An attitude significantly influences not only how a person will be disposed to a new stimulus or situation, but also whether or not he will even perceive the very existence and texture of the new stimulus or situation.[18] This psychological fact holds true for persons of virtually every age and condition, making the teaching in and for attitudes central for the religious instruction of preschoolers,[19] of youth[20] and of adults.[21] An attitude, of course, is a process of personally perceiving and orienting. But an attitude is also a product, because the attitude which has been processively formed and which then itself undergoes modification is itself a produce content.

Attitude is part and parcel of religion. There is even a valid (though perforce limited) sense in which religion can be said to be a lived set of attitudes toward God and his creation. Indeed, an individual who lacks a deep and pervasive set of religious attitudes is not likely to lead much of a religious lifestyle. Consequently, attitude in its product as well as in its process dimension is crucial for the preservation and enhancement of the overall substantive content of religious instruction.

Just as a person's affects are composed of process and product contents, so too his lifestyle behaviors consist in a living amalgam of process and product contents. While it is of course true that a person's lifestyle *en marche* is a process content, nonetheless there are vital product contents which go to make up lifestyle content. To be sure, the way in which a person has already lived his life does represent a product content—a product content which not only abides in that individual's self-perception but also a product content which forms the relatively stable base and context out of which he self-integratively engages in present and future lifestyle activities.[22]

Religion, the overall substantive content of religious instruction, is, above all, a lifestyle content. Religion is a way of life. Because product content is indispensable in lifestyle content, it is therefore indispensable for religious instruction endeavor.

Religion is the substantive content of religious instruction. Like all existential, ontological contents, religion has its product and process components. As a substantive content, religion is brought into existence by the mediational activity whereby relevant product contents (religious knowledge, biblics, psychology of religion, attitudes, lifestyle, and so forth) are joined to relevant process contents (experiencing, for example) to form a new entity. Naturally the distinctive tints of both the process contents and the product contents will have an effect on the coloration of the newly-formed substantive content. It is in this way that religion as substantive content can take on a conservative or liberal coloration, an immanentist or transcendist coloration, and so forth. Because the social-science approach is itself value-free, it can accomodate all sorts of product-content colorations. By value-free I do not mean, nor have ever meant, that the substantive content of religious instruction contains no values or does not lean to one value or another.[23] Rather, by value-free I mean that the religious instruction act itself can facilitate learning outcomes toward one system of values more or less as readily as toward a different system of values. The general pedagogical process, the laws of learning, and the laws of teaching remain basically the same regardless of whether the desired learning outcomes are Catholic outcomes, Mainline Protestant outcomes, Evangelical Protestant outcomes, Fundamentalist Protestant outcomes, Jewish outcomes, Shinto outcomes, or whatever. The religious instruction act, precisely because it is a social-science endeavor, can take on as many colorations as there are theologies and religious experiences while still remaining fully potent. The value-free nature of religious instruction as described above is a particularly important feature of the social-science approach, because no macrotheory which purports to explain, predict, verify, and enhance *all* religious phenomena can be theologically, politically, socially, or religiously particularistic. The religious instruction act might assume a variety of religious or theological colorations, but it remains the religious instruction act.

Religion as Experience

Religion is the substantive content of religious instruction. Subsumed into religion is a vast number of product contents including theology. Precisely because of this subsumptional operation, *theology as product content has no place in the religion lesson as pure theology, but rather insofar as theology is logically related to and existentially bonded to religion according to religion's manner of existence in the religious instruction act itself.* Theology, therefore, is not brought into the religion lesson according to the mode of theology, but according to the mode of religion.[24] Put another way, in the religious instruction act, theology is religious instruction's theology and not theology's theology. Since religion is first and foremost an experience, the product content of the religion lesson can be nothing less than experiential in the full human sense of this term.

Though not tightly controlled or systematically researched, the available empirical data would seem to suggest that religion teachers typically regard product content in terms of providing the learners with cognitive theological inputs rather than as facilitating religious experience. On the American Protestant scene, John Westerhoff cogently comments that "conversations with church school teachers reveal that they understand education as primarily imparting information. They believe that children, youth, and sometimes adults need to be told what the Bible says, what occurred in the history of the church, what Christians believe, and what right or wrong behavior is."[25] My own conversations with Catholic religious educators indicate that the vast majority, though by no means all, of Catholic religion teachers have a similar opinion as the subjects in Westerhoff's unscientific sample. A pilot scientific research study of Catholic and Protestant adolescents from sixteen to nineteen years of age in the Frankfurt-Wiesbaden area of the German Federal Republic indicates that these youth perceive that religious instruction is typically conducted in the theological information mode, despite the fact that these youth wish the program to be more life-oriented.[26] My personal visitations to selected religious instruction home/church/school lessons in France, Belgium, Germany, and Austria from 1970 through 1980 revealed that the overwhelming majority of the lessons centered around transmitting theology rather than facilitating religious experience, notwithstanding the fact that several eminent European religious educationists over the years have suggested that a more subjective, personalized element be infused into the lesson.[27] Doubtless one major factor contributing to this state of affairs in both the United States and in Europe is the lack of awareness on the part of many religion teachers of the basic difference between religious instruction and theological instruction.[28] Religious instruction is geared to facilitating desired religious behaviors in the learner whereas theological instruction aims to induce cognitive theological outcomes.[29] Further, one can only wonder whether many religion teachers consciously or unconsciously seek to have the learner behave as a specialist in theology behaves—at a much lower level, of course. The implicit assumption in such cases would appear to be that the learner will go on for increasingly more advanced work in theology, culminating in a major specialization at the university, or at least to a vigorous pursuit of theological knowledge lasting well into old age. But religious instruction does a disservice both to itself and to theological instruction by becoming, or trying to become, something which it is not.

Because of its formal object, it is religious behavior far more than theology per se which acts as the source of vitality for religious instruction. When all is said and done, theology is nothing more than generalized inferences and abstractions derived from an analysis of religious behavior as it was lived by biblical figures, by men of the past, and by persons today.[30] To value religious behavior is not to disvalue theology in the religious instruction act, but rather to make theological abstractions properly subordinate to the concrete revelational realities from which they derive.

The great significance of religious instruction's focus on the facilitation of religious behavior or religious experience is further attested to by many religious counselors and psychotherapists.[31] Though they operate from a different educational vantage point and have somewhat different goals from those of other kinds of religious educators, religious counselors and psychotherapists nonetheless have also discovered the supreme importance of religious experience for the individual. Writing from the dual perspective of a seasoned religious psychotherapist and a recognized spiritual writer, Morton Trippe Kelsey concludes that direct, concrete, personal, intense experience constitutes the most powerful and most meaningful thing which an individual can undergo. Kelsey adds that religious experience constitutes the most personally moving and deeply touching of all forms of human experience. For Kelsey, religious experience enables an individual to make significant breakthroughs in taking hold of reality.[32] From years of clinical practice, Carl Jung concludes that there is a natural and deep-seated need in every person for religious experience; if a person ignores this urge, he will be in danger of losing his psychic health.[33]

Theological product content per se is impotent in directly generating religious outcomes. Theology and religion, after all, are two distinct ontic entities. An ontic entity can directly generate effects only within the sphere of its own actuality. But in the religious instruction enterprise, theology can and should provide *an* important cognitive explanation, interpretation, and meaning for religious experience and religious behavior.

As one of the product contents in the religious instruction act, theology functions at two levels. At the first and lower level, theology can serve to open up for the learner an adequate understanding of theological concepts and truths. At the second level, theology can provide *a* plausible cognitive grounding for religious behavior. Both levels should find fruition in the religion lesson. However, it is at the second level that theology's role in religious instruction is more significant, for it is at this level that theology is the more potentially illuminative of religious experience. Indeed, this is precisely the role which theology has played throughout the entire history of God's dealings with humanity. Fundamentally, the bible is not a theological treatise but rather a selected account of people's religious experience over the centuries. By means of various events and through a series of prophets, God provided his people with a progression of theological concepts which were intended to help the people of those times to bring their own experiences into greater congruence with authentic religious behavior.[34] As Edward Schillebeeckx cogently reminds us, theological truths are always an intellectual, verbal expression of the whole church's experience of faith as this is made continually present from the religious experience of the apostles down through the whole history of the church. Thus, for example, a cognitive dogma is just a formulation, relating to a particular situation, of the mystery of salvation experienced in the church. A cognitive dogma, at bottom, is an intellectual statement about "the church's *actualized experience* of faith."[35]

The test, therefore, of the value of theological product content in a particular religion lesson can be discovered by ascertaining the degree to which this kind of content makes religious behavior or experience more meaningful. From a somewhat different though related perspective the value of theological product content in the religion lesson is determined by the degree to which it meshes with the other contents so that, operating in a complementarily interactive fashion, religious behavior is promoted in the learner. Thus theology in a religion lesson is far more than simply a point of view; it represents a new vision or cognitive perspective for enabling the learner to more meaningfully encounter God in experience.[36] The religion teacher uses theological product content not so much to acquaint the learner with doctrinal facts as to make it possible for him to come to a progressively deeper cognitive *consciousness* of his present and potential religious experience.[37] Just as theological consciousness is significant to the extent to which it facilitates the having of religious experience, so too are doctrinal facts significant to the extent to which they promote enhanced religious consciousness.[38] By being more consciously aware of the fact that in each and every act of his existence he stands in a personal relationship with God through actual ongoing revelational encounter, the learner is in a better position to continually enrich the quality of his religious experience.[39]

If it is to be promotive of a deepening of that kind of theological conscidusness which itself illuminates religious experience, theological content must be of such a character that it is personally *significant* to the learner. By this I mean that the learner must perceive theological product content as an opening toward, or even possibly the answer to basic questions which he himself is asking of life and experience.[40]

If it is to be valid for religious instruction, theological product content must be of the type which enhances personally significant religious consciousness in the learner. It is this type of theological content which most effectively furthers religious experience outcomes in the learner. Theological product content which exists for itself is thus inappropriate for the religion lesson; moreover, this kind of theological content may actually serve as a dampener or even as a deterrent to facilitating religious experience outcomes. Both factual theological knowledge and theological consciousness untargeted to religious experience can easily serve as a wall of defense which prevents the learner from breaking through and touching his own experiences. In every person there is a tendency which motivates him to be his experience as well as a tendency which fears this "being one's experience."[41] Theological product content should play its appropriate role in enabling the learner first to cognitively touch his religious experience and then to become that experience insofar as this is possible for theological product content to accomplish. Otherwise, theological product content will become such that correctness of formula replaces personally significant religious consciousness, and memorization will be held to be the essence of learning.[42]

The experiential or behavioral orientation of theological product content espoused in this section in no way minimizes or demeans the signal significance of the theological product content in the religious instruction act. What this orientation implies is that insofar as religious instruction is concerned, theological product content ought to be targeted toward facilitating a deeper understanding of religious experience on the part of the learner. Now this has important practical ramifications in that it provides a basis for a curricular or instructional decision on which theological product content should be included in the religion lesson and which should be excluded. What the experiential or behavioral orientation clearly suggests is that theological product content should be selected on a psychological basis rather than on a logical basis. By this I mean that theological content should be selected for and inserted into the lesson primarily on the basis of the degree to which it can be incorporated by the learner into his religious lifestyle rather than on the basis of the logical order inherent in the development of theology as a science. For example, the theology of Jesus should be situated in the religion lesson in terms of how the various aspects of this theology are relevant to facilitating the learner's knowing or experiencing Jesus rather than on the basis of the logical discipline of Christology considered in itself. Put another way, the religious instruction act means that theological content is ordered according to how it can be psychologically related by the learner to significant religious knowledge and experience rather than how theological content is ordered to theology as a rational series of the different aspects of theological content, an ordering which results from theological science itself.[43]

Grounding theological product content in its relevance to religious experience or Christian living (psychological basis) rather than in its relevance to the intrinsic nature of theological science (logical basis) not only provides the foundation for decisions concerning which kind of theological content to include in the religion lesson, but also indicates the manner in which this product content is to be placed and arranged.[44] The laws applying to the psychological organization of learning are the laws governing how a person engages in meaningful learning and retention, whereas the laws dealing with the logical organization of learning are derived from the logic of classification intrinsic to theological content itself. Hence the selection and arrangement of theological product content ought to proceed according to the way in which the learner acquires this content in terms of his religious knowledge and experience.

The empirical research on learning strongly indicates that all learning begins with the learner and proceeds according to the psychological structure of the way in which he actually learns. The primacy of the subjective in this regard clearly suggests that the learner is the starting point for any effective religious instruction act. This is true, not only for product content which is factual in nature, but for product content which constitutes significant learning. One social scientist describes significant learning as "more than an accumulation of facts. It is learning which makes a difference—in the individual's behavior, in the course of action he chooses in the future, in his attitudes and in his personality. It is a pervasive learning which is not just an accretion of knowledge, but which interpenetrates every portion of his existence."[45] Significant learning tends to occur when the religion lesson starts with the learner where he is, and when it is perceived by the learner as having relevance to his own purposes. When these two conditions are met, learning takes place very rapidly and is retained. There is some research evidence to suggest that if these two conditions are met, one-third to one-fifth of the present time allotment is sufficient to produce the desired product content outcomes.[46]

To assert that the religion curriculum and the religion lesson must be architected around the way in which the learner learns in no way implies a disvaluation or denigration of product content as a key outcome in religious instruction. Rather, this assertion highlights the fact that in the religious instruction act learning takes place according to the way learning takes place and not according to the way theology or any other product content is structured *in se.*

The psychological versus the logical arrangement of theological product content implies that the religious educator proceed simultaneously along two levels in building his curriculum or lesson. First, he considers how a person does in fact learn theological product content (as contrasted to how theological science is intrinsically ordered according to its own laws of development). Second, he takes into careful account how this theological product content is in fact learned as an opener to or an expander of religious experience (as contrasted to how theological product content serves to enrich the science of theology). The practical consequence of the simultaneous application of these two principles would be to cause a total reordering of a great many religion curricula and lessons around the world. It would also have the effect of rescuing religious instruction from the clutches of the theological approach and bringing it into the precincts of the social-science approach.

At an international convention sponsored by the Religious Education Association, I overheard one Catholic secondary-school religion teacher telling another, "Children don't come to religion class as well-prepared as they do for other subjects." It is safe to assume that this teacher thought of the religion class primarily or even exclusively in terms of imparting theological product content. If this teacher had grounded her class in the facilitation of religious experience and Christian living, then she would not have had any serious problem, since every individual is always prepared for a religious experience which is relevant to him. If, as Jerome Bruner maintains, "the foundations of any [academic] subject may be taught to anybody at any age in some form"[47] then *a fortiori* an individual is always ready for religious experiencing. Religious experiencing is the very stuff of life; one never needs to get prepared or ready for some type of this ever-present mode of human activity. Quite obviously, various kinds of religious experiences can be quickened or blunted by the specific situation in which the learner finds himself, but this is far different from asserting that the learner is not ready for some form or other of religious experiencing. A six-year-old girl might not be ready for that level of religious experience attained by a Zen master or by a Christian mystic; nonetheless she certainly is ipso facto ready for religious experiencing appropriate for her as a particular six-year-old girl coming from her milieu. Indeed, there has been a growing body of psychological thought which holds that the traditional view of readiness as a blanket construct is unnecessary and probably erroneous.[48] Within the broad boundaries of developmental levels of the person, the pedagogical situation in which an individual is placed has been shown by the research to help make the individual ready.[49] This also holds true for moral and religious development.[50] This suggests, among other things, that the religion teacher so structure the learning situation that theological product content plays its appropriate role both in enriching the learner's present religious lifestyle and in fostering in him increasingly higher levels of this lifestyle.

SOME PRACTICAL CONSEQUENCES

Product content is not identical to subject matter. Subject matter content is wider and more comprehensive than product content. Subjective matter content can be equated with substantive content as the latter is considered in its objective aspect. Product content, therefore, is one form of subject matter content. Other forms of subject matter content include process content, affective content, unconscious content, and so on.

The subject matter content of religious instruction is religion, notably religion as it is operationalized in Christian living. The subject matter content of religious instruction is not theology. Theology, as Cornelius Ernst reminds us, is a reflection on the meaning of the event, a cognitive searching of the scriptures, and an intellectual searching of the historical life of the church. The chief task of theology is to search and explore that meaning in and for itself.[51] Religion, on the other hand, is a total way of life engaging the whole person.

If the subject matter content of religious instruction is not identical to theology, neither is it the same as social ethics or group dynamics or the like. The subject matter content of religious instruction contains product contents of *religious* knowledge and *religious* experience so suffused with religious theory and enriched living as to make it quite distinct from social ethics or group dynamics or the like. Because the religious instruction provided in many Christian denominations contains such meager religious product content, many contemporary youth and adults are finding that the content of their experiences in a specifically nonreligious setting has more religious product (and process) content than is the case in the denominational program. Thus, for example, one Christian leader participating in the activities of a group development laboratory at Bethel, Maine, noted his chagrin and humiliation at hearing participants in this nonspecifically religious environment report: "This is the greatest religious experience of my life."[52]

A general pedagogical rule governing the proper way to utilize product content in the religion lesson is this: *The product content must be appropriate to and must further the ends of the subject matter content (substantive content).* Thus, for example, the introduction of theology into the religion lesson is determined by how appropriate this theological product content is to the acquisition of the fundamental subject matter outcome. The following excerpt from the secondary school religion program developed by the Higher Catechetical Institute of Nijmegen (Holland) clearly illustrates a violation of this basic pedagogical rule: "Besides explaining such topics and answering the questions, we should find place every year for a series of classes devoted to the exegesis of some scriptural texts. In this way the students will be confronted with the undiluted wine of God's word and will get some understanding of the methods of exegesis."[53] Product content is not an end in itself, but rather one means through which the achievement of the subject matter is facilitated. Thus theological product content, or any other kind of product content, should not be taught as an end in itself, but as a means to enhance the manner in which the subject matter content is understood, felt, and lived by the learner.

Expanding the Cognitive Dimension of Product Content

Product content has a cognitive dimension, an affective dimension, and a lifestyle dimension. In one important sense, the cognitive dimension of product content is more salient and more pervasive than the affective and lifestyle dimensions of this content.

One of the major constituents of the cognitive dimension of product content is meaning. Meaning is the agreement, significance, or relevance of a particular content to the nature of the product content itself, to the nature of kindred substantive contents, or to the nature of the person or reality in which the meaning resides. Meaning is determined or constructed according to the nature of the particular product content, communication, or system of signs.[54] In terms of religious instruction, "meaning" typically connotes purpose—purpose directed inward toward the learner or outward toward other contents (including fruitful living). When any kind of product content is taught "irrespective of present purpose," then this content becomes meaningless to the learner.[55] Yet the significance of product content is the extent to which it is charged with meaning for the learner.

If the product content of religious instruction is to be meaningful, it must have significance or meaning in relation to: (1) the basic subject-matter content of religious instruction, namely religion; (2) other kindred disciplines, sciences, and fields; (3) the learner's own life.

In terms of the first of these, the product content must be taught so that its intrinsic meaning shines forth. That this is not always perceived as important by teachers in general can be seen by one empirical investigation which discovered that a majority of British grammar-school teachers surveyed thought that their students would gain something from the discipline of studying product content even when they did not understand it.[56] The intrinsic meaning of product content will not shine forth if the teacher places an undue emphasis on factual knowledge, since facts isolated from understanding tend to decay into meaninglessness. Finally, the various ingredients of product content must be taught in such a way that the learners grasp their organic relationship. Gregory Baum's comments are germane here:

> The church's teaching is not a summary of doctrines or a collection of true propositions about the divine; it is, rather, a single witness, through the interrelation of many doctrines, to God's self-communication in Jesus Christ. All the doctrines of the church are therefore interconnected and qualify one another. They do not have a meaning as such, looked upon in isolation from the whole; they derive their meaning from their coherence with the whole and their manner of serving God's self-communication to his people.[57]

The American Catholic Church's document *Sharing the Light of Faith* is rightfully insistent on the necessity of teaching product content in such a way as it relates integrally, not just with doctrinal propositions of various kinds, but with the liturgical, ecclesial, historical, and service activities of Christians.[58]

Unless the religion teacher enhances the cognitive aspect of the product content of religious instruction so that its relationships with other disciplines, sciences, and fields are made manifest, he runs the danger of reducing the product content to irrelevance. The more the religion teacher can structure the learning situation so that the product content is seen in its true living form as relational to other forms of reality, the more relevant will that product content become to the learners. "Relational" has much in common with "relevant."

Finally, the product content of religious instruction must be meaningful to the learner's own life. There is a wealth of empirical research investigations which conclude that a very high correlation exists between the meaningfulness of the learning task and the attainment of the desired learning outcome.[59] Conversely, the acquisition of meaningful material constitutes one of the most powerful factors in augmenting the probability that the individual will integrate the learning outcome into his own life. In this vein, Maria Montessori notes that when people, both children and adults, learn something meaningful, they tend to frequently repeat the learned behavior just for the pleasure of it.[60] Repetition in this case is, of course, a form of positive reinforcement, and positive reinforcement tends to increase the probability that the learned behavior will recur.

An Illustration. A cardinal product content of all religious instruction is God.[61] To be sure, God is a pivotal product content regardless of the setting in which religious instruction is enacted (e.g., home, school, church, recreational area, peer-group situation) and regardless of who the religious educator might happen to be (e.g., parent, school-teacher, clergyman, youth leader, friend).[62]

The religious educator endeavoring to teach God as a product content could center part of his teaching on the *via positiva* and the *via negativa.*

Throughout the history of Christianity, there have been two basic but distinct cognitive ways of acquiring a knowledge and understanding of God, namely the *via positiva* and the *via negativa.*[63]

The *via positiva,* sometimes referred to as the way of perfection or excellence, enables a person to come to a knowledge of God by taking each and every good quality of creatures and affirming this quality to exist in God in a perfect or excellent manner. The *via positiva* is based on the premise that whichever positive attributes one is able to ascribe to creatures can *ipso facto* be ascribed in the very highest and perfect degree to their Creator. Thus, for example, because an individual is just, loving, or wise, then God as the absolute uncreated author of the world and its creatures must therefore be perfectly just, perfectly loving, perfectly wise, and so forth. The *via positiva* tends to be used more frequently by the religious studies specialist, the theologian, the philosopher, and the man-on-the-street than does the *via negativa.*

By contrast, the *via negativa,* sometimes referred to as the way of removal or exclusion, enables a person to come to a knowledge of God by removing or excluding all imperfections which exist in creatures and affirming that the "distilled" good qualities which remain provide a glimpse of the nature of God's attributes. The *via negativa* is based on the premise that God is infinitely more powerful and "other" than his creatures, and hence the only way to come to an adequate, unmarred understanding of God is to remove all the imperfections of creatures so as to come to a glimpse of naked perfection itself. The *via negativa* tends to be used more frequently by the mystic than by the religious studies specialist, the theologian, the philosopher, or the man-in-the-street.

Religious studies specialists, theologians, and philosophers usually suggest that a more full—or perhaps a less inadequate—knowledge of God results when the learner employs both the *via positiva* and the *via negativa* instead of relying on the exclusive use of one or the other. Nevertheless, the nature of God is such that it is especially difficult for the religious educator to teach God to the learner in even a minimally adequate fashion. The major—and some would say the insurmountable—problems in the use of religious knowledge or other kinds of cognitive product content as the avenue to gain an understanding of God is that God is both a transcendent being as well as a being who is immanent in each creature by his presence, a presence which is required for the very existence and development of this creature. God, then, not only is the goal of knowledge; he also suffuses with his being the very knowing process itself. God is not and cannot be an "object" of knowledge, because he is at once the presupposition of this knowledge and infinitely beyond the capabilities of a person's finite intellect. Inasmuch as God is both transcendent as well as totally immanent in the most profound sense (as the very grounding of all creation), an individual cannot know God directly but only by analogy.[64] This means that when all is said and done our knowledge of God is inferential—which is why God's existence and attributes can be only cognitively demonstrated and not cognitively proved. Hence, while a certain limited analogical knowledge *about* God and *about* his perfections is legitimately acquired through the *via positiva,* nonetheless such a knowledge is extraordinarily inadequate because it lacks a basic criterion of adequate knowledge.[65] This criterion is that human knowledge contains and circumscribes, in a cognitive fashion, the object known. But the knowledge of God which we gain analogously from an analysis of the perfections of his creatures neither encloses nor embraces the divine reality, but leaves it uncontained and uncircumscribed. From the epistemological viewpoint, God can indeed be known, but it is the way in which we know him that is the incredibly defective aspect.[66] Jacques Maritain expresses this point with his customary lucidity: "In God what is signified by them [our concepts] breaks loose—we don't know how—from the manner of *conceiving.* The divine essence is known in some fashion—and truly known—but it does not surrender itself; its own mystery remains intact, unpierced. To the very extent to which we know it, it escapes our grasp, infinitely transcends our knowledge. As Thomas Aquinas put it after Augustine and Boethius, 'Whatever form our intellect may conceive, God escapes it through his own sublimity'."[67] God is such that he simply cannot be caught in anyone's conceptual nets.

In view of the foregoing analysis, what can the religious educator do to facilitate in the learner the acquisition of cognitive product content about God? The fundamental operative pedagogical principle which should guide the religious educator in this case is that of structuring the pedagogical variables in such a way that the learner acquires a cognitive analogical experience about God. Even though this kind of learning experience constitutes the ultimate in analogical pedagogy, still such an experience does represent that tiniest bit of cognitive product content—and a little content in this case is about all that can be legitimately sought. This instructional experience should be of such a type that it is as deeply religious as is possible for any cognitive experience to be. This experience, therefore, should not be primarily theological; the learner can reflect on the theological (and other relevant) interpretations of the experience once this experience has occurred. Furthermore, this cognitive analogical experience should be such that it is meaningful to the learners in terms of the learner's here-and-now developmental level. This implies that the cognitive experience will often be significantly different if the learner is a child or an adolescent or an adult, if the learner is socioeconomically disadvantaged or advantaged, and so forth—though there are some cognitive analogies which appeal to learners of all ages and conditions.

The religious educator can tell a story analogy, such as a progressive *via negativa* journey into the furthermost reaches of the soul's increasing darkness to find God. At bottom, a story is primarily a cognitive experience which invites the listeners to vicariously participate in the events narrated in the story.[68] Because a story is a cognitive invitation to a vicarious experience, it tends to be one of the most effective kinds of verbal pedagogical devices.[69]

A straightforward experience-based meaningful cognitive analogy can also prove useful in teaching the learner a product content about God. In this connection I still recall the straightforward experience-based cognitive analogy used by my fifth-grade elementary schoolteacher. This man wished to teach us learners one of the properties customarily attributed to God, namely his eternity. Since no person here on earth has ever experienced eternity, it is manifestly impossible to adequately conceive what eternity is or how it operates. One can only know eternity through the use of analogy. Teaching ten-year-old learners a never-experienced and directly inconceivable concept surely presented the teacher with a formidable pedagogical challenge. The teacher began by asking us to imagine that the school building in which we were then sitting was one solid hard stone. This was quite easy for us children to imagine, because the school was a former castle perched nobly on a hill, a castle which only the year before had been purchased by a religious congregation of brothers for the use as a small boarding school. Then the teacher continued: "Imagine that once every year a single drop of water fell on the school building. When enough drops of water have fallen that the entire solid rock building had been completely eroded, then eternity has just begun."

Expanding the Affective Dimension of Product Content

Though product content seems to enjoy a greater affinity to cognitive content than to either affective content or lifestyle content, nonetheless product content definitely does possess an affective dimension.

One of the major constituents of the affective dimension of product content is attitude. An attitude is an affective, acquired, and relatively permanent disposition or personality-set to respond in a consistent manner toward some physical or mental stimulus.[70] The acquisition of attitudes is one of the most crucial of all product outcomes in religious instruction because an attitude selects and interprets what an individual will learn and how he will learn it.[71] Indeed, perceptive religious educationists and educators are beginning to regard religious attitudes as one of the most important learning outcomes they can consciously and systematically facilitate.[72]

An Illustration. A cardinal product content of religious instruction is faith in God. Though some religious educationists claim that faith in God is experienced by human beings only in a cognitive theological form,[73] other religious educationists contend that faith in God does contain an affective dimension.[74]

In an important book, Erich Fromm distinguishes between faith-as-having and faith-as-being. For Fromm, faith-as-having suggests "the possession of an answer for which one has no rational proof. It consists of formulations created by others—usually a bureaucracy. It carries the feeling of certainty because of the real (or only imagined) power of the bureaucracy. It is the entry ticket to join a large group of people." Faith-as-being, on the other hand, is not so much a belief in certain ideas or in other kinds of cognitive contents, but a whole felt personal orientation, an attitude. Thus it is more accurate to say that a person *is in* faith rather than asserting that one *has* faith. For Fromm, "the God of the Old Testament, is first of all, a negation of idols, of gods whom one can *have*." Faith in God rests on the ability and the actuality of the person to have faith in himself and faith in others. Faith implies certainty, "but certainty based on my own experience and not on my submission to an [external] authority that dictates a certain belief." For Fromm, an individual is in the certainty of faith because of personal experiential, subjective evidence.[75]

If a religious educator takes the position that faith in God involves an affective dimension, then he will naturally wish to teach the learner to have a favorable product attitude toward God.[76] Of the many specific favorable attitudes toward God, trust is one of the most important.[77] Trust possesses the major characteristics of attitude—characteristics summarized in the definition of attitude given near the beginning of this subsection. Trust is not innate or maturational, but is learned from experience and instruction. Trust is comparatively stable, rather than changing from moment to moment. Trust reflects a disposition toward an activity rather than either a verbalization of it or the activity itself. Trust is a more-or-less coherent way in which a person orders data or experience. Trust is selective in that it provides a basis for discriminating between alternative courses of action. Trust is a felt orientation toward others, toward objects, and toward situations. Trust is primarily affective; it is a psychologically organized feeling-tone about a stimulus, together with a preconceived judgment about that stimulus and a prepared reaction toward it.[78]

Over the years social scientists have carefully examined trust from a wide variety of theoretical positions. Particularly fruitful research investigations of trust have been made by social scientists operating out of a psychotherapeutic framework and by social scientists embracing the quite different social-learning perspective.

The neo-Freudian social scientist Erik Erikson has placed great emphasis on what he terms "basic trust." For Erikson, "basic trust is the cornerstone of a healthy personality."[79] Conversely, basic trust is noticeably absent or defective in a neurotic individual.[80] Indeed, Erikson places basic trust as the very first major component of a healthy personality, a component upon which all other stages of the human life cycle are subsequently built. Erikson conceptualizes the "trust" dimension of basic trust as a molar attitude of confident acceptance of oneself and one's environment, an attitude of appreciating the worth and integrity both of oneself and others. Erikson regards the "basic" dimension of basic trust as meaning that "neither this component nor any of those that follow [in the life-cycle maturational process] are, either in childhood or in adulthood, especially conscious. In fact, all the criteria, when developed in childhood and integrated in adulthood, blend into the total personality.'' Basic trust brings with it confidence and initiative. In Erikson's view, if the person fails to develop an attitude of trust in infancy, then the other subsequent progressive stages of his life-cycle maturation will be seriously impaired. Indeed, a person who does not develop a positive attitude of trust in infancy will tend to have an attitude of mistrust in adulthood.[81]

Basic trust is also a pivotal construct in the theory and practice of psychotherapy advocated by Carl Rogers. For Rogers, self-fulfillment necessitates a basic trust or fundamental faith in oneself and especially in the validity of one's own personal experience. This basic trust in oneself is also necessary for healthy and fulfilling relationships with others. In a celebrated passage, Rogers writes: "I can trust my experience. One of the basic things which I was a long time in realizing, and which I am still learning, is that when an activity *feels* as though it is valuable or worth doing, it *is* worth doing. Put another way, I have learned that my total organismic sensing of a situation is more trustworthy than my intellect. All of my professional life, I have been going in directions which others thought were foolish, and about which I have had many doubts myself. But I never regretted moving in directions which 'felt right,' even though I have often felt lonely or foolish at the time. I have found that when I have trusted some inner nonintellectual sensing, I have discovered wisdom on the move.''[82]

Some social-learning theorists have also empirically investigated trust.[83] Whereas psychotherapeutically oriented social scientists conceptualize trust from the viewpoint of healthy personality, social-learning theorists conceptualize trust from the perspective of generalized expectancy.[84] In this view trust may be defined as the generalized expectancy that the cognitive statements, affective assurances, and lifestyle activities of others can be relied upon.[85] To investigate an individual's level of trust, Julian Rotter devised the Rotter Interpersonal Trust Scale which has since become the most widely used standardized instrument for assessing trust.[86] The Rotter Interpersonal Trust Scale describes the trust variable in this way: "This person expects others to be honest. She is not suspicious of others people's intentions, she expects others to be open and that they can be relied upon to do what they say they will do.''[87]

The overall social-scientific investigation and theorizing on trust

obviously has signally important consequences for the religious educator who wishes to teach the learners trust in God as a vital product
content. Basic trust is needed if a person is to adequately *feel* his
proper relationship of complete dependence and utter reliance upon
God. Such a feeling is necessary for the individual to attain a correct
existential position with respect to God. An attitude of basic trust is
required if an individual is to respect and love and rely upon himself in
a proper manner. It is impossible to respect and love and rely on others
without first respecting and loving and relying on one's own self.[88]
This social-scientific observation is clearly consonant with the command of Jesus to love one's neighbor as much as one loves oneself (Mk.
12:31), a comment which implies that the ability to love one's neighbor clearly is contingent upon the ability to love oneself.

Basic trust also seems necessary if a person is to be psychologically
nondefensive, that is to say, open to the experiences and feelings and
ideas of others as well as of himself. As Rogers observes, basic trust
enables an individual to permit his total organism to consider, weigh
and balance each stimulus, need and demand, together with the relative worth and intensity of each.[89] Anent this point, an empirical
research investigation conducted by Sasi Misra and Amar Kalro concluded that persons who lack an attitude of trust exhibited a tendency
to be blind toward the true variability and uniqueness of people and
things. Persons with a trusting attitude tend to display more hetero-
geneity in their judgments of people and things.[90]

Basic trust in oneself and also in others seems essential if one is to
risk being oneself.[91] Theologians and other scholars of religion, especially among the Protestants, observe that risk lies at or near the
essence of faith—the risk involved in the leap of faith, and the risk
involved in both totally being oneself and appropriately opening
oneself to others (and to God). A deep life of faith, a full religious
existence, and a robust encounter with reality, all seem to necessitate
that kind of basic trust which not only tolerates personal risk but which
indeed encourages it.

From the viewpoint of trust-as-expectancy, a trusting attitude seems
definitely helpful for a vigorous faith life and a mature religious life.
The Christian conceptualization of the church as a family with Jesus as
the head and individual Christians as the members can only be successfully operationalized if the individual trusts the family members and
avoids hurting them (sin). Empirical research has shown that trust is

needed in order to develop adequate family relations, to produce proper conduct in children, and to avoid delinquency.[92] One research study found that persons whose parents had different religious affiliations tended to possess lower levels of trust than those who came from homes in which both parents had the same religious affiliation. Commenting on this finding, the investigator remarked that "it seems reasonable that a child subjected to two different kinds of adult interpretations in such an important area as religion would grow up to be more cynical of the verbal communications of authority figures."[93]

The ability to defer immediate worldly pleasures and to endure present suffering in order to gain the later reward of eternal life with God constitutes a major goal of Christian religious instruction. Empirical studies on trust-as-expectancy suggest that individuals who have high levels of trust are also able to more willingly and more meaningfully defer immediate gratification than those persons with lower levels of trust.[94] This finding makes sense. After all, if one cannot trust in the worth of the deferred reward, in the surety that the deferred reward will someday be forthcoming, and in the reliability of the person or group promising the future reward, then obviously one cannot possess either the capacity or the interest to defer gratification until a later time.

In view of the foregoing analysis of trust, what can the religious educator do to facilitate in the learner a product content attitude of trust? The fundamental operative pedagogical principle which should guide the religious educator is that of structuring the pedagogical variables in such a way that the learner acquires the attitude of trust.[95] If the learner is able to develop trust in himself and others as a product outcome, then the necessary groundwork has been laid for him to develop and enhance trust in God. The instructional experience which the religious educator provides should be as personalized and as fraught with productive risk as possible, since a deep attitude of trust involves much personal involvement and considerable risk.

One pedagogical technique[96] which might prove effective in teaching the learner to have or develop trust is the trust fall. In this technique, the religious educator asks the learner to stand up if he is not doing so already. Then the educator asks another person to stand directly behind the learner. The religious educator then tells the learner that at the count of three, the learner will fall backward from the heels.

This pedagogical technique tends to facilitate the development and enhancement of trust because the learner must trust the other person enough to believe that this person will surely catch him when he falls. The trust fall involves the learner personally because he makes an existential commitment of his whole self, body and spirit, to the activity of falling. To be sure, the personal dimensions of the trust fall are magnified because the learner cannot see what the person behind him is doing, whether that person is positioning himself properly for the catch, whether he is idly looking the other way, and so forth. The trust fall involves considerable risk because the learner could suffer considerable bodily injury if he were not caught before hitting the ground.

There are all sorts of variations of the trust fall technique which the religious educator can employ as pedagogically appropriate. For example, the religious educator could devise a developmental trust fall procedure in which the learner first entrusts his fall to a relative or close friend, and then gradually over the weeks entrusts his fall to persons increasingly removed from his affectional circle or personal acquaintance.

If it is true that one's attitude of trust in God is to some degree contingent upon his trust in himself and in others, then the pedagogical technique of trust fall does indeed enjoy a distinct instructional advantage. If the learner cannot trust one who is on earth, then it probably will be difficult for him to place total trust in One who is not so palpably present.

Expanding the Lifestyle Dimension of Product Content

Though product content seems to enjoy a greater affinity to cognitive content than do either affective content or lifestyle content, nonetheless product content definitely does possess a lifestyle dimension.

One of the major constituents of the lifestyle dimension of product content is experience. In this connection, it is important to make the logical distinction between experience as a substantive product content and experience as a substantive process content. As a substantive product content, experience constitutes the totality of what is had in the act of experience. As a substantive process content, experience is the act or dynamic by and through which one encounters reality. This distinction can perhaps be rendered clearer by using the term ''experience'' to denote substantive product experience content and by using the term ''experiencing'' to denote substantive process experience content. This logical distinction points up, from another vantage point,[97] the invalidity of the alleged dichotomy between so-called "content-centered" religious instruction and so-called "experience-centered" religious instruction. In the real order, experience is simultaneously a substantive product content and a substantive process content. Indeed, in the real order, experience is also a substantive content and a structural content. It is only in the conceptual order that a distinction can be legitimately made between experience as a substantive product content and experience as a substantive process content, or between experience as a substantive content and experience as a structural content.

An Illustration. A cardinal product content of religious instruction is the experience of God. To be sure, the personal experience of God is, in my own version of the social-science approach at least, the most important of all substantive product contents. If a person does not have recurring personal experiences of God in one way or another, then he is very likely either not religious or his religious life is shallow and arid. Religion is by its very nature the existential communion which a person has with and in God. Religion above all is a certain shared experience which takes place between God and the individual human being.[98]

The preeminent dilemma which has confronted institutional churches and individual religious educators down through the centuries is this: how can a human being have an experience of God when by definition God is absolutely transcendent? If God is God, then he is totally transcendent and hence not amenable to being experienced by human beings. If a human being could experience God, then God's transcendence would thereby be automatically destroyed. Transcendence, after all, means something or someone wholly other, wholly outside of whatever can be presented in human experience. If God is indeed transcendent, then perforce he is a God unexperienced by humans.

Many churches and scholars of religion have endeavored to extricate themselves from this dilemma by noting that while God is indeed transcedent, he is also immanent. Ian Knox skillfully summarizes the immanentist dimension of God when he states that creation and the incarnation are simultaneously a once and ongoing activity of God, and that every reality which a person experiences is to one degree or another a revelatory outpouring or enfleshment of God.[99] Religious educationists emphasize that God's immanence is the only way in which his transcendence can be preserved. Immanence thus makes it possible for a person to have an experience of God. This experience must be veiled (1 Cor. 13:12) and very indirect (Ex. 33:20), but still it is a religious experience as full as a person in the human condition can bear.

The immanentist dimension of God thus makes it possible for the religion teacher to directly facilitate a pedagogical situation which will be conducive to an experience of God on the part of the learner. Donald Gray's observation about God's immanence in all reality as related to one's personal experience of God is quite useful to the religion teacher. Gray notes that while God is indeed omnipresent, he is present to a person primarily through that person's experience in the world, in the church, and for some Christians, in the sacraments.[100] Following this principle, a religion teacher helps rather than hinders the facilitation of an experience of God when he structures the pedagogical situation in such a way that the learner encounters any and all reality in as experiential a manner as possible. (Somewhat akin to this point is the empirically verified fact that belief in a loving, accepting God is most likely to occur in an atmosphere in which persons themselves receive acceptance and love in a fully experiential fashion.)[101] All other things being equal, the more God-filled is the reality which the learner encounters, the greater will be the probability that he will have a religious experience as a product content outcome of that encounter. Thus, for example, a sacramental encounter is more likely to facilitate a religious experience in a learner than walking home—all other things being equal, which often is not the case. In the final analysis, of course, it is the learner's here-and-now existential readiness at a particular moment in a particular situation which enables him to experience the ever-present immanent God. Hence, a learner whose marriage is floundering might have no religious experience during Sunday morning worship service but have an intense encounter with God as he watches the sun slowly set over the rolling surf on Sunday evening.

In light of the foregoing analysis of religious experience, what can the religious educator do to facilitate religious experience as a product content? The fundamental operative pedagogical principle which should guide the religious educator is that of structuring the pedagogical variables in such a way that the learner comes to an experience of or with God as the divine presents himself in one or another of his manifestations. The instructional activity which the religious educator provides should be as fully experiential as possible. Furthermore, this instructional activity should be freighted with as much religious content as possible—religious not just in the objective sense of this term but far more importantly in the subjective sense of religion as a personal encounter with God how and where the learner in his present existential developmental moment can enter into such an encounter. Unfortunately many religious educators regard the facilitation of religious experience by the religious educator as either impossible or as destructively manipulative.[102] Such views are incorrect and inaccurate. Many church groups have carefully and successfully structured liturgies, retreats, revival meetings, and the like for the express purpose of facilitating religious experience with God. This type of instructional activity is generally highly beneficial, and not destructive or wrongly manipulative. Furthermore, expertly conducted social-scientific research experiments have been able to facilitate mystical experiences.[103] In the narcomedical and narcopsychological fields, certain kinds of drugs taken by members of so-called "primitive religions," by some groups of Oriental and Latin American natives, and by affluent Occidentals seeking altered states of consciousness have also been successful in facilitating religious experience, regardless of how one judges the worthwhileness of this kind of facilitation or this kind of religious experience.

To enhance the probability of successfully facilitating religious experience, the religion lesson should be taught as a present, living experience rather than as a preparation for future religious experiences. If the religion lesson is not a living religious experience, then it quite obviously is a dead, areligious nonexperience. Furthermore, rich sensory experiences should be utilized, as appropriate, during the religion lesson. As I have written elsewhere[104] "inspired writers like the author of the Canticle of Canticles, and great mystics such as Bernard of Clairvaux saw the necessity of . . . rich sensory experiences as a powerful and indispensable means not only in attaining knowledge but in attaining God."

Liturgically based or liturgically integrated lessons offer the religious educator manifold opportunities for facilitating religious experience. In this connection let me recount a pedagogical incident in which I attempted to facilitate a noninstitutionally anchored and nonenculturated type of Eucharistic experience in a group of doctoral students I was then teaching in the Notre Dame graduate religious education program.[105] This incident took place in the very early 1970s.[106] There were about twelve students in this class. These men and women were quite intelligent, came from diverse national and confessional backgrounds, and varied in their position on a continuum of religious conservatism-liberalism. The students and I jointly devised a structured learning situation which we tentatively predicted would afford us all a personal religious experience which would be meshed in the lesson with desired cognitive and attitudinal outcomes. We decided to hold one of our classes in a modest local restaurant, and to have a Roman Catholic Mass in the restaurant as part of the lesson. The group agreed. At a pedagogically propitious moment in the restaurant setting, as we were all sitting around a regular dining table, the lesson was switched to the divine liturgy. One of the doctoral students, a priest from The Netherlands, then said a Mass of his own construction right on the dining table, using the regular restaurant whole-wheat bread for the host and the table wine as well. After the Mass we had dinner and then reflected, refelt, and reexperienced what had taken place at the restaurant liturgy. All the students indicated that the restaurant lesson/Mass did indeed facilitate a religious experience of some kind. In almost all of the students, this religious experience was more-or-less of the type I had intended, namely one not anchored to ''normal'' institutional forms and not situated in the accustomed cultural milieu. For me as the teacher/learner, the religious experience was particularly profound because at that restaurant liturgy I encountered Jesus in the form of a plain, stale, restaurant brown bread and not in the form of a round fresh white host. This experience revealed to me how institutionally and culturally conditioned my own religion was with respect to the Eucharist—a particularly moving and self-disclosing experience for me since I had been an outspoken and regionally leading advocate of so-called ''radical'' liturgical reform in the late 1950s and early 1960s. (Indeed, I had been formally censored by the religious authorities in the New England Catholic college in which I was teaching in the late 1950s and early 1960s.) Little did I realize, feel, or experience myself as an institutionally anchored and culturally conditioned Catholic vis-à-vis the Eucharist until that restaurant Mass. At the opposite end of the spectrum, a conservative religious brother from another country was also experientially moved by the restaurant lesson/Mass, but in a very different way than I was. This fine man, who is now one of his country's leading religious educationists, experienced personal religious revulsion at the restaurant liturgy. The restaurant Mass confirmed him in his own convictions and feelings and experience that the Eucharist is experienced authentically and religiously, for him at least, in the regular church setting with the "normal" institutionally prescribed liturgical paraphernelia. This religious brother, the other learners, and myself each had our separate religious experiences in terms of where we were developmentally at the existential moment in which the restaurant Mass took place in our lives.[107]

To end this short section on expanding the lifestyle dimension of product content, I would like to again emphasize the point that religious experience of God in any of his manifestations is a bona fide product content; it is not merely an instructional avenue to be traveled on the way to a product content (usually regarded as some form of cognitive theological content). Any attempt to restrict the comprehensiveness of product content to religious knowledge, and a fortiori to theological knowledge, is as myopic as it is invalid. Indeed, religious experience is typically a more fruitful product content than is religious knowledge. Through religious knowledge, the religion teacher can only teach about God, whereas through religious experience he can teach God. Nonetheless, as a practicing social scientist, the religion teacher should facilitate these two product contents not so much on the basis of their intrinsic worth as on the extent to which each of these contents furthers the behavioral goals of the lesson or the curriculum. For some learners at their present developmental level, the path to God lies primarily through the intellect, with relatively little affective influence. For others, God is most fruitfully met through affect. For still others, the encounter with God best takes place in here-and-now experience, with the intellect and affect playing a supporting role. For each person, God is sought and found according to his personality type, developmental level, and the environment in which he finds himself. Starting with the learner where he is, the effective religion teacher deliberatively structures the learning experience in such a way as to help the learner find God in a manner best suited to that particular learner.

CONCLUSION

Product content is a vital and indeed an indispensable part of the overall substantive content of any religion lesson, whether that lesson takes place in a formal or an informal setting. There is no lesson which is totally devoid of product content. Indeed, product content is always present throughout the religion lesson, as are all the other contents which go to form the overall substantive content. For religious instruction, therefore, the basic issue is not product content versus some other type of content. Rather, the issue is to successfully devise and enact that kind of product content which is most productive of Christian living.

While product content is vital and indispensable, the other constituent forms of substantive content are also of crucial worth. Any religious instruction program which attempts to focus exclusively on product content will produce a learner who is just that—a product.

NOTES

1. Fulke Grenville, Lord Brooke, *Chorus Sacerdotum.*
2. See my treatment of product and process contents in James Michael Lee, "The Thrust of the Three Strategies in Religious Education," in *Today's Catholic Teacher,* n.v. (October, 1969), pp. 14–19.
3. James Michael Lee and Nathaniel J. Pallone, *Guidance and Counseling in Schools: Foundations and Processes* (New York: McGraw-Hill 1966), p. 130.
4. Gilbert Ryle, *The Concept of Mind* (London: Hutchinson, 1949), pp. 149–153. With respect to the last sentence in the body of the text in which this footnote appears, Aristotle notes that the product content of happiness is acquired only at the termination of the process of a completed life. See Aristotle, *Ethics,* I.9.
5. *Ibid.,* pp. 27–32.
6. While this is common sense, nonetheless it seems too sophisticated a concept for some religious educationists and educators to grasp. These well-meaning individuals insist that this fusion is done according to the mode of product content. For a representative example of this view, see Christian P. Ceroke, "Training Religious Education Teachers: An Interview," edited by Carl Balcerak and Cherry Wyman, in *Momentum: Journal of the National Catholic Educational Association* IV (February 1973), p. 24.
7. On this point, see James Michael Lee, "The Authentic Source of Religious Instruction," in Norma H. Thompson, editor, *Religious Education and Theology* (Birmingham, Ala.: Religious Education Press, 1982).
8. Process and product content are discussed a bit, though not too much *in se,* in the general education literature. Even here there is no clear agreement on the terms and thrust. Thus Nathaniel Gage uses process content to equal teacher behaviors and product content to equal those consequent learner behaviors which have been produced by the teacher's antecedent instructional practice. Barak Rosenshine and Norma Furst refer to process and product much in the way Gage does. Cecil Parker and Louis Rubin treat of product and process content almost exclusively from the vantage point of the learner. These conceptualizations, while accurate, are nonetheless incomplete. See N. L. Gage, *The Scientific Basis of the Art of Teaching* (New York: Teachers College Press, 1978), pp. 69–94; Barak Rosenshine and Norma Furst, "Research on Teacher Performance Criteria," in B.

Othanel Smith, editor, *Research in Teacher Education* (Englewood Cliffs, N.J.: Prentice-Hall, 1971), pp. 42–66; also J. Cecil Parker and Louis J. Rubin, *Process as Content* (Chicago: Rand McNally, 1966).

9. George Albert Coe, "The Administration of Religious Education in a Parish," in *Religious Education* X (June, 1915), pp. 277–279.

10. James Michael Lee, "The Teaching of Religion," in James Michael Lee and Patrick C. Rooney, editors, *Toward a Future for Religious Education* (Dayton, Ohio: Pflaum/Standard, 1970), p. 76. I have substituted the words "religious instruction" for "catechetical" in the original text.

11. For a treatment of religious instruction as a subsumptional mediator, see James Michael Lee, "The Authentic Source of Religious Instruction," pp. 165–172.

12. For these definitions, and an expansion of them as they pertain to religious instruction, see James Michael Lee, *The Shape of Religious Instruction,* (Birmingham, Ala.: Religious Education Press, 1971), pp. 94–100.

13. Because it is a field of activity, it can be studied scientifically; in this sense there can be the *intellectual* field of religious studies.

14. Berard Marthaler claims that faith can only be experienced as theology. This claim is, of course, as theologically imperialistic as it is absurd. At the time he made this astounding claim, Marthaler was a highly placed official in the academic apparatus of the Central Cathechetical Establishment. See Berard L. Marthaler, "Socialization as a Model for Catechetics," in Padraic O'Hare, editor, *Foundations of Religious Education* (New York: Paulist, 1978), p. 75.

15. For a clear, uncompromising equating of theology with all cognitive product, see Roger Lincoln Shinn, *The Educational Mission of Our Church.* (Boston: United Church Press, 1962), p. 39.

16. V. Bailey Gillespie, *Religious Conversion and Personal Identity* (Birmingham, Ala.: Religious Education Press, 1979), pp. 44–123.

17. Letty M. Russell, "Handing on Traditions and Changing the World," in Padraic O'Hare, editor, *Tradition and Transformation in Religious Education* (Birmingham, Ala.: Religious Education Press, 1979), pp. 73–86.

18. Robert B. Cialdini, Richard E. Petty, and John T. Cacioppo, "Attitude and Attitude Change," in Mark R. Rosenzweig and Lyman W. Porter, editors, *Annual Review of Psychology,* volume 32 (Palo Alto, Calif.: Annual Reviews, 1981), pp. 357–404; Kenneth H. Andrews and Denise B. Kandel, "Attitude and Behavior: A Specification of the Contingent Consistency Hypothesis," in *American Sociological Review* XLIV (April, 1979), pp. 298–310; Norman Kirby, "Learning to Care," in *Childhood Education* LIII (November–December, 1976), pp. 59–65; Bernard Berelson and Gary A. Steiner, *Human Behavior: An Inventory of Scientific Findings* (New York: Harcourt, Brace, and World, 1964), pp. 557–585.

19. Lucie W. Barber, *The Religious Education of Preschool Children* (Birmingham, Ala.: Religious Education Press, 1981), pp. 17–24.

20. Robert E. Poerschke, "Adolescents in the Family and Subculture." in G. Temp Sparkman, editor, *Knowing and Helping Youth* (Nashville, Tenn.: Broadman, 1977), pp. 31–42; Edward A. Wynne, "Adolescent Alienation, the Catholic Family and Catholic School Policy," in Berard L. Marthaler and Marianne Sawicki, editors, *Catechesis, Realities and Visions: A Symposium on the Catechesis of Children and Youth* (no place, no publisher, no date), pp. 39–48.

21. David O. Moberg, "The Nature and Needs of Older Adults," in Roy B. Zuck and Gene A. Getz, editors, *Adult Education in the Church* (Chicago: Moody, 1970), pp. 56–72.

22. Morton Kelsey, *Can Christians be Educated?* (Birmingham, Ala.: Religious Education Press, 1977), pp. 7–22.

23. Richard McBrien's simplistic and sloganeering type of analysis fails to grasp this point, as I duly note in James Michael Lee, "The Authentic Source of Relgious Instruction," pp. 132–133. See Richard P. McBrien, "Toward an American Catechesis," in *Living Light* XIII (Summer, 1976), p. 174.

24. For a further discussion of this point, see James Michael Lee, "The Authentic Source of Religious Instruction," p.172.

25. John H. Westerhoff III, *Values for Tomorrow's Children* (Philadelphia: Pilgrim, 1970), p. 25.

26. See Karl Ernst Nipkow, "Beyond the Bible in Religious Education," in Alois Müller, editor, *Catechetics for the Future* (New York: Herder and Herder, 1970), pp. 46–47.

27. See Herman Lombaerts, "Reciprocal Relationships Between Moral Commitment and Faith Profession in Worship," in Christiane Brusselmans and James A. O'Donohoe, editors, *Toward Moral and Religious Maturity* (Morristown, N.J.: Silver Burdett, 1980), pp. 252–275; see also Alfonso M. Nebreda, "Living Faith: Major Concern of Religious Education," in Johannes Hofinger and Theodore C. Stone, editors, *Pastoral Catechetics* (New York: Herder and Herder, 1964), pp. 136–137.

28. See, for example, Matthew J. Hayes, "How Much Theology Should Coordinators and DRE's Know?" in *Living Light* XIV (Fall, 1977), pp. 360–365.

29. See James Michael Lee, *The Flow of Religious Instruction* (Dayton, Ohio: Pflaum/Standard, 1973), pp. 14–27.

30. See, for example, Helmut Thielicke, *The Evangelical Faith*, volume II, translated and edited by Geoffrey W. Bromiley (Grand Rapids, Mich.: Eerdmans, 1977), p. 3; Bernard J. F. Lonergan, *Method in Theology* (New York: Herder and Herder, 1972), p. 144; Paul Tillich, *Systematic Theology*, volume I (Chicago: University of Chicago Press, 1951), p. 28.

31. See, for example, Morton Kelsey, *Can Christians Be Educated?* (Birmingham, Ala.: Religious Education Press, 1977).

32. Morton Kelsey, *Encounter with God: A Theology of Christian Experience* (Minneapolis: Bethany Fellowship Press, 1972), pp. 10, 162–170.

33. Carl G. Jung, *Psychology and Religion* (New Haven, Conn.: Yale University Press, 1938).

34. The bible, of course, tells us that God: (1) typically used events and other experiences from which theological concepts could be deduced, and (2) used events and experiences more for religious purposes than for theological deployment.

35. Edward Schillebeeckx, *Revelation and Theology*, volume II, translated by N. D. Smith (New York: Sheed and Ward, 1968), pp. 24–25. Italics mine.

36. Compare this with Rudolf Bultmann, *Jesus and the Word*, translated by Louise Pettibone Smith and Erminie Huntress Lantero (New York: Scribner's, 1934), p. 15.

37. On this point, see Morton T. Kelsey, *The Other Side of Silence* (New York: Paulist, 1976), pp. 125–184.

38. In the view of cognitivist liberationist religious education writers like Thomas Groome, this progressively deeper cognitive consciousness is necessary for a person to achieve liberation from oppressive forces of divers sorts. Thomas H. Groome, *Christian Religious Education* (San Francisco: Harper & Row, 1980), pp. 121–126, 184–188.

39. The Higher Institute of Catechetics of Nijmegen, *Fundamentals and Programs of a New Catechesis,* revised by Henry J. Koren, translated by Walter Van de Putte (Pittsburgh: Duquesne University Press, 1966), pp. 129–132.
40. While I conceptualize significance as providing both openings and answers, Hubert Halbfas regards significance exclusively in terms of providing answers. This divergence in viewpoint is possibly due to the difference between the American and German mentalities. See Hubert Halbfas, *Theory of Catechetics* (New York: Herder and Herder, 1971), p. 106.
41. This sentence is a metaphorical expression of a truth, and should not be construed as a careful description of motivation theory or drive theory. These hotly debated psychological theories are quite complicated and are outside the purview of my treatment here. More appropriate to my thesis are Matthew Fox, *On Becoming a Musical Mystical Bear* (New York: Paulist Deus, 1976), pp. 75–95; Gregory Baum, *Man Becoming: God in Secular Experience* (New York: Herder and Herder, 1970), pp. 43–45; and Carl R. Rogers, *On Becoming a Person* (Boston: Houghton Mifflin, 1961), pp. 103–106.
42. Thomas O'Dea contends that more often than not this was the state of affairs in much of American Catholic schooling until, at least, the late 1950s. See Thomas F. O'Dea, *American Catholic Dilemma: An Inquiry Into the Intellectual Life* (New York: Sheed and Ward, 1958), p. 110; see also James Michael Lee, "Professional Criticism of Catholic High Schools," in the *Catholic World* CIII (October, 1961), pp. 7–12. This unfortunate situation had largely changed by the onset of the 1980s.
43. On this last point, see Jean Le Du, "Language Problems and Catechetics," translated by Lancelot Sheppard, in Alois Müller, editor, *Catechetics for the Future,* pp. 64–66. Le Du calls the psychological ordering of content the "logic of relation" and the logical ordering of content the "logic of content."
44. For a further discussion of this point, see James Michael Lee, "The Authentic Source of Religious Instruction," pp. 100–197.
45. Carl R. Rogers, "Significant Learning: In Therapy and In Education," in *Educational Leadership* XVI (January, 1959), p. 232.
46. See Carl R. Rogers, "The Facilitation of Significant Learning," in Laurence Siegel, editor, *Instruction: Some Contemporary Viewpoints,* (San Francisco: Chandler, 1967), p. 42.
47. Jerome S. Bruner, *The Process of Education* (Cambridge, Mass.: Harvard University Press, 1960), p. 12.
48. An important salvo in the readiness controversy was fired in Fred T. Tyler, "Issues Related to Readiness to Learn," in the National Society for the Study of Education, *Theories of Learning and Instruction,* Sixty-third Yearbook (Chicago: University of Chicago Press, 1964), pp. 210–239.
49. For a review of the pertinent research, see James Michael Lee, *The Flow of Religious Instruction,* pp. 65–73, 79–89. For a short but comprehensive review of the research as it applies to infancy development, see Lucie W. Barber, "The Infancy Design in Relation to Other Infancy Research: A Search of the Literature," in *Character Potential* V (February, 1971), pp. 107–111. On this point, see also Lucie W. Barber, *The Religious Education of Preschool Children* (Birmingham, Ala.: Religious Education Press, 1981), pp. 5–12; Lucie W. Barber, *Celebrating the Second Year of Life* (Birmingham, Ala.: Religious Education Press, 1978), pp. 1–17.
50. James Michael Lee, *The Flow of Religious Instruction,* pp. 119–141. The experiments of Lawrence Kohlberg, B. F. Skinner, and the behavioral modifica-

tion psychologists are particularly germane to this point. See also Linda Rosenzweig, "Kohlberg in the Classroom: Moral Education Models," in Brenda Munsey, editor, *Moral Development, Moral Education, and Kohlberg* (Birmingham, Ala.: Religious Education Press, 1980), pp. 359–380; Charles Bailey, "The Notion of Development and Moral Education," in Donald B. Cochrane, Cornel M. Hamm, and Anastasios C. Kazepides, editors, *The Domain of Moral Education* (New York: Paulist, 1979), pp. 205–219.

51. Cornelius Ernst, "Introduction," in Karl Rahner, *Theological Investigations,* volume I, 2d edition, translated by Cornelius Ernst (New York: Herder and Herder, 1965), p. vii.

52. Theodore O. Wedel, "Group Dynamics and the Church," in *Theology Today* X (January, 1954), p. 513.

53. The Higher Institute of Catechetics of Nijmegen, *Fundamentals and Programs of a New Catechesis,* p. 298.

54. This conceptualization of "meaning" is intended to be a working one rather than an encapsulation of the enormous amount of scholarship and controversy on the subject.

55. See John Dewey, *Democracy and Education* (New York: Macmillan, 1916), p. 233.

56. Frances M. Stevens, *The Living Tradition* (London: Hutchinson, 1960).

57. Gregory Baum, *Man Becoming: God in Secular Experience,* pp. 166–167.

58. National Conference of Catholic Bishops, *Sharing the Light of Faith* (Washington, D.C.: The Conference, 1979), pp. 18–21 (#s 32–37).

59. For a review of some of the relevant research in this regard, see James Michael Lee, *The Flow of Religious Instruction,* pp. 75–79.

60. Maria Montessori, *The Montessori Method,* translated by Anne E. George (Cambridge, Mass.: Bentley, 1965), pp. 357–358.

61. In making this statement I am not taking a position for or against process theology. Rather I am simply taking God—one's knowledge of him, one's affects toward him, and one's lifestyle participation in him—as a pivotal product content in all religious instruction.

62. In the following pages of this chapter, I interweave a great deal of my own religious and theological concepts in treating God as a product content; to be sure, I do this to a certain extent throughout all the volumes of my trilogy, as Ian Knox has skillfully shown. Other religious educationists and educators can be equally strong advocates of the social-science approach even though they adopt a religious or theological stance somewhat or even greatly at variance with my own. Indeed, one of the wellsprings of the seemingly inexhaustible richness and applicability of the social-science approach to religious instruction is that it can include myriad kinds of substantive contents and religious contents and theological product contents while still remaining true, authentic, and fruitful participants in the social-science approach. Persons like Françoise Darcy-Bérubé who advocate their own special brand of theology as the only one which can serve as wellspring and ultimate explanation of religious instruction endeavor are as incapable of understanding the theological neutrality of the social-science approach as they are of devising a macrotheory which can apply validly to all religious instruction including those forms whose theological product contents are at variance with their own. See Ian P. Knox, *Above or Within?: The Supernatural in Religious Education* (Birmingham, Ala.: Religious Education Press, 1976); Françoise Darcy-Bérubé, "The Challenge Ahead of Us," in Padraic O'Hare, editor, *Foundations of Religious Education,* pp. 115–119.

63. Adolphe Tanquerey claims that there is yet a third way, namely the way of causality. This posited way suggests that the very encounter which an individual has with creation itself yields a knowledge of God (See Romans 1:19–20). However, it would appear that this posited way is really an aspect of the *via positiva* and the *via negativa*, especially if one extends both of these *viae* from simply the ratiocinational mode of knowing to the intuitional and the experiential modes as well.

64. Thus Karl Rahner writes that "we can speak about transcendental experience only by means of what is secondary to it." (p. 71). For Rahner, our analogical knowledge of God is "the tension between the categorical starting point and the incomprehensibility of the holy mystery, namely, God" (p. 73). Karl Rahner, *Foundations of Christian Faith,* translated by William V. Dych (New York: Seabury, 1978).

65. Thomas Aquinas holds this position. See his *Summa Theologica,* I, qq. 12–13. For other illuminating views on this subject, see Gordon D. Kaufman, *God the Problem* (Cambridge, Mass.: Harvard University Press, 1972), pp. 41–71; Frederick Ferré, *Language, Logic and God* (New York: Harper & Row, 1961), pp. 105–120; John Baillie, *Our Knowledge of God* (New York: Scribner's 1939), pp. 155–177.

66. For a helpful examination of this point, see Helmut Thielicke, *The Evangelical Faith,* pp. 94–100.

67. Jacques Maritain, *Man's Approach to God* (Latrobe, Pa.: Archabbey Press, 1960), p. 33.

68. See John Shea, *Stories of God* (Chicago: Thomas More, 1978); Sallie McFague TeSelle, *Speaking in Parables* (Philadelphia: Fortress, 1975).

69. Michael Benton, "Children's Response to Stories," in *Children's Literature in Education* X (Summer, 1979), pp. 68–85; Brian Sutton-Smith, Gilbert Botvin, and Daniel Mahoney, "Developmental Structures in Fantasy Narratives," in *Human Development* XIX (January, 1976), pp. 1–13; Brian Sutton-Smith, "Importance of the Storytaker: An Investigation of the Imaginative Life," in *Urban Review* VIII (Summer, 1975), pp. 82–95.

70. This definition is patterned after what probably is the most influential definition of attitude, namely that devised by Gordon Allport. See Gordon W. Allport, "Attitudes," in Carl A. Murchison, editor, *Handbook of Social Psychology* (Worcester, Mass.: Clark University Press, 1935), p. 806.

71. James Michael Lee, *The Flow of Religious Instruction* (Birmingham, Ala.: Religious Education Press, 1973), p. 107; Alice H. Eagly and Samuel Himmelfarb, "Attitudes and Opinions," in Mark R. Rosenzweig and Lyman W. Porter, editors, *Annual Review of Psychology,* volume XIX (Palo Alto, Calif.: Annual Reviews, 1978), pp. 517–554.

72. Lucie Barber is among the contemporary leaders with respect to the advocacy of attitudinal learning as central in religious instruction. See Lucie W. Barber, *The Religious Education of Preschool Children* (Birmingham, Ala.: Religious Education Press, 1981), pp. 17–24; Lucie W. Barber, *Celebrating the Second Year of Life: A Parent's Guide for a Happy Child* (Birmingham, Ala.: Religious Education Press, 1978), pp. 3–4.

73. Berard Marthaler takes this position. See Berard L. Marthaler, "Socialization as a Model for Catechetics," in Padraic O'Hare, editor, *Foundations of Religious Education,* p. 75.

74. See, for example, Thomas H. Groome, *Christian Religious Education,* pp. 61–63, 75. Groome's proper advocacy of the affective dimension of faith, however,

is seriously flawed because he assumes rather than proves or demonstrates his claim. For example, he simply assumes the characteristics of affectivity rather than proceeding in the manner typically favored by scholars, namely that of adducing empirically proven characteristics of that empirical phenomenon called affectivity and then showing how faith possesses these characteristics. Furthermore, Groome waffles throughout his book on whether the core of faith is cognition, affect, or conduct. Despite his outward denials, Groome's deliberate appropriation of a cognitively based model of faith (Piaget/Kohlberg/Fowler), his expressed preference for the highly cognitive system of David Ausubel, and his decidedly cognitive method of shared-praxis instruction all seem to suggest that Groome *de facto* regards the essence of faith as cognitive. Such a position, of course, is a venerable one with strong and abiding roots in the history of Catholic theology. It should be emphasized, however, that the cognitive core of faith which Groome seems to *de facto* espouse is active and liberating rather than static and oppressive.

75. Erich Fromm, *To Have or To Be?* (New York: Harper & Row, 1976), pp. 41–44. Two additional points are in order here. First of all, Fromm distinguishes between faith and love as two distinct ways of personal orientation. I mention this to underscore a point I make near the beginning of my lengthy article "The Authentic Source of Religious Instruction," namely that religion is not identical to faith and that faith is of a different order of reality than love. Second, Fromm's reference to the bureaucracy as a major cause for undermining genuine faith underscores, albeit from a different perspective, another point I develop in "The Authentic Source of Religious Instruction." I am referring here to my distinction between the *ecclesia* and the *ecclesiasticum*. The *ecclesia* is a generalized community of Christian persons in which the individual thinks through and feels and operationalizes his faith and hope and love, while the *ecclesiasticum* is the bureaucracy which properly provides important and significant and pivotal guidelines for a Christian's faithful life in faith and in hope and in love. The *ecclesiasticum* is a political network and apparatus. This conception of the nature and function of the *ecclesiasticum* is, of course, quite at odds with that of Berard Marthaler and many other functionaries operating within the executive and academic wings of the Central Catechetical Establishment. See James Michael Lee, "The Authentic Source of Religious Instruction," in Norma H. Thompson, editor, *Religious Education and Theology*, p. 191.

76. Jeffrey Keefe, "The Learning of Attitudes and Values," in James Michael Lee and Patrick C. Rooney, editors, *Toward a Future for Religious Education* (Dayton, Ohio: Pflaum, 1970), pp. 30–54.

77. Many Christian theologians, notably among the Protestants but also among some perceptive Catholics, conceptualize trust as occupying a central place in the galaxy of faith. See, for example, Hans Küng, *On Being A Christian,* translated by Edward Quinn (Garden City, N.Y.: Doubleday, 1976), pp. 73–79; David Tracy, *Blessed Rage for Order* (New York: Seabury, 1975), pp. 134–135; Dietrich Bonhoeffer, *Letters and Papers From Prison,* third edition, edited by Eberhard Bethge, translated by Reginald Fuller (New York: Macmillan, 1967); Paul Tillich, *The Courage To Be* (New Haven, Conn.: Yale University Press, 1952), pp. 160–190; Søren Kierkegaard, *Concluding Unscientific Postscript,* translated by David F. Swenson (Princeton, N.J.: Princeton University Press, 1941), pp. 185–188.

78. In Chapter Five, I discuss at some length the various social-scientific conceptualizations and empirical research studies on attitude.

79. By healthy personality Erikson means an individual who actively masters his environment and is able to perceive the world and himself correctly.
80. Anent this point, it seems that religious bureaucracies have the innate tendency to become neurotic and to cause its leading functionaries to become tainted with neuroticism as well. After all, one of the first laws of a typical religious bureaucracy is to close itself in and to prevent persons or individuals who disagree with it from entering the bureaucracy or influencing it in any significant way. In short, religious bureaucracies almost inevitably move to a position of basic mistrust, a position which renders impossible the actualization of a healthy and open institutional organism. The Central Catechetical Establishment in its executive and academic wings, together with its official organ *Living Light,* exemplifies a bureaucracy where basic self-trust seems woefully lacking. Thus, the Central Catechetical Establishment almost never sponsors nonclergy to represent it at official Vatican gatherings, almost never employs leadership persons with basically differing though complementary religious views (e.g., Protestants, liberal Catholics), and only very seldom invites to its official conferences scholars or practitioners holding views at variance with Establishment operatives. Its chief organ, *Living Light,* almost never publishes articles which its compliant Establishment editor believes disagrees significantly with his own ecclesiastically approved views.
81. Erik H. Erikson, *Identity and the Life Cycle* (New York: International Universities Press, 1959), pp. 50–56, quotations on p. 56.
82. Carl R. Rogers, *On Becoming A Person* (Boston: Houghton Mifflin, 1961), p. 22, some italics deleted.
83. While many social-learning theorists appear to regard trust as an attitude, they are inclined to classify attitude as belonging more to the cognitive realm than to the affective domain. I disagree with the social-learning theorists on this point.
84. Julian B. Rotter, "Generalized Expectancies for Interpersonal Trust," in *American Psychologist* XXVI (May, 1971), pp. 443–452. The relevant empirical research of Rotter and many other social-learning theorists concerns itself with interpersonal trust. Since psychotherapeutically oriented social scientists regard basic trust and interpersonal trust as simply dimensions of the same basic phenomenon, and social-learning theorists regard basic trust as either implied in or irrelevant for interpersonal trust, my treatment of trust from both the intensely and the socially interpersonal vantage points seems warranted.
85. This definition is an expanded version of that offered by Julian Rotter. However, I should note that in the article cited in this note, Rotter explicitly restricts the scope of general expectancy to verbal statements. However, it should be remembered that in that article Rotter is defining trust principally from the standpoint of his own instrument and its deployment. A careful perusal of this article and the other writings of Rotter, together with a detailed examination of the writings of other social-learning theorists who investigate trust, reveals that in actuality these scholars consider affective and lifestyle behaviors to also fall within the purview of that generalized expectancy involved in trust. Julian B. Rotter, "A New Scale for the Measurement of Interpersonal Trust," in *Journal of Personality* XXXV (December, 1967), pp. 651–665.
86. This Rotter scale should not be employed to predict specific behaviors in specific situations, since this kind of prediction is out of step with the theoretical foundations of the instrument. On this point, see Betty A. Walker and Rick Robinson, "Utilizing Dimensions of the Rotter Interpersonal Trust Scale in Investigations

of Trust: Validation of Suggested Methods,'' in *Psychological Reports* XLIV
(April, 1979), pp. 423–429; W. Barnett Pierce, "Trust in Interpersonal Com-
munication,'' in *Speech Monographs* XLI (August, 1974), pp. 236–244; Julian
B. Rotter, "Generalized Expectancies for Interpersonal Trust,'' pp. 443–452.

87. Julian B. Rotter, "A New Scale for Measurement of Interpersonal Trust,'' p.
661. The instrument's description of the contrary of the trust variable is as
follows: "This person is cynical. She thinks other people are out to get as much
as they can for themselves. She has little faith in human nature and in the
promises or statements of other people.''

88. Anna Gourevitch remarks that a person not in touch with his own feelings would
not seem to be able to trust others. This lack of being in touch with one's own
feelings seems to restrict one's capacity for communication and for fully experiencing life and love. On the basis of the relevant empirical research as well as on
her own theoretical orientation. Gourevitch maintains that this capacity to be in
trusting touch with one's own feelings arises from the original trust relationship
which the individual had with his mother when he was a young child. Like many
other psychotherapeutically oriented social scientists, Gourevitch contends that
basic trust implies the ability to be separate and still to belong—an important
insight for religious educators wishing to teach faith in God and also faith in the
church. Anna Gourevitch, "On Encounter and Communication,'' in *Contemporary Psychoanalysis* XV (April, 1979), pp. 214–225.

89. Carl R. Rogers, *On Becoming a Person,* p. 118.

90. Sasri Misra and Amar Kalro, "Triangular Effect and the Connotative Meaning
of Trust in Prisoner's Dilemma: A Cross Cultural Study,'' in *International Journal of Psychology* XIV (December, 1979), pp. 255–263. The Prisoner's Dilemma referred to in this study is the celebrated game developed by Morton Deutsch.
See Morton Deutsch, "Trust, Trustworthiness, and the F. Scale,'' in *Journal of
Abnormal and Social Psychology* LXI (July, 1960), pp. 138–140.

91. Gerard Egan, *Encounter* (Belmont, Calif.: Brooks/Cole, 1970), pp. 229–230.

92. Julian B. Rotter, "A New Scale for Measurement of Interpersonal Trust,'' p.
651; see also William J. Doherty and Robert G. Ryder, "Locus of Control,
Interpersonal Trust, and Assertive Behavior Among Newlyweds,'' in *Journal of
Personality and Social Psychology* XXXVII (December, 1979), pp. 2212–2220.

93. Julian B. Rotter, "A New Scale for the Measurement of Interpersonal Trust,'' p.
658.

94. *Ibid.,* p. 653.

95. There is a fundamental conceptual disagreement among some social scientists
about the locus of interpersonal trust. One group of social scientists (including
Morton Deutsch, for example) proposes an internal attitude model for interpersonal trust. Another group of social scientists (including Julian Rotter, for example) offers a situational model. My own position has always been that the self is
forged and altered through an ongoing dynamic interaction with the environment
as this environment is localized in the particular here-and-now situation in which
the person finds himself. My position in this matter vis-à-vis interpersonal trust
is that such trust is the dynamic compound of the individual's generalized at-
titude/specific trust attitude on the one hand and the particular existential situation in which he finds himself *hic-et-nunc* on the other hand. My person-interact-
ing-with-environment model with respect to interpersonal trust is supported by
the research studies on interpersonal trust conducted by James Driscoll and
Cuthbert Scott. See James W. Driscoll, "Trust and Participation in Organiza-

tional Decision-making as Predictors of Satisfaction,'' in *Academy of Management Journal* XXI (March, 1978), pp. 44–56; Cuthbert L. Scott III, "Interpersonal Trust: A Comparison of Attitudinal and Situational Factors,'' in *Human Relations* XXXIII (November, 1980), pp. 805–812; James Michael Lee, *Principles and Methods in Secondary Education* (New York: McGraw-Hill, 1963), pp. 162–183; James Michael Lee and Nathaniel J. Pallone, *Guidance and Counseling in Schools: Foundations and Processes* (New York: McGraw-Hill, 1966), pp. 259–272, 439–488; James Michael Lee, "Christian Religious Education and Moral Development,'' in Brenda Munsey, editor, *Moral Development, Moral Education, and Kohlberg* (Birmingham, Ala.: Religious Education Press, 1980), pp. 343–349.

96. Technique is a technical term indicating one specific level in the taxonomy of the teaching act. For a discussion of this taxonomy and its constituents, see James Michael Lee, *The Flow of Religious Instruction*, pp. 32–38.

97. The first vantage point was treated in Chapter One.

98. This sentence expresses one of the major difficulties which I have with Thomas Groome's highly cognitivist instructional method of shared praxis. For Groome, knowledge is the core and axis of all Christian religious instruction. In his view a praxis knowledge is "a relational, reflective, and experiential way of knowing in which by critical reflection on lived experience people discover and name their own story and vision'' (p. 149). The key and instructionally operative words in Groome's characterization of what knowledge is and how knowledge occurs in Christian religious instruction are, of course, "critical reflection.'' Thus despite his earlier allusions to what he interprets to be a biblical way of knowing, Groome's clear-cut conceptualization of knowledge is unmistakably very cognitivist as cognition is understood by most classical and modern philosophers and psychologists.

As Groome describes the specific pedagogical movements in which his instructional method of shared praxis is enacted *in concreto*, the primary emphasis is decidedly on knowing about God and his actions in human beings in the hope that this knowledge will *itself* somehow *directly* generate religious conduct. But knowledge and lifestyle are different orders of being. Hence knowledge is not lifestyle, nor can knowledge itself directly generate lifestyle. Groome's gratuitous and empirically unproved attempts to directly equate knowledge and lifestyle (p. 221) are as unconvincing as they are contradictory of his own earlier descriptions of praxis knowledge. The history of religious instruction endeavor is littered with the debris of the denominational and individual efforts of those who attempted to teach theological truths or biblical knowledge in the fervent expectation that such cognitive truths and knowledge are themselves religious lifestyle or could directly generate religious lifestyle outcomes. Because of the inextricable cognitive core and matrix necessarily inherent in every phase of Groome's highly cognitivist shared-praxis instructional method, he seems to have accorded relatively little emphasis on directly facilitating a personal experience of God as a central axis of the here-and-now lesson itself. Indeed, Groome's instructional method is primarily targeted toward bringing the learner *hic-et-nunc* to newer and more liberating cognitive knowledge, knowledge which Groome hopes will inform the learner's future decisions.

As Groome delineates his pedagogical method, the major and indeed exclusive emphasis is placed on God and God's actions by means of critical cognitive reflection. This cognitive reflection is facilitated by such activities as cognitive sharing, cognitive dialogue, cognitive research, cognitive questions, and teacher cognitive lecturing. The central function of religious instruction as facilitating a religious experience of God seems to be relegated to something which occurs after the lesson has been completed, or at best a kind of support function for cognition during the lesson itself. See Thomas H. Groome, *Christian Religious Education*, pp. 207–232; Pleasant R. Hightower, *Biblical Information in Relation to Character* (Iowa City, Iowa: State University of Iowa, 1930).

99. Ian P. Knox, *Above or Within?: The Supernatural in Religious Education*. Knox's book is probably the finest work available on the immanentist and transcendist views in religious education.

100. Donald P. Gray, *Where is Your God?* (Dayton, Ohio: Plaum, 1966), pp. 56–66, 106–116.

101. For a good review of the pertinent pre-1960 empirical research, see Charles Homer Ellzey, "Relationships among Acceptance of Self, Acceptance of Others, and Belief in an Accepting God," unpublished doctoral dissertation, Teachers College, Columbia University, 1961.

102. For a representative example of this mentality, see Françoise Darcy-Bérubé, "The Challenge Ahead of Us," pp. 118–119.

103. See, for example, the splendid and widely acclaimed empirical research conducted by Ralph Hood.

104. James Michael Lee, *Principles and Methods of Secondary Education*, p. 145.

105. The Notre Dame graduate religious education program was later suspended by the University's subsequently-deposed provost, James Tunstead Burtchaell. No satisfactory reason was ever advanced by Burtchaell for his unilateral and abrupt suspension of this program. Indeed, this program per capita produced more outstanding leaders in the church than any other academic program in Notre Dame during any comparable time span.

106. I mention the time because by the late 1970s and early 1980s, noninstitutionally anchored and situated Masses became more prevalent and accepted. In the late 1960s and very early 1970s, however, such activities as restaurant Masses were rather unusual.

107. I was "allowed" to report this restaurant Mass in *Living Light,* the ecclesiastically approved official organ of the American Roman Catholic Church's Central Catechetical Establishment. I was dismayed but not surprised at the Central Catechetical Establishment's subsequent negative reaction to this restaurant liturgy. Rather than being highly pleased that desirable religious experiences had been effectively facilitated in some learners during the lesson, the Central Catechetical Establishment reprimanded me in a special notation for, in its opinion, not strictly adhering to the official ecclesiastical directives then nationally in force for the setting and circumstances in which to celebrate Mass. The Central Catechetical Establishment's stance in this matter clearly points to what is basically wrong with this Establishment, namely its almost neurotic preoccupation with squeezing all religious instruction activities and outcomes within the confines of current official ecclesiastical pronouncements and concomitantly disvaluing and attempting to ban all religious instruction activities and outcomes which, though highly relevant and revelatory in the lives of learners, do not seem to fall within the borders of one or another set of formal ecclesiastical pronouncements. The Central Catechetical Establishment would do well to read Matthew 23:23 and also Matthew 12:9–14 in this regard. See James Michael Lee, "Prediction in Religious Instruction," in *Living Light* IX (Summer, 1972) pp. 44–45.

CHAPTER THREE

PROCESS CONTENT

"O chestnut tree, great rooted blossomer,
Are you the leaf, the blossom or the bole?
O body swayed to music, O brightening glance,
How can we know the dancer from the dance?" [1]

—William Butler Yeats

THE NATURE OF PROCESS CONTENT

Process content refers to a generalized, dynamic, and usually "intangible" content. "Intangible" here does not mean abstract or ethereal; it means a content in motion rather than one which is congealed into a fixed state. To illustrate: in the example two times two equal four, the process content is the getting of the four and the ability to arrive at four again when another somewhat similar arithmetical problem arises. [2]

Process content consists in the actual moving progressively from one point or another on the road to completion. (Upon completion of the movement, product content is produced.) Process content is the hitting of the bull's-eye; product content is the hit bull's-eye. A vital feature of process content is its developmental nature and thrust: process content consists of the act of passing through continuing development from some beginning to some projected end. Process content is a content *in via*. It is *"realité en marche."*

Process content, then, is a content characterized by becomingness. Qua process content, this becomingness must be referred to itself in order to properly assess its intrinsic meaning or worth. Qua broader subject-matter content, this becomingness must be referred not only to itself but also to other kinds of subject-matter content (including product content as a completed ending of the becoming process) in order to correctly gauge its meaning or worth. This dually-referenced nature of process content suggests that while all process contents do indeed have intrinsic worth, nonetheless some process contents are more meaningful and more valuable than others.

Many religious educators and educationists seem to regard process as a means of arriving at or attaining content rather than as a valid content in its own right. This mentality is perhaps largely due to a preconceived notion of content as static and tangible. But process content is a content which is flowing, and therefore slips out of the grasp of any attempt to seize it in any sort of concrete fashion. Process content is like the motion in a motion picture film, whereas product content is like the pictorial representation in a particular frame of that selfsame motion picture film. In short, process content is a progressively continuing operation which features instant changes which succeed one another—or, more accurately, pass through one another—on the way toward some ending or completion.

An important distinction must be drawn between process content and instructional practice.[3] The two are not identical; they are not separate notations for the selfsame reality. Process content is wider than instructional practice. Instructional practice, it will be recalled, is structural content. As such, it represents a form of sheer process. Thus the pedagogical approach, styles, strategies, methods, techniques, and steps which the religion teacher uses are process contents in themselves. But over and above its presence in instructional practice, process content also inheres in the substantive content of religious instruction, namely in religion. Religion as a way (process) of think*ing,* a way (process) of lov*ing,* and a way (process) of liv*ing* also has its own process contents separate from (but in the religion lesson, not independent of) instructional practice or structural content.

Because of its flowing, nonstatic, "intangible" nature, process-as-content is not always understood or appreciated by religious educators. Many of these individuals have never been accustomed to regard process as a content but rather to view process as some sort of means to enable the learner to acquire content. It might be instructive, therefore, to give some illustrations of process-as-content. Toward the end of the previous paragraph I indicated that thinking, loving, and living are simultaneously process forms of reality and also key contents in religious instruction. Certainly no religious educator would hold that thinking, loving, and living are not key contents in the lesson and key outcomes of the lesson.[4] One of the key content outcomes which a religious educator seeks to facilitate is the transfer of what is learned in the religion lesson to other areas of the learner's life. Indeed, acquisition of the ability or skill of transfer quite possibly represents the most important learning the individual can gain from the religion lesson. Transfer of learning is a process content.[5]

The entire thrust of Marshall McLuhan's celebrated thesis that "the medium is the message"[6] is that process (the medium) is a content (the message). McLuhan frequently uses one of this favorite examples, the electric light bulb, to illustrate his point. For McLuhan, the electric light coming from the bulb is pure process. But this electric lighting process is surely a genuine content in itself; if it were not a true content, then there would be no difference between a switched-on bulb and a switched-off one. It is precisely because process is a content that a switched-on bulb contains something, yields some outcome which a switched-off bulb does not. When the light bulb is off, the process content, that is, the light*ing*, disappears.

The Relation of Process Content to Product Content

In Chapter Two I treated the relationship between process content and product content primarily from the standpoint of product content. In this section I will explore the relationship between these two contents chiefly from the perspective of process content.

Process content is targeted to itself simultaneously as a discrete kind of content and also to the achieving of a product content which lies outside itself. Perhaps an example drawn from the sports world will illustrate this very important point. In the offensive side of the game of basketball, there are both the playmaking and the attainment of the basket. The playmaking constitutes both a process content in itself and a process content pointed toward the realization of a product content outside itself (the attainment of the basket). Process content is thus at once a content which serves as a means to the attainment of an end outside itself and also a content which is an end in itself. Process is both the getting of a product outcome and an outcome in its own right. In the latter sense, process content can be regarded as a product. It can be regarded as a product outcome in the sense that it is something which is produced. In the basketball example, the playmaking is a process content which, taken by itself without reference to the ball swishing through the hoop, is a product, an attainment. It is this double targeting of process content both to itself as a content and to an external product content which helps give process such great worth as a content.

It is this necessary dual thrust of process content which makes process at once a means and an end. The medium is simultaneously a medium for an external message and a message itself. Therefore process content in its proper and authentic sense can never neglect "what" is communicated.[7] In its aspect as an instrumental content, process cannot even exist without a "what" to communicate. In its aspect as a goal content, process is as much a "what" as the end product of the communication. In the latter connection, it is important to note that all "whats" are not *eo ipso* product contents.

Many children and adults are involved in learning one or another of the sciences. But what is the content these individuals are learning? A science is not only a body (product content) of knowledge; it is also the organization (process content) of knowledge.[8] The success which a person has in learning a science is in direct proportion to the degree to which he has learned the organization or configuration (process content) of that science.[9] Let us say, for example, that an individual wishes to learn a foreign language. Once he grasps the organization or configuration (process content) of a sentence, he is in a position to generate many other sentences based on this process content even though these new sentences differ in product content from the product content in the original sentence learned. Thus he can say "John goes home," "John has gone home," "the house is green," "the moon is made of green cheese," and so forth. Scholars have discovered that in any science, the product content tends to be congruent both with the way in which that content is inwardly organized and the way in which that product content is used.[10] Now "inner organization" and "use" are both process contents. Thus, there began in the 1960s an accelerated effort on the part of curriculum builders in the nonreligious instruction sciences to shift from inventory to transaction. This shift was occasioned by the realization that while inventory might result in the accumulation (product content) of inert knowledge, transaction enables the learner both to understand (process content) the science and to control (process content) some part of his environment through the discovery (process content) of the structure of the science and the manipulation (process content) of facts and their relationships.[11]

Just as the product content of any learning experience shapes the process content of that experience, so does the process content shape the product content. Religious educators and educationists have long recognized that product content shapes process content (especially process content qua instructional practice) but they have usually failed to realize that process content also shapes product content.[12] Marshall McLuhan provides a keen insight into this failure when he remarks that it is very typical that the product content of any activity blinds people to the process character of the medium. "It is not until the electric light is used to spell out some brand name that it is noticed as a medium. Then it is not the light [process content] but the '[product] content' (or what is really another medium) that is noticed."[13]

Let me use an example from the pictorial arts to illustrate how process content does in fact shape product content. Assume that there are two paintings depicting Jesus' agony in the Garden of Gethsemane. Both paintings show Jesus in a kneeling position before a rock, the angel, the chalice, the sleeping apostles—in short, both paintings have the same product contents. However, one of the pictures has been executed in the style of Renaissance Italian art, while the other was done after the manner of late nineteenth-century French impressionism. What makes each of these paintings significantly different from the other is its style, a process content. Indeed, the distinctive process content (style, in this case) of each of these paintings not only makes each painting as a whole different from the other but also influences and shapes their very product contents. What Roger Shinn writes concerning the impact of style on the total message or subject-matter content of a picture can also be said of the influence of any process content on product content (or on any other kind of content for that matter):

> Art communicates, not only through *what* it portrays but also through its *style*. Pictures, whether of "religious" or of "secular" subjects convey moods of warmth, austerity, playfulness, dignity, or wonder. Paul Tillich has shown convincingly that some supposedly religious pictures (for instance, of bible characters) are actually irreverent because their style is flaccid or trivial, while other pictures of presumably secular subjects are deeply religious in style. The motion pictures are the irrefutable proof of the point. Many a spectacular biblical film is offensive to Christian faith.[14]

Process content does not simply receive its purpose from the product content to which it is conjoined; process content also generates its own purpose. Process content is for its own outcomes as much as it is for the attaining of a product content. A melody is not just for the lyrics or for a hit song; it is also for itself. The medium is a message too. Maria Montessori gives a touching illustration of this point that process content generates its own purpose. One day she was in the Pincio Gardens in Rome. There she saw a beautiful, smiling, one-and-a-half year old baby who was working away trying to fill a little pail by shoveling dirt into it. His governess, who was very warm and affectionate to the tot, was coaxing him to leave his work so she could put him into the baby carriage. When her efforts proved to be of no avail, she herself filled the pail with dirt and set both pail and the little child into the carriage firmly convinced that she had given him what he wanted, namely product content. But instead of being pleased, the little fellow made loud cries of protest. Montessori immediately grasped the pedagogical import of the situation. The child did not wish to have the pail full of dirt. He was not striving to attain product content. What he wanted were the motions necessary to fill it, thus satisfying a process need of his own vigorous organism. The little boy's nonconscious aim was his own self-development, his own processing as a person. The process content (filling) generated its own purpose and its own objective. Commenting on this incident, Montessori sadly concludes that all too often an individual is "persecuted" by a teacher for seeing process content as having its own purpose and objective, rather than as merely a means toward the attainment of some product content.[15]

As I have taken pains to indicate in Chapter Two, there is no such thing as process content existing in itself. Process content cannot be separated from product content in the real, concrete, existential order.[16] Let me again take McLuhan's example of the light bulb to bring out this point. I am using this illustration because the illumination from a switched-on light bulb constitutes one of the clearest examples of a content which is as close to being pure process as one can find.[17] Light is a visible form of electromagnetically radiating energy which travels through space or matter. In and of itself energy can be conceptualized as pure process. However, in the real here-and-now world, energy is in fact the process which, *when united to a body* (product content), enables that body to work. Put another way, energy represents a particular body (product content) in a state of working (process content). In terms of the switched-on light bulb, energy of an electromagnetically radiating kind so acts in and through the filament (product content) that there is light. Light, in this case, is a filament in a certain form of process. The light waves which travel out from the filament are themselves processing particles,[18] i.e., product contents in that special kind of process which gives them the characteristics of constituting light.[19] This example of the illumination from a switched-on light bulb once again demonstrates the point that I have frequently been making in this chapter and the previous one, namely that every real being (as distinguished from a so-called "logical being") has both its product and process contents. Only in the conceptual order can a person hypothetically create a pure process content devoid of any conjoined product content.

A few additional examples might serve to further clarify the nature, structure, and thrust of process content as these are related to product content. Let us take the case of a person chewing. Surely one cannot say that chewing (process content) exists totally in and by itself. After all, when a person is chewing (process content), he is chewing something (product content). There is no chewing without something chewed; there is no process content in the real order without an existentially conjoined product content. It is only when the person wishes to analyze his act of chewing that he can isolate the process content (chewing) from the product content (what is being chewed). Further, the chewing (process content) exercises a determining influence upon what is being chewed (product content); conversely, what is being chewed (product content) exercises a determining influence on the chewing (process content). What happens to that which is being chewed (product content) is far different than if it were being thrown; what happens to chewing (process content) is far different if that which is being chewed (product content) is a soft pudding or a hard nut. Finally, chewing can be a means to an end or an end in itself. Chewing is a means to an end when it is an instrumental step in the digestive process. Chewing is an end in itself when it is done for its own sake, such as to experience the act of chewing.[20] Process content, then, can be: (1) a means to an end; (2) an end in itself; (3) a means and an end.

Divine revelation is yet another illustration of a process content which is simultaneously an end and a means. Revelation partakes of substantive process content. Indeed, one of the major emphases in modern Catholic and Protestant theology is the insistence that revelation is not simply product content (namely, a set of salvifically-oriented truths found in the bible), but is also a process content (namely, an ongoing process of God reveal*ing* himself to a person in and through that person's day-to-day existence).[21] As an end, revelation as process content represents the encounter*ing* of God and the person in the revelatory dynamic—the existential bond*ing* of God's initiat*ing* and man's respond*ing* to this initiat*ing*. As a means, revelation as product content is God's manifest*ing* of himself and of his saving action in history in order that the person can come to salvation. (Parenthetically, revelation is also a product content, as the older Christian theologians recognized, albeit in an excessive and unduly restrictive way. The fact that revelation is at once a product content and a process content lends still further support to my assertion that in the here-and-now real order, process content and product content are so intertwined that they cannot exist apart as totally separate entities.[22] The fact that the same noun "revelation" is used for both revelatory product content and revelatory process content is regrettable in that religion teachers are thereby blinded to the realization that revelation is both a product content and a process content. To clarify the situation, it might help if the noun "revelation" were reserved for revelatory product content, while the gerund "revealing" were used to denote revelatory process content.)

The Importance of Process Content

Process represents one of the most important types of substantive content. This fact should not be surprising because the substantive content of religious instruction, namely religion, is, after all, a process of experiencing, a process of living.

It would appear that process content is a much more important and significant learning outcome than is product content. Product outcomes are particularized and consequently can only be transferred to identical situations. Because of their generalized and generalizable nature, process outcomes are readily transferrable. To continue with the arithmetic example I have been using in this chapter and the previous one, the product outcomes in the mathematical problems two times two, three times one, five times three, and four times four are: four, three, fifteen, and sixteen respectively. These results hold true only when the numbers in the problems are exactly the same. But the process outcome, skill in multiplying, can be generalized far beyond these specific examples to all other arithmetic problems involving integers.[23] A product outcome is simply the sum of the workings, for example, that two times two equal four. A process outcome, on the other hand, indicates how a person muliplies these integers. A process outcome indicates that multiplying two numbers is not the same as adding these same two numbers, that nine times four is not thirteen. Let me take another example from mathematics to further illustrate my point. "Algebra," remarks Jerome Bruner, "is a way of arranging knowns and unknowns in equations so that the unknowns are made knowable. The three fundamentals involved in working with these equations are commutation, distribution, and association. Once a student grasps the ideas embodied by these three fundamentals, he is in a position to recognize wherein 'new' equations to be solved are not new at all, but variants on a familiar theme."[24] What Bruner is suggesting here is that the critical and indeed the basic content involved in algebra is process content. Arranging knowns and unknowns, commuting, distributing, and associating are all process contents.

One of the most fundamental affirmations which can be made about religious instruction is that it is a process, both structurally and substantively. From the teaching perspective, religious instruction is the process of facilitating a desired change in the learners by which their cognitive, affective, and lifestyle behaviors are modified along religious lines. From the vantage point of learning, religious instruction is the process through which religiously oriented cognitive, affective, and lifestyle behaviors are changed. The term "process content," therefore, not only describes the pedagogical structure of religious instruction but it describes one of its substantive outcomes as well.

Substantive process outcomes seem to be far more significant and important for all kinds of instruction than do product outcomes. This is not only my view; it is one shared by almost every modern educator and facilitator, regardless of his orientation or his ideology of his setting. Carl Rogers, a nondirective psychotherapist, regards the primary outcome of instruction as the facilitation in the learner of an openness to the process of change.[25] Asahel Woodruff, an educational psychologist with certain behavioristic tendencies, considers the major outcome of instruction as enabling the learner to make wise choices and causing him to constantly strive to make manifest in his life the finest qualities of his culture.[26] Jerome Bruner, a cognitive learning psychologist, maintains that the primal outcome of instruction is grasping the structure of subject-matter content, seizing it in the way that this total content is processing, understanding it in a way that permits many other realities to be related to it meaningfully, learning how to learn.[27] Paulo Freire, a Brazilian educational philosopher and theorist of pedagogical revolution, asserts that the principal desired outcome of instruction is to empower the learner to perceive through his relations with reality that reality is really a process undergoing constant transformation.[28] And virtually all educators, irrespective of their convictions or outlooks, stoutly maintain that a cardinal instructional outcome is transfer of learning—which is, of course, a process outcome.

The *General Catechetical Directory* seems to suggest, perhaps unwittingly, that process content is far more important than product content in terms of religious instruction outcomes. The *Directory* defines religious instruction[29] as that form of ecclesial pastoral action which leads Christian communities and Christian individuals to a maturing of faith.[30] This definition underscores the primacy of process content: after all, "leads," "action," "maturing,"[31] and "faith" are all words denoting and describing a process. This last-mentioned process content, namely faith, once again illustrates how in the *hic-et-nunc* world, process content and product content are distinct but inseparable. The *Directory* makes the classic Catholic distinction between faith as a process content and faith as a product content. Faith as a process content is the believing, the faithing, the *"fides qua"* in the language of the *Directory*. Faith as a product content, on the other hand, is the corpus of Christian truths or data, the *"fides quae."* In the last few centuries Catholic religion teachers typically taught faith as a product content, a *fides quae,* often consciously or unconsciously minimizing or even attempting to obliterate the process content dimension of faith. Since the mid-1950s the process content element of faith has rightfully assumed the ascendancy it had in the apostolic and subapostolic periods of the church.[32] But there is a danger that the laudable efforts of religious educators and educationists to restore faith-as-process-content to pride of place will be accompanied by attempts to denigrate or even totally erase faith-as-product-content. Such a task is existentially impossible, for as the *Directory* itself states, the faith-as-process-content and faith-as-product-content are inseparable, "and a normal maturing of faith assumes progress of both together."[33] Only for purposes of investigative analysis or of exposition can the two be separated, and then artificially so.[34]

To be a Christian means that an individual incorporates both the product content and the process content of Christianity. To be a Christian is not so much *what* is done in given situations as it is a *way* of doing all things in all situations.[35] Put another way, to be a Christian is not so much product content as it is process content. To be a Christian is essentially a process: Christian liv*ing*. It embodies a processing goal, namely the construction of a meaningful and deeply felt world for himself, plus the living out of that world in his own lifestyle. To be a Christian is to enact a processing posture: a way of encountering God, and living within the personally expanding dimensions which this encounter empowers one to act.

It is because process is a full-fledged substantive content in itself that a Christian may not do evil so that good might thereby come about. A "means" is a substantive process content, a content which *in itself* has positive or negative valence.[36] If a "means" had no existence in itself, but had existence *only* insofar as it is related to and targeted to an end outside itself, then a religiously good end would justify any means, no matter how evil that means might be. As I observed earlier, substantive process content (such as a means) is at once ontically related both to itself as an end unto itself and to some other end outside itself. Hence there can be no such thing in Christian living as an evil means yielding an outside good end to which that means directly and heavily contributes. One might speculate as to whether the frequent failure of Catholic and Protestant religious leaders to place a high premium on process-as-content has been largely responsible for some of these leaders employing evil means (substantive process contents) in an attempt to attain good ends. A Christian might figuratively slit the throat of another person for the sake of Jesus, but that person's throat is slit nonetheless.

Substantive process content has important and far-reaching effects on the other substantive contents to which it is conjoined. Thus Marshall McLuhan observes that process content radically alters both the product content to which it is conjoined as well as the effect of this combined process-product content. According to McLuhan, the development of print typography, with its uniform characters and linear dimensionalities, in and of itself caused a radical revolution in the way Western civilization learned both what the typography "contained" and its total worldview. McLuhan further notes that the texture of the process content, its "hotness" or "coolness," affects both the product content for which it is a medium and civilization itself. For McLuhan, it is the total framework itself that changes with new process content, and not just the picture within the frame.[37] Any subject-matter content, composed as it is of many contents, is itself radically affected by a substantial change or thrust in any one or more of its component contents. Thus, as Thomas Luckmann can observe, the subject-matter content called "religion" is shaped by interpersonal encounter.[38] What John Dewey notes about society can, in the same vein, be applied also to religion, namely that religion not only continues to exist *by* communication but also may be said to exist *in* communication.[39]

It is a fact of life that people "learn from the patterns and forms of their experiencing as well as from explicit articulation of ideas, relationships, and meanings."[40] In a religion lesson, learners deal with process contents as well as product contents. As a product content, the word "tonight" has but one meaning; yet Stanislavsky used to ask his young actors to pronounce and inflect this word in fifty different ways, while other acting students wrote down the different shades of feeling and meaning conveyed by this one word. In terms of the learner as a person, it should never be forgotten that every person is a maker, an artist. From this perspective, the important thing for the learner is not so much the finished product itself but rather the process or act of making it.[41] In terms of the learner as a person who wishes to learn something, process content is of tremendous importance. Apropos of this, John Lancaster Spalding, toward the beginning of the twentieth century, observed that education is a process, and the universal failure of educators is attributable chiefly to the teachers' belief that their task is to turn out products, whereas in point of fact their role is to start, stimulate, and direct processes of self-activity that will last as long as life itself.[42]

Process Content and Christians

There seems to be a strong, inbuilt denigration and even rejection of process-as-content on the part of many Christians, especially Catholics. Any one or more of five possible underlying reasons might explain this strong resistance to process-as-content. The first of these is the still prevalent conception held by the Christian in the street that revelation is a product content rather than a process content. In this conceptualization, revelation is regarded solely as a fixed, stable, unalterable body of product truths contained in the bible. Revelation is the God revealed, not the revealing God. Revelation is not a present process—and most certainly it is not a form in process. According to this view, revelation can be held, possessed. Revealed truths dwell in the believer; the believer does not dwell in truths which are both revealed and revealing.[43] Revelation is looked at in terms of a variety of existential conditions which took place in former times and under certain historical circumstances. Revelation is not considered as an act of present emergence; indeed such a notion might be considered to constitute a form of revelational Darwinism.[44] I hasten to add that there tends to be a strong anti-process-content bias among product-centered Christians who see revelation as continuous. For such persons, continuous revelation often means that God is continuously revealing to human beings a fixed body of product truths or variations thereof. Such a viewpoint implies rejection of God revealing truths which are in themselves processing, as well as rejection of truths which are processed by the person who in encountering them at once transforms these truths and is transformed by them.

A second reason accounting for a strong, inbuilt anti-process-content bias on the part of so many Christians is their view of the development of doctrine. For these persons, doctrine is a product content which either remains permanently fixed and immutable, or which, while remaining fundamentally unalterable, is still capable of being adapted or interpreted in different ways to meet the needs of different people or eras. Such a product-centered view of doctrine tends to reject the notion that Christian doctrine does not and cannot exist as immutable doctrinal product contents but as living, processing *credenda*— *credenda* which become articles of belief only by being transformed in texture and hue by each believing Christian living in a certain era and subject to certain sociocultural conditions.[45] Product-centered Christians typically regard doctrine as product content which is external to the individual, rather than as a process of personalized ''saving Eventing'' in which doctrine consists of a set of abstract product contents which become religious only in the living, changing, salvific, transformational process occurring in the Christian's life.

A third point which might suggest the reason why so many Catholics and other Christians have an anti-process-content bias is the all too prevalent opinion that religious doctrine, religious culture, and indeed religion itself must be transmitted faithfully from sender to receiver. In this conception, religious instruction is transmissive with tremendous emphasis on the product content which is transmitted. In transmission-oriented religious instruction, process is not only a non-content; it is also an inherently troublesome affair since it can only hinder and never really substantially help the effective transmission of product content.[46]

A fourth reason why so many Christians are oriented against process-as-content seems to be a highly extrinsicist view of what is a religious goal and what is a pedagogical goal.[47] For these persons, a goal is basically and essentially something outside the processes used to attain it. Thus a goal is not an organic outgrowth of a series of interactive processes, nor another form of the totality of the processes themselves. In this view, the processes are not contents in themselves, nor is anything of these processes contained in the final goal (since the goal is basically extrinsic to the series of processes). Quite possibly it is this mentality which prompts product-centered learners who participate in process-oriented religion lessons to exclaim: "But we are not going anywhere!" For these learners, this so-called "anywhere" is some product which is almost completely extrinsic to the processes in and of the lesson. These learners regard "anywhere" to be anywhere outside the lesson and outside the growing, the interacting, and the expanding which help comprise the lesson's process content. Quite opposed to this anti-process mentality is the following statement made by a member of a back-to-the-land religious community located in a rural area in Pennsylvania: "We aren't searching for some 'thing' up here [in Pennsylvania]. When you do that you wake up one day and find yourself dead and you still haven't found it. To us, the searching for it, the finding of it, and the 'it' are one and the same."[48]

A final factor which might explain why so many Christians in general and religious educators in particular denigrate process content is the known fact that clergymen, religious, and lay religionists tend to be somewhat more authoritarian than other persons.[49] Studies have found that the following traits (which are labeled as "authoritarian") tend to occur in combination: great concern with external authority, particularly in terms of deference to superiors and assertion over underlings; need for closure; conventionality, conformity, and lack of "individuality"; intolerance, superstition, and bigotry; stereotyped, inflexible "black-and-white" thinking; rigidity; self-righteousness. Authoritarian personalities seem to prefer order over change, stability over processing. It is very difficult for individuals with authoritarian personalities to tolerate ambiguity, especially with regard to ends and means. Consequently, such individuals are seldom truly creative or innovative. It is quite obvious, then, that the fluidity, tentativeness, ambiguity, and nuanced character of process content would be quite unpalatable to the authoritarian personality.

The blindness of so many Christians and theologically oriented religious educators to process as a content in its own right has quite possibly been a major factor in giving rise to numerous Christian failures. It may well be that a fundamental reason why Christians are frequently lacking in Christlike charity is that they practice the "thats" (product contents) of their religion while simultaneously neglecting to live out the "ways" (process contents) of Christianity.

One tragic result of the neglect of process content on the part of religious educators is that those whom they teach so often emerge from their lessons knowing the bible but not being biblical.

THE FORM OF PROCESS CONTENT

Basic Principles

The form which a specific process content takes is determined at the first level by its dynamic relationship to the substantive content of which it is an integral constituent, and at the second level by the way in which this substantive content is fused with the structural content in that new subsumptional entity. Applying this basic principle to religious instruction, we can say that at the first level, the process contents of religious instruction such as religious understand*ing*, religious lov*ing*, religious feel*ing*, religious liv*ing*, and so forth, are utilized in such a way that they contribute to the creation and enhancement of the overall substantive content, namely religion. At the second level this overall substantive content (religion) with its component contents (including process content) takes on the form given to it by virtue of its dynamic fusion with structural content (instructional practice) as subsumed into that new entity we call the religious instruction act.

While each of the eight contents I deal with in this book operates at these two levels, the situation with respect to process content is more complicated than is the case with any of the other seven. The reason for this complication lies in the fact that unlike any of the other seven forms of substantive content, process is simultaneously a substantive content *and* structural content.

Level 1. One of the key points I have been making throughout this chapter is that process content is a legitimate and indeed a very powerful form of substantive content. Because process content is a form of substantive content, the accusation so frequently hurled at process-oriented religion teachers ("Where is the doctrine in your lesson?") becomes meaningless and irrelevant.[50] To emphasize process content in a religion lesson in no way implies that doctrine thereby disappears; to be sure, doctrine is itself a process content as well as a product content. Doctrine is a living, processing, interactive reality.[51] To regard it in any other way is to de-doctrinalize doctrine.[52] In addition, living, processing doctrines are not isolated entities unto themselves but are situated in a definite overall configuration. Unless one learns the overall configuration, unless one learns the way doctrines are interactively related to one another, one cannot really acquire a proper or adequate knowledge of these doctrines. Thus, for example, the learner who knows certain cognitive doctrines about the Incarnation event does not really know these doctrines unless he also knows how these doctrines interactively relate to the global structure of redemption. Now, configuration or inner organization, as I demonstrated earlier in this chapter, is a process content—a process content which does not automatically flow simply from an accumulation of specific doctrinal product contents. Furthermore, it should be underscored that Christian doctrine is not simply cognitive. Christian doctrine is fully human, that is, affective and lifestyle as well as cognitive.

There are levels or gradations of worth in process content. The worth of any process content is gauged by two criteria, internal and external. Internal criteria are those which relate to the nature of the particular process content itself, without reference to any reality outside it. For example, in the process content called "knowing" Benjamin Bloom and his associates have examined this process content in itself and have discovered various levels or gradations at which this process content operates. Thus, evaluating is posited to be a higher-order process content than synthesizing, synthesizing a higher-order process content than analyzing, and so forth.[53] David Krathwohl and his associates have examined the process content "feeling" and have located various gradations at which that process content functions. Thus, for example, receiving (attending) is of a lower level of affective process content than is responding, responding is of a lower order than valuing, and so forth.[54]

The worth of a particular process content is also gauged by external criteria. In terms of religious instruction these external criteria comprise the totality of those behaviors known as religion. Accordingly, the worth of a particular process content in religious instruction is the extent to which it enhances the individual's learning of religion.

Religion, as I have previously indicated, is the substantive content of religious instruction. Substantive content is composed of the fusion of many subcontents of which process content is one. This conceptualization suggests the deep and inseparable interrelatedness of both the external and internal criteria of the worth of process content. It further reinforces the notion that process content is a legitimate content which in no way can be downplayed or separated from substantive content.

Because the worth of process content can be judged by both internal and external criteria,[55] there is no truth in the charge that religion teaching which is thrusted toward process content is by that very fact lacking in or devoid of moral or dogmatic standards. Process content has its own internal levels of quality; to emphasize process content is therefore not to neglect the quality of teaching. Process content has its own external levels of quality (religion, in the case of religious instruction): to emphasize process content is therefore not to detract from the quality of the religion taught to the learners.

For religious instruction the question is not: "Should process content be emphasized in the teaching act?" but rather "How can the teacher heighten the use of process content so as to enhance the deepest purpose of the religious instruction experience?" To paraphrase Cecil Parker and Louis Rubin, there are three major tasks which the religion teacher must successfully negotiate if he wishes to make the process content in his lesson eminently worthwhile. First, he must identify which substantive process contents are valuable in terms of the optimal attainment of the desired subject-matter goals. Second, he must effectively design a set of instructional practices (structural process contents) which bring out the richness of the substantive process contents. Finally, he must dovetail the substantive process contents and the structural process contents so that they are mutually enhancing and reinforcing.[56]

As I stress continually throughout this chapter, the religion teacher simply cannot teach pure process content alone because there is no such thing as subsistent process content. Furthermore, process content is not taught or learned in a vacuum; it is bound up inextricably with all the other seven substantive contents. Process content is always learned in a particular context—a context of the other substantive contents and the context of the varying elements in the religious instruction act itself.[57] Indeed, the very fact that process content is taught within a given context serves to again point up the legitimacy and validity of process as a content. For after all, context itself is an overall interactive process. Context, in short, is the medium; it is process content writ large.

Level 2. The religion teacher decides which substantive process contents he will use in the lesson primarily on the basis of the way in which these process contents combine with other appropriate substantive contents so as to effectively promote the desired learning outcomes. For example, the religion teacher might select such process contents as valuing and attending when the desired learning outcomes are affective in nature. Or again, the teacher might choose to stress process contents like analyzing and evaluating when the desired learning outcome is a cognitive grasp of religion.[58]

A religion lesson should not merely supply a continuity with the broader ecclesial community or with everyday experience in the "world." A religion lesson represents a special purposive activity which endeavors to provide a focused, enriched, and directional set of experiences to attain a desired learning outcome. This suggests that the successful religious educator is one who brings about an efficacious meshing of substantive content with structural content on the one hand, and of substantive process content with other substantive contents on the other. In terms of the latter, the religion teacher carefully examines the implications of the various forms of substantive process content for the immediate and overall desired learning outcomes. There is no effective activity—and this includes the teaching activity—which does not conform to the requirements of inner relationship; indeed, any activity can be considered intelligent and informed to the degree to which these relational requirements are both conformed to and consciously borne in mind.[59] Thus, as Marshall McLuhan notes, "the painter learns how to adjust relations among things to release new perception, and the chemist learns how other relations release other kinds of power."[60] It is each individual process content which gives meaning, form, vitality, and direction to the product content or other individual substantive contents to which it is conjoined. In a more global perspective, it is overall process content, namely the pattern or configuration of the overall substantive content, which gives the totality of substantive content both its own internal relevance as well as its relevance to the life of the learner. To be sure, the subject-matter content of religious instruction, namely religion, is basically a systematized pattern or configuration—in other words, overall process content—of one's cognitive, affective, and lifestyle relation to God. Indeed, it is precisely the teaching-learning of overall process content, rather than of specific product or cognitive contents, which is at the center of the learner's ability to transfer the outcomes gained in one situation to other areas of life. As I repeatedly demonstrate throughout this trilogy, transfer of learning is perhaps the most important single outcome of any religion lesson.

Process content is both *a* substantive content and *the* structural content of religious instruction. Just as effective teaching necessitates the meshing of process-as-substantive-content with the other forms of substantive content, so also does effective teaching require the meshing of process-as-substantive-content with process-as-structural-content (instructional practice). The texture and form of process-as-instructional-practice help or hinder the attainment of process-as-substantive-content outcomes. For example, if the intended process outcome of a particular religion lesson is the demonstrated skill of correctly evaluating the morality of designated actions against specified moral criteria derived from the eighth commandment, then the religion teacher ought to select the problem-solving pedagogical method rather than the lecture technique.

Process-as-instructional-practice should be selected so as to mesh with both specific substantive process contents and overall substantive process content. Apropos of the latter point, James Loder observes that since instructional practice can shape the outcomes of the religion lesson by fashioning "the general frame of reference within which all one's hearing, speaking, and learning takes place, then it behooves us to take a long look at it."[61] Indeed, the entire religion curriculum can be regarded as a general frame of reference in which the instructional act takes place. Viewed from this perspective as an overall process content, the religion curriculum should be so constructed and deployed that it is optimally promotive of both specific and overall substantive process contents.

A Cautionary Note. Process content, both substantive and structural, possesses tremendous educational value because of its inherent dynamism and generalizability. But the inestimable value of process content can be minimized and even canceled out by misguided attempts to create religion lessons which do not consciously and overtly join it with other substantive contents, such as, for example, product content. Indeed there were some Protestant and Catholic religion teachers in the 1960s and 1970s, who, upon discovering for the first time the great worth of substantive process content, went completely overboard by attempting to create the impossible religion lesson, that is, a process lesson totally devoid of any other substantive content. These religion lessons were dubbed by their devotees as "happening lessons," "experience catechetics," and similar catchy names. But these foolhardy attempts could never have existential viability because, in the real order, process content simply cannot exist in and by itself. Process content comes into here-and-now real existence only when it is conjoined with a product content of one sort of another. Processing has no existence apart from some product in process. There is no such thing as experiencing without something which is experienced. Interaction without product content is barren. As I shall indicate in the next section, religion is very much a substantive process content; but it is also a substantive product content as well. To teach religion is to teach substantive content, and substantive content is more than simply sheer process content.

Religion as Process Content

Religion is the substantive content of religious instruction. Like all existential, ontic contents, religion has its product and its process components. In Chapter Two, I consider religion from the perspective of a product content; in this chapter, I deal with religion from the standpoint of process content.

Religion is a field of personal and/or communal activity. Religion, then, is the encountering of God either in the arena of one's own selfhood or in some communal situation such as in the church. With respect to meeting God in one's own selfhood, it should be underscored that a Christian is a dynamic, not a static, creature. "To be man is a process of becoming man . . ." remarks Edward Schillebeeckx, from a theological vantage point.[62] From a more focused psychological perspective, the Austrian religious educationist Michael Pfliegler notes that "man's personality is always in the state of becoming."[63] Man, then, is basically a person in process, a person who matures and learns from experiencing life and its events.[64] Gregory Baum goes so far as to say that "man is created through the ongoing communication with others.''[65] One of the milieux in which this ongoing communication takes place is the church. It would be myopic and inaccurate to consider the church as primarily a place or an institution. The church is a community of believers, a community which at a particular time in history or in a particular setting might be congruent with a place or an institution. In Karl Rahner's words, "the church is not a substance." For Rahner, the church is a living event, one which is constantly growing and being renewed in human beings.[66] Whether the church is a place or an institution or a living event—or all three—one thing is clear: the church is a dynamic organism. The church is a reality in process. The church is *in via*. The church is a processing community on pilgrimage—and as John Giles Milhaven so touchingly puts it, the church is a dusty pilgrim at that.[67]

Religion is, I repeat, a field of personal and/or communal activity. The Christian is one kind of organism, the church another kind of organism. But both realities are organisms. In this connection it must be underscored than an organism maintains its vitality as well as its identity by changing, by processing. If an organism is not processing, it loses its identity, forfeits its dynamism, and dies.[68]

To be a Christian is to be a person always in process, to be a person eternally changing. Growth, change, dynamism, processing—all these do not cease when the Christian departs this life to abide with God in heaven. Heaven does not mean an end to a Christian's processing. Quite the contrary; heaven, if it means anything, means a more elevated, more enriched, more undiluted form of processing, growing, loving, encountering. Unfortunately, most Christians seem to lose sight of this axial point. The kingdom is not the end, the final resting point at which everything done on earth is concluded. The kingdom is just the beginning of new and more robust Christian living. This old, commonly held notion of heaven as being a completion, an end—a kind of product outcome—flows from the typical Christian disvaluation of process-as-substantive content. In a statement which I believe is fraught with great import for the work of religious instruction, John Dewey notes that from the traditional educational outlook, "growth is regarded as *having* an end, instead of *being* an end."[69] In terms of my analysis of process content in this chapter, I take a broader position than Dewey by averring that processive growth is both a means to an end and an end in itself. But I believe Dewey's point is highly germane since it indicates that for a Christian, whether in heaven or on earth, growth is, among other things, an end in itself. The typical failure of religious educationists to appreciate this point has led to absurdities which are as ludicrous as they are incredible. Thus Gabriel Moran, for example, regards Christianity as an adult religion because he claims that it is only in adulthood that Christians can be said to have arrived as persons. Children, Moran states, are merely "on the way" and so the only religion these unfortunates can have is an "on the way" sort of religion.[70] But the fact of the matter is that every individual—child, adolescent, and adult—is always "on the way," always processing here on earth and in heaven too. Growth and process are their own ends, are their own contents, as well as ways to the getting of other contents. The follies of so many American Catholic religious educators in the 1970s who attempted to liquidate children from the religious instruction enterprise because of a mistaken notion that Christianity is an arrival (adult) religion can be directly traced to a blindness to process-as-substantive-content, to a blindness of growth as an end to be prized for itself. Possibly it is this same blindness which prompted one Protestant religious educationist to tell me once that "nothing really occurs" in a lesson conducted on a process-content axis.

An essential aspect of Christian religious behavior is loving God. Yet as François-Xavier Durrwell reminds us, "man loves God when he desires to love him."[71] What Durrwell is accentuating here is that praying is a process behavior, a desir*ing* to love God. The desiring, the process—this is prayer. And prayer is a substantive content. Durrwell follows up his statement by observing that the Christian's heart is made pure through his desire for purity. The process (desiring), then, yields its own fruit. Process content is its own end as well as a means to other ends.

Virtually all Christian denominations underscore the importance of conscience as at once a regulatory function of and a directional guide for authentic religious living. But conscience is not a "thing"; it is not some sort of entity residing within the recesses of the human person.[72] Conscience is basically a conceptual construct used to tentatively explain specific attitudinal or value responses. In other words, conscience is a way of explaining a basic human process.[73] This value-oriented regulatory and directional process is, for Christians, an important substantive-content of religious living.

I find it paradoxical that some religious educationists who seem so resistant to the conceptualization of religion as being a substantive process content are nonetheless quite enamored, on religious grounds, of Paulo Freire's notion of *conscienticação*. At bottom, *conscienticação* is "the deepening of the attitude of awareness characteristic of all emergence."[74] Consequently, *conscienticação* can be properly characterized as a substantive process content. *Conscienticação* is a progressive deepening of awaring—a substantive process content if ever there was one. Indeed, the substantive process content of the deepening of awaring is placed by Freire within an even more overarching substantive process content, namely emergence. Freire hypothesizes that the exclusive identification of life with product content (objects) represents the principal obstacle to achieving *conscienticação*. From this perspective, *conscienticação* is, for Freire, a substantive process content " by means of which men, through a true praxis, leave behind the status of objects to assume the status of historical Subjects."[75] If emphasis on "Subject" means anything, it means emphasis on the human being who is a processing person.[76] It is at this deeper level of person-as-substantive-process-content that I see Paulo Freire having much to offer the religious instruction enterprise.

Central to every Christian's religious life is the whole matter of divine revelation. Revelation is at once a product content as well as a substantive process content.[77] It is from the latter vantage point that I am briefly treating it at this juncture. (As I observed earlier in this chapter, the process dimension of revelation would be rendered more salient by using the gerund "revealing" with greater frequency.)

Revelation, both as recorded in the bible and as occurring continuously throughout the world from the dawn of time to the present day, occurs in history. There is no such thing on this earth as God revealing himself outside of history.[78] Now, history is that which takes place in time. In other words, revelation is always a process content because it is done within the context of temporal processing.

Revelation is accomplished in and through history, in and through a temporally processing state. As I suggested in the foregoing paragraph, revelation can be either a revelation-in-word (the bible) or a revelation-in-reality. In terms of the latter form of revelation (sometimes referred to as "general revelation"), revelation is always a meeting, never just a product-content message.[79] Revelation is the person encountering God in highly focused forms (such as in the Eucharist), moderately focused forms (such as in other human beings in their gracefulness and sinfulness), and in not-too-sharply-focused forms (such as in nature). Hence revelation is not simply the unfolding of a set of religious product contents called "religious truths." Revelation is the unfolding of God himself; it is the meeting and greeting of God and the human being in a personal though somewhat indirect fashion. Revelation is a substantive process content because the essence of revelation is an unfolding, an encountering, a meeting. The Christian is not just the recipient of some product content called "revelation"; he stands within the very context and flow of the revealing process. Revelation, then, is a processing series of events between God and the person.[80] Revelation refers not simply to a deposit of divinely revealed product contents; revelation is the relational encounter between God and the person.[81] Indeed, it may be argued with some qualification that even revelation as a set of divinely revealed truths (product contents) does not become operatively revelatory until a human being encounters God in these truths, until the human being is engaged in a relational process with these truths. It is only when the human being has a living, processing *engagement* with this set of truths that these truths can be operative in his life, can be revealing to him. For religious instruction, this conceptualization of revelation as a substantive process content suggests that revelation can never be "presented" or "handed on"[82] by the religion teacher as some religious educationists would have us believe. If revelation is at bottom a process encounter, then the most effective way to teach revelation is to teach it as a process content. This pedagogical principle suggests that the religion teacher employ a process-oriented instructional strategy such as the structured-learning-situation strategy rather than a product-oriented strategy like the transmission strategy.

In terms of the bible (sometimes referred to as "special revelation"), the process character of scripture is again an invaluable key to unlocking its privileged nature and operative power. Emil Brunner observes that it is the verb (a process word), rather than the noun (a product word), which is the chief part of speech used in the bible. He notes that it was the old, Platonically influenced Christian theology which converted verb-theology into noun-theology. The bible, concludes Brunner, is actualistic and processing rather than static or product.[83] Rudolf Bultmann similarly underscores the actualistic, process structure of the bible by remarking that "the now of the New Testament is both timeless and temporal. . . . The now of the New Testament implies that the supratemporal reality becomes an event for each particular individual only by virtue of an encounter in time; it has itself the character of encounter."[84] As for myself, I distinguish between the bible as the revealed word (product content) and the revealing word (process content). The bible *in se* is the inspired, revealed word of God. But the bible becomes operatively revealing only when a person reads it or otherwise encounters it. This position flows from the definition of divine revelation as a personalistic disclosure of God to a human being. (If one defines revelation differently, of course one is bound to reach a conclusion other than the one I reach.) Suppose, for example, that one defines revelation as nothing more than the act of God disclosing himself, irrespective of any encounter with this disclosure on the part of man. Were this so, then the bible *in se* would be both the revealed word of God and the operatively revealing word of God. My adherence to a conceptualization of revelation as a processing encounter between God and a human being precludes any valid comparison between the bible in a world where no person exists to read it, on the one hand, and the celebrated psychological debate as to whether there exists the "sound" of a tree falling in a forest with no person around to hear it, on the other hand.

Process Theology

The overt attention accorded to substantive process content on the part of a few twentieth-century religious educationists has a certain parallel in theological circles. I am referring here to the development of process theology. Though the religious instruction conceptualization of substantive process content is in no way dependent upon or necessarily linked with process theology, nonetheless religious educators can broaden and deepen their understanding of substantive process content by looking at process theology.

With certain notable exceptions like Pierre Teilhard de Chardin, process theology by and large grew out of process philosophy. There does not presently exist any integrally united "school" or highly developed global system of process theology. Thus process theologians often differ significantly among themselves. Important process theologians (and philosophers) include Alfred North Whitehead,[85] Charles Hartshorne,[86] Schubert Ogden,[87] John Cobb, [88] Daniel Day Williams,[89] Norman Pittinger,[90] Bernard Loomer, [91] Walter Stokes,[92] the empirical theologians such as Henry Nelson Wieman[93] and Bernard Meland,[94] and finally Pierre Teilhard de Chardin[95] and the Chardinians.[96] There have been some religious educationists who have been highly influenced by process theology. The most notable of these is Randolph Crump Miller.[97] Gloria Durka and Joanmarie Smith have also written sympathetically about the relationship of process theology and religious instruction.[98]

At least six basic principles or touchstones of process theology can be identified: becoming; change; continuous perfecting; time; relation; and experience. *First,* becoming, not being, is the ultimate reality. The most real reality is not existing substance, thing, or person, but rather the actually occurring event, state, or experience. Only becoming, process, really exists; the notion of "being" represents a kind of abstraction, an inference drawn from the ongoing, becoming reality.[99] The human person lives in a changing, moving, active world which has to do with dynamic processes rather than with inert "substances," with events rather than things. Process theology typically does not totally reject the notion of being. What process theology asserts is a doctrine of being in and through becoming. This is a reversal of the typical theological conceptualization of becoming as a mode of being. *Second,* the basic, all-encompassing actuality is change. The world is change; the world is not a substance which changes. The universe is not a substance but a process. Hence evolution is not an hypothesis but a general condition of reality which all hypotheses (including theological hypotheses) must successfully satisfy. *Third,* all reality, including God, is a perpetual state of continuous and continuing perfecting. Reality is always overfilling itself, extending itself by perfecting itself. Because becoming and change are the ultimate reality, to be perfect necessitates change and becoming. In the old Platonic-Aristotelian conception of reality, change or perfecting were held as signs of intrinsic weakness because to change or to perfect denoted "becoming better" or "filling up what was lacking." The only value of changing or perfecting, according to Platonic-Aristotelian thought, must be to remedy a prior defect. However, in Charles Hartshorne's words, "there is nothing in the religions (unless in Hinduism or Buddhism) to indicate that change simply as such is a weakness; and the only sense in which 'perfection' is used biblically is the ethical sense. 'Be ye perfect' does not mean 'be ye immutable'! Nor is any immutability attributed to deity in the Scriptures save what the context implies or is purely ethical."[100] *Fourth,* time is at the essence of reality rather than being a property of reality. Reality does not consist of inert substances passing through successive temporal instances; rather, reality consists of processes having temporal extension. *Fifth,* reality is at bottom relational. The universe is an interrelated, ongoing organism. This dynamic interrelation stems from the universe as essentially a process; substances have their being and texture to the extent to which they are interactively processing. The world is not a collection of self-contained objects related only externally to each other. Because the stuff of reality is process and becoming, the world is a network of mutual influences spread through time and space. Thus the universe is a single overarching process without interruption.[101] Hence Whitehead rejects "simple location" on the grounds that this is a mechanistic assumption which posits the existence of independent particles of reality which are basically "apart from any essential reference to the relations of that bit of matter to other regions of space and to other durations of time."[102] *Sixth,* experiencing is of the essence of reality. Experiencing is the ongoing process whereby one reality dynamically interacts with another reality. In terms of the human person, what is experienced is a "substance" only to the extent that it is a form or extension of another reality-as-process. Hence in the human domain, that which is experienced derives its meaning, worth, and validity from the way in which the person is experiencing his own experiencing as he here-and-now processively interacts with some external ongoing reality.

The import and consequences of process theology for the Christian view of reality are considerable. For example, process theology conceptualizes God as the divine activity through which and in which the creative process is at work. God thus is process rather than an entity outside of process. All reality is grounded in God who is quintessentially divine activity; hence God is intimately related to the processing ongoing world. God is not some sort of external fashioner of an essentially static, substantialist system, but the creative processing influence immanent in evolutionary development. Consequently, process theology stands in stark opposition to pristine Thomism and all other forms of Aristotelian-derived theistic positions. Process theologians believe that those positions result in a doctrine of God as a changeless absolute who is wholly unrelated to the world.[103] Aristotle denied God's knowledge of the contingent (the world) because whatever is known cannot be independent of the knower. The Stagirite similarly rejected any involvement with the contingent (the world) on the grounds that for God, to know a changing reality is automatically to be totally involved with that reality. These Aristotelian conceptualizations were difficult for many Christian theologians to accept. (For example, the Aristotelian and Thomistic view of God makes it very difficult to adequately explain the efficacy of prayer.) Theologians holding to an Aristotelian (and Thomistic) conceptualization of God felt obliged, for what Charles Hartshorne calls "religious reasons," to affirm God's knowledge of (and involvement with) the contingent and changing world.[104] The image of an unchanging God, an unmoved mover, an aloof deity is not supported by the testimony of biblical revelation. Indeed, the classical affirmation that God is not temporal, relative, changing, and involved stands in utter contradiction to the bible's representation of God as "the eminent Self or Thou."[105] Norman Pittinger further observes that the bible suggests that "God *is* self-giving love, who lives and moves and has His being not so much as First Mover . . . but in relationship with that in and through which His love is working."[106] Process theologians generally assert that to make the triple affirmation that God is involved with the world, is self-giving to the world, and loves the world leads to the inevitable conclusion that God is essentially processing and changing. God, then, can be influenced. Since God interacts with the world in time, he is influenced by that with which he temporally interacts. This view of God as one who both expansively changes and is dynamically influenced provides a fresh and perhaps a satisfying insight into a problem which has always been particularly vexing for classical theologians, namely the problem of how God could possibly be influenced by the prayers of human beings. Because God is conceptualized as both the eternal ground of and supreme participant in an essentially changing world, process theology has particularly warm and rich implications for the whole area of redemption. It is because God is both the eternal ground of and supreme participant in the processing world that Alfred North Whitehead can state that "God is the great companion—the fellow-sufferer who understands."[107]

Whether he takes a position for or against or neutral to process theology, there are several things which the religious educator can learn from process theology. *First,* to even minimally understand process theology the religious educator must turn aside from his typical substantialist position, reverse his field, and plunge into a basically different way of looking at God and his creatures. A plunge into a world in which process is *the* substantive content quite possibly will

enable a substantistically oriented religious educator to further appreciate how, in the religious instruction act, process can at least be *a*
substantive content. *Second,* a grasp of process theology might enable
the religious educator to take experience more seriously as a process
content rather than as something which just happens. Process theology
is a way of thinking grounded in the act of experiencing. Religious
instruction, for its part, is an activity in which experience is at once a
ground and a content. *Third,* as process theology implies a processing
God, so does religious instruction suggest a processing religion. Religion is not static; religion is the growing with God unto God. The
process content of religious instruction is simultaneously a means and
an end: "caring, loving, suffering, forgiving, creating, redeeming."[108] *Fourth,* process theology suggests to the religious educator
that if religion is to remain itself, it must become. A lack of understanding of the processing nature of religion, and indeed of all reality,
has doubtless caused some religious educators who readily perceive
the inadequacy of a static, totally substantialist world to fall prey to a
naive and simplified form of Existentialism. Such an Existentialism
has not infrequently resulted in an attempt by these persons to
dereligionize religion as a way out of the static, substantialist religion
in which they find themselves trapped and suffocated. Yet this very
self-defeating attempt at dereligionizing religion flows from a failure
on the part of these individuals to adequately appreciate religion as that
very ongoing, upsurging force which sweeps away all the anguish-
generating uncertainties spawned by this brand of naive Existentialism. *Fifth,* process theology might provide some added insights to
the religious educator on how God interacts with the world in a fashion
that the human being processively finds redemption in and through
God's activity. Commenting on Hegel's concept of history as the
process of the progressive unfolding of God's self-realization (the so-
called "unfinished God"), John Dunne pointedly remarks that "the
story of God's awakening to himself through man is really the story of
man's [progressive] awakening to God."[109]

SOME PRACTICAL CONSEQUENCES

Process Content as Substantive and Structural

Process is a content. Indeed, process partakes of two distinct overarching forms of content, namely structure and subject matter. Process

content is thus the way in which the subject matter is taught, and also an essential component of the subject matter itself. Process is both instructional practice and an object of that selfsame practice. It is this dual nature of process content which makes it so axial and so rich in the religious instruction enterprise.

A brief mention of structural process content is in order here—but only a brief word, because Volume II of this trilogy is devoted exclusively to structural process content, that is to say, instructional practice.[110] No consideration of substantive process content can leave out or even minimize structural process content. The interrelationship and congruence between structural process content and substantive process are absolutely indispensable for effective religious instruction. In its structural aspect (namely, in its nature as teaching practice), process content is value-free;[111] it receives its value from the subject-matter content to which it is conjoined in the existential here-and-now religious instruction act. In its substantive aspect, however, process content is value-laden; in the case of religious instruction, the value coloration of substantive process content is determined by the kind and form of that religion which comprises the totality of the subject-matter content. It is precisely here that the congruence of structural process content and substantive process content is most easily seen. Different instructional practices tend to generate different subject-matter outcomes. Put another way, certain instructional practices are more conducive to yielding a specified learning outcome than are other instructional practices. The principle underlying this is: *the nature and texture of various forms of structural process contents (instructional practices) are organically related to the substantive process content ingredient of subject-matter content—and ingredient which radically shapes and colors the other contents which go to form that compound known as subject-matter content. Hence, the more the structural process contents (instructional practices) of a religion lesson are congruent with the substantive process contents of that lesson, the more effective will the teacher tend to be in that situation.* This is an extremely important and fecund point because it enables the religious educator to (1) tap more deeply the riches of both forms of process content in his efforts to improve his religion teaching, and (2) free himself from falling into such pedagogically untenable, yet frequently held positions as "structural process content is the handmaid of substantive process content," or "method receives its norms, validation, and directions from [theological] content."

Perhaps two illustrations, one speculative and the other practical, might serve to further illuminate this crucial principle. I draw my speculative illustration from Marcel van Caster and Jean LeDu who observe that while religious educators strive to teach their students that faith is a dynamic process which is in no way alien to human life, these teachers often use instructional practices which are decidedly un-lifelike in character.[112] For the practical example, we are all familiar with religious educators who use lecture method or other teacher-centered, transmissive instructional practices in a lesson which aims to teach the learners the process outcome of active participation in the liturgy or in parish affairs.

Expanding the Cognitive Dimension of Process Content

Like substantive product content, substantive process content also has a cognitive dimension, an affective dimension, and a lifestyle dimension.

Substantive process content is an integral and indispensable aspect of cognition. After all, cognition is an operation, a process.

One of the major constituents of the cognitive dimension of process content is meaning. As I observe in Chapter Two, meaning in one of its aspects is a substantive product content. But meaning in another of its essential aspects is a substantive process content. As a substantive process content, meaning is the correspondence or the grasp of the relatedness/significance of realities. Objectivist philosophers such as Aristotle[113] and Thomas Aquinas[114] stress the objective correspon-dence of meaning. In this view, meaning inheres in and thus is derived from the truth in all its dimensionalities. Truth in this conceptualiza-tion is the conformity of the mind with what actually exists.[115] This correspondence (or better still, this corresponding) between mind and object is substantive process content. Relationship *in se* is substantive process content, of course. Subjectivist philosophers like the Kan-tians,[116] the pragmatists,[117] and the phenomenologists[118] emphasize the subjective awaring or personal construction of meaning. Thus meaning is that significance and understanding which a person out of his subjectivity gives or attaches to reality. This personal subjective giving, this personal subjective attaching is substantive process content.

Some religionists, especially those with either/both a social-scien-tific orientation or a liberationist posture seem to be aware that substantive process content represents a vital dimension of faith-as-meaning. For Ana-Maria Rizzutto, faith is always a developmental event which depends on the duality of synthetic meaning which a person is capable of making. Faith, then, is a substantive process content.[119] In James Fowler's view, faith is a basic way (process) in which a person structures foundational personal meaning.[120] Thus Fowler can write: "To have faith, then, is not primarily to hold certain beliefs about reality. To have faith is to engage all life in relation to a unifying center of meaning and value."[121] That faith for Fowler is very much an ongoing substantive process content rather than simply a finished product content is highlighted by his frequent use of the process-oriented word "faithing" rather than the more product-directed word "faith." Liberationist writers like Thomas Groome[122] and Malcolm Warford[123] believe that at the center of all religious instruction lies the process of personally reconstructing meaning. In this view, meaning as substantive process content is necessary to liberate persons from the shackles of oppression of every sort.

In view of the foregoing analysis, what can the religious educator do to facilitate in the learner the acquisition of cognitive process content? The most effective general thing he can do is to adopt an authentic teaching model such as the one I outlined in *The Flow of Religious Instruction*.[124] This model, which is anchored to the social-science approach, indicates that the learner represents the only valid starting point for the religious instruction act. This approach is in marked contrast to the theological approach to religious instruction which typically takes theological product content, rather than the learner, as the starting point.

The learner learns as the learner is—and as I have demonstrated in this chapter, the learner is fundamentally, though not exclusively, a person in process. (Indeed, process philosophers and process theologians might well say that the learner is not so much a person in process as a process of a person kind.) The learner is in process in time and space; he is in the process of becoming more and more a person; he is involved in the process of salvation. As a Christian, the learner is essentially a person on pilgrimage, *in via*, in processing Christianly.

The assertion "the learner learns as the learner is," while accurate is nonetheless incomplete. A more adequate fundamental statement would be that the learner learns as he is situated within a certain set of circumstances or conditions with which he interacts. Prescinding from its maturational aspects, human behavior is learned behavior—and learned behavior is the result of the learner's interaction with one or more aspects in a given set of circumstances or structure of conditions. From this fundamental empirical law of learning it is possible to deduce the following basic statement about the facilitation of process content in learners: *The learner most effectively learns process content in those learning situations which are so structured as to put him in a process mode of behaving.*

Though the teaching act is not an inverse form of the learning event, nonetheless it is an antecedent reciprocal task. Consequently, all teaching starts with the learner and how he learns. Thus the basic *pedagogical* (as contrasted with learning) principle in terms of process content is: *To most effectively facilitate substantive process content outcomes, the teacher should so structure the learning situation that all the elements in that situation, as well as the interaction among these elements, are heavily process-oriented.*

An Illustration. One pedagogical procedure which is oriented to cognitive process content is the discovery strategy.[125] The discovery strategy is that in which the teacher withholds from the learners those concepts, principles, and laws which constitute the objective of the lesson, while providing them with instances, exemplars, concrete materials, or problem situations which are intended to lead the learners to induce for themselves those very concepts, principles, and laws. At bottom, then, the objective of the discovery strategy is to enable the learners to find out for themselves the process contents which make up those laws and theories which underlie and explain the various product contents involved in the lesson.[126] For Jerome Bruner, a proponent of this strategy, discovery is a matter of rearranging information or transforming evidence.[127]

There are many teaching methods and techniques through which the discovery strategy is enacted, ranging from almost complete teacher direction of the learning steps through which a learner must proceed, to virtually no direction at all.[128] In other words, there is a continuum between totally guided discovery and totally unguided discovery. Richard Suchman's discovery strategy, which falls somewhere on the guided end of the continuum, is carried out in three procedural stages. First, the learner is introduced to a prepared set of learning materials which represent puzzling situations or seemingly inconsistent data.

Second, the learner is led through a series of steps by which he "inquires" into these puzzlements and inconsistencies so that in the end he "discovers" the principles or laws by which these apparent puzzlements can be explained. Finally, the learner is prompted by the teacher to examine his own process of inquiry and discovery, so as to ascertain the basic reasons why that which he discovered is indeed the underlying concept, principle, or law.[129]

The discovery strategy can generate a wide variety of pedagogical methods and techniques.[130] For example, a religious educator can teach the learner to come to a deeper analogical understanding of eternity-as-a-process-content by having him personally discover the meaning of time-as-a-process-content. Many effective techniques for experientially discovering the meaning of time-as-a-process-content have been developed by Gestalt psychologists, encounter psychologists, rehabilitation psychologists, human potentialists, and the like. One technique is to place the learner in a structured environment in which external distractions are removed. The learner's task is to enter into himself and reflect on himself as he is in his here-and-now situation. Denuded of external distractions, the learner is thereby led to encounter himself as a person-in-time. In this heightened, often newly experienced realization of self-in-time, the learner gradually comes to a deeper realization of the meaning and significance of time. With the help of a skilled religious educator, the learner can then be helped to draw a processive analogy between time and eternity.[131]

Expanding the Affective Dimensions of Process Content
Substantive process content is an integral and indispensable aspect of affect. After all, affect is an operation, a process. Thus it is not surprising that post World War II psychologists and educationists who specialize in affective education place great theoretical and practical stress on the process dimension of affect.

One of the major constituents of the affective dimension of process content is attitude. To assert that an attitude is a disposition or personality set to respond in a consistent manner is to assert two fundamental processive characteristics of attitude. First, an attitude is a general affective orientation which a person has toward one or another reality. As affective orienting, an attitude involves seeing a reality positively or negatively, favorably or unfavorably.[132] Second, an attitude is the way in which various personality elements are organized into a relatively consistent affectively valenced personality set.[133] Orientation and organization—or more accurately personal orienting and personal organizing—are substantive process contents.

An attitude can be properly regarded as a mediating process. Indeed, attitudes have been found by the research to be among the most effective of all kinds of mediating processes in determining the texture and success which new and novel stimuli will have on the individual.[134]

There is even a significant number of social scientists who hold that attitudes are purely process to which are necessarily conjoined the product contents of beliefs and opinions.[135] This conceptualization is related to James Fowler's view of faith as primarily a substantive process content which is conjoined to the substantive product contents of beliefs, etc.[136]

As fundamentally or even as wholly a substantive process, attitudes are in constant flux. At times a person's attitudes change drastically, at other times only slightly. Even a person's deepest attitudes set in infancy undergo some modification. Attitudes, like the times and the persons living in the times, are always changing in one way or another.[137] To be sure, attitude change can be linked to the person's processive and continual adaptation to the changing processing world.[138]

An Illustration. Faithing is a cardinal affective process content of religious instruction. Consequently, one of the important processive dimensions of faithing, namely trusting, is also a key affective substantive process content of religious instruction endeavor. Trusting in God or in religiously charged realities is, above all, a confident feeling in, a confident feeling with, and a confident feeling for God or some religious reality.

Trusting is an ongoing and processive activity. In effective religious instruction, the strength of a person's trusting in God should grow, and the contours of this trusting should also enlarge. This is true whether the religious educator conceptualizes trusting as a processive operationalizing of a healthy personality or as a processive enfleshment of general expectancy.

Trusting is keyed to affect far more than to cognition. Thus depth psychologists have found that a well-developed affective life is a necessary grounding for the development and exercise of a robust trusting attitude. Conversely, religious instruction activity which is targeted to the development and enhancement of a trusting attitude must do so within the broader parameters of affect as a whole.

One pedagogical technique which might prove effective in teaching the learner to have or to develop trust is the trust walk.[139] The trust walk is more processive than the trust fall described in the previous chapter because in the trust walk the learner is extend*ing* his trust vertically with himself and horizontally in time. A trust fall happens very quickly. In a trust walk, however, the learner must go on keeping trust; he must engage in continuous trusting.

In the trust walk, the learner is blindfolded and is lead by the religious educator around furniture, in and out of rooms, up and down stairs, through and across busy streets, and so forth. An effective instructional procedure in this regard is for the religious educator to start the walk in a situation in which only a little trust is required, such as walking through a familiar room. Gradually the educator leads the learner into situations requiring the exercise of an increasingly greater trusting relationship, such as walking through an unfamiliar room filled with furniture, then down stairs, and finally across a busy street intersection.

Trust walking requires the learner to continuously trust the teacher not to lead him into places and situations in which he would be frightened, hurt, or even injured. The trust walk is highly personalistic and grounded in the learner's total affective system because the learner must continuously and continually be giving of himself totally and confidently into the hands of the religious educator.

Expanding the Lifestyle Dimension of Process Content

A thoroughly Christian lifestyle is surely the most important dimension of process content, just as it is the most important dimension of every content of religious instruction. Central to a thoroughly Christian lifestyle is the process content of religious experiencing.

Religious experience, as I indicate in Chapter Two, is a product content of religious instruction. Religious experienc*ing,* on the other hand, represents a substantive process content in religious instruction.[140] There is an intrinsic and necessary relation between the process of experiencing and religious instruction. Indeed, all religious instruction takes place within the existential framework of the experiential process.[141] It is in this sense that personal experiencing can be said to be the most educationally significant of all process contents. Lifestyle, after all, is the way in which a person dynamically orders and experientially lives out his present personal experiencing.

An Illustration. A cardinal substantive process content of religious instruction is an expansion of self-experiencing, an openness of self to both present and new experiencing.[142] To be sure, this ongoing openness to being and becoming, this dynamic transparency of one's self to everything in the world, good and evil alike, constitutes one of the most educative of all process contents. In a moving passage, Morton Trippe Kelsey, summing up his nearly thirty years as a facilitator of religious experiencing, comments: "In fact, God is most polite. He seldom breakes in upon us until we open ourselves to him. . . . Since it is up to us to bring what we are, like it or not, to the meeting, this takes honesty. Few men allow themselves to know what they are, what lies within them, and when men do not face themselves, they cannot meet God."[143] The degree to which a person is open to his present and potential experiencing appears to be directly proportional to the degree to which he has achieved personhood. Put more operationally, the degree to which a person manifests openness-to-experiencing behaviors represents an adequate gauge of the degree to which he has self-actualized as a person—and from the religious perspective, the degree to which he has self-actualized as a person of religion. It is probably not an exaggeration to state that many of the cruel and malicious actions performed by so-called religious individuals in the name of religion were consequences of their lack of transparency and openness to the full gamut of their own personal experiencing of the entire spectrum of reality.

One pedagogical technique which might prove helpful in teaching the learner to expand his openness to present religious experiencing is that called "contacting the actual."[144] The goal of this technique is to assist the learner to make genuine personal contact and then to engage in a processive experiencing of present actuality.

Using this technique, the religious educator spends some minutes creating an atmosphere conducive to present experiencing, one not cluttered with extraneous cognitive content. Then the educator says the following to the learner: "Try for a few minutes to make up sentences stating what you are aware of at this very moment. Be sure to begin each and every sentence with the words 'now' or 'at this moment,' or 'here and now.' " The religious educator should emphasize that when the learner speaks of the present, he should mean the immediate, here-and-now present—the time of his present attention span, the time that is right now.

The objective of this instructional technique is not the help learners live for present experience but rather to live in and with present experiencing.[145]

If the pedagogical technique of contacting-the-actual is successful, the learner will experience himself as he is presently experiencing reality. He will expand and open his experiencing so that he more fully and more consciously experiences himself in his here-and-now activity. This activity even includes dull and prosaic experiences such as "Now my nose itches. Now I am scratching it." When experiencing memories, the learner will become aware that he is experiencing these memories not as past and inert product contents, but rather as ongoing present experiences of past events, experiences which are given a particular present coloration and a particular present force on the developmental basis of the learner's own present circumstances and here-and-now exigencies.

Once the learner has gained proficiency in opening himself to actual present experiencing, the religious educator can structure a religiously valenced activity such as a liturgy, a group prayer experience, a mini-retreat, and the like. Then at pedagogically appropriate times during this situation, the educator can say the following to the learner: "Try for a few minutes to make up sentences stating what you are aware of religiously at this very moment. Be sure to begin each and every sentence with words 'now,' or 'at this moment,' or 'here and now.' "

The pedagogical technique of "contacting the actual" has been found to produce several important and beneficial outcomes. In some learners, the effort to experientially contact present actuality tends to rouse anxiety (often masked as boredom, annoyance, and impatience). This anxiety seems to be brought on by one's felt realization that his present secular and religious here-and-now experiencing has been split off from his everyday personality functioning. In other learners, the successful experiential contact with present reality sharpens the sense of the immediacy and the concreteness of here-and-now experiencing. This sharpened sense enables the learner to more existentially appreciate the difference between concrete experiencing, on the one hand, and abstractions drawn from this experiencing, on the other hand. Such an existential appreciation is essential for successful religious instruction.

After all, the primary goal of religious instruction is immediate concrete experienced religious living, and not removed generalized abstractions (theology) drawn from immediate concrete experienced religious living. In still other learners, the successful experiential contact with ongoing present reality is strenuous but rewarding work. For this type of learner, the quality and texture of here-and-now concrete experiencing becomes rich and real and exciting. His capacity to *be his experiencing* and to open himself to that which his experiential self is actually contacting makes life at once whole and wholesome.

The pedagogical technique of "contacting the actual" might seem deceptively and even fatuously simple. Yet it can be a very useful pedagogical procedure in religious instruction endeavor because it teaches many learners a basic human verity which they may have unlearned in the journey of life. One of the prevalent barriers to fruitful religious living is a personal detachment from here-and-now experiencing. Regrettably, religion programs and religion lessons often erect such barriers by teaching learners abstractions about reality rather than teaching them to processively and immediately experience reality. Theology is helpful as one aid in interpreting religious experiencing, but it is no substitute for religious experiencing. There seems to be in some persons—child, youth, and adult—a mystic strain.[146] One of the most salient characteristics of the religious mystic is that such persons have an extraordinarily well-developed immediate experiential contact with here-and-now actualities around them and in them. Indeed, the writings of most religious mystics are typically rich in concrete, here-and-now, sensuous imagery which pulsates with immediacy.[147]

CONCLUSION

To emphasize substantive process content in no way weakens or destroys religion, whether this religion is of an older or newer cast. All too often process content is regarded as something totally new and therefore intrinsically inimical to the older, more traditional forms of religion. True it is that my own heavy and overt emphasis on the great worth of process-as-substantive content is relatively new in religious instruction theorizing. I believe history shows that the most sensitive and most effective religious instruction in every century was that which placed strong stress on process content. It does not matter that religious educators of these bygone eras often did not formally recognize that what they were emphasizing was the process content of religious instruction. What does matter is the way they interwove process content into their lessons. Process content has always been a deep and very significant aspect of meaningful religion, effective religious instruction, and fecund theology. Perhaps one of the most helpful services which twentieth-century scholars in many fields are performing is to consciously mine the rich ore of process content so as to contribute toward a more abundant treasury of religion, religious instruction, and theology.

NOTES

1. William Butler Yeats, *Among School Children.*
2. See James Michael Lee, "The *Teaching* of Religion," in James Michael Lee and Patrick C. Rooney, editors, *Toward a Future for Religious Education* (Dayton, Ohio: Pflaum/Standard, 1970), pp. 76–78.
3. A great many religious educators and educationists do not seem to recognize that process is a substantive content. And those who do, typically tend to equate process content with instructional practice. See, for example, J. Gordon Chamberlin, *Freedom and Faith: New Approaches to Christian Education* (Philadelphia: Westminster, 1965), pp. 118–119. Berard Marthaler seems to embrace a fuller, more mature view of process than does Chamberlin when he writes: "Process is more than [pedagogical] methods. It is the interaction of all the factors involved in a learning experience." Berard Marthaler, *Catechetics in Context* (Huntington, Ind.: Our Sunday Visitor, 1973), p. 211.
4. The first part of this statement assumes that the religion teacher is adopting an integralist position with regard to religious instruction. A teacher having an intellectualist view or a moralist view might well restrict his process contents to thinking or loving respectively. The second part of this statement is in line with what I remark earlier in the book about total content being simultaneously part of the teaching act and an outcome of it.
5. Henry C. Ellis, *Transfer of Learning* (New York: Macmillan, 1965), pp. 32–38, 61–74.
6. See Marshall McLuhan, *Understanding Media: The Extensions of Man* (New York: McGraw-Hill, 1964), p. 129.
7. This point can be illustrated by disorders in human speaking. Various speaking disorders are defects in the speaking (process) of some word or sound (product). While the cure for such disorders centers around remediating the process content (speaking), such remediation typically takes place with the accompaniment of product content (words or sounds). See James F. Curtis, editor, *Processes and Disorders of Human Communication* (New York: Harper & Row, 1978); Donald E. Mowrer, *Methods of Modifying Speech Disorders* (Columbus, Ohio: Merrill, 1977).
8. Thus Jacob Bronowski defines science as "the organization of our knowledge in such a way that it commands more of the hidden potential in nature." J. Bronowski, *Science and Human Values,* rev. ed. (New York: Harper & Row Torchbooks. 1965), p. 7.

9. On this point, see Jerome S. Bruner, *The Process of Education* (Cambridge, Mass.: Harvard University Press, 1960), pp. 6–10. The following example in the text is drawn from Bruner.

10. Marc Belth, *Process of Thinking* (New York: McKay, 1977), pp. 126–154; Thomas S. Kuhn, *The Structure of Scientific Revolutions,* 2d edition (Chicago: University of Chicago Press, 1970), pp. 23–42, 92–110.

11. See Ole Sand, "Bases for Decisions," in Robert R. Leeper, editor, *The Role of the Supervisor and the Curriculum Director in a Climate of Change* (Washington, D.C.: Association for Supervision and Curriculum Development, 1965), pp. 30–49.

12. Harold William Burgess has superbly catalogued and collected the views of many religious education writers who fail to properly appreciate process as a substantive content. See Harold William Burgess, *An Invitation To Religious Education* (Birmingham, Ala.: Religious Education Press, 1975), p. 35–41. Religious educationists who have adopted the social-science approach, or who have been strongly influenced by this approach, recognize and prize process as a substantive content. See, for example, Lucie W. Barber, *The Religious Education of Preschool Children* (Birmingham, Ala.: Religious Education Press, 1981); Donald E. Bossart, *Creative Conflict in Religious Education and Church Administration* (Birmingham, Ala.: Religious Education Press, 1980); Thomas H. Groome, *Christian Religious Education* (San Francisco: Harper & Row, 1980); Morton Kelsey, *Can Christians Be Educated?* (Birmingham, Ala.: Religious Education Press, 1977).

13. Marshall McLuhan, *Understanding Media: The Extensions of Man,* p. 9.

14. Roger Lincoln Shinn, *The Educational Mission of Our Church* (Boston: United Church Press, 1962), p. 98.

15. Maria Montessori, *The Montessori Method,* translated by Anne E. George (Cambridge, Mass.: Robert Bentley, 1965), pp. 355–356.

16. Unfortunately, imprecise formulations on the part of quite a few religious educationists who do in fact agree on this point lead readers or hearers to precisely the opposite conclusion. Thus Morton Trippe Kelsey can write: "Process and content cannot be separated, however." Kelsey, a Jungian psychotherapist frequently involved in religious education, is a staunch advocate of substantive process content. Were Kelsey and likeminded persons to more carefully frame their conceptualizations of process as (1) itself a content (2) which exists in the real order only in conjunction with product content and other contents, the import and impact of their theses would doubtless be even further enhanced. See Morton Kelsey, *Encounter with God* (Minneapolis, Minn.: Bethany Fellowship, 1972), p. 226.

17. Because the physics of light is so complicated when compared to the physics of sound, it would have been easier for me to have used sound as my illustration. However, since McLuhan has so popularized the light-bulb example in connection with process content, I have decided to follow through with his illustration.

18. All electromagnetic radiation is energy brought about by the acceleration of charged particles.

19. It is beyond my concern here to discuss the corpuscular theory and the wave theory in terms of explaining or describing the action of light. Suffice it to say in a somewhat oversimplified fashion that the corpuscular theory explains light as particles which move, while the wave theory explains light as particles which are moved.

20. Of course every "end" in one sense is never a total end but rather a means to some more terminal, more all-embracing end.
21. Presumably to emphasize revelation as a substantive process content, one religious educationist has titled his book *The Present Revelation*. I am tempted to observe that this writer's point might have been even further strengthened had he used as his title *"The Present Revealing."* See Gabriel Moran, *The Present Revelation* (New York: Herder and Herder, 1972)
22. For my treatment of revelation as both process content and product content I am utilizing the concise conceptualization of revelation made by Sacra Congregatio pro Clericis, *Directorium catechisticum generale* (Città del Vaticano: Libreria Editrice Vaticana, 1971), p. 38 (#37). With more careful wording, the Sacred Congregation could have brought to an even higher degree of precision and salience its view of revelation as both process content and product content.
23. See James Michael Lee, "The *Teaching* of Religion," pp. 76–77.
24. Jerome Bruner, *The Process of Education*, pp. 7–8.
25. Carl R. Rogers, "The Facilitation of Significant Learning," in Laurence Siegel, editor, *Instruction: Some Contemporary Viewpoints* (San Francisco: Chandler, 1967), p. 43.
26. Asahel D. Woodruff, *Basic Concepts of Teaching*, concise ed. (San Francisco: Chandler, 1961), p. 43.
27. Jerome Bruner, *The Process of Education*, p. 7.
28. Freire's celebrated term "conscienticação" is most fruitfully and authentically interpreted within this overall context. Paulo Freire, *Pedagogy of the Oppressed*, translated by Myra Bergman Ramos (New York: Herder and Herder, 1970), p. 61, italics deleted. Freire elaborated on his views of the outcomes of instruction in a lengthy conversation I had with him in his Geneva office in March, 1971.
29. The precise term used by the *Directory* is *"catechesis,"* a term denoting that form of religious instruction directly controlled by the Vatican and local ecclesiastical hierarchies.
30. Sacra Congregatio pro Clericis, *Directorium catechisticum generale*, p. 28 (#21); see also p. 37 (#36). Curiously, the American translators of the *Directorium* render *"maturatio"* in #21 as "maturity," while in #36 *"maturatio"* is rendered as "maturing." From a pedagogical, psychological, and theological standpoint, the second rendition is the more accurate.
31. It is unfortunate that the *Directory* uses the words "maturity," "maturation," and "maturating" (*"maturatio"*) because the construct "maturation" is a precise term in educational circles. Maturation refers to the relatively *automatic* process of the cellular, organic, and functional development of the person. Thus "maturation" is sharply contrasted to the construct of "learning" which is defined as that form of self-activity through which, by means of *experience,* the person's behavior is changed. It would have been less confusing pedagogically and more accurate psychologically had the *Directory* used the terms "growth" or "growing" instead of "maturation" or "maturing." Quite possibly the original *Directorium* would have employed more precise and careful terminology if scholars representing a social-science approach to religious instruction had been on the drafting and reviewing committees; as it happened, these committees were made up exclusively of theologians and members of various theologically oriented Central Catechetical Establishments.
32. This statement can be especially appreciated when viewing the fundamental conceptualization of and research on faith by persons such as James Fowler.

33. Sacra Congregatio pro Clericis, *Directorium catechisticum generale,* p. 37.
34. The *Directory* makes this same point: "The two can, however, be distinguished for reasons of methodology," p. 37 (#36). Berard Marthaler's commentary on this entire passage (#36) of the *Directory* seems to be ambiguous and confusing. He initially states that faith-as-process-content (*fides qua*) *can* be "distinguished in *life* as well as in thought" from faith-as-product-content (*fides quae*). Two sentences later, he notes that "Speculative theology can and must emphasize the difference, but the catechist in the field *cannot.*" The immediate context of Marthaler's statements seem to agree with my own conceptualization of the relationship of product and process content; however, Marthaler's wording of the two relevant passages on page 55 of his *Catechetics in Context* does cause some confusion in this regard. (Note: For the sake of emphasis, italics have been added to the quote from Marthaler.) In fairness to Marthaler, however, it must be noted that the *Directory* is verbally lax in that it fails to place a needed qualifying adjective before the word "methodology" (*ob rationes methodologicae*), thus generating confusion as to whether the proper qualifying adjective should be "pedagogical" or "investigative." Because of the immediate context of the passage in question, together with the broader context of the *Directory* as a whole, the qualifying adjective "investigative" definitely appears to be the one implied.
35. For a relationship of this point to the religious instruction act, see Didier-Jacques Piveteau and J. T. Dillon, *Resurgence of Religious Instruction* (Birmingham, Ala.: Religious Education Press, 1977), pp. 173–182; Robert E. Rumer, "Christian Education is Spiritual Nurture," in J. T. Dillon, editor, *Catechetics Reconsidered* (Winona, Minn.: St. Mary's College Press, 1968), p. 20.
36. In this discussion I am using "means" in its dimensionality of a substantive process content. When taken in a structural content sense, "means" has a neutral valence with respect to value.
37. Marshall McLuhan, *Understanding Media: The Extensions of Man.*
38. Thomas Luckmann, *The Invisible Religion* (New York: Macmillan, 1967).
39. John Dewey, *Democracy and Education,* (New York: Macmillan, 1916), p. 5.
40. J. Gordon Chamberlain, *Freedom and Faith,* p. 123.
41. See George B. Leonard, *Education and Ecstasy* (New York: Dell, 1968), p. 97. For a liberationist conceptualization of this point, see James John Jelinek, "The Learning of Values," in James John Jelinek, editor, *Improving the Human Condition* (Washington, D.C.: Association for Supervision and Curriculum Development, 1978), pp. 192–194.
42. J. L. Spalding, *Glimpses of Truth* (Chicago: McClurg, 1903), p. 56.
43. On this last point, see Emil Brunner, *Truth as Encounter,* translated by Amandus W. Loos and David Cairns (Philadelphia: Westminster, 1943), p. 28.
44. Much of the difficulty which Pierre Teilhard de Chardin had with the Vatican authorities had its roots sunk deep in the question of whether revelation is a stable product content or a process content in emergence.
45. See Karl Rahner, *Theological Investigations,* volume XIV, translated by David Bourke (New York: Seabury, 1976), pp. 24–46; Karl Rahner, *Theological Investigations,* volume I, 2d edition, translated by Cornelius Ernst (Baltimore, Md.: Helicon, 1965), pp. 43–48.
46. Albert Shamon is on target when he observes that "during his life on earth, Christ showed himself to be the perfect communicator, for the medium was the message: the Word was made flesh." Albert J. Shamon, *Catching Up on Catechetics* (New York: Paulist, 1972), p. 43.

47. On this point, see James Michael Lee, "Christian Religious Education and Moral Development," in Brenda Munsey, editor, *Moral Development, Moral Education, and Kohlberg* (Birmingham, Ala.: Religious Education Press, 1980), pp. 343–347.

48. "In a Search for Simplicity," *Life* LX (January 9, 1970), p. 20. It well might be that this man's awareness of the organic interrelationship of process content and product content enabled him to remark: "I am a philosophy major and here I am with calf's blood up to my elbows. But this work is very real, sacred to me. It makes you understand that veal chops don't grow in cellophane bags."

49. Doyle P. Johnson, "Religious Commitments, Social Distance, and Authoritarianism," in *Review of Religious Research* XVIII (Winter, 1977), pp. 99–113; Richard D. Kahoe, "Intrinsic Religion and Authoritarianism: A Differentiated Relationship," in *Journal for the Scientific Study of Religion* XVI (June, 1977), pp. 179–182; Andrew D. Thompson, "Open-Mindedness and Indiscriminate Antireligious Orientation," in *Journal for the Scientific Study of Religion* XIII (December 1974), pp. 471–477. For a broad review of the relevant pre-1970 empirical research, see Merton P. Strommen, editor, *Research on Religious Development* (New York: Hawthorn, 1971).

50. Gerard Pottebaum cogently addresses himself to this issue. See Gerard A. Pottebaum, "Where is Your Doctrine?" in *New Book Review*, n.v., n.d., p. 9.

51. For a superb and pithy discussion of doctrine as interactively processive, see Bernard Lonergan, *The Way to Nicea*, translated by Conn O'Donovan (Philadelphia: Westminster, 1976), pp. 1–17.

52. Thus Benkt-Erik Benkston contends that if it is to be authentic, doctrine must not be so much fixed but rather on pilgrimage because persons, like the church, are essentially on pilgrimage. Benkt-Erik Benkston, *Dogma als Drama* (Stuttgart: Calwer, 1976), pp. 13–15.

53. Benjamin S. Bloom, editor, *Taxonomy of Educational Objectives: Handbook I: Cognitive Domain* (New York: McKay, 1956).

54. David R. Krathwohl, Benjamin S. Bloom, and Bertram B. Masia, *Taxonomy of Educational Objectives: Handbook II: Affective Domain* (New York: McKay, 1964).

55. See, for example, Henry P. Cole, *Process Education* (Englewood Cliffs, N.J.: Educational Technology Publications, 1972), pp. 58–121, 190–234.

56. J. Cecil Parker and Louis J. Rubin, *Process as Content* (Chicago: Rand McNally, 1966), p. 44.

57. See Howard Grimes, *The Church Redemptive* (Nashville, Tenn.: Abingdon, 1958), pp. 90–91.

58. Regrettably, not a few advocates of process-as-content, such as Jerome Bruner on the one hand, or Cecil Parker and Louis Rubin on the other, limit process content to simply the cognitive domain. A considerable amount of fine research has been done on cognitive process content because academic researchers have a natural affinity for such research. See, for example, Jack Lochhead and John Clement, editors, *Cognitive Process Instruction* (Philadelphia: Franklin Institute Press, 1979).

59. John Dewey, *Experience and Education* (New York: Macmillan, 1938), p. 104.

60. Marshall McLuhan, *Understanding Media: The Extensions of Man* (New York: McGraw-Hill, 1964), p. 148.

61. James E. Loder, "A Medium for the Message," in John H. Westerhoff III, editor, *A Colloquy on Christian Education,* (Philadelphia: Pilgrim, 1972), p. 71.

62. Edward Schillebeeckx, *Christ: the Sacrament of Encounter with God*, translated by Paul Barrett, revised by Laurence Bright and Mark Schoof (New York: Sheed and Ward, 1963), p. 19.
63. Michael Pfliegler, *The Right Moment*, translated by M. Veronica Riedl (Notre Dame, Ind.: University of Notre Dame Press, 1966), p. 70.
64. On this point, see C. Ellis Nelson, *Where Faith Begins* (Richmond, Va.: Knox, 1967), pp. 87–93.
65. Gegory Baum, *Man Becoming* (New York: Herder and Herder, 1970), p. 42.
66. Karl Rahner, *The Christian Commitment*, translated by Cecily Hastings (New York: Sheed and Ward, 1963), p. 117.
67. John Giles Milhaven, *Toward a New Catholic Morality* (Garden City, N.Y.: Doubleday, 1970), p. 12.
68. See John A. T. Robinson, *The Difference in Being a Christian Today* (Philadelphia: Westminster, 1972), p. 12.
69. John Dewey, *Democracy and Education*, p. 60.
70. Gabriel Moran, *Catechesis of Revelation* (New York: Herder and Herder, 1966), p. 127.
71. François-Xavier Durrwell, "The Efficacy of Petitionary Prayer," in *Lumen Vitae* XXIII (September, 1968), p. 414.
72. See Robert Sears, Eleanor Macoby [sic] and Harry Levin, "How Conscience Is Informed," in C. Ellis Nelson, editor, *Conscience: Theological and Psychological Perspectives* (New York: Newman, 1973), p. 296.
73. Walter E. Conn, *Conscience: Development and Self-Transcendence* (Birmingham, Ala.: Religious Education Press, 1981).
74. Paulo Freire, *Pedagogy of The Oppressed*, p. 101.
75. *Ibid.*, p. 158, italics deleted.
76. See, for example, Quentin Lauer, *The Triumph of Subjectivity* (New York: Fordham University Press, 1958).
77. See Sara Little, *The Role of the Bible in Contemporary Christian Education* (Richmond, Va.: Knox, 1961), pp. 158–162; Vatican Council II, *The Dogmatic Constitution on Divine Revelation,* translated by George A. Tavard (New York: Paulist, 1966), pp. 58–61 (#'s 2–6).
78. In this connection, Wolfhart Pannenberg holds the following: "The self-revelation of God in the biblical witnesses is not of a direct type in the sense of a theophany, but is indirect and brought about by means of historical acts of God (p. 25). Revelation is not comprehended completely in the beginning, but at the end of revealing history (p. 131). In distinction from special manifestations of the Deity, the historical revelation is open to anyone who has eyes to see. It has universal character (p. 135). The universal revelation of the Deity of God is not yet realized in the history of Israel, but first in the fate of Jesus of Nazareth, insofar as the end of all events is anticipated in his fate (p. 139). The Word relates itself to revelation as foretelling, forthtelling, and report" (p. 152). Wolfhart Pannenberg, "Dogmatic Theses on the Doctrine of Revelation," in Wolfhart Pannenberg, editor, *Revelation as History*, translated by David Granskov (New York: Macmillan, 1968), pp. 123–158.
79. See Wayne Rood, *On Nurturing Christians* (Nashville, Tenn.: Abingdon, 1972), p. 57; see also, Heinrich Stirnimann, "Language, Experience, and Revelation," in Edward Schillebeeckx and Bas van Iersel, editors, *Revelation and Experience* (New York: Seabury, 1979), pp. 117–130.
80. See Gabriel Moran, *Catechesis of Revelation*, p. 13; see also Gabriel Moran, *Theology of Revelation* (New York: Herder and Herder, 1966), p. 120.

81. See Gabriel Moran, *The Present Revelation*, p. 117.
82. Harold Hatt is quite critical of propositional theology in this connection. One of the chapters in his stimulating book, for example, is entitled "The Non Sequitur of Propositional Theology" (pp. 150–175). See Harold E. Hatt, *Encountering Truth: A New Understanding of How Revelation as Encounter Yields Doctrine* (Nashville, Tenn.: Abingdon 1966). Hatt rests heavily on Martin Buber and Emil Brunner.
83. Emil Brunner, *Truth as Encounter*, p. 155.
84. Rudolf Bultmann, "A Reply to the Thesis of J. Schniewind," in Hans Werner Bartsch, editor, *Kerygma and Myth*, rev. ed. (New York: Harper & Row Torchbooks, 1961), pp. 114–115.
85. See, for example, Alfred North Whitehead, *Religion in the Making* (New York: Macmillan, 1926); Alfred North Whitehead, *Process and Reality* (New York: Macmillan, 1929); Alfred North Whitehead, *Adventures of Ideas* (New York: Macmillan, 1933).
86. Hartshorne was Whitehead's student and is probably the most notable exponent of Whitehead's doctrine of God. See, for example, Charles Hartshorne, *The Divine Relativity* (New Haven, Conn.: Yale University Press, 1948); Charles Hartshorne, *A Natural Theology for Our Time* (La Salle, Ill.: Open Court, 1967); Charles Hartshorne, *Creative Synthesis and Philosophical Method* (La Salle, Ill.: Open Court, 1970).
87. Ogden is a former student of Hartshorne. See, for example, Schubert M. Ogden, *The Reality of God and other Essays* (New York: Harper & Row, 1966); Schubert M. Ogden, "Toward a New Theism," in Delwin Brown, Ralph E. James, Jr., and Gene Reeves, editors, *Process Philosophy and Christian Thought* (Indianapolis, Ind.: Bobbs-Merrill, 1971), pp. 173–187.
88. See, for example, John B. Cobb, Jr., *A Christian Natural Theology* (Philadelphia: Westminster, 1965); John B. Cobb, Jr., *God and the World* (Philadelphia: Westminster, 1969); John B. Cobb, Jr., *Christian Natural Theology Based on the Thought of Alfred North Whitehead* (Philadelphia: Westminster, 1979); John B. Cobb, Jr., *The Structure of Christian Existence* (New York: Seabury, 1979).
89. See, for example, Daniel Day Williams, *God's Grace and Man's Hope* (New York: Harper & Row, 1949); Daniel Day Williams, *The Spirit and The Forms of Love* (New York: Harper & Row, 1968).
90. See, for example, W. Norman Pittinger, *The Word Incarnate* (New York: Harper & Row, 1959); W. Norman Pittinger, *God in Process* (London: SCM Press, 1967); W. Norman Pittinger, *Process-Thought and Christian Faith* (New York: Macmillan, 1968); Norman Pittinger, *The Christian Church as A Social Process* (London: Epworth 1971); Norman Pittinger, *The Divine Triunity* (Philadelphia: Pilgrim, 1977); Norman Pittinger, *Cosmic Love and Human Wrong* (New York: Paulist, 1978).
91. See, for example, Bernard M. Loomer, "Empirical Theology within Process Thought," in Bernard E. Meland, editor, *The Future of Empirical Theology* (Chicago: University of Chicago Press, 1969), pp. 149–173; Bernard M. Loomer, "Christian Faith and Process Philosophy," in Delwin Brown, Ralph E. James, Jr., and Gene Reeves, editors, *Process Philosophy and Christian Thought*, pp. 70–98.
92. See, for example, Walter E. Stokes, "God for Today and Tomorrow," in Delwin Brown, Ralph E. James, Jr., and Gene Reeves, editors, *Process Philosophy* and *Christian Thought*, pp. 244–263; Walter E. Stokes, "A Whiteheadian

Reflection on God's Relation to the World," in Ewert H. Cousins, editor, *Process Theology* (New York: Paulist, 1971), pp. 137–152.

93. See, for example, Henry Nelson Wieman, *Religious Experience and Scientific Method* (New York: Macmillan, 1926); Henry Nelson Wieman, *The Source of Human Good* (Chicago: University of Chicago Press, 1946); Henry Nelson Wieman, *Religious Inquiry* (Boston: Beacon, 1968); Henry Nelson Wieman, *Seeking a Faith For A New Age*, edited by Cedric L. Hepler (Metuchen, N.J.: Scarecrow, 1975).

94. See, for example, Bernard E. Meland, *Seeds of Redemption* (New York: Macmillan, 1947); Bernard E. Meland, *The Realities of Faith* (New York: Oxford University Press, 1962); Bernard E. Meland, "Can Empirical Theology Learn Something from Phenomenology?" in Bernard E. Meland, editor, *The Future of Empirical Theology*, pp. 283–305; Bernard E. Meland, *Fallible Forms and Symbols* (Philadelphia: Fortress, 1976).

95. Pierre Teilhard de Chardin, *The Phenomenon of Man*, translated by Bernard Wall (New York: Harper & Row, 1959); Pierre Teilhard de Chardin, *The Future of Man*, translated by Norman Denny (New York: Harper & Row, 1964); Pierre Teilhard de Chardin, *Christianity and Evolution*, translated by René Hague (New York: Harcourt Brace Jovanovich, 1971).

96. See, for example, Eulalio R. Baltazar, *Teilhard and the Supernatural* (Baltimore, Md.: Helicon, 1966); Eulalio R. Baltazar, *God Within Process* (New York: Paulist, 1970); Eulalio R. Baltazar, *The Dark Center* (New York: Paulist, 1973).

97. Randolph Crump Miller, *The American Spirit in Theology* (Philadelphia: Pilgrim, 1974); Randolph Crump Miller, *This We Can Believe* (New York: Hawthorn, 1976); Randolph Crump Miller, *The Theory of Christian Education Practice* (Birmingham, Ala.: Religious Education Press, 1981).

98. Gloria Durka and Joanmarie Smith, *Modeling God* (New York: Paulist, 1976).

99. Christopher Mooney claims that this is not true for Teilhard's process theology. For Teilhard, asserts Mooney, the dynamism of the processing reality itself forces one to recognize the primacy of being over becoming. Teilhard's absolute, according to Mooney, is outside the process, present both at its beginning and at its end. Christopher F. Mooney, "Teilhard de Chardin and Christian Spirituality," in *Thought* XLII (Autumn, 1967), p. 398.

100. Charles Hartshorne, *A Natural Theology for Our Time*, pp. 18–19.

101. See Ian G. Barbour, "Teilhard's Process Metaphysics," in Ewert H. Cousins, editor, *Process Theology*, p. 326.

102. Alfred North Whitehead, *Science and the Modern World* (New York: Macmillan, 1925), p. 84.

103. In the Aristotelian-Thomistic view, the world is related to God because of its contingency. God, however, is totally unrelated to the world ontologically for this very same reason (contingency).

104. Charles Hartshorne, "The Development of Process Philosophy," in Ewert H. Cousins, editor, *Process Theology*, p. 48.

105. Schubert M. Ogden, *The Reality of God and Other Essays*, p. 65.

106. W. Norman Pittinger, "Process Thought: A Contemporary Trend in Theology," in Ewert H. Cousins, editor, *Process Theology*, p. 31.

107. Alfred North Whitehead, *Process and Reality*, p. 532. I should note that there is a range of views among process thinkers concerning the nature of God. For one group of process theologians, Alfred North Whitehead's conceptualizations are

seminal, while for another group, Pierre Teilhard de Chardin provides the *point de départ.*

108. Wayne R. Rood, *On Nurturing Christians* (Nashville, Tenn.: Abingdon, 1972), p. 131.
109. John S. Dunne, *A Search for God in Time and Memory* (New York: Macmillan, 1967), p. 196. This notion of man's progressive awakening to God by journeying with open eyes and with open heart is a central theme in John Dunne's books. See, for example, John S. Dunne, *The Way of All the Earth* (New York: Macmillan, 1972); John S. Dunne, *Time and Myth* (Garden City, N.Y.: Doubleday, 1973); John S. Dunne, *The Reasons of the Heart* (Notre Dame, Ind.: University of Notre Dame Press, 1979). Dunne's form of human-development theology which is grounded in coming to God by empirically coming to self is most congenial with the social-science approach to religious instruction. Dunne's writings show that the empirical need not be "cold."
110. Howard Grimes, "Review," in *Religious Education* LXVIII (November–December, 1973), pp. 757–758.
111. See Abraham Edel, "Discussion," in C. M. Beck, B. S. Crittenden, and E. V. Sullivan, *Moral Education: Interdisciplinary Approaches* (Toronto: University of Toronto Press, 1971), pp. 347–348.
112. Marcel van Caster and Jean LeDu, *Experiential Catechetics,* translated by Denis Barrett (Paramus, N. J.: Newman, 1969), p. 21.
113. Aristotle, *Metaphysics,* #s 1010–1012, 1027B.
114. Thomas Aquinas, *Summa Contra Gentiles,* I, 59; Thomas Aquinas, *Summa Theologica,* I, q. 16, a.2.
115. In the Scholastic formula familiar to some religious educationists, this is *adequatio rei et intellectus.*
116. For Immanuel Kant, the mind does not conform to reality, but rather reality conforms to the mind. The person, thus, in large measure, determines something about realities both prior to experiencing them and also in the act of experiencing them. A person, then, in a sense constructs reality, or more precisely, constructs his own reality. Immanuel Kant, *Critique of Pure Reason,* 2d edition, translated by F. Max Müller (Garden City, N.Y.: Doubleday Anchor, 1966), p. xxxiii–xxxv (Kant's "Preface," #s Bxvi–xix).
117. For philosophical pragmatists like John Dewey, meaning comes from and in the way in which a person successfully works through and solves personally felt problems in a manner which is satisfying and productive for him. John Dewey, *Democracy and Education* (New York: Macmillan, 1916), pp. 117–129.
118. Michael Polanyi, for example, stresses that meaning, like all forms of knowledge, possesses an essential phenomenological dimension in that the person attaches to a sensed object or mental idea a quality and meaning that the sensed object or mental idea does not have in itself. Even natural science, therefore, necessitates personal involvement, not personal detachment. There is no such thing as meaning in itself. Meaning is always someone's meaning. Michael Polanyi and Harry Prosch, *Meaning* (Chicago: University of Chicago Press, 1975), pp. 33–45, 57–63.
119. Ana-Marie Rizzuto, "The Psychological Foundations of Belief in God," in Christiane Brusselmans, convenor, *Toward Moral and Religious Maturity* (Morristown, N.J.: Silver Burdett, 1980), pp. 116–133.
120. James W. Fowler, "Faith and the Structuring of Meaning," in *ibid.,* pp. 52–84.

121. James W. Fowler, "Introduction," in James W. Fowler and Robin W. Lovin, editors, *Trajectories in Faith* (Nashville, Tenn.: Abingdon, 1980), p. 19.

122. Thomas H. Groome, *Christian Religious Education*.

123. Malcolm L. Warford, *The Necessary Illusion* (Philadelphia: Pilgrim, 1976). Warford and Groome underwent much the same doctoral training at basically the same time and hold fundamentally the same positions. One notable divergence between them, however, is that Warford claims that pedagogical procedure can only hurt the teaching of liberation, while Groome contends that liberation-oriented pedagogical procedure is necessary to facilitate the product outcome of liberation. For a variety of reasons including philosophical and psychological evidence, I believe Groome is eminently correct in this regard.

124. James Michael Lee, *The Flow of Religious Instruction* (Birmingham, Ala.: Religious Education Press, 1973), pp. 233–240.

125. The twentieth-century roots of the discovery strategy include John Dewey's philosophy of the thinking process, empirical research in cognitive psychology, and the continued exploration into the structure of natural science and natural-science education by scientists and science educators. The contemporary pedagogical development of the discovery strategy is generally credited to J. Richard Suchman as first encapsulated in full-blown form in his United States Office of Education project, *The Elementary School Training Program in Scientific Inquiry* (Urbana, Ill.: University of Illinois, 1962). As it was propounded in the 1960s, the discovery strategy was the fruit of careful empirical research investigation. On this point, see Graham Nuthall and Ivan Snook, "Contemporary Models of Teaching," in Robert M. W. Travers, editor, *Second Handbook of Research on Teaching* (Chicago: Rand McNally, 1973), pp. 59–68.

126. R. M. Di Vincenzo, "Forming A Theoretical Synthesis for Viewing Discovery Learning Instruction," in *School Science and Mathematics* LXXX (March, 1980), pp. 218–226. Two helpful empirical investigations illuminating this point are Aletha Solter and Richard E. Mayer, "Broader Transfer Produced by Guided Discovery of Number Concepts with Preschool Children," in *Journal of Educational Psychology* LXX (June, 1978), pp. 363–371; Shirley M. DeShields, "The Traditional Approach versus the Process-Discovery Approach to the Teaching of Science to Urban Youth," in *Journal of Negro Education* XLIV (Winter, 1975), pp. 1–5.

127. Jerome S. Bruner, "Some Elements of Discovery," in Lee S. Shulman and Evan R. Keisler, editors, *Learning by Discovery: A Critical Appraisal* (Chicago: Rand McNally, 1966), pp. 101–103.

128. A helpful book is Harold Morine and Greta Morine, *Discovery: A Challenge to Teachers* (Englewood Cliffs, N.J.: Prentice-Hall, 1973).

129. See Bruce Joyce and Marsha Weil, *Models of Teaching* (Englewood Cliffs, N.J.: Prentice-Hall, 1972), p. 139.

130. The terms "strategy," "method," and "technique" are technical ones, and refer explicitly to the successive decending stages in the taxonomy of the instructional process which I devised in *The Flow of Religious Instruction*, pp. 32–35.

131. This instructional technique has been practiced for centuries in the strictly contemplative orders of Western monasticism.

132. Martin Fishbein and Icek Ajzen, *Belief, Attitude, Intention and Behavior* (Reading, Mass.: Addison-Wesley, 1975), pp. 1–16.

133. Charles A. Kiesler, Barry E. Collins, and Norman Miller, *Attitude Change* (New York: Wiley, 1969), pp. 1–5.

134. Joseph E. Grush, "A Summary Review of Mediating Explanations of Exposure Phenomena," in *Personality and Psychology Bulletin* V (April, 1979), pp. 154–159.

135. Martin Fishbein and Icek Ajzen, *Belief, Attitude, Intention and Behavior*, pp. 1–16.

136. James W. Fowler, *Stages of Faith*, pp. 9–15.

137. Thus, for example, one national social survey found that in the 1970s changes in persons' attitudes toward racial integration took place. Depending on the circumstances and individuals' reaction to these circumstances, these attitudinal changes sometimes were rapid (1970–1972) and at other times proceeded at a slow but steady rate. D. Garth Taylor, Paul B. Sheatsley, and Andrew M. Greeley, "Attitudes toward Racial Integration," in *Scientific American* CCXXXVIII (June, 1978), pp. 42–49.

138. Anne Ruggles Gere and Eugene Smith, *Attitudes, Language, and Change* (Urbana, Ill.: National Council of Teachers of English, 1979), pp. 22–23.

139. See Harold C. Lyon, Jr., *Learning to Feel—Feeling to Learn* (Columbus, Ohio: Merrill, 1971), pp. 159–160.

140. Because of the sloppy and imprecise way the word "experience" is so frequently used in educational literature, the meaning of the term "experience" is often equivocal, referring either to product content or to process content. Thus when encountering the word "experience" in literature on general education or on religious education, the religious educator must be constantly attentive to the referent of this term.

141. John Dewey, *Experience and Education*, pp. 7–11.

142. For a discussion of this point, albeit from a somewhat different perspective, see James Michael Lee and Nathaniel J. Pallone, *Guidance and Counseling in Schools: Foundations and Processes* (New York: McGraw-Hill, 1966), pp. 41–42, 108–109, 345–346.

143. Morton Kelsey, *Encounter with God*, p. 199. Kelsey is a transcendist.

144. For a more expanded treatment of this technique as used in a psychotherapeutic setting, see Frederick Perls, Ralph F. Hefferline, and Paul Goodman, *Gestalt Therapy* (New York: Delta, 1951), pp. 30–41.

145. In this connection, Perls, Hefferline, and Goodman write: "The wish to seize the present and pin it down—to mount it, as it were, like a butterfly in a case—is doomed to failure. Actuality forever changes. In healthy persons the feeling of actuality is steady and continuous but, like the view from a train window, the scenery is always different. . . . When actuality seems fixed, permanent, unchanged and unchangeable, this is fictional actuality which we *continuously build anew* because it serves some present purpose of our own to preserve the fiction." *Ibid.*, p. 33.

146. Charles T. Tart, editor, *Transpersonal Psychologies* (New York: Harper & Row, 1975); Walter H. Clark, "Intense Religious Experience," in Merton P. Strommen, editor, *Handbook on Religious Development* (New York: Hawthorn, 1971), pp. 521–550. Cultural environments seem to enhance or depress the incidence of mystical experience. On this point, see Ralph W. Hood, Jr. and James R. Hall, "Comparison of Reported Religious Experience in Caucasian, American Indian, and Two Mexican American Samples," in *Psychological Reports* XLI (October, 1977), pp. 657–658.

147. This statement holds true even for the introverted mystics who contend that the attainment of mystical union is contingent upon emptying the mind of all sensa-

tions, images, and thoughts so as to more immediately and purely experience God in his manifestations. John of Ruysbroeck describes the ultimate mystical union of the soul with God in this manner: "And in this [mystical union] there is a delectable passing-over and flowing-away and a sinking down into the essential nakedness." Teresa of Avila describes God's grace and favors as "this rain which comes from Heaven to fill and saturate the whole of this garden with an abundance of water." John of the Cross likens the genuine mystical experience to a spiritual marriage and in this spirit writes: "My Beloved, The mountains, The solitary wooded valleys, The strange islands, the sonorous rivers, The whispering of the amorous breezes, The tranquil night, At the time of the rising dawn, The silent music, the sounding solitude, The supper that recreates and enkindles love. Our flowery bed, encompassed with dens of lions, Hung with purple and Builded in peace, Crowned with a thousand shields of gold." Indeed, some Christian (and Islamic) mystics have gone much further, and used passionate sexual language to describe the mystical union of the person with God. See Jan van Ruysbroeck, *The Spiritual Espousals,* translated by Eric Colledge (London: Faber and Faber, 1952), p. 190; Teresa of Avila, *Complete Works,* volume I, translated by E. Allison Peers (New York: Sheed and Ward, 1950), p. 108; John of the Cross, *Complete Works,* volume II, translated by E. Allison Peers (Wheathampstead, England: Clark, 1953), p. 27.

CHAPTER FOUR

COGNITIVE CONTENT

"The wisdom of others remains dull till it is writ over with our own blood. We are essentially apart from the world; it bursts into our consciousness only when it sinks its teeth and nails into us." [1]

—Eric Hoffer

THE NATURE OF COGNITIVE CONTENT

Cognitive content refers to any kind or type of intellectual content. It encompasses both the process content of intellectualizing and the product content which is yielded by the intellectualizing process.

It should be underscored that cognitive content embraces all the diverse ways in which persons think as well as all the various intellectual fruits obtained from basically different modes of intellectualizing. I mention this important point because so often cognitive content is regarded as solely conceptual or ratiocinative, while in fact nonconceptual thought, intuitive thought, or the other ways and fruits of thinking also constitute valid and rich cognitive contents. In terms of cognitive content, the general role of the religion teacher thus is to select from among the various modes of intellectualizing that particular mode which is most appropriate to the texture of the cognitive content which he seeks to introduce into the lesson.

The nature of the cognitive act has always been a controverted point among philosophers and psychologists. At a global level [2] there are two major disparate positions, namely the substantialist theory and the functionalist theory. Each of these larger theories explains the cognitive act very differently. Substantialism posits the existence of an independent entity or substance called "intellect" as the source of cognition. Intellectualizing takes place when this substance or independent entity is activated. Nonmaterialistic substantialism views this substance as a kind of qualitative entity, while materialistic substantialism claims that this substance is located in some part of the body, for example, in the brain. Functionalism, on the other hand, regards intellectualizing simply and solely as a particular way of human functioning. Functionalism holds that any positing of a separate substance or independent entity called "intellect" is a gratuitous assumption which can be denied just as gratuitiously. Functionalism, then, regards cognition as a special kind of personal activity which is coordinated with other kinds of human functioning such as affect. Substantialism claims that cognition emanates from some material or nonmaterial entity within an individual, while functionalism asserts that it is the very actualization of a person's intellectual powers which is at once the root and the activity of cognition. Substantialism conceptualizes cognition as an activity flowing from a separate substance, while functionalism regards cognition as a mobilization of conditions.[3]

It is probably safe to maintain that most religion teachers, especially in the Roman Catholic community, implicitly or explicitly hold the substantialist position. Christians in general, and Catholics in particular, seem prone to make substances out of constructs and processes, as for example, "supernatural," "grace," "faith," and the like. Religion teachers of the substantialist persuasion might well wish to reexamine their position in light of the deeply Christian concept of *homo integer*. This concept, which has the backing of the biblical view of the human person, and also of the findings of modern psychology, looks on each activity of a person as confluently flowing from that individual's entire self rather than as emanating from separate "substances" such as the intellect, will, and so forth. This holistic viewpoint claims that to state "Here is Mr. Smith's *cognition*" is not really accurate; what is accurate is to state "Here is *Mr. Smith's* cognition." The first of these two statements is more in keeping with the substantialist theory, while the second is more congruent with functionalism. Indeed, the functionalist theory is the more fruitful in terms of religious instruction because it places emphasis on the cognitive behaviors of the learner rather than on some posited substance called the intellect.[4] Thus substantialist theory would say to the religion teacher: "Try to reach the learner's intellect in order to get him to know and to understand," while the functionalist theory says to the religion teacher: "Facilitate the production of actual cognitive behavior(s) in the learner in order to enable him to know and to understand."

It should be noted that a holistic functionalism in no way denies (or affirms) that cognition is a spiritual activity. Rather, functionalism stresses that cognition is a certain kind of human activity in which all the aspects of one's personality are involved to the degree appropriate for the type and texture of the intellecting taking place at a given moment. Conversely, a holistic functionalism denies that cognition inheres in some separate, independent entity or substance within a person and operates independently of a person's other personality functions.

The character and thrust of cognition can be contrasted to affect. Cognition refers to intellectual functioning, whereas affect has to do with the feeling and emotional aspects of human activity. For example, to understand the difference between the Calvinist and the Arminian position on depravity represents a cognitive activity or behavior. On the other hand, to feel compassion for a starving child in the ghetto is an affective activity or behavior.

The holistic concept of *homo integer* suggests that no human function or activity exists independent of other key aspects of the person. Thus, as George Brown comments, it should be apparent that there is no intellectual activity without some sort of concomitant affect, and there are no affective functions taking place without cognitions being somehow involved.[5] Cognition is a mobilization and actualization of particular human conditions; however, this mobilization and actualization take place within the context of the individual's total personality system. Cognitive behavior is enacted as a *person's* cognitive behavior, and not as a disempersoned—I do not say merely disembodied— activity. It certainly is valid to speak of a sphere of personal activity called "cognitive" which can legitimately be distinguished by virtue of its functional characteristics from another sphere of personal activity called "affective." However, it is not valid to speak of cognitive activity as ever being untouched by the human organism's affective and psychomotor functioning. Cognitive activity is never un-affected. In short, every human behavior has its cognitive component, its affective component, its psychomotor component, and so forth. What makes one activity cognitive and another affective is the basic mode and axial thrust of the particular human behavior or set of behaviors.

The fruitful notion of *homo integer* also enables the religious educationist and educator to dispose of the old fallacy that a person's cognitive and affective functions cannot exist in potentially equal strengths with one another. To be sure, there do not appear to be any empirical data to support the old fallacy that an individual's cognitive capacities are in inverse proportion to his affective potential, and vice versa. As a matter of fact, quite the opposite seems to be true. The higher a person's cognitive abilities are, the deeper his affective capacities will be. Cognition is one of the most potent factors enabling the affective to enlarge, while affect constitutes one of the most powerful forces enabling the cognitive to soar. What I have noted thus far in this paragraph has important practical implications for religious instruction because time and time again teachers assume that when a learner is very intelligent, then his affective nature is by this very fact incapable of a depth of feeling commensurate with the level of his cognitive powers. If indeed a particular learner consistently displays high-level cognitive behaviors and low-level affective behaviors, it is typically because he has oriented his self-system in such a way as to give undue weight to the deployment of his cognitive functions while not allowing his affective energies to likewise exert themselves. When dealing with such a learner, the astute religion teacher structures that type of instructional situation which evokes responses which are at once highly cognitive and deeply affective. Conversely, when dealing with a learner who has attained a deep level of authentic affect, the teacher should structure the pedagogical situation in such a way that the type of cognitive content which is provided is commensurate with and, above all, congruent with his affective attainments. It should always be borne in mind that cognition and affect are confluent functions of the human personality. Hence any instructional practice which aims to produce a certain kind or level of learning outcome in one of these zones of human activity must perforce give appropriate weight and emphasis to the other sector, in accordance, of course, with the basic objectives of the lesson.

A holistic view of cognition affirms that all cognition is personal cognition. Put another way, all cognition takes place according to the mode of the cognitor. Whether in a religion lesson or in any other form of human activity, there is no cognitive content which is totally impersonal and "out there." Cognitive content is someone's cognitive content. Cognitive content always bears the imprint and coloration of the person who has learned this content. Cognitive content is always inserted into the prior existential personality system of the cognitor. According to functionalist theory, cognitive content is always operational in the person, achieving a degree of salience and potency directly proportional to: (1) how it is integrated into the total matrix of intersecting personality functions, and (2) the extent of its usefulness to the particular activity in which the person is engaged at any given moment.

Personal knowledge implies a knowledge which is basically tentative. All cognitive content grasped by an individual, no matter what its external source or referent, is tentative. All religious knowledge, all theological knowledge, all knowledge whatever is tentative. The religion teacher, therefore, should eschew treating cognitive religious content or cognitive theological content or any other cognitive content in the lesson as anything but tentative, lest he teach the learner to regard cognitive content with an absolute certainty which it does not possess. One of the tragedies in the history of religious instruction is that persons have been sucked into the erroneous rationalist belief that somehow cognitive content represents absolute and certain truth, and that cognitive content suffices to set a person on the sure path to beatitude.

Since cognition constitutes one mode of personal functioning, it is accompanied by a personal commitment on the part of the person who is doing the thinking. A person can acquire cognitive content only by being committed, however slightly, to its worth and its validity. In Michael Polanyi's words, "[cognitive] truth is something that can be thought of only by believing it."[6] Polanyi shows over and over again throughout his book that the degree of "passionate commitment" which a person has toward the knowing process is directly related to the depth and the daring of his cognitive functioning. It should be underscored that commitment as such belongs to the affective domain. Commitment is a feeling, a valuing, and consequently is an affective process. But on an even deeper affective level, commitment represents a form and a thrust of love. To have an intellectual commitment does not mean, therefore, that this commitment is a form of knowing, but rather that the commitment (affective process) is directed toward a cognitive object.

The foregoing analysis of commitment as a necessary accompaniment shows clearly that a person's cognitive acts are not the cold, dispassionate operations which some religion teachers imagine them to be. Perhaps in themselves cognitive functions are cold and dispassionate. But holistic functionalism suggests that all cognitive functions originate, are worked out, and are produced out of the total framework of a human being's entire personality structure. Hence there is always a degree of affect (and a degree of psychomotor processes) accompanying an individual's cognitive activity.[7]

One task of the religion teacher is to enable the learner to more consciously perform his cognitive functions in deliberative concert with the other noncognitive aspects of his personality. Holistic functionalism indicates that the more a person performs his cognitive functions in interactive harmony with his affective and psychomotor activities, the more subjectively and objectively fruitful these cognitive functions will thereby be rendered.

The Importance of Cognitive Content

Cognitive content is important in religious instruction because it is indispensable to it. Without cognitive content of all shades and textures there could be no religious instruction. There are countless reasons for the crucial importance of cognitive content in religious instruction. I shall detail below only a few of the more salient ones.

By exercising his cognitive function, the learner can unlock many of the doors to the universe, including the religious nature of the universe. Cognition allows the learner to *know* reality—know, after a fashion, what reality is, why reality is, how reality is, and the way reality operates. Through the use of his *memory* and *imagination*, the learner becomes, in a sense, eternal, because all things in the past are immediately present to him and he can leap into the future. By means of his power of *creativity,* the learner is able to rearrange already existing elements so as to form new modes of reality to serve and enrich him. Cognition enables the learner to *explain* his experiences. After all, experiences are by themselves simply raw, nude phenomena. Explanation enables the learner to make sense out of these phenomena, to understand them. Explanation offers basic reasons for specific experiences being what they are, how they are, and especially why they are. Cognition also gives *meaning* to experiences. Meaning helps the learner discover the agreement, significance, or relevance of a particular experience both in terms of kindred experiences and in terms of himself as person and learner. Cognition, when architected into a broad intellectual network, provides a *system of thought* into which the learner can integrate his experiences. An organized network of this kind is not foreign or antithetical to experience; rather, it is necessary to bring order and fruitfulness into what would otherwise be a chaotic mass of singular, isolated experiences.[8] Closely related to this point is that cognition enables the learner to make his religious behavior *intelligent*. Intelligent behavior is that which is deliberatively arranged in goal-directed systems whose parts are interconnected. "The opposite of intelligent behavior is random or disorganized behavior, sequences of behavior which bear no relation to each other. A behavior system may not be effective—that is, it may not attain its goal—but at a fixed point in time the behavior is intelligent from the viewpoint of the person acting, if it is a systematic plan to attain a goal."[9] Cognitive activity typically has a *heuristic* effect on the learner. It helps him discover aspects of reality which are not immediately apparent or manifest. Further, mental effort also serves to stimulate exploration into sectors of reality which are as yet experientially unverified or which are purportedly not amenable to direct empirical verification. Cognition also plays a major role in helping the learner[10] become *socialized* into the "secular," the religious, and the denominational environments—or to assist the learner to become liberated from these environments, as the case may be. Successful socialization into contemporary civilization demands a host of cognitive competencies ranging from an understanding of how everyday technology works, to the knowledge of basic Christian principles, to the meaning of liturgical symbols.[11] Cognition enables the learner to come to an intellectual *validation* for his religious behavior. Without such a validation—however hypothetical[12] and tentative it might be—the learner has no mental anchor for what he believes and does.

Some Limitations of Cognitive Content

The religious educator should be acutely aware, not only of the crucial importance of cognitive content, but also of its limitations with regard to the total work of religious instruction.

The first major limitation of cognitive content is that it represents just one content—albeit an extremely important one—of religious instruction. There are also many other important and indispensable contents which the religion teacher must use effectively in the pedagogical situation. Consequently, in facilitating the goal of religious instruction, namely Christian living, cognition can never serve as the total content or the complete guide.[13] This is particularly true of the lower levels of cognition such as the sheer accumulation of facts[14] or the more abstract and indirect modes of cognition such as ratiocination.

The second major limitation of cognitive content is that it provides the learner with only tentative knowledge of reality. This tentativeness is underscored by the fact that all cognitive content is acquired by specific methods and from different points of view.[15] *A person's truth,* therefore, is never final, but is alive and constantly growing just as each person constantly grows.

The third major limitation of cognitive content is that it constitutes incomplete learning. The person acquires learnings from other than his cognitive activities. Affective activities and psychomotor activities yield learnings not accessible through cognitive means, as any person in love or as any ballet dancer will be quick to affirm. What cognition does do vis-à-vis learnings gained from affective and psychomotor activities is to enlarge the scope, meaning, and significance of these noncognitive learnings by cognitively reflecting upon them. George Kneller observes that life is indeed far larger than logic or cognition; human existence cannot be captured merely by a concept or some other form of cognition of human existence.[16] Cognitive learning represents, after all, the possession of some reality in an immaterial manner,[17] and therefore is always intrinsically defective.

The fourth major limitation of cognitive content is that it provides a relatively weak starting point and energizer for an authentic and profound Christian understanding of basic religious realities. Such an authentic Christian understanding arises from and is fecundated by the learner's own religious experiences, particularly his experiences of worship, whether this worship takes place at a church service or in the privacy of his own heart. The role of cognitive content is to clarify religious experiences and to offer tentative, enlightening, intellectual explanations of individual or community religious experiences. In this vein Monika Hellwig observes: "What we hand on from generation to generation is an experience of God's grace in our lives and a way of life that is a response to that grace."[18]

The fifth major limitation of cognitive content is that while it provides the learner with a valid grasp of the Christian message, it does not supply him with a content which is wholly congruent with this message. Cognitive content is basically content *about* the Christian message rather than the living Christian message itself. The Christian message is first and foremost a person, Jesus Christ.[19] The Christian message, therefore, is not a content about Jesus but rather the living, existential Jesus. The learner acquires the Christian message not primarily by intellecting about Jesus, but by experientially encountering Jesus as he is in the church and in the "world."[20] *All learning is fundamentally a union of the learner with that which is learned, and love constitutes a more perfect union than cognition, especially in an instance where that which is learned is a person.* Alfonso Nebreda claims that even John Henry Newman, a staunch intellectualist, realized this in terms of how the Christian message is best learned.[21] Certainly this pivotal point did not escape the notice of Thomas Aquinas, another cognitive hard-liner, who states: "Knowledge is perfected when the object known is united, through its likeness, to the knower. Love is perfected when the object itself is, in a certain way, united to the lover. Consequently the union of the lover with that which is loved is more intimate than the union of the knower with that which is known."[22]

This brief examination of the limitations of cognitive content should put religious educationists and educators on their guard against an overemphasis on cognitive content. In past centuries, religious instruction seemed to place excessive stress on cognitive content, often to the exclusion of other more fruitful forms of content. In Protestant circles, this overemphasis tended to take the form of religion lessons consisting largely of rote memorization of biblical texts, with some tangential forays into their practical applicability. In the Catholic quarter, undue stress on cognitive content manifested itself in a catechism-centered pedagogy. Indeed, advocates of the Munich Method proudly announced that this Method was revolutionary because it replaced the "text-explanatory method" with the "text-developing method."[23] After a brief flirtation in the 1960s with experientially grounded and affectively oriented religious instruction[24] there is mounting pressure from certain elements within mainline Protestantism and particularly within Catholicism to return to a cognitive exclusivism. This mentality has its roots sunk deeply in rationalism. Proponents of cognitive exclusivism would do well to heed the warning of Léon Elchinger who unequivocally calls rationalism "the great danger" facing religious instruction.[25] Carl Jung calls rationalism "the disease of our time" because it pretends to have all the answers.[26] Even when the religious educationist or educator eschews rationalism he must ever be aware of the limitations as well as the strong points of cognitive content. Jung contends that nothing is more damaging and dangerous to immediate experience than cognition.[27]

Christian Doctrine

Christian doctrine contains a great deal of cognitive content. Put even more forcefully, Christian doctrine is suffused with cognitive content. Indeed, virtually every Christian denomination has devised doctrinal formulae or propositions about its *credenda*. Formulae and propositions are, naturally, relatively pure forms of cognitive content.

Revelation constitutes a vital principle of Christianity. In one sense, Christianity is the embodiment of a historical and focused form of God's revelation to humanity. Revelation is, of course, "to be found in God's saving activity," as Edward Schillebeeckx reminds us. But having made this point, Schillebeeckx hastens to add that "it is only *as understood by* the people of God that this saving history acquires the full significance of revelation."[28] In other words, a cognitive grasp of the content of the revelation experience is essential if this experience is to achieve the total degree of saving effect of which it is capable. Hence revelation as personally experienced, revelation as felt and loved—these, together with revelation-as-cognitively-understood—form the pillars supporting the religion of revelation.

What kind and manner of cognitive contents are woven into the fabric of Christian doctrine? Certainly theology is one of the most important and indispensable of these contents. There can be no Christian religion without theological interpretations and theories. I would like to make two observations concerning the role of theology in religious instruction. First, the kind of theology which is employed should be first-rate theology, not the ersatz variety of fuzzy and often gooey thinking which has so often masqueraded as theology, particularly in the decade following Vatican II. Theology is a science, and as such has its definite norms and canons of investigation. The theology which forms an aspect of the religious instruction given to persons of any age level should be that kind of theology which is suitable for that level, rather than a watered-down theology. There is a great deal of difference between a watered-down theology and a sound, integral theology which the religion teacher deliberatively renders appropriate for the kinds and levels of people he is teaching.

The second observation I would like to make concerning the role of theology in religious instruction is that the theology introduced into the religion lesson should be a theology-for-religion rather than a theology-for-theology. By a theology-for-religion I mean that a theology which is infused into the religion lesson should be done in a way which clarifies, enhances, and promotes Christian living. This kind of theology is different from a theology-for-theology which has as its purpose the exploration and refinement of specifically theological data.[29] I hasten to add that theology-for-religion is in no way an ersatz or watered-down theology; rather it is a robust and integral theology which is thrusted toward religious goals rather than toward theological goals. A theology-for-religion endeavors to assist the learner to discover the relevance of Christian knowledge for his own personal lifestyle.

The foundation upon which Christianity rests is not theology but religious experience. Peter's religious experience, not his level of theological knowledge, is the rock upon which Jesus decided to build his church. The celebrated biblical passage of Matthew 16:13–20 basically represents Peter's vocal testimony of the sum total of his own personal religious experiences, most notably those he had after having first met Jesus.[30] My view here in no way denies that Peter theologized. Rather, it accents the primacy of religious experience and the role which theology properly plays in Christian living.[31]

It cannot be overemphasized that the cognitive aspect of Christian doctrine is not simply theology, but rather comprises all the cognitive aspects contained in Christian living. Put another way, *the cognitive content in Christian doctrine is not derived just from theological speculation, but more importantly is derived from the lived phenomenon called religion.*[32] Thus one cardinal goal of religious instruction is to teach the learner to think religiously, and not just to think theologically.[33]

Teaching for cognitive religious outcomes does not suggest a kind of instructional practice which is radically or fundamentally different from teaching for any other kind of cognitive outcome. Thus Ronald Goldman's carefully conducted empirical research investigation concluded that religious thinking uses the same modes and methods of cognition as does thinking in any other cognitive area.[34]

What is Christian doctrine with respect to cognition? Christian doctrine is religion, the personal human relationship which an individual has with God as that individual operationalizes this relationship in daily living. Christian doctrine in its fullness and integralness is Christian living. Therefore, it is not accurate to conceptualize Christian doctrine as consisting solely of cognitive content. Christian doctrine encompasses all eight basic kinds of substantive content dealt with in this book. *A fortiori,* then, Christian doctrine is not even equivalent to theological content, since theological content comprises only one aspect of the totality of cognitive content.

Etymologically, doctrine means that which is taught, the sum total of the teaching—and surely the doctrine of Jesus and hence of his church is a way of living. In this doctrine, in this Christian living, cognitive content plays a vital part, but so do all the other seven contents. The cognitive aspect plays an indispensable, but nonetheless supporting role in the totality of Christian doctrine. Christian doctrine is the whole of the Christian message, and, as I indicated earlier in this chapter, cognitive content is basically content *about* the Christian message rather than the living Christian message in its fullness and its livingness. If it is to be faithful to its purpose with respect to Christian doctrine, cognitive content can never be made the sum total of the religion lesson, or even its primary element.

Inasmuch as it is a single aspect of religious living and not its ground of being, cognitive content can be more accurately described as accompanying religious living rather than as causing it. Put another way, a person behaves in a certain manner *with* a reason. (Often in everyday speech, we say that an individual does something *for* a reason; however this is sloppy linguistic usage in terms of the basic personality operations involved.) Religious instruction must take into account and utilize as fully as possible the cognitive content of Christian living. Yet, according to Philip Phenix, it is simply not true that cognitive content is a sure and sufficient ground for religion.[35] A purely cognitive religion is a dead religion, one disemboweled of all the other contents which make it living and vibrant. Indeed, a purely cognitive religion is hard to imagine, since it has neither a univocal relationship to unconscious and instinctive content[36] nor any intimate tie with the other contents which comprise the total Christian doctrine.

Theology, as contrasted to religion, is wholly and completely an intellectual enterprise. Therefore it is not surprising that persons holding the theological approach to religious instruction wittingly or unwittingly tend to view the task of religious instruction as basically one of imparting only the cognitive content of Christian doctrine. Many of these individuals consider it outside the province of religious instruction to facilitate noncognitive outcomes such as affective behavior, lifestyle behavior, and the like. Thus Joseph Colomb, a leading European Catholic religious educationist and advocate of the theological approach to religious instruction, maintains that the work of religious instruction is only a cognitive "commentary" on religion, only "the grasping by the mind in a more or less rational way" of flesh-and-blood religion. Colomb further asserts that the religious instruction enterprise exists in order that the learner can more effectively grasp the cognitive aspects of Christian doctrine so that, as a result, he can at some later time more intelligently live out the total, existential Christian message.[37] Religious educationists like Colomb who espouse the theological approach to religious instruction forget that there is a major difference between the goals and objectives of theological instruction on the one hand and religious instruction on the other. Theological instruction properly and legitimately has cognitive content as its primary proximate goal. However, religious instruction has all the contents involved in Christian living as its primary proximate goal.

The difference between the goals of theological instruction and religious instruction was graphically illustrated for me by an incident which occurred while I was recording a set of twelve cassette tapes which comprise a widely-used training program for preservice and inservice religion teachers in Catholic schools as well as those engaged in CCD work and adult education.[38] In one of the tapes I devote considerable time to a discussion of Jesus. After I had completed the recording of that particular tape, the publishing company's recording specialist who is himself particularly well-versed in Christian culture called me aside and remarked: "Your treatment of Jesus in that tape is most intriguing. During the past few years we have had many great and not-so-great theologians from Europe and North American make tape recordings for us about Jesus. These persons all centered their discussions around the quest for the historical Jesus, the relationship of Jesus to the Trinity, the cosmic Christ, the Logos and the church, the connection between the crucifixion and the resurrection, and so on. You are the first one who ever defined and talked about Jesus as a lifestyle." To which I responded, "That exemplifies one of the major differences between a theologian and a religious educationist."

Cognition and Overt Activity

What is the relationship between cognitive content and overt activity? Or, put in a somewhat more focused form, what is the functional relationship between cognitive content and Christian living?

Cognitive content does not itself produce overt activity. This is so because cognition and overt activity are different orders of being, and one order of being is not capable of directly giving rise to another order of being.[39] What cognitive content can do is to inform overt activity, to help make overt activity something which is done intelligently. The relation of theory to practice illustrates this point at one of the highest levels at which cognition and overt action functionally relate. A theory does not directly produce practice. What a theory does is to provide a well-integrated cognitive framework from which intelligent and effective practice can be deduced.

The most effective way to insure that overt activity will take place in an intelligent fashion, and that cognition is not done in its own sealed-off world, is to devise a learning situation in which overt activity and cognition are joined. When the goal of an enterprise is Christian living, then it is obvious that the cognitive content learned in this enterprise should be acquired within the context of Christian living. Cognitive content built around and thrusted toward Christian living is most effectively learned in the very living of Christianity, in the very here-and-now forging of a Christian personality.[40] John Dewey comments that there is no such thing as genuine and fruitful cognitive content "except as the offspring of doing. The analysis and rearrangement of facts which is indispensable to the growth of knowledge and power of explanation and right classification cannot be attained purely mentally—just inside the head. Men have to *do* something to things when they wish to find out something."[41] From a distinctly Christian perspective, Marcel van Caster emphasizes that faith cannot come from pure speculation, but rather from a person being engaged in overt activity. "By faith we know in participation and communion." Using theological language and conceptualizations, van Caster observes that the act of religious belief (faith) "finds its source in the contact between the interior action of the Holy Spirit in our soul and the exterior action of God who makes his word known to us in the 'signs' of his revelation."[42]

Cognitive content brings intelligence to overt activity. Without its cognitive component, overt activity would not be human overt activity. Man and animals engage in overt activity; however, one of the principal distinguishing characteristics which sets people apart from animals is that people can join intelligence to their overt activity. The less the cognitive domain functions within the matrix of overt activity, the less human is that overt activity. In terms of religious instruction, cognitive content thus enriches the entire unified fabric of Christian living.

In religious instruction, cognitive content should not be taught for its own sake. On the contrary, cognitive content should find its place in the religion lesson only in the manner and to the extent that it contributes to a richer and deeper form of Christian living.[43]

Is there any direct "causative" relationship between religious cognitive content and overt religious behavior (religious conduct)? Does religious knowledge directly produce religious conduct? If an individual has a high level of cognitive content about Christianity, can it be taken for granted that he will, on this account, have a high level of religious lifestyle behaviors?

From the philosophical perspective, it must be remembered that cognition and overt activity represent two discrete and very different realms of reality. Cognitive content yields only cognitive content; it does not directly yield overt activity or affect. Knowing what an elephant is does not of itself directly produce an elephant. Cognition is a function. As such it correlates with and accompanies overt activity and affective activity. I believe that one philosophically accurate way of expressing the relationship between cognition and overt activity is to say that cognitive content provides an intellectual base and framework for overt activity while itself not directly producing this overt activity.

The available research data suggest that any posited, direct, significant, causal relationship between cognitive content and religious conduct simply does not exist. The advantage of the empirical research evidence in terms of our present discussion is that it bypasses the philosophical issues of "distinct realms of reality" on the one hand, and "independent reified substances" on the other. In other words, empirical research evidence enables us to assess the actual influence which moral and/or religious cognitive content does or does not in fact exert on moral and/or religious conduct. Summing up the pertinent empirical research data gathered from a very broad range of studies,[44] Bernard Berelson and Gary Steiner conclude that there is a clear differentiation between what a person knows is morally right and how he comports himself morally.[45] Thus the weight of the research evidence strongly indicates that a person may know what is right, and even profess belief in what is right, and still do what is wrong. Experimental studies as well as other forms of empirical investigations disclose that the discrepancies between moral concepts and overt moral conduct are greater than are popularly acknowledged. Virtually all the empirical research conducted since the classic Hartshorne and May experimental studies in the 1920s[46] have confirmed these investigators' conclusion that cognitive content of what is wrong does not prevent a child from cheating when a particular situation arises which induces that individual to cheat. Indeed, one review of the research notes that the relevant empirical data reveal a correlation of approximately .25 between moral cognitive content and moral conduct in children.[47] Mary Delafield Fite's research study discovered that there was not a consistent relationship between a child's moral cognitive judgment of the "rights" and "wrongs" of aggressive activity and the actual aggressive acts which he perpetrated on other children in the playground.[48] Studies made of juvenile delinquents[49] indicate that these children and youth are seldom unaware that their misdeeds are morally wrong. To be sure, these research investigations reveal that the moral knowledge of delinquents is markedly similar to that of nondelinquents. In this connection Hans Eysenck, on the basis of the existing research evidence, makes the pointed comment that "the delinquent child as well as the criminal adult is usually only too well aware of the fact that his conduct is contrary to moral precept; his evil-doing is not by and large due to ignorance."[50]

More directly focused on the relationship between specifically religious cognitive content and specifically religious conduct are the research investigations conducted by Pleasant Hightower, and by Martin Maehr. In a classic and frequently cited study, Hightower designed his experiment in such a way that his 485 adolescent research subjects were not only evaluated on the degree of their biblical information, but also were given opportunities to lie and cheat—opportunities which were so constructed by the investigator as to be amenable to empirical measurement. This study found "no relationship of any consequence" between biblical information and truthfulness or cheating.[51] Maehr's study discovered that only a low correlation exists between the level of biblical information possessed by upper elementary school Missouri Synod Lutheran children and statements by these same pupils of how they would actually act in hypothetical, concrete situations.[52]

Two correlative major global findings run through the empirical research investigations conducted in virtually every sector of human behavior. The first of these is that *the most effective way to learn a particular behavior is to engage in that behavior in as direct and as immediate a fashion as possible.* The second major global finding is that a relatively ineffective and chancy way to learn a particular behavior is to acquire a cognitive content about that behavior on the assumption that this cognitive content will somehow of itself bring about the desired behavior. *To learn religious conduct, therefore, the individual must learn to perform specific overt behaviors in specific situations.* Cognitive content plays its role here in significantly helping the learner to intelligently choose the most worthwhile kinds and levels of overt behaviors he will perform; further, cognitive content enables the learner to more accurately assess the meaning and personal significance for himself of these overt behaviors after these overt behaviors have been completed.

I take pains to emphasize that what I have written in this section in no way suggests that cognitive content, such as religious knowledge and moral judgment, is totally or basically unrelated to religious conduct. To be sure, all religious conduct contains cognitive content because such content is at once human and religious. Indeed, one of the prime fruits of mature cognitive content is that it enables religious conduct to be more fully human and religious particularly by elevating religious conduct both to a deeper personal meaning and to a closer congruence with God's revelatory activities. What this section does emphatically point out, however, is that religious cognitive content of itself does not directly produce religious conduct. Thus Pleasant Hightower's previously mentioned empirical investigation concluded that while biblical knowledge is not worthless in terms of its impact on religious conduct, nonetheless biblical cognitive content is not of itself sufficient to insure religious conduct.[53]

If overvaluation of cognitive content seriously disrupts the wholeness and integralness of the substantive content of religious instruction, so also does a disvaluation of cognitive content lead to a distorted and twisted form of religious teaching. *There are at least eight contents which go to make up religion as substantive content. Overemphasis or denigration of any one of these contents as that content is interactively and organically situated within the entire substantive-content context in a manner appropriate to that entire context will upset the exquisitely tensioned balance among all eight of the constitutive contents. An upsetting of this balance—a balance which represents religion in its dynamic integralness—will ultimately lead to the warping or even the destruction of religion as substantive content.*

The disvaluation of cognitive content is commonly called anti-intellectualism, and it has been a particularly seductive temptress throughout the long history of the Christian church. Richard Hofstadter states that the common strain which binds together anti-intellectualist ideas and attitudes is "a resentment and suspicion of the life of the mind and of those who are considered to represent it; and a disposition constantly to minimize the values of that life."[54] Many and deeply-rooted are the causes of anti-intellectualism within the Christian church; I will simply identify ten of the most salient among them.[55] *First,* there is a distinct residue of anti-intellectualism among some ecclesiastical officials, notably in the Catholic church, in certain evangelical Protestant churches, and in fundamentalist Protestant churches. This anti-intellectualistic residue often takes the form of a basic and deep-seated distrust of the intellectual life. These officials seem firmly convinced that when people acquire sophisticated cognitive content they will begin to question the validity, the relevance, or at least the formulation of some of the church's religious tenets and disciplinary measures.[56] *Second,* there seems to be an inbuilt fear and anxiety on the part of many Christians that the intellectual life by its very nature involves a threat to their own religious life and convictions. It is true that the element of risk is inseparable from the intellectual life. But these Christians seem to forget that mature religion is neither a security blanket nor a set of safety rules. Rather, mature religion is a great human adventure which perforce involves risk. It is this adventure which shakes the very depths of the soul; but it is this very shaking which enables the Christian to experience a Good Friday and an Easter in his own life. *Third,* an erroneous notion of "blind faith" inclines some Christians to think that it is more religious to do the right things in the absence of any reason for doing them than it is to have solid cognitive grounding for those things which one believes in or does. *Fourth,* an overly narrow view of revelation as that which is contained exclusively in one book or as a "deposit of faith" which closed at the death of John the Evangelist blunts a person's natural tendency to acquire relatively sophisticated cognitive content about the post-first-century world, to say nothing of today's world in which God is constantly revealing himself in new and ever-fresh ways. *Fifth,* the notion that cognitive content is somehow opposed to religion, or at best is unrelated to religion, tends to have a crippling effect on the degree to which many Christians value cognitive content. Thus one representative of this mentality can write that we should not worry so much about educating a poor, devout, intellectually backward man in some distant land who has been converted to Christianity because "he has in his will charity, which is superior to all knowledge in this life." This same anti-intellectualist also remarks that "Parents and teachers should never forget that a boy of twelve with a knowledge of the essential truths of faith is on a loftier pinnacle than a Steinmetz, an Edison, an Einstein without faith."[57] *Sixth,* the conflict which has been going on between ecclesiastical officials (I do not say "religion") and natural science since the sixteenth century has made Christian churches and Christians hesitant to place high value on cognitive content. After all, it was the cognitive content of natural science to which ecclesiastical officials, especially in the sixteenth century and the nineteenth centuries, took great exception on the erroneous grounds that there was a legitimate conflict between science and religion. *Seventh,* the hyperintellectualism over the centuries on the part of many Christian seminary professors,[58] theologians, and philosophers—a hyperintellectualism which was as disdainful of the common man as it was removed from the day-to-day life of that same common man—resulted in many ordinary Christians reacting adversely to the whole of the intellectual life rather than just to the distortion of that life as represented by the hyperintellectualists. *Eighth,* the persistently recurrent tendency within the Christian churches toward hyperaffectivity, especially as manifested in one-sided, unsophisticated, and distorted "religion of the heart" movements, sharply denigrated the intellectual life. For hyperaffective persons and movements, cognitive content has been falsely regarded as the implacable foe of a warm Christian life which stresses a personal, intimate encounter with God. *Ninth,* the anticognitive stance taken by many psychotherapists in the twentieth century, particularly since World War II, has had widespread effect among Christian clergymen and religious educators, some of whom are not too well-endowed intellectually. For such persons, cognition is regarded as the natural enemy of feelings, emotions, and love. These individuals forget that true affectivity is one which is wholesome, robust, and in no way disjointed from one's concomitant cognitive functioning. It is no wonder, then, that those Christian clergymen and religious educators who maintain a hyperaffective stance toward Christianity tend to wallow in a sloppy sentimentality, debase virile religion into a "touchy-feely" affair, and regard careful, rigorous, and sophisticated cognitive functioning as the ultimate in dehumanization. *Tenth,* the cultural milieu in which American Catholicism and Protestantism operate is decidedly anti-intellectual.[59] Prominent intellectuals in the United States are often contemptuously referred to by both politicians and persons-in-the street as "egg heads," or in another age, "brain trusters." This anti-intellectual attitude on the part of Americans is hardly surprising. The seventeenth-, eighteenth-, and nineteenth-century immigrants were rarely intellectuals or men of culture. On the frontier, shooting a bullet straight to kill an enemy, or felling a tree to construct a house were more important than engaging in intellectual or cultural pursuits. Christianity is often greatly influenced by the intellectual milieu in which it operates, and the history of the churches in America has proved to be no exception.

Nothing less than a genuine respect for cognitive content in its fullness, its thrust, its many forms, and its limitations can preserve religious instruction (and Christianity) against the onslaughts of hyper-intellectualism and anti-intellectualism. This kind of well-rounded respect will safeguard religious instruction from falling prey to the age-old temptations of rationalism on the one side and gooey sentimentality on the other. Cognitive content should be used, as appropriate, in facilitating growth in Christian living. Hyperintellectualists must come to appreciate the limitations of cognitive content. Anti-intellectualists must discover the indispensability of cognitive content in Christian living and come to a recognition that cognitive content enhances rather than diminishes the overall quality of religious living. The important thing is not to overvalue or undervalue cognitive content, but rather to employ it wisely and well in the achievement of the goals and objectives of the religion lesson. Cognitive content should be organically integrated into the entire dynamic fabric of the religious instruction act. This integration suggests that cognition is not the "regulator" or the "basic guide" to religious behavior as some religious educationists and theologians would have us believe. It is the whole person, functioning cognitively, affectively, and in conduct, which taken together as a dynamic whole, forms the only solid, humanistic "regulator" and "basic guide" to religious behavior. After all, what a person finds out about reality through his affective life or through his overt activity often provides him with more accurate regulator-data or guide-data than do the fruits of cognitive functioning. Hence no one of these functions in isolation is an adequate or sufficient "regulator" or "guide" to full religious living; it is only the dynamic integration of these three functions which can serve as an holistic, personalistic, and fruitful "regulator" and "guide."

THE FORM OF COGNITIVE CONTENT

It is not the purpose of this section to present a comprehensive overview of all the major cognitive maps, much less of all the myriad minor ones currently in existence. Rather, my purpose here is to present just a few cognitive maps which might be helpful and significant to religion teachers and curriculum builders.

Rational and Extrarational Cognitive Knowing

Rational cognitive knowing is that power by which, through the use of an objective system of intellectual logic, inferences are made and conclusions are drawn from phenomena, premises, or various kinds of data. There are many forms which rational cognitive knowing takes, a few of which will be treated in some of the sections following this one. Suffice it to state at this juncture that in the West, most systems of logic are based on ascertaining cause-effect relationships, whereas in the East far more stress is placed on acausal logic.[60] Hence it is quite erroneous to identify rationality with only one system or sub-system of logic.

Extrarational cognitive knowing is that power by which, through the use of means which lie outside of any objective system of intellectual logic, inferences are made and conclusions drawn from phenomena, premises, or various kinds of data. It is important to note that the extrarational is quite different from the irrational. The irrational is that which is in diametrical opposition or contradiction to the rational and the extrarational. Rational knowing and extrarational knowing are authentic cognitive contents, while irrational activity (one cannot properly speak of "irrational knowing") represents the overturning and hence the absence of cognitive content.

Two important types of extrarational knowing which are important for religious educators are symbol and myth. Both are deeply personal and subjective types of cognitive content. It is primarily the intensive subjective character—and therefore supreme uniqueness—of all forms of extrarational knowing which places this form of cognitive content outside that objective system of logic known as the rational.[61]

Symbol. Psychologically speaking, a symbol is any reality which serves as a token of something else.[62] Frequently a symbol assumes an immaterial or spiritual form. Depth psychologists tend to reserve the term "symbol" for outward signs of a very deep form of spiritual or personal reality, as contrasted to the common usage of the word in everyday life and business. For Sigmund Freud, a symbol stands for deep, primary material which an individual has repressed into the unconscious. Carl Jung, who devotes a great deal of attention to the nature and function of symbol, asserts that a symbol represents the best possible formulation of a reality which is unknown or relatively unknown rationally and which cannot on this very account be clearly or accurately represented in rational categories. For St. Paul and the early Christian mystics, Jung states, the Cross was a living and true symbol which cognitively represented a reality which was inexpressible in conventional, nonsymbolic form. Today the Cross more often than not is merely an object on top of a church, a token rather than a symbol.[63] For most depth psychologists, the symbol represents a rich, dynamic, and potent form of knowing because much of it (for some depth psychologists, all of it) arises from the unconscious where all the elements which gave it birth enjoy unfettered interplay with all the other aspects of one's individual personality, both profound and shallow. Thus to be in touch in some way with one's own process of symbolization, together with the fruits of this process, especially as revealed in one's dreams, fantasies, artistic and literary productions, and religious experiences enables one to explore and utilize the very depths of one's personhood. Because it represents an aspect of the dynamic and unfettered intermingling with other deeper aspects of man's personality, symbol tends to be a creative force within the person. In symbolic thinking, the mind is flooded with all sorts of images and other data not known by the person's rational processes, or which have been forgotten, suppressed, or repressed.[64] Jung claims that once a symbol is known by rational processes, once it becomes a rational formulation of that which it represents, it is then no longer a true symbol. Now this in no way suggests that symbol stands in diametrical opposition or contradiction to rational means of knowing. The rational and the extrarational are complementary, not contradictory.[65] True symbols in the depth-psychology sense of the term, are not chosen arbitrarily by a person; rather they grow or erupt quite naturally out of his entire personality structure. The living symbol is not merely a matter of dreams or fantasies; by its very nature, symbol is lived by the person. The way in which a person engages in or withdraws from the world tends to be revealed in the type of symbol which is formed within him. Anent this, Jung remarks that symbols of the deeper sort are far from being simple. Indeed, a symbol is an extremely complex entity, since it issues from a meshing of data proceeding from every psychic function.[66]

Avery Dulles observes that, aided by the findings of depth psychology, "the twentieth century has given renewed attention to symbol, considered as yielding a special but authentic type of religious knowledge."[67] Hence it behooves the religion teacher as well as the curriculum builder to insure that symbolic cognitive content finds an appropriate place in the religion lesson. Indeed, symbol is one of the most religiously fecund of all cognitive contents because of its dynamic, spiritual, living, and personality-encompassing character. Much of religious instruction in the liturgical sector could be vastly improved if it accentuated deep and living symbol rather than remain a scissors-and-paste operation of adding or subtracting a hymn or rearranging some rubrics.[68]

Myth. A myth is a narrative, a story, or an exposition which portrays a phenomenon or a series of phenomena in an extrarational manner. More often than not, a myth consists of a story about events. A myth is an extrarational device used to supply information and interpretation of the most basic and ultimate questions about life and human existence, questions for which rational knowing can supply only inadequate answers or insights. A myth, Julius Schniewind states, is "the expression of unobservable realities in terms of observable phenomena."[69] A myth is typically a story about some aspect of the holy. Hence so much of ancient religious literature, especially the most profound parts of this literature, is written in the form of myth rather than in a rational, logical mode. It is therefore not surprising that every religion, and indeed all religious worship and ritual are at home in myth.[70] That reality which is beyond ordinary everyday experience— that reality which is characterized by transcendence and ultimacy—is effectively communicated through myth, symbol, and rite.[71] Myths are prized by religion because they provide a cognitive opening to the superhuman world, a world characterized by transcendence and absolute values. Hubert Halbfas contends that "myth, symbol, and rite are therefore not available for their own sakes, but refer beyond their sensuously perceptible form and actualize the unconditioned in everything that is conditioned."[72] Myth is subjective, impressionistic, extrarational truth. In myth one communicates about reality in a way which is untranslatable into another language. Halbfas claims that "the very depths of reality, from which men live, and therefore love and suffer, strive, see, sacrifice, believe, and hope, is revealed through myth. . . . It [myth] is the kind of knowledge that reveals itself to a man who surrenders himself to its power in a real situation, and surrenders himself with all his individuality."[73] In one sense, myth can be considered as a kind of symbol. Thus for Morton Trippe Kelsey, myth is the symbolic description of a person's encounter with spiritual and holy reality, a description characterized by color and drama.[74]

One scholar contends that there are four functions of myth: (1) to elicit a sense of awe in the face of the mystery of being; (2) to provide a meaningful cosmology; (3) to support the current social order; (4) to initiate the individual into his own psyche, guiding him to his own spiritual enrichment and realization.[75]

Myth is not *eo ipso* fictitious or false. The terms "fictitious" and "false" typically have as their referent that which is rationally factual or true.[76] But myth is a form of extrarational knowing, not of rational knowing. The criteria of fact and truth are quite different for extrarational knowing than for rational knowing. A myth has extrarational criteria, not rational criteria, on which its factualness and truth are based. The factualness and truth of a myth do not reside in the objective reality or logic of the myth, but rather in its appropriateness to and congruence with the religious or other profound reality which it is representing.[77] Verification of the factualness and truth of a myth is not made against a set of rational, logical, objective categories, but in accordance with its accuracy in portraying extrarational, subjective reality. Consequently, the cognitive content of an authentic myth is just as factual and true as a piece of authentic rational, logical data. That many religious myths deal with history is quite evident from the sacred literature of a number of world religions, including Christianity. It is cognitively erroneous to employ the canons of rational, logical historiography to judge mythical stories whose canons for veracity and verification are of a very dissimilar cognitive order. It is also erroneous to search in myths for rational truths which these myths are supposed to hide in some "mysterious" or "enigmatically sacred" form. Myths convey their own truths which are extrarational. It is only the rankest kind of rationalism which claims that myths are simply primitive, quaint, esoteric, or earthy ways of communicating rational, logical truths. The profound religious truth of mythic communication is betrayed if its very extrarational nature is interpreted by means of rational, logical categories.

Myth is one special way in which a learner can grasp religious cognitive content of a deep and profound variety.[78] Consequently, myth is of great importance in the work of religious instruction. Myth is a legitimate and indeed for human beings a necessary way of looking at reality in a fashion which complements and completes that kind of rational cognitive content which every age and culture makes its own. One great foe of myth is not so much false myths but myths misunderstood as rational knowing. The religious educator should enable the learners to acquire a basic understanding *in* the mythic and *with* the mythic, rather than merely a grasp *of* the mythic. Thus, for example, in teaching the bible from the perspective of cognitive content, the religion teacher should treat its mythic elements, not just in terms of literary imagery or as culturally conditioned ways in which Neareasterners of those days communicated, but rather in a manner which will help the learner gain a deeper understanding of the structure and workings of that kind of reality which the mythic language portrays. Or to use another example, when teaching the learner to understand the liturgy better, the religious educator should endeavor to enable him to come to an appreciation of how the symbolic and mythic elements of liturgy are neither distractors from nor mere ornaments of the eucharistic celebration, but are instead cognitive modes for grasping some of the more profound dimensions of the worship service. In one sense, all liturgy is worship enacted in mythic form. Thus for a number of reasons Randolph Crump Miller can observe that myth is necessary in any profound worship.[79]

My abbreviated treatment of extrarational knowing clearly indicates that cognitive content is far more than a mere accumulation of various kinds of rational knowing. Extrarational cognitive content has its own form and genre, and supplies cognitive insights and understandings unattainable by rational knowing. Any attempt to rationalize the extrarational is an undertaking which is intellectually doomed to failure before it begins. In religious instruction, it should be underscored that exclusive or even extended concentration on rational cognitive content will tend to corrupt and shrink the full range of the learner's intellective functions. There must be an interweaving in the religion lesson of both rational and extrarational cognitive content in a manner appropriate to the objectives of the lesson.

Varieties of Rational Cognitive Knowing

Philosophers, psychologists, religious thinkers, and other astute students of the cognitive process have, over the centuries, claimed that there are two basic varieties of rational knowing, namely ratiocination and intuition.

Ratiocination. Often referred to as "reasoning," ratiocination is the mode of rational knowing most frequently used by religious educators and indeed by other kinds of educators as well. There seems to be a widespread notion among teachers that ratiocination is all there is to rational thinking; the result is that the intuitive knowing process is often neglected or completely overlooked. Ratiocination can be defined as the gathering into the mind of the intelligible forms of reality and the subsequent judgment and reasoning about these forms by means of a successive interplay among the various functions of the mind.[80] This definition suggests that ratiocination takes place in three basic stages. The first stage, abstraction, is that by which the idea or concept is generated. In the abstractive process, the external, individual impressions are reduced to internal, universal ideas or concepts. The concept, together with the properties, accidents, and various relations of the essence, forms the basis for ratiocination. The second stage of ratiocination takes place through judgment. Judgment is the intellectual discernment by means of composition and division of the identity or diversity between two concepts. In every judgment there are three steps: apprehension of the concepts, comparison of the concepts, and awareness of their agreement or disagreement. Basically, every act of thought at its deepest ontological level is an act of judgment. Joseph Donceel notes that judgment is the central point of an individual's ratiocinative life precisely because a person's intellect seeks the dynamic, not the static (the concept merely being a static representation of reality).[81] The third stage of ratiocination is reason (in the precise sense of the term). Reason is the mental operation in which two judgments are compared through the medium of a third judgment, and a new judgment is derived from this comparison. The two most common types of reason are induction and deduction. Induction is synthetic reasoning, while deduction is analytic reasoning.

Ratiocination is very important in acquiring and effectively using cognitive content. Abstraction or concept-formation constitutes an indispensable anchor for reflective direction of human activity. Concrete events or situations happen once and never repeat themselves exactly. By means of abstraction, a universal concept is formed from the original concrete individual situation or event, thus enabling the essence or subject matter of that original concrete individual situation to be available to a person for further use. Abstraction emancipates a concrete experience from everything which is purely personal and strictly immediate; it detaches that which one experience has in common with other experiences so as to render each experience generalizable and therefore highly usable in future experiencing. The abstractness of abstraction makes it remote from life but at the same time accounts for the genesis and development of new, innovative, practical activities.[82] The judgment aspect of the ratiocinative process is very much at the heart of the work done by cognitive psychologists such as Ronald Goldman and Lawrence Kohlberg who are interested in moral development and moral education. These cognitive psychologists believe that the stage of moral judgment at which a person is developmentally appears to constitute the most important cognitive element correlating with the type and level of religious conduct which that person engages in. Both Goldman and Kohlberg have constructed curricula which aim to sharpen and raise the level of the learner's moral judgment. Reason, the third feature of the ratiocinative process, is used by many of the more effective curriculum builders and teachers. The Bloom taxonomy of cognitive educational objectives gives prominent place to analysis and synthesis.

While ratiocination is important in enabling the learner to acquire religious cognitive content, it should not be used to the exclusion or downgrading of the intuitive process. Over the centuries, intuition has proved more congenial to a deeply religious way of knowing than has ratiocination. The great Christian mystics have been inclined to use intuitional knowing rather than ratiocinative knowing. Because it tends to seize the total person, and because it is a direct rather than a mediated process, intuition is a higher form of rational knowing than is ratiocination.

Intuition. Intuition is the direct, nonsensory, immediate, intellectual apprehension of a reality without any intermediary. Intuition is direct and immediate knowing, as contrasted with ratiocination which slices up reality by abstraction, judgment, and reasoning. Intuitive knowing is not nonrational or extrarational; it is only nonconceptual. Intuition leads a person to discover areas of reality which are quite often hidden from ratiocinative gaze. Due in no small measure to the influence of philosophical phenomenology, there has been renewed interest in cognitive intuition in the twentieth century.

There are many advantages of intuitive knowing as contrasted to ratiocinative knowing. *First,* intuition affords a person a deeper cognitive grasp of reality than does ratiocination because intuition is an immediate and direct intellectual grasp of reality. Intuition provides the learner with a cognitive knowledge from within the object to be learned, as it were, rather than from the outside as tends to be the case with ratiocinative knowledge.[83] Cognition of every sort, including intuition, is "knowledge about," as I observe earlier in this chapter. However, ratiocination represents a greater "aboutness," that is to say a greater removal from the withinness of the known reality than is true of intuition. *Second,* intuition represents a more personal form of knowing than ratiocination. Intuition tends to involve the *homo integer,* the whole person to a greater degree than does ratiocination. For example, intuitive knowing is more amenable to a synapse with a person's affective activity than is ratiocinative knowing. *Third,* intuition seems more at home with religious ways of thinking than ratiocination seems to be. A Christian way of thinking is one which is primarily directed to knowing a person (Jesus) in a personal manner. This kind of knowledge brings about a cognitive attachment and intellectual bonding, an attachment and bonding which are integral aspects of faith. Intuition makes available a newer, deeper, and hence a more faith-full grasp of another person's subjectivity. This richer cognitive grasp is basic for a profound cognitive connection to Jesus, an I-Thou relationship rather than the areligious I-it.[84] Intuitive knowledge of Jesus (or of any person) tends to emphasize the "whoness," while ratiocinative knowledge of Jesus (or any person) typically focuses on the "whatness" or the quiddity. Once again, then, we see that intuition is more "I-Thou" oriented, while ratiocination is more directed to an "I-it."[85] *Fourth,* intuition affords a certain sense of intellectual security which ratiocination does not supply in as great an abundance.

When a person grasps reality through his intuitive powers, "he *knows* it is true." Sarvepalli Radhakrishnan remarks that "intuitive truths as simple acts of mental vision are free from doubt. They do not carry conviction on the ground of their logical [ratiocinative] validity. We cannot help assenting to them as soon as we intuit them. Doubts occur when [ratiocinative] reflection supervenes."[86] *Fifth,* intuition brings a certain sense of intellectual insecurity and uneasiness which ratiocination does not furnish in as great a profusion. The empirical research, for example, shows that intellectual uneasiness and dissatisfaction with conventional solutions tend to produce more creative thinking than do intellectual security and contentment.[87] Indeed, the relevant empirical research studies indicate that creative persons are overwhelmingly intuitive rather than ratiocinative, and that creative persons are more open to experiences both within and without.[88] Since openness to experience appears to be a critical variable in religious development, it might be well for religious educators to place greater emphasis on promoting intuitive cognition.

Intuition is a rational function which is complementary to, not opposed to ratiocination. As in all rational functioning, there must be a harmonious balance of complementaries between ratiocination and intuition.[89] Intuitive knowing, Jerome Bruner states, may invent and discover realities which ratiocination does not; yet it is ratiocinative thought which gives the fruits of intuition the proper formalism. "The rightness or wrongness of an intuition is finally decided not by intuition itself but by the usual methods of [ratiocinative] proof."[90] Intuition is not some sort of magic, spooky process of "just suddenly happening on something." Fruitful intuition rests upon (1) solid rational foundations, and (2) a rather well-developed understanding of the ratiocinative aspects of the particular reality on which the person focuses his intuitive powers. Albert Einstein frequently asserted that his greatest scientific discoveries were achieved through intuition. But it is quite obvious that Einstein had a marvelously well-developed ratiocinative command of his subject-matter content, a command which furnished the ground and framework out of which he intuited.

Because of its great importance in expanding religious growth, the teacher should structure learning activities which require intuitive thinking as well as those which involve ratiocination. If one is to judge by much of the Catholic and Protestant curricular materials, the promotion of intuition is quite neglected in religious instruction.

Infused Cognitive Knowing

Infusion is a mode of rational and/or extrarational knowing by which God is said either to directly provide a person with cognitive data or to directly augment his intellectual powers so he can acquire cognitive data not otherwise accessible to him. Over the centuries, two major theories have been proposed concerning the type of cognitive content which infusion supplies. One theory maintains that God supplies a person with knowledge by directly pouring cognitive data into his thinking processes. The second theory holds that God directly illumines a person's cognitive powers so that he can thereby be enabled to exercise his intellectual abilities in such a drastically enriched way as to gain cognitive content not normally or naturally attainable. Infused cognitive content can be either rational or extrarational. What sets infusion apart from purely rational or purely extrarational knowing is that it proceeds along the distinctively processive and intellective lines of divine illumination. Further, in the case of infusion the person tends to be passive, while in much of extrarational knowing and in all of rational knowing the person is intellectually active.

Christian theologians and religious thinkers usually assert that infused cognitive content comes about as part and parcel of a living faith-relationship which a person has with God.[91] Put metaphorically, infused cognitive content is the light provided by a person's living relationship with God. Since religious faith and divine grace are necessary for infusion, it is not possible to have infused cognitive content unless its recipient is in a state of faith and grace,[92] or so many Christian theologians claim.

What can the religious educator do to hasten and enrich infusion, assuming that this kind of cognitive content does indeed exist? If one is to believe the classical authors on this subject, there is much a human being can do to promote and cultivate the possibilities for infusion to take place.[93] Inasmuch as infusion typically occurs according to the depth of the religious lifestyle of the individual, the most fruitful instructional practices are those which are centered around enriching the learner's religious lifestyle behaviors. Most of the authors who treat of infused cognitive content further suggest that some other kinds of effective practices which the religion teacher can employ to enhance the possibilities of infusion taking place include frequent engagement in intuitive thought, opening the self to the mythic and the symbolic in reality, and attempting to consciously choose those kinds of activities which are most congruent with the higher-order spiritual counsels given in the bible.

Levels of Cognitive Content

There are three levels of cognitive content. In ascending order, they are knowledge, understanding, and wisdom.

Knowledge is the simple apprehension of truth. It is information concerning the facts basic to a given reality. Knowledge tells a person the *that* of a given reality. Knowledge is oriented toward the particulars of a given reality.

Understanding is the grasp of the elementary and the penultimate principles underlying a given reality. Understanding tells a person the *immediate why* of a given reality. Understanding is oriented toward general principles or universals and not toward particulars. Because understanding is targeted toward underlying general principles, it enables a person to come to a discerning and penetrating judgment about a given reality. Understanding perfects knowledge and is superior to knowledge because understanding yields the ''why'' and not just the ''that,'' and because it supplies a deeper insight and awareness of the nature and operations of a given reality.[94]

Wisdom is the comprehension of the ultimate principles underlying a given reality. Wisdom tells a person the *ultimate why* of a given reality. Because it yields cognitive content about the ultimate causes and explanations of a given reality, wisdom perfects both knowledge and understanding. In virtually every philosophical system[95] and religion, wisdom is considered as the highest, most sublime, and most finished form of cognitive content. Wisdom is the summit of cognitive achievement, a goal which draws a person higher and ever higher in its pursuit. Aristotle comments that the wise person not only knows what flows from ultimate principles, but also posseses truth about these ultimate principles themselves.[96] Since the most ultimate principle of reality—a principle so radically ultimate and fundamental that it suffuses all reality and is the ground for the very existence of all reality—is God, wisdom puts a person in a more profound cognitive contact with God than is possible for either knowledge or understanding to do. Wisdom enables a person to relate all things to God, to link all effects to their divine cause, and to connect all finite reality to the God who is the living, sustaining ground for everything which is. Wisdom, then, brings a person cognitive content of the deepest human and divine things. It is on this account that wisdom is the peak of cognitive achievement.

In both the Aristotelian and the Platonic traditions, it is wisdom which supplies the cognitive superstructure and direction for intelligent and fruitful activity in every sector of reality. Aristotle observes that because wisdom deals with ultimate principles and causes, it is able to correctly judge all things and place them in proper order and perspective, since there can be no perfect and universal judgment which is not based on ultimate principles.[97] Aquinas states that an effect is judged according to the cause or principle which underlies it. Furthermore, a lower effect is properly judged on the basis of a higher cause or principle. Thus, concludes Aquinas, wisdom, which is the highest intellectual activity, is the supreme judge of all intellectual activities and operations. Indeed, wisdom directs and architects all cognitive activity.[98] Plato, for his part, teaches that wisdom suggests a unified view of ends and means, a view which results from an examination of reality and oneself. Hence there arose the celebrated Platonic maxim: "It belongs to the wise person to order."

Christian wisdom is decidedly Christocentric—which should indeed be expected, since Christian wisdom is, after all, *Christian* wisdom as well as Christian *wisdom*. Paul the Apostle calls Jesus "the power and the wisdom of God" (1 Cor. 1:24). All truly human and Christian wisdom, then, must be grounded in the person of Jesus. As Paul further observes, "God has made you members of Christ Jesus and by God's doing he has become our wisdom, and our virtue, and our holiness, and our freedom" (1 Cor. 1:30). The deeply religious person, the individual who has joined himself to Jesus by living a religious lifestyle, is one who is thereby in existential union with Jesus and hence in a sense of one mind with that Lord who is himself the most ultimate of all causes or principles.

To teach religious knowledge is important and indeed indispensable in the work of religious instruction. But it is far more important to teach religious understanding and religious wisdom. Religious understanding and religious wisdom are not mere speculative finery adorning the Christian's life; they are the most practical aspects of his daily living. Understanding a given reality, knowing the principles by which it operates, enables a person to utilize that reality to the fullest extent and under the widest range of conditions. It is from understanding and particularly from wisdom that intelligent and fruitful practice is drawn. Decades of research in educational psychology have disclosed that when a person learns the underlying principles or theoretical components of a reality, he will be able to utilize that reality far more effectively than if he simply acquires a knowledge of the raw, brute facts. Furthermore, transfer of learning is greatly facilitated when the underlying principles of reality are understood by the learner. This research finding is of capital importance, since the overall and lasting effectiveness of religious instruction is so heavily tied up with transfer of learning.[99] Wisdom ought to be given pride of place in cognitive curricular materials and in everyday cognitively oriented instruction. Wisdom can be taught,[100] particularly if the religion teacher focuses attention on the acquisition of the ultimate principles and "whys" of the Christian religion by engaging in lifestyle activities. Fostering intuitive thinking in the learners effectively facilitates their acquisition of wisdom, as Aristotle discovered many centuries ago.[101]

The Guilford Classification System

Utilizing an empirical approach, and employing factor analysis, J. P. Guilford devised a "structure of intellect" model which attempts to place in an orderly, comprehensive framework the various multifaceted, interacting cognitive operations of the human person.[102] Guilford was spurred on to erect his celebrated model because empirical investigations which made use of extensive factor analysis "have proved wrong" the widely held assumption that the same intellectual function is involved regardless of the kind of information with which a person deals.[103]

Like many models which represent a social-science theory, Guilford's highly influential and eminently respected model takes the form of a three-sided cube. One side of this cube has four elements; the second side has five elements; and the third side has six elements. Thus there are $4 \times 5 \times 6$ or 120 cells in the model. Each cell specifies the way in which a particular cognitive function actually takes place. Guilford's comprehensive model thus has the advantage of teasing out and specifying which kind of cognitive functioning is actually going on when an individual is engaged in a particular act of knowing. Such specification is of signal practical benefit to the religious educator because it helps him (1) to enlarge his overall curricular and instructional goals so as to require for their attainment the use of the learner's entire 120 cell repertoire of cognitive abilities, and (2) to sharpen his instructional practices so that in any given teaching situation he employs that pedagogy maximally conducive to enabling the learner to use the cognitive function (cell) most appropriate to the achievement of the desired cognitive outcome.

Guilford gives to the first side of his three-sided cubed structure-of-intellect model the label "content category."[104] In this category are four discrete kinds of intellectual contents, namely, figural, symbolic, semantic, and behavioral. Figural content is represented by geometric patterns or designs which convey no intrinsic meaning. Symbolic content is made up of signs and signals which convey meaning by representing other things, for example, numbers or formulae. Semantic content represents meaning as conveyed in spoken and written language; it is verbal in character. Behavioral content is identified as the physical actions and overt social behaviors of the individual; most nonverbal content falls under behavioral content.

To the second side of his three-sided cubed structure-of-intellect model Guilford gives the name "operation category." In this category are five discrete types of intellectual operations, namely, evaluation, convergent-production, divergent-production, memory, and cognition. Evaluation is the intellectual operation of comparing a product of information with known information according to logical criteria, reaching a decision concerning criterion-satisfaction. Convergent production is the intellectual operation of generating information from given information with stress on rigorous deduction from and pointed analysis of the original information: convergent production yields a definite answer or end-result precisely because of the tightness of the logical structure through which it is enacted. Divergent production is the intellectual operation of generating information from given information, with an emphasis on the variety and output from the same source: divergent production indicates an intellectual operation wherein the person is relatively free to generate his own information within an information-poor structure, or to derive new directions or new perspectives from given information. Memory is the intellectual operation involving the retention or storage, with some degree of availability, of information in the same form in which it was committed to storage and in connection with the same cues with which it was learned; examples of memory include recognition, selective recall, and rote memory. Cognition is the intellectual operation which consists of: (a) awareness, immediate discovery or rediscovery, or recognition of information in divers forms; (b) comprehension or understanding.

To the third side of his three-sided cubed structure-of-intellect model, Guilford assigns the term "product category." A product, in Guilford's system, pertains to the form in which any information occurs. In this category are placed six discrete kinds of intellectual products, namely, unit, class, relation, system, transformation, and implication. A unit is a chunk of reality, a segregated whole, a figure on a ground; a unit is a type of reality to which a noun normally applies. A class is a set of objects with one or more common properties; however, it is more than just a set since, for a class, idea is involved. A relation is some kind of connection between two realities, a connecting link having its own character which is not identical to the realities it joins. Prepositions typically express relations, such as "son of," "harder than." A system is a complex, a pattern, or an organization of interdependent or interacting parts, such as a verbally stated arithmetic problem, a program, or an outline. A transformation is a change, a revision, a redefinition, or a modification by which any product of information in one state passes over into another state. An implication is something predicted, expected, or anticipated from the given information; implication is akin to the frequently used term "association."

Guilford's structure-of-intellect model has myriad uses in the improvement of religion teaching. It suggests to religious educators that there are at least 120 structurally distinct varieties of cognitive content. Awareness of this large number of cognitive operations shows the teacher that there is a wide diversity of cognitive outcomes which can be facilitated in the learners. A diversity of this magnitude will go a long way in reducing the sameness and staleness which characterize the cognitive content offered in some religion lessons. Guilford's model also provides convenient and easily usable points of concentration for those religious educators involved in the preparation and improvement of religion teachers. Each of Guilford's 120 cells pinpoints a particular kind of cognitive activity. By focusing the attention of the preservice or inservice teacher on the acquisition of selected cells, the educator who is professionally preparing religion teachers will learn to turn his attention to highly specified instructional outcomes rather than to devote the bulk of his energies to more global (and hence less attainable) learning outcomes. As I underscore in *The Flow of Re-*

ligious Instruction, one of the keys to the acquisition and improvement of effective teaching skills is to specify as finely and as tightly as possible both the desired learning outcome and the pedagogical practice which most successfully yields this outcome.

The Bloom Taxonomy

Benjamin Bloom and his associates devised a formal taxonomy of educational objectives for the cognitive domain of the teaching endeavor.[105] The Bloom taxonomy places its emphasis on obtaining evidence about the level and extent to which the desired and intended cognitive behavior has been actually acquired by the learner.

The practical benefits of the Bloom taxonomy are at least six. *First,* the taxonomy separates what could easily remain an undifferentiated mass of cognitive content into categories of intellectual activity classified according to internally related groupings of disparate (though sometimes overlapping) ways of intellectual behavior. Consequently, the taxonomy enables the educator to see with some degree of clarity the various kinds and levels of cognitive behavior which do in fact exist. *Second,* the taxonomy enables the teacher to sharpen and refine the type and level of cognitive behavior which he intends the learner to acquire. Using the taxonomy, the teacher selects that particular cognitive behavior most appropriate to the goals of the lesson or wider instructional unit. *Third,* the taxonomy helps the educator to achieve optimum vertical articulation[106] between the cognitive behavior he is attempting to facilitate in the lesson and the other cognitive components classified in the taxonomy. Vertical articulation is essential in insuring that the cognitive behavior being facilitated does indeed work in harmony rather than at cross-purposes with the other types of cognitive behavior being facilitated in the lesson or in the wider instructional unit. *Fourth,* the taxonomy assists the teacher to achieve optimum horizontal articulation between the cognitive behavior he is facilitating and the other noncognitive pedagogical objectives he intends to enact in a particular lesson or wider instructional unit. This meshing of mutually appropriate cognitive behaviors is essential if these behaviors are to reinforce and harmoniously expand each other rather than cancel each other out. *Fifth,* the taxonomy is suggestive of kinds of learning experiences which might prove fruitful in bringing about the desired cognitive objectives of the lesson.[107] *Sixth,* the taxonomy provides the teacher with adequate criteria by which to accurately assess the type and level of cognitive outcomes actually acquired by the learner during the lesson or wider instructional unit.

Because of its great utility, the Bloom taxonomy has exerted a great influence on teachers and especially on curriculum builders in general education. Religious educators, for their part, would do well to make extensive and appropriate use of the Bloom taxonomy both in teaching and in curriculum construction.[108]

There are six major categories of cognitive behaviors listed in the Bloom taxonomy. The first of these, namely knowledge, is conceptualized by Bloom and his associates as a product content, to utilize the terminology I employ in my trilogy on religious instruction. The remaining five categories in the Bloom taxonomy are process contents. (Parenthetically, this 1:5 ratio in favor of process content serves to again reinforce my observation in Chapter Three that process content is educationally more significant than is product content.)

The first category of the Bloom taxonomy is knowledge. Knowledge is defined in the taxonomy as the recall of specifics and universals, the recall of methods and processes, or the recall of a pattern, structure, or setting. Major divisions of knowledge include knowledge of specifics, knowledge of ways and means of dealing with specifics, and knowledge of the universals and abstractions in a field. Each of these major divisions have subdivisions.

The second category of the Bloom taxonomy is comprehension. Comprehension is defined in the taxonomy as a type of apprehension such that the person knows what is being communicated and can make use of whatever is being communicated without necessarily relating it to other material or grasping the full extent of its implications. Major divisions of comprehension include translation, interpretation, and extrapolation.

The third category of the Bloom taxonomy is application. Application is defined in the taxonomy as the employment or utilization of abstractions in particular situations. There are no divisions or subdivisions listed for this third category.

The fourth category of the Bloom taxonomy is analysis. Analysis is defined in the taxonomy as the dissection of a communication into its component elements or parts in such a way that the relative hierarchy of ideas is laid bare and/or that the relations between the ideas expressed are made explicit. Major divisions of analysis include analysis of elements, analysis of relationships, and analysis of organizational principles.

The fifth category of the Bloom taxonomy is synthesis. Synthesis is defined in the taxonomy as the combining or putting together of elements and parts so as to form an integrated, coherent whole. Major divisions of synthesis include production of a unique communication, production of a plan or proposed set of operations, and derivation of a set of abstract relations.

The sixth category of the Bloom taxonomy is evaluation. Evaluation is defined in the taxonomy as a judgment about the pertinence, appropriateness, relevance, or value of the material and practices for given purposes or tasks. Major divisions of evaluation include judgments in terms of internal evidence and judgments in terms of external criteria.

The Bloom taxonomy attempts to examine the whole of intellectual activity and to classify the structure of this activity on the basis of differential cognitive behaviors. Viewed from this perspective, the taxonomy indicates that there are six broad categories of cognitive operations. Knowledge focuses on cognitive *recall*. Comprehension focuses on cognitive *apprehension*. Application focuses on cognitive *use*. Analysis focuses on cognitive *dissection*. Syntheses focuses on cognitive *integration*. Evaluation focuses on cognitive *value-judgment*.

As I observed previously, the Bloom taxonomy is an eminently useful device for helping religious educators in sharpening, enacting, and evaluating the cognitive content of the religion lesson. History has shown that religion teachers have typically formulated instructional objectives and goals which are fuzzy and hence ill-suited for effective pedagogy. The Bloom taxonomy classifies cognitive behaviors into operational categories in terms of the intended learning outcomes. Consequently, use of the Bloom taxonomy will decrease fuzziness and increase focused precision in instructional practice (and in curriculum construction as well). To make things even easier for the teacher, the Bloom taxonomy book provides concrete, operational, instructional examples for each of its divisions and subdivisions.

Ideogenesis in Aristotelian-Thomistic Philosophy
The Aristotelian-Thomistic philosophy of ideogenesis has exerted considerable influence throughout the history of Protestant and especially

Catholic religious instruction. This statement holds true even for many of these persons who, since the close of Vatican II in 1965, purport to reject this philosophy.

In the section of this chapter captioned "Varieties of Rational Cognitive Knowing," I indicated that the Aristotelian-Thomistic system regards ratiocination as taking place in three stages, namely abstraction, judgment, and reason (in the precise Scholastic sense of this last term). Ideogenesis, that is, the birth of an idea or the formation of a concept, takes place in the first of these stages, namely in abstraction. In the abstractive process, the external, individual impressions are reduced to internal, universal ideas. There are five successive steps postulated to occur during ideogenesis. *The first step* is that of sensation, namely, the stimulation of a sense receptor by an external stimulus. This is a crucial step indeed, for as the famous Scholastic maxim states, "there is nothing in the mind that was not first in the senses." In sensation, an external stimulus impinges upon a sense receptor in the human body. This stimulus then becomes a neural impulse which is transmitted via interlinking nerve connections to the cerebral cortex of the brain. *The second step* in abstraction is that of perception, namely, the immediate and automatic cognitive coordination of a given sensation and of related sensations into a sensorily meaningful whole. Thus, for example, a man instantly perceives a house, a perception which arises from the coordination of many individual sensations about the house, such as the color of the roof and siding, the reflection from the windows, and so forth. There is no sensation without perception also. *The third step* in abstraction is that of phantasm, namely, the construction by the imagination of the objects perceived. The phantasm retains the individual, concrete attributes of the perception. *The fourth step* in abstraction is the activation of the agent intellect. The agent intellect is the intellectual process which abstracts the individual, concrete notes of the phantasm and reveals the nonmaterial, universal essence of the object perceived. The essence is the substantial nature of the object, that which makes it to be what it is. This essence is universal, that is, common to all objects of a similar kind. It is through the intellectual activity called the agent intellect that cognition is transformed from the physical to the nonphysical. The *fifth and final step* in abstraction is the activation of the possible intellect. The possible intellect is the intellectual process which, having been fecundated by the active intellect with the essence of the perceived object, forms a concept, constructs an idea. The process called the possible intellect thus enables a person to bring to fruition his power to know. It does this by becoming, in a cognitive fashion, the very object it knows.

In terms of philosophical science, the Aristotelian-Thomistic system does offer a highly plausible hypothesis of how a person acquires cognitive content. However, despite its emphasis on sensation as the necessary starting point for all abstraction, the Aristotelian-Thomistic perspective places its major stress on the processes of the agent intellect and the possible intellect. The natural consequence of this stress on the agent intellect and the possible intellect is that the value and role of the more abstract orders of the cognitive process are magnified to such a great extent that the value of concrete activity is sharply lessened if not actually denigrated. Therefore, the Aristotelian-Thomistic explanation of knowing, while appealing in varying degrees to professional philosophers down through the centuries, never seems to have been embraced to any large extent by post-Renaissance natural scientists or engineers as the philosophical matrix for their efforts to investigate and harness physical phenomena. With reference to religious instruction, the Aristotelian-Thomistic postulations about the cognitive process are perhaps largely responsible for the fact that traditional religious instruction curricula and lessons have often shied away from any attempt to operationalize instructional objectives in concrete performance terms. This avoidance of operationalization seems to have frequently led religion teachers and curriculum builders into amorphousness of pedagogical purpose, haphazardness of pedagogical practice, and fuzziness of pedagogical evaluation.[109]

The Cognitive Process in Deweyan Philosophy

By various subjective and introspective observations, John Dewey formulated his well-known five states involved in the process of reflective thinking: "(1) suggestions, in which the mind leaps forward to a possible solution; (2) an intellectualization of the difficulty or perplexity that has been *felt* (directly experienced) into a *problem* to be solved, a question for which the answer must be sought; (3) the use of one suggestion after another as a leading idea, or *hypothesis* to initiate and guide observation and other operations in collecting factual material; (4) the mental elaboration of the idea or supposition as an idea or supposition (*reasoning,* in the sense in which reasoning is a part, not the whole, of inference); and (5) testing the hypothesis by overt or imaginative action.''[110] Dewey takes pains to point out that these five phases or functions of reflective thinking are of general applicability. By this he means that in every act of reflective thought the five steps do not necessarily follow one another in a set of immutable sequence. Thus, for example, elaboration of the hypothesis (phase #4) need not always wait until the problem has been defined (phase #2) and until an adequate hypothesis has been constructed (phase #3); the hypothesis might be elaborated at any intermediate point, depending on the nature of the problem, person, or circumstance.

It should be evident that reflective thinking is for Dewey basically a process of problem solving.[111] Knowing for Dewey, then, is instrumental. It arises from a felt difficulty and proceeds in a total problem-solving manner until the difficulty (which the person refashions into a problem by use of his cognitive processes) has been definitely solved. Because reflective thinking is basically problem solving, it is experimental in character. Reflective thinking is experimental in two ways: cognitively, by reshaping the difficulty into an intellectual problem and then generating an hypothesis which serves as a guide to finding a satisfactory solution; concretely, by actively testing through overt activity whether the hypothesized solution to the problem does, in fact, represent a satisfactory solution.

The Deweyan conceptualization of the cognitive process is one of problem solving carried out by means of hypothesizing, experimenting, and empirical testing. Consequently, Deweyan theory has been regarded by most natural scientists and social scientists as being more fruitful for their work than the Aristotelian-Thomistic system. In religious instruction, for example, the Deweyan notion of hypothesis construction and empirical verification provides a helpful tool for the teacher in making his pedagogical objectives more precise and his evaluation more accurate. The Deweyan view of the cognitive process also seems in many ways to be more useful to the learner than does the Aristotelian-Thomistic system.[112] Let us say, for example, that the learner encounters a particular moral problem which is quite difficult for him. The Aristotelian-Thomistic system, with its sensation—perception—phantasm—agent intellect—possible intellect, followed by judgment and reason, does not provide much practical, down-to-earth assistance to the learner on what he should do in the face of the moral problem with which he is presently confronted. The Deweyan theory, on the other hand, offers the learner a plan of cognitive action whereby he can most fruitfully deploy his thought processes to come to a satisfactory intellectual solution to the moral difficulty.[113]

Moral Judgment

One of the most important and significant cognitive contents in religious instruction is that of moral judgment. In the Aristotelian-Thomistic system, judgment represents the second stage of ratiocination. From this philosophical standpoint, judgment is the central point of a person's ratiocinative life. Certainly moral and religious judgment is one of the central foci for religion teaching.

Much of the interest in moral judgment on the part of Catholic and Protestant religious educators since the 1960s has revolved around the theoretically anchored empirical research of Lawrence Kohlberg. As a result of his investigations, Kohlberg has constructed six discrete, developmental stages of moral judgment which he asserts his research has demonstrated to be more-or-less universally applicable to all persons.[114] Kohlberg takes the moral principle of justice as the norm for his hierarchical ranking of the six stages and the subdivisions within each stage. The more a stage of moral judgment is congruent with the principle of justice, the higher will that stage be in Kohlberg's six-storied edifice.[115] These six stages are, in ascending order, (1) punishment and obedience orientation; (2) instrumental relativist orientation; (3) interpersonal concordance or "good boy—nice girl" orientation; (4) "law and order" orientation; (5) social-contract legalistic orientation; (6) universal ethical-principle orientation.

Kohlberg's basic point is that the heart of moral development resides in cognition, namely a person's judgment about the morality of a particular action. There are three fundamental features of the Kohlbergian map of moral judgment, namely development, structure, and cognition.

The *first fundamental aspect* of Kohlberg's model of moral judgment is that it is developmental. By this I mean that for Kohlberg moral judgment takes place according to a developmental sequence. This stream of human development has six discrete levels hierarchically ordered from the lowest stage (punishment and obedience orientation) to the highest (morality of individual principles of conscience). Moral judgment is a learned behavior, and thus develops and is refined as a person grows from infancy to adulthood. Kohlberg's schema represents a charting of the course in which the structure of moral judgment is built up in an individual, describing the successive stages of evolution from the simpler levels of moral judgment to the more complex, more differentiated ones.

Because of the developmental, evolutionary manner in which a person's moral judgment advances, the developmentally earlier (and lower) stages are prerequisites for the attainment of the developmentally later (and higher) stages. Stages are sequenced in a definite order because the earlier stages are less difficult and hence more readily attainable than the later stages. The later the developmental stage, the more it can adequately reflect a person's congruence with and sensitivity to the nuanced character of the principle of justice as this principle operates in a given set of circumstances. A religion curriculum which adopts Kohlberg's developmental model endeavors to continually structure the learning situation over an extended period of time so that it stimulates the growth of moral judgment step by step upward through the stages. Viewed in this light, religion teaching has a twofold task with respect to moral judgment: (1) to speed up the normal process of the development of moral judgment in the learner, thus hastening his attainment of higher stages of development; (2) to facilitate the possibility that a higher stage will be reached by a person who, were he not in a religion program of one sort or another, might otherwise never reach that stage of moral judgment. To fulfill this twofold task of moral education, Kohlberg proposes a pedagogical procedure termed "+1 match." A +1 match means that the teacher ascertains the learner's present stage of moral judgment and then presents him with a set of learning experiences which are one stage higher.[116]

The *second fundamental aspect* of Kohlberg's model of moral judgment is that it is structural. In other words, Kohlberg's model deals with the structure or the form of moral judgment rather than with the actual rules or precise virtues contained within the overall structure. As a cognitive developmentalist, Kohlberg is interested in the structural organization of moral judgment, that is, in questions such as: "How does the learner organize stimulus inputs in terms of categories or concepts?" or "What integrating principles or synthesizing operations are used to make moral judgments?" Because his is a structural model, Kohlberg contends that moral-judgment instruction should not be directed specifically or exclusively toward teaching a particular set of correct/incorrect moral judgments, but rather should concern itself with enabling the learner to develop the organizational structures by means of which he can analyze, interpret, and judge moral issues.[117] Because of its structuralist emphasis, the Kohlberg model in itself is relatively value-free. Employing the Kohlberg approach in its intended manner therefore means that the teacher does not attempt to undertake the transmitting of a fixed moral truth, but rather engages in a process of stimulating the learner to cognitively restructure his experience.[118] Thus the religion teacher is not an "answer man" or a dispenser of product content, but rather a process facilitator.

The *third fundamental aspect* of Kohlberg's model of moral judgment is that it is cognitive. To make a moral judgment is to engage in a cognitive process. The ability to make a moral judgment, like all other cognitive skills, is a competency which must be acquired. As did other developmentally oriented social scientists, Kohlberg first attempted to analyze fully developed (I do not say "mature") competence in terms of the intellectual discriminations, thought operations, and rule systems which go to form cognitive competence; in short, Kohlberg sought to discover the cognitive structure of moral judgment. In Kohlberg's model, higher stages are said to be superior to lower stages on cognitive grounds, namely that the higher stages demand a more advanced cognitive organization of the structure of moral judgment, are more effective in both analyzing moral problems and in tracing out their far-reaching implications, and integrate diverse data and inferences in a more intellectually sophisticated manner.

Kohlberg-type curricula are typically based on the presentation by the teacher of a moral problem. To come up with a solution to this problem the learner must engage in a cognitive search for the reasons and the factors which suggest one solution to him rather than some other solution.[119] It is the combination of these reasons and factors prompting the learner to select a particular kind of solution that gives the teacher a clue as to which stage of moral judgment the learner is currently at. Problem-posing situations, not a few of which are controversial in their product content, are the staple of a Kohlberg-type lesson. When the teacher wishes to introduce a +1 match into the lesson, he presents a moral problem whose solution can be attained only by employing principles embodied in the stage which is one level higher than that at which the learner is at developmentally in the here-and-now pedagogical moment.

As I observe in *The Flow of Religious Instruction*,[120] Kohlberg's model, like that of the Swiss cognitive developmentalist Jean

Piaget,[121] situates moral judgment within the broad framework of overall cognitive development. However, as Kohlberg himself carefully notes, maturity of moral judgment, while positively correlated with cognitive maturity, nonetheless is clearly distinguishable from it.[122] General cognitive development is a necessary but not a sufficient condition for moral-judgment development. In other words, all persons who have attained a given developmental level of moral judgment have also attained a corresponding level of general cognitive development, but not all persons who have achieved a given level of general cognitive development have also achieved a corresponding level of moral-judgment development. Moral judgment, then, is not simply the application of an individual's general cognitive functioning to moral situations or problems. Making a moral judgment requires an appropriate level of general cognitive development, but it also demands the cultivation and refinement of the moral-judgment function of this overall general cognitive development.[123] This observation is important for the religion teacher, because it suggests that teaching merely for general cognitive gain in matters religious will not automatically insure a corresponding growth in the learner's moral-judgment skills. If the religion teacher intends that improvement in the learner's level and facility in moral judgment constitutes an outcome of the lesson or the course, then he must architect a lesson or curriculum which provides structured learning experiences that are directly geared to inducing moral-judgment behaviors.

Creative Thinking

There is no definition of creativity which is generally agreed upon by social scientists.[124] Consequently there are no measures of it which are as widely accepted or used as the I.Q.[125] Of the many categories of measures used to assess creativity, that of divergent thinking has been the most extensively used. This emphasis on divergent thinking stems primarily from J. P. Guilford's seminal structure-of-intellect model which I discussed earlier in this chapter. It will be recalled that the second side of Guilford's three-sided cube model consists of the operation category. Of the five discrete types of intellectual operation contained in this category, one is of especial relevance to the process of creative thinking, namely divergent production. To be sure, divergent production, for Guilford, is the intellectual substratum of creative thinking. Divergent production stands in contrast to convergent production. In Guilford's structure-of-intellect model, there are twenty-four cells (varieties) of divergent production,[126] thus bringing to salience the many different kinds of creativity which can be tapped by persons in their own daily lives.

On the basis of biographical correlates with actual creative accomplishment, the research evidence[127] indicates that as compared with average or with noncreative performers, a person who has made an outstanding or highly significant creative contribution to the world tends to possess the following set of personal characteristics.[128] A creative individual has a strong achievement orientation.[129] He is independent, autonomous, relatively free, and not rigidly controlled. He possesses initiative; he does not wait for people to tell him what to do. He is free to fail; when one of his ideas or projects does not work out, he loses no self-respect as a result. He exercises independent judgment, and is highly resistant to group pressure. He has little hesitation about proffering ideas or suggesting practices which are not consensual. The creative person is dynamic, self-assertive, dominant, aggressive, and self-sufficient. He has persistence of motive, self-discipline, perseverance, and a high-energy output as well as a capacity and a liking for work. He rejects repression or suppression. He is uninhibited and highly acceptant of his own inner impulses. He is unconventional, iconoclastic, and radical (in the nonpolitical sense of this term). He is unconcerned about whether his behavior is regarded by others as hyper-individualistic or even bohemian; however, he is not a bohemian. He is a nonconformist, and is his own man. The creative individual is less contented and more dissatisfied with the way things are than the average person; however, his is a constructive criticism. He is marked by a sense of originality. He displays, not only an interest in, but, more significantly, a preference for novelty, complexity, and some degree of apparent asymmetry in perceptual phenomena. He has an intrinsic interest in situations which require some resolution in preference to those which are cut-and-dried. He enjoys exploring and rearranging possibilities; he finds pleasure in variety and in speculating on "what would happen if . . . ?" Many of his ideas are fresh, unusual, and "off the beaten track." He is stimulus-free rather than stimulus-bound, that is, he frees himself from a given stimulus or set of stimuli, juxtaposing irreconcilables or purported irreconcilables to form surprising associations.

When confronted with a problem-solving situation, the creative person usually works slowly and cautiously while he is analyzing the problem and gathering his data. But once he has accumulated his basic data and approaches the point of synthesis, he works rapidly.[130] He is playful. He does not regard any single probe or trial as comprising the "be all" or "end all." His creative accomplishments emerge from large amounts of "wasted time" as judged by conventional standards or by convergent-thinking criteria. He spends a great deal of time "playing with the data or with the reality," and enjoys this playing process. He has a sense of humor, often of a subtle and wildly associative type. He can see the humorous and wry aspects in what is real, pressing, and earnest for others.

The creative person is more concerned with ideas than with persons. He has little interest in cultivating a wide circle of interpersonal relationships, or in attending gatherings involving a high degree of social activity on his part. He is asocial, low in need for social affiliation, individualistic, introverted, and reserved in his own way. However, he is socially aware and possesses a good deal of social insight. He is open to feelings and emotions, especially his own. He is intuitive, empathic, and highly subjective. He is characterized by vitality and enthusiasm. The creative individual is psychologically well-adjusted in the broad sense of feeling happy in his work, socially useful, congruent with his inner self, and relatively fulfilled as a person. He is emotionally unstable as measured by average standards of emotional stability; however, he uses this instability effectively and productively in the service of his self and of his work. He is decidedly aesthetic in his judgment and orientation. Concomitantly, he often places a relatively low value on the acquisition of wealth.

The creative person has a high curiosity need. He typically is widely informed, has a broad range of interests, and is versatile. He is motivated by a need for order, harmony, and form. He is more self-assured and less critical of himself than is the average person. He takes risks where he feels they are warranted. He is less authoritarian in his attitudes than is the average person; he is also less anxious. There is a significant tendency for a creative person to be either an only child or a first-born child. In the Northern Hemisphere, there is a slight tendency for the creative individual to be born from August through November.[131] The childhood patterns of creative persons tend to be characterized by parents or extended family members who were independent, and who provided the child with emotional support, encouragement, respect, value-direction, and a relative degree of freedom. The creative person is well aware that he is creative. Finally, the creative person tends to make a greater impact on others.

This empirically supported profile of the personality characteristics of the creative performer probably is not very appealing to many Catholic or Protestant ecclesiastical officials in terms of what these officials wish to see as the fruit of their religious instruction programs. To be sure, institutional religion, particularly as it is enfleshed in the form of ecclesiastical officials, has always seemed to be ill at ease with divergent thinkers and creative performers. History has shown that divergent and creative Christians, especially those of the outspoken or more visible sort, have frequently been rewarded by their churches by being clapped into prison, burned at the stake, run out of town, placed on the *Index of Forbidden Books,* denounced, formally condemned, excommunicated, censored, banned, or otherwise ostracized. In the more immediate area of religious instruction, one needs only to recall the repressive activities by which the Central Cathechetical Establishment and like-minded local diocesan catechetical establishments have censored, banned, or otherwise ostracized religious educationists whose views were not consonant with the Central Cathechetical Establishment's official party line.[132] It is interesting that in the monumental *Research on Religious Development* there is a notable scarcity of items on creativity listed in the index, and there is not a single entry listed for creativity in religious instruction.[133]

If religion is to be fluid rather than frozen, bold rather than timorous, expanding human life rather than restricting it, pushing forward into the frontiers of the still fully unexplored Jesus rather than retreating into tight little bastions of safety—then it must allow and indeed encourage the full expression of divergent thinking and creative production from outside and especially from inside its own ranks. In the past, religious instruction typically consisted in transmitting doctrinal formulae or creedal beliefs to others. This view of religious instruction naturally stressed "correct," conventional answers which emphasized convergent thinking. But religious instruction surely is more than helping the learner to become a glorified Xerox machine, reproducing totally faithful copies of formulae and beliefs in as short a time as possible. Religious instruction should enable the learner to become religious, to use his cognitive, affective, and lifestyle behaviors to reconstruct himself, society, the church, and religion itself. If religion is to be a living, expanding, authentic force in the life of the learner, then it must play this reconstructionist role. Hence what is urgently needed in religion lessons is more emphasis on promoting and rewarding divergent thinking and creativity. Human creation is reconstruction. To state all this is in no way to approve or advocate the education of radical-type rebels, persons who claim to completely reject all formulae, beliefs, and all of the past as well. (Indeed, one might legitimately argue that such rebels are usually noncreative individuals who see the limitations of a pattern of exclusively convergent thinking and noncreative living, but who are not themselves sufficiently divergent or creative to devise truly creative solutions or stances.)[134] The religion teacher can indeed teach both a genuine appreciation for those standard formulae, legitimized beliefs, and data from the past which are objectively and subjectively valuable; but he can and should also teach the learner to see how things can be done differently and made better.

SOME PRACTICAL CONSEQUENCES

Cognition is an indispensable content within the larger galaxy of the substantive content of religious instruction. The religious educator must both be familiar with the nature and various forms of cognitive content and also skilled in the pedagogical procedures of teaching cognitive content if he is to successfully structure that kind of pedagogical experience in which learners can encounter truly the richness and multidimensionality of the cognitive content of religious instruction.

Because cognitive outcomes are so many and varied, different pedagogical procedures are necessary to facilitate the acquisition of different kinds of cognitive outcomes. As I observe in Chapter One, substantive content and structural content are not totally distinct molar contents which are simply laminated on to one another in the religious instruction act. Rather, substantive content and structural content are so fused and mediated in the religious instruction act that the two become a new and distinct ontic entity.[135] Consequently, substantive content and structural content not only affect each other, but in the religious instruction act are each other in one very real sense.

In this final section of the chapter, I will very briefly deal with some practical consequences involved in teaching two related representative process cognitive contents, namely understanding and wisdom.

Earlier in this chapter I delineated three levels of cognitive content, namely knowledge, understanding, and wisdom.[136] All three are essential outcomes in religious instruction. Thus it is crucial that the religious educator not simply be satisfied with facilitating knowledge outcomes, but press on and teach for understanding and wisdom outcomes as well. After all, one of the touchstones of genuine solid religious living is that a person frequently relates in a conscious fashion the phenomena of his experience with the penultimate principles (understanding) and the ultimate principles (wisdom) of these phenomena.

Understanding and wisdom consider reality in terms of its penultimate and ultimate *meanings* respectively.[137] Understanding judges and orders knowledge; wisdom judges and orders both knowledge and understanding.[138] The potency of wisdom to judge and to order all truths and all cognitive awareness of reality arises from the fact that there can be no perfect or universal judgments about reality except those which flow from and are unceasingly tethered to the ultimate cause (and in the case of religion, to the Ultimate Cause).[139] Wisdom is the perfect[140] and complete cognitive content, not only because it judges and orders all other cognitive contents, but also because it involves both ratiocination and intuition.[141]

In my view, understanding and wisdom, unlike knowledge, can be gained only through firsthand experience. If God is indeed the ultimate cause and ground of all phenomena, then one must consciously experience God in some manner in all reality if one is to become truly wise. Religion allows us this wisdom, so that a religiously wise person is empowered to connect all the reality which he experiences with the ultimate cause of that reality.[142]

If religious instruction is to be a mode of religious education rather than a mode of religious training, then a cardinal cognitive outcome of religious instruction courses[143] surely must be understanding and most especially wisdom.[144]

The ideal religious educator, like any ideal practitioner, understands and is wise with respect to both the substantive content and the structural content of that which he is teaching. The religious educator understands and is wise in the basic principles of the teaching process. Over and above this, the teacher is an artist, namely, one highly skilled in facilitating desired pedagogical outcomes in the learners.[145] This understanding and wisdom, plus the accompanying artistry which is fused to them in the religious instruction act, is one of the main features distinguishing the artist from the hack not only in religion teaching but in all facets of life.[146]

One fruitful pedagogical procedure which the religious educator might wish to use in facilitating understanding and wisdom outcomes in learners is the technique of higher-order questions.

Higher-order questions are those which endeavor to facilitate more advanced and more sophisticated cognitive behaviors on the part of the learner. Higher-order questions are typically operationalized by contemporary educational specialists to be the three highest levels elaborated in the Bloom taxonomy, namely analysis, synthesis, and evaluation. Thus a religious educator seeking to induce cognitive responses from learners which are analytic in nature might ask higher-order questions designed to enable the learner to distinguish factual from normative statements made by church officials (#4.10 in the Bloom taxonomy, namely, analysis of elements), to grasp the relationship among the various ideas presented in several biblical passages (#4.20 in the Bloom taxonomy, namely, analysis of relationships), or to find out how the *ecclesiasticum* is organized with respect to the oppression-liberation continuum (#4.30 in the Bloom taxonomy, namely, analysis of organizational principles).[147]

Though one of the many signal instructional benefits of the Bloom taxonomy is that of hierarchically ordering and specifying the various forms and subforms of higher-order cognitive processes, it should not be thought that higher cognitive activities did not exist in the pre-Bloom era. To be sure, the core of the teaching technique used by Socrates was that of higher-order questions. The pedagogical technique favored by Socrates is called maieutic teaching because in the *Thaeatetus*[148] Socrates categorizes his own instructional procedures as midwifery,[149] a process of bringing others' thoughts to the birth through higher-order questioning.[150] Maieutic teaching stresses process content far more than product content. Socrates does not have certain cognitive conclusions to impart to others, but rather wishes to teach learners a process of cognitively investigating reality, a cognitive process which for Socrates is far more important than cognitive product content because this process involves testing cognitive product content, revising cognitive product content, and going beyond cognitive product content.[151]

Socratic higher-order questioning inexorably forces the learner to

separate the particulars of experience from the search for more universal and more profound truths[152]—in short, to arrive at understanding
and wisdom. Maieutic teaching, then, is targeted, not to specific and
immediate concrete practice, but rather to general and long-range theory,[153] especially as theory relates to understanding and to wisdom.[154]
An examination of Plato's *Dialogues* clearly shows that in Socrates'
view understanding and wisdom are not the result of occasional insightful ideas or "immediate-happening" pedagogy but only come
about through carefully planned, systematic, and unrelenting teaching
activity. Socrates did not present learners with a cognitive product;
instead he involved them deeply and personally in the process of
higher-order cognition. Commenting on this central feature of maieutic
teaching, the German philosopher Leonard Nelson observes that while
presenting or telling can sometimes stimulate persons to think, especially in the case of more mature learners, still such a pedagogical
stimulus is not irresistible to the learner. In Nelson's view, one great
strength of the Socratic teaching technique is that "only persistent
pressure to speak one's mind, to meet every counter-question, and to
state the reasons for every assertion transforms the power of
[pedagogical] allure into an irresistible compulsion."[155] The maieutic
pedagogical procedure introduces tension into the instructional process
since this teaching practice deliberately loosens the learner from the
perceived security of his cognitive (and sometimes dogmatic) anchorages and places him in a state of perplexity and bewilderment.
Consequently, patience on the educator's part and endurance on the
learner's part are essential requirements for successful maieutic instruction. Endurance is not simply a requirement for maieutic teaching;
it is also one of maieutic teaching's firstfruits since it forcefully brings
home to the learners that they deceive themselves if they believe that
understanding and wisdom are obtained easily and without long, hard
work. Maieutic teaching requires courage on the part of the learner.
The teacher should help the learner gain this courage.[156]

There is a growing corpus of empirical research evidence which
suggests that higher-order cognitive questions definitely tend to induce
higher-order cognitive learning outcomes. Francis Hunkins' empirical
investigation concludes that higher-order questions tended not only to
elicit critical thinking outcomes on the part of learners but also tended
to yield significantly higher scores on a standardized achievement
test.[157] George Ladd's study found that teachers who asked a greater

proportion of higher-order cognitive questions tended to produce a greater percentage of higher-order cognitive outcomes in learners as contrasted to teachers who did not ask as high a proportion of higher-order cognitive questions.[158] Beatryce Newton's research investigation discovered that students who were taught by an instructional procedure which emphasized higher-order cognitive questions showed a statistically significant mean gain in scores on a standardized test of critical thinking, while students who were taught by a pedagogical technique which did not emphasize higher-order cognitive questions failed to show a statistically significant mean gain.[159] Of especial importance is a sophisticated review by Doris Redfield and Elaine Waldman Rousseau of twenty experimental research investigations on questioning. These twenty investigations included the use of higher-order and lower-order cognitive questions by the teacher. Using a meta-analysis technique for reviewing these experimental research studies, Redfield and Rousseau found that the preponderance of these studies indicated that gains in both product cognitive achievement and process critical thinking occur when higher-order cognitive questions assume a predominant role in the pedagogical event.[160]

On the basis of their own respective empirical research investigations, two different sets of scholars hypothesize that teachers' use of lower-order cognitive questions as contrasted to higher-order cognitive questions is often dependent upon the type of educational materials being used.[161] Meridith Gall, for example, hypothesizes that teachers ask more higher-order cognitive questions about primary sources (e.g., poems, the bible) then about secondary sources (e.g., most school textbooks, news accounts in diocesan or jurisdictional newspapers). If this last-mentioned hypothesis is true, then there is empirical support for the contention advanced by most biblical scholars and some religious educationists,[162] namely, that learners of all ages should spend far more time encountering the bible text directly than reading textbook commentaries on the bible or listening to teachers and preachers talk about the bible.

If religious educators working in every kind of setting are to significantly improve their pedagogical skills in facilitating cognitive outcomes such as higher-order cognitive questioning, then they must learn both the theory underlying these pedagogical skills and the practice of these skills. An especially effective milieu in which to directly practice a particular pedagogical procedure and to experientially link this practice to the theory which undergirds it is the teacher performance center.[163] The teacher performance center is a laboratory setting which provides the religious educator with the facilities and the opportunities for actually practicing a particular pedagogical skill, for assessing the degree of his effectiveness in deploying that skill, and for examining the theoretical bases and extensions of that skill in order that he can thus optimize the wider application of the skill.

Summarizing the pertinent professional literature, Willis Copeland has found three major types of activities conducted in the teacher performance center, namely microteaching, protocol materials, and simulation.[164]

Microteaching is a laboratory-based procedure designed to teach educators how to significantly improve one or other specific pedagogical skill. Interfacing the pedagogical technique of higher-order cognitive questioning with the seven major characteristics of microteaching delineated by Copeland,[165] the religious educator would learn the following. First, he would learn the characteristics of the pedagogical technique of higher-order cognitive questioning. This learning would include both an explanation of the higher-order cognitive questioning as well as exhibition of this technique in actual use. Second, the religious educator teaches a religion lesson to a small number of learners, generally four to six. During this teaching episode, the religious educator concentrates on using higher-order cognitive questions. Third, the lesson is of short duration, lasting six to ten minutes as a general rule. Fourth, the lesson is videorecorded. Fifth, within a few minutes after conducting the lesson, the religious educator receives feedback on his performance by viewing a replay of the lesson. The religious educator, with the assistance of one of the teachers conducting the teacher performance center, reviews the lesson with the religious educator, centering his attention primarily on scientific analyses of the teaching event using such devices as the Flanders Interaction Analysis System.[166] Sixth, within a short time after viewing the videorecording, the religious educator replans and then reteaches the lesson to a new group of learners, again centering attention on higher-order cognitive questioning. Seventh, this teach-review-reteach cycle continues until both the teacher performance center coordinator and the religious educator are satisfied that the religious educator has mastered the pedagogical technique of higher-order cognitive questioning.

There is empirical support for the use of microteaching in teaching religious educators to improve their repertoire of pedagogical skills. Surely every diocese and central religious education office should have a teacher performance center in which such procedures as microteaching are used to upgrade the pedagogical skills of religious educators in the area.

CONCLUSION

Though cognitive content is relatively less important in the religious domain than affective content or lifestyle content, nonetheless cognitive content is a vitally important and indeed indispensable substantive content in religious instruction. Cognitive content will only assume its full potential in the religious instruction enterprise when intuition is taught as well as ratiocination, when creative or divergent thinking is taught as well as convergent thinking, and when higher-order cognitive behaviors such as evaluation are taught as well as lower-order cognitive behaviors. Furthermore, cognitive content can only become a truly yeasting force in religious instruction when it is structurally inserted into the learner's own personal day-to-day living.

NOTES

1. Eric Hoffer, *The Passionate State of Mind* (New York: Harper & Row Perennial Library, 1954), p. 106.
2. A host of theories has been proposed both in philosophy and in psychology to explain how thinking does in fact take place. In philosophy, there are well-developed theories such as Platonism, Aristotelianism, Thomism, Kantianism, Humeanism, Hegelianism, and Husserlianism. Psychology also has advanced its varying theories among which are the Watsonian, Thorndikean, Hullian, Gestaltist, and Skinnerian. It is beyond the purview of this book to do more than simply mention these theories. More useful, I believe, is to pursue the polarization in the overarching macrotheory between what I term the substantialists and the functionalists.
3. This short paragraph obviously represents a simplication, and to some extent an oversimplification, of two very profound and complex philosophical and psychological macrotheories.
4. When I use the word "intellect" in my writings, I typically do so in the functionalist meaning of this term.
5. George Isaac Brown, *Human Teaching for Human Learning* (New York: Viking, 1971), p. 4.
6. Michael Polanyi, *Personal Knowledge* (Chicago: University of Chicago Press, 1958), p. 305, italics deleted.
7. See Carl R. Rogers, *Freedom to Learn* (Columbus, Ohio: Merrill, 1969), p. 273.
8. See John Dewey, *Experience and Education* (New York: Macmillan, 1938), pp. 102–103.

9. Frederick J. McDonald, "A Concept of Heuristics," in B. Othanel Smith, editor, *Research in Teacher Education* (Englewood Cliffs, N.J.: Prentice-Hall, 1971), p. 74.

10. This does not apply only to young children, but to persons of any age bracket.

11. See Susan W. Gray and James O. Miller, "Early Experience in Relation to Cognitive Development," in *Review of Educational Research* XXXVII (December, 1967), p. 475.

12. See Kenneth Barker, *Religious Education, Catechesis, and Freedom* (Birmingham, Ala.: Religious Education Press, 1981).

13. See George F. Kneller, *Existentialism and Education* (New York: Wiley, 1958), p. 158.

14. On this point, see John Dewey, *Democracy and Education* (New York: Macmillan, 1916), pp. 185–187.

15. See Karl Jaspers, *Reason and Anti-Reason in Our Time*, translated by Stanley Godman (New Haven, Conn.: Yale University Press, 1952), pp. 26–28. There is, of course, a difference between the validity and adequacy of knowledge on the one hand, and its absoluteness and certainty on the other.

16. George F. Kneller, *Existentialism and Education*, p. 157.

17. Thomas Aquinas, *De Veritate*, q. 2, a. 2. Indeed Aquinas holds that the immateriality of cognition constitutes the basic reason why knowledge is the noblest way of possessing a given reality. Modern Existentialists like Gabriel Marcel contend that it is this very immaterial character of cognitive content which makes knowledge so ignoble, unlifelike, and unreal.

18. Monika Hellwig, *The Christian Creeds* (Dayton, Ohio: Pflaum/Standard, 1973), p. 43.

19. "Revelation is not the communication of a list of [cognitive] truths. It is the communication of a person." William J. Duggan, *Myth and Christian Belief* (Notre Dame, Ind.: Fides, 1971), p. 32.

20. I disagree fundamentally with Randolph Crump Miller on this point. For Miller, "Revelation is a theological position." For me, revelation is a personal experience. A theological position is cognitive; experience is lifestyle. See Randolph Crump Miller, *The Theory of Christian Education Practice* (Birmingham, Ala.: Religious Education Press, 1980), p. 7.

21. Alfonso Nebreda, "Living Faith: Major Concern of Religious Education," in Johannes Hofinger and Theodore C. Stone, editors, *Pastoral Catechetics* (New York: Herder and Herder, 1964), p. 142.

22. Thomas Aquinas, *Summa Theologica*, I–II, q. 28, a. 1, ad 3. Translation mine.

23. See Josef Andreas Jungmann, *Handing on the Faith*, translated and revised by A. N. Fuerst (New York: Herder and Herder, 1959), pp. 174–193.

24. This is more applicable to the Catholic sector than to mainline Protestantism. The latter has been working on this type of religious instruction since the 1950s.

25. Léon Arthur Elchinger, "The Bible and Catechesis," in Johannes Hofinger, editor, *Teaching All Nations: A Symposium on Modern Catechetics*, revised and partially translated by Clifford Howell (New York: Herder and Herder, 1961), p. 143.

26. C. G. Jung, *Memories, Dreams, and Reflections*, recorded and edited by Aniela Jaffé, translated by Richard and Clara Winston (New York: Pantheon, 1963), p. 300. Jung links rationalism with "doctrinairism."

27. C. G. Jung, *Psychological Reflections*, edited by Jolande Jacobi (New York: Harper & Row, 1953), p. 174.

28. E. Schillebeeckx, *Revelation and Theology*, volume 1, translated by N. D. Smith (New York: Sheed and Ward, 1967), p. 172.

29. See James Michael Lee "The Authentic Source of Religious Instruction," in Norma H. Thompson, editor, *Religious Education and Theology* (Birmingham, Ala.: Religious Education Press, 1982), pp. 144–146.

30. John McKenzie shares my point of view in this regard. See John L. McKenzie, "The Gospel According to Matthew," in Raymond E. Brown, Joseph A. Fitzmyer, and Roland Murphy, editors, *The Jerome Biblical Commentary*, volume 2 (Englewood Cliffs, N.J.: Prentice-Hall, 1968), pp. 91–92. Some biblical scholars contend that certain portions of Matthew's account of Peter's testimony of his religious experiencing, notably "the son of the living God," probably reflect the more developed religious experience of the post-resurectional church community which formed the existential milieu in which Matthew wrote his gospel. This view is, of course, conjecture. But even if this conjecture is true, it would serve to strengthen, rather than diminish the force of my argument.

31. Theologies change, as the history of persons and the ecclesia amply demonstrate; religious experience remains firm and in a sense absolute.

32. For an elaboration of this point, see James Michael Lee, "The Authentic Source of Religious Instruction," pp. 100–110.

33. I would like to think that the *General Catechetical Directory* deliberately chose to use the phraseology "of a religious way of thinking" (*"religiosi modi cogitandi"*) in preference to "of a theological way of thinking" to describe one of the most important cognitive process contents of religious instruction. Sacra Congregatio pro Clericis, *Directorium catechisticum generale* (Città del Vaticano: Libreria Editrice Vaticana, 1971), p. 81 (#88).

34. Ronald Goldman, *Thinking from Childhood to Adolescence* (London: Routledge and Kegan Paul, 1964), p. 66.

35. Philip H. Phenix, "Education for Faith," in John H. Westerhoff III, editor, *A Colloquy on Christian Education* (Philadelphia: Pilgrim, 1972), p. 43.

36. See James Hillman, *Insearch: Psychology and Religion* (New York: Scribner's, 1967), p. 67.

37. Joseph Colomb, "A Modern Approach to Catechesis in the Church as a Whole," in Alois Müller, editor, *Catechetics for the Future* (New York: Herder and Herder, 1970), pp. 30–31.

38. James Michael Lee, *Forward Together: A Preparation Program for Religious Educators* (Chicago: Thomas More Association, meditape program, 1973).

39. Thus Josef Goldbrunner can remark: ". . . although knowledge is part of faith it does not engender it." Josef Goldbrunner, *Realization: The Anthropology of Pastoral Care*, translated by Paul C. Bailey and Elizabeth Reinecke (Notre Dame, Ind.: University of Notre Dame Press, 1966), p. 36.

40. For a brief discussion of this point, see William Bedford Williamson, *Language and Concepts in Christian Education* (Philadelphia: Westminster, 1970), pp. 54–55.

41. John Dewey, *Democracy and Education*, p. 321.

42. Marcel van Caster, *The Structure of Catechetics*, translated by Edward J. Dirkswager Jr., Olga Guedetarian, and Nicolas Smith (New York: Herder and Herder, 1965), p. 119. The sharp difference of opinion I have with van Caster concerning the nature and operation of this "interior action of the Holy Spirit" does not diminish the force of van Caster's argument in this instance, to my mind at least.

43. For a nice illustration of this point, see Jackie M. Smith, "Kairos and Youth: A Call for Community," in D. Campbell Wyckoff and Don Richter, editors, *Religious Education Ministry with Youth* (Birmingham, Ala.: Religious Education Press, 1982), pp. 166–207.

44. The phrase "a very broad range of studies" is used to indicate that these studies deal not only with correlations between religious cognition and religious conduct, but with moral cognition and moral conduct which the investigators did not frequently valence specifically in terms of what is typically conceptualized as "religious."

45. Bernard Berelson and Gary A. Steiner, *Human Behavior: An Inventory of Scientific Findings* (New York: Harcourt, Brace, and World, 1964), pp. 576–577.

46. Hugh Hartshorne and Mark A. May, *Studies in Deceit*, volume 1 (New York: Macmillan, 1928); Hugh Hartshorne, Mark A. May, and Julius B. Maller, *Studies in Service and Self-Control*, volume 2 (New York: Macmillan, 1929); Hugh Hartshorne, Mark A. May, and Frank K. Shuttleworth, *Studies in the Organization of Character*, volume 3 (New York: Macmillan, 1930).

47. Bernard Berelson and Gary A. Steiner, *Human Behavior: An Inventory of Scientific Findings*, p. 577.

48. Mary Delafield Fite, "Aggressive Behavior in Young Children and Children's Attitudes toward Aggression," in *Genetic Psychology Monographs* XXII (April, 1940), p. 306. That Fite is here writing primarily about the relationship of moral *cognitive* judgments and moral conduct seems borne out by her frequent use of the phrase "consciousness of morals" in connection with the particular finding I am here citing from her study. On this last point, see, for example, p. 196 of the Fite study.

49. See, for example, Edward R. Bartlett and Dale B. Harris, "Personality Factors in Delinquency," in *School and Society* XLIII (May 9, 1936), pp. 653–656; George E. Hill, "The Ethical Knowledge of Delinquent and Non-delinquent Boys," in the *Journal of Social Psychology* VI (February, 1935), pp. 107–114; Sheldon Glueck and Eleanor Glueck, *Unraveling Juvenile Delinquency* (New York: Commonwealth Fund, 1950); and Albert K. Cohen, *Delinquent Boys* (New York: Free Press, 1955).

50. H. J. Eysenck, "Symposium: The Development of Moral Values in Children: VII—The Contribution of Learning Theory," in *British Journal of Educational Psychology* XXX (February, 1960), p. 11, italics deleted.

51. Pleasant Roscoe Hightower, *Biblical Information in Relation to Character and Conduct* (Iowa City, Iowa: University of Iowa, 1930), pp. 33.

52. Martin J. Maehr, "The Relationship of Bible Information to Certain Specific Beliefs and Practices," unpublished doctoral dissertation, University of Nebraska, 1955. The correlation was .351 which, especially when taking into account both the population and the hypothetical (rather than the real life) nature of the situations, is in keeping with the .25 figure cited earlier in the text.

53. Pleasant Roscoe Hightower, *Biblical Information in Relation to Character and Conduct*, pp. 33–34.

54. Richard Hofstadter, *Anti-Intellectualism in American Life* (New York: Knopf, 1963), p. 7.

55. Though published in 1958, Thomas O'Dea's short but meaty book is still relevant today. See Thomas F. O'Dea, *American Catholic Dilemma: An Inquiry into the Intellectual Life* (New York: Sheed and Ward, 1958).

56. See, for example, the splendid treatment of this issue in Andrew M. Greeley, *The Communal Catholic* (New York: Seabury, 1976). It is regrettable that this important book is so much neglected in religious education circles—quite possibly because it hits so close to home.

57. Kevin J. O'Brien, *The Proximate Aim of Education* (Milwaukee: Bruce, 1958), pp. 167 and 165.

58. I am here speaking of a hyperintellectual *mentality* on the part of many seminary professors. This is a different issue than the cognitive *caliber* of the courses taught by these professors.

59. See J. Gordon Chamberlin, *Freedom and Faith* (Philadelphia: Westminster, 1965), pp. 15–19.

60. The *I Ching* is an example of a highly influential work utilizing acausal relationships. See *The I Ching*, the Richard Wilhelm translation, rendered into English by Cary F. Baynes, 3rd edition (Princeton, N.J.: Princeton University Press, 1967).

61. Thomas Groome's pedagogical method which he labels "shared praxis" is almost entirely rational; virtually no attention is paid by his instructional method to extrarationality. Furthermore, Groome's instructional method is almost totally ratiocinative, with relatively scant attention given to intuition. Thus Groome's highly cognitive teaching method is not only narrow with respect to the range of substantive contents it includes, but is also narrow with respect to the range of cognitive subcontents it involves. This last point is significant for accurately assessing the value of Groome's overall approach, since he de facto identifies his overall approach with only one single pedagogical procedure. See Thomas H. Groome, *Christian Religious Education* (San Francisco: Harper & Row, 1980), pp. 207–232.

62. In this section I am treating symbol exclusively from the perspective of depth psychology.

63. For a pithy treatment of Jung's theory of symbol, see C. G. Jung, *Psychologische Typen*, zehnte, revidierte auflage, Band VI in *Gesammelte Werke* (Zürich: Rascher, 1967), pp. 515–523, #'s 894–908. For a more extended treatment, see C. G. Jung, *Psyche and Symbol*, edited by Violet S. de Laszlo, translated by Cary Baynes and R. F. C. Hull (Garden City, N.Y.: Doubleday Anchor, 1958).

64. See Morton T. Kelsey, *Dreams: The Dark Speech of the Spirit* (Garden City, N.Y.: Doubleday, 1968), p. 198.

65. Note should be made here of Jung's singular terminology. Words like "rational," "irrational," and the like, have meanings for Jung which are quite different than the way in which such terms are used in this book and indeed in much of the social sciences and human sciences.

66. C. G. Jung, *Psychologische Typen*, p. 520 (#903).

67. A. Dulles, "Symbol in Revelation," in *New Catholic Encyclopedia*, volume 13 (New York: McGraw-Hill, 1967), p. 862.

68. John Westerhoff seems to recognize the importance of the concept expressed in this statement. See Gwen Kennedy Neville and John H. Westerhoff III, *Learning Through Liturgy* (New York: Seabury, 1978), pp. 107–135.

69. Julius Schniewind, "A Reply to Bultmann," in Hans Werner Bartsch, editor, *Kerygma and Myth*, revised edition, translated by Reginald H. Fuller (New York: Harper & Row Torchbooks, 1961), p. 47.

70. Thus Albert Cook observes: "Religion as a social institution makes myth accessible to the individual psyche through ritual." Albert Cook, *Myth and Language* (Bloomington, Ind.: Indiana University Press, 1980), p. 55.
71. Mircea Eliade, *Myth and Reality,* translated by Willard R. Trask (New York: Harper & Row, 1963), pp. 139–143.
72. Hubert Halbfas, *Theory of Catechetics* (New York: Herder and Herder, 1971), p. 169. Halbfas's book seems to lean quite heavily on the thought of Karl Jaspers. See, for example, Karl Jaspers, *Von der Wahrheit* (München: Piper, 1947), pp. 1022–1054.
73. *Ibid.,* pp. 134–135.
74. Morton Kelsey, *Encounter with God* (Minneapolis, Minn.: Bethany Fellowship, 1972), pp. 43–46.
75. Joseph Campbell, *The Masks of God* (New York: Viking, 1964), pp. 519–521. This is a celebrated and respected formulation among scholars of myth.
76. See Raphael Patai, *Myth and Modern Man* (Englewood Cliffs, N.J.: Prentice-Hall, 1972), pp. 28–30.
77. On this point, see David Bidney, "Myth, Symbolism, and Truth," in John B. Vickery, editor, *Myth and Literature: Contemporary Theory and Practice* (Lincoln, Neb.: University of Nebraska Press, 1966), pp. 11–13.
78. Joseph Strelka states that "True myth is connected with genuine religion, although it might be explained psychoanalytically. . . . False myth, on the other hand, rests upon a total secularization of the mythical realm. In other words, true myth by its very nature transcends the logical sphere or the realm of outward manifestations, while false myth either reduces the infinite to the finite or applies infinite qualities to the second." Joseph P. Strelka, "Preface," in Joseph P. Strelka, editor, *Literary Criticism in Myth* (University Park, Pa.: Pennsylvania State University Press, 1980), pp. viii–ix.
79. Miller further states that ritual and emotion are also necessary elements in profound worship. See Randolph Crump Miller, *The Language Gap and God* (Philadelphia: Pilgrim, 1970), p. 16.
80. I am here following the Aristotelian-Thomistic view of ratiocination, because this view lies at or near the foundation of most current theories of ratiocination. Though these theories differ, sometimes markedly, from the Aristotelian-Thomistic analysis, especially with respect to method and process, nonetheless many of them do, in fact, have the Aristotelian-Thomistic view as a prime manifest or latent referent. Further, and perhaps even more germane, Christian theological and religious thought, Protestant as well as Catholic, has been more strongly influenced in one way or another by the Aristotelian-Thomistic view than by any other competing system. For a fuller treatment of the Aristotelian-Thomistic view of ratiocination, see Thomas Aquinas, *Summa Theologica*, I, q. 12, a. 4; q. 55, a. 2; q. 84, a. 6–8; q. 85, a. 5. See also Robert E. Brennan, *Thomistic Psychology* (New York: Macmillan, 1941).
81. Joseph Donceel, *Philosophical Anthropology* (New York: Sheed and Ward, 1967), p. 361.
82. See John Dewey, *Democracy and Education*, pp. 264–265.
83. See Wayne Rood, *The Art of Teaching Christianity* (Nashville, Tenn.: Abingdon, 1968), pp. 16–17.
84. On this point, see Gerald A. McCool, "The Primacy of Intuition," in *Thought* XXXVII (Spring, 1962), pp. 57–73.

85. On this point, see P. De Letter, "The Encounter with God," in *Thought* XXXVI (Spring, 1961), pp. 5–24.

86. S. Radhakrishnan, *An Idealist View of Life*, 2d edition (London: Allen and Unwin, 1937), p. 146.

87. Bernard Berelson and Gary A. Steiner, *Human Behavior: An Inventory of Scientific Findings*, p. 229; also J. W. Getzels and J. T. Dillon, "The Nature of Giftedness and the Education of the Gifted," in Robert M. W. Travers, editor, *Second Handbook of Research on Teaching* (Chicago: Rand McNally, 1973), pp. 700–702.

88. See, for example, Helen Rowan, "The Creative Person," in *Carnegie Corporation of New York Quarterly* IX (July 1961), pp. 2–5.

89. See William Bedford Williamson, *Language and Concepts in Christian Education*, pp. 47–48.

90. Jerome S. Bruner, *The Process of Education* (Cambridge, Mass.: Harvard University Press, 1960), pp. 58–60.

91. I should observe that infusion is something quite different than the philosophical explanation of "knowing through illumination" offered by some thinkers such as Augustine.

92. On this point, see Jacques Maritain, *The Degrees of Knowledge*, translated under the supervision of Gerald B. Phelan (New York: Scribner's, 1959), pp. 254–260.

93. See, for example, Adolphe Tanquerey, *The Spiritual Life: A Treatise on Ascetical and Mystical Theology*, 2d edition, translated by Herman Branderis (Westminster, Md.: Newman, 1930), pp. 601–699.

94. See Thomas Aquinas, *Summa Theologica*, I–II, q. 57, a. 2; also I–II, q. 68, a. 4.

95. Plato considered wisdom as the highest form of intellection. For Plato, wisdom consists in the harmony of the intellect and the will (*Laws* 689d) based on self-knowledge (*Charmides*, 164d). Aristotle maintains that wisdom is the chief among the intellectual virtues (*Ethics*, VI. 7).

96. *Ibid.*

97. Aristotle, *Metaphysics*, I. 1 and 2.

98. Thomas Aquinas, *Summa Theologica*, I–II, q. 66, a. 5.

99. See James Michael Lee, *The Flow of Religious Instruction* (Birmingham, Ala.: Religious Education Press, 1973), pp. 141–148.

100. See, for example, Aristotle, *Metaphysics*, I. 2. I know of no social-science data which indicate that wisdom is incapable of being taught.

101. Aritotle, *Ethics*, VI. 7.

102. J. P. Guilford, "The Structure of Intellect," in *Psychological Bulletin*, LIII (July, 1956), pp. 267–293; J. P. Guilford, *The Nature of Human Intelligence* (New York: McGraw-Hill, 1967), pp. 60–68. Guilford uses the word "cognitive" in a different sense than I do; for him it is one specific kind of mental functioning while in my terminology cognition is any sort of intellectual functioning.

103. *Ibid.*, p. 61.

104. The definitions given in this treatment of Guilford are drawn directly or indirectly from Guilford. *Ibid.*, *passim*. In not a few instances, I employ terminology differently than does Guilford.

105. Benjamin S. Bloom et al., *Taxonomy of Educational Objectives: Handbook I: Cognitive Domain* (New York: McKay, 1956).

106. Articulation is the relationship and interdependence existing among the different elements or components of an educational program. Vertical articulation is the functional relationship and interdependence existing within some internally similar group in the educational program, while horizontal articulation is the functional relationship and interdependence existing within dissimilar groups in the educational program. See James Michael Lee, "New Directions in Articulation," in *National Catholic Guidance Conference Journal* XIII (Fall, 1968), pp. 44–53.

107. Teaching is not a form of applied learning; teaching is a procedure, while learning is an event, as I underscore in *The Flow of Religious Instruction* (pp. 39–55). However, a knowledge of various types and levels of cognitive objectives as detailed in the Bloom taxonomy constitutes a starting point and a target point for the teacher when he sets about devising fruitful pedagogical experiences.

108. Bloom and his associates note that a taxonomy is, at bottom, a kind of super-classification system. A taxonomy embodies certain structural rules which are more complex than the rules of an ordinary classification system. A classification system may or may not have many arbitrary elements; a taxonomy may not have any arbitrary components. A taxonomy, therefore, must be constructed in such a fashion that the order of its terms must have a necessary and integral correspondence with some real, existential order among the phenomena represented by the terms. "A classification scheme may be validated by reference to the criteria of communicability, usefulness, and suggestiveness; while a taxonomy must be validated by demonstrating its consistency with the theoretical views in research findings of the field it attempts to order." (p. 17 of Bloom's *Taxonomy*).

109. I should add that my observations in the previous paragraph are not intended as an attempt to deprecate or discard Aristotelian-Thomistic philosophy, but rather to illustrate that for religious instruction the usefulness of its explanation of the cognitive process is to some extent limited.

110. John Dewey, *How We Think,* revised edition (Boston: Heath, 1933), p. 107. Compare Dewey's reformulation of these five states of thinking with those proposed by him in his first edition (1910), p. 72.

111. Because for Dewey the nature of all learning is reconstruction through self-construction, the problem-solving process is eminently descriptive of the way Dewey believes a person learns. For a fine pithy treatment of this point with specific relation to religious instruction, see Leon McKenzie, *The Religious Education of Adults* (Birmingham, Ala.: Religious Education Press, 1982), pp. 178–180.

112. The fact that Dewey did not believe in supernatural religion while Aquinas did believe in divinely revealed religion does not radically affect the worth or utility of the theory of knowledge advanced by these two philosophers. All too often Christian religious educationists have condemned *in toto* the theories of philosophers simply because these philosophers were not Christian or because their theories did not directly incorporate Christian beliefs. For a representative example of this mentality, see Cornelius van Til, *Essays on Christian Education* (Phillipsburg, N.J.: Presbyterian and Reformed Publishing, 1979), pp. 49–55.

113. My remarks in the foregoing paragraph in no way imply that I regard the Deweyan theory of reflective thinking as the "best" of all such theories. To be sure, the Deweyan theory has many weaknesses, several of a debilitating nature

in terms of an adequate general theory of knowing. By far the most serious weakness of the Deweyan view is that it is not imbedded in any thoroughgoing, overall, systematic theory of reality. Indeed, as Patrick Suppes observes, "Dewey himself did not properly recognize the importance of deep-running systematic theories." The greatest strength and ultimate fecundity of the Aristotelian-Thomistic system of knowing is that this system is precisely that, a system. Patrick Suppes, "The Place of Theory in Educational Research," in *Educational Researcher* III (June, 1974), p. 72.

114. Kohlberg vigorously denies ethical relativity, and on the basis of his research claims that there are developmental stages of moral judgment which are universal. Lawrence Kohlberg, "Stages of Moral Development as a Basis for Moral Education," in C. M. Beck, B. S. Crittenden, and E. V. Sullivan, editors, *Moral Education: Interdisciplinary Approaches* (Toronto: University of Toronto Press, 1971), pp. 30–42.

115. Kohlberg settled on justice as the norm for moral judgment on the basis of both his own empirical research and because his reading of the philosophical literature persuaded him that, at bottom, justice is held as the central principle of morality by almost all classical and contemporary philosophers.

116. James Michael Lee, "Christian Religious Education and Moral Development," in Brenda Munsey, editor, *Moral Development, Moral Education, and Kohlberg* (Birmingham, Ala.: Religious Education Press, 1980), pp. 326–355.

117. James Rest contends that Kohlberg's emphasis on facilitating an understanding and use of general structure places his model at odds with educators who emphasize behavioral or performance objectives. I do not believe that Rest's allegation is legitimate. The point at issue is not *whether* behavioral objectives are emphasized in a Kohlberg-type curriculum, but rather *how* they are utilized. To be sure, Kohlberg-type curricula tend to make pervasive, imaginative, and highly operational use of behavioral objectives. It is to be expected that Kohlberg-type curricula employ behavioral objectives in a manner quite different from the way they are utilized in nonstructuralist curricula. See James Rest, "Developmental Psychology as a Guide to Value Education: A Review of "Kohlbergian' Programs,' in *Review of Educational Research* XLIV(Spring, 1974), p. 242.

118. Lawrence Kohlberg, "Stages of Moral Development as a Basis for Moral Education," p. 43.

119. Bernard Rosen, "Moral Dilemmas and Their Treatment," in Brenda Munsey, editor, *Moral Development, Moral Education, and Kohlberg,* pp. 232–265.

120. James Michael Lee, *The Flow of Religious Instruction,* p. 125.

121. Jean Piaget, *The Moral Judgment of the Child,* translated by Marjorie Gabain (New York: Free Press, 1965). For a helpful—and creative—look at Piaget with particular reference to religious instruction, see John H. Peatling, *Religious Education in a Psychological Key* (Birmingham, Ala.: Religious Education Press, 1981), pp. 144–211.

122. Lawrence Kohlberg, "Stages of Moral Development as a Basis for Moral Education," p. 45. Part of the problem here is that I.Q. tests are, by their very nature, not geared to assess the level of total, overall cognitive development. Yet it is on the basis of these very I.Q. tests that an individual's level of total, overall cognitive development is typically assessed. Small wonder it is, then, that correlations between I.Q. and moral maturity usually run from 0.35 to 0.50 in various samples.

123. For an especially fine treatment which incorporates the theories of Lawrence

Kohlberg, Jean Piaget, and Bernard Lonergan into a new view of conscience, see Walter E. Conn, *Conscience: Development and Self-Transcendence* (Birmingham, Ala.: Religious Education Press, 1981).

124. Most of the leading definitions or conceptualizations of creativity can be classified on the basis of the emphasis accorded to any one of four criteria, namely product, subjective experience, social context, and process.

125. What George Klein, Harriet Linton Barr, and David Wolitsky wrote in 1967 on this matter still holds true today: "When we turn to the issue of creativity, we find almost complete chaos. Psychologists use widely different criteria [measures] in studies purporting to deal with creativity, ranging from careers of eminent people (who are obviously worthy of consideration), to the idea of creativity in interpersonal relationships (which makes one wonder whether this is really 'creativity'), down to measures of sales productivity and customer service (which can be cheerfully ignored)". George S. Klein, Harriet Linton Barr, and David L. Wolitsky, "Personality," in Paul R. Farnsworth, Olga McNemar, and Quinn McNemar, editors, *Annual Review of Psychology*, volume 18 (Palo Alto, Calif.: Annual Reviews, 1967), p. 536.

126. For a pictorial representation of this twenty-four cell matrix, see J. P. Guilford, *The Nature of Human Intelligence*, p. 139.

127. In this paragraph I am summarizing the empirical research on creativity. Some of the noteworthy reviews of this research include Jack Getzels and George F. Madaus, "Creativity," in Robert L. Ebel, editor, *Encyclopedia of Educational Research*, 4th edition (Chicago: Rand McNally, 1969), pp. 267–275; Morris I. Stein, "Creativity," in Edgar F. Borgatta and William W. Lambert, editors, *Handbook of Personality Theory and Research* (Chicago: Rand McNally, 1968), pp. 900–942; Richard S. Mansfield and Thomas V. Busse, "Creativity," in Harold E. Mitzel, editor, *Encyclopedia of Educational Research*, volume 1 (New York: Free Press, 1982), pp. 385–394; Morton Bloomberg, editor, *Creativity: Theory and Research* (New Haven, Conn.: College and University Press, 1973); George S. Welsh, *Creativity and Intelligence: A Personality Approach* (Chapel Hill, N.C.: University of North Carolina at Chapel Hill, 1975); Silvano Arieti, *Creativity: The Magic Synthesis* (New York: Basic, 1976), pp. 3–98; 293–383.

128. Two points are germane in this connection. First, biographical analysis data give information regarding *creative accomplishment,* while *creative thinking* test data supply information on *creative intellecting.* Second, while the research reveals that not all persons judged to be outstanding in terms of creative accomplishment possess every one of the personality characteristics listed in the text, nonetheless the research suggests that there are *patterns* of personality characteristics which seem quite systematically to distinguish persons of acknowledged accomplishment in their fields.

129. Morris Stein ("Creativity," p. 928) notes that the creative individual tends to score higher on a self-descriptive test of need achievement than on a projective test of the same variable, possibly because his achievement need is fulfilled in actuality and hence his need does not have to be converted into fantasy.

130. The less creative person, in contrast, spends less time in analyzing the problem, but more time than the creative person in attempting to synthesize his data.

131. The research also reveals a significant tendency of only children and first-born children, and a slight tendency for children conceived in the cold months, to enjoy an advantage in I.Q. scores, scholastic achievement, and career success.

132. For this reason, members of the Central Catechetical Establishment and their sycophants have eagerly embraced socialization theory and practice, since the prime intent of socialization is to form individuals according to the prescriptions, mores, and folkways of the controlling society. For an advocacy of socialization from the foregoing perspective, see Berard L. Marthaler, "Socialization as a Model for Catechetics," in Padraic O'Hare, editor, *Foundations of Religious Education* (New York: Paulist, 1978), pp. 64–92.

133. Merton P. Strommen, editor, *Research on Religious Development*, (New York: Hawthorn, 1971), p. 884. There is a total of only two entries on creativity, one dealing with Jung's concept of religion as symbolic creativity and the other having reference to a clause in the text which suggests that Pentecostal tongue-speaking might not be a neurotic activity but rather an eruption of unconscious creativity.

134. Some of the most ridiculous—and pathetic—spectacles in religious instruction during the 1965–1975 decade, particularly in the Catholic sector, was the attempt by highly convergent-type teachers and curriculum builders to construct highly creative, divergent lessons. The results were almost always ludicrous, incongruous, superficial, and totally lacking in authentic creative fire.

135. For a fuller treatment of this mediatorship, see James Michael Lee, "The Authentic Source of Religious Instruction," in Norma H. Thompson, editor, *Religious Education and Theology* (Birmingham, Ala.: Religious Education Press, 1982), pp. 165–172. Mediatorship is a key feature of my religious instruction theory.

136. While I am borrowing heavily from Aristotle and Thomas Aquinas in my treatment of understanding and wisdom, nonetheless in certain respects I am departing from the treatments of the two molar cognitive contents made by the Stagirite and the Angelic Doctor.

137. John of St. Thomas, *The Gifts of the Holy Ghost,* translated by Dominic Hughes (New York: Sheed and Ward, 1951), III. 1–23 (pp. 76–86).

138. Understanding and wisdom are eminently judgmental. As understanding judges knowledge and subsequently corrects and illumines knowledge as a result of this judgment, so too does wisdom judge understanding and subsequently corrects and illumines it. With respect to the judgmental, corrective, and illuminative functions of wisdom, see Etienne Gilson, *The Philosophy of Thomas Aquinas,* translated by Edward Bullough and edited by G. A. Elrington (Cambridge, England: Heffer, 1924), pp. 252–253.

139. Thomas Aquinas, *Summa Theologica,* I–II, q.57, a.1.

140. Knowledge is perfected by understanding; knowledge and understanding are perfected by wisdom. Understanding and wisdom are not directed toward a simple apprehension of the nature and activities of phenomena, but rather toward a judgment of phenomena in terms of the basic principles which govern and explain these phenomena. For example, knowledge of an unjust act is the cognitive content *that* the act is unjust in its here-and-now manifestations. Understanding an unjust act is the cognitive content *why* the act is unjust penultimately.

141. Aristotle, *Ethics,* VI. 7.5.

142. John of St. Thomas, *The Gifts of the Holy Ghost,* IV. 1–10 (pp. 123–128).

143. A course is an organized set of learning experiences which lasts several days, weeks, months, or years. A course need not be academic or occur in a formal setting. It would appear that Gloria Durka does not understand this elemental point.

144. The wisdom of which I am discussing here is both means and end, namely, wisdom in daily living rather than wisdom as a disembodied end. See Douglas E. Lawson, *Wisdom and Education* (Carbondale, Ill.: Southern Illinois University Press, 1961), pp. 10–15.

145. The principle of instruction as artistry, and the teacher as an artist, has always been central in my macrotheory, as *The Flow of Religious Instruction* clearly indicates. I was disappointed, but not very surprised, to find that the teaching process as artistry was given such short shrift in a book entitled *Aesthetic Dimensions of Religious Education*. See James Michael Lee, *The Flow of Religious Instruction* (Birmingham, Ala.: Religious Education Press, 1973), pp. 206–229 (teaching as orchestration, and teaching as an art-science). See also Gloria Durka and Joanmarie Smith, editors, *Aesthetic Dimensions of Religious Education* (New York: Paulist, 1979).

146. George Howie, "Introduction Note," in George Howie, editor, *Aristotle on Education* (New York: Macmillan, 1968), pp. 136–139.

147. For a helpful treatment of pedagogical principles and procedures involving higher-order cognitive behaviors, see Benjamin S. Bloom, J. Thomas Hastings, and George F. Madaus, *Handbook on Formative and Summative Evaluation of Student Learning* (New York: McGraw-Hill, 1971), pp. 19–41, 177–223. See also Francis P. Hunkins, *Questioning Strategies and Techniques* (Boston: Allyn and Bacon, 1972), pp. 49–61.

148. Plato, *Thaeatetus*, 148E–151D.

149. Maieutic, from the Greek *maia* (midwife) and *maievesthai* (to act as a midwife), means performing the services of a midwife, in this case a midwife with respect to the birthing of higher-order cognitive content.

150. In this connection Francis MacDonald Cornford writes: "Like the midwife who is past childbearing, Socrates' [pedagogical] function is not to produce his own ideas and impart them to others, but to deliver their minds of thoughts with which they are in labor, and then test whether these thoughts are genuine children or mere phantoms." Francis MacDonald Cornford, "Commentary," in Plato, *Thaeatetus,* translated by Francis MacDonald Cornford (Indianapolis, Ind.: Bobbs-Merrill, 1957), p. 17.

151. Gregory Vlastos, "Introduction: The Paradox of Socrates," in Gregory Vlastos, editor, *The Philosophy of Socrates* (Garden City, N.Y.: Doubleday Anchor, 1971), pp. 12–18. Vlastos adds, however, that the principal shortcoming of Socratic cognition is that is has excessively little interest in facts (p. 16). A religious educator using maieutic teaching can, of course, surmount this difficulty.

152. Leonard Nelson, *Socratic Method and Critical Philosophy,* translated by Thomas K. Brown III (New York: Dover, 1949), p. 16. Nelson is a neo-Kantian.

153. It goes without saying, therefore, that hyperpracticalists in religious instruction such as Marie McIntyre or Elizabeth McMahon Jeep are basically uninterested in maieutic teaching.

154. Alan F. Blum, *Socrates* (London: Routledge and Kegan Paul, 1978), p. 113.

155. Leonard Nelson, *Socratic Method and Critical Philosophy,* p. 15.

156. Paul Friedländer, *Plato,* volume 3, translated by Hans Meyerhoff (Princeton, N.J.: Princeton University Press, 1969), p. 154.

157. Francis P. Hunkins, "The Influence of Analysis and Evaluation Questions on Achievement in Sixth Grade Social Studies," in *Educational Leadership* XXV (January, 1968), pp. 326–331.

158. George T. Ladd, "Determining the Level of Inquiry in Teachers' Questions," unpublished doctoral dissertation, Indiana University, 1969.

159. Beatryce T. Newton, "Theoretical Bases for Higher Cognitive Questioning: An Avenue to Critical Thinking," in *Education* LXXXXVIII (March–April, 1979), pp. 286–291.

160. Doris L. Redfield and Elaine Waldman Rousseau, "A Meta-analysis of Experimental Research on Teacher Questioning Behavior," in *Review of Educational Research* LI (Summer, 1981), pp. 237–245.

161. Fred A. Sloan and Robert Thomas Pate, "Teacher-Pupil Interaction in Two Approaches to Mathematics," in *Elementary School Journal* LXVII (December, 1966), p. 167; Meridith D. Gall, "The Use of Questions in Teaching," in *Review of Educational Research* XL (December, 1970), p. 713.

162. James Michael Lee, "Religious Education and the Bible: A Religious Educationist's View," in Joseph S. Marino, editor, *Biblical Themes in Religious Education* (Birmingham, Ala.: Religious Education Press, 1983), pp. 1–61.

163. For a treatment of the teacher performance center, see James Michael Lee, *The Flow of Religious Instruction*, pp. 288–289.

164. Willis D. Copeland, "Laboratory Experiences in Teacher Education," in Harold E. Mitzel, editor, *Encyclopedia of Educational Research* 5th edition, volume 2, pp. 1008–1019.

165. *Ibid.*, p. 1009.

166. For a description of the Flanders Interaction Analysis System, see James Michael Lee, *The Flow of Religious Instruction*, pp. 256–260.

CHAPTER FIVE

━━━━━━━━━━━━━━━━━━━━━━

AFFECTIVE CONTENT

"We have all been shaped and reshaped by those who have loved us." [1]

—François Mauriac

THE NATURE OF AFFECTIVE CONTENT

Basic Principles of Affective Content

Affective content refers to any kind of content which is characterized by feeling — emotions, attitudes, values, love, and the like. Affective content can be a positive sort (such as trust, feeling accepted, love) or of a negative type (such as fear, anxiety, hatred). "How a child or adult feels about wanting to learn, how he feels as he learns, and what he feels after he has learned are included in the affective domain."[2] Affective content encompasses both the process content of feeling[3] and the product content which is yielded by this feeling process. In popular usage, the affective domain is linked with the heart while the cognitive domain is associated with the head. Without in any way suggesting that cognition is necessarily cold, it should be noted that affect is usually regarded as being warm and at times even hot. Positive affect is a heat which warms and soothes, while negative affect is a heat which burns and frequently injures.

While affect is a content considered apart from the bodily changes which frequently accompany it, nonetheless it should be underscored that there is a close connective interaction between affect and the body. Commonly used verbal idioms often reflect the deep-flowing ties which a person's feeling-function has with his body or body movement, such as, for example, "butterflies in my stomach," and "lost my head."[4] Hence affective content is usually related to nonverbal content while cognitive content has an affinity for verbal content.

I must emphasize the fact that affect is a legitimate content in its own right. Affect is not a way to content, a sugared path to content. It is not a motivational tool to get at content. Affect is a content with its own distinctive structure and operations. In this connection Iris Cully observes that the affective content so frequently depicted in the bible is typically ignored by religious educators who seem to regard biblical content basically in terms of cognitive knowledge or theological (cognitive) meaning.[5] I strongly maintain that a person not only can know about God (cognitive content), but also, and in many ways more significantly, can feel the presence and the action of God in his own life (affective content). Knowing about God provides a very indirect and, in one sense, a very inaccurate view of God. Feeling God's action provides a more direct — or much better yet, a less indirect — grasping of God. Small wonder it is, then, that conversions to and within Christianity seem to be more highly correlated with affective content breakthroughs than with cognitive content breakthroughs.

Because affect is a content in its own right with its own distinctive existential structure, it describes reality in a radically different manner than does cognitive content or any other kind of content. Cognitive content is the intellectual representation of a reality. Cognitive content, therefore, is never the same as the reality itself; it is only a mental abstraction *of* or intuition *about* this reality. Consequently, cognitive content is perforce tentative and always subject to adjustment and revision as new features about this reality emerge. Affective content, in contrast, is not a description of a reality, but rather a person's actual, direct feeling-reaction to a reality which he encounters. Hence affective content is certain because it is its own reality. When a person intellectually explores his affective content, this affective content remains certain and nontentative.

The certainty of affective content as contrasted to the tentativeness of cognitive content suggests why the fully functioning person tends to trust his deepest feeling of a reality more than his cognitive content about that reality, particularly in momentous matters or when the "chips are down" for him. An important task in religious instruction is to help the learner trust and indeed to rely on his own feeling-function, especially where manifestly religious realities are concerned. As a child, every person relies on his feeling-function. Yet, unfortunately, in Western society the individual is repeatedly told that his feeling-function yields emphemeral and transitory data and hence is not to be trusted. Small wonder, then, that persons in Western culture make mistake after mistake about the reality they encounter. Small wonder too that persons in Western culture fail so frequently to fully resonate with reality and to be totally united to it as far as their human condition will permit.

I should emphasize that affective content is capable of being directly facilitated by a parent, a schoolteacher, a youth minister, or any other kind of religious educator. There is a common misconception, one particularly prevalent in religious circles, that attitudes, values, love, and other forms of affective content "can be caught but not taught." This misconception arises from both an ignorance of the nature of teaching and an unfamiliarity with the research evidence, two failings not infrequently found among religionists in general and religious educators in particular.[7] To teach is not simply to use verbal, transmissive pedagogy. Teaching is a far wider activity than this. In its proper and accurate meaning, teaching consists in so structuring a learning situation that the four key variables[8] interact in such a way that the desired learning outcome is thereby effected.[9] All behavior which can be learned, therefore, is capable of being taught. Affective content is primarily learned behavior, and hence is able to be taught. Affective curricula and affectively oriented instructional practices have been shown by the research to yield many and various kinds of affective content.[10] Indeed, some of the affects which the research has demonstrated to have been successfully facilitated are the very affects that proponents of the "caught, not taught" position claim are incapable of being taught.

Affective instruction is of a distinctly different educational genre than counseling or psychotherapy. The goals of affective instruction differ sharply from the goals of counseling and psychotherapy; affective instruction is used with any and all kinds of learners to assist them to acquire desired learning outcomes, while counseling and psychotherapy are typically employed in cases of individuals experiencing personal problems or significant blockages in their affective functioning.[11] The practices of affective instruction diverge considerably from those of counseling and psychotherapy; affective instruction, for example, is a judgmental process facilitated in a relatively structured fashion while counseling and psychotherapy are nonjudgmental processes facilitated in a relatively unstructured manner.

It was the ancient Greek philosophers who defined the human being as a rational animal. This definition was accepted uncritically until modern times. From what we know today about a person's distinctive nature, it is possible to say that this ancient Greek definition is seriously deficient. A more adequate definition of a human being's essential and distinctive nature is that a person is a cognitive *and* an affective animal. Affect is not simply an *additum* or an appendage to an individual's basic nature; it is part and parcel of his very essence. A person's nature as human denotes immediately a life of both feeling and cognition.[12] Cognition and affect, though two discrete functions, interact with each other to color human behavior, and indeed to make the behavior human. Not to regard a human being in his feeling dimension, or not to give this dimension its full sweep in a definition of human nature is to strip a person of his humanity. From both the Christian perspective and the psychological vantage point, a strong case can be made for affirming that affect, especially in its love modality, is more distinctively human than is cognition. It was the Greek philosophers who asserted that God is pure cognition; the apostle John, on the other hand, defines God as love (1 Jn. 4:8). The Evangelist points out that a person who loves is begotten of God and knows God, while a person who does not love does not know God (1 Jn. 4:7–8). It is significant to note here that John does not state that a person who knows is begotten of God. Love is the vital and essential feature of human nature according to John. To be sure, love produces awareness of a dynamic, relational, and saving sort. John also writes that anyone who lives in love lives in God and God lives in him (1 Jn. 4:16).[13] It is love which gives a person eternal life. In this connection I am not aware of any classical Christian theologian or classical Christian writer who has ever consigned to hell a real or fictitious person who had great love for God or his fellow human beings. But many of these authors do remand to the inferno some individuals whose cognitive content about God was impressive. From the psychological vantage point, there seems to be evidence that when an individual's feeling-function grows deeper and more mature, the unity of the human person becomes more apparent. This unity is not simply a unity of the various complementary functions of one's personality (the unity of the *homo integer*) but also the unity of the individual with other persons (the brotherhood of humanity).[14]

The Relation of Affective Content to Cognitive Content

The foregoing paragraph brings us quite naturally to a consideration of the dynamic and structural relationship between affect and cognition. It is generally agreed that this relationship is undeniably and indestructibly symbiotic. What has been controverted for centuries is the nature of the form of affect and cognition as well as the nature of their interaction. One aspect of this controversy[15] can be cast into question form: Does cognition enter into the very form and structure of affective behavior, or does affect have its own unique structure and set of rules not *internally* controlled or influenced by cognition? Does affect have cognitive elements within its very own structure? Carrying this last question one step further: Is affect basically situated in cognitive housings? Does affect operate separately on rules of its own, merely being tied to cognition by some kind of associative functioning within the organism? Or, on the other hand, is there a basic cognitive structure of, is there a series of essential cognitive elements within, affect itself? Two conflicting responses have historically been given to this knotty issue. One response is that affect is totally separate and distinct in form and structure from cognition. Moreover, the interaction between affect and cognition is such that cognition dynamically works with and on affect in an ongoing, interactive function, a function which is separate, external, unique, and complementary to affect. This response typically implies that human conduct, including religious conduct, is either controlled on the one hand by a single basic function such as cognition or affect, or on the other hand by the totality of fundamental human functions working together in concert.[16] The second response to this basic issue at hand is that affect contains essential cognitive elements within its very form and structure; these cognitive elements become more salient and influential vis-à-vis affect as the individual advances from childhood to adolescence to adulthood. In other words, affect either is a unique kind and distinctive form of cognition, or it contains within its very structure cognitive elements so basic and necessary that without these elements affect would not be affect. This response suggests that all human conduct, including religious conduct, is cognitively controlled and not affectively controlled.[17] I underscore the fact that neither response denies that affect has its own distinct form and structure apart from pure cognition in and of itself; the controverted issue deals with the nature of this form and the degree to which cognition interacts with it and is an aspect or basis of it.

The critical question, then, is not whether affect and cognition are coupled in human functioning but rather the manner in which they are coupled.[18] This problem will be definitively settled only when a satisfactory metaphysic and a satisfactory psychology are developed concerning the affect-cognitive relationship in human life. A satisfactory metaphysic and a satisfactory psychology must be based, not simply on philosophy, but even more importantly on the findings and constructs of the social sciences. As for my part, I tend to side with the first of the two previously mentioned responses to the controverted issue, with, however, an exception to one possible implication of this response. I believe the notion of *homo integer* suggests that a person's conduct is not controlled by either his cognition or by his affect as isolated functions, but rather by the individual's total personality structure as this total structure is functionally mobilized in a particular activity. The final validation of all the speculation detailed in this paragraph and in the preceding one awaits the conclusions of intensive and sophisticated social-science research on this highly complicated issue, research which is consciously meshed with appropriate high-level philosophical reflection.[19]

While the structural relationship of their coupling is controverted, the fact that affect and cognition are coupled in some way represents a point of agreement among the overwhelming majority of social scientists (and philosophers).[20] Abstract thinking, remarks George Isaac Brown, is joined with affect on the part of the thinker, even in experiences of pleasure, boredom, or pain.[21] Berard Marthaler reminds us that social-science research suggests that cognitive content is necessary but not sufficient for yielding morality, and I might add, for yielding effective Christian living. Affective content is so essential that there can be no true or authentic religious lifestyle without it.[22] Cognitive content brings to Christian living an intelligence, a reflective awareness, an understanding and wisdom, and a descriptive view of what phenomena are and what the world can be and ought to be. For its part, affective content endows Christian living with a human and humane feeling-tone, passion, attitudes, values, and a personal immediacy and significance.[23] Both contents are essential, just as both act as complementary reinforcers of each other as well as checks against each other.

To assert that affective content is both indispensable to and tremendously important for religious instruction in no way implies a disvaluation of cognitive content, much less an anti-intellectualism. At bottom, disvaluation of the intellect or anti-intellectualism debases affective content and renders it impotent. That the truth of this observation has not always been grasped is borne out, for example, by the fact that in pre-Civil War America, the Sunday School relegated cognitive content to a decidedly inferior position because it regarded its mission as being one "of the heart" to which the intellect perforce had to be subjugated.[24] To this very day there exists in some religious instruction circles what Gabriel Moran terms "a certain kind of salesmanship of religion" which plays on the learner's affective functioning without bringing to bear knowledge or understanding.[25] Now all this attempted polarizing of affective content on the one side and cognitive content on the other side tends to be injurious not only to the learner's religious life specifically considered, but to the overall fabric of his personality development. Summing up the relevant empirical research, Eli Bower observes that successful affective development does not by itself produce an affectively functioning or free individual unless such development is linked to the acquisition of significant cognitive content and lifestyle tasks. For a healthy personality, a person must know as well as feel.[26]

The Importance of Affective Content

The process of becoming a person can be described in terms of three dimensions: conversation, communion, and collaboration. Conversation refers chiefly to the cognitive aspects of a person's dealings with his environment. Communion constitutes principally the individual's affective encounter with the reality he meets and greets. Collaboration consists in all of one's basic human functions working together (*co-laborare*) in harmony as one encounters and interacts with one's environment. Both conversation and communion are vital and indispensable to mature fruitful living; however, I believe that affect is more important in this respect than is cognition. To be sure it is communion, it is affect, which imbues conversation with added richness, robust humanness, and existential congruity. A person's feeling-function is central to that kind of Christian living which can be characterized as vital and vibrant. Existence is not simply *knowing* "I am"; more profoundly, it is *feeling* "I am." Authentic feeling, contends Ross Snyder, "is sensing with the *all* of us. Such feeling is the last — and perhaps the greatest — freedom of man."[27] To have affect is to have a certain richness of heart, a quality which engenders loyalty, devotion, compassion, empathy, and self-sacrifice.

The greatest and noblest of all affective content is love. The bible defines God as love (1 Jn. 4:8). Thus, as Emil Brunner pointedly remarks, the bible really means that love is God's nature and not merely his disposition or some secondary aspect of his divinity.[28] Alfred North Whitehead observes that Aristotle conceived of God as the unmoved mover; the Hebrews saw him as the avenging moralist; Caesar regarded him as the ruling monarch; while the Galilean vision was that of tender love operating quietly and creatively in the world. (Whitehead sardonically comments that the church rendered to God those attributes which belonged to Caesar and to Caesar's conception of God.)[29] For his part, Daniel Day Williams states that "in the biblical faith man's greatness is understood in the light of the image of God which he bears. If God is love the image in man defines the forms of love in human existence."[30] Those persons generally regarded as most clearly mirroring God's nature, namely the mystics, are characterized most accurately as persons caught up in and seized by an intense and terribly human love for God as he is in himself and how he is in the world which he suffuses. In their deepest religious moments mystics encounter God in seizures of religious ecstasy, seizures which they speak of in erotic behavioral terms describing a love-communion with God or with Jesus under the aspect of the union of bride and bridegroom. If, as some perceptive church officials and religious educationists tell us, God and Jesus constitute the subject-matter content of religious instruction, then it would appear that love lies at the very heart of the work of every religion teacher. For Jesus — and by way of analogy, for God too — love is the lifestyle. If God is love, if God and Jesus are love in action, then the primary and overarching content of religious instruction must be a lifestyle of love. "Education ought to teach us how to be in love always, and what to be in love with. The great things in history have been done by the great lovers, by saints and men of science and artists."[31] There is a goodly amount of empirical research data which indicate the necessity of love for a person not only if he is to achieve maturation but if he is to live. The celebrated research investigation by René Spitz, for example, found that in the absence of love or love-related behaviors, the babies studied exhibited a strong tendency to become severely underdeveloped in personality configuration, and in about one-third of the cases actually died.[32] Sandor Ferenczi states: "The unloved child dies, and if it does not die maybe it were better that it did."[33] In light of the relevant empirical research on this matter, Theodore Reik is able to remark: "Be loved or perish."[34] Religious thinkers explain the root cause of these conclusions by noting that a person has life and its fullness only to the extent that his nature and actions effectively participate in the divine nature. Since the divine nature is love, one's personality growth and indeed one's very life are dependent upon the amount of love he gives and receives, love which puts him into existential unity with God. Because God is love, he cannot be caught in a human being's cognitive nets. To the extent to which God can be caught, he can be caught only in the nets of love. This love of, with, and for God is not gooey or "touchy-feely," but rather a lifestyle of affective self-surrender and mutual union. The *Directorium catechisticum generale* states that since God is love, and since his plan consists in communicating his love in Jesus and in uniting persons in love for one another, it follows that the Christian enacts a life of love by living both the joy and the law of *caritas*.[35] Commenting on this and related passages in the *Directorium,* Berard Marthaler writes: "Love transposes the routine of life in a new key. . . . A Christian is concerned about the moral virtues but they are not the hallmarks of a Christian . . . .For the Christian the ideal is no longer to be simply a moral person, but a lover."[36]

Very frequently one hears a religion schoolteacher stress the importance of facilitating personalized religion in the lesson. But what does that person do pedagogically to enable this learning outcome to be acquired? Does that person architect the instructional situation in such a way as to help the learner to be in touch with his own affects, with his own religious feelings? Does that person structure the pedagogical environment in such a way that the learner can know himself but not feel himself? Indeed, is it psychologically possible to really know oneself without also feeling oneself? Is it possible to facilitate personalized religion without also enabling the learner to be deeply aware of and in constant touch with the affective domain of his personality? It is readily apparent that a major factor accounting for the home being such an all-powerful educative force is that the parent(s) structure the home in such a deliberative fashion that both child and parent(s) engage in self-awared and shared affectivity.

Since the end of World War II, and particularly since the late 1950s, there has been much emphasis placed by religious educationists on the necessity of facilitating in the learner a deeper understanding and meaning of his own existence.[37] Can a learner actually grasp the meaning of his own existence, much less come to a gripping awareness of his own existential predicament, without a heavy amount of affective content? Answers to the deeper existential questions of life, as Michael Pfliegler points out, can hardly be reduced to intellectual formulae or be adequately encapsulated in cognitive content.[38] In terms of an individual's personal response to reality, affect seems to play a larger, more pervasive, and more potent role than does cognition.

Self-knowledge and self-understanding have long been held as very important learning outcomes in religious instruction. But to know and to understand oneself, as well as to be oneself, a person must be able not only to think but to feel.[39] Real self-knowledge and self-understanding come about when the learner is congruent with his total functioning self, his cognitions, his feelings, and his lifestyle. Thus, authentic self-knowledge and self-understanding is a total, personal response.

Being congruent with one's own feeling-function, allowing one's feeling-function to seep into and surge through the inner recesses and the outer manifestations of his personality in harmonious, balanced manner — these empower one to imbue one's religious life with a deep, personal character. There is a wisdom inbuilt in one's own organism, say some social scientists.[40] This is organismic wisdom. Through organismic wisdom, an individual is aware from the depths and from the resonating functions of his personhood of what is right and good for him and why it is this way. Organismic wisdom can only come about when the individual places deep, personal trust in the ultimate accuracy and reliability of his organism as a totality.

In learning, as in all of living, the lions of affect tend to be stronger than the horses of cognition. A learner's affective reaction toward an object or situation often has more effect on his judgment of and behavior toward the reality to be learned than mere cognition or intellectual apprehension of it. An affective base must be laid before any kind of goal-directed learning can successfully occur. For example, if a learner is beset with unmet emotional needs, or if he is affectively insecure, little purposive learning, especially of a pervasive religious type, will ensue. If an individual is affectively constricted or rigidly defensive, it is very difficult for that person to freely experience and "hear" reality in such a way as to learn from it. An important empirical investigation of Belgian teenage boys by Georges Van Driessche found that the affective guilt feelings experienced by these youths proved to exert a more powerful influence on their cognitive view about and lifestyle reactions toward religious penitential practices than did their religious knowledge or beliefs.[41]

It is fairly safe to say that religious malfunctioning is more closely bound up with deficient affective content than with defective cognitive content. Religious conflicts, doubts, blockages, exaggerations, and aberrations tend to arise not so much from lack of knowledge or intellectual understanding as from inadequate or unbalanced affective content.[42] It would be an anachronism for a religious educator in this century to utilize mainly cognitive content (such as theology) for assuaging a learner's religious anxieties, unblocking his religious frustrations and conflicts, or touching the real locus of his religious doubts. Affective mechanisms, so frequently minimized or regarded as having no religious significance, play a much larger and more integral role with respect to well-developed or warped religious functioning than most religious educationists have typically allowed. Consequently, the religious educator who wishes to facilitate mature, fully functioning religious living must inject a goodly amount of various kinds of affective content into the lesson, in a manner appropriate to the attainment of the desired instructional objective.[43]

Rollo May, a social scientist, is of the opinion that affectlessness is a dominant mood or spirit which has surfaced in our age. For May, affectlessness and apathy are basically the same thing. If authentic love has become so difficult and scarce in our time, claims May, it is because of the affectlessness which is beginning to pervade modern civilization. Hate is not the opposite of love; apathy or affectlessness is. May notes that the post-World War II era is an anxious age: apathy, lack of feeling, and being "cool" serve as a protective barrier against anxiety. When an individual continually faces dangers which he believes he is powerless to overcome, his final line of psychological defense is to avoid even feeling the danger. But, observes May, the post-World War II age is becoming more violent as it is also becoming more affectless. There is a dialectical relationship, contends May, between affectlessness (or apathy) and violence. To live affectlessly promotes violence. Violence for its part fosters affectlessness.[44] If the religion teacher is to facilitate love of God and a minimizing of self-directed or other-directed violence, then he had better structure the learning situation so that it is rich in appropriate affective content.

It is a common lament of religion schoolteachers not only in the United States but also around the Western world[45] that many learners become bored with or even resistant to the religion lesson because they believe that "we already had this before." This reaction seems to be more typical of religion lessons conducted in formal settings than those which take place in informal settings. What these learners are complaining about is the repetition of cognitive content, often in altered or sometimes in a slightly more advanced form. It is only natural for normal, healthy individuals to turn away from previously studied material and seek fresh new content. Here is where affective content plays a vitalizing role in the religion lesson. Affective content is always subjectively new to the learner, even when "objectively" it might seem to be repetition of previously experienced affects. Each moment of joy or sadness or warmth always has something new and significantly different about it. This is the underlying reason why persons of every age-level can listen to the same affectively laden song over and over again. This is also the reason why a person in love never wearies of receiving the same affective communication, "I love you," coming from the lips or eyes of the beloved. By lacing the religion lesson with appropriate and goal-directed affective content, the teacher can do much to reduce if not totally eliminate the age-old complaint of learners: "But we've had all that before."

Since over the centuries religious instruction has been regarded by both theologians and theologically trained religious educationists as a branch of theology, it was quite natural for affective content to receive short shrift in religion teaching.[46] Theology is a speculative science and consequently resides entirely in the cognitive domain. The task of the theologian is to cognitively interpret the religious experience of the church, writes Gregory Baum, a theologian who is quite congenial to the importance of affective content in Christian living.[47] Edward Schillebeeckx, an internationally recognized master of theological method, observes that affective content and personal piety are extraneous to the work of theology *in se,* however helpful these qualities may be as an "inspirational power" to the theologian. Theology is a cognitive science, while affective content resides in another domain; "we must be careful not to confuse these issues," cautions Schillebeeckx. Theology is "formally a question of scientific activity and insight, of research and methodological precision." As a holy person, Thomas Aquinas apparently lived a life which had much affectivity to it; but as a theologian "Aquinas in fact banished the entire affective aspect from his methodology."[48]

Some Limitations of Affective Content

Notwithstanding its inestimable importance in the work of religious instruction, affective content is not without its limitations. I should like to touch on some of the more conspicuous of these.

Though it furnishes the learner with a crucial, highly personal contact with reality, affective content is simply not equipped to provide him with the whole truth. The whole truth comes to the human being only by the coordinated and integrated activities of his cognitive, affective, psychomotor, and lifestyle behaviors. Each of these activities provides its own unique and individual encounter with reality; only in harmonious concert can they all together provide a balanced and unified grasp of the real. Affective content, out of balance with its cognitive, psychomotor, and lifestyle complementarities, can easily reel out of control, leaving a person utterly naked to his own feeling-function, unable to ground it or interpret it from within the total context of his holistic functioning. A person's feeling-function is existentially meaningful and useful to him only when it is properly situated within the overall matrix of his situation and human condition.

While affective content is necessary for Christian living, it is not sufficient for it. Cognitive content and lifestyle content must play their indispensable and appropriate roles else affective content, detached from its referent of total personhood, can easily become psychologically and religiously destructive.[49] Peter Bertocci's review of some of the relevant empirical research investigations conducted by Gordon Allport concludes that when an individual relies totally and fundamentally on religious affect to furnish him with certainty, to rid him of insecurity, to endow him with privileged status among God's children, then the personality structure of that individual is apt to be of a prejudiced and authoritarian sort. Such a person uses his religious feelings as a fortress against any aspect of reality which tends to reduce his certainty, erode his privileged status, or challenge his security.[50] In cases of this kind, affective content serves to close a person off from free encounter with all reality, a freedom which is so essential to full, mature, and vibrant Christian living.

Affective content is limited precisely because it is affective content.

To feel Christianly is not to live Christianly. An individual's feeling-function is a necessary component in the doing of his Christianity, but the part does not equal the whole. It is not enough to feel Jesus; a person must live a Jesus kind of life. Affective content does not of itself directly produce Christian living, because affect and lifestyle are two different orders of being.

Of all the forms of affective content, surely love is at the pinnacle. But even love is not sufficient for Christian living. The learner cannot "go out there" and just love. What to love, how to love, why to love, where to place love — these are existential questions for which affective content by itself cannot supply an holistic, totally personalistic answer. Affective content does contribute a goodly measure to the answer to these ever-so-pressing questions; it does not, however, give the learner those nonaffective dimensionalities so necessary for him to make either a wholly Christian or an integrally human existential response to these questions. The scriptures do not speak of love only; they speak also about the law. Love and law, dynamic complementarities — this is the message of Jesus and Paul. Cognitive content of what the law is, the living of this law, all done in and for love — this is to put on the Lord Jesus Christ. By itself, love is not enough; when properly integrated with cognitive and lifestyle contents, love is empowered to become more than enough.

THE FORM OF AFFECTIVE CONTENT

A person's feeling-function, like a rich, well-cut ruby, is many faceted. Some facets, like the emotions, are fiery and smoldering; some, like feelings, give forth a softer glow. Others, like attitudes and values, seem to yield deep and formative colorations. But it is love, at once a facet and the convergence of all the facets, which endows the gem with radiance, elegance, beauty, and grace.

The feeling-function is as luminous as it is warm, as robust as it is fragile, as strong as it is vulnerable. A person's feeling-function is one of his most whole-some characteristics. It brings contrasting affective states into a personalistic wholesomeness, as, for example, enabling an individual to feel the sufferings of the daily crosses each Christian must bear in Jesus's name as well as the contrapuntal joys one experiences when one encounters some aspect of reality which reflects in a particularly luminous way the glorified, risen, cosmic Christ. The affective dimension of the human personality is laced with sentiment.

But this sentiment is deep-seated, vigorous, and sturdy; it is not that sloppy, mushy kind of sentimentality which is the corrupter of any soft faith just as fanaticism and absolutism despoil hard faith.

Many psychological explanations have been advanced to elucidate the inner functions and purpose of a person's affective activities. Carl Jung and his disciples claim that feeling is basically a feminine function.[51] From this perspective, the development of affective content leads to a growth of inner femininity.[52] The cultivation of this inner femininity, the "*anima*" in Jungian terminology, is necessary for both a man and a woman. For a man, the flowering of his *anima* is necessary in order to actualize the more gentle, tender characteristics of his personality. For a woman, the cultivation of her *anima* is necessary to enable her to encounter reality from a fundamentally womanly grounding, with her *animus* (masculine side) tethered to and working for her feminine nature. Whether the religious educationist or educator takes a Jungian or Freudian view of affectivity, whether he finds himself in the camp of a Carl Rogers or an Albert Bandura, or whether he embraces any other particular social-science viewpoint on feeling-function is not the main issue in this section on the form of affective content. Rather, what I seek to accomplish here is to highlight some key facets in the ruby of affect, so that the religious educator can have an improved understanding of why affect is so precious and so priceless.

As is the case with cognitive content and with lifestyle content, affective content has its product and process aspects. In other words, affective process is as much a full-fledged content as is affective product.[53] There are as many forms of affective process contents as there are of feeling. Similarly, there are numerous kinds of affective product contents. I will restrict myself in this section to a consideration of five major kinds of affective product contents, namely, feelings, emotions, attitudes, values, and love. I would like to think it superfluous to indicate that each of these affective product contents also has its process dimensionalities without which none could exist as a real, actual, here-and-now affective content.

Feelings

While "feeling" is a term used more or less synonymously with "affective," the category "feelings" has reference to a definite and particular form of affective content. "Feelings" is not the plural of "feeling"; they are of a different order of specificity. In other words, the category "feelings" constitutes one aspect or kind of feeling. This distinction should be borne in mind while reading this section and indeed the entire chapter.

There is notable lack of precision in social-science literature on the definition and composition of feelings. Often the words "feelings," "emotions," and "affects" are used interchangeably with seemingly little regard for pinpointing, to say nothing of nuancing, these terms. This disregard for clear-cut, well-defined terminology has led to inconsistencies within and among those who investigate both the entire affective domain as well as its various forms, particularly emotion and love.[54]

Since those who have been lifelong students of various aspects of affective content seem unwilling or unable to satisfactorily define feelings, emotion, love, and the like, I will not venture to do so. What I will do, however, is to offer some of the more commonly agreed-upon conceptualizations of these affects in a way which will be of significance and utility to religious educationists and educators.

Feelings are customarily distinguished from emotion on the basis of intensity. Feelings are typically described as mild forms of emotion. Feelings are simple experiences of pleasantness or unpleasantness associated with warm or mildly distasteful memories, anticipations, food, drink, fatigue, and so on. Feelings are distinguished not only from emotion, but also from interest, mood, and temperament. An *interest* is an affective state which is valenced toward the concern for and the pursuit of a task, an object, a person, or any class of reality. A *mood* is a chronic affective condition in which one set of feelings and emotions predominates for an indeterminate length of time. *Temperament* is a term used to describe the characteristic or habitual affective state of a person, such as vivacious, depressed, and so on. Although temperament is relatively stable, it has been known to change to a certain degree with alterations in health, age, and environmental conditions.

Feelings are associated with many realms of reality. For example, feelings are associated with the aesthetic realm, such as a feeling for art or beauty or music. Feelings can also be associated with ethics and values, as for example, a feeling for what is right, or a feeling that such-and-such is good for me or good in itself.[55] I should like to make two points about what I have just written. First, the feelings which I mention here are intuitive in character. Intuitive feelings are affective, and as such are distinctly different in both kind and texture from the cognitive type of intuition I discuss in Chapter Four. Affective intuition is even more immediate than is cognitive intuition. Further, it seizes the person more totally than does cognitive intuition, and gives the individual directly a definite feeling of security, a feeling which differs significantly from the intellectual certainty which cognitive intuition bestows on the intuitor. However, because affective intuition and cognitive intuition are both modes of the intuitive process, they are more mutually congenial and complementary than are most other types or "pairs" of cognitive and affective content. The second point I wish to make about the first two sentences in this paragraph is that in this instance, I use the terms "feeling for art" and "feeling for what is right" to indicate specific kinds of feelings. Yet earlier in this section, I made the definite observation that the category "feelings" represents one specific kind of feeling. This confusion in terminology,[56] plus the fact that feelings are described with reference to emotion rather than with reference to feeling, has done much to make the category "feelings" fall into disuse with many psychologists.

Emotion

Emotion is generally acknowledged to be one of the most complex of all phenomena known to psychology. Its complexity derives from the fact that emotion involves so many aspects of the organism at so many levels of psychological, neural, and chemical integration.[57] Both subjectively and objectively, the workings and consequences of emotion are diffuse and intertwined with a great many other psychophysiological processes.[58] Perhaps therein lies the major significance of emotion for an individual's well-being and for religious instruction as well.

Many people have tried to define emotion. At present there is no definition of emotion which is agreed upon by social scientists. Quite possibly one major source of difficulty in arriving at a satisfactory *definition* of emotion lies not only in the great complexity of this phenomenon, but also in the failure of investigators to carefully distinguish between the workings of emotion and the dynamic mechanisms underlying it. While the *workings* of emotion are indeed highly complex, they seem to fall into three major classifications or groupings: (1) a consciously experienced affect, such as a feeling of anger, joy, or grief; (2) an observed overt activity, such as terrified flight or friendly vocalizing; (3) a physiological behavior, such as marked activity in the autonomic nervous system and viscera, blushing, and so forth. The dynamic *mechanisms* of emotion, in contrast, are psychological constructs postulated to explain these three major groupings, such as, for example, unconscious defense mechanisms.[59]

Emotion is generally recognized as a process which is quite distinctive from, but tied in with, cognitive and physiological activities.[60] As holistic functionalism suggests, any experienced emotion is intermingled with cognitions, physiological changes, and overt activities consonant with the character of the particular emotions or set of emotions being felt.

One of the major reasons accounting for the fact that emotion is so potent in an individual's daily living is its massiveness. But as James Hillman notes, this massiveness, this molar character of emotion should not only be understood as a psychophysiological totality in the sense of a *big* event, but also, and even more importantly, as a totality in the sense of a *kind* of event. The psychophysiological totalness of emotion, then, does not simply describe its size, but also, and more crucially, its potent pervasiveness throughout the total organism. An emotion is capable of convulsing one's entire personality.[61]

Philosophers and psychologists over the centuries have attempted to distinguish or otherwise tease apart different emotions. Paul Thomas Young provides a nice historical précis. René Descartes suggests that there are six primary emotions, namely, admiration, love, hate, desire, joy, and sadness. Baruch Spinoza is more parsimonious, listing only three primary emotions: joy, sadness, and desire. In more recent times John Broadus Watson specifies three primary emotions: fear, rage, and love. Mehran Thomson enumerates dozens of "compound emotions" which he then attempts to reduce to their principal components. Alexander Shand catalogs seven primary emotions: fear, anger, joy, sorrow, curiosity, repugnance, and disgust. For William McDougall, the primary emotions consist of fear, disgust, wonder, anger, subjection, elation, and tenderness. George Stratton describes a network of emotions including undifferentiated excitement, elation, depression, together with differentiated fear, anger, and affection. Robert Yerkes has constructed a scale of moods, weak emotions, strong emotions, and passions. William James distinguishes between the "coarser emotions" (grief, fear, rage, and love) and the "subtler emotions" (including moral, intellectual, and aesthetic feelings). Floyd Allport reduces the facial expression of emotion to six elementary roots, namely, pain-grief, surprise-fear, anger, disgust, pleasure, and attitudes such as doubt. As Young concludes, "So it goes. There is some agreement but there are more discrepancies!"[62]

In contemporary psychology there is a strong trend away from defining or conceptually isolating specific emotions. Concomitantly, there is also a tendency toward attempting to describe behaviorally what happens during different emotional states. Thus, for example, Joel Davitz used a critical-incident, word-checklist research technique in order to arrive at behavioral descriptions of what a person experiences while involved in one or another emotional state. On the basis of his research data, Davitz found twelve clusters of generalized behaviors into which he cautiously suggests emotions can be grouped: (1) activation; (2) hypoactivation; (3) hyperactivation; (4) moving toward; (5) moving away; (6) moving against; (7) comfort; (8) discomfort; (9) tension; (10) enhancement; (11) incompetence/dissatisfaction; (12) inadequacy. Factor-analyzing these clusters, Davitz discovered that each one seemed to have a particularly strong valence toward one or another of what he then identified as the four different major dimensionalities of emotion, namely, level of activation, relatedness to the environment, hedonic tone, and sense of personal competence in dealing with the environment.[63]

Emotion is more closely tied in with bodily changes than is any other form of affect. Ten of the more significant of these bodily changes include observable (and in some instances very pronounced) alterations in heartbeat, blood distribution, galvanic skin response, respiration, pupillary response, gastrointestinal motility, muscle tension and tremor, blood composition, and pilomotor response ("goose pimples"). While psychologists have been successful in identifying the bodily changes which accompany emotion, they have been unsuccessful in pinpointing which human emotions are specifically correlated with given bodily changes.

The inability of either speculative or empirical investigators thus far to adequately define emotion or to satisfactorily tease apart discrete emotions has led many social scientists to concentrate their efforts on examining the behaviors which occur in conjunction with emotions commonly labeled as fear, sadness, disgust, and so forth.[64] Thus, for example, on the basis of empirical research, Robert Plutchik has formulated a useful schema in which he correlates words used by people (subjective language) to describe emotions with corresponding activities (behavioral language) and with the equivalent global roles (functional language) which these emotions play in the person's here-and-now living.

The following is Plutchik's chart of three languages used to describe emotional states:[65]

SUBJECTIVE LANGUAGE	BEHAVIORAL LANGUAGE	FUNCTIONAL LANGUAGE
Fear, Terror	Withdrawing, Escaping	Protection
Anger, Rage	Attacking	Destruction
Joy, Ecstasy	Mating, Possessing	Reproduction
Sadness, Grief	Losing Contact	Deprivation
Acceptance, Greed	Eating	Incorporation
Disgust, Loathing	Vomiting, Defecating	Rejection
Expectancy, Watchfulness	Sensing	Exploration
Surprise, Astonishment	Stopping	Orientation

LANGUAGE OF EMOTIONAL STATES

Many years ago Carney Landis drew an important distinction between two separate kinds of expression of emotions. The first kind is the involuntary expression of emotions and includes observable changes in muscles and glands. These bodily correlates of emotion are involuntary and maturational. The second kind of bodily expression of emotion is voluntary. Of great significance to the religion teacher is that these voluntary bodily expressions of emotion are the result of learning and not of maturation — or more precisely, are superimposed on the "natural" expression resulting from maturation in such a way as to modify and partially shape the manner in which the emotion is overtly expressed.[66] Learned bodily expressions are socially appropriated; hence it is far easier to differentiate them by the conventionalized expressions which people learn to use for conveying the particular emotion(s) they are expressing. Now all this suggests that the religious educator must learn to become sensitive to detecting differential bodily expressions of the same emotion.

Mature, personalistic Christian living demands the full development of the emotions and their appropriate expression. Suppression, excessive control, or a blunting of the emotions, whether self-imposed or exerted by a religious educator, can result in apathy. Apathy congeals and freezes Christian living, for when a person is apathetic he becomes incapable of love or of courage or any of the necessary Christian virtues.

Emotional development and expression for mature Christian living should be adequate, appropriate, and goal-directed. It should be adequate in terms of the degree of affective strength and fullness of an individual's temperament. The level and force of emotional expression for a person of mild temperament may be far too little — and hence inadequate — for a person with a more full-blooded temperament. An individual's emotional expression should be appropriate to the task in which one is engaged and to the circumstances in which one finds oneself. What might be an appropriate emotional expression with one's own children might be inappropriate when dealing with adult peers. Emotional expression should be goal-directed rather than indiscriminate. Emotions constitute one integral aspect of a person's holistic functioning, a functioning which in its totality is goal-directed immediately toward personal fulfillment and eschatologically toward a more existential union with God.

In his deliberate deployment of emotional content for instructional purposes, the religious educator should always bear in mind its great power and long-lasting effects. Emotional experiences can do much to help form or unform an attitude, value, or belief. Abraham Lincoln was said to have been so emotionally distressed at seeing slaves being auctioned at a New Orleans slave market that he resolved if ever he had the opportunity he would come down very hard on slavery. Emotion can be a great boon or a great hindrance to cognitive learning.

Emotion is not so much a way to gain content as it is a full-fledged content in its own right.[67] Emotion is a powerful content, for it provides the learner with an experience of the heat of God's dynamic action in his life and in the whole cosmos, a heat which kindles or warms or scorches or reduces to ashes or, paradoxically, freezes. The religion teacher should deal with emotion as a content of great worth, to be taught wisely and well — and skillfully.

Attitudes

Because attitudes condition all of a person's learning, they are one of the most important, pervasive, and influential of the substantive contents of religious instruction. It is difficult to imagine any truly effective and perduring religious instruction taking place without the educator placing a major emphasis on the acquisition of desired attitudes.[68]

An attitude is an affective, acquired, and relatively permanent disposition or personality-set to respond in a consistent manner toward some physical or mental stimulus.[69] This definition incorporates the six major characteristics which most social scientists agree are basic to the attitude construct. These six are: (1) an attitude is not innate or maturational, but is learned from experience and teaching; (2) an attitude is comparatively stable, rather than changing from moment to moment; (3) an attitude reflects a disposition toward an activity rather than either a verbalization of it or the activity itself; (4) an attitude is a more-or-less coherent way in which data or experiences are ordered; (5) an attitude is selective in that it provides a basis for discriminating between alternative courses of action; (6) an attitude is an orientation toward others, toward objects, and toward situations. My definition contains a seventh characteristic, one which is still controverted among social scientists, namely, the basic affective nature of an attitude. It would appear, however, that there is a growing trend among social scientists to recognize the fundamentally affective nature of an attitude.[70]

That an attitude is basically affective in nature in no way implies that its functioning precludes the involvement of cognitive processes.[71]

Holistic functionalism suggests that no one human operation works independently of the others. An individual's attitude structure does indeed contain cognitive components which are shaped by and mesh with its affective core. The attitude an individual has to some degree alters his cognitive content about a person or object.[72]

From the structural point of view, an attitude is one way in which an individual organizes his psychological processes. There are many other complementary ways in which an individual organizes his psychological processes, such as ratiocination, intuition, valuing, loving, and so on.[73]

An attitude is a psychologically organized feeling-tone about a stimulus, together with a preconceived judgment about that stimulus and a prepared reaction toward it. In this vein, Stansfeld Sargent and Robert Williamson note that "an attitude defines one's position toward a given aspect of his perceptual world. An attitude is either for or against an object, situation, person, or group."[74] This strongly valenced character of an attitude is part and parcel of its motivational tendency. An attitude involves a continual potential toward overt activity. The force, direction, and texture of an individual's attitudinal motivation at any given moment depends on many factors including the kind of stimulus, the frequency and force with which the attitude was deployed in the past, the present psychophysiological state of the individual, situational factors, and so forth.

It is the prepared "for" or "against" direction of an attitude — a direction grounded in affect and accompanied by a cognitive prejudgment — which accounts for much of the almost awesome importance of attitudes in the work of religious instruction. Attitudes largely account for a person's approach and subsequent response to virtually all of reality. Attitudes influence and condition nearly all learning. "Attitudes will determine for each individual what he will see and hear, what he will think and what he will do."[75]

It is its twin function of selector and interpreter that makes an attitude so crucially important in religious instruction. As I note in *The Flow of Religious Instruction*,[76] an attitude is far more potent than an objective fact because an individual tends to acquire facts which concur with his attitudes while excluding or blunting facts which are at variance with one or more of his attitudes (selector function).[77] Or again, when a new objective fact enters a person's perceptual and cognitive fields, it frequently does so in such a way as to be rendered congruent with the individual's previously held attitude complex, often to the destruction or at least to the diminution of the objective content of the new fact (interpreter role).[78] In religious instruction, the learner's attitudinal content exerts a major determining influence on (1) *which* cognitive doctrinal content he will acquire, and also (2) *how he will perceptually shape* the cognitive doctrinal content he does acquire. An attitude is typically much more enduring than facts or concepts. Further, an attitude contains a basic intrinsic motivational thrust, something relatively or perhaps even totally absent from cognitive content. For these reasons, the "let's stay with pure cognitive doctrine" movement, or any other reductionist form of religious instruction which downplays or neglects the learner's (and the teacher's) attitudes is doomed to failure at the outset.

Another major reason why attitudes are so very important in religious instruction is the strong inbuilt linkage between attitudes and overt conduct, between attitudes and lifestyle.[79] A review of the large mass of empirical research studies on the relationship between attitudes and conduct concluded that researchers are no longer questioning *if* attitudes predict and give rise to conduct; rather, researchers are examining *when and how* attitudes predict and generate conduct.[80]

The relevant empirical research indicates that there are three critical periods in attitude formation, namely, early childhood, adolescence, and early adulthood.[81] Of these three periods, early childhood is by far the most important. An individual's deeper attitudes are formed primarily (and some of the data suggest almost exclusively) in early childhood in the home environment. It is not an exaggeration to maintain that by and large the deeper attitudes which are acquired in later childhood, adolescence, and adulthood typically are amplifications or directional modifications of those fashioned in early childhood. This conclusion has all sorts of implications for the religious instruction enterprise. For example, if religious education officials truly regard religious attitudes as an extremely important content, then they should commit a disproportionately high percentage of their financial and personnel resources to instructional programs for young children, adolescents, and young adults, in formal as well as informal settings. Such a commitment, of course, would require a drastic — and a salubrious — reversal of the traditional Catholic (and Protestant) overemphasis on the denominational/religious instruction of boys and girls from six to thirteen years of age.

Throughout the twentieth century, social scientists have attempted to more clearly etch the nature and properties of attitudes by comparing them to other related psychological constructs. While differences of opinion do exist among social scientists about the specific nature and properties of these other constructs, nevertheless there is enough general agreement to be able to briefly describe them here.

A *belief* is composed of three principal processes, namely, cognition, affect, and motivation. Some social scientists, like the cognitively oriented Milton Rokeach, claim that belief is more basic than attitude. Thus, for Rokeach, an attitude is simply an organization of beliefs.[82] Other social scientists contend that attitude, not belief, is the more fundamental: in this conceptualization, belief is a kind of attitude which contains a great deal of cognitive structuring.[83] The first view would make an attitude basically a cognitive affair, whereas the second adheres to the view that an attitude is basically affective in nature. The second view seems more consistent with the motivational force of a belief, since at its base motivation, like overt activity, is deeply intertwined with affect; in contrast, a basically cognitive activity *in se* lacks motivational or overt-action thrust. This is not to deny or even to minimize the affective component of belief, as some social scientists were prone to do at one time. Rather, the second view offers a more ready explanation than the one Rokeach supplies for the affective potency of beliefs, notably of strong beliefs such as those associated with religion. Empirical measures of belief tend to assume its attitudinal (and hence affective) base, concentrating instead on assessing an individual's cognitive concept about a stimulus. This is done because belief is regarded as a kind of attitude, and it is the "kind of" — the "specific difference" in Scholastic terminology — which is being subjected to empirically controlled scrutiny. Measures of attitude tend to restrict themselves to an appraisal of the underlying affective structure and texture of one's attitudes.[84] Operationally, then, one has an attitude *toward,* and a belief *about* or *in* a person, object, or situation.[85]

Related to belief by virtue of its primary (but not exclusive) cognitive nature is *opinion.* An opinion is a tentative viewpoint or judgment about a particular stimulus. An opinion has less depth, less affective grounding, less firmness, and less perdurance than a belief.

A predisposition to choose one stimulus over another is termed a *preference.* Like belief and opinion, preference is more cognitively based than affectively grounded; however, preference typically contains affective elements. Preference, like opinion, is often correlated with attitude. Thus, for example, if a person has a highly favorable attitude toward Methodism, he is very likely also to prefer Methodism over Lutheranism and to have the opinion that Methodism is more suitable for him than Lutheranism.

An important kind of attitude is *prejudice.* Prejudice has four main characteristics. First, it is generalized, and indeed overgeneralized. Second, it is positively or negatively valenced toward a stimulus. Third, it is based on insufficient or inaccurate data about the stimulus. Fourth, it is highly resistant to being reversed, even in the presence of new and objectively compelling data.[86] While prejudice can be for or against a stimulus, nonetheless it usually means an overgeneralized, ill-founded attitude against a stimulus. In this sense, prejudice is a warped or unfair attitude. *Bias* is weak prejudice. An individual frequently is aware of, and even admits his biases; this is rarely the case with his prejudices, however.

Value is a psychological construct closely related to an attitude. I shall devote the next section of this chapter to the crucial subject of value.

Attitude, belief, opinion, prejudice, and bias are all extremely important contents of religious instruction. Indeed, these contents are frequently more influential and enduring in the life of the learner than is the bald cognitive content of "basic doctrine" in the conventional sense of this term. It is clearly erroneous to view attitude, belief, and so forth, simply as entry vehicles or helpful adornments to the content of religious instruction. Attitude, belief, opinion, prejudice, and bias are full-fledged contents in their own right, and should receive due emphasis in the religion lesson. It is far more important for the learner to have acquired a favorable attitude toward the bible and the biblical *Weltanschauung* than just to have mentally stored all sorts of cognitive data about the bible, to the stultification and possibly the jeopardy of this attitude.

An awareness of the various properties of an attitude can assist the religious educator to heighten the effectiveness of his teaching for attitude formation or re-formation. There are seven major properties of an attitude. *Kind* refers to the nature of the stimulus. For example, one can have an attitude about religion, about political events, about economics, and so forth. *Content* has to do with the cognitive aspects with which a particular attitude is concerned. For example, the conception of "church" in the religious attitude structure of a Catholic Christian might be quite different from the conception of "church" in the attitude pattern of a member of the United Missionary Church. *Clarity* deals with the precision of an attitude; it deals with the sharpness with which the content of an attitude is perceived. For example, a clergyman with a highly favorable attitude toward religion might perceive the nature, parameters, and consequences of religion far more accurately than would a casual churchgoer who has a moderately favorable attitude toward religion. *Direction* refers to the positive or negative valence of an attitude — the "for" or "against" aspect. For example, a Catholic Christian might have a "pro" attitude toward ecclesiastical authority. *Strength* pertains to the intensity of an attitude. For example, a Christian clergyman might have a much more intense positive attitude toward ecclesiastical authority than the average person in the pew. *Importance* is concerned with the centrality or salience of one attitude as compared with the other attitudes in one's overall attitudinal constellation. For example, a daily communicant's attitude toward religion might be a far more crucial one for him than his attitude toward economics. *Coherence* has to do with the consistency with which various attitudes are integrated into the individual's overall attitude structure. For example, a Caucasian might have favorable attitudes toward all nonwhites except Asians. It should be noted that these properties tend to bear a significant correlation with each other. Thus, for example, the research shows that strong attitudes are also clear and important.[87]

Since a person's attitudes are so pervasive, so influential, and so wide-ranging, it is obvious that they must satisfy some fundamental needs in his psychological makeup. Sigmund Freud claims that attitudes serve primarily extrarational and ego-defensive functions.[88] One of the most commonly accepted formulations of the functions performed by attitudes is that made by Daniel Katz.[89] According to Katz, an attitude has one or more of four functions. *First,* the instrumental, adaptive, or utilitarian function disposes the individual toward stimuli which are instrumental in achieving his valued goals. To change an instrumental attitude, the religion teacher alters the individual's evaluation of the goal to which it is instrumental, or more easily, the individual's perception of its usefulness for that goal. *Second,* the ego-defensive function assists the individual in: dealing with his inner conflicts by shaping his perception, estimation, and valence toward a particular helpful/hurtful stimulus; protecting himself from acknowledging the basic truths about himself or the world; and enabling him to successfully work out his principal psychological needs while at the same time coping with his environment. To change an ego-defensive attitude, the religion teacher assists the individual to engage in catharsis (preferably one involving overt behavior) and in activities aimed at facilitating self-insight and affective reorganization. *Third,* the value-expressive function enables the individual to derive affective satisfaction from expressing attitudes which he feels are congruent with his personal values, with his self-concept, and with his need for self-expression. To change a value-expressive attitude the religion teacher presents the learner with other stimuli which provide opportunities for him to express his values and his self-concept more fully and more congruently. *Fourth,* the knowledge function helps the individual to give personal meaning, structure, and consistency to a world which would otherwise be for him an undigested mass of complex and unrelated phenomena. To change a knowledge attitude, it is not enough to expose the learner to new information since attitudes are not too sensitive to new cognitive data; rather, the teacher should structure the pedagogical situation so that the learner is put into that kind of overt-activity mode in which he can feel (and not just think about) the inconsistency and incongruity between his basic attitude structure and the attitude to be changed.

These four functions of an attitude do not operate in isolation. They are not mutually exclusive. Nor are they rival contenders to explain the acquisition and/or operation of attitudes. A particular attitude might serve several or all four of the functions. Indeed, these functions possibly are variations on one overarching functional theme.

Attitude Formation. Because attitude is one of the most important contents of religious instruction, the teacher should have a knowledge of how an attitude is formed. In his classic article on attitudes, Gordon Allport identifies four general sources of attitude formation.[90] The first of these sources is the integration of numerous specific responses of a similar type. Second, attitudes are formed by the individual, especially in the early stages of his life, in order to help him become significantly differentiated from other persons, to gain a kind of personal or group individuation.[91] Third, attitudes are formed as a result of a particularly intense or traumatic experience.[92] Finally, attitudes are adopted ready-made from parents, teachers, spouses, subculture peers, and the like. It is common knowledge, for example, that a child will adopt uncritically and ready-made the religious, political, ethnic, and cultural attitudes of its parents.

In their attempts to refine and more directly pinpoint the four major sources of attitude as postulated by Allport, social scientists have found that the following also play a significant role in the formation of attitudes: genetic factors, personality characteristics, direct experience, interpersonal attraction, group influence, cultural impact, and experience in a total institution.

Some social scientists claim that genetic factors, namely those inherited from one's parents or from the human race as a whole, play a part in the formation of attitudes. Carl Jung's notion of archetypes and the collective or racial unconscious represents an example of one such claim for genetic sources of attitudes. Inherited characteristics such as intelligence, sex, physiological constitution, and the like appear to be sources or conditioners of attitudes, despite the modifications in each of these brought about by the individual's interaction with his environment.

Personality characteristics appear to play a significant role in attitude formation.[93] As holistic functionalism suggests, no human operation remains unaffected either by any one of the individual's functions or by the totality of these functions working in concert. The celebrated study by Theodor Adorno and his associates on authoritarianism discovered that an authoritarian personality structure was positively correlated with attitudes of ethonocentrism. Authoritarianism, in turn, represents one manifestation of insecurity and ego-defensiveness. Psychological imbalance was also found to be positively correlated with attitudes; thus, for example, persons, especially women, having a high anxiety level were more prejudiced than the average individual.

Direct experience with the stimulus tends to shape and modify attitudes.[94] Experience of this kind can be of a single, dramatic, and even traumatic sort on the one hand, or it can be a collection or accumulation of direct encounters with the stimulus on the other hand. Psychoanalytic and depth psychology research suggests that the single-incident direct experience is especially potent in early childhood; this is particularly true for attitudes of the deeper, more personal sort. There is also some empirical research which suggests that single traumatic incidents occurring in late adolescence might shape or at least drastically modify an individual's politically- or ideologically-oriented attitudes.[95] The attitudinal effect of accumulated direct experience has been the subject of considerable research. In short, the research suggests that it is not simply accumulated direct experiences *in se* which change or modify an individual's attitude; rather, what counts is the quality, force, and texture of these experiences as they interact with the individual's personality characteristics, reference-group membership, and the like.

It is possible that interpersonal attraction might play a role in the formation of attitudes. One review of the research concludes that the empirical studies do not as yet give firm support for many of the commonsense hypotheses concerning the attitudinal effects of interpersonal attraction. What the research has consistently discovered, however, is a positive correlation in most circumstances between interpersonal attraction on the one hand and a similarity of attitudes, beliefs, values, personality characteristics, and the like on the other hand.[96] Similarity of attitudes, values, and the like, therefore, might possibly underly interpersonal attraction and thus constitute a more potent factor than interpersonal attraction considered in itself.

There is abundant empirical evidence to indicate that an individual's attitudes are shaped, formed, and modified by group influences. The research data suggest that a reference group (that is, one with which the individual closely identifies regardless of whether or not he is formally a member) exerts more impact on a person's attitudes than does a membership group (namely, one in which the individual is a member).[97] The family is the individual's first, most pervasive, and in many instances his most enduring reference group; this is a further explanation for the tremendous influence of the family on attitude formation.

Both the broad culture and the particular subculture in which an individual lives have a potent effect on the shaping of his attitudes. A learner from a Presbyterian culture will likely have different attitudes toward Jesus and toward Zionism than a learner coming from a Jewish cultural background. How these attitudes in turn will be modified depends on the particular kind of religious and socioeconomic subculture to which the Presbyterian or Jewish learner belongs. Of interest to religious educators is the suggestion made by one researcher that learners from socioeconomically underprivileged environments actually are influenced more by a schoolteacher than are those from middle-class or upper-class families precisely because the lower-class learners have fewer potent sources of adult warmth and support at home.[98] Yet the tragic thing is that in so many well-intentioned religious and "secular" instructional programs designed to help the socioeconomically disadvantaged, the primary emphasis typically is put on providing enriched cognitive content rather than on the affective content for which these learners hunger and which is frequently a prerequisite to attain the cognitive content offered.

Finally, a total institution has marked influence on attitude formation and modification. From the sociological perspective, a total institution is a place of residence or work where a person, cut off from the wider society for an appreciable length of time, lives together with like-minded individuals in an enclosed, formally administered round of life.[99] From the psychological point of view, a total institution is an environment which pervasively and purposively programs for the person "what stimuli he receives, what response possibilities are available to him, and what rewards and punishments are administered to him."[100] Typical of all total institutions is the aim of forming the person or the new person, of generating pervasive attitudes or of bringing about attitudinal change. There are two types of total institutions, namely, the almost universal and usually benign total institution of childhood within a family setting, and the voluntary or involuntary total institution enrolling people during adolescence or adulthood. The first of these aims at making the person, the second at making the new person. It should be borne in mind that as a general rule, the more the total institution partakes of a voluntary character, the more impact it will have on the positive attitudinal structure of its residents. This is one reason why Taizé is more attitudinally successful in the positive sense than Sing Sing. Voluntary retreats lasting a week or more in an isolated setting and featuring divers kinds of purposive, goal-directed stimuli can be effective in attitudinal modification. The same holds true for religiously oriented summer camps, the educational potential of which is yet to be fully exploited even by Fundamentalist and Evangelical Protestant denominations.

Values

Virtually all social scientists agree that attitudes and values are closely related psychological constructs. The nature of this relationship, however, is a subject of considerable disagreement.

Two main schools of thought have arisen concerning the relationship of attitude and value. The first school sees value as being intimately related to but yet significantly different from attitude. Adherents of this line of thought tend to regard value as attitude plus some critical *additum*. Typical of this school is the conceptualization of opinion, attitude, interest, and value as successive points along a single continuum.[101] Jeffrey Keefe who shares essentially the same view states: "Values are more general than attitudes. Attitudes are limited to a fairly specific class of objects (such as Negroes) or to an abstraction (such as foreign aid), while values on the other hand encompass generalities."[102]

The second school of thought about the relationship of attitude to value regards value as being a configuration or a component of attitude. Value, then, is a special case of the attitude construct. Thus, for example, Theodore Newcomb, Ralph Turner, and Philip Converse define value as a configuration of inclusive attitudes. As the individual grows and develops, he builds up generalized attitudes which in turn may come to be integrated into a few broad patterns. These inclusive attitudes — values as they are called — frequently serve as axes around which his cognitive, affective, and lifestyle behaviors tend to revolve.

The difference between the two schools of thought concerning the attitude-value relationship has not yet produced many far-reaching practical consequences.[103] But this state of affairs does indeed have a significant practical ramification for religious educationists and educators, since it underscores my oft-repeated point that religious instruction should not rivet its immediate attention on constructs *per se,* but rather on specific behaviors. By hitching their priorities and energies to such constructs or logical beings as "faith," for example, religious educationists and educators have seriously neglected the more important pedagogical issue of religious behaviors. A construct is "constructed" to explain a behavior; its worth and utility consist in no more than this. Behavior, phenomena, data — these are real beings, and are the primary stuff of the religious instruction act. Constructs are simply inferences from behavior, and are accepted, modified, or rejected on the basis of how well they explain the behavior and how well they fit into the overarching theory. The religion teacher can no more teach faith than he can teach attitude, for faith and attitude are constructs and hence only logical beings with no real existence.

Value, I contend, is primarily an affective content. Thus when we say that a person values something, we mean that he has a special kind of affective attachment for that particular reality. Value represents a deep affective bond between the person and that which he values. To assert that value is basically affective in nature does not imply that it is without cognitive accompaniments.[104] Every person functions holistically. In the valuing process there are a great many cognitive components, components which are shaped by and meshed with its affective core. When we say that a certain individual has a "distorted value" we never question whether that which he possesses is an authentic value. What we question in such an accusation is twofold: the objective accuracy of the cognitive accompaniments of this value, and the degree of existential congruity between the subjective personal valuing of a reality and the objective *in se* value of that reality.

Elsewhere[105] I define value as "the worth of a reality." In the same place I further state that value is at once subjective and objective. This latter point represents one theoretical position in the long history of values as this construct has been examined by sages, philosophers, theologians, litterateurs, and social scientists over the centuries.[106] Those twentieth-century scholars who are positivists, including virtually all behaviorists and many psychotherapists (especially of the psychoanalytic variety) emphatically repudiate my contention that value is objective as well as subjective. Such positivistic scholars and practitioners reject the objectivity of value chiefly by attempting to reduce it to motivation, drives, repressed emotions, rewards and punishments, and the like.[107] But to deny that any worth resides in the stimulus, and to affirm that the worth of the stimulus is only a function of the way a person deeply feels about it, goes counter to our own validated experience. To deny intrinsic value or worth to a stimulus is equivalent to declaring that kitchen-sink art is as value-laden as Michelangelo's masterpieces,[108] or that it is all right to offer no help to a little boy being beaten up by a teenage bully. From a Christian perspective, every reality has value in itself. This value is determined by the fullness of its being, a fullness which is in direct proportion to the degree to which it participates in God. The objective pole of value acts as a needed safeguard against an otherwise exclusive, subjective orientation of one's valuing process. The objective side of value rescues a person's value functioning from an exclusive subjectivism which can easily degenerate into egocentricism and even affective solipsism. All affect needs cognitive accompaniments and existential congruity; this is preeminently true of valuing.

Social scientists have made various attempts to formulate classifications of human values.[109] Charles Morris, for example, suggests that value preferences can be placed into three basic categories: Dionysian (valuation for the expression of and indulgence in certain ego-centered, often hedonistic, wants); Promethean (valuation of planning, managing, and altering environmental stimuli); and Buddhistic (valuation of self-control through the control of one's desires).[110] Cultural as well as individual differences have been shown to lead to various combinations of these three basic value clusters.[111] The most celebrated and widely-used psychological value classification system is the Allport-Vernon-Lindzey *Study of Values* instrument.[112] Using as its starting point and springboard Eduard Spranger's earlier classification of the human personality into six major types,[113] the Allport-Vernon-Lindzey instrument is based on the hypothesis that there are six basic life values: the theoretical (discovery of truth as the central value); the economic (utility as the central value); the aesthetic (form and harmony as the central value); the social (love for people as the central value); the political (power as the central value); and the religious (unity of the cosmos as the central value). While every individual embraces a number of these six major life values to some degree, nevertheless empirical results derived from this instrument suggest that an individual develops a personality structure which employs one or another of these categories as his dominant value framework. Surveying philosophical and social-science research, Milton Rokeach concludes that a value may either be a desirable mode of conduct (instrumental values) or desirable end-states of existence (terminal values). In Rokeach's classification, there are two major types of instrumental values, namely moral values and competence values. Similarly, there are two major kinds of terminal values, namely personal values and social values. There is a vital functional relationship between instrumental values and social values.[114]

Whether values are conceptualized as being part of or somewhat distinct from attitudes, social scientists typically agree that they are directional and goal-oriented with respect to the attitudes to which they are related. Put differently, values exert a determining influence over attitudes.[115] Values further serve as benchmarks and touchstones determining the pattern and texture of a person's interaction with various realities.[116] As Lawrence Frank observes, each individual "lives primarily by investing all situations and events, all persons and activities, with meaning he has learned to give them, imputing to them the value, the significance, the highly individualized worth they have for him alone."[117] Consequently, it is of crucial importance that the religion teacher devote much of his pedagogical efforts to teaching desired values. Values are not innate or inborn; they are learned. Consequently, values can be taught, and taught directly.[118] The most successful way to teach values is to deliberately plan and enact the pedagogical event in such a way that specified values constitute an outcome. If these specific values are to be teachable and learnable, then they must be put into concrete behavioral form.[119]

Love

"God is love," the bible says (1 Jn. 4:16). Herein lies the centrality of love in religious instruction. Because each person is made in the image and likeness of a God whose very being is love,[120] the perfection and fulfillment of the human being lies in loving. If religious instruction is anything, it is an activity which is permeated with love in both its procedures and its outcomes.

Definition of Love. The answer to the question "What is love?" seems more elusive than the answer to "What is truth?" Over the centuries, in all civilizations and climes, wise persons and plain have grappled with devising a satisfactory definition of love, but thus far none of the definitions has seemed adequate or pleasing.[121] In the Christian tradition, philosphers and theologians have typically defined love in relation to the good. For the Scholastic philosophers and theologians, love consists in an appetency toward the good.[122] This theme is echoed by many spiritual writers, especially Catholics. Thus, for example, François de Sales conceptualizes love as the movement, effusion, and advancement of the heart toward the good.[123] Such definitions fall short of the mark because "good" is a transcendental and therefore lacks that specificity which is part of every satisfactory definition.[124] Karl Rahner and Herbert Vorgrimler state that in Christian (especially Catholic) usage, love is "the free fulfillment of man's being which orientates the whole man — as God actually wills and summons him — to God, thus establishing him in God's grace (justification) and in salvation."[125] This definition is so general and vague as to be seriously limited in its helpfulness. Psychologists and other social scientists have not as yet offered satisfactory definitions. Some psychologists claim that love is an emotion.[126] But this definition is reductionist, transforming one element of love into its whole essence.[127] Many other psychologists define love as an attitude,[128] as do some theologians.[129] "Love," states Erich Fromm, "is an attitude, an orientation of character which determines the relatedness of a person to the world as a whole, not toward one 'object' of love."[130] While considerably less reductionist than the conceptualization of love as an emotion, nevertheless the definition of love as an attitude serves to reduce the multifaceted nature of love to one of its features. Quite a few psychologists[131] define, or at least assume a definition of love as one or another type of interpersonality — interpersonal attraction, interpersonal attitude, interpersonal relationship, and so forth.[132] This definition is less than adequate because interpersonality seems to be an attribute of love rather than its nature. Finally, there are those philosophers, theologians, and social scientists who simply give up any attempt to achieve an adequate definition of love.[133]

Perhaps the major reason accounting for the unsatisfactory definitions of love proffered over the centuries is that love has usually been conceptualized either as totally unidimensional or as a series of unidimensional forces operating independently or quasi-independently of each other. But love is a highly complex affect and so can admit only of a multidimensional definition. There are several dimensions of love each of which must be defined in a somewhat different manner. The latter point, of course, has been recognized by thinkers down through the ages.[134] But the major task confronting humanity in terms of adequately conceptualizing love is to coalesce the varying dimensionalities of love into one comprehensive definition which allows dynamic interaction among the varying dimensionalities while at the same time meshing them into a coherent whole.

Any adequate definition of love must necessarily include four elements which are fundamental to its nature. *First,* love is a function. Love is not a "thing," a substance, or a *res* located somewhere in a person's physical nature or somehow in his spiritual dimensionalities. Love delineates a function, namely, the way in which a person mobilizes and deploys any or all of his personality characteristics at a given moment.[135] *Second,* love is more of a process content than a product content. Love is the term given to a particular type of processing relationship between lover and the beloved.[136] It is this process element which explains why love is dynamic rather than static. *Third,* love is affective. Its taproot is sunk into the deepest and most authentic aspects of an individual's affective functioning. A person does not think love, nor can he will love; he feels love. This is not to imply that love consists only of affect but rather that all the contents or ingredients of love are radically colored by, and indeed are subsumed into the affective. If affectlessness or apathy is emerging as a dominant feature of our civilization, writes Rollo May, we can understand at a deeper level why love has become so difficult.[137] "Hate is not the opposite of love; apathy is."[138] *Fourth* and finally, love is deeply intermingled with lifestyle content. There is no love that is not bound up with lifestyle. Indeed, one test of the depth of a person's love is the degree to which it is integrated into his lifestyle.[139] Love is not just feeling — it is feeling which is organically incorporated into the person's behaviors.[140] More than any other affect, more than any other human function, love involves the whole person, what the person is and what the person does. It is the goal of religious instruction to enable the learner to develop a lifestyle permeated with Christian love.

Kinds of Love. In order to expose more clearly the anatomy of love, scholars throughout the ages have endeavored to distinguish various major fibers which go to make up this anatomy. Of the many forms or kinds of love which have been suggested for consideration, I shall briefly treat only four.

Possibly the most well-known and well-accepted typology of love in the Western tradition is the fourfold classification of love into sex, eros, philia, and agapé. *Sex* is that form of love in which bodily desire, lust, or libido, for the sake of pleasure itself, predominate.[141] *Eros* is that physiopsychological kind of love in which the impulse to procreate or create is in the ascendancy. Eros is passion, while sex is sensation. Eros is the longing to establish union, a full relationship. It is eros, not sex, which is the occasion for human tenderness. For sex to be personally fulfilling and to achieve its potential as a form of love, it should be undertaken within the context of eros.[142] *Philia* is that type of love in which the element of friendship plays the leading role.[143] As sex is rescued from self-destruction by eros, so eros can be long-lived only when accompanied by philia. Philia empowers the individual to relax from the tension created by the heat and passion of eros. Philia is the relaxation in the presence of the beloved; it is the state which accepts and rejoices in the other's being as being. "Philia gives a width to eros; it gives it time to grow; time to sink its roots deeper."[144] In mature love, a person not only has an erotic relationship with the other but a philic relationship as well.[145] A beautiful expression of the nature of philia was articulated by the Roman poet Horace on learning of the death of his dear friend Virgil: "I have lost the half of my soul."[146] *Agapé,* or *caritas* is that variety of love characterized by love for another for the other's sake.[147] While eros pushes toward self-fulfillment, agapé seeks the fulfillment of the other. Agapé, then, is that self-giving love which seeks no gain or recompense from the beloved. Agapé, or *caritas,* is the highest form of love, the kind of love which Jesus continually taught and lived.[148] With respect to the four kinds of love mentioned in this paragraph, it should be underscored that genuine human love does not consist in any single one of these four.[149] Rather, "every human experience of authentic love is a blending, in varying proportions, of these four."[150] A Christian who strives to live agapé while attempting to simultaneously banish philia or eros or sex from his life will probably attain neither agapé nor love.[151] In Paul Tillich's words, "If eros and agapé cannot be united, love of God is impossible."[152] The history of the church is littered with the dry bones of those who sought agapé alone and along the way lost the fire, oil, and balm with which sex, eros, and philia imbue love. This is a lesson from the past which the religion teacher would do well to remember. A major task of religious instruction is to help the learner to integrate these four kinds of love in such a manner that God is best served and that the learner himself is most fulfilled. "Love your neighbor as yourself" (Mt. 22:39) suggests that agapé and self-love go hand in hand — indeed, in this biblical quotation, self-love is made the *point de départ* for love of neighbor. It is a truism in social science that a person can love another for that other's sake only to the extent to which he truly, authentically, and humanly loves himself. This is doubtless also true for one's love of God.

A second major typology of love is the Thomistic division between *concupiscent love (amor concupiscentiae)*, and *benevolent love (amor benevolentiae)*. This twofold classification which has exerted great influence on Catholic as well as on Protestant spiritual writers, theologians, and religious educators down the centuries shares many of the features of the sex-eros-philia-agapé typology. The main difference between these two typologies is that the Thomistic typology categorizes love on the basis of the essential metaphysical polarity within human love, while the sex-eros-philia-agapé schema classifies love according to its operations.[153] Put in the starkest metaphysical terms, *amor benevolentiae* is the love of being, while *amor concupiscentiae* is the love of well-being.[154] *Amor concupiscentiae* is that kind of love in which the individual seeks to achieve happiness and perfection for himself, while *amor benevolentiae* is that kind of love in which he seeks to achieve happiness and perfection for the sake of the beloved person. *Amor concupiscentiae* is primarily directed to the self; *amor benevolentiae* is basically directed to the beloved. *Amor consupiscientiae* is the love of desire and seeks affirmation of the self; *amor benevolentiae*, the love of generosity, seeks affirmation of the other. *Amor concupiscentiae* seeks the good *through and from* the beloved; *amor benevolentiae* seeks the good *in and for* the beloved. Since Aquinas defines love as the attraction a person has for some good *(amare est velle alicui bonum)*, both *amor concupiscentiae* and *amor benevolentiae* represent appetencies toward a worthwhile goal. *Amor benevolentiae* constitutes a higher form of love than *amor concupiescentiae* because, in metaphysical terminology, the former is a variety of love which goes straight to the term willed in and for itself and rests there, while the latter is a kind of love which implies a further reference in its term to something outside itself.[155] *Amor benevolentiae* is thus direct love while *amor concupiscentiae* is indirect. Both types of love seek the union of the lover and the beloved. Both forms of love are complementary and are not reducible to the other. *Amor concupiscentiae* should not be regarded as egoism or selfishness since it is normal, proper, and indeed necessary for a person to love himself. For Aquinas, as for Aristotle before him, direct love for another person is an extension of the direct love which every being has for itself. The latter form of love is basic and primary. Self-love is always prior. "It is, as it were, the root and the archetype of all *amor benevolentiae,* so that direct love for another is, in relation to this fundamental love for self, simply derivative, simply an analogue."[156] This fundamental character of *amor concupiscentiae* calls into question, from a philosophical perspective,[157] the possibility of pure and disinterested love which is posited to constitute *amor benevolentiae* in its highest form. Some mystical theologicans (notably in the Middle Ages) and some philosophers advocate disinterested love, particularly that directed toward God, as the only genuine form of love. Yet this solution to the problem of the possibility of the existence of disinterested love (and especially disinterested love of God), while seeking to preserve the person from any taint of egoism, also tends to wrench the human element from love. Other philosophers, including most probably Aquinas, consider authentic self-love in its truest and finest form to be a pure and great love for God since to love oneself is simultaneously and deeply to promote the whole in which the self finds and has its being. Neither of these two positions is wholly satisfactory in explaining, from the philosophical standpoint, the problematic of disinterested love. The second solution appears to have greater merit, not only because it is philosophically more reasonable, but also because it is more congruent with the research findings of social science, especially psychology. In any event, no real opposition can exist between authentic love of self and authentic love of others (including God), something which has clear and unmistakable ramifications for the work of religious instruction.

Perhaps the typology most familiar to religionists in general and religious educators in particular is that of human love and divine love — natural and supernatural love as they are sometimes termed.[158] This typology is theological in nature and inspiration. According to traditional theology, *human love* is that by which a person is drawn to union with other human beings and with all creation, while *divine love* is that by which an individual dwells in union with God. Human love is natural to every human being by virtue of that person's existence qua human being, while divine love is a grace freely given by God and wholly unmerited by any individual. A person can harden himself to human love, or can refuse divine love — the words "harden" and "refuse" indicate respectively that which is part-and-parcel of a person's bald human existence and that which is freely given over-and-above his bald human existence. Advocates of this typology claim that human love is a natural virtue while divine love is a supernatural virtue. Divine love is thus an infused virtue. Divine love does not undermine, destroy, or go counter to authentic human love; rather it enlarges, elevates, and perfects it.[159] Love of God as a state of being is termed sanctifying grace by classical Catholic authors, while a particular dynamic act executed out of the existential context of this state is said to be a manifestation of the effects of actual grace.[160] Divine love is enmeshed in grace and redemption; it represents a divinizing of human love. A person's sanctity or holiness, regardless of his state of life or profession, ultimately consists in the advancement and perfection of the divine love which God gives him and in which he dwells in grace.[161] Although this classical theological formulation I have just sketched still consciously or unconsciously undergirds much of contemporary theological speculation and most of religious instruction, serious questions have been raised concerning its accuracy and utility. "Natural" and "supernatural" are not substances or ontological entities; they are only logical beings, theological constructs devised as conceptual and analytical tools to better investigate God's dealings with human beings.[162] There is really no ontological dualism between natural and supernatural in this world. There is no such creature as a "natural" person since it is precisely God's "supernatural" grace which created that person, which sustains him at every moment of his existence, and empowers him to do what he does. A human person, as Protestant theologians have been asserting for centuries, is a supernatural being by his very nature as God's creation, as a being made in God's image and likeness — an image and likeness which is love, as the bible tells us (1 Jn. 4:16). Supernature, then, is really part of human nature; it is not something added on to human nature in an extrinsic manner.[163] A human being can choose to resonate with this supernatural aspect which flows in and around him, or he can opt to be out of tune; in either case the supernatural hymn is there present.

A fourth typology of love is that of an *integrated mutidimensional set of affectional systems*. Drawn from the results of empirical investigations rather than from philosophical or theological speculation, this typology affirms that love is a multidimensional function served by at least five distinct but interacting affectional systems, each aroused by its own stimulus conditions and expressed through its own response patterns. As elaborated by Harry Harlow, a social scientist who has spent much of his career empirically studying love and other affective functions,[164] each affectional system proceeds in a series of orderly, progressive developmental stages characterized by somewhat different underlying variables and mechanisms. In order of development, the first is the *infant-mother affectional system*. This stage is initially marked by reflex sucking and clinging in which bodily contact plays at least as important an affective role as does nursing. As this stage progresses, the infant's affective attachment to the mother gradually comes under voluntary control. The sight and sound of the mother provide it with a feeling of comfort and security, both of which color the nature of the infant's love for the mother. The development of voluntary control together with its feeling of comfort and security enables the infant to be away from the mother for increasingly longer periods of time to explore its physical and social environment.

The second system to develop is that of the *infant-infant or peer stage* in which the infant comes to play and otherwise associate with age-mates, thereby developing affectional ties with them. The mother fosters the development of this system by encouraging peer association for the child plus consciously or unconsciously discouraging exclusive attachment to her. She accomplishes the latter by performing such activities as withdrawing her immediate presence from the infant for increasingly longer periods of time. The infant-infant or peer affectional system is characterized by liking through similarity and affective acceptance. This system serves as the basis of friendship and close acquaintanceship, and continues to function throughout the individual's lifetime.

The foundations for the third affectional system, namely that of *heterosexual love*, are grounded in the previous stage. The warm and positive affect which is felt in the infant-infant or peer system becomes more and more accepted, desired, and extended to members of the opposite sex. At puberty, the heterosexual affectional system takes on added emotional and physical dimensions so that the heterosexual love is typified by the warmth brought on by physical and psychological attachment, arousal, esteem, comfort, and what in its finest sense is termed "romantic love."

The fourth and fifth affectional systems, namely, the *maternal affectional system* and the *paternal affectional system* normally become operative at the same developmental time in an adult's life, the nature of the system being determined, obviously, by the gender of the parent. The maternal affectional system is marked initially by continuous physiopsychological care, providing nursing, contact, protection, and grooming; as the child grows older maternal care becomes more psychological and less physical, a condition which perdures throughout the mother's lifetime. Mother love is quite possibly the very ultimate in deep affection and warm care; indeed, when painters and artists in virtually every age, civilization, and clime wished to portray the deepest level of personhood and human affectivity, they have depicted mother and child. For its part, the paternal affectional system[165] is characterized by the development in the father of such affects as tenderness, sympathy, and protection, affects which are reinforced and enlarged by the infant's responsive behaviors. The paternal affectional system differs most markedly from the maternal system in that it lacks the underlying physical changes which accompany pregnancy and parturition which doubtless shape maternal behavior and love. Harlow's typology is limited, though by no means negated[166] by the fact that his observations and experiments were conducted with rhesus monkeys rather than with human beings.

Besides Harlow's typology, other empirical typologies have been formulated for love. The two foremost classes of these typologies are those drawn from psychotherapeutic practice and those derived from learning research. The most celebrated of the psychotherapeutic typologies is that developed by Sigmund Freud. For Freud and likeminded psychonanalysts, love is an all-inclusive sexual drive[167] termed the libido.[168] Love, in the Freudian typology, is the process and the product of the relief of libidinal urgings and strivings.[169] Though the libido is a function of the person from cradle to grave, it is shaped principally in the very early childhood years when the infant progresses through two primary stages, the oral and the anal. These stages are followed in the childhood period by the phallic stage which provides satisfaction by urination and masturbation. The phallic stage becomes latent and sublimated at about five or six years of age, awakening dramatically at the onset of puberty. In contrast, typologies developed from learning research have typically been drawn from experimental laboratory studies of selected emotional activities and psychophysiological responses to deliberately induced stimuli. The heyday for this research seeking to directly link emotions and induced psychophysiological responses to love was in the Watson and immediate post-Watson era. From that day until the 1970s learning research on love was in limbo — or to give a more benign interpretation, in its own latency period. The principal defect of typologies elicited from psychotherapeutic sources is the relative lack of rigorous research data on which they are based, and the sometimes fanciful and bizarre interpretations given to even the most simple phenomena. Typologies drawn from learning investigations are deficient in that they come mainly from research conducted in laboratory settings, and also that they tend to become so locked into purely physical stimulus-response patterns as to skirt or miss the deeper, more global, and more personalistic aspects of love. Harlow's typology in many ways parallels both psychotherapeutic and learning typologies, while adding to them common sense, breadth, and a measure of integration.

Some Characteristics of Love. Delineating a few key characteristics of love in no way suggests that each characteristic separately, or that all the characteristics collectively, operate with equal or identical salience, force, and texture in every one of the various types of love which I treated in the foregoing subsection of this chapter. Each of the various types of love exhibits these characteristics in a manner and shape distinctive to its own special type.[170] In one sense, the very reason why the various types of love are different lies in the fact that a particular set or configuration of characteristics is more operative in one type of love than in another.

The first characteristic of love is that it is a term describing a certain set of *behaviors*. Love is a term naming a particular pattern of human functions. Love interacts with and to an extent works through a wide variety of other more-or-less congruent human functions. Love, then, is not some sort of amorphous or vague kind of feeling, but a description of a particular way of behaving.[171]

The second characteristic of love is that it is a set of *learned* behaviors. Love has to be learned by experience and instruction. Whether a person loves at all, whether a person loves a great deal or a very little, whether a person loves in this way or that way — all these depend on the way the person has learned to love. And the way a person learns to love is by being loved, and in such a context, by himself engaging in love behaviors. The way a person is loved, the degree to which he is loved greatly affect the way and the degree of his own loving.[172] For this reason psychologists place great stress on the manner and degree in which the infant is loved by its parents.[173] Excessive deprivation of the love-needs of the infant has been shown by the research to lead to a lack of hope, a withering of the personality, depression, and even death.[174]

The third characteristic of love is that it is a set of learned behaviors of an *interpersonal* variety. While love is not identical with interpersonal attraction, nonetheless love has a measure of interpersonalness about it.[175] One can really only like a thing; one cannot love it. For love is an interpersonal relationship, a dynamic affect of one person for and with another person. "And love in the fully personal sense is not just any relationship between two persons who meet in some third thing, whether this *tertium quid* is a task, a truth or anything else; it is the ceding and the unfolding of one's inmost self to and for the other [person] in love."[176] Love is interpersonal because it is done in relationship with another person; hence love is deeply personal. Love is the most personal thing one can think of, states Emil Brunner.[177] Since it is personal and interpersonal, love involves the whole person, body and soul.[178] As Jean Mouroux remarks, love in human beings is both spirit and flesh.[179]

The fourth characteristic of love is that it is a set of learned behaviors which seeks *union* with the beloved.[180] Love is a force which impels a person to become one with the beloved insofar as possible. Love "has perhaps no more accurate or descriptive antonym than the word separation."[181] Paul Tillich puts it succinctly: "Love is the drive toward the reunion of the separated."[182] Addressing himself to this issue from the psychological perspective, Alexander Lowen writes: "All relationships in which love enters are characterized by the desire for closeness, both spiritually and physically with the love object. 'Closeness' may not be a strong enough word. In its more intense forms, the feeling of love includes the desire for fusion and union with the love object."[183] From the standpoint of classical Thomism, both cognition and love represent a person's striving for union with the other. In cognition, the term or end of this union is the object in the subject (knower) while in love, the term or end process is the object (the beloved). Put somewhat differently, the term or end of the cognitive union is the object with intentional existence; in the case of love it is the object with real existence. "Cognition is brought to fulfillment when that which is known is united, through its likeness or intentional form, to the knower. Love, on the other hand, is brought to completion when that which is love is itself united to the lover. Consequently, the union of the lover with that which is loved is closer and more intimate than the union of the knower and the object known."[184] Love as union meets and fulfills one of a person's deepest needs — the need to overcome his feeling of separateness from reality outside himself. It is through the union which love brings that a person transcends the confines and limitations of his own separateness. Love is a force that breaks down the walls which separate persons from each other. Love unites an individual to other(s). The solution to the problem of human existence, Erich Fromm observes, "lies in the achievement of interpersonal union, of fusion with another person, in love."[185] Because love affords a person a greater union with the other than is possible through cognition, love brings with it a greater human fulfillment and thus a greater degree of happiness than is possible through cognition.

The fifth characteristic of love is that it is a set of learned behaviors which features a large measure of *self-giving and self-emptying* to the beloved.[186] In its noblest forms, love represents the total giving and emptying of self.[187] In love, a person gives and expends himself prodigiously because love is a reproductive force, not so much in essence as in action.[188] Love qua self-emptying implies commitment to the person loved. Love is the union with the beloved on what the lover perceives to be the beloved's terms; the greater the love, the more totally the lover gives and pours himself forth.[189] It is for this reason that many persons are reluctant and afraid to fall deeply in love, for to fall deeply in love means basically to die to self. "Death is always in the shadow of the delight of love."[190] A person consciously or unconsciously fears that a prospective love relationship will eventually destroy him, for when he deeply loves, he gives up the center of his own existence. His new center of existence becomes the beloved person, or more properly the new reality formed through the reciprocal giving of selves by the lover and the beloved.[191] Love converts the "I am" into "us is." Relinquishing the "I am" is a painful prospect for any normal human being. Yet a paradox of love is that it is through this very emptying of the self that a person finds his own true and best self.[192] Thus Pierre Teilhard de Chardin, writing from the cosmic vantage point, observes: "At what moment do lovers come into the most complete possession of themselves if not when they say they are lost in each other?"[193] The bible puts it clearly when it states that whoever loses his life for love of Jesus will find it (Lk. 9:24).

The sixth characteristic of love is that it is a set of learned behaviors which seeks union with the beloved *as the beloved is in himself*. Love accepts the beloved as the beloved is, not as the lover wants him to be. It is a sham love which attempts to mold or refashion essential features of the beloved's personality to conform to the needs or desires of the person professing to be the lover. Therefore, as Karl Rahner and Herbert Vorgrimler state, "human love must come soberly to terms with the limitations of the beloved, and while necessarily and unquenchably hoping for infinite fulfillment does not make the beloved suffer for its disillusionment but accepts its own human limitations as the point at which God, by the very pain of his absence, shows that he is infinite fulfillment"[194] and the only totally-satisfying of all love objects. "Love," maintains Marcel van Caster, "is not content merely to appreciate what another person has; it encounters the other person in what he is."[195] Daniel Day Williams holds the same view: "To love another is to seek that person as he is, in all the dimensions of his life and in all that makes him a person."[196] Love has the power of effecting a transformation of the individual according to the concrete existence and demands of the beloved without forcing the lover to lose any of his own dignity, integrity, or unconditional validity. To love means to respect the beloved. As Erich Fromm reminds us, "respect is not fear or awe; it denotes, in accordance with the root of the word (*respicere*, to look at), the ability to see a person as he is, to be aware of his unique individuality. Respect means the concern that the other person should grow and unfold as he is. Respect, thus, implies the absence of exploitation. I want the loved person to grow and unfold for his own sake, and in his own ways, and not for the purpose of serving me."[197]

The final characteristic of love with which I wish to deal in this section is that love is a set of learned behaviors marked by personal *freedom*. Love is the free bestowal of a person, as Karl Rahner aptly remarks.[198] In the same vein, Emil Brunner states that "enforced love is not love at all. To be anything else except free contradicts the nature of love — precisely that love depicted in the bible as the right kind of love. Love presupposes an even higher degree of freedom than the acknowledgment (in obedience) of God as Lord.''[199] But because love is the free bestowal of a person, mature and full personal love can come about only when a person possesses himself and, therefore, has the capability to bestow himself or to refuse himself.[200] Freedom to love, then, is grounded in a person's self-possession, self-awareness, and self-love.[201] A person has the power to love only when he authentically possesses himself, is aware of who and what he is, and loves himself.[202] In the last connection, Erich Fromm remarks: "If an individual is able to love productively, he loves himself too; if he can love only others, he cannot love at all."[203]

The Importance of Love. A person's supreme perfection, as Jacques Maritain observes, consists in loving.[204] Loving perfects an individual in two ways: it perfects him as he is a person, and it perfects him as he is a God-created, God-suffused, and God-directed person.[205]

Love perfects a person qua person because, as I mentioned earlier, love is in a certain sense the cause of everything a person does. A person performs noble deeds or even plain ones because he loves an ideal, another person or set of persons, or himself. Love enables a person to bear sufferings, hardships, and pain to a degree unattainable by cognition or other kinds of human functioning. Love bears all things and endures all things (1 Cor. 13:7).[206] In this connection one is reminded of the true story of the Catholic nun laboring as a missionary in a leper colony in the Pacific during World War II. One day a journalist watched the nun bathing the decayed, diseased stump of what was once the leper's foot. "I wouldn't do that for a million dollars," the journalist remarked. The nun looked up at him and replied: "Neither would I."

In love, a person opens his whole being to himself and to others to a depth and degree found in no other form of human functioning.

Love perfects a person as that person is God-created, God-suffused, and God-directed because, as Rudolf Bultmann observes, it is Christian love through which faith operates.[207] This is true regardless of whether faith is viewed as notional or existential assent. In a highly significant article on love, Robert Johann states that it is through love that a human being is somehow already in union with the infinite, unchanging God, and indeed with all reality.[208] As the mystics were deeply aware, the whole universe can be seen and experienced fully and accurately when it is grasped as a form of love. Everything is physically and even literally lovable in God, which also means that God can be encountered and loved in everything around us. God, especially Jesus, is at once the source, the ongoing evolver and the Omega of all reality, including human beings. By this very fact, Pierre Teilhard de Chardin observes, a person's charity is existentially synthesized. As the ongoing evolver, Jesus is the directional flow*ing* of all reality. As Omega, he is the focal point toward which and in which all reality converges. Jesus, then, is not simply a divine person, but the line in which the dynamic center of every reality lies. "This can mean but one thing," Teilhard continues, "that every operation, once it is directed toward him, assumes, without any change of its own nature, the psychic character of a center-to-center relationship, in other words, an act of love."[209] The central, and indeed the essential Christian message is one of love, a love in which, by which, and through which a human being is redeemed, reconciled, and opened to the world.[210] The history of Israel in the Old Testament, and of Christianity down to this day is the familiar cycle: a human being, who bears the image and likeness of God who is love, falls into disorder and spurns this love; God's love restores the person's love to a fulfilling orientation; after a time the person again falls out of a relationship with God; once again God's love restores the individual to integrity and communion; and so on.[211] The best way one can return to God, however feebly, that which one has received from God is to offer love and compassion to one's fellow human beings, especially those who are not lovable.[212] Faith is active through love of neighbor, a love which seeks no return or reward.[213]

Love is so terribly important because it so intimately and so totally binds a person to God and to all reality as well.

Love is the touchstone of the Christian religion. It is the measure of all religious conduct.[214] The primacy in moral theology and practical theology belongs to love. "If a man really loves," remarks Rudolf Bultmann, "he knows already what he has to do."[215]

A Final Note. Love, whether human or divine, is the most powerful force in this world and the next.[216] It was in love that we were created and it is through love that we have been redeemed.[217] And it is through love that we will eventually be saved. It is the love of one person for another which inspires the greatest heroism, the greatest sacrifices, and the greatest happiness of which a person is capable.

It is love, more than any other human functioning[218] or cosmic power, which is capable of bridging the otherwise unbridgeable abyss between here and eternity, between mortality and immortality. To love unconditionally is to say to the beloved person: "You will never die." At bottom, it is because a person is created, sustained, and shot through and through with God's unconditional love that he is immortal. The inextricable connection between love and immortality is graphically illustrated, for me at least, in the story of the bell in Račić Memorial Chapel located in the old town cemetary at Cavtat (the Roman Epidaurus) on the Dalmatian coast just south of Dubrovnik in Yugoslavia. This lovely burial ground is perched at the end of town on the brow of a promontory directly overlooking the azure Adriatic waters. As I stood there on several July afternoons, the golden summer sunlight which mingled with the apparently endless breeze blowing off the sea seemed to bestow on this graveyard a breath of that kind of newness and freshness and cleanness which we associate with eternity and immortality. It was in this cemetery that the great Croatian sculptor, Ivan Meštrović erected the world-famous mausoleum for the Račić family. This family had known Meštrović for several years and was one of his most generous patrons. It is said that once the young Račić daughter asked Meštrović if he believed life to be immortal. Meštrović reflected long and meditatively on her question. In the inscription which he placed on the bell of the mausoleum chapel Meštrović gave his answer: "Know the secret of love," it reads, "and you solve the secret of death." Whenever this bell tolls it carries Meštrović's response over the tombs of the dead and far out on the shining sea.

Love is the greatest reality in all the world. It is the ultimate touchstone and measure of every individual's being, strivings, and deeds. In the evening of our day, one Christian hero of bygone days remarked, we shall be judged by our loving. All human achievements, all joys and sorrows, all moments of triumph and tragedy and doldrums will all eventually fade away, but love remains. "There are three things which endure," states Paul, "faith, hope, and love, and the greatest of these is love" (1 Cor. 13:13).

The Krathwohl Taxonomy

David Krathwohl and his associates devised a formal taxonomy of educational objectives for the affective domain of the teaching endeavor.[219]

There are numerous advantages accruing to the religious education and curriculum builder who use the Krathwohl taxonomy. *First,* the taxonomy situates a large number of affective contents within a broad, hierarchically ordered, overall general matrix or schema. Thus each content is placed in a form in which its role and usefulness in affectively oriented instruction are enhanced. *Second,* the taxonomy provides the religious educator with a vitally necessary form or structure out of which he can operationalize his affective objectives. *Operationalizing instructional objectives in performance terms which can be taught and evaluated on the basis of observable evidence of achievement is, of course, the key to successful teaching.* *Third,* the taxonomy enables the religious educator to sharpen his own instructional objectives in the affective domain. Thus pedagogically fuzzy, vague, and useless objectives such as: "the learner should develop an appreciation of sacred music," or "the learner should come to value his neighbor" can be made more precise and thus more serviceable, thanks to the taxonomy. *Fourth,* the taxonomy makes it possible for the religious educator and the curriculum worker to make pedagogically necessary distinctions between affective and cognitive content, as, for example, between values and knowledge. (Amazing as it might seem in this day and age, there are even some religious educators and educationists who claim that affect does not really exist as a function independent of cognition.)[220] *Fifth,* the taxonomy helps the religious educator to achieve optimum vertical articulation between the affective behavior he is attempting to facilitate in the lesson and those other affective behaviors which are classified in the taxonomy. *Sixth,* the taxonomy assists the religious educator to attain maximum horizontal articulation between the affective behavior he is facilitating and the other nonaffective pedagogical contents he intends to teach in a particular lesson or wider instructional unit.

There are five major categories of affective behaviors listed in the Krathwohl taxonomy.[221]

The first category of the Krathwohl taxonomy is receiving (attending).[222] Receiving or attending is defined in the taxonomy as the sensitization to the existence of certain phenomena and stimuli. This category deals with a willingness to receive and attend to phenomena and stimuli. Major divisions within this category include awareness, willingness to receive, and controlled or selected attention.[223]

The second category of the Krathwohl taxonomy is responding. Responding is defined in the taxonomy as the individual's reaction to a given stimulus. The responding category contains three divisions, namely acquiescence in responding, willingness to respond, and satisfaction in response.

The third category of the Krathwohl taxonomy is valuing. Valuing is defined in the taxonomy as the voluntary prizing of a stimulus because of its perceived worth. Major divisions within this category include acceptance of a value, preference for a value, and commitment.

The fourth category of the Krathwohl taxonomy is organization. Organization is defined in the taxonomy as the arrangement of values so that they form a system which delineates the interrelationships among the different values within this system and at the same time pinpoints those values which are regarded as dominant and pervasive. Major divisions within the organization (of values) category include the conceptualization of a value and the organization of a value system.

The fifth category of the Krathwohl taxonomy is characterization by a value or value complex. Characterization by a value or value complex is defined in the taxonomy as the way in which an organized value system operates in an individual's lifestyle. "At this level of internalization the values already have a place in the individual's value hierarchy, are organized into some kind of internally consistent system, [and] have controlled the behavior of the individual for a sufficient time that he had adapted to behavior in this way."[224] Major divisions within the characterization by a value or a value complex category include generalized set and characterization.

From my examination of the nature and varieties of affective content as detailed in this chapter, it is obvious that the Krathwohl taxonomy has quite a few shortcomings, some of which are serious. To be sure, the taxonomy needs considerably more refinement in both breadth and depth. Even the authors of the taxonomy admit that they are far from being totally satisfied with the result of their labors. Nonetheless, the usefulness of the taxonomy should in no way be minimized, since at long last religious educators and curriculum builders have at their disposal a workable tool for significantly enhancing the facilitation of affective content.

SOME PRACTICAL CONSEQUENCES

Without a doubt, affective content is one of the most radiant jewels in the regal diadem of the substantive content of religious instruction. If the religious educator is to effectively teach affective content, then such a person perforce must be familiar with the nature and various forms of affective content. Furthermore, such a person must be skilled in the pedagogical procedures involved in successfully teaching affective content.

Because affective outcomes are so many and varied, different pedagogical procedures are necessary in order to facilitate the acquisition of different kinds of affective content. In this final section of the chapter I will very briefly deal with some practical consequences involved in teaching a representative affective content, namely attitudes.

So often in the past religious educators in all settings and curriculum builders in formal settings have failed to devise adequate pedagogical practices for teaching attitudes because of two basic misunderstandings. *First,* they lacked the basic scientific understanding concerning the nature, characteristics, and formation of attitudes. Their comprehension of attitudes was typically based on well-meaning hunches, guesses, or plain probes in the dark rather than on the theories and data which the social sciences have devised and discovered. *Second,* these teachers labored under the erroneous impression that attitudes are incapable of being taught directly. "Attitudes are caught, not taught" was, and still is, a distressingly frequent cliché voiced by many religious educators in an effort to gloss over their failure to teach — or even attempt to teach — desired attitudes. Yet as the research evidence has overwhelmingly indicated, an attitude is learned; it is not innate.[225] Furthermore, even though attitudes are not momentarily transient, they are susceptible to change — and it is the religion teacher's task to facilitate that change.[226] The remainder of this section will treat of the dynamics of attitude change and one pedagogical practice designed to foster attitude learning and change.

What are the conditions correlated to attitude change? Following the molar pedagogical model for the teaching act which I develop in *The Flow of Religious Instruction,*[227] the conditions bearing upon attitude change can be grouped into four major categories: the teacher/teaching category, the learner/learning category, the environment category, and the subject-matter content category. Usually the conditions of attitude change are treated by social-science authors in simple, unitary fashion.[228] The advantage of the Lee model is that it not only groups unitary conditions into the overall class to which they belong, but it also performs this task in a way consistent with a teaching model. The signal benefits of this categorization for the workaday religion teacher and curriculum builder are obvious.

The first of the Lee categories correlated to attitude change is that of teaching/teaching. I shall first deal with teacher factors and follow this by teaching factors.

There are at least four principal teacher-related conditions correlated with the facilitation of attitude change, namely, credibility, attractiveness, power, and the teacher's own attitudes. The perceived *credibility* of the facilitator or other source has been shown to enhance the probability of desired attitude change, but in a selective, not in any across-the-board fashion. Thus the relevant empirical research indicates that the facilitator's perceived high credibility does indeed bring about the desired attitude change but does not bring about any noticeable increase or modification in the cognitive content of the particular attitude which has been changed.[229] This interesting finding reveals in yet another way that attitude is basically affective in structure. The *attractiveness* of the facilitator or other source appears to be positively correlated with attitude change in the desired direction. Attractiveness in this case includes at least three ingredients, namely similarity, familiarity, and liking. There are considerable empirical data that the more the individual perceives that he and the facilitator enjoy a basic similarity in personality characteristics, interests, and so forth, the higher is the probability that attitude modification will take place.[230] Familiarity has been shown to be positively correlated with attitude change; this holds true not only for familiarity with persons but also for familiarity with other forms of stimuli as well.[231] Liking seems definitely correlated with attitude change, so that the more a person likes a person or object, the more will that individual's attitude be amenable to change.[232] The *power* which the teacher or other source has over the individual exerts an effect on attitude change. The research indicates that overt compliance brought about by the facilitator's power tends under most conditions to eventuate in relatively significant, internalized attitude change.[233] In general, the more the facilitator administers positive or negative sanctions, the more the facilitator cares whether the individual conforms or not, and the more the facilitator is in a position to observe whether the individual has demonstrated attitudinal compliance — the greater is the facilitator's power and the greater is his potential for bringing about desired attitude change. But this power does not exist in a vacuum. Rather, power is a variable which both changes and is changed by the concrete situation in which it is enacted.[234] The *teacher's own attitudes* have been shown over and over again in the research literature to exert a marked influence on forming and changing the attitudes of learners. Stronger teacher attitudes toward the learner tend to be more potent in modifying the learner's attitudes than weaker teacher attitudes. This holds true for both positive and negative teacher attitudes.[235]

There are at least two principal teaching-related conditions correlated with the facilitation of attitude change, namely immediacy of experience and mode of teaching. *Immediate and direct experiences* are more conducive to facilitating the formation and change of attitudes than remote or indirect encounters with a stimulus.[236] Quite probably the reason for the power of immediate and direct experience as contrasted with remote and indirect experience comes from the fact that immediate and direct experience involves more aspects of the individual's total personality than does remote and indirect experience. The *mode of teaching* employed is significantly correlated to attitude change. For example, the research indicates that the discussion technique is superior to the lecture in bringing about attitude change; however, both methods are equally effective as to the extent of cognitive learning produced.[236] The empirical data generally indicate that attitudes are modified more by the spoken word than by the written word, though written communications yield greater cognitive retention and comprehension.[237] Face-to-face encounters with significant others tend to be more potent in modifying attitudes than are mass-media communications.[238] In short, the way a teacher teaches — the general and specific instructional practices he deploys — has a definite and marked effect on bringing about the desired attitude change.

The second of the Lee categories correlated with attitude change revolves around the learner. As in the case of the teacher category, the learner category can be divided for the sake of analysis into two parts, namely what the learner is and what the learner does.

What the learner is as a person — in other words, personality factors — bears a marked correlation with attitude change. *Age,* both chronological and psychological,[239] is intimately related to attitude change. One review of the relevant research concludes that the older a person becomes, the more conservative and resistant to change his attitudes become.[240] The learner's *gender* has been repeatedly shown to enjoy a definite correlation with attitude change. The data suggest that boys hold less favorable attitudes toward school[241] and reject their teachers more[242] than do girls. Females generally seem to be more susceptible to influences leading to attitude change; however, there is disagreement among social-science theorists as to why this is so.[243] *Physical appearance* seems to be correlated with attitude formation and change. Psychologists frequently speak of the "little man syndrome" to indicate that a noticeable number of shorter men hold attitudes which are more aggressive, more vain, and more rooted in insecurity than those of average-sized males.[244] One experimental study showed that a physically attractive girl tends to be more successful in deliberatively persuading an audience than is a physically unattractive female.[245] An individual's *self-esteem* seems to be more likely to produce attitude change when the stimulus is multidimensional and complex than when it is unidimensional and simple.[246] Attitudes which are deeply *ego-imbedded* are far less amenable to change than those which are not directly enmeshed in the more central aspects of the self.[247] The texture and strength of the learner's *needs* appear to play a significant role in advancing or retarding attitude change. *Socioeconomic status* is positively correlated with the formation and change of attitudes. For example, the research evidence suggests that learners who live in upper socioeconomic areas tend to hold more positive attitudes toward authority figures and authority institutions than do their counterparts from lower socioeconomic milieux.[248]

In general, the real or perceived effects of the learner's conduct will tend to reinforce in his self-system the attitude to which the conduct is related, or to diminsh the attitude's potency to such an extent as to render a change in his attitude more probable. If a particular pattern of conduct leads to success, achievement, or fulfillment, then a person will be likely to retain or to acquire a favorable attitude toward these actions and the milieux in which they are situated. Thus, for example, the research suggests that if a learner achieves well in a formal instructional setting, then he will tend to have favorable attitudes toward that setting, and vice versa.[249]

The third of the major Lee categories correlated with attitude change deals with the subject-matter content of the attitude. It stands to reason that it is impossible to form or change an attitude without supplying additional or revisional stimuli. For example, studies of primary and secondary textbooks used in schools in the 1950s and 1960s failed to depict the position and role of minority groups and women in the way in which contemporary civil rights leaders and feminists believe is just and fair.[250] Small wonder, then, that the attitudes of white students toward minority groups and the attitudes of males toward females tended to be what they were. It should be underscored, however, that the content of a stimulus is not coextensive with cognitive content. The cognitive content of a stimulus devoid of congruent affective content, process content, and so forth, is not very potent in bringing about attitude change. Thus one review of the research on prejudice concludes that the acquisition of more cognitive content tends to result in a lessening of prejudice but not to any great extent.[251] To be sure, the affective content of a stimulus (such as, for example, its pleasantness, its resonance with the learner's ego-defensive functions, and so forth) appears to be correlated with attitude change. Verbal content also seems to have a bearing on attitude change. Thus one investigation discovered that speeches heavy in satirical words and phrases are singularly unsuccessful in producing attitude change in the general mass of population.[252] This might well be due to the affective texture of satire, including its threat-producing aspects. The available empirical evidence suggests that metaphors produce significantly more attitude change than do straightforward, literal words and phrases.[253] In general, a person's attitude toward a stimulus object is more vulnerable to change when that individual's existing mass of stored content (cognitive, affective, product, and so on) is small.[254] For example, the research suggests that the effects of one-sided versus two-sided communication in changing attitudes varies with the individual's original attitudes and level of knowledge. One-sided communications (that is, arguments solely in favor of the content of the "message") appear to be more effective than two-sided communications if the learner's attitude, beliefs, or opinions are already in accord with the content, or if a previous information about the content is lacking.[255]

The fourth and final of the major Lee categories correlated with attitude change is environment. (In *The Flow of Religious Instruction* I define environment as "that aggregate of external physical, biological, cultural, and social conditions or stimuli to which an individual consciously or unconsciously responds.")[256] In the same volume I review the relevant empirical research literature, the conclusion of which is that the particular environment in which an individual develops, matures, and interacts exerts an extraordinarily powerful influence on his learning, including the learning and alteration of attitudes.[257] Environmental settings are crucial to attitude development and change: contrast, for example, the potency of a family setting, a peer-group setting, a hostile-group setting, and an institutional setting to alter one's attitudes. The social environment has also been shown to constitute a critically important variable in facilitating or hindering attitude change. Learning milieux characterized by an atmosphere of intensive indoctrination or by pressure to conform, especially when these environmental factors are linked to the learner's needs for achievement and affiliation, have been shown by the research to have a marked effect on attitude change.[258] The socioemotional climate of the learning environment, regardless of whether this environment is a formal one[259] or an informal one,[260] plays a significant role in forming and reforming attitudes. Most societies, cultures, and organizations which in the past have proved successful in modifying attitudes have paid a great deal of attention to the learning environment. Religious educators could profit from this example.

In concluding this treatment of attitude change I would like to emphasize one point of capital importance: attitude change comes about neither automatically nor simply.[261] Rather, the religion teacher must consciously and deliberatively work for it by structuring the pedagogical situation in a way that will enhance the probability that the desired attitudinal change will take place.[262] Operationalizing any one or more of the pedagogical and learning principles or findings which I have mentioned in no way automatically insures that attitude change will thereby result. For example, I offered data to indicate that personal contact and direct experience tend to be positively correlated with attitude change. Yet other data show that personal contact or other kinds of direct experience with ethnic minorities do not automatically increase or reduce tensions; they can do either or neither.[263] What is important in facilitating desired attitude change, then, is that the religion teacher weave the variables of personal contact and direct experience into a total pedagogical fabric which also contains other goal-directed instructional variables known to correlate with facilitating a particular kind of attitude change in a particular situation. Attitude change is not the result of any one of the many variables reviewed in this section; rather, it is the consequence of a series of interacting conditional variables and behavioral events. To successfully change a learner's attitudes is no easy matter; it requires, as does all pedagogy, that the teacher be a practicing social scientist.

The pedagogical technique of role playing holds considerable promise in terms of forming and changing a learner's attitudes. Before briefly treating role playing, I must reiterate in slightly different form that which I noted in the previous paragraph, namely that role playing or any other teaching technique in and of itself is not effective in forming or changing attitudes. If role playing or any other pedagogical procedure is to yield the desired learning outcomes, then it must be enacted in such a manner that it is actively congruent with and adequately reinforced by each of the four major pedagogical variables necessarily involved in the teaching-learning dynamic.

One of the teaching techniques mentioned most frequently in connection with attitude change is role playing.[264] Role playing is an unrehearsed dramatization of a problem in which a group of learners, without scripts, extemporaneously portray how they would act in a given situation. By its nature, role playing does not stress attitudes toward a general class of persons or objects; rather, it emphasizes these attitudes precisely in so far as they relate to the particular individual or stimulus the role player is dealing with in the simulation experience. In role playing the individual takes the other's role as the other himself experiences it — not a generalized other but this very other.[265] (Consequently, the religious educator would do well to structure the role-playing situation and its follow-up in such a way as to enable the learner to generalize his present and newly altered attitudes.)[266]

The explanatory and predictive power of role playing flows from its place in role theory.[267] Role theory, as its name implies, is concerned with roles, namely those kinds of patterned behaviors which are characteristic of and expected from persons within contexts.[268] When persons interact in a social milieu, they interact not solely as a self but as a self-in-role. In order to be a social being, then, a person must necessarily take on various kinds of roles. Social relations, then, consist in the reciprocal interplay among persons in social roles. In one milieu an individual has one role, in a second milieu a second role, and so forth. Role taking and role enactment are virtually indispensable for social action, since groups can only exist if their members behave in somewhat predictable ways — ways more-or-less defined and circumscribed by their roles.[269] Roles which persons necessarily play in varying social situations make human relationships possible and rewarding because roles entail two major clusters of behaviors on the part of both the self-in-role and the other person(s). First, every role is endowed with a set of norms which the person in a role is required by himself and by others to fulfill. Second, every role is endowed with a set of expectancies which the person in a role and others believe he will fulfill. For example, a person occupying the role of a religious educator is expected to behave knowledgeably in the religious domain of life. Every person, then, plays many roles in everyday life. The teaching technique of role playing is a pedagogical procedure through which the learner's self contacts his own self and another's self by existentially placing his own self into the roled self of another person. It is precisely this kind of realistic yet highly personalistic contact with the self of another person, a self which is necessarily a roled self, that enables role playing to be a potentially powerful technique for attitude change.[270]

Attitudes are among the most pervasive, most powerful, and most internalized of a person's entire self-system. In order to touch one's attitudes at all, and in order to touch one's attitudes deeply enough to reinforce or alter these attitudes, it is necessary to become existentially enmeshed in one's self-system. Because the self is a social self, because the self is so deeply intertwined in the roles which the self necessarily plays, it stands to reason that any pedagogical device which deals entirely with self-in-role will necessarily deal deeply with the self and with the attitudes held by the self. The self is developed and continuously reevaluated by the role(s) which the self plays in ordinary life; furthermore, the way in which an individual interacts with others is heavily influenced by the role in which the individual finds himself at a given moment.

In terms of role theory, the pedagogical technique of role playing calls for a learner to step out of his own self and to immerse himself into the self of another person.[271] This transfer of selves is accomplished by stepping out of one's own role and plunging into the role of another person.

Role playing can improve interpersonal relations among learners. It can enhance or change an individual's self-concept.[273] Role playing enables an individual to feel, perceive, and behave toward the world as other persons feel, perceive, and behave toward the world. In role playing, values are examined, defended, and sometimes even changed — all in a concrete existential situation in which affective content is on center stage. Role playing provides valuable feedback to an individual on his own attitudes, and how his attitudes affect other persons.

Role playing can improve interpersonal relations among learners. It can enhance or change an individual's self-concept.[273] Role playing enables an individual to feel, perceive, and behave toward the world as other persons feel, perceive, and behave toward the world. In role playing, values are examined, defended, and sometimes even changed — all in a concrete existential situation in which affective content is on center stage. Role playing provides valuable feedback to an individual on his own attitudes, and how his attitudes affect other persons.

There are two major forms of role playing currently in use, namely, procedure-centered role playing and developmental role playing. Procedure-centered role playing is higher in specific structure than developmental role playing. Procedure-centered role playing places emphasis on desired skills to be acquired, while developmental role playing features attitudes as the central ingredient. Procedure-centered role playing is generally not as useful for attitude learning as is developmental role playing.[274]

The empirical research evidence suggests that role playing can be an effective pedagogical procedure for inducing attitude learning.[275] One reason for this appears to be the fact that teaching procedures which require learners to engage in concrete overt behaviors or activities tend to yield much more attitude change than those procedures which are rooted simply in abstracted comprehension or feeling. Role playing takes place in a concrete situation and involves overt behaviors — two conditions in which an individual's deeper attitudes are manifested and hence more available for alteration.[276] The studies indicate that role playing tends to be successful when the player finds his role rewarded or rewarding, when he gains some new insight regarding the attitude object, and when he so fully invests himself with a particular role that he becomes that role.[277] Pedagogical steps which reinforce the learner tend to be effective in modifying attitudes; such reinforcers include praise, social or symbolic rewards, acceptance of feeling, and so forth.[278] It should be noted, however, that the research suggests that role playing is not always effective in producing attitude change.[279] Therefore, the religious educator should not be dismayed when role playing does not always work in facilitating attitudinal learning.

How can religious educators learn and improve skills involved in the role playing technique? Guided work in the teacher performance center is one of the best ways a religious educator can learn and improve this kind of pedagogical skill. In the previous chapter, I indicated that a teacher performance center is a laboratory setting which provides the religious educator with the facilities and the opportunities for actually practicing a particular pedagogical skill, for assessing the degree of his effectiveness in deploying that skill, and for examining the theoretical bases and extensions of that skill in order that he can thus optimize the wider application of that skill.

In addition to using microteaching situations to improve his pedagogical skills in conducting role playing sessions, the religious educator might well wish to avail himself of protocol materials on role playing. Protocol materials are records of pedagogical events of instructional significance which illustrate those broader educational laws and theory which underlie the pedagogical event. The records may be written, audio-recorded, video-recorded, or even filmed. The basic principle upon which the validity and utility of protocol materials hangs is that a teacher can only be successful when he consciously grounds his pedagogical practice in relevant educational laws and theory. As one major document which advocates the development of protocol materials puts it, "teachers fail because they have not been trained calmly to analyze new [instructional] situations against a firm background of relevant theory. Typically, they base their interpretations of behavior on intuition or common sense."[280]

The available empirical research evidence suggests that well-prepared protocol materials can significantly enhance a teacher's ability to relate what occurs in a pedagogical event with the relevant educational laws and theory which underlie such an event.[281]

An effective set of protocol materials is one which focuses on all four major variables in the teaching-learning dynamic, namely the learner, the teacher, the subject-matter content, and the environment. Thus a protocol material is defective if it centers simply on teacher behavior.[282] Furthermore, a protocol material should center primarily on the relevant laws and theory underlying a teaching procedure or event, rather than focus chiefly on developing competence in a particular pedagogical skill. It seems reasonable that all diocesan and local religious education offices which are serious about religious instruction should have in place protocol materials for various teaching procedures like role playing. These protocol materials should be genuine protocol materials, and not simply little outlines or a short list of pedagogical steps to take when teaching role playing.[283]

CONCLUSION

Affective content is one of the key substantive contents in the work of religious instruction. In whatever setting it may be enacted, religion teaching will be lacking in human and divine qualities to the extent to which it is deficient in affective content. If such a great emphasis is placed on power and politics in contemporary civil and religious society, then it is small wonder that both state and church are so unfeeling and unloving. The path to humanity and to divinity lies not through power or politics or cognition, but through affect and value and love. Thus it behooves the religious educator to center a good deal of his attention on the affective content of religious instruction.

NOTES

1. François Mauriac, *Le Désert de L'Amour* (Paris: Grasset, 1925), p. 75, translation mine.
2. George Isaac Brown, *Human Teaching for Human Learning* (New York: Viking, 1971), p. 4.
3. As I shall indicate later in this chapter, feelings are a particular variety of affective content as contrasted to other types, notably emotion. Feeling (as contrasted to feelings) is the term usually taken to be somewhat synonymous with affect.
4. See William C. Schutz, *Joy: Expanding Human Awareness* (New York: Grove, 1967), pp. 25–26.
5. Iris V. Cully, *Change, Conflict, and Self-Determination* (Philadelphia: Westminster, 1972), p. 131.
6. See Walter H. Clark, "Intense Religious Experience," in Merton P. Strommen, editor, *Research on Religious Development* (New York: Hawthorn, 1971), pp. 531–534.
7. For a representative example of this mentality, see Catherine M. Gannon, "Hallowing," in *Religious Education* LXXV (July-August, 1980), p. 435. Curiously enough, Gannon in one sentence declares that reverence, consecration, faith, and a sense of the sacred can only be caught and cannot be taught, while in the next four sentences she gives specific instructions on how to teach in such a way that the above-mentioned contents can be effectively taught.
8. These variables are, of course, the teacher, the learner, the subject-matter content, and the environment.
9. For a more extensive treatment of the nature of teaching, see James Michael Lee, *The Flow of Religious Instruction* (Birmingham, Ala.: Religious Education Press, 1973), pp. 206–268.
10. In nearly every issue, the major psychology journals carry articles reporting empirical research investigations on the deliberative facilitation of divers sorts of affective content. See, for example, *Journal of Transpersonal Psychology, Journal of Humanistic Psychology, Journal of Applied Behavioral Analysis, Journal of Applied Psychology, Journal of Personality,* and *Journal of Consulting and Clinical Psychology.* .
11. There has been for many years now, a movement afoot to regard counseling as essentially a means to help the client self-actualize rather than solely a means of assisting persons with problems. However, this movement has not been very successful for a wide variety of reasons. For an advocacy of the goal of counsel-

ing as self-actualization, see James Michael Lee and Nathaniel J. Pallone, *Guidance and Counseling in Schools: Foundations and Processes* (New York: McGraw-Hill, 1966), pp. 244–245.

12. On this last point, see James Hillman, *Insearch: Psychology and Religion* (New York: Scribner's, 1967), p. 15.

13. Some biblical commentators like Bruce Vawter seem to suggest that the love of which John is here speaking is "not the love that is natural to man, but [that which] has been revealed by God and is perceived by faith." However, the biblical passage itself simply mentions love, with no textual or immediate contextual implication of one particular kind of love, namely, love specially given by God or love directed specifically toward God. I would agree with Vawter *if* the Vincentian scholar conceives revelation and faith in an expansive, immanentistic, general-revelation sense as well as in a more restricted sense. See Bruce Vawter, "The Johannine Epistles," in Raymond E. Brown, Joseph A. Fitzmyer, and Roland E. Murphy, editors, *The Jerome Biblical Commentary*, volume II (Englewood Cliffs, N.J.: Prentice-Hall, 1968), p. 410.

14. On this point, see William C. Schutz, *Here Comes Everybody* (New York: Harper & Row, 1971), p. 221.

15. I am restricting my comments solely to the aspect of the "cognitive-in-the-affective" since the scope of this chapter is limited to affective content.

16. On this last point, see Justin Aronfreed, "Comments," in C. M. Beck, B. S. Crittenden, and E. V. Sullivan, editors, *Moral Education: Interdisciplinary Approaches* (Toronto: University of Toronto Press, 1971), pp. 391, 393.

17. See David P. Ausubel, "Psychology's Undervaluation of the Rational Components in Moral Behavior," in *ibid,.* pp. 200–227; also Lawrence Kohlberg, "Comment," in *ibid.*, p. 392.

18. On this point, see Lucie W. Barber, "The Dichotomies of Thinking and Feeling," in *Religious Education* LXXVI (September-October, 1981), pp. 497–504.

19. In a contribution of great importance to religious educators, Robert Zajonc states that affect is more primary than cognitive in that a person's affective response to a stimulus preceeds that individual's cognitive response to that same stimulus. Zajonc also makes other insightful statements about the relation of cognition to affect. R. B. Zajonc, "Feeling and Thinking: Preferences Need No Inferences," in *American Psychologist* XXXV (February, 1980), pp. 151–175.

20. This coupling occurs not only with complex higher order cognitive behaviors such as intellectual synthesis but also for relatively simple, lower-order cognitive behaviors like memory. On this latter point, see the experimental studies recorded and discussed in Satrajit Dutta and Rabindra Nath Kanungo, *Affect and Memory: A Reformulation* (Oxford, England: Pergamon, 1975).

21. George Isaac Brown, *Human Teaching for Human Learning*, p. 11.

22. Berard L. Marthaler, *Catechetics in Context* (Huntington, Ind.: Our Sunday Visitor Press, 1973), pp. 121, 123. Marthaler's observation would have been significantly strengthened if he had cited some relevant empirical research findings to buttress his empirically derived statement.

23. There is a sense in which cognitive content is geared to reality as object while affective content is geared to reality as subject. See Paul Tournier, *The Gift of Feeling*, translated by Edwin Hudson (Atlanta, Ga.: Knox, 1979), pp. 8–15.

24. Robert W. Lynn and Elliott Wright, *The Big Little School*, 2d edition, revised and enlarged (Birmingham, Ala.: Religious Education Press, 1980), pp. 76–78.

25. Gabriel Moran, "Adolescents and Today's Crisis of Faith." in J. T. Dillon, editor, *Catechetics Reconsidered* (Winona, Minn.: St. Mary's College Press, 1968), p. 132.
26. Eli M. Bower, "Mental Health," in Robert L. Ebel, editor, *Encyclopedia of Educational Research*, 4th ed. (New York: Macmillan, 1969), p. 814.
27. Ross Snyder, "Toward Foundations of a Discipline of Religious Education," in *Religious Education* LXII (September-October, 1967), p. 401.
28. Emil Brunner, *The Christian Doctrine of God: Dogmatics*, volume I, translated by Olive Wyon (Philadelphia: Westminster, 1950), p. 191.
29. Alfred North Whitehead, *Process and Reality* (New York: Macmillan, 1929), pp. 519–521.
30. Daniel Day Williams, *The Spirit and the Forms of Love* (New York: Harper & Row, 1968), p. 131.
31. Arthur Clutton-Brock, quoted in Jacques Maritain, *Education at the Crossroads* (New Haven, Conn.: Yale University Press, 1943), pp. 23–24.
32. René A. Spitz, "Hospitalism," in *The Psychoanalytic Study of the Child*, volume I (New York: International Universities Press, 1945), pp. 53–74.
33. Sandor Ferenczi, quoted in Theodor Reik, *The Need to Be Loved* (New York: Farrar, Straus, 1963), p. 22.
34. *Ibid.*
35. Sacra Congregatio pro Clericis, *Directorium catechisticum generale* (Città del Vaticano: Libreria Editrice Vaticana, 1971), p. 60 (#64).
36. Berard L. Marthaler, *Catechetics in Context*, p. 125.
37. See, for example, The Higher Institute of Catechetics of Nijmegen, *Fundamentals and Programs of a New Catechesis*, revised by Henry J. Koren, translated by Walter Van De Putte (Pittsburgh, Pa.: Duquesne University Press, 1966), p. 101.
38. Michael Pfliegler, *The Right Moment*, translated by M. Veronica Riedl (Notre Dame, Ind.: University of Notre Dame Press, 1966), p. 66.
39. On this point, see Arthur T. Jersild and Kenneth Helfant, *Education for Self-Understanding* (New York: Bureau of Publications, Teachers College Columbia University, 1953), p. 9.
40. See, for example, Carl R. Rogers, *Freedom to Learn* (Columbus, Ohio: Merrill, 1969), p. 250.
41. More globally, Van Driessche found that in general, affective "psychological" forces tended to be a more powerful stimulus to the adolescent's conduct vis-à-vis the Sacrament of Penance than cognitive "religious" forces. Georges Van Driessche, "Confession and Adolescents," in *Lumen Vitae* XXII (September, 1967), pp. 503–528.
42. This close, interactive relationship between affect and religion explains why Carl Jung could claim that serious psychological/affective aberrations could not be successfully resolved until the person came to a religious attitude toward life. C. G. Jung, *Zur Psychologie westlicher und östlicher Religion*, Band XI, in *Gesammelte Werke* (Zürich: Rascher, 1963), p. 362 (#509), and p. 369 (#523).
43. For a leading contemporary tractarian's plea for the inclusion of affective content in the work of religious instruction, see John H. Westerhoff III, "What Has Zion To Do with Bohemia?" *Religious Education* LXXVI (January-February, 1981), pp. 5–15.
44. Rollo May, *Love and Will* (New York: Norton, 1969), pp. 27–30.

45. Dutch religious educationists, for example, testify that this holds true in their country. The Higher Institute of Catechetics of Nijmegen, *Fundamentals and Programs of a New Catechesis,* p. 269.
46. Examples of this point are as notorious as they are numerous. For example, not a single one of Richard McBrien's "basic questions for religious educators" deals with affect. (Indeed, none of them even deals directly with religion; all of them deal cognitively with theological issues.) McBrien is a theologian with a sometime interest in religious instruction. See Richard P. McBrien, *Basic Questions for Religious Educators* (Winona, Minn.: St. Mary's College Press, 1977).
47. Gregory Baum, *Man Becoming* (New York: Herder and Herder, 1970), p. xii.
48. E. Schillebeeckx, *Revelation and Theology,* volume I, translated by N. D. Smith (New York: Sheed and Ward, 1967), pp. 102–103, 252.
49. In one study of life in American communes the researchers found that the emphasis in these counterculture settings was exclusively on the affective domain. Communal parents wanted an affective well-being for their children. For example, children were free to learn cognitive material or not to learn it; most children chose not to learn it. Susan Wolf and John Rothchild, *The Children of the Counterculture* (New York: Doubleday, 1976), pp. 204–207.
50. Peter A. Bertocci, "Psychological Interpretations of Religious Experience," in Merton P. Strommen, editor, *Research on Religious Development,* p. 30.
51. See, for example, Josef Goldbrunner, *Realization: The Anthropology of Pastoral Care,* translated by Paul C. Bailey and Elisabeth Reinecke (Notre Dame, Ind.: University of Notre Dame Press, 1966), p. 174. Goldbrunner, a Jungian pastoral psychotherapist, at one time turned some of his professional attention to religious instruction.
52. See James Hillman, *Insearch: Psychology and Religion,* pp. 95–126.
53. In sharply setting off feelings as functions from feelings as contents, James Hillman seems thereby to suggest that functions are not contents. Hillman claims to be interpreting Carl Jung in this regard. I strongly disagree with the Hillman-Jung position. As I indicate in my chapter on process content, functions or processes are contents in their own right. The implication that process is not a content is completely unwarranted and has resulted in seriously hampering the progress of an integral, optimum facilitational practice in many fields. See James Hillman, "C. G. Jung's Contributions to 'Feelings and Emotions': Synopsis and Implications," in Magda B. Arnold, editor, *Feelings and Emotions* (New York: Academic Press, 1970), pp. 128–129.
54. On this point, see K. T. Strongman, *The Psychology of Emotion* (New York: Wiley, 1973), pp. 6–7.
55. See Ernest Harms, "A Differential Concept of Feelings and Emotions," in Martin L. Reymert, editor, *Feelings and Emotions* (New York: McGraw-Hill, 1950), p. 156.
56. Magda Arnold, for example, seems to equate — or confuse — feelings and feeling in a way that is not altogether clear. See Magda B. Arnold, *Emotion and Personality,* volume I: *Psychological Aspects* (New York: Columbia University Press, 1960), pp. 19–21.
57. For a good overview of the complex and integrated activity between psychology and physiology in the dynamic fabric of emotion, see William W. Grings and Michael E. Dawson, *Emotions and Bodily Response: A Psychophysiological Approach* (New York: Academic Press, 1978).

58. On this point, see K. T. Strongman, *The Psychology of Emotions*, pp. 36–65.
59. Paul Thomas Young, *Emotion in Man and Animal*, 2d edition (Huntington, N.Y.: Krieger, 1973), pp. 37–39.
60. On this point, see Ira J. Gordon, "Social and Emotional Development," in Robert L. Ebel, editor, *Encyclopedia of Educational Research*, 4th ed., p. 1222; Paul Thomas Young, "Emotion," in David L. Sills, editor, *International Encyclopedia of the Social Sciences*, volume V (New York: Macmillan and Free Press, 1968), p. 35; D. O. Hebb, *The Organization of Behavior: A Neuropsychological Theory* (New York: Wiley, 1949), p. 147.
61. James Hillman, *Emotion* (London: Routledge & Kegan Paul, 1960), pp. 87–89.
62. Paul Thomas Young, *Emotion in Man and Animal*, 2d ed., p. 20.
63. Joel R. Davitz, *The Language of Emotion* (New York: Academic Press, 1969).
64. For a fine overview of the empirical research on emotions commonly labeled joy, surprise, anguish, anger, depression, fear, and so on, see Carroll E. Izard, *Human Emotions* (New York: Plenum, 1977), pp. 239–452.
65. Robert Plutchik, "Emotions, Evolution, and Adaptive Processes," in Magda B. Arnold, editor, *Feelings and Emotions*, p. 11; Robert Plutchik, *The Emotions* (New York: Random House, 1962), pp. 108–125.
66. Carney Landis, "Studies of Emotional Reactions: 2: General Behavior and Facial Expression," in *Journal of Comparative Psychology* IV (October, 1924), pp. 447–501.
67. Jean-Paul Sartre, the Existentialist philosopher, contends that emotion is an authentic content of life because emotion is one of the major ways a person seeks to transform the world — an individual's attempt to so change the world that he can thereby deal with it effectively in a way that was previously inaccessible to him. See Jean-Paul Sartre, *Sketch for a Theory of Emotions*, translated by Philip Mairet (London: Methuen, 1962), pp. 56–91.
68. Every attitude appears to have cognitive, motivational, and affective components working together in concert. These components have not yet been satisfactorily teased apart empirically or classified in a functionally hierarchical order of importance largely because of their pervasive and influential character. Some definitions make attitude primarily a cognitive function subsuming but still preserving affective and motivational components. Other definitions suggest that attitude is primarily a motivational operation on the one hand and an affective process on the other hand. However, research tends to confirm the conclusion drawn by Martin Fishbein and Icek Ajzen whose own review of the pertinent studies concludes that "evidence for the convergent validity of standard attitude scales and *other affective measures* continues to accumulate." For this as well as for other reasons of a more theoretical cast, I believe it is relatively safe to assert that attitude is basically an affective process, one which possesses motivational qualities and which organizes and inflames cognitive content. See Martin Fishbein and Icek Ajzen, "Attitudes and Opinions," in Paul H. Mussen and Mark R. Rosenzweig, editors, *Annual Review of Psychology*, volume XXII (Palo Alto, Cal.: Annual Reviews, 1972), p. 494, italics added.
69. This definition represents a greater elaboration and refinement of the one I give in *The Flow of Religious Instruction* (p. 106). Both definitions state basically the same thing.
70. For example, in the *Second Handbook of Research on Teaching*, the discussion of attitudes is placed in the chapter on affectivity. See S. B. Khan and Joel

Weiss, "The Teaching of Affective Responses," in Robert M. W. Travers, editor, *Second Handbook of Research on Teaching* (Chicago: Rand McNally 1973), pp. 760–761.

71. A review of some pertinent research studies concludes that an attitude has been found to be capable of influencing cognitions as well as being influenced by cognitions. However, this review of the research is careful to avoid the claim that cognition by itself, unaccompanied by affect or other noncognitive variables, directly and solely causes attitude formation or change. Of importance to my discussion of attitude as an affective content is the assertion made by these reviewers that attitudes and cognitive responses are quite different. These reviewers go on to state that "cognitive responses are the specific products of information-processing activity that occurs at a particular moment in time, whereas an attitude represents a favorable or unfavorable feeling about an object or issue." John T. Cacioppo, Stephen G. Harkins, and Richard E. Petty, "The Nature of Attitudes and Cognitive Responses and Their Relationships to Behavior," in Richard E. Petty, Thomas M. Ostrom, and Timothy C. Brock, editors, *Cognitive Responses in Persuasion* (Hillsdale, N.J.: Erlbaum, 1981), pp. 48–49.

72. For example, the relevant empirical research suggests that persons tend to make significantly less reliable and less objective cognitive judgments about stimuli which are highly related (either positively or negatively) to their established attitudes than about stimuli which are not objects of their embedded attitudes. See Muzafer Sherif and Carolyn W. Sherif, *Social Psychology*, 3rd edition (New York: Ronald, 1969), pp. 337–354.

73. There is a major sense in which religious conversion can be regarded as a change in basic attitude, a change in the way in which an individual organizes his psychological processes. For an in-depth examination of conversion from this perspective, see V. Bailey Gillespie, *Religious Conversion and Personal Identity* (Birmingham, Ala.: Religious Education Press, 1979).

74. S. Stansfeld Sargent and Robert C. Williamson, *Social Psychology*, 3rd edition (New York: Ronald, 1966), p. 244, italics deleted.

75. Gordon W. Allport, "Attitudes," in Carl A. Murchison, editor, *A Handbook of Social Psychology* (Worcester, Mass.: Clark University Press, 1935), p. 806.

76. James Michael Lee, *The Flow of Religious Instruction*, pp. 107–108.

77. The potency of attitudes in this regard is modified by the degree to which other psychological and situational factors are simultaneously operating. Such factors include the person's interest, attention, belief system, proximity to significant or prestigious others, economic or bodily needs, and so forth.

78. A major task of authentic instruction is to empower the learner to be aware of his attitudes and to use his other psychological processes in an attempt to allow the objective facts to remain as objective as is humanly possible.

79. For a helpful series of analyses of the relationship between attitudes and conduct, with a recurring emphasis on the theoretical foundations of the attitude-conduct relationship, see Donald P. Cushman and Robert D. McPhee, editors, *Message—Attitude—Behavior Relationship* (New York: Academic Press, 1980).

80. Robert B. Cialdini, Richard E. Petty, and John T. Cacioppo, "Attitude and Attitude Change," in Mark R. Rosenzweig and Lyman W. Porter, editors, *Annual Review of Psychology*, volume 32 (Palo Alto, Calif.: Annual Reviews, 1981), p. 366.

AFFECTIVE CONTENT 263

81. For a review and discussion of the pertinent empirical research, see James Michael Lee, *The Flow of Religious Instruction*, pp. 108–111.
82. Milton Rokeach, *Beliefs, Attitudes, and Values* (San Francisco: Jossey Bass, 1968), p. 113.
83. See, for example, Joseph B. Cooper and James L. McGaugh, *Integrating Principles of Social Psychology* (Cambridge, Mass.: Schenkman, 1963), p. 34.
84. Martin Fishbein and Icek Ajzen, "Attitudes and Opinions," p. 495.
85. For an interesting examination of the relationship between belief and faith, see James W. Fowler, *Stages of Faith* (San Francisco: Harper & Row, 1981), pp. 9–15.
86. See Gordon W. Allport, *The Nature of Prejudice* (Cambridge, Mass.: Addison-Wesley, 1954), pp. 6–15, 68.
87. On this point, see Joseph B. Cooper and James L. McGaugh, *Integrating Principles of Social Psychology*, p. 247.
88. Sigmund Freud, *Civilization and Its Discontents*, translated and edited by James Strachey (New York: Norton, 1962).
89. Daniel Katz, "The Functional Approach to the Study of Attitudes," in *Public Opinion Quarterly* XXIV (Summer, 1960), pp. 163–204.
90. Gordon W. Allport, "Attitudes," pp. 810–812.
91. Empirical studies of prejudiced attitudes among religious people indicate that these prejudices appear to stem from notions of a unique revelation, or special election to membership in a divinely chosen group, or both. See James E. Dittes, "Religion, Prejudice, and Personality," in Merton P. Strommen, editor, *Research on Religious Development* (New York: Hawthorn, 1971), p. 363.
92. The particularly intense experience of Saul on the road to Damascus (Acts 9:1–22) is a case in point.
93. Robert B. Cialdini, Richard E. Petty, and John T. Cacioppo, "Attitude and Attitude Change," pp. 371–372; Alice H. Eagly, "Attitudes and Opinions," in Mark R. Rosenzweig and Lyman Porter, editors, *Annual Review of Psychology*, volume 29 (Palo Alto, Calif.: Annual Reviews, 1978), p. 531.
94. Dennis T. Regan and Russell Fazio, "On the Consistency of Attitudes and Behavior: Look to the Method of Attitude Formation," in *Journal of Experimental Social Psychology* XIII (January, 1977), pp. 28–45; Elaine Songer-Nocks, "Situational Factors Affecting the Weighting of Predictor Components in the Fishbein Model," in *Journal of Experimental Social Psychology* XII (January, 1976), pp. 56–69.
95. In *The Flow of Religious Instruction* (p. 109) I briefly indicate the compatibility of the data showing that deeper attitudes are virtually all formed in early childhood with the evidence suggesting that significant attitudes can be formed or drastically modified in adolescence and young adulthood.
96. Martin Fishbein and Icek Ajzen, "Attitudes and Opinions," pp. 510–513.
97. See Muzafer Sherif and Carolyn W. Sherif, *Reference Groups* (New York: Harper & Row, 1964). I cannot agree with George McCall and J. L. Simmons who claim that reference groups are merely abstract social anchorages. Indeed, reference-group theorists assert that the potency of a reference group is greater than that of a membership group precisely because a reference group involves the individual at a more intimate, personal — and hence more concrete — level than does a membership group. See George J. McCall and J. L. Simmons, *Identities and Interactions* (New York: Free Press, 1966), pp. 7–8.

98. Albert H. Yee, *Factors Involved in Determining the Relationship between Teachers' and Pupils' Attitudes* (Austin, Tex.: University of Texas, 1966); Albert H. Yee, "Source and Direction of Causal Influence in Teacher-Pupil Relationships," in *Journal of Educational Psychology* LIX (August, 1968), pp. 275–282.

99. Erving Goffman, *Asylums* (New York: Doubleday, 1961), p. xiii.

100. William J. McGuire, "The Nature of Attitudes and Attitude Change," in Gardner Lindzey and Elliot Aronson, editors, *Handbook of Social Psychology*, 2d edition, volume III (Reading, Mass.: Addison-Wesley, 1969), p. 167.

101. On this point, see *ibid*, p. 151.

102. Jeffrey Keefe, "The Learning of Attitudes, Values, and Beliefs," in James Michael Lee and Patrick C. Rooney, editors, *Toward a Future for Religious Education* (Dayton, Ohio: Pflaum, 1970), p. 35.

103. Whether the negligible amount of serious and sustained psychological research on values (as compared to the amount of such research on attitudes) is due to the lack of agreement concerning the attitude-value relationship, or whether it is, in fact, the reason accounting for this lack of agreement is an open question. In any event, the main practical consequence of this controversy seems to be that the topic of values does not receive much attention in the textbooks or in other psychological literature; possibly this is due to the relative dearth of psychological research on the value construct.

104. In attempting to accentuate the cognitive component or accompaniment of value, James Shaver and William Strong have unnecessarily belittled the overriding affective nature of value. James P. Shaver and William Strong, *Facing Value Decisions: Rationale-Building for Teachers* (Belmont, Calif.: Wadsworth, 1976), pp. 16–17.

105. James Michael Lee, *Principles and Methods of Secondary Education* (New York: McGraw-Hill, 1963), p. 179.

106. Ralph Barton Perry, in his classic book *Realms of Value*, defines value in terms of interest. For Perry, interest is a paraphrase of "motor-affective attitudes" or "attitudes of favor and disfavor." Ralph Barton Perry, *Realms of Value* (New York: Greenwood, 1968), p. 7.

107. For a critique of such positivistic views, see Solomon E. Asch, *Social Psychology* (Englewood Cliffs, N.J.: Prentice-Hall, 1952), pp. 353–363.

108. I, for one, would like to engage in business transactions involving art with such persons.

109. For what I regard as a lovely holistic integration of various domains of value, see Pitirim A. Sorokin, "Reply to Professor Weisskopf," in Abraham H. Maslow, editor, *New Knowledge in Human Value* (Chicago: Regnery Gateway, 1970), pp. 224–232. Sorokin is a social scientist specializing in the sociology of culture.

110. Charles Morris, *Varieties of Human Value* (Chicago: University of Chicago Press, 1956), pp. 188–190.

111. Charles Morris and Lyle V. Jones, "Value Scales and Dimensions," in *Journal of Abnormal and Social Psychology* LI (November, 1955), pp. 523–535.

112. Gordon W. Allport, Philip E. Vernon, and Gardner Lindzey, *Study of Values*, 3d ed. (Boston: Houghton Mifflin, 1960). See also its forerunner, Philip E. Vernon and Gordon W. Allport, "A Test for Personal Values," in *Journal of Abnormal and Social Psychology* XXVI (October-December, 1931), pp. 231–248.

113. Eduard Spranger, *Lebensformen* (Halle, Deutschland: Niemeyer, 1922).

114. Milton Rokeach, *The Nature of Human Values* (New York: Free Press, 1973), pp. 7–9. In Rokeach's view, the research of Jean Piaget and Lawrence Kohlberg deals with instrumental values, while the research of Abraham Maslow and Allport-Vernon-Lindzey deals with terminal values.

115. This is true whether one holds that values determine attitudes either as being somehow external to attitudes (first school) or as comprising the determinational aspect of the attitude itself (second school).

116. The religious educator should be acutely aware that the religious values of his denomination have been heavily influenced by the Western cultural milieu in which that denomination was born, grew, and currently flourishes. The learner can profit much by being judiciously exposed to non-Western value systems, systems which can fecundate Christianity and daily Christian living. See, for example, Shanti Nath Gupta, *The Indian Concept of Value* (Columbia, Mo.: South Asia Books, 1978).

117. Lawrence K. Frank, "On Loving," in Ashley Montagu, editor, *The Meaning of Love* (New York: Julian, 1953), p. 27.

118. Religious educationists of the superficial sort erroneously claim that I hold that the concrete teaching act is devoid of value because I assert that the social-science approach to relgious instruction is value-free. Such a claim by these religious educationists is patently absurd as even a casual look at the grammar will readily reveal. My assertion is, and has always been, that the social-science *approach* is value-free. An approach is obviously different than the reality which it approaches, namely the teaching act in this case. I have never asserted, nor will research allow me to assert, that the concrete teaching act is value-free. It is well worth noting that if the social-science *approach* were indeed value-laden particularistically, then it would be useless as a macrotheoretical approach. After all, the nature of a macrotheoretical approach is such that it enables this approach to adequately explain, predict, and verify all kinds of diverse teaching acts regardless of the specific values which these acts enflesh.

119. Michael Bargo Jr. has developed a concrete, behavioral pedagogical procedure which endeavors to link here-and-now value decisions with the lifestyle process of valuation. Bargo claims that his procedure is superior to values clarification which, according to Bargo, falls short of effecting a link between the here-and-now and the more far-reaching lifestyle. Michael Bargo, Jr., *Choices and Decisions: A Guidebook for Constructing Values* (San Diego, Calif.: University Associates, 1980).

120. Consciously reflecting a Thomistic perspective, M. D. Chenu writes: "By the mystery of the creative act [of God] we are elevated to the mystery of gratuitous and free love. The identity of Being and of Love, there lies the meaning of the creative genesis. Our being is born of love. The ontological dependency is handed on by the certitude of love." M. D. Chenu, "Body and Body Politic in the Creation Spirituality of Thomas Aquinas," translated by Madeleine Doerfler, in Matthew Fox, editor, *Western Spirituality: Historical Roots, Ecumenical Routes* (Notre Dame, Ind.: Fides/Claretian, 1979), p. 211.

121. For a famous history of viewpoints on love proposed by ancient Greek philosophers, see L. Dugas, *L'Amitié Antique: D'apres les Moeurs Populaires et les Théories des Philosophes* (New York: Arno, 1976).

122. "*Ipsa autem aptitudo sive proportio appetitus ad bonum est amor.*" Thomas Aquinas, *Summa Theologica*, I-II, q. 25, a.1.

123. François de Sales, *Traité de l'amour de Dieu*, I, 7.

124. Every satisfactory definition contains both the genus and the specific difference of the reality being defined.

125. Karl Rahner and Herbert Vorgrimler, *Theological Dictionary*, edited by Cornelius Ernst and translated by Richard Strachan (New York: Herder and Herder, 1965), pp. 265–266.

126. Love, in the psychological literature, "sometimes designates a mood or an emotion." Paul Thomas Young, *Emotion in Man and Animal*, 2d ed., p. 421.

127. Paul Tillich writes, "The emotional element cannot be separated from love; love without emotional quality is 'good will' toward somebody or something, but it is not love. This is also true of man's love of God, which cannot be equated with obedience, which some antimystical theologians teach." Paul Tillich, *Systematic Theology*, volume III (Chicago: University of Chicago Press, 1963), p. 136.

128. Among psychologists, "the term love is used in several senses to mean an attitude or a motive or a state of conflict." Paul Thomas Young, *Emotion in Man and Animal*, 2d ed., p. 421, italics deleted.

129. Rudolf Bultmann, *Jesus and the Word*, translated by Louise Pettibone Smith and Erminie Huntress Lantero (New York: Scribner's, 1934), p. 117. For Bultmann, love is "a definite attitude of the will."

130. Erich Fromm, *The Art of Loving* (New York: Harper, 1956), p. 46, italics deleted.

131. See, for example, Zick Rubin, "Measurement of Romantic Love," in *Journal of Personality and Social Psychology* XVI (October, 1970), pp. 265–273.

132. Lawrence Frank is particularly strong in linking love with interpersonal relationship, though he stops short of totally equating the two. Lawrence K. Frank, "On Loving," pp. 25, 30.

133. See, for example, Robert Johann, *The Meaning of Love* (New York: Paulist Deus, 1966), p. 11.

134. In our own time, Silvano Arieti and James Arieti hold that there are four major strands of, or perhaps more accurately four major interpretations of, love, namely love as biological, love as psychological, love as a cosmic force, and love as a spiritual force. Silvano Arieti and James A. Arieti, *Love Can Be Found* (New York: Harcourt Brace Jovanovich, 1977), pp. 198–210.

135. Some scholars regard love as *the* central function of the human personality. See, for example, Lawrence K. Frank, "On Loving," p. 35.

136. Thus Martin Buber writes: "Love does not cling to the *I* in such a way as to have the *Thou* only for its 'content,' its object, but love is *between I* and *Thou*. The man who does not know this, with his very being know this, does not know love." Martin Buber, *I* and *Thou*, 2d ed., translated by Ronald Gregor Smith (New York: Scribner's, 1958), pp. 14–15.

137. Rollo May, *Love and Will*, p. 27.

138. *Ibid*. p. 29.

139. This is one of the great themes of the New Testament. See, for example, Jn. 15:13; Eph. 5: 2; 1 Jn. 2:10.

140. Conversion is a major change in lifestyle content, a change in which love assumes a prominent role. On the relation between love and conversion see Walter E. Conn, *Conscience: Development and Self-Transcendence* (Birmingham, Ala.: Religious Education Press, 1981), pp. 185–194.

141. Sex, of course, can be loveless. While love between a postpubescent male and female typically involves sex, not all sexual relations between such persons is love. On this point, see Alexander Lowen, *Love and Orgasm* (New York: New American Library Signet, 1965), pp. 27–53.

142. These last few points are drawn from Rollo May, *Love and Will*, pp. 65–98.

143. For a medieval treatment of friendship which can be of profit to contemporary religious educators, see Aelred of Rievaulx, *De spirituali amicitis*.

144. Rollo May, *Love and Will*, p. 317.

145. In a happy marriage, each partner is a genuine friend and not just a lover. Similarly, genuine love of God means that one treats God as a friend rather than just as a loving or adorable being.

146. Horace, *Odes*, I.iii.8 ("animae dimidium meae").

147. Agapé also is the technical term for a love feast in the early Christian church. For a short summary of agapé as love feast, see A. J. Maclean, "Agapé," in James Hastings, editor, *Encyclopedia of Religion and Ethics*, volume I (New York: Scribner's, 1908), pp. 166–175; also C. Bernas, "Agapé," in *New Catholic Encyclopedia*, volume I. (New York: McGraw-Hill, 1967), pp. 193–194.

148. Paul Tillich maintains that agapé forms the basis of Christian ethics. See Horst Bürkle, "Paul Tillich," in Leonhard Reinisch, editor, *Theologians for Our Time* (Notre Dame, Ind.: University of Notre Dame Press, 1964) p. 74.

149. Vladimir Solovyev, *The Meaning of Love*, translated by Jane Marshall (New York: International Universities Press, 1947), pp. 54–57.

150. Rollo May, *Love and Will*, p. 38.

151. "Neither eros nor agapé, taken separately, would seem to be equal to love's total drive, for the distinction between self and other is a distinction within being. A love, therefore, looking to Being Itself could not exclude either without falling short." R. O. Johann, "Love," in *New Catholic Encyclopedia*, volume VIII (New York: McGraw-Hill, 1967), p. 1039.

152. Paul Tillich, *Systematic Theology*, volume I (Chicago: University of Chicago Press, 1951), p. 281, italics deleted.

153. R. O. Johann, "Love," p. 1039. This emphasis on operation is characteristic of the social-science approach to religious instruction as contrasted (but not opposed) to the centrality which being assumes in the theological approach. On this point, see James Michael Lee, *The Shape of Religious Instruction* (Birmingham, Ala.: Religious Education Press, 1971), pp. 65–74.

154. Thomas Aquinas, *Summa Theologica*, I-II, q. 28, a.1., ad 2 et ad 3.

155. On this point, see Robert Johann, *The Meaning of Love* (New York: Paulist Deus, 1966), p. 18.

156. *Ibid,*, p. 30, footnote numbers deleted and the words *"amor benevolentiae"* substituted for "friendly relations."

157. From a social-science vantage point, this issue is investigated quite differently.

158. Something of a classic work in the Christian conception of love is Anders Nygren, *Agapé and Eros*, parts I and II, translated by Philip Watson (Philadelphia: Westminster, 1953).

159. Love, natural and supernatural, often peaks in ecstasy. In supernatural love, this ecstasy sometimes assumes the form of divinely oriented mysticism. See Arthur D. Colman and Libby Lee Colman, *Love and Ecstasy* (New York: Seabury, 1975), pp. 6–43.

160. For a treatment of this point by a contemporary Catholic theologian, see Bernard J. F. Lonergan, *Method in Theology*, 2d edition (New York: Herder and Herder, 1972), pp. 288–291.

161. See Sacra Congregatio pro Clericis, *Directorium catechisticum generale*, p. 60 (#64); also Gérard Gilleman, *The Primacy of Charity in Moral Theology*, translated by William F. Ryan and André Vachon (Westminster, Md.: Newman, 1959).

162. The nature and relationship of natural and supernatural is one of the major theological issues which impinge upon religious instruction. For an admirable treatment of this issue, see Ian P. Knox, *Above or Within?: The Supernatural in Religious Education* (Birmingham, Ala.: Religious Education Press, 1976).

163. I discuss the relation between "natural" and "supernatural" in *The Shape of Religious Instruction,* pp. 258–297.

164. Harry F. Harlow, *Learning to Love* (New York: Aronson, 1974), pp. 1–102.

165. This system has been found to be significantly stronger in human males than in animal males.

166. Because the higher animals, especially monkeys, have a physiological system not very dissimilar to that of humans, the data from animal studies bear a certain relevance to human beings.

167. Some neo-Freudian and non-Freudian psychotherapists expand (minimize?) Freud's pansexualism to a broad life force.

168. Sigmund Freud, *An Outline of Psychoanalysis,* translated by James Strachey (New York: Norton, 1969), p. 22. In classic psychoanalytic theory, libido is both sexual and aggressive.

169. See Martin S. Bergmann, "On the Intrapsychic Function of Falling in Love," in *Psychoanalytic Quarterly* XLIX (January, 1980), pp. 56–77.

170. See Erich Fromm, *The Art of Loving,* pp. 46–47.

171. When I write that "love is a set of behaviors," or "attitude is a predisposed readiness," and so forth, I do not thereby imply that love or attitude or the like are substantive or real entities. They are, of course, psychological constructs. Human language being what it has become, the simpler and less complex course is to write "love is *x* or *y*" than always to state that "love is a construct naming and describing a set of *x* or *y* behaviors."

172. On this point, see Lawrence K. Frank, "On Loving," p. 33.

173. See, for example, Jeffrey Keefe, "The Learning of Attitudes, Values, and Beliefs," pp. 43–45.

174. One empirical study, for example, found that rigidity in personality among male college students was significantly related to the mother's withdrawal of love and the father's power/assertive form of discipline. Lakshmi K. Singh, "Rigidity and Parental Discipline," in *Indian Journal of Clinical Psychology* VII (March, 1980), pp. 63–65.

175. On this point, see Abraham Tesser and Delroy L. Palhus, "Toward a Causal Model of Love," in *Journal of Personality and Social Psychology* XXXIV (December, 1976), pp. 1095–1105; P. M. Bentler and G. J. Huber, "Simple Minitheories of Love," in *Journal of Personality and Social Psychology* XXXVII (January, 1979), pp. 124–130.

176. Karl Rahner, *Theological Investigations,* volume I, 2d edition, translated by Cornelius Ernst (Baltimore, Md.: Helicon, 1965), p. 123.

177. Emil Brunner, *Truth as Encounter,* translated by Amandus W. Loos and David Cairns (Philadelphia: Westminster, 1943), p. 98.

178. One empirical study sought to ascertain if romantic love is more predictive of the development of self-disclosure than self-disclosure is predictive of the development of romantic love. The research investigation concluded that the strongest causal association suggests that romantic love precedes self-disclosure in males, while for females self-disclosure leads to love. Gerald R. Adams and Judy A. Shea, "Talking and Loving: A Cross-Lagged Panel Investigation," in *Basic and Applied Social Psychology* II (June, 1981), pp. 81–88.

179. Jean Mouroux, *The Meaning of Man,* translated by A. H. G. Downes (New York: Sheed and Ward, 1948), p. 205.
180. W. Norman Pittinger, *Love Looks Deep* (London: Mowbray, 1969), pp. 43–49.
181. C. F. Kelly, *The Spirit of Leve* (New York: Harper, 1951), p. 1, italics deleted.
182. Paul Tillich, *Systematic Theology,* volume III, p. 134. As a theologian, Tillich uses the word "drive" in an nonpsychological sense.
183. Alexander Lowen, *Love and Orgasm,* p. 28.
184. Thomas Aquinas, *Summa Theologica,* I-II, q.28, a. 1, ad 3, translation mine.
185. Erich Fromm, *The Art of Loving,* p. 18.
186. Theological thinkers often regard this characteristic of human love as an echo of or a participation in the all-giving love which typifies God. On this point, see W. H. Vanstone, *The Risk of Love* (New York: Oxford University Press, 1978), pp. 57–74.
187. The point I am making here suggests that sacrifice is part and parcel of love, regardless of whether one considers love from the perspective of the professedly nonreligious or the professedly religious. See James Michael Lee, "Discipline in a Moral and Religious Key," in Kevin Walsh and Milly Cowles, *Developmental Discipline* (Birmingham, Ala.: Religious Education Press, 1982), pp. 149–242; Evelyn Underhill, *Anthology,* edited by Lumsden Barkway and Lucy Menzies (London: Mowbray, 1953), p. 199.
188. Wayne R. Rood, *On Nurturing Christians* (Nashville, Tenn.: Abingdon, 1972), p. 104.
189. It is for this reason that Rosemary Haughton believes that the authentic religious mystic provides contemporary civilization with the standard of true love which is urgently needed today. Rosemary Haughton, *Love* (Baltimore, Md.: Penguin, 1971), p. 175.
190. Rollo May, *Love and Will,* p. 101.
191. George H. Tavard, *A Way of Love* (Maryknoll, N.Y.: Orbis, 1977), pp. 72–76.
192. Many social scientists hold that the ability to love unselfishly is one of the hallmarks of a self-actualized, mature, well-adjusted human being. See Kenneth L. Jones, Louis W. Shainberg, and Curtis O. Byer, *Emotional Health,* 2d edition (San Francisco: Canfield, 1975), p. 16.
193. Pierre Teilhard de Chardin. *The Phenomenon of Man,* translated by Bernard Wall (New York: Harper, 1959), p. 265. That self-emptying is a correlate of love-as-union is reaffirmed by Teilhard who states: "Love alone is capable of uniting living human beings in such a way as to complete and fulfill them, for it alone takes them and joins them by what is deepest in themselves. This is a fact of daily experience." (*Ibid.*)
194. Karl Rahner and Herbert Vorgrimler, *Theological Dictionary,* pp. 266–267.
195. Marcel van Caster, "Mutual Love: Insights from Phenomenology and from the Gospel," in *Lumen Vitae* XXIII (June, 1968), p. 237.
196. Daniel Day Williams, *The Spirit and the Forms of Love,* p. 140.
197. Erich Fromm, *The Art of Loving,* p. 28.
198. Karl Rahner, *Theological Investigations,* volume I, 2d ed., p. 123.
199. Emil Brunner, *Truth as Encounter,* p. 98.
200. Karl Rahner, *Theological Investigations,* volume I. 2d ed., p. 123.
201. The research has shown that much of a person's self-possession is formed in the early years of life in a family context. Thus, for example, one empirical investigation found that the most important factors involved in determining who is or will be one's ideal beloved person are, in addition to the obvious factor of sex,

the factors of religion, mother's marital happiness, and father's education. These conclusions were true of both males and females. Theodore D. Kemper and Roslyn W. Bologh, "The Ideal of Love Object: Structural and Family Sources," in *Journal of Youth and Adolescence* IX (February, 1980), pp. 33–48.

202. In this connection, Rollo May writes: "We receive love—from our children as well as others—not in proportion to our demands or sacrifices or needs, but roughly in proportion to our own capacity to love. And our capacity to love depends, in turn, upon our prior capacity to be persons in our own right. To love means, essentially, to give; and to give requires a maturity of self-feeling." Rollo May, "A Preface to Love," in Ashley Montagu, editor, *The Practice of Love* (Englewood Cliffs, N.J.: Prentice-Hall, 1975), p. 118.

203. Erich Fromm, *The Art of Loving*, p. 60, italics deleted.

204. Jacques Maritain, *Education at the Crossroads* (New Haven, Conn.: Yale University Press, 1943), p. 7.

205. My division of these two types of perfection is conceptual and is used for the sake of analytically probing the perfection which love offers an individual. Hence this division should in no way be reified. A person by his very nature as a created being is God-created, God-suffused, and God-directed.

206. Theologians typically interpret 1 Cor. 13:1–13 as referring to "supernatural" love. I believe on both theological and psychological grounds that most of the statements in this biblical passage refer to so-called "natural" love too.

207. Rudolf Bultmann, "New Testament and Mythology," in Hans Werner Bartsch, editor, *Kerygma and Myth*, revised edition, translated by Reginald H. Fuller (New York: Harper & Row Torchbooks, 1961), p. 26.

208. Robert O. Johann, "Charity and Time," in *Cross Currents* IX (Spring, 1959), p. 143.

209. Pierre Teilhard de Chardin, *Science and Christ*, translated by René Hague (New York: Harper & Row, 1968), p. 170.

210. Wayne R. Rood, *On Nurturing Christians.* p. 10.

211. See Daniel Day Williams, *The Spirit and the Forms of Love*, pp. 130–131.

212. See Morton Kelsey, *Encounter with God*, p. 201.

213. The Higher Institute of Catechetics of Nijmegen, *Fundamentals and Programs of a New Catechesis*, p. 96.

214. For a helpful treatment of education in Christian love, see Morton Kelsey, *Can Christians Be Educated?* (Birmingham, Ala.: Religious Education Press, 1977), pp. 39–75.

215. Rudolf Bultmann, *Jesus and the Word*, p. 94.

216. Some Christian religious educators have attempted to make justice more primary than love. For a discussion of this point, see Gene Outka, *Agapé* (New Haven, Conn.: Yale University Press, 1972), pp. 75–92. I contend that while justice may stress giving only love can emphasize giving and forgiving. On love as forgiving, see Philip Potter, *The Love of Power or the Power of Love* (New Malden, England: Fellowship of Reconciliation, 1974), pp. 17–18.

217. I have always held that love is superior to faith. Some persons disagree. See, for example, George M. Newlands, *Theology of the Love of God* (Atlanta, Ga.: Knox, 1980); Vladimir Solovyev, *The Meaning of Love*, pp. 58–61.

218. Because love is essentially and integrally a mode of human functioning, it is necessary (but not sufficient) to understand the psychological dimension of the human being. On this point, see Morton T. Kelsey, *Caring: How Can We Love One Another?* (New York: Paulist, 1981), pp. 133–147.

219. David R. Krathwohl, Benjamin S. Bloom, and Bertram B. Masia, *Taxonomy of Educational Objectives: Handbook II: Affective Domain* (New York: McKay, 1964).

220. Michael Warren, for example, holds this strange position. For Warren, affect is at bottom cognitive. Warren believes that affect operates as an intellectual device for mentally investigating and clarifying human rationality. Warren and those of his persuasion do not seem to realize that the accompaniment of affect with cognition and psychomotor behaviors in the moment-to-moment activities of *homo integer* is precisely that, an accompaniment, rather than a merging or an identification. See Michael Warren, "All Contributions Cheerfully Accepted," in *Living Light* VII (Winter, 1970), p. 31. Gabriel Moran denied the existence of affect as a distinct human function.

221. A taxonomy, by its very nature, is a hierarchical structuring of similar elements around a single ordering principle. It is the ordering principle which gives meaning and integration to the taxonomy. Further, it is the ordering principle which lies at the basis for determining at which hierarchical level a particular element of the taxonomy is to be properly placed. In the Bloom taxonomy, the ordering principle is complexity, with hierarchical stages proceeding from the more simple intellectual operations to the more complex. In the Krathwohl taxonomy, the ordering principle is internalization, with hierachical stages based on the progressive degree of internalization which a particular affective content represents.

222. I am using the Krathwohl taxonomy numbering system.

223. The three divisions within this category represent a continuum from more passive behaviors to less passive ones.

224. David R. Krathwohl, Benjamin S. Bloom, and Bertram B. Masia, *Taxonomy of Educational Objectives: Handbook II: Affective Domain*, p. vii.

225. In this connection, two of the most highly respected scholars observe that virtually every theorist and researcher on attitude agrees with the statement that attitudes are learned. Indeed, a considerable portion of the research on attitudes is concerned with exploring teaching procedures which best produce attitudinal learning. Martin Fishbein and Icek Ajzen, "Introduction," in Martin Fishbein and Icek Ajzen, editors, *Belief, Attitude, Intention and Behavior* (Reading, Mass.; Addison-Wesley, 1975), pp. 9–10.

226. For a clear delineation of some of the basic pedagogical processes involved in teaching attitudes, see Lucie W. Barber, *The Religious Education of Pre-school Children* (Birmingham, Ala.: Religious Education Press, 1981), pp. 17–24. Many of the pedagogical processes proposed by Barber are applicable, with appropriate modification, to learners of all ages.

227. James Michael Lee, *The Flow of Religious Instruction*, pp. 233–240.

228. One notable exception to this is the splendid categorization formulated by William J. McGuire, "The Nature of Attitudes and Attitude Change," in Gardner Lindzey and Elliot Aronson, editors, *The Handbook of Social Psychology*, 2d edition, volume III (Reading, Mass: Addison-Wesley, 1969), pp. 172–258. Much of the remainder of this section draws heavily, though not completely, from his work.

229. Carl I. Hovland, Irving L. Janis, and Harold H. Kelley, *Communication and Persuasion* (New Haven, Conn.: Yale University Press, 1953), pp. 19–55; William A. Watts and William J. McGuire, "Persistence of Induced Opinion Change and Retention of Inducing Message Contents," in *Journal of Abnormal and Social Psychology* LXVIII (March, 1964), pp. 233–241.

230. Ezra Stotland, Alvin Zander, and Thomas Natsoulas, "Generalization of Interpersonal Similarity," in *Journal of Abnormal and Social Psychology* LXII (March, 1961), pp. 250–256; Ezra Stotland and Martin Patchen, "Identification and Changes in Prejudice and in Authoritarianism," in *Journal of Abnormal and Social Psychology* LXII (March, 1961), p. 265–274; Ezra Stotland and Robert E. Dunn, "Identification, 'Oppositeness,' Authoritarianism, Self-Esteem and Birth Order," in *Psychological Monographs* LXXVI, number 9, 1962, pp. 1–21; Ezra Stotland, "Exploratory Investigations of Empathy," in Leonard Perkowitz, editor, *Advances in Experimental Social Psychology,* volume IV (New York: Academic Press, 1969), pp. 271–314.

231. See, for example, Herbert E. Krugman, "Affective Responses to Music as a Function of Familiarity," in *Journal of Abnormal and Social Psychology* XLVII (July, 1943), pp. 388–392; see also Robert B. Zajonc, "The Attitudinal Effects of Mere Exposure," in *Journal of Personality and Social Psychology* IX (June, 1968), pp. s1–s2.

232. The direction and valence of liking are controverted among some social scientists, as for example the interpretations made by symmetry theorists versus those made by dissonance theorists.

233. William J. McGuire, "The Nature of Attitudes and Attitude Change," pp. 194–196.

234. The Lee multidimensional model of the teaching act illustrates the overall way in which the major variables change and are changed by the other variables in the course of the instructional act. See James Michael Lee, *The Flow of Religious Instruction,* pp. 233–240.

235. For a review of some of the more pertinent studies, see S. B. Khan and Joel Weiss, "The Teaching of Affective Responses," pp. 774–776; see also, Edwin Wandt, "A Comparison of the Attitudes of Contrasting Groups of Teachers," in *Educational and Psychological Measurement* XIV (Summer, 1954), pp. 418–422; Henry Clay Lindgren and Gladys May Patton, "Attitudes of High School and Other Teachers toward Children and Current Educational Methodology," in *California Journal of Educational Research* IX (March, 1958), pp. 80–85; Larry J. Brandt and Mary Ellen Hayden, "Male and Female Teacher Attitudes as a Function of Students' Ascribed Motivation and Performance Levels," in *Journal of Educational Psychology* LXVI (June, 1974), pp. 309–314. As Brandt and Hayden remark, the Rosenthal-Jacobson study found that the performance of a learner is conditioned by the teacher's *attitude* of how he (the teacher) expects him to perform. Robert Rosenthal and Lenore Jacobsen, *Pygmalion in the Classroom: Teacher Expectation and Pupils' Intellectual Development* (New York: Holt, Rinehart and Winston, 1968); Sherry Willis and Jere Brophy, "Origins of Teachers' Attitudes toward Young Children," in *Journal of Educational Psychology* LVI (August, 1974), pp. 520–521.

236. David C. Dietrick, "Review of the Research: Appendix A," in Richard J. Hill, *A Comparative Study of Lecture and Discussion Methods* (White Plains, N.Y.: Fund for Adult Education, 1960), pp. 90–118. See also James Michael Lee, *Principles and Methods of Secondary Education,* p. 299.

237. William J. McGuire, "The Nature of Attitudes and Attitude Change," p. 226.

238. *Ibid.,* p. 231.

239. I avoid the term "mental age" here because "psychological age" is more comprehensive including as it does not only mental age but also affective age and, if it exists, conative age.

240. Paul B. Maves, "Religious Development in Adulthood," in Merton P. Strommen, editor, *Research on Religious Development*, pp. 782–790. Possibly data such as these will have a sobering effect on those religious educators who are making wildly optimistic and uncritical *a priori* claims for the presumed incredible efficacy of adult religious instruction as over against religious instruction for young children and adolescents.

241. One of the most famous studies in this connection is Carroll H. Leeds and Walter W. Cook, "The Construction and Differential Value of a Scale for Determining Teacher-pupil Attitudes," in *Journal of Experimental Education* XVI (December, 1947), pp. 149–159.

242. Gayle F. Gregersen and Robert M. W. Travers, "A Study of the Child's Concept of the Teacher," in *Journal of Educational Research* LXI (March, 1968), pp. 324–327.

243. William J. McGuire, "The Nature of Attitudes and Attitude Change," pp. 251–252.

244. It has often been pointed out by historians that a disproportionately large percentage of dictators down through the centuries have been men who are short of stature. A few examples of this include Julius Caesar, Napoleon Bonaparte, Benito Mussolini, Adolf Hitler, and Josef Stalin.

245. Judson Mills and Elliot Aronson, "Opinion Change as a Function of the Communicator's Attractiveness and Desire to Influence," in *Journal of Personality and Social Psychology* I (February, 1965), pp. 173–177.

246. William J. McGuire, "The Nature of Attitudes and Attitude Change," p. 250.

247. In my observations of religion lessons in the United States and Europe, I have noticed that effective teachers often operationalize this principle, especially in cases where they wish to facilitate a change in one or another motivational aspect of the learner's attitude.

248. Theodore M. Newcomb, Ralph H. Turner, and Philip E. Converse, *Social Psychology: The Study of Human Interaction*, p. 143.

249. Lewis R. Aiken Jr., "Attitudes toward Mathematics," in *Review of Educational Research* XL (October, 1970), pp. 551–596; Benjamin S. Bloom, "Affective Consequences of School Achievement," in James H. Block, editor, *Mastery Learning* (New York: Holt, Rinehart and Winston, 1971), pp. 19–21. The relationship between attitudes and performance is quite possibly reciprocal. Social scientists hypothesize, but for reasons I suggest earlier in this section have not yet conclusively demonstrated, that attitudes are in some way predictive of future overt behavior.

250. Loretta Golden, "The Treatment of Minority Groups in Primary Social Studies Textbooks," unpublished doctoral dissertation, Stanford University, 1965; Lloyd Marcus, *The Treatment of Minorities in Secondary School Textbooks* (New York: B'nai Brith Anti-Defamation League, 1961)

251. Bernard Berelson and Gary A. Steiner, *Human Behavior: An Inventory of Scientific Findings* (New York: Harcourt, Brace, and World, 1964), p. 517.

252. Charles R. Gruner, "An Experimental Study of Satire as Persuasion," in *Speech Monographs* XXXII (June, 1965), pp. 149–153.

253. John Waite Bowers and Michael M. Osborn, "Attitudinal Effects of Selected Types of Concluding Metaphors in Persuasive Speeches," in *Speech Monographs* XXXIII (June, 1966), pp. 147–155.

254. Theodore M. Newcomb, Ralph H. Turner, and Philip E. Converse, *Social Psychology: The Study of Human Interaction*, p. 91.

255. Paul F. Secord and Carl W. Backman, *Social Psychology*, 2d edition (New York: McGraw-Hill, 1974), pp. 104–106.

256. James Michael Lee, *The Flow of Religious Instruction*, p. 65.

257. *Ibid.* pp. 65–73.

258. For a review of some of the pertinent literature, see David Marlowe and Kenneth J. Gergen, "Personality and Social Interaction," in Gardner Lindzey and Elliot Aronson, editors, *Handbook of Social Psychology*, volume III, pp. 608–621.

259. For a review of some of the research literature, see S. B. Khan and Joel Weiss, "The Teaching of Affective Responses," pp. 777–778.

260. The classic study in this area is Kurt Lewin, Ronald Lippitt, and Ralph K. White, "Patterns of Aggressive Behavior in Experimentally Created 'Social Climates,'" in *Journal of Social Psychology, X: Bulletin of the Society for the Psychological Study of Social Issues* (May, 1939), pp. 271–299.

261. For a nice treatment of the attitude of trusting, a treatment infused by a Christian perspective, see Carolyn Gratton, *Trusting* (New York: Crossroad, 1982). Gratton delineates some ways for teaching the attitude of trusting.

262. Summarizing their research data, Gordon Allport and Bernard Kramer assert: "Religious training in itself does not lessen prejudice. But religious training which successfully stresses tolerance and brotherhood does tend to lessen prejudice." Gordon W. Allport and Bernard M. Kramer, "Some Roots of Prejudice," in *Journal of Psychology* XXII (July, 1946), p. 38.

263. Bernard Berelson and Gary A. Steiner, *Human Behavior: An Inventory of Scientific Findings*, p. 510.

264. Role playing was originally developed as a group psychotherapeutic technique. Later it began to be used widely by teachers and other kinds of non-psychotherapeutic facilitators seeking to bring about affective and attitudinal outcomes.

265. See James Michael Lee and Nathaniel J. Pallone, *Guidance and Counseling in Schools: Foundations and Processes* (New York: McGraw-Hill, 1966), pp. 328–329.

266. Joseph Weitz and Seymour Adler, "The Applied Optimal Use of Simulation," in *Journal of Applied Psychology* LVIII (October, 1973), p. 224.

267. The threefold molar task of all theory is to explain, predict, and verify phenomena. On this point, see James Michael Lee, "The Authentic Source of Religious Instruction," in Norma H. Thompson, editor, *Religious Education and Theology* (Birmingham, Ala.: Religious Education Press, 1982), pp. 117–121.

268. Bruce J. Biddle, *Role Theory* (New York: Academic Press, 1979), p. 4.

269. Melvin L. DeFleur, William V. D'Antonio, and Lois DeFleur Nelson, *Sociology: Human Society* (Glenview, Ill.: Scott, Foresman, 1977), p. 37.

270. The almost exclusively cognitive emphasis adopted by proponents of the religious-education-for-liberation movement has blinded these persons to giving due weight to attitude learning and to attitudinally oriented pedagogical procedures to bring about liberation outcomes. (There is not a single index entry for attitudes in Thomas Groome's *Christian Religious Education*, for example.) Were liberationist religious educators ever to discover attitude learning, these persons would be astounded to find the potentiality of the role-playing technique to yield liberation attitudes.

271. Mark Chesler and Robert Fox, *Role-Playing Methods in the Classroom* (Chicago: Science Research Associates, 1966), p. 3.

272. It is for this reason that role playing is so highly prized in training programs for management and leadership practice. See, for example, Norman R. F. Maier, Allen R. Solem, and Ayesha Maier, *The Role-Playing Technique* (La Jolla, Calif.: University Associates, 1975).

273. Fannie R. Shaftel and George Shaftel, *Role-Playing for Social Values* (Englewood Cliffs, N.J.: Prentice-Hall, 1967), pp. 31–47.

274. Wallace Wohlking and Patricia J. Gill, *Role Playing* (Englewood Cliffs, N.J.: Educational Technology Publications, 1980), pp. 6–8.

275. While the research does indeed support the efficacy of role playing, nonetheless the research is not as totally conclusive as the more ardent supporters of role playing would probably prefer. See Jay A. Mathis et al., "Psychodrama and Sociodrama in Primary and Secondary Education," in *Psychology in the Schools* XVII (January, 1980), pp. 96–101. On a major methodological issue in research on role playing, see C. D. Spencer, "Two Types of Role Playing: Threats to Internal and External Validity," in *American Psychologist* XXXIII (March, 1978), pp. 265–268.

276. For a review of the research on attitude alteration with specific reference to religious instruction, see James Michael Lee, *The Flow of Religious Instruction*, pp. 106–119; see also Mary D. Atwood, K. Britton, and Frances L. Everett, "The Effects of Modeling and Role Playing on Children's Delay of Gratification Behavior," in *Child Study Journal* VIII (Third Quarter, 1978), pp. 149–163.

277. This research suggests a point which I make continually throughout the trilogy, namely that a learning is made more potent when it is inserted into one's lifestyle behavior.

278. For a review of the research on the pedagogical potency of reinforcement, see James Michael Lee, *The Flow of Religious Instruction*, pp. 78–89, 317–318.

279. Anthony G. Greenwald, "When Does Role Playing Produce Attitude Change? Toward an Answer," in Samuel Himmelfarb and Alice Hendrickson Eagly, editors, *Readings in Attitude Change* (New York: Wiley, 1974), p. 576.

280. B. Othanel Smith et al., *Teachers for the Real World* (Washington, D.C.: American Association of Colleges for Teacher Education, 1969), p. 28.

281. See, for example, David C. Berliner et al., *Protocols on Group Process* (San Francisco: Far West Laboratory for Educational Research and Development, 1973); J. C. Kleucker, "Effects of Protocol and Training Materials," in *Acquiring Teacher Competencies* (Bloomington, Ind.: National Center for the Development of Training Materials in Teacher Education, Indiana University, 1974); R. C. Pugh and David Gliessman, *Measuring the Effects of a Protocol Film Series* (Bloomington, Ind.: National Center for the Development of Training Materials in Teacher Education, Indiana University, 1976).

282. Willis D. Copeland, "Laboratory Experiences in Teacher Education," in Harold E. Mitzel, editor, *Encyclopedia of Educational Research*, 5th edition, volume II (New York: Free Press, 1982), p. 1013.

283. The latter may be useful as a pedagogical aid, but it is no substitute for protocol materials. Pauline Furness gives fifty-two different short lesson plans each of which uses role playing to develop attitudes and wider affectivity. These are not protocol materials. Pauline Furness, *Role Playing in The Elementary School* (New York: Hart, 1976).

CHAPTER SIX

VERBAL CONTENT

*"Ever since the Greeks, we have been drunk
With language! We have made a cage of words
And shoved our God inside, as boys confine
A cricket or a locust, to make him sing
A private song!"* [1]

—Morris West

THE NATURE OF VERBAL CONTENT

Verbal content refers to all the linguistic elements and units used during the course of the teaching-learning dynamic. Thus verbal content includes not only the sum total of the words expressed by the religious educator and the learners, but also the written words contained in the instructional materials themselves, together with whichever words go to form the here-and-now pedagogical environment.

In order to come to a correct understanding and appreciation of verbal content, it is necessary to realize that *verbal content is an authentic substantive content in its own right and not simply a bearer of some other substantive content.* This is a key point, one which cannot be emphasized sufficiently. Verbal content is the fusion of a word-qua-joined letters[2] and some other particular content. In this fusion, a new reality is born, a reality basically different both from the joined letters existing before this fusion and from the other content prior to the latter's being placed in a verbal mode. In the concrete order, of course, there is no such thing as a word qua word unalloyed with some other particular content.

Verbal content, then, is a distinctive substantive content formed by the fusion of word-qua-joined-letters-or-sound and some other particular content. That verbal content is not just a transparent bearer of this other particular content, but is indeed a fusion-formed substantive content in its own right, can be easily seen by comparing the results of placing a particular content in words with placing that selfsame content in a painting. If words were simply a transparent carrier of the other content, then verbal content would not differ from pictorial content when each of these contents serves as a medium for the identical particular other content. There is a vast difference in the substantive content of the word "Madonna" and the substantive content of a Raphael Sanzio painting of the Madonna.

The points I have treated of thus far in this chapter are of great practical import in the work of religious instruction. If the religion teacher wishes to use verbal content purposively and effectively, he ought not to regard it merely as a medium for some "deeper" message. The words which the educator and learner use *are* themselves the message—or at least the verbal part of it. Words, then, do not just carry revelation; they are in themselves revelatory in so far as it is possible for words to be revelatory. Unless the religion teacher recognizes verbal content as an authentic substantive content in its own right, he will almost of necessity fail to properly or fully utilize his and the learner's verbal behavior.

Verbal content is inclined to have a natural affinity for cognitive content rather than for affective content or lifestyle content. One explanation for this phenomenon is that both words and cognitions tend in a greater or lesser degree to be abstractions. Affective behavior and lifestyle behavior, however, lie more in the zone of the tangible and the concrete. When an individual wishes to communicate a great deal of significant cognitive content, that person quite naturally is prone to augment the quantity and quality of his verbal content. But if an individual desires to communicate affective or lifestyle contents, that person will typically reduce his verbal behavior, employing instead nonverbal behavior or silence.

Why is it vital for a religious educator to have a working knowledge of the nature and theory of language? It is vital because, at least in its present stage of development, teaching is done largely in the verbal mode. Verbal content forms a very sizable portion of the lesson.

Definition and Characteristics

Verbal content is that linguistic form of conventional, patterned, and symbolic human communication which conveys meaning. This definition suggests and implies that all varieties of verbal content have the following general characteristics.

Verbal content is a *learned behavior*. Language is not instinctive. Nor is it infused by the Holy Spirit. Rather, verbal behavior is a process and a skill which is acquired.[3] An individual typically acquires his verbal behavior from the members of the immediate or proximate social group(s) with which he is affiliated as a child. "Language depends upon, but is not determined by, the biological constitution of man, and differences among languages are not linked with physical differences among men. Any person can learn any language as his mother tongue."[4]

Verbal content is *arbitrary*. Language is symbolic, and there are "no preordained reasons for any (linguistic) symbol to possess a particular meaning."[5] There is "no direct necessary connection between the nature of things or ideas language deals with and the linguistic units or combinations by which these things or ideas are expressed."[6] A verbal symbol is artificially constructed by human beings; it is not natural, it is not in the nature of things.

Verbal content is *conventional*. A culture or a society attaches a specific, arbitrary denotation or connotation to a particular linguistic symbol. The verbal unit, then, is meaningless in itself; it gains denotative or connotative sense only when a culture or a society invests it with meaning. Verbal behavior consists in "culturally ordained forms or categories."[7] Because intrinsically meaningless linguistic units are given particular denotations and connotations by a culture or a society, particular verbal units, constructions, and expressions have the same *in se* meaning and set of rules.

Verbal content is *systematic*. Verbal content is a patterned or arranged set of linguistic symbols intended to cognitively handle all references and meanings of which a culture is capable.[8] The placing of various linguistic units into a system is of significant assistance in properly encoding and decoding the intended meaning of specific verbal units and expressions.

Verbal content is *symbolic*. A symbol is a token of some other reality, rather than that other reality itself.[9] A symbol, insofar as it is a symbol, represents only an aspect of that for which it stands. "The symbols of language are simultaneously substitute stimuli and substitute responses and can call forth further stimuli and responses, so that discourse becomes independent of an immediate physical stimulus."[10] A society or a culture arbitrarily decides which verbal symbols may substitute at a given time for particular realities. Because of its symbolic character, language cannot point to any reality, cannot convey any desired meaning except by the aid of conventions to which a society or a culture has agreed to attach a specified denotation and connotation.[11] Verbal behavior basically consists in the purposive control and manipulation of linguistic symbols.[12] It is the manner and skill with which linguistic symbols are employed by the communicator which account for the accuracy, flavor, and creativeness of the communication. By effective use of linguistic symbolic stimuli and symbolic responses, both the communicator and the receiver can create a new world through verbal behavior. This new world can stimulate breakthroughs in our understanding of reality and the world, or it can deceive us by catching us in a web of words which are made to exist more for themselves than for the realities they betoken. In the final analysis, understanding and wisdom do not come through dealings with linguistic symbols alone, but rather with the realities for which they stand.[13]

Verbal content conveys *meaning*. Indeed, meaning is at once the most significant characteristic of language and its *raison d'être*. Language is, after all, that formal symbolic system whose purpose is to embody and express meaning. To be sure, verbal behavior is regarded as the linguistic organization of meaning. The use of words represents a particular arrangement and combination of meaningful symbols. The rules of verbal behavior exist largely in order to facilitate the formation and transformation of linguistic symbols in such a manner as to convey the most accurate and richest meaning possible. Verbal behavior is the connection by symbols to some reality; it is by virtue of this connection that any given verbal behavior is meaningful. But this connection is objective and subjective. It is objective because meaning has been attached to symbols by a society or a culture. Thus the meaning of linguistic symbols is objectively the same for all users of this language. The objective meaning of verbal symbols is encoded in a dictionary. The connection is subjective because at bottom both the communicator and the receiver attach their own special and personal meaning(s) to a given linguistic symbol. Thus in one sense it is even possible to assert that in the concrete, existential order, linguistic symbols mean nothing: it is only the person (communicator and receiver) who means something by the linguistic symbols.[14] It is meaning in its subjective aspect that largely accounts for the slipperiness and ambiguity of naked linguistic symbols—why they are misunderstood, why the same symbol has different meanings for different people and at different times, and so forth.

Verbal behavior is *pedagogical*. Linguistic symbols are formed and transformed so that a person can explore reality in different fashions, can vicariously try out and try on diverse realities, and through symbols can communicate these efforts and their meanings to himself and to others. By converting a flower or a tree or a house into linguistic symbols, an individual can explore the nature and characteristics of these realities in a way which teaches him and those who share his communication new aspects and insights into these realities.[15]

Religious Language

Religious language is that kind of linguistic behavior which one uses in one's private and/or communal encounters with God, or in verbalizing about these encounters.[16] Religious language is also that type which God uses or causes to be used when he deals with human beings linguistically. There is a fundamental distinction between religious language and theological language.[17] *Religious language* is that set of linguistic symbols used in a person's verbal encounters with God or in linguistically reliving, refeeling, or reflecting upon these encounters. *Theological language* is that set of linguistic symbols employed in the cognitive, scientific reflection about God and his workings in the world. Unhappily, this distinction is seldom recognized by those American and British scholars writing in the fields of religious language and theological language.[18] An illustration of religious language is the recitation or invocation of the Lord's Prayer. An illustration of theological language is the set of verbal symbols used in the cognitive investigation of the elements of praise and petition in the Lord's Prayer.

"Religious language and theological language are two basically different types of language," observes Valerio Tonini. Both these languages deal with the domain of the sacred, continues Tonini, but each is quite different from the other in the manner of discourse, in the structure of immediacy of symbols, in the texture of substantive content, and in objective. "Religious language and theological language are a complementary duality resembling the duality we find between 'communication' and 'information.' There is no communication without information nor is there information without communication." Using this comparison Tonini remarks that religious language and theological language make use of each other and need each other. Neither can exist without the other. However, making use of the other, even needing the other, in no way implies a lack of fundamental difference between the two. "The one is not the other." Religious language and theological language "are two different things, and each must be analyzed and treated with different techniques." Religious language and theological language are complementary, but are by no means the same. At bottom, Tonini asserts, *"religious language is essentially a normative language while theological language is essentially a predicative language."*[19] There is a vast difference, and in some ways an existential chasm, between normative language and predicative language, particularly in what each symbolizes. Almost all of the scholarly investigation of linguistic behavior thus far undertaken has concentrated on predicative language. "But in terms of the investigation of normative language, we are practically at zero."[20] Elaborating on a point made by Tonini I would like to suggest that religious language is a language of communication, while theological language is a language of information. Thus, religious language is basically existential and direct, while theological language is basically logical and inferential.[21] Religious language sometimes makes use of theological language, but theological language draws upon and receives its sustenance from religious language.

Religious language is a special language. As such, it is in a sense a technical language[22] expressing a person's thoughts, feelings, and actions with respect to his encounters with God. In other words, religious language (and even theological language) appropriates a culture's regularly employed words and puts them to special use.[23] Words like "salvation" and "communion" are common human words which take on a somewhat different and more charged meaning when used in religious language. At least three reasons can be adduced to explain why religious language employs ordinary human words in a special way. First, religion represents a certain kind or form of human experience. Such an experience must be reflected in and symbolized by an appropriate language.[24] Second, a special language uses common words in a distinctive and sometimes unusual manner[25] as a pedogogical device to (1) jog people out of the regular meaning-framework suggested by common words, and (2) serve as a linguistic cue or pointer to the fact that religious words and phrases do indeed have a meaning somehow different from words used regularly or in common combinations. Finally, religious language reflects private experience and therefore must use common words not in a common way but in a special way reflecting the privateness and the personalness of this experience.[26]

The two most important characteristics of language in general, and of religious language in particular, are that verbal content embodies meaning and that it is symbolic.

Religious Language as Meaningful. At the outset, one crucial question must be raised about the meaningfulness of religious language: "Is it possible to talk meaningfully with God?" Put differently, "Does my verbal behavior with God (and about God) have any meaning?"[27] The traditional Thomistic position on this question (a position which has influenced much of classical Protestant as well as Catholic thinking) is that the God-aspect of a person's discourse with and about the divine is meaningful only in an analogical sense and not in a real sense. "We can never mean God literally, but only somehow indirectly."[28] The explanation for this is that owing to God's total otherness, a person cannot know God directly. "We are just simply not able to know what God is. Rather we can only know what God is not. We have no capability or means for considering how God is, but only how he is not."[29] Summarizing Aquinas's treatment of our knowledge of God, George Klubertanz states that "St. Thomas repeatedly rejected any pretended proper human concept of God. The assertion that we have a concept of God's essence appeared to him to be simply false. Surely whatever man can clearly conceive is by that very token finite. Our natural abstractive concepts are knowledges of formal natures— and to build a knowledge of God out of such concepts, be it by addition or subtraction, is nothing short of idolatry."[30] Because God as God is totally other, it is also impossible to encounter him directly. We encounter God only as he is immanent in all his creation, particularly in such enriched immanent forms as the sacraments. Human knowledge of, and existential encounter with, God takes place only in an indirect fashion.[31] Does this basic and irreducible indirectness of a person's verbal behavior with (and about) God indicate that discourse with the divine is devoid of any real meaning? "If our human words, when used (with and) of God, cannot have literal meaning, how do they come to have any meaning at all? How can we mean them? What—on earth—makes them meaningful for us?"[32]

A satisfactory solution to the question of the parameters of meaning inherent in a person's verbal behavior with God is of significant concern to every Christian and to every religious educator. Therefore I shall now briefly review first the position of Aquinas and then the basic tenets of some of the most influential twentieth-century linguistics scholars in terms of the problem here posed.

For Aquinas, religious language is meaningful because analogy is meaningful. Those of our words to God which treat of God express something of what we perceive God to be and of how we perceive God to act. These perceptions arise from our empirical encounters with the world around us. Such analogous, indirect perceptions, while by no means perfect, nonetheless do at least contain some meaning—a meaning which a person arrives at whether he realizes it or not, by virtue of the *via positiva* or *via negativa*.

In the twentieth century the work of various philosophers of language has been examined by certain religious educationists[33] and by many theologians.[34] The most skeptical view of the meaningfulness of human verbal discourse with God is that derived from *logical positivism*. This stance, especially as championed by Alfred Jules Ayer, delimits all language to that which is either analytic or synthetic. Altering and refining a distinction made famous by Immanuel Kant, Ayer argues that a proposition is analytic "when its validity depends solely on the definitions of the symbol it contains, and synthetic when its validity is determined by the facts of experience."[35] Analytic statements are tautological because they state only what was previously known and "are devoid of factual content." Consequently, analytic propositions really say nothing and are basically meaningless. The only way in which analytic propositions can be said to provide some new knowledge and meaning resides in the fact that they "call attention to linguistic usage, of which we might otherwise not be conscious, and they reveal unsuspected implications in our assertions and beliefs."[36] Religious language, in this view, is cognitive nonsense since it is tautological and unverified (as well as unverifiable) through sense experience. Hence the only meaning which religious language possesses is "emotive."[37]

Less skeptical than logical positivism is that view of religious language embraced by the followers of Ludwig Wittgenstein's later form of *functional analysis*.[38] According to functional analysis, the real meaning of verbal behavior is found not only in its logical make-up but also (and, in a way, more crucially) in its initial usage. Language, particularly in its spoken form, is part-and-parcel of ongoing life. Therefore the meaning of language cannot be sought simply in the analysis of its logical components and aspects, but even more importantly in the way it functions in both the immediate and broader context in which it is used.[39] The purpose of language analysis, therefore, is to clarify the use of any form of verbal behavior and to point to whatever use which might occur due either to improper internal logical structure or to a clash between the internal logical structure of the verbal behavior and the manner and context in which this behavior is employed. The meaning of religious language is, therefore, basically (but not totally) to be sought in its performance. "Grace," as used in everyday speech, means "a dignified kind of charm." But "grace" can also mean "thanks to," or "God's self-communication in love." Its meaning is located in the way in which it is used at any given time.

The position of *broader logical empiricism* developed by Ian Ramsey quite possibly is the most overtly congenial stance toward the meaning of religious language formulated by any major twentieth-century philosopher of language.[40] For Ramsey, hard-nosed empirical philosophy and logical positivism present healthy challenges to Christians to elucidate the empirical anchorage of their religious language.[41] Language at once refers back to its own internal logical structure and to that external reality to which it points. The very way in which a phrase or sentence is structured suggests one or more meanings. The choice, placement, and form of linguistic units are capable of disclosure. Religious language is that which points to and indeed highlights cosmic disclosures, including disclosures of transcendent realities. The possibility that religious language can evoke such disclosures is enhanced by the use of linguistic units in unusual, "odd," and "extraordinary" ways and combinations. Verbal behavior, then, can lead to a "Christian disclosure situation," a situation which provides religious meaning. However, "a Christian disclosure situation can only be evoked; it can never be described (by verbal behavior) nor can its occurrence be guaranteed by a formula."[42] Situations which are capable of disclosing Christian meaning are common in everyday life. These situations "when they occur, have an objective reference and are, as all situations, subject-object in their structure."[43] Disclosure suggests an objective reference. The task of religious language is to point to those situations, to break them free in our awareness from other situations not so pregnant with disclosure possibilities, and to plumb these situations to an appropriate depth. God, the transcendent, the "cosmic more," is disclosed "in discernment-commitment situations in analogy to the manner in which the moral and personal dimensions are mediated through empirical situations."[44]

Religious language is a frequently used and very important avenue of a human being's encounter with God. Consequently it is important for religious educationists, theologians, philosophers of religion, and linguistics scholars interested in religious phenomena to probe more deeply into the question of how and in what manner religious language is meaningful.[45] If religion teachers and curriculum builders wish to continue to work toward expanding the religious language repertoire of the learner, then these educators had better be aware of the capabilities and limitations of religious language.

Religious Language as Symbolic. Religious language is a symbolic expression of religious experience. Religious language arises from religious experience and/or points to religious experience and/or describes religious experience and/or seeks to clarify and interpret religious experience. The past, present, and future primacy must therefore rest ultimately on religious experience, not on religious language. The religious educator never ought to allow religious language to get in the way of religious experience. Words fail to express adequately[46] the reality to which they point and which they symbolize. Because any human symbol *reflects* another reality rather than *is* that reality, a symbol is always ambiguous and analogous. This is particularly true of verbal symbols which tend to be more abstract than symbols which are more existentially congruent and hence point more directly to the reality they reflect. Due to its highly abstract and ambiguous nature, religious language is a very dim and flickering taper with which to explore and make personal such profound religious realities as God, grace, redemption, and sacrament.

Despite their serious limitations, religious symbols are not only necessary but also helpful to human communication with God. Symbolic forms are significant and useful (some would go so far as to say necessary)[47] in apprehending religious meaning within the context of religious experience as a whole. Indeed, linguistic symbols can suggest and indicate, after a fashion, the deeper currents and dynamisms in an individual's religious experience. Because God is God and humans are humans, words to or about God are, in the final analysis, helpful rather than descriptive of God.

The problem and the power of religious language qua symbol can be demonstrated by taking a quick look at the most important word in all of religious language, "God." To some persons, the word "God" is a word which symbolizes a person's ultimate concern; to other individuals, "God" is a term symbolizing the ground of all being; to others, "God" is an expression symbolizing total self-giving love; and to still others, "God" is a symbol of a human being's need to invent nonsense. Paul Tillich, for whom symbol is at the center of his theological system, asserts that the only nonsymbolic statement a person can make about or to God is that all statements made about or to God which express God or treat of him are symbolic. Religious language, like any other religious symbol, "uses the material of ordinary experience in speaking of God, but in such a way that the ordinary meaning of the material used is both affirmed and denied. Every religious symbol negates itself in its literal meaning, but affirms itself in its self-transcending meaning."[48] Using the word "God" as our focus at this juncture, I believe that the power of religious language derives both from the extent to which its symbolism participates in God's nature and ongoing activity, and from the degree to which it draws the individual to the referent of the symbol. The problem of religious language with respect to God results from its total existential and logical inadequacy to properly symbolize the great God, the totally Other. The power of religious language stems from the concrete here-and-now existential depth and involvement which this language reflects for the person who is communicating with God via religious language. The problem of religious language arises from our overwhelming inability to adequately conceptualize or otherwise grasp the God with whom the communicating is being done.

The Usefulness of Religious Language. Given the ambiguous, highly abstract, and fragile character of religious language, we can readily sympathize with the religious educator who seriously questions the utility of religious language in terms of furthering the attainment of his primary pedagogical objective of facilitating Christian living. To be sure, one of the major themes of my trilogy is that religious verbal behavior represents a much lower ontological and pedagogical level than religious nonverbal behavior, particularly when the latter is of the lifestyle variety. We are saved by our deeds far more than by our words.

Despite its limitations, religious verbal behavior is quite useful in the religion lesson just as it is useful throughout one's entire life span. A highly illuminating perspective from which to view the value and practicality of religious verbal behavior is that offered by John Langsham Austin in his seminal distinction between performative utterances and constative utterances. I will treat of this important notion in the section dealing with the form of verbal content. Suffice it to state at this juncture that a performative utterance is one which does something, while a constative utterance is one which describes something.[49] For example, when a Christian says: "I understand the role of baptism as a sacrament of initiation," his verbal behavior simply describes a certain kind of cognitive content. But when this same Christian declares "I baptize you" while he is pouring water on the head of another person, those words, when properly received by the other person in the prescribed situational context, actually in themselves do something.

One of the most important zones setting off religious language from theological language is precisely the conceptualization of performative language and constative language. Theology is a cognitive science. Consequently, all theological language is perforce constative. Theological language can only describe religious events and experiences; it can only speak *about*. Theological language can never perform some religious act by means of its words. Religious language, on the other hand, is both constative and performative. Religious language such as "I felt the presence of God while I watched the rolling thunderclouds pass overhead" describes experienced religious feelings. Statements like "I believe in the bible" are acts of performative commitment. Religious instruction is not theological instruction; it is religious instruction. Consequently the teacher cannot be content to just stay at the level of theological descriptive words. Rather, he must endeavor to see that, when appropriate, the verbal behavior of the learners is religious language, that is, both constative and performative.

Religious language has utility and value for the task of religious instruction primarily to the degree that it: (1) reflects and expresses the realities it symbolizes; (2) provides deeper and more educational meaning to experience; (3) evokes cognitive, affective, and lifestyle responses in the learner; (4) describes significant religious understandings, events, and experiences, in addition to performing religious acts in and through the very words themselves.

Religious language is verbal behavior *to* or *with* God. Theological language is verbal behavior *about* God. Theological language is thus seriously tied down and restricted to the tremendous existential inadequacy which is necessarily attendant upon any attempt to catch God in humanity's conceptual nets. Religious language breaks through these nets, to some extent at least, because religious language only partially deals with the individual's conception or perception of God. Religious language, from the subjective standpoint, consists not only in the individual's cognitive awareness of the God to whom or with whom a person is speaking, but even more importantly in the expression of affective impulses and lifestyle strivings of that person to and with God. It is the personal subjective affective and lifestyle dimensions of religious language which, in the final analysis, imbue religious language with such rich and personal meaning and with such efficacy. It is the affective and lifestyle dimensions of religious language which make communication to and with God possible. Lacking the rich flow of affective and lifestyle currents, theological language can do little more than remain moored to that existential inadequacy and, to some extent, inaccuracy which is the lot of any of human being's efforts to cognitively speak to God.

Theological language, expressing as it does the cognitive character of theology, treats of God as an object. To speak about one's investigation *of* God or of one's thinking *about* God is, in effect, to treat God as an object. This is what theological language must inevitably do. But religious language treats God as a subject, as a person. To speak to God and with God is to treat God as a subject. Religious language is thus typically more personally satisfying and fulfilling than theological language. We need theological language to express and develop conceptualizations and theories of God and of his workings in the world. We need religious language to praise God, to thank him, to petition him, and, in short, to have converse with him as he shines in and through all creation.

The Importance of Verbal Content

Verbal language enables an individual to accomplish two tasks which are essential to his existence as a human being. First, it makes it possible for him to communicate his thoughts to others. Second, verbal language forms a major basis on which internal mental images and concepts are organized and classified in the process called cognition.[50] Despite this tremendous importance of verbal language in the lives of human beings and in the work of religious instruction, religious educators have seldom given sufficient attention to the phenomenon of language.[51]

Verbal language and cognition, then, are highly interconnected. "In a way every word is a symbol and all our thinking may be described as thinking in symbols."[52] As Marshall McLuhan observes, "Language does for intelligence what the wheel does for the feet and the body. It enables them to move from thing to thing with greater ease and speed and ever less involvement. Language extends and amplifies man."[53] One of the major reasons accounting for human dominance in the world is that, unlike animals, a person can intimately link cognitions in linguistic symbols in such a way as to be able to (1) extricate from cognitions new implications and (2) combine different verbal symbols to eventually produce new leaps forward in cognitions.

From the psychological perspective, Jerome Bruner argues that language is a process which not only symbolically represents experience, but also transforms it.[54] From the linguistics perspective, the most forceful advocacy of the highly influential, if not indeed the determinable, role of language on experience and particularly on culture is the Sapir-Whorf hypothesis.[55] The foundation, or at least the guiding spirit of the Sapir-Whorf hypothesis, is psychological. According to this hypothesis, language is a form of an individual's perception of phenomena. In other words, language is a certain way of viewing and interpreting experience. As an infant, an individual is initiated, not only into a particular culture, but into the verbal language which that culture employs. If culture is a set of experiences freely flowing into an individual's personality, then language is a categorization or system of rules by which these experiences are classified and interpreted. No person ever directly experiences the basic, pristine stimuli of reality in its naked form; an individual experiences reality only through the filter of perception, a filter whose mesh is composed of many kinds of categories and classification systems, one of the most potent of which is language. A person classifies according to the names, according to the verbal labels which that individual knows, tending to discard everything else. One perceives in reality those things which the rules of one's particular linguistic system have made one sensitive to. This kind of slanted but completely normal perception is very powerful because to a large extent a person is typically unaware of the effects which his native language as a system has on the objectivity of his perception.[56] (Thus, for example, certain advocates of the theological approach to religious instruction tend mistakenly to criticize the structured-learning-situation strategy which I have proposed as the optimum pedagogical model, alleging that the SLS minimizes the learner's freedom. What these advocates of the theological approach fail to grasp, among many other things, is that their beloved verbal transmission/proclamation strategy affords the learner far less freedom because the transmitter/herald is locking up the learners in the cells of his (the herald's) own individual linguistic categories. (According to the Sapir-Whorf hypothesis we are imprisoned in a house of language).[57]

Verbal language enables an individual to engage in vicarious experiences, albeit on a highly abstract and symbolic level. By means of verbal content a person can learn *about* the experiences of others without being present when these experiences happen. For example, it is because of the verbal content which is the bible that persons down through the centuries can vicariously share the experiences of the sufferings of Jesus, the dreams of Peter, and the apostolic labors of Paul.

Human existence is welded to language. If a person lacks the ability to use language, that individual is not considered normal. Handling verbal content is regarded as much a part of the human condition as seeing or feeling or loving. No other form of animal life is known to possess the ability to communicate verbally; such a skill as far as we know at present is a uniquely human one.

Because language is so intimately tied in with the human condition, it is an important element of the fabric binding persons together in relationships of association or community. Thus Gabriel Moran comments that a community uses a common core of verbal content for its existence. This common language serves two functions, one thrusted outward and the other inward: it manifests the common ties of experience and purpose, and it serves as a linking force helping to bind the members of the group more closely together.[58] In terms of the second function, it was Edward Sapir who observed that verbal language is one of the greatest forces of socialization which exists.[59] Most religious denominations have their own special language which tends at once to show the world that they are a group and to bind them more closely together.

Language is very important for intellectual activity. Psychologists specializing in cognitive development claim that "meaningful verbal learning is the human mechanism *par excellence* for acquiring and storing the vast quantity of ideas and information represented in any body of knowledge."[60]

Some verbal content falls into the category of performative language. In other words, some words or phrases do something. For example, when a judge states: "I sentence you to four years in prison" his words exert a performative function. As I shall discuss more at length later in this chapter, while all performatives do something, not all performatives cause something. Thus, if an ecclesiastical official states, "I believe your views on the Eucharist are inaccurate," these words do not cause the views to be inaccurate. Some performative words, such as the "I do" or "I will" by the bride and bridegroom are clearly causative. Religious educators ought to be particularly attentive to those verbal contents which are directly or indirectly causative. Just as the very mention of the word "cancer" has been said to sometimes hasten the death of some patients with this disease, it has also been shown that telling learners they are dull or bright tends sometimes to make them so.[61]

Religious instruction is a social activity involving the teacher and the learners. Verbal content exerts a highly significant role in the development and control of a person's thoughts, affects, and conduct. Persons are educated to be responsive to verbal code words such as "Stop!" "Listen!" "Do this!" and so forth. Some important contingencies of reinforcement are verbal.[62] Parents and other religious educators teach a child to name religious realities by reinforcing what they believe to be correct responses. If the child says "crucifix" when the object before him is a crucifix, the parent or teacher says "good!" But if the object is a bible, the parent or teacher says "wrong!"[63] Words, then, are used to educate in any desired direction. As such, words can either enhance the learner's freedom or do violence to it.

A human being is so tied up with the verbal content he mentally or orally uses that to examine a person's language is, to a certain extent, to examine the person using the language. An important way to find out about a person is in and through the language which that individual employs. Verbal content is one of the houses of a person's being. Indeed, verbal content outers some of the deeper and unconscious aspects of an individual's personality. Differences in language have been found to exist between persons with high anxiety and those with low anxiety, between schizophrenics and normal individuals, between those whose heart is filled with love and those whose heart is bitter, and so forth.[64] For the religion teacher, therefore, verbal content is not only a crucial pedagogical tool but it also provides valuable insights into the learner's personality and lifestyle behavior.[65]

Some Limitations of Verbal Content

One of the most serious limitations of verbal content arises not so much from the nature of verbal content itself, but from what religious educationists and educators imagine verbal content is and what it can do. For these individuals, especially for those adhering to the theological approach to religious instruction, verbal content is claimed to comprise the whole, or at least the essence of teaching. To teach is to speak—this is the contention. In support of their position, religious educationists and educators typically cite the biblical text: "Faith comes from hearing" (Rom. 10:17). The goal of religious instruction, according to these persons, is faith, and, as the bible says, faith is brought about by listening to the verbal content of and about God's word. For Protestants, this text is decisive because it is in the bible. For Catholics, this text has been cited over and over again by popes and theologians. Thus, for example, Thomas Aquinas writes: "In its essence, faith comes from infusion and is given through baptism; however, the shape and degree which faith assumes come from hearing, and so a person is taught his faith by catechetics."[66] Catholics even today—principally Catholics advocating the theological approach to religious instruction—typically use the term "catechetics" instead of religious instruction. The word "catechetics" comes from the Greek meaning "to inform by word of mouth," or "to sound down," and has been traditionally used to indicate "the act of informing and instructing by oral tradition; the idea being that children in school were instructed by making them 'sing out' in chorus the answers to the questions asked by the teacher."[67] To be sure, the Catholic word "catechetics" not only means exclusive verbal content but also directly denotes that set of words officially approved by the Catholic *ecclesiasticum*.[68]

That teaching is fundamentally verbal content constitutes the prime pedagogical principle of the vast majority of Protestant and Catholic theologically oriented religious educationists down to the present. Alfonso Nebreda puts it plainly and directly: "So God has decided that his Word should prolong the line of incarnation and be transmitted through human words. *Fides ex auditu.*"[69] For Nebreda, a religion teacher is "a carrier of the word of God."[70] Hubert Halbfas, a German, extravagantly claims that "we can examine the world only through language" because, in the final analysis, "the category of reality is defined in terms of language." Because language is "the basic expression of existence," it naturally follows that "introduction to reality is therefore essentially instruction in language."[71] Actually, "language decides what existence means." Tjeu van den Berk, a Dutchman, writes that catechetics can be described "as the verbal expression of the ultimate meaning of our existence."[72] Paul Brunner forges a very close link between catechetics and homiletics, stating that they are both addressed to the question of how liturgy and the faith should be explained to the faithful.[73] For William Reedy, catechetical method is basically linguistic: "All during our catechizing, we should be explaining." The catechist, in a step-by-step-manner, prepares, presents, explains, summarizes, and applies, all in the verbal mode.[74] For Marcel van Caster, a Belgian, "catechesis, the ministry of the word of God, consists in proclaiming and interpreting the word of God." To be sure, proclamation "constitutes the most important catechetical operation." Faith comes from hearing; hence in catechetics, the learner's prime function is to be the hearer while that of the teacher is to be the proclaimer or transmitter of the word. The most effective form of catechesis consists in active verbal dialogue "between him who transmits the word of God and him who receives it."[75] The Higher Institute of Catechetics of Nijmegen (Holland) defines catechetics as witnessing to the mystery of Jesus through the proclamation of verbal content. The primacy of verbal content in catechesis has biblical roots: "He who hears you hears me" (Lk. 10:16), and "faith comes from hearing" (Rom. 10:17). Catechesis represents a special form of witness, namely a witness by means of the word. Thus it can be concluded that "proclamation is the means *par excellence* for imparting Christian meaning to man's existence."[76] For Joseph Colomb, a Frenchman, catechesis is basically a process in which the teacher speaks and the learner listens. If the learner perchance does not correctly or fully understand the verbal content transmitted to him, then the catechist will find it necessary to state the verbal content more clearly and in proper terms.[77] Berard Marthaler places himself in full agreement with the position that catechesis is "a form of the ministry of the word." While in no way gainsaying the importance of the catechist's living Christian witness, he agrees with the theological approach's contention that "the primary form of catechesis is the spoken word—faith comes from hearing" (Rom. 10:17).[78] Marianne Sawicki, a former student of Marthaler, strongly contends that catechetics is essentially the ministry of the word, and that catechists are fundamentally ministers of the word.[79]

The thesis that teaching in general and religion teaching in specific is fundamentally verbal content has many deficiencies. Four of the most glaring of these are that it gives to words a wider range of effectiveness than they actually possess; it constitutes an overly restrictive notion of teaching, thus shriveling the scope of teaching and crippling its effectiveness; it places a premium on teacher dominance and learner passivity; and it is based on the transmissionist or proclamation "theory" of religious instruction.

Advocates of the "verbal-content-is-teaching" theory ascribe to words a much greater power and a wider range of effectiveness than they possess. Hubert Halbfas, for example, holds that language decides what existence means. This empirically unsupported claim is obviously extravagant. Almost all verbal content can directly and of itself only yield more verbal content. Only in an indirect fashion can verbal content of itself typically give rise to outcomes or behaviors which are not verbal. Language, after all, is simply a verbal content, an abstract symbol. Language is just an intermediary, and often an opaque one at that. Jean Le Du pointedly warns religious educators never to sacralize the intermediacy of language.[80]

The assertion that verbal content equals teaching constitutes an overly restrictive notion of the pedagogical process. Teaching is a mode of intentional, goal-directed communication. A basic error of the advocates of the "teaching-is-verbal-content" position is that they fail to see that verbal language is only one kind of communication. But communication is far wider than just the verbal. Roy Buehler and Jo Richmond have constructed a taxonomy of communicative behaviors of which the verbal constitutes only a part. Their categories are: (1) biochemical communication, including body contact and noncontact body reactions such as laughing or sighing; (2) motor-movement communication such as posture, facial movement, and gestures; (3) speech communication, including verbal utterances and simple sound utterances (oral utterances without verbal form); and (4) technological communication like drawings and charts.[81]

To claim that teaching equals the heralding of verbal content is to place a premium on teacher dominance and learner passivity. Thus Josef Goldbrunner, a German, states that because the essence of catechetics is to verbally herald the message, the religion teacher should not encourage initiative and independent work as is done in "secular" subjects, but rather should transmit the message "with authority." The catechetical message "cannot be found by itself [as in discovery teaching], it cannot be grasped through the 'learning by doing' principle. It must be proclaimed and heard."[82] Unhappily, teacher dominance and learner passivity ignore the basic pedagogical principle that teaching is a cooperative art-science, and not an operative one.

Finally, the thesis that teaching is basically verbal content naturally flows from the transmission "theory" of religious instruction. Because I treat of this pseudo-theory at some length in *The Flow of Religious Instruction,*[83] it is unnecessary at this juncture to detail the reasons why the transmission "theory" is incapable of serving as an adequate or fruitful wellspring from which effective pedagogical practices can flow.

To interpret the biblical text "faith comes from hearing" as meaning that faith and its enlargement come exclusively or even primarily from listening to oral transmissions of God's word represents an unduly restrictive and myopic exegesis. In Romans 10:14–17, Paul the Apostle is speaking specifically of preaching. In biblical times there were no books, movies, television, or multi-media devices available to the vast majority of the population. Hence the only way in which most persons of those days could hear the linguistic word of God was through the mouth of a preacher. Moreover, the bible is explicitly a book of religion and religious instruction;[84] it is not a manual on how to teach. Furthermore, enormous advances in teaching practice have been made since biblical times, advances unknown in Paul's day and age. To restrict all religion teaching practice to the kind of pedagogical practice known by biblical personages is not only ludicrous but in a real sense unbiblical.

Those religious educationists who equate or at least identify the word of God with words are in error biblically, revelationally, existentially, and pedagogically. As Roger Shinn rightly emphasizes, the biblical word is never just verbal words. The biblical word is God's total and living communication. Most decisively of all, Shinn observes, the word of God is "the Word made flesh in Jesus Christ."[85] Edward Schillebeeckx notes that the Hebres *dābhār* meant simultaneously a spoken/written word and also an event in nature and in history. *Dābhār* was something which was not just spoken; it was something which was done. No distinction seems to have been made in ancient Israel between the word and the person speaking. Speaking was simply one symbolic way of expressing the being of the person; the importance of the word was in direct proportion to the person and to the deeds it pointed to. For ancient Israel, the word of God included every activity with humanity and the world, and not linguistic activity alone.[86] In the bible, God spoke much more frequently and much more powerfully through deeds than through words. If the bible is itself a collection of inspired words it is because by means of parchments and books, words can be communicated from epoch to epoch whereas people die and cannot be communicated, and events pass and cannot be relived. The word of God is not solely or even basically a linguistic unit; it is the totality of God's living communication to us. Verbal content is one of its segments—and, I would argue, not at all the most important or most fruitful segment. Gabriel Moran comments that if God's word were simply a linguistic unit, then a person could control this kind of word and pass it on merely by communicating verbal content. But if the word is the communication of a person, then there are no words which can adequately express the word of God.[87] Revelation ought never to be regarded as restricted to revelation-in-word; revelation is also, and more importantly, revelation-in-reality.[88] Revelation for us is our human existential encounter with the entire reality of God as this reality permeates and soaks all of creation. Revelation, then, is not simply the encounter of an individual's cognitive powers with the verbal dimension of God's revelation. Revelation ought never to be made identical with words.

An analysis of the bible will, by and large, show that God typically encased his words in the broader, more fruitful context of a major person, a major event, or a major encounter.

To teach religion is not to transmit words about God or spread the Christian cognitive message, as theologically oriented transmission theorists would have it. Rather, to teach religion is to structure a pedagogical situation in which the learner acquires a personalized religous lifestyle. Lifestyle, not verbal content, should be the *terminus a quo* and the *terminus ad quem* for all religion teaching. Christianity is a lifestyle, not a collection of words. The object of the act of faith is not words or even the understanding of them; the object of faith is a lived relationship with God. James Smart comments that God did not entrust his gospel to a book but to a fellowship of disciples who lived a gospel lifestyle. Scripture takes on its revelatory power and meaning when it is incarnated in the life of the church, in the lifestyles of the men and women who comprise the church:[89] "The Word became flesh," not word. More important than verbal content is sacrament, that encounter between a person's fullness and God.[90]

One of the primary reasons why religious instruction has so often been unduly constricted to verbal content alone is because religious instruction has been under the direct seignory of theology. It must be remembered that words are all that theology really has. Without words, theology would cease to exist. Theology is fundamentally a verbal affair. While theology can be deduced or induced from nonverbal behavior, for example, theology can never be nonverbal in nature. Religious instruction, on the other hand, deals primarily with religious experience and religious lifestyle. To the extent that verbal content (and theology) are relevant to experiencing and to Christian living, to that extent and only to that extent may verbal content and theology be legitimately brought into the religion lesson. Religious instruction, then, is far richer, far broader, and far more holistically experiential than theology. Not until religious instruction frees itself from the seignory of theology and becomes an autonomous field will it be able to broaden its base to include nonverbal contents of all sorts, including affect and lifestyle. I strongly suspect that one of the major underlying motives of people like Berard Marthaler who strive so fiercely to restrict religious instruction to verbal messages is to make sure that religious instruction remains firmly under the control of theology rather than becoming an autonomous field.[91]

Today's religious instruction is, unhappily, the meetingplace of the scribes and the word mongers. Religion teachers are not infrequently calcified in their verbal arrogance as if the world and the Christian message are fundamentally verbal in nature. Yet even a casual glance at the world shows us that words are not the most productive or fruitful content. Words are an important content of religious instruction, to be sure, but far more important, far more foundational, and far more revelational are lifestyle and affective contents. It is through our love for Jesus, it is by following Jesus in our daily lives—and not just talking about Jesus—that we truly live and learn the Christian way.

THE FORM OF VERBAL CONTENT

Verbal behavior is not coextensive with language. Rather, verbal behavior is a type or an instance of language. In addition to verbal behavior, language includes graphs, maps, gestures, music—in short, a wide variety of communication modes. If verbal behavior is a type of language, then language is a type of communication.

All communication, whether verbal or nonverbal, is composed of at least six elements. First there is a *source* or sender. The source *encodes* that which he intends to communicate. This encoded *message* is then sent through some particular *channel*. The encoded message is picked up by a *receiver* who in turn *decodes* the original encoded message.[92]

Verbal communication is so fragile and so open to misunderstanding for many reasons, including the following: (1) the original linguistic symbol is encoded by the sender not simply in accord with the conventional meaning attached by society to that symbol but also with his own particular understanding of the meaning of that symbol; (2) in the very act of sending, the linguistic symbol takes on additional symbols which heighten or modify the referent of the original symbol; (3) the kind of channel through which the symbols are sent serves to shape and mold the original linguistic symbol; and (4) the received symbol, already altered in the ways indicated above, is further changed by the receiver in the decoding process. As an upshot of all this, the religion teacher and curriculum builder need to be acutely aware of the danger of the misunderstanding which is inherent in the communication of verbal content. The religious educator, in speaking and in writing, should use words with utmost care and with consummate precision. A general pedagogical rule to follow is that verbal content should be used only when other, less indirect forms of communication are either impossible, unfeasible, or unsuitable to the desire learning outcome.

It is most important for the religion teacher and the curriculum builder to constantly bear in mind that their verbal content does not transmit truth or truths to the learner. What their verbal content does is simply to place before the learner an abstract linguistic symbol or set of symbols. These symbols mediate the desired learnings to the extent to which the learner's understanding of and frame of reference for the particular linguistic symbols match those of the teacher. Hence when the teacher or curriculum builder uses verbal content the effect is not direct but indirect. There is no transfusion of linguistic message from sender to receiver in the way there is for a transfusion of blood.

Linguistics

Linguistics is the formal study of verbal language as a system of communication.[93]

At least five general fields of specialization exist within linguistics.[94] *General linguistics* (sometimes referred to as theoretical linguistics) deals with the parameters and delimitations of the area of linguistics. *Descriptive linguistics* is concerned with the conditions and operations required for effective language use. Thus, for example, phonology and grammar are forms of descriptive linguistics. *Comparative linguistics* examines similar language structures and operations in two or more languages, while *historical linguistics* gives precise accounts of the temporal development of a language or languages. Both comparative linguistics and historical linguistics utilize the methodology of descriptive linguistics. *Applied linguistics* consists in putting general linguistics and descriptive linguistics to concrete, here-and-now use in a particular situation.

The effective religion teacher utilizes applied linguistics in the fashioning and reception of words, word forms, and word structures during the course of the lesson.[95] He draws on the findings of historical and comparative linguistics when he teaches the bible. In order to sharpen and enhance his pedagogical analysis of and control over his own verbal behavior and that of the learners, the effective religious educator draws from the theories advanced in general linguistics and from the language procedures detailed in descriptive linguistics. The study of linguistics serves to heighten the teacher's awareness of the nature and use of verbal content, thus yielding more fruitful instructional practice.[96] Consequently, linguistics is of considerable practical import and relevance for the religion teacher as well as for the curriculum builder.

In the twentieth century, notably since the conclusion of World War II, linguistics has become increasingly scientific. Whereas the traditional approach to linguistics was primarily speculative and consequently subjective, the contemporary thrust is empirical and hence objective. Commenting on this, the Jesuit scholar Francis Dinneen remarks that the linguistician is dissatisfied with the traditional approach because deficiencies in its methodological procedures have consistently led to a lack of precision. The most important claim linguistics makes, Dinneen notes, is that it is scientific and hence employs scientific methodology. Such methodology includes "the use of controlled experiment, in which the variable factors involved have been precisely identified in an objective way, as well as the requirement that the methods used be made public, so that the results of an experiment can be verified. Thus a scientific study should be empirical, exact, and, therefore objective."[97] The battle to free linguistics from the speculative and the subjective, and to set it on the firmer footing of empirical methodology can be fruitfully compared to the current struggle to emancipate religious instruction from the strangling grip of theological speculation and subjectivity. Once linguistics embraced the social-science perspective and utilized social-science procedures, significant new advances began to proliferate. So also, when religious instruction fully and consciously embraces the social-science approach, exciting breakthroughs can be expected.

Psycholinguistics. One of the zones in which linguistics has most discernibly moved in the direction of social science is that of psycholinguistics. Psycholinguistics is that interdisciplinary field in which the theories, laws, constructs, and research procedures of psychology are applied to linguistic phenomena. Psycholinguistics may be defined as the study of linguistic behavior as influencing and influenced by psychological factors. The fruitful friction generated by the meshing of linguistics and psychology is inherently productive not only of important new insights into the nature and processes of verbal behavior, but also of a crossfertilization of these two sciences themselves. Thus, for example, when it was discovered that the Navajos could not distinguish green from blue, psychologists gave these Indians tests for color blindness, while linguisticians adhering to the Sapir-Whorf hypothesis claimed that the fact that there exists only one word for blue/green in the Navajo language itself imposes the faulty color perception.[98]

Six major approaches to psycholinguistics have been distinguished. These approaches are complementary; they are ways of investigating and clarifying verbal processes. (1) The *normative approach* focuses on spoken or written linguistic units in order to ascertain developmental norms concerning usage, to categorize verbal behavior in terms of usage, or to develop new categories of linguistics for the purpose of adequately describing usage. Much of the empirical research in this approach deals with nonsense syllables or words. (2) The *material approach* investigates language as the content or matter which is being learned by an individual. A great deal of the research in this area centers around word associations and rote.[99] (3) The *mediational approach* concentrates on the physiological or psychological processes which are hypothesized to productively intervene between stimuli and verbal responses, between responses and verbal responses, and between verbal stimuli and responses. Thus, for example, "justice" and "war," though not directly or intrinsically associated, might become so if a person who thinks "justice" also thinks "peace." The latter may lead to the word "war," thus serving to mediate between "justice" and "war."[100] Verbal mediators, for their part, are, in a sense, a covert language. (4) The *linguistic approach* examines the language aspect of verbal behavior, and then applies these data and findings to human verbal behavior. For example, the linguistic form and structure of preverbal stages of infant vocalization are compared to the vocalizations of adult speech. (5) The *behavioral approach* seeks to better understand, explain, predict, and control human behavior in general by studying linguistic behavior in particular. The behavioral approach takes as its point of departure the notion that verbal behavior is a kind or instance of a more generalized flow of human behavior. (6) The *methodological approach* seeks to locate the bases and the operative processes of verbal dysfunction. Scholars utilizing this approach seek explanations of verbal deficiency in order that such explanations will eventually lead to a remedying of (or at least a coping with) such deficiencies, and that such explanations will contribute in their own right to a more complete knowledge of human behavior in general and of verbal behavior in particular. Difficulties in verbal comprehension, impaired skills in reading or writing, and other linguistic problems are of particular concern to religious educators working with psychologically handicapped learners or with learners experiencing permanent or temporary verbal blockages.

The Structure of Linguistics. It is generally recognized that there are five principal branches of linguistics: phonology, morphology, syntax (grammar), semantics, and etymology. Through the study of these five specializations linguisticians endeavor to: (1) elucidate and bring out more clearly the meaning of linguistic units and their combinations; (2) enhance linguistic competence; and (3) develop more fruitful theories of language, theories which will possess a high degree of explanatory power and which will generate more effective and more motile verbal behavior. Because these three goals of linguistics are intimately related to the task of religious instruction, the teacher and curriculum builder can profit from the findings of the scientific study of language.

Phonology is the study of the nature and use of vocal sounds, with special focus on the phoneme.[101] A phoneme is defined as the smallest unit of speech that distinguishes one utterance from another in all the variations it exhibits in the speech of one particular person.[102] The number of phonemes in world languages ranges from thirteen to fifty-five. Examples of an English language phoneme would be such as Go*d*, *d*aring, and loa*d*. Phonemes form the basic building blocks of speech, as it were.[103]

Morphology is the scientific study of the morpheme. A morpheme is the smallest formal unit of a language. Put in a negative fashion, a morpheme is a unit which is formally kept apart from all other such units in a given language. A morpheme is not the same as a word. Rather, a morpheme may be a whole word or a formal part of a word.[104] The word "God" is a single morpheme; it cannot be broken down into smaller formal parts. The word "gods," however, is composed of two morphemes, the second of which (the "s") means, in English, plural. The letter "s" is a morpheme, but not a word. C. E. Bazell suggests that a morpheme "serves less to express a meaning than to express a distinction in meaning."[105]

Syntax (grammar) is the arrangement of morphemes in larger units. The function of syntax is to provide a systematized deployment of morphemes so as to express meaning. Rules for the correctness of syntax or grammar exist in order that the same structure of morphemes will express basically the same meaning regardless of the person using them or the external circumstances in which they are employed. In English, syntactic units are inflectional morphemes, words, phrases, clauses, and, according to some linguisticians, sentences. Thus in syntax there is a kind of hierarchical linguistic organization into units of progressively larger size and increased complexity.

Three fundamental schools of explanation or broad clusters of theory have been advanced by linguisticians to explain and predict syntax. The oldest theory, and probably the most familiar to Christian religious educators, is that of *traditional grammar*. This theory finds its roots in the work by the Hellenistic scholar from Alexandria, Dionysius Thrax, called *Technē grammaticē* (*The Art of Grammar*) written about 100 B.C.[106] Traditional grammar is basically normative and prescriptive. To speak good or correct grammar, a person must learn and use certain rules. For example, in English, the preposition "during" takes the accusative (objective) case, while the German equivalent of "during" (*während*) takes the genitive. Grammar rules in traditional grammar are frequently arbitrary, such as the distinction in English between "shall" and "will," or in German, the use of the genitive after "*während*."

With the posthumous publication in 1916 of Ferdinand de Saussure's book *Cours de Linguistique Générale* (*A Course in General Linguistics*), *structural grammar* can be said to have begun. Saussure held the thesis that language has both an inner and an outer form. The French linguistician contended that *langue* ("word" in the sense of language system) comprises the sum total of the regularities and patterns (rules) of formation which characterize a language, while *parole* ("word" in the sense of language behavior) is the actual language performance itself. *"Parole"* plugs into *"langue"* and both of these, taken together, go to form *langage* (language). In the United States, structural grammar had its heyday from the end of the First World War until the mid-1950s. The most influential book of this period was Leonard Bloomfield's *Language,* published in 1933. Structuralism is opposed to the atomism of traditional grammar. For Bloomfield and his followers, syntax is the study (and use) of free forms that are composed entirely of free forms. "The free forms (words and phrases) of a language appear in larger free forms (phrases), arranged by taxemes of modulation, phonetic modification, selection, and order. Any meaningful recurrent set of such taxemes is a syntactic construction."[107] The bases of all syntax are form classes and form constituent structure. Bloomfield's approach to language is positivistic and aims at eliminating any purely mental features from language use.[108] Post-Bloomfieldians tend to downplay the role of meaning in their analysis of language.[109]

A form of generative grammar, *transformational grammar,* was founded in 1957 by Zellig Harris[110] and his student Noam Chomsky.[111] Since 1957 the views of Harris and Chomsky have become increasingly divergent, with most of the transformationalists supporting Chomsky. While traditional grammar is prescriptive, both structural grammar and transformational grammar are purely descriptive.[112] Whereas structural grammar is empirical and inductive, transformational grammar is speculative and deductive. The structuralists take as their point of departure the bottommost fundamental sounds (phones), while Chomsky begins at the top with the "undefined primitive, the sentence 'S.'" Traditional grammar starts with the word, structural grammar with the phoneme, and transformational grammar with the sentence. Bloomfield asserts that a child learns grammar by imitation, while Chomsky claims that grammar is innate in every child. Bloomfield is a physicalist, Chomsky a mentalist.[113] Chomsky breaks down grammar into four sections or components: the phrase-

structure component; the transformational component; the mor-
phophonemic component; and the semantic component.[114] Syntax or
grammar is, in a sense, a theory of a particular language. Chomsky's
theory seeks to generate "all and only the grammatical sentences of a
language."[115]

Protestant missionaries desirous of translating the bible faithfully
into other languages, or of preaching biblical texts in accurate translation, have intensively studied both structural grammar and transformational grammar to assist them in their tasks.

Semantics considers the meaning of linguistic forms. An artificial or
logically constructed reality such as a linguistic form derives its meaning from (1) the actual reality to which it points, (2) the cultural reality
which society has accorded to it, (3) the personal reality with which an
individual has psychologically invested it, and (4) the structure of the
language in which it is situated.

Linguistic meaning is not an actual reality; it is a referent. Meaning
is not an entity but rather is a derivation or an inference from an entity.
Meaning, in a sense, is an interpretation. Thus meaning can never be
anything more than an hypothesis used to explain the reality to which it
refers. As soon as a person discovers a superior or more fruitful hypothesis (meaning), he discards the previous one. For, after all, a
hypothesis is only valuable when it possesses the power to explain
something usefully and simply.[116]

There are two major vantage points from which to view semantics,
namely from linguistics and from the philosophy of language.

From the linguistic standpoint, semantics is concerned with the investigation and communication of meaning by the grammatical and
lexical devices of a language.[117] The linguistician asks not merely
"What does language mean?", but perhaps even more importantly,
"How does language mean?" At least four different classes of linguistic meaning are typically identified by linguisticans.[118] (1) Referential
meaning is the literal, descriptive meaning of a linguistic unit. (2)
Figurative meaning is the metaphorical or allegorical meaning of a
linguistic unit. (3) Spiritual meaning is the nonphysical or supernatural
meaning of a linguistic unit. (4) Tautological meaning is the meaning
of a linguistic unit which is automatically expressed in its very formulation. Differences among these four meanings flow not so much
from their product content as from the verbal description employed.

Both how words mean and how sentences mean affect what words and sentences mean. In the here-and-now existential context, process content exerts an interactive impact on product content.

How a word means typically depends on how it is used. A word can function as a designator or as an expressor. Most words are used as designators. A designator is a word which points to, or "designates," the reality it purports to verbally stand for. There are two basic forms of designators, namely indicators and predicators. An indicator is a word which designates or "indicates" that about which the person wishes to speak. A predicator is the second kind of designator. A predicator is a word which designates or "predicates" a characteristic. An expressor is a word which describes one's personal, subjective relation to a reality. While the word "pain" designates pain, the word "ouch" expresses pain.

How do sentences mean? Many semanticists contend that the meaning of sentences can be more effectively found in their function than in their form (or perhaps more accurately, in the conceptualization of their form). The traditional formal classification suggests that there are four basic sentence forms: declarative, interrogative, imperative, and exclamatory. Viewed functionally, a sentence is either informational (cognitive), expressive (affective), or directive (the overt-action thrust of lifestyle). Though most persons operate on the basis of these form-function pairings, nevertheless one form may at times hide a function other than those with which it is paired. This disguised usage often causes difficulties in meaning. For example, when a priest or minister tells his congregation, "Sinners will go to hell," he might really be saying (meaning) "Stop your sinning!"[119]

In improving the semantic quality of the lesson, the religious educator should be mindful not only *what* his verbal behavior means, but perhaps more importantly *how* this behavior means. Process content (*how* it means) not only shapes the product content (*what* it means) but bestows upon the product content a new mode of existence and a new shape of meaning.

Thus far I have treated of semantics from the linguistic standpoint. Now I shall briefly touch on semantics from the aspect of the philosophy of language.

From the perspective of the philosophy of language, semantics considers the meaning of verbal behavior from the point of view of logic.[120] As a branch of logic, semantics investigates the relationship between verbal behavior and the realities to which this behavior points, with special emphasis on the interrelated problems of meaning, truth, and denotation. While philosophers over the centuries have wrestled with the question of verbal meaning, much of the new intensive and highly focused investigation of semantics from the philosophical-logical perspective can be said to have originated in the Vienna Circle. It then developed in Cambridge (England) and subsequently gained a strong foothold in the United States.

The importance of semantics in contemporary philosophy of logic grows out of the contention that all problems in philosophy are due to a misunderstanding or a confusion in language.[121] Hence the job of ascertaining the real meaning of verbal behavior becomes the central task of philosophy. But what is meaning? What does meaning mean? Margaret Gorman has nicely summed up some of the important explanations of meaning given down through the years.[122] First, meaning is the reality of which the sign is name-denotative. This is the notion accepted by most nonsemanticists and nonphilosophers. Second, meaning is an intricate property of realities. John Stuart Mill appears to hold this view. Third, meaning is an ideal reality. This is the Platonic conception. Fourth, meaning is the relation between linguistic units. Thus lexical meaning is obtained by finding another linguistic unit which is synonymous with the original one. Fifth, meaning is the set of operations which a person can perform with linguistic units. P. W. Bridgman espouses this conceptualization. Sixth, meaning consists in one's overall reaction to the linguistic unit. This reaction might be the practical consequence of the linguistic unit for one's own future life (William James), or the habit it produces in an individual (Charles Peirce), or the reflex conditioning which the person has to sign or signal (Ivan Pavlov). Seventh, meaning is the total personal encounter with linguistic units and the realities to which they point. This conceptualization of meaning stresses the personal element far more than does the sixth hypothesis. Eighth, meaning flows directly from the relationship between thought and the reality which is thought, and only indirectly between the linguistic unit and the reality to which it points. Charles Ogden and Ivor Richards support this view.

Two of the most prominent contemporary philosophers of language who are vitally concerned with semantics are Alfred Tarski and Rudolf Carnap. Tarski, a mathematician and logician, developed a precise set-theoretical description of basic semantic notions, together with a very careful treatment of the language in which linguistic units are expressed and expressible. Through the use of these analytical tools, Tarski discovered both general properties of these semantic notions and ways in which these notions could be applied.[123] Carnap, though generally a representative of logical positivism, nonetheless contends that philosophy, far from being devoid of meaning, is rather "fulfilled by semantics." The task of philosophy is semantic analysis, states Carnap. Indeed, formalized propositional logic represents a semantic system.[124] If indeed there is a grain of truth in Carnap's contention that the task of philosophy is semantic analysis, then could it not also be true that the task of both religious thought and of theology[125] is also inextricably bound up with semantic analysis, with the search for linguistic meaning? The implications of this tentative hypothesis for religious instruction, especially for its cognitive side (and even for its human relations aspect)[126] are far-reaching. For example, as Thomas McPherson pointedly asks: "Is religious belief expressible in a set of meaningful assertions?" McPherson goes on to state that this question has two halves, namely, is an expression of religious belief meaningful and is an expression of religious belief an assertion?[127]

Etymology investigates the origins and history of a linguistic unit such as a morpheme or a word. Etymology traces both the structural and the substantive components of a linguistic unit back to its earliest usage, and then explores how and under what conditions this unit was used in the verbal behavior of previous ages and cultures. One branch of etymology is concerned with identifying cognate linguistic units or forms among various contemporary languages.[128] Another branch of etymology attempts to track similar linguistic units or forms of related languages back to a common ancestral origin.

Use of relevant findings from etymology can be singularly beneficial to the religion teacher. The introduction of the etymological meaning of a word or a morpheme can trigger a deeper awareness in the learner of the reality which a particular unit symbolizes. The learner's grasp of the sense of the word "holy," for example, might well be enhanced when he finds out that this word is derived from an Old English linguistic form meaning "whole, healthy, perfect."

Functions of Language

What language is perceived to do, or what it actually might do depends on the vantage point from which one examines linguistic function.

One useful perspective from which to view linguistic function is that of *performative-nonperformative* language. Toward the conclusion of my treatment of religious language, I observed that performative language is that which itself brings something to pass, while nonperformative (constative) language simply describes phenomena.[129] Thus in marriage ceremony, the words ''I do'' or ''I will,'' if freely uttered by the man and the woman, ratify the marriage. These words are performative; they do something.

John Langsham Austin, who appears to have invented or at least to have made salient the distinction between performative and constative language, identifies five types of performatives.[130] First, a *verdicative* gives a judgment or verdict about a phenomenon. Examples of verdicatives include estimate, analyze, appraise, reckon, grade, value, and judge. The judgment expressed by a verdicative need not be final, such as is the case with estimate or appraise. A verdict has an effect, in the law, on oneself and on others. Second, an *exercitive* consists in the exercise of power, influence, or a right. ''It is the giving of a decision in favor of or against a certain course of action, or advocacy of it.''[131] An exercitive is a decision that something is to be so, rather than a judgment that something is so. Exercitives include order, decree, appoint, excommunicate, annul, resign, urge, advise, and dedicate. Third, a *commissive,* as its name suggests, commits a person to do something. However, this category also includes ''declarations or announcements of intention, which are not promises, and also rather vague things, which we may call espousals.''[132] Illustrations of commissives include promise, covenant, contract, plan, intend, favor, bet, agree, and propose to. Fourth, a *behavitive*[133] encompasses ''the notion of reaction to other people's behavior and fortunes and of attitudes and expressions of attitudes to someone else's past conduct or imminent conduct.''[134] Thus for greetings, there is ''welcome''; for wishes, ''bless'; for challenges, ''protest''; for apologies, ''apologize''; and for sympathy, ''commiserate.'' Fifth, an *expositive* is a word ''used in acts of exposition involving the expounding of views, the conducting of arguments, and the clarifying of usages and of references.''[135] Expositives include inform, state, report, and identify.

''To sum up,'' Austin writes, ''we may say that the verdicative is an exercise of judgment, the exercitive is an assertion of influence or exercising power, the commissive is an assuming of an obligation or declaring of an intention, the behavitive is the adopting of an attitude, and the expositive is the clarifying of reasons, arguments, and communications.''[136]

Donald Evans observes that words in two of these performative categories entail the self-involvement of the person uttering them. These categories are the commissive and the behavitive.[137] In a commissive, the person commits himself to do something. A commissive is an intention, a pledge. For its part, a behavitive implies that the person has a particular reaction or attitude.

Most proponents of the conceptualization of performative language claim that this form of speech or writing is neither true nor false.[138] Instead, it is felicitous or infelicitous. According to this notion, a performative simply does something. To do something merely indicates that some action was undertaken or completed; it does not indicate truth or falsity. At bottom, truth and falsity are cognitive judgments, and hence can be predicated only in a cognitive way. An overt performance is an overt performance; it is not a cognitive activity. To say "I do" or "I will" in a marriage ceremony is not true or false; truth or falsity are not intrinsically germane to this performative utterance. But to say "I do" or "I will" can have happy or unhappy consequences, depending on how well the marriage develops. Happiness or unhappiness, not truth or falsity, are associated with performatives.

It is important to distinguish, as Donald Evans does, between the performative function and the causal function of a linguistic act. All performatives do something, but not all performatives cause something.[139] For example, a verdicative expression such as "I judge your statement to be inaccurate" does not cause the statement to be inaccurate. A performative can have a wide variety of direct or indirect causal functions. Thus, the performative "I do" or "I will" freely uttered by the bride at a wedding ceremony may not only produce the ratification of the marriage (direct causality) but may also bring about rage and frustration in a rejected former suitor in attendance (indirect causality). Often the performative function of a linguistic act is independent of its causal power. For example, John Jones might thank Richard Catanzaro for a favor, but the performative might not cause any feeling of gratitude in Jones. Or a person might utter words of alarm, but his hearers might not be thereby alarmed. When trying to bring about a desired effect, the religion teacher should consider the pedagogical advisability of carefully choosing those performatives which are most closely associated with the causal function which he would like these performatives to achieve. Exercitives tend to be reasonably well correlated with the causal function of linguistic acts. An exercitive, it should be noted, is not an inherently authoritarian or imperious kind of performative.

Perhaps the most familiar function of language is the declarative. A declarative performs a cognitive task; it informs. A declarative gives new information, or serves to reinforce or illumine previously held information. All declaratives have truth-value.

Yet another pivotal function of language is the expressive. Language expresses one's affects. Michael Polanyi points out that language is primarily interpersonal; consequently, to some degree language is the expression of a person's loves and hates, his emotions, attitudes, and so forth.[140] Expressive language, like all other kinds of language, has a revelatory power—it reveals the person's inner life. Yet expressive language tends to be more revelatory of the person's inner life than declarative language since it suggests where the individual is situated psychologically at any given moment. Expressives thus are particularly important in the religious instruction enterprise. The religion teacher should listen with the third ear to the learner's declaratives, for often they are expressives in declarative disguise. Declaratives are the language of the head; expressives are more closely linked to the language of the heart. Theological words are typically declaratives; religious words are typically expressives.

Some Important Verbal Forms

Words are not the reality to which they point. Rather, words are simply linguistic representations of one or another reality. Hence people all over the world use different verbal forms in an attempt to capture some particular aspect of the reality which they represent. Each form catches some aspect, some attribute of the reality which other verbal forms do not reflect nearly so well. Each of these forms has its own structure which must be understood in order to adequately grasp the meaning of the form. The bible and the liturgy are rich in their variety of verbal forms: proverbs, idioms, allegories, myths, parables, and metaphors, to name just a few. There is deep truth embodied in each of these verbal forms, and the important thing is to get at the truth embodied in any given verbal form. As James Smart reminds us, "failure to recognize the [verbal] form in which the truth is expressed may result in a failure to hear the truth itself."[141]

Idiom. An idiom is a linguistic expression which is peculiar to itself in grammatical construction (as "ain't"), or in possessing a meaning which cannot be put together as a whole from the combined or conjoined denotations of its elements (as "pass away" for "die").[142] An idiom is a word or expression which is proper, peculiar, and idiosyncratic to a particular culture, subculture, language, or dialect.[143] The creation of idioms represents an attempt by a culture or a subculture to enrich the standard language by making it more descriptive of what the idiom is intended to symbolize, by fashioning it more closely to the psychological contours of the group, or by making it more nuanced and more precise than standard linguistic expressions. An idiom is a rich and powerful verbal content, one which can enliven religious instruction.

Metaphor. A metaphor is a figure of speech in which two or more verbal symbols denoting quite different realities are juxtaposed in such a manner that each becomes identified with the other. I constructed this definition because virtually all the definitions of metaphor which one finds in dictionaries or in encyclopedias presume and enflesh one or another particular theory about the nature of metaphor.

The term "metaphor" comes from two Greek words meaning "a movement beyond." This "movement beyond" indicates that the basic nature and function of a metaphor is the movement beyond the conventional denotation of each of the key terms contained in the metaphor. A metaphor, then, is a linguistic clash between syntax and semantics. Syntactically, it is meaningless to say "The Lord is my shepherd." Semantically, however, this sentence is charged with deep and fruitful meaning. A metaphor, consequently, is a semantic movement (*phora*) which goes beyond (*meta*) the meaning denotatively indicated by the syntactic composition of the sentence. "The test of essential metaphor is not any role of grammatical form, but the quality of semantic transformation brought about."[144] A metaphor moves beyond normal syntactic meaning by "effecting instantaneous fusion of two separated realms of experience into one illuminating, iconic, encapsulating image."[145] In Victor Turner's words, "metaphor is, in fact, metamorphic, transformative."[146] A metaphor represents a shift in meaning. The verbal symbol jumps from one context to a completely different one.[147]

A metaphor triggers a psychological process in the person who encounters it. A metaphor presents the person with a cognitive conflict, a conflict generated by the juxtaposition of terms which seem to clash semantically because they typically clash grammatically. The psychological conflict produced in the person by means of this conflict provides an inner impulsion for him to resolve the conflict and come to semantic peace. Semantics, quite naturally, is far more important to the person than is syntax. Therefore his search for the meaning of the metaphor propels him to move (*phora*) beyond (*meta*) the meaning denoted by the metaphor's syntactical structure.

A metaphor juxtaposes two seemingly opposed verbal symbols in order to move beyond ordinary meaning to the realm of enriched meaning. A metaphor is thus a linguistic unit characterized by a struggle between the terms it contains.[148] Philip Wheelwright holds the theory that at bottom a metaphor is a vital form of what he calls "tensive language," language which is characterized by built-in structural tensions. Viewing metaphor as an instance of tensive language serves to reveal something of its nature.[149]

Metaphor is admirably suited to religious language. Indeed, when religious experience is expressed or described verbally, it frequently assumes the form of a metaphor. This is particularly noticeable with regard to those religious experiences of the deeper sort. A metaphor is alive. It attempts to catch the dynamism and the freshness of the real. It is impregnated with the vital juices of subjectivity, juices which contribute so greatly to making the metaphor such a fecund literary device.[150]

The very reasons which make metaphor so appropriate for religious language are the selfsame reasons why metaphor is so unsuitable for theological language. Theology is a science, a metaphor is a notoriously inappropriate way of expressing thoughts in a highly precise, scientific manner. Theology proceeds by way of a definitive series of interconnected arguments, but metaphor, by its very nature, is no argument.[151] Any science, be it theology or biology, must proceed according to the rules of logic; logicians regard metaphor as a great foe of logic. A metaphor, after all, is literally false—theological statements, especially ones concerning doctrinal propositions, are misleading at best if they are literally false.

One way of viewing language is to divide it into two categories, the experiential and the scientific. Experiential language is primarily subjective and affective. Scientific language is fundamentally objective and cognitive. Religious language is a form of experiential language, while theological language is an instance of scientific language. In experiential language, such as religious language, the predication finds its verification (its validated truth) within the lived interiority of the person, especially in his felt experiences. In scientific language, such as theological language, the predication finds its verification in some reality outside the person.[152] The purpose of experiential language, as for example religious language, is to enable a person to experience and to feel; the purpose of scientific language, such as theological language, is to enable a person to adequately know. Theological knowledge aims at definite meaning. But "metaphor does not aim at definite meaning and therefore does not stop there. Unlike literal predication, whose term is the mind's seizure of reality, the term of metaphor remains outside the mind wholly."[153] Scientific language, such as theological language, seeks to describe reality as it is in itself; experiential language, such as religious language and metaphor, attempts to make reality come alive by infusing it with the ego.[154] Scientific language, such as theological language, is rooted in a "ground" which is objective, public, and yields the same basic meaning to all who read or hear it.[155] On the other hand, experiential language, such as religious language, is not rooted in any simple, hard-and-fast "ground"; its "ground" is subjective, private, and yields somewhat different meanings to those who encounter it.[156] It is the complex, subjective, private "ground" which accounts for the shift of meaning requisite to a metaphor—there is no blanket reason why some metaphors are meaningful and others nonmeaningful to an individual.[157] Scientific language is the language of truths; experiential language is the language of the arts.[158] "The language of truths is the language of concepts and beliefs, of theories and opinions, of judgments and evaluations, of systematic discourse, of explanations. It is the language in which ideas are expressed. It is the language of the intellect. It is the language we use when we talk about 'the meaning of life'; it is the language we used to 'explain' a pattern of realities and to rationalize human experience. . . . It is the language of metaphysics, of moral philosophy, of esthetics, of [transmissive] education, of theology. . . . There is another language which we may call the language of the arts. . . . It is the language of imaginative literature. It is the language of the prophetic writings of religion. It is the language of poetry. In its effect it goes beyond representation or duplication; it is not about something. It has its own life, its own being, its own permanence and perfection. Some miracle of transformation gives this language a will of its own. Some magic transforms mere words into living creations. It is, as has been said before, the language of the gods."[159]

The bible is replete with metaphors.[160] This is particularly true of its most sublime and most religious passages. The abundant use of metaphor in the bible is to be expected because the bible is essentially a piece of religious writing. The bible is an account of religious experiences written both to relate these experiences and to generate in its readers/listeners new religious experiences. The bible, then, is a religious document, not a theological one.[161] The bible's utility for theology is to provide a corpus of divinely inspired religious experiences which can serve as a source for theological reflection. The worth of any theological reflection is determined largely by the worth of the religious experiences from which it draws. Despite the fact that metaphor is unscientific language and should be used only when necessary in theological science, nevertheless there is a significant role which it can play in the course of theological reflection.[162] The usefulness of metaphor for theology flows from the nature of the cognitive process and even more importantly from the nature of theology. As I show in Chapter Four, all cognition is personal cognition, and metaphor is part-and-parcel of the human condition. While metaphor is inappropriate for use in the development and elaboration of theological theses, it is nonetheless very useful to the theologian in his search for the meaning of the divine. Meanings, especially those which are divinely impregnated, are often subtle and not readily apparent. Imagination is needed in such cases. Metaphor can crack open the barriers to creative imagination, can free it to soar, can lead it to an awareness of theological insights not otherwise attainable.[163] "Imagination could hardly do without metaphor, for imagination is, literally, the moving around in one's mind of images, and such images tend commonly to be metaphoric. Creative minds, as we know, are rich in images and metaphors, and this is true in science and art alike. The difference between scientist and artist has little to do with the ways of creative imagination; everything to do with the manner of demonstration and verification of what has been seen or imagined."[164]

A metaphor is well suited for use in the pedagogical act as well as in the religious act because of what it does to verbal behavior.[165] Metaphor enriches verbal behavior by introducing vital images which make language live and pullulate with meaning. Metaphor involves the injection of heavy doses of personal experience into the bloodstream of language; herein lies its chief utility for the instructional act. Experience has two poles: the object which is experienced and the subject who is experiencing. In terms of the object, a metaphor focuses the subject's attention on the dynamic real, the processing existence of the object. By their very nature, abstractions, words, and phrases tend to rob the real of its vigor and here-and-now actuality. Metaphor restores, as much as possible, these quintessential characteristics. In terms of the subject who is experiencing, metaphor imbues language with deep personal and affective meaning. In this connection Philip Wheelwright maintains that "what really matters in a metaphor is the psychic depth at which the things of the world, whether actual or fancied, are transmuted by the cool heat of the imagination."[166] What a metaphor does is to enrich a person's experience, or perhaps more accurately the meaning of his experience. Metaphors are born because we continually feel the need to stretch the range of words as we accumulate new concepts and abstract relationships—concepts and relationships whose meaning and implication have to be illuminated by metaphor if they are to say something to us.[167] But beyond this, metaphor represents "an attempt to express in terms of experience thoughts lying beyond experience, to express the abstract in terms of the concrete, to picture forth the unfamiliar by means of the familiar, to express insensuous thought by senuous terms."[168]

The religion teacher, of course, should be ever mindful of the limitations of metaphor. Metaphor is no substitute for logic; neither should it be used in the development of a logical train of thought except in cases of "open logic." A metaphor is syntactically false; its two terms represent each other rather than equal each other. "Therefore," Anatol Rapoport observes, "the linguistically hygienic use of metaphor depends on the full recognition of its limitations, that is, on critical consciousness of the generalizations, analogies, and abstractions involved."[169]

In ultimate meaning, the world is a metaphor. It is a metaphor in the consciousness of humanity. It is a metaphor in the consciousness of God. I like to think that persons who are in deep contact with the world and with God live their lives metaphorically.

Hyperbole. A hyperbole is an overblown exaggeration which represents something as much greater or less, much better or worse than it actually is. Because religious instruction deals with God, with Jesus, and with the most enriched dimensions of reality, there almost is an inbuilt tendency to use hyperbole. The main advantage of hyperbole is that it is arresting. It startles the listener or reader, causing him to bring to salience in his awareness the meaning encased in the hyperbole.

Hyperbole, then, is used for emphasis. The drawbacks of hyperbole are many. For example, it often unduly exaggerates the worth or the defects of a reality, thus presenting a somewhat falsified picture of it. A hyperbole remains fresh for a short time only; when it is used with any degree of frequency, it not only grows stale but, what is worse, it trivializes words and phrases which have impact in themselves.[170] But the verbal content in the religion lesson is represented by the teacher, by the parish, and by the church to be basically true and devoid of undue exaggeration. Hence the religion teacher should recognize that while hyperbole can be an effective linguistic tool, nonetheless its wise use must be regulated by great care and discretion.[171] Not a few young adults have been thrown into serious doubt of faith because one day they discovered that what they had been fed in religion lessons in their childhood and adolescent days was hyperbole—hyperbole which masked and obscured the truth rather than illuminating it.

Slogan. A slogan is a catchy word, phrase, or sentence typically designed to encapsulate a position or goal held to be of significant subjective or objective worth. Linguisticians and philosophers of language tend to regard slogan as a form of emotive language intended to invite enthusiasm, engender loyalty, or achieve a unity of feeling and spirit.

Religious instruction, like preaching, is chock-full of slogans.[172] That teachers and preachers substitute slogans for logic or for authentic affective procedures suggests that these persons might not understand how a slogan actually functions in pedagogical discourse.[173]

Two basic uses of the slogan have been identified: ceremonial and nonceremonial.[174] A slogan is employed in a ceremonial fashion at such events as a dedication, a consecration, a convocation, an inauguration, and the like. On such occasions a slogan is used either as a rallying cry, as an affectively charged appeal to hold fast to some goal or position, or as a way of helping people feel comfortable and secure in that adherence. Nonceremonial use of a slogan includes statements of educational objectives, pedagogical discourse in the instructional act itself, advertising, preaching, and so forth. In terms of educational activity, a slogan generates all sorts of logical difficulties when it is used in a manner basically suited to a ceremonial setting. In a religious instruction milieu, a slogan is typically employed to provide information and direction to pedagogical activity.

Few people really take ceremonial slogans with much logical seriousness. Most persons recognize them for what they are, exhortations and high-sounding rhetoric intended more for export than for logical content.[175]

The educationally important uses of slogans, therefore, are not of the purely ceremonial variety. Rather, the important uses of slogans are those which purport to mean something. Any slogan which is meaningful has two primary logical functions: to serve as a summarizing assertion, and to provide an interpretation.

A slogan encapsulates or synthesizes several assertions in such a way that these assertions are not explicitly stated in the slogan itself. Therefore to tease out the logical meaning of a slogan from its affective overtones, it is necessary to see just what assertions it summarizes.[176] A slogan, then, can be compared to a *generalization*. It should be emphasized, however, that a generalization is more logically structured than a slogan. This suggests one reason why it is more highly esteemed than a slogan. Much of the misuse of slogans in nonceremonial settings results from the fact that people knowingly or unknowingly attempt to palm them off as generalizations.

Virtually all educational slogans are directly or indirectly prescriptive. Thus educational slogans purport to give prescriptions and directions to instructional matters, to give information on why and how to do things—in short, to prescribe procedures. The trouble with this prescriptive function is that educational slogans provide only catchy words; they do not supply any specific behaviors or activities. For example, the slogan "The only true Christian education is that which has Christ as its center"[177] fails utterly to give any specific help to the religious educator or curriculum builder.

In addition to summarizing sets of assertions, a nonceremonial slogan has a second important logical function, namely to provide interpretation. It is in this second realm that slogans can be of some benefit to religious instruction. Because it is deliberately amorphous, a slogan is capable of a host of interpretations, which gives one explanation for its frequent effectiveness with mass audience. But if a teacher or a curriculum builder uses a particular slogan always in one way with one particular meaning, then such a slogan will tend to almost automatically yield a certain interpretation in the minds of those who hear or read it. In this manner a slogan can be recycled and brought to a state in which it is pedagogically serviceable. Its usefulness in such a recycled state ensues because now the slogan both summarizes some proposals and is always applicable to them. Recycled slogans are frequently used in major political movements: for example, the slogan "manifest destiny" carried with it a summary of an implied set of procedures of American domestic policy.

Pedagogically, slogans should be used judiciously and with great care. They are fraught with risks which typically far outweigh their advantages. When used, they should be employed to reinforce a behavior, heighten motivation, emphasize a point, or rephrase some outcome in order to enhance its appeal. Slogans should not be used as a substitute for logic or for authentic affective procedures. When slogans are employed, they should be utilized in such a way that the ambiguity of interpretation is reduced to a minimum.

Sign

A sign is anything which points to or represents a reality other than itself. The scholarly discipline which investigates sign phenomena is called semiotics.

A sign is composed of three necessary components: (1) the perceptible reality which does the signifying; (2) the reality which is signified, namely, that which is distinct and other from the sign but is adequately represented by the sign; and (3) the power of signifying, that is, the suitability or capacity of that which does the signifying to evoke in a person the cognitive awareness that it is pointing to a reality other than itself.[178]

Signs have been classified in various ways, often along different axes. The traditional classification identifies six types of sign, namely, natural or unnatural, formal or instrumental, imaging or nonimaging. A natural sign receives its significative force from nature itself, as smoke is a sign of fire. An artificial sign gains its significative force from cultures or subcultures, as white is a sign of joy for Christians and a sign of sadness for Chinese. A formal sign is one in which the sign is known together with the thing which is signified, as a baby's shrieking cry signifies his sense of danger even though such a cry had never been previously heard. An instrumental sign is one which must be known apart from and in advance of the thing signified, as one must have previously learned the connection between smoke and fire in order to grasp the significative force of smoke. An imaging sign is one which pictures the thing signified, such as the drawing of a halo around a head to signify holiness. Finally, a nonimaging sign is one which uses representations other than pictures, such as written alphabetical language. Obviously, a particular sign frequently intersects these three categories. Thus a natural sign may be instrumental or formal, imaging or nonimaging.

The mid-1970s witnessed an attempt by Thomas Sebeok to devise an all-inclusive categorization of sign arranged in hierarchical order. From lowest to highest, from more concrete to more abstract, Sebeok's classes of sign are: signal, symptom, icon, index, symbol, and name. A signal is that type of sign which mechanically or conventionally triggers some reaction on the part of the receiver. A symptom is a compulsive, automatic, nonarbitrary sign, such that the signifier is coupled with the signified in the manner of a natural link.[179] An icon is a sign in which there is topological similarity between a signifier and its denotata. An index is a sign in which the signifier is contiguous with that which it signifies, or is a sample of it. A symbol is a sign with a conventional or arbitrary link between the signifier and its denotata, and with an intentional class for its designatum.[180] Finally, a name is a sign which has an extensional class for its designatum.[181]

Verbal content, or language, is a sign. Specifically, it is a symbol, one of the generally accepted classes of sign. Language as a symbol-sign points to something other than itself. In other words it is a sign of something else; it signifies another reality. Language is an arbitrary sign born of and ratified by convention.[182]

The overarching purpose of linguistic sign, like that of all other kinds of sign, is to point to meaning.[183] Words are significant when they signify the meaning of another reality. Verbal language, then, is a coherent, ordered system of signs designed to arrive at and enhance meaning. Since verbal language is a sign-symbol, it operates according to rules. Viewed from this perspective, language is a set of signs linked together by syntactic, semantic, and pragmatic rules.

The nature and theory of sign form the very superstructure around which the edifice of Catholic sacramental theology is constructed. Many books and treatises on the sacraments begin with an explanation of signs. To be sure, the commonly accepted Catholic definition of a sacrament is: ''a sensible *sign*, instituted by Christ, to signify and produce grace.'' A sacrament is a sign, and the sacramental system is a sign system.[184] So vital are the existence and the personal cognitive awareness of signs that John Richard Quinn, a sacramental theologian, claims: ''Only he who understands the language of signs can speak intelligently in his prayer and give himself fully to God in Christ.''[185]

The concept and the power of sign are ever present throughout the history of the Judaeo-Christian tradition. All of scripture is itself a sign of God's saving activity. Furthermore, both the Old Testament and the New are filled with accounts of particular signs of God's working in and through the world.[186] During the desert years, God provided manna to the children of Israel as a sign of his special care. Prophets were "raised up" in the midst of Israel as a sign to the people of God's presence, judgment, and will. The last of the prophets was Jesus who often taught by signs and wonders. As the last of the prophets and God's only-begotten son, Jesus himself is God's supreme sign, a sign who both points to the Father and who is himself the divine reality to whom all other signs point. As Jesus is the sign of the Father, so too is the church the sign of Jesus.[187] Because a sacrament is a sacred sign, we can say that Jesus is the sacrament of God and that the church is the sacrament of Jesus.[188]

Perhaps the period in which sign received the greatest attention from Catholic religious educationists and educators was the 1960s. At the International Catechetical Conference held at Antwerp in 1956, "three great routes" (les trois grandes lignes) in authentic religion teaching were postulated: the bible, the liturgy, and Christian doctrine.[189] A "fourth great route," namely personal Christian witness, was added during the International Catechetical Conference at Eichstätt (Germany) in 1960.[190] These great routes were identified as great routes because in the minds of those who formulated and accepted them they constituted the four major signs through which God taught his people in the Old and New Testaments. In the 1960s as well as in previous decades, it was widely believed that the religious educator should follow the same teaching procedures and sources which God used; hence the four principal signs took on enormous prestige and weight. During the 1960s many Catholic religion curricula, teacher-training programs, and treatises on religious instruction were organized around the four major signs.[191] By the 1970s, however, Catholic emphasis on the four major signs declined noticeably, principally because of the growing recognition that while these four might possibly constitute the major religious pedagogical signs in the past history of the world, they often are not the most effective signs for facilitating religious outcomes in the here-and-now instructional situation.

The decline in emphasis on the four major signs ought not to hasten a sharp drop in the awareness and effective use of signs on the part of religion teachers and curriculum builders. To be sure, the recognition of the supreme importance of effecting a congruence and a point of contact between sign and learner should spur religious educators on to sharpen their understanding and use of sign.[192] Because of the nature and transcendence of God, no person can encounter him directly. One encounters God only through a sign or set of signs of one sort or another. The more the sign or set of signs points to God, the richer can be the experience of the person grasping the sign. In many ways religious instruction is teaching with and through signs. This is especially true on those occasions when it is neither possible nor feasible for the learner to be provided with direct or firsthand experiences.

The issue confronting the religious educator with respect to signs is not whether or not to use them, since the verbal behavior which the teacher employs during the lesson are cognitively pointing signs. Hence the real issue confronting the religion teacher is how to make more effective use of signs.

Two cautions should be sounded with respect to the effective pedagogical use of signs in religious instruction. First, the teacher should never allow the sign to become confused with the reality to which it points.[193] There seems to be an inbuilt tendency among Christians, particularly among Catholic Christians, to equate that which signifies with the reality which is signified. Second, the teacher should be aware of the ambiguity inherent in signs. The cross (a sign) on a church steeple signifies one thing to a devout Methodist, something else to a Catholic adult who was maltreated by nuns in her childhood years, and quite another to a Jew. The sign is the same in all three cases, but that which is signified is vastly different.

Symbol

Words are linguistic symbols. They are artificial signs. Words symbolize some other reality; they point to another thing.[194]

As I indicate in the preceding section, a symbol is one type or class of sign. From the linguistic perspective, symbol is an artificial sign, one whose referent and meaning are bestowed upon it by convention or usage. But from the viewpoint of depth psychology, symbol is a natural sign, one whose referent and meaning flow out of some form of nature itself.[195] In this section I will treat of symbol from the linguistic perspective; much of what I write will, however, apply to all symbols nonpsychologically considered.[196]

There are at least seven characteristics of symbol which contribute toward making it somewhat different from other kinds of sign.[197] First, a symbol is more abstract than most other kinds of signs, and consequently demands more discrimination and subjective self-involvement by the symbol's user or consumer. A dog can become accustomed to verbal symbols like "food" or "shake hands"; however, at the human level, such verbal symbols acquire a much wider set of meanings influenced by the context in which they are used.[198] Second, a symbol tends to be more subjectively charged than many other kinds of sign. Because of its abstractness, an individual has to invest the symbol with a great deal of his own personal perceptions. Third, a symbol is usually more artificial than most other signs. Due to its abstract and subjective character, a symbol is very much reflective of the referent given to it by society or by an individual. The song "Lili Marlene" became a symbol to the troops in Erwin Rommel's Afrika Korps, a symbol to which this particular group of men attached a certain meaning. But the same song would become a different symbol (with a different meaning) to a soldier of the Korps who, on furlough, proposed marriage to a girl as the band played "Lili Marlene" ("our" song). Fourth, a symbol is usually more abstract and more subjectively charged than most other kinds of sign. Consequently it can typically evoke a greater degree of personal or group participation in it and in its referent. Fifth, a symbol is generally a more adequate representation of another reality than are other varieties of sign because it is selected and repeatedly confirmed by convention for the purpose of providing adequacy.[199] For example, a poem symbolizing the horrors of war might well afford a more precise pointer to battlefield suffering than some nonsymbolic sign of war. Linguistic symbols are, of course, chosen to give precision and force to one's representation of experience.[200] Sixth, a symbol often enhances the personal or group meaning of an experience more than other kinds of sign. Seventh, a symbol frequently, though by no means always, tends to point to a higher or a more different reality than do other varieties of sign. In this context, the word "reality" is used as subjective and relational only, without any judgment as to the objective existence of this reality.[201]

If interpreted with caution and with due reservation rather than in a universal and apodictic fashion, the following two statements can prove helpful in suggesting how symbol is a special kind of sign. A sign usually provides notification while a symbol gives inspiration.[202]

A sign announces its objects to an individual, while a symbol leads the individual to its objects.[203]

There are many kinds of symbol besides linguistic symbol. As a general rule, admitting of some notable exceptions, it is accurate to assert that the more nonverbal a symbol is, the more powerful, the more evocative, and the deeper its referent is. Also, within the linguistic domain itself, there are many gradations of verbal symbol. A continuum in depth and power exists from bald words at the one pole to sensuous image-filled verbal myth at the opposite pole.

A symbol is an attempt to capture the spiritual in sense-ible fashion.[204] It also seeks to form a bridge between the known and the unknown in a way which ever increasingly extends the frontiers of the known, thereby resulting in a shrinking of the land of the unknown. A symbol endeavors to bring darkened and hidden depths to view by incarnating them in some existential representation such as bread and wine, or a doxology. Because a symbol is so frequently a part standing in place of a whole, it focuses one's attention on a particular feature of a symbol, which thus brought to salience, illumines the whole.

A symbol becomes a symbol only when a person perceives it as such and makes it such. For something to be a symbol and to act as a symbol, an individual must participate in it.[205] A symbol cannot point to a reality unless the person adds his own human dimension to that which the symbol suggests.[206]

A verbal symbol has two facets, namely the external facet (that reality to which the word points) and a semantic facet (that reality which the word signifies for the speaker/writer and for the listener/reader).[207] The semantic facet suggests that a symbol cannot function as a symbol unless it is made so by the persons using it. Persons give verbal symbols their meaning. There is no meaning without a meaning-maker. As Alfred North Whitehead observes, in terms of symbolic quality, the mere sound or appearance of a word is indifferent or neutral. The word becomes a symbol, and its meaning is constituted by the ideas, images, and emotions which it raises in the speaker/writer and listener/reader.[208] Personally appropriated and constructed, symbol systems enable a person to make much of reality intelligible and comfortable. Neil Postman and Charles Weingartner remark: "A symbol system is, in effect, a [personal] point of view."[209]

How real is a verbal symbol? After all, a symbol is not the reality to which it points; it is only a representation of that reality. Notwithstanding, it should be noted that while a verbal symbol is a representation, still it is real as a representation.[210] A verbal symbol has its own reality—a reality not totally separate from the thing in which it participates but in its own existence as a special and distinct way of participating in the thing. There are even instances when a symbol can be more psychologically real for a person than the object which it symbolizes.[211] As a general rule, however, symbols, particularly verbal symbols, do not have as powerful or as immediate an impact on a person as does firsthand experience. A verbal symbol can help enhance, explain, deepen, or ripen a firsthand experience. While a symbol takes the place of firsthand experience, it can never really replace it.

Because it is highly improbable that God can be experienced directly by any human being, signs and symbols are utilized by religious individuals as helpful substitutes for such direct experience. Thus faith is expressed in a wide variety of signs and symbols, such as special postures (for example, kneeling), objects (for example, the crucifix), realities (for example, baptismal water), and formulae (for example, creedal statements). Such signs and symbols, if understood and internalized properly, can point to that Reality which we on earth are in all probability not able to encounter directly.

A symbol in and of itself has little or no meaning. Rather, a symbol acquires meaning when a person inserts it into a symbol system. There are all sorts of symbol systems. For example, there is the verbal symbol system and the imaginal symbol system, each with its own character and high points.[212] There is a religious symbol system, a family symbol system, a sports symbol system, and so forth. "Bread and wine" or "God" have different symbolic referents in a religious symbol system than they have in a family symbol system.

The religion teacher should not allow symbol systems to become ends in themselves for the learner, but rather use them as contents leading to a deeper understanding of and a more fruitful firsthand encounter with the realities which they represent.[213]

Over the years, various typologies of symbol have been proposed. One of the most useful of these for religious educators is that devised by Arnold Whittick.[214] This scholar divides symbol into five classes or types. First, there is symbolism of a concrete reality by approximate or conventional imitation, and of a part of a reality to represent the whole.

Second, there is symbolism of a reality by some object directly associated with it. Third, there is symbolism of a reality by an object which by its nature, analogous character, function or purpose suggests the reality. Fourth, there is symbolism of a reality by the relationship of two or more objects. Finally, there is symbolism of a reality by shapes incorporated in the very design which suggest or express the reality.[215]

Symbols are of inestimable importance in the life of every individual. Symbols occur in virtually all human activities; indeed it is difficult to imagine a zone of human thought, feeling, or conduct in which symbolization does not occur in one form or another.[216] Thomas Carlyle claims that "it is in and through symbols that man, consciously or unconsciously, lives, works, and has his being."[217] A person does not live only in a world of concrete things; one also lives in a world of signs and symbols.[218]

A human being, to be truly human, must create symbols. A human being is, among other things, a symbol-maker, a symbolizing animal. To be sure, there cannot be cognition without the use of symbols, for a person cannot think except in symbols. Symbol is not only important for cognition, it is essential to it.

In the religious sphere, symbol is supremely important.[219] Symbol, both linguistic and psychological, is the verbal language of religion; together with sign, it is the only way in which religion can at least ever so faintly reduce the tremendous indirectness of its expression. Encounters with God on this earth often take place through a glass darkly, in symbol and in sign.

Religion tends to be organized around certain master signs and master symbols.[220] The cross, the sacraments, creedal or confessional statements and the like are signs and symbols which not only serve to point to other realities but also constitute both the structure around which Christianity is built and the necessary preconditions for effective religious communication and community/fellowship.[221]

There is an important sense in which *homo religiosus* is automatically *homo symbolicus*. A linguistic symbol is a verbal attempt to make another or a higher reality more accessible and more readily understandable. This is precisely what religion attempts to do—to bring a person into contact with God in ways an individual can know God more clearly, love him more ardently, and serve him more faithfully. Thus the primary, the deepest, and the most illuminating form of religious linguistic expression is the symbol—the symbol in itself, in metaphor, in myth, and so forth. Symbol is not a substitute for religious knowledge; it is religious knowledge in one of its richest forms.[222]

Religious symbolism, like anything else of great value, can be misused. It is important for the religion teacher to be aware of two of the major misuses which can be made of religious symbolism, namely magic and avoidance. Magic involves the use of religious symbols, linguistic or nonlinguistic, in an attempt to strongly persuade, pressure, or compel God to do or to refrain from doing something.[223] Often linguistic religious symbols, notably of the mythic variety, represent an attempt by man to avoid the constraints and constrictions imposed on him by virtue of his finite, human condition. Religious symbol should not be an escape from the human, but rather a flight into the divine and into the deepest sectors of the human.

A symbol only points to reality; it represents it somehow. Thus a symbol is inherently ambiguous, a fact which must be faced squarely by the religious educator. Thomas Carlyle once wrote that a symbol simultaneously conceals and reveals.[224] The religion teacher needs to know how the linguistic symbols he employs conceal and reveal, lest they reveal what is misleading and conceal what is helpful. Verbal symbols are slippery. They can be used to great advantage or with quite the opposite effect. Whether they work to enhance or to sidetrack the religious lifestyle of the learner depends on the pedagogical awareness and the pedagogical skill of the teacher.

Allegory

Etymologically, the word "allegory" is derived from two Greek words meaning "to speak other than plainly and openly." An allegory presents a theme, an idea, or an implication which is not directly expressed in its wording, as for example, a Christian's pilgrimage through life expressed by a narrative relating a traveler's journey through a new land.[225] "In the simplest terms, allegory says one thing and means another. It destroys the normal expectation we have about language, that our words 'mean what they say.' "[226] An allegory is thus a brief narrative or a long story in which the real theme is revealed only by suggestion and often in an intricate fashion.[227]

There are many different kinds of allegories. Some are simple, like fables. Others are more complex, such as extended literary allegories like Dante Alighieri's *Divine Comedy*. An important class of allegory is that which speaks of deep psychic experience under the guise of describing something else. Quest, pilgrimage, search for self, redemption, and participatory religious realities are among the most frequent themes of the allegory of psychic experience.[228] The allegory of psychic experience was a highly developed literary form in the Middle Ages. Many of these allegories of psychic experience were used by their authors and by the church as devices to instruct the people in religion.[229] The twentieth century, however, has witnessed a great revival of the allegory of psychic experience, thanks to the pervasive influence of the depth-psychology movement and such figures as Sigmund Freud and Carl Jung. Indeed the allegory of psychic experience in many ways has been the dominant form of allegory used in literary and religious circles since the end of World War I; certainly it seems to be the most popular form of allegory with youth, young adults, and persons of refined religious sensibilities.

An allegory serves at least seven separate but related functions—functions which have made it an important religious education tool from biblical times down to the present day. *First,* an allegory conveys more than one level of meaning simultaneously.[230] Thus allegory enables a person to discover that life can be understood and lived on several different planes. *Second,* an allegory implies a dominance of theme over action, events, and characters. Hence an allegory helps a person to grasp the importance of the deeper thematic strands running throughout his life, strands which are more self-revelatory than many of the individual persons or events he encounters. *Third,* an allegory typically portrays a vital abstract truth in symbolic form, thus clothing the abstraction in a garb which is at once more interesting and more readily assimilable. *Fourth,* an allegory is frequently expressed in an enchantingly literary—and at times even a somewhat surrealistic—form. Because of this, an allegory is capable of touching a person's sensibilities in a manner not always possible with some other literary devices. *Fifth,* an allegory typically situates polarities either in direct conflict with each other or at least in immediate juxtaposition so that the deepest paradoxes inherent in life can be planked out side by side, and that a subsumptional reconciliation of these paradoxes or a tranquil reconciliation of them can be evoked in the hearer/reader. The cross and the circle, darkness and light, evil so prevalent in a church which is the bride of him who is all good—these are some of the polarities with which allegory deals. *Sixth,* an allegory invests a basic theme, series of events, or cast of characters with an authority fundamentally different from the kind they are typically perceived to have. This new authority enables the hearer/reader to view familiar themes, events, and characters in a new and often more illuminating light. *Seventh*, an allegory embodies a free though purposeful play on and with the familiar. This freedom typically results in a new configuration of events and characters; it also stimulates imaginativeness in the hearer/reader to make his own fresh construction or interpretation of inner and deeper meanings of the phenomena he encounters.

Allegories usually are written to provide both entertainment and instruction. This is particularly true of moral and religious allegories.[231] Perhaps it is not too much to say that moral and religious allegories are created in order to teach individuals in a manner which is entertaining and which at the same time structures the basic material in a way that evokes different kinds of learning than that stimulated by a more prosaic presentation.[232]

An allegory is purposeful; it consists in the deliberate architecting of a number of details, characters, and events of varying figural density all of which work together to make a point. In the better allegories, this point is no cheap moralizing lesson; nor is it intended to achieve some momentary or narrow purpose. Rather, the goal-directedness of a good moral or religious allegory is to make some point which is basic to human nature, universal to all persons, and expansive of mature, authentic moral or religious development.

Authors and storytellers frequently compose or narrate moral or religious allegories because they believe that virtue is more closely related to allegorical art than it is to straightforward prose art.[233] This belief gains some credence in view of the empirical research data I cite in Chapters Four and Five which indicate that affectivity is more closely related to conduct than is cognition. (Allegory, of course, contains a great deal of affective content of both the conscious and unconscious varieties). In terms of yielding certain deeper religious outcomes, allegory is not indirect but indeed rather direct. James Wimsatt finds himself in agreement with the contention that "allegory is the most forthright method we know of conveying an ethical message in representational form."[234]

A good moral or religious allegory "fulfills a religious ideal imaginatively—that is, renews it in the rebirth of consciousness, so that the fiction finally eludes absorption or parody in any dogma."[235]

The use of allegory in the bible is of great importance, of great concern, and in some instances of great anxiety to parents, schoolteachers, and other kinds of religious educators. The bible contains many allegories, the number of which often depends on the reader's degree of religious fundamentalism or liberalism. To a goodly number of modern Christians, many Old Testament stories are not so much factually true as they are allegories given to us for our instruction. For example, the stories of the six-day creation, the Garden of Eden, the parting of the Red Sea waters, and Jonah's three-day stay in the stomach of the great fish are taken by many Christians to be allegorical rather than factual.

The foregoing creates a problem for the religion teacher: How should he deal with allegory? How much allegory is there in the bible? Does biblical allegory destroy or seriously qualify the truth of the scriptural narrative?

The theory of Thomas Aquinas still remains one of the most influential and seminal in Protestant as well as Catholic biblical circles on the types or levels of meaning in the bible. In this theory there are four types or levels of meaning in the bible: (1) the historical or literal, which expresses the reality of that which the words directly speak, and which supplies the foundation and the source for all other meanings; (2) the allegorical, in which the reality expressed in words also refers to a reality on another plane; (3) the moral, in which the words literally expressed also touch an individual directly and urge him on to activity; (4) the anagogical, which expresses realities beyond time and space.[236] Most orthodox commentators on the bible reiterate Aquinas's contention that the allegorical sense, the moral sense, and the anagogical sense are based on the literal sense. This in no way denigrates the worth, distinctiveness, or the utility of the allegorical sense.

Though the literal statement has significance on its own account, nonetheless the allegorical sense of the bible remains an authentic and vital meaning of the inspired text. In allegorical passages, the real sense gains, not loses, meaning when an allegorical sense is suggested. Words only symbolize the reality to which they point; allegory often acts as a more enriched pointer than the words taken literally. To be sure, to confine all the meaning of the bible solely to the literal sense is to betray the multitiered richness which the word of God perforce must contain if indeed it is truly the word of God.

Myth

While there is no universally accepted definition of myth, nevertheless many of the prevalent definitions tend to share certain points of commonality.[237] A myth is a tale, a narrative, a poem.[238] A myth is "a story or a complex of story elements taken as expressing and therefore, as implicitly symbolizing, certain deep-lying aspects of human and transhuman existence."[239] Myth typically, though by no means exclusively, treats of the superhuman or transhuman, especially that which is not known about each of these forms of existence. For John Dunne, "myth is an interpretation of mystery."[240] In the words of Millar Burrows, myth is "a symbolic, approximate expression of truth which the human mind cannot perceive sharply and completely but can only glimpse vaguely, and therefore cannot adequately or accurately express."[241] Myth tends to force deeply awared but dimly known segmented glimpses of and strivings toward the primordial in personal and universal existence into a unity of reference. This unity of reference typically occurs in the symbolic mode. Myth is usually composed of a more-or-less united and internally coherent set of symbols.[242]

In one way or another, directly or indirectly, suggested or implied, a myth is a tale of beginnings. It gives an account and an interpretation of origins. In myth, a condition or an order is introduced and is accomplished in a foundation. Because myth relates beginnings and origins, it is deeply bound up in history.[243]

If myth is indeed tied up in history, it is even more closely linked to sacred history.[244] Myth is not just a story—it is at once a story of the sacred (past reality) and a sacred story (present reality). It is the story of primordial event(s) and/or of primordial person(s) who constituted and inaugurated a reality which determined and still determines the human concrete existential situation in a universe-as-sacred-world.[245] Myth deals with the basic historico-sacred situation in which every person finds himself: birth, redemption, death, initiation. Myth points out and highlights these situations as sacred. Myth is not merely a story about the gods or about God: it is a story about the holy. Myth is a verbal celebration of a once and still abiding religious event.[246] Myth is a present reality, one meant to be experientially participated in. In Thomas Altizer's words, "myth, like ritual, is a mode of encounter with the sacred which makes possible the continuous re-presentation or re-evocation of a primitive sacred event."[247]

Myth ought not to be equated with narrative forms related to it in one way or another, such as, for example, etiological tale, saga, legend, fairy tale, or dream. What is it that fundamentally distinguishes myth from all other kinds of sacred or past-related narratives? Mircea Eliade claims that myth relates that which concerns present-day people directly, while the other forms of narrative refer to persons or events which, even when they have caused changes in the universe, have not altered the human condition as such.[248]

Myth has three basic functions: cognitive, affective, and lifestyle. Thus from the perspective of an holistic religious instruction, myth is a form of verbal content which breaks through, however feebly, many of the limitations inherent in the nature and structure of verbal content.

The cognitive functions of myth are many and varied. First, myth provides a kind of primitive epistemic, a fundamental way or path of knowledge. Myth is first and foremost a variety or type of cognition, a way of intellectually approaching and interpreting reality. Second, myth provides a straightforward answer to the basic intellectual questions about causes. From a rationalistic or literalistic mentality, answers provided by myth are anything but straightforward. But from a mythic point of view, the answers are straightforward indeed, or as straightforward as is possible, given the nature of the cause(s). Third, myth provides an explanation of important events and basic human/cosmic verities.[249] Fourth, myth relates "how one state of affairs became another: how immortals became mortal; how the seasons came to replace a climate without seasons; how the original unity of mankind became a plurality of tribes and nations," and so on.[250] Fifth, myth brings the unknown into relation with the known.[251] Sixth, myth reveals insights and glimpses into what we customarily regard as mystery.[252] Seventh, myth describes a world which a person has never seen for himself and which he believes that he can never see, at least not in the here-and-now. Eighth, myth is an "effective means of awakening and maintaining consciousness of another world, a beyond, whether it be the divine world or the world of ancestors. This 'other world' represents a superhuman 'transcendent' plane, the plane of absolute realities."[253] Ninth, the world of myth serves as a continuous source of the knowledge needed for crucial problems facing humanity during life: war and peace, life and death, suffering and redemption, good and evil, and so forth. Tenth, myth furnishes structure and meaning to each person's experience of his private self.

The affective functions of myth are freighted with importance. Indeed, Cecil Maurice Bowra contends that a mythic explanation is fundamentally more affective than it is cognitive because it associates, at the level of feeling, one kind of deep inner experience with another in a manner which establishes a personally felt link or connection between them.[254] First, myth evokes emotions and existentially thrusted feelings in those who hear/read it or who otherwise partake in the mythic. Second, myth expresses attitudes—attitudes which it endeavors to teach. Third, myth names basic needs and thus brings them to salience—needs of a person or of a people. Fourth, myth is a verbal form or expression of a deeply felt belief or belief-system. Fifth, myth places basic attitudes, beliefs, information, worldview, and patterns of conduct into an affectively oriented literary structure, the poetic-artistic. This literary structure points the hearer/reader in the direction of affective content as well as accents the affective nonlinguistic product content of the myth's foundation.

Finally, myth has important lifestyle functions. "The foremost function of myth," writes Mircea Eliade, "is to reveal the exemplary models for all human rights and all significant human activities—diet, marriage, work or education, art or wisdom."[255] A myth, then, presents a model for human conduct.[256] Second, myth points to a lived-out commitment to policies of action and to religious or moral norms. Third, myth encourages decision and personal involvement.[257] Fourth, the crucial and critical problems in life have their theoretical solutions in myth. Thus to live in and with the mythic is to be enabled to satisfactorily resolve life's fundamental problems. Fifth, myth has important social functions. It promotes the integration of society. It serves as "a cohesive force binding the community together and contributing to social solidarity, group identity and communal harmony." It encourages cultural stability, since it is an active force which is intimately related to virtually every aspect of culture.[258] Sixth, myth functions as a theoretical basis for a way of life. For those who live in and with the mythic, myth is not merely a story but a reality which is lived. It is not an ornamental tale, but a hard-worked active force.[259] The mythic comes to total power when it is inserted into a person's holistic lifestyle.

Many persons, including not a few religionists, view myth as a purely fictional and fictitious narrative. To be sure, it was only in the twentieth century that the action of myth as fiction began to be seriously challenged and then toppled. Serious twentieth-century students of myth, such as Mircea Eliade, realize that myth is a genuine form of knowing and possesses its own special kind of truth-value.

The ancient Greeks made a distinction between *mythos* and *logos*. *Mythos* or myth denoted "word" in the sense of a decisive, final pronouncement. *Logos* (from which the English "logic" derives) meant a word whose truth and validity can be rationally known, argued, and demonstrated. Myth is not irrational; it is extrarational, and hence the canons of rational truth and falsity cannot be legitimately applied to it. Myth lies beyond logical or rational truth and falsity. But, as Claude Lévi-Strauss concludes, the form of cognition which is used by mythic thought "is as rigorous as that of modern science, and that difference lies not in the quality of the intellectual process, but in the nature of the things to which it is applied."[260]

One sector in which myth plays a visible and highly important role in religion is that of ritual.[261] In religious worship, myth and ritual dynamically interact with each other. This interaction occurs because myth and ritual each express, in complementary fashion, a personal encounter with the divine. So deeply intertwined are myth and ritual in overall worship that scholars of comparative religion seem uncertain whether, historically, myth preceded ritual or ritual antedated myth. There often is a fecundating circularity involved in the interaction of myth with ritual.[262] If myth was historically prior to ritual, then it gave rise to ritualistic celebration, and in turn this celebration confirmed myth. If, on the other hand, ritual was historically prior, then it generated myth which in turn confirmed ritual. One thing seems certain, however: There appears to be no ritual without myths, but there do appear to be many myths without ritual. The encapsulation or enactment of myth in the form of ritual makes divine deeds infinitely repeatable. Thus in the Catholic Mass, for example, the ritualistic celebration repeats not only the story of Jesus and his redemption of humanity, but even more importantly repeats, in a somewhat altered form, the redemption process itself. For myth to truly realize its nature and to achieve its purpose, it must be deeply embedded in the religious life of a people. When myth is severed, or if it drifts away from this existential religious life, it tends to disintegrate by expanding to include within itself bizarre details and elements incongruous with it.[263]

Important as it is for the religious educator to teach learners the mythic in various cultures, it is even more important to teach them about the mythic in which and with which they themselves presently live. Every individual, whether that person realizes it or not, lives in and with the mythic.[264] The religion teacher should encourage the learners to talk about the myths they live. The other learners, together with the teacher, should spur them on to interpret these myths in terms of their own religious existence. No attempt should be made, at least in the beginning, to evaluate the myths. What should be sought is insight into the conscious and unconscious product and process contents of the myths rather than judgment about them. The myth should be allowed to speak for itself. It must be allowed to address the learners from its own unique vantage point, namely the extrarational. Therefore the religion teacher should not try to ratiocinatize myth for, as Gabriel Moran observes, the introduction of the rational element is not likely to improve myth but rather to corrupt it, changing it into mythical fiction.[265] Myth is in one sense logically prior to any rational assertion. The religion teacher will sometimes be sorely tempted to try to rationally evaluate, logic-ify, and clean up religious myths such as original sin. Attempts along this line will serve only to reduce myth to the fictional. A myth is extrarational; therefore the logical categories of truth and falsity are inapplicable to it. The mythic has its own categories of, and criteria for, truth and falsity. As a myth, original sin might (or might not) be rationally false, but it certainly is not extrarationally false. To be sure, placing the cognitive doctrine of original sin in mythic instead of rational form was probably the most effective thing the sacred writer(s) could have done to pedagogically convey the authentic texture, true meaning, and facticity of original sin. Myths such as original sin and the resurrection compel the learner to envision the horizons of time and space into which these myths reach.[266] But to appreciate this fact requires the development and refinement of a person's consciousness of the mythic. In order to help the learner to become aware of the real earth-shattering dimensions of the resurrection and original sin, the religion teacher must assist him to expand his capability of thinking in and with the mythic. Myth blows one's mind—one's rational mind, but not one's mythic mind. When a person thinks, feels, and lives in the mythic, he will not only significantly deepen his appreciation of religious reality, but will also greatly enhance the quality of his religious life, most notably in the direction of mysticism.[267]

Hermeneutics

Hermeneutics is that branch of linguistics which studies the methodological principles involved in the interpretation of verbal content. Hermeneutics is thus the "body of principles which govern the interpretation of any statement."[268] It is that branch of linguistics consisting of the methods of true interpretation of verbal content, with particular attention to research and reflection on the nature and principles of these methods.[269] Hermeneutics makes verbal content comprehensible and understandable, thereby rendering this content serviceable in sense and significance. Appreciation of the significance of verbal content leads to an appraisal of its worth.[270] Of particular importance to hermeneutics is that language is itself interpretation, and not merely the object of interpretation.[271]

Though some theologians and would-be theologians appear to regard hermeneutics as part of theology, such is definitely not the case. Hermeneutics is a branch of linguistics which is utilized by theology. To be sure, linguistics is far more akin to social science than to theology. Many of the new advances in linguistics, such as psycholinguistics, have been made by placing linguistics into the framework of social science.

For religious educationists and educators one of the most relevant fields to which hermeneutics has been applied is that of biblics.

One of the oldest and most traditional uses of hermeneutics lies in the attempt by scholars and laypersons to interpret the bible. The hermeneutical objective, then, is by no means new; it has been around for as long as human beings have sought to discover what the bible really means.

When the religious educator, the learner, or anyone else reads the bible, that person encounters the text from within an interpretive context, through an interpretive filter. Whether an individual realizes it or not, to read the bible is to awaringly or unawaringly apply some set of hermeneutical principles to that which is being read. It is the application of these hermeneutical principles and methods to the bible passage being read which actually provides the reader with the meaning which that person claims to derive from the passage.[272]

The fundamental task of hermeneutics is to find out the meaning of the inspired author's text, and thereupon to convey that meaning in such a way that people will understand this meaning.[273] Hermeneutics, therefore, concentrates on bringing out the true meaning or meanings which the bible contains.[274] Hermeneutics focuses on the examination of biblical texts without making them say anything other than what they do say. Hermeneutics strives as far as possible for clarity of interpretation. It is questionable hermeneutics which attempts to give a vague and cloudy interpretation to those biblical texts which, for the time being or to a particular hermeneuticist, seem obscure or opaque.[275]

Much as religious instruction is not the blind application of fixed procedures to any and all pedagogical situations, neither is hermeneutics a set of mechanical rules to be unswervingly applied to biblical texts. Religious instruction is grounded in religioeducational theory; hermeneutics is grounded in linguistic interpretive theory.

The traditional biblical manuals customarily divide hermeneutics into three subdivisions or sectors: (1) moematics, the study of the various senses of the bible; (2) heuristics, the investigation of how to discover the sense of a text; (3) prophoristics, the exploration of the principles, rules, and guidelines for accurately communicating the sense of a biblical text to others.

Closely allied to hermeneutics is *exegesis*. While hermeneutics is regarded as the theory of interpretation, exegesis is considered to be the practice of the scholarly discipline of interpretation.[276] Exegesis is the practical application of the theoretical rules supplied by hermeneutics.[277] Exegesis, therefore, critically examines the biblical text, considers the question of authorship, inspects earlier sources, and provides a scholarly commentary on scripture. The exegete performs his task by integrating a wide variety of other sciences and disciplines into the matrix of his own basic operative framework of linguistic theory. These sciences and disciplines include history, geography, anthropology, theology, archeology, and the like.[278]

In working to establish the true and authentic meaning of a biblical text, the exegete is bedeviled with a host of formidable difficulties. There is a wide diversity in the literary structure of the bible, including, for example, prose and poetry, history and apocalyptic, proverbs and legal codes, allegory and myth. Each of these forms of verbal content has its own structure and must therefore be interpreted according to the rules of that structure.[279] Then there is the matter of the literal and nonliteral senses of the bible. Yet another problem consists in the additions to a biblical book by later authors or editors—how are the later author's additions and editorial revisions to be dealt with in terms of literary consistency, of determining meaning, and of divine inspiration? But by far the most thorny and perplexing problem facing the exegete and the hermeneuticist is that uniquely dual authorship of every passage of the bible, a dual authorship which Christianity has always fiercely contended is the fundamental feature of holy writ. The bible, Christians believe, has both a human author and a divine author. Both are truly the composers of each passage. Protestants and Catholics differ between and among themselves on how this dual authorship is to be explained. Be this as it may, the fundamental exegetical and hermeneutical problem arising from the bible's dual authorship is this: What did the divine author intend in a particular text? And, secondarily, did the divine author's intention exceed in breadth and depth the intention of the human author? Such problems lead to many crucial issues, not the least of which is that of the literal and nonliteral senses of scripture.

What are the basic hermeneutical principles involved in the interpretation of the bible? Reginald Fuller classifies these hermeneutical principles into two main categories, namely, general principles and special principles.[280] There are four *general hermeneutical principles:* (1) the historical and cultural background in which the particular biblical text was written; (2) the human author of the text, taking into consideration his literary style, his own particular circumstances, his temperament, and so forth; (3) the book or part of the book in which the text appears—each book has its own purpose and characteristics so that, for example, a prophetical book must be interpreted in a somewhat different manner from a law-giving book; (4) the vocabulary and the context of a text, taking into account a word's denotation and connotation, its meaning at different periods of history and in various localities, and so forth. The *special hermeneutical principles* are four in number. The first special hermeneutical principle is harmony between the testaments, namely the unity, congruity, and confluence which must perforce flow through both major divisions of holy writ. The second principle is inerrancy, that is, the bible as the inspired word of God is necessarily free from any formal error. The third principle is that of analogy of faith, namely accord with the faith of the church as this faith has been handed down to us by sacred tradition and as it once was and now is lived by the believing and praying community which is the *ecclesia.* The fourth special hermeneutical principle is concurrence both with the church's authority to interpret and with its actual pronouncements or official interpretations.

It is quite apparent that there is a significant divergence of opinion between Protestants and Catholics on the third, and most especially on the fourth of the special hermeneutical principles.

Because the bible occupies so central a place in Christianity, it is incumbent on the religious educator to have a working knowledge of the basic principles of hermeneutics, a knowledge which he is able to utilize during the religious instruction act.

Hermeneutics is especially helpful to religious instruction not only because it deals with attaining a "correct" interpretation of the bible, but also because it is vitally concerned with the way in which God's word becomes clear to human beings. The learners not only have the God-given right to know what the scripture means, but also to discern its significance for their own personal, everyday lives. Hermeneutics thus helps the religion teacher in both a positive and a negative fashion. Positively, hermeneutics enables the teacher to grasp the genuine interpretation of a biblical passage, and to assist the learners to obtain from that passage a meaning and a significance which are deeply personal and yet in harmony with the passage. Negatively, hermeneutics provides an objective and subjective check to the religion teacher lest he either impose on the learners an erroneous textual interpretation or foist on them some meaning which might be personally relevant for the teacher but not relevant or helpful to them.

The religious instruction act constitutes one of the principal hermeneutical places where the bible speaks most authentically and most compellingly to the human being. It is in the religious instruction act that the learner acquires much of his biblical knowledge and outlook. If the religious instruction act is holistic, like the liturgy or in genuine experiential teaching, then this act becomes a setting in which the learner comes to feel and live the bible as the fully human face of hermeneutics. If neither the religious educator nor the learners encounter the bible from within an hermeneutical perspective, then the bible will be indeed a closed book.[281]

Hermeneutic

The term "hermeneutic" in the singular is used to designate another and newer way of looking at the principles of textual interpretation.[282] This newer way differs from, yet is intimately related to the more traditional and still widely used approach of hermeneutics.[283] While traditional hermeneutics is concerned with the theoretical aspects of the science of textual interpretation, hermeneutic focuses its primary attention on the way in which (1) verbal content was and particularly is (2) understood by the person.[284] Proponents of hermeneutic see their investigations as leading to a satisfactory solution to what has become known as the hermeneutical problem, namely, the gap between the life-understanding and the total existential situation of the here-and-now person on the one hand, and the message of the biblical (or nonbiblical) text written long ago in a variety of existential situations quite different from and in some cases alien to the modern condition on the other hand.

Three principal strands are typically interwoven throughout the fabric of hermeneutic: history, ontology, and phenomenology. In hermeneutic, history is treated in terms of previous ontological existence which has been codified and congruently outered in linguistic form; ontology is considered as necessarily including the great and living chain of being which binds past and present reality, particularly as this linkage is effected by words; phenomenology is the way to approach and to help interpret the historical ontology and the ontological historicity which present or past verbal content represents.[285]

The goal of hermeneutic is to bridge the gap between object and subject.[286] In terms of interpreting a biblical text, for example, there exists the classic and frequently unresolved tension between the proper interpretation of the biblical text as it is the written word of God (object), on the one hand, and the contemporary reader attempting to understand the text from his own inescapable cognitive framework and existential situation (subject), on the other hand. Hermeneu*tics* typically focuses primarily and indeed perhaps exclusively on attaining the most accurate and most penetrating interpretation of the object itself (the biblical text). Hermeneu*tic*, on the other hand, constitutes an attempt to bring together object and subject, biblical text and modern human beings in one interacting matrix of interpretation.[287] In other words, a hermeneutic of the bible endeavors to both bring contemporary human beings into an understanding-relationship with the biblical message and to enable the *total* biblical message to be grasped.[288]

Hermeneutic seeks to focus much of its attention on the broader historical contexts of verbal content, such as a biblical text, for example. This broader context necessarily includes the person whose verbal behavior was recorded as well as the sociocultural context in which it was recorded. The thread connecting the recorded verbal content and the modern reader/listener is thus human experience—the experience of the author and the experience of the reader/listener.[289] In hermeneu*tics*, the interpreter scrutinizes the text; in hermeneu*tic*, the text scrutinizes the interpreter at the same time that the interpreter is scrutinizing the text. This twofold scrutiny, it is claimed, helps hermeneu*tic* to erase the object-subject duality which typically characterizes hermeneu*tics*.[290]

The shift in the thrust and scope of hermeneutic from an emphasis on rules of literary and textual analysis to a much broader base of interpretation is by common consent traced back to Friederich Schleiermacher.[291] Ever the personalist, Schleiermacher contends that in addition to this objective, external, logico-linguistic analysis, there must be a subjective, intuitive awareness into a text or book as the unique expression of the author's existence, life, and condition.[292] For Schleiermacher, the subjective factor in hermeneutic is fully as important as the objective factor; indeed, proper interpretation weds the two. It is the conjoining of psychological interpretation to the traditional logical-grammatical-historical approach which makes Schleiermacher the founder, so to speak, of hermeneutic.

The radical introduction of the psychological into the hermeneutical was carried forward by Wilhelm Dilthey.[293] Dilthey's hermeneutical formula can be summarized in three words: experience, expression, and understanding.[294] Thus all textual interpretation involves some lived experience that is ex-pressed in some verbal content which subsequently must be understood by an interpreter. Can a person's lived experience (as expressed in verbal content, for example) be re-constructed and understood in such a faithful manner that the original purpose of a text reappears once more?[295] Yes, Dilthey would respond, because all past historical writings are ex-pressions of the human spirit in whose psychological structures and capacities the interpreter should also participate.[296]

Interestingly enough, Karl Barth stands in the developmental line of hermeneutic. In his celebrated *Römerbrief* commentary, the great Swiss theologian emphasized that all interpretation, and especially theological interpretation, must continually bear in mind that its object (a biblical text) was once subject. The interpreter's task is to enable this former subject to become subject again in our day.

Martin Heidegger placed hermeneutic squarely within the realm and operation of ontology.[297] In working out his philosophy, Heidegger differentiates particular entities or "beings" (*Seiendes*) from the "to be" (*das Sein*) and from "being-in-presence" (*Dasein*). The importance of *Dasein* lies in its sense that the human person is the only being (*Sein*) who existentially deals with the "to be" in its presence (*da*).

The phenomenology of *Dasein* is hermeneutic. To the extent that *Dasein* has ontological priority over every other entity, to that extent is hermeneutic as the interpretation of *Dasein* philosophically primary. Thus hermeneutic is more than simply the interpretation of language; it is the interpretation of existence—the "analytic of the existentiality of existence."[298] Because ontology is fundamental, hermeneutic is fundamental.[299]

Drawing on Heidegger, Rudolf Bultmann used the principle and the process of the existential analytic in seeking to understand the meaning and present-day relevance of biblical texts. Bultmann "aims to interpret the text in such a way as to get at the reality that is prior to and more permanent than the [linguistic] expression of that reality."[300] To his hermeneutic, Bultmann gave the term "demythologizing."

While Bultmann drew heavily on the early Heidegger, Ernst Fuchs relied more on the later Heidegger (and on Bultmann as well) to provide himself with the basic structures out of which to develop his own hermeneutic. For Fuchs, being is bodied forth in language. Being is revealed in a language event (*Sprachereignis*). Language is important because it is the house of being, a house in which each person lives and comes to understanding. Language is "the primal, nonobjectifying voice of being."[301] To understand the human person one must understand his language. "Language lets being in."[302] The basic hermeneutical problem is twofold: that the interpretation call forth from the text the being which it houses, and, even more importantly, that the text call forth from the interpreter that insight into and understanding of being which the text embodies.[303] Verbal content is not simply the language of words; it is the language of being.[304]

Like Ernst Fuchs with whom he is often linked, Gerhard Ebeling incorporated Bultmann's existential interpretation into a wider vision of the word of God in human history.[305] The word of God that outers itself in a biblical text is a "word event" (*Wortgeschehen*). As such, a biblical text is a more existential content than mere words and therefore can open the way for a reader/listener to existentially resonate in living faith with the one God who speaks to that individual in the scriptural word-event. The word (*Wort*) of God arouses faith, to which faith is the response (*Ant-wort*). The biblical text is a word-event because human existence is first and foremost a linguistical, historical existence. Thus through verbal content, our present existence enjoys a natural ontological bond with persons and activities in the past as well as in the future.[306] "Theology constitutes a science, proclamation constitutes the church," writes Gerhard Ebeling.[307] Thus there is an inbuilt tension between theology and proclamation, a tension which can only be fruitfully resolved when theology helps proclamation proclaim itself. This is the task of hermeneutic, states Ebeling.[308]

Some scholars assert that in the writings of Hans-Georg Gadamer hermeneutic entered an important new phase.[309] Hermeneutic seeks understanding; however, understanding is not a subjective activity of the human person over against some object like a biblical text. Instead, understanding is the way of being of the person as a person. Thus hermeneutic is not a discipline seeking to illumine science, but far more importantly it is "a philosophical effort to account for understanding as an ontological—*the* ontological—process in man."[310] Gadamer's hermeneutic is oriented to language and to subject-matter rather than to what he believes is a Dilthey-like psychologism.[311] Gadamer rejects the classic philosophical and linguistic principle that language is a symbol, a sign pointing to another reality.[312] Instead, language is disclosure or representation of a reality. A person does not invent a word or bestow meaning upon it; rather one experiences a word as disclosing or revealing a world. A word is not made meaningful; a word is always itself already meaningful. Meaning lies in the word itself.[313] There is an undeniable gap between past documents and the here-and-now interpreter; hence interpretation is always a translation from one situation to another. Consequently the subject-matter of hermeneutic is the dynamic relation between the interpreter and the text.[314]

Two other influential German scholars who have dealt with hermeneutic deserve to be mentioned. Building upon Gadamer, Wolfhart Pannenberg regards universal history as the horizon wherein understanding occurs.[315] There is a radical historical distance between the horizon of the text and the horizon of the interpreter. These two horizons can be bridged by the interpreter only if that person seeks to understand the text within the context of universal history, through the continuum of history which binds text and interpreter.[316] For Pannenberg, history is the most comprehensive horizon of Christian understanding, a horizon which makes truthful interpretation possible. Jürgen Habermas, another German scholar, regards hermeneutic as a creative praxis[317] opening up new dimensions or horizons for human understanding,[318] dimensions which are closed or inaccessible to an excessive historicism or ontologism.[319]

Of the numerous criticisms directed against hermeneutic, nine are in my opinion particularly serious. *First,* the attempt to resolve the complicated hermeneutical problem in terms of just one dimension, namely verbal language, is, as Carl Braaten cogently argues, "an almost unbelievable over-simplification." Such a purported solution must necessarily suffer from "the tyranny of reduction in a single principle."[320] *Second,* endless confusion, and possibly invalidity, is created by indiscriminately lumping together verbal meaning and significance (meaningfulness for me or for us). As Emilio Betti notes, *Bedeutung* (meaning) must be kept separate from *Bedeutsamkeit* (significance), else linguistics collapses; furthermore, any possibility of obtaining objective and valid results from the interpretive process will evaporate.[321] To merge meaning and significance is to preclude the possibility of developing or utilizing objective canons of interpretation. Eric Hirsch points out that hermeneuticists frequently are self-contradictory when they attempt to explain how "the meaning of a text has remained the same, while the significance of that meaning has shifted."[322] *Third,* hermeneutic fails to provide a stable normative principle by which the correct or proper meaning of a text can be ascertained. *Fourth,* hermeneutic overextends itself by attempting to be one universal ontology. Hermeneutic can be of assistance in metaphysics, but it cannot act as a legitimate or valid substitute for it.[323] *Fifth,* hermeneutic is quite restricted in validity, scope, and potency because it labors under the combined limitations of critical-historical method and existentialist theology. In addition, it relies too heavily on only one philosophical group instead of seeking to also incorporate the principles and insights of other important philosophical traditions, such as that of Ludwig Wittgenstein, for example.[324] *Sixth,* critics of hermeneutic contend that it fails to successfully bridge the gap between object and subject, between text and interpretation. The historical (to say nothing of the existential) gulf between the author's then-present and the interpreter's now-present simply cannot be bridged by a psychological act on the part of the interpreter or by his plunge into that great ocean of being which purportedly merges past and present into an eternal "here." *Seventh,* proponents of hermeneutic exaggerate the importance and effectiveness of verbal content while at the same time failing to recognize its limitations. Words simply do not have the power which the hermeneuticists claim. One wonders whether the hermeneuticists have allowed their speculations to run rampant in this regard. Hermeneuticists present little, if any, empirical evidence to support their heady claims for the power of language—indeed, not a few hermeneuticists would undoubtedly attempt to disparage, on *a priori* grounds, any empirical testing of their claims. *Eighth,* advocates of hermeneutic assign to their discipline far too many tasks and powers for it to be optimally useful or effective. Its proponents give to hermeneutic the mantles of history, ontology, and psychology, to name but three. Now it is plain that hermeneutic cannot do the work of history plus that of ontology plus that of psychology, or even the work of just one of these. *Ninth,* hermeneuticists, notably the post-Bultmannians, tend to give awesome responsiblity and power to the perceptions of the individual interpreter. Concomitantly, the interpretive role of the believing and praying *ecclesia* is minimized.

When parents, schoolteachers, pastors, and other kinds of religious educators lament, as they often do, that one of their greatest difficulties lies in enabling the learner to realize that religion is relevant for him in the here-and-now, these persons are actually stating the hermeneutical problem. The hermeneutical problem, on the one hand, is the gap between the life-understanding and the total existential situation of the learner, and, on the other hand, the lifeway and imperatives of a Christianity shaped in former times by cultures and by persons quite foreign to the modern context and to modern human beings. A helpful way of bridging this gap on the verbal and cognitive levels is by hermeneutic, namely, in so structuring a pedagogical situation that religion, the bible, and Christian tradition will be interpreted by the learner as important and meaningful and significant for that individual.

Though hermeneutic has limitations, nonetheless it has some value in religious instruction, most notably in the verbal dimension of religion teaching. The whole impetus and texture of hermeneutic thrusts the religious educator into the role of cognitive interpreter—specifically, the interpreter of the learner's verbal behavior.[325] Hermeneutic suggests that the religious educator interpret the verbal materials such as books used in the religious instruction act from a subjective as well as from an objective perspective. These two perspectives are in existential dialogue. Hermeneutic also suggests that the religious educator dialectically interpret the verbal behavior of the learners and the religious educator as these behaviors oscillate in give-and-take activity.[326]

Hermeneutic is personalistic, and so suggests to the religious educator that if he is ever to arrive at a true interpretation and understanding of both the text and the learner's verbal behavior it is imperative that he grasp the personal and social existential situation which at once suffuses and encases the text and the verbal behavior.

SOME PRACTICAL CONSEQUENCES

The available empirical research suggests that for better or for worse a great deal of teaching is exercised in the verbal mode. Teaching done in the formal setting of the classroom is heavily verbal. Indeed, two-thirds of all the time spent in classroom interaction is accomplished in the verbal mode—and this figure does not even include the amount of time spent in studying print materials.[327] While the teaching which occurs in informal settings possibly does not utilize as much verbal content as that done in formal settings, nonetheless the amount of verbal content in such milieux is formidable. Regardless of the setting in which they work, therefore, religious educators ought to give considerable attention to the nature, structure, and effects of verbal content. All too often, it would seem, verbal content is taken for granted and not sufficiently heeded by the religious educator.

Words-as-content are verbal symbols. To teach verbal content, then, is to so structure and manipulate words that they embody as intended meaning and force. Verbal content is not so much a vehicle of meaning as it is an embodiment of meaning. Verbal content symbolizes a particular meaning or set of meanings.

Because verbal content is a substantive content in its own right, each verbal symbol *eo ipso* is targeted to some operation. For example, some verbal symbols are targeted to performative operations, some to explanatory operations, some to judgmental operations, and so forth. The successful religious educator selects that verbal symbol or combination of verbal symbols whose operation is most congruent with the instructional outcome he wishes to facilitate.

If religious educators are to successfully utilize verbal content, they should be adequately steeped in both the theory and the practice of words-as-content.

With respect to theory, the religious educator utilizing verbal content should operate out of a theory of language, conjoining this to a theory of instruction.[328] For teaching purposes, a theory of language should adequately explain the nature of verbal content, its strengths and limitations, together with direct implications for pedagogical use.

With respect to practice, the religious educator utilizing verbal content should be well-prepared in the actual pedagogical skills of teaching religion in the linguistic mode. The first stage in such skill-preparation is that of being trained in what has become known as verbal content analysis.[329] Proficiency in content analysis will enable the religious educator to become more sensitive to the color, texture, interactivity, and valence of the verbal content used during the religious instruction act. For example, content analysis will help the religious educator find out why one set of words attracts learners and brings them to examine their deeper convictions while another set, having basically the same logical structure as the first, repels learners and does little or nothing to make them engage in what is occurring in the religious instruction act. The second stage in skill-preparation for the effective use of verbal content is that of assisting the religious educator to expand the repertoire of his actual verbal behaviors. A rich-textured learning outcome tends to be facilitated by rich-textured pedagogical stimuli, in this case verbal stimuli. The research suggests that nondifferentiated, blanket verbal responses tend to be used by the least effective teachers, while successful educators typically employ a wider repertoire of verbal content, a repertoire which perforce is more varied, more discriminating, and more nuanced.[330] The research has also shown that the patterns of a teacher's verbal behavior do definitely affect the learner's response. Verbal behavior which is interpretive and confrontive, for example, produces different effects than does verbal behavior which is reflective or interrogative.[331] The third stage in skill-preparation for the effective use of verbal content is that of assisting the religious educator to make his verbal behavior congruent with the other types of pedagogical communication he employs in the religious instruction act. If the teacher's verbal content is at variance with his nonverbal content, for example, the learner will be faced with an unclear, confusing, and often internally contradictory set of stimuli. The religious educator must learn to mesh three complementary instructional activities which are more-or-less directly related to verbal content: (1) the pedagogical moves he is making in the verbal domain, such as responding, initiating, reacting, soliciting; (2) the substantive content of his verbal behavior, such as the effects of baptism, the brotherhood of all humanity; and (3) the texture, potency, interactivity, and valence of his verbal behavior. These three verbally oriented complementary activities, when meshed with one another, ought then to be melded with other substantive contents such as nonverbal content and lifestyle content so that a fully rounded holistic religious instruction act can thereby ensue.

One way in which the teacher can help the learner to mine more fruitfully the meaning of his religion is to use that kind of verbal communication called interpretive refraction.[332] In this mode of verbal behavior, the teacher offers the learner a tentative hypothesis about the meaning of the learner's experience of his self. This kind of tentative analysis serves as a prism through which the learner's experience of his self can be verbally refracted. The learner uses the teacher's interpretive verbal refraction as a jumping-off place for arriving at a deeper meaning of his own experience of self. In employing interpretive refraction, the religious educator must always keep his comments tentative, resisting any tendency to become definitely judgmental. Tentativeness will help the learner clarify and deepen the meaning of his own personal experience of self, in contrast to definitive judgmental statements which of their very nature tend to exert a freezing effect on the flow of exploration into the meaning of one's experience of self. The educational procedure of interpretive verbal refraction tends to move the verbal content of the religious instruction act toward the zones of personal experience, affect, and lifestyle

Above all else, religion is an experience and a lifestyle. While words can tilt toward the experiential, all too often they are made to serve nonexperiential functions. But even more basically, as the gifted Protestant author Ross Snyder reminds us, "words are not the fundamental reality" but rather are a secondary process. What is primary is existence and the experiencing of existence. Snyder urges that the Reformation theology of the word be replaced by the expansive, existentially interpretive character of the incarnation-redemption events. In Snyder's view, the Gutenberg consciousness underlying much of the verbal approach to religion ought to be replaced by a personally lived experiential religion.[333]

The religious educator can tilt verbal content toward the experiential in any one of three ways. Use and encourage the learners to use words, phrases, and sentences which are concrete, sensuous, imaginal, performative, or which are otherwise closely pegged to rich firsthand experience. Place the verbal content squarely within the context of a firsthand experiential context—the structured-learning-situation (SLS) teaching strategy which I have long advocated is especially potent in this regard. Finally, accompany and/or follow up the teaching act with additional firsthand experiences.

The base and the summit of Christian living is lifestyle. Surely Christianity is a way of life, not a set of words. There is a strong sense in which words are inimical to a Christian lifestyle in that words tend to lead a person to believe that the essence of Christianity is knowing or speaking verbal content rather than leading a devout Christian life. To attempt to teach solely via verbal content a message so fraught with individual affective and lifestyle behavior is not only a problem—it is an impossible task. No verbal content by itself, however rich in religious symbolism, can contain or directly produce religious feelings or religious conduct. The most that verbal content can do is to point to affectivity and to a way of life. Some kinds of verbal content are more effective pointers or representers than others. But whenever the religion teacher employs verbal content, he should not forget that the content which ultimately supports all the verbal content used in the lesson is not a sign but the presence and the activity of God himself[334]—not an ethereal presence or a spooky activity, but rather a presence and an activity which immanently reside in the persons of teacher and learners and which immanently work in the religious instruction act itself.

Many religious educationists seem to be aware of the point made in the beginning of the previous paragraph, at least on the cognitive level. Alfonso Nebreda, for example, states that "the force of Christ's preaching resides in his words and in his whole personality more than his words. The same applies to the church."[335] John Westerhoff comments that Christianity cannot be really understood by asking Christians to state in words what they believe. Christianity can be adequately understood in a person living his own life in a Christian manner.[336] Gabriel Moran is fond of speaking of revelation happening in the learner's experience of the present community.[337]

In endeavoring to relate his verbal content to lifestyle, the religious educator should select words which have a relatively high degree of lifestyle pointedness. Words with a high image density, metaphors, poetic language—these are the varieties of verbal content which enjoy an inherent affiliation with lifestyle content.[338] Verbs seem to be more intrinsically bound up with lifestyle than are nouns. If theology is a language of nouns, then religious instruction is a language of verbs.

The point made in the preceding paragraph also suggests that the verbal symbols which the religious educator and the learner use should be more religious than theological. Religious language directly addresses the learner's Christian lifestyle, while theological language by definition speaks only to the learner's cognitive dimension or, in certain cases, says something *about* his Christian lifestyle. Religious language is not a watered-down version of theological language. Rather, theological language is a cognitivization of religious language. Religious language ought not to be equated with overly pious, soupy, formal, stilted, goody-goody words. Religious language is that which grips the Christianness of the learner insofar as it is possible for verbal symbols to grip anything. Religious language is theologically accurate, though it may assume forms at which some theologians might bridle. Religious language is keyed into revelation. Thus, while being in living contact with bygone manifestations of the Christian deposit, religious language is born in the present and targeted toward the future, all within the context of the learner's present style of development.

Hubert Halbfas argues that theological vocabulary, born of church tradition and scientific theology, is inappropriate for persons in contemporary society. Worse still, contends Halbfas, is that theological language alienates the learner from religion because of its sterility, its lifelessness, its datedness, and its lack of congruity with everyday language.[339] Whether one agrees with Halbfas or not, nonetheless it surely must be admitted that religious language is far closer to an individual's here-and-now existence and to the concrete revelational dynamic than is theological language.

Myth is a form of verbal content which, if used knowledgeably and skillfully, holds great potential for bringing verbal content into the domains of holistic personal experiencing and of Christian lifestyle—or at least into the vestibules of these domains. Furthermore, myth offers splendid expansive opportunities for both the teacher and the learner to engage in interpretive refraction of self.

Helmut Thielicke observes that myth is the "only adequate expression of religious truth." The reason for this, claims Thielicke, is that myth offers a particularly profound dimension of reality, a dimension inaccessible to scientific thought since it deals with the underlying significance of events, persons, and things.[340] While I cannot go so far as to assert that myth is the only adequate expression of religious truths, I do nonetheless assert that myth is one of the least inadequate verbal encapsulations of religious truth. Myth is experiential- and life-style-oriented because it deals with the inner dynamic and flow of religious reality on the reality's own terms and not so much on a human being's own cognitive terms. To be sure, myth is not intended to be a logical piece of work; it is literature, it is the genuine story of a person's life and therefore, as Richard Chase notes, "must be considered as an aesthetic creation of the human imagination."[341]

At this juncture, a clarification of language might prove helpful for the religious educator. *Logic* is the language of the analytic, the discursive. *Mythic* is that special form or imaginative language, frequently symbolic, about those basic verities in life which cannot be adequately or exactly expressed in logical form—verities such as ultimate beginnings and foundations, love and hatred, life and death, God and the human person. *Mythical* is the language of the unreal, of a fancifulness detached from the world of which it purports to speak.[342] Logical language speaks of what we can know; mythic language speaks of what we ultimately do not know or cannot know on this earth; and mythical language speaks of an unreality which it itself creates.

There are two basic theories on how the dramatic world of myth originated: the rationalistic and the depth-psychological. The religious educator using myth in the religious instruction act should be aware of these theories.

The rationalistic theory holds that myth is primitive, prescientific thought, a way of coping with a world which is perceived hostile, or at least threatening. Myth in ancient days and in modern times is rooted in people's fear of hostile or threatening forces beyond their control. To assuage this fear, people create myths to give them solace and comfort.[343]

In contrast to the rationalistic theory, the depth-psychological theory claims that it is not just the need but it is even more importantly the subject-matter content of myth which is intrinsic to human nature. Sigmund Freud believes that myth is an individual or societal attempt to return to those all-important realities which a person or a group has previously repressed. These repressed elements, present and active in the unconscious, are brought to consciousness by myth. Myth, like the psyche through which it flows, is a transhistorical mechanism based not on cultural history but on a biological conception of the human person. But it was Freud's one-time student, Carl Gustav Jung, who has probably delved into myth more profoundly and more seminally than any other depth psychologist. Jung holds that myth is first and foremost a manifestation which mirrors or represents the basic nature of the psyche. A myth is the symbolic, objectified expression of the inner, unconscious drama occurring deep and dark within each person. This drama is rendered accessible to human consciousness by the psychological mechanism of projection. Myth typically deals with occurrences of nature; in myth, the unconscious projects its hidden workings on to nature. Thus the workings of nature mentioned in myth are basically the projected images of the unconscious. For Jung, persons or cultures do not invent myth; they experience myth.[344] In myth, they experience the primordial images or archetypes buried deep within the collective unconscious. Jung's theory of the collective unconscious lies at the very foundation of his theory of myth.[345]

Myth has an intrinsic experiential and lifestyle pull for learners of varied backgrounds and psychological ages. "The world of myth," states Ernst Cassirer, "is a dramatic world—a world of actions, of forces, of conflicting powers. In every phenomenon of nature it sees the collision of these powers."[346] Myth tells the tale of this dramatic experiential and lifestyle world—and specifically how the human person grapples with this world.

There are two basic approaches which a religious educator can follow in teaching myth. The first approach is teaching the learners about the mythic in various cultures. The second approach is teaching the learner about the mythic in which and with which they themselves live.

In teaching about myths in various cultures, the religious educator should himself take seriously the myths he is teaching.[347] The myths which the learners study should be examples of the finest, not of the marginal, myths which various religions or cultures have to offer. The myths chosen for study should be interesting and attractively told. A myth should be typically read aloud or better yet enacted dramatically, since myth fully lives only in its re-telling and re-enactment, in the interaction of the teller or actors with the audience. Because myth is the communication of encoded conscious and unconscious messages, the religious educator should so structure the pedagogical situation that the learner is enabled to decode the real and possibly hidden messages of the myth. Because the fundamental conscious and unconscious content are deliberately coded into the language of a myth in a definite specific fashion, the myth-tellers or myth-enacters are required to adhere to an unchanged form.[348] The religious educator, therefore, should not alter the words or the form of the original myth, for such misguided attempts to make the myth "relevant" will, in actuality, destroy its exquisitely interworked form and structure, thereby making it genuinely irrelevant. The religious educator should be aware that the more religious the myth, the more people in various cultures tended to act it out in special ceremonies as well as in their own lives.

The second approach to teaching the mythic can only be adequately accomplished by so structuring the pedagogical situation that the learner actually lives in and with the mythic here-and-now. In a very real sense, each learner lives his own myth, a myth formed and nourished and modified by a variety of intersecting realities including home, church, and society. Each family, each church, and each society purposively socializes the individual into its living myth about its beginnings, its heroes, and its mighty deeds. It is into and with these intersecting myths that a Christian grows up and lives in adulthood, myths which gradually become part-and-parcel of a person's self-system and in a major sense one primal grounding and fundamental explanation of each individual's behavior pattern.

The mythic enjoys a natural appeal for each learner because the mythic places the individual in close interactive relationship with the latent conditions of his own existence and personhood. Myth deals with the most basic realities involved in the human situation, realities with which each person must come to grips in his own personal life— realities like life, death, suffering, love, evil, meaning, and heroism. Myth enriches the world and world-events by viewing them as they are, open—open to the eruption or irruption (depending on whether one is an immanentist or a transcendist) of God into the workings of the universe.[349] It places religion in somewhat of an affective atmosphere inasmuch as one of the most vital sources of myth lies in a person's feeling-functions. Because myth has a very creative dimension, it can help liberate an individual from the cage of the exclusive here-and-now, allowing that person to range to all reality, to the existentially dynamic, the extrarational, the transcendent.[350]

An apparently promising pedagogical technique for teaching learners to enter and befriend their own personal myth through verbal content is that of the personal journal.[351] A personal journal is an intimate record of one's deepest human moments as one passes on pilgrimage through time. A personal journal is an account of the most intimate thoughts, feelings, and experiences which an individual has had during a given period of time—a day, a week, a month, a year, and so on.[352]

The journey of self and into self which constitutes the fundamental axis of genuine personalistic living is a process of coming into close contact with that which one is so that one might become fully that which one truly can be.[353] One's personal journey is, then, essentially a process. James Olney nicely encapsulates the centrality of process with respect to life, to the self, and to the personal journal when he writes: "Form, which in the language of scholastic philosophy is closely related to soul or essential being, is not of the order of facts but the order of process: an activity exercised continuously outward from a center. Tracing form back from manifestation to source, one sees it recede into a finer and finer point, and there, where it disappears into its own center, is the spiritual mind of man, a great shape-maker impelled forever to find order in himself and give it to the universe."[354]

As it is viewed by most of its proponents, a personal journal is not a recounting of the "external" facts of one's life such as one's marriage day or a quarrel which one had last Thursday with one's best friend. Rather, a personal journal is an account of what is happening personalistically to the individual as that individual experiences the facts of daily life such as a marriage day or a quarrel with a best friend. In the personal journal procedure, then, the writer comes into close contact with his deepest self and with some of the basic myths in which and with which he lives. A personal journal is really a processive search for self and a search for the self-in-process. A personal journal is thus one potentially fruitful response to Socrates' famous dictum and challenge: "The unexamined life is not worth living."[355]

A personal journal is typically written by the individual in the humanistic solitude of deep existential contact with one's actual authentic self-in-process.[356] It is in the silence of solitude, the withdrawal from group interaction, that the person is enabled to explore, wrestle, and find his processing self. Plunging into the aloneness-of-self in an environment of solitude is not easy for some Christians whose life is characterized by a plethora of group activities.[357] Nonetheless, the intimate existential contact with self, a contact made in the solitude which at bottom is the self-in-real-life, tends to have a freeing and healing effect. From the Christian perspective, after all, redemption and reconciliation to self, to others, and to God is possible only to the extent to which one sees, feels, and lives one's actual here-and-now self.

There are quite a few highly specific pedagogical techniques through which personal journaling may be done, including the somewhat directive procedure advocated by Milt Hughes,[358] the psychosynthetic practice advanced by Roberto Assagioli,[359] and the Gestalt-inspired and feminist-oriented procedure proposed by Christina Baldwin.[360] One of the most widely used personal journal techniques is that of the intensive journal pioneered and developed by Ira Progoff.[361] Progoff began his career as a scholar and devotee of Carl Jung, and the intensive journal technique in one large sense can be viewed as *a* kind of pedagogical objectification of the Jungian perspective. Because Carl Jung was a firm believer in the force and omnipresence of the mythic in human existence, it is only natural that Progoff's intensive journal technique has as one of its faces the encounter between the person with the mythic in general and with his own individual myth in particular. In one major sense, the intensive journal technique is oriented around myth, in this case exploring the process contents and the product contents of the dominant image of that life-stage in which the person is currently situated. When the person makes contact with this dominant image, then the individual proceeds back in personal time to uncover the markers he found there and the paths he took then in arriving at his present state of existence—as well as the markers not heeded and the paths not taken. The intensive journal technique makes considerable use of images and consciousness-relaxing procedures to structure the learning situation in such a way that the person's unconscious functions can seep into some kind of open view for himself. Though verbal content tends to be intrinsically linked to cognition, the intensive journal technique is deliberately designed to use words in such a manner as to bypass ratiocinative cognition in order to get at the unconscious and the mythic. Progoff gives the term "process meditation" to the way in which the intensive journal technique is carried out. Process meditation is not free-floating, but is carried out by certain exercises designed to facilitate process flow and process outcomes in the learner. Progoff views the intensive journal technique as "indeed a species of prayer and meditation, but not in isolation from life and not in contrast to active life involvement. Rather, it is meditation in the midst of the actuality of our life experiences. It draws upon the actualities of life for new awarenesses, and it feeds these back into the movement of each life as a whole. The fact is that the fundamental *process* in process meditation is each life itself."[362]

In terms of empirical support for the effectiveness of the intensive journal technique, I am not aware of any formal research studies made to evaluate this procedure. However, a significantly high percentage of persons who have taken the Progoff workshops who use the intensive journal technique report that this pedagogical tool is effective in their own lives.

Probably the most effective way in which a religious educator can learn the skills involved in the intensive journal technique is to take one of the intensive journal workshops conducted by Ira Progoff or by one of his professionally prepared collaborators. These workshops are conducted at many different times and sites around the country. Once the religious educator has taken one of these workshops and has practiced the intensive journal technique in his own life, he is at least minimally prepared to use this kind of journaling technique with the learners in his care.[363]

CONCLUSION

Verbal content will always occupy an important place in the galaxy of religious instruction activities. While recognizing the richness which verbal content gives to the work of religious instruction, still we should also be mindful of the limitations which verbal content has.

One of the principal tasks of religious instruction is to put revelation into focus. It endeavors to make more meaningful the revelational elements already present in life. Finally, religious instruction works toward facilitating congruence between the learner's personal development and God's ongoing presence in the universe, since it is through the facilitation of this kind of congruence that religious instruction is able to help expand the boundaries of revelation for the learner. If religious instruction is to achieve this threefold task, it must ultimately pass to the supraverbal level where both the teacher and the learner recognize the incapability of words to adequately express the personal force and meaning of revelation. To put revelation into focus for the learner, to make revelation more meaningful for him, to enable the learner to become more existentially congruent with the ongoing revelational dynamic, the religious educator's lessons must ultimately pass from the zone of verbal content into the richer regions of nonverbal content and of lifestyle content.

NOTES

1. Morris West, *The Heretic* (New York: Morrow, 1969), p. 37.
2. I am using "letters" here to include words spoken, written, and thought, as well as those words which are alphabetic, ideogrammic, and so forth.

3. See Edward Sapir, *Language* (New York: Harcourt, Brace, 1921), p. 27. I should add that both spoken and most nonspoken verbal content are learned.

4. John Lotz, "Symbols Make Man," in Lynn White, Jr., editor, *Frontiers of Knowledge in the Study of Man* (New York: Harper, 1956), p. 207.

5. Harold J. Vetter, *Language Behavior and Communication* (Itasca, Ill.: Peacock, 1969), p. 18.

6. Francis P. Dinneen, *An Introduction to General Linguistics* (New York: Holt Rinehart and Winston, 1967), pp. 8–9.

7. Benjamin Lee Whorf, *Language, Thought, and Reality*, edited by John B. Carroll (Cambridge, Mass.: M.I.T. Press, 1956), p. 252.

8. Edward Sapir, "The Nature of Language," in David G. Mandelbaum, editor, *Selected Writings of Edward Sapir* (Berkeley, Calif.: University of California Press, 1949), p. 10.

9. Depth psychologists, for their part, tend to reserve the term "symbol" for outward signs of a very deep form of spiritual reality, as I note in Chapter Four. In this chapter, I consider symbol in its verbal dimensionality.

10. Archibald A. Hill, *An Introduction to Linguistic Structures* (New York: Harcourt, Brace, and World, 1958), p. 9.

11. See Samuel Butler, "Thought and Language," in Max Black, editor, *The Importance of Language* (Englewood Cliffs, N.J.: Prentice-Hall, 1962), p. 18.

12. For an especially illuminating treatment of this and related points, see Charles E. Osgood, "What is Language?" in Doris Aaronson and Robert W. Rieber, editors, *Psycholinguistic Research: Implications and Applications* (Hillsdale, N.J.: Erlbaum, 1979), pp. 189–227.

13. See S. I. Hayakawa, *Language in Action* (New York: Harcourt, Brace, 1941), p. 55.

14. This sentence, of course, must be balanced against the objective aspect of linguistic symbols. Even Michael Polanyi seems to concede this, as is suggested by his distinction between factual words and assertion words. See Michael Polanyi, *Personal Knowledge* (Chicago: University of Chicago Press, 1958), pp. 252–254.

15. There is some controversy in linguistic circles about whether audible speech is an essential characteristic of verbal behavior. Most linguisticians hold that language is sound, or at least is primarily sound. The strongest argument in behalf of such a position is that spoken language is prior in time to written language, both in terms of a contemporary child's acquisition of verbal behavior and in terms of the fact that oral language preceded written language in the history of humanity. Written language, in this view, represents the attempt to capture or imitate in another medium the sounds or sound patterns contained in oral language. A written word or ideogram should be cast in such a fashion that it represents the spoken word. See Edward Sapir, "The Nature of Language," p. 15; also Francis P. Dinneen, *An Introduction to General Linguistics*, pp. 6–7.

16. These encounters are interpreted by a person as taking place either directly or indirectly, depending on his standpoint—whether transcendist or immanentist. For an illuminating and penetrating treatment of the role of the transcendent and the immanent metaperspectives in religious instruction theory, see Ian P. Knox, *Above or Within?: The Supernatural in Religious Education* (Birmingham, Ala.: Religious Education Press, 1977).

17. Some scholars disagree with my distinction. See for example, Earl R. MacCormac, *Metaphor and Myth in Science and Religion* (Durham, N.C.: Duke University Press, 1976), pp. 61–62.

18. As a broad generalization admitting of some notable exceptions, social scientists tend to view religious discourse as strictly applying to the person-God encounter (or perception of such an encounter), while theologians appear to lump religious language and theological language together. For an example of a social-science treatment of religious language which does not deal with theological language, see Charles A. Ferguson, "Some Forms of Religious Discourse," in Günther Dux, Thomas Luckmann, and Joachim Matthes, Herausgeber, *Zur Theorie der Religion: Religion und Sprache* (Oplader, Bundesrepublik Deutschland: Westdeutscher, 1973), pp. 224–235.

19. In logic, a predicate is that which is affirmed or denied of the subject in a proposition.

20. Valerio Tonini, "Commentaire," dans Stanilas Breton, redacteur, "Langage Religieux, Langage Théologique," dans Enrico Castelli redacteur, *Débats sur le Langage Théologique* (Paris: Aubier, 1969), pp. 127–128, translation mine, italics mine.

21. The writings of Johannes Hofinger, an advocate of the traditional theological approach, are a case in point. Because Hofinger views religious instruction as essentially a theological discipline, he regards the verbal content of the religious educator as primarily informational and cognitive rather than existential. For Hofinger, catechesis is a logical informational step-by-step arrangement and development of the point(s) to be proclaimed. See, for example, Johannes Hofinger, *Our Message is Christ* (Notre Dame, Ind.: Fides/Claretian, 1974), pp. 17–22.

22. On the use of technical language, see James Michael Lee, *The Shape of Religious Instruction* (Birmingham, Ala.: Religious Education Press, 1971), p. 135.

23. See Robert Butterworth, "On Theological Language," in *The Way* XII (April, 1972), pp. 114–115.

24. This statement in no way suggests that religious experience is necessarily apart from the general texture of human experience. Nor does it affirm or deny that all of human experience is, or potentially is, religious.

25. Some scholars refer to religious (and theological) language as "odd, peculiar, and unusual." See Ian T. Ramsey, *Religious Language* (London: SCM, 1957), p. 19. Ramsey tends to uncritically lump religious language together with theological language.

26. Robert Butterworth, "On Theological Language," pp. 110–112.

27. See William T. Blackstone, "The Status of God-Talk," in Robert H. Ayers and William T. Blackstone, editors, *Religious Language and Knowledge* (Athens, Ga.: University of Georgia Press, 1972), pp. 1–17.

28. *Ibid.*, italics deleted.

29. Thomas Aquinas, *Summa Theologica,* Ia, q. 3, intro. See also David B. Burrell, "Aquinas on Naming God," in *Theological Studies* XXIV (June, 1963), pp. 192–210.

30. George P. Klubertanz, *St. Thomas on Analogy* (Chicago: Loyola University Press, 1960), p. 151.

31. I treat this issue in Chapter Three of this volume.

32. Robert Butterworth, "On Theological Language," p. 113, italics deleted.

33. See, for example, Randolph Crump Miller, *The Language Gap and God* (Philadelphia: Pilgrim, 1970.)

34. See, for example, Langdon Gilkey, *Naming the Whirlwind: The Renewal of God-Language* (Indianapolis, Ind.: Bobbs-Merrill, 1969).

35. Alfred Jules Ayer, *Language, Truth and Logic*, 2d ed. (New York: Dover, 1952), p. 78.
36. *Ibid.*, pp. 79–80.
37. *Ibid.*, pp. 114–120.
38. I say "later" because functional analysis or usage analysis characterizes Wittgenstein's later writings, notably his *Philosophical Investigations*. His earlier conceptualizations, especially as formulated in his *Tractatus Logico-Philosophicus*, lean in the direction of asserting that every proposition has (1) one and only one complete analysis, and (2) a definite sense, regardless of the manner and context of its usage.
39. Ludwig Wittgenstein, *Philosophische Untersuchungen*, with facing translation as *Philosophical Investigations* made by G. E. M. Anscombe (New York: Macmillan, 1953), pp. 1 (1ᵉ) − 14 (14ᵉ).
40. Terrence Tilley calls Ian Ramsey and Dallas High "personalist empiricists." (pp. 71–95). Tilley's book is an important introductory attempt to show how analytical-empirical philosophy can be helpful in understanding religious language. Unfortunately, Tilley does not adequately distinguish between religious language and theological language. Terrence W. Tilley, *Talking of God* (New York: Paulist, 1978).
41. Ian T. Ramsey, *On Being Sure in Religion* (London: Athlone, 1963), p. 3.
42. Ian T. Ramsey, *Religious Language*, p. 167. "To know what hypostatic unity is *in fact*, there must be evoked a Christian disclosure situation with Jesus Christ as the occasion and object of it; a situation where we wish to speak of the object as 'Jesus Christ' and yet also as 'God.' " *Ibid.*
43. *Ibid.*, p. 25, italics deleted.
44. Edmund J. Dobbin, "Religious Language," in *New Catholic Encyclopedia*, volume XVI (New York: McGraw-Hill, 1974), p. 383.
45. Sociolinguistics is helpful in this regard. For one application of sociolinguistics to religious language, see William J. Samarin, "The Language of Religion," in William J. Samarin, editor, *Language in Religious Practice* (Rowley, Mass.: Newbury, 1975), pp. 3–13.
46. I am using the term "express adequately" in its fulsome existential sense rather than in its logical sense.
47. See, for example, Langdon Gilkey, *Naming the Whirlwind: The Renewal of God-Language*, p. 419.
48. Paul Tillich, *Systematic Theology*, volume II (Chicago: University of Chicago Press, 1957), p. 9.
49. J. L. Austin, *Philosophical Papers* (London: Oxford University Press, 1961), pp. 220–239.
50. When a person perceives certain stimuli relating to a holy place having physical features such as an altar and a pulpit and pews, then the person tends to immediately organize and classify these stimuli as "church."
51. Notable exceptions to this include Randolph Crump Miller, Gabriel Moran, and Kieran Scott.
52. Th. P. van Baaren, "Religious Symbols: Their Essence and Their Function," in H. W. Obbink, A. A. van Ruler, and W. C. van Unnik, editors, *Verbum: Some Aspects of the Religious Function of Words* (Utrecht, The Netherlands: Kemink, 1964), p. 22.
53. Marshall McLuhan, *Understanding Media* (New York: McGraw-Hill, 1964), p. 79.

54. Jerome S. Bruner, "The Course of Cognitive Growth," in *American Psychologist* XIX (January, 1964), pp. 1–15.

55. Edward Sapir postulated that language determines culture, while Benjamin Lee Whorf, a student of Sapir, held, a bit more restrainedly, that language exerts a highly influential role on culture. See Edward A. Sapir, *Culture, Language and Personality*, edited by David G. Mandelbaum (Berkeley, Calif.: University of California Press, 1966); and Benjamin Lee Whorf, *Language, Thought, and Reality*.

56. Sam Glucksberg and Joseph H. Danks, *Experimental Psycholinguistics* (Hillsdale, N.J.: Erlbaum, 1975), pp. 175–207.

57. Though the Sapir-Whorf hypothesis is held by a great many linguisticians, still it should be remembered that this hypothesis is easier to accept intuitively and deductively than to prove in a rigorous scientific way. No correlations can be said to exist between language and perceptual frameworks until the specific perceptual frameworks are themselves defined in terms of observable behaviors. Of interest also is that some Soviet scholars such as Aleksandr Luria have been researching the regulatory function of verbal content in a different but somewhat complementary way to the Sapir-Whorf hypothesis. On this last point, see David Bloor, "The Regulatory Function of Language," in John Morton and John C. Marshall, editors, *Psycholinguistics: Developmental and Pathological* (Ithaca, N.Y.: Cornell University Press, 1977), pp. 73–97.

58. Gabriel Moran, *The Present Revelation* (New York: Herder and Herder, 1972), p. 314.

59. Edward A. Sapir, *Selected Writings of Edward Sapir*, p. 15.

60. David P. Ausubel, "A Cognitive-Structure Theory of School Learning," in Laurence Siegel, editor, *Instruction: Some Contemporary Viewpoints* (San Francisco: Chandler, 1967), p. 219.

61. See, for example, Robert Rosenthal and Lenore Jacobson, *Pygmalion in the Classroom: Teacher Expectation and Pupils' Intellectual Development* (New York: Holt, Rinehart and Winston, 1968).

62. For a brief discussion of the nature and function of reinforcement, see James Michael Lee, *The Flow of Religious Instruction* (Birmingham, Ala.: Religious Education Press, 1973), pp. 79–89.

63. See B. F. Skinner, *Beyond Freedom and Dignity* (New York: Knopf, 1971), pp. 105–106.

64. On this last point, see Ole R. Holsti, *Content Analysis for the Social Sciences and Humanities* (Reading, Mass.: Addison-Wesley, 1969), p. 15.

65. The religious educator would do well to recall, however, B. F. Skinner's observation that the size of a child's vocabulary or the grammatical forms the child employs are not so much a function of his age but of the verbal contingencies which have prevailed in the community in which he grew up. B. F. Skinner, *Beyond Freedom and Dignity*, p. 139.

66. Thomas Aquinas, *Scriptum Super Sententiis*, 1.4, d.4, q.2, a.2, ad. 3:1, translation mine.

67. Joseph P. Christopher, translator's annotation, in Aurelius Augustinus, *De Catechizandis Rudibus*, translated and annotated by Joseph P. Christopher (Westminster, Md.: Newman, 1962), pp. 93–94. In this annotated passage, Christopher gives a brief but meaty etymological overview of the word "catechetics." In my short treatment of the role of verbal content in the theory and practice of certain Catholic theologically oriented religious educationists and educators, I will em-

ploy the terms "catechetics," "catechesis," and "catechist" in order to preserve the flavor of the writings of these persons.

68. See Kieran Scott, "Collapsing the Tensions," in *Living Light XVIII* (Summer, 1981), pp. 167–169. For an especially lucid summary of some pertinent pros and cons of the term "catechetics," see Mary C. Boys, "The Standpoint of Religious Education," in *Religious Education* LXXVI (March–April, 1981), pp. 129–133.

69. Alfonso M. Nebreda, "The Theological Problem of Transmission," in *Lumen Vitae* XX (June, 1965), p. 317.

70. *Ibid.*, p. 319.

71. Hubert Halbfas, *Theory of Catechetics* (New York: Herder and Herder, 1971), pp. 51, 53, 54.

72. Tjeu van den Berk, "Language in the Dutch Catechism," in Alois Müller, editor, *Catechetics for the Future* (New York: Herder and Herder, 1970), p. 84.

73. Paul Brunner, "Liturgical Pastoral Theology," in Johannes Hofinger and Theodore C. Stone, editors, *Pastoral Catechetics* (New York: Herder and Herder, 1964), p. 20.

74. William Reedy, "The Mystery of Christ," in *ibid.*, pp. 116–117. Reedy combines the verbal with the witness theory, hoping that the catechist's personal witness will somehow teach the learners.

75. Marcel van Caster, *The Structure of Catechetics,* translated by Edward J. Dirkswager, Jr., Olga Guedetarian, and Nicolas Smith (New York: Herder and Herder, 1965), pp. 185, 195–196.

76. The Higher Institute of Catechetics of Nijmegen, *Fundamentals and Programs of a New Catechesis,* revised by Henry J. Koren, translated by Walter Van de Putte (Pittsburgh, Pa.: Duquesne University Press, 1966), pp. 51, 87–91, 106–107, 127. For a discussion of the witness "theory" of religious instruction, see James Michael Lee, *The Flow of Religious Instruction,* pp. 164–174.

77. Joseph Colomb, "A Modern Approach to Catechetics in the Church as a Whole," in Alois Müller, editor, *Catechetics for the Future,* p. 27.

78. Berard L. Marthaler, *Catechetics in Context* (Huntington, Ind.: Our Sunday Visitor Press, 1973), pp. 3, 36. For an even more pointed elaboration of his position of catechetics-equals-verbal-transmission, see Berard L. Marthaler, "Evangelization and Catechesis: Word, Memory, Witness," in *Living Light* XVI (Spring, 1979), pp. 33–45. The task of witness, for Marthaler, is to reinforce the central verbal content—a content which must be perfectly faithful in every detail to the official pronouncements of the Catholic *ecclesiasticum.*

79. Marianne Sawicki, "The Power and Ministry of the Word," in *Living Light* XVII (Summer, 1980), p. 150.

80. Jean Le Du and Marcel van Caster, *Experiential Catechetics,* translated by Denis Barrett (New York: Newman, 1969), p. 76.

81. Roy E. Buehler and Jo F. Richmond, "Interpersonal Communication Behavior Analysis: A Research Method," in *Journal of Communication* XIII (September 1963), pp. 150–151.

82. Josef Goldbrunner, "Catechetical Method as Handmaid of Kerygma," in Johannes Hofinger, editor, *Teaching All Nations,* revised and partly translated by Clifford Howell (Freiburg, Bundesrepublik Deutschland: Herder, 1961), pp. 112–113.

83. James Michael Lee, *The Flow of Religious Instruction,* pp. 188–194.

84. For a development of this point, see James Michael Lee, "Religious Education

and the Bible: A Religious Educationist's View,'' in Joseph S. Marino, editor, *Biblical Themes in Religious Education* (Birmingham, Ala.: Religious Education Press, 1983), pp. 3–8.

85. Roger Lincoln Shinn, *The Educational Mission of the Church* (Boston: United Church Press, 1962), p. 31.

86. Edward Schillebeeckx, *Revelation and Theology,* volume I, translated by N. D. Smith (New York: Sheed and Ward, 1967), pp. 33–37.

87. Gabriel Moran, *Theology of Revelation* (New York: Herder and Herder, 1966), p. 81.

88. Edward Schillebeeckx, *Revelation and Theology,* volume I, p. 74.

89. James D. Smart, *The Teaching Ministry of the Church* (Philadelphia: Westminster, 1954), pp. 35–36.

90. See Jakob Laubach, ''Heinrich Schleir,'' in Leonhard Reinisch, editor, *Theologians of Our Time* (Notre Dame, Ind.: University of Notre Dame Press, 1964), p. 136.

91. I also suspect that one of the prime motives for Marthaler's interest in the catechist as Christian witness stems from his apparent desire to make sure that catechesis is always subject in every detail to the *ecclesiasticum,* an organization which typically contends that it is the sole determinant of authentic Christian witness.

92. This schema does not imply that communication takes place in what I earlier termed ''the radio model.'' The radio model is an instance of only one of the many specific ways in which this schema, this communicative process, actually happens.

93. One of the surprising things is that advocates of the religious-instruction-equals-verbal-content position never seem to have made a serious sustained scientific study of linguistics. If these people, such as Berard Marthaler, are truly sincere in their position, then they ought to deeply explore linguistics and place linguistics near the center of their writings and speeches.

94. I am following here the division suggested in Francis P. Dinneen, *An Introduction to General Linguistics,* pp. 1–4.

95. I find it interesting, and a little sad too, that religious educationists like Gabriel Moran and Kieran Scott who forcefully declare that language is so all-important in religious education do not seem to believe that language is important enough for them themselves to study its structure carefully or scientifically.

96. See Frederick Ferré, ''Paul M. van Buren's A-Theology of Christian Education,'' in *Religious Education* LX (January–February, 1965), pp. 22–23.

97. Francis P. Dinneen, *An Introduction to General Linguistics,* p. 4. See also p. 5. There is one aspect of linguistics, however, which can be legitimately called a branch of mathematics.

98. Feminists are inclined to lean in the direction of the Sapir-Whorf hypothesis (even though a goodly number of them might be unaware of this crucial hypothesis in psycholinguistics). Thus, for example, Gloria Durka argues that what she terms ''sexist religious language'' with respect to God distorts both woman's proper image of God and man's image of God. See Gloria Durka, ''The Religious Journey of Women: The Educational Task,'' in *Religious Education* LXXVII (March–April, 1982), pp. 166–168.

99. Perhaps the most celebrated form of the material approach is that used by B. F. Skinner and his followers. See, for example, B. F. Skinner, *Verbal Behavior* (New York: Appleton-Century-Crofts, 1957). For Skinner, verbal behavior is a

dependent variable. "Meaning is not a property of behavior as such but of the conditions under which behavior occurs" (p. 14). This concept has significant import for the religious educator.

100. Charles N. Cofer, "Language: The Psychology of Language," in David L. Sills, editor, *International Encyclopedia of the Social Sciences*, volume IX (New York: Macmillan and The Free Press, 1968), p. 2.

101. For a brief account of the relationship of phonology to descriptive linguistics, see Martin Joos, "Phonology: Phonetics and Acoustic Phonetics," in Archibald A. Hill, editor, *Linguistics Today* (New York: Basic, 1969), pp. 18–19.

102. A diaphone is similar to a phoneme except that it deals with minimum speech units of one person compared to those of other persons. Daniel Jones, "The Theory of Phonemes and Its Importance in Practical Linguistics," in Eric A. Hamp, Fred W. Householder, and Robert Austerlitz, editors, *Readings in Linguistics II* (Chicago: University of Chicago Press, 1966), pp. 31–32.

103. For a relatively comprehensive and favorable treatment of phoneme, see Daniel Jones, *The Phoneme: Its Nature and Use* (Cambridge, England: Heffer, 1962). See also Martin D. S. Braine, "On What Might Constitute Learnable Phonology," in *Language* L (June, 1974), pp. 270–279.

104. Though almost all grammars make use of the word as a fundamental syntactical unit, no generally accepted definition of the word-unit exists. Joseph H. Greenberg, "The Linguistic Approach," in Alfred G. Smith, editor, *Communication and Culture* (New York: Holt, Rinehart and Winston, 1966), p. 129.

105. C. E. Bazell, "On the Problem of the Morpheme," in Eric A. Hamp, Fred W. Householder, and Robert Austerlitz, editors, *Readings in Linguistics II*, p. 217. See also Eugene A. Nida, *Morphology: The Descriptive Analysis of Words* (Ann Arbor, Mich.: University of Michigan, 1946), pp. 166–167.

106. One of the most influential books in the entire history of the world, Thrax's *Technē grammaticē* proved to be the principal pillar of Roman grammar and was regarded as definitive for more than a thousand years. Its impact on grammar, notably school grammars, can still be felt down to the present day.

107. Leonard Bloomfield, *Language* (New York: Holt, 1933).

108. Bernard Bloch, "Obituary Notice," in Charles F. Hockett, compiler, *A Leonard Bloomfield Anthology* (Bloomington, Ind.: University of Indiana Press, 1970), p. 531.

109. A classic textbook explaining structural grammar is W. Nelson Francis, *The Structure of American English* (New York: Ronald, 1958).

110. Zellig S. Harris, "Co-occurrence and Transformation in Linguistic Structure," in *Language* XXXIII (July–September, 1957), pp. 283–340.

111. Noam Chomsky, *Syntactic Structure* ('s-Gravenhage, The Netherlands: Mouton, 1957). This work was Chomsky's doctoral dissertation.

112. A useful textbook explaining transformational grammar is Emmon Bach, *An Introduction to Transformational Grammars* (New York: Holt, Rinehart and Winston, 1964).

113. Noam Chomsky, *Language and the Mind*, 2d ed. (New York: Harcourt Brace Jovanovich, 1972).

114. Chomsky added the semantic component to the previous three in his book *Studies on Semantics in Generative Grammar* (The Hague: Mouton, 1972).

115. Robert B. Lees, "Review," in *Language* XXXIII (July–September, 1957), p. 391.

116. Lažló Antal, *Content, Meaning, and Understanding* (The Hague: Mouton, 1964), pp. 34–57.

117. For a witty and somewhat trenchant view of how certain modern movements ranging from advertising to feminism to education have bent linguistics to their respective semantic purposes, see Mario Pei, *Weasel Words: The Art of Saying What You Don't Mean* (New York: Harper & Row, 1978).

118. See Robert L. Benjamin, *Semantics and Language Analysis* (Indianapolis, Ind.: Bobbs-Merrill, 1970), pp. 16–19. I am following Benjamin in my treatment of semantics.

119. See Louis B. Salomon, *Semantics and Common Sense* (New York: Holt, Rinehart and Winston, 1966), pp. 65–67. By and large, religious educationists have also neglected semantics in their writings and speeches. Gabriel Moran seems to be one of the few persons writing on religious education who recognizes the crucial value of semantics in the instructional setting. Gabriel Moran, *Religious Body* (New York: Seabury, 1974), pp. 21–22.

120. See, for example, Gareth Evans, "Semantic Structure and Logical Form," in Gareth Evans and John McDowell, editors, *Truth and Meaning: Essays in Semantics* (Oxford, England: Clarendon, 1976), pp. 199–222.

121. In their investigations of the structure of language and its meaning, "ordinary-language philosophers have by and large tended to occupy themselves with the study of the use of words, while [linguistic] positivists have been primarily concerned with the analysis of sentences and their inference relations." Jerry A. Fodor and Jerrold J. Katz, "Introduction," in Jerry A. Fodor and Jerrold J. Katz, editors, *The Structure of Language* (Englewood Cliffs, N.J.: Prentice-Hall, 1965), p. 3, italics deleted.

122. M. Gorman, "Semantics," in *New Catholic Encyclopedia,* volume XIII (New York: McGraw-Hill, 1967), p. 67. Charles Ogden and Ivor Richards also give a helpful review of the nature of meaning in the theories of some key thinkers. See C. E. Ogden and I. A. Richards, *The Meaning of Meaning,* 8th ed. (New York: Harcourt, Brace, and World, 1946), pp. 267–290.

123. See Alfred Tarski, *Logic, Semantics, and Metamathematics,* translated by J. N. Woodger (Oxford: Clarendon, 1956).

124. See Rudolf Carnap, *Introduction to Semantics* (Cambridge, Mass.: Harvard University Press, 1942); Rudolf Carnap, *Formalization of Logic* (Cambridge, Mass.: Harvard University Press, 1943); and Rudolf Carnap, *Meaning and Necessity,* 2d ed. (Chicago: University of Chicago Press, 1964).

125. Religious thought and theology, while related, are not identical.

126. Alfred Korzybski's system, called "general semantics," was proposed largely to bring meaning back into life and living. For Korzybski, society is riddled through and through with mental and emotional disease. This disease, contends Korzybski, has been brought about by linguistic and indeed by semantic maladjustment. This approach to semantics is one of the most influential in the twentieth century. See Alfred Korzybsky, *Science and Sanity* (Lakeville, Conn.: International Non-Aristotelian Library, 1948).

127. Thomas McPherson, "Assertion and Analogy," in Douglas M. High, editor, *New Essays on Religious Language* (New York: Oxford University Press, 1969), pp. 211–212.

128. For an illustration of this, see Mario Pei, *The Families of Words* (New York: Harper, 1962).

129. J. L. Austin maintains that the distinction between performative and constative words is related to locutionary and illocutionary operations in the total linguistic act much as special theory stands to general theory. J. L. Austin, *How to Do Things with Words*, edited by J. O. Urmson (Cambridge, Mass.: Harvard University Press, 1962), p. 147.
130. *Ibid.*, pp. 150–162.
131. *Ibid.*, p. 154.
132. *Ibid.*, p. 157.
133. After the word "behavitive" in his preliminary listing, Austin adds: "(a shocker this)." One can only wonder why words which stress personal behavior would be considered as "a shocker." *Ibid.*, p. 150.
134. *Ibid.*, p. 159.
135. *Ibid.*, p. 160.
136. *Ibid.*, p. 162.
137. Donald D. Evans, *The Logic of Self-Involvement* (New York: Herder and Herder, 1963), pp. 257–262.
138. Certain linguisticians such as Ingemar Hedenius and Edward John Lemmon claim that performatives have truth value. Lennart Åqvist also believes that performatives are bound up with truth and falsity for the following reasons: "If, in accordance with the characterization agreed upon, we do sometimes succeed in making a promise just by uttering the sentence 'I promise to pay you $5,' couldn't this very fact as well be conveyed by saying that we sometimes succeed in making that sentence true just by uttering it? But then, far from its being characteristic of performatives that they lack truth-value, that is, on the contrary, quite essential for them to be capable of truth: how else could they sometimes be made true by their production in appropriate contexts of linguistic communication?" Lennart Åqvist, *Performatives and Verifiability by the Use of Language* (Uppsala, Sweden: University of Uppsala, 1972), p. 2.
139. Donald D. Evans, *The Language of Self-Involvement*, pp. 70–71.
140. Michael Polanyi, *Personal Knowledge*, p. 77.
141. James D. Smart, *The Teaching Ministry of the Church*. (Philadelphia: Westminster, 1954), p. 149.
142. For a variety of views of the types and structure of idioms, see Adam Makkai, *Idiom Structure in English* (The Hague: Mouton, 1972), pp. 23–58.
143. Logan Pearsall Smith, *Words and Idioms* (Boston: Houghton Mifflin, 1925). pp. 167–169.
144. Philip Wheelwright, *Metaphor and Reality* (Bloomington, Ind.: University of Indiana Press, 1967), p. 71.
145. Robert A. Nisbet, *Social Change and History* (New York: Oxford University Press, 1969), p. 4.
146. Victor Turner, *Dramas, Fields, and Metaphors* (Ithaca, N.Y.: Cornell University Press, 1974), p. 25.
147. Hugh R. Walpole, *Semantics* (New York: Norton, 1941), pp. 148–149.
148. Paul Ricoeur uses this struggle, this tension inherent in the nature of metaphor as a basis for the development of his concept of metaphorical truth. Paul Ricoeur, *The Rule of Metaphor*, translated by Robert Czerny (Toronto: University of Toronto Press, 1977), pp. 245–256.
149. Philip Wheelwright, *Metaphor and Reality*, pp. 45–69.
150. In the field of religious instruction, Maria Harris has shown herself as one who is vitally interested in metaphor. See, for example, Maria Harris, "Word, Sacra-

ment, Prophecy,'' in Padraic O'Hare, editor, *Tradition and Transformation in Religious Education* (Birmingham, Ala.: Religious Education Press, 1979), pp. 35–57.

151. Theology, of course, employs metaphor. However, theology uses metaphor not to prove a truth but (1) to illustrate a truth or (2) to point to an ineffable truth which cannot be conclusively proved in a rational manner.

152. On this point, see R. Boyle, "Metaphor," in *New Catholic Encyclopedia,* volume IX (New York: McGraw-Hill, 1967), p. 725.

153. Robert Boyle, "The Nature of Metaphor: Further Considerations," in *Modern Schoolman* XXXIV (May, 1957), p. 294.

154. Martin Foss, *Symbol and Metaphor in Human Experience* (Princeton, N.J.: Princeton University Press, 1949), pp. 60–62.

155. Though not as objective as the social sciences or the natural sciences, theology nonetheless is still somewhat objective.

156. In contrast to Aristotle who proposed that metaphors should be derived from beautiful words (objectivity), Robert Rogers contends that psychoanalytic practice shows that the finest metaphors are derived from significant verbal imagery of the body (subjectivity). In Rogers' view, a metaphor is "the flesh made word." Aristotle, *Rhetoric,* III.2.13; Robert Rogers, *Metaphor: A Psychoanalytic View* (Berkeley, Calif.: University of California Press, 1978), pp. 77–112.

157. See Max Black, *Models and Metaphors* (Ithaca, N.Y.: Cornell University Press, 1962), p. 45.

158. Religion is an art—the art of living in a certain manner.

159. Weller Embler, *Metaphor and Meaning* (DeLand, Fla.: Everett/Edwards, 1966), pp. 134–136.

160. For an interesting exploration of the religious metaphors in Matthew's gospel from two contemporary social-science perspectives (synectics and psychosynthesis), see Daniel O'Connor and Jacques Jiminez, *The Images of Jesus* (Minneapolis, Minn.: Winston, 1977).

161. For a fuller development of this point, see James Michael Lee, "Religious Education and the Bible: A Religious Educationists's View," in Joseph S. Marino, editor, *Biblical Themes in Religious Education* (Birmingham, Ala.: Religious Education Press, 1983), pp. 1–61.

162. See, for example, Herwi Rikhof, *The Concept of Church: A Methodological Inquiry into the Use of Metaphors in Ecclesiology* (London: Sheed and Ward, 1981).

163. See Sallie McFague, *Metaphorical Theology* (Philadelphia: Fortress, 1982).

164. Robert A. Nisbet, *Social Change and History,* p. 5.

165. Thomas G. Sticht, "Educational Uses of Metaphor," in Andrew Ortony, editor, *Metaphor and Thought* (Cambridge, England: Cambridge University Press, 1979), pp. 474–485.

166. Philip Wheelwright, *Metaphor and Reality,* p. 71.

167. On this point, see Colin Cherry, *On Human Communication,* 2d ed.(Cambridge, Mass.: M.I.T. Press, 1966), p. 74. The dedication in the first edition of this work is "*To my dog, Pym*"; the dedication in the second edition reads: "*To all those human beings who have enquired so kindly after my dog Pym.*"

168. Stephen J. Brown, *The World of Imagery* (London: Kegan Paul, Trench, Trubner, 1927), p. 33.

169. Anatol Rapoport, *Operational Philosophy* (New York: Harper, 1954), p. 206.

170. See Dwight Bolinger, *Aspects of Language* (New York: Harcourt, Brace and World, 1968), p. 112.

171. Maurice Monette has written a nice little introductory-type article on the sometimes hyperbolic use of the word "need" in education in general and in adult education particularly. Maurice L. Monette, "The Language of Need in Adult Religious Education," in *Living Light XV* (Summer, 1978), pp. 167–179.

172. About the only element which seems to be missing from such religious instruction slogans is music. Indeed, some religious instruction slogans would make ideal jingles. The slogans rife in religious instruction can be compared to those used in advertisements by the business world. In the latter connection, see Valerie Noble, *The Effective Echo: A Dictionary of Advertising Slogans* (New York: Special Libraries Association, 1970).

173. Preaching, quite obviously, is a mode of religious instruction. It is equally apparent that religious instruction is not a form of preaching, as Domenico Grasso erroneously contends it is. See Domenico Grasso, *Proclaiming God's Message* (Notre Dame, Ind.: University of Notre Dame Press, 1965), pp. 222–246.

174. B. Paul Komisar and James E. McClellan, "The Logic of Slogans," in B. Othanel Smith and Robert R. Ennis, editors, *Language and Concepts in Education*, pp. 195–215. In my treatment of slogan, I am relying heavily on this source, as well as on an engaging book written by William Bedford Williamson, one of Komisar's students. See William Bedford Williamson, *Language and Concepts in Christian Education* (Philadelphia: Westminster, 1970).

175. Gabriel Moran and his disciples, as well as Dwayne Huebner and his disciples, have done much to unmask some of the empty slogans which have dominated religious instruction for so long. The tacks which Moran and Huebner have taken are more philosophical and political than linguistic.

176. Sometimes a slogan synthesizes other slogans. These sub-slogans, in turn, can be reduced to more specific assertions.

177. Lois E. LeBar, *Education that is Christian* (Old Tappan, N.J.: Revell, 1958), p. 20. Caught up in the emotion of her slogan, LeBar claims that a Christ-as-the-center curriculum will do wondrous things: "And lo, what an amazing thing we have now! A curriculum that is centered not in sinful human life, but in divine Life Himself, eternal life, fullness of life, the Living Word revealed by the written Word!" *Ibid.*

178. Some scholars like Thomas Sebeok claim that only the first two of these characteristics are necessary for a sign, while other specialists like Henri Grenier assert that all three are necessary. I lean toward Grenier's position because it takes into account the psychological processes involved in bringing a stimulus to significational status. See Thomas A. Sebeok, "Six Species of Signs: Some Propositions and Strictures," in *Semiotica* XIII (Fall, 1975), pp. 237–252; also Henri Grenier, *Thomistic Philosophy:* volume I, *Logic* (Charlottetown, Canada: St. Dunstan's University Press, 1950), p. 31.

179. Sebeok classifies a syndrome as a rule-governed configuration of symptom signs having a stable designatum.

180. Thomas A. Sebeok, "Six Species of Signs: Some Propositions and Strictures," pp. 237–252.

181. David Burrell claims that Thomas Aquinas insists that the names we give to God actually signify him. But Burrell also allows that this is a position made intriguing by the following problem: "How can we signify something distinctly of God

when there is no residual meaning connecting the world and its principle—no rapport, no proportion, no common givens?'' In other words, can our naming of God have any genuine sign-ificance for the nameless essence of God? I should add that Burrell's seeming lack of recognition of the sign character of symbol does not detract from the skill with which he treats this problematic. David B. Burrell, "Aquinas on Naming God," pp. 206–210.

182. M. A. K. Halliday, *Language as a Social Semiotic* (Baltimore, Md.: University Press, 1978), pp. 8–35, 108–126.

183. F. Allan Hanson and Louise Hanson, "The Cybernetics of Cultural Communication", in Robert T. De George, editor, *Semiotic Themes* (Lawrence, Kan.: University of Kansas Publications, 1981), pp. 251–273.

184. Jared Wicks observes that "sacraments serve as signs of the single mystery of God's saving love." Jared Wicks, "The Sacraments: A Catechism for Today," in Michael J. Taylor, editor, *The Sacraments* (Staten Island, N.Y.: Alba, 1981), p. 25.

185. J. R. Quinn, "Sacraments, Theology of," in *New Catholic Encyclopedia*, volume XI, p. 807.

186. I suppose a transcendist would write "on the world" rather than "in" it and "through" it. For a discussion of immanence and transcendence in religious education, see Ian Knox, *Above or Within?: The Supernatural in Religious Education* (Birmingham, Ala.: Religious Education Press, 1976).

187. See Karl Rahner, *The Church and the Sacraments,* translated by W. J. O'Hara. (New York: Herder and Herder, 1963), pp. 11–19; Raymond Vaillancourt, *Toward a Renewal of Sacramental Theology,* translated by Matthew J. O'Connell (Collegeville, Minn.: Liturgical Press, 1979), pp. 68–69.

188. One of the most important, and indeed one of the most controverted issues in sacramental theology is how sacramental signs actually do function. Put differently, how does causality work in that kind of sign we call a sacrament? The core of the official Catholic teaching on sacraments is that a sacrament is a *signum efficax gratiae,* a sign which actually bestows the grace it signifies. Thus, for example, the sacrament of baptism, a sign of initiation into faith, actually confers santification upon its recipients. The major theoretical difficulty in the proposition that a sacrament bestows that which it signifies lies in the issue of whether a sign simply points to another reality or whether, in some cases, it is possible for a sign to contain the very reality to which it points. Can a sacramental sign really exert causality, or is it solely a pointer or a representation? The prevailing theory attempting to explain sacramental causality is called "*res et sacramentum*," namely "reality and sign."

189. The most important documents of this conference can be found in *Lumen Vitae* XI (October–December, 1956), pp. 564–654.

190. "Basic Principles of Modern Catechesis," in Johannes Hofinger, editor, *Teaching All Nations,* revised and partly translated by Clifford Howell (Freiburg, Deutschland: Herder, 1961), pp. 398–399.

191. See, for example, Mark J. Link, editor, *Faith and Commitment* (Chicago: Loyola University Press, 1964), pp. 1–97.

192. Ultimately, this point of contact may be fruitfully understood from either the immanentist or the transcendist views of revelation. For an admirable treatment of these two contrasting views, see Ian P. Knox, *Above or Within?: The Supernatural in Religious Education.*

193. For a discussion of this point in a somewhat different though related context, see

Karl Barth, *Dogmatics in Outline* (New York: Harper & Row, 1959), p. 62.

194. See Marcel Cohen, *Synchronie?*, *Beiträge zur Sprachwissenschaft, Volkskunde und Literaturforschung* (Berlin: Akademie, 1965), p. 75.

195. See John L. Elias, "A Cultural Approach to Religious Moral Education," in *Living Light* XVII (Fall, 1980), pp. 238–240.

196. It is important to bear in mind this distinction of symbol as used in linguistics on the one hand and in depth psychology on the other. Not a few theologians, religious educationists, and religious educators indiscriminately lump together these two distinct kinds of symbol, with the result that the proper understanding and use of symbol are blunted. William Alston faults Paul Tillich on this point, asserting that the "failure to draw the proper sort of distinctions between symbols and symbolic language leads Tillich into various confusions." William P. Alston, "Tillich's Conception of a Religious Symbol," in Sidney Hook, editor, *Religious Experience and Truth* (New York: New York University Press, 1961), p. 16. For an example of uncritically combining the varieties of symbol in religious education, see John Dale Foerster, "Symbolism and Its Use in Religious Education," unpublished doctoral dissertation, School of Theology at Claremont, 1967, pp. 127–128.

197. These characteristics are not ironclad, nor do they hold true in every case. They are more indicative than determinative.

198. Hugh R. Walpole, *Semantics*, pp. 79–80.

199. Jörg Splett, "Symbol," in Karl Rahner et al., editors, *Sacramentum Mundi: An Encyclopedia of Theology*, volume VI (New York: Herder and Herder, 1970), p. 199.

200. On this last point, see H. Gordon Hullfish and Philip G. Smith, *Reflective Thinking: The Method of Education* (New York: Dodd, Mead, 1964), pp. 139–140.

201. See Th. P. van Baaren, "Religious Symbols: Their Essence and Their Function," p. 24.

202. J. M. Somerville, "Symbol," in *New Catholic Encyclopedia*, volume XIII, p. 860.

203. John Dale Foerster, "Symbolism and Its Use in Religious Education," p. 82.

204. Cyrille Vogel calls a symbol an attempt to give tangible form to that which is intangible. Cyrille Vogel, "Symbols in Christian Worship: Food and Drink," in Luis Maldonado and David Power, editors, *Symbol and Art in Worship* (New York: Seabury, 1980), p. 67.

205. Abner Cohen, "Symbolic Action and the Structure of the Self," in Ioan Lewis, editor, *Symbols and Sentiments* (New York: Academic Press, 1977), pp. 117–128.

206. *Ibid.*, p. 128.

207. Stephen Ullmann, *The Principles of Semantics*, 2d ed., p. 31.

208. Alfred North Whitehead, *Symbolism.* (New York: Capricorn, 1927), p. 2.

209. Neil Postman and Charles Weingartner, *Teaching as a Subversive Activity* (New York, Delacorte: 1969), p. 121.

210. Archibald A. Hill, *An Introduction to Linguistic Structures*, p. 9.

211. See Leopold Caligor and Rollo May, *Dreams and Symbols: Man's Unconscious Language* (New York: Basic, 1968), pp. 9–10. Unfortunately, the otherwise fine treatment by Caligor and May is seriously marred by a lack of awareness of the scholarly work done on sign and symbol in fields other than psychotherapy. The lack of awareness of, or even the blocking out of, data and theory supplied

by nonpsychotherapeutic fields seems to be an all too prevalent state of affairs in the psychotherapeutic community.

212. "Imagery is relatively better than the verbal system for representing and coping with the concrete aspects of a situation, with transformations, and with parallel processing in the spatial sense. The verbal system is superior in abstract and sequential processing tasks." Allan Paivio, *Imagery and Verbal Processes* (New York: Holt, Rinehart, and Winston, 1971), p. 30.

213. Michael Lawler makes and important pedagogical linkage between the findings of cognitive developmental psychology and the capacity of a person to meaningfully deal with symbols. Michael G. Lawler, "Symbol and Religious Education," in *Religious Education* LXXII (July–August, 1977), pp. 366–372.

214. Paul Tillich's conceptualization of symbol as discursive or representative is also useful for religious educators. Paul Tillich, "The Meaning and Justification of Religious Symbols," pp. 3–6.

215. Arnold Whittick, *Symbols,* 2d ed. (Newton, Mass.: Branford, 1971), p. 5.

216. Herbert Musurillo, *Symbol and Myth in Ancient Poetry* (New York: Fordham University Press, 1961), p. 3.

217. Thomas Carlyle, *Sartor Resartus* (London: Bell, 1898), p. 254.

218. Bernard Kaplan, "Symbolism: From the Body to the Soul," in Nancy R. Smith and Margery B. Franklin, editors, *Symbolic Functioning in Childhood* (Hillsdale, N.J.: Erlbaum, 1979), pp. 219–228.

219. Thus Didier-Jacques Piveteau and James Dillon are most likely correct when they place the development of symbolic functioning as a major developmental task of adult faith. Didier-Jacques Piveteau and J. T. Dillon, *Resurgence of Religious Instruction* (Birmingham, Ala.: Religious Education Press, 1977), pp. 202–203.

220. Some critics, such as the Freudians, regard religion itself as one grand regressive symbol encapsulating personal and cultural wish-fulfillment. See Hans-Günter Heimbrock, *Phantasie und christlicher Glaube* (München: Kaiser, 1977), pp. 46–57.

221. A ritual in general, and the liturgical rite in particular, is a lived integration of various symbols and a symbolic living out of various major religious themes. Werner Jetter, *Symbol und Ritual* (Göttingen, Bundesrepublik Deutschland: Vandenhoeck und Ruprecht, 1978), pp. 115–121.

222. Of interest here is that Bernard Lonergan links symbol to value and feeling. Bernard J. F. Lonergan, *Method in Theology* (New York: Herder and Herder, 1972), pp. 64–69.

223. In this connection Michael Fuchs writes: "The educator can not hope to share the power of the symbol if the symbol is presented as something magical." Michael Fuchs, "The Church and the Task of Inhabiting the Symbol," in *Religious Education* LXXVI (March–April, 1981), p. 169.

224. Thomas Carlyle, *Sartor Resartus,* p. 254.

225. Gay Clifford writes that the use of symbols is fundamental to allegory. Gay Clifford, *The Transformations of Allegory* (London: Routledge and Kegan Paul, 1974), p. 11.

226. Angus Fletcher, *Allegory* (Ithaca, N.Y.: Cornell University Press, 1964), p. 2.

227. Walter Russell Bowie, "The Teaching of Jesus: The Parables," in George Arthur Buttrick et al., editors, *The Interpreter's Bible,* volume VII (Nashville, Tenn.: Abingdon-Cokesbury, 1951), p. 167.

228. See John MacQueen, *Allegory* (London: Methuen, 1970), pp. 62–65.

229. Paul Piehler, *The Visionary Landscape: A Study in Medieval Allegory* (Montreal: McGill—Queen's University Press, 1971).

230. Maureen Quilligan holds that "a sensitivity to the polysemy of words is the basic component of the genre of allegory." Maureen Quilligan, *The Language of Allegory* (Ithaca, N.Y.: Cornell University Press, 1979), p. 33.

231. See Northrop Frye, "Allegory," in Alex Preminger, editor, *Encyclopedia of Poetry and Poetics* (Princeton, N.J.: Princeton University Press, 1965), p. 12.

232. For a fine discussion of the structure of allegory in the bible, see Hans-Josef Klauck, *Allegorie und Allegorese in synoptischen Gleichnistexten* (Münster, Bundesrepublik Deutschland: Aschendorff, 1978).

233. One study concludes that this is Edmund Spenser's underlying belief in the composition of the fifth book of *The Faerie Queene*. See John A. Lopach, "Educative Allegory: Poet and Reader in *The Faerie Queene,V,*" unpublished doctoral dissertation, University of Notre Dame, 1969.

234. James I. Wimsatt, *Allegory and Mirror* (New York: Pegasus, 1970), p. 27.

235. Edwin Honig, *Dark Conceit: The Making of Allegory* (Evanston, Ill.: Northwestern University Press, 1959), p. 100.

236. Thomas Aquinas, *Summa Theologica*, I, q. 1, a. 10. It would appear that this fourfold distinction was first made by John Cassian in the fifth century.

237. For reasons of space, I am unable to treat at sufficient length the role of myth in modern depth psychology (e.g., Sigmund Freud and especially Carl Jung) or myth in modern biblical theology (e.g., Rudolf Bultmann).

238. Richard Chase, *Quest for Myth* (Baton Rouge, La.: Louisiana State University Press, 1949), p. 73.

239. Philip Wheelwright, "Myth," in Alex Preminger, editor, *Encyclopedia of Poetry and Poetics*, p. 538. Wheelwright claims that this definition is so framed as to embrace both the Kant-Cassirer view of myth and the opposite extreme which regards myth as mere story—and usually a fictitious one at that.

240. John S. Dunne, *The City of the Gods* (New York: Macmillan, 1965), p. 1.

241. Millar Burrows, *An Outline of Biblical Theology* (Philadelphia: Westminster, 1946), p. 115. Burrows notes that this is a view of myth increasingly shared by many theologians.

242. Albert Cook observes that metaphor and parable are verbal symbols ideally conducive to myth. As Cook also notes, Jesus' parables were something entirely new in rabbinic literature. Albert Cook, *Myth and Language* (Bloomington, Ind.: Indiana University Press, 1980), pp. 234–259, 305.

243. Victor Larock, *La Pensée Mythique* (Bruxelles: Lebégue, 1945), p. 6. "Relative" here is meant to be the contrary of "absolute."

244. Albert B. Lord, "The Mythic Component in Oral Traditional Epic: Its Origins and Significance," in Wendell M. Aycock and Theodore M. Klein, editors, *Classical Mythology in Twentieth-Century Thought and Literature* (Lubbock, Tex.: Texas Tech Press, 1980), pp. 146–147.

245. Walter Brenneman argues that myth is a fundamental aspect of the personal existential *conjunctio* which an individual makes among himself, other persons, the universe, and the divine. Walter L. Brenneman Jr., *Spirals: A Study in Symbol, Myth and Ritual* (Washington, D.C.: University Press of America, 1979), pp. 107–120.

246. G. van der Leeuw, *Religion in Essence and Manifestation*, translated by J. E. Turner (London: Allen and Unwin, 1938), p. 413.

247. Thomas J. J. Altizer, *Truth, Myth and Symbol* (Englewood Cliffs, N.J.: Prentice-Hall, 1962), p. 150.
248. Mircea Eliade, *Myth and Reality*, translated by Willard Trask (New York: Harper & Row, 1963), p. 11.
249. Mauricio H. Usher, "Towards an Understanding of Myth," in *Religious Education* LXXVI (September–October, 1981), pp. 553–561.
250. Victor W. Turner, "Myth and Symbol," in David L. Sills, editor, *International Encyclopedia of the Social Sciences,* volume X, p. 576.
251. For a lovely expansion of this point, see William James O'Brien, *Stories to the Dark: Explorations in Religious Imagination* (New York: Paulist, 1977).
252. Shirley Park Lowry, *Familiar Mysteries: The Truth in Myth* (New York: Oxford University Press, 1982), pp. 11–12. By understanding myth, one can learn to accept these mysteries.
253. Mircea Eliade, *Myth and Reality,* p. 139, italics deleted.
254. C. M. Bowra, *The Greek Experience* (London: Weidenfeld and Nicolson, 1957), p. 10.
255. Mircea Eliade, *Myth and Reality,* p. 8.
256. See Ann Brennan, "Myth is Personal Spirituality," in *Religious Education* LXXV (July–August, 1980), pp. 441–451. Some of Brennan's religious instruction prescriptions, unfortunately, lack rigorous empirical support as to their worth.
257. In the view of Janet Dolgin and JoAnn Magdoff, myth functions as a rhetorical mode articulated as part of a people's reification of itself—and, I might add, of a people's deepest self. Janet L. Dolgin and JoAnn Magdoff, "The Invisible Event," in Janet L. Dolgin, David S. Kemnitzer, and David M. Schneider, editors, *Symbolic Anthropology* (New York: Columbia University Press, 1977), pp. 351–363.
258. Ian Barbour, *Myths, Models and Paradigms* (New York: Harper & Row, 1974), p. 23.
259. See Bronislaw Malinowski, *Magic, Science and Religion and Other Essays* (Boston: Beacon, 1948), pp. 74–79.
260. Claude Lévi-Strauss, "The Structural Study of Myth," in Thomas A. Sebeok, editor, *Myth: A Symposium* (Philadelphia: American Folklore Society, 1955), p. 66.
261. Gwen Kennedy Neville and John H. Westerhoff III, *Learning Through Liturgy* (New York: Seabury, 1978), pp. 129–135.
262. K. K. Ruthven, *Myth* (London: Methuen, 1976), pp. 35–38.
263. See Gabriel Moran, *The Present Revelation,* p. 199.
264. The Stewards contend that a person's own name and the process of being named by a family or group insert that individual into a personal myth. David S. Steward and Margaret S. Steward, "Naming into Personhood: The Church's Educational Ministry," in Iris V. Cully and Kendig Brubaker Cully, editors, *Process and Relationship* (Birmingham, Ala.: Religious Education Press, 1978), pp. 49–56.
265. Gabriel Moran, *The Present Revelation,* p. 199.
266. On the implications of this sentence, see Guilford Dudley III, *The Recovery of Christian Myth* (Philadelphia: Westminster, 1967), p. 15.
267. For an especially fine book which views transcendence and mysticism as the goals of all education, and especially of religious instruction, see David Arthur

Bickimer, *Christ the Placenta* (Birmingham, Ala.: Religious Education Press, 1983).

268. Karl Rahner and Herbert Vorgrimler, *Theological Dictionary,* edited by Cornelius Ernst, translated by Richard Strachan (New York: Herder and Herder, 1965), p. 204.

269. René Marlé, *Introduction to Hermeneutics,* translated by E. Fromment and R. Albrecht (New York: Herder and Herder, 1967), p. 12.

270. Henry S. Nash, "Exegesis and Hermeneutics," in Samuel Macauley Jackson, editor, *The New Schaff-Herzog Encyclopedia of Religious Knowledge,* volume IV (Grand Rapids, Mich.: Baker, 1963), p. 237.

271. James M. Robinson, "Hermeneutic Since Barth," in James M. Robinson and John B. Cobb Jr., editors, *The New Hermeneutic* (New York: Harper & Row, 1964), p. 3.

272. James D. Smart, *The Strange Silence of the Bible in the Church: A Study in Hermeneutics* (Philadelphia: Westminister, 1970), pp. 52–56.

273. See A. Berkeley Michelsen, *Interpreting the Bible* (Grand Rapids, Mich.: Eerdmans, 1963), p. 5. It should be noted that I write "to find out the meaning of the inspired author's text," and not "to find out what the inspired author meant." There is a body of biblicists which asserts that inspiration extends to the full meaning of the text, a meaning which conceivably might be above and beyond what the scriptural writer consciously meant or realized at the time he dictated or wrote the words.

274. Religious educators often teach parables. For a succinct illuminative treatment of the hermeneutics of parable, see Pheme Perkins, "Interpreting Parables: The Bible and the Humanities," in Gloria Durka and Joanmarie Smith, editors, *Emerging Issues in Religious Education* (New York: Paulist, 1976), pp. 149–172.

275. On this point, see E. D. Hirsch Jr., *Validity in Interpretation* (New Haven, Conn.: Yale University Press, 1967), pp. ix–x.

276. This distinction between hermeneutics and exegesis appears to be a modern one. James Robinson notes that in Greek, "one meaning of *hermēnia* is synonymous with *exēgēsis,* a synonymity carried over into their Latin translations, *interpretatio* and *expositio* respectively." James M. Robinson, "Hermeneutic Since Barth," in James M. Robinson and John B. Cobb Jr., editors, *The New Hermeneutic* (New York: Harper & Row, 1964), p. 5. Italics added.

277. Raymond E. Brown, "Hermeneutics," in Raymond E. Brown, Joseph A. Fitzmyer, and Roland E. Murphy, editors, *The Jerome Biblical Commentary* (Englewood Cliffs, N.J.: Prentice-Hall, 1968), p. 606. Daniel Patte claims that exegesis is concerned with establishing the actual meaning of the text itself while hermeneutic involves the construction of a reader's relationship with the text. Daniel Patte, "Preface to the American Edition," in Entrevernes Group, *Signs and Parables,* translated by Gary Phillips (Pittsburgh, Pa.: Pickwick, 1978), pp. xvi–xvii.

278. Karl Rahner and Herbert Vorgrimler are guilty of theological imperialism when they erroneously assert that exegesis is a theological discipline. Exegesis is, of course, a branch of linguistics. The biblicist who uses exegesis does so primarily on the basis of the linguistics canons of exegesis. See Karl Rahner and Herbert Vorgrimler, *Theological Dictionary,* p. 159.

279. See John T. Wilkinson, *Principles of Biblical Interpretation* (London: Epworth, 1960), pp. 9–10.

280. R. C. Fuller, "The Interpretation of Holy Scripture," in Bernard Orchard et al., editors, *A Catholic Commentary on Holy Scripture* (London: Nelson, 1953), pp. 58–60.

281. On this point, see James Michael Lee, "Religious Education and the Bible: A Religious Educationist's View," pp. 11–19.

282. Alla Bozarth-Campbell proposes that the art of interpretation is a threefold progressive process of creation, incarnation, and transformation, that is, "a process involving the *creation* of a new being by bringing two separate beings together in an *incarnation* and that this process leads to an event which constitutes a *transformation* of all who participate in it, including, to an extent, the literary work itself." Alla Bozarth-Campbell, *The Word's Body* (University, Ala.: University of Alabama Press, 1979), p. 13.

283. The use of the English singular "hermeneutic" doubtless reflects the fact that hermeneutic was primarily developed and elaborated on by German scholars, in whose language *"Hermeneutik"* is singular.

284. For a fine, scholarly book which integrates both hermeneutics and hermeneutic, see Mary C. Boys, *Biblical Interpretation in Religious Education* (Birmingham, Ala.: Religious Education Press, 1980).

285. This summary, and that which follows throughout the remainder of this section, is far too brief to do justice to the complexities of, the nuances in, and the divergencies among various approaches to hermeneutic, or to the disagreement which exists among the different proponents of hermeneutic.

286. One thorny issue which arises from hermeneutic is whether the basis of interpretation has moved from the past to the present and from the objective text to the subjective interpreter. Anthony C. Thiselton, *The Two Horizons* (Grand Rapids, Mich.: Eerdmans, 1980), pp. 17–23. Hans-Georg Gadamer in his important book *Wahrheit und Methode* attempts to confront this issue squarely by arguing that hermeneutic is *Horizontverschmelzung,* namely a fusion of horizons.

287. One inference from this statement is that a student or a proponent of hermeneutic must also be well-versed in psychology and even in physiological psychology. See Walter L. Brenneman Jr., Stanley O. Yarian, and Alan M. Olson, *The Seeing Eye: Hermeneutical Phenomenology in the Study of Religion* (University Park, Pa.: The Pennsylvania State University Press, 1982), pp. 72–85.

288. In one view of hermeneutic, the message of the bible is not the words of the bible but the word-event in and of and through the bible. Language-event, not language, is the reality. See Edgar V. McKnight, *Meaning in Texts* (Philadelphia: Fortress, 1978), pp. 72–84.

289. Gerhard Maier puts it this way: *"Schriftauslegung fordert vom Ausleger eine Kongenialität (Geisteswanderschaft) mit den Texten. Der Ausleger muss sich dessen bewusst sein, dass er von der Schrift in ein Gespräch hineingenommen wird, das auf seinen Glauben hinzielt."* Gerhard Maier, *Wie legen wir die Schrift aus?* (Giessen, Bundesrepublik Deutschland: Brunnen, 1978), p. 34.

290. A. Berkeley Michelsen, *Interpreting the Bible,* p. 173.

291. Fr. D. E. Schleiermacher, *Hermeneutik* (Heidelberg, Bundesrepublik Deutschland: Universitätsverlag, 1959).

292. See Carl E. Braaten, "How New is the New Hermeneutic?" in *Theology Today* XXII (July, 1965), p. 221.

293. Wilhelm Dilthey, *Der Aufbau der geschichtlichen Welt in den Geisteswissenschaften*, Band VII in *Gesammelte Schriften* (Leipzig, Deutschland: Teubner, 1942), pp. 205–207.

294. See Richard E. Palmer, *Hermeneutics* (Evanston, Ill.: Northwestern University Press, 1969), pp. 106–115.

295. Karl Lehmann, "Hermeneutics," in Karl Rahner et al., editors, *Sacramentum Mundi*, volume III, p. 24.

296. Carl Braaten, "How New Is the New Hermeneutic?" p. 222.

297. In Heidegger's view, understanding is not reason. Rather, understanding is the work of life and so in a sense is life itself. *Dasein ist sein Erschlossenheit.* See Zygmunt Bauman, *Hermeneutics and Social Science* (New York: Columbia University Press, 1978), pp. 148–171.

298. Martin Heidegger, *Being and Time*, translated by John Macquarrie and Edward Robinson (New York: Harper & Row, 1962), p. 62.

299. "When Heidegger says: 'Understanding of Being is itself a definite characteristic of Dasein's Being,' he means that one of the determining ways that Dasein can be said to be is to understand what it means to be." Michael Gelver, *A Commentary on Heidegger's Being and Time* (New York: Harper & Row, 1970), p. 27.

300. Berard L. Marthaler, "The New Hermeneutic, Language and Religious Education," in *American Ecclesiastical Review*, p. 75.

301. Carl E. Braaten, "How New Is the New Hermeneutic?" p. 226.

302. Berard L. Marthaler, "The New Hermeneutic, Language and Religious Education," p. 77.

303. D. Ernst Fuchs, *Hermeneutik* (Bad Cannstadt, Bundesrepublic Deutschland: Müllerschön, 1963), pp. 103–111.

304. D. Ernst Fuchs, *Zum hermeneutischen Problem in der Theologie: die existentiale Interpretation* (Tübingen, Bundesrepublik Deutschland: Mohr, 1959), pp. 126–131. "*Auch der Grund, in welchem die Sprache wurzelt, ist nicht etwa Gott . . . Der Grund, in welchem die Sprache wurzelt, ist—das Sein*" (p. 127).

305. D. Gerhard Ebeling, *Wort und Glaube*, Band I (Tübingen, Bundesrepublik Deutschland: Mohr, 1960), pp. 90–160.

306. It is from this perspective that I like to interpret Ebeling's statement that "the linguistic utterance normally mediates understanding itself and does not have to be made understandable. It is only when the normal function of word is disturbed that interpretation is required. The aim of such interpretation cannot, however, be anything other than the removal of the obstacle which prevents the word from mediating itself." Gerhard Ebeling, *God and Word*, translated by James W. Leitch (Philadelphia: Fortress, 1967), pp. 40–41.

307. Gerhard Ebeling, *Theology and Proclamation*, translated by John Riches (Philadelphia: Fortress, 1966), p. 20.

308. I resonate with this emphasis of Ebeling's, though I would not identify the work of the church as essentially verbal or proclamatory. Theology is at the service of religious instruction in the religious instruction task—this is a basic thesis of my trilogy in religious instruction.

309. See, for example, Richard E. Palmer, *Hermeneutics*, p. 163. Palmer, in fact, dedicated his book to Gadamer.

310. *Ibid.*
311. Hans-Georg Gadamer, *Wahrheit und Methode* (Tübingen, Bundesrepublik Deutschland: Mohr, 1960), pp. 229–240.
312. Hans-Georg Gadamer, *Philosophical Hermeneutics,* translated and edited by David E. Linge. (Berkeley, Calif.: University of California Press, 1976), pp. 3–17, 69–81.
313. *Ibid.,* p. 394.
314. James M. Robinson, "Hermeneutic Since Barth," p. 75.
315. Wolfhart Pannenberg, "Hermeneutics and Universal History," translated by Paul J. Achtemeier, in Robert W. Funk, editor, *History and Hermeneutic* (New York: Harper & Row, 1967), pp. 122–152.
316. See E. Frank Tupper, *The Theology of Wolfhart Pannenberg* (Philadelphia: Westminster, 1973), pp. 119–121.
317. That Habermas' context and goal is social-scientific is clearly etched by Josef Bleicher. As Bleicher notes, Habermas's critical hermeneutic is a dialectical social science which "attempts to mediate the objectivity of historical processes with the motives of those acting within it" in order that emancipatory potential might be liberated. The essential social-science context and thrust of Habermas seems to have been conveniently (or politically?) overlooked by Thomas Groome and Kieran Scott. Josef Bleicher, *Contemporary Hermeneutics* (London: Routledge and Kegan Paul, 1980), pp. 152–164. Quotation on p. 152.
318. Jürgen Habermas, *Knowledge and Human Interests,* translated by Jeremy J. Shapiro (Boston: Beacon, 1971).
319. The hermeneutic of Gadamer and Habermas has been injected with some modification into the bloodstream of religious instruction by Thomas H. Groome, in *Christian Religious Education.* The basis of Groome's position is verbal, cognitive, interpretive, and dialectical.
320. Carl E. Braaten, "How New is the New Hermeneutic?" p. 227. While Braaten addresses himself specifically to Fuchs and Ebeling in this context, his critique can be legitimately extended, I believe, to most proponents of hermeneutic.
321. Emilio Betti, *Die Hermeneutik als allgemeine Methodik der Geisteswissenschaften* (Tübingen, Bundesrepublik Deutschland: Mohr, 1962), pp. 28–29.
322. E. D. Hirsch Jr., *Validity in Interpretation,* pp. 213–214.
323. Karl Lehmann, "Hermeneutics," in Karl Rahner et al., *Sacramentum Mundi,* volume III, p. 26.
324. Carl E. Braaten, "How New is the New Hermeneutic?" pp. 229–230, 233.
325. Thomas H. Groome, *Christian Religious Education,* pp. 184–232.
326. As a verbal exclusivist by and large, Berard Marthaler naturally favors hermeneutic. While I applaud Marthaler's interest in hermeneutic, still I take serious objection to his conclusion that hermeneutic bids the educator to focus on substantive content rather than on the learner. The thrust of hermeneutic is a mutual interplay between subject and object. Berard L. Marthaler, "The New Hermeneutic, Language and Religious Education," pp. 73–83.
327. This figure is the conclusion of a wide variety of empirical studies. Two representative research investigations on this issue are Ned A. Flanders, *Interaction Analysis in the Classroom: A Manual for Observers,* rev. ed. (Ann Arbor, Mich.: School of Education, University of Michigan, 1966); John I. Goodlad, "A Study of Schooling: Some Findings and Hypotheses," in *Phi Delta Kappan* LXIV (March, 1983), pp. 466–467.

328. *The Flow of Religious Instruction* is a book wholly directed toward advancing a viable theory of instruction explicitly for religious educators.
329. Ole R. Holsti, *Content Analysis for the Social Sciences and Humanities* (Reading, Mass.: Addison-Wesley, 1969); Klaus Krippendorff, *Content Analysis* (Beverly Hills, Calif.: Sage, 1980).
330. John Withall and W. W. Lewis, "Social Interaction in the Classroom," in N. L. Gage, editor, *Handbook of Research on Teaching* (Chicago: Rand McNally, 1963), p. 691.
331. On this point, see James Michael Lee and Nathaniel J. Pallone, *Guidance and Counseling in Schools: Foundations and Processes* (New York: McGraw-Hill, 1966), p. 262.
332. *Ibid.,* pp. 259–261.
333. Ross Snyder, "Religious Education as a Discipline: Toward Foundations of a Discipline of Religious Education," in *Religious Education* LXII (September–October, 1967), p. 404. For Snyder's lovely operationalizing of experience-centeredness in religious education, see Ross Snyder, *Contemporary Celebration* (Nashville, Tenn.: Abingdon, 1971).
334. On this last point, see Wayne R. Rood, *The Art of Teaching Christianity* (Nashville, Tenn.: Abingdon, 1968), p. 36.
335. Alfonso Nebreda, "The Role of Witness in Transmitting the Message," in Johannes Hofinger and Theodore C. Stone, editors, *Pastoral Catechetics,* p. 78. Unhappily, Nebreda uses this to advocate the witness "theory" of religious instruction, rather than to draw the logical conclusion from his text—the logical conclusion, of course, being that it was the entire lifestyle situation in which Christ placed the apostles, and not just the witnessing aspect of this lifestyle, which effectively taught the apostles.
336. John H. Westerhoff III, *Values for Tommorrow's Children* (Philadelphia: Pilgrim, 1970), pp. 27–28.
337. Gabriel Moran, *Catechesis of Revelation,* p. 145; Gabriel Moran, *Interplay* (Winona, Minn.: St. Mary's Press, 1981), pp. 53–64.
338. On this point, see F. H. Drinkwater, "The Use of Words: A Problem of Both Content and Method," in Gerard S. Sloyan, editor, *Shaping the Christian Message* (New York: Macmillan, 1958), pp. 266–277.
339. Hubert Halbfas, *Theory of Catechetics,* pp. 111, 198.
340. Helmut Thielicke, "The Restatement of New Testament Mythology," in Hans Werner Bartsch, editor, *Kerygma and Myth,* translated by Reginald H. Fuller (New York: Harper & Row, 1961), pp. 158–159.
341. Richard Chase, *Quest for Myth,* p. 73.
342. See Philip Wheelwright, *The Burning Fountain,* pp. 149–150; also Tjeu van den Berk, "Language in the Dutch Catechism," pp. 84–85.
343. See, for example, E. E. Kellet, *The Story of Myths* (New York: Harcourt, Brace, 1927), pp. 23–47.
344. C. G. Jung and C. [*sic*] Kerény, *Essays on a Science of Mythology,* translated by R. F. C. Hull (New York: Pantheon, 1949), pp. 101–103.
345. Robert Creegan declares that the most widely rejected of all Jung's tenets is that of the collective unconscious. Geoffrey Kirk states that analyses of various cultural sets of myth clearly show that the construct of the collective unconscious is fallacious. Robert F. Creegan, "Carl G. Jung," in Philip Lawrence Harriman, editor, *Encyclopedia of Psychology* (New York: Philosophical Library, 1946), p. 316; G. S. Kirk, *Myth* (Cambridge, England: Cambridge University Press, 1970), pp. 275–276.

346. Ernst Cassirer, *An Essay on Man* (New Haven, Conn.: Yale University Press, 1944), p. 76.
347. David Bidney, "Myth, Symbolism, and Truth," in Thomas Sebeok, *Myth: A Symposium,* p. 14.
348. Elli Miranda, *Myth and Art as Teaching Materials* (Cambridge, Mass.: Educational Services, 1965), pp. 12–15.
349. See David Cairns, *Gospel Without Myth?* (London: SCM, 1960), p. 85.
350. See Victor Larock, *La Pensée Mythique,* p. 5.
351. For a good introduction to the personal journal and the various forms which a journal may take, see George F. Simons, *Keeping Your Personal Journal* (New York: Paulist, 1978); see also Morton T. Kelsey, *Adventure Inward: Christian Growth Through Personal Journal Writing* (Minneapolis, Minn.: Augsburg, 1980).
352. Consequently, a personal journal can well serve as a devotional aid to the journal-keeper. Daniel Aleshire, "Keeping a Religious Journal," in *Review and Expositor* LXXI (Summer, 1974), pp. 359–364.
353. Ron Gestwicki, "Autobiographical Journals," in *Perspectives in Religious Studies* III (Summer, 1976), pp. 203–216.
354. James Olney, *Metaphors of Self: The Meaning of Autobiography* (Princeton, N.J.: Princeton University Press, 1972), p. 17.
355. Plato, *Apology,* XXVIII A.
356. This statement tends to hold true even when one's personal journal is composed in a workshop setting.
357. George F. Simons, *Keeping Your Personal Journal,* pp. 19–20.
358. Milt Hughes, *Spiritual Journey Notebook* (Nashville, Tenn.: National Student Ministries, 1976).
359. Roberto Assagioli, *Psychosynthesis* (New York: Hobbs, Dorman, 1965).
360. Christina Baldwin, *One To One: Self-Understanding Through Journal Writing* (New York: Evans, 1977).
361. Ira Progoff, *At a Journal Workshop: The Basic Text and Guide for Using the Intensive Journal Process* (New York: Dialogue House, 1975).
362. Ira Progoff, *The Practice of Process Meditation: The Intensive Journal Way to Spiritual Experience* (New York: Dialogue House, 1980), pp. 18–19. Three major aspects of the personal, subjective process are, in the Progoff scheme of things, cycles, integrations, and emergents.
363. Progoff apparently does not smile with favor on persons whom he has not trained to conduct intensive journal teaching activities. While it may be true that Progoff-trained personnel are in a favored position to teach the fullness of the intensive journal technique, nonetheless it seems to me that a sufficient degree of the spirit and substance of this kind of journaling may be fruitfully taught by religious educators who have gone through a Progoff workshop and who practice the intensive journal technique in their own lives.

CHAPTER SEVEN

NONVERBAL CONTENT

"Oh, how one wishes sometimes to escape from the meaningless dullness of human eloquence, from those sublime phrases, to take refuge in nature, apparently so inarticulate, or in the wordlessness of long, grinding labor, or sound sleep, of true music, or of human understanding rendered speechless by emotion." [1]

—Boris Pasternack

THE NATURE OF NONVERBAL CONTENT

Nonverbal content refers to all those other-than-linguistic elements and units used during the course of the teaching-learning dynamic. Thus nonverbal content includes not only the sum total of the nonverbal activities used by the teacher and the learners, but all those other-than-linguistic aspects of the instructional materials used during the lesson together with all the other-than-linguistic features of the here-and-now pedagogical environment.

In order to come to a correct understanding and appreciation of nonverbal content, it is necessary to realize that *nonverbal content is an authentic substantive content in its own right and not simply a bearer of some other substantive content*. This fact suggests that if the religious educator wishes to use nonverbal content purposively and effectively, he ought not to treat it simply as a medium for some "deeper" message. The nonverbal activities occurring during the lesson are themselves the message—or at least the nonverbal part of it. Nonverbals, then, do not just carry revelation; they are in themselves revelatory.

Nonverbal content tends to enjoy more of a natural affinity for affective content and for lifestyle content than for cognitive content.

One explanation for this phenomenon is that affective content and lifestyle content to a great extent lie in the zone of the tangible and the concrete—a zone particularly congenial and natural for nonverbal behavior. When a person wishes to communicate a significant affective content, that person will tend to augment his nonverbal content while at the same time reducing the amount of his verbal behavior. Activities which are suffused with a high degree of affective content—painting, sculpting, dancing, music-making, loving—tend to employ primarily nonverbal content.

Over the centuries in Western civilization there has been a great deal of seminal and sophisticated research on human verbal communication. However, until the middle of the twentieth century, research of a comparable profusion and caliber in the area of human nonverbal communication has been scarce.[2] For centuries, Christian moral theologians and spiritual writers frequently relegated nonverbal behavior to the zone of untoward self-disclosure, temptations, and occasions of sin.

Despite the great importance of nonverbal behavior in the teaching-learning dynamic, empirical research and serious scholarly attention to this critical pedagogical substantive content is minimal. This unhappy situation is graphically illustrated by the fact that neither the *Handbook of Research on Teaching*[3] nor its successor the *Second Handbook on Teaching*[4] contains as much as a single index entry for nonverbal communication. The multivolume fifth edition of the *Encyclopedia of Educational Research*[5] has no article on nonverbal behavior in education. Textbooks on the teaching process typically make some perfunctory comments about nonverbal behavior in the instructional context, but this is about the extent of their treatment of this vital substantive content of teaching. The situation in the field of religious instruction is even more shocking. I have been able to locate only one article in a serious religious education journal which deals at length and expressly with nonverbal behavior in religious instruction.[6] Major religious educationists of such widely diverse views as Johannes Hofinger, Randolph Crump Miller, and Gabriel Moran, to name just a few, virtually never accord serious extended attention to nonverbal content in religious education.[7] To be sure, nonverbal behavior is a substantive content essentially at variance with a few foundational positions in religious education, especially with the views of Dwayne Huebner and his disciples, such as Thomas Groome, Kieran Scott, and Malcolm Warford. These persons argue forcefully that dialectical cognitive content of the verbal sort constitutes the fundamental axis and thrust of religion teaching.[8] Some religious educationists even go so far as to directly declare that the essence of religion teaching is verbal behavior.[9]

Despite the serious neglect and even disvaluation of nonverbal content in the teaching-learning dynamic, several important empirical investigations have been conducted on nonverbal behavior in teaching. Two notable examples of such research studies are those conducted by Charles Galloway, on the one hand, and by Barbara Grant and Dorothy Grant Hennings, on the other hand. Galloway developed and tested an observation schedule for ascertaining teacher nonverbal communication.[10] Grant and Hennings empirically examined nonverbal communication occurring in the pedagogical act by inserting their data into the Bellack four-functional framework of structure, solicit, respond, and react.[11]

Definition of Nonverbal Content

The very term "nonverbal content" is itself a poor one. A term should describe or denote in a positive way the reality to which it points. But the term "nonverbal content" in itself does not point in a positive way to the reality which it represents; the term points only to a reality which it does not represent. "Like the term 'nonhuman' which covers an infinity of life forms from protozoas to gorillas, 'nonverbal' denotes that which is *not* included in the concept 'verbal,' but it tells little about what *is* included."[12] Researchers and practitioners have long recognized the inadequacy of the term "nonverbal." In the first half of the twentieth century, some researchers gave the term "expressive behavior" to nonverbal activity. In the 1960s the term "body language" was frequently employed, especially by writers and speakers eager to turn the growing research on nonverbal behavior into cash profit for themselves. Nonetheless, the term "nonverbal" still remains as the only generally accepted one among theoreticians and researchers. So until a generically inclusive, positively oriented term is devised, "nonverbal" will continue to prevail.

Nonverbal content is a term referring to a human, humanly produced, or situational reality which typically communicates in a fashion or channel outside the verbal domain. This definition contains five essential elements. First, nonverbal content is a concrete reality. It thus differs substantially from verbal content which is a linguistic symbol. Second, nonverbal content can refer to directly human behavior such as a smile or a head nod; it can also refer to a humanly produced reality such as music. Third, nonverbal content can refer to concrete situations such as the particular arrangement of furniture or the proximity of people to each other. Fourth, nonverbal content typically conveys information to an individual. Fifth, nonverbal content lies outside the verbal domain. In this sense, all human communication can be grouped into two primary classes: verbal and nonverbal.

Relation of Nonverbal Content to Verbal Content

To better appreciate the nature of nonverbal content, it might be helpful to compare it with verbal content. Before doing this, however, I believe that it is important to emphasize that human communication usually—though by no means always—takes place in a complex, multidimensional, overlapping, and intersecting form in which both verbals and nonverbals are freely intermixed and conjoined. Verbal and nonverbal behaviors thus are infracommunicational modes that are frequently merged interdependently.[13] Thus, for example, a person venting his rage verbally is usually also communicating in a nonverbal mode both bodily (such as clenching his fists) and situationally (as by moving furniture so as to allow for the full expression of his rage). Religious worship services typically represent a purposeful form of communication in which verbal and nonverbal content are deliberatively intermixed and interdependently conjoined. While it is generally true that verbal content is used to embody cognitive content such as facts or theories, and nonverbal content is employed to express affects, nonetheless each can substitute for the other to a limited extent and under certain conditions.[14] Verbal behavior and nonverbal behavior exert influence on each other, doubtless because they are so frequently conjoined in complementarily embodying the same kind of content and because each is a potent form of communication in its own right.

When verbals and nonverbals are conjoined in any given communication episode, they can either be congruent or incongruent with each other. When they are congruent, the communication achieves clarity and potency. When there is an incongruency between verbal and nonverbal behavior, the communication becomes ambiguous and possibly loses force. When such an incongruency does exist, persons usually believe that the nonverbal content represents a more accurate and a more authentic communication of basic feeling and intent than the verbal content. Michael Argyle explains this generally recognized fact by asserting that most people realize that an individual's nonverbal behavior is much more difficult for a person to control than his verbal behavior. For example, a nervous young preacher may manage to smile and sound relaxed as he delivers his sermon, but he may also be perspiring visibly and shaking all over his body.[15]

Nonverbal behavior is more functionally related to affect, to the unconscious, and to lived-but-unreflected-upon forces than is verbal behavior. Indeed, the available psychological evidence suggests that nonverbal communication is more consonant with the real feelings and inmost thoughts of the person than is verbal communication. Any discrepancy between a person's verbal and nonverbal content has definite communicative significance. An individual who detects such discrepancies is able to obtain more accurate data and more reliable meaning on the real underlying human forces motivating the communicator.

The differences between nonverbal and verbal behavior can be divided into five basic types: (1) general; (2) semantic; (3) neurophysiological and developmental; (4) perception and evaluation and transmission; (5) spatiotemporal.[16]

General characteristics are those which refer to broad or generic properties. A nonverbal act is typically governed by principles and forces which largely flow from physical and biological wellsprings, as for example, the nonverbal behaviors communicating fright or panic. A verbal act, on the other hand, is governed by arbitrary, conventionally agreed-upon, humanly constructed principles. For example, grammatical and linguistic rules differ among various cultural groups. Furthermore, nonverbal acts are absolutely necessary for human existence; a person cannot continue life if that individual stops altogether in engaging in nonverbal behavior. Verbal acts, on the other hand, are not absolutely necessary in human existence; a person can continue life if that individual stops engaging in verbal behavior.[17]

Semantic characteristics of content are those which are concerned with reference and meaning. A nonverbal behavior has concrete existence in itself and thus can fill a practical as well as a symbolic function. A verbal behavior, on the other hand, exists not as a concrete reality but a sign or symbol reality. A nonverbal behavior is subject-oriented while a verbal act is predicate-oriented. A nonverbal behavior is affectively rooted and affectively charged, while a verbal behavior is primarily cognitively rooted and cognitively charged.[18]

Neurophysiological and developmental characteristics of a content refer to the degree to which a content is sunk into the physical structure and ongoing process of the human organism. A nonverbal behavior involves complex physiological networks and includes the effector organs. A verbal act, on the other hand, involves the central nervous system only. A nonverbal behavior frequently involves a great many concurrent physiological activities, while a verbal behavior usually involves only a few concurrent physiological activities.

Characteristics referring to perception, evaluation, and transmission are those which are concerned with the subjective impact which a communicated content has. A nonverbal behavior can be perceived by distance and proximity receptors alike; for example, bodily action may not only be seen and heard, but may also produce physical effects. Verbal behavior, on the other hand, can be received by distance receptors only, that is, it can only be heard or read. Furthermore, a nonverbal act influences perception, coordination, and integration; it leads to the acquisition of psychomotor, affective, and lifestyle outcomes. A verbal act, in contrast, influences thinking and leads to the acquisition of cognitive outcomes. Additionally, in a nonverbal act evaluation is based on the appreciation of similiarities and differences. In a verbal act, on the other hand, evaluation is governed by the principles and rules of logic.[19]

Spatiotemporal characteristics of a content refer to the way in which that content is itself situated in time and space. A nonverbal act can comprise several behaviors or events simultaneously; for example, a person can communicate warning and stop behaviors simultaneously. A verbal act, on the other hand, must by its very nature indicate simultaneous events successively; for example, a spoken or written report consists of words which are aligned serially. A nonverbal act can represent space adequately and sometimes superbly, as for example in a drawing or three-dimensional model. A verbal act, in contrast, is unable to directly represent space successfully except for a conceptual description of boundaries and distances.

Classification

Before treating some of the major ways in which nonverbal behavior can be classified, it is necessary to draw an important distinction between nonverbal behavior and nonverbal communication. The parameters of nonverbal behavior are wider than those of nonverbal communication. Not all nonverbal behavior exercises a communicative function. A person alone in a dark room might experience a subtle facial twitch which he does not feel or even perceive. Such a nonverbal behavior would become a form of nonverbal communication to himself if this person would be able to feel or perceive the twitch; it would become a form of communication to others if the light were turned on in that room and another individual saw the twitch.

Classification by Form. Jurgen Ruesch and Weldon Kees classify nonverbal behavior on the basis of what they perceive to be its form, shape, or structure. Their classification enjoys the advantage of being one of the simplest and easiest to grasp of all the many classifications of nonverbal behavior which have been proposed since World War II. Ruesch and Kees[20] place all nonverbal behavior into three categories, namely, sign language, action language, and object language. *Sign language* is the substitution of gestures for words, numbers, and punctuation signs. The complexity and completeness of nonverbal sign language runs the gamut from the gestural system used by deaf persons to simple substitutions for verbal phrases such as the thumbs-down signal signifying "no" or "I disapprove." Sign language is perceived exclusively through the eye. *Action language* consists in all those bodily movements which are not employed exclusively as signals. Eating, drinking walking, clenching one's fists are examples of action language. Action language is perceived through the eye and the ear, and to a lesser degree through the sense of touch. Action language represents the principal way in which emotions and other affects are expressed. *Object language* is the display of material things such as clothes, furniture, architectural arrangements, implements, art objects, machines, and the like. Object language is perceived through all five senses. Critics of the Ruesch-Kees classification system claim that placing the entire spectrum of nonverbal behaviors into just three categories results in grouping together widely dissimilar phenomena; a more discriminating system of classification is obviously necessary for optimal study and deployment of the many diverse kinds of nonverbal behavior.

Classification by Code. Randall Harrison[21] classifies nonverbal behavior on the basis of what he perceives to be the fundamental way in which it is coded in a sign system. He places all nonverbal behavior into four categories, namely, performance codes, artifactual codes, mediational codes, and contextual codes. *Performance codes* are those in which nonverbal signs emanate from bodily activities. Examples include gestures, facial expressions, eye meovements, bodily posture, tactile contact, and olfaction. A special subcategory of performance codes includes paralinguistic and extralinguistic behaviors such as voice tone, speech nonfluencies, sighs, laughter, grunts, and so forth. *Artifactual codes* are those in which nonverbal signs emerge in the arrangement of dress, cosmetics, furnishings, art objects, architecture, and the like. *Mediational codes* are those in which nonverbal signs arise from selections, arrangements, and inventions within communication media. Examples of mediational codes are motion pictures in black-and-white or in color, with music and special sound effects, and a close-up or long-shot film sequence. *Contextual codes* are those in which nonverbal signs arise in the deployment of space and time, through spatial and temporal location of communication systems, and in the arrangements of communicators and their artifacts. Like the Ruesch-Kees system, Harrison's is open to the criticism that his classification unduly squeezes widely dissimilar nonverbal behaviors into an excessively small number of categories.

Classification by Manifestation. Many of the systems which classify nonverbal behavior do so on the basis of the manifestations or appearances which various kinds of nonverbal behaviors assume. The system devised by Mark Knapp[22] is representative of the parsimonious classifications by manifestation, while that delineated by Larry Barker and Nancy Collins[23] is illustrative of the more detailed types of this kind of classification. Knapp's system includes the following categories, each of which is relatively self-explanatory: (1) kinesic behavior, that is, body motion; (2) physical characteristics; (3) touching behavior; (4) paralanguage; (5) proxemics, that is, the use or arrangement of space; (6) artifacts; (7) environmental factors.

The category system favored by Barker and Collins includes eighteen areas in which nonverbal communication takes place in the world: (1) animal and insect; (2) culture; (3) environment; (4) facial and kinesic activity; (5) human behavior of all sorts not included in any other category and which is not verbal; (6) interaction patterns; (7) learning; (8) machine; (9) media; (10) those mental processes, perception, imagination, and creativity which are not verbally encoded; (11) music; (12) paralanguage; (13) personal grooming and apparel; (14) physiological activities which occur naturally; (15) pictures; (16) space; (17) tactile and cutaneous; (18) time.

Classification by Combined Bases. It is fairly well agreed that each bit of nonverbal behavior consists in the interplay or merging of various kinds of activities, thrusts, and dimensions. Consequently, some theorists and researchers argue that any valid and adequate classification of nonverbal behavior must be constructed in a manner which includes these diverse kinds of activities, thrusts, and dimensions. Only in this way can the classification system be adequate to and reflective of the phenomena it is endeavoring to categorize. The classification system developed by Paul Ekman and Wallace Friesen[24] represents one attempt to classify nonverbal behavior on the basis of combined aspects. Ekman and Friesen maintain that if any instance of a person's nonverbal behavior is to be properly understood, one must learn how that behavior became part of the individual's repertoire, the circumstances of its use, and the rules which explain how the behavior conveys information. These three fundamental features, then, are origin, usage, and coding. Employing these fundamental features as the basis or matrix from which to examine the spectrum of nonverbal behavior, Ekman and Friesen identify five major classes of nonverbal activity, namely, emblems, illustrators, regulators, affect displays, and adaptors.

Emblems are those nonverbal acts which have a direct verbal translation, one which is well known by virutally all members of a particular group. class, or culture. Sign language for the deaf, secret signs in fraternal orders, and the twirling of the forefinger around the temple to indicate ''crazy'' are examples of an emblem. In terms of their usage, an emblem may repeat, substitute, or even contradict some part of the corresponding verbal symbol. People typically employ emblems intentionally. While emblems are the most easily understood nonverbal behavior, they nonetheless seem to carry less personal information than any of the five major classes of nonverbal behavior.

Illustrators are acts which are directly conjoined to speech; they serve to illustrate what is being said verbally. Six kinds of illustrators can be identified, namely batons, ideographs, deictic activities, spatial activities, kinetographs, and pictographs. Batons are movements which accent or emphasize a particular word or phrase. Ideographs are movements which sketch a path or direction of thought; deictic activities are movements which point to a here-and-now present object. Spatial activities are movements which depict a spatial relationship of one kind or another. Kinetographs are movements which portray a bodily action. Pictographs are movements which draw a picture of a bodily action. The illustrator class of nonverbal behavior is not exclusive of the others; thus a nonverbal behavior which might fall within this category might also fall into another category, depending on usage in a particular instance.

Regulators are acts which maintain and regulate the back-and-forth character of speaking and listening in human interaction. Regulators inform the speaker to continue, elaborate, hurry up, become more interesting, give others an opportunity to talk, and so forth. Regulators include head nods, eye contacts, slight movements forward and other postural shifts, eyebrow raises, looking at one's wristwatch, and the like. Regulators seem to operate on the periphery of the behaver's awareness.

Affect displays are acts which embody or reveal one's feeling-functions. Facial expressions are among the most important bodily sites for affect displays. Muscle tenseness is another important site. In terms of usage, an affect display can repeat, qualify, or contradict a verbally stated affect, or be totally unrelated to a concomitant verbal behavior. Affect displays carry more personal information than do illustrators or most emblems. Affect displays are typically affect blends, that is, a combination of multiple emotions, attitudes, and the like.

Adaptors are acts which were originally learned as part of the individual's efforts to satisfy one's physical or psychological needs to perform bodily actions, to manage the emotions, to develop and maintain prototypic interpersonal contacts, or to learn instrumental activities. These behaviors were acquired by a person early in life as part of the adaptive efforts of the organism to satisfy its needs. Three kinds of adaptors can be identified, namely self-adaptors, alter-directed adaptors, and object adaptors. Self-adaptors are those which are geared to the mastery or management of a variety of problems or needs in order to facilitate or block sensory input. Personal-grooming behaviors represents a form of self-adaptor. Alter-directed adaptors are those related to interpersonal contacts. Nonverbal movements necessary in giving to or taking from another person, in establishing successful affection or intimacy, and in withdrawal or advancement are examples of alter-directed adaptors. Finally, object adaptors are those related to the performance of some instrumental task. Driving a car, washing dishes, wielding a tool are examples of object adaptors. All adaptors usually operate at a rich and variegated level of idiosyncratic meaning, though they also contain shared meanings especially as the individual advances in age. Because adaptors are generally automatic and physiologically rooted, they tend to be nonintentional.

Theoretical Frameworks

The relation of theory to practice is a crucial one. Theory explains what a practice really is, and why a practice operates the way it does. Theory helps us make sense out of a practice; it also helps us derive maximum benefit and advantage from a practice or set of practices. Theory enables a person to decide when a particular practice will work and when it will not work. Theory enables an individual to decide when to put a practice into operation and when not to. Theory explains why, when, how, and under what circumstances a practice works.[25] Consequently, if a religious educationist or educator wishes to derive optimum benefit from his knowledge or understanding of nonverbal behavior, he should look to one or another of the theories which claim to be at the basis of this kind of human activity.

Theory is the set of grand hypotheses inferentially derived from a study of practice. The more carefully an individual studies practice, the firmer foundation that person will have for constructing an adequate theory. The name ''research'' is given to that systematic, consistent, reliable, and valid study of practice. The kind of research conducted on a particular practice or set of practices plays a large role in influencing the nature, type, and thrust of the theory which is eventually constructed on the basis of this research.

I must emphasize that research in and of itself does nothing more than simply provide data. While empirically validated data are absolutely necessary for the genuine improvement of practice, nonetheless data are not sufficient for improving practice. The insufficiency of research for understanding and improving practice flows from the fact that data just are; data have no meaning in and of themselves. It is theory which draws or infers meaning, generalizability, and applicability from the data. Thus if the religious educator wishes the data mined from research in nonverbal behavior to be truly useful for pedagogical practice, then this teacher must insert these data into an adequate and fruitful theory of nonverbal behavior.[26]

Randall Harrison and Mark Knapp identify two principal research strands which have been used to investigate nonverbal behavior, namely the anthropological strand and the psychological strand.[27] Both strands are social-scientific in nature and structure.

The anthropological research tradition in nonverbal behavior has two major representatives. The first is that derived from traditional anthropological concerns and deals with the investigation of the nonverbal behavior of persons in a wide variety of cultural settings. David Efron is an investigator working in this tradition. The second representative of the anthropological tradition is that of the language-framed approach to research on nonverbal behavior.[28] Ray Birdwhistell's research on kinesics and Edward Hall's investigations of proxemics are examples of that tradition.

The psychological research tradition in investigating nonverbal behavior has three major branches. The first started with the clinical point of view, and is very much tied in with psychotherapy. Jurgen Ruesch exemplifies this branch. The second branch is linked in scope and methodology to experimental psychology. Paul Ekman is a representative of this branch. The third branch is related to the work of social psychology with its focus on human interaction. Albert Mehrabian works primarily in this frame of research.

The two basic strands of research on nonverbal behavior—the anthropological and the psychological, with their different infravariations—have been used as bases to develop five major kinds of theory claiming to explain, predict, and verify nonverbal behavior. These five major theoretical approaches to nonverbal behavior are the biological, the language-framed, the sociological, the social-psychological, and the psychotherapeutic.

The biological theory of nonverbal behavior holds that the basic explanation accounting for a person's nonverbal activities can be found in one's own physiological origins, structure, and operations. Culture and society modify physiology, to be sure, but the roots lie in the physiology of the human organism. Desmond Morris claims that the rhythmic side-to-side motions of a lecturer or after-dinner speaker frequently take place at the same speed as the heartbeat. This confluence affords the speaker a very comforting motion at a time of a discomforting situation.[29]

The language-framed theory of nonverbal behavior holds that the basic explanation accounting for a person's nonverbal activities can be found in the communication nature of nonverbal behavior. Advocates of this theory claim that nonverbal communication is itself a language, with its own rule-governed hierarchical structure in which smaller nonverbal units are grouped so as to form larger nonverbal units. In such a language-framed conceptualization, nonverbal behavior is in many respects analogous to verbal behavior in that each has its own distinctive syntax, grammar, and semantic. Ray Birdwhistell's development of kinelogical, kinemorphological, and kinesyntactic forms exemplifies the language-framed theory.[30]

The sociological theory of nonverbal behavior holds that the basic explanation accounting for a person's nonverbal activities can be found in the meaning and function which these activities have in a particular culture or subculture. Each culture and subculture has its own set of rules for conduct and communication; it is within, or from, this rule-framework that nonverbal behavior operates and has meaning. In Italian culture, for example, the children learn to give full rein to their facial expressions. In Bali, on the other hand, the children learn to restrain their facial expressions and not to be especially emotive.[31]

The social-psychological theory of nonverbal behavior holds that the basic explanation accounting for a person's nonverbal activities can be found in the way in which an individual's personality reciprocally influences and is influenced by the structure, dynamics, and behavior of the persons or groups with whom he interacts. Advocates of this theory contend that while biology, language, and culture all do exert a certain influence on nonverbal behavior, nonetheless the basic confluent factors involved in nonverbal behavior are the individual's personality (psychological) as it is developmentally interactive in the social setting (sociological).

The psychotherapeutic theory of nonverbal behavior holds that the basic explanation accounting for a person's nonverbal activities can be found in the person's unconscious experience. For example, the way in which a person holds his body during sleep is said to express the individual's unconscious wish to return to the womb. According to psychotherapeutic theory, for example, a speaker who cleans his spectacles or drinks water during his lecture is not so much cleaning his spectacles or drinking water as he is expressing a denial of danger. Such mannerisms represent a clinging to inanimate objects since the other person representing security, notably the mother, is not available.[32]

Is Nonverbal Behavior Learned or Instinctive?

One school of thought contends that all nonverbal behavior is learned and that none is instinctive. According to this school of thought, each culture and society has its own distinctive, peculiar, and learned symbols of nonverbal behavior.[33] The findings of David Efron's classic investigation of the gestures of traditional and assimilated Jewish and Italian immigrants to the United States "certainly do not bear out the contention that this form of behavior [gestures] is determined by biological descent."[34]

Another school of thought holds that although most nonverbal behaviors are indeed learned, nonetheless there are some which appear to be instinctive. Summarizing the pertinent research, Michael Argyle states that there is solid empirical evidence indicating that some bodily signals are innate.[35] Though conceding that their contention is not yet a definitely proven fact, nonetheless Paul Ekman and Wallace Friesen maintain that cross-cultural research does tentatively suggest that "there are distinctive movements of the facial muscles for each of a number of primary affect states, and these are universal to mankind."[36]

The Importance of Nonverbal Content

The importance of nonverbal content in religious instruction, in general education, and in all of life is very great. One review of the pertinent research concludes that "in the development of each human being, nonverbal communication precedes and perhaps structures all subsequent communication."[37]

Unfortunately, the awareness of the great importance of nonverbal content is dimmed by the naturalness with which a person learns how to use nonverbal behavior. The appreciation of its importance is also obscured by the apparent ease with which a person is able to encode and decode highly complex sequences of verbal behaviors. With specific reference to religious educationists and educators, the great importance of nonverbal content is blurred and often hidden by the extreme and often exclusive emphasis which is placed on verbal content, particularly by the proponents of the theological approach to religious instruction.

There is something of a regrettable *grande hauteurisme* in certain otherwise sophisticated circles which suggests that nonverbal content is a refuge of the person who is either too lazy or too stupid to couch his ideas or feelings in verbal form. The facial expressions, the hand movements and other forms of gesture—these are the forms of communicative content used by the uneducated and the unlearned, and are low-level forms of communicative content. Persons holding such a superficial view can possibly be excused for not being conversant with the research which demonstrates the superiority of nonverbal content over verbal content in the facilitation of many of humanity's deepest and most personalistic behaviors. But it is difficult to grasp how such individuals can be so blind as to have utterly failed in seeing the tremendous importance and significance of nonverbal content in their own personal lives and in their own social interaction. Most persons trust their own nonverbal behavior far more than their verbal behavior to encapsulate their feelings and deeper experiences. Conversely, most persons will tend to trust another individual's nonverbals more than the verbals to provide accurate data on the other individual's real feelings and profound experiences. To assert that nonverbal content is the refuge of a lazy or stupid individual is to assert nonsense.

Nonverbal content occurs far more frequently than does verbal content, even with the most loquacious of persons or religious educators. Verbals occur some of the time, nonverbals occur virtually all of the time. The absence of nonverbal content in life or in the lesson is almost impossible. In contrast, the absence of verbal content in life or in the lesson does indeed occur. Except in moments when everyone is talking at once, there is only one set of verbal stimuli occurring at any given time. But in the case of nonverbal content, there are many different forms of nonverbal behavior all simultaneously taking place: facial expressions, gestures, voluntary and involuntary body movements, silence when not talking and paralanguage when talking, and so forth. If a religious educator were to have his lesson videotaped, he would find that the frequency and range of his nonverbal content far exceeded those of his verbal content.[38]

Evidence from commonsense observation, from focused instructional awareness, and from carefully conducted empirical research investigations indicates that persons tend to place more reliance upon the authenticity and frequently upon the accuracy of another's nonverbal behavior than upon that individual's verbal behavior. John Westerhoff, the tractarian, advises religion teachers that "a person call tell a group of black and white children that they are all loved equally, but if that person puts her arms around a white child and unconsciously holds back contact with a black child, a different message is communicated, a different lesson is learned."[39] Othanel Smith remarks that a learner is quick to pick up nonverbal cues which reveal whether or not a teacher likes and respects him. For example, the learner might notice that the teacher shrugs his shoulders or frowns when the learner is responding to a question.[40] On the basis of his research, Paul Torrance concludes that even though a teacher vocalizes the "right words" purportedly representing certain attitudes, nevertheless his "real attitude" is likely to show through, thereby affecting the learner's emotional responses as well as their conduct.[41] Charles Galloway's research investigation revealed that "the meanings inherent in nonverbal expressions [of the teacher] are used by pupils to check on the fidelity of [the teacher's] communicative act. . . . By interpreting and inferring from nonverbal expressions, pupils may attempt to obtain the full import of a teacher's perceptions and motivations." Galloway observes that when a teacher communicates conflicting verbal and nonverbal behaviors, the learner quite frequently places greater store in the validity of the nonverbal communication. For example, a teacher may verbally utter approval of a particular learner behavior, yet the learner might pick up nonverbal cues which suggest disapproval.[42] A research experiment conducted by Michael Argyle and his associates on the relative impact of verbal and nonverbal cues for dominance-submission found the nonverbal cues to be superior to the verbal ones.[43] In one of several research experiments conducted by Albert Mehrabian and some associates it was found that when an attitude which was communicated with positive verbal content was accompanied by negative nonverbal voice tone, the entire message was perceived as communicating a negative attitude.[44]

As a result of his research, Mehrabian concluded that "the combined effect of simultaneous verbal, vocal, and facial attitude communication is a weighted sum of their independent effects—with the coefficients of .07, .38, and .55 respectively."[45] Placed into an equation, this conclusion would be expressed as follows: perceived attitude = .7 verbal + .38 paralanguage + .55 facial expression. Findings like this are vitally important for religious educators.

It is quite possible that nonverbal behavior is generally a more powerful communicator than verbal behavior because of its greater directness and apparently deeper link to the more organic in the human person. Michael Argyle, for example, states that verbal behavior is arbitrarily coded by a society or a culture, while nonverbal behavior is "mostly iconic (fragments of the real things) or uncoded (i.e., are themselves the very emotions or acts indicated)."[46] Though a forceful advocate of verbal content (as contrasted to nonverbal content) in the work of religious instruction, Augustine nonetheless holds that verbal language is symbolized and therefore subject to arbitrary custom and indirectness of expression, while nonverbal behavior is often unsymbolized and direct. Indeed, for Augustine, nonverbal behavior is sometimes so powerfully direct that words are incapable of either adequately expressing nonverbal behavior in linguistic form or dealing with it effectively during the teaching act.[47] The nonsymbolized aspects of experience are largely nonverbal. Direct experience, obviously, tends to exert a greater and deeper pull on a person than indirectly-valenced experiences such as language.

Religious educators are fond of saying that the world, and especially the religious world, is an unspeakable world. Why, then, does so much speaking take place in the religion lesson? The deepest and most profound realities in life are indeed unspeakable and so should be expressed in nonverbal form. Religion, after all, tends to "deal with" and "live out" rather than "talk about." Religion is a deeply personal activity, one pulsing with intimacy, warm affect, and human significance. Dimensions such as these can be grasped adequately only in a nonverbal form. The verbal somehow diminishes the depth, cools the affectivity, and subtracts from the intimacy of one's expression of profound realities like religion. Theology is most effectively expressed in verbal form. Religion is most effectively expressed in nonverbal form. Religion seems most at home when it assumes the form of nonverbal content; religion seems least at home when it assumes verbal garb.

Because the bible was recorded in a verbal mode, theologians have tended to downplay or even neglect totally the nonverbal dimension of revelation. It would be well to remind theologians that though the bible is indeed a verbal record, nonetheless many if not most of the significant revelation-events which it records are nonverbal realities. The crossing of the Red Sea, the incarnation, the transfiguration, the crucifixion, the descent of the Holy Spirit upon the Apostles—all these were supremely nonverbal events.[48] The once-and-still continuing revelation which God provides to each individual establishes a personal relationship between God and the human being, a relationship which is nonverbal at its base. Revelation in nonverbal form does not simply consummate and seal the revelation given by word, as some theologians would tell us.[49] Rather, revelation in nonverbal form usually antedates in time, precedes in importance, and succeeds in effect revelation in the verbal mode.

Religion has always been closely tied in with ritual, with rites, and with ceremonies. While verbal and nonverbal behaviors are conjoined in many rituals, nonetheless the nonverbal is often predominant. Indeed, some rituals are almost totally enacted in the nonverbal mode. Ritual appears to be an indispensable aspect of humanity and of culture. It is deeply and inextricably embedded in personality development, in cultural values, in social structure, and in social change.[50] Ritual typically is architected to place a person or group in deep existential touch with the more profound dimensions of reality.

Michael Argyle contends that nonverbal behavior is more basic and more characteristic of ritual than is verbal behavior for the following reasons. Nonverbal behavior communicates realities of the inner world, while verbal behavior is designed to communicate events pertaining to the external world. Second, nonverbal behavior is capable of evoking powerful affects, of bringing about changes in social relationships, and in producing physical and psychological healing. Verbal behavior is relatively weak in all these areas. Third, nonverbal behavior is linked to the unconscious processes far more than is the case with verbal behavior. It is in the unconscious that flow so many functions deeply related to religion, including love and hate, dependence and self-assertion, identity and individuation, and so forth.[51]

One of the most powerful forms of religious instruction is art. Indeed, art was the principal form of religious instruction in church and societal settings until the widespread acquisition of literacy. Art communicates the deeper, the more personal, the more mystical, and the more divine aspect of human existence. Religion has always been intimately bound up with art, from the days of the image of the fish being scrawled on catacomb walls to contemporary churches. Art takes on many forms: painting, sculpture, dance, music, and so forth. Art has a special quality which takes a person out of himself and plunges him into a world which many characterize as divine. Music, perhaps more than any other form of creative art, has this capacity. Art is nonverbal, of course. In view of the role which art plays in the religious act,[52] and in view of the effects which all forms of art have in facilitating religious outcomes, it is indeed regrettable that religious educators do not make wider use of all the various modes of creative art available to them.

Religion is a deeply personal matter. And nonverbal behavior is one of the most person-freighted of all the contents of religious instruction. Nonverbal content is an integral embodiment of the deeper self, the self which must be touched and taught if the fruits of religious instruction are to become permanent in the learner. An individual's deepest affects, convictions, and thoughts about religion are conveyed nonverbally in a manner far more frequent and far more authentic than they are verbally. Thus to ignore nonverbal content is to ignore some crucial dimensions of religious instruction. Nonverbal leakage—that nonverbal content which is communicated unawaringly and sometimes unconsciously by the communicator—often provides an excellent clue to the perceptive educator as to where the learner is religiously.

Religion is not only deeply personal; it is also profoundly interpersonal. Theologians are increasingly maintaining that divine revelation is fundamentally an interpersonal communion.[53] Revelation between persons is also a deeply interpersonal relationship. Nonverbal content is personally revelatory because it contains and conveys affects, attitudes, and values. While verbal content is helpful in discussing aspects about persons, nonverbal content communicates the ongoing dynamics of the interpersonal encounter itself.[54] "A person's relationship to others is often defined by action."[55] While verbal behavior usually just symbolizes or points to action, nonverbal behavior frequently is action. The voice tone one uses, the gestures, the posture and gait, the muscle tensions, the way one arranges one's clothes and furniture—these are all actions which establish, maintain, change, and signal a particular quality of interpersonal relationship.

Nonverbal behavior is an important feature of an individual's life in society. For example, it provides an individual with important cues on whether or not to react to another person, to walk away from him or embrace him, to smile at him or to frown, to give him food, and so forth. Or again, nonverbal behavior can be used to be prophetic to society, such as Mohandas Gandhi's hunger strikes or Martin Luther King, Jr.'s sit-ins and marches. These strikes, sit-ins, and marches were nonverbal behaviors whose effect was more powerful and more prophetic than speeches and verbal harangues.

One of the tragedies in so much of religious instruction is the relative neglect of the body. Largely due to Puritan and Jansenistic influences, Christians for the past three centuries have customarily regarded the body as unclearn, a source of moral temptation, and a barrier to rapid and clear learning. It was not always so, however. Though Augustine held a negative view of the body due to a residual Manicheanism with which he was afflicted, Thomas Aquinas was quite positive. Aquinas contends that the sensory quality of different persons' bodies is the prime explanation for the difference in their intelligence.[56] In his view, all human souls of themselves are of equal intellectual power; it is the bodies to which they are joined that enables this ability to be exercised. It has only been in the second half of the twentieth century that Protestants and especially Catholics have come to embrace that kind of positive and wholesome regard for the body which was characteristic of much of Christianity from the Middle Ages until the seventeenth century.[57] Schubert Ogden, the process theologian, squarely faces the role of the body when he writes: "To exist as a self, as each of us does, is always to be related, first of all, to the intimate world constituted by one's own body." As Ogden observes, a person's cognitive and affective functions are enacted in and through brain cells, nerve connections, and the entire corporeal apparatus, for that matter. In and through the body, a person dynamically relates and is related to his own self and to the world outside himself.[58] If a person wishes to find the truth about himself, he will learn just as much, and even sometimes more, by existentially consulting his body as by consulting his mind or soul. How does a person feel about himself, about others, about God, for example? If that person would carefully examine and relate to his bodily functions when he is reflecting, when he is interacting with others, or when he is praying, he would find the answers to these questions—answers which are often different and more accurate than what his mind tells him. His muscle tension, his inner smile, his facial expression (especially around the mouth), his gestures, his postures, the feeling in his stomach—these reveal to a person who he really is and how he really operates when he confronts himself, other people, and God. A person's life history is located fully as much in a person's body as in his soul. Nonverbal content allows a person's body and a person's corporeal thrust to be taught.

There is an accumulation of research studies which conclude that psychotherapy and counseling have not proved to be more effective in curing patients and clients than the miscellaneous processes of time and experience.[59] I maintain that a major factor accounting for the relative lack of success of psychotherapy and counseling is the heavy and almost exclusive reliance on verbal behavior in the psychotherapeutic hour and in counseling interview. Personality disorders are typically linked far more to nonverbal content than to verbal content. Consequently, it is only at such time as psychotherapy and counseling are conducted primarily in a nonverbal fashion that any real and permanent cures can be expected. Both religion teachers and religious counselors might profit from an incident which William Schutz relates. It seems that a well-regarded psychiatrist logged 100 hours of individual therapy with a patient. In his final report, the therapist concluded that possibly his most effective act in all that time was when, in the final psychotherapeutic hour, he inadvertently placed his hand on the patient's shoulder.[60]

One final point is especially noteworthy. The substantive content of religious instruction is religion. Some perceptive philosophers maintain that words are unsuitable for expressing religious content, and that nonverbal behavior such as ritual and music are more appropriate and more powerful in this regard.[61] It is interesting to note that the research suggests that the right hemisphere of the brain appears to be the dominant one for aesthetic, analogical, nonverbal, and intuitive processes, while the left hemisphere is dominant for cognitive and verbal functions.[62] When these data are linked to the empirical evidence which indicates that religious persons tend to be right-hemisphere dominant,[63] the conclusion is obvious. Thus speculative nonempirical observations that religion is more intimately connected to nonverbal content than to verbal content is given empirical support. (By way of contrast, theology of course is linked to the verbal and to the cognitive.)

Limitations of Nonverbal Content

The denotative referent of verbal behavior is objective, namely an arbitrary but nonetheless culturally agreed-upon set of meanings. The denotative referent of verbal behavior is found in the dictionary. Everyone, for example, knows the denotative meaning of the words "mother," "church," "bible," and so on. However, the denotative meaning and/or act of nonverbal behavior is generally subjective.[64] It is the person's unique physiological structure, social enculturation, and psychological structure which comprise the denotative referent and/or act. One person's hand gesture might denote or be something quite different than a similar hand gesture made by another person. The denotation or act of proxemic arrangement varies from culture to culture. Consequently, nonverbal behavior can be, and frequently is, misunderstood cognitively. One cannot always trust one's cognitive interpretation of nonverbal content. Thus, for example, white schoolteachers sometimes report that children from certain black ghettos are surly and disrespectful in class because they roll their eyes and gaze upward while being reprimanded. However, upon further examination it was found that in these black ghettos, rolling one's eyes and gazing upward nonverbally indicates a person's feelings of guilt, shame, and inferiority.

Many theorists and researchers in the area of nonverbal behavior assume that nonverbal content can be trusted because it reveals information, feelings, and attitudes which are deeply held by an individual and which evade the person's efforts to censor. Nonverbal leakage— the unconscious or unwitting betrayal of withheld information or feelings—allows the other person to discover the true state of affairs. While this statement is generally true, nonetheless it does not always obtain. Nonverbal behavior can reveal false information, not only because of the referential and behavioral ambiguity to which I alluded in the previous paragraph, but also because a person can train himself to deliberately use nonverbal content in such a way as to withhold information from others as well as to deceive others.[65] Thus many of the more popular books on nonverbal behavior teach a person how to fake his own nonverbal behavior so as to deceive others.[66] The important point for the religious educator to remember in this connection is this: While nonverbal leakage is unwitting and unconscious, nonetheless there are some nonverbal behaviors which a person can control for his own purposes. Nonverbal behavior is not tantamount to nonverbal leakage. In other words, some nonverbal behavior is wittingly controlled, while other nonverbal behavior is unwittingly leaked. Thus the religious educator should attempt to develop criteria and discriminatory skills to ascertain when an individual's nonverbal content truly reveals his inner self and when it is consciously or unconsciously being used for purposes of withholding or deceiving.[67]

Nonverbal content is sometimes incomplete, and needs to be supplemented with verbal content. For example, while liturgical rituals are often nonverbal in content, yet they are sometimes conjoined to verbal content to bring out the fullness of meaning and purpose. Put differently, the right hemisphere of the brain cannot function alone, but needs the left hemisphere to attain human completeness.

Nonverbal content does not seem to be as successful as verbal content for the encapsulation of certain kinds of cognitive content, such as knowledge and the higher ratiocinative processes. Perhaps this is due to the differential information function of nonverbal and verbal content. Nonverbal content basically provides information about the subject, while verbal content appears geared to providing information about the object. Nonverbal content, however, might well afford superior existential understanding than does verbal content.[68]

THE FORM OF NONVERBAL CONTENT

In this section on the form of nonverbal content, I am restricting my attention to some principal varieties or types of nonverbal content, such as paralanguage, facial expressions, gestures, and the like. Structuring the section in this way enhances its usefulness by allowing each of the discrete types of nonverbal content to be placed into any one or more of the classification systems identified earlier in this chapter.

This section only treats some of the more prominent varieties of nonverbal content and is in no way intended to exhaust either the entire repertoire of nonverbal types or the depth of research conducted on any one of the types.

In reading this section it will be helpful to bear in mind that many of the nonverbal types herein discussed are sometimes taken for granted. Nonverbal behavior frequently acts as covert content. The smile when talking, the slightly sarcastic tone of voice, the manner in which a learning environment is physically structured, one's posture while conversing or walking, the pauses between words—these and many other nonverbal contents often go unnoticed by the learner who is typically focusing on the teacher's words or on some other behavioral feature which society has conditioned him to regard as more salient and more important. Consequently, nonverbal content often acts in an almost subliminal fashion, penetrating in a relatively unobtrusive and unfiltered manner into a person's awareness and unconscious. Much of the power and force of nonverbal content arises from its covertness and subliminality. Nonverbal content tends to confirm, expand, and validate the deepest and most personal communications which occur between persons in relationship.

Paralanguage

Paralanguage is the term generally given to those vocal characteristics occurring during speech which are nonverbal in form and structure. Examples of paralanguage include volume, tone, pitch, and tempo. Paralanguage can also apply to those nonverbal but mechanical features of handwritten or printed materials. Examples of this include typeface size and thickness, spacing, contour, and so forth. Specialists in nonverbal behavior generally investigate the spoken form of paralanguage almost to the exclusion of the written variety.

Paralanguage is used to change, direct, conceal, flavor, nuance, or otherwise manage the spoken or written word. In a certain sense, paralanguage constitutes a set of specific instructions consciously or unconsciously given by the speaker or writer/typesetter about the way the message ought to be interpreted and felt. Paralanguage adds valuable information about the verbal activity in progress by clarifying the performance, specifying the context—or by increasing the ambiguities.

Put in a somewhat oversimplified manner, language refers to what is said while paralanguage refers to how it is said.[69]

Paralanguage, notably the spoken variety, provides others with important information on one's mood, attitudes, values, and indeed on one's basic personality configuration. A soft, low, and breathy voice typically connotes warmth and affection, while a hurried, strident, moderately blaring voice tends to suggest impatience. A monotonous voice tone might imply a boring personality.

Paralanguage adds a necessary personal dimension to language. Spoken words in themselves have an impersonal quality about them; but the tempo, tone, pitch, timbre, rhythm, and so forth, with which each person invests the spoken word bestows a deeply personal character on what would otherwise be impersonal or "objective" speech. It is the individual's paralinguistic pattern which largely results in no two persons sounding the same, and which makes each person's speech pattern so unique. When a person wishes to sound objective and impersonal, such as a radio announcer, he will try as hard as possible to standardize and otherwise regulate his paralanguage.

Most persons seem to know the uses of paralanguage. When a person tries to sound religious, he will generally lower his voice tone and make it more resonant, all the while slowing the tempo of the words. To sound animated, a person will raise his voice tone, decrease its resonance, increase its tempo, and so forth.

Michael Argyle proposes a category system which classifies paralanguage according to its relation to language. There are two major categories in this system. First, there are those paralinguistic behaviors which are basically unrelated to the linguistic content of what is uttered, such as voice tone. Behaviors in this category reveal data about an individual's unconscious states, personality configurations, social class, and group affiliation. Second, there are those paralinguistic behaviors which in one way or another tend to be directly related to the linguistic content of what is uttered, as for example, pitch, stress, and so forth. Behaviors in the second category tend to work hand-in-hand with the linguistic content so as to deliberately provide another person or group of persons with as complete and as accurate information as possible about what one wishes to say.[70] I should note, however, that this classification system is not always clear-cut or even correct. For example, the pitch, tempo, and stress in one's voice might be more the result of an individual's anxious or angry psychological state at the moment than it is of any intentions he might have to accurately accentuate in paralinguistic form the linguistic content of his utterances.[71]

Charles Galloway's research study discovered that a teacher's paralinguistic behavior was a factor in encouraging or inhibiting learner responses and initiative.[72] In another empirical research investigation, it was found that in those therapeutic sessions perceived by psychotherapists to be successful, the facilitator tended to use a medium or normal amount of vocal intensity and stress combined with a soft, relaxed, warm tone.[73]

The degree to which a person varies the pitch of his voice appears to be correlated with perceived pleasantness or unpleasantness. For example, a study by Paul Vitz concluded that the pleasantness ratings of a particular speech act bears a curvilinear relationship to the amount of pitch variation used in that speech act. Moderate variation in pitch was perceived to be the most pleasant.[74]

The research suggests a distinct correlation between pitch and affective states.[75] Studies by Grant Fairbanks and his associates found that anger and fear were expressed with a much higher-pitched voice than were grief or contempt. Of all the affective states investigated, indifference was the one expressed with the lowest pitch. Voices manifesting anger, fear, and contempt exhibited a wider range of changes in pitch and inflection than voices manifesting grief and indifference.[76] The empirical data also suggest that voice pitch constitutes a basis on which individuals perceive and evaluate another's personality characteristics.[77]

Loudness of voice has been shown to exert a measurable effect upon one's perceptions and attitudes. The studies indicate that persons typically associate loud voice tones with dominance, power, self-assurance, and assertiveness—and vice versa for a soft voice. That such subjective associations have some basis in objective reality is borne out by Albert Mehrabian and Martin Williams' experimental investigation which found that more submissive persons tend to indeed speak in a softer voice during interactions with a stranger.[78]

Rate of speech is generally correlated with animation and extraversion. People who speak rapidly are frequently regarded as animated, extraverted, and interesting. On the other hand, persons who speak quite slowly are typically perceived as lacking in animation, introverted, and dull.[79] The research also suggests that rate of speech tends to be associated with emotional reactions and responses. The experimental studies conducted by Grant Fairbanks and his associates found that the affective states of fear, anger, and indifference are expressed at a much faster speaking rate than contempt and grief. Contempt was expressed in a slow, steady rate of speech.[80] The research study conducted by Albert Mehrabian and Martin Williams concluded that individuals who are deliberately attempting to be persuasive typically speak faster, louder, and with more intonation than speakers who are trying to be neutral,[81] as anyone who has watched late-night, one-person television commercials will readily corroborate. The research has discovered that in an act of deceitful communication, a speaker tends to talk more slowly than one engaged in truthful communication. (The person who engages in deceitful communication also tends to talk less, make more speech errors, smile more, and take more distant positions from persons to whom they are speaking.)[82]

Speech disruptions such as pauses, interruptions, and hesitations are significant paralinguistic phenomena which impinge upon the perceptions of others. One research study found that utterances containing a large number of filled pauses ("ums" and "ers") were perceived as indicating anxiety and boredom, while utterances having a large number of unfilled pauses were interpreted as reflecting anxiety or contemptuousness.[83] Another research study discovered that the speech of persons expressing grief displayed a particularly large number of pauses, both between phrases and within phrases.[84]

Rhythm is another important feature of paralanguage. Rhythmic speech tends to be perceived as indicating activity, fear, and surprise, while speech which is not rhythmic suggests (and possibly induces) boredom.

Accent is a paralinguistic feature which serves as a basis for making judgments or drawing inferences about another person. It is common observation that a teacher whose speech reflects a foreign, regional, or class-related accent is, by that very reason, evaluated somewhat differently than a teacher who talks with no discernable accent. The listener's evaluation of accent-laden communication is influenced by his attitudes toward the group which uses such an accent. Michael Argyle contends that the research indicates that accents are typically rated along three main dimensions, namely competence, integrity, and attractiveness.[86] Competence is generally associated with what is regarded to be both standard pronunciation and upper-class pronunciation of the language being used.[87]

How well can another person's affective state be judged from that individual's paralanguage? Summarizing the research on this issue, Joel Davitz states that, for adults, affective meaning can be accurately communicated and thus can be accurately perceived by a listener.[88] How accurate is accurate? One review of the research states that adults can accurately identify affective states 30 to 45 percent of the time if a range of fourteen affective states is presented. This is a significant percentage for accuracy, and ranks only slightly lower than the corresponding percentage for facial expression.[89] In an especially fine series of programmatically related experimental studies on paralanguage, Joel Davitz and seven associates concluded that persons were able to judge with 20 to 50 percent accuracy the affective states of others solely on the basis of paralanguage.[90] The empirical research indicates that there seems to be a significant positive correlation between the ability to encode and decode paralanguage. In other words, persons who have the capacity to skillfully communicate desired affective states to others by means of paralanguage are also those who have the ability to accurately judge the affective states of others on the basis of their paralanguage, and vice versa.[91]

Extralanguage

Extralanguage consists of those vocal behaviors which occur in episodes in which no verbal content is simultaneously occurring. Extralanguage is not used in direct structural connection with words. Rather, extralinguistic behaviors stand on their own. They are used as a separate kind of language which is not occurring at the exact time in which words are being spoken. Extralanguage, then, is significantly different from paralanguage. A paralinguistic behavior like pitch occurs in direct and immediate association with words. Thus what is being pitched is a word or set of words. An extralinguistic behavior like crying, on the other hand, occurs independently of words. Crying is a language in its own right and does not occur in conjunction with a word or sentence which is being uttered. Extralanguage can be voluntary, such as some kinds of laughing, or it can be involuntary, such as most belching. Extralanguage communicates affective, cognitive, and psychomotor states. Extralanguage is typically used to convey one's feelings, deeper thoughts, and bodily states in a manner generally regarded as more forceful than is possible with words or paralanguage. For example, hissing is a more potent form of communicating one's displeasure than saying: "I don't like this," in an angry tone of voice.

Laughter. Laughter is an important aspect of almost every person's extralinguistic repertoire. Some scholars suggest that the basis of laughter lies deep in a human being's biological structure, and that therefore laughter is a very vital and necessary feature of a person's behavior.[92] Many scientists believe that laughter (extralinguistic behavior) and smiling (facial behavior) have different phylogenetic origins and have converged to a considerable extent in the human being.[93]

There are different forms of laughter, each communicating one or another meaning.[94] A belly-laugh and a sarcastic laugh are both laughter, but the meaning each communicates varies greatly from the other. Differential patterns of laughing are frequently accompanied by differential facial expressions, as for example, the broad-smile laugh (the so-called "cheese" smile) with intense baring of teeth on the one hand, and the wide-open-mouth laugh so favored by children on the other.

The origins and source of laughter are disputed, and no satisfactory, generally agreed view appears to prevail. One review of the relevant philosophical and literary theories indicates that three principal theoretical explanations of laughter can be identified, namely superiority, conflict, and relief.[95] Immanuel Kant, Herbert Spencer, and Sigmund Freud regarded laughter primarily as a means to discharge surplus physical tension or excessive mental excitement. Charles Darwin considered laughter in its original form to be the expression of joy, happiness, and high spirits. For Paul Carus, the origins of laughter can be found in the primitive shout of savage triumph, a loud vocal trumpet-ting of victory, and a cruel mocking over a conquered enemy.[96] Boris Sidis holds that one of the principal roots of laughter lies in the amusement one takes in the misfortunes of other people whom one treats with contempt and possible hatred.[97] Laughter can also result from perceiving incongruities in life and in the behavior of persons attempting to deal with these incongruities.[98]

Christian thinkers in the second half of the twentieth century have been giving an increasing amount of attention to the religious dimension of laughter and play. Peter Berger notes that Christianity has a basically comic character on two accounts. First, the hero (Jesus, and with him the entire redeemed human race) is the victor over sin and so can laugh at sin. Second, the redeemed Christian can mockingly laugh at such otherwise fear-producing aspects of life such as suffering, pain, misfortune, and death.[99] Jürgen Moltmann views Easter as the central Christian event, an event which gives a comic base to Christianity. With Easter, there "begins the laughter of the redeemed, and the creative game of the new, concrete concomitants of the liberty which has been opened for us, even if we still live under conditions with little cause for rejoicing."[100]

It is interesting to note that empirical research on laughter in infants and young children offers confirmation of some of the speculations made by Christian thinkers and theologians on the communal and comic bases of Christian existence. Two examples illustrate this point. First, one study of the beginnings of laughter concludes that situations which evoke laughter in a baby are those which combine the fear-producing stimulus of rough handling with the pleasure-producing stimulus of the familiar parent.[101] Second, the empirical research suggests that young, post-infant children almost never laugh when by themselves: they seem to laugh only in the presence of others.[102] This finding takes on additional force when juxtaposed with the renewed Catholic and Protestant emphasis on community as a vital source and locus for the effective education and living out of one's Christian religion.

Crying. Crying is an extralinguistic behavior which is deeply prized in the Judaeo-Christian tradition.[103] In the Old Testament, weeping was frequently connected with a personal search for Yahweh[104] because, in large measure, weeping was thought to express sorrow for sin and a sense of contrition.

Especially in the affective domain, the psychological correlates of crying are typically of greater interest to the religious educator than the physiological stimuli of tears.[105] On the basis of careful speculative analysis, Balduin Schwarz identifies five types of crying which he places on a progressive scale advancing from the purely physical through the subjective and culminating in what he calls the truly personal level. The first stage is purely physical, one's direct response to physical pain. The second stage is also purely physical, but unlike the first stage in which crying occurs simultaneously with physical stimuli, crying follows painful stimuli as an independent act. An example of second-stage crying is that which follows nervous anxiety or exhaustion. It is at the third stage in which the affective or subjective type of weeping begins. In this stage a person cries because of subjective events such as inner excitation or emotional surrender in the face of the superior power of misfortune. The fourth stage is the weeping of peripeteia which is triggered when an individual steps out of one personal stance into another existential posture. In the fourth stage one weeps because one perceives oneself freed, liberated, or granted deliverance—in contrast to the third stage in which one cries because one sees oneself as a powerless victim of misfortune or as one imprisoned helpless within one's body. An example of fourth-stage crying is weeping for remorse. The fifth and highest stage is rooted in what Schwarz calls the truly personal. Crying in the fifth stage is the response of one's whole being to value, the existential way in which one evaluatively responds to the qualities of what is found moving, touching, lovable, or holy as these qualities are values per se and not as these qualities relate to the individual or to any other person. In the first four stages, a person can be deceived, as for example, when an individual cries because of self-pity or oversentimentality or even in remorse for something about which one should not be remorseful. But in the fifth stage, one weeps not in and for one's personal relationship to misfortune or to value, but because the value (like holiness or goodness or love) is in itself moving or touching.[106]

Giggling. Giggling is an extralanguage content well known to anyone working with children and adolescents. The perceptive religious educator does not dismiss giggling as immature nonsense, or unduly rebuke the giggler. Rather, the discerning religious educator considers giggling as an extraverbal content and seeks to grasp its meaning in a particular situation so as to better understand the learner and to more effectively communicate with that individual. Irenäus Eibl-Eibesfeldt has filmed individuals in Europe, Africa, and the South Seas. This researcher discovered that at different times, in different situations, and in combination with different nonverbal contents, giggling can signal embarrassment, coyness, flirting, or a real conflict.[107]

Hissing. Hissing is an extralanguage content used in the Western World to signify displeasure, derision, scorn, or even hatred. Hissing is a powerful extraverbal content and sometimes has profound social and psychological effects.

"Mm-Hmm" and "Uh-Huh." The "Mm-Hmm" and the "Uh-Huh" are two extraverbal contents much favored by counselors, psychotherapists, and those religious educators seeking to focus on the affective content of an educational episode. The religion teacher employs these two nonverbal contents for one or more of the following reasons: to assure the learner that his communication is really heard; to give the learner the feeling that he is being affectively understood, sympathized with, and even empathized with; and to provide the learner with a nondirective, noncoercive, nonjudgmental communication. The religious educator's use of "Mm-Hmm" and "Uh-Huh" tends to enhance the socioemotional climate of the lesson and to enrich the amount and quality of the affective content being learned. The "Mm-Hmm" and the "Uh-Huh" are positive cues to the learner, and if used skillfully and purposively, can also be of assistance in helping the learner talk more about himself and even about the subject-matter content. Reviews of the research suggest that the "Mm-Hmm" and the "Uh-Huh" extralanguage behavior not only tends to lead to dramatic increases in the length of the speaking intervals of an individual[108] but also accelerates the individual's verbal and nonverbal communication of affectively laden material.[109]

Silence

Silence is not language. Nor is it paralanguage, or even extralanguage. Yet silence does have a definite nonverbal communicatory function. It is an authentic nonverbal content.

Thomas Bruneau identifies three major forms of silence, namely psycholinguistic silence, interactive silence, and sociocultural silence.[110]

Psycholinguistic silence is that occasioned or characterized by the interplay of the speaker's and the hearer's psychological processes with their linguistic behavior. A host of psychological variables impinge upon the speaker and the hearer during the communication dynamic, thus occasioning various forms of silence. There are two subtypes of psycholinguistic silence, namely fast-time silence and slow-time silence. Fast-time silences are those of short duration. They consist of "imposed mental silences closely associated with the temporal-horizontal sequencing of speech in mind. Fast silences vary in mind-time, but are relatively low in intensity and duration of mind-time. They are, however, high in frequency. Their duration is usually less than two seconds of mechanical time."[111] Slow-time silences are those of longer duration than fast-time silences. They consist in "imposed mental silences closely associated with the semantic (and metaphorical) processes of decoding speech. These silences are more signalic than symbolic. It is suggested that slow-time silences relate to organizational, categorical, and spatial movement through levels of experience and levels of memory.

Interactive silence is any pausal, unfilled interruption in conversation, dialogue, debate, and so forth. Interactive silence differs from psycholinguistic silence mainly in each participant's conscious recognition of the degree and manner in which that individual is expected to participate in communicative speech exchange. Bruneau identifies six main functions of interactive silence: making decisions, drawing inferences, exerting control, reacting to diversity, expressing or receiving intense emotions, and maintaining or altering interpersonal distance. Interactive silence exerts considerable control: It is a means of commanding the decoder's attention; it is a method for snubbing and interdicting another person and giving him the nonperson treatment; it is a device whereby a person who desires no interpersonal relationships can so manage his silences that no relationship ever develops; it is a procedure to punish norm violators following an alleged or real violation, as for example the Amish practice of shunning. Interactive silence can promote interpersonal closeness, promote interpersonal distance, or even be a form of interpersonal attack.[112] Silence is a way of both expressing and receiving intense emotion: It is a way of expressing affective states (such as great grief or sorrow) where words seem feeble or hard to come by, and it is a way of receiving another individual's expression of intense emotion when such an expression comes unexpectedly.

Sociocultural silence refers to "the characteristic manner in which entire social and cultural orders refrain from speech and manipulate both psycholinguistic and interactive silence."[113] Indeed, sociocultural silences might well define and set forth the cultural patterns of communications much more clearly and forcefully than do the verbal behaviors of a culture or a society. It would appear that Western culture is characteristically noisy with sounds and speech, while Eastern culture tends to prize silence, with both general and lengthy silences not uncommon.[114] Thomas Bruneau contends that silence is an age-old device used by Christian ecclesiastical leaders to promote or force respectful acceptance of orthodox doctrine as the current ecclesiastical leadership interprets and enforces this doctrine.[115]

There appears to be a rather high positive correlation between silence and affectivity, even in the Western world. Christian mystics down through the centuries frequently report that their greatest moments of love for and in God occurred during peak experiences in which they were silent and outwardly passive. On the basis of his career of practicing psychotherapy with Christian patients, Morton Trippe Kelsey writes that deeply disturbing emotions often arise in periods of silence. These emotions, which are difficult to control, "can range from vague apprehension to terror and panic, or they may vary from bitterness and indignation to aggressive hatred and rage."[116] On the basis of his analysis of silence and speech, Bruneau concludes that "moments of high sensation, whether pleasant or unpleasant, seem almost to demand silence and absence of cognitive control."[117]

Religious counselors and psychotherapists seem to be far more aware of the communicative nature, function, and effects of silence than are religion teachers. Indeed, religion teachers seem to fear silence in the lesson. They apparently believe that in moments or times of silence, nothing is taking place—nothing of value or of learning anyway. This erroneous view is probably a result of the false conception that teaching is conducted primarily if not exclusively in the verbal mode.[118] Actually, there are a great number of pedagogical and psychological benefits of productive silence.[119]

Silence cannot be taught by simply having the teacher discuss silence verbally, or by assigning readings on silence, or by requiring the learners to take paper-and-pencil examinations on silence. Silence can only be effectively utilized in the religious education lesson by structuring the pedagogical situation in such a way that the learners can be silent in a productive, fulfilling manner. Ways in which the religious

educator can utilize silence for productive purporses include structuring times for silence depending on the shape and contour of the here-
and-how pedagogical dynamic, positioning the external features of the
instructional environment in such a way as to facilitate productive
silence, preparing that kind of affectively oriented teaching milieu
which tends to promote silence, use of silence-evoking stimuli such as
music, refraining from a great deal of teacher-talk, and the like.

Facial Expressions

Many social scientists would probably agree with Michael Argyle's
statement that the face constitutes the most important area of nonverbal
communication.[120] Many factors account for the importance of the
face in nonverbal communication. Facial expression represents one of
the most visible of all nonverbal communicators of affect. The face
generally is the area of the body which is most closely observed during
interpersonal interaction. An individual's reactions to another's behavior are often reflected in facial expression.

Studies conducted by Albert Mehrabian conclude that "the combined effect of simultaneous verbal, vocal, and facial attitude communications is a weighted sum of their independent effects—with the
coefficients of .07, .38, and .55 respectively."[121] These studies give
some inkling of the importance of facial expressions in the galaxy of
nonverbal communication. The face is one of the richest personal
zones for exhibiting the entire spectrum of human affects and reactions, a fact capitalized upon by mimes and movie actors.

Why is it that the human face provides such a relatively telling
display of personal reactions and affect? Social scientists often point to
the physiology of the face as a major factor in this regard. The face is
the site for the sense receptors of sight, hearing, smell, and taste.
Furthermore, the face contains the intake organs for food, water, and
air. It is also the output location for speech. In short, then, the face is
the location for many of the essential and most important human functions: sensory receptors, life-necessity intake, and verbal communication output. The autonomic nervous system has a particularly ready
outlet in the face, as for example in blushing, blanching, weeping, and
pupil dilation/contraction. Because autonomic activities are involuntary, the face is a revealing site for personal reactions and affect
display.[122]

For religious educators, doubtless the most significant issue with regard to facial expression is this: "What do various facial expressions *mean?* What can I tell about the learner from the facial expressions which that individual uses?" The professionally aware religious educator also wants to know: "What is it that I communicate to the learner when I use one or another facial expression?" The issue of the meaning of facial expressions is important for religious educators because to a certain extent facial expressions disclose the quality, texture, and changes in interpersonal relationships. The facial expressions used by teacher and learner are, in part, a function or at least a concomitant of the interactive behavior taking place in the pedagogical dynamic. Facial activity is especially sensitive to the nuances and intricacies of human interaction and the degree to which people are getting along.[123]

It is also well worth noting that certain social settings and environments have rules governing the "correct" facial expressions to be used. Though these rules are seldom written down, nevertheless they exert a significant regulatory force over the participant's facial expressions. A liturgical service is one example of a structured social environment in which hidden rules governing facial expression are operative.[124] These rules are typically organized along two axes, namely type and stage. The type of liturgical service itself prescribes rules for "correct" facial expression. For example, a person's face ought to express cheerfulness during weddings, sadness during funerals, and attentiveness during the minister's regular Sunday sermon. There is also a hidden set of rules governing the "correct" facial expression to be used during successive stages of the liturgical ritual. In the Catholic Mass, for example, the facial expression of the members of the congregation should reflect joyful expectancy during the entrance procession, contrition during the confession of sins, receptive attentiveness during the scripture readings, agreement during the sermon, generosity during the collection or free-will offering, adoration during the consecration, sharing during the kiss of peace, fulfillment during communion, thanksgiving during the prayers after communion, and successful celebration at the end of the service. If any member of the congregation (and also the presiding minister) deviates from the hidden set of rules, he will usually be regarded by the rest of the worshipers as being out of joint with the liturgical service and indeed disrespectful to the Mass and to God—as for example, a happy facial expression during the confession of sins and a bored facial expression during the sermon.

The face is a multicontent system. By this I mean that the face conveys expressions from which many kinds of physiological and psychological information can be inferred, including age, race, sex, attitudes, emotion, overall personality, character, attractiveness, intelligence, and so forth. [125]

Paul Ekman's careful research on the face has led him to identify eight different styles of the facial expression of affect. These eight styles are: revealing, withholding, unwitting expressive, blanked expressive, substitute expressive, frozen-affect expressive, ever-ready expressive, and flooded-affect expressive. These styles are by no means exclusive of one another. Typically any given facial expression includes one or more of the other styles, such as, for example, revelaing, unwitting, ever-ready, and flooded-affect. [126]

The research suggests that facial expressions which manifest two or more simultaneously occurring affects tend to occur with greater frequency than facial expressions exhibiting only a single affect. [127] Specific attitudes, emotions, values, and other affects are experienced not only singly, but more often than not in conjunction with one another. There are facial-expression blends just as there are general affect blends. [128] As I observed earlier in this section, the face is a multicontent message system capable of simultaneously expressing a variety of physiological and psychological states.

The important issue, "What do various facial expressions mean?" is necessarily linked to the question of the accuracy by which single or multiple facial expressions can be judged. In this connection it is vital to bear in mind the distinction between intention to communicate and the actual communication itself. A person may or may not intend to communicate that which his facial expressions actually do communicate.

Can the religious educator make relatively accurate judgments about the meaning of the learner's facial expressions? The research evidence suggests a "yes" to this question. One careful analysis of the experiments conducted from the 1920s onward concludes that there is "consistent and conclusive evidence that accurate judgments of facial expression can be made." [129] Indeed, accurate judgments of meaning can be made both with spontaneous facial expressions and with deliberate facial expressions which people employ intentionally to convey a particular affect.

The key to accurately gauging the affective dimensions of an individual's facial expressions is to carefully attend to the particularities of the other person's behavior. Behavioral interaction is the fundamental characteristic of the religious instruction dynamic. Thus if the religious educator wishes to improve the quality of his teaching, he must continually keep the focus of his attention on specific learner behaviors— what these behaviors are, and how these behaviors specifically flow and ebb during the process of ongoing interaction with the teacher, with the subject-matter content, and with the environment. The available empirical research suggests that by carefully attending to the behavioral components of the learner's facial expressions, the religious educator can significantly heighten his chances of drawing correct inferences about the current affective state of the learner. Two studies have suggested that fear can be best seen in the eyes/eyelids, disgust in the cheeks/mouth, anger from both cheeks/mouth and brows/forehead, happiness in both cheeks/mouth and eyes/eyelids, sadness in both brows/forehead and eyes/eyelids, and surprise with equal accuracy in any of the three major facial areas (brows/forehead, eyes/eyelids, and cheeks/mouth).[130] In what is probably one of the most massive and thoroughgoing studies on facial behavior, Ekman and Friesen found that the face expresses several affects which can be classified as primary affects. These primary affects include surprise, fear, disgust, anger, happiness, and sadness. Each of these primary affects is expressed in a different combination of facial expression. For example, surprise is typically manifested by raised curved eyebrows, long horizontal forehead wrinkles, wide-opened eyes, signs of skin stretched above the eyelids, a dropped-open mouth, little or no stretch or tension in the corners of the lips but the lips parted, and opening of the mouth in varying degrees.[131]

The empirical research suggests that just as individuals vary markedly in their ability to nonverbally express their own affective states in a manner in which these expressions will be correctly recognized,[132] so also do they differ in their capacity to recognize accurately the nonverbal expressions of other individuals.

Social scientists have devised instruments to enable persons to accurately judge the meaning of facial expressions. Dale Leathers has developed the Facial Meaning Sensitivity Test (FMST), an instrument which contains many series of photographs of different facial expressions. This instrument postulates ten classes of meaning.[133] Albert Mehrabian has put together a scoring criterion scale for assessing three major categories of facial expression, namely pleasantness, activity, and dominance.[134] Probably the most sophisticated instrument is the Facial Affect Scoring Test (FAST) devised by Paul Ekman and his associates. In using FAST, the observer decides which one of the three basic facial areas is to be examined: the forehead/brows, the lids/eyes, and the lower face. After one of these facial areas is isolated for intensive study and examination, the observer goes through two separate steps, namely location and classification.[135] The Ekman and Friesen model has been used successfully to train persons to accurately identify various affects expressed in the face.[136]

Both empirical research and fruitful theory suggest some guidelines to assist the religion teacher in translating a set of facial wrinkles or muscle movements into an accurate judgment about the affective state of another individual. *First,* center attention on specific facial *behaviors.* Judgments are inferences from behavior. If facial behaviors are not carefully observed, then the judgments made about the meanings of these behaviors will quite likely be false or inaccurate. *Second,* watch and observe the face with *great care.* Some of the most revealing facial expressions are those which are micromomentary or which occur in rapid succession. Such fast-moving expressions are likely to be overlooked unless the observer is watching the face with great care. *Third,* concentrate on the learner's facial *expressions.* Every individual uses communication barrage—verbal, facial, gestural, postural, and so forth. Unless the religious educator focuses on the learner's expression, it is likely that he will be thrown off the track when attempting to judge accurately the meaning of facial behavior. *Fourth,* attend to the specific kind of *signal* the learner's face is displaying. Rapid signals often encode different or more nuanced messages than do slow signals.[137] *Fifth,* work at successfully teasing apart the *proper referent* of a particular facial behavior or set of behaviors. There are facial expressions which point to realities or to referents other than affects. In successfully teasing out the proper referent of facial expression, it is helpful to note that various facial areas ''probably differ in terms of the ratio of nonaffective movements to affect-specific components which can occur. The brows/forehead probably have a smaller number of nonaffective movements and also of affect-specific components than the lower face.''[138] *Sixth,* situate the learner's facial behavior in the *contextual framework* of the entire repertoire of his other simultaneously occurring nonverbal behaviors. *Seventh,* be sensitive to the *cultural configuration* in which any facial expression is enacted. The religion teacher runs the constant risk of interpreting the learner's facial expression in terms of its meaning in his (the teacher's) own cultural background. While crosscultural studies do indeed suggest that certain facial (and other nonverbal) displays seem to be universally understood across cultures, nonetheless these and other investigations also show that there is a great deal of dissimilarity in the way people of various cultures and subcultures facially express themselves.[139] *Eighth,* be on the lookout for possible *facial deceit.* Because the face generally is, and also is perceived to be, the most proficient and revelatory of all nonverbal communicators, it is for this reason probably the most effective nonverbal liar, capable not only of withholding information but of simulating or otherwise faking the facial behavior associated with an affective state which the person is in no way experiencing.[140]

The empirical research evidence suggests that there are at least three major procedures which persons employ in order to control and manage their facial expressions: qualifying, modulating, and falsifying.[141] *Qualifying* a facial expression is accomplished by adding a further expression as a comment or addendum on the expression just displayed. The most frequently used qualifier is the smile added as a comment to any expression of negative affect. The smile qualifier provides a nonverbal hint about the probable limits or consequences of the negative affect. *Modulating* a facial expression is accomplished through adjusting the intensity of the original expression to show either more or less than what is actually felt or experienced. A modulating expression, then, acts either as an intensifier or a deintensifier. There are three primary ways in which facial expression can be modulated: variation in the number of the facial areas involved in the original expression, variation in the duration of the original expression, or variation in the excursion of the facial muscles. If, for example, a person wishes to deintensify his facial expression of fear, he typically does one or more of the following: attempt to eliminate fear from either the mouth area or from the eyes; try to shorten the duration of the fear expression; endeavor to stretch the mouth less and avoid lifting or drawing together the brow. *Falsifying* a facial expression is accomplished in one of three ways, namely simulating, neutralizing, and masking. *Simulating* a facial expression is accomplished by displaying an affect when in fact this affect is not being experienced. Successful simulation necessitates being sensitive to what particular affects actually feel like on the face, and then being able to voluntarily control the face in such a way that it accurately expresses the desired affect. *Neutralizing* a facial expression is accomplished by showing nothing on the face when in fact a particular affect is being personally experienced. Neutralizing, then, is the opposite of simulating. It represents the extreme of deintensifying. In endeavoring to neutralize one's affects, one attempts to engage in some or all of the following: keep the facial muscles relaxed and inhibit muscular contractions; freeze the facial muscles into a poker-face pattern; set the jaw; tighten the lips without pressing them; stare but avoid tensing the eyelids; camouflage the face by employing distracting behaviors of a neutral sort such as wiping the eyes, rubbbing the face, and so forth. *Masking* a facial expression is accomplished by simulating an affect which is not experienced in order to cover or conceal another affect which is being felt. The smile is most often used to mask one's true affective state, particularly if this state is a negative one. There is a physiological basis for using the smile as a masking behavior. After all, the muscular movements involved in smiling are most different from the muscular movements which express the negative affect. Thus the smile best conceals the appearance in the lower face of anger, fear, disgust, and sadness.

Thus far in this section I have been treating of facial behavior and facial expression in general. In the remaining portion, I will deal with specific facial manifestations.

Blushing. The psychological and pedagogical significance of blushing lies not simply in the fact that this kind of facial reddening graphically expresses inner affect and reactions, but also in the fact that blushing is an involuntary behavior. Blushing usually cannot be prevented or controlled. It occurs quite rapidly. Because of its involuntary and quick-fire character, blushing tends to leak important data about how an individual is feeling and otherwise reacting. Blushing therefore carries with it a greater degree of truth value than many other specific forms of facial expression. The affective referent of facial behavior will vary in some measure from person to person. In general, however, blushing appears to indicate embarrassment,[142] anxiety, and discomfort.[143]

Eyebrows. Movements of the brow are indicative of internal affective states and other psychological reactions. The biological and physiological bases underlying the meaningfulness of eyebrow movement can be seen, at least rudimentarily, in the fact that both human beings and some of the higher primates typically raise their eyebrows in surprise and fear, and lower their eyebrows in moments of anger and threat.[144] Irenäus Eibl-Eibesfeldt's extensive research has found that eyebrow-flash appears to be universal throughout the world as an indication of friendly greeting.[145] When greeting a friend, people tend to quickly and maximally raise their eyebrows, holding them in this position for about one-sixth of a second. Because of the impact of culture display rules, the particular way in which the eyebrow-flash is employed in the act of friendly greeting varies from culture to culture. Besides their use in greeting and in flirting, eyebrow-flashes are also used in approving (a nonverbal equivalent of the verbal "yes"), in seeking (a nonverbal way of asking), in confirming, in thanking, and in emphasizing a statement (calling for attention). Eibl-Eibesfeldt contends that the common denominator in all these is a "yes" to social contact. Hence the eyebrow-flash is used either in requesting this kind of contact or in approving a request for contact.

Eyebrow movements are important to the religious educator for two major reasons. First, any sort of movement in the eyebrow indicates that a change of one kind or another is taking place during the course of social interaction.[146] A second major reason why the religion teacher should carefully observe the ongoing positioning and repositioning of the learner's eyebrows is that this very positioning and repositioning provide clues on the learner's inner affective state at the moment.[147] Surprise is probably an affect which people generally correlate with raised eyebrows.[148]

Looking. If visual behavior does not rank as the most important of all facial behaviors, then certainly it can be counted as one of the most important. In terms of duration, there are two principal types of looking: glance (short duration), and gaze (longer duration). Glance and gaze can be either active or interactive. Active glance and gaze consist simply in looking at other persons or objects. Interactive glance or gaze, sometimes called eye contact by psychologists and educators, consists in people looking into each other's eyes. Visual behavior is used to receive information about other persons or objects, to send information about oneself, and to regulate the behavior of others.[149]

As with other nonverbal behaviors, looking has a biological base in the lower animals as well as in human beings. Visual behavior, particularly gaze, is often used or reacted to as a threat signal in much of the animal kingdom.[150]

The use and pattern of gaze are not only determined by innate physiological processes such as those governing pupillary dilation, but also are acquired as a result of the influences of the specific culture or subculture in which a child is raised. Empirical research suggests that gaze usage is significantly affected by an infant's early interaction and other socialization experiences with its mother during the first year of life.[151] Later learning is affected by cultural rules and traditions both about the proper use of gaze and the meanings of particular kinds of gaze. Arabs, Southern Europeans, and Latin Americans tend to look into each other's eyes more than do Asians, Northern Europeans, and Indians-Pakistanis. The research evidence further suggests that gaze patterns learned from the family and the culture during childhood remain relatively fixed throughout life and thus are only slightly modified by later experience.[152] Cultural and societal rules tend to circumscribe and at times even prescribe the way in which one person may legitimately gaze at another individual.[153]

A common use of gaze and glance is to obtain information about other people, events, and external reality in general. On the basis of the information a person receives as a result of glancing or gazing, he is in a position to make the necessary adjustments in his own behavior so as to achieve that which he is seeking to achieve.[154]

Visual behavior is also used for regulatory purposes. Looking at another individual regulates interpersonal communication in that it signals a willingness to enter into a relationship, while looking back in return indicates the readiness of the other to enter into the relationship as well. Continued plentiful eye contact shows a willingness to prolong the communicatory relationship. Breaking eye contact, when coupled with an unpleasant facial expression, serves to indicate rejection or disapproval of the other person.[155]

Some individuals seem to control their gaze patterns for psychologically defensive reasons, such as a fear of being rejected by the other person, anxiety about social intimacy, concealment, and fear of exposure.[156] Sexual repression, as well as fear of sexual arousal, also appear to motivate people to control their visual behavior.[157]

The stare is a form of gaze which has a variety of purposes. Staring can be used to express hatred. Political and racial oppressors often use the hate stare on whom they exercise power. The hate stare is insulting partly because it conveys the implication to the person being stared at that the latter has little or no worth as a human being.[158] But staring can also be a sign or manifestation of love. On the matter of the lover's stare,

Harvey Sarles states that by staring into each other's eyes, the lovers are perhaps busy "transfiguring each other's bodies, and the eyes diminish in interactional importance. It may also be that the dilation of female eyes during courting has to do with a 'willingness' to relax some of the eye focus movements."[159] Then there is the blank stare, which often indicates boredom and the clear impression of: "I'm looking at you but not listening."[160] A blank stare is sometimes associated with mental deficiency. There is also a kind of staring into space which characterizes artists, intellectuals, and scientists during moments of deep thought or creative intuition. Staring may also convey hostility and interpersonal conflict.[161] The "eyeball-to-eyeball" confrontation, the mutual glare, is an example of the conflict stare. In situations of this sort, each starer assiduously attempts to avoid losing eye contact with the other, since such a behavior tends to signal defeat or fear on the part of the person who breaks the stare.[162] There seems to be a positive correlation between winning a staring contest and dominance.[163] A stare can also indicate aggression. There is some research evidence suggesting that aggressive people tend to stare more than nonaggressive persons.[164] Probably the stare is used more for controlling, regulating, and dominating purposes than for any other reason or set of reasons. A person being stared at tends to perceive the starer, on account of the staring itself, to be more dominant and potent than he.[165] In terms of a person's actual conduct being modified as a result of staring, one experimental study found that motorcyclists who stared at motorists when both were waiting at a red stoplight seemed to cause the motorists to accelerate their vehicles with especial rapidity once the signal had turned green.[166]

Blinking the eyes is another visual behavior which can provide clues about an individual's internal states, especially that person's affective states. The research indicates that there is a positive correlation between the rate of eye-blink and the level of a person's affective excitation and arousal.[167] Frequent blinking appears to be tied in with self confidence: The more confident a person is, the less that individual tends to blink.[168] Frequent blinking can also be part of a fear reaction. When an elevated frequency of blinking occurs during normal conversation, it may suggest weakness and submissiveness.[169] Blink-rate has been found to correlate with both manifest anxiety and neuroticism.[170]

There is abundant research evidence which indicates that liking is positively correlated with looking in general and with gaze in particular. (Liking is described in terms of interpersonal attraction.) A study by Jay Efran and Andrew Broughton found that an individual tends to look more at a friendly, familiar person than one who is a stranger.[171] An investigation by Adam Kendon and Mark Cook discovered that persons engaged in friendly, dyadic conversations evaluated their partners more positively the longer these partners gazed at them.[172]

Sex differences in visual behavior are pronounced. One summary of the research puts the matter succinctly: "Females look more than males on all measures of gaze."[173] In dyadic interactions, females gaze at their partners more than do males.[174] Females also engage in more eye contact while speaking,[175] while listening,[176] and during silences.[177] The same results seem also to hold true in groups larger than two persons.[178] Two major explanations have been offered for the greater incidence of gaze on the part of females. Neither interpretation is necessarily exclusive of the other. The first explanation is based on the research finding that females have greater affiliative needs than men, and appear to regard gaze as an affiliation signal.[179] The second explanation for the greater incidence of female looking is linked to the nature and workings of the sexual function itself. Sexual attraction leads to both gaze and pupil dilation as a result of the stimulation of the autonomic nervous system.[180] To be sure, female eyes do dilate during courting.[181] It is well known that consciously or unconsciously, females typically tend to be more existentially congruent with their sexual functions than are males. Because of the sexual overtones involved in gazing, it is hardly surprising that females attach more value to gaze and, in fact, do gaze more.

Mouth. An important area of nonverbal behavior is the mouth, including, of course, the lips. In their carefully conducted research investigations, Ekman and Friesen found a correlation between human mouth movements and affective states. These findings frequently bore a resemblance to mouth behaviors of other mammals. When a person is experiencing happiness, the mouth typically breaks into a smile; the lips can be open or closed, depending on the type and intensity of the happiness being felt. In moments of sadness, the lips are usually (but not always) loose, and the corners of the mouth are generally turned downward. In fearful moments, the mouth opens, while the lips tense up and may be drawn back tightly.[182]

The mouth is a difficult facial area for a person to control completely and effectively. The mouth typically moves, trembles, and even contorts when certain affects and reactions are being experienced. Individuals who are aware of their own nonverbal behavior tend to be cognizant of this fact. One frequently used strategy to mask the expression of emotion occurring in the mouth area is the smile.

Smile. Smiling is generally regarded as an active display of a positive attitude, of enjoyment, and of a certain tranquility.[183] The research also indicates that smiling seems to be associated with personal or interpersonal affinity, more so than laughing. Laughing, on the other hand, appears to be more closely associated with playfulness than does smiling.[184] Smiling also seems to be a manifestation of affiliative behavior. People frequently use and interpret a smile as a form of interpersonal affiliation.[185] Persons whose dependency needs are higher than normal tend to respond more to smiles than do persons with normal or little dependency needs.[186] Smiling seems to be related to social status. One study found that children low in peer social status or power tend to smile more when initiating an interaction with high-ranking children than do high-rankers when initiating interactions with those who rank low in social status or power. Smiling in response to smiles, however, tends to be more common in those children enjoying high peer social status or power.[187] It is quite possible that smiling is an important function of interpersonal intimacy.[188] Along this general line, the research strongly suggests that smiling enjoys a high positive correlation with liking. People tend to smile more at and with persons they like. Smiling also tends to convey warmth and a positive attitude.[189]

Smiling is frequently used as a signal. Smiling can serve as a signal for positive reinforcement. It can indicate to another person that he and/or his behavior is accepted.[190] A smile can signal reassurance. It can act as a breaker of barriers or of distance at a social gathering. It can help relieve another's discomfort in an awkward social situation. It can relieve tension and even placate another individual. Smiling makes communication more efficient by providing the communicator with feedback on a number of levels simultaneously.[191]

Tongue. The tongue is a form of nonverbal behavior which can be considered separately from its more obvious role in verbal activity. Tongue-showing can consist of a single brief flick in and out, or the tongue can be kept visible for a few seconds or even minutes. Investigators report that tongue-showing in one form or another seems to be universally employed in all cultures and age-groups.[192] One researcher suggests that "the tongue is actively tracking during interaction and might contribute to or be part of the mentation process."[193] Activity of the tongue seems to be intimately associated with affective and psychomotor activities. For example, a dry tongue often accompanies states of anxiety, fear, and nervousness. Intracultural and crosscultural studies have discovered a variety of uses to which tongue-showing is put. John Smith and his colleagues have found tongue-showing to sometimes take place involuntarily or at least without too much awareness during tasks which require concentration because they are difficult (such as threading a needle or working out a complex problem), or risky (such as physical balancing or other precarious activities), or both. These tasks may be enjoyable or unpleasant, but they are usually not more than moderately distressing. Smith and his colleagues interpret most forms of human tongue-showing as probably "evidencing some form of rejection behavior, with respect to any social interaction or to particular aspects of interaction."[194] Henry Seaford contends that while tongue-showing is often a rejection signal, nonetheless tongue-showing is also used for many nonrejection displays such as manifesting positive states of friendliness, liking, and sexual interest.[195] Irenäus Eibl-Eibesfeldt's crosscultural data lend support to Seaford.[196]

Kinesic Behavior

Kinesic behavior is the term which many specialists in nonverbal communication use in referring to body activity. The branch of social science which studies body activity as a form of nonverbal communication is generally referred to as kinesics.

Kinesicists generally consider any bodily activity to fall under their purview. But for pedagogical reasons, I have decided that in this chapter I would treat separately certain bodily activities normally associated with kinesics, such as the face and posture.

For the most part, theoretical formulations and empirical research on kinesics have proceeded along two main lines, namely the anthropological-linguistic line and the psychological-sociological line. Both lines seek to understand what is intrinsic in body movement, and also how body movement as a whole and in its parts operates as a communication process.[197] The anthropological-linguistic line tends to examine kinesic behavior from the standpoint of structure, while the psychological-sociological line typically investigates kinesic behavior experimentally from the perspective of personal dynamics and interpersonal interaction.

The anthropological-linguistic approach to kinesics is well represented by Ray Birdwhistell. It is Birdwhistell who is generally considered to be the founder of kinesics, and it is he who originally gave the name "kinesics" to the scientific study of body movement as a form of human communicatory behavior. In Birdwhistell's view, kinesic behavior functions in a manner analogous to linguistic behavior. Thus kinesics, like linguistics, has its own unique structure and grammar. Kinesic behavior represents an internally structured and systematically ordered form of a discrete communication system. There are, then, separate and distinct channels of communication. In actually communicating with another person, an individual might use several of these channels simultaneously. Verbal behavior and kinesic behavior represent two of the major channels. "Communication is a multichannel system emergent from, and regulative of, the influenceable multisensory activity of living systems. The spoken and body motion languages thus are infracommunicational systems that are interdependently merged with each other and with comparable codes that utilize other channels; they are operationally communicative."[198] As verbal behavior is a combination of linguistic building blocks, so also is kinesic behavior a combination of body-movement building blocks. A phoneme in verbal language corresponds to a kineme in body language. A kineme cannot stand alone, any more than a phoneme can. In order for a kineme to become communicatively meaningful, it must be situated in one or another context. To adequately analyze body movement, Birdwhistell has developed an elaborate kinesic notation system. This system classifies the body into seven basic categories: (1) total head; (2) face; (3) trunk and shoulders; (4) wrist, arm, and shoulder; (5) hand and fingers; (6) hip, upper leg, lower leg, and ankle; (7) feet.[199]

The psychological-sociological approach to kinesics is the one held by the majority of researchers in nonverbal behavior. This approach regards kinesic behavior, not as having its own special set of internal linguistic-type rules, but rather as being bodily expressions of internal states. Kinesics, then, does not take its shape and structure from any set of rules somehow inherent in body movement; it takes its shape and structure from the functioning of internal psychological and physiological states as these states manifest themselves bodily in an existential context of interaction with one's immediate environment (including persons, objects, and space). It is this natural, organic connection of kinesic behavior with one's internal states in dynamic environmental action which gives nonverbal behavior its force and authenticity.

Different parts of the body act as modes of nonverbal communication in different ways. Kinesic behavior appears to be one of the primary modes, along with paralanguage, facial expression, gaze, bodily contact, proxemic behavior, and personal appearance. Each communication mode qua communication mode seems to operate in a somewhat distinctive manner. Also, one area of the body may be used simultaneously by two or more of the primary communication modes.[200]

Bodily gestures and other kinds of kinesic behavior play a prominent and often essential role in religious rituals and activities. In several Roman Catholic sacraments, the appropriate and prescribed kinesic behavior of the confector is considered as an essential part of the sacrament itself, and therefore indispensable for its validity. In Confirmation, for example, the anointing of the comfirmand with chrism—a kinesic behavior on the part of the confector—is essential for validity. In Holy Orders, the imposition of hands on the ordinand by the bishop is essential for validity.[201]

For religious educators, the issue of the meaning of kinesic behavior assumes paramount importance. What does kinesic behavior mean? What can the religious educator find out about learners from the kinesic movements they use? What can learners discover about the teacher from the kinesic behaviors he uses? Two basic pivot points of the entire issue of kinesic meaning are germane here, namely the overall relationship of one's gestures to one's personality, and the specific relationship of one's kinesic behaviors to certain patterns of response.

While it is indeed possible that particular kinesic movements do correlate with basic overall personality characteristics, still the available empirical research suggests that linking certain kinesic behaviors to particular affective states appears to be more reliable and more valid than a judgment about the relationship between a given kinesic movement and a molar personality characteristic.

The empirical evidence suggests that affect is reflected in kinesic movements.[202] The research further suggests that there seem to be at least five conclusions which can be validly drawn concerning the relationship of kinesic behavior and affect.[203] *First,* the face carries information about the identity of the particular affect being experienced (disgust, for example), while kinesic cues issuing from parts of the body other than the face communicate information chiefly about the intensity of the affect being experienced. *Second,* kinesic acts carry and communicate different types of affect than do kinesic positions. (Kinesic acts are body movements of some duration, while kinesic positions are nonmoving body sets or postures of some duration.) Kinesic acts, like facial expressions, communicate specific affects, while kinesic positions (including head orientations) usually communicate a very global affective state such as pleasantness or unpleasantness. *Third,* kinesic acts are capable of displaying only a limited range of affect intensity (moderate to high), while kinesic positions can display the full range of affect intensity. *Fourth,* kinesic behaviors which express a person's emotions consist by and large of self-touching, while kinesic behaviors which reveal one's attitudes toward others involve touching the bodies of others or of making bodily movements in the direction of the other person's body. *Fifth,* kinesic acts which are directed toward oneself merely serve to release physiological or psychological tension, while kinesic movements oriented toward objects and linked with speech generally are intended as acts of communication.

A number of studies have found correlations of one degree or another between certain kinesic behaviors and particular affects. Paul Ekman and Wallace Friesen found that face-touching movements frequently take place in experiencing shame or other negative affects about oneself. For example, a person tends to cover the eyes when experiencing shame.[204] An attitude of rejection is often shown by crossed arms or legs, tilting the head forward, touching or rubbing the nose, rubbing the eye, or scratching behind the ear. Readiness is frequently displayed by hands on hips while standing, hands on knees while seated, sitting on the edge of the chair, or moving forward to speak confidently. Cooperation is many times exhibited by sitting on the edge of the chair, leaning forward while seated, putting the hand to the face, unbuttoning the jacket or top of the shirt, or tilting the head. Acceptance is often shown by placing the hand to the chest, touching, or moving closer.[205]

Gesture. A gesture can range all the way from a simple flick of the finger to a complex kinesic movement involving the hands, arms, head, and posture. Most gestures involve the use of the hand in one way or another.

In terms of its direct relation to speech, a gesture can either substitute for speech or accompany it. Using the highly important and frequently used Ekman-Friesen classification of nonverbal behaviors treated near the beginning of this chapter, a gesture which accompanies speech and is directly conjoined with it is called an illustrator, while one which substitutes for it is called an emblem. It will be recalled that six kinds of illustrators were identified: (1) a baton, namely, a gesture which accents or emphasizes a particular word or phrase; (2) an ideograph, namely, a gesture which sketches a path or direction of thought; (3) a deictic activity, namely, a gesture which points to a here-and-now present object; (4) a spatial activity, namely, a gesture which depicts a spatial relationship of one kind or another; (5) a kinetograph, namely, a gesture which portrays bodily action; (6) a pictograph, namely, a gesture which draws a picture of bodily action. An illustrator, then, illustrates gesturally what is being uttered linguistically or paralinguistically.

Jurgen Ruesch and Weldon Keys state that when used in conjunction with speech, gestures are used to illustrate, emphasize, point, explain, or interrupt what is being said verbally. When gestures are used to accompany speech, it is not always easy to isolate gesture from verbal content in terms of meaning. To understand spoken contents, it is often necessary to heed both the verbal and the gestural contents.[206]

Gestures are also used in conjunction with paralanguage. For example, three important types of intonation appear to have corresponding gestures as accompaniments. These three are: (1) rising intonation, indicating a question; (2) falling intonation, indicating completion; (3) level intonation, indicating that the speaker intends to continue. For example, at the end of a sentence or train of thought, the speaker frequently lowers both his intonation and his head.[207] One carefully conducted study revealed that the head, hands, and feet produce movements directly related to paralanguage, the hands and feet conforming more closely than the head.[208]

A gesture is typically culture-bound since it is a learned rather than an innate behavior.[209] A particular culture, then, assigns or recognizes a certain gesture as associated with a consensually agreed-upon meaning. Some gestures admit of a direct verbal translation, such as the upward or downward circular gesture of the index finger signifying the words "spiral staircase." Other gestures used and understood throughout a culture may have a meaning not readily or even possibly translatable directly into a verbal equivalent, such as shaking hands, gestural dancing, and certain gestures used in rituals.[210] The Christian religion employs a wide variety of special gestures, such as the sign of the cross for blessing and palms together for praying.

Partly because religious instruction is deliberatively targeted toward effectively bringing the learner into the world of God's fellowship, there is a strong element of direct and indirect persuasion throughout much of religion teaching. (Persuasion, of course, is quite different from coercion.) The teacher, the subject-matter content, and the instructional environment all serve as educational forces of persuasion designed to help the learner become convinced about why and how he should live in God's blessed fellowship. No matter how high-keyed or low-keyed are the religious educator's efforts at persuasion, it is quite likely that he will consciously or unconsciously use gestures in his attempts to be persuasive. Howard Rosenfeld's frequently cited experimental investigations found that persons tend to use certain types of gestures when they seek to persuade others. For example, men and women attempting to be persuasive tend to use more gesticulations than individuals seeking not to be persuasive. Persons intending to be persuasive appear to increase the incidence of positive head nodding (up and down).[211] In short, people generally seem to agree that the amount and type of gesticulation is directly correlated to the effectiveness of persuasion efforts. Of interest in this connection is that Rosenfeld's data disclosed that gesticulations (and smiles) were less effective persuaders than people believe, and that positive head nods and gestural self-manipulations tend to be perceived as more effective persuasive devices than people normally imagine.[212]

From the all-important vantage point of theory, the question emerges: "Why do certain gestures enhance the persuasiveness of communication?" On the basis of the available research data, Albert Mehrabian offers two separate but complementary hypotheses. First, certain gestures tend to be persuasive because they convey to the other person the notion that he is liked. An individual who perceives that he is liked generally tends to be open to persuasive communication from the one whom he perceives has a liking for him. Second, certain gestures tend to be persuasive because they convey to the listener that the communicator is responsive to him. People need to be existentially heard and responded to. Hence a person who perceives that the communicator is responsive to him tends to become open to persuasive communication from the one whom he perceives is responding to him. Mehrabian suggests that from the interpersonal perspective, the communicator's gestures can be considered in a large sense to be measures of the communicator's response to the person with whom he is communicating. Put in terms of person-perception theory, gestures are persuasive or nonpersuasive largely because the individual perceives another's gestures directed at him as positive, negative, or neutral responses. Reviewing the pertinent research data, Mehrabian comments that "the strongest effects by far showed that a communicator's responsiveness to his listener was a monotonically increasing function of his intended persuasiveness, and that perceived persuasiveness was correlated with communicator responsiveness. The results . . . showed that a communicator's responsiveness was an even more important factor in his positiveness in a persuasive situation."[213]

Head Kinesics. Head kinesics, like most kinesic behaviors, are of two basic types, namely positions and acts. Head positions consist of keeping the head in a raised or lowered attitude, or of maintaining it in a frontal or sideways position. Head acts, often termed head movements, typically comprise nodding or shaking behaviors.

Summing up the pertinent research, Michael Argyle states that while head positions and head movements are highly visible, nonetheless the amount and range of information they can convey is limited.[214]

Of especial importance to the religion teacher is the response to the question: "What do head kinesics mean?" This question can only be adequately answered by addressing two separate but existentially related issues, namely (1) what is the meaning-capability of head kinesics in general, and (2) what is the situational context in which a specific head kinesic or set of head kinesics is enacted? Because of the relative recency of extensive social-scientific investigation into nonverbal behavior, there are not yet enough empirical data to confirm the various hypotheses made to explain or delimit the meaning-capability of head kinesics. Albert Mehrabian, for example, hypothesizes that in terms of affects, nonverbal communication (including head kinesics) possesses the capability of communicating meaning along three independent dimensions: like-dislike; potency or status (domination and control versus submission and dependence); responsiveness (awareness of and reaction to another).[215] Other social scientists like Paul Ekman and Wallace Friesen offer somewhat different hypotheses. The religion teacher, then, should know the major theoretical hypotheses, and use these as basic overall guides to the interpretation of the learner's head kinesics.[216] The religious educator should also seek the meaning of head kinesics within the overall existential context of the particular social and environmental situations in which these behaviors are taking place. Head kinesics are part of the coordinated pattern of human interaction and must be interpreted as such. For example, in terms of Mehrabian's hypothesis, a teacher's head nod might indicate responsiveness to a learner, it might indicate a liking for the learner, it might indicate a dominance over the learner, or all three. The overall interpersonal, interactional, and situational context tells the learner which one (or more) of these dimensions the teacher is communicating.

Head positions are of several kinds, including the turned head, the tilted head, the raised head, the lowered or bowed head, the erect head, and so forth.

The turned head occurs when the head has been moved sideways on a horizontal plane. The turned head takes place in order to see a stimulus which is not presently in one's line of vision, to attend to a third person, or to avoid the intensity of eye contact with the individual with whom one is interacting. In the first two cases, the turned head might indicate attention to or even liking of the other stimulus or other person. In the latter instance, the result is to cut off visual communication with the original interactor.[217]

The tilted head is one in which the head is slightly inclined from a vertical or horizontal plane. A tilted head can have quite a few rather different meanings. Females appear to be especially adept at using and interpreting the various functions and attitudes of the head tilt.[218]

The raised head occurs when a person elevates the head on a vertical plane. An experimental investigation by Michael Argyle and his associates found that when told to adopt a superior role, persons typically raise their heads and hold their heads in that position.[219]

The bowed head occurs when a person lowers the head on a vertical plane. A bowed head is frequently interpreted as action-receiving and not action-giving.[220] Depending on the extent to which the head is bowed, and depending on the gaze direction and other accompanying nonverbal behaviors, a bowed head is perceived as signaling subordination, insignificance, and humanity on the one hand, or withdrawal, self-concern, and receiving on the other hand. A bowed head can indicate withdrawal from interpersonal contact and, in certain circumstances, even disdain for this contact.[221]

The erect head is one which is straight and in proportional axis to the spine. An erect head of itself is often a weak nonverbal communicator, since it is the normal, regular physiological position of the head.

Head movements are important nonverbal behaviors. The head nod is used frequently by religious educators and learners. In terms of function, a head nod can serve as an indicator, a reinforcer, a regulator, and so forth. A positive attitude toward another person is conveyed by appropriate head nodding.[222] When one wishes to signal to another that one is attentively listening to that other person, a head nod will suffice.[223] Head nodding conveys a sense of increased liking for the person at whom the head nodding is directed.[224] Especially when used frequently, head nodding tends to communicate affiliation for the other person.[225] Indeed, a head nod, like a pat on the back, suggests approval of another person's behavior and/or the other person as a self.[226] Head nodding also exercises an important regulatory function in human interaction. When it is regulatory, the head nod operates as an attention signal at interactional junctures. The head nod plays an important role in what Michael Argyle terms "floor apportionment[227] because the nod gives the other person permission or approval to continue speaking.[228] The regulatory function of some kinds of head nodding is often related to dominance.[229] Irenäus Eibl-Eibesfeldt states that head nodding can be interpreted as ritualized submission. A person nods regularly during conversation as a signal of agreement and reassurance, thus communicating his submission to the ideas of the speaker.[230]

Arm and Hand Kinesics. Like other forms of nonverbal behavior, arm and hand kinesics can be classified as emblems, illustrators, regulators, affect displays, and adaptors. Arm and hand kinesics predominate among the various kinds of nonverbal emblems. But it is in their role as illustrators that arm and hand kinesics are most familiar to the average person. Indeed, when one thinks of arm and hand kinesics, one tends to think of their use as illustrators. How often we hear the expression, "He talks with his hands," or "If you tied her hands behind her back, she wouldn't be able to talk." Arm and hand kinesics are often used as emotive accompaniments of speech, as anyone who has observed people from Mediterranean regions is well aware. As regulators, arm and hand kinesics include such behaviors as using a pointed finger or outstretched hand to command a person to betake himself to a particular place, or an extended index finger to the mouth as a signal for silence. The clergy use arm and hand regulators during worship service. Arm and hand positions and movements without speech are widely used as affect displays.

Arm and hand kinesics tend to be culture-bound, except for those behaviors of the autistic kind.[231] Consequently, the religious educator must exercise due caution when attempting to ascertain the proper meaning of a learner's arm or hand movements and positions.

It is perhaps indicative of the naturalness and humanness of nonverbal behavior that a person can more easily and more quickly learn the correct meaning of the nonverbal behaviors of another culture than that individual can acquire the verbal language of that culture.[232]

Arm and hand kinesics, like other forms of nonverbal behavior, are used in and of themselves as well as in conjunction with speech. Three major types of arm positions can be identified: arms extended, arms down at side, and arms covering the body.

When an individual fully extends his arms, he is defining the outer limits of his personal space insofar as he can physically control this space.[233] Personal space as defined by fully extended arms or legs can be called radial space.[234] Radial space is one's own and is generally perceived as such. The familiar expression "keep him at arm's length" nicely encapsulates the point I am making about personal space and interpersonal distance. Depending on both the circumstances attendant upon arm-and-hand movement and the way in which the arms are extended (total or partial, straight or curved, rigid or flexible), extended arms may indicate initiation of an action or activity (in contrast to being on the receiving end), determination (in contrast to uncertainty), psychological strength (in contrast to psychological weakness), aggressiveness and assertiveness (in contrast to passivity and timidity), and even imperiousness (in contrast to humility).[235] At other times, extended arms, especially when partially extended and curved, may indicate an invitation to interaction, interpersonal attraction, liking, warmth, freedom from constraint or inhibition, eroticism, and immodesty.[236] Extended arms can also suggest a concern for other persons.

When a person's arms are down at his side, he is knowingly or unknowingly defining his personal space as open. Arms down at one's side signal open access, unless contradicted by other nonverbal positions and acts. Open access connotes interpersonal approachability, receptivity, and a willingness to authentically encounter other persons and events. The arms-down position contrasts in many respects to the arms-extended position. Depending upon circumstances and conditions, the arms-down position may indicate receipt of action (in contrast to initiation of action), passivity (in contrast to activity), lack of aggressiveness and of assertiveness, and even humility (in contrast to self-assuredness and arrogance). At other times, the arms-down position may indicate constraint or coldness. Or again, depending upon the situation and other concurrent nonverbal behaviors, the arms-down position may express naturalness, calmness, and relaxation.[237] An arm dangling between the legs, with the hand open, frequently signals frustration.[238]

Crossing one's arms on one's chest defines one's personal space as closed. This position of the arms denies the other person access to one's own personal or private space. Arms folded across the chest closes one individual off from the other, thereby nonverbally placing the other person in the position of an outsider or even, in some cases, of an opponent. When an individual covers his chest with his arms, he is blocking the approach to his body, so that his body is thereby signaling that kind of inner-directedness which tends to exclude openness or a free and total communication with the other.[239] Frequently an individual with arms crossed on the chest is perceived as a person hiding somewhere behind the arms, a person lodged within the barriers, a person taking refuge inside the walls of his limbs.

Hand positions can be of several different varieties, ranging from partially open to completely open. The open hand position, especially when the hands are slightly flexed and the palms face upward, is often associated with sincerity and openness.[240] Hands held in such a way that they are drooping tend to be correlated with weakness, submissiveness, and shyness. Hands with palms up and in a cupped position are often judged as passive and entreating.[241] The steepled hand position, in which the palms are open but are joined at the fingertips, frequently designates confidence—and sometimes even a smug, pontificational, egotistical, and proud attitude. The more important a person feels in a particular situation, the higher he tends to hold his hands while steepling. This hand kinesic is reputedly prevalent in superior-subordinate relationships. Clergymen, lawyers, academicians, and business executives seem to steeple their hands often.[242] Clasping one's hands together is a typical hand kinesic used by Christians while praying in a formal manner.[243]

Hand acts have been placed by one experimental investigation into four fundamental types based on the kind of dimensions they tend to elicit or suggest. Type I includes the dimensions of active-passive, sharp-dull, interesting-uninteresting, tense-sleepy, exciting-boring, curious-indifferent, and intentional-unintentional. Dimensions comprising Type II are pleasant-unpleasant, friendly-unfriendly, good-bad, and beautiful-ugly. Type III dimensions are dominant-submissive, strong-weak, armed-unarmed, certain-doubtful, brave-shy, and fast-slow. Among the dimensions in Type IV are controlled-uncontrolled, mature-immature, deliberate-compulsive, functional-superfluous.[244] There are many different kinds of hand movements; indeed, Paul Ekman and Wallace Friesen found thirty-four kinds of hand acts displayed by one person just in a single interview.[245] The hand-shrug rotation movement is frequently associated with expressions of uncertainty, confusion, defensiveness, helplessness, and inability to cope.[246] The hand-toss movement is often indicative of frustrated or exasperated anger.[247] The open-hand reach movement, in which the hand goes out palm up to the other person who is the directive partner in the interaction, sometimes suggests uncertainty and a call for assistance.[248]

Finger positions and movements are important kinesic behaviors which are woven into the fabric of culture, psychophysiological functioning, and interpersonal activities. Finger kinesics can be classified on the basis of physiology, psychology, and culture. Physiologically, a single finger may be extended lax, extended tense, hooked, curled, or closed. When several fingers are involved, combinations of these positions occur.[249] From the psychological viewpoint, the finger has both interpersonal and personal dimensions. As an interpersonal kinesic, the finger has many functions including regulation, referencing, reassurance, and reinforcement. The personal dimension of finger positions and acts is manyfold. Culturally, finger positions and movements have great communicative power and symbolic significance.[250] The finger is the point at which an individual's total personal energies are most intensely focused and under control as an individual physically encounters and joins the world outside the self.[251] In this sense the finger is an individual's prime gateway to physically greet the world outside the self and thus to shape that world, as well as to be physically greeted by the outside world and thus to be affected by it.

The finger has quite a few important functions other than those pertaining to psychomotor tasks. The finger exerts a regulatory function. It commands another person to turn his attention to something or someone. When a finger is used as a regulator, it is usually the index finger which is called upon to do the job. The finger can also serve in a referencing capacity, that is, to refer to objects or persons about whom one is speaking.[252] Various finger behaviors sometimes convey an individual's anxieties, inner conflicts, or apprehensions. In such instances, a child needing reassurance may suck his thumb, a teenager may bite his nails, an adult may pick at his cuticles until they are sore. At times, adolescents and adults bite or suck finger substitutes such as pens and pencils to gain self-reassurance.[253]

The hand has long been regarded as one of the most personalistically charged and humanistically oriented parts of the human body. A key ingredient in making and creating is the hand. A person's hands execute paintings and sculpture.[254] A person's hands play the piano and the violin. Some of the most fundamental human affects are expressed through the hands. Hence the religious educator would do well to use and interpret hand acts and positions with accuracy and sensitivity.

Leg and Foot Kinesics. There are many kinds of leg positions and leg movements. The major leg position clusters are erect leg (standing), bent leg (sitting, squatting, and kneeling), and prone leg (lying). Within each of these three major position clusters are somewhat specific leg positions. For example, in the sitting leg position, there is the crossed and the uncrossed, the fully and the partially extended, the touching and the nontouching of the legs or of some other object, and so forth. Leg movements are numerous, including running, walking, swinging, jerking, pulsating or trembling, rotating, and so forth. Each of these leg movements admits of many varieties. For example, walking behavior includes the bent knee walk, the straight knee walk, the bounce, the glide, the tip-toe, the high step, the foot drag, the shuffle, the duck walk, and the Indian walk.[255]

Foot positions and foot movements are many and varied. Important foot positions include foot pointing (straight, outwards, inwards), foot balancing (standing on toes, or on balls of foot, or on sides of foot, or on entire foot), and toe extension (full or partial). The foot admits of many kinds of movements both while standing and walking. Ray Birdwhistell identifies eight different kinds of foot movements which can take place while standing but not walking, such as the toe teeter (standing, rising on toes and flopping back on heel and toe), the full teeter (standing, rocking back on forth from toe to heel to toe), the foot shuffle (feet move back and forth but do not move the body away), and the toe dig (the toes of one foot scratch the ground while the other foot supports the person's weight).[256] Ekman and Friesen found eight different kinds of foot movement which took place when a research subject was sitting. These foot movements include the one-foot floor slide (forward and/or back), the two-foot floor slide (forward and/or back), the sole show (with the legs being crossed or uncrossed), the ankle cross or cross-uncross or uncross-cross or cross-uncross-cross or cross-recross, and the ankle lateral bend (one- or two-feet), and the foot tap (repetitious or one tap, with one foot or both feet).[257]

What do leg and foot kinesics mean? This is a question of considerable concern to the alert religious educator.

There is scientifically controlled empirical evidence which suggests that psychological states and reactions are communicated through leg and foot kinesics.[258]

Legs, like arms, help define the outer limits of one's personal space insofar as one can physically control this space. Radial space is one's own and is generally perceived as such. Persons whose legs and feet are most extended from the body often are engaged in active or initiating behaviors, while those whose legs and feet are not extended are frequently involved in passive or receiving activities.[259] People in dyads or in small groups often position themselves in such a way that their legs, feet, and arms define the perimeter of their social group. Inside the perimeter is the social space or territory of the group.[260]

Of all the specific seated leg positions, probably none is more common than the legs-crossed and the legs-open position, for the simple reason that virtually all specific seated leg positions can be considered variants of these two basic ones. From the standpoint of radial space, the legs-open position suggest open personal space while the legs-crossed position signifies closed personal space. However, this general statement can be modified and even at times be contradicted by the particular kind of open- and crossed-leg behavior, by what the legs are doing while they are open and crossed, and by what the head, face, arms, hands, and torso are communicating. Thus, for example, if the body muscles are rigid or even tremble, then crossed legs may indicate defensiveness or nervousness. But if the body muscles are not tense, crossed legs may suggest a psychological state of relaxation and comfortableness. Gerard Nierenberg and Henry Calero found that crossed legs are part of the cluster of behaviors which a person uses while rejecting another person or group. Other nonverbal behaviors in the rejection cluster include folded arms, moving the body away, and tilting the head forward in a quizzical or skeptical manner. Crossed legs, when accompanied by arms folded over the chest, tend to indicate defensiveness.[261] The meaning of crossed legs and parallel legs can be accurately ascertained only with caution and with attention to the individual's simultaneously occurring nonverbal and verbal behaviors, as well as to the overall situational context. After all, a person might cross or uncross the legs simply to attain a greater degree of physical comfort at the moment.[262]

Meaning can also be communicated on the basis of whether leg positions are symmetrical or asymmetrical. An asymmetrical leg position is often regarded as being positively correlated with relaxation. For a seated person, asymmetrical leg (and arm) positions, especially when combined with greater-than-normal reclining or sideways lean, have been found to be frequently indicative of the higher status of that person relative to another individual—this is particularly true if the person with the asymmetrical leg position is the speaker and the other individual is the listener. Of special interest to the religion teacher is the body of research data which suggest that persons who are attempting to be persuasive tend to keep their legs in symmetrical position.[263]

Foot positions sometimes provide a basis for deriving meaning. For example, the ankles-locked position, especially when accompanied by clenched hands, often suggests that a person is anxious, defensive, and making an effort to control himself or hold himself back. People frequently lock their ankles when sitting or lying in the dentist's chair.[264]

Thusfar in this subsection, I have dealt with the meaning of leg and foot positions. Now I wish to briefly consider the meaning of leg and foot acts or movements. Frequent movements involving the crossing and recrossing of one's legs may mean that the person is nervous or ill at ease.[265] Frequent foot movements of any sort may suggest anxiety. The rhythmic beating or tapping of one's foot on the ground or in the air (as when seated with the legs crossed) in synchronization with another person's verbal or nonverbal behaviors is sometimes indicative of one's here-and-now psychological compatability or congruity with the other person. If the rhythmic use of the foot (or other body part) is consciously or unconsciously adopted by the other person also, rapport is often indicated.[266]

The legs and feet are the most reliable kinesic sources of nonverbal leakage and deception clues, with the arms and hands placing next, and the face ranking last—quite possibly because in terms of sending capacity, external information, and internal information, the face ranks highest, the arms and hands next, and the legs and feet the lowest. People tend to pay relatively little attention to their own leg/foot positions and movements because these positions and movements rank so low in sending capacity, external information, and internal information. Therefore the leg and foot area is the sector of the body which a person is least likely to use deliberately for deception purposes since an individual generally exercises little vigilance over what the nonverbal behaviors occurring in this area might be communicating.

Posture. Posture is the relative arrangement and alignment of different parts of the body at any given moment. Posture includes the combination of such things as the set of the head upon the shoulders, spinal carriage, stance, and so forth.

From the strictly physiological point of view, there are three main types of posture: standing, geniculating (sitting, squatting, and kneeling), and lying. This typology reveals the physiological centrality of legs in posture. Each of the three main postural types admits of many variations corresponding to different angles of the body, varying positions of the torso and arms and head, diverse placement of the body extremeties (crossing each other, apart, on furniture), degree of muscle tonus in the entire body or in any of its parts, and so forth.

One of the most important postural typologies representing the combined physical and psychological perspectives is that devised by William T. James.[267] From a series of experimental studies in which several individuals judged 347 different postural sets, James was able to identify four basic postural categories, namely approach, withdrawal, expansion, and contraction. The approach category is characterized by a general forward lean of the body, while the withdrawal category is typified by physically drawing back or turning away. Expansion features an expanded chest, erect or backward-leaning trunk or head, and raised shoulders; contraction is marked by a drooping, shriveling, cowering, cringing posture which is evidenced in such acts as a forward-leaning trunk, bowed head, drooping shoulders, and sunken chest. The psychological correlates of these four main postural categories are as follows. The approach posture tends to convey attention, readiness, interest, scrutiny, or curiosity. The withdrawal posture typically suggests negation, refusal, repulsion, or disgust. The expansion posture generally suggests mastery, self-esteem, pride, conceit, arrogance, or disdain. Finally, the contraction posture usually indicates that the person is dejected, downcast, crestfallen, depressed, or abased. For each of these four generic postural categories, the head and trunk positions reveal themselves as the most important indicators. However, specific discriminations within each category were determined by the position of the hands and arms. For example, within the overall basic configuration of the approach posture, the palms facing up tend to suggest acceptance, offering coaxing, supplication, pleading, or humility. The palms facing downward generally indicate disapproval, opposition, active repulsion, avoidance, or opposition. The palms facing down usually point to soothing, calming, blessing. James emphasizes that the meaning of any of the four basic posture types is somewhat affected and altered, not only by the contextual situation in which the postural behavior takes place, but also by the coordinating relationship which overrall posture bears to any and all of its constituent parts (such as facial acts, kinesic behaviors, and so forth).

Because of its deeply human quality, posture has played an important and vital role in the history of Eastern and Western religion. Postural positions and movements occupy a central place in Christian worship services. This is especially true in Catholicism and Eastern Orthodoxy. In the liturgy, posture signals the onset of a new phase of the worship activity. Even more, posture serves as the embodiment and enfleshment of that phase of the worship activity. To kneel or to bend over in adoration is to humbly adore, to stand is to expansively praise, to sit is to rest and be attentive to God's focused grace coming from within and from without. Posture is a religiously valenced content in its own right and not just simply a curious concomitant of content.

As a result of his carefully conducted, classic cross-cultural study of posture, Gordon Hewes concluded that "the English [and American] postural vocabulary is mediocre—a fact which in itself inhibits our thinking about posture." Quite the opposite is true in India, where the religious tradition gave birth to and nourishes yoga which contains what is probably the world's richest set of postural configurations.[268] As an integral aspect of its realization, yoga features postural activities, breathing patterns, and other nonverbal behaviors whose goal is to attain a self-less communion and/or union with God.[269]

Do the learner's postural configurations tell anything about his personality structure? J. C. Brengelmann's review of the pertinent empirical research indicates that correlations between certain personality characteristics and posture have been shown to be both significant and reliable.[270]

The correlation between posture and personality has been explored by social scientists coming from the psychoanalytic tradition.[271] In Sigmund Freud's view, for example, postural changes and other bodily movements are physical manifestations of simultaneously occurring emotional activity. Quite often postural activity occurs as a reaction to former experiences associatively stimulated.[272] Summarizing the interpretations of posture offered by various psychoanalytic studies, Michael Argyle found the following. A stiff bearing among males and a prim upright carriage among females indicates an imprisoning of anxiety. An affected snooty posture suggests a conflict between flirtation and shyness. A drooping, listless, and seemingly immobile posture points to a deep sense of helplessness and quite possibly an anguished cry for help. A standing posture in which the body is held rigid and the arms folded on the chest signifies self-protection, repression, and withdrawal. A nestling, languid posture while seated represents an expression of sexual impulses.[273]

Posture tends to be directly correlated with status and power. Postural relaxation typically conveys high status and potency. The research has shown that a communicator generally adopts a more relaxed posture with an interactant of lower status, and a less relaxed posture with an interactant of higher status.[274]

Posture is a form of communication. Put somewhat differently, posture is a nonverbal content which does, in fact, communicate. Posture communicates the degree of an individual's attentiveness. The attentive person typically adopts an alert, congruent posture, with the head slightly cocked.[275] Posture communicates information about the affective warmth or coldness of an individual. Warmth is frequently communicated by a shift of posture toward the other person, accompanied by a smile, direct gaze, and hands remaining still. Coldness is often communicated by a listlessly slumped posture, accompanied by a lack of smiling, looking around the room, and a drumming of the fingers.[276]

Posture communicates in the following broad ways. First, it demarcates the components of personal behavior which each individual manifests when alone or in a group. Second, it indicates how the various components of one's personal behavior are related to each other. Third, it defines the steps and the order—that is, the "behavioral program"—in both one's inner activities and in one's social interaction.[277]

Body lean is one of the most important and revealing features of posture. There are three major types of body lean, namely forward lean, sideways lean, and backward lean.

Forward lean can be measured by the number of degrees that a plane from the interactant's shoulders to the hips deviates ventrally from the vertical plane.[278] The relevant empirical research data suggest that forward lean is an approach posture which indicates a positive attitude on the part of the interactant, particularly if the interactant is the one who is talking at the same time.[279] Forward lean by a listener tends to convey an attitude of receptivity and attentiveness to the speaker.[280] Forward lean seems to act as a nonverbal reinforcer. Empirical research suggests that a forward lean and congruent limbs on the part of persons in dyads are significant contributors to rapport.[281]

Sideways lean can be measured by the number of degrees that a plane cutting the interactant's torso in half deviates from the vertical.[282] The relevant empirical research data suggest that sideways lean is indicative of relaxation.[283] Sideways lean can also convey other positive attitudes such as warmth and liking in those situations in which the sideways-leaning communicator is standing or seated at an angle to the other interactant(s).

Backward lean can be measured by the number of degrees that a plane from the interactant's shoulders to the hips dorsally deviates from the vertical plane.[284] The relevant empirical research data suggest that backward lean indicates a negative attitude on the part of the interactant.[285] Backward lean by a listener tends to convey an attitude of unreceptivity and aloofness to the speaker.[286] Backward lean is a withdrawal posture; it is a negative, refusing, repulsed posture communicated by drawing back and away.[287] Backward lean suggests a greater degree of negative attitude when it is combined with a bodily orientation away from rather than toward the other interactant, physical distance, lengthier duration of the interaction itself, relatively low rates of head movement, and infrequency of eye contact or smiling.[288]

Proxemics

Proxemics can be defined as the way an individual interacts with personal, social, and environmental space.[289] The research suggests that each person consciously, and even more unconsciously, structures his personal space, his social space, his environmental space, and even his cities and towns.[290] Conversely, personal, social, and environmental space constitute very important influences on personal behavior and social interaction.[291] Thus, for example, different kinds of interpersonal interactions tend to occur when individuals are located at different spatial distances from one another. Closer proxemic distances inherently tend to promote more intimate interpersonal transactions. Individuals wishing more intimate interpersonal transactions tend to reduce the proxemic distance between or among themselves.[292]

So important is proxemics in shaping and influencing human behavior that Robert Sommer rightly calls it "the axiology of space."[293] The way that personal, social, and environment space is structured, then, exerts significant direct impact on the kinds of values a person who lives and learns in such a space will acquire.[294]

One well-known classification of proxemic arrangement categorizes spatial organization into three groups, namely, fixed feature, semi-fixed feature, and informal.[295] Fixed-feature space refers to an arrangement of environmental space such as houses, rooms, and even cities and towns. Semi-fixed space refers to movable objects such as tables, chairs, and the like. Informal space refers to interpersonal distance. There are four kinds of informal space, namely, intimate distance, personal distance, social distance, and public distance. Intimate distance is used in comforting, protecting, loving, and other kinds of close physiological and psychological encounters. Intimate distance ranges from actual total contact up to eighteen inches. Personal distance "may be thought of as a small protective sphere or bubble that an organism maintains between itself and others."[296] Personal distance ranges from one-and-a-half feet to four feet. Social distance is that in which most interpersonal transactions take place between individuals under normal circumstances. Social distance is from four feet to twelve feet. Public distance is that in which a person is dealing with a group of individuals at such a proxemic interval that there is no real involvement of a deeply interpersonal nature, as for example, a public speaker or a priest from the pulpit. Public distance is from twelve feet and beyond. Each of the four distinct kinds of informal space contains two phases, namely, the close phase and the far phase. Each distance exerts influence on a wide variety of personal behaviors, ranging from voice loudness and tone to the degree of cognitive/affective output. The greater the proxemic distance between the interactants, the louder and the more formal will the voice become, and the more cognitive will be the verbal output.[297]

Of the four major categories of informal space, the one most researched by social scientists is probably that of personal space. The use of personal space seems to be significantly affected by many factors including culture and gender. Mideasterners such as the Arabs tend to enjoy and employ personal space to a far greater extent than does the typical Anglo-Saxon.[298] One review of the pertinent empirical research found that as a general rule, females have a smaller personal space zones than do males, and persons in heterosexual pairs have smaller personal space zones than do those individuals in same-gender pairs.[299]

Personal space is closely related to but is not the same as personal territory. Personal space refers simply to that area immediately around the body which the individual inhabits as his own. Personal territory, on the other hand, is that area around the body which the individual perceives himself as owning, controlling, or having exclusive use of.[300] When one individual crosses into the personal space of another individual, regardless of whether such a crossing is physical or is by gaze, the first individual normally signals that he is crossing the boundaries and the second individual normally grants or withholds approval. The way in which one individual crosses into the personal territory of another typically requires some adherence to the cultural conventions of interpersonal passage into that territory.[301]

The liturgies of virtually every Christian denomination make extensive use of structured proxemics for deliberative worship and instruction purposes. The sanctuary, for example, is proxemically demarcated from the rest of the church building. In Catholic church buildings, the altar of sacrifice, the altar of repose, the pulpit, the pews, the baptismal font, the stained glass windows, and so forth, are deliberatively structured in such a proxemic fashion as to achieve the desired learning outcome. When a new liturgical and religious awareness of "altarness" and sacrifice swept over the Catholic Church in the years immediately following the Second Vatican Council,[302] the tabernacle was moved from the altar of sacrifice to an altar of repose, and the altar of sacrifice was dramatically repositioned to allow for more direct contact between the rite enacted on the altar and the congregation.

Religious educators who wish to enhance the effectiveness of their instructional activities would do well to accord due importance to the proxemics of the setting in which they teach, be that setting in a family milieu, a youth group, or in a school classroom. In terms of teaching religion in a formal setting such as in a classroom, the following points are germane. In most classrooms, the teacher has a great deal of proxemic space while the students have little. Robert Sommer remarks that the typical classroom teacher has about fifty times more space than each of the students.[303] The implications of such a proxemic state of affairs with respect to religious educators wishing to teach the goals of social liberation and individual independence are quite obvious.[304] The research shows that students in classroom situations will conduct themselves differently depending on the way in which they are seated.[305] Seating arrangements exert a definite effect on the degree and texture of group collaboration, interaction, initiative in productive tasks, and so forth.[306] Proxemic arrangements and structures do not operate magically in terms of producing the desired learning outcomes; the religion teacher must be professionally prepared in proxemic sensitivity and then must go ahead and skillfully utilize space for desired pedagogical results. Thus in his examination of the research, Robert Sommer found that though most classroom environments featured movable chairs, in actual fact the teachers seldom used pedagogical processes in which the chairs were moved, but treated furniture as fixed.[307]

SOME PRACTICAL CONSEQUENCES

The range of the nonverbal content of religious instruction is so rich and so varied that space will allow treatment of some practical consequences of only one of these contents, namely that of touch.

The scientific study of touch is called tacesics. The purpose of tacesics, among other things, is to chart, analyze, predict, and verify the range of touching behaviors in which an individual engages.

The importance of touch in human life and development can scarcely be exaggerated. Because the human person is *homo integer,* everything that the person is and will become necessarily involves both physiological functioning intertwined with psychological functioning.

This theme will run throughout my treatment of touch, as indeed it runs throughout everything I have ever written.

Ashley Montagu calls touch "the mother of the senses" in that it is the earliest to develop in the human embryo. To be sure, the skin is "the oldest and the most sensitive of a person's organs, the first medium of human communication, and the most efficient of protectors." In Montagu's view, the skin with its capacity to give and to receive touch is an organ whose importance ranks second only to the brain.[308]

Touching is probably the most basic form of social communication throughout the whole animal kingdom, including human beings. Touch of one kind or another is found in very simple organisms, and is absolutely fundamental in infants and in young children.[309] Because of its primary place in both the human species and throughout human development, touch enables the most essential forms of interpersonal affect and attitude to be communicated successfully.

Throughout the animal kingdom, notably in primates (including human beings), acts of touching are probably more important than any other kinds of acts in the early development of infants and the very young. This fact is of utmost practical importance to religious educators since there is an abundance of empirical research which suggests that the texture and quality of one's early development enormously influences the personality configurations of that individual's later life. The research of Harry Harlow on rhesus monkeys—research which has done so much to cast helpful light on human development and affectional systems—suggests that contact-clinging can be postulated as the primary variable that binds mother to infant and infant to mother. Maternal affection appears to be at its maximum during face-to-face touching contacts between mother and infant. Maternal affection appears to wane progressively when this type of tactile interchange decreases.[310]

The research evidence rather clearly suggests that the skin is the primary sense organ of the human infant. During the infant's reflex attachment period, tactile experience is the most important kind of experience for the infant's continued healthy growth and development.[311] Classical Freudianism claims that the tactile activity of the infant's lips at the mother's breast is an important foundation stone in that infant's present and future sexuality.[312] For both advocates and opponents of Freud, touch is generally recognized as the infant's most important means of communication with the outside world, human and nonhuman.[313] Communication implies relationship of one sort or another, and by tactilely communicating with the outside world, the infant develops a personal relationship to that world, a relationship which conditions the contours of the infant's growth and development. Montagu puts it this way: "It is the interpersonal relationship with the mother, exteroceptively and proprioceptively, especially involving the rectors of the gastrointestinal tract—and this is very important—that the child establishes its first communicative relationships."[314] The quality, duration, and frequency of interpersonal touch between parents on the one hand and the infant on the other hand go a long long way in promoting or impeding physical and psychological health later on in life. Montagu's review of the research suggests that quite possibly poor tactile experiences by the infant and to the infant leads to all sorts of physical hypersensitivity issuing in colitis, ulcers, and psychogenic cardiovascular disturbances.[315] Dan Millar and Frank Millar assert that psychological health is advanced or retarded through tactile experiences in infancy and childhood. "By being touched, cuddled, caressed, and stroked, the child learns he is loved and wanted—an important beginning in the development of self-esteem."[316] Tactile deprivation leads to a loss or weakening of self-esteem and even worse results. Thus the research suggests that children in nursing homes who are touched extremely infrequently or not at all tend to die because of acute tactile deprivation.[317] In the later nineteenth and early twentieth centuries, children in "progressive" homes where rationality and cognition were enthroned, while touching and other kinds of affectivity were downplayed, frequently suffered from a disease then called marasmus, which means a kind of wasting away.[318] A review of the pertinent research by Lawrence Rosenfeld and Jean Vivikly indicates that a lack of touch early in a person's life may result in a variety of health problems, including allergies and eczema. It may also cause learning problems with speech, symbolic recognition, and a relative incapacity for later more highly developed sensitive tactile communication.[319]

Most persons-in-the-street, most religious educators, and indeed most researchers in human development, seem to have failed to grasp adequately the deep significance of touch, especially active touch. It is well to remember that a person makes constant contact with the outside world by means of a vast conglomeration of perceptual fields, including a perceptual field which is sight-oriented and a perceptual field which is touch-oriented. It is common knowledge that the touch-oriented perceptual field is more immediate, more warm, and more friendly than the sight-oriented field.[320] It is the immediacy, the warmth, the friendliness of the perceptual field of touching which, among other things, renders touch so interpersonally powerful. Touch, after all, "requires an invasion of one's personal space, the space we use to protect ourselves from others. The permission of invasion itself becomes a 'giving' to the other person. Touching is powerful also because each participant is mutually stimulated" to some degree in one or another way.[321] In one experimental research investigation, a library clerk was trained to "accidentally" brush the hand of students in the process of returning a library card to those students. The experiment found that, in general, touching by the library clerk resulted in more positive evaluations by students not only of the touches, but of the library setting as well. This effect held true even when the students were not immediately aware of being touched. The researchers concluded that their investigation suggested that the act of touching another person is amazingly potent; a touch of less than a second appears to have the power to make people feel better, and this effect can be transferred even to an evaluation of associated stimuli (such as the library setting, in the case of this experiment).[322] It might well be that tactile sensations lie in some way at or near the root of other kinds of sensory experiences. Thus in a well-regarded scholarly contribution in the field of tacesics, Lawrence Frank states that "the potency of music, with its rhythmical patterning and varying intensities of sounds, depends in large measure upon the provision of an auditory surrogate for the primary tactile experiences in which . . . rhythmic patting is peculiarly effective in soothing the baby."[323]

Touching behaviors are important features of every religion, and play a prominent and sometimes even an essential place in religious ceremonies. In the sacrament of Orders, for example, the laying on of hands by the bishop is fundamental. Nancy Henley, a tacesiologist, writes that in the New Testament, "of 25 miracles of healing attributed to Jesus, 19 occur within touching range and tell the method of healing. Fourteen of these are accomplished through touch, in all but one case of Jesus' touch to the afflicted rather than vice versa."[324]

In Western culture, there are many different kinds of touching behaviors, including patting, squeezing, slapping, pinching, punching, stroking, shaking, kissing, licking, holding, guiding, embracing, linking, laying-on of hands, kicking, grooming, and tickling.[325] Each type of touch conveys a somewhat different kind of affective stimulus and meaning, and evokes a related kind of response under normal conditions. For example, squeezing hands, when not done with excessive force, usually means affection and friendliness.[326]

David Edwards identifies nine major uses of touch in interpersonal relationships, namely (1) informational pick-up, (2) movement facilitation, (3) prompting, (4) aggressive, (5) nurturant, (6) celebratory, (7) sexual, (8) cathartic, and (9) ludic.[327] Michael Argyle's summary of the available empirical research combines this list somewhat into five basic uses of touch, namely, interaction signals, sex, aggression, affiliation, and nurturance-dependence.[328]

The touching behaviors which are used as interactional signals do not primarily communicate interpersonal attitudes, though attitudes are often implicit in these signals. Some of the more common touch interaction signals are greetings and farewells as conveyed by a handshake or a kiss, congratulations as expressed by a handshake or by embracing, attention signals such as touching a person on the shoulder to gain attention, and guiding a person as by holding an elderly bishop's arm while mounting the altar steps.

Touching often has a sexual meaning whether intended or not. Consequently, in Western society, especially in Anglo-Saxon society and in some religious circles, touching is avoided except in professional cases as physicians, hairdressers, and clerics in sacramental or ceremonial duties.

Touching constitutes one of the most prevalent and widely recognized forms of aggression. Slapping, punching, and kicking are examples of the aggressive use of touch. As a general rule, persons in a lower socioeconomic class tend to manifest their aggression by touching behaviors more than do individuals in a higher socioeconomic stratum.

For religious educators, those touching behaviors which primarily convey affiliation are especially important. As an affiliative device, touch communicates care and affection and love—all of which are essential ingredients in a holistic religious instruction of the type I am proposing in this trilogy. Both touching and being touched constitute extremely powerful, intimate, and all-embracing forms of relating to another person and in disclosing oneself to the other. Hence the import and helpful utility of touching behaviors in the task of a humanistic religious instruction are obvious.

One researcher notes that it is possible to validly correlate the level of intimacy implied by a touching behavior with the intensity, frequency, and duration of that touching behavior.[329] For example, an embrace ranks above a handshake in intimacy, and a long handshake ranks above a short handshake in intimacy.

In addition to, or perhaps more accurately, as a corollary to the major uses of interpersonal touch described above, Nancy Henley stoutly contends that touch is used for power.[330] Henley views touch in terms of what she calls "tactual politics." She maintains that there is a "network of touch privileges by which the social order is maintained, particularly its expression in the control of women."[331] Henley points out that during interactions between pairs of persons of differing social status, the person of superior social status is the one touching the person of inferior social status, rather than vice versa. As examples of this she gives the interactions between teacher and student, master and servant, police officer and accused person, doctor and patient, minister or priest and parishioner, foreman and worker, businessman and secretary. Thus we can see, comments Henley, in what she terms a "hierarchical-ridden society," touch, especially between the sexes, is used to maintain and reinforce the social hierarchy.[332] In an observational field study, Henley discovered that males touched females much more often than females touched males—and much more than people touched others of the same sex. She interpreted these data not as indicators of demonstrations of intimacy or affection, but rather of assertion of male power.[333] Commenting on this study, Michael Argyle points out that dominance is not the only reason why males touch females. Males might and do touch females for a wide variety of reasons, ranging from affection[334] to interaction signals such as greetings, attention signals, lucid demonstrations, sex, and so forth. Politics may be part of human interaction, but it is not the whole of human action, and probably is not the most important dimension of human action.[335] Weakening the all-inclusiveness of Henley's contention that touch is largely an expression of male dominance over females is the fact that the empirical research suggests that far from being unwillingly subdued or dominated by touch, females seem to enjoy touching and being touched, more so in fact than do males.[336] For example, Robert Harper and his associates report on one study which found that in response to touching in crowded situations, males became more uncomfortable while females became more comfortable.[337] While many explanations might be legitimately offered for the superiority of American females over males in tactile maturity, Ashley Montagu offers one of the most intriguing. Montagu's review of the research found that female infants tend to be weaned later and receive more early tactile stimulation than male children. Montagu concludes that "perhaps this difference in [early] tactile experience, at least in part, accounts for the American female being so much less uptight about tactuality than the American male."[338] Even Henley acknowledges that there is research evidence to suggest that women deprived of human touch tend to seek it through sex.[339]

While some meanings of touch seem to be innate, still a great many other meanings of a particular touch are learned from the culture in which a person lives. Thus Thomas Benson and Kenneth Frandsen observe that "our sense of touch develops early. Our disposition to touch and be touched persists. However, we seem to regulate this form of nonverbal activity more carefully than any other. That these regulations vary substantially from family to family, from nation to nation, and from time to time is obvious even to the casual observer."[340] Put even more specifically, each culture either promotes or specifically teaches children and adolescents "to develop different kinds of thresholds to tactile contacts and stimulation so that their organic, constitutional and temperamental characteristics are accentuated or reduced."[341] Social scientists have classified cultures into two major groups on the basis of the degree to which their members touch each other. Contact cultures include the Arabs, Latin Americans, Southern Europeans, and a number of African groups. Noncontact cultures include Northern Europeans, Americans, and Indians/Pakistanis.[342]

Northern Europe, and especially the countries north of the Mexican border, seem to be tactile-starved societies. Indeed, it would appear that persons from these cultures by and large are even opposed to touching behaviors outside carefully prescribed limits. This seems to be borne out "by the extreme lengths to which we sometimes go to avoid touching others in public. A person who accidentally touches another generally takes pains to apologize; persons forced into close proximity, as in a crowded elevator, uncomfortably constrict their bodies and movements to avoid touching."[343] From the mid-1960s onward, quite a few Americans have paid large sums of money to go to encounter groups just to touch strangers. This is surely an astounding phenomenon. The frequently seen bumper sticker displayed on American automobiles: "Have you hugged your child today?" would be impossible in Mediterranean cultures. It is only recently that the omnipresent proscription *"Noli me tangere"* ("Do not touch me") has begun to fade from prominence in the Catholic Church—with some of its members, it would appear, going to the opposite extreme.

Though by no means conclusive, there is some empirical evidence which suggests that touching behaviors bring about beneficial effects in education, including counseling as well as instruction. For example, Donna Conant Aguilera found that nurses who touched psychotic patients were more effective in eliciting verbal responses from them than nurses who did not touch.[344] Indeed, one researcher observed that "the extraordinary frequency with which one comes upon accounts of breakthroughs brought about by body contact in reaching schizophrenics who had for years been inaccessible to other therapeutic approaches is striking."[345] In one experimental study, Joyce Pattison trained counselors to touch the hands of their clients when more information was sought. This experiment found that this kind of touching resulted in greater depth of psychological self-exploration by the clients, even though the touching did not alter the clients' perception of their relationship with the counselor.[346] Writing on the positive effects which touching another person can have on facilitating interpersonal relations, Jean Wilson notes that touching a learner can possibly encourage his self-disclosure, enhance his self-acceptance, and develop mature interpersonal relationships with others.[347] Of course those touching behaviors in which an educator engages must be done in such a fashion as to lessen and even obviate any possible sexual misinterpretation on the part of the learner.

Religious educators who are serious about their work should be actively aware of their own nonverbal behaviors in teaching, and also seek to sharpen their skills in the area of nonverbal communication. Specifically, religious educators might profitably ask themselves some pointed questions such as: Am I aware of the nonverbal content present in my teaching? Am I willing to take responsibility for the influences and effects which my nonverbal behaviors have on learners? Am I cognizant of the nonverbal effects communicated by the learners? Am I genuinely willing to attend to and be influenced by the nonverbal content communicated by the learners? Do I really want to read and study about nonverbal behavior as an integral part of my ongoing inservice preparation? Am I prepared to actively sharpen my nonverbal skills such as by working in a teacher performance center or being pedagogically monitored by a colleague trained in nonverbal communication?[348]

Religious instruction is a social activity: It is done with other persons. Sensitivity and appropriate response to other persons' nonverbal behavior appears to constitute an important dimension of every individual's competence as a person and as a professional.[349] It is therefore especially important for a religious educator to cultivate a refined sensitivity to the nonverbal behaviors of the learners and also to develop a heightened skill in effectively communicating nonverbally to them. Furthermore, there is some empirical research which suggests that there is a definite correlation between interpersonal effectiveness and the ability to decode nonverbal messages.[350] Consequently, if the religious educator is defective in the ability to properly decode the nonverbal messages of learners and other individuals, his effectiveness as a teacher is significantly lessened.

There is a great deal of talk, especially among religious educators working with youth and young adults, that learners often feel out of touch with them and with the whole ecclesia for that matter. I wonder whether persons who get out of touch with religious educators and with fellow Christians might possibly be out of psychological touch because they are already out of tactile touch? Persons in interpersonal contact with others typically are physically touched by these other individuals in the course of their interpersonal relationship.

In skillfully fusing nonverbal content and verbal content in the religion lesson, the religious educator would do well to remember that it is vitally important to coordinate these two major substantive contents in such a harmonious manner that these contents are communicated consistently to the learners. Bella DePaulo and Robert Rosenthal report one study which found that parents who sent conflicting communications tended to have children who were less pleasant and more anxious as persons. This finding held true not only for children in normal families but even for children in schizophrenic families.[351] Another study found that boys whose mothers produced relatively more discrepant communications tended to engage in more aggressive behavior than the sons of mothers who were more consistent in their communications.[352] In a role-play study of counselors engaging in consistent or inconsistent cues, it was discovered that the clients of inconsistent counselors sat further away.[353]

There are a great many nonverbal pedagogical experiences which religious educators can fruitfully use in the lesson in order to help learners sharpen their awareness, their sensitivity, and their use of touch.[354] Unfortunately but predictably, most of these pedagogical experiences were not originally developed by general educators or by religious educators. Rather, these experiences were pioneered by persons working with encounter groups, human potential movements, and the like.[355] Though the four teaching techniques I will mention in the succeeding paragraphs have not been sufficiently researched so as to enjoy confident empirical support, nonetheless many persons who have used them as educators and as learners claim that these techniques have proved fruitful in raising their tactile consciousness as well as helping them to enter into a more holistic encounter with reality.

In the first pedagogical technique, the religious educator asks the learners to remove all the furniture from the room in which they are in, or if this is not possible, to place the furniture against the walls. The the religious educator requests the learners to take off their shoes and put blindfolds over their eyes. He then suggests that the learners very slowly walk around the room, concentrating all their attention as they walk on the tactile contact which their feet are making with the floor. The learners are invited to try as hard as possible to be existentially in touch with what these tactile contacts are telling them, and what their feelings are as they are in awared experience of their tactile contacts with the floor. After ten minutes or so, the religious educator terminates the exercise. The learners then share their experiences with the rest of the group, if the religious educator deems this pedagogically appropriate. Because most learners take for granted their everyday foot contacts with the floor, this exercise often proves quite revealing for learners, and helps them to become in more continual awareness of the tactile avenues with which they directly encounter reality. This technique can be especially beneficial for adult learners.

In the second pedagogical technique, the religious educator leads the learners into the church building. The learners remove their shoes and place blindfolds over their eyes. They then proceed to touch the sacred vessels used during the service, the altar and its linens, the tabernacle, the pulpit, the statues, the candles, the stations of the cross, the pews, and so forth. As in the previous exercise, the religious educator asks the learners to concentrate all their attention on the tactile contact which their hands are making with the objects they touch. The learners are invited to endeavor to become existentially aware of what these tactile contacts are communicating to them, and what they are affectively feeling during these tactile experiences. After the exercise is concluded, the learners can share their feelings and other experiences with the rest of the group, if this is pedagogically appropriate. This technique is aimed at helping learners gain a greater existential awareness of and a more deeply personal feeling for the physical environment of the church building and its artifacts so that these persons' future liturgical participation might be therefore rendered more human and moving.

In the third pedagogical technique, the religious educator asks the learners to place themselves in dyads. The learners take off their shoes and don blindfolds. Facing each other, one member of the dyad feels first the head, and then successively the shoulders, arms, and hands of the other member. This procedure occurs slowly, and should take at least ten minutes. When the process has been completed, the other member of the dyad engages in the same tactile communications with the individual who originally did the touching. The person doing the touching as well as the person being touched are invited by the religious educator to try as hard as possible to be in heightened existential awareness of what these tactile communications are revealing to them, and what their feelings are during this time. After the exercise is completed, the members of the dyad share their experiences and feelings with each other and later with the whole group, if the religious educator judges this to be pedagogically appropriate. One primary objective of this nonverbal exercise in tactile communication is to assist learners to become more personally aware that what they know about another individual cognitively and verbally might possibly be superficial or even somewhat different than what they experience in nonverbal tactile relationships with that other individual.

In the fourth pedagogical technique, the religious educator requests that the learners place themselves in dyads. The learners remove their shoes and put blindfolds over their eyes not simply to avoid distracting variables from entering their perceptual awareness, but also to avoid receiving any visual feedback from each other. The religious educator then asks one member of the dyad to communicate tactilely to the other member one particular affect or other human experience such as caring. This tactile communication should be done slowly and not rushed. When this has been completed, the religious educator asks the same member of the dyad to tactilely communicate to the other member a second affect or human experience such as anguish. When this has been completed, then a third affect such as love. In all, five different affects or other fundamental kinds of human experience are tactilely communicated. When this entire process is finished, the other member of the dyad engages in the same kinds of tactile communications with the individual who originally did the touching. From the outset and at pedagogically opportune moments during this nonverbal exercise, the person doing the touch as well as the one receiving the touch are invited by the religious educator to concentrate on what they are feeling and experiencing during these tactile communications. After the entire exercise is completed, the members of the dyads share their experiences and feelings with each other and later with the whole group, if pedagogically appropriate. Some important objectives of this nonverbal exercise in tactile communication include developing one's skill in effective nonverbal communication, being able to openly receive another individual's nonverbal expressions of affect, becoming aware that we are sometimes constricted and "uptight" when it comes to open nonverbal communication with other individuals including members of what is sometimes called "the community of faith," and improving interpersonal relationships.

CONCLUSION

Because of reasons of space, I am reluctantly forced to omit from this chapter a host of nonverbal contents which are essential in the ongoing activity of religious instruction. For example, music, sculpture, painting, architecture—none of which were specifically treated in this chapter—all contain in eminently human form the living record and present force of Christianity in general and of religious experience in particular.

The deliberative inclusion of a healthy profusion of pedagogically productive nonverbal content into the religion lesson will help make religious instruction more holistically experiential and so more genuinely human. Religious instruction is done in a human context with human beings. Hence religious instruction should be as fully and as widely human as possible. By human here I do not mean a force or stress somehow opposed to the scientific. I have long advocated[356] that the scientific is not only a very human enterprise in itself but indeed is necessary to preserve the human in creation from being overwhelmed by personal fantasies and delusions and skewed needs masquerading as the optimally human.[357] My point here is put very well by one specialist in nonverbal communication in teaching who observes that the scientific study of nonverbal communication "converts you toward the humanistic tradition whether you like it or not. When you come close to the variables that influence nonverbal understanding, you see the frailty of the human condition and the powerlessness of human beings to be understood well, if at all. The cries and calls of nonverbal messages scream out to an unperceptive and insensitive world that you are here, you exist, you need to be recognized, and you want to be given a chance to live your life with meaning."[358]

NOTES

1. Boris Pasternack, *Doctor Zhivago,* translated by Max Hayward and Manya Harari (New York: Pantheon, 1958), p. 139.
2. From classical times until the mid-nineteenth century there were some scattered treatments of nonverbal behavior. Aristotle dealt with nonverbal behavior in his *Physiognomia, Historia Animalium, De Anima,* and the *Parva Naturalia.* In 1586, Giovanni Battista della Porta in his *Humana Physiognomia* dealt with the face and its capacity to communicate nonverbally. Though the vast bulk of major research on nonverbal behavior has occurred since the mid-twentieth century, still it was the second half of the nineteenth century which witnessed the beginning of serious investigations of nonverbal behavior with the research studies carried out by G.-B. Duchenne, Charles Bell, Charles Darwin, and Wilhelm Wundt.
3. N. L. Gage, *Handbook of Research on Teaching* (Chicago: Rand McNally, 1963).
4. Robert M. W. Travers, editor, *Second Handbook of Research on Teaching* (Chicago: Rand McNally, 1973).
5. Harold E. Mitzel, editor, *Encyclopedia of Educational Research,* 5th edition (New York: Free Press, 1982), 4 volumes.
6. Michael Francis Pennock, "Non-verbal Communication and the Religion Teacher," in *Living Light* XI (Winter, 1974), pp. 523–528. Liturgists seem to be a bit more directly aware of nonverbal content in their work. See, for example, Secretariat of the Bishops' Committee on the Liturgy, *Environment and Art in Catholic Worship* (Washington, D.C.: National Conference of Catholic Bishops, 1978); John P. Mossi, "Building the Non-verbal," in John P. Mossi, editor, *Modern Liturgy Handbook* (New York: Paulist, 1976), pp. 112–119.
7. In a statement which I find to be truly astounding, Gabriel Moran states absolutely and unequivocally that "religious education is a combination of silence and paradoxical speech." If Moran had ever examined any religious education act in even the most cursory fashion, he would have discovered that these acts contain far more nonverbal behaviors than silence. (Moran goes on to make a

few perfunctory and unverified comments on the basis of religious education as bodily and social ritual, remarks which leave basically untouched his linchpin comment that religious education is a combination of speech and paradoxical silence.) Gabriel Moran, "Teaching Within Revelation," in Gloria Durka and Joanmarie Smith, editors, *Aesthetic Dimensions of Religious Education* (New York: Paulist, 1979), p. 162.

8. For an example of this, see the significant book by Thomas H. Groome, *Christian Religious Education* (San Francisco: Harper & Row, 1980). See also Malcolm L. Warford, *The Necessary Illusion* (Philadelphia: Pilgrim, 1976). Groome's book is written in the scholarly tradition, while Warford's slim volume is written as a tract.

9. Thus Mary Boys unabashedly declares that "the essence of good teaching lies in the ability to pose questions." Boys' reductionist unidimensional view of teaching not only squeezes the essence of all pedagogy into the verbal domain to the exclusion of nonverbal content but also seriously fails to take into account that the questioning technique comprises only one basic form of verbal content—a form which is pedagogically inappropriate in quite a few teaching situations in which verbal content forms the dominant substantive content. Mary C. Boys, "Questions 'Which Touch on the Heart of Our Faith,' " in *Religious Education* LXXVI (November-December, 1981), p. 637.

10. Charles M. Galloway, "An Exploratory Study of Observational Procedures for Determining Teacher Nonverbal Communication," unpublished doctoral dissertation, University of Florida, 1962.

11. Barbara M. Grant and Dorothy Grant Hennings, *The Teacher Moves* (New York: Teachers College Press, 1971). For a brief description of the Bellack framework, see James Michael Lee, *The Flow of Religious Instruction* (Birmingham, Ala.: Religious Education Press, 1973), pp. 263–265.

12. Abne M. Eisenberg and Ralph R. Smith Jr., *Nonverbal Communication* (Indianapolis, Ind.: Bobbs-Merrill, 1971), p. 20.

13. See Ray L. Birdwhistell, "Kinesics," in David L. Sills, editor, *International Encyclopedia of the Social Sciences,* volume VIII (New York: Free Press, 1968), p. 380.

14. Michael Argyle, *Social Interaction* (New York: Atherton, 1969), p. 120.

15. *Ibid.*, p. 119.

16. I am here following the category analysis and distinctions developed in Jurgen Ruesch, "Nonverbal Language in Therapy," in *Psychiatry* XVIII (November, 1955), pp. 324–325.

17. C. David Mortensen, *Communication: The Study of Human Interaction* (New York: McGraw-Hill, 1972), p. 210.

18. *Ibid.*, p. 217; Abne M. Eisenberg and Ralph R. Smith, *Nonverbal Communication,* p. 22; Michael Argyle, *Social Interaction,* pp. 74–75.

19. With respect to all these characteristics, and especially of the evaluation characteristic, what is being considered is the nonverbal content in itself and the verbal content in itself.

20. Jurgen Ruesch and Weldon Kees, *Nonverbal Communication* (Berkeley, Calif.: University of California Press, 1956) pp. 181–192.

21. Randall Harrison, "Nonverbal Communication," in Ithiel de Sola Pool et al., editors, *Handbook of Communication* (Chicago: Rand McNally, 1973) p. 94.

22. Mark L. Knapp, *Nonverbal Communication in Human Interaction* (New York: Holt, Rinehart & Winston, 1972), pp. 5–8.

23. Larry L. Barker and Nancy B. Collins, "Nonverbal Behavior and Kinesic Research," in Philip Emmert and William D. Brooks, editors, *Methods in Research in Communication* (Boston: Houghton Mifflin, 1970), pp. 345–352.
24. Paul Ekman and Wallace V. Friesen, "The Repertoire of Nonverbal Behavior: Categories, Origins, Usage, and Coding," in *Semiotica* I (Spring, 1969), pp. 49–95. Ekman and Friesen note that their classification system is derived from that originally developed by David Efron, though they have redefined or otherwise altered some of his terminology here and there for greater precision, increased clarity, or to avoid seeming contradictions. Efron's book is a landmark volume in the history of scholarship on nonverbal behavior. See David Efron, *Gesture and Environment* (New York: King's Crown, 1941).
25. For a further discussion of theory, see James Michael Lee, "The Authentic Source of Religious Instruction," in Norma H. Thompson, editor, *Religious Education and Theology* (Birmingham, Ala.: Religious Education Press, 1982), pp. 117–121.
26. Judee K. Burgoon, "Nonverbal Communication Research in the 1970s: An Overview," in Dan Nimmo, editor, *Communication Yearbook,* volume IV (New Brunswick, N.J.: International Communication Association, 1980), pp. 179–197.
27. Randall P. Harrison and Mark L. Knapp, "Toward an Understanding of Nonverbal Communication Systems," in *Journal of Communication* XXII (December, 1972), pp. 340–341.
28. The language referred to here is nonverbal language, of course—namely attempting to derive a nonverbal "grammar" or language-structure from nonverbal behavior.
29. Desmond Morris, *The Naked Ape: A Zoologist's Study of the Human Animal* (New York: McGraw-Hill, 1967), p. 109.
30. Ray L. Birdwhistell, *Introduction to Kinesics* (Louisville, Ky.: University of Kentucky Press, 1952).
31. Gregory Bateson and Margaret Mead, *Balinese Character: A Photographic Analysis,* volume II, edited by Wilbur G. Valentine (New York: New York Academy of Sciences, 1942), pp. 3–5.
32. S. S. Feldman, "Mannerisms of Speech: A Contribution to the Working Through Process," in *Psychoanalytic Quarterly* XVII (July, 1948), p. 367.
33. See, for example, Weston La Barre, "The Cultural Basis of Emotions and Gestures," in *Journal of Personality* XVI (September, 1947), pp. 49–68.
34. David Efron, *Gesture and Environment,* p. 137.
35. Michael Argyle, *Bodily Communication* (New York: International Universities Press, 1975), p. 73.
36. Paul Ekman and Wallace V. Friesen, "The Repertoire of Nonverbal Behavior: Categories, Origins, Usage, and Coding," p. 71.
37. Randall P. Harrison and Wayne W. Crouch, "Nonverbal Communication: Theory and Research," in Gerhard J. Hanneman and William J. McEwen, editors, *Communication and Behavior* (Reading, Mass.: Addison-Wesley, 1975), p. 77.
38. Barbara M. Grant and Dorothy Grant Hennings, *The Teacher Moves,* pp. 3–4.
39. John H. Westerhoff III, "Toward a Definition of Christian Education," in John H. Westerhoff III, editor, *A Colloquy on Christian Education* (Philadelphia: Pilgrim, 1972), p. 64.
40. B. Othanel Smith, *Teachers for the Real World* (Washington, D.C.: American Association of Colleges for Teacher Education, 1969), p. 160.

41. E. Paul Torrance, "Teacher Attitudes and Pupil Perception," in *Journal of Teacher Education* XI (March, 1960), pp. 97–102.
42. Charles M. Galloway, "Nonverbal Communication in Teaching," in *Educational Leadership* XXIV (October, 1966), pp. 55–63.
43. Michael Argyle, *Social Interaction,* p. 142.
44. Albert Mehrabian and Morton Wiener, "Decoding of Inconsistent Communication," in *Journal of Personality and Social Psychology* VI (January, 1967), pp. 109–114.
45. Albert Mehrabian and Susan R. Ferris, "Inference of Attitudes from Nonverbal Communication in Two Channels," in *Journal of Consulting Psychology* XXXI (June, 1967), p. 252.
46. Michael Argyle, *Social Interaction,* p. 75.
47. Aurelius Augustinus, *De Catechizandis Rudibus,* translated by Joseph P. Christopher (Westminster, Md.: Newman, 1962), pp. 15–16.
48. Could it be that when Pilate asked "What is truth?" Jesus decided not to answer verbally but instead to respond nonverbally by his presence? Is it possible that by his nonverbal response to Pilate's position, Jesus was indicating that truth is to be found more in the nonverbal than in the verbal, more in the personal than in the abstract?
49. See, for example, René Latourelle, *Theology of Revelation* (Staten Island, N.Y.: Alba, 1966), p. 318.
50. James D. Shaughnessey, editor, *The Roots of Ritual* (Grand Rapids, Mich.: Eerdmans, 1973).
51. Michael Argyle, *Bodily Communication,* pp. 188–189.
52. Norma Thompson rightly contends that art is simultaneously a lure into religious experience and an interpreter of religious experience. I believe that Thompson's position, while correct as far as it goes, does not go far enough. I maintain that art is itself often a religious experience, and that religious experience is especially congenial to artistic form. Norma H. Thompson, "Art and the Religious Experience," in Gloria Durka and Joanmarie Smith, editors, *Aesthetic Dimensions of Religious Education,* pp. 31–46.
53. See for example, Emil Brunner, *The Divine-Human Encounter,* translated by Amandus W. Loos (Philadelphia, Pa.: Westminster, 1943), pp. 45–71; Karl Rahner, "Observations on the Concept of Revelation," in Karl Rahner and Joseph Ratzinger, *Revelation and Tradition,* translated by W. J. O'Hara (New York: Herder and Herder, 1966), pp. 9–25; David Tracy, "The Particularity and Universality of Christian Revelation," in Edward Schillebeeckx and Bas van Iersel, editors, *Revelation and Experience* (New York: Seabury, 1979), pp. 106–116.
54. Paul Ekman, "Communication through Nonverbal Behavior: A Source about an Interpersonal Relationship," in Silvan Tomkins and Carroll E. Izard, editors, *Affect, Cognition, and Personality* (New York: Springer, 1965), pp. 435–441.
55. Abne M. Eisenberg and Ralph R. Smith Jr., *Nonverbal Communication,* p. 6.
56. Thomas Aquinas, *Summa Theologica,* I, q. 85, a. 7.
57. I suspect that the abject ignorance of and strong bias against both the empirical mentality and empirical research which characterize the work of a great many Catholic religious educationists are ultimately rooted in a residual negative attitude toward the body and toward terrestrial reality. Thus, for example, Mary Boys believes that an empirical mentality and empirical research constitute "technology and outer space" as contrasted to "humanism and inner space."

The highly humanistic and nontechnological character of, for example, depth psychology, person perception research, proxemic studies, attitudinal investigations, and the like seem to elude her. Mary C. Boys, *Biblical Interpretation in Religious Education* (Birmingham, Ala: Religious Education Press, 1980), pp. 238–239.

58. Schubert Ogden, *The Reality of God* (New York: Harper & Row, 1966), p. 58.

59. Buford Stefflre and Kenneth Matheny, "Counseling Theory," in Robert L. Ebel, editor, *Encyclopedia of Educational Research,* 4th edition. (New York: Macmillan, 1969), pp. 262–263; Bernie Zilbergeld, *The Shrinking of America* (Boston: Little, Brown, 1982).

60. William C. Schutz, *Here Comes Everybody* (New York: Harper & Row, 1971), pp. 243–244.

61. See, for example, Susanne K. Langer, *Philosophy in a New Key,* 3rd edition (Cambridge, Mass.: Harvard University Press, 1957), pp. 45–52, 150–160.

62. Robert E. Ornstein, *The Psychology of Consciousness* (San Francisco, Calif.: Freeman, 1973), pp. 50–73. For some other helpful material on this topic, see Julian Jaynes, *The Origin of Consciousness in the Breakdown of the Bicameral Mind* (Boston: Houghton Mifflin, 1976); Paul E. Bumbar, "Notes on Wholeness," in Gloria Durka and Joanmarie Smith, editors, *Aesthetic Dimensions of Religious Education,* pp. 47–68.

63. Paul Bakan, "The Eyes Have It," in *Psychology Today* IV (April, 1971), pp. 64–67, 96.

64. I am excluding here any consideration of nonverbal sign language such as that used by the deaf and dumb.

65. For further discussion, including research, on this point, see Daniel Druckman, Richard M. Rozelle, and James C. Baxter, *Nonverbal Communication* (Beverly Hills, Calif.: Sage, 1982), pp. 177–228.

66. See, for example, Julius Fast, *Body Language* (New York: Evans, 1970).

67. Some researchers have developed such criteria to assist them in their own studies. See, for example, Paul Ekman and Wallace V. Friesen, "The Repertoire of Nonverbal Behavior: Categories, Origins, Usage, and Coding," p. 52.

68. In Chapter Four I differentiated among knowledge, understanding, and wisdom.

69. Patrick W. Miller, *Nonverbal Communication* (Washington, D.C.: National Education Association, 1981), p. 16.

70. Michael Argyle, *Bodily Communication,* p. 345.

71. Another frequently cited categorization of paralanguage is George L. Trager, "Paralanguage: A First Approximation," in *Studies in Linguistics* XIII (Spring, 1958), pp. 1–12.

72. Charles M. Galloway, "An Exploratory Study of Observational Procedures for Determining Teacher Nonverbal Communication," pp. 129–134.

73. Starkey Duncan Jr., Laura N. Rice, and John M. Butler, "Therapists' Paralanguage in Peak and Peer Psychotherapy Hours," in *Journal of Abnormal Psychology* LXXIII (November, 1968), pp. 566–570.

74. Paul C. Vitz, "Affect as a Function of Stimulus Variation," in *Journal of Experimental Psychology* LXXI (January, 1966), pp. 74–79.

75. When considering the empirical data contained in this paragraph, it will be well to keep in mind that the research suggests that pitch variability tends to increase with age, and that males typically have a greater variability in pitch than do females.

76. Grant Fairbanks and Wilbert Pronovost, "An Experimental Study of the Pitch Characteristics of the Voice during the Expression of Emotion," in *Speech*

Monographs, research annual, V, 1939, pp. 87–104; Grant Fairbanks and LeMar W. Hoaglin, "An Experimental Study of the Voice During the Expression of Emotion," in *Speech Monographs,* research annual, VIII, 1941, pp. 85–90.

77. Norman N. Markel and Gloria L. Roblin, "The Effect of Content and Sex-of-Judge on Judgments of Personality from Voice," in *International Journal of Social Psychiatry* XI (Autumn, 1965), pp. 295–300.

78. Albert Mehrabian and Martin Williams, "Nonverbal Concomitants of Perceived and Intended Persuasiveness," in *Journal of Personality and Social Psychology* XIII (September, 1969), pp. 37–58.

79. Klaus R. Scherer, "Acoustic Concomitants of Emotional Dimensions: Judging Affect from Synthesized Tone Sequences," in Shirley Weitz, editor, *Nonverbal Communication* (New York: Oxford University Press, 1974), p. 109.

80. Grant Fairbanks and Wilbert Pronovost, "An Experimental Study of the Pitch Characteristics of the Voice During the Expression of Emotion," pp. 87–104; Grant Fairbanks and LeMar W. Hoaglin, "An Experimental Study of the Voice During the Expression of Emotion," pp. 85–90.

81. Albert Mehrabian and Martin Williams, "Nonverbal Concomitants of Perceived and Intended Persuasiveness," pp. 37–58.

82. Albert Mehrabian, "Nonverbal Betrayal of Feeling," in *Journal of Experimental Research in Personality* V (March, 1971), pp. 64–73.

83. Michael Argyle, *Bodily Communication,* p. 348.

84. Grant Fairbanks and Wilbert Pronovost, "An Experimental Study of the Pitch Characteristics of the Voice During the Expression of Emotion," pp. 87–104.

85. Klaus R. Scherer, "Acoustic Concomitants of Emotional Dimensions: Judging Affect from Synthesized Tone Sequences," p. 109.

86. Michael Argyle, *Bodily Communication,* p. 352.

87. William Labov, "On the Mechanism of Linguistic Change," in John J. Gumperz and Dell Hymes, editors, *Directions in Sociolinguistics* (New York: Holt, Rinehart & Winston, 1972), pp. 516–537.

88. Joel R. Davitz, "A Review of Research Concerned with Facial and Vocal Expressions of Emotion," in Joel R. Davitz, editor, *The Communication of Emotional Meaning* (New York: McGraw-Hill, 1964), p. 23.

89. Michael Argyle, *Bodily Communication,* p. 348.

90. Joel R. Davitz, editor, *The Communication of Emotional Meaning.*

91. Franklin H. Knower, "Studies in the Symbolism of Voice and Action: V. The Use of Behavioral and Tonal Symbols as Tests of Speaking Achievement," in *Journal of Applied Psychology* XXIX (June, 1945), pp. 229–235; Phyllis Kempner Levy, "The Ability to Express and Perceive Verbal Communications of Feeling," in Joel R. Davitz, editor, *The Communication of Emotional Meaning,* pp. 43–55; Susan F. Zaidel and Albert Mehrabian, "The Ability to Communicate and Infer Positive and Negative Attitudes Facially and Vocally," in *Journal of Experimental Research in Personality* II (March, 1969), pp. 233–241.

92. There is empirical support for the view that laughter is the most prevalent and most frequent of all affective responses among mental idiots and imbeciles. See Charles Darwin, *The Expression of the Emotions in Man and Animals* (Chicago: University of Chicago Press, 1965), p. 197.

93. J. A. R. A. M. van Hooff, "The Facial Displays of Catarrhine Monkeys," in Desmond Morris, editor, *Primate Ethology* (London: Weidenfeld and Nicolson, 1967), pp. 7–68.

94. All laughter, of course, does not fall within the normal psychological range.

There are also various types of pathological laughter. See Donald W. Black, "Pathological Laughter: A Review of the Literature," in *Journal of Nervous and Mental Disease* CLXX (February, 1982), pp. 67–71.

95. D. E. Berlyne, "Laughter, Humor, and Play," in Gardner Lindzey and Elliott Aronson, editors, *The Handbook of Social Psychology*, 2d edition, volume III (Reading, Mass.: Addison-Wesley, 1969), pp. 799–803.

96. Paul Carus, "On the Philosophy of Laughter," in *Monist* VIII (January, 1898), pp. 261–264.

97. Boris Sidis, *The Psychology of Laughter* (New York: Appleton, 1913).

98. Lambert Deckers, Jerry Edington, and Gary Van Cleave, "Mirth as a Function of Incongruities in Judged and Unjudged Dimensions of Psychological Tasks," in *Journal of General Psychology* CV, pt. 2 (October, 1981), pp. 225–233.

99. Peter L. Berger, *The Precarious Vision* (New York: Doubleday, 1961), pp. 209–218.

100. Jürgen Moltmann, *Theology of Play*, translated by Reinhard Ulrich (New York: Harper & Row, 1972), p. 29.

101. Anthony Ambrose, "The Age of Onset of Ambivalence in Early Infancy: Indications from the Study of Laughter," in *Journal of Child Psychology and Psychiatry* IV (December, 1963), pp. 167–181.

102. N. G. Blurton Jones, "Communication in Children," in R. A. Hinde, editor, *Non-verbal Communication* (Cambridge, England: Cambridge University Press, 1972), p. 280.

103. See, for example, Flemming Friss Hvidberg, *Weeping and Laughing in the Old Testament*, translated by Niels Haislund (Leiden, The Netherlands: Brill, 1962), pp. 138–146.

104. See, for example, Jer. 50:4.

105. For an interesting study relating crying to gender and to possible gender-related affectivity, see D. G. Williams, "Weeping by Adults: Personality and Sex Differences," in *Journal of Psychology* CX (March, 1982), pp. 217–226.

106. Balduin V. Schwarz, "*Untersuchungen zur Psychologie des Weins*," unpublished doctoral dissertation, Universität München, 1928.

107. I. Eibl-Eibesfeldt, "Similarities and Differences between Cultures in Expressive Movements," in R. A. Hinde, editor, *Non-verbal Communication*, pp. 302–303.

108. Joseph D. Matarazzo et al., "Speech and Silence Behavior in Clinical Psychotherapy and Its Laboratory Correlates," in John Schlien, editor, *Research in Psychotherapy*, volume III (Washington, D.C.: American Psychological Association, 1968), pp. 358–359.

109. James Michael Lee and Nathaniel J. Pallone, *Guidance and Counseling in Schools* (New York: McGraw-Hill, 1966), pp. 265–266.

110. Thomas J. Bruneau, "Communicative Silences: Forms and Functions," in *Journal of Communication* XXIII (March, 1973), pp. 23–42.

111. *Ibid.*, p. 26.

112. Mary Ritchie Key, *Male/Female Language* (Metuchen, N.J.: Scarecrow, 1975), pp. 107–116.

113. Thomas J. Bruneau, "Communicative Silences: Forms and Functions," p. 36.

114. Robert T. Oliver, *Communication and Culture in Ancient India and China* (Syracuse, N.Y.: Syracuse University Press, 1971), p. 264.

115. Thomas J. Bruneau, "Communicative Silences: Forms and Functions," pp. 37–40.

116. Morton T. Kelsey, *The Other Side of Silence* (New York: Paulist, 1976), p. 105.
117. Thomas J. Bruneau, "Communicative Silences: Forms and Functions," p. 21.
118. For a representative example of this mentality, see Christiane Brusselmans, "Key Faith Communities: Family, Parish, School," in *National Catholic Reporter* XIII (August 12, 1977), p. 11.
119. It should be noted, of course, that not all silence is productive.
120. Michael Argyle, *Bodily Communication*, p. 211.
121. Albert Mehrabian and Susan R. Ferris, "Inference of Attitudes from Nonverbal Communication in Two Channels," p. 252.
122. For an example of this, see Eckhard H. Hess, "Attitude and Pupil Size," in *Scientific American* CCXII (April, 1965), pp. 46–54.
123. On this last point, see Paul Ekman, "Communication through Nonverbal Behavior: A Source of Information about Interpersonal Relationship," p. 391.
124. Michael Argyle, *Bodily Communication*, p. 223.
125. In addition to being a multicontent system, the face is also a multisignal system. See Paul Ekman and Wallace V. Friesen, *Unmasking the Face* (Englewood Cliffs, N.J.: Prentice-Hall, 1975), pp. 10–11.
126. *Ibid.*, pp. 154–157.
127. Paul Ekman, "Cross-Cultural Studies of Facial Expression," in Paul Ekman, editor, *Darwin and Facial Expression* (New York: Academic Press, 1973), pp. 204–208.
128. Paul Ekman, Wallace V. Friesen, and Phoebe Ellsworth, *Emotion in the Human Face* (New York: Pergamon, 1972), p. 25.
129. Paul Ekman and Wallace V. Friesen, *Unmasking the Face*, p. 22.
130. Paul Ekman, Wallace V. Friesen, and Silvan Tomkins, "Facial Affect Scoring Technique (FAST): A First Validity Study," in *Semiotica* III (First Quarter, 1971), pp. 37–58; Jerry D. Boucher and Paul Ekman, "Facial Areas of Emotional Information," in *Journal of Communication* XXV (Spring, 1975), pp. 21–29.
131. Paul Ekman and Wallace V. Friesen, *Unmasking the Face*, pp. 34–128. This fine book also has many photographs of faces to graphically illustrate the verbal descriptions of the facial attributes of the various emotions.
132. See, for example, Diana Frumkes Thompson and Leo Meltzer, "Communication of Emotional Intent by Facial Expression," in *Journal of Abnormal and Social Psychology* LXVIII (February, 1964), pp. 129–135.
133. Dale Leathers, *Nonverbal Communication Systems* (Boston: Allyn and Bacon, 1976), pp. 26–32.
134. Albert Mehrabian, *Nonverbal Communication.* (Chicago: Aldine, 1972), p. 195.
135. Paul Ekman, Wallace V. Friesen, and Silvan S. Tomkins, "Facial Affect Scoring Technique (FAST): A First Validity Study," pp. 37–58; Paul Ekman, "Universals and Cultural Differences in Facial Expressions of Emotion," in James K. Cole, editor, *Nebraska Symposium on Motivation*, volume XIX (Lincoln, Neb.: University of Nebraska Press, 1971), pp. 246–260.
136. Fred Stickle and Dominick Pellegrino, "Training Individuals to Label Nonverbal Facial Cues," in *Psychology in the Schools* XIX (July, 1982), pp. 384–387.
137. Michael Argyle, "The Syntaxes of Bodily Communication," in Jonathan Benthall and Ted Pohlemus, editors, *The Body as a Medium of Expression* (New York: Dutton, 1975), p. 155.
138. Paul Ekman, Wallace V. Friesen, and Phoebe Ellsworth, *Emotion in the Human Face*, pp. 125–126.

139. Henry W. Seaford Jr., "Facial Expression Dialect: An Example," in Adam Kendon, Richard M. Harris, and Mary Ritchie Key, editors, *Organization of Behavior in Face-to-Face Interaction* (The Hague: Mouton, 1975), pp. 151–155.

140. Paul Ekman, Wallace V. Firesen, and Phoebe Ellsworth, *Emotion in the Human Face,* pp. 23–24.

141. Paul Ekman and Wallace V. Friesen, *Unmasking the Face,* pp. 140–153. Much of the material in this paragraph closely follows this Ekman and Friesen material.

142. Abne M. Eisenberg and Ralph Smith, *Nonverbal Communication,* p. 68.

143. Albert Mehrabian, *Silent Messages* (Belmont, Calif.: Wadsworth, 1971), p. 127.

144. Michael Argyle and Mark Cook, *Gaze and Mutual Gaze* (Cambridge, England: Cambridge University Press, 1976), p. 6.

145. I. Eibl-Eibesfeldt, "Similarities and Differences between Cultures in Expressive Movements," pp. 299–302.

146. Gerard I. Nierenberg and Henry H. Calero, *How to Read a Person Like a Book.* (New York: Hawthorn, 1971), pp. 24–26.

147. Michael Argyle, "The Syntaxes of Bodily Communication," p. 150.

148. I. Eibl-Eibesfeldt, "Similarities and Differences between Cultures in Expressive Movements," pp. 300–301.

149. More empirical research has been conducted on gaze than on glance, especially since 1965.

150. Michael Argyle and Mark Cook, *Gaze and Mutual Gaze,* p. 1.

151. *Ibid.,* pp. 15–16, 26.

152. O. Michael Watson, *Proxemic Behavior: A Cross-Cultural Study* (The Hague: Mouton, 1970), pp. 62–100.

153. Edward T. Hall, "A System for the Notation of Proxemic Behavior," in *American Anthropologist* LXV (October, 1963), p. 1012. This article also offers a good summary of Hall's categories of proxemic behavior.

154. Robert Deutsch and Carl Auerbach, "Eye Movement in Perception of Another Person's Looking Behavior," in *Perceptual and Motor Skills* XL (April, 1975), pp. 475–481; Richard M. Harris and David Rubinstein, "Paralanguage, Communication, and Cognition," in Adam Kendon, Richard M. Harris, and Mary Ritchie Key, editors, *Organization of Behavior in Face-to-Face Interaction,* pp. 245–255.

155. A. Morrison and D. McIntyre, *Teachers and Teaching* (Baltimore, Md.: Penguin, 1969), pp. 162–163.

156. Michael Argyle and Mark Cook, *Gaze and Mutual Gaze,* p. 144.

157. Lester Luborsky, Barton Blinder, and Jean Schimek, "Looking, Recalling, and GSR as a Function of Defense," in *Journal of Abnormal Psychology* LXX (August, 1965), pp. 270–280.

158. Michael Argyle and Mark Cook, *Gaze and Mutual Gaze,* p. 74.

159. Harvey B. Sarles, "A Human Ethological Approach to Communication: Ideas in Transit Around the Cartesian Impasse," in Adam Kendon, Richard M. Harris, and Mary Ritchie Key, editors. *Organization of Behavior in Face-to-Face Interaction,* p. 33.

160. Gerard I. Nierenberg and Henry H. Calero, *How to Read a Person Like a Book,* p. 120.

161. Michael Argyle and Mark Cook, *Gaze and Mutual Gaze,* pp. 1–2.

162. Gerard I. Nierenberg and Henry H. Calero, *How to Read a Person Like a Book,* p. 24.

163. K. T. Strongman and B. G. Champness, "Dominance Hierarchies and Conflict in Eye Contact," in *Acta Psychologica* XXVIII (November, 1968), pp. 376–386.
164. H. T. Moore and A. R. Galliland, "The Measurement of Aggressiveness," in *Journal of Applied Psychology* V (June, 1921), pp. 97–118.
165. Mark Cook and Jacqueline M. C. Smith, "The Role of Gaze in Impression Formation," in *British Journal of Social and Clinical Psychology* XIV (February, 1975), pp. 19–25.
166. The motorcyclists in this case were confederates with the experimenters. Phoebe C. Ellsworth, J. Merrill Carlsmith, and Alexander Henson, "The Stare as a Stimulus to Flight in Human Subjects: A Series of Field Experiments," in *Journal of Personality and Social Psychology* XXI (December, 1972), pp. 302–311.
167. Eric Ponder and W. P. Kennedy, "On the Act of Blinking," in *Quarterly Journal of Experimental Physiology* XVIII (August, 1927), pp. 89–110; Elliott A. Wiener and Paul Concepcion, "Effects of Affective Stimuli on Eyeblink Rate and Anxiety," in *Journal of Clinical Psychology* XXXXI (April, 1975), pp. 256–259.
168. Gerard I. Nierenberg and Henry H. Calero, *How to Read a Person Like a Book,* p. 90.
169. Albert Mehrabian, *Silent Messages,* p. 29.
170. C. Stanley Harris, Richard I. Thackray, and Richard W. Schoenberger, "Blink Rate as a Function of Induced Muscular Tension and Manifest Anxiety," in *Perceptual and Motor Skills* XXII (February, 1966), pp. 155–160.
171. Jay S. Efran and Andrew Broughton, "Effect of Expectancies for Social Approval on Visual Behavior," in *Journal of Personality and Social Psychology* IV (July, 1966), pp. 103–107.
172. Adam Kendon and Mark Cook, "The Consistency of Gaze Patterns in Social Interaction," in *British Journal of Psychology* LX (November, 1969), pp. 481–494. In an experiment of role-play conflict between dating couples, it was found that reduced eye contact variously conveyed disapproval, cues of lower interpersonal power, and a reduction of intimacy. John E. Lochman and George Allen, "Nonverbal Communication of Couples in Conflict," in *Journal of Research in Personality* XV (June, 1981), pp. 253–269.
173. Michael Argyle and Mark Cook, *Gaze and Mutual Gaze,* p. 147.
174. William L. Libby Jr., "Eye Contact and Direction of Looking as Stable Individual Differences," in *Journal of Experimental Research on Personality* IV (October, 1970), pp. 303–312.
175. Ralph V. Exline et al., "Visual Interaction in Relation to Machiavellianism and an Unethical Act," in Richard Christie and Florence L. Geis, editors, *Studies in Machiavellianism* (New York: Academic Press, 1970), pp. 53–75.
176. Ralph V. Exline and Lewis C. Winters, "Affective Relations and Mutual Glances in Dyads," in Silvan S. Tomkins and Carroll E. Izard, editors, *Affect, Cognition, and Personality,* pp. 319–350.
177. Ralph Exline, David Gray, and Dorothy Schuette, "Visual Behavior in a Dyad as Affected by Interview Content and Sex of Respondent," in *Journal of Personality and Social Psychology* I (March, 1965), pp. 201–209.
178. Ralph V. Exline, "Explorations in the Process of Person Perception: Visual Interaction in Relation to Competition, Sex, and the Need for Affiliation," in *Journal of Personality* XXXI (March, 1963) pp. 1–20.
179. Michael Argyle and Mark Cook, *Gaze and Mutual Gaze,* p. 149. Ralph Exline's

investigation concluded that there tends to be a strong interaction among sex, strength of affiliation motivation, and gaze. Ralph V. Exline, "Explorations in the Process of Person Perception: Visual Interaction in Relation to Competition, Sex, and the Need for Affiliation," pp. 1–20. See also Samuel Juni and Tobi Hershkowitz-Friedman, "Interpersonal Looking as a Function of Status, Self-Esteem, and Sex," in *Psychological Reports* XLVIII (February, 1981), pp. 273–274.

180. Michael Argyle and Mark Cook, *Gaze and Mutual Gaze*, p. 81.

181. Harvey B. Sarles, "A Human Ethological Approach to Communication: Ideas in Transit around the Cartesian Impasse," p. 33.

182. Paul Ekman and Wallace V. Friesen, *Unmasking the Face*, pp. 103–105, 119–121.

183. J. A. R. A. M. van Hooff, "A Comparative Approach to the Phylogeny of Laughter and Smiling," in R. A. Hinde, editor, *Non-verbal Communication*, p. 211.

184. *Ibid*, p. 229.

185. Albert Mehrabian, *Silent Messages*, p. 61; Albert Mehrabian, "Verbal and Nonverbal Interaction of Strangers in a Waiting Situation," in *Journal of Experimental Research in Personality* V (June, 1971), pp. 127–138.

186. Michael J. Gatton and John D. Tyler, "Nonverbal Interview Behavior and Dependency," in *Journal of Social Psychology* XCII (August, 1974), pp. 303–304.

187. N. G. Blurton Jones, "Non-verbal Communication in Children," in R. A. Hinde, editor, *Non-verbal Communication*, p. 282.

188. Michael Argyle and Mark Cook, *Gaze and Mutual Gaze*, p. 64.

189. Albert Mehrabian, *Nonverbal Communication*, pp. 12, 21.

190. This is especially true if the smiling behavior of the first person is done in direct response to a second person's smiling at that first person. On this point, see Dale O. Jorgenson, "Nonverbal Assessment of Attitudinal Affect with the Smile-Return Technique," in *Journal of Social Psychology* CVI (December, 1978), pp. 173–179.

191. On this last point, see Lawrence J. Brunner, "Smiles Can be Back Channels," in *Journal of Personality and Social Psychology* XXXVII (May, 1979), pp. 728–734.

192. I. Eibl-Eibesfeldt, "Similarities and Differences between Cultures in Expressive Movements," in R. A. Hinde, editor, *Non-verbal Communication*, pp. 303, 311–312; W. John Smith, Julia Chase, and Anna Katz Lieblich, "Tongue Showing: A Facial Display of Humans and Other Primate Species," in *Semiotica* XI (Fall, 1974), p. 202.

193. Harvey B. Sarles, "A Human Ethological Approach to Communication: Ideas in Transit Around the Cartesian Impasse," p. 37.

194. W. John Smith, Julia Chase, and Anna Katz Lieblich, "Tongue Showing: A Facial Display of Humans and Other Primate Species," pp. 201–246.

195. Henry W. Seaford Jr., "Facial Expression Dialect: An Example," p. 154.

196. "In Central Europe also the [playful tongue-showing] pattern can be observed, but it is loaded with sexual meaning and therefore considered indecent." I. Eibl-Eibesfeldt, "Similarities and Differences between Cultures in Expressive Movements," p. 303.

197. Martha A. Davis, "Towards Understanding the Intrinsic in Body Movement," unpublished doctoral dissertation, Yeshiva University, 1973.

198. Ray L. Birdwhistell, "Kinesics," p. 380, italics deleted.
199. Ray L. Birdwhistell, *Kinesics and Context* (Philadelphia: University of Pennsylvania, 1970), pp. 257–302.
200. Michael Argyle, "The Syntaxes of Bodily Communication," pp. 143–161.
201. On this last point, see Pius XII, "Sacramentum Ordinis," in *Acta Apostolicae Sedis* XL (29 Januarii, 1948), pp. 6–7.
202. Mark L. Knapp, *Nonverbal Communication in Human Interaction*, p. 101.
203. These studies are summarized in Paul Ekman and Wallace V. Friesen, "The Repertoire of Nonverbal Behavior: Categories, Origins, Usage, and Coding," pp. 50–52, and also in Norbert Freedman and Stanley P. Hoffman, "Kinetic Behavior in Altered Clinical States: Approach to Objective Analysis of Motor Behavior during Clinical Interviews," in *Perceptual and Motor Skills* XXIV (April, 1967), pp. 527–539.
204. Paul Ekman and Wallace V. Friesen, "Hand Movements," in *Journal of Communication* XXII (December, 1972), pp. 362–364; see also Paul Ekman and Wallace V. Friesen, "Nonverbal Behavior in Psychotherapy Research."
205. James J. Thompson, *Beyond Words: Nonverbal Communication in the Classroom* (New York: Citation, 1973), pp. 156–157.
206. Jurgen Ruesch and Weldon Kees, *Nonverbal Behavior*, p. 37.
207. Mary Ritchie Key, *Paralanguage and Kinesics*, pp. 36–37.
208. Allen T. Dittmann and Lynn G. Llewellyn, "Body Movement and Speech Rhythm in Social Conversation," in *Journal of Personality and Socal Psychology* XI (February, 1969), p. 101.
209. David Efron, *Gesture and Environment*.
210. This last point is made in Michael Argyle, *Bodily Communication*, p. 260.
211. Data such as these constitute a sharp empirically supported repudiation of Françoise Darcy-Bérubé's extraordinarily naive claim that religious instruction of the truly Christian sort is somehow exempt or ought to be exempt from elements of persuasion. If one were to adopt Darcy-Bérubé's views, human communication would cease, since all human communication by its very nature is inherently bound up with persuasive behaviors, quasimanipulative behaviors, and even with manipulative behaviors. Indeed, Albert Scheflen's well-regarded empirical research has convincingly shown that by its very nature, human communication, especially nonverbal communication, involves a significant degree of behavioral control. Françoise Darcy-Bérubé, "The Challenge Ahead of Us," in Padraic O'Hare, editor, *Foundations of Religious Education* (New York: Paulist, 1978), pp. 118–119. Albert E. Scheflen and Alice Scheflen, *Body Language and Social Order: Communication as Behavioral Control* (Englewood Cliffs, N.J.: Prentice-Hall, 1972).
212. Howard M. Rosenfeld, "Approval-seeking and Approval-inducing Functions of Verbal and Nonverbal Responses in the Dyad," in *Journal of Personality and Social Psychology* IV (December, 1966), p. 603; also Howard M. Rosenfeld, "Nonverbal Reciprocation of Approval: An Experimental Analysis," in *Journal of Experimental and Social Psychology* III (January, 1967), pp. 102–111. In these studies, Rosenfeld gauged the effectiveness of persuasion on the basis of the degree to which the individual interacting with the persuader perceived this persuasive attempt to be.
213. Albert Mehrabian, *Nonverbal Communication*, pp. 78–79.
214. Michael Argyle, *Social Interaction*, p. 104.
215. Albert Mehrabian, *Nonverbal Communication*, p. 179.

216. Gene Davis found that first-grade general education teachers were basically unaware of the influence of their nonverbal behaviors on their students. If this result holds true for religious educators in school and nonschool settings, then the need to professionally prepare these religious educators in nonverbal behavior is all the more imperative. Gene L. Davis, "Nonverbal Behavior of First Grade Teachers in Different Socio-economic Level Elementary Schools," unpublished doctoral dissertation, Oklahoma State University, 1973.

217. Michael Argyle, *Social Interaction,* p. 104; Albert Mehrabian, *Nonverbal Communication,* p. 180.

218. Adam Kendon and Andrew Ferber, "A Description of Some Human Greetings," in Richard P. Michael and John H. Crook, editors, *Comparative Ecology and the Behaviour of Primates* (London: Academic Press, 1973), pp. 591–668; Gerard I. Nierenberg and Henry H. Calero, *How to Read a Person Like a Book,* p. 54; Mary Ritchie Key, *Paralanguage and Kinesics,* p. 152.

219. Michael Argyle, *Social Interaction,* p. 104.

220. John Spiegel and Pavel Machotka, *Messages of the Body* (New York: Free Press, 1974), p. 273.

221. *Ibid.,* pp. 266, 273–274.

222. Albert Mehrabian, *Silent Messages,* p. 129.

223. In this respect, a head nod is roughly equivalent to the "Mm-Hmm" in a telephone conversation. See Michael Argyle, "Non-verbal Communication in Human Interaction," p. 256; also I. Eibl-Eibesfeldt, "Similarities and Differences Between Cultures in Expressive Movements."

224. Albert Mehrabian, *Nonverbal Communication,* p. 83.

225. Albert Mehrabian, *Silent Messages,* p. 61.

226. *Ibid.,* p. 119.

227. Michael Argyle, "Human Social Interaction," p. 249.

228. On the head as a component of offering and accepting the floor, see Andrew P. Thomas and Peter Bull, "The Role of Pre-speech Posture Change in Dyadic Interaction," in *British Journal of Social Psychology* XX (June, 1981), pp. 105–111.

229. Albert Mehrabian, *Nonverbal Communication,* pp. 58–61, 81.

230. I. Eibl-Eibesfeldt, "Similarities and Differences between Cultures in Expressive Movements," p. 304.

231. Mary Ritchie Key, *Paralanguage and Kinesics,* pp. 90–91.

232. Wilhelm Wundt, *The Language of Gestures,* translated by J. S. Thayer, C. M. Greenleaf, and M. D. Silberman (The Hague: Mouton, 1973), p. 67.

233. This outer limit of personal space can, of course, be subsequently modified or constricted by the individual. For a discussion of personal space from the perspective of extended arms, see John Spiegel and Pavel Mochotka, *Messages of the Body,* pp. 119–124.

234. Spiegel and Machotka prefer the term "axial space."

235. John Spiegel and Pavel Machotka, *Messages of the Body,* pp. 220–221, 282, 284–285.

236. *Ibid.,* pp. 182–183, 195, 219–221, 285–286, 290, 320.

237. *Ibid.,* pp. 194–195, 220–221, 278, 282–287, 290.

238. Chris L. Kleinke, *First Impressions* (Englewood Cliffs, N.J.: Prentice-Hall, 1975), p. 57.

239. John Spiegel and Pavel Machotka, *Messages of the Body,* pp. 193, 202, 220.

240. Gerard I. Nierenberg and Henry H. Calero, *How to Read a Person Like a Book,* p. 37.

241. Chris L. Kleinke, *First Impressions*, p. 58.
242. *Ibid.*, p. 92.
243. Wayne E. Oates, *The Psychology of Religion* (Waco, Tex.: Word, 1973), p. 142.
244. Sharon R. Gitlin, "A Dimensional Analysis of Manual Expression," in *Journal of Personality and Social Psychology* XV (July, 1970).
245. Paul Ekman and Wallace V. Friesen, "Nonverbal Behavior in Psychotherapy Research," p. 202.
246. *Ibid.*, p. 207, 210–211.
247. *Ibid.*
248. *Ibid.*
249. Mark L. Knapp, *Nonverbal Communication in Human Interaction*, p. 191.
250. This fact has not been lost on artists painting religious themes down through the centuries.
251. The eye and the ear do not directly encounter the world outside the self in the sense of immediate contact.
252. Albert E. Scheflen, *Body Language and Social Order: Communication as Behavioral Control*, p. 41.
253. Gerard I. Nierenberg and Henry H. Calero, *How to Read a Person Like a Book*, pp. 74–75.
254. For a discussion of the role of the hand in art as well as in the communication of attitudes, see Ernst Jokl, "The Human Hand," in *International Journal of Sport Psychology* XII (Number 2, 1981), pp. 140–148.
255. On this last point, see Mark L. Knapp, *Nonverbal Communication in Human Interaction*, pp. 191–192.
256. Ray Birdwhistell, *Kinesics and Context*, p. 278.
257. Paul Ekman and Wallace V. Firesen, "Nonverbal Behavior in Psychotherapy Research," p. 199.
258. *Ibid.*, p. 200; Robert J. Edelmann and Sarah H. Hampson, "The Recognition of Embarrassment," in *Personality and Psychology Bulletin* VII (March, 1981), pp. 109–116.
259. John Spiegel and Pavel Machotka, *Messages of the Body*, p. 282.
260. Albert E. Scheflen, *Body Language and Social Order: Communication as Social Control*, pp. 30–31.
261. Gerard I. Nierenberg and Henry H. Calero, *How to Read a Person Like a Book*, pp. 14–15, 39, 47–50, 62.
262. On this point, see Julius Fast, *Body Language*, pp. 145–146.
263. Albert Mehrabian, *Nonverbal Communication*, pp. 71, 153, 63–64.
264. *Ibid.*, pp. 1, 63–64, 112–115.
265. George F. Mahl, "Gestures and Body Movements in Interviews," in John M. Shlien, editor, *Research in Psychotherapy*, volume III (Washington, D.C.: American Psychological Association, 1968), p. 305.
266. Albert E. Scheflen, *Body Language and Social Order: Communication as Behavioral Control*, p. 68.
267. William T. James, "A Study of the Expression of Bodily Posture," in *Journal of General Psychology* VII (October, 1932), pp. 405–436. This researcher is not the William James (died 1910) who wrote *The Varieties of Religious Experience*.
268. Gordon W. Hewes, "World Distribution of Certain Postural Habits," in *American Anthropologist* LVII (April, 1955), p. 242.
269. *"This is the Whole, That is Whole, Whole emerges from Whole, Whole subtracted from Whole results in Whole.* The invisible, the cosmic consciousness, is

the Whole; the visible, the phenomenal universe, too, is the Whole. From the Whole, the Whole has come. The Whole remains the same, even after the Whole comes out of the Whole.'' Ajit Mookerjee, *Yoga Art* (Boston: New York Graphic Society, 1975), p. 19.

270. J. C. Brengelmann, "Expressive Movements and Abnormal Behavior," in H. J. Eysenck, editor, *Handbook of Abnormal Psychology* (New York: Basic Books, 1960), p. 63.

271. See, for example, Felix Deutsch, "Analysis of Postural Behavior," in *Psychoanalytic Quarterly* XLV (Summer, 1947), pp. 195–213.

272. Sigmund Freud, *Psychopathology of Everyday Life,* translated by A. A. Brill. (London: Benn, 1921), pp. 124–150.

273. Michael Argyle, *Bodily Communication,* p. 281.

274. Albert Mehrabian, *Nonverbal Communication,* pp. 16–30.

275. Michael Argyle, "Non-verbal Communication in Human Social Interaction," p. 256.

276. Michael M. Reece and Robert N. Whitman, "Expressive Movements, Warmth, and Verbal Reinforcement," in *Journal of Abnormal and Social Psychology* LXIV (March, 1962), pp. 234–236.

277. Albert E. Scheflen, "The Significance of Posture in Communication Systems," in *Psychiatry* XXVII (November, 1964), p. 316.

278. Albert Mehrabian, *Nonverbal Communication,* p. 192.

279. Albert Mehrabian, "Inference of Attitudes from the Posture, Orientation, and Distance of a Communicator," in *Journal of Consulting and Clinical Psychology* XXXII (June, 1968), p. 307.

280. Albert Mehrabian, *Nonverbal Communication,* pp. 19, 67.

281. Deborah L. Trout and Howard M. Rosenfeld, "The Effect of Postural Lean and Body Congruence on the Judgment of Psychotherapeutic Rapport," in *Journal of Nonverbal Behavior* IV (Spring, 1980), pp. 176–190.

282. Albert Mehrabian, *Nonverbal Communication,* p. 193.

283. *Ibid.,* pp. 11, 26, 79.

284. *Ibid.,* p. 193.

285. Albert Mehrabian, "Inference of Attitudes from the Posture, Orientation, and Distance of a Communicator," p. 307.

286. Albert Mehrabian, *Nonverbal Communication,* p. 67.

287. *Ibid.*

288. Albert Mehrabian and Martin Williams, "Nonverbal Concomitants of Perceived and Intended Persuasiveness," p. 44.

289. Such interaction includes both the individual's use of these spaces as well as the individual's perception of these spaces. On this point see Howard A. Smith, "Nonverbal Communication in Teaching," in *Review of Educational Research* XLIX (Fall, 1979), p. 644.

290. Miles S. Patterson, "The Role of Space in Social Interaction," in Aron W. Siegman and Stanley Feldstein, editors, *Nonverbal Behavior and Communication* (Hillsdale, N.J.: Erlbaum, 1978), pp. 266–268.

291. *Ibid.* p. 268.

292. Edward T. Hall, *The Hidden Dimension* (Garden City, N.Y.: Doubleday Anchor, 1969), pp. 113–129.

293. Robert Sommer, *Personal Space: The Behavioral Basis of Design* (Englewood Cliffs, N.J.: Prentice-Hall, 1969), p. 3.

294. Françoise Darcy-Bérubé seems to imply that religious educators who use prox-emics and other deliberative structurers of the learning situation in order to facilitate desired outcomes are manipulative. She seems to prefer the untram-meled blowing of the Spirit instead, a Spirit which makes religious instruction essentially uncontrollable and unpredictable. What Darcy-Bérubé fails to under-stand is that *all* proxemic arrangements and activities, whether structured or simply "there" in an unstructured fashion, *eis ipsis* tend to yield some set of general or specific values. Thus the religious educator who ignores or deprecates deliberative proxemic arrangements is not eliminating manipulativeness by fail-ing to attend to proxemics, but rather is thereby directly promoting undesirable manipulativeness by allowing space to generate values which might be antitheti-cal both to the outcomes of the lesson and indeed to the Christian message. Furthermore, the burden of proof falls clearly on Darcy-Bérubé with respect to her connotation that the Holy Spirit does (and should!) operate magically in ways other than through the creation which this selfsame Spirit once created and continues to create. Françoise Darcy-Bérubé, "The Challenge Ahead of Us," in Padraic O'Hare, editor, *Foundations of Religious Education*, p. 119.

295. Edward T. Hall, *The Hidden Dimension*, pp. 101–129.

296. *Ibid.*, p. 119.

297. One can hardly imagine, for example, a highly cognitive pedagogical method like either lecturing or Thomas Groome's shared-praxis being enacted at a per-sonal distance, to say nothing of an intimate distance.

298. Robert T. Hall, *The Hidden Dimension*, pp. 131–164.

299. Lawrence J. Severy, Donelson R. Forsyth, and Peggy Jo Wagner, "A Multi-method Assessment of Personal Space Development in Female and Male, Black and White Children," in *Journal of Nonverbal Behavior* IV (Winter, 1979), p. 71.

300. Michael Argyle, *Bodily Communication*, pp. 312–320.

301. Norman Ashcraft and Albert E. Scheflen, *Personal Space: The Making and Breaking of Human Boundaries* (Garden City, N.Y.: Doubleday Anchor, 1976), pp. 73–74

302. Though this liturgical reform was originally pioneered by forward-looking litur-gists prior to the Second Vatican Council, it was not given universal approbation until Vatican II's Constitution on the Sacred Liturgy (*Sacrosanctum Concilium*, promulgated December 4, 1963), and more particularly the document *Inter Oecumenici* (September 26, 1964, especially chapters five and six). The latter document was the first instruction by the Sacred Congregation of Rites on the implementation of the Constitution on the Sacred Liturgy. For an important article of this era, see Godfrey Diekmann, "Altar and Tabernacle," in *Worship* XL (October, 1966), pp. 490–509. For a European view shortly after the Coun-cil, see Joseph Pascher, "Augenblicklicher Stand der Liturgiereform und Aus-blick auf das Kommende," in Franz Hentrich, Herausgeber, *Studien und Berichte der Katholischen Akademie in Bayern*, Band XLII (Würzburg, Bun-desrepublik Deutschland: Echter, 1968), pp. 57–58.

303. Robert Sommer, *Personal Space: The Behavioral Basis of Design*, p. 99.

304. For a book dealing with religious education for personal and cultural freedom, see Kenneth Barker, *Religious Education, Catechesis, and Freedom* (Bir-mingham, Ala.: Religious Education Press, 1981).

305. Howard A. Smith, "Nonverbal Communication in Teaching," pp. 644–645.

306. Robert G. Harper, Arthur N. Wiens, and Joseph D. Matarazzo, *Nonverbal*

Communication: The State of the Art (New York: Wiley, 1978), pp. 277–282.
307. Robert Sommer, *Personal Space: The Behavioral Basis of Design*, p. 102.
308. Ashley Montagu, *Touching: The Human Significance of the Skin* (New York: Columbia University Press, 1971), p. 1.
309. Michael Argyle, *Bodily Communication*, p. 286.
310. Harry F. Harlow, Margaret K. Harlow, and Ernest W. Hansen, "The Maternal Affectional System in Rhesus Monkeys," in Harriet Lange Rheingold, editor, *Maternal Behavior in Mammals* (New York: Wiley, 1963), pp. 267–268.
311. Ashley Montagu, *Touching: The Human Significance of the Skin*, p. 188.
312. Sigmund Freud, *Drei Abhandlungen zur Sexualtheorie und verwandte Schriften* (Frankfurt: Fischer, 1979), pp. 28–29, 54–57.
313. Michael Argyle, *Bodily Communication*, p. 288.
314. Ashley Montagu, *Touching: The Human Significance of the Skin*, p. 93, italics deleted.
315. *Ibid.*
316. Dan P. Millar and Frank E. Millar, *Messages and Myths: Understanding Interpersonal Communication* (Port Washington, N.Y.: Alfred, 1976), p. 93.
317. Ron Adler and Neil Towne, *Looking Out/Looking In.* (San Francisco, Calif.: Rinehart Press, 1975), pp. 225–226.
318. *Ibid.*
319. Lawrence B. Rosenfeld and Jean M. Civisky, *With Words Unspoken: The Nonverbal Experience* (New York: Holt, Rinehart & Winston, 1976), p. 122.
320. Ashley Montagu, *Touching: The Human Significance of the Skin*, p. 213.
321. Dan P. Millar and Frank E. Millar, *Messages and Myths: Understanding Interpersonal Communication*, pp. 93–94.
322. This research is reported in Robert G. Harper, Arthur N. Wiens, and Joseph D. Matarazzo, *Nonverbal Communication*, p. 301.
323. Lawrence K. Frank, "Tactile Communication," in *Genetic Psychology Monographs* LVI (November, 1957), p. 227.
324. Nancy M. Henley, *Body Politics: Power, Sex, and Nonverbal Communication* (Englewood Cliffs, N.J.: Prentice-Hall, 1977), p. 96.
325. Michael Argyle, *Bodily Communication*, p. 287.
326. Lawrence B. Rosenfeld and Jean M. Civisky, *With Words Unspoken: The Nonverbal Experience*, pp. 126–127.
327. David J. Edwards, "The Role of Touch in Interpersonal Relations: Implications for Psychotherapy," in *South African Journal of Psychology* XI (First Quarter, 1981), pp. 29–37.
328. Michael Argyle, *Bodily Communication*, pp. 290–296.
329. *Ibid.*, p. 287.
330. Henley conceptualizes power as most social scientists do, namely the ability and the means to influence other persons to do what one wants. Power is manifested by such things as control, dominance, authority, and status. Nancy M. Henley, *Body Politics: Power, Sex, and Nonverbal Communication*, pp. 19–21.
331. *Ibid.*, p. 101.
332. *Ibid.*, p. 95. In the field of religion, Henley states, "the touch of 'holy men' throughout the ages, including Jesus and the apostles down through the popes, and 'faith healers' everywhere, has been believed to cast out devils and disease" (p. 96). Jesus, apostles, holy men, and faith healers enjoy superior hierarchical status in the society of believers.
333. Nancy M. Henley, "Status and Sex: Some Touching Observations," in *Bulletin of the Psychonomic Society* II (August, 1973), pp. 91–93.

334. Michael Argyle, *Bodily Communication*, p. 291.
335. Some religious educationists would disagree with me on this point. Thomas Groome, for example, believes that the product and process essence of religious education is politics. Thomas H. Groome, *Christian Religious Education*, p. 15.
336. For a summary of some of the pertinent research, see Robert G. Harper, Arthur N. Wiens, and Joseph D. Matarazzo, *Nonverbal Communication*, pp. 300–302.
337. *Ibid.*, p. 298.
338. Ashley Montagu, *Touching: The Human Significance of the Skin*, p. 182.
339. Nancy M. Henley, *Body Politics: Power, Sex, and Nonverbal Communication*, p. 99.
340. Thomas W. Benson and Kenneth D. Frandsen, *An Orientation to Nonverbal Communication* (Chicago: Science Research Associates, 1976), p. 22. The primary cause for such regulations stems from the fact, in Benson and Frandsen's words, that touch "dissolves" interpersonal space and therefore requires crossing personally established boundaries.
341. Lawrence K. Frank, "Tactile Communication", p. 241.
342. O. Michael Watson, *Proxemic Behavior: A Cross-Cultural Study*. (The Hague: Mouton, 1972). See also Dean C. Barnlund, "Communicative Styles in Two Cultures: Japan and the United States," in Adam Kendon, Richard M. Harris, and Mary Ritchie Key, *Organization of Behavior in Face-to-Face Interaction*, pp. 444–447.
343. Nancy M. Henley, *Body Politics: Power, Sex, and Nonverbal Communication*, p. 98.
344. Donna Conant Aguilera, "Relationship between Physical Contact and Verbal Interaction between Nurses and Patients," in *Journal of Psychiatric Nursing and Mental Health Services* (January-February, 1967), pp. 5–21.
345. Ashley Montagu, *Touching: The Human Significance of the Skin*, p. 212.
346. Joyce E. Pattison, "Effects of Touch on Self-Exploration and the Therapeutic Relationship," in *Journal of Consulting and Clinical Psychology* XL (April, 1973), pp. 170–175.
347. Jean Wilson, "The Value of Touch in Psychotherapy," in *American Journal of Orthopsychiatry* LII (January, 1982), pp. 65–72.
348. See Charles M. Galloway, "Teaching and Nonverbal Behavior," in Aaron Wolfgang, editor, *Nonverbal Behavior* (New York: Academic Press, 1979), p. 197.
349. Dana Cristensen, Amerigo Garina, and Louis Boudreau, "Sensitivity to Nonverbal Cues as a Function of Social Competence," in *Journal of Nonverbal Behavior* IV (Spring, 1980), pp. 146–156.
350. Robert Rosenthal et al., "The PONS Test: Measuring Sensitivity to Nonverbal Cues," in Shirley Weitz, editor, *Nonverbal Communication*, 2d edition. (New York: Oxford University Press, 1979), pp. 357–370.
351. Bella M. DePaulo and Robert Rosenthal, "Ambivalence, Discrepancy, and Deception in Nonverbal Communication," in Robert Rosenthal, editor, *Skill in Nonverbal Communication* (Cambridge, Mass.: Oelgeschlager, Gunn, and Hain, 1979), p. 205.
352. Daphne E. Bugental et al., "Verbal-nonverbal Conflict in Parental Messages to Normal and Disturbed Children," in *Journal of Abnormal Psychology* LXXVII (February, 1971), pp. 6–10.
353. James R. Graves and John D. Robinson II, "Proxemic Behavior as a Function of Inconsistent and Consistent Verbal and Nonverbal Messages," in *Journal of Counseling Psychology* XXIII (July, 1976), pp. 333–338.

354. Some helpful books exist which provide a wide variety of nonverbal pedagogical experiences which religious educators can fruitfully use with learners. See, for example, Kenneth T. Morris and Kenneth M. Cinnamon, *A Handbook on Nonverbal Group Exercises* (Springfield, Ill.: Thomas, 1975).
355. See, for example, Frederick S. Perls, Ralph F. Hefferline, and Paul Goodman, *Gestalt Therapy* (New York: Delta, 1965).
356. One of my earliest writings on this subject is James Michael Lee, "The Place of Science in the High School Curriculum," in *Catholic Educational Review* LVII (May, 1959), pp. 302–307.
357. It would appear that this terribly important point is not grasped by some religious educationists such as Françoise Darcy-Bérubé, Mary Boys, Gabriel Moran, and Mary Perkins Ryan.
358. Charles M. Galloway, "Teaching and Nonverbal Behavior," p. 199.

CHAPTER EIGHT

UNCONSCIOUS CONTENT

*"It's not really much good tearing out a page, because
you can see the place where it's been torn."*[1]

—Graham Greene

THE NATURE OF UNCONSCIOUS CONTENT

Unconscious content refers to that kind of content which falls outside
one's own awareness.[2]

Though a great deal of the powerful force and all-pervasiveness of
unconscious content stems from its heavy affective texture and its
symbolized lifestyle, nonetheless it would be erroneous to regard unconscious content as noncognitive. There is a considerable degree of
cognition present in unconscious content. This cognition is not of the
ratiocinative variety; it is extrarational. (I deal briefly with extrarational cognition in Chapter Six of this book.)

Unconscious content is an authentic substantive content in its own
right and not simply a path on the way to conscious content. Though
one important aim of the religious educator is to make unconscious
content manifest in the conscious life of the learner, nonetheless a
significantly large portion of the substantive content which the learner
encounters and eventually acquires in the religious instruction act is
unconscious in nature and in hue. (Indeed, a significant portion of
structural content is also unconscious. By this I mean that much of the
pedagogical transaction which a learner has with the religious educator, with other learners, with the subject matter, and with the environment is and will remain at the level of the unconscious.) Consequently,
to ignore or to denigrate unconscious content is to ignore or to denigrate an important and highly influential substantive content.

Though the existence of processes described as unconscious seems fairly well established, the nature and operations of the unconscious remain extremely controverted, to say the least. Natalino Caputi's extensive review of the literature reveals that the construct of the unconscious is in a state of great confusion, not only at the psychological and philosophical levels, but at the imaginal and verbal levels as well.[3] To be sure, "unconscious" is one of the most troublesome, disputed, and ambiguous terms in all of social science.

One of the major reasons why the nature and operations of the unconscious are so disputed lies in the fact that the unconscious is not a substance but rather a social-scientific construct. A construct is that kind of concept which is deliberately invented or "constructed" for one or more special scientific or heuristic purposes. The principal aim of a construct is to put a certain class of observable phenomena into a viable theoretical framework so that these phenomena can be most fruitfully explained and verified and that future phenomena belonging to the same class can be predicted. Constructs have proven extremely important in social science's mission of more adequately understanding human behavior and of helping persons live more fruitful lives. For example, social-scientific constructs such as learning, attitude, socialization, and the like, are of signal value in assisting us to understand more truly certain activities of the human being and human group.

Why is the unconscious a construct? Why does it have to be "constructed," that is to say, invented? The answer to these questions lies in the very definition of the unconscious given in the opening sentence of this chapter. Because the unconscious by definition lies outside one's awareness, we cannot know through direct observation how it operates, or even that it is actually "there." Thus the only clues we can get about the unconscious are through inferences drawn from direct observation of a person's behavior. I can directly observe myself having a headache, for example, or being emotionally agitated in the stomach. But I cannot observe myself being unconscious or doing this-or-that in a state of unconsciousness. As Carl Jung wrote: "Of the unconscious we can know nothing directly, but indirectly we can perceive the effects that come into consciousness."[4] It was through careful, deliberate, social-scientific work using direct observation through such devices as free association, slips of the tongue, and most notably the dream that scholars such as Sigmund Freud[5] and Carl Jung[6] were able to develop and elaborate on their versions of the construct they termed the unconscious. James Hillman puts the whole matter nicely when he writes: "The unconscious is not proved logically. The idea of an unconscious mind has been held to be a logical contradiction; for what is mind if not consciousness? So the proof of the unconscious is experiential; it is a hypothesis, an inference, derived from living experience as this experience is observed in some manner."[7]

Regardless of the school of depth psychology to which one adheres, the task of the facilitator is to so structure the learning situation that stimuli are introduced or evoked in such a manner that unconscious content is somehow brought to conscious awareness and thus to direct observation.

Because the unconscious is a construct rather than an empirically proven process, there is the natural and almost inevitable tendency for the unconscious to be invented or constructed in a variety of different ways. A construct, after all, is simply the encapsulation of an hypothesis. It is a "best guess" about the nature or operations of a reality. As a hypothesis, a construct is invented in order to permit the imagination of the social scientist to go beyond present scientifically verified explanations and currently orthodox but inadequate theories. (Thus, for example, the construct of the unconscious enabled Freud to go beyond the then-prevalent orthodox theories of insanity such as possession by a supernatural entity called the devil.) To be legitimate and workable, a construct should rest on some measure of empirical support and also contain an element of testability. The more empirical support a construct enjoys, the more fruitful and adequate it will be. By admitting of testability, a construct may subsequently be further buttressed by the acquisition of new empirical support by means of experimentation and the like. The accumulation of increasingly greater amounts of supporting empirical evidence may enable a construct to become transformed into an admissible, operationally valid intervening variable, the kind of construct upon which scientific thinking is based.[8] Depth psychologists try to adduce layer upon layer of empirical support for the construct of the unconscious and attempt to test the adequacy of this concept in a variety of ways. Since this testing cannot usually be experimental but is typically only a variation of recalled events, social scientists outside the depth psychology community often dismiss the results of this testing as not rigorously scientific and hence inadmissable as evidence. Those social scientists inside the depth psychology community, on the other hand, produce their own divergent evidence which supports one or another conflicting view on the nature of the construct they call the unconscious.

Another major factor accounting for widely divergent constructions of the unconscious is the intimate organic relationship which a construct necessarily bears with theory. Since a construct is constructed in order to more adequately explain, predict, and verify phenomena, it naturally follows that a construct is intimately and organically tied in with one or another specific theory.[9] A workable and fruitful construct seldom stands isolated. Rather, a workable and fruitful construct is inserted into a wider theoretical framework and thus becomes structurally related to other constructs, concepts, postulates, facts, and laws.[10] Each theory has a different set of explanations and verifiers, and looks for different predictions. Consequently, each separate theory instinctively tends to invent a different construct or different versions of the same construct.[11] Ruth Munroe, an advocate of the Freudian view of the unconscious, encapsulates the major point made in this paragraph: "Psychology is a young science," she observes, "and how close it is still to deductive philosophy, despite the heavy emphasis on observation and experimentation. Each school erects its own basic principles, which are then used to establish the smaller codification of events necessary for scientific ordering of observational data. Since the principles of all the major schools are derived from important [empirical] observations and are reapplied with sensitive intelligence, good results are attained by all—up to a point."[12]

Despite the considerable variation in the ways in which various theories devise and interpret the construct they call the unconscious, all the theories do concur that this construct is necessary in order to explain and verify a human process. It is in this light that I like to interpret the following statement by Natalino Caputi: "The unconscious is probably more a symbol for the unknown factors in human behavior than anything else."[13]

It is vitally important that the religious educator keep in mind that the unconscious is a logical construct and not a real entity. To reify a construct, to make a real being of the unconscious is unwarranted logically and possibly existentially. The unconscious is not some *res,* not some thing deep inside the human being. Unfortunately, the term "the unconscious" tends to mislead some persons into thinking that the unconscious is a noun and therefore a substance. Actually, the proper use of the term "the unconscious" is adjectival, and is an abbreviated form of "unconscious psychological processes." Ira Progoff puts this point nicely when he states: "The use of the term, *the unconscious,* which seems to be the weakest and may be expected to pass out of usage the soonest, places emphasis upon the *'the.'* Speaking of *the* unconscious presents the term as a noun and carries the implication that the unconscious is a fixed entity."[14]

Like the term unconscious, the term learning and the term attitude are constructs. Learning does not exist as an ontic entity. Attitude does not exist as an ontic entity. Both these terms are constructs used to fruitfully explain and verify certain molar forms of human functioning.

Virtually all major schools of depth psychology agree that the unconscious is a construct which stands for a process and not a product, for an activity and not for a *res.*[15]

Because the unconscious is a logical construct, and because it is a term referring to a hidden process which is revealed obliquely and symbolically rather than directly, there is a natural tendency to use images and metaphors to describe the process. This tendency should not be viewed as a weakness of the construct, but rather as an attempt to describe, however feebly, the nature and operations of a very clouded process. Some of the images and metaphors used to describe the unconscious include: storehouse of memories; dark field; 2,000,000-year-old person within us; seething cauldron; dark continent; internal guru; guardian angel; the other me; the eternally, living, creative, germinal layer.[16]

Since the unconscious is a deeply hidden process, and since the unconscious is construed quite differently by the various theories seeking to explain it, there is a plethora of definitions of the unconscious. These definitions are of considerable practical import because the religious educator or psychotherapist will deal with a learner's unconscious processes according to the way he defines the process, according to the way he construes the process. In his well-known comparative analysis, James Grier Miller found sixteen significantly different definitions of unconsciousness: (1) inanimate, subhuman; (2) absent-minded, daydreaming, unresponsive to stimulation; (3) not mental; (4) undiscriminating; (5) conditioned, acting sheerly on the basis of conditioning; (6) unsensing; (7) unnoticing or unattending; (8) insightless; (9) unremembering; (10) acting instinctively; (11) unrecognizing; (12) acting involuntarily; (13) unable to communicate; (14) ignoring; (15) unavailable to awareness; (16) dynamically repressed away from consciousness, involuntary, made available to consciousness only by special techniques.[17] In their review of some of the pertinent professional literature, Horace English and Ava Champney English observe: "It is said that there are no less than 39 distinct meanings of *unconscious;* it is certain that no author limits himself consistently to one. And nearly all meanings are closely linked to debatable theories. Any user of the term therefore risks suggesting agreement with theories he may deplore."[18]

Schools of depth psychology not only significantly differ on the definition of unconscious; they also significantly differ on the kinds of unconsciousness and/or the levels of unconsciousness. Sigmund Freud distinguishes between what he terms the preconscious and the unconscious. Material which is easily brought to awareness is preconscious. Material which cannot be brought to awareness by means of effort at a designated time but later was found to have been retained by the person is called the unconscious.[19] Carl Jung distinguishes between what he terms the personal unconscious and the collective unconscious. The personal unconscious consists of those materials below awareness which are wholly related to the experience of that individual. The collective unconscious consists of those archetypal materials below awareness which are wholly related to the ancestral experience of the human race.[20] Viktor Frankl distinguishes among what he calls the instinctual unconscious, the spiritual unconscious, and the transcendent unconscious.[21] Roberto Assagioli distinguishes among what he labels the lower unconscious, the middle unconscious, the higher unconscious or superconscious, and the collective unconscious.[22] And so it goes.

There is considerable empirical evidence to suggest that the unconscious is intimately intertwined with a person's physiological functioning, specifically with the structure and operation of the brain. Direct physical stimulation of parts of the brain both in psychophysiological research and in necessary surgical operations while the person is conscious have enabled the individual to bring long-forgotten and nonawared (unconscious) experiences back to the level of awareness. Furthermore, necessary surgical operations which have removed specific parts of the brain have the effect of eliminating any retention of specific conscious or unconscious experiences in one's memory. These empirical findings suggest that the notion advanced by some depth psychologists that previous experiences persist throughout one's lifetime in one's unconscious simply is not true. In terms of the holistic position advanced in the present trilogy on religious instruction, such findings are to be expected. The human person functions as an integer, and not in separate parts each in isolation from the other.

History of the Construct Unconscious

The construct unconscious did not make its first appearance with the publication in 1900 of Sigmund Freud's *The Interpretation of Dreams.* As a matter of fact, physicians, philosophers, theologians, psychologists, and litterateurs had for millenia inferred some kind of psychological activity which takes place outside of conscious life.[23] Galen (c. 130–c. 200 A.D.), the Greek physician and founder of experimental physiology, seems to have recognized that individuals make inferences about the unconscious from their perceptions. Plotinus (c. 205–c. 270 A.D.), an ancient philosopher whose teachings exerted very great influence, clearly indicated that a considerable amount of a person's psychological activity takes place without that individual being aware of it. Augustine (354–430) appears to indicate that human memory contains a spreading limitless room which a person cannot totally grasp by conscious activity. Thomas Aquinas (1224–1274) noted the importance of unconscious functions when he observes that there are processes in the soul of which we are not aware.

Mystics in medieval times and later seem to have been especially cognizant and appreciative of the unconscious. Persons like Meister Eckhart (c. 1260–c. 1327), John of the Cross (1542–1591), and Jakob Böhme (1575–1624) suggested, among other things, that the mystical path to the inmost soul takes a person on a journey to a region of which he is unaware, a region which is at once dark, foreboding, and a locus of the hidden God.

Paracelsus (c. 1493–1541), the Swiss physician, implied in some of his writings that each person is guided by deep biological and spiritual influences of which the individual is seldom aware. Michel de Montaigne (1533–1592), the French essayist, mused on the limited role which awareness plays in life, and discussed the power of inner activity lying outside the realm of consciousness. William Shakespeare (1564–1616) is well known for his allusions to the importance of personal memories and experiences which remain active below the threshold of awareness.

Réné Descartes (1596–1650), the French philosopher, regarded dreams as the physiological activity of the sleeping person's organism, activity which connotes and translates desire. Blaise Pascal (1623–1662), the French mathematician and philosopher, believed that the inner nonlogical core of the person constitutes the seat of the deepest humanity, knowledge, and will. John Milton (1608–1674) put unconscious processes (in the form of imagination) as second only to reason in the galaxy of human powers. Gottfried Wilhelm von Leibnitz (1646–1716), the German philosopher, taught that ordinary human perceptions are composed of countless smaller perceptions which fall below the threshold of awareness. Christian von Wolff (1679–1754), another important German philosopher, stated unequivocally that full human functioning requires the individual to bring hidden psychic material to light by drawing inferences from that of which one is unconscious.

Jean Jacques Rousseau (1712–1778), the French philosopher, contended that the source of many of his motives past and present lie below the threshold of awareness. Johann Gottlieb Fichte (1762–1814), the German philosopher, regarded the unconscious as the ultimate basis of all consciousness even though it never comes to consciousness itself. Franz Anton Mesmer (1734–1815), a German-born physician, believed that underlying the conscious level in each person is a mysterious fluid called animal magnetism. Friedrich Wilhelm Joseph von Schelling (1775–1854), the philosophical link between Fichte and Hegel, contended that in all human activity the conscious and the unconscious cooperate in a dynamic and interplaying fashion. Johann Wolfgang von Goethe (1749–1832), the greatest of all German poets, stated that a person's roots lie in his unconscious rather than in his conscious life. Friedrich von Schiller (1759–1805), the German poet and dramatist, wrote that poetry begins from the unconscious and can be set into motion through the technique of free association. William Wordsworth (1770–1850), the British lyrical poet, rhapsodized on the hidden sources of his thoughts with lines like, ''I held unconscious intercourse with beauty.''

Georg Wilhelm Friedrich Hegel (1770–1831), the German philosopher, viewed the unfolding of the Absolute Spirit as beginning from a most profoundly hidden unconscious instinct and proceeding dialectically to increasingly higher levels of consciousness. Arthur Schopenhauer (1788–1860), the German philosopher, touched on a great many dimensions of the unconscious as the present age understands this construct. Johann Friedrich Herbart (1776–1841), the German philosopher and educationist, held that all mental activity results from the interaction of conscious ideas with unconscious ones. Søren Kierkegaard (1813–1855), the Danish philosopher, sought to penetrate the layers of unconscious distortions of reality in order to ultimately attain the redeeming vision of the Christian message. Carl Gustav Carus (1789–1869), an influential German physician, wrote in the opening sentence of his great work: "The key to understanding the nature of the soul's conscious life lies in the zone of the unconscious."

William Benjamin Carpenter (1813–1885), an Englishman, coined the term "unconscious cerebration" for the action of the brain which produces results which might never have been produced by conscious thought. Henri Frédéric Amiel (1821–1881), a world-renowned Swiss literary critic, strongly believed in the power and omnipresence of the unconscious in daily living. Immanuel Hermann Fichte (1797–1879), the son of the famous philosopher and himself a psychologist, wrote that there are two intimately interconnected fundamental dimensions of mental life, namely the conscious and the unconscious. Eduard von Hartmann (1842–1906), a German, published a very famous three-volume work on the unconscious, a work which is still cited in modern times. Gustav Theodor Fechner (1801–1887), a German and the father of psychophysics, found from experimental research studies that the difference between the waking state and the sleeping state can be compared to mental activities alternately displayed on different theater stages. Wilhelm Max Wundt (1832–1920), the father of experimental psychology, believed that the unconscious mind is the genesis of creative activity. Jean-Martin Charcot (1835–1893), a French neurologist, did research into hysteria and hypnosis which he contended pointed to the existence of unconscious "fixed-ideas" as the nuclei of certain neuroses. Friedrich Nietzsche (1844–1900), the German philosopher, believed that every major advance in knowledge ultimately comes from bringing unconscious materials to consciousness. Nietzsche even invented the term "id" which was later taken over by Freud.

The year in which Nietzsche died, 1900, was the same year that Freud published his first major book. The era of full-blown scientific attention to the unconscious had arrived.

The next year, 1901, the famous French philosopher Henri Bergson forthrightly stated that the main task of psychology in the twentieth century would be to explore the unconscious with particularly sophisticated scientific methods. Whether religious educationists and educators believe Bergson's statement or not, surely they would be foolish if they were to neglect the unconscious.

Conscious and Unconscious

A major recurring leitmotif in my trilogy on religious instruction, and indeed in all of my writings, is holism. Each person is *homo integer*. As applied to the dynamic relationship between conscious human functioning and unconscious human functioning, holism asserts that it is difficult, and indeed highly inaccurate, to draw a rational line or indeed a hard boundary of any sort between conscious and unconscious processes. The conscious and the unconscious are *human* processes and hence function together. It is holistically and scientifically unwarranted to divide the conscious and the unconscious into tight, separate compartments.

Alfred Adler rarely uses the term "unconscious" because he explicitly regards any contrived division between conscious and unconscius as an artificial one. The personality always functions as a unit, states Adler.[24] For Carl Jung, the human psyche is transformed or developed by the dynamic oscillating relationship of consciousness to the contents of the unconscious processes.[25] Even Sigmund Freud, whom some unfriendly critics accuse of tending to dichotomize conscious and unconscious into almost separate unrelated processes, is adamant in uniting conscious and unconscious during psychoanalytic therapy. In Freud's view, successful psychoanalysis takes place when the patient consciously recognizes and consciously deals with those repressed elements in the unconscious dynamic. Neuroses, and especially psychoses, occur when the conscious and unconscious dimensions of the person are cognitively and especially affectively disjointed.[26]

In a foray into a consideration of the unconscious and nonrational dimensions of human experience, Gabriel Moran regards the conceptualization of conscious/unconscious as a helpful device for more totally understanding human life. Moran puts it this way: "One must be careful to understand from the start that this conceptualization [conscious/unconscious] is an attempt to describe the relationship that *is* man. The advance which this description represents is that conscious and unconscious are not metaphysical entities. . . . We are therefore not introducing under slightly altered terms the former [dualistic] division into parts. Rather, we are describing the relational character of human experience and looking for distinguishable poles of activity within a growing unity.''[27] Moran goes on to say that in an organic (holistic) model of the human person, it is really not accurate to state that material is dredged up from the unconscious and transferred to consciousness. Instead, the conscious and the unconscious grow together. Quoting another author, Moran writes: ''As the islands of consciousness grow broader the surrounding seas of the unconsciousness grow deeper.''[28]

As a result of his superb overview of the history of the construct unconscious, Lancelot Law Whyte concludes that ''the antithesis conscious/unconscious probably does not hold the clue to the further advance of psychological theory''[29] because such an antithesis is dualistic and therefore fatal. ''We require a single method of approach which avoids the partly verbal problem of the relations of 'matter' and 'mind' and deals with the changing structure of experienced and observed relationships. It will therefore be assumed that a unified theory [of the human person] is possible, and lies ahead, in which 'material' and 'mental,' 'conscious' and 'unconscious' aspects will be derivable as related components of one primary system of ideas.''[30]

In short, then, the conscious processes and the unconscious processes work together—not necessarily in harmony, but together. This confluent but nonetheless separate functioning of conscious and unconscious processes stands in radical opposition to psychic dualism.[31] One of Sigmund Freud's greatest, though frequently most unheralded achievements, was to break the disastrous dualism which gave rise to concepts like foreign demons substantively inhabiting the person, to escape from the disastrous dualistic split which has wreaked havoc on every individual and culture (including church groups) that has flirted with or even embraced this facile disruption of experience. ''No difficulties have been so profound or so persistent as those which reason has made for itself by its hasty separation of the conscious self from everything else.''[32]

At this juncture in my discussion of the relationship of conscious and unconscious, it should be noted that consciousness or awareness, like unconsciousness, is a logical construct rather than a substantive entity of one sort or another. At our present stage of social-scientific knowledge, the conscious is nothing more than a construct which is built up or constructed on the basis of inferences drawn from observable behaviors such as verbal reports.[33] As a construct, the conscious remains distinct from the responses from which it is inferred.

The unconscious and the conscious, then, are constructs used to describe and somehow conceptually encapsulate two discrete kinds of major fundamental processes which function in an individual's personality system. What, then, is the ongoing dynamic relationship between these two basic human processes we call the unconscious and the conscious? Sigmund Freud calls the unconscious "primary process" and the conscious "secondary process" because in his view the unconscious in human growth and development occurs first, and is therefore primary. Though primary and secondary processes always occur together in human functioning, nonetheless the primary process is present in the person from the very beginning, while the secondary process occurs later when the person orders and controls the primary processes by means of rational thought and voluntary action.[34] For Carl Jung, the conscious arises from the unconscious in human functioning.[35] Jung contends that the unconscious is older than the conscious. The unconscious is the primal datum out of which the conscious arises ever fresh. Therefore consciousness is only a secondary process which is built upon and flows from the fundamental psychic activity, namely the unconscious.[36] Taking the broad view, Jung regards consciousness as phylogenetically and ontogenetically a secondary phenomenon. Just as the human body evolved and shows in its parts evident traces of this evolution, so also the human psyche evolved and reveals evidences of earlier stages. Consciousness in general and in each particular person began its own evolution from the preexistent unconscious state.[37]

The temporal and existential priority of the unconscious over the conscious accounts for what depth psychology claims is the ultimate governance by the unconscious of our here-and-now lives. Sigmund Freud holds that the unconscious demands immediate gratification precisely because it is the primary human process. The secondary process of consciousness depends on primary process. In Freud's view, the basic motivations and "intentions" of a human being arise from that person's unconscious, not from his conscious. The unconscious has its own fundamental inbuilt drive for meaning and for personal goals, a drive which can function with or without conscious awareness. A person deceives himself if he believes that the basic motivations and goal-orientations are primarily the result of the activities of his rational consciousness.[38] In Carl Jung's view of things, it is undeniable that in every important situation in a person's life the individual's consciousness is fundamentally dependent upon the unconscious. The unconscious is "that fundamental stratum or core of human nature where the instincts dwell. Here are those preexistent dynamic factors which ultimately govern the ethical decisions of our consciousness. This core is the unconscious and its contents, concerning which we cannot pass any final judgment."[39] The requisite for fully functioning consciousness is unconscious wholeness. For Jung, unconscious wholeness is "the true *spiritus rector* of all biological and psychic events. Here is a principle which strives for total realization—which in man's case signifies the attainment of total consciousness."[40]

"Know yourself!" is a constant admonition of every religious educator worthy of the name. In the view of depth psychology, self-knowledge can take place only when a person attempts to existentially integrate both unconscious and conscious processes. Such holistic integration requires that a person live on and mesh two planes simultaneously, namely the conscious which attempts to understand truly and cannot, and the unconscious which endeavors to express that which it understands truly and can do so only indirectly such as in dreams and in symbols.[41]

Holistic integration of conscious and unconscious processes is only possible when an individual recognizes that these two processes operate on very different axes. Consciousness typically operates around a logical axis. This logic is both cognitive and affective. (It is a mistake to regard consciousness as synonymous with cognition.) Cognitive logic consists in the logic of ratiocination and intuition, as well as the various modes of logic discussed in Chapter Six. The affective domain has its own particular kind of logic, a point not often recognized by members of the psychotherapeutic community on the one hand and by ultrarationalists on the other hand. Carl Rogers is a deservedly celebrated champion of affective logic, the organismic logic of one's feeling-functions.[42] This organismic logic enables the person to affectively discern or feel what is "right" for him, namely what processes and products advance the development of his personality and which processes and products retard such development.[43] I like to describe this kind of logic as "affective fit." In marked contrast to consciousness, the unconscious operates around a nonlogical or extrarational axis.[44] Put somewhat more conventionally, secondary process (consciousness) has one form of logic, while primary process (unconsciousness) has another quite different form of logic. Unconscious processes are nonlogical only when conscious processes are made the benchmark for logic. As Freud and Jung both agree (though for profoundly different reasons), the unconscious is in a large sense time-less and space-less. Consequently, time gets "mixed up logically," so that in a dream, for example, all sorts of logically bizarre time sequences take place. From the perspective of the unconscious, these apparently odd juxtapositions of time sequences are quite "logical" when the benchmark for such logic is the unconscious. Similarly, all sorts of "strange" spatial configurations take place in unconscious activity—strange when the benchmark is conscious logic. One moment in a dream we are in New York, the next moment with no apparent "logical" connection we are in Singapore.[45] Depth psychologists do not regard the nonlogic of the unconscious as a liability to a person's capacity for understanding or for overt activity. On the contrary, depth psychologists regard nonlogic, including spatio-temporal relativity, as a richer and far more authentic source for understanding and overt activity precisely because conscious logic is limited to sense perception while unconscious nonlogic can transcend the confines of sense perception.[46] The greater breadth and depth of nonlogic—especially in dream, symbol, and image—hold considerable promise in religious instruction, notably in significantly enriching and personalizing one's prayer life.[47]

During the first part of the twentieth century, the study of consciousness very much receded into the background, primarily because of two major factors. First, the exciting and adventuresome discoveries into the new realm of the unconscious as pioneered by such social-scientific giants as Sigmund Freud, Carl Jung, and Alfred Adler had the effect of turning attention away from the anatomy and functions of consciousness. Second, the phenomenal rise and spread of behaviorism tended to ignore or deny constructs such as consciousness which did not readily fit in with their methods of inquiry or with their conception of the human person.[48] In this respect, behaviorism was reinforced, albeit not intentionally, by the philosophical school of logical positivism.[49]

Since the middle of the twentieth century, and especially since the 1960s, there has been a rapid growth in the attention paid to consciousness. Three primary reasons account for this fact. First, a natural tendency arose to explore the other side of the unconscious more deeply and more scientifically. Second, both research and the widespread consumption of consciousness-expanding drugs led to increasingly sophisticated attempts to examine and chart that consciousness which was being expanded by drugs. Third, a fallout of philosophical Existentialism—a fallout probably neither intended nor envisioned by the great European Existentialist philosophers—led a good number of well-educated individuals to take refuge in certain great Eastern religio-philosophical systems like Zen Buddhism or Hinduism, systems which place consciousness and its direct expansion at the heart of their way of life.

Almost all of the remainder of this section will be devoted to summarizing a few scholarly explorations into the nature and functions of consciousness. This information should enable religious educators to better situate the unconscious within the totality of human holistic functioning.

In his careful and in some ways landmark study, Julian Jaynes maps the conscious in terms of what he states are its six fundamental structural features, namely spatialization, excerption, the analog "I," the metaphor "Me," narratization, and conciliation.[50] *Spatialization* is the first and most primitive structural feature of consciousness. The conscious makes and arranges spatial images of everything which a person encounters, including both those realities which have a spatial quality about them and those realities which do not possess a spatial quality. (Spatialization here refers to putting things into some kind of mental or conscious order, and thus includes not only area extension but temporal extension or time, as well.) *Excerption* refers to that feature of consciousness in which a person never "sees" any experienced reality in its entirety, but rather excerpts a portion of that reality. The variables which affect and control excerption merit careful examination since it is upon these variables that depend a person's whole awareness of the world and the persons with whom he interacts. *The analog "I"* refers to that feature of consciousness in which the conscious self is aware of itself thinking this or that, doing this or that. In consciousness, I am aware that I am doing such and such. *The metaphor "Me"* refers to that structural feature of consciousness in which the conscious self catches a glimpse of itself in a kind of autoscopic image. In the metaphor "Me," consciousness enables the person to step outside self a bit and see himself almost as a kind of "other" walking along a street or making an important point in a discussion with fellow religious educators. *Narratization* refers to that feature of consciousness in which a person sees his vicarial self as the main figure in the story of his life. Of especial importance to religious educators is that consciousness chooses to attend and to be aware of those experienced realities which are congruent with one's own narratized stories until the picture which one has of oneself in one's narratized life story veritably determines how a person will decide and act in novel situations as they arise.[51] It is not just my own analog "I" that I am narratizing; it is everything else in my consciousness. *Conciliation* is that structural feature of consciousness in which a person assimilates various data encountered in experience in such a manner as to make these data compatable with the way in which that individual's consciousness has previously ordered the world. For example, when traveling south in the summertime from Paris through the rolling plains of the Beauce, a person gradually sees the great steeples of Chartres on the horizon. The person's consciousness automatically conciliates the rolling plains and the steeples by having the steeples rise from the plains rather than being plunked on the plains from the sky.

A useful description and mapping of consciousness has been proposed by Charles Tart.[52] This description and mapping emphasizes the psychological approach to consciousness. Tart's work is basically a theoretical framework of the sort which stresses a systems approach to the exploration of discrete states of consciousness. In addition to being deliberately anchored in theory, Tart's systems approach to examining consciousness can quite easily be translated into behavioral and into neurophysiological terms, thus giving his work the added potency of interdisciplinary convertibility.

Tart's view takes as its central axis the position that consciousness involves three fundamental elements, namely attention/awareness, psychological structures, and the interaction between attention/ awareness and psychological structures.

Awareness is the recognition that something is happening, together with some ability to direct this recognition to one reality or another. Hence awareness is intimately and inextricably tied in to attention. Awareness involves the process content of consciousness as definitely distinct from the product content(s) of consciousness. Consciousness also implies the awareness of being aware, in other words self-awareness. Awareness can be volitionally directed to some extent. The major phenomenal energy of the consciously experienced mind is attention/awareness. The total amount of attention/awareness available to a person varies from time to time; however, there might well be some fixed upper limit on it for a certain time period, such as an hour or a day.

Psychological structure refers to a relatively stable organization of constituent parts which performs one or more related psychological functions. Structures are hypothesized or constructed explanatory entities tightly drawn from psychological, behavioral, or experiential data. A psychological structure may show variation in the intensity and/or the quality of its activity while still retaining its basic patterns and its basic system function. Thus a psychological structure can remain recognizably the same despite ongoing changes which occur in any of its parts or even as a whole. Some structures primarily or even totally arise from a person's unique developmental history. However, permanent structures create limits on as well as add qualities to what can be done with the input which comes from an individual's own personal developmental history.

While some human structures, notably physiological ones, function almost autonomously with respect to attention/awareness, others must use a certain amount of attention/awareness energy. Such interaction between attention/awareness and structure is necessary for some new structures to be formed, to operate, to have their operation inhibited, to have their structure or operation modified, or to be destructured and dismantled. The interaction between structure and attention/awareness is not always ready or easy. Once a structure has been formed and is operating, the attention/awareness energy required for its operation may be intermittent or continuous. Since structures have their own properties, structures may interact with other structures.

In Tart's view, any particular discrete state of consciousness is made up of a certain number of psychological structures or subsystems, each with its own characteristics and each interacting with the other in a particular pattern. Tart contends that there are ten major subsystems in any discrete state of consciousness, plus an undetermined number of latent psychological functions which may come into operation. These ten major subsystems are: (1) exteroceptors; (2) interoceptors; (3) input processing; (4) memory; (5) sense of identity; (6) evaluation and decision making; (7) subconscious; (8) emotion; (9) time sense; (10) motor output. Exteroceptors refer to those senses for perceiving energies in the external world. Interoceptors refer to those senses for perceiving the conditions of our own bodies. Input processing refers to the vast collection of perceptual learnings which a person receives from exteroceptors and interoceptors. Input processing makes a person's perception highly selective in that it discards an estimated 99 percent of the sensory data reaching the individual, passing on to awareness only instantaneous abstractions of what is "important" in the stimuli reaching the person at any given moment. Memory refers to that collection of specialized memories which store information received from input processing. Sense of identity, sometimes referred to as the ego or sense of "my-ness," is a quality which gets added to other information within one's state of consciousness rather than being information in itself. Evaluation and decision making refer to a person's cognitive processes, namely the various learned and possibly partially innate rules and procedures used in analyzing and manipulating information according to one or more kinds of logic. Subconscious refers to the unconscious as this construct is understood in depth psychology, but also includes many of the qualities which some other psychologists identify as the subliminal self. Emotion refers to the totality of an individual's affects. Time sense refers to the general awareness a person has for the rate of the flow of time and the structuring of experience in terms of psychological time. Motor output refers to an individual's voluntarily controlled skeletal muscles, and also to various internal effects on the person's body involved in certain kinds of actions, e.g., glandular secretions.[53]

Drawing directly on the work of Donald Lindsley,[54] David Klein has devised a useful continuum of consciousness which ranges from an intense level of consciousness at one pole to a lack of consciousness at the other pole.[55] Of especial interest to religious educators is the fact that Klein correlates each level of consciousness with a person's behavioral pattern in that level, his brain waves[56] in that level, and the behavioral efficiency which a person enjoys in that level of consciousness.

In level 1, the state of consciousness is characterized by restricted awareness, divided attention, and a certain haziness and diffuseness. The brain waves are desynchronized, with low to moderate amplitude and with fast, mixed frequencies. The person's overt behavioral state is that of strong excited emotion, as in fear or rage. His overt behavioral efficiency is poor, with a lack of control, freezing-up, and disorganization.

In level 2, the state of consciousness is characterized by selective attention which may vary or shift; there is also concentration, anticipation, and set. The brain waves are partially synchronized, with mainly fast, low amplitude waves. The person's overt behavioral state is that of alert attentiveness. His overt behavioral efficiency is organized for serial responses and is good in terms of reactions which are efficient, selective, and quick.

In level 3, the state of consciousness is characterized by a certain wandering in attention, with a tendency toward free association. The brain waves are synchronized with an optimal alpha rhythm. The person's overt behavioral state is that of relaxed wakefulness. His overt behavioral efficiency is good, with routine reactions and creative thought.

In level 4, the state of consciousness is characterized by borderline, partial awareness, imagery and reverie, and almost "dreamlike" conditions. The brain waves are reduced alpha and occasional low-amplitude slow waves. The person's overt behavioral state is that of drowsiness. His overt behavioral efficiency is poor in that it is uncoordinated, sporadic, and lacking in sequential timing.

In level 5, the state of consciousness is characterized by markedly reduced consciousness or even a loss of consciousness; it is in this state that dreams occur.[57] The brain waves are in spindle bursts and are slow (larger), with a loss of alphas. The person's overt behavioral state is that of light sleep. His overt behavioral efficiency is absent.

In level 6, the state of consciousness is characterized by a complete loss of awareness, with no memory for stimulation or for dreams. The brain waves are large and very slow synchronous, with a random, irregular pattern. The person's overt behavioral state is that of deep sleep. His overt behavioral efficiency is absent.

In level 7, the state of consciousness is characterized by a complete loss of awareness, with little or no response to stimulation, and amnesia. The brain waves are isoelectric to irregular large slow waves. The person's overt behavioral state is that of a coma. His overt behavioral efficiency is absent.

In level 8, the state of consciousness is characterized by a complete, total, and irreversible loss of awareness as death ensues. The brain waves are isoelectric, with gradual and permanent disappearance of all electrical activity. The person's overt behavioral state is that of death. His overt behavioral efficiency is absent.

One singular benefit to religious educators directly accruing from

Klein's correlation between states of consciousness and their intimate tie-ins with overt behaviors is that this approach wittingly or unwittingly suggests a holistic view of consciousness and indeed of all human functioning. By a holistic view of consciousness I specifically mean a standpoint which incorporates at the most fundamental levels both the physical and the psychological features of the human person. If materialists typically neglect the nonphysical psychological functions of the human person with such notions as "the ghost in the machine," religious educationists and educators tend to severely downplay and almost denigrate the physical components of human functioning in general and of conscious functioning in particular. Yet with each passing year sophisticated physiological research, especially in neurology and in brain functions, indicate the centrality of the physiological in all human endeavor, including cognition and affect. For religious educationists who work out of an Aristotelian or even a Thomistic grounding, the sophisticated physiological research to which I am alluding comes as no surprise and is to be fully expected. After all, both the Stagirite and the Patron of the Schools held that all terrestrial beings are essentially composed of matter as well as form (body and soul in humans), that the soul can only perform in congruence to the body to which it is joined (the matter must be apt for the form), and that it is the body and not the soul which accounts for differences in cognitive and affective ability in persons. Because there is a strong tilt in the religious instruction community away from the physical, an eerie air of etherealness, amorphousness, and unrealness hangs like a spooky pall over the field. If it is to be truly effective, the field of religious instruction must abandon its ensnarement in philosophical mentalism and angelism, and come to a flesh-and-spirit, a blood-and-sweat Christianity. One of the reasons I lean toward performance objectives in religious instruction is precisely because performance objectives are holistic and involve the lifestyle fusion of body and spirit in their execution.[58]

Much of the current interest in the dynamic relationship between a person's consciousness and his physiological functioning stems from brain research, especially that having to do with localization of functions in the brain and with the role of the two hemispheres of the brain. Beginning with the experimental work of Pierre Flourens (1794–1867), continuing with the pioneer work of Pierre Broca (1824–1880) and John Hughlings Jackson (1835–1911), and gaining great momentum since the close of the World War II with the highly significant research of persons like Wilder Penfield and Roger Sperry,[59] we now have a reasonably good idea about those parts of the brain which are physiologically responsible for a wide variety of brain functions.

Brain research has shown that consciousness and the brain are somehow intimately related.[60] The nature of this relationship between brain and consciousness in particular, and brain and mind in general, is still not adequately understood. We understand quite well *that* the brain exercises a wide variety of mental functions, but we do not adequately understand *how* and even more fundamentally *why* specific brain activities function as they do with respect to mental processes and consciousness. Though modern physiological research has refined the physiological elements operative in the brain-mind relationship, it has not solved the brain-mind problem itself. (The brain-mind problem, of course, refers to the nature of the reciprocal action between brain events and mental events.) How do the coded performances of our cortical modules interact with perceptual experiences?[61] How can a brain mechanism readily transform nerve impulses into subjective experience? Conversely, how can subjective experience alter brain structure and function? Though this double-barreled issue is admittedly one of great complexity, religious educationists and educators ought to come to grips with it, lest their fundamental epistemology of the religious instruction act rest on shaky or even nonexistent grounds. The religious educationist or educator can satisfactorily begin to approach the formulation of such an epistemology, however tentative and amenable to revision this epistemology might be, by gaining a minimally adequate knowledge of brain physiology.[62] Such knowledge will help prevent the religious educationist or educator from the falling into glaring errors[63] which could seriously impair his understanding and enactment of the religious instruction act.

Historically and presently, there are two major conflicting views on the brain-mind problem with respect to consciousness. In the first view, consciousness is directly tied in with protoplasm. The conscious mind is no more than a direct read-out from the spatiotemporal patterned operation of the brain. In the second view, the brain is necessary but not sufficient for consciousness. In this view, there is a self-conscious mind associated with the brain, a mind which interacts with the neural machinery of the brain. The self-conscious mind is a subsistent function actively engaged in the process of working on, interpreting, and in some way adding information to the tremendously diverse energy of the brain.[64]

Our understanding of some of the structures and operations of the physiological side of the brain-mind controversy has been enormously enriched and possibly even transformed by ground-breaking research on the two hemispheres of the brain.[65] Despite the almost undeniable fact that our greatly enhanced knowledge of the functions of the hemispheres of the brain will significantly expand our understanding of the *that* in the brain-mind problem, such knowledge is not likely to completely answer the issues of *how* and *why* the brain and the mind dynamically interact as they do.[66]

There is a body of convincing physiological and psychological research evidence which indicates that the brain is bicameral. In other words, there are two major hemispheres in the brain. Surgical stimulation of the hemispheres, and more dramatically, surgical separation of the hemispheres reveal that there are two distinct domains of brain activity and in this sense two distinct domains of consciousness. The research data clearly support the contention that the human brain is asymmetrical both structurally and functionally.[67] It should be underscored, however, that the existence of two distinct and different domains of consciousness says nothing directly about *self*-consciousness, about whether self-consciousness is identical to the sum total of the functions of both hemispheres or is some other separate subsistent functional entity.

The two hemispheres of the brain appear to operate independently of one another. This highly probable view is supported by the present research evidence which indicates that surgical or other kind of separation of the hemispheres creates two independent spheres of consciousness within a single cranium.[68] "It is possible to think of the two hemispheres of the brain almost as two individuals, only one of which can overtly speak, while both can listen and both understand."[69] It seems that the two hemispheres have complementary functions, thus allowing each hemisphere to operate independently while still being enabled to be combined in an integrated fashion.[70] Though the two hemispheres work independently of each other, nonetheless they each share the fruits of their independent operation with one another. Thus the two hemispheres work in a kind of harmony to give an overall unity to consciousness.[71]

At the physiological level, the overall unity of consciousness is maintained by the corpus callosum, a tract of about 200 million nerve fibers which provides an enormous commissural linkage[72] among almost all regions of the two cerebral hemispheres.[73] There is an exceedingly rich and intense traffic of neural impulses in the corpus callosum, traffic which enables both independent hemispheres of the brain to function as an overall unity. The overall functional unity of the two hemispheres through the access of the corpus callosum means that even though both hemispheres are independent, they function together in the performance of any particular task such as speech or musical activity. "Only the person whose corpus callosum has been surgically disconnected is confronted with the choice of utilizing the right or left hemisphere for a particular attention-demanding task."[74] The overall functional unity of the two hemispheres through the corpus callosum suggests a fundamental physiological cause accounting for the overall unified personality style which typically belongs to a normal individual.

Though the normal brain functions as a unity, nonetheless each hemisphere has specific inbuilt abilities and functions.[75] These specific functions are of significance for persons engaged in diverse kinds of religious education ministry, including schoolteachers, counselors, administrators, curriculum builders, youth workers, parents, and so on.

Before proceeding with a discussion of specific abilities and functions of each hemisphere of the brain, it is well to recall from the outset something we all learned in high-school biology, namely that each hemisphere is crossed in a functional X pattern with each of the two sides of the body. Thus the left hemisphere of the brain is linked to the right side of the body, while the right hemisphere of the brain is linked to the left side of the body. Thus when we talk about "right" in everyday speech, we are alluding to the right side of the body but the left side of the brain.

The left hemisphere of the brain, the one connected to the right side of the body, is predominantly involved in cognitive, analytical, and logical activities. The left hemisphere is primarily concerned with verbal and mathematical functions. Stimuli coming into the left hemisphere appear to be processed sequentially and convergently.[76]

The right hemisphere of the brain, the one connected to the left side of the body, is predominantly involved in affective, extrarational, and holistic kinds of activities. The right hemisphere is primarily concerned with spatial relationships. artistic endeavors, music, crafts, body image, and the like. The linguistic abilities of the right hemisphere are extremely limited; to be sure, the right hemisphere is the one dealing with nonverbal behavior. Stimuli coming into the right hemisphere appear to be processed holistically, relationally, simultaneously, and divergently.[77]

Drawing on material presented by other researchers as well as from his own reflections, John Eccles indicates that the following specific performances are characteristic of the left hemisphere of the brain: liaison to consciousness, verbal, linguistic description, ideational, conceptual similarities. analysis over time, analysis of detail, arithmetical and computer-like. The following specific performances are characteristic of the right hemisphere of the brain: no liaison to consciousness, mostly nonverbal, musical, pictorial and pattern sense, visual similarities, synthesis over time, holistic and imaginal, geometrical and spatial.[78]

Distilling a wide variety of sources, Robert Ornstein presents the following table which contrasts two distinct modes of consciousness in a way which can be correlated with the left and right hemispheres of the brain. Ornstein takes pains to state that he created this table for purposes of suggestion and clarification, and not as a final categorical statement. ''Many of the poles are, of course, tendencies and specializations, not at all binary classifications.''[79]

In terms of the substantive contents of religious instruction dealt with in the various chapters of this present volume, we can say that cognitive content and verbal content are typically linked to the left hemisphere of the brain. Affective content, nonverbal content, and unconscious content are typically linked to the right hemisphere.

Persons and cultures which had no specific knowledge of left and right hemispheric functioning in the brain nevertheless were aware of the fact that there are different modes of consciousness. Jerome Bruner, a very important cognitive psychologist whose best work was done around the middle of the twentieth century, wrote: ''Since childhood, I have been enchanted by the fact and the symbolism of the right hand and the left—the one the doer, the other the dreamer. The right is order and lawfulness. . . . Of the left hand we say that it is awkward and, while it has been proposed that art students can seduce their proper hand to more expressiveness by drawing first with the left, we nonetheless suspect this function.''[80] The French word for law, an

MODES OF CONSCIOUSNESS

ORIGIN	FIRST MODE	SECOND MODE
Many sources	Left hemisphere	Right hemisphere
W. Domhoff	Right side of body	Left side of body
Many sources	Day	Night
T. Blackburn	Intellectual	Sensuous
R. Oppenheimer	Time, History	Eternity
A. Deikman	Active	Receptive
M. Polanyi	Explicit	Tacit
J. Levy, R. Sperry	Analytic	Gestalt
J. Bogen	Propositional	Appositional
D. Lee	Lineal	Nonlineal
A. Luria	Sequential	Simultaneous
J. Semmes	Focal	Diffuse
I Ching	The Creative	The Receptive
I Ching	Masculine	Feminine
I Ching	Yang	Ying
I Ching	Light	Dark
I Ching	Time	Space
Many sources	Verbal	Spatial
Many sources	Rational	Intuitive
Vedanta	Buddhi	Manas
C. G. Jung	Causal	Acausal
F. Bacon	Argument	Experience

extremely linear and rational and convergent activity, is *droit,* which literally means "right." The French also speak of socially illegitimate biological descent as being *à la gauche.*[81] French nobility who were of illegitimate descent often featured on their coats of arms the famous *barre sinistre* (in medieval French, the left-hand bar). Indeed, the English word "sinister" is carried over wholesale from the Latin word *sinister* which means "left." The Hopi Indians of the American Southwest distinguish the function of each of the two hands, the right for writing and the left for making music.[82] William Domhoff's survey of myth and symbolism as each of these is connected with left and right concludes that the left is often the zone of the sacred, the taboo, the unconscious, the feminine, the intuitive, and the dreamer.[83] (The visible corporeal left is, of course, linked to the right hemisphere of the brain.)

I wish to again reiterate one of the major points I have been making in this whole section, namely the fundamental unity of consciousness. Though the left and right hemispheres function differently and have different specializations, both do indeed collaborate to operate as one unit. Let me illustrate this pivotal point by alluding to a pertinent finding of physiopsychological research. When a tachistoscope[84] is employed in order to provide stimuli to the right hemisphere alone, and either a nonverbal or verbal response is required, the nonverbal response comes more rapidly than the verbal response. A verbal response requires the information to be sent across the corpus callosum to the left hemisphere, which takes some time. This finding shows that the normal brain does indeed make use of lateral specialization, selecting the appropriate area for differential information processing.[85] The brain, then, operates as a whole utilizing the appropriate hemispheres and local areas to do the job. Another illustration might further clarify the important point I am making about the overall unity of consciousness. It would appear from the available empirical research that the area of creative problem-solving involves the active collaboration of both hemispheres of the brain. The left hemisphere formulates the problem and gives it to the right hemisphere to develop and work out. When the right hemisphere has creatively worked out the problem, it relays its response to the verbal left hemisphere.

Physiopsychological research of the hard-data variety strongly suggests that there are important innate differences between males and females with respect to hemispheric functions. Jerre Levy's comprehensive review of the research literature indicates that boys tend to surpass girls on tests of spatial function by four years of age. For their part, females tend to be superior to males in relating verbal language to nonverbal aspects of communication and in interhemispheric integration of remotely related information. These are just two representative examples of gender-related differences in hemispheric operations.[86] Some individuals, notably a certain segment within the feminist community, argue that sex differences in hemispheric functions stem not from biological or other kinds of innate factors, but rather from culture in general and from differential patterns of social reinforcement in particular. This line of argument suggests, for example, that the left hemisphere of girls matures rapidly because of the reward which society tends to give girls for verbal behavior. Furthermore, this argument continues, the right hemisphere of boys matures rapidly not because of any innate factor but rather as a result of the reward which society tends to give boys for spatial-mechanical performance. In contrast to this line of reasoning propounded by some members of the feminist community, the large corpus of well-conducted research studies adduced by Levy suggests rather strongy that while sex differences in hemispheric functions are partially the effect of social reinforcement, nonetheless there does exist a strong set of sex-related dissimilarities due to biological or other innate factors. The differential performances of males and females on a wide variety of tasks indicate that within-hemisphere organization is profoundly different in the two sexes. One study cited by Levy concluded that irrespective of the nature of cognitive specialization, the left hemisphere of girls and the right hemisphere of boys mature earlier.[87] Thus, arguments which attempt to dismiss the proven neuropsychological differences between the sexes do not seem permissible on the basis of the available research evidence. Levy puts the entire matter very nicely when he states: "A recognition that there are biologically based differences in the neuropsychology of males and females should, in a just society, lead both to an appreciation of the special skills brought to the social system by each sex as well as to an acceptance and encouragement of those with sex-atypical abilities and values."[88] To be genuinely helpful to society and to individuals arguments should be based on research rather than on ideology.

One area in which culture has conditioned our views on brain functioning, however, is that of the major and minor hemispheres of the brain. Clinical reports and neurological research on the brain tend to speak of the left hemisphere as the major or dominant one, and the right hemisphere as the minor one. This notion of hemispheric dominance appears to have developed from Pierre Broca's rule that right-handedness is associated with cortical representation of verbal language in the left hemisphere.[89] Yet as Robert Ornstein pointedly observes, each hemisphere is the major or dominant one depending on the mode of consciousness under consideration. For a linguistician, a mathematician, or a theologian, the left hemisphere is dominant. But for a musician, an artist, or a religious mystic, the right hemisphere is the major one. It is quite possible then, that the terms "major" and "minor" are more of a cultural distinction than a neurological one. The major or dominant mode of Western culture is verbal and cognitive, and this cultural emphasis can have a decided effect on what we label "dominant" and what we call "minor."[90] To be sure, culture might well have exerted a significant influence on the specializations of each hemisphere in the human brain. There is no empirical evidence which indicates that the two cerebral hemispheres in other nonhuman primates are specialized. Two brain research scholars have even suggested that human beings evolved in a manner in which the left hemisphere of the brain is dominant because the sequential, convergent information processes which undergird rational cognition are not readily compatable with the more simultaneous divergent information processes which undergird extrarational or nonrational cognition and affect.[91]

It is highly probable that left and right hemisphere functioning of the brain has direct consequences for religion. Put more directly and more forcefully, religion appears to be a part of brain functioning in general and of right hemispheric functioning in particular. Religion, then, has a physiological foundation, which is as it should be since anything pertaining to a human being's nature must be organically rooted in both body and spirit. Julian Jaynes suggests that the essence of religion resides primarily in the right hemisphere. The history of civilization, Jaynes contends, is a gradual dissolution of the unity of consciousness in the breakdown of the bicameral mind. As humanity became more and more civilized with the passing of the centuries, the left hemisphere came into increasing prominence and the right hemisphere fell into decline. For Jaynes, the hemispheric difference in brain functioning echoes the fundamental difference between God and man. In the Old Testament, as well as in religions of every sort, the role of God and of the gods was the creative planning and guidance of human action in novel situations. Thus the role of God and the gods was in the domain of the right hemisphere. (In my view, the Old Testament had an added right hemisphere function, namely that of intertwined compassion, care, and forgiveness.) God and the gods thus gave these right-hemisphere kinds of directions to humanity's left hemisphere. Even today, Jaynes contends, the right hemisphere of the brain exhibits a vestigal godlike function. Jaynes traces the steady erosion of devout religion and a religious view of humanity to the breakdown of the bicameral mind, to the decline in prominence of the right hemisphere.[92]

It seems to me that the gradual erosion of religion into theology which has taken place in Western civilization over the centuries represents an example of the breakdown of the bicameral mind. As the rational (left hemisphere) more and more triumphed and replaced the extrarational (right hemisphere), so did theology more and more triumph and replace religion. Like any human activity, religion partakes of both hemispheres of the brain. Nonetheless, religion partakes much more fundamentally in right hemisphere functions than in left hemisphere functions. Theology, on the other hand, is almost exclusively an activity of the left hemisphere.[93] Religion is a full-blooded human experience in all its dimensions; it cannot be reduced to the domain of the verbal and the cognitive (left hemisphere). A person can engage in theology at a high level, but this activity in itself will not make that individual religious. Religion has its own existence quite independent of theology. Theology is nothing more than a cognitive, verbal, primarily left-hemispheric reflection upon religion.[94]

If we are to prevent religion from being strangled by theology, if we are to prevent religion from disintegrating into theology, then we must pay much more heed to the right hemisphere which seems to be the primary neurological seat for religious activity. The right hemisphere is highly developed; however it cannot express itself in verbal language and so is not able to disclose any experience of consciousness that is recognized by rational knowledge or words. Roger Sperry goes so far as to suggest that there is another consciousness in the right hemisphere, but that its existence is obscured by a lack of linguistically expressive rational knowledge. The depth psychologists contend that this other consciousness of the right hemisphere is the unconscious. In any event, the religious educator who wishes to teach religion as the overarching substantive content of the lesson must always heed the messages of the right hemisphere. He can do this by attuning himself to the special extrarational manner in which the right hemisphere expresses itself. The burden of this entire chapter is to assist the religious educator in doing just that.

The period following World War II has witnessed one of the greatest emphases the world has ever known on rational consciousness and on the supremacy of the left hemisphere of the brain. In the postwar period, peaking in the 1960s and 1970s, a sharp reaction to this highly rationalistic way of life arose among some people. This reaction against rationalism with its dry husks of human existence took many forms, including philosophical Existentialism and altered states of consciousness.

An altered state of consciousness is "any mental state, induced by various physiological, psychological, or pharmacological maneuvers or agents, which can be recognized by the individual himself (or by an objective observer of the individual) as representing a sufficient deviation in subjective experience or psychological functioning from certain general forms for that individual during alert, waking consciousness. This sufficient deviation may be represented by a greater preoccupation than usual with internal sensations or mental processes, changes in the formal characteristics of thought, and impairment of reality testing to various degrees.''[95] Basically, then, an altered state of consciousness results from agents or maneuvers which in one way or another interfere with the normal inflow of sensory or proprioceptive stimuli, with the normal outflow of motor impulses, with normal affective tone, or with normal activity and organization of cognitive processes. The research suggests that there is a certain range of exteroceptive stimulation which is necessary for maintaining regular, normal, waking consciousness. Stimulation by agents or maneuvers which fall above or below this range, such as in sensory overload or sensory deprivation, seem to be conducive to bringing about an altered state of consciousness.[96]

An altered state of consciousness tends to be typified by a set of general characteristics.[97] It is because an altered state of consciousness possesses these general characteristics in greater or lesser degree that it is attractive to many persons who wish to existentially enter the extra-rational dimension of their personality. The general characteristics of an altered state of consciousness include alterations in thinking, disturbed time sense, loss of control, change in affective expression, alteration of body image, distortions in perception, change in meaning or significance, sense of the ineffable, feelings of rejuvenation, and hypersuggestibility.

Alterations in thinking include subjective disturbances in concentration, memory, attention, and judgment. Primary process thought predominates, and cognitive reality testing tends to become impaired in varying degrees.

Disturbed time sense is that in which the sense of time and chronology become greatly altered. Common expressions of this are subjective feelings of timelessness and the acceleration or deceleration of the pace of time.

Loss of control means that the individual experiences a loss of his normal grip on reality. In some individuals, the loss of control may arouse feelings of powerlessness and anxiety, while in other individuals this loss of control may give rise to feelings of heightened power which paradoxically is achieved precisely because the person is experiencing a loss of rational control. The latter phenomenon is quite common in mystical, ecstatic, or revelatory forms of altered states of consciousness.

Change in affective expression is brought about because of a diminution of rational control and inhibition. Sudden and often unexpected displays of more primal and intense emotion than normal may appear.

Body image is altered in that one's body tends to appear subjectively to oneself other than it is, as for example, weightless, disconnected, enlarged, and so forth. When an altered state of consciousness is mystical or religious, the alteration of body image might take on the added dimension of an experience of oneness or oceanic feelings.

Distortions in perception are among the most common characteristics of an altered state of consciousness. The content of these perceptual distortions might be heavily influenced by cultural, group, individual, or neurophysiological factors. Distortions in perception include increased visual imagery, illusions of all sorts, and subjectively awared hyperacuity of vision.

Change in meaning and significance is an especially important and attractive feature of an altered state of consciousness. In such a state, a person attaches weighty, momentous, and sometimes even cosmic importance and meaning to phenomena which the rational mind normally regards as relatively unimportant or commonplace.

A sense of the ineffable is associated with those altered states of consciousness which tend to be mystical, transcendental, aesthetic, and creative. In an altered state of consciousness which is religious in cast, the person tends to be swept away into the universe of the Godhead, into a kind of first-hand experience of the *numinosum et tremendum,* into the oneness of the One, into a God-drenched reality which oozes divinity immanentially from every speck of phenomena.

Feelings of rejuvenation refer to those emotions which a person experiences subjectively during and after an altered state of consciousness in which that individual feels he is somehow reborn, given a new sense of hope, and otherwise rejuvenated.

Hypersuggestibility refers both to the susceptibility and even propensity of a person in an altered state of consciousness to accept statements made by a leader, as well as to the increased tendency to misperceive or misinterpret various stimuli because of inner fears or wishes.

On the basis of his review of the relevant research, Arnold Ludwig has classified the entire range of altered states of consciousness according to the different ways in which each is induced.[98] Ludwig emphasizes that there may be much overlap among the various types.

Type I is produced by a reduction of exteroceptive stimulation and/or motor activity. Type I includes mental states resulting chiefly from the absolute reduction of sensory input, the change in patterning of sensory data, or constant exposure to repetitive, monotonous stimulation. Examples of a Type I altered state of consciousness include sleep and related phenomena such as dreaming and somnambulism, highway hypnosis, kyack disease, temple sleep, and so forth.

Type II is produced by an increase of exteroceptive stimulation and/or motor activity and/or emotion. Type II includes excitatory mental states resulting principally from sensory overload or bombardment, which may or may not be accompanied by strenuous physical exercise or exertion. Examples of a Type II altered state of consciousness include brainwashing, intensive ''grilling,'' healing trance experiences during revival meetings, spirit possession states, shamanistic trance states during tribal ceremonies, and mental aberrations associated with certain rites of passage.

Type III is produced by greatly increased mental alertness or mental involvement. Type III includes mental states which appear to result primarily from focused or selective hyperalertness over a sustained period of time. Examples of a Type III altered states of consciousness include prolonged sentry duty trance, prolonged radar screen trance, and intense mental absorption states.

Type IV is produced by decreased alertness or relaxation of critical faculties. Type IV includes mental states which appear to occur mainly as a result of what might be described as ''a passive state of mind'' in which active goal-directed thinking is minimal. Examples of a Type IV altered state of consciousness include daydreaming, mediumistic and autohypnotic trances, profound aesthetic experiences, creative and illuminatory states, mental states associated with profound cognitive and muscular relaxation such as during sun-bathing, and Far Eastern mystical states such as in Zen, Zazen, Yoga, and Sufism.

Type V is produced in the presence of somatopsychological factors. Type V includes mental states resulting from alterations in body chemistry or neurophysiology. These alterations may be deliberately induced such as by ingesting consciousness-altering drugs or may occur from conditions over which the person has little or no control. Examples of a Type V altered state of consciousness include hyperglycemia, extreme dehydration, sleep-deprivation states, and pharmacologically induced states resulting from narcotic, sedative, stimulant, or psychedelic drugs.

In terms of religion, the overarching substantive content of religious instruction, I would like to comment somewhat briefly on two of the above-mentioned types of altered states of consciousness, namely type IV and type V. Both of these have found favor with some religionists as a way to facilitate heightened religiousness in their own experience and the experience of others.

The kind of type IV altered state of consciousness which is identified with the Far Eastern mode of awareness manifested itself in the West in the postwar period and peaked in the 1960s and 1970s. This kind of altered state of consciousness is that advanced by Zen Buddhism, Hinduism, or a concocted combination of these two. A leading and influential proponent of this kind of type IV consciousness is Ram Dass, an American.[99] This man is a prototype of an individual who has attempted to integrate the Western mentality into a broader perspective of Far Eastern consciousness, a perspective which Ram Dass claims does not destroy the Western mentality but rather enables it to be elevated to a higher plane.[100] Ram Dass contends that the Western view of consciousness arises from what he terms philosophical materialism which is best exemplified in René Descartes' celebrated maxim *"Cogito, ergo sum"* (I think, therefore I am.). The Cartesian emphasis on a person as existentially identified with rationality is the foundation of Western consciousness. Ram Dass observes that a person is more than his rationality. "I am my extrarationality, my feelings, my desires—and not just my rational processes and products," asserts Ram Dass. Rationality is part of a person's self-definition, but it is not a person's entire self-definition, nor is it even the most important part of his self-definition. To be sure, Zen Buddhism places great emphasis on the rational mind in the form of a *kōan*—but for the explicit purpose of emptying consciousness of rationality.[101]

The overarching goal of the Eastern way to personal and religious perfection is the attainment of the highest possible state of consciousness.[102] This kind of consciousness brings with it enlightenment. The fundamental characteristic of the highest state of consciousness is that of unity.[103] Higher states of consciousness have the eminently practical advantage of enabling a person to transmute himself and other persons spiritually so that everyone can move forward together spiritually, unifying these relationships on higher and higher plateaus of consciousness. At these higher plateaus, a person's attachment to reality is jettisoned so he can be genuinely liberated to become one with God and with self.[104] In attaining higher states of consciousness, all dualism between mind and body must be rejected and cast aside. The mind and body must work together, not separately, if higher states of consciousness are to be attained.[105] Thus there are definite ways of eating, of breathing, and so forth—ways in which the body can best work cooperatively with the mind so as to attain higher levels of consciousness. A person can only attain fulfillment when that individual enjoys an experience which overrides rationality, namely the experience of being with his own existential consciousness.[106]

To attain higher states of consciousness, the person must be existentially congruent with his chakra centers. A chakra is an energy center in the body. Ram Dass calls chakra centers "psychic localizations of psychic energy."[107] There are seven principal chakras. From the first chakra to the seventh, they are located, respectively, at the bottom of the spine, in the genital area, at the navel, in the heart region, at the throat, between the eyebrows, and on top of the head. Each chakra is a power center for a particular ego function. For example, the first chakra, *Muladhara,* is concerned with the survival of the individual as a separate being. The third chakra, *Manipura,* is primarily concerned with power, mastery, and ego control. A person's spiritual occupations are determined by the chakra out of which that individual tends to operate at the moment and habitually. The higher the chakra, the higher is a person's conscious life. Increased consciousness enables an individual to understand his own nature more fully. The higher the level of consciousness, the more creative will be the solutions which an individual offers to problems with which he is confronted. To advance in one's chakra level, the person must transmute his energy from the lower chakras to the higher ones.[108] One of the most effective devices a person can use to become congruent with which chakra is operating at the moment and over the long term in his life is the double-barreled process of tuning and centering. Tuning means to become existentially resonant with one's here-and-now functioning, with the chakra source presently at work. Centering means to position oneself existentially so that a person becomes his consciousness as far as possible.

Tuning and centering are the two primary axes around which Ram Dass and many other Far Eastern oriented practitioners revolve their specific techniques for attaining higher states of consciousness. As a person tunes into different planes of himself, he meets various beings ranging from saints to ghosts, heroes to villains. As a person centers himself around one particular plane, he finds himself moving into that plane.

Two specific techniques which Ram Dass and like-minded Far Eastern devotees use in attaining higher levels of consciousness are the *mantra* and the *mandala*.

A *mantra*[109] is a particular sound or phrase which a person repeats over and over again. One of the most widely used of all mantras is *Om Mani Padme Hum,* which means "God in unmanifest form is like a jewel in the middle of a lotus, manifest in my heart."[110] The goal of ceaselessly repeating the *mantra* is to empty the mind of all rational thought. As a person recites a *mantra* over and over again, he begins to reflect on the meaning of the *mantra.* Slowly the person begins to sift out the relevant meanings from the irrelevant ones. After a while, the individual begins to feel the *mantra* and its vibrations. After another while, the person becomes the *mantra,* so that all rational thoughts are banished and the individual breaks through to attain a higher level of consciousness in which he is in harmony with the eternal present and indeed with the universe.[111]

A *mandala*[112] is a symbol of the universe, a concentrated area where the forces of the universe are gathered. While some *mandalas* are in the form of a circle, most *mandalas* are square or rectangular in shape, and are divided into various sections or "courts." A *mandala* is based on the belief that mind manifests itself in matter, and that there is no ultimate duality between mind and matter. The goal of a *mandala* is that by concentrating on the image of the *mandala,* a person becomes centered in his own being. As the person focuses his attention on the *mandala,* various meanings come to him, as for example the relation of the inner circle to the inmost circle in a *mandala* which has circles in its design. As the individual concentrates on that inner circle, he perceives it as a long tube. Looking more intently, his consciousness plunges down through that tube so that the person gets drawn through the tube into, literally, another frequency of vibration, another level of consciousness.

Far Eastern views on education, especially as exemplified by Ram Dass, have a direct bearing on religious education. After all, all education is in one sense fundamentally religious education, and all religious education is essentially that of raising the learner's level of consciousness. Ram Dass' view of religious education is remarkably similar in many of its fundamental features to the social-science approach to religious instruction, notably stress on the environment, on the teacher, and on learner-centeredness. A structured environment is very important in Ram Dass' way of thinking because he believes that consciousness can only be discovered and advanced in an environment which supports the being of consciousness. An *ashram* is one such structured environment. An *ashram* provides several vital ingredients for the optimum facilitation of learning outcomes including a community of learners to live and commune, a religious educator or spiritual leader to teach the personal existential relevance of consciousness, and the cooperation of everyone to keep the learning environment flourishing both spiritually and financially.[113] Of course it should be emphasized that a religious educator teaches everywhere, and not just in an *ashram*. At many, though not all, states of development in consciousness, a person needs the help of a religious educator. A religious educator is called a *guru*. A *guru* is not a religion teacher in the sense of a person who presents or imparts material. Rather, a *guru* is a religion teacher who takes the learner where the learner is developmentally, and helps the learner attain higher states of consciousness. Each learner finds his *guru* when he is ready. The fundamental thing which a *guru* has to offer the learner is not a presentation or a heralding of subject-matter content, but rather the *guru*'s own state of being. The *guru* offers the learner his own state of being, his own consciousness which has evolved to a higher state. A religious educator, a *guru*, offers the learner the universe because he offers the learner the infinite possibilities of his own higher state of consciousness, according to Ram Dass' view of a *guru* and of a *guru*'s educational activity.

A type V altered state of consciousness, namely that produced by pharmacological substances, seems to be effective in facilitating intense religious experience in some persons who ingest these substances. Individuals who take consciousness-altering drugs for the purpose of heightening their own religious experience include persons who are creative, somewhat daring, and who tire of the institutional and societal banalities with which religion is often admixed. To illustrate the profoundly religious effects which pharmacological substances can have on some persons, I will simply recount two reports of such effects.

David Arthur Bickimer once went to the International Foundation for Advanced Study in California, where under the supervision of researchers and psychologists, he was administered a large dosage of LSD together with psilocybin and mescaline. In order to optimally profit from his experience, Bickimer had spent many months of assiduous preparation studying and talking to qualified individuals about his forthcoming trip. After he ingested the pharmacological substances, he found himself in a type V altered state of consciousness in which he suddenly experienced, among other things, a shining chalice before which he bowed in transfixed adoration.[114]

When Ram Dass was still Richard Alpert, he and some colleagues conducted a scientific experiment at Harvard and Boston University Chapel. The experiment was of a double blind variety. Ten of the twenty theological students in the experiment took a placebo, and the other ten ingested psilocybin. Of the ten divinity students who ingested the pharmacological substance psilocybin, nine had a mystical religious experience. Ram Dass concluded his report by some statements which are highly relevant for those religious educators who contend that religious experience cannot be directly facilitated because it is a totally free gift of God.[115] "Now they had it with psilocybin, but it's in a church, in a regular religious setting, so we're learning something about what rituals of religion are necessary for it to be a religion that brings man into the Spirit, which is what religion is supposed to be about in the first place. So it's entirely possible it can be. It behooves us to have a very, very open mind about all of this at all times."[116]

I wish to make it perfectly clear that I do not recommend persons of any age or station ingesting pharmacological substances in order to attain intense mystical experiences. But neither do I condemn this practice. The fact that persons sometimes feel impelled to ingest pharmacological substances in order to provide themselves with intense religious experiences is itself a condemnation of those religious educators and ecclesiastical officials who do not structure religion lessons and other kinds of ecclesially oriented learning experiences in such a way that learners will thereby attain profound religious experiences of the mystical and nonmystical variety.[117]

I have devoted a considerable portion of this chapter to the topic of consciousness because it is difficult to properly appreciate either the unconscious itself or the role of the unconscious in religious instruction unless one has an adequate grasp of consciousness. The unconscious does not occur in or by itself, but always in existential association with the conscious. One significant task of religious instruction is to help the unconscious become revealed in and through conscious processes. If the religion teacher does not understand consciousness in its contours and depths, then it will be difficult for that educator to deal effectively with unconscious phenomena.

Importance of Unconscious Content

There are many features of the unconscious which make it an important substantive content for religious instruction. Because of limitations of space, I shall list only five reasons why the unconscious constitutes an important substantive content of religious instruction.

Motivation. It is the contention of the overwhelming majority of depth psychologists and psychotherapists that the unconscious is the fundamental seat of human motivation. This statement holds especially true for Freudianism, although most other schools of depth psychology would also admit to this proposition in greater or lesser degree. For classical Freudianism, the id, which in some ways forms the core of the unconscious, is the reservoir of instinctual needs which press toward immediate and total fulfillment.[118] The id contains and is the fundamental source of the person's two basic sets of motives, namely the sexual and the aggressive. Sexual motivation promotes the survival of the species while aggressive motivation promotes the survival of the individual. These two basic motives comprise in Freud's view everything a person really wants in life.[119] The unconscious, primarily through the id, is a person's fundamental source of drive energy[120] empowering his motivations to be put into action. This drive energy which is fueled by both sexual and aggressive instincts is given the name libido in Freudian psychoanalytic theory.[121] Even depth psychologists who are not Freudians, persons of the caliber of Carl Jung, for example, readily admit that the unconscious is the primary source of motivation in human beings.

In his work of facilitating the acquisition of all kinds of substantive content, the religious educator surely must not neglect the role of the learner's powerful unconscious motivation. The religious educator, especially the educator who wishes to teach the learner in and for freedom,[122] ought to be ever mindful of the enormous power of unconscious motivation over the exercise of one's free choices and free actions. Unconscious motivation also constitutes a significant factor in one's search for self-fulfillment. From a personalistic perspective, the unconscious is like an insatiable hunger that drives the learner "to find food for his spirit and nourishment for his growth, that leads him to a constant activity by which he endeavors to fulfill himself."[123] Commenting on the depth psychology view of human motivation from an explicitly Christian vantage point, James VanderVeldt and Robert Odenwald remark that it might well be that basic inner motivations do indeed flow from or through the unconscious. But, as VanderVeldt and Odenwald remind us, a person operates at both conscious and unconscious levels at the same time. A person is conscious of what he is doing.[124] Thus one of the tasks of the religious educator is to so deal with the learner's unconscious that the materials in this hidden process can be brought to consciousness so that they can be dealt with in a pedagogically productive manner.

Creativity. Most depth psychologists hold that human creativity fundamentally springs from the unconscious. Nineteenth-century precursors of depth psychology often believed that the phenomenon of creative inspiration can be compared to a "second personality" which often works dynamically but in a hidden fashion underground, and then bursts through in an eruption of creativity.[125] Carl Jung contends that every worthwhile idea and all creative work are the offspring of unconscious processes.[126] In Jung's view, the ultimate genesis of human creativity lies in the archetypes of human existence which an individual encounters in his unconscious, archetypes which are encased in myriad images and symbols. For Sigmund Freud, creativity, especially when creativity takes artistic form, is intimately tied in with fantasy. Fantasy has its roots in the unconscious. The child lives a rich life of fantasy. This fantasy recedes in adulthood, but the creative person is able to retain some of this fantasy and convert it to imaginative use.[127] Writing from a Freudian point of view, John Hill states: "All creative work is done by the unconscious mind. Poets, artists, and musicians, for example, have to keep their intellectual and critical faculties in abeyance while the unconscious mind creates.''[128] It should be emphasized, however, that eruptions of creativity from the unconscious probably do not just come out of the blue, with no relation to the conscious dimension of one's life. What possibly happens in creativity is that during hours, days, weeks, and months of consciously grappling with a problem and thereby making that problem one's very own, the unconscious mind works on this problem and applies its own unique processes to this problem. The result is a creative solution, a solution which is related yet novel to the conscious mind.[129] It is of interest to note that both Sigmund Freud and Carl Jung suffered what Henri Ellenberger aptly calls "creative illness," namely a protracted period of time (for Jung it lasted from 1913–1919) in which they were emotionally troubled. This "creative illness" in both men followed a time of intense preoccupation into the depths and breadth of the human soul.[130]

As far as I am aware, there is no definitive empirical proof that creativity exclusively or even primarily resides in the unconscious. Indeed, depth psychologists sometime offer what seem to be extremely fanciful and indeed wild explanations of unconscious forces operating in the creative process.[131] Nonetheless, there appears to be some convincing introspective and empirical evidence supporting the limited hypothesis that creativity is at least in part linked to the unconscious.

From the standpoint of religious instruction, creativity is very important because in and through creativity, an individual shares in the work of God's creation. In and through creativity, a person helps unlock the inestimable treasures which God has placed in hidden form throughout the depths of the cosmos and in the human heart as well, treasures which enable the individual to come closer to God. In and through creativity, a person actively cooperates with God in bringing the universe to Point Omega.

Though creativity should be prized in religious instruction, it is often severely neglected and sometimes even despised throughout Christianity in general and Catholicism in particular. This indisputable fact in large measure stems from the heavy socialization emphasis which pervades the institutional church and its officials. This socialization emphasis does not allow for much genuine creativity. Socialization, of course, is that process whereby persons are educated to follow as completely as possible the mores and folkways of the society into which they are being socialized. To use a powerful and perfectly correct image employed by Berard Marthaler (a socialization advocate and devoted apologist for the *ecclesiasticum*), the goal of religious education (catechetics) in the church is "to impress its institutionalized meanings and values powerfully and unforgettably on its members."[132] The image of the medieval seal and the wax is, for me at least, quite revelatory. It is by no accident, then, that the Roman Catholic Church's universal directory on catechetics contains no index entry and, as far as I can detect, no treatment of creativity.[133] The same holds true for the Catholic catechetical directory governing this segment of religious education in the United States.[134] To be sure, the latter document takes pains to quote Paul VI to the effect that any Catholic religious content which is communicated to others "must remain the content of the Catholic faith just exactly as the ecclesial magisterium has received it and transmits it."[135] However, I firmly believe that if religious instruction is to move forward and be prophetic, as well as to be faithful to the Lord of continuous creation, then religious educators must ceaselessly strive to inject heavy and persistent dosages of creativity into the structural content and into the substantive content of religious instruction. To do this, the religious educator must come into living contact with his own unconscious processes, as well as those of the learners.

Working with Learners. In the religious instruction act, the whole person of the teacher interacts with the whole person of the learner. Thus it is not only the educator's and the learner's conscious lives which intersect each other in the religious instruction act; it is also the unconscious lives of each. Teacher and learner meet each other not only in the conscious realm, but in the unconscious realm.[136] As Anna Freud notes, the learner's "unconscious mind, its innate contents as well as its dynamic energies, provides the significant material with which teachers have to deal and which they have to respect."[137]

If the religious educator is to be genuinely cognizant of the learner's unconscious processes, and if he is to effectively deal with these processes, then it would be quite helpful for him to be in active touch with his own unconscious. He can do this by attending to what his dreams are communicating, what happens during moments of free association, and so forth. The words of Morton Trippe Kelsey are instructive here: "If the teacher is aware of his own unconsciousness and of the forces that can play upon him from the spiritual world, he can begin to know what other attitudes he is imparting to his students along with his conscious ones. The teacher needs to know whether he is reinforcing his teaching unconsciously, or if he sometimes imparts unconsciously the opposite of what is intended; particularly is this true for the teaching of religion."[138]

Personal Wholeness. To achieve personal wholeness is to successfully integrate the various areas of one's personality structure into a harmonious melody in which the various human notes and chords collaborate in one way or another. If a person avoids a molar area of human experience such as the unconscious, he makes it difficult for himself to achieve optimum personal wholeness.[139] In this connection Carl Jung writes that the richness of human living derives from the fact that personal existence is both law-abiding and lawless, rational and extrarational. Consequently, rationalism and rationally directed volition can take us only part of the way in the journey of life. If a person allows rational consciousness to become the entire way, then such an individual will have missed a very important part of life's journey.[140] Indeed, by remaining blind to the unconscious and its manifestations, the person condemns himself to an enfeebled journey through life, since the unconscious exerts such a powerful influence on the conscious.[141] Being open to the existence and operation of unconscious processes does not make life easier, since unconscious processes are not predictable and controllable rationally. Being open to the existence and operation of unconscious processes tends to round out the totality of the human equation, and helps the person admit and deal with all his needs, unconscious as well as conscious.[142]

Life might be considerably easier if unconscious processes were not a molar aspect of the human condition. But still it is the unconscious which accounts for much of the essential humanity of the human condition. Depth psychologists claim that the unconscious, with all its dark and troublesome forces (as judged by rational consciousness) is absolutely necessary for wholeness and holiness.[143] Quoting Rainer Maria Rilke, the religious education writer Gabriel Moran states: "If my devils are to leave me, I am afraid my angels will take flight as well."[144] As Moran notes, it is far better in terms of personal wholeness and growth to integrate the unconscious with the conscious in human functioning than attempting to ignore or banish the unconscious.

When the conscious and the unconscious are holistically integrated, both gain increased potency since each becomes less unidimensional and more rounded. Depth psychologists agree that when a person is in touch with his unconscious, he is enabled to live a deeper, more holistic life than were he to be in contact only with the conscious side of his personality. Emotional development, and emotional blockages also, are intimately connected with unconscious processes, and not so much with conscious processes.[145] Emotional blockages often result when conscious processes function in a manner which ignores, smothers, represses, or suppresses the unconscious. In Carl Jung's view, unconscious processes bring with them a greater and deeper sort of knowledge than rational processes, namely "knowledge in eternity, usually without reference to the here and now, not couched in language of the intellect."[146] In Jung's perspective, the more that cognitive rationality dominates, the more impoverished life becomes. "Over-valued reason has this in common with political absolutism: under its domination the individual is pauperized."[147]

Since the unconscious is so necessary for full human and religious living, it becomes a major task of the religious educator to assist learners to be on close terms with their unconscious processes. Being on close existential terms with the unconscious is a difficult undertaking for many individuals, as depth psychologists testify.[148] The religious educator should assist the learner to come to existential grips with his unconscious, not to escape from it.[149] In accomplishing this task, the religious educator should help the learner to go through that moment of twilight, through that crack in the learner's personal universe between the light and the darkness into another world of being, a world which, though of a very different order of reality than what he is used to, is still very much his own. Passing through this crack in his personal universe, the learner will be able to begin to travel, however falteringly at first, on the exciting journey into the depths of his soul.

Religion. As I indicated earlier in this chapter, recognition and acceptance of unconscious processes steadily mounted in Europe during the period from 1700 until the publication of Sigmund Freud's first major book in 1900. During this period, rationalism grew so powerful that it controlled much of religion, and especially theology. Rationalists of all sorts during this period, including well-educated religionists and particularly theologians, came to regard the unconscious as the realm of uncontrollable, irrational forces threatening the social, religious, and theological order which rational consciousness—or so they imagined— had built up over the generations. "Day was challenged by Night, the enlightenment of reason by the tempests and conflicts of intuition and instinct, the soul of man by a dark and frightening, but desperately attractive, inner spirit of temptation and surrender."[150] With the onslaught of Sigmund Freud and scientific depth psychology, the worst fears of the well-educated religionists and especially the rationalistic theologians were confirmed. Until the 1960s, only a few courageous Christian depth psychologists dared to openly challenge the barrage of condemnation directed at depth psychology by many theologians and the ecclesiastical apparatus in which they wielded singular political influence.[151]

Freud's critique of religion caused such an infantile negative and prolonged reaction among most theologians and ecclesiastical officials that one can legitimately wonder whether Freud might not have been correct in his claim that the roots of religion lie in repressed libido. Even now, theologians often seem to be frightened of Freud. This fear extends to almost all of depth psychology, unless that depth psychology is somehow explicitly couched in theological terms and is made an explicit extension of standard theological concepts. Yet, as Hans Küng remarks, Christian theologians can learn a great deal from Freud, not only from his explorations into the unconscious but also from his attempt to deal with religion honestly rather than to deal with it unrealistically or with kid gloves.[152]

Religion is an illusion, writes Sigmund Freud.[153] Religion is a universal compulsive neurosis of the human race.[154] Freud contends that religion is a huge illusion because people have created it in order to shield themselves from primary process (the unconscious), a shielding which makes life basically unreal and hence illusory.[155] Instead of integrating the unconscious with the conscious, people live on a rational conscious plane (secondary process), and consign primary process to a segregated other world they call religion. Freud claims that all the drives which people cannot handle, all the seething inbuilt needs for total self-gratification which are sovereign in primary process are placed in a Holy Grail called religion, a Grail which people claim is wholly other and Other in order to avoid the fact that primary process is a necessary basic dimension of self which must be integrated into one's personalistic functioning. In this perspective, "religion lets us go on being children forever, projecting our wishes for satisfaction and our need for safety onto a sort of divine Santa Claus who rewards us every time we promise to be good. Our infantile fantasies of omnipresence are allowed to continue unchecked by reality through manipulating prayers and obeisances to an all-powerful diety.''[156] By praying to a God out there, we keep our unconscious out there as well. Because religion prevents the unconscious from being integrated with the conscious, the latter is severely debilitated and never becomes sturdy enough to encounter the totality of one's psychic reality. People escape to an illusion which promotes the split between primary and secondary process. For Freud, religion is a sublimation of our raging aggressive and sexual instincts which require total immediate gratification, a sublimation which is illusory.[157]

Religion is very important and indeed necessary, states Carl Jung. Indeed, Jung's voluminous writings represent some of the most significant and far-reaching studies of religious experience ever written.[158] Jung contends that by nature the soul has a religious function. He maintains that the unconscious contains the equivalent of everything that has been formulated in the dogmas of all the churches, and a good deal more to boot.[159] In Jung's view, religion is directly connected with the contents of what he terms the collective unconscious, namely the deeper layer of the unconscious which is impersonal, universal, and common to everyone because it comes down from the human race's psychic past. God is not so much revealed through the churches as through psychological archetypes, the *imago Dei* or image of God which lies in the unconscious. For Jung, then, a person should not seek God above, but rather below—below in the depths of his unconscious processes. John Dunne refines this concept somewhat when he states that in the unconscious, especially in its shadow side, lies the hidden God and the darkness of faith. The human soul has a natural affinity for the darkness of the unconscious because it is there that God dwells and it is there that the person can unite himself with the hidden God.[160] In Jung's view, then, the unconscious offers a host of new and ever fresh possibilities for enriching the life of the spirit[161] because the unconscious is the door through which a person passes to find God, to find his soul, and to find himself. In this vein James Hillman, one of the world's foremost interpreters of Jung, declares that ''it is through the unconscious that many people have found a way into love and a way into religion and have gained some small sense of soul. This is confirmed again and again in analytic [psychotherapeutic] practice.''[162] Because God dwells in the unconscious, all psychological illnesses are ultimately illnesses of a defective religion. Hence to cure psychological illness requires a person, at the most basic level of his existence, to discard a defective or an irreligious mentality and to adopt a mentality which is patterned to an extent after the God archetype within his unconscious. Jung holds that religion fundamentally means that the person is holistically in touch with God and with the other archetypes in unconscious functioning and in this holistic contact achieves that wholeness necessary for human living.[163] Jung regards religious dogma as essentially ''in here'' and not ''out there''—dogma in the unconscious and not in the propositional formulae advanced by church denominations. Genuine religious dogma consists in the immediate experience of meeting the God archetype or other religious reality in the unconscious; denominational propositional dogma by its very nature excludes immediate experience.[164] Jung is none too sympathetic to the Christian churches with their centuries-old emphasis on consciousness in general and on conscious teachings (propositional dogmas) in particular. This is how he puts it: ''Christian civilization has proved hollow to a terrifying degree: it is all veneer, but the inner man has remained untouched and therefore unchanged. His soul is out of key with his external beliefs; in his soul the Christian has not kept pace with external developments. Yes, everything is to be found outside—in image and in word, in Church and in Bible—but never inside. Inside reign the archaic gods, supreme as of old.''[165]

Other depth psychologists and persons knowledgeable in depth psychology have also written sympathetically about the relationship of the spiritual in general and of religion in particular. Viktor Frankl, for example, believes that while spiritual phenomena may be conscious as well as unconscious, nevertheless the spiritual basis of human existence is ultimately unconscious. Hence the center of the human person in the deepest and ultimate sense is unconscious. The spirit is intimately tied in with religion—religion considered in the broad sense of the relationship of a person to God rather than in the sense of the narrow concepts of God promulgated by many representatives of denominational and institutional religion.[166] Rudolf Allers contends that depth psychology shows how truly all-pervasive God is in the universe, all-pervasive down to fundamental unconscious processes. Thus an appreciation of the unconscious reveals more clearly the totality of religion and its privileged place at the core of the human condition.[167] Hinting strongly about the insights and findings of depth psychology, Lewis Sherrill, the Christian religious educationist, boldly declares that sinners have learned "the bitterest lesson which modern Christianity teaches, namely that it has a remarkable metaphysical theory of redemption which in practice, in the hands of many of its servants, cannot reach down into the recesses of the human soul and set that soul free from guilt."[168]

Unless one takes a hard-bitten positivistic or right-wing behaviorist stance, one is forced to admit that depth psychology has proven quite helpful in illuminating some of the ways in which unconscious processes are operative in piety, in theology, and in religious education.[169] Speaking from a theological perspective, Gregory Baum declares that "the insights of depth psychology and in particular the discovery of the unconscious, including the death impulse, have considerably modified the traditional understanding of how men enter into growth and holiness."[170] Placing the construct unconscious squarely within our conceptualization and actualization of religion surely produces a radical change in the way religion has traditionally been conceived and lived.[171] Perhaps, as depth psychology asserts, God is indeed found more in darkness and personal difficulty than in light and in good times.[172] At any event, authentic religious instruction must, if it is to be personalistic, take into account the contours and findings of depth psychology.[173]

In the view of many depth psychologists, most notably Carl Jung and the Jungians, a symbol constitutes a privileged way in which the religious-in-the-unconscious reveals itself to the human person. A symbol is polyvalent. In other words, a symbol can and does contain a variety of meanings. This fact suggests that the meaning and reality of a symbol are not exhausted when a person discovers this or that particular meaning in it. This fact also suggests that symbol is subjective as well as objective, namely that it is a reality which is felt and experienced as well as thought about.[174] Jung underscores the subjective nature of symbol when he states that cognitive rationalists who attack the allegedly magical effects of symbol and symbolically charged activities such as rite miss the essential point, namely the subjective effect of symbol.[175] Though symbols are subjective, they have a certain objectivity of content, as I have previously noted. The objectivity of the content of a symbol enables persons of all cultures to gain some common meanings from the symbol, in addition to their own particular subjective meanings. For the Jungians, archetypes contain deep primordial and often religious meanings. One Jungian, Edward Edinger, claims that in addition to being objectively real as an historical personage, Jesus is "a model for an ideal ego that separates itself from the larger, unconscious 'objective psyche' and, once firm in its own ego identity, finds a way back into relationship with the larger self."[176] For depth psychology, myth and symbol are intimately related, since both have unconscious roots and since both are to a large extent manifestations of unconscious processes. For Jung, myth and symbol are more prototypically religious than any of the particularities of religion such as Christianity. Hence it is a mistake, a deeply religious mistake, for Christianity to attempt to purge from its rites and beliefs that which it contends are non-Christian myths and symbols. This kind of purging will probably cut Christianity off from one of its basic dynamic sources, namely the prototypical and foundational religion found in the unconscious.[177] Ignace Lepp, a depth psychologist, profoundly laments the efforts of the rationalists to rid the world of myth and symbol. Lepp writes that one of the major causes of psychic disorders in the modern world stems from the malevolent influence of rationalism which has caused human beings to lose their whole understanding of the nature and workings of symbol. Rationalists and other kinds of hard-line cognitivists degrade ritual symbolism, liturgical ceremony, biblical parable, and the like, into expressions of magic and a magical mentality. Lepp continues that "even if we had no other reason for wanting to see Jung's psychology spread over a larger domain of professional influence, the fact that it can reeducate us to the language of symbolism is reason enough in itself."[178]

Because religion flows from both the unconscious and the conscious, it is in a uniquely favored position to integrate both processes into the quintessential whole person, into the quintessential fully functioning person.[179] To be sure, this integration of conscious and unconscious is one of religion's greatest strengths, and probably is a major factor accounting for the incredible durability of religion in the face of onslaughts both from persecution and from worldy success. If a person is to gain fulfillment in his life, then one of the first requisites is an integrative functional relationship between his conscious and his unconscious processes.[180] This integrative functional relationship between the conscious and the unconscious is not always smooth or trouble-free, since the relationship between these two basic human processes contains the inbuilt dynamic tension inherent in any set of contraries. This explains why saints and other devout Christians have not always been free from psychological difficulties. Integration in human functioning means working together as a whole; it does not necessarily mean that this working together is effortless, frictionless, or trouble-free. The important point to keep in mind is that religion offers a privileged and in many ways a uniquely favored basin for the conscious and the unconscious to work together integratively.

In past centuries, especially in the ancient and medieval worlds, religion typically served to integrate the conscious with the unconscious in the practical routine of everyday living. Indeed, it frequently happened that religion ascribed a higher cognitive status to extrarational activities of the unconscious such as dreams than to rational activities of the conscious such as discursive reasoning. The rise of rationalism in the post-Cartesian modern world has tried mightily to replace religion's integration of the conscious and the unconscious[181] with a solely rational, conscious explanation and treatment of reality. No wonder there is such a deep fissure in, and often even a complete breakdown of, integration in so many modern individuals and in so many modern societies.

One of the most imperative goals of contemporary religion ought to be the restoration of holistic integrity between the unconscious and conscious processes in the daily lives of its adherents. For example, when striving to make the sacrament of penance as deeply religious as possible for its participants, the church should incorporate into the rite itself the fruits of depth psychology as well as the speculations of theology.[182] (Depth psychology probes into the unconscious, while theology is primarily concerned with the conscious rational exploration of the workings of God in the world.) To use another example, when religious educators attempt to teach God to learners, they ought not to restrict themselves to fruits of theological speculation, but also incorporate into the substantive content of the lesson the findings of depth psychology concerning the representation of God which the learner possesses.[183] Among the many reasons why religious instruction should never be turned over to the theologians is that theologians tend to banish the unconscious or at best relegate it to a minor role in religious activity. Modern history bears this out. Religion can never be restricted to the conscious; rather religion must fulfill its basic nature and integrate unconscious and conscious processes as dynamically and as holistically as possible. As no person can successfully banish either the unconscious or the conscious from his life no matter how hard that individual tries to do so, similarly no religion can successfully banish either the unconscious or the conscious from its own structure and operations.

There probably are some religious educationists and educators who will assert that it might be terribly dangerous to deal with the dark, extrarational, symbolic forces of the unconscious during the religion lesson. Morton Trippe Kelsey forcefully addresses this question by indicating that there is indeed a certain danger in dealing with the unconscious. "But which is more dangerous," Kelsey continues, "a dead religion or a dangerous one; neurotic, unconscious people or those dealing with the depths of themselves? When religion is dead, the involuntary and unconscious forces are either projected out upon others . . . or else they break forth in the individual in depression and anxiety and psychosomatic illness."[184] Those religious educationists and educators who might not wish to deal with unconscious substantive content because of fear of what this might do to learners would do well to heed Viktor Frankl's words: "Fear tends to bring about precisely that which one is afraid of."[185]

Limitations of Unconscious Content

Unconscious content has many limitations. In this section, I will briefly deal with a few of the more important of these limitations.

The unconscious is a construct, and this presents a whole set of difficulties with respect to religious instruction. Because the unconscious is a construct, at least for the present, it contains within itself the possibilities of an enormous variety of interpretations. As a result, religious educators are confronted with a bewildering array of choices about what is and what is not unconscious content, about which one of a vast multitude of interpretations of the unconscious is best, and so forth. Is the unconscious a valid construct to explain the psychic forces which this construct purports to explain and encapsulate? There is abundant empirical and nonempirical evidence which suggests that some kind of hidden and deep-running psychic forces do indeed exist; however, is the correct or even adequate explanation for these forces to be found in the construct unconscious? David Klein, for example, contends that "it is possible to provide for a scientific account of unconscious thinking without having to invoke a *deus ex machina* in the form of a mythical entity called the unconscious."[186] Interpretations of hidden and deep-running psychic forces are legion, ranging all the way from the hard-headed formulations offered by brain researchers to some of the mushy-headed views presented by some members of the psychotherapeutic community. Academic psychologists often dismiss psychotherapeutic explanations of the unconscious, claiming that psychotherapeutic theories are basically untestable and therefore scientifically unacceptable, that psychotherapeutic research and practical procedures are mushy, and that psychotherapeutic descriptive language is chocked full of gibberish.[187] Even some staunch members of the psychotherapeutic community openly acknowledge that there are enormous splits in both theory and practice within the psychotherapeutic community, especially within Freudianism.[188]

Another limitation of unconscious content—or more accurately, in the way unconscious content is interpreted by some members of the psychotherapeutic community—is that it is sometimes used as a basis for bizarre explanations of phenomena. Classical Freudians, and even some neo-Freudians, have the tendency to invest even the most commonplace realities with all sorts of direct sexual meanings. Some of these sexual explanations have historically been so fanciful and even downright weird that Sigmund Freud, an avid cigar smoker, was forced to remark that there are times when a cigar is only a cigar. Even those psychotherapeutic explanations which are not preposterous nonetheless are frequently prone to be unidimensional with respect to the unconscious as if conscious processes exist only as an appendage to human functioning. Thus Antonio Moreno accuses Carl Jung of over-psychologizing symbol, of making the foundation of symbol reside totally in unconscious processes in a way which minimizes and possibly even eliminates the conscious components of symbol in itself and of symbol as rendered meaningful by learners.[189]

The final limitation of unconscious content which I wish to discuss concerns the relatively poor practical results attained by those who are the most steeped and well-versed in the nature and operation of the unconscious, namely the psychotherapists. As I have indicated previously in this book the overwhelming mass of research over the years strongly suggests that the results of psychotherapy are relatively poor. Some patients do make improvement in the basic way in which their unconscious processes function; such improvement, however, is usually marginal. Indeed, there is no research to suggest that psychotherapy attains results with patients which cannot be just as satisfactorily explained by that great healer of us all, time. If the unconscious exists in the way the psychotherapists say it exists, then why is it that their clinical treatment of the unconscious has such dismal results? As I suggest in the previous chapter, part of the relative lack of success attained by psychotherapists can be legitimately explained by the fact that they typically employ a verbal procedure to cure an aberration of nonverbal content. Still, one is tempted to inquire whether the poor success rate enjoyed by psychotherapists might possibly have a deeper and more far-reaching cause, namely that the unconscious does not at all exist in the way that psychotherapy claims it exists.

THE FORM OF UNCONSCIOUS CONTENT

Earlier in this chapter I devoted considerable space to the form of conscious content. My purpose in doing so was to provide the necessary backdrop and juxtaposition for properly understanding the contours and form of unconscious content. It should be underscored that unconscious content does not function in isolation, but always within the existential holistic context of the person. Conscious processes, then, are always linked existentially in one way or another with conscious processes. In both understanding and appreciating the form of unconscious content, it is imperative that we always keep the form of conscious content firmly fixed in our minds.

Just as there are many sharply contrasting interpretations of the form of conscious content, so also are there many widely divergent views on the form of unconscious content. In an admirable attempt to introduce some measure of conceptual order into the seemingly myriad diverse views on the form and operations of unconscious processes, Natalino Caputi has devised a helpful category system into which most if not all the major interpretations of unconscious content fall. These four categories of unconscious content are the bio-physical view, the psycho-personal view, the socio-cultural view, and the transpersonal-spiritual view.[190] Each category represents a very different fundamental principle underlying the nature and operations of unconscious processes. While each category is necessarily quite discrete, nonetheless the persons represented in each category are not necessarily as discrete. While a particular theorist might primarily be an adherent of one category, nonetheless some of his doctrines might also partake of another category. In ascertaining the proper category in which to place a theorist, the principal tenets and overriding spirit of a theorist determines the category in which that theorist most properly belongs.[191]

Bio-Physical View

The bio-physical view regards the unconscious as a direct function of biological and physiological processes. From this perspective, all unconscious processes are basically biological and physiological in nature and operation. Because the activities of the unconscious fundamentally deal with bio-physical processes, it is therefore unnecessary and unwarranted to posit the unconscious either as a separate spiritual entity or even as a separate spiritual function.[192] The bio-physical view of the unconscious satisfies two major requirements for every adequate scientific explanation,[193] namely parsimony and subsidiarity. Parsimony is that criterion of science which seeks to explain phenomena in the simplist, most economical manner possible. Subsidiarity is that criterion of science which never attributes to a higher order of being an explanation which can be adequately offered by a lower order of being.

It is important for religious educators to note that the bio-physical view does not deny that unconscious processes exist or that they operate in a potent manner. Rather, the bio-physical view states that these processes are not spiritual but instead are part-and-parcel of a person's biological and physical apparatus.

There have been some efforts among proponents of the bio-physical view to discover the physiological locus of the unconscious. Justin Neuman claims that there are two basic types of nerve tissue, the kind which is connected to conscious processes and the kind which is linked to unconscious processes.[194] Gert Heilbrunn contends that repressed unconscious processes are connected to certain areas of the brain. When these areas are given electrical stimulation, repressed unconscious processes are brought to awareness.[195] Conrad Chyatte and his associates believe that unconscious repression is a function of the partial atrophy of unactivated neurons which receive inadequate nourishment from the blood.[196] Some brain researchers assert that investigations on the two hemispheres of the brain hold the key to unconscious as well as conscious processes. In this view, unconscious processes are direct functions of the right hemisphere of the brain.[197]

Some advocates of the bio-physical view suggest that most, if not all, of the substantive content of unconscious processes are actually stored in the person's memory. Memory contains both conscious and unconscious (unawared) remembrances. Both types of remembrances can be brought to present awareness by electrical stimulation of the brain. Conscious memory can also be stimulated by deliberative conscious procedures. Memory of unconscious (unawared) happenings can also be stimulated by purposive techniques aimed at eliciting remembrances from this kind of memory. These techniques include free-association devices, hypnotism, and the like.

Other advocates of the bio-physical view consider unconscious processes to be basically a form of automatic behavior.[198] Thus the unconscious is seen as that conglomerate of processes which occur automatically without a person's volitional control, such as the Freudian slip, dreams, free associations, and the like. All these automatic processes can be adequately explained by biological and physiological mechanisms.

Subliminal perception constitutes yet another form of the bio-physical view of unconscious processes.[199] (Subliminal perception refers to all those perceptions falling below the threshold of awareness.) From this vantage point, subliminal perception can satisfactorily account for those unawared processes associated with unconscious activity.[200] Hence there is no need to posit a discrete entity or separate process called the unconscious.[201]

Some proponents of the bio-physical view contend that conditioning can satisfactorily explain unconscious processes without the necessity of constructing a separate entity or function called the unconscious.[202] There are two major types of conditioning, namely classical conditioning and operant conditioning.[203] One feature of *classical conditioning* is interoceptive conditioning. The basic principle underlying interoceptive conditioning is this: Any variation of one's internal environment associated with an unconditioned activity may become a conditioned activity.[204] Interoceptive conditioning is that mode of classical conditioning in which a conditioned stimulus or an unconditioned stimulus, or both, are delivered to the mucous membrane of some particular internal organ. Supporters of interoceptive conditioning state that empirical research suggests that these stimuli to the mucous membrane, which can be considered subliminal, can indeed become signals for higher neural activities.[205] Proponents of interoceptive conditioning argue that interoceptive phenomena adequately account for those processes which depth psychologists assign to the unconscious.[206] For their part, proponents of *operant conditioning* claim that all behavior, including so-called "unconscious behavior," is nothing more than the response of a person to certain events which have happened to him in his life. Neurotic or psychotic activities of the individual are not manifestations of some hidden entity or process called the unconscious, but rather manifestations of events in the person's life which exercise a conditioning effect upon that individual.[207] By examining the facts in which these neurotic or psychotic activities are grounded, it is usually possible to identify the contingencies of reinforcement which account for these activities.[208] Advocates of operant conditioning do not reject the unconscious totally. What they reject is the unconscious as agent.[209] The unconscious is a human process, a particular way of behaving. Proponents of operant conditioning declare that at bottom depth psychology is unwittingly based on their operant position, since depth psychology believes that the unconscious can only be known and treated when elements of the unconscious are rendered conscious and observable, and when the person is helped to identify and deal with those events of his past which have shaped the unconscious dimension of his behavior.

In assessing the worth and effect of the bio-physical view of the unconscious, Natalino Caputi provides a helpful guideline when he states that the bio-physical view serves well as the devil's advocate regarding the other major views of the unconscious. In other words, when faced with some behavior which should be explained, the religious educator should first eliminate the possibility (or evaluate the degree) of it being accounted for by memory, automatic behavior, subliminal perception, and conditioning, before he entertains other explanatory views of unconscious processes.

The bio-physical factors involved in unconscious processes are always present. After all, each human being is a composite of physical and spiritual. None of the other three categories purporting to explain the unconscious denies the role of bio-physical processes. What the proponents within each category do assert, however, is that bio-physical factors have only limited utility in explaining the origin and workings of unconscious processes.

Psycho-Personal View

The psycho-personal view regards the unconscious as a primary human process whose origin and functioning flow from a person's most basic affective and cognitive maturation and development.

Of all the representatives of the psycho-personal view of the unconscious, none has been more influential and more pervasive than Sigmund Freud. Whether one agrees or disagrees with Freud's position, the fact of the matter is that Freud's stance on the unconscious is the one to which all other viewpoints are inevitably compared. This statements holds true even for the other three major views of the unconscious presented in this chapter.

In order to appreciate Freud's view of the unconscious and its interactions with other domains of human personality, it is helpful to examine three of the major perspectives which he himself used at various times to examine the fundamental structure of personality as a whole. These three approaches are the topographical perspective, the structural perspective, and the economic perspective.

The *topographical perspective* crosscuts the entire personality in terms of the conscious-unconscious continuum.[210] This perspective places the processes involved in the conscious-unconscious continuum into three major zones of differing depth.[211] In Freud's terminology, these three zones are the conscious, the preconscious, and the unconscious. The *perceptual conscious,* to use Freud's exact term, consists in that which we are aware of at any given moment. Only a relatively small portion of a person's present experience is conscious at any given moment. The conscious may be compared to that small portion of a vast field which is illuminated at the moment by a moving narrow-focused beam from a searchlight. The *preconscious*[212] consists of those materials which, though falling below the threshold of immediate conscious awareness, can nonetheless be brought to awareness without excessive difficulty if a person's attention or needs so demand. The scope of materials contained in the preconscious is vast.[213] Some preconscious material is readily available to consciousness, such as, for example, experiences we have forgotten. Other preconscious material can only be brought to consciousness with some difficulty because it has been insulated from immediate awareness by various psychological maneuvers designed to make the person look good to himself.[214] The *unconscious* consists of those materials in psychological experience which cannot be brought to conscious awareness when the occasion demands because they have been actively repressed or have otherwise been kept from awareness. Most of the materials in the unconscious at one time or another were present in the conscious or in the preconscious. The unconscious is inexhaustible. Even if some material from the unconscious is made manifest, nonetheless most of the unconscious material will never and indeed can never be made manifest.[215]

The conscious and preconscious are secondary processes, namely processes which have developed secondarily as a result of the formative impact of external demands of other persons and of society. The unconscious domain, however, is primary process, namely one which grows according to its own impulsive demands, demands which are temporally, existentially, and causatively prior to secondary process. As secondary process, the conscious and the preconscious domains follow the *reality principle,* namely a rational and practical set of behaviors appropriate to the environment which the individual is encountering.[216] As primary process, the unconscious domain follows the *pleasure principle,* namely the immediate total gratification or discharge of all its wants and tensions no matter how contradictory and no matter what the consequences of such immediate gratification may be to the person himself or to other individuals. The only impulse and concern of primary process is to seek and maintain an optimal level of internal impulsive energy.

The *structural perspective* crosscuts the area of instinct. This perspective places all psychic processes into three discrete institutions or provinces. These three provinces of the mind grow and become crystalized during the course of one's life, especially during one's early life. Though these three provinces constantly interact during human functioning, nonetheless they are processive structures which are independent of one another. In Freudian terminology, these three independent interactive structures are the id, the ego, and the superego.[217] The *id* is always unconscious. Though the ego and the superego are largely conscious, nonetheless there are large expanses of the ego and especially of the superego which operate at the unconscious level. The id is primary process, and as such is prior to and outside of conscious control. As primary process the id is the basic condition and force in psychic functioning. The id is the dynamic reservoir of instinctual needs which vigorously press upward for immediate fulfillment. Somatic in origin, the id is the major source of drive energy. It operates extrarationally and alogically rather than rationally and logically. The *ego* is the processive organization of one's psychological systems arising from the dynamic interaction of somatic reality with the external world. The ego is primarily secondary process. It tends to operate rationally and logically. The prime function of the ego is to fruitfully incorporate for the optimum benefit of the person the incessant demands made on the psyche by what Freud calls "the three tyrannical masters,'' namely the id, the superego, and external reality.[218] This key role of the ego in synthesizing the demands of the ''three tyrannical masters'' is not easy.[219] The id demands total and immediate fulfillment of its seething tumultuous impulses. The superego demands immediate tight control and offers total suppression of the surging impulses flowing from the id. External reality imposes a host of demands, some of which are extraneous to and even destructive of one's personality. Hence there is considerable strain placed upon the ego. The ego employs a wide variety of psychological tricks to play off one area of personality against the other in order to achieve its goals. The *superego* is the sum total of the demands placed on the personality by society (most especially the parents) which are introjected into the psyche. The superego is an organization of psychological systems whose primary functions include examining ego activity at all levels and supplying various imperatives to the psyche such as approval and disapproval, self-criticism and self-esteem. The superego carries out these functions in relation to internalized moral standards and in relation to an ego-ideal which is the superego's measuring stick.[220] Though the superego is largely conscious, nonetheless a considerable portion of the superego operates at the unconscious level, something which accounts for its great force and power. Participating as it does in primary process, the superego typically demands immediate gratification. In order to appreciate how the superego operates, it is vital to understand how it is formed. The superego develops in early childhood as a direct consequence of the utter biological helplessness of the infant and its total dependence upon its immediate family. At birth the infant is amoral, with no inhibitions counteracting the impulses of its id. The parents are the main sources of satisfaction for the infant, and the main restrictions on the infant as well. The infant and young child at first conform to parental dictates because of ''objective anxiety,'' namely the conditioned fear of unpleasant consequences flowing from giving full rein to the uninhibited id. Later on in early childhood, notably during the period of the Oedipus complex or the Electra complex, a new process takes place in which the young child identifies with its parents. Their commands, their image of themselves and of the child, become introjected into the child's own psyche. The child personally identifies with the commands and the ideals of its parents. Parental dictates become internalized and the superego becomes gradually crystalized. Once formed, the superego tends to function with all the force of parental imperatives and ideals as the child understood these imperatives and ideals during the process of introjection. Though the superego functions directly with the primal energies of the id, it is often organized in such a manner as to constitute a psychic force fundamentally opposed to the id. For Freud, the superego operates as conscience which strives to direct the person toward higher standards and values as opposed to the sexual and aggressive forces of the id. Sometimes these superego forces are too idealistic or too extrarational for the pragmatic, logical ego. On the negative side, anxiety or guilt arise when the ego excessively compromises the superego, or when the person surrenders to the surging impulses of the id. On the positive side, helpful self-esteem, sacrifice, noble ideals, and even heroism are gifts which the superego offers the personality.

The *economic perspective* crosscuts the personality in terms of the force or valence of one or more psychic processes. The particular psychic organization of internal forces and counterforces depends to a large extent upon the strength of various psychic zones and factors active at any given moment. Freud stresses the importance of the quantitative distribution and balance of psychic energy as the key to understanding the functions of a particular individual's personality. Conversely, Freud sharply downplays qualitative distribution and balance of psychic energy, asserting that there is not a very great qualitative difference between normal and pathological disturbances of the psyche. Pathological disturbances are not a simple extension of normal disturbances, however; rather, when a particular psychological trend becomes excessively intensified quantitatively, it may upset the person's entire psychic equilibrium.[221]

In order to gain a firmer purchase on the bases and essential spirit of the Freudian view of the unconscious, it might be helpful to very briefly mention some key terms and concepts in Freudian depth psychology.

Libido is the name given to a person's drive energy. The course of the libido lies primarily in the unconscious, particularly in the id. The libido's energy is primarily sexual, though it also includes aggression. The sexual energy of the libido is not restricted solely to the more patent genital instincts, but includes two basic sexually inspired and sexually tinged forces, namely eros and thanatos.[222] *Eros,* or life wish, is geared to self-preservation. Eros is that totality of primal forces in the organism which seeks to unify, bind together, preserve, and to build up.[223] *Thanatos,* or death wish, is geared to self-destruction. Thanatos is that totality of primal forces which seeks to disintegrate, separate, disrupt, and destroy. In the depths of each person's unconscious there is an ongoing struggle between the instinctual life-wish of eros and the instinctual death-wish of thanatos.[224]

The growth and development of the libido normally takes place in three successive stages, the oral stage, the anal stage, and the phallic stage.

The *oral stage* is that period in human growth and development when the energy of the libido primarily flows through the mouth. This is the first stage in the growth of the libido. Freud discovered that the mouth is not only an organ used to meet hunger needs; it is also a pleasure organ coordinate with other zones of libidinal satisfaction.[225] Nipple sucking, putting everything within grasp into the mouth—these and other activities in the early oral stage are simultaneously the major outlet for libidinal energy and a primary building block in the development of one's personality. The libidinal energy in the early oral stage is passive and receptive. In the late oral stage, the infant enters a cannibalistic phase in which the mouth is used to bite with all the infant's strength. The mother's nipple, objects, toys—all are bitten with a vengeance. While not all biting at the oral stage has a sadistic cast, nevertheless the late oral stage is characterized by the release of the libido's aggressive impulses. The libidinal energy in the late oral stage is active and aggressive.

The *anal stage* is that period in human growth and development when the energy of the libido normally but not exclusively flows through the anus. This is the second stage in the growth of the libido. The anal stage usually begins at about eighteen months of age. Freud discovered that the anus is not only an organ to meet defecational needs; it is also a pleasure zone coordinate with other zones of libidinal satisfaction. As the child identifies his mouth with himself during the oral stage, so also he identifies himself with his anus and his feces in the anal stage.[226] During the anal stage and also the oral stage, the ego is still weak and in its early phase of development. The boundaries between self and not-self, between subject and object, between people and things, are highly fluid in the anal and oral periods. In the early anal stage, the child freely and with little or no control expels feces from the anus. The libidinal energy in the early anal stage is passive. In the late anal stage the child enters a more active phase in which the anus is used to express power, will, or mastery in deciding when to release the fecal matter when he impulsively feels like doing so, or when to defecate because of parental or societal demands. Toilet training in this period is an extremely important factor in the development of personality because it represents the first major clash between the child's libido and growing ego on the one hand and the demands of parents and society on the other hand.

The *phallic stage* is that period in human maturation and development when the energy of the libido normally but not exclusively flows through the genital organs.[227] This is the third and final stage in the growth of the libido. The phallic stage normally begins at about three years of age. There are three levels within the phallic stage. At the first level, the child noticeably experiences pleasurable sexual sensations in the genitalia. Masturbation, frequent erection in male children, and sex play with other children, are typical. In the second level, the child enters into what Freudians call the latency period when the sex drive subsides markedly and virtually goes into hibernation. In the final level, called the genital level, the full-blown phallic stage appears and remains for the rest of the individual's life. This level begins with the onset of puberty.

Several major depth-psychological occurrences take place during the first phase of the phallic stage, notably the onset of the Oedipus complex and castration fear in boys, and the onset of the Electra complex and penis envy in girls. The *Oedipus complex*[228] develops because of the irresistible libidinal attraction the young boy has for his mother. Like Oedipus of old, each boy is fated to murder his father in fantasy and marry his mother. The murder must take place because the little boy perceives his father as the archrival for the love of his mother. The Oedipal murder of the father is especially important because of its large role in the development of the phallic stage, especially in its genital phase. Attendant upon the Oedipus complex is the *castration fear*. To be sure, castration fear constitutes the crisis of the phallic stage, for obvious reasons. On the female child's side, the *Electra complex* is in some ways comparable to the Oedipus complex in boys. Under the influence of her libido, the girl is fated to murder her mother in fantasy and marry her father. Attendant upon the Electra complex is *penis envy*. To be sure, it is penis envy which constitutes a major motivational force driving her into the Electra complex.[229] When the little girl comes to the extremely painful realization that she lacks a penis, she passionately wishes to regain what she deeply feels is a lost or cut-off penis. She desires to regain the lost penis from the only one who possesses a penis, namely a male. She fantasizes that having a child by her father will enable her to restore the lost precious organ.[230]

The theory of the libido has the twin advantage of accounting for the dynamic unity of psychic life and of revealing the purposive goal-directed character of psychic life as interactive with basic biological needs. The constructs of fixation and regression provided Freud with useful and discriminating tools for attaining a differentiated under-standing of the actual ongoing complexities of personality. Fixation and regression block or retard normal personality development with infelicitous psychological consequences. Fixation and regression are possible because the various stages of libidinal growth are inherently characterized by a considerable degree of overlap and interaction. No phase of libidinal development is ever given up totally. *Fixation* is the tendency of the personality to preserve and cling to the thoughts, feelings, and actions which that person perceives to have served him well at one particular past stage of growth. For example, a forty-year-old man might have a personality fixated at the anal stage. *Regression* is the process in which an individual reverts to some earlier stage of libidinal development. It might well be that fixation actually facilitates regression.[231] Alcoholism is regarded as an example of regression to the oral stage.[232]

General defense mechanisms play a central role in Freud's depth psychology and his view of the unconscious.[233] The three most impor-tant and most pervasive defense mechanisms are repression, suppres-sion, and sublimation. *Repression* is the unconscious psychological process which prevents certain impulses seething in the id from reach-ing the individual's conscious level. The cause of repression lies in the fact that some impulses in the id are dangerous to the person's psychic equilibrium, or are unacceptable to his personal code and to that of society. Repression operates at the unconscious level. To be sure, repression is the primary general defense mechanism operating at the level of the unconscious. A great and continuing battle occurs at the unconscious level between the surging impulses of the id demanding total immediate gratification and the forces of repression opposing the entry into consciousness of certain impulses of the id. In the depths of each person, then, there is a raging ongoing unconscious conflict whose exact nature the person is not aware of. *Suppression* is the conscious psychological process which endeavors to force certain libidinal strivings or otherwise unwanted memories and desires into the preconscious zone of the psyche. The cause of suppression lies in the fact that some libidinal strivings or unwanted memories and desires are perceived as dangerous to the person's psychic equilibrium, or are unacceptable to his personal code and to that of society. Suppression operates at the conscious level, and at this level can induce considerable strain in the individual. *Sublimation* is the conscious or unconscious process which transforms and/or channels libidinal energy into forms or activities acceptable and productive for the individual or for society.[234] Sublimation operates at both the conscious and the unconscious levels, and is the root cause of many of humanity's most noble and most heroic achievements. Repression and suppression are frequently unhealthy defense mechanisms, while sublimation is often but not always a healthy mechanism of defense.

Specific defense mechanisms are also important in Freudian scheme of things. There are a host of defense mechanisms. I shall only briefly mention some of the most important of these.[235] *Denial* is the psychological process in which unacceptable unconscious impulses or threatening conscious perceptions are refused recognition, that is, the individual simply refuses to believe that he is experiencing such impulses or perceptions.[236] *Rationalization* is the psychological process in which unacceptable unconscious impulses or threatening conscious perceptions are attributed to rational, credible, ego-inflating motives, thus glossing over the real bases of these impulses or perceptions.[237] *Projection* is the psychological process in which unacceptable unconscious impulses or threatening conscious perceptions are attributed to or projected on to another person as that other person's set of impulses or perceptions. *Displacement* is the psychological process in which unacceptable unconscious impulses or threatening conscious perceptions are relocated to other psychological forces or physiological states which bear no intrinsic connection to the unacceptable impulses or perceptions. *Reaction formation* is the psychological process which unacceptable unconscious impulses or threatening conscious perceptions are manifested in behaviors which are directly opposite to the unacceptable impulses or threatening perceptions. *Isolation* is the psychological process in which unacceptable unconscious impulses or threatening conscious perceptions are placed into watertight psychic compartments untouced by the normal psychic elaboration in associative connections and in affect.[238] *Undoing* is the psychological process in which unacceptable unconscious impulses or threatening conscious perceptions are reversed into positive behaviors so as to undo and heal the harm which the psyche imagines has been visited upon self or others by these impulses and perceptions. *Compromise* is the psychological process in which unacceptable unconscious impulses or threatening conscious perceptions are allowed some kind of partial and frequently masked form of direct expression.

The pervasiveness and utter purposiveness of the unconscious form the foundation of Freud's interpretation of human freedom and motivation. Put simply if perhaps a bit starkly, Freud believes in psychological determinism. All psychological phenomena from the most important such as dreams and repression to the most trivial such as slips of the tongue are rooted in highly purposive unconscious processes. Personal freedom is really an illusion. A person's motivations and parameters of action are determined by unconscious forces outside that individual's awareness. Human activity is the inevitable consequence of the processes of the id as interactive with ego and superego. A person might like to believe that he is free and in control of his motivations. However, because that individual is unaware of his unconscious processes, he is therefore unaware of the determinative and finalistic role which these fundamental unconscious processes play in his everyday activity.[239]

I will now briefly mention nine ways in which Freud's theories of the unconscious can be of significant assistance to religious educators, even if these educators disagree with some or possibly with all of Freudianism.

A requisite for gaining insight and assistance from Freud's views is to take his position seriously. All too often religious educators shut themselves off from major helpful advances by flicking off positions and persons whose views do not at first sight seem to be congruent with their own. Such an intolerant, narrow-minded attitude only hurts the cause of religious education and cripples the otherwise fine instructional efforts by religious educators.

First, the religious educator can learn from Freud to be deeply aware of the role which unconscious forces play in the life of both the learner and himself. Unconscious processes constitute an important and indispensable aspect of the learner's personality, an aspect which the religion teacher simply cannot afford to neglect. Furthermore, a significant degree of interpersonal communication between the religious educator and the learner occurs at the unconscious level.

Second, the religious educator should constantly bear in mind that unconscious content is a key substantive content in religious instruction. If this substantive content is missing or neglected in the lesson, to that extent will the lesson be watered-down religious content. The teacher should so structure the pedagogical situation that religion is integrated with primary process. Any divorce of religion from the unconscious will result in debasing religion into an artificial buffer against the realities of life, a buffer which will crumble and turn in upon the learner should that individual come to maturity.

Third, the religious educator should be ever aware of the role which wish fulfillment plays in religion. Freud is not as incorrect as he might at first seem when he states that the human psychogenesis of religion lies in wish fulfillment.[240] The religious educator should actively assist the learner to insert religion-as-wish-fulfillment into an integrated eschatologically oriented religion of hope. Such a religion does not deny that much of its origins lie in wish fulfillment, but affirms that this wish fulfillment is a necessary psychic dimension of every human being's fundamental hope for resurrection and the beatific encounter. If the wish-fulfillment orientation in religion is not positively cathected to eschatological hope and to the Christian promise, then this human orientation to wish fulfillment will become free-floating. Consequently, the learner in his religious life will be tempted to regress to the infantile level, with his religion being transmogrified into a magical affair in which God magically satisfies all the learner's wishes. Persons operating at this regressive level—and there seem to be many Christians who fall into this category—tend to attribute to an "out there" Holy Spirit matters which are really outgrowths of their unconscious processes.

Fourth, the religion teacher should help the learner deal constructively with his libido rather than urge the learner to repress or suppress this primal force. It might well be that Paul the Apostle wittingly or unwittingly alludes to the forces of the libido when he speaks about the war raging within himself (Rom. 7:23). A realization that libido and sin are an intrinsic part of the human condition is crucial to psychological maturity and wholesome holiness. Sublimation is generally a healthy way of dealing with certain libidinous urges.

Fifth, the religious educator should assist the learner to integrate the sexual function into his everyday life.[241] Typically there is no such thing as a neuter person. One's gender permeates and definitively colors all of one's conscious and especially unconscious processes. Not to be in intimate touch and harmony with one's deepest sexuality is to abdicate one's very own personhood and therefore to depersonalize one's own religion. Since sexuality is so intimately bound up with the unconscious, the religious educator must perforce consider the unconscious processes of the learners during the instructional act.

Sixth, the religious educator should help the learner to come to grips with eros and thanatos, the life wish and the death wish within him. This is especially important for religious educators working with youths and young adults. Achieving a working relationship between these two fundamental orientations will assist the learner in deciding when to hang on and when to let go, when to rise to self and when to die to self.

Seventh, the religious educator should neither underestimate nor neglect the great practical importance of the superego. Freud's concept of the superego means that morals and ideals are not "out there" somewhere, but are deeply and inextricably imbedded in the core of the human personality. If learners can be assisted in realizing that morality is a permanent dimension of their selfhood—constricting though it might be at times—rather than some negative set of imperatives imposed from outside their self-system, then perhaps they can cognitively understand and affectively accept the fact that morality is not opposed to self but advances and fulfills self from within.

Eighth, the Freudian perspective assists the religious educator to recognize a learner's immature behavior, be this behavior a regression of one sort or another or a specific defense mechanism. A learner sometimes laminates his regression or specific defense mechanisms on to religion, with the result that his religious life becomes psychologically diseased and counterproductive not only to this religious life but to his entire mental health as well.

Ninth, Freud's psychological determinism should spur on the religious educator to clarify his concepts of motivation, desire, and freedom. Perhaps the learners are not as free as the religious educators think they are. Perhaps this or that undesirable (or desirable) learner behavior during the lesson has unconscious roots beyond his immediate control. Perhaps it is well to teach learners about unconscious drives and motivations so that they will come to a greater appreciation of the basic constituents of their own human behavior and thence to the saving power of God's grace.

Socio-Cultural View

The socio-cultural view regards the unconscious as a primary human process which is essentially a function of some collectivity.

Natalino Caputi contends that one fundamental thesis common to the various and sometimes divergent standpoints within the socio-cultural view is transcendent collectivism.[242] Transcendent collectivism states that the whole is more than the sum of its parts, and that the whole determines the nature of its parts.[243]

Of all the representatives of the socio-cultural view of the unconscious, none has been more influential and pervasive than Carl Gustav Jung. Whether one agrees or disagrees with Jung's position, the fact of the matter is that modern religionists and religious educators must come to grips with Jung in one way or another.

Though many of Jung's views can be fruitfully understood within the overall context of both the psycho-personal view and the transpersonal-spiritual view, nonetheless he properly belongs to the socio-cultural school because of the centrality of the collective unconscious and archetypes in his theory.

A few background factors might throw some helpful light on Jung's view of the unconscious. He came from a long line of physicians and theologians; indeed, his father was a clergyman. As a youth, he had a desire to study archeology. He eventually became a physician, specializing in psychiatry. He made field expeditions to study primitive cultures in Arizona, Mexico, North Africa, and Kenya. He traveled to India to ingest the culture and thought patterns of that ancient civilization. These background factors all manifested themselves in his theory of the unconscious, with its intense attention to religious essentials, to archeological shapes, to medical empiricism, to ancient myths and primitive history, and to the Eastern way of approaching reality. The assimilation of these widely diverse background factors helps explain why Jung's influence extends far beyond depth psychology. Furthermore, these background factors also account for the fact that Jung's theory tends to seek a kind of synthetic union of opposite poles or schools such as extrarational and rational, scientific and personal, mythic and empiric, occult and realistic.

Jung's theory of the unconscious comes into especially clear light when contrasted to that of Freud. Jung began his career in depth psychology as a follower of Freud. After some years, he broke with the master, and started his own school of thought which he called analytical psychology to distinguish his system from that of Freud who used the term psychoanalysis.[244] Whereas Freud stresses causality, Jung emphasizes teleology. Whereas Freud stresses the biological basis of personality, Jung emphasizes racial and phylogenetic factors. Whereas Freud stresses sexuality, Jung emphasizes symbolism. Whereas Freud focuses exclusively on medicine and psychology, Jung broadens his attention to include not only medicine and psychology but also philosophy, religion, cultural anthropology, mysticism, history, and literature.[245] In most persons who revolt against a person or system, a considerable residual amount of the essence, structure, and valence of the original person or system remains in the person who revolted. This familiar principle of life holds true for Jung in his revolt against Freud. Though Jung drastically changed some of Freud's basic emphases, though Jung significantly reworked some of Freud's major concepts, and though Jung greatly broadened some of Freud's cardinal interpretations, nonetheless the fundamental spirit and essence of Freud play a considerable role in Jung's system. There is a sense in which Jung stands in the shadow of Freud, a fact which Jung himself seems to have recognized judging by the frequency with which references to Freud appears in his works.[246]

The *topographical perspective* in Jung's depth psychology crosscuts the entire personality in terms of the conscious-unconscious continuum.[247] (Jung gave the name *psyche* to what many contemporary social scientists call personality. The psyche consists of all an individual's psychological processes.)[248] The topographical perspective places the processes involved in the conscious-unconscious continuum into three major zones of differing depth. In Jung's terminology, these three zones are the conscious, the personal unconscious, and the collective unconscious. The *conscious* refers to awareness.[249] Conscious processes develop out of unconscious processes.[250] Consciousness is "the relation of psychic contents to the ego in so far as this relation is perceived as such by the ego."[251] The *personal unconscious* is that upper dimension[252] of the unconscious which comprises two discrete kinds of material. The first kind of material consists of those contents which have been set aside by conscious processes. (It should be remembered that consciousness can contain only a few contents at any given time. Hence the conscious processes must set aside some material to which it cannot attend.) The second kind of material consists of those contents which have been forgotten, repressed, or subliminally perceived.[253] The first kind of material in the personal unconscious can be returned to consciousness at will, while the second kind can only be brought to awareness by the use of psychotherapeutic techniques.[254] The personal unconscious is also called the subjective unconscious because it comprises the acquisition of an individual's own subjective personal life—everything subjectively forgotten, everything subjectively repressed, everything subjectively perceived subliminally, everything subjectively thought and felt, and so on.[255] The structural contents of the personal unconscious are what Jung calls "feeling-toned complexes," namely clusters of affectively charged psychological processes. Compared to the activity of the collective unconscious, this is a superficial function of the psyche. The *collective unconscious* is the residual history of the human race and of the race's animal ancestors in which each individual existentially participates at the unconscious level.[256] The collective unconscious is inherited by the individual and is embedded in the pathways and structures of the brain itself.[257] The collective unconscious is not simply a storehouse of unconscious ideas passed down through the history of the race; it is also, and indeed far more significantly, an accumulation of predispositions and potentialities which, in its totality, forms the most fundamental frame of reference from which an individual views and encounters the world. The collective unconscious is the foundation for every person's psyche.[258] The collective unconscious is fundamental in human existence because the base of each individual's own personal experience is the collective experience of the human race.[259] Jung views the collective unconscious with its archetypes as "the mind of our unknown ancestors, their way of thinking and feeling, their way of experiencing life and the world, gods and men. . . . Just as the human body is a museum, so to speak, of its phylogenetic history, so too is the psyche. We have no reason to suppose that the specific structure of the psyche is the only thing in the world that has no history outside its individual manifestations. Even the conscious mind cannot be denied a history reaching back at least five thousand years. . . . [The collective unconscious] molds the human species and is just as much a part of it as the human body, which, though ephemeral in the individual, is collectively of immense age."[260] The collective unconscious is universal and is common to everyone.[261] Jung writes: ''I have chosen the term 'collective' because this part of the unconscious is not individual but universal; in contrast to the personal psyche, it has contents and modes of behavior that are more or less the same everywhere and in all individuals. It is, in other words, identical in all men and thus constitutes a common psychic substrate of a suprapersonal nature which is present in every one of us.''[262] The personal unconscious ''comprises contents which are integral components of the individual personality and therefore could just as well be conscious; [the collective unconscious] forms, as it were, an omnipresent, unchanging, and everywhere identical quality or substrate of the psyche per se. . . . The deeper 'layers' of the psyche lose their individual uniqueness as they retreat farther and farther into darkness. 'Lower down,' that is to say, as they approach the autonomous functional systems, they become increasingly collective until they are universalized and extinguished in the body's materiality, i.e., in chemical substances. The body's carbon is simple carbon. Hence 'at bottom,' the psyche is simply 'world.' ''[263] There are two major structural components of the collective unconscious, namely inherited instincts[264] and archetypes. Some material in the collective unconscious can be brought to consciousness in dreams, through certain psychic symbols, and by the techniques of analytical psychology. Other material in the collective unconscious can never be brought to consciousness.[265] The collective unconscious is also called the objective unconscious because it is independent of one's own individual experience and impervious to the critical and ordering activity of consciousness. In the objective unconscious, the person responds to the call of the universal, and hears the voice of uninfluenced primal nature.[266]

The *structural perspective* of Jungianism is not nearly as clear-cut as it is in classical Freudianism. For Jung, the psyche exhibits certain relatively independent structures which dynamically interact with one another in human functioning.[267] The most important of these structures are the intellect, the ego, and the soul. The *intellect* is the purely rational side of an individual. The intellect is best conceived of as directed thinking ''because it arranges the contents of ideation under concepts in accordance with a rational norm of which I am conscious.''[268] The intellect functions wholly in the sphere of consciousness. The *ego* comprises the conscious perceptions, memory contents, thoughts, and feelings which permit the person to fruitfully and adaptively interact with the environment. In Jung's words, the ego is "a complex of ideas which constitutes the center of my field of consciousness and appears to possess a high degree of continuity and identity."[269] The ego is at once the center of consciousness and the subject of consciousness.[270] The ego gives stability to consciousness and to human functioning in general.[271] While the ego is the center of consciousness it also relates to the unconscious realm as well. Depending on how the psyche is functioning at any given moment, the ego can deal more with the conscious than the unconscious, or vice versa.[272] The ego is a structure which develops with time and experience, and gradually incorporates at the conscious level all experienced phases of conscious and unconscious activity into a new conscious whole.[273] A well-developed ego thus represents the personal achievement in consciousness of all aspects and levels of the psyche, especially an integration of conscious and unconscious processes.[274] Ego-consciousness is a somewhat undifferentiated awareness of the "I," of an awareness of personal identity. The *soul* is a "definite, circumscribed functional complex which might be characterized as a kind of 'inner personality,' as the 'subject' to whom the ego-consciousness is related in the same way as to an outward object."[275] By the subject of ego-consciousness Jung means the unconscious. The subject of the soul is the unconscious, and most especially the collective unconscious.[276] The soul is the living force which simultaneously "lives of itself and causes life" in each person.[277] The primal source of the soul's life flows from its unconscious base. Thus the task of every person becomes that of the psyche seeking and finding the soul. The soul is naturally religious, that is to say, possesses a religious function.[278]

Foundational and fundamental to the function of the psyche are *archetypes*. Archetypes are found in the collective unconscious. Archetypes are the structural elements of the collective unconscious. Also called primordial images, archetypes "are the pictorial forms of the instincts, for the [collective] unconscious reveals itself to the conscious mind in images which, as in dreams and fantasies, initiate the process of conscious reaction and assimilation."[279] Archetypes or primordial images "express material derived from the collective unconscious and indicate at the same time that the factors influencing the conscious siutation of the moment are collective rather than personal."[280] Archetypes are objective forms preexistent to the individual, archaic[281] universal images existing since ancient times. Archetypes originate from the historical experiences of the human race which have occurred repeatedly over long periods of time.[282] Archetypes are inherited by each person from the history of the human race and constitute the foundation upon which the whole edifice of the psyche is built.[283] Consequently each individual's psyche reflects and in a sense encapsulates the collective wisdom and experience of the ages.[284] Archetypes thus are inherited universal dispositions which incline the individual to experience and conduct himself in eternally recurring situations in somewhat the same way as his ancestors experienced and conducted themselves in these same kinds of situations, as for example, in death, parenthood, and danger. The chief evidence for the existence of archetypes is that highly complex representations of this nature appear in almost all cultures, in virtually all eras, and may be dreamed about and painted by modern persons who possess no conscious knowledge of the ancient symbols and myths.[285] In this connection Jung writes that fantasies, including dreams, "undoubtedly have their closest analogues in mythological types [and motifs]. We must therefore assume that they correspond to certain collective (not personal) structural elements of the human psyche in general, and, like the morphological elements of the human body, are inherited."[286] Archetypes are essentially unconscious contents which are altered by becoming conscious and by being personally perceived; thus archetypes take their color from the individual human consciousness in which they appear.[287] It is precisely in this way that Jung attempts to avoid psychic determinism by the archetypes. The archetypes are, after all, objective. Hence they do not determine an individual's psychic contents, since the archetypes are necessarily colored by each person's own experiences and view of life.[288] Depending on an individual's own personal history and operative mode of consciousness, the archetype of a supreme being, for example, may express itself in sun worship, in metaphysical speculation, in the Catholic Mass, or whatever.[289] Archetypes are extremely important in human functioning because they are motive forces and organizers of experience which help account for, but do not determine, the way a person thinks, feels, and conducts himself. Some archetypes are so well-developed and expressive that they constitute autonomous personality systems, such as, for example, the persona, the shadow, and the animus/anima.[290] *Mandalas,* which are extremely important and central archetypal patterns, offer rich material of incalculable help in more profoundly understanding human nature.[291] In a *mandala,* the individual is shown to be a plurality of psychic forces, both conscious and unconscious, which sometimes block each other, but which may also be reinforcing too. Since *mandalas* typically have four parts in the whole, Jung believes that quaternity rather than trinity is the symbol of wholeness. This view has major consequences not only for his position on human nature, but on religion as well.

There are quite a few central constructs in Jung's analytical psychology which are integral to his notion of archetype. Three of the most important of these constructs are the self, the shadow, and the animus/anima.

The *self* represents the integration of both the conscious and the unconscious aspects of the psyche.[292] Thus the self is at once an empirical reality (known contents in consciousness) and an archetype (unknown material in the collective unconscious).[293] The self is the realization of each person's individual subjective psyche; it also partakes in the universal objective archetypes as well.[294] Self is the central archetype, the archetype of order, the totality of personality.[295] The self, then, is a mediator between conscious and unconscious processes. As a mediator, it is a center of tension between conscious and unconscious processes.[296] As the integration of conscious and unconscious processes, the self is expressed in the inborn strivings of the individual toward psychic wholeness, a central activity which Jung calls individuation or striving toward self-realization.[297] The self is a person's life goal,[298] a goal which only a few persons achieve. As an archetypal ideal of a person's developed nature, there is a sense in which the self both includes the other archetypes and presupposes the integration of these other archetypes.[299] "Empirically, the self appears in dreams, myths, and fairytales in the figure of the 'supraordinate personality" such as the king, hero, prophet, or savior."[300] A person cannot adequately know the self, since much of the self is unconscious. The only content of the self a person can adequately know is the ego, which is conscious. A person, therefore, can only experience the self.[301] The relation of the self to the ego is very important in Jungian depth psychology. The self is far broader than the ego. As the ego is at once the center of consciousness and the subject of consciousness, so the self is at once the center of the entire psyche and the subject of the entire psyche. In this sense the self is an ideal entity which includes the ego.[302] The ego is the integration of conscious processes, while the self is the integration of the entire psyche conscious as well as unconscious.[303] The ego is the only psychic content that a person knows.[304] "The individuated ego senses itself as the object of an unknown and supraordinate subject."[305]

The *shadow* is the dark and generally negative dimension of the psyche. If one major dimension of the psyche is the conscious and bright and upward-striving ego, then the opposite dimension of the psyche is the unconscious and dark and downward-striving shadow. The shadow is the other side of the ego, the ego's dark brother, a brother which is inseparable from a person's psychic totality. The shadow is literally a shadow, the unconscious obverse of whatever trends the person has emphasized in his ego-consciousness, in the active orientation and trend of his living. The shadow is intensely related to the person as the dark reflection of his conscious efforts. The development of the shadow runs parallel to that of the ego.[306] Jung holds that the shadow, what he calls "the inferior part of the personality," is made up of the "sum of all the personal and collective psychic elements which, because of their incompatability with the chosen conscious attitude, are denied expression in life and therefore coalesce into a relatively autonomous 'splinter personality' with contrary tendencies in the unconscious."[307] Qualities which the ego does not need or cannot utilize are set aside or repressed, and so the shadow lengthens. The shadow is composed of all those dark elements of personality which are hidden, unexpressed, or repressed because they are not consistent with the orientation or attitude of consciousness. In Jung's words, the shadow is "that hidden, repressed, for the most part inferior and guilt-laden personality whose ultimate ramifications reach back into the realm of our animal ancestors and so comprise the whole historical aspect of the unconscious."[308] Shadow, the dark side of the psyche, is the "inborn collected predisposition which we reject for ethical, aesthetic, or other reasons, and repress because it is in opposition to our conscious principles."[309] The shadow is an integral part of the individual, a split-off portion which nevertheless always follows him around and thus remains attached to him "like his shadow."[310] The shadow reflects the objective universal of the collective unconscious; it becomes personal only insofar as each person draws differently upon the primitive human which is archetypally present in each human being.[311] The shadow thus partakes of both the collective unconscious with its archetypes and the personal unconscious with its repressed materials.[312] As an empirical concept, the shadow refers primarily to Jung's larger psychology of opposites; the shadow, after all, is the unconscious antithesis or opposite of whatever overt trends in personality have developed in a particular given direction.[313] For psychic wholeness, it is imperative that each person acknowledge and then deal effectively with his shadow. The inability of a person to successfully come to grips with his shadow represents a major danger to the psyche. The more the shadow is repressed and isolated from consciousness, the blacker, denser, and more wayward it tends to become.[314] The shadow can be raised to consciousness, but not fully since its roots and primal functioning lie in the collective unconscious. In dealing effectively with the shadow, one major Jungian has this to say: "The cure of the shadow is a problem of love. How far can our love extend to the broken and the ruined parts of ourselves, the disgusting and the perverse? How much charity and compassion have we for our own weakness and sickness? How far can we build an inner society on the principle of love, allowing a place for everyone?"[315] It should be emphasized that the shadow has its decidedly positive aspects as well as its dark negativities. Every living form needs a shadow if it is to be motile and real. A reality without a shadow is nothing more than a two-dimensional phantom.[316] Psychic wholeness is impossible without the shadow; to be sure, the individuation process typically begins when a person becomes aware and then acceptant of his shadow. The shadow might be the dark brother, but it is one's brother nonetheless, a part of the nuclear psychic family in which the individual necessarily lives and grows. Jung takes pains to note that the shadow "does not consist only of morally reprehensible tendencies, but also displays a number of good qualities, such as normal instincts, appropriate reactions, realistic insights, creative impulses, etc."[317] From the moral point of view, the shadow offers wonderful possibilities for genuine personal and moral growth. Jung holds that personal and moral growth is possible only when an individual comes to authentic self-knowledge. Authentic self-knowledge necessarily involves recognizing the dark aspects of the personality as present and real in one's life, that is to say coming to grips with the shadow side of one's own psyche.[318] From the religious perspective, the shadow provides an especially fresh and highly illuminating insight into the age-old religious problem of evil. Largely because much of classic Christian theology has been based on Hellenistic philosophy, the Christian churches have typically regarded evil simply as a privation of the good. In such a view, evil really does not exist in itself; evil is the lack of something which should be present in a given reality. Furthermore, under the influence of Hellenistic philosophy, classic Christian theology typically asserts that evil should be totally extirpated from one's life. Jung holds that these two conceptions of evil are nonsense. First of all, anyone who has genuinely experienced evil can testify that it is an actual force and not simply a lack of something. Evil exists; it is not nonbeing.[319] Second, there is a major sense in which evil should not be stamped out but rather integrated into everyone's life in a positive fashion so that the full dimension of humanity can be operatively present in each person. The shadow exists, and should be dealt with in such a manner that its beneficial aspects can be assimilated into daily life.[320]

The *anima and animus,* globally speaking, comprise the inner personality, the way in which the individual behaves in relation to his inner psychic processes, notably the unconscious.[321] The anima and animus, specifically speaking, comprise the "personification of the feminine nature of a man's unconscious and the masculine nature of a woman's."[322] The anima is the feminine imprint on a man's unconscious, while the animus is the masculine imprint on a woman's unconscious. Thus each male has certain necessary feminine attributes while each female has certain necessary male attributes. Consequently, anima and animus are contragender. The animus is related to logos while the anima is related to eros.[323] For Jung, logos is the principle of reason, a principle which forms and differentiates, which brings order out of chaos, which strives for mastery and competence. Eros, on the other hand, is the principle of relatedness and receptivity, of love, and of nurturance of the essentials of life. The anima gives to the male psyche an essential touch of extrarationality, of feeling, of tenderness, and of love. The animus endows the female psyche with an essential touch of rationality, of thinking, of mastering, and of ordering. As orienters and regulators of behavior, anima and animus are powerful archetypes. "Jung did not by any means conceive the anima/animus as an idea which could be grasped intellectually, but rather a naturally grown symbol which represented the life-giving aspect of the psyche in general."[324] In Jung's own words, the anima/animus is "a natural archetype that satisfactorily sums up all the statements of the unconscious, of the primitive mind, of the history of language and religion . . . it is always the a priori element in [a person's] moods, reactions, impulses, and whatever else is spontaneous in psychic life. It is something that lives of itself, that makes us live; it is a life behind consciousness that cannot be completely integrated with it, but from which, on the contrary, consciousness arises."[325] Jung also writes that the anima/animus is a function "mediating between conscious and unconscious; the unconscious contains pictures which are transmitted, that is, made manifest, by the anima/animus, either as fantasies, or, unconsciously" in the person's own life and actions.[326] Each male carries an archetypal image of the ideal woman, and each female carries an archetypal image of the ideal man. For psychic wholeness, each male and each female must keep a proper wholesome balance between the orientations of his or her gender on the one hand and between his or her anima/animus on the other hand. Any upsetting of this balance tends to result in psychic disorder (imbalance). Thus, for example, when a male attempts overmasculine or so-called "macho" consciousness and thereby rejects his anima, he will tend to become cold, overbearing, and lacking in the basic tenderness which is essential to genuine masculinity. When a female attempts to significantly escalate her animus and significantly downplay the psychic character inherent in her feminine gender, then she will tend to become a ruthless, calculating, cold person who has paradoxically renounced both her own femininity and a balanced masculinity.[327] Jung contends that any true religion must embody both anima and animus. He believes that one of the great strengths of Catholicism is that it has stressed the anima,[328] and that one of the impoverishments of Protestantism is that it has cut itself off from the anima.[329]

The *persona,* globally speaking, comprises the outer personality, the way in which the individual behaves in relation to the outer world. As a general rule, then, the persona is the complementarity of the anima; the former is outer, the latter is inner.[330] The persona, specifically speaking, is "the individual's system of adaptation to, or the manner he assumes in dealing with the world."[331] The word persona is deliberately taken from the name of the mask worn over the faces of actors in antiquity. The persona is the socially accepted and socially imposed mask behind which dwells the true ego.[332] It is the role a person plays. The persona is formed both consciously and unconsciously. The persona is formed consciously as the individual develops specific personal ideals, goals, and a sense of his social roles. The persona is formed unconsciously as the individual identifies with significant others and as he subtly adopts the social values of the environment without being aware of this process.[333] The persona is exclusively concerned with the relation to the subject.[334] While the persona is an unavoidable necessity of life, nonetheless it brings with it certain potential dangers. For example, the ego can fail to achieve self-realization either by identifying itself too strongly with its persona or by not developing an adequate persona at all. Every calling or profession has its own characteristic persona; this general statement is almost protypically true in the case of schoolteachers and clergymen. In a particularly revealing observation, Jung remarks that "one could say, with a little exaggeration, that the persona is that which in reality one is not, but which oneself as well as others think one is."[335]

Symbol is extremely important in Jung's system of depth psychology. Since I discuss symbol earlier in this chapter as well as in Chapter Six, I will make only a few additional observations. Jung defines a symbol as "an indefinite expression with many meanings, pointing to something not easily defined and therefore not fully known. . . . The symbol therefore has a large number of analogous variants, and the more of these variants it has at its disposal, the more complete and clear-cut will be the image it projects to its object." Jung sharply contrasts symbol with sign. For Jung, sign "always has a fixed meaning because it is a conventional abbreviation for, or a commonly accepted indication of, something known."[336] Sign is thus dead, while symbol is living.[337] The symbol is always extremely complex and multilayered in nature because material flowing from every psychic function flows into its making.[338] The tremendous importance of the symbol ultimately flows from the fact that the materials of the collective unconscious are revealed not directly but in symbols. Archetypes clothe themselves in symbols. Symbols are revelations to the conscious of the prima materia of the unconscious. The collective unconscious, then, is the *Urquelle* and fundamental matrix of symbol.[339] The important aspect of symbol in terms of human functioning and self-realization is that the symbol is a mediator unifying the opposites of consciousness and unconsciousness. The symbol unites in mediatorship the prima materia of the collective unconscious with the person's rational consciousness.[340] The symbol allows the prima materia of the collective unconscious to be understood by rational consciousness. This understanding takes place not rationally but symbolically, that is, both extrarationally and rationally. In Jung's words, "the symbol is neither abstract nor concrete, neither rational nor irra-tional, neither real nor unreal. It is always both."[341] The symbol thus has a unifying psychic function which creatively guides the individual to the deepest psychological truths.[342] Jung calls the symbol a libido analogue because it is a transformer of energy from the collective unconscious to the conscious.[343] Common symbols include the wise old man, the hero, the withered tree of life, and so forth. Dreams, myths, and *mandalas* are precious because they are primary functional repositories or channels for symbol. Since symbols have an archetypal foundation, they can never be reduced to anything else. Every living religion necessarily revolves around living symbols, because every living religion is necessarily in touch with fundamental religious real-ities, realities which flow from the collective unconscious and are mediated to human beings by symbol. In Jung's view, most Christians have not adequately grasped the meaning of the symbols used in their religion, and have failed to establish a connection between the sacred figure of the symbol and their own soul. Such Christians have debased living symbol into dead sign. Whereas the foundation of Christian belief should rest on living symbols, ecclesiastical officials have re-placed these symbols with dogmas. Dogmas, states Jung, are dead signs, and thus are barriers to immediate religious experience of the deeper sort.[344]

The *libido* is the undivided vital energy which flows through the psyche.[345] Psychic energy for Jung denotes a broader life energy which includes both mental and biological energy, both of which flow through the psyche.[346] Life energy—Jung's preferred term for the libido—is equivalent to the intensity with which the contents of the psyche are charged.[347] The libido is essentially creative. Life energy, that is to say libidinal energy, courses ceaselessly through the psyche, sometimes escalating, sometimes diminishing. This fact makes possi-ble a functional approach to psychic events. This important point can be put somewhat differently. The individual's personality dynamics derive their basic energy from the libido, an energy which can flow in one direction or another. In the case of the individual who has attained complete self-realization, the basic life energy is evenly distributed throughout the various developed systems. Ordinary persons who have not attained this state of equilibrium tend to develop one side of their personality at the expense of others, something which creates a greater or lesser degree of inner strain and tension.

Psychological attitude refers to the fundamental personality direction which the libido takes in an individual.[348] Psychological attitude is basically reactive, that is to say reactive to the libido. There are two basic psychological attitudes or orientations, namely introversion and extraversion.[349] One or the other of these two fundamental psychological attitudes or orientations constitutes the "reaction habitus" that largely determines the generalized way in which a certain individual will tend to respond to outer or inner objects, to the nature and value of his own subjective experience, and even to the compensatory action of the unconscious.[350] So decisive are personality attitudes that Jung calls them "the central switchboard from which, on the one hand, external behavior is regulated and, on the other, specific experiences are formed."[351] *Introversion* is that psychological attitude which is directed toward the subjective, inner world of the psyche. Introversion tends to manifest itself in introspection. Introversion is the withdrawal of the libido from the external object; consequently, a heightened significance of the internal object results. "This leads to a particularly intense development laid down by the primordial image. In this way, the primordial image comes to the surface indirectly."[352] Introversion is characterized by a negative reaction to the environment; consequently a poor adjustment to external objects results. An introvert is more apt to withdraw from external reality, to be less sociable, and to be more absorbed in his own inner life. The introvert's "first move in every situation that confronts him is to recoil 'as if with an unvoiced no,' and only then does his real reaction set in."[353] In Jung's words, introversion "is normally characterized by a hesitant, reflective, retiring nature that keeps itself to itself, shrinks from objects, is always slightly on the defensive and prefers to hide behind mistrustful scrutiny."[354] *Extraversion* is that psychological attitude which is directed to the objective world, to reality external to the psyche. Extraversion is the outward turning of the libido. It is characterized by a manifest positive relation of subject to object; consequently a good adjustment to external objects results. A person in the extraverted state "thinks, feels, and acts in relation to the object, and moreover in a directly and clearly observable fashion, so that no doubt can remain about his positive dependence on the object."[355] Extraversion is active when it is intentional, and passive when the object compels it. The extravert is apt to be sociable, outgoing and optimistic. In both adjustment and pattern of reaction, the extravert orients himself predominantly to societal norms, the spirit of the times, and so forth.[356] In Jung's words, extraversion "is normally characterized by an outgoing, candid, and accommodating nature that adapts easily to a given situation, quickly forms attachments, and setting aside any possible misgivings, will often venture forth with careless confidence into unknown situations."[357] Each person possesses tendencies to both introversion and extraversion, but one of them is usually dominant and conscious while the other is subordinate and unconscious. There is a certain conflict between the dominant and the subordinate attitudes. The more consciously and exclusively the person develops his natural dominant psychological attitude, the greater will be the unconscious development of its opposite.[358] Put somewhat differently, a particular individual tends to exhibit introversion and extraversion at different times and under different circumstances, depending on whether conscious or unconscious processes are more potent at the moment.

Psychological function refers to the fundamental process or way of operating within a personality. Psychological function, then, refers to the process content and not the product content of psychic activity. As process, psychological function refers solely, for example, to the overall way of thinking or intuiting rather than to the product content of thought or intuition. Jung identifies four major psychological functions,[359] namely thinking, feeling, sensation, and intuition.[360] The thinking and the feeling functions are essentially rational processes because they utilize one or another kind of evaluation and judgment. The sensing and intuiting functions are essentially extrarational because they circumvent evaluation and judgment and deal instead with brute perceptions which are neither evaluated nor judged. *Thinking* is the psychological function which deals with the world in a cognitive manner. It evaluates the world on the basis of true or false. If thinking is carried on excessively or in isolation from other functions, it may lead the individual away from reality rather than toward it. When combined with strong sensation, thinking can lead to pedantic attention to raw fact or to abstract theory divorced from practice. *Feeling* is the psychological function which deals with the world in an affective manner.[361] It evaluates the world on the basis of pleasantness or unpleasantness, acceptance or rejection. If feeling is carried on to excess, it can lead to a blind acceptance or rejection of a reality on no broader base than personal whim.[362] When combined with strong sensation as an auxiliary function, feeling may lead to infantile or even deviant behavior. At any particular given moment, the thinking function and the feeling function are mutually exclusive; one or the other is dominant. *Sensation* is the psychological function which perceives the world as it really is and not otherwise. It is the person's sense of reality par excellence; it concerns the present, the now. *Intuition* is the psychological function which perceives not so much through consciousness but even more importantly through its capacity for an unconscious "inner perception" or "inner vision" of the world.[363] Intuition deals with the potential, namely that which a reality will be or has been rather than what it is. Like the thinking-feeling pair, the sensation-intuition pair is a set of opposites and cannot operate simultaneously. When one member of the pair is highly developed, the other tends to be submerged. One representative of each pair is generally observable as the *dominant function,* with a representative of the other pair as an *auxiliary function.* The auxiliary function modifies and colors the dominant function.[364] Thus, for example, a person might be described as a feeling-intuitive type or as a thinking-sensation type.[365]

Personality type, properly considered, is the actual ongoing constellation of interactive personality attitudes and personality functions. In every human being, personality attitudes combine with psychological functions. Introversion/extraversion interpenetrate thinking/ feeling/ sensation/intuition. Thus there are eight molar personality types representing different combinations of psychological attitude and psychological function. The degree to which conscious processes and unconscious processes are developed in both the predominant attitude-function combination and in the other more-or-less submerged combinations accounts for the major personality differences among individuals. Because a psychological attitude (introversion/extraversion) is rooted in a person's biological make-up, it can be changed only by a fundamental inner reconstruction of such a magnitude as to significantly modify the structure of the psyche.[366] Although a psychological function (thinking/feeling/sensation/intuition) is to a certain extent biological, it is also to a certain extent the result of learning. Hence a psychological function can be modified considerably or even repressed by conscious effort.[367]

Individuation is the process by which the psyche comes to wholeness.[368] Individuation is the process through which the conscious and the unconscious are integrated.[369] "Individuation is closely connected with the transcendent function [such as symbol], since this function creates individual lines of development which could never be reached by keeping to the path prescribed by [society's] norms."[370] In the process of individuation, the archetypes appear both as structural elements and as regulators of unconscious psychic material. In individuation, then, the archetypes are especially potent and dynamic factors. The phases in the process of individuation are characterized by the encounter of the unconscious with some typical components of the unconscious such as the great mother, the wise old man, the shadow, anima/animus, and so forth.[371] In this ongoing encounter of conscious and unconscious, wholeness can emerge.[372] Jung chooses the term "individuation" deliberately because he is thereby lexically emphasizing the process by which a person becomes a psychological "individual," that is, a separate, indivisible entity or whole.[373] Individuation stresses growing unto selfhood, existentially realizing the self—the self, of course, as Jung's theory views it. Individuation thus places great store in each person's uniqueness. Individuation takes place not only in a manner through which a person's own wholeness develops, but simultaneously in a manner in which the person becomes authentically differentiated from the general societal mentality. There are two key elements contained in this last sentence. First of all, individuation means growing to self positively by integrating conscious and unconscious processes, and negatively by divesting the self of the false wrappings of the persona.[374] Second, individuation inherently involves the process of differentiation. Differentiation encompasses a striving toward personal uniqueness so that one's vital activity is not leveled down or injured by societal standards. But differentiation also encompasses that relationship to society which leads not to isolation but to more intense and broader relationships to other persons.[375] Societal norms and relationships are not antagonistic to individuation, but only differently oriented.[376] In a statement of much significance for religious educators, Jung states: "Under no circumstances can individuation be the sole aim of psychological education. Before it can be taken as a goal, the educational aim of adaptation to the necessary minimum of [societal] norms must first be attained. If a plant is to unfold its specific nature to the full, it must first be able to grow in the soil in which it is planted."[377]

Because religion is of major importance in Jungianism, I shall devote the remainder of this section to that topic. However, it must be constantly borne in mind that the reality of religion is somewhat different for Jung than it is for much of so-called orthodox Christianity.

For Jung, *religion* is embedded in the psyche. Put differently, the psyche has a basically religious function. Therefore, psychic processes are not only psychic but also are religious.[378] Religion originates in psychic processes, flows through psychic processes, and culminates in psychic processes.[379] Consequently, religion cannot be separated from the psyche. Conversely, the psyche cannot be separated from religion. Any attempt to separate religion from the psyche necessarily results in psychic disturbances because such an attempt represents the splitting off from the psyche of one of its necessary essentials, namely religion. All psychic problems in this sense are basically religious problems. A neurosis is the splitting or disintegration of the personality; therefore, separating or even neglecting religion from the psyche inevitably leads to neurosis. No psychic problem can really be handled until the religious function is restored to and made operative in the psyche. Healing of the psyche is basically a religious problem.[380]

Because religion is so essential to each person, one major task of psychology is to explain how a person's nature and functions respond to personal events normally described as religious.[381] This point naturally leads one to ask: "What is religion in Carl Jung's view?" This is not an easy question to answer. It would seem that for Jung, religion consists in an immediate experience of the numinosum.[382] Jung's religion is wholly experiential rather than rational. There is no way in which religion can be either reduced to the rational or even described in a rationally adequate manner. Religion is simply a subjective experience of the numinosum; it is neither an experience of the reality of the numinosum-in-itself nor an existential affirmation of the objective reality of the numinosum. With perhaps a touch of Kant's epistemological agnosticism,[383] Jung keeps religion wholly within the bounds of a human being's phenomenal psychic life and free from specific theological commitments or entanglements.[384] Because religion is totally in the psyche, it has spacious room for all divers manner of sects, confessions, and personages: Jesus and Buddha, Protestantism and Islam, and even God and the devil, are united in the psyche.[385] In a major sense, religion is essentially the process of individuation:[386] it is a process of being receptive to the inbreaking of the numinosum from the collective unconscious, and it is a personal awareness that the psyche has been altered by the experience of the numinosum.[387] Religion, or more properly religious experience, is essentially *"extra ecclesiam,* subjective, and liable to boundless error."[388] For Jung, no one can know the nature of the numinosum, of ultimate things. "We must therefore take them as we experience them. And if such experience helps to make life healthier, more beautiful, more complete and more satisfactory to yourself and to those you love, you may safely say: 'This was the grace of God.' "[389]

Religious experience is not directed outwardly to the church or to society or to one's neighbor. Rather, religious experience is directed inwardly, especially to the archetype God.[390] Religious experience is what Jung calls "a living mythlogem."[391] People have a strong need for religious experience because in religious form persons are able to encounter and accept the contents of the collective unconscious. The essential elements of religion, and especially God, are personally experienced in archetypes.

God, for Jung, is found in the collective unconscious.[392] While Christians typically affirm that God is a personal or transpersonal ontic entity, Jung declares that God is an archetype. The reality of the archetype God is totally unrelated to any claim of the absolute existence of God.[393] God antedates the human being because all basic archetypes antedate the purposeful use of the mind. As archetype, God can break into a person's psyche at any time. God, then, exists in the collective unconscious and is available to any person at any time.[394] God is the archetype in which wholeness most abundantly shines. Since, as I have indicated earlier in this section, the number four has been shown to be the empirical indication of wholeness both in dreams and in the myths of various cultures, Jung states that quaternity, not trinity, is the ideal symbol of God.[395] For Jung, the trinity is an incomplete God archetype, a God lacking the necessary fourth dimension. This fourth dimension is also necessary for there to be two sets of opposites and hence for a total reconciliation of the opposites into the wholeness of the archetype.[396] It is not altogether clear what the missing fourth dimension of the archetype God is. In some trinity/quaternity discussions Jung speaks of the missing fourth dimension as the feminine, while in other trinity/quaternity discussions Jung speaks of the missing fourth dimension as evil.[397]

Jung's views on religion have met with praise by some Christians[398] and with condemnation by other Christians. In the latter connection,

some critics have bitterly denounced what they claim is Jung's fundamental Christian irreligiosity, and have called Jung a greater enemy of
religion than Freud.[399] Other Christian critics observe that Jung is
popular with some Catholics "who confuse the inspirational value of
much of Jung's thought with the basic accuracy required of such thinking."[400] In fairness to Jung, however, it must be noted that he cannot
be held responsible for the naivete and overcredulity exhibited by some
of his religious followers who seem to regard him primarily as a great
or near-great religious thinker. Jung typically denied this kind of trib-
ute, repeating almost ad nauseam that he was only a psychologist. It
might well be that the considerable—and in some cases manic—support given to Jung by some religionists represents the enfleshment of a
basic defense mechanism against Freud who held that religion is the
supreme illusion whereby human beings seek to soften the essential
harshness of the human condition.

I will now briefly mention nine ways in which Jung's theories of the
unconscious can be of significant assistance to religious educators,
even if these educators disagree with some or possibly with all of
Jungianism.

First, the religious educator can learn from Jung that religion is far
more than just a conscious process. Religion necessarily involves the
dynamic oscillation between rational and extrarational, conscious and
unconscious. In some ways, the unconscious is a higher "intelligence," a reality more compatable with religion. If the religion
teacher neglects the unconscious substantive content of religion, he
runs the risk of depriving the learners (and himself) of a goodly portion
of religion's greatest profundities and richest blessings.

Second, the religious educator ought to be aware of the depth to
which general traditions and religious traditions have markedly influenced his own life and the lives of the learners. The learner might not
live in the past, but the past surely lives in the learner. It is existentially
impossible for a religious educator to deal adequately with the learner
without simultaneously dealing with the learner's history as that history is even now affecting the learner.[401]

Third, Jungianism suggests that the religious educator ought to realize that conflict can be productive psychically. For Jung, opposites and
their reconciliation form a basis of psychical activity. Psychological
wholeness is not the eradication of conflict but the successful integration of conflict, e.g., the conflict between conscious and unconscious,

between rational and extrarational, between light and shadow, and so forth. Hence the religious educator should not try to banish conflict from the religion lesson, but rather help the learner deal with conflict in an integrative fashion.

Fourth, the religious educator should emphasize the deeper psychological aspects of Christian symbol when teaching. Symbol mediates extrarational and rational processes and thus is simultaneously a deep human source and inexhaustible divine wellspring for religious experience. If symbol is so often a dead sign in Christianity, then part of the blame must be placed at the door of religious educators who have denuded symbol of its unconscious roots.

Fifth, the religious educator can help learners immeasurably if he assists them to work with their shadow. Religious instruction in the past often endeavored to help learners subjugate or even repress their shadow. No wonder that so many devout religionists and religious educators were so two-dimensional in their personal and religious lives. The shadow is necessary for three-dimensional religion. When individuals learn how to live with their shadow, they can paradoxically make evil work to their spiritual betterment by gaining that sense of humility so necessary for genuine holiness and wholeness.

Sixth, the religious educator should so structure the pedagogical situation that the anima of the male learner and the animus of the female learner gain appropriate expression in whatever context is either religious or related to religion. In this way learners will accomplish their total sexuality, and will not be unduly restricted to either a hyper masculinity/femininity or a defective masculinity/femininity, a scourge which has affected so many religionists, especially within the Catholic celibate community.

Seventh, the religious educator should deal effectively with his own persona and with the persona of the learners. If religious instruction is to be human and humane, then it should become an encounter between teacher-as-person and learner-as-person, and not simply between teacher-as-role and learner-as-role. Furthermore, learners should be taught to be as honest as possible to themselves and to others, especially in religious matters. There is too much phoniness in religion because there is too much unresolved persona in religionists.

Eighth, the religious educator should be aware that while in one sense learners can be effectively grouped, still in another major sense each learner is basically different. Personality types represent profound differences in existential orientation and are not simply degrees of difference on some similar scale. Hence the religious educator should not fall prey to using a pedagogical procedure which does not differentiate among learners (e.g., the transmission strategy) or to using a highly restricted repertoire of pedagogical procedures.

Ninth, one cardinal goal of religious instruction ought to be personal wholeness. This is not the only goal of religious instruction, but it is a major and necessary one. The religious educator should always keep in mind that the so-called "basics" in religious instruction are not restricted solely to cognitive outcomes, but also include affective outcomes, unconscious outcomes, and so forth. But even more than this, personal wholeness suggests that a major goal of religious instruction is not simply to assist learners to acquire these outcomes, but to integrate them into an individuated religious lifestyle, into effective Christian living.

Transpersonal-Spiritual View

The transpersonal-spiritual view regards the unconscious as a function of some transpersonal or spiritual entity. From this perspective, the unconscious is a privileged medium through which an individual makes contact with a transpersonal being of one kind or another. Because the activities of the unconscious have as their core the contact with the transpersonal-spiritual world, the unconscious can be properly regarded as essentially spiritual in nature. Some advocates of the transpersonal-spiritual view claim that the essential spiritual nature of the unconscious is, in fact, a nature which is basically religious in character.

At least four major groups have adherents who espouse the transpersonal-spiritual view of the unconscious. These four groups include some romantics, some transpersonalists, some tangential followers of Jung, and an assortment of writers and depth psychologists.

The *romantics,* in the context of this chapter, are those persons who adhere to that kind of philosophy of nature espoused by the philosophical and literary Romantic Movement of the eighteenth and nineteenth centuries.[402] This movement regarded nature as a kind of unified collective being whose organic and developing parts are held together by an inner primal sympathy. Nature as a collective and each human being as a singular are tied together in a sort of *Einfühlung* or empathy. Nature is also the oversoul, an oversoul which is in intimate contact with the depths of each person's own soul. The person's unconscious is a prime medium whereby the individual can come into contact with, and be nourished by, the oversoul.[403] Thus a major task confronting each person is to commune as fully as possible with nature so that his unconscious can thereby relate to the oversoul, an oversoul which possesses a significant unconscious dimension.

Carl Gustav Carus and Eduard von Hartmann are two highly influential psychological writers from the romantic tradition who deal with the unconscious. For Carus, the unconscious is the primordial source of life and is instinctively merged with the life of the universe. The life of the universe, the life of nature, is a kind of immanent revelation of the divine, a revelation which assumes intelligent but unconscious form in the silent and essentially spiritual workings of nature.[404] Eduard von Hartmann was especially influenced by the romantic philosophy of Friedrich Wilhelm Joseph von Schelling.[405] Von Hartmann contended that the unconscious, when viewed from the perspective of the world as a whole, is not just a process unitary to each person but is an ongoing collective process springing from and unified in One Absolute Subject. The unconscious, both in each person and in nature, is an ongoing crystalization of the nucleus of the unified expanding Cosmos.[406]

The *transpersonalists,* in the context of this chapter, are members of a brand of third-force or humanistic psychology.[407] Third-force psychology, or the psychology of being as it is sometimes called, contends that psychologically healthy persons are existentially propelled toward what Abraham Maslow calls self-actualization, namely the dynamic ongoing fulfillment of human potential. A self-actualized person is dynamically realizing his capacities, fulfilling his personal mission (or call or destiny or vocation), is becoming more fully alive to his own personal human nature, and is progressing toward personal unity and integration and synergy. Self-actualized persons also have peak experiences in which the individual transcends himself in an experience of cosmic unity, mysticism, and awe. Peak experiences, transpersonal experiences, and self-transcending experiences constitute the individual's psychologically healthiest moments.[408]

Ken Wilber, and to an extent Kenneth Ring, are two prominent writers who take a transpersonal stance with respect to the unconscious. For Wilber, the human unconscious is composed of many layers proceeding along a dynamic upward-oriented axis from the lowest level of "ground unconscious" to the highest level of "emergent unconscious." It is the emergent unconscious which has the potential for transpersonal experiences, peak experiences, and transcendental experiences.[409] Ring contends that there are eight regions of unconscious "inner space" ranging from the preconscious at the most outward region of "inner space" to the extraterrestrial unconscious and the superconscious and the void at the inmost regions. The extraterrestrial unconscious includes out-of-the-body experiences wherein one encounters entities and guides for traveling to other parts of the universe. At this unconscious level there occur mediumistic phenomena, telepathy, clairvoyance, and spirit possession. The superconscious is that level in which the person travels to the very edge of awareness, where experiences become increasingly ineffable, where ecstatic experiences occur and in which the person can merge with the Universal Mind. The void is that state which is beyond any content whatever.[410]

The *tangential followers of Jung,* in the context of this chapter, are those persons who have taken selected portions of Jung's analytical psychology and combined these elements with their own religious, cultural, educational, and theological views.[411] Like Jung—and very much unlike Jung—the tangential followers see the collective unconscious as a privileged medium to directly contact the spiritual world, to experience a personal ontic God, and to encounter the God-derived and God-opposed realities of good and evil.

Morton Trippe Kelsey and John Sanford, both Episcopal clergymen appropriately living in California, are among the best known representatives of the tangential followers of Jung. Kelsey regards the unconscious as the principal place where God directly "breaks into" human experience. The spiritual world's archetypal forces of good and evil, forces which radically affect our psyche, are encountered and dealt with more powerfully and more directly in the unconscious realm than in any other dimension of human life.[412] Authentic Christian experience is possible only when and as a person experiences God and oneself-in-God as God reveals himself directly in the unconscious, especially in dreams.[413] In Kelsey's view, most contemporary Christian theology, with its strong emphasis on rationalism, is leading believers up a blind alley in which God can never be adequately known much less experienced. The only way out of this blind alley is for theology to shuck its rationalism and set its course toward elaborating the theological bases of directly contacting the transcendent God and the spiritual world via the unconscious.[414] Like Morton Trippe Kelsey, John Sanford is not a theologian but rather a social scientist interested in the unconscious. Religious experience, not theology per se, is his metier. Thus Sanford writes that he is not concerned with "a theological God possessing a whole string of metaphysical attributes. By saying that our dreams [in our unconscious] are from God I mean that they are, from the point of view of the ego, purposively directed, and seem to revolve around a central authority in the psyche."[415] Unlike liberation theologians and those religious educators who seek the kingdom of God "out there" in economic and political reforms, Sanford's work is directed to the "kingdom within," to the unconscious where the transcendent God breaks in upon the person and encounters the individual in symbol and religious myth.[416]

An *assortment of serious writers and depth psychologists,* in the context of this chapter, comprises those persons whose writings in whole or in part espouse the transpersonal-spiritual view of the unconscious. Because the persons falling under this category are widely diverse in background and in viewpoint, it is manifestly impossible to delineate any common core or thread of their beliefs. In short, this category serves as a kind of catch-all.

Ernest White and, to an extent, Viktor Frankl are two widely known representatives of their category. For White, God and Christ dwell in the human heart as well as in the transcendent spiritual world. Therefore God dwells in each person, and most especially in the person's heart of hearts, in the unconscious. Evil, guilt, salvation—all these begin and work through the depths of the human heart, the unconscious. It is in and from the unconscious, ultimately, that these spiritual forces transmogrify a person to the bad or transform him to the good. It is in and through the unconscious that faith flourishes and that charity joins us to the transpersonal transcendent God.[417] Viktor Frankl is the founder of logotherapy, an existentially oriented form of depth psychology which focuses on the basic meaning of human existence as well as on the person's own concrete search for this meaning.[418] Meaning is satisfactory and significant only to the extent to which it is found and fulfilled by the person. Existence has three levels: biology, which is oriented just to bald human existence itself; psychology, which is oriented to the general meaning of existence; noölogy, which is oriented to the ultimate meaning of one's concrete here-and-now personal existence. Ultimate meaning is necessarily bound up with religion.[419] In Frankl's view, religion "certainly goes far beyond the narrow concepts of God promulgated by many representatives of denominational and institutional religion."[420] Religion is "ultimately man's experience of his own fragmentariness and relativity against a background which must properly be called 'the Absolute'—although it is somewhat arrogant to do so, *so* absolutely must the Absolute be conceived."[421] God is absolutely transcendental. Because God is also ultimate meaning, religion, the path to ultimate meaning, is vitally present in the core and foundation of the human person, namely the unconscious.[422] The unconscious has a basic transcendent orientation; indeed, one may properly speak of a transcendent unconscious. The unconscious is intrinsically religious. God, the transcendent, is somehow contacted and encountered in the unconscious. The unconscious God is one who has simply not yet become conscious to the person; the task of logotherapy is to assist the person to become existentially aware of his unconscious religiousness. Frankl sharply criticizes Jung's view of religion, stating that the great Swiss psychiatrist failed "to locate the unconscious God in the personal and existential region [of the unconscious]. Instead, he allotted it to the region of drives and instincts, where unconscious religiousness no longer remained a matter of choice and decision. . . . For Jung, unconscious religiousness was bound up with religious archetypes belonging to the collective unconscious. For him, unconscious religiousness has scarcely anything to do with a personal decision, but becomes an essentially impersonal, collective, 'typical' (i.e., arche-typical) process occurring in man. . . . For Jung and the Jungians unconscious religiousness has always remained something more-or-less instinctual."[423] Deliberately distancing himself from Jung with respect to unconscious religiousness, Frankl forthrightly asserts that "unconscious religiousness stems from the personal center of the individual man rather than an impersonal pool of images shared by mankind."[424]

SOME PRACTICAL CONSEQUENCES

Unconscious Content in the Instructional Process

I must emphasize that unconscious content does not belong to psychotherapy alone. Unconscious content belongs to the religious instruction process as well. Psychotherapists deal with unconscious content in a psychotherapeutic way, while religious educators work with unconscious content in an instructional manner. The goals of psychotherapy in dealing with unconscious content are significantly different from the goals of instruction in working with unconscious content. Psychotherapeutic procedures and goals in dealing with unconscious content properly complement rather than exclude instructional procedures and goals in dealing with unconscious content.

While psychotherapists deal with the learner's unconscious in a far deeper manner than do religious educators, nonetheless religious educators do in fact work with the learner's unconscious whether these educators like it or not. Teachers and learners encounter each other, not only at the conscious level, but at the unconscious level as well. The teacher's unconscious existentially addresses the learner's unconscious, and vice versa.[425] Some dimensions of this constant unconscious teacher-learner interchange are hidden; other dimensions flow subtly but nonetheless visibly in and through the outward behavior of both teacher and learner. While this last-mentioned fact holds eminently true for nonverbal behavior, it also obtains for verbal behavior.[426]

It would appear that a great deal of an individual's most significant religious learning occurs at the unconscious level. Hence the religious educator should attempt to pedagogically reach rather than block out vibrations from the deep regardless of whether these vibrations are harmonious or discordant.[427] For religious instruction to be optimally effective, it must be targeted toward the total personal environment of the learner, an environment which perforce includes the unconscious as well as the conscious.[428]

One of the principal tasks of the religious educator is to help the learner unite the conscious and the unconscious realms in a holistic fashion. This is a creative process; it is also a demanding one.

The religious educator who wishes to deal fruitfully with the unconscious content of both religion and the learner would do well to get into personal existential touch with his own unconscious as far as this is possible. The religious educator should constantly strive to be aware of the manifestations of his own unconscious in the teaching-learning dynamic.[429] In the pedagogical process, the learner selects from the teacher and the rest of the instructional environment those elements which have personal meaning for him on his own existential terms—elements which often do include communicated materials from the teacher's own unconscious. What Carl Jung remarks about a psycho-therapist also holds equally true for a religion teacher: "The therapist must at all times keep watch over himself, over the way he is reacting to his patients. For we must always be asking ourselves: How is our unconsciousness experiencing this situation? We must therefore observe our dreams, pay the closest attention and study ourselves just as carefully as we do the patient. Otherwise the entire treatment may go off the rails." [430] For example, it might well be that the religion teacher's unconscious needs are getting in the way of a really effective lesson or instructional procedure. [431]

Is the religious educator entering into dangerous territory by dealing with unconscious content? Of course he is. The religion teacher might possibly do some harm to the learner. This is an unavoidable risk in the great adventure which is religious instruction. Religion teaching is, or ought to be, a grand journey into unexplored religious territory rather than a search for rules of safety. Even psychotherapists have been known to do psychological damage, sometimes severe, to their patients. [432] It should be emphasized that the religious educator is possibly even more dangerous if he fails to deal with the learner's unconscious content. At any event, the religious educator can minimize the danger by carefully studying scholarly treatises on the unconscious and also by assiduously monitoring the manifestations of his own unconscious processes through dreams, free associations, and the like. The religious educator should be guiding and helping the learner with courage and humility, "rather than hiding away from life in the cabin or the fo'c'sle and pretending there is no storm and no danger." [433]

Dreams

Despite their highly diverse and frequently conflicting theoretical positions, almost all depth psychologists would agree with Sigmund Freud's statement that "the interpretation of dreams is the royal road to a knowledge of the unconscious activities of the mind." [434] Almost all depth psychologists, regardless of persuasion, would also tend to agree with Carl Jung's statement that "dream-analysis is an eminently educational activity, whose basic principles and conclusions would be of the greatest assistance in curing the evils of our time." [435] Whatever else the dream is, it at least reveals what is occurring in an individual's personality and unconscious—if, of course, one admits the possibility that dreams have a deeper meaning. [436]

A dream is a series of cognitive, affective, or lifestyle behaviors which occur in the form of imagery during sleep. "In this condition," claims Carl Jung, "the mind is to a large extent withdrawn from our voluntary control. With the small portion of consciousness that remains to us in the dream state we apperceive what is going on, but we are no longer in a position to guide the course of psychic events according to our [conscious] wish and purpose."[437]

Beginning in 1953, there has been a spate of sophisticated physiological research conducted on the interrelationship between dreaming as a physiological state and the processes/products of dreaming.[438] A good deal of this research relates to the connection between dreaming and rapid eye movements (REM). The empirical research indicates that when a sleeper is awakened during a period of REM, he typically reports that he had just been dreaming.[439] The empirical research also indicates that "the degree of physiological activation during REM sleep, no matter what the particular parameter may be, is substantially greater and resembles the waking state considerably more than the amount of physiological arousal associated with NONREM sleep."[440] Thus the overwhelming mass of empirical research reveals that (1) REM is very much associated with the dreaming process, and (2) during REM the person's whole physiological state is greatly transformed as contrasted to NONREM. Two contrary conclusions from these data invite themselves for consideration. First, a dream can be reduced to basic biological processes operating in REM. Second, a dream is an independent process separate from but intimately associated with REM.[441] As yet, neither conclusion has been indisputedly proved right or wrong.

In an admirable attempt to mesh the wide corpus of empirical findings on sleep, Ernest Hartmann proposes a comprehensive theory which endeavors to combat dualism by integrating psychology and physiology. Hartmann's theory states that REM sleep restores psychological functioning after prolonged conscious activities and strains during wakefulness. REM accomplishes this task by providing recuperation of catecholamine-dependent neuronal systems in the brain which have become depleted in the course of one's activities during wakefulness.[442]

The dream was regarded as highly significant in ancient cultures. The Babylonians and Assyrians believed that the dream is a medium whereby devils and spirits of the dead exert bad influences on the dreamer.[443] The ancient Egyptians regarded dreams as messages from the gods.[444] The gods were believed to intervene in a person's life in three different kinds of dream: the unsolicited dream in which the gods appear in order to demand some act of piety toward themselves; the dream in which the gods give a spontaneous warning; the dream in which the gods grant the dreamer an answer to a particular question or provide guidance on a specific problem which the dreamer had.[445] The ancient Chinese believed that the origin of the dream lies not in sources external to the person but from within the person's own spiritual soul (*hun*) itself. The spiritual soul is involved with dreams; while temporarily separated from the body during sleep, the spiritual soul can communicate with the souls of the dead and return to the body with impressions of these communications. The *Vedas* or sacred scriptures of ancient India connected dream content with the temperament of the dreamer. The ancient Greeks viewed the dream as a visit paid to the sleeping person by a God or otherworldly ghost. Later, Hippocrates emphasized the astrological features or pointers of the dream. Aristotle, on the other hand, rejected both astrological interpretations of the dream and the contention that the dream had divine origin (animals were discovered to dream as well). Primitive noncivilized tribes throughout the world have tended to regard the dream as possessing an especial real reality. Dreams have exerted a very practical influence over the lives of these tribesmen ranging from decisions on war to sacrificial acts, religious ceremonies, living sites, inventions of material objects, and so forth.

Without a doubt the dream played a highly prominent and influential role in both the Old Testament and the New Testament.[446] Regrettably, most theologians, including biblical theologians, neglect this patent fact—something doubtless caused by the cognitivism and rationalism imbedded in theology. With respect to the foundation of the theory of dreams in the Old Testament, Morton Trippe Kelsey states that "the word dream (*chalom*, or the verb *chalam*) is related to the Aramaic and Hebrew verb 'to be made healthy or strong.' "[447] More often than not, Kelsey states, the ancient Hebrews did not separate dream and vision.

A brief mention of a few representative passages in the bible will indicate how important and decisive a role the dream has played in the religious life of biblical Israel and biblical Christianity.

The convenant which Yahweh made with Abraham originated when the latter had fallen into a deep sleep, most probably in a dream (Gen.

15: 12–21). Joseph clearly regarded dreams as, among other things, the revelation of God to the dreamer. Thus, for example, Joseph told Pharaoh that by means of Pharaoh's dreams God told the Egyptian ruler what he (God) was going to do (Gen. 41:25). In Numbers 12: 5–6 it is recorded that Yahweh called Aaron and Miriam telling them: "If anyone among you is a prophet, I shall make myself known to him in a vision, I shall speak with him in a dream."[448] It was during the night, presumably in a dream, that Yahweh spoke to Nathan instructing him (2 Sam. 7: 4–17) to tell David to build the center of Jewish worship (the Temple) and to assure David that Yahweh would establish the House of David (which would culminate in the birth of Jesus).

Joseph's doubts about Mary were removed when an angel of the Lord appeared to him in a dream informing him of the divine origin of Jesus (Mt. 1: 18–23). The Magi were warned in a dream to take another route home to their native lands (Mt. 2:12). While in Egypt, Joseph was told by an angel of the Lord in a dream that he should return to the land of Israel (Mt. 2: 19–20). There is a sense in which the Book of Revelation can be regarded as the record of the Apostle John's dreams and visions. This book has a dream-like quality about it, and the principles of dream interpretation provide an especially fruitful hermeneutical framework for ascertaining the meaning of this last book of the bible.

The relevant empirical research indicates that dreaming is a universal process. Everyone dreams. The empirical research also reveals that dreaming appears to be a process which is adaptive with respect to the individual and functional with respect to the group.[449] The fact that everyone dreams suggests that dreaming is not a process which is minor or tangential to the human condition. Hence social science in general, and religious instruction in particular, should devote due attention to the phenomenon and meaning of dreams.

Prior to using dreams productively in the religious instruction act, the religious educator must satisfactorily answer two major questions which have always puzzled human beings. First, what is the actual meaning or significance of the dream? Second, what is the relationship between one's experiences during the dream and one's experiences during wakefulness, or put somewhat differently, what degree of reality can one properly attach to the dream?[450] To answer these questions, the religious educator must delve as deeply as possible into the various theories of the dream, because only from theory can come adequate explanations about the nature and practical operations of the dream. There are, of course, highly conflicting theories of dream origin and dream interpretation.[451] I shall treat very briefly two of these disparate theories, namely that of Sigmund Freud and that of Carl Jung. The religious educator can choose between these two, or from among the many other theories of dream, on the basis of both the fruitfulness of the theory and the practical data which he gleans from the research and his own teaching practice.

It is important to note that dreams are not necessarily linked to spontaneous unconscious processes. Some dreams seem to be the simple conscious-related result of stimuli which occur during one's waking hours. For example, a particular experience such as encountering an unavailable beloved person in a restaurant, or a generalized experience such as stress, seem to trigger a dream reaction at times.[452] Other dreams seem to be caused by physiological stimuli impinging upon the sleeping person. For example, dreams involving the element of cold can be the result of the sleeper being exposed to cold stimuli while in the dormant state. Still other dreams appear to be linked with unconscious processes of one type or another. It is this last-mentioned type of dream which is my concern in this section.

Before proceeding to my extremely brief summary of the Freudian and Jungian interpretations of the dream, I would like to highlight three cardinal principles of dream interpretation with which virtually every school of depth psychology would agree. First, dreams are orderly, psychologically nonrandom events which reflect day-to-day changes in the life of an individual.[453] Thus the dream is an especially valuable indicator of what is really happening to a person not only at the deepest levels but throughout his entire personality holistically considered. Second, the image or symbol in which a dream is encased is real. The dream image or symbol is not half-real or quasi-real, but fully real. Though a symbol might be different kind of reality than the reality which one regularly encounters in daily wakefulness, nonetheless the symbol is eminently real.[454] Third, a dream takes place in, and encapsulates, multiple levels of awareness. Any proper explanation of the meaning of a dream must perforce recognize two or more levels of awareness which occur in the dream.[455]

For Sigmund Freud, every dream has a basic biological function, namely to preserve and continue sleep. This is the foundation of Freud's dream theory. Dreams are attempts to relieve emotional tensions which interfere with complete rest. These tensions proximately originate and develop in the needs and desires which have been repressed into unconsciousness or have otherwise been radically unfulfilled during the preceding day. In adults, these repressions and radical unfulfillments arise because of inner conflicts. These inner conflicts are frequently the continuing result and active residue of seething libidinous desires which the person originally repressed during childhood because these desires were unacceptable to parental attitudes. Sleep cuts the person off from most external stimuli and from the critical inhibitory cognitive functions of waking consciousness. In such a passive state, the repressed and radically unfulfilled unconscious material is freed from inhibitions to find vicarious expression in the symbolism of the dream.[456] The essence and thrust of the dream, then, is wish fulfillment. This wish fulfillment is a compromise formulation—it does indeed express a basic fulfillment of deep-seated unconscious wishes but in such a disguised symbolic fashion as not to conflict sharply with the ego and thus interrupt sleep. This compromise expression of repressed unconscious wish fulfillment is the result of the dream censor which significantly tones down and reshapes the original repressed desires raging in the unconscious. The dream censor, then, attempts to prevent the pristine unconscious from emerging into consciousness. Because of the dream censor, every dream has a double aspect, namely manifest content and latent content. Manifest content is the symbolism or external garb of imagery in which the dream is clothed. The latent content is the basic but hidden meaning of the dream, the real essential meaning of the dream. Since sex, and to a lesser extent aggression, constitute the essence of the unconscious, the censor refashions this surging latent content of the dream into nonthreatening manifest content.[457] At least four major mechanisms occur in the formation of a dream, that is to say in the process of transforming latent content into manifest content. These four mechanisms are condensation, displacement, dramatization, and symbolization. Condensation takes place when several elements or meanings of the latent content are combined into a single image of the manifest content. Displacement occurs when the emotional charge is detached from its natural object and directed to a secondary object. Dramatization happens when conceptual ideas or emotional valences are expressed in concrete plastic images. Symbolization occurs when a concrete hidden dimension of the unconscious takes on the form of a particular representational image. Many symbols which appear in dreams are independent from any exclusive individual interpretation and possess a universal (but not archetypal) meaning, such as an empty house or an empty shoe symbolizing a vagina.[458] Recalling the dream aloud to a dream consultant is vitally important not simply because this process enables the dreamer to become more consciously aware of the key mental forces operating in his life,[459] but even more importantly because this process extends dream work. This extension, which Freud calls secondary elaboration,[460] consists in attempts by the ego to further refashion the manifest content of the dream into a semblance of rational logic and coherence—and ego acceptability. Secondary elaboration thus provides a further clue as to the latent content of the dream, to the identity of the repressed materials hiding in the unconscious, and to the way in which an individual's personality functions.[461]

For Carl Jung, every dream has a basic holistic function, namely to advance the person toward wholeness or individuation. The dream is not so much a wish striving to be fulfilled as a continuing attempt to resolve personality problems and blockages on terms available to the organism. Because of its holistic personality thrust, the dream often acts as a compensatory mechanism to balance lopsided feelings about a person, event, or object.[462] Compensation is a mechanism innate in the psyche, a mechanism geared to produce holistic adjustment or rectification. The compensatory mechanism also functions to activate via the dream those significant personality tendencies which might have been overlooked, neglected, or downplayed during wakefulness. Since each person is simultaneously an individual in the here-and-now and an individual who is existentially immersed in the entire history of the race, the dream deals not only with the dreamer's here-and-now life but also with everything that has been of significance in the entire history of the human race. A dream is especially valuable because it is only in a dream that the unconscious is made readily available to the conscious. Thus it is only in the dream that the basic structures of one's personality are revealed. In a dream, writes Jung, a person does not dream; a person is dreamt. The dreamer suffers the dream, is the object of the dream.[463] Because the dream is targeted toward achieving present and future individuation, it deals only with present and future situations in the life of the dreamer.[464] Dreams also have the power to foretell future events.[465] Dreams contain all sorts of conscious and unconscious material, all kinds of known and unknown realities. There are two basic kinds of dream, both of which are connected to the unconscious. There is the dream which arises as a direct reaction by the unconscious to some event of the day which took place during conscious waking life. Then there is the dream which arises or erupts spontaneously from the unconscious. Such a dream naturally brings the unconscious into conflict with those conscious forces still operating in the dreamer. When the conscious forces are stronger, a certain psychic balance between the conscious and the unconscious is achieved. But when the unconscious forces are stronger, then come the most psychically significant dreams, dreams which can sometimes greatly alter or even reverse a person's conscious orientation. The essence and thrust of the dream is simply this: a dream is what it is and not something else. A dream is real in itself; it is not a facade hiding or disguising some deeper reality.[466] Rejecting Freud's distinction between manifest and latent content, Jung states forthrightly that the so-called manifest content is the dream itself and contains the whole meaning of the dream.[467] The dream, then, is literal. There is no dream censorship; the dream always says exactly what the unconscious means. The dream represents what Jungians call a "true and living symbol," namely an expression in imagery of a reality not yet recognized or formulated in awareness. A true and living symbol is "an image which describes in the best possible way the dimly discerned nature of the spirit."[468] These symbols are polyvalent, admitting to a wide variety of meanings. To be sure, the meaning of dream symbols depends on the context in which they occur as well as on the specific external and internal situation of the dreamer. Symbols are used creatively in dreams to further one's ongoing process of individuation. Thus there is, strictly speaking, no "objectively correct" interpretation of dreams with regard to the meaning of the symbol for a particular dreamer. This statement even holds true for those dreams which feature universal symbols of the collective unconscious. Jung does not analyze dreams; rather, he reads dreams and makes hypothetical tentative interpretations from this reading. A proper reading of a dream demands that the dream be viewed not as an isolated phenomenon but instead as one interconnected unit in a sequential series of dreams. In this manner each dream can be dealt with as part of an organic meaningful whole and read with an eye to internal consistency. If another person reads one's dream, then such a person perforce must be familiar with the life and existential aspirations of the dreamer. Whereas Freud analyzes the dream with the method of free association, Jung reads the dream by the process of amplification. Amplification denotes the "examination of all possible connotations of a given image, among which many might be related to the person's past or present experiences, while others will perhaps elucidate the significance of an archetypal dream. Great importance is ascribed to archetypal dreams; they must be studied carefully and in sequence as milestones marking the path of individuation."[469] There are two levels to the Jungian reading of dreams, namely the objective level and the subjective level. In the objective level, dream images are broken down into memory complexes that refer to external situations or actual objects. In the subjective level, the memory complexes are separated from external causes and related back to the dreamer. The first level is analytic, the second synthetic.

The following practical principles and suggestions will aid the religious educator in assisting learners to come into fruitful contact with their dreams and with the basic meanings of these dreams. These principles will generally hold true regardless of which dream theory is guiding the religious educator.

First, establish a warm socioemotional climate in the instructional group. This is obviously easier to do when religious instruction is conducted in family settings than in institutional settings like the classroom. If the classroom climate is heavily cognitive, rationalistic, or authoritarian, it will be difficult to achieve that warmth, honesty, and acceptance so necessary for dealing productively with dreams in a group situation.[470]

Second, structure the pedagogical situation in such a way that the group understands and appreciates that its purpose in dream lessons is to openly explore the dream both for the benefit of the dreamer and of themselves as well. Everyone should profit spiritually from the sharing and investigation of dreams.

Third, undertake the exploration of dreams with seriousness of purpose. If dream lessons are regarded by learners (and by the religious educator) as simply a game, as a pleasant diversion, or as a respite from "serious" cognitive product content, then these lessons will bear scant pedagogical fruit.[471]

Fourth, encourage learners to share their dreams with others. Because dreams are a highly private and personal affair, learners are often understandably reluctant to disclose them. A warm and acceptant socioemotional group climate, together with some judicious pump-priming by the religious educator in the form of revealing some of his own dreams, can help break the ice and facilitate the flow of shared dream material.[472]

Fifth, help each learner trust the dream—his own dreams and the dreams of other group members. While dreams are the dark speech of the spirit, they are the speech of the spirit nonetheless, and hence are of signal importance to each person's own psychic welfare and fulfillment. A dream is an important dimension of the intrinsic process of self-awareness, self-healing, and self-actualization.

Sixth, befriend the dream. Both the religious educator and the learners should befriend their own dreams and the dreams of others in the group. To accomplish this, each person in the group should be-friend the dream, that is to say, to *be* the dream and to form a genuine *friendship* with the dream. A learner should not simply treat his dream or the dreams of other group members as objects to be studied. Rather, learners should try to move into the dream and attempt to make that dream their own.[473] As Carl Jung once wrote, "there is no knowledge *about* the psyche, but only *in* the psyche."[474]

Seventh, make no a priori assumptions about the meaning of a dream, whether this dream is one's own or that of another group member. While there may exist certain general flexible guidelines available to the religious educator and to the learners about how to explore the meaning of dreams, these guidelines should not be transmuted into fixed a priori assumptions of what a dream should definitely mean or not mean.[475]

Eighth, assist learners to listen carefully to their own dreams and to the dreams of others in the group. Only by careful, empathic listening will the learners be enabled to come into tune with the main themes of the dream, with the less-than-obvious meanings of the dream, and with materials which are consistent from one dream to another.

Ninth, encourage learners to be open, honest, and forthright when sharing their dreams with the group. Again, a warm and acceptant socioemotional climate is a requisite precondition for an open disclosure and an honest discussion of dream material. Since much dream material is erotic, aggressive, bizarre, and socially unacceptable, the religious educator should do all in his pedagogical power to insure that dreams are received by the group in a spirit of Christian love and understanding.

Tenth, suggest to the learners that they keep a journal or other kind of record of their dreams. Dreams are important features of one's psychic life, of one's spiritual journey. Hence it is well worth the little extra effort it takes to maintain a log of one's dreams. The best time to record one's dreams in a journal is immediately upon awakening. People who keep a journal of their dreams usually find that they dream far more frequently than they had realized, and that the content of their dreams is far more important than they had previously imagined.[476]

Eleventh, sensitize the learners to look for leitmotifs in their dreams. The onset, recurrence, and ebbing of dream leitmotifs can serve as important indicators to learners about the shape and direction of their psychic and religious journey.[477]

Twelfth, empower the learners to confront the dream when it is recalled and presented to the group—their own individual dreams as well as the dreams of other members of the dream group. There may be varying degrees of resistance to such confrontation. In such instances, the religious educator as instructional facilitator helps elicit a readiness to come to terms with the material presented in the dream.[478]

Thirteenth, assist the learners to use their imagination when encountering their own dreams, and the dreams of others in the group. Whether one views the basic meaning of dreams as hidden in latent content, as present in an archetypal symbol, or whatever, the basic meaning of the dream is not couched in obvious or direct form. Learners must be taught to use divergent thinking, extrarational thinking of the conscious variety, imagination, empathy, and a feeling-for-the-dream in order to come to the essential message brought by this visitor in the night.

Fourteenth, remind learners that the dreamer is the expert on his own dream. Other groups members can assist the learner to come to grips with his own dream. Indeed, other group members can appropriate another person's dream as their own. But when it comes to interpretation, the whole group, including the religious educator, must pay special heed to what the dreamer thinks and especially feels his dream means and is.

Fifteenth, structure the pedagogical situation in such a manner that the learners can make useful theoretical and practical application in their own personal lives of the dreams dealt with in the dream group. The purpose of religious instruction, after all, is to facilitate a deeper religious lifestyle. Hence dreams should be integrated into each learner's lifestyle as far as possible. Each learner should listen to his own dreams and try to live more in harmony with what his dreams are telling him. Each learner should also listen to the dreams of others in the group so that they can use that dream material to enrich their own dreams and fructify their own Christian lifestyle.

Dreams can be a valuable help to the religious educator in improving certain pedagogical procedures, especially those kinds which are tied in with personality variables. What Carl Jung once wrote concerning the blockage and subsequent improvement of his own psychotherapeutic procedures has relevance for religious educators in their unremitting efforts to significantly improve their own pedagogical practice. Jung had a female patient with whom he at first enjoyed considerable psychotherapeutic success. After a while he noticed that his procedures were losing their effectiveness. He resolved to discuss this with his patient. The night before he was to mention this matter to his patient, he had a dream which gave him a major clue as to why his psychotherapeutic practices had become relatively ineffective. Through the dream, Jung discovered, to his surprise, that he was practicing psychotherapy with the patient in such a manner that he was looking down on her rather than respecting her. The next day he told his patient of the dream. Jung reported that this produced an immediate beneficial change in the situation, and that the procedures once more began to be effective.[479]

CONCLUSION

In this chapter I have presented a wide variety of divergent views on both consciousness and unconsciousness without expressing a preference for any particular one of these disparate perspectives. My reason for doing this flows from the fact that there does not yet exist a corpus of convincing empirical evidence leading to the conclusion that any one or more of these views is indeed correct.[480]

The overarching purpose of this chapter has been to identify unconscious processes as a major indispensable substantive content of religious instruction. Until religious educationists and educators come to a realization that the teaching-learning dynamic contains a great deal of unconscious content, they will continue to grossly neglect this essential ingredient of the instructional act.

Revelation both human and divine constitutes the warp and woof of religious growth and development. This chaper has shown, I think, that expanded consciousness and also unconscious processes are especially rich loci in which significant human and divine realities are revealed to the learner.

NOTES

1. Graham Greene, *The Heart of the Matter* (New York: Viking, 1948), p. 166.
2. Though full of loopholes and ambiguities, this is a definition of the unconscious with which virtually every school of depth psychology and physiological psychology can agree. Ernest Jones, the official biographer of Freud, considers this to be Freud's own definition of the unconscious. Carl Jung also agrees to the definition of the unconscious. Even physiological psychologists, who disagree with the basic tenets of depth psychology, also by and large agree to this definition. See Judd Marmor, "Foreword," in D. B. Klein, *The Unconscious: Invention or Discovery?* (Santa Monica, Calif.: Goodyear, 1977), p. xiv; C. G. Jung, *Aion,* 2d edition, in C. G. Jung, *Collected Works,* volume IX, part II, translated by R. F. C. Hull (Princeton, N.J.: Princeton University Press, 1959), p. 3.
3. Natalino Caputi, *Guide to the Unconscious* (Birmingham, Ala.: Religious Education Press, 1984).
4. C. G. Jung, *The Development of Personality,* in C. G. Jung, *Collected Works,* volume XVII, translated by R. F. C. Hull (Princeton, N.J.: Princeton University Press, 1954), p. 59.
5. On slips of the tongue, see Sigmund Freud, *The Psychopathology of Everyday Life,* translated by Alan Tyson, edited by James Strachey (New York: Norton, 1960), pp. 230–279; on dreams, see Sigmund Freud, *New Introductory Lectures on Psychoanalysis,* translated by James Strachey (New York: Norton, 1965), pp. 7–56.
6. C. G. Jung, *Memories, Dreams, Reflections,* recorded and edited by Aniela Jaffé, translated by Richard and Clara Winston (New York: Pantheon, 1963), p. 223.
7. James Hillman, *Insearch: Psychology and Religion* (New York: Scribner's 1967), pp. 50–51.
8. Carter V. Good, editor, *Dictionary of Education,* 2d edition (New York: McGraw-Hill, 1959), p. 124; Fred N. Kerlinger, *Foundations of Behavioral Research,* 2d edition (New York: Holt, Rinehart & Winston, 1973), pp. 28–41.
9. For short summaries of the nature and function of theory with specific reference to the work of religious instruction, see James Michael Lee, *The Shape of Religious Instruction* (Birmingham, Ala.: Religious Education Press, 1971), pp. 152–161; James Michael Lee, "The Authentic Source of Religious Instruction," in Norma H. Thompson, editor, *Religious Education and Theology* (Birmingham, Ala.: Religious Education Press, 1982), pp. 117–121.
10. The process of validating a construct is densely intertwined with theory. Thus Lee Cronbach notes that there are three phases of construct validation: suggesting which construct or constructs primarily account for a particular behavior, deriving hypotheses from the guiding theory involving the construct or constructs, and finally testing the hypotheses empirically. Commenting on Cronbach's statement, Fred Kerlinger observes that construct validation is far deeper and more elegant than those bald unsophisticated empirical approaches which deal with a construct simply in terms of its predictive power. Construct valida-

tion seeks explanation and verification, two essential ingredients of theory. Lee J. Cronbach, *Essentials of Psychological Testing*, 3rd edition. (New York: Harper & Row, 1970), p. 143; Fred N. Kerlinger, *Foundations of Behavioral Research* (New York: Holt, Rinehart & Winston, 1973), pp. 461–462.

11. It is fundamentally for this reason that David Klein can properly remark that "just as those who are convinced of God's existence differ among themselves about the nature of God, so those persuaded of the reality of the unconscious differ among themselves about the nature of the unconscious." D. B. Klein, *The Unconscious: Invention or Discovery?* p. 2.

12. Ruth L. Munroe, *Schools of Psychoanalytic Thought* (New York: Holt, Rinehart & Winston, 1955), p. 601.

13. Natalino Caputi, *Guide to the Unconscious*, p. 166.

14. Ira Progoff, *The Symbolic and the Real* (New York: Julian, 1963), p. 68. In an attempt to make sure that his readers would not yield to the temptation of reifying the unconscious, James Grier Miller pointedly and expressly employs the word "unconsciousness." James Grier Miller, *Unconsciousness* (New York: Wiley, 1942), pp. 77–78. Because the term "the unconscious" is so imbedded in usage, I use this somewhat unfortunate term in this chapter.

15. See, for example, C. G. Jung, *Memories, Dreams, Reflections*, p. 209.

16. Natalino Caputi, *Guide to the Unconscious*, pp. 5–6.

17. James Grier Miller, *Unconsciousness*, pp. 16–44.

18. Horace B. English and Ava Champney English, *A Comprehensive Dictionary of Psychological and Psychoanalytical Terms* (New York: Longmans, Green, 1958), p. 569.

19. Sigmund Freud, *New Introductory Lectures on Psychoanalysis*, p. 111.

20. Carl Jung also writes as follows: "Theoretically, no limits can be set to the field of consciousness, since it is capable of indefinite extension. Empirically, however, it always finds its limit when it comes up against the *unknown*. This consists of everything we do not know, which, therefore, is not related to the ego as the center of the field of consciousness. The unknown falls into two groups of objects: those which are outside and can be experienced by the senses, and those which are inside and are experienced immediately. The first group comprises the unknown in the outer world; the second the unknown in the inner world. We call this latter territory the *unconscious*." C. G. Jung, *Aion*, p. 3.

21. Viktor E. Frankl, *The Unconscious God* (New York: Simon and Schuster, 1975); see also Viktor E. Frankl, *The Doctor and the Soul: From Psychotherapy to Logotherapy* (New York: Vintage, 1973).

22. Roberto Assagioli, *Psychosynthesis* (New York: Hobbs, Dorman, 1965), pp. 17–18. There is a sense in which these three Assagioli categories compare to Freud's categories of id, preconscious, and superego respectively.

23. Three especially helpful sources on this topic include Lancelot Law Whyte, *The Unconscious Before Freud* (London: Tavistock, 1959); Henri F. Ellenberger, *The Discovery of the Unconscious* (New York: Basic, 1970); Franz G. Alexander and Sheldon Selesnick, *The History of Psychiatry* (New York: New American Library, 1966). I have used all three of these books in my distillation of the history of the construct unconscious.

24. To be sure, one of Adler's principal objections to psychoanalytic (Freudian) theory is that he believed that this theory fails to properly emphasize that the personality always functions as a unit. See Alfred Adler, *The Social Interest*, translated by John Linton and Richard Vaughan (London: Faber and Faber, 1938), p. 93.

25. C. G. Jung, *Memories, Dreams, Reflections,* p. 209.
26. For a discussion of this point, see A. C. MacIntyre, *The Unconscious* (Atlantic Highlands, N.J.: Humanities Press, 1958), pp. 63–66.
27. Gabriel Moran, *The Present Revelation* (New York: Herder and Herder, 1972), p. 97. I regard this volume as the best book Moran has written to date (1984).
28. *Ibid.,* p. 99.
29. Lancelot Law Whyte, *The Unconscious Before Freud,* p. x.
30. *Ibid.,* p. 19, italics deleted.
31. One of the more egregious errors in Françoise Darcy-Bérubé's assessment of the social-science approach to religious instruction lies in the heavy and pervasive dualistic view which she seems to have toward human functions in particular and to the natural/supernatural in general. See Françoise Darcy-Bérubé, "The Challenge Ahead of Us," in Padraic O'Hare, editor, *Foundations of Religious Education* (New York: Paulist, 1978), pp. 112–120.
32. Lancelot Law Whyte, *The Unconscious Before Freud,* p. 29.
33. See Charles T. Tart, "Discrete States of Consciousness," in Philip R. Lee et al., editors, *Symposium on Consciousness* (New York: Viking, 1976), pp. 91–105.
34. Sigmund Freud, *The Interpretation of Dreams,* translated by James Strachey (New York: Avon Discus, 1953), pp. 626–648.
35. C. G. Jung, *The Development of Personality,* p. 115.
36. C. G. Jung, *Psychological Reflections,* edited by Jolande Jacobi (New York: Harper & Row, 1953), pp. 22–35.
37. C. G. Jung, *Memories, Dreams, Reflections,* p. 348.
38. George Klein makes an interesting observation when he notes that the behaviorists seized upon Freud's notion that attendant consciousness is necessary for meaningful and goal-directed behavior. But, Klein continues, the behaviorists ignored the central import of Freud's teaching on this matter, namely that non-awared or uncomprehended meaning is active and has a definite controlling influence upon human behavior. George S. Klein, *Psychoanalytic Theory* (New York: International Universities Press, 1976), p. 247.
39. C. G. Jung, *Memories, Dreams, Reflections,* p. 331.
40. *Ibid.,* p. 324.
41. *Ibid.,* p. 242. Later, Jung writes: "What happens within oneself when one integrates previously unconscious contents with the consciousness is something which can scarcely be described in words. It can only be experienced. It is a subjective affair quite beyond discussion; we have a particular feeling about ourselves, about the way we are, and that is a fact which is neither possible nor meaningful to doubt. Similarly, we convey a particular feeling to others, and that too is a fact that cannot be doubted. So far as we know, there is no higher authority which could eliminate the probable discrepancies between all these impressions and opinions." (p. 287).
42. For example, Rogers pointedly remarks that "man is wiser than his intellect." Carl R. Rogers, The Humanistic Conception of Man," in Richard E. Farson, editor, *Science and Human Affairs* (Palo Alto, Calif.: Science and Behavior Books, 1965), p. 23.
43. Carl R. Rogers, *On Becoming a Person* (Boston: Houghton Mifflin, 1961), pp. 107–124.
44. Sometimes in the professional literature the terms "alogical," "nonlogical," and "extrarational" are used synonomously. Sometimes in my own writings, including this book, I also use these terms more-or-less interchangeably.

45. For a fine, succinct, and meaty explanation of Freud's view of unconscious nonlogic, see Ruth L. Munroe, *Schools of Psychoanalytic Thought*, pp. 55–57.

46. See, for example, C. G. Jung, *Memories, Dreams, Reflections*, p. 316.

47. This is a favorite theme of Morton Trippe Kelsey, an ardent disciple and popularizer of Jung. See Morton Kelsey, *Can Christians Be Educated?* (Birmingham, Ala.: Religious Education Press, 1977), pp. 23–38.

48. It seems to me that persons like Richard McBrien and certain of his protegées witlessly equate behaviorism with all of social science—an error comparable to equating, for example, Jansenism or Thomism with all of theology. See Richard P. McBrien, "Toward an American Catechesis," in *Living Light* XIII (Winter, 1976), pp. 174–175; Mary C. Boys, "Supervision in Religious Education: Selected Models," in *Living Light* XIII (Winter, 1976), pp. 505–507. (Parenthetically, I have reason to question whether persons like McBrien or Boys even know what behaviorism really is.)

49. Robert E. Ornstein, *The Psychology of Consciousness* (San Francisco: Freeman, 1972), p. 5.

50. Julian Jaynes, *The Origin of Consciousness in the Breakdown of the Bicameral Mind* (Boston: Houghton Mifflin, 1977), pp. 48–66.

51. It seems to me that in this aspect of Jaynes' conceptualization of the structural features of consciousness, the unconscious intersects the conscious. I suspect that Jaynes would not even admit this point. After all, there is not even a single index entry in his book for the unconscious, nor does he really treat the unconscious even on the occasions which might well warrant such a treatment.

52. One of the great strengths underlying Tart's description and map of consciousness is the truly wide variety of diverse sources which he utilizes in devising his formulation. These sources include such poles-apart positions as Sigmund Freud and Carl Jung, Ernest Hilgard and Gardner Murphy, Thomas Kuhn and Idries Shah—with persons like Carlos Castaneda, George Gurdjieff, Robert Ornstein, Peter Ouspensky, and Claudio Naranjo thrown in for good measure.

53. Charles T. Tart, "Discrete States of Consciousness," pp. 91–105, 126–131.

54. Donald B. Lindsley, "Psychological Phenomena and the Electroencephalogram," in *Electroencephalography and Clinical Neurophysiology* IV (November, 1952), pp. 443–456.

55. D. B. Klein, *The Unconscious: Invention or Discovery?*, p. 7.

56. Brain waves are here measured by an electroencephalogram.

57. It is primarily at this level that advocates of the unconscious claim that the unconscious most forcefully and most tellingly manifests itself.

58. It would seem that Richard McBrien does not appreciate this point. It well might be that McBrien has a defective understanding and appreciation of the centrality of the physical in all human functioning, including mysticism and art. See Richard P. McBrien, "Toward an American Catechesis," p. 175.

59. For a short history of the development of modern research on cortical localization, see Edwin Clarke and Kenneth Dewhurst, *An Illustrated History of Brain Function* (Berkeley, Calif.: University of California Press, 1972), pp. 113–142. I found the illustrations in this book to be especially helpful.

60. Karl H. Pribram, "Problems Concerning the Structure of Consciousness," in Gordon G. Globus, Grover Maxwell, and Irwin Savodnik, editors, *Consciousness and the Brain* (New York: Plenum, 1976), pp. 297–313. Pribram regards consciousness as a property by which organisms achieve a special relationship with their environment.

61. See John C. Eccles, *The Human Mystery* (Berlin: Springer, 1979), pp. 177–179.
62. Karl R. Popper and John C. Eccles, *The Self and Its Brain* (Berlin: Springer, 1977), pp. 429–436.
63. Gabriel Moran is a case in point. In a public conference on religious instruction sponsored by a major northeastern Catholic university in April of 1977, Moran announced that there is no real difference between the cognitive domain and the affective domain, declaring further that they are not two distinct domains at all. Had Moran familiarized himself with the physiological research on the left-hemisphere and right-hemisphere brain activities (to say nothing of the numerous psychological research on cognitive and affective functioning), he never would have committed so basic an error.
64. See John C. Eccles, *The Human Mystery*, pp. 210–234; John C. Eccles, *The Understanding of the Brain* (New York: McGraw-Hill, 1977), pp. 226–228.
65. John C. Eccles, *The Human Mystery*, p. 222.
66. Sally P. Springer and Georg Deutsch, *Left Brain, Right Brain* (San Francisco: Freeman, 1981), p. 101.
67. Richard J. Davidson, "Consciousness and Information Processing: A Biocognitive Perspective," in Julian M. Davidson and Richard J. Davidson, editors, *The Psychobiology of Consciousness* (New York: Plenum, 1980), pp. 26–32.
68. Michael S. Gazzaniga, "The Split Brain in Man," in *Scientific American* CCXVII (August, 1967), p. 29. Gazzaniga continues: "This conclusion is disturbing to some people who view consciousness as an indivisible property of the human brain. . . . It is entirely possible that if a human brain were divided in a very young person, both hemispheres could as a result separately and independently develop mental functions of a high order at a level attained only in the left hemisphere of normal individuals."
69. Julian Jaynes, *The Origin of Consciousness in the Breakdown of the Bicameral Mind*, p. 113. The left hemisphere, of course, is the one which can overtly speak—in linguistic fashion, that is.
70. John C. Eccles, *The Human Mystery*, pp. 222–224.
71. R. W. Sperry, "Mental Phenomena as Causal Determinants in Brain Function," in Gordon G. Globus, Grover Maxwell, and Irwin Savodnik, editors, *Consciousness and the Brain*, pp. 170–174.
72. A commissure is a connecting band of nerve tissue, especially in the brain and the spinal cord.
73. John C. Eccles, *The Human Mystery*, pp. 217–219.
74. Marcel Kinsbourne, "Cognition and the Brain," in M. C. Whittrock, editor, *The Brain and Psychology* (New York: Academic Press, 1980), pp. 334–335.
75. Experimental testing procedures have been developed in which stimuli are introduced into one or the other hemisphere and in which the responses of either hemisphere can be observed independently.
76. Robert E. Ornstein, *The Psychology of Consciousness*, p. 54.
77. Julian Jaynes writes as follows concerning the fact that we hear and appreciate music with our right hemispheres: "Such lateralization of music can be seen even in very young infants. Six-month-old babies can be given EEG's [electrical stimulation to the brain] while being held in the laps of their mothers. If the recording electrodes are placed directly over Wernicke's area on the left hemisphere and over what corresponds to Wernicke's area on the right, then when tape recordings of speech are played, the left hemisphere will show the greatest activity. But when a tape of a music box is played or of someone singing, the

activity will be greater over the *right* hemisphere.'' Julian Jaynes, *The Origin of Consciousness in the Breakdown of the Bicameral Mind*, pp. 367–368.

78. John C. Eccles, *The Human Mystery*, p. 222.

79. Robert E. Ornstein, *The Psychology of Consciousness*, p. 67. I have changed the order of Ornstein's original presentation slightly.

80. Jerome S. Bruner, *On Knowing: Essays for the Left Hand* (Cambridge, Mass.: Belknap, 1964), p. 2.

81. *Ibid.*

82. Robert E. Ornstein, *The Psychology of Consciousness*, p. 64.

83. G. William Domhoff, ''But Why Did They Sit on the King's Right Hand in the First Place?'' in *Psychoanalytic Review* LVI (Winter, 1969–1970), pp. 586–596.

84. A tachistoscope is an instrument for the brief exposure to visual stimuli. It is used to investigate learning, perception, and attention.

85. R. A. Filbey and M. S. Gazzaniga, ''Splitting the Normal Brain with Reaction Time,'' in *Psychonomic Science* XVII (Number 6, 1969), pp. 335–336.

86. Jerre Levy, ''Cerebral Asymmetry and the Psychology of Man,'' in M. C. Whittrock, editor, *The Brain and Psychology*, pp. 284–296.

87. *Ibid.*, p. 286.

88. *Ibid.*, p. 296.

89. Edwin Clarke and Kenneth Dewhurst, *An Illustrated History of Brain Function*, p. 132.

90. Robert E. Ornstein, *The Psychology of Consciousness*, p. 54.

91. Jerre Levy-Agresti and Roger Sperry, ''Differential Perceptual Capacities in Major and Minor Hemispheres,'' in *Proceedings of the National Academy of Sciences* LXI (November 15, 1968), p. 1151.

92. Julian Jaynes, *The Origin of Consciousness in the Breakdown of the Bicameral Mind*, pp. 107–125, 433–446.

93. Michael Lawler's claim that theology is essentially a function of the right hemisphere is clearly false. Theology is essentially a cognitive science which is performed in the verbal mode. Thus theology is fundamentally and inextricably linked to the left hemisphere of the brain. One fatal flaw in Lawler's reasoning is that he erroneously identifies theological language with religious language. Another fatal flaw is that he apparently believes that theological reflection upon right hemisphere activities automatically makes such cognitive reflection itself a right hemisphere activity. At any event, Lawler's article nicely illustrates the main point I am making in this paragraph of the text, namely, that the breakdown of the bicameral mind has produced attempts to submerge both hemispheres into one, to make primarily right hemisphere religion into left hemisphere theology. Michael G. Lawler, ''Right-Lobe Religion, Theology and Religious Education,'' in Gloria Durka and Joanmarie Smith, editors, *Aesthetic Dimensions of Religious Education* (New York: Paulist, 1979), pp. 167–184.

94. For a further treatment of this point, see James Michael Lee, ''The Authentic Source of Religious Instruction,'' pp. 100–197.

95. Arnold M. Ludwig, ''Altered States of Consciousness,'' in Charles T. Tart, editor, *Altered States of Consciousness* (New York: Wiley, 1969), pp. 9–10.

96. Donald B. Lindsley, ''Common Factors in Sensory Deprivation, Sensory Distortion, and Sensory Overload,'' in Philip Solomon et al., editors, *Sensory Deprivation* (Cambridge, Mass.: Harvard University Press, 1961), pp. 174–194.

97. Arnold M. Ludwig, ''Altered States of Consciousness,'' pp. 13–18.

98. *Ibid.*
99. Ram Dass was born Richard Alpert. Of Hebraeo-American ancestry, Alpert received his doctorate in psychology, and taught psychology and also education at Stanford, the University of California at Berkeley, and Harvard. His experience in frequent consumption of consciousness-altering substances eventually led to a trip to India where he became a convert to Eastern religion. He was given the name Ram Dass by his guru in India. See Ram Dass, *Remember: Be Here Now, Now Be Here* (San Cristobal, New Mex.: 1971), first part (pages not numbered).
100. Ram Dass asserts that in converting to Far Eastern consciousness he did not give up his Western mode of consciousness but rather his *attachment* to that mode of consciousness Alpert sees himself renouncing his attachment to Western consciousness and embracing Eastern consciousness so that he can thereby bring back to Western consciousness the transforming power of Eastern consciousness. See Ram Dass, *The Only Dance There Is* (Garden City, N.Y.: Doubleday Anchor, 1973), p. 54.
101. *Ibid.,* pp. 54, 117. On the place of the *kōan* in the Zen system, see James Michael Lee, "Discipline in a Moral and Religious Key," in Kevin Walsh and Milly Cowles, *Developmental Discipline* (Birmingham, Ala.: Religious Education Press, 1982), pp. 161–162.
102. The third eye of the god *Śiva* illustrates this point. The god *Śiva* is commonly represented as having a third eye in the middle of his forehead. The dark side of *Śiva* is that of the destroyer-god. The light side of *Śiva* is tied in with consciousness and is the inward look. (The other two eyes look to external things.) *Śiva's* third eye is a constant reminder to Hindus to elevate their own personal consciousness. To be fully conscious is to be. See Troy Wilson Organ, *The Hindu Quest for the Perfection of Man* (Athens, Ohio: Ohio University Press, 1970), pp. 65–70.
103. In Zen Buddhism, enlightenment or *satori* "consists in a luminously clear personal experience or intuitive vision of the original oneness of all reality." James Michael Lee, "Discipline in a Moral and Religious Key," p. 160.
104. Ram Dass summarizes this point nicely; "From a Zen Buddhist point of view, once you are in the One, there's no one. Of course, you don't see the One; you only see the One if you're two. Once you are in the One it's non-dualism." Ram Dass, *The Only Dance There Is,* p. 14.
105. The goal of this way of life is not to *know* the truth, but to *realize* it, to become one with it. Being one with truth is to attain a higher state of consciousness. See Sarvepalli Radhakrishnan and Charles A. Moore, "General Introduction," in Sarvepalli Radhakrishnan and Charles A. Moore, editors, *A Source Book in Indian Philosphy* (Princeton, N.J.: Princeton University Press, 1957), p. xxiv.
106. An overriding purpose of Zen is to provide the seeker "with a deep experiential awareness of his own consciousness and also with a being-with his own consciousness." James Michael Lee, "Discipline in a Moral and Religious Key," p. 160. See also T. P. Kasulis, *Zen Action/Zen Person* (Honolulu: University Press of Hawaii, 1981), pp. 116–124.
107. Ram Dass, *The Only Dance There Is,* p. 28.
108. *Ibid.,* pp. 28–34, 89–91.
109. *Mantra* is a Sanskrit word meaning "sacred utterance." In the Vedic period, the *mantras* were words used in the ritual. Some scholars claim that the Roman Catholic lesser doxology is a mantra. On this last point, see Heinrich Zimmer,

Philosophies of India, edited by Joseph Campbell (Princeton, N.J.: Princeton University Press, 1951), p. 586.

110. This particular *mantra* is a feature of Tibetan Buddhism, a religious system which exerted significant influence on Ram Dass. Many Hindu *mantras* include the sacred syllable OM, which is a synthesis of the three sounds A U M. These three sounds are believed by classical Hinduism to contain all basic sounds and thus to symbolize the universe. Hence by repeating OM, it becomes possible to realize one's identity with the One.

111. In later Hindu theory, the continuous recitation of the *mantra* makes present that which it symbolizes.

112. This word comes from the Sanskrit for "circle." In Vedic days, the *mandala* was a power zone consisting of a circle of political states, some of which did not have sovereign powers. The *mandala* later evolved into a more spiritual symbol. See Dhirendra Mohan Datta, "Some Philosophical Aspects of Indian Political, Legal, and Economic Thought," in Charles A. Moore, editor, *The Indian Mind* (Honolulu; East-West Center Press, 1967), pp. 261, 282.

113. Ram Dass, *The Only Dance There Is,* pp. 2–6.

114. David Arthur Bickimer, *Christ the Placenta* (Birmingham, Ala.: Religious Education Press, 1983), pp. 100–101; also interviews with Bickimer.

115. Elsewhere, I describe the "blow theory" of religious instruction, the operative theory for proponents of the view that religious experience and indeed all religious learning cannot be directly facilitated by the religious educator. See James Michael Lee, *The Flow of Religious Instruction* (Birmingham, Ala.: Religious Education Press, 1973), pp. 174–180.

116. Ram Dass, *The Only Dance There Is,* p. 47.

117. Speaking for myself, I have never had the slightest need to ingest pharmacological substances in order to come to intense religious experience, since a good deal of my life is a "religious high." As far as I can recall, however, not a single intense religious experience I have ever had was the result of a school-based religion lesson or a liturgy. Surely this ought not to have been the case.

118. To properly situate Freud's theory of motivation, it is well to recall that Freud was originally a neurologist. On this point, see Benjamin Wolman, *The Unconscious Mind* (Englewood Cliffs, N.J.: Prentice-Hall, 1968), p. 29.

119. These basic sets of human motives may not be readily apparent; however they become manifest once surface motives are scraped away to reveal the fundamental motives. For a brief discussion of his point, see D. B. Klein, *The Unconscious: Invention or Discovery?* p. 142.

120. The term "drive" is a technical one in psychology and means somewhat different things in different psychological systems. In Freudianism, drive is more or less equivalent to instinct, and more specifically to instinct flowing from the id. For a clear discussion of drives in Freudianism, see Charles Brenner, *An Elementary Textbook of Psychoanalysis* (Garden City, N.Y,: Doubleday Anchor, 1955), pp. 16–32.

121. As Brenner correctly notes, the original psychoanalytic usage of libido included both instincts, namely aggression and sexuality, and not just sexuality alone. *Ibid.,* p. 32.

122. For a book dealing with religious education for freedom, see Kenneth Barker, *Religious Education, Catechesis, and Freedom* (Birmingham, Ala.: Religious Education Press, 1981). Barker has a very short section on the unconscious (pp. 109–111).

123. John C. Hill, *Teaching and the Unconscious Mind* (New York: International Universities Press, 1971), p. 54.

124. James H. VanderVeldt and Robert P. Odenwald, *Psychiatry and Catholicism* (New York: McGraw-Hill, 1952), p. 152.

125. Henri F. Ellenberger, *The Discovery of the Unconscious,* p. 169.

126. For a nice collection of some of Jung's more important comments on the creative process, see C. G. Jung, *Psychological Reflections,* pp. 163–186. For Jung, creativity typically does not go far afield from the basic reality of things because it is too closely bound with the taproot of all human and animal instinct.

127. While Freud is here treating specifically of creativity in poets, his concept of creativity as expressed in this material can be legitimately extended to other forms of creativity.

128. John C. Hill, *Teaching and the Unconscious Mind,* p. 157.

129. For an extension of this point, see James Grier Miller, *Unconsciousness,* pp. 183–209.

130. Henri F. Ellenberger, *The Discovery of the Unconscious,* p. 672.

131. For example, Sigmund Freud claims that pubic hair inspired the creative invention of weaving. Sigmund Freud, *New Introductory Lectures on Psychoanalysis,* p. 132.

132. Berard L. Marthaler, "Socialization as a Model for Catechetics," in Padraic O'Hare, editor, *Foundations of Religious Education,* p. 77.

133. Sacred Congregation for the Clergy, *General Catechetical Directory* (Washington, D.C.: United States Catholic Conference, 1971).

134. National Conference of Catholic Bishops, *Sharing the Light of Faith* (Washington, D.C.: United States Catholic Conference, 1979).

135. *Ibid.,* p. 163.

136. James Hillman, *Insearch: Psychology and Religion,* p. 38.

137. Anna Freud, "Foreword," in John C. Hill, *Teaching and the Unconscious Mind,* pp. ix-x. Italics deleted.

138. Morton Kelsey, *Encounter with God* (Minneapolis, Minn.: Bethany Fellowship, 1972), p. 237. Like most psychotherapists, Kelsey is deficient in his knowledge of the teaching process. Specifically, he errs in asserting that attitudes can be imparted. Attitudes can and are taught, but they are not imparted. Imparting denotes a transmission strategy of teaching.

139. Morton Kelsey, *Can Christians be Educated?* (Birmingham, Ala.: Religious Education Press, 1977), p. 90.

140. C. G. Jung, *Psychological Reflections,* p. 228.

141. Many members of the psychotherapeutic community would put this stronger. Thus Morton Trippe Kelsey, for example, writes that unconscious forces "possess our lives, determining at will how we react to the outer world." Morton Kelsey, *Encounter with God,* p. 210.

142. James Hillman, *Insearch: Psychology and Religion,* p. 20.

143. This is the central theme in Morton Kelsey's book, *Can Christians Be Educated?*

144. Gabriel Moran, *The Present Revelation,* p. 100.

145. See William C. Schutz, *Joy* (New York: Grove, 1967), p. 57.

146. C. G. Jung, *Memories, Dreams, Reflections,* p. 311. While admitting that unconscious knowledge is superior to conscious knowledge from the human perspective, Sigmund Freud sees the unconscious as far more related to the *hic-et-nunc* and to repressed needs seeking immediate gratification than does Jung.

147. *Ibid.,* p. 302.

148. See, for example, the testimony of Carl Jung in his *Memories, Dreams, Reflections*, p. 228.

149. Rollo May writes that in his judgment the most crucial issue in the practice of depth psychology with individuals is whether "to help the person gain freedom from anxiety or rather to help him confront anxiety experiences with the aim of enlarging his freedom." The first is geared to gaining relief, while the second is targeted toward attaining authentic selfhood and self-reflection. Rollo May, "Foreword," in Henry Gutrip, *Psychotherapy and Religion* (New York: Harper and Brothers, 1957), p. 7.

150. Lancelot Law Whyte, *The Unconscious Before Freud*, p. 71.

151. From the 1960s onward, Christian depth psychologists have become less unfriendly to Freud. Some of these persons are even beginning to interpret the Bible from a psychoanalytic perspective. See, for example, Arnold Uleyn, "A Psychoanalytic Approach to Mark's Gospel," in *Lumen Vitae* XXXII (Number 4, 1977), pp. 479–493.

152. Hans Küng, *Freud and the Problem of God*, translated by Edward Quinn (New Haven, Conn.: Yale University Press, 1979), p. 93.

153. Sigmund Freud, *The Future of an Illusion*, translated by W. D. Robson Scott, revised and edited by James Strachey (Garden City, N.Y.: Doubleday Anchor, 1961).

154. Anent this viewpoint of Freud, Viktor Frankl writes that he is "tempted to reverse Freud's statement and dares to say that compulsive neurosis may well be diseased religiousness. In fact, clinical evidence suggests that atrophy of the religion sense in man results in a distortion of his religious concepts." Viktor E. Frankl, *The Unconscious God* (New York: Simon and Schuster, 1975), p. 69.

155. Anent this, Eckhart Wiesenhütter writes: "*Ein solches Gebot stammt nicht von Gott, ein solches stammt vom Menschen. Ja, es wird an dieser Stelle erkennbar, dass Gott ein Produkt des Menschen ist und dass der Mensch ihm nur zuschreibt, was er sich selbst an Wünschen nicht erfüllen kann oder was ihm absolut verboten ist.*" Eckhart Wiesenhütter, "Verdrängter Glaube—Freuds Ende einer Illusion," in Heinz Zahrnt, Herausgeber, *Jesus und Freud* (München: Piper, 1972), p. 69. For an interesting article on the topic of Freud as theologian, see Johannes Schreiber, "Sigmund Freud als Theologe," in Eckhart Nase und Joachim Scharfenberg, Herausgeber, *Psychoanalyse und Religion* (Darmstadt, Bundesrepublik Deutschland: Wissenschaftliche Buchgesellschaft, 1977), pp. 233–263.

156. Ann Ulanov and Barry Ulanov, *Religion and the Unconscious* (Philadelphia: Westminster, 1975), p. 33.

157. Attempting to answer this Freudian critique, Viktor Frankl writes: "No one will be able to make us believe that man is a sublimated animal once we can show that within him there is a repressed angel." Viktor E. Frankl, *The Unconscious God*, p. 59.

158. For this reason some religionists and theologians have latched on to Jung in the belief that here is one major depth psychologist who presents what they apparently believe is an acceptable or at least a nonthreatening view of the Christian religion and of Christian theology. However, Jung's views of religion are frequently dissimilar to the orthodox ecclesiastical position. Certainly the way Jung looks at God, the Christian mysteries, and especially theology is often quite opposite to the positions espoused by the vast majority of Christian theologians, especially those who are "approved" by denominational *ecclesiastica*. On this

point, see Antonio Moreno, *Jung, Gods, and Modern Man* (Notre Dame, Ind.: University of Notre Dame Press, 1970), pp. 70–101. Moreno states, for example, that "Jung is agnostic with respect to the existence of a transcendent God" (p. 82).

159. C. G. Jung, *Psychology and Alchemy,* in C. G. Jung, *Collected Works,* volume XII, 2d edition, translated by R. F. C. Hull (Princeton, N.J.: Princeton University Press, 1968), pp. 12–13.
160. John S. Dunne, *A Search for God in Time and Memory* (New York: Macmillan, 1967), p. 173.
161. Ann Ulanov and Barry Ulanov, *Religion and the Unconscious,* p. 57.
162. James Hillman, *Insearch: Psychology and Religion,* p. 50.
163. Victor White, *God and the Unconscious* (Cleveland: World Meridian, 1952), p. 162.
164. Carl Gustav Jung, *Psychology and Religion* (New Haven, Conn.: Yale University Press, 1938), pp. 56–57.
165. C. G. Jung, *Psychological Reflections,* edited by Jolande Jacobi (New York: Harper & Row, 1953), p. 304.
166. These individuals "often depict, not to say denigrate, God as a being who is primarily concerned with being believed in, by the greatest possible number of believers, and along the lines of a specific creed at that." Viktor E. Frankl, *The Unconscious God,* pp. 9–14, 31.
167. Rudolf Allers, "Psychiatry and the Role of Personal Belief," in Francis J. Braceland, editor, *Faith, Reason, and Modern Psychiatry* (New York: Kenedy, 1955), pp. 52–58.
168. Lewis J. Sherrill, *Guilt and Redemption* (Richmond, Va: Knox, 1945), p. 14.
169. R. P. Casey, "The Psychoanalytic Study of Religion," in Orlo Strunk Jr., *The Psychology of Religion,* 2d edition. (Nashville, Tenn.: Abingdon, 1971), pp. 61–62. Casey properly reproaches Freudianism for its persistent failure "to realize as yet the full scope of religion as the instrument of the manifold unconscious motives" (p. 62).
170. Gregory Baum, *Man Becoming* (New York: Herder and Herder, 1970), pp. 145–146.
171. Peter A. Bertocci, "Psychological Interpretations of Religious Experience," in Merton P. Strommen, editor, *Research on Religious Development* (New York: Hawthorn, 1971), pp. 36–37.
172. Morton Kelsey, *Encounter with God,* p. 192.
173. This is the theme of Adolphe Ferriére's book *Éducation religieuse et psychologie de l'inconscient* (Genève: Labor et Fides, 1951).
174. Victor White, *God and the Unconscious,* p. 233.
175. C. G. Jung, *The Undiscovered Self,* translated by R. F. C. Hull (Boston: Little, Brown, 1958), p. 27.
176. Ann Ulanov and Barry Ulanov, *Religion and the Unconscious,* p. 110.
177. Antonio Moreno, a Dominican scholar who views and many times judges Jung from a certain kind of Thomistic perspective, takes a less positive view of myth. As a champion of conscious cognition and also to a large extent of ratiocination, Moreno forthrightly declares that "myth always distorts the sacred images, for emotions and irrational elements bear an important part of its formation. [Cognitive conscious] dogma is much more perfect than myth; it will always describe the nature of God better." Jung, as I have shown in this section, would disagree vehemently with this analysis. Antonio Moreno, *Jung, Gods, and Modern Man,* p. 181.

178. Ignace Lepp, *The Depths of the Soul: A Christian Approach to Psychoanalysis* (Staten Island, N.Y.: Alba House, 1965), p. 268.

179. A major goal of psychology, including depth psychology, is remarkably similar to a major goal of religion, namely homo integer, uniting the divided and sometimes broken person. See Charles A. Curran, *Psychological Dynamics in Religious Living* (New York: Herder and Herder, 1971), pp. 190–221.

180. James Bissett Pratt, *The Religious Consciousness* (New York: Macmillan, 1927), p. 60.

181. On this point, see Peter L. Berger, *The Sacred Canopy* (Garden City, N.Y.: Doubleday, 1967), p. 43.

182. For a discussion of this point from a somewhat different perspective, see Gregory Zilboorg, "Some Denials and Assertions of Religious Faith," in Francis J. Braceland, editor, *Faith, Reason, and Modern Psychiatry*, p. 119.

183. For a fine discussion of this last point, see Ana-Maria Rizzuto, "The Psychological Foundations of Belief in God," in Christiane Brusselmans and James A. O'Donohoe, editors, *Toward Moral and Religious Maturity* (Morristown, N.J.: Silver Burdett, 1980), pp. 116–135.

184. Morton T. Kelsey, *Dreams: The Dark Speech of the Spirit* (Garden City, N.Y.: Doubleday, 1968), p. 237.

185. Victor E. Frankl, *The Unconscious God*, p. 85.

186. D. B. Klein, *The Unconscious: Invention or Discovery?* p. xviii. Klein's scientific explanation rests upon what he calls "a somewhat neglected distinction between sensory and nonsensory ideation."

187. See, for example, Seymour Fisher and Roger P. Greenberg, *Scientific Credibility of Freud's Theories and Therapy* (New York: Basic Books, 1977).

188. See, for example, Joel Kovel, "Things and Words: Metapsychology and the Historical Point of View," in *Psychoanalysis and Contemporary Thought*, I (Number 1, 1978), pp. 21–88. "When experienced analysts within the American Psychoanalytic Association cannot agree in practice as to what they are or should be doing, then what hope is there for adequate research?" (p. 24). And again, "psychoanalysis itself remains both troubled internally and without a solid external relationship to the rest of thought" (p. 26).

189. Antonio Moreno, *Jung, Gods, and Modern Man*, pp. 130–132.

190. Natalino Caputi, *Guide to the Unconscious*. My treatment in this section follows Caputi.

191. The Caputi category system is not etched in stone. It is more of a heuristic device than an absolutely objective procedure.

192. By spiritual here I mean nonphysical rather than religious or supernatural.

193. These two requirements hold true for all the sciences, ranging all the way from biology to psychology to history to philosophy to theology.

194. Justin Neuman, "The Existence of the Freudian Unconscious in the Structure and Functions of the Nervous System," in *Psychoanalytic Review* XXXVI (October, 1949), pp. 355–364.

195. Gert Heilbrunn, "The Neurobiological Aspect of Three Psychoanalytic Concepts," in *Comprehensive Psychiatry* II (October, 1961), pp. 261–268.

196. Conrad Chyatte et al., "Brain Blood-Shift Theory: Verification of a Predicted Gradient in Tactual-Auditory Rivalry," in *International Journal of Neuropsychiatry* III–IV (Number 1, 1967–1968), pp. 360–364.

197. Rhawn Joseph, "Awareness, The Origin of Thought, and the Role of Conscious Self-Deception in Resistance and Repression," in *Psychological Reports* XLVI (June, 1980), pp. 767–788; see also Rhawn Joseph, "The Neuropsychology of

Development: Hemispheric Laterality, Limbic Language, and the Origin of Thought," in *Journal of Clinical Psychology* XXXVIII (January, 1982), pp. 4–33.

198. Some Soviet scholars are pursuing this tack.

199. For a helpful treatment of unconscious processes as subliminal, see James Grier Miller, *Unconsciousness,* pp. 135–158.

200. For a fine summary statement of this position, see Charles W. Erikson, "Unconscious Perception," in David L. Sills, editor, *International Encyclopedia of the Social Sciences,* volume XI (New York: Macmillan, 1968), pp. 575–581.

201. Some opponents of the bio-physical view use subliminal perception in a way quite opposed to the manner in which advocates of the bio-physical standpoint do. For example, some of these adversaries believe that the reception, retention, and subsequent manifestation of subliminal perception in awareness does in fact point to the existence of a discrete entity or separate process called the unconscious. Commenting on the experimental research of Lloyd Silverman, Virginia Adams maintains that external subliminal messages are flashed into the unconscious, an unconscious which she implicitly suggests is of a far different order than the mere functioning of bio-physical processes. Virginia Adams, " 'Mommy and I Are One': Beaming Messages to Inner Space," in *Psychology Today* XVI (May, 1982), pp. 24–36. For the Silverman research, see Lloyd Silverman, "An Experimental Method for the Study of Unconscious Conflict, " in *British Journal of Medical Psychology* XLVIII (December, 1975), pp. 291–298. One is tempted to comment that the subtitle of the Adams article appears to have much in common with Mary Boys' theory of human functioning in general and with her view of the teaching process in particular. See Mary C. Boys, *Biblical Interpretation in Religious Education* (Birmingham Ala.: Religious Education Press, 1980), pp. 239–244.

202. Psychologists who make conditioning central to their theoretical formulations are usually, but not always, behaviorists. Psychologists of this variety typically reject all kinds of mentalistic notions such as mind, consciousness, unconsciousness, atttiude, personality, self, and so forth.

203. I summarize the major features of classical conditioning and operant conditioning in *The Flow of Religious Instruction* (Birmingham, Ala.: Religious Education Press, 1973), pp. 317–318. Ivan Pavlov is the person most closely identified with classical conditioning, as is B. F. Skinner with operant conditioning.

204. An unconditioned activity, e.g., a stimulus, is one which is independent of learning and which tends to be innate in the organism. For example, a tap on a certain point on the knee is the unconditioned stimulus for knee-jerking. A conditioned activity is one associated with learning or training.

205. See, for example, Gregory Razran, "The Observable Unconscious and the Inferable Conscious in Current Soviet Psychophysiology," in *Psychological Review* LXVIII (March, 1961), pp. 81–147.

206. See, for example, E. Airapetyantz and K. Bykov, "Physiological Experiments and the Psychology of the Subconscious," in *Philosophy and Phenomenological Research* V (June, 1945), p. 581. It should be noted that some post-1960 Soviet social scientists are less antagonistic toward Freudian depth psychology than was previously the case. See Nancy Rollins, "The New Soviet Approach to the Unconscious," in *American Journal of Psychiatry* CXXXI (March, 1974), pp. 301–304.

207. B. F. Skinner, *Science and Human Behavior* (New York: Macmillan, 1953), pp. 359–383.

208. B. F. Skinner, *About Behaviorism* (New York: Vintage, 1974), p. 170.

209. *Ibid.*, p. 169.
210. See Ruth Munroe, *Schools of Psychoanalytic Thought*, p. 82.
211. Freud even constructed a topographical sketch indicating these zones graphically. See Sigmund Freud, *New Introductory Lectures on Psychoanalysis*, p. 78.
212. In psychoanalytic literature, the preconscious is sometimes called the foreconscious.
213. Sigmund Freud, *The Ego and the Id*, translated by Joan Riviere, revised and newly edited by James Strachey (New York: Norton, 1960), pp. 5–10.
214. "Some of the preconscious includes material which once was conscious or readily available, but has since been reshaped and assimilated so as to make it *ego-syntonic*, that is, acceptable in terms of social approval or the image a person has of himself." Norman Cameron, *Personality Development and Psychopathology* (Boston: Houghton Mifflin, 1963), p. 165.
215. See David Bakan, *The Duality of Human Existence: An Essay on Psychology and Religion* (Chicago: Rand McNally, 1966), p. 11.
216. In technical Freudian terms, the reality principle indicates how and why the conscious and preconscious domains are able to bind cathexes into stable organizations of personality. These two domains have an energy of organization.
217. These three structural processes, though developed by Sigmund Freud later than his three topographical zones, represent not simply a refinement of the topographical zones but perhaps more importantly, another way of looking at psychic phenomena.
218. Sigmund Freud, *New Introductory Lectures on Psychoanalysis*, p. 77.
219. In a sense, the ego is primarily a kind of helpless mediator at the service of the demands of the id and the superego. It possesses the capability of successfully performing its mediatorship function for the benefit of the total organism because its superior knowledge of reality and its control of the pathways of memory, attention, and action endow it with a certain degree of expedient action.
220. See Norman Cameron, *Personality Development and Psychopathology*, p. 188.
221. Sigmund Freud, *New Introductory Lectures on Psychoanalysis*, pp. 74–75.
222. In typical Freudian fashion, both eros and thanatos are tethered to, but not restricted to, biology.
223. Sigmund Freud, *An Outline of Psycho-Analysis*, translated and edited by James Strachey (New York: Norton, 1949), pp. 5–8.
224. Franz Alexander and Sheldon Selesnick remark that in the history of the development of Freud's thought, the life-versus-death instinct constituted his last dualistic theory. Franz G. Alexander and Sheldon T. Selesnick, *The History of Psychiatry*, p. 255.
225. Sigmund Freud, *An Outline of Psycho-Analysis*, pp. 10–11.
226. Such identification, of course, is not exclusive. Ruth Munroe writes that in many primitive societies children are taught to hide their feces because the discovery or attack upon these feces by an enemy would be tantamount to the discovery or attack upon the whole person. Ruth Munroe, *Schools of Psychoanalytic Thought*, p. 196.
227. In Freudian theory, the mouth and the anus still provide sexual pleasure. One reason why eating and certain kinds of defecation are pleasurable is because these two activities give sexual enjoyment by releasing sexual tensions and energies.
228. The term derives from Greek mythology in which Oedipus unwittingly (unconsciously?) kills his father Laius and marries his mother Jocasta, with dire consequences. Oedipus was in the grip of Fate, and so in a large sense could not be held morally responsible for his actions.

229. For an examination of Freud's overall position on women, see Lucy Freeman and Herbert S. Strean, *Freud and Women* (New York: Ungar, 1981).
230. Despite the testimony from psychoanalysts that penis envy is a recurrent theme in their female patients, militant feminists have bestowed upon the notion of penis envy some of their most blistering denunciations and scorching accusations. Of course, the classic Freudians could respond by noting that the very bitterness of the denunciations heaped by feminists upon the notion of penis envy is itself de facto proof that these feminists have neurotically repressed their own penis envy and allowed the energy of this repression to be discharged into the feminist cause in general and into harsh statements about penis envy in particular. And so it goes.
231. For an advocacy of this last point, see Charles Brenner, *An Elementary Textbook of Psychoanalysis,* p. 204.
232. James H. VanderVeldt and Robert P. Odenwald, *Psychiatry and Catholicism,* p. 113.
233. Freud's followers have since developed and significantly advanced the theory of defense mechanisms first developed by Freud. For an especially important and influential treatment of defense mechanisms, see Anna Freud, *The Ego and the Mechanisms of Defense,* revised edition (New York: International Universities Press, 1966). Anna Freud was Sigmund Freud's daughter.
234. For this reason some Freudians like Charles Brenner claim that sublimation is not so much a defense mechanism as it is a normal function of the ego. Charles Brenner, *An Elementary Textbook of Psychoanalysis,* pp. 106–107.
235. For a somewhat expanded but still succinct treatment of specific defense mechanisms, see James Michael Lee and Nathaniel J. Pallone, *Guidance and Counseling in Schools: Foundations and Processes* (New York: McGraw-Hill, 1966), pp. 348–352.
236. See Paul Mussen et al., *Psychology* (Lexington, Mass.: Heath, 1973), pp. 223–225.
237. A further distinction might be made between the "sour-grapes" and the "sweet-lemon" forms of rationalization. In the former, the person convinces himself that an unattainable goal is not worth having anyway. In the latter, the person rationalizes that a substitute goal is superior to the unattainable one. See James C. Coleman, *Abnormal Psychology and Modern Life,* 2d edition (Chicago: Scott, Foresman, 1956), pp. 91–92.
238. For a fine, succinct treatment of isolation, see Ruth L. Munroe, *Schools of Psychoanalytic Thought,* pp. 254–255.
239. Sigmund Freud, *The Psychopathology of Everyday Life,* pp. 230–279.
240. Two points are worth noting here. First, when I myself (as distinct from Freud) assert that *a* psychogenesis of religion lies in wish fulfillment, I am not also asserting that the *entire* psychogenesis of religion lies in wish fulfillment. Rather, my assertion states that a person's wishes constitute a necessary feature of his religious life and the origin of that life. Second, my assertion (as distinct from Freud's) that the psychogenesis of religion lies in wish fulfillment in no way subtracts or undercuts God or his grace as the *Urquelle* of religion in the human being.
241. In his book *Totem and Taboo,* Freud maintains that religion is also based on the Oedipus complex of the human race as a whole.
242. Caputi's term for this fundamental thesis is systems theory. I avoid using this term because not all instances of systems theory encapsulate this fundamental thesis. See Natalino Caputi, *Guide to the Unconscious,* p. 89.

243. For a fine, pithy summary of the major arguments pro and con of this position, see May Brodbeck, "Logic and Scientific Method in Research on Teaching," in N. L. Gage, editor, *Handbook of Research on Teaching* (Chicago: Rand McNally, 1963), pp. 51–55.

244. The term depth psychology covers all divergent schools of thought, which is why I am employing it in this chapter. Psychotherapy is a general term applying to the depth-psychological treatment of patients, regardless of what particular school of depth psychology is being utilized— Alfred Adler and Viktor Frankl to the contrary notwithstanding.

245. One of Jung's closest collaborators writes that a particular goal for Jung was to uncover the existential analogies "between the unconscious psychic contents of modern Western man and certain manifestations of the psyche in primitive peoples, as well as of their myths and cults." Jolande Jacobi, "Jung, Carl Gustav," in David L. Sills, editor, *International Encyclopedia of the Social Sciences*, volume VIII (New York: Macmillan & Free Press, 1968), p. 327.

246. One is tempted to wonder whether, in Jungian terminology, Freud might be Jung's shadow.

247. Of paramount importance for religious educationists and educators, especially those adhering to the theological approach to religious instruction, are these words of Jung: "The concept of the *unconscious* is for me an *exclusively psychological* concept, and not a philosophical concept of a metaphysical nature." C. G. Jung, *Psychological Types*, in C. G. Jung, *Collected Works*, volume VI, translated by R. F. C. Hull (Princeton, N.J.: Princeton University Press, 1971), p. 483.

248. In a statement having significant practical ramifications for religious educators, Jung states unequivocally that "the psyche is indistinguishable from its manifestations." C. G. Jung, *Psychological Reflections*, p. 8.

249. In the psychotherapeutic act, Jung was generally more concerned with consciousness than was Freud.

250. Thus Jung writes: "For indeed our consciousness did not create itself—it wells up from unknown depths. . . . It is like a child that is born daily out of the primordial womb of the unconscious." C. G. Jung, *Memories, Dreams, Reflections*, p. 394.

251. C. G. Jung, *Psychological Types*, in C. G. Jung, *Collected Works*, volume VI, translated by R. F. C. Hull (Princeton, N.J.: Princeton University Press, 1971), p. 421. Conversely, the unconscious consists in "relations to the ego that are not perceived as such."*Ibid.*

252. By "upper" here is meant the psychic section of the unconscious closer to consciousness. The use of the spatial term "upper" in no way implies or suggests that Jung conceives the personal unconscious as an entity as contrasted to a process or function.

253. Jolande Jacobi, *The Psychology of C. G. Jung,* translated by Ralph Manheim (New Haven, Conn.: Yale University Press, 1962), p. 8. This book is, in my view, one of the finest, and indeed possibly the finest, introduction to the theory and practice of Jungianism.

254. The Jungian personal unconscious is analogous but not identical to the Freudian preconscious. The Freudian preconscious consists only of material which can be brought to consciousness at will.

255. C. G. Jung, *Psychological Types*, p. 485.

256. I am using the word "participate" here somewhat in the sense in which Plato uses it, since it seems to me that there is a certain similarity in the way Jung

regards a person participating in the collective unconscious and the way Plato regards a person participating in the world of forms. Like contents in the world of forms, contents in the collective unconscious are essences which are objective in character. Like the contents in the world of forms, the contents in the collective unconscious exist apart from immediately experienced sensible realities. Like the contents in the world of forms, the contents of the unconscious are the most important and foundational of all realities both objectively and for each individual person. The doctrine of every individual's participation in the objective world of forms is key for Plato. The doctrine of every individual's participation in the objective world of the collective unconscious is key for Jung.

257. C. G. Jung, *Psychological Types*, p. 485.

258. The collective unconscious is also the most controverted and most rejected of all the molar aspects of Jungianism.

259. Freud had this to say about Jung's tremendous stress on the collective unconscious: "I fully agree with Jung in recognizing the existence of this phylogenetic heritage; but I regard it as a methodological error to seize on a phylogenetic explanation before the ontogenetic possibilities have been exhausted. I cannot see any reason for obstinately disputing the importance of infantile prehistory while at the same time freely acknowledging the importance of ancestral prehistory." Quoted in Liliane Frey-Rohn, *From Freud to Jung*, translated by Fred E. Engreen and Evelyn K. Engreen (New York: Putnam's, 1974), p. 129.

260. C. G. Jung, *The Archetypes and the Collective Unconscious*, 2d edition, in C. G. Jung, *Collected Works*, volume IX, part I, translated by R. F. C. Hull (Princeton, N.J.: Princeton University Press, 1968), pp. 286–287.

261. C. G. Jung, *Memories, Dreams, Reflections*, p. 138.

262. C. G. Jung, *The Archetypes and the Collective Unconscious*, pp. 3–4.

263. C. G. Jung, *Memories, Dreams, Reflections*, p. 402, italics deleted.

264. Jung defines such instincts in the collective unconscious as "impulses to carry out actions from necessity." *Ibid.*, p. 401.

265. Jolande Jacobi has a striking diagram of this on page 9 of her book, *The Psychology of C. G. Jung*.

266. *Ibid.*, p. 35.

267. I must emphasize that the structural perspective and the way I am setting it up represents a somewhat inadequate and highly oversimplified attempt to order what Jung maintains are highly complicated and integral functional relationships. Indeed, severe limitations of space make my brief treatments of both Freud and Jung very meager and perforce oversimplified.

268. C. G. Jung, *Psychological Types*, pp. 481–482. Contrasted to directed thinking is undirected thinking. Undirected thinking is an extrarational function because "it arranges and judges the contents of ideation by norms of which I am not conscious and therefore cannot recognize as being in accord with reason." Cognitive intuition, especially of the creative variety, is an example of undirected thinking. Jung follows these remarks by a statement of supreme theoretical and practical importance for religious educators: "Thinking that is governed by *feeling* I do not regard as intuitive thinking, but as a thinking dependent on feeling; it does not follow its own logical principle but is subordinated to the principle of feeling. In such thinking the laws of [rational] logic are only ostensibly present; in reality they are suspended in favor of the aims of feeling." *Ibid.*, p. 482.

269. *Ibid.*, p. 425.

270. Jolande Jacobi, *The Psychology of C. G. Jung*, p. 7.
271. Commenting on the stabilizing function of the ego, Morton Trippe Kelsey writes that "there is no mystical doctrine in Jung's thought of the ego being swallowed by the unconscious as is found in Eastern mysticism." Morton Kelsey, *Encounter with God* (Minneapolis, Minn.: Bethany Fellowship, 1972), p. 115.
272. Jolande Jacobi's diagrams and explanations are quite illuminative in helping one to understand this important point. See Jolande Jacobi, *The Psychology of C. G. Jung*, pp. 6–8.
273. The key here is "*conscious* whole." This Jungian view of the ego contrasts sharply with that of Freud. For Freud, the ego is battered and torn between a set of primal instinctual drives (id) on the one hand, and a set of moral principles and social customs (superego) on the other hand.
274. The key here is "achievement *in consciousness.*"
275. Jolande Jacobi, *The Psychology of C. G. Jung*, p. 5.
276. C. G. Jung, *Psychological Types*, p. 466.
277. C. G. Jung, *The Archetypes and the Collective Unconscious*, p. 26.
278. In Jung's words: "I do not attribute a religious function to the soul, I merely produced the facts which prove the soul is *naturaliter religiosa.*" C. G. Jung, *Psychology and Alchemy*, 2d edition, in C. G. Jung, *Collected Works*, volume XII, translated by R. F. C. Hull (Princeton, N.J.: Princeton University Press, 1968), p. 13.
279. Erich Neumann, *The Origins and History of Consciousness*, translated by R. F. C. Hull (Princeton, N.J.: Princeton University Press, 1954), p. xv.
280. C. G. Jung, *Psychological Types*, p. 443; italics deleted; two singular words changed to plurals.
281. For Jung, the word archaic is a technical term specifically designating the "oldness" of psychic contents or functions. Archaic for Jung does not mean outdated. *Ibid.*, p. 413.
282. For example, in the history of the human race people at different eras and in varying cultures have experienced the effect of the sun on life and growth and famine, a historical experience which gave rise in bygone days to the archetype of a supreme being.
283. This conception of archetypes being inherited has interesting ramifications for the classical Christian doctrine that original sin is actually transmitted to different generations as an inheritance of the race's first parents.
284. Jung carefully distinguishes between archetypes and archetypal ideas. "The archetype as such is a hypothetical and irrepresentable model, something like the 'pattern of behavior' model in biology." C. G. Jung, *The Archetypes and the Collective Unconscious*, p. 5.
285. For a particularly illuminating examination of ancient myth from a Jungian perspective, see Erich Neumann, *The Origins and History of Consciousness*.
286. C. G. Jung, *The Archetypes and the Collective Unconscious*, p. 155.
287. *Ibid.*, p. 5.
288. Jung writes: "Again and again I encounter the mistaken notion that an archetype is determined in regard to its content, in other words that it is a kind of unconscious idea (if such an expression is admissible). It is necessary to point out once more that archetypes are not determined as regards their content, but only as regards their form and then only to a very limited degree. A primordial image is determined as to its content only when it has become conscious and is therefore filled out with the material of conscious experience. . . . The archetype itself is

empty and purely formal, nothing but a *facultas praeformandi,* a possibility of representation which is given a *a priori.* The representations themselves are not inherited, only the forms, and in that respect they correspond in every way to the instincts, which are also determined in form only.'' *Ibid.,* p. 79.

289. Jung is very careful to distinguish the archetype in itself, as hinted at in the previous footnote. In this vein Jung writes: ''The archetypal representations (images and ideas) mediated to us by the unconscious should not be confused with the archetype as such. . . . It seems to me probable that the real nature of the archetype is not capable of being made conscious, that is transcendent. . . . Moreover, every archetype, when represented to the mind, is already conscious and therefore differs to an indeterminable extent from that which caused the representation.'' C. G. Jung, *The Structure and Dynamics of the Psyche,* 2d edition, translated by R. F. C. Hull (Princeton, N.J.: Princeton University Press, 1969), p. 213, one uppercase added.

290. Jung spent a great deal of his life in attempting to uncover the mythological roots of modern human beings. Some of the archetypes which Jung studied the most include the primordial images of the earth mother, the hero, the demon, the elder wise man, unity, magic, power, and death.

291. Jolande Jacobi claims that *mandalas* are among the oldest religious symbols of the human race. Some *mandalas,* she states, date as far back as the paleolithic age. Jolande Jacobi, *The Psychology of C. G. Jung,* p. 130.

292. C. G. Jung, *Psychology and Alchemy,* 2d edition, in C. G. Jung, *Collected Works,* volume XII, translated by R. F. C. Hull (Princeton, N.J.: Princeton University Press, 1968), p. 41.

293. C. G. Jung, *Psychological Types,* p. 460.

294. ''It would be wildly arbitrary and therefore unscientific to restrict the self to the limits of the individual psyche, quite apart from the fundamental fact that we have not the least knowledge of these limits, seeing that they also lie in the unconscious.'' C. G. Jung, *Psychology and Alchemy,* p. 182.

295. C. G. Jung, *Two Essays on Analytical Psychology,* 2d edition, in C. G. Jung, *Collected Works,* volume VII, translated by R. F. C. Hull (Princeton, N.J.: Princeton University Press, 1966), p. 177.

296. On the last point, see Jolande Jacobi, *The Psychology of C. G. Jung,* p. 127.

297. For a treatment of individuation and self-realization from a combined Jungian and Christian perspective by a man who was involved in religious education during the mid-twentieth century, see Josef Goldbrunner, *Realization: The Anthropology of Pastoral Care* (Notre Dame, Ind.: University of Notre Dame Press, 1966).

298. C. G. Jung, *Two Essays on Analytical Psychology,* p. 240.

299. Of additional interest to religious educators is the contention in Jungian psychology that the increase of energy which sometimes occurs in the process of religious conversion is a sign that the integration of diverse archetypes into the self is possible.

300. C. G. Jung, *Psychological Types,* p. 460.

301. Jolande Jacobi, *The Psychology of C. G. Jung,* p. 126.

302. C. G. Jung, *Psychological Types,* p. 425.

303. A leading Jungian interpreter writes: ''Here we may remember how the ego grows. The ego develops its focus from infancy onward by gathering to itself the more diffuse light of general consciousness. Its growth is at the expense of the

whole being, of the Self. On the one hand, this development gives the ego its force for specialized directed attention and action. But on the other hand, this development robs consciousness from the psyche as a whole, leaving much of it in the dark. (Archetypal ego-figures showing how the ego-complex often gains its consciousness are frequently thieves: Eve, Jacob, Hermes, Prometheus)." James Hillman, *Insearch: Psychology and Religion*, p. 114.

304. "The self is a quantity that is superordinate to the conscious ego. It embraces not only the conscious but also the unconscious psyche, and is therefore, so to speak, a personality which we *also* are. . . . There is little hope of our ever being able to reach even approximate consciousness of the self, since however much we may make conscious there will always exist an indeterminate and indeterminable amount of unconscious material which belongs to the totality of the self." C. G. Jung, *Two Essays on Analytical Psychology*, p. 177.

305. *Ibid.*, p. 240.

306. Thus "a child has no real shadow but his shadow becomes more pronounced as his ego gains in stability and range." Jolande Jacobi, *The Psychology of C. G. Jung*, p. 107.

307. C. G. Jung, *Memories, Dreams, Reflections*, pp. 398–399. Jung also notes that in dreams the shadow figure is always of the same gender as the dreamer.

308. C. G. Jung, *Aion*, p. 266.

309. Jolande Jacobi, *The Psychology of C. G. Jung*, p. 107.

310. *Ibid.*, p. 106. In the same place Jacobi writes: "The shadow is an archetype figure which among primitive peoples still makes its appearance in a wide range of personifications."

311. Ruth Munroe, *Schools of Psychoanalytic Thought*, pp. 562–563.

312. C. G. Jung, *The Archetypes and the Collective Unconscious*, p. 284.

313. In Jung's words: "As in its collective, mythological form, so also the individual shadow contains within it the seed of an enantiodromia, of a conversion into its opposite." *Ibid.*, p. 272.

314. Jolande Jacobi, *The Psychology of C. G. Jung*, p. 109.

315. James Hillman, *Insearch: Psychology and Religion*, p. 76. Hillman also observes that loving the shadow may begin with carrying it.

316. The unreality of a person with a weak or with no apparent shadow is evident in the colorlessness of so-called "goody-goody" persons in real life and in the theater.

317. C. G. Jung, *Memories, Dreams, Reflections*, p. 399.

318. C. G. Jung, *Aion*, p. 8.

319. In attempting to circumvent this insuperable ontological difficulty, Hellenistically oriented philosophers tried to erect a category of being called "privative being." This new category has never been convincing.

320. For a treatment of evil, the shadow, and Christian theology, see Victor White, *Soul and Psyche* (New York: Harper, 1960), pp. 141–165.

321. C. G. Jung, *Psychological Types*, p. 467.

322. C. G. Jung, *Memories, Dreams, Reflections*, p. 391. Jung was a medical man, and his training shows. For example, he claims that anima/animus are not just archetypes totally "out there"; they are also rooted in biological facts very much "in here." Anima/animus means that each person is psychologically bisexual much as this same person is physiologically bisexual. Each individual possesses masculine and feminine genes. The larger number of male or female genes is

what determines a person's gender. "The smaller number of contrasexual genes seems to produce a corresponding contrasexual character, which usually remains unconscious." *Ibid.*

323. Logos is paternal, eros maternal.
324. Liliane Frey-Rohn, *From Freud to Jung,* p. 264.
325. C. G. Jung, *The Archetypes and the Collective Unconscious,* p. 27, /animus added.
326. *Ibid.,* p. 197, anima/ added, person substituted for patient.
327. Some Jungians believe that this is the case with some nuns and feminists.
328. Possibly this is because Catholicism has tended to be a male religion.
329. On this point, see Victor White, *Soul and Psyche,* pp. 115–140. From a Jungian perspective, the overriding animus in Protestant feminism will only exacerbate this unfortunate situation.
330. C. G. Jung, *Psychological Types,* pp. 467–468.
331. C. G. Jung, *The Archetypes and the Collective Unconscious,* p. 122.
332. The counterweight to the individually exposed and socially accepted persona is the shadow.
333. Ruth Munroe, *Schools of Psychoanalytic Thought,* p. 558.
334. "The relation of the individual to the object must be sharply distinguished from the relation to the subject." C. G. Jung, *Psychological Types,* pp. 465–466.
335. C. G. Jung, *The Archetypes and the Collective Unconscious,* p. 123.
336. C. G. Jung, *Symbols of Transformation,* 2d edition, translated by R. F. C. Hull, in C. G. Jung, *Collected Works,* volume V (Princeton, N.J.: Princeton University Press, 1967), p. 124.
337. A symbol which is no longer living typically degenerates into a sign.
338. C. G. Jung, *Psychological Types,* p. 478.
339. C. G. Jung, *Psychology and Alchemy,* pp. 432–435.
340. Liliane Frey-Rohn, *From Freud to Jung,* pp. 265–269.
341. C. G. Jung, *Psychology and Alchemy,* p. 283.
342. For Freud, the symbol has a definite compromise function. For Jung, the symbol has the function of a creative transition from one attitude to another. C. G. Jung, *Psychological Types,* pp. 475–481.
343. Jolande Jacobi, *The Psychology of C. G. Jung,* p. 91.
344. J. G. Bishop, *Jung and Christianity* (London: SPCK, 1966), p. 16.
345. C. G. Jung, *Two Essays on Analytical Psychology,* pp. 52–53.
346. C. G. Jung, *The Structure and Dynamics of the Psyche,* pp. 15–16.
347. Jung's concept of the libido is thus much wider than that of Freud.
348. The nature, structure, and workings of psychological attitude can be fruitfully considered as an instance of Jung's more global view of the centrality of opposites in the depth of reality.
349. For Jung, "attitude is a readiness of the psyche to act or react in a certain way. To have an attitude means to be ready for something definite, even though this something is unconscious; for having an attitude is synonymous with an *a priori* orientation to a definite thing, no matter whether this be represented in consciousness or not." C. G. Jung, *Psychological Types,* p. 414.
350. Jolande Jacobi, *The Psychology of C. G. Jung,* p. 18.
351. *Ibid.*
352. C. G. Jung, *Psychological Types,* p. 445.
353. Jolande Jacobi, *The Psychology of C. G. Jung,* p. 19.
354. C. G. Jung, *Two Essays on Analytical Psychology,* p. 44.

355. C. G. Jung, *Psychological Types*, p. 427.

356. Jolande Jacobi, *The Psychology of C. G. Jung*, p. 18.

357. C. G. Jung, *Two Essays on Analytical Psychology*, p. 44.

358. Ruth Munroe, *Schools of Psychoanalytic Thought*, p. 545. I should also note that in Jungian analytical psychology, the basic psychological attitude which is subordinate will tend to be expressed in dreams and fantasies if it is denied appropriate expression in reality.

359. Again we see the centrality of quaternity, rather than of trinity, in Jung's system—a fact with definite ramifications for Jung's conception of religion. See Marie-Louise von Franz, "The Inferior Function," in Marie-Louise von Franz and James Hillman, *Jung's Typology* (New York: Analytical Psychology Club, 1971), p. 1.

360. C. G. Jung, *Psychological Types*, p. 483.

361. For a fine description of the feeling function from a Jungian perspective, see James Hillman, "Feeling Types," in Marie-Louise von Franz and James Hillman, *Jung's Typology*, pp. 96–103.

362. Ruth Munroe, *Schools of Psychoanalytic Thought*, p. 548.

363. C. G. Jung, *Psychological Types*, p. 145.

364. In more complex personalities, two functions and very occasionally three functions may dominate; however there always will be at least one personality function which is submerged or neglected.

365. A psychometric test has been devised to assist counselors to ascertain which type an individual represents. This test, called the Myers-Briggs Type Indicator, is sometimes used with seminarians and clergy. For an overview of the validation of this instrument, see "Myers-Briggs Type Indicator," in Oscar Krisen Buros, editor, *The Eighth Mental Measurements Yearbook*, volume I (Highland Park, N.J.: Gryphon, 1978), pp. 970–975 (#630).

366. This is one major purpose and goal of psychotherapy.

367. Jolande Jacobi, *The Psychology of C. G. Jung*, p. 19.

368. Jung states that whenever an instinct for wholeness appears, it begins by revealing itself under the symbolism of incest. See James Hillman, *Insearch: Psychology and Religion*, p. 123.

369. Psychic disturbances are instances of a dis-integration in conscious and unconscious processes. This dis-integration retards and indeed injures individuation and the coming to wholeness. Jung's analytical psychotherapy aims at restoring the natural process of integrative development.

370. C. G. Jung, *Psychological Types*, p. 449, italics deleted.

371. Jolande Jacobi, "Jung, Carl Gustav," p. 328.

372. This Jungian notion of the integration of conscious and unconscious stands in marked contrast to Freud's emphasis on the attainment of conscious control by the ego and the mature expression of the libido.

373. C. G. Jung, *The Archetypes and the Collective Unconscious*, p. 275.

374. C. G. Jung, *Two Essays on Analytical Psychology*, pp. 173–175.

375. C. G. Jung, *Psychological Types*, p. 448.

376. *Ibid*, p. 449.

377. *Ibid*.

378. Thus Jung acerbically criticizes those religionists, especially theologians, who assert that it smacks of blasphemy to regard religious experience as a psychic process. C. G. Jung, *Psychology and Alchemy*, p. 9.

379. "It is a telling fact," Jung writes, "that two theological reviewers of my book

Psychology and Religion—one of them a Catholic, the other Protestant—assiduously overlooked my demonstration of the psychic origin of religious phenomena.'' *Ibid.*

380. C. G. Jung, *Psychology and Religion: East and West*, 2d edition, in C. G. Jung, *Collected Works*, volume XI, translated by R. F. C. Hull (Princeton, N.J.: Princeton University Press, 1969), p. 341.

381. This position is, of course, diametrically opposed to that of Freud who believed that psychology would eventually succeed in explaining religion away in much the same way as any neurosis can be cured. For Freud, humanity needs to be cured of the neurosis of religion. For a discussion of this point, see G. Stephens Spinks, *Psychology and Religion* (Boston: Beacon, 1963), p. 101.

382. C. G. Jung, *Psychology and Religion*, p. 300.

383. There is, of course, a major difference between epistemological agnosticism and religious agnosticism.

384. See Peter A. Bertocci, ''Psychological Interpretations of Religious Experience,'' in Merton P. Strommen, editor, *Research on Religious Development*, p. 17.

385. Pedro V. Salgado, *Psychology of the Unconscious* (Manila: University of Santo Tomas Press, 1966), p. 51.

386. ''Perhaps the most puzzling question is this: How does Jung, to begin with, identify a religious experience *as* religious as compared with one which is aesthetic or ethical? What in the experience, what in the expression within the person, makes a particular experience religious—given the presumable neutrality of Jung's epistemic stance and his unwillingness to favor any one overbelief? Jung must, it would seem, here rely somewhat parasitically and externally on what others, who do not take his epistemic and ontological stance, do hold as 'their religion.' '' Peter A. Bertocci, ''Psychological Interpretations of Religious Experience,'' p. 19.

387. On this point, see Edward Glover, *Freud or Jung?* (New York: Meridian, 1956), p. 155.

388. C. G. Jung, *Psychology and Religion: West and East*, p. 105.

389. *Ibid.*

390. Edward Glover, *Freud or Jung?*, p. 165.

391. C. G. Jung, *Psychology and Religion: West and East*, p. 300.

392. ''Nun sagt aber Jung, und damit sichert er sich sofort wieder ab: ich rede ja nicht über Gott, soweit sein Bild in den Träumen meiner Patienten mir immer wieder begegnet und auch in meinen eigenen Träumen, insofern er sich also mir erfahrbar macht. Für den Seher Jung wird Gott also zu einer Erfahrung. Gott ist für Jung eine erfahrbare Grösse.'' Ulrich Mann, ''Die Gotteserfahrung des Menschen bei C. G. Jung,'' in Wolfgang Böhme, Herausgeber, *C. G. Jung und die Theologen* (Stuttgart: Radius, 1971), p. 15.

393. Jung always stresses that he is dealing with psychology and not with metaphysics or theology. As a psychologist, Jung is concerned not with God as he is or might be as an absolute being in himself, but rather with the archetype God as experienced in the psyche. See Victor White, *Soul and Psyche*, pp. 48–53.

394. This sentence provides what I believe is an authentic Jungian interpretation of the inscription over the entrance to Jung's Swiss villa: ''Called or not, God is present.''

395. C. G. Jung, *Psychology and Religion: West and East*, pp. 164–200.

396. This wholeness of the archetype is necessary for personal individuation, that is to say, individual psychic wholeness.

397. Wallace B. Clift, *Jung and Christianity: The Challenge of Reconciliation* (New York: Crossroad, 1982), pp. 129–134.
398. Morton Trippe Kelsey and John Sanford are notable cases in point.
399. For an example of this mentality, see Pedro V. Salgado, *Psychology of the Unconscious*, p. 53.
400. This line is Cyril Connolly's as expressed in a conversation with Edward Glover. Glover himself remarks that after studying Jung's writings closely, he (Glover) could not find in Jung's thought any inspirational value that is not at the same time illusory. Edward Glover, *Freud or Jung?*, p. 9.
401. Jewish religious education, especially since the Holocaust, seems to be more aware of this point than is most of Christian religious education.
402. The Romantic Movement originated in Germany and later spread, though in weakened form, to France and England.
403. Henri F. Ellenberger, *The Discovery of the Unconscious*, pp. 199–223.
404. Carl Gustav Carus, *Psyche* (New York: Spring, 1970). This book was originally published in 1846.
405. He was also deeply influenced by the philosophies of Hegel and Schopenhauer. See Dennis N. Kenedy Darnoi, *The Unconscious and Eduard von Hartmann* (The Hague: Nijhoff, 1967), pp. 10–20.
406. Eduard von Hartmann, *Philosophy of the Unconscious*, translated by William Chatterton Coupland (New York: Harcourt, Brace, 1931), pp. 3–5. This book first appeared in 1869, and went through twelve editions.
407. Third-force psychology is proposed by its adherents as an alternative to objectivist behaviorist psychology on the one hand and depth psychology on the other hand. Abraham Maslow is generally credited as the founder of humanistic psychology. I should note that some transpersonalists contend that transpersonalism is really fourth-force psychology, one significantly different from third-force psychology, one which gives primacy to the occult and to the spiritual.
408. See Abraham Maslow, *Toward a Psychology of Being* (Princeton, N.J.: Van Nostrand, 1968); Abraham Maslow, *Religions, Values, and Peak Experiences* (New York: Penguin, 1964); Abraham Maslow, *The Farthest Reaches of Human Nature* (New York: Viking, 1970).
409. Ken Wilber, "A Developmental View of Consciousness," in *Journal of Transpersonal Psychology* XI (Number 1, 1979), pp. 1–21.
410. Kenneth Ring, "A Transpersonal View of Consciousness: A Mapping of Farther Regions of Inner Space," in *Journal of Transpersonal Psychology* VI (Number 2, 1974), pp. 125–155; Kenneth Ring, "Mapping the Regions of Consciousness: A Conceptual Reformulation," in *Journal of Transpersonal Psychology* VIII (Number 2, 1976), pp. 77–88.
411. These persons can best be thought of as tangential rather than direct followers of Jung because, unlike Jung's direct followers, they have discarded a good portion of Jung's teachings which do not fit in with their religious and theological views. The tangential followers generally have received limited rather than extensive training in Switzerland, are often not fully licensed analytical psychologists, and are usually popularizers rather than serious Jungian scholars or scholar-practitioners.
412. Morton Kelsey, *Can Christians Be Educated?* (Birmingham, Ala.: Religious Education Press, 1977), p. 30.
413. Morton T. Kelsey, *Dreams: The Dark Speech of the Spirit* (Garden City, N.Y.: Doubleday, 1968). This is by far the best book which Kelsey has written on dreams.

414. Morton Kelsey, *Encounter with God,* pp. 26–41. For some of Kelsey's views on the transcendent God and the way in which persons can encounter this God through the unconscious, see Morton T. Kelsey, *Transcend* (New York: Crossroad, 1981).

415. John A. Sanford, *Dreams: God's Forgotten Language* (New York: Lippincott, 1968), p. 7.

416. John A. Sanford, *The Kingdom Within* (Philadelphia: Lippincott, 1970).

417. Ernest White, *Christian Life and the Unconscious* (New York: Harper, 1955).

418. In contrast to the pleasure principle of Sigmund Freud, the archetypal principle of Carl Jung, and the power principle of Alfred Adler, logotherapy stresses what Frankl terms "the will to meaning." Viktor E. Frankl, *Man's Search for Meaning: An Introduction to Logotherapy,* revised edition, translated by Ilse Lasch (Boston: Beacon, 1962), pp. 97–137.

419. Viktor E. Frankl, *The Unconscious God,* p. 13.

420. *Ibid.*

421. Viktor E. Frankl, *The Doctor and the Soul,* 2d edition, translated by Richard Winston and Clara Winston (New York: Knopf, 1965), p. 270.

422. Meaning, it must be remembered, forms a basis for human existence and is therefore quintessentially present and active at the core of each human being.

423. Viktor E. Frankl, *The Unconscious God,* pp. 64–65.

424. *Ibid.,* p. 65.

425. John C. Hill, *Teaching and the Unconscious Mind,* pp. 117–118.

426. J. Gordon Chamberlin, *Freedom and Faith* (Philadelphia: Westminster, 1965), p. 120.

427. In a statement having great practical importance to religion schoolteachers, Carl Jung writes that "the things which have the most powerful effect upon children do not come from the conscious state of the parents but from their unconscious background." C. G. Jung, *The Development of Personality,* p. 41.

428. This statement also applies to the God met in a nonrational manner, including the unconscious. Rachel Henderlite decries the tendency of Protestant Christian education to teach God as though he were the object of intellectual inquiry only. The same holds true of much Catholic religious education, especially since the 1970s. Rachel Henderlite, *Forgiveness and Hope: Toward a Theology for Protestant Christian Education* (Richmond, Va.: Knox Aletheia, 1961), p. 23.

429. C. G. Jung, *The Development of Personality,* p. 55.

430. C. G. Jung, *Memories, Dreams, Reflections,* p. 133.

431. James Dillon's remark takes on added force when applied to the educator's unconscious needs: "One wonders how much students suffer in order to satisfy teacher goals or needs." J. T. Dillon, "Why Discussion?" in J. T. Dillon, editor, *Catechetics Reconsidered* (Winona, Minn.: St. Mary's College Press, 1968), p. 190.

432. Viktor Frankl is not hesitant in remarking that psychotherapists have caused neuroses. Viktor E. Frankl, *The Unconscious God,* pp. 111–112.

433. John C. Hill, *Teaching and the Unconscious Mind,* p. 158.

434. Sigmund Freud, *The Interpretation of Dreams,* p. 647.

435. C. G. Jung, *The Development of Personality,* p. 104.

436. Morton T. Kelsey, *Dreams: The Dark Speech of the Spirit,* p. 226.

437. C. G. Jung, *The Development of Personality,* p. 59.

438. Most specialists in the "new psychobiology of dreaming" credit the beginning of this movement to the publication in 1953 of Eugene Aserinsky and Nathaniel

Kleitman, "Regularly Occurring Periods of Eye Motility and Concomitant Phenomena During Sleep," in *Science* CXVIII (September 4, 1953), p. 273–274.

439. "Since the discovery of REM sleep in man, nearly every physiological variable which can be [empirically] recorded from the surface of the body has been measured during sleep. Most of these measures show distinct and characteristic changes in REM sleep compared to their levels or patterns in NREM stages." Harold L. Williams, Frank A. Holloway, and William J. Griffiths, "Physiological Psychology: Sleep," in Paul H. Mussen and Mark R. Rosenzweig, editors, *Annual Review of Psychology*, volume XXIII (Palo Alto, Cal.: Annual Reviews, 1973), p. 284.

440. Harry Fiss, "Current Dream Research: A Psychobiological Perspective," in Benjamin B. Wolman, editor, *Handbook of Dreams: Research, Theories, Applications* (New York: Van Nostrand, 1979), pp. 26–27. This review of the research shows that respiration, heart rate, and blood pressure are more elevated and more irregular in REM sleep as compared to NONREM sleep. Also, oxygen consumption, brain temperature, and cortical blood flow increase in REM sleep but decrease in NONREM sleep. Finally, penile erections, middle ear muscular activity, and twitches of the small muscles of the face and limbs are all very much in evidence during REM sleep but are either rare or totally absent during NONREM sleep. *Ibid.,* p. 27.

441. One possible fallout from these findings in terms of research procedure is that the dream might possibly be studied as both an independent variable and as a dependent variable. See Wilse B. Webb and Rosalind D. Cartwright, "Sleep and Dreams," in Mark R. Rosenzweig and Lyman W. Porter, editors, *Annual Review of Psychology,* volume XXIX (Palo Alto, Calif.: Annual Reviews, 1978), pp. 243–245.

442. Ernest L. Hartmann, *The Functions of Sleep* (New Haven: Yale University Press, 1973).

443. For a concise summary of ancient dream theories, see Robert L. Van de Castle, *The Psychology of Dreaming* (Morristown, N.J.: General Learning, 1971), pp. 3–9.

444. The Egyptians even had a special god for dreams, namely Serapis. Several serapeums (temples) were located in various localities in Egypt.

445. Jackson Steward Lincoln, *The Dream in Primitive Cultures* (New York: Johnson, 1970), p. 4. This is a classic work on the subject.

446. The finest scholarly account which I have found on this topic is Morton T. Kelsey, *Dreams: The Dark Speech of the Spirit.*

447. *Ibid.,* p. 19.

448. Of interest in connection with the views of modern depth psychologists on dream form is Yahweh's statement that a dream is a riddle and not a direct unambiguous kind of communication (Num. 13:8).

449. Dorothy Eggan, "Dream Analysis," in Bert Kaplan, editor, *Studying Personality Cross-Culturally* (New York: Harper & Row, 1961), p. 555.

450. Roger Caillois, "Logical and Philosophical Problems of the Dream," in G. E. von Grunebaum and Roger Caillois, editors, *The Dream in Human Societies* (Berkeley, Calif.: University of California Press, 1966), p. 23.

451. For a helpful elaboration of this point, see Norman MacKenzie, *Dreams and Dreaming* (New York: Vanguard, 1965), p. 11. As MacKenzie observes, the dream debate, fortunately, has been steadily moving from sheer speculation to science.

452. See, for example, Louis Breger, Ian Hunter, and Ron W. Lane, *The Effect of Stress on Dreams* (New York: International Universities Press, 1971).
453. This principle was verified by at least one experimental research investigation. See Milton Kramer et al., "Do Dreams Have Meaning?: An Empirical Inquiry," in *American Journal of Psychiatry*, CXXXIII (July, 1976), pp. 778–781.
454. On this point, see Rollo May, "Introduction," in Leopold Caligor and Rollo May, *Dreams and Symbols: Man's Unconscious Language* (New York: Basic, 1968), pp. 9–10. The purpose of the dreaming process itself, writes May, is to experience symbol rather than to explain it. The explanation of symbol comes during wakefulness, in the process of dream interpretation.
455. Ernest Lawrence Rossi, *Dreams and the Growth of Personality* (New York: Pergamon, 1966), pp. 138–142.
456. One review of the pertinent empirical research concludes that the Freudian hypothesis that dreams operate in order to gratify forbidden impulses in acceptable ways has not yet been tested experimentally. The reviewers further state that due to the considerable design problems inherent in experimentally testing the Freudian hypothesis, a scientifically valid conclusion on this issue may not be forthcoming for some time. Wilse B. Webb and Rosalind D. Cartwright, "Sleep and Dreams." p. 244.
457. The interpretation of a dream by Géza Róheim, a Freudian psychoanalyist, illustrates this point. The dreamer was a businessman forty years of age. He had not been in business for many years because of severe anxiety flowing from an unresolved Oedipus complex. "In his dream, the man was on top of a mountain. He was trying to get off the top and could do so by getting into a hollow shaft. But he found that the jump from the top into the shaft is dangerous. Two strong men helped him with a rope." Now that was the manifest content of the dream, the content which the businessman recalled. The latent content of the dream, in Róheim's view, is as follows: "The top of the hill—his mother's bosom. The two helpers—his testicles. The rope—his penis. The shaft—his potential wife's (mother's) vagina. The business deal means being potent, making a lot of money, killing father, getting married" to mother. Géza Róheim, *The Gates of the Dream* (New York: International Universities Press, 1952), p. 27.
458. In Freudian psychology, many fairy tales are narrative symbols containing latent sexual meaning, such as, for example, Cinderella and the slipper.
459. Sándor Ferenczi, *Further Contributions to the Theory and Technique of Psycho-Analysis*, compiled by John Richman, translated by Jane Isabel Suttie et al. (London: Hogarth, 1926), p. 348.
460. Charles Brenner, *An Elementary Textbook of Psychoanalysis*, p. 186.
461. In an obvious slam at Jungian dream analysis, Edward Glover states: "Admittedly Freud's functional approach to dream psychology, involving as it does the concept of the dynamic unconscious, of the primary processes that govern the unconscious system, of a repression-barrier, of the superego or unconscious conscience, and of unconscious conflict and of unconscious resistance, is inevitably disappointing to those who seek hopefully in dreams for evidence of man's occult and magical powers." Edward Glover, *Freud or Jung?* p. 113.
462. For a helpful discussion of this point, see Ann Faraday, *Dream Power* (New York: Berkeley, 1972), pp. 119–120.
463. Jolande Jacobi, *The Psychology of C. G. Jung*, p. 71.
464. Though the dream symbol often includes material from a person's past and from the human race's past, it does so not in order to resolve or undo the past

experiences but simply to put past experiences to that kind of future use promotive of individuation. Freud, in contrast, views dreams as primarily oriented to the past, that is to repair unresolved tendencies or make up for poorly worked-through infantile urges.

465. Morton Trippe Kelsey told me on several occasions that Barbara, his wife and co-therapist, had dreams whose content actually came to pass sometime after the dream took place. Jung's claim about the foretelling power of dreams runs into many formidable obstacles, including the psychological difficulty of self-fulfilling prophecy and the even more formidable philosophical difficulty of free futurables.

466. Jung states: "The so-called facade of most houses is by no means a fake or a deceptive distortion; on the contrary, it follows the plan of the building and often the interior arrangement. . . . What Freud calls the 'dream-facade' is the dream's obscurity, and that is really only a projection of our own lack of understanding." C. G. Jung, *The Practice of Psychotherapy*, 2d edition, in C. G. Jung, *Collected Works,* volume XVI (Princeton, N.J.: Princeton University Press, 1966), p. 149.

467. *Ibid.*

468. C. G. Jung, *The Structure and Dynamics of the Psyche*, p. 336. Jung continues: "A symbol does not define or explain; it points beyond itself to a meaning that is darkly divined yet still beyond our grasp, and cannot be adequately expressed in the familiar words of our language."

469. Henri F. Ellenberger, *The Discovery of the Unconscious*, pp. 716–717.

470. For a review of some pertinent empirical research on the relationship of a warm socioemotional climate to effective religion teaching, see James Michael Lee, *The Flow of Religious Instruction*, pp. 98–106.

471. Morton T. Kelsey, *Encounter with God*, pp. 175–176.

472. A helpful essay for religious educators is Montague Ullman, "The Experiential Dream Group," in Benjamin B. Wolman, editor, *Handbook of Dreams: Research, Theories and Applications*, pp. 406–423.

473. *Ibid.*, p. 414.

474. C. G. Jung, *The Development of Personality*, p. 87.

475. *Ibid.*, p. 103.

476. Morton T. Kelsey, *Dreams: The Dark Speech of the Spirit*, pp. 232–235.

477. For a review of some of the pertinent research on thematic approaches to dream content, see Carolyn Winget and Milton Kramer, *Dimensions of Dreams* (Gainesville, Fla.: University Presses of Florida, 1979), pp. 208–219. An earlier and highly regarded book on dream content is Calvin S. Hall, *The Meaning of Dreams* (New York: McGraw-Hill, 1966).

478. Montague Ullman, "The Experiential Dream Group," p. 509.

479. C. G. Jung, *Memories, Dreams, Reflections*, p. 133.

480. With respect to empirical research on consciousness, see Ernest R. Hilgard, "Consciousness in Contemporary Psychology," in Mark R. Rosenzweig and Lyman W. Porter, editors, *Annual Review of Psychology*, volume XXXI (Palo Alto, Calif.: Annual Reviews, 1980), pp. 2–26.

CHAPTER NINE

LIFESTYLE CONTENT

"But God's own descent
Into flesh was meant
As a demonstration
That the supreme merit
Lay in risking spirit
In substantiation." [1]

—Robert Frost

THE NATURE OF LIFESTYLE CONTENT

Lifestyle content refers to the overall pattern of a person's activities. Put somewhat more personalistically, lifestyle content consists of the way in which a person organizes his self-system and lives out his life. [2] Lifestyle, then, is the all-inclusive shape and operational flow of the totality of a person's behavior. By virtue of its complete inclusivity, lifestyle delineates, demarcates, orients, pervades, and colors all of an individual's general activities as well as all of his specific behaviors. Thus in a major sense all human functioning more or less represents or embodies a person's own individual lifestyle. This holds true for the most global comportment through various levels of general activities right down to highly specific behaviors.

The foregoing brief explanation reveals that lifestyle has at least two fundamental and interrelated characteristics, namely totality and integrativeness.

Lifestyle content is total in that it includes the entire repertoire of a person's human functioning from the most general to the most specific. Thus every single behavior in which a person engages is existentially incorporated into his lifestyle or pattern of living. This incorporation takes place on its own terms as well as on the terms of the person's entire lifestyle broadly considered. For example, the incorporation of a particular cognitive behavior into one's living functional self-system (that is to say into his lifestyle) occurs in a manner which simultaneously is true to the objective structure and operation of that cognitive content and is true to the subjective structure and operation of the person's own unique lifestyle.

Lifestyle content is integrative in that it meshes the myriad kinds of human activities and behaviors into one overall relatively congruent pattern of personal functioning. It is lifestyle which accounts for the order and harmony in personal functioning. By virtue of its integrative power, lifestyle enables diverse kinds of human behavior both to attain objective completion and to be incorporated into that wider form of life we call human activity. Thus, for example, lifestyle enables a particular affect, such as liking, to be joined to other affects, such as affiliation, and to psychomotor behaviors, such as touch, so that liking may achieve fullness in itself and thus be completed; lifestyle also enables liking to productively interact with other affects, with available range of cognitions, and with various psychomotor behaviors so that liking is thereby elevated from a simple affect to an eminently personal affect, that is to say, an affect which functions primarily in a personal way for a personal purpose. In the ultimate analysis, it is the integrative character of lifestyle which situates the enormous expanse of individual human behaviors into that kind of overall pattern which enables one or another behavior to be meaningful with respect both to the person himself and to other human beings. Thus the adequacy, understandability, and reference of any particular human behavior is judged on the twin bases of how well this behavior fits in with the person's own lifestyle and how well this behavior fits in with the idealized lifestyle which a particular cultural group views as appropriate and acceptable. If one or another of an individual's behaviors is incongruent or unharmonious with respect to that person's lifestyle, then this individual usually suffers one or more of the typical pains of such dis-integration, as for example a sense of personal instability, an awareness of disequilibrium, feelings of guilt, an inability to adequately cope, and so forth.

Holistic Functionalism

Correlative to, and in some ways a consequence of, the totality and the integrativeness of lifestyle is holistic functionalism. As I have repeatedly stressed throughout my writings, and again in this book,[3] each person operates as an integral whole, as *homo integer*. This operational unity of the varying activities and diverse behaviors of a human being is, of course, holistic functionalism. Lifestyle represents personal holistic functionalism par excellence because lifestyle comprises that overall pattern of total human action which integrates the entire repertoire of human behavior into one more or less operationally unified whole which can be recognized by self and others. Holistic functionalism suggests that no one kind of human process can change without both involving and having some effect on the other basic kinds of human processes, since no single human process operates in total independence from the others. Holistic functionalism further suggests that the degree to which a person learns is directly contingent upon the degree to which all his human processes are interactively engaged and undergo appropriate change during a given learning activity.[4] For example, the degree to which a person learns a particular cognitive behavior directly depends upon the degree to which his affective processes and his psychomotor processes are *appropriately*[5] involved in and change during the time in which the individual is endeavoring to acquire that cognitive behavior.[6] This statement holds especially true for what Carl Rogers terms ''significant learning,'' namely that kind of learning which holds personal significance for us and thus enjoys the capacity to change our lives in some significant way.[7]

Lifestyle is the way in which holistic functionalism in its entirety achieves operational concretization—or, more accurately, holistic functionalism is an especially apt concept to describe the workings and ongoing nature of lifestyle in the latter's entirety. Lifestyle constitutes the zenith of holistic functionalism because it operationally coordinates in one overall unified pattern the various discrete though somewhat interrelated human processes such as those which occur in the cognitive, affective, and psychomotor domains. Lifestyle is thus the most global, most integrated, and most synthesized form of holistic functionalism. In earlier chapters I show that holistic functionalism necessarily occurs in the workings of cognition, of affect, and of bodily activities. What I am now asserting is that holistic functionalism achieves total actualization and fullness when it assumes the form of lifestyle. Lifestyle displays how holistic functionalism works in its entirety. Lifestyle reveals the orientation which holistic functionalism takes in a particular human being. Lifestyle shows how holistic functionalism coordinates cognitive, affective, and psychomotor processes—a coordination which corrects and modifies the otherwise full flow of each process. Lifestyle demonstrates how holistic functionalism enables human beings to open themselves up to new opportunities for synthesized personal growth.[8]

An especially fruitful instructional consequence of the concept of holistic functionalism is that it can assist religious educators to avoid a one-sided emphasis on the cognitive, on the affective, or on the psychomotor. Any one-sided pedagogical endeavor almost necessarily has the regrettable effect of introducing new compartmentalization or reinforcing old fragmentation in the lives of learners and thus skewing their lifestyles.[9] By organismic necessity, every person strives to achieve wholeness. By organismic necessity, every person innately works toward attaining a workable functional balance among his basic human processes. Hence any attempt to skew the learner's lifestyle in the direction of the cognitive or the affective or the psychomotor perforce introduces a destructive conflict into the learner's lifestyle. Such conflict can distort, cripple, and in extreme cases even destroy the health of the learner's personality and his religious life.

The religious educator should be especially alert lest he unwittingly skew the learner's lifestyle away from the psychomotor domain of human functioning. After centuries of neglect and of disvaluation, the tremendously pervasive and powerful impact of the body and of psychomotor activity in holistic human life and in holistic religion began to reappear in the last third of the twentieth century. Professionally trained Christian counselors, exposed as they have been to the body-affect axis as interpreted by diverse groups ranging from Esalen devotees to neo-Rogerians, originally took the lead in bringing the body out of the closet, so to speak. Christian artists, especially those working in religious dance and in religious sculpture, have also contributed significantly to restoring the body to its proper place in a holistic Christian lifestyle. In theological circles, there has been a predictably slow but nonetheless growing acknowledgement of the great worth of psychomotor activity in daily Christian living. Thus Schubert Ogden, a leading process theologian, writes: "To exist as a self, as each of us does, is always to be related, first of all, to the intimate world constituted by one's own body. What I think and feel has as its most direct effects on my own brain cells and central nervous system, and thence on the rest of the organism in which I as a self am incarnate."[10] In the religious instruction community, recognition of the pivotal role of psychomotor processes in Christian lifestyle has sometimes been slow, sometimes excessively enthusiastic, and sometimes has received major setbacks. In the hypermoralistic phase of religious instruction (before the mid-1960s), the axial role of psychomotor processes in the Christian lifestyle was typically disvalued or ignored. Partly as a direct reaction to this narrow hypermoralistic phase, a touchy-feely phase settled in upon much of religious instruction (mid-1960s until late 1970s). In this phase, every corporeal flutter, no matter how insignificant or outrageous, was viewed as a matter of utmost spiritual importance and of inestimable lifestyle worth. Quite possibly as a direct reaction to both the negative excesses of the hypermoralistic phase and the superficial gushiness of the touchy-feely phase, an ultracognitive emphasis with respect to Christian lifestyle made its appearance toward the end of the 1970s.[11] Like the hypermoralistic phase of which it is a very close relative (a converse relative, but a close relative nonetheless—*les extrêmes se touchent*), the ultracognitivist emphasis in religious instruction ignores and neglects the body, and thus in effect disvalues the body's central place in an holistic Christian lifestyle.[12] For example, one looks in vain for any significant inclusion of the body or of psychomotor processes in the well-conceptualized writings of Thomas Groome, a leading ultracognitive religous educationist of the 1980s.[13] It has long been my hope that religious instruction will move toward a truly balanced phase, a phase in which the psychomotor domain is accorded its proper central role and function. In this ultimate phase, which I call integralism, the psychomotor domain takes its place together with the cognitive and the affective domains in the fluid center of a genuinely holistic Christian lifestyle. In my view, a genuine and therefore a holistic Christian lifestyle is one in which all domains are operationally confluent, in which none is downplayed, and in which all are given that weight appropriate to the learning/living task at hand.[14]

While psychomotor activity in particular and overt behavior or conduct in general are inextricably central characteristics of lifestyle, nonetheless lifestyle is the here-and-now dynamic integration of cognitive, affective, and psychomotor behaviors. The more these behaviors are totally integrated, the more holistic and the more personalistic will be the quality of one's lifestyle. Let me use cognition to illustrate this pivotal point. Cognition in human functioning takes place in a decidedly lifestyle context rather than as a totally isolated process.

Francis of Assisi put the issue this way: "A person has as much knowledge as he lives out."[15] Thomas Aquinas, who is by and large a staunch cognitivist, makes a similar point, though in a backdoor manner, when he writes that a person cannot come to a knowledge of himself except through his overt behaviors.[16] My point here is that while cognition and affect and psychomotor activity are in themselves separate processes each with its own particular mode of being and special axis of functioning, nonetheless these separate processes always function together and never in complete isolation from one another. Any total separation of cognition or affect or psychomotor activity from one another occurs only in the logical order for the sake of intellectual analysis; such a total separation never occurs in the real order. In the real order, cognition and affect and psychomotor activity all take place in some degree of holistic harmony in a lifestyle behavior or series of lifestyle behaviors.[17] In human functioning, there is no such thing as internal activities which are totally separate or wholly isolated from overt behavior of one kind or another, be that overt behavior extremely subtle or highly manifest. *Homo integer* is precisely that, namely *homo integer*.

"Inner" and "Outer" Behavior

A person's overt behavior does not "reveal" some inner element or activity as if that element or activity were some hidden entity or substance "in there" somewhere. Rather, as holistic functionalism suggests, a person's so-called "inner life" constitutes an inextricable dimension of that individual's entire personalistic pattern of behaving as well as each single one of that individual's overt behaviors. This inextricable dimension is a less manifest dimension to be sure, but it is still a dimension which forms an inseparable aspect of an individual's overall lifestyle as well as of that person's particular overt behaviors. To deny this point is to maintain that each person suffers from an almost infinite number of split personalities. No overt behavior is simply external because the whole person and nothing less than the whole person is engaged in a particular overt behavior. The whole person is a functional integration of many confluent dimensions, both internal and external (if one must use these terms). It is common sense, and indeed an empirically proven fact, that there is a significant correlation between overt behavior and the less manifest dimensions of human behavior such as motivation.[18] This statement holds especially true when the overt behavior forms a discernable pattern. After all, we can only judge the character, the virtue, the motivation, and indeed the whole personality of another individual from that person's observable behaviors, his so-called "external life." If the "inner" dimension of one's conduct were cut off from one's "external" conduct, there would be no way of making any valid cognitive judgments about another individual, and there would be no way of entering into any kind of authentic affective relationship with another individual. A major goal of both general instruction and religious instruction is to enable all dimensions of the learner's personhood to shine forth radiantly, so that whatever might have formerly been less manifest may now become as fully manifest and as fully actualized as possible.[19] Pedagogical, psychological, and religious problems tend to increase in direct proportion to the degree to which the less manifest dimensions of one's life are cut off from the more manifest ones and are relegated to a separate, isolated "inner life."[20] Any attempt to teach the "inner person" primarily and exclusively will have little effect other than to destructively separate from one another the various functions and domains of human personality.[21] For example, efforts to teach the bible primarily to the "inner" cognitive person typically results in at least two pedagogically deleterious consequences: the "inner" person attains and retains little of the biblical cognitive content, and the biblical cognitive content which does remain tends to exert relatively little impact on the learner's lifestyle behavior.[22]

Since lifestyle consists in a more-or-less[23] holistic here-and-now integration of the various dimensions of human existence, lifestyle therefore implies an ongoing transformation of an individual's entire personality. This ongoing transformation of one's entire personality occurs because lifestyle necessarily involves and to a greater or lesser[24] extent functionally meshes the different zones of an individual's existence. Consequently, any kind of religious instruction which is targeted toward the enhancement of lifestyle content must be such as to actively involve the appropriate integration of all the dimensions of a person's lifestyle in a performance manner.

Lifestyle is the integrated living out in behavioral form of all the molar substantive contents mentioned in this third volume of the trilogy. The actualization of lifestyle content is directly contingent upon the degree to which its various components are existentially realized and integrated in behavioral form. This cardinal point cannot be emphasized too strongly. I hasten to note that the term behavior is neither identical to nor coextensive with overt behavior. Rather, as I take pains to note in *The Flow of Religious Instruction,* behavior "is the generic term used to indicate any activity of the organism."[25] For example, a specific cognitive activity is a cognitive behavior, a specific affective activity is an affective behavior, and so forth. If religious instruction is to enhance both the general quality and the specifically religious texture of the learner's lifestyle, then it must necessarily involve placing learners in that kind of instructional situation which involves the actual behavioral performance of lifestyle activities. Just as a person's cognitive behavior cannot be modified unless he engages in appropriate cognitive performances, so too a person's lifestyle behavior cannot be modified unless he engages in appropriate lifestyle performances.[26]

Operationalizing through Performance

In order for Christian lifestyle content to be effectively taught it must be rendered as fully operational as possible. In using the term operational I do not mean bringing a so-called "inner" activity to "outward" form, since there is no such thing as an inner behavior which is not in some way or another intrinsically and inextricably bound up with its outer component. When I use the term operational I mean the placement of the lifestyle content to be taught into that kind of pedagogical form which necessarily involves the actual here-and-now accomplishment of those specific behaviors that comprise the lifestyle content to be taught.[27] The lifestyle content to be taught should not be put into an abstract state such as a construct or a concept, but rather should be operationalized into demonstrable behaviors which are observable both to the learner and to the religious educator.[28]

Perhaps an illustration will shed additional light on the basic point I am making about rendering lifestyle content as fully operational as possible. Let us suppose that a religious educator wishes to teach learners the lifestyle content known as faith. Now faith is a construct and so is an abstraction. Faith is simply a logical being; it does not have any real substantive existence in itself. Faith is just a label given to a certain set of behaviors which share a common function and which have a somewhat similar orientation. To teach faith *in se* as a lifestyle content, therefore, is impossible since faith is a construct belonging to the logical order while lifestyle content *x* or *y* or *z* are activities belonging to the real order. To make faith teachable, therefore, the religious educator should isolate one or another component contained in the construct faith, and then operationalize this component by placing it into a situation in which the learner will have to perform a faith act. Since lifestyle content perforce involves the active integration of all the domains of human activity, the particular faith behavior which the learner performs must therefore include the confluent performance of all these domains as appropriate. The omission of any major human domain in the performance of the behavior will alter the character of that behavior to such an extent that its holistic lifestyle texture will be significantly reduced or even that it will cease to be a lifestyle behavior at all. In the latter instance, the desired lifestyle behavior would, in reality, be a cognitive behavior, a psychomotor behavior, or the like.

The operationalizing of lifestyle content does not take place automatically. On the contrary, the religious educator must plan, structure, and implement that kind of lesson which of itself facilitates the operationalizing of lifestyle content. Since operationalizing is typically tied in with performance, operationalized lifestyle content almost necessarily entails a performance-type curriculum, a curriculum in which the learner actually performs those lifestyle behaviors which comprise the content he is endeavoring to acquire.[29] A person learns to live a Christian lifestyle by performing those behaviors which comprise a Christian lifestyle. Conversely, a person will not learn to live a Christian lifestyle simply by cognitively reflecting on this lifestyle or just by entertaining warm feelings for this lifestyle. Contemporary social scientists as far apart theoretically as B. F. Skinner[30] and Carl Rogers[31] agree that in order to acquire a particular behavior the learner must engage in that behavior. Any successful performance of a behavior necessarily entails the inclusion of the overt dimension of that behavior, at least in pedagogical situations.[32] This theoretical statement flows not just from common sense, but from empirical research as well. Thus, for example, one review of the pertinent empirical research concludes that all in all people learn less from incidental content than from content upon which overt responses are contingent.[33]

In his religious educational ministry, Jesus the Christ exhibited a marked penchant for performance-based learning. In order to appreciate the fact that Jesus typically enacted a performance-based mode of teaching which generally included overt learner behaviors, one only has to pick up the gospels at any point one wishes and begin reading.

After I wrote this last paragraph, I picked up my bible to re-check the correctness of what I had just stated. Quite by chance I began with the fifth chapter of Matthew and ended with the eleventh. Here are a few of the many pertinent things which I found. In Matthew 7:20, Jesus makes performance the basis of the Christian lifestyle (''By their fruits they shall be known''). In social-scientific language, this sentence means that Jesus is identifying learning with performance. Possibly to reinforce, specify, and indeed operationalize the basic performance-referenced principle which he had just enunciated, Jesus immediately follows up this sentence with a statement to the effect that in order to attain salvation it is not sufficient just to verbalize "Lord, Lord"; rather, what is needed is to do or to perform God's will (7:21). Jesus seems to be so wedded to the concept that lifestyle is inseparable from performance that he explicitly frames his own personal identity as redeemer and as religious educator in overt, observable, performance terms when he responds as follows to John the Baptist's identity question: ''Go and tell John what you have seen with your own eyes and heard with your own ears, namely that the blind see, the lame walk, the lepers are healed, the deaf hear, the dead are raised to life, and the poor have the gospel preached to them'' (11:2–6). When two blind men seek to be cured, Jesus first asks them to perform an overt demonstrable, observable act of faith. When they do so, Jesus cures them (9: 27–29). When Jesus teaches people to love each other, he tells them that this love has to be put in performance terms, namely doing good deeds to those who hate them and by praying for those who insult them. The performance of these kinds of behaviors, Jesus goes on to state, is important if persons are to become true children of God (5:43– 46). In the language of religious instruction, Jesus is once again making affiliation with God contingent upon the performance of certain kinds of behaviors. In the sixth chapter of Matthew, Jesus tells people which behaviors to eschew and which behaviors to perform while praying (6:5–15). The instructions Jesus gives to the twelve apostles upon beginning their ministry (10:5–15) clearly suggest that he views the religious educator's task primarily in performance terms. Thus we read that Jesus tells the apostles that their religious education ministry consists of, among other things, the following kinds of performances: preaching the gospel, healing the sick, cleansing lepers, casting out devils, and so forth.[34]

Behavioral objectives represent *one* way in which the religious educator can effectively operationalize lifestyle content through the actual performance of lifestyle activities.[35] To be sure, behavioral objectives are often called performance objectives because they consist of the here-and-now observable and verifiable performance of one or another specific behavior. Behavioral objectives enjoy the distinct pedagogical advantage of placing the purposes and goals of a religion lesson into teachable form. An instructional purpose or goal is in itself not teachable since it typically is a religious, philosophical, or theological ideal.[36] For example, the goal of teaching the learner to love God is a religious ideal which, in itself, is not teachable. In order to render this eminently worthwhile instructional purpose or goal teachable, two processes must initially take place. First, the purpose or goal must be translated into general social-scientific form. By this I mean that the instructional purpose or goal must be fundamentally reworked in such a manner as to revolve around the twin axes of how, in general, learners learn and how, in general, teachers teach.[37] Second, the newly translated purpose or goal must then be placed into operational form. By this I mean that the instruction purpose or goal, which has already been translated into social-scientific form, must now be further refashioned in such a manner that the learners will actually perform the outcomes or behaviors which they seek to acquire. Behavioral objectives represent one way of successfully operationalizing an instructional purpose or goal. Behavioral objectives, then, are essentially statements of instructional purpose placed in operational form.[38]

Behavioral objectives enable an instructional purpose or goal to attain maximum potency precisely because behavioral objectives represent one final step in the process of converting the original purpose or goal from an abstract ideal into an actual set of behaviors which the learner can and does actually perform.[39] There are many varieties of behavioral objectives, as, for example, open objectives and closed objectives. The religious educator chooses that kind of behavioral objective which holds the greatest promise for effectively operationalizing the desired instructional purpose or goal.[40]

Laboratory for Christian Living

Thus far in this chapter I have been highlighting some major features of lifestyle content. Inserting these features into a single overall configuration, it can be said that lifestyle content is the operationalized integration of all domains of personal existence as actually performed in a holistic pattern of general activities and specific behaviors.

What constitutes the optimal set of conditions for learning Christian lifestyle content as summarized in the preceding paragraph? Put in direct pedagogical form, what kind of instructional context tends to optimally facilitate the acquisition of lifestyle content?[41] For many years now I have consistently taken the position that the most effective way to teach Christian lifestyle content is to so structure the learning situation that what eventuates is nothing less than a laboratory for Christian living.[42]

A laboratory for Christian living is that kind of structured pedagogical situation in which a learner is enabled to existentially experiment with and actually perform one or another desired lifestyle activity or lifestyle behavior.

There are at least seven major elements which go to make up a laboratory for Christian living. These elements are not wholly discrete, but overlap each other to some degree.

First, a laboratory for Christian living features concrete here-and-now performance. In the laboratory, the learner does not simply study cognitively about the Christian lifestyle or feel affectively for the Christian lifestyle. Rather, the laboratory is so structured that the learner actually performs general lifestyle activities and specific lifestyle behaviors. The laboratory enables the learner to actually and concretely "put on the new self," and to actually and concretely "do the truth." Laboratory performance is of the actual concrete lifestyle variety and not simply a cognitive or affective experience which is supposed to somehow help the learner engage in robust Christian lifestyle activities and behaviors later on outside the confines of the instructional situation. But as everyone knows, these prior cognitive and affective experiences really do not constitute an adequate or potent preparation for later lifestyle situations. Furthermore, the very fact that these cognitive and affective experiences are essentially preparatory doom such experiences at the outset to pedagogical feebleness. Real religious instruction is not a mere preparation for Christian living, but rather Christian living itself.[43] Because the laboratory is architected around the actual here-and-now performance of Christian lifestyle activities and behaviors, it possesses the inherent capacity to facilitate the transfer of Christian lifestyle learnings far more effectively than any other form of religious instruction.[44]

Second, a laboratory for Christian living necessarily involves first-hand experience. First-hand experience is primary human experience[45] and as such is of utmost significance to the personality and perceptions of the learner. If the clue to the considerable ineffectiveness of most past and present religious instruction lies in the second-handedness of the experiences it has typically provided,[46] the clue to the great potential success of the laboratory form of religious instruction lies in the immediacy and first-handedness of the experiences which it necessarily offers.

Third, a laboratory for Christian living perforce requires for its enactment the holistic integration of all the major domains of human functioning. Laboratory learning revolves around the actual living out of lifestyle content, content which of its very nature is composed of holistically integrated domains of human functioning. What laboratory learning does, therefore, is to make deliberative provision for the complete operationalization and total concretization of the holism intrinsic to lifestyle content. Furthermore, a laboratory for Christian living directly promotes the full personal extension of lifestyle content, an extension which favors the amplification of the holism which necessarily characterizes lifestyle content.

Fourth, like every laboratory, a laboratory for Christian living is typified by controlled conditions. A laboratory for Christian living does not denote a place or an actual site. Rather, a laboratory for Christian living denotes a set of controlled conditions. (The term conditions refers exclusively to those factors upon which learning depends. The term controlled conditions refers solely to the contoured and ordered character of the contingencies of learning themselves. The term controlled conditions, therefore, deals with a reality belonging to a different ontic and functional order than political power or authoritarian force.)[47] In the ultimate analysis, the term controlled conditions refers to that arrangement of teaching-learning variables which are deemed productive in terms of the successful acquisition of the desired content. Actually, of course, every instructional transaction necessarily involves some sort of controlled conditions. One of the unique features of a laboratory for Christian living is that the axis around which the controlled conditions revolve is the operationalizing of lifestyle activities and behaviors through the concrete performance of these selfsame activities and behaviors. The arrangement of the controlled conditions must be such as to allow for the enactment of the full range of possibilities inherent in the laboratory, including the fifth and sixth categories which will be discussed briefly in the following two paragraphs. A laboratory for Christian living should afford the learner the freedom to become, not in a blurred or amorphous way, but in a situation whose controlled conditions optimize the possibility of authentic personal religious growth. The various Christian liturgies of divine worship, and most especially the Catholic Mass, are fine examples of the nature and structure of laboratory controlled conditions. From the pedagogical perspective, a liturgy is a laboratory for Christian living. The instructional potential of a liturgy depends on how fully it incorporates and actualizes the major elements which comprise a laboratory for Christian living.[48]

Fifth, a laboratory for Christian living, like every laboratory worthy of the name, involves experimentation. A laboratory, be it a social laboratory or a physical laboratory, is essentially a *labora-torium*, namely a situation which features working through experimentation under controlled conditions. Experimentation is essentially a way of purposively and fruitfully discovering the truth and workability of a reality through an ongoing process of both testing the validity and workability of previous ways of doing things and trying out new ways of doing things—all through the medium of first-hand experience. Experimentation is fundamental to all worthwhile religious instruction because, as an earlier writer put it so well, ''the educational process is one of continued reorganizing, reconstructing, transforming.''[49] After all, the learning process is not a passive activity in which new content is somehow poured into the learner like water into a waiting receptacle. On the contrary, the learning process is one in which the learner actively manipulates the relevant variables[50] in such a manner that these variables are recombined into a new configuration, a configuration which is true both to the variables themselves and to the learner's own self-system. The fresher, the finer, and often the more original the new configuration, the deeper and the more personally moving will the learning process and product tend to be. Furthermore, a radical new configuration often results in radical new learning, as, for example, in the process of religious conversion. Most, though not always all, of this manipulation of variables into a new configuration occurs within the learner's own self-system. What all this means is that the learning process is inherently an ongoing act of deeply personal experimentation in which the learner, as he encounters new content, so reshapes and refashions his self-system as to incorporate this new content in a manner which is at once faithful to the ''objective'' content and authentic to his own subjective self-system. At bottom, learning means that the learner has changed, has been reconstructed. This is just as true for simple learnings as for profound ones. After learning has taken place, the learner is no longer exactly the same person he was before; he has changed to a certain extent. The degree of change is, of course, contingent upon the nature and freshness of the new configuration both objectively and subjectively. The change process, the learning process, is effected through experimentation with new content. The more a learner is personally and deeply involved with any new content, the more he will tend to experiment with it. A central purpose of a laboratory for Christian living is to provide that kind of purposive and fruitful structure which will tend to optimally promote successful experimentation with various kinds of Christian lifestyle activities and behaviors.

Sixth, a laboratory for Christian living includes the ongoing performance-based validation of Christian lifestyle activities and behaviors. The Christian lifestyle activities and behaviors which are subjected to laboratory validation include those in which the learner is presently engaged as well as those which he has newly discovered through experimentation in the laboratory. The ongoing validation of Christian lifestyle activities and behaviors is accomplished by empirically testing the processes and products of these activities and behaviors here-and-now in the laboratory situation itself. Accurate validation is possible because both the enactment and the testing of Christian lifestyle activities/behaviors occur in a situation characterized by controlled conditions. Such conditions are, of course, highly conducive and indeed in a certain sense necessary for adequate validation. Some Christian churches, notably Roman Catholicism, urge their members to validate their lifestyle activities and behaviors through a practice known as the examination of conscience. Such a practice, while commendable in many respects, nonetheless affords a less than adequate validation of the lifestyle activities and behaviors it is supposed to validate. For example, the examination of conscience is only a cognitive reflection upon lifestyle activities. Adequate validation requires that the mode of validation be of the same ontic or functional order as the reality being evaluated. Or again, the examination of conscience takes place after the performance of the original lifestyle activity or behavior, thus allowing intervening and occasionally confounding variables to inject themselves into the evaluation process. The more immediately linked the evaluation is to the reality being evaluated, the more valid the evaluation tends to be, other things being relatively equal. The laboratory for Christian living is an admirable structure for the adequate testing and evaluation of Christian lifestyle activities/behaviors because the laboratory structure inherently enables learners and significant others to evaluate lifestyle activities/behaviors in a directly lifestyle manner, and because the laboratory structure intrinsically affords the opportunity for immediate assessment. I should add that from the instructional standpoint, it is important that the results of present and newly-discovered lifestyle activities/behaviors be done in a situation characterized by controlled conditions. The pervasive presence of controlled conditions during the ongoing testing and evaluation process enables the learner not only to accurately assess the state of his Christian lifestyle activities/behaviors, but even more importantly to be able to make those kinds of fruitful adjustments which will bring his lifestyle performances to the desired level and tone.

Seventh, a laboratory for Christian living inevitably intertwines theory and practice in a mutually expansive and corrective fashion.[51] A theory is an abstraction drawn from practice. A theory is a tentative statement which attempts to make molar sense out of the practice from which it is necessarily constructed. Theory is constructed out of practice and tested by practice. Practice simply is. Practice has no meaning in itself. Without theory, practice would be meaningless and without past or present or future significance. Each learner has his own personal theory and practice of Christian lifestyle. His theory of Christian lifestyle was constructed from many sources, including parental influences, societal forces, personal interests and needs, culture, the bible, religion, theology, and first and foremost his own personal experience of living the Christian lifestyle. His practice of Christian lifestyle was conditioned by a host of factors, the two most important of which were his own theory of the ideal Christian lifestyle and his own personal experience in endeavoring to make his Christian practice congruent with this ideal theory. A laboratory for Christian living enables the learner to broaden, deepen, and in some cases to alter his theory of the ideal Christian lifestyle through here-and-now theoretical reflection upon those concrete lifestyle activities and behaviors which he is currently performing in the laboratory. Complementarily, a laboratory for Christian living directly enables the learner to broaden, deepen, and in some cases to alter his Christian lifestyle practices by more reflectively, more awaringly, and more holistically bringing them into congruence with his theory of the ideal Christian lifestyle. A laboratory is one of the few instructional situations which intrinsically provides the opportunity for the direct, immediate, and here-and-now conjunction of theory and practice in the learner's life.

My advocacy of a laboratory for Christian living as an ideal situation to intentionally teach lifestyle activities and behaviors is drawn from many sources.[52] Though they typically did not use the term "laboratory for Christian living," many Christian religious leaders proposed and in some cases established educational milieux which incorporated many of the features of a laboratory situation. For example, Benedict of Nursia (c.480 − c.546), the founder of monasticism in the West, regarded the monastery as "a school for the Lord's service," that is to say, a school for sanctity. (One serves the Lord best by being holy and following the Lord's way.)[53] Some of the most outstanding educational reformers in the modern era transformed the traditional cognitive-based, transmissionist-oriented schools into laboratory situations. Foremost among these individuals were the Swiss educationist Johann Pestalozzi (1746–1827),[54] the German educationist Friedrich Froebel (1782–1852),[55] the Italian educationist Maria Montessori (1870–1952),[56] and the American educationist John Dewey (1859–1952)[57]

To some people the word laboratory connotes an essentially cold and antiseptic atmosphere, one which is inimical to personal expression and human activity. To be sure, this kind of cold and antiseptic atmosphere is characteristic of certain kinds of laboratories in some of the natural sciences, notably in particular sectors of biology and chemistry. However, the kind of laboratory I am advocating is by intrinsic necessity anything but cold and antiseptic. Owing to its definition and nature, a laboratory for Christian living is a social situation, a situation which necessarily involves the widest possible range of personal expression and human authority. A laboratory for Christian living is not some sort of huge hermetically-sealed enclosure. On the contrary, a laboratory for Christian living is a purposively oriented situation in which learners personalistically try on various kinds of lifestyle behaviors, experiment with those behaviors which seem to hold developmental promise, perform various lifestyle behaviors, and finally verify them in terms of both their own personal lives and the ideal Christian lifestyle.

A laboratory for Christian living is essentially a clinical situation.

But it must be emphasized that a clinical situation is not one in which personal expression and free human activity are necessarily reduced or altogether eliminated.[58] Rather, a clinical situation is one in which the major independent variables are so controlled as to allow for a relatively unimpeded examination and concomitant/subsequent performance of desired activities or behaviors. A clinical situation exists precisely to enable the independent variable—dependent variable relationship (cause-effect) to come into clear, unimpeded, and accurate view. Clinical social laboratories are growing in number and effectiveness, especially in counseling and psychotherapeutic situations. Such social laboratories which are essentially clinical situations include pyschodrama, encounter groups, Esalen-type workshops, and the like. Surely clinical laboratories like these are not cold situations in which personal expression is dampened and free human activity expunged. Indeed, one prevalent criticism of the above-mentioned clinical laboratories is that they encourage too much personal expression and human activity.

Nothing in life is irrelevant to a person's overall religious education. To be sure, each person learns a great deal from situations and from events which lie outside the sphere of religious instruction per se. But life experience does not necessarily produce desirable religious outcomes in an individual. Even in those instances in which life experience does yield desirable religious outcomes, it may not do so in the most effective or efficient manner.[59] The supreme advantage of religious instruction is that it directly and purposively seeks to facilitate the acquisition of desired religious outcomes in the most effective and efficient manner possible. Religious instruction fulfills this task by selecting, organizing, and deploying life experiences in a relatively focused manner so as to achieve a definitive educative purpose. Religious instruction constitutes a planned, systematic, and deliberative activity which has as its main overall goal the sharpening, the codification, and the enhancement of the educational process. Purposiveness and intentionality lie at the heart of the teaching endeavor. The presence of controlled conditions goes a long way to insure that a pedagogical situation will optimize the actualization of purposiveness and intentionality, and thus render the situation as instructionally fruitful as possible. The more that a teaching activity becomes a clinical situation with controlled conditions, the more effective it is able to become. The structural tightness or fluidity of the controlled conditions vary in direct proportion to the nature and contours of the learning objective sought. In a clinical situation such as a laboratory for Christian living in which lifestyle outcomes are sought, there will be varying degrees of structural tightness or fluidity. Let me use the home to illustrate this point. The home is, par excellence, a clinical situation involving controlled conditions. Exemplary Christian homes are exemplary precisely because they are built around controlled conditions which are purposively ordered toward the attainment of Christian learning outcomes. The parents vary the tightness or fluidity of the controlled conditions according to the kind of desired learning outcome, the present developmental state of the child, and so forth. One outstanding feature of a home is that, more than any other situation, it permits and indeed encourages full personal expression and free human activity of its members.

The Direct Teaching of Lifestyle Content

Can a lifestyle content be taught directly? Is it possible for a lifestyle content to be a consequence of a particular pedagogical activity?[60] Or can a lifestyle content only be indirectly caught and never directly taught?

The answer to these questions is simple. A lifestyle outcome cannot be directly taught when the substantive content and/or the structural content of the teaching act are ontically different or pedagogically disjointed from the desired lifestyle outcome.[61] For example, a teaching act which employs lecture/telling, discussion, action-reflection, and the like, can never directly yield a lifestyle outcome because its substantive content is almost exclusively verbal and cognitive, while its structural content centers primarily on the teacher and on one aspect of the subject matter. However, a lifestyle outcome can be directly taught when both the substantive content and the structural content of the teaching act are ontically similar and pedagogically connected to these outcomes. The structured-learning-situation strategy in general,[62] and the laboratory for Christian living in particular, represent concrete examples of the ontic and pedagogical meshing of that kind of holistic substantive content and structural content which are intrinsically tied in with lifestyle outcomes.

It is imperative for the successful teaching of lifestyle outcomes that both the substantive content and the structural content of the lesson are such as to be ontically and pedagogically related to these outcomes as

directly and as immediately as possible. This important point is sometimes not grasped by advocates of the theological approach to religious
instruction. Thus, for example, Ferdinand Kopp argues that while the
substantive content of religion teaching should be kept cognitive and
verbal and theological, the structural content should be congruent with
that of a laboratory for Christian living. Speaking specifically of religion teaching in a formal setting, Kopp writes: "The school can
become a laboratory of social awareness, not through the instruction
itself, but through the very method of instruction. It should become the
school of living together."[63] What Kopp fails to realize is that in the
religious instruction act itself, substantive content and structural content are of a piece. If the substantive content and the structural content
are thrusted in opposite directions, then one will win out over the
other, or pedagogical chaos will ensue. Furthermore, in the religious
instruction act itself, substantive content and structural content lose
whatever ontic separateness they might once have had and become
mediated into a new entity, namely the religious instruction act.[64]
Thus it is ontically impossible for any effective religious instruction act
to have a substantive content which is incongruous with or contrary to
structural content.[65]

If Christian lifestyle is to be taught directly, then the substantive
content must necessarily consist of Christian living itself. Each lesson
or series of lessons ought to embody one or more specific aspects of
Christian living. Thus the substantive content of the lifestyle-oriented
religion lesson is not talking about or reflecting on Christian living, but
actually engaging in one or another dimension of Christian living
itself. The substantive content of many traditional religion lessons has
all too often been existentially alien to daily Christian living, or at least
existentially estranged from it. Small wonder that such lessons have
not been successful in directly effecting Christian lifestyle outcomes.
If a religion lesson is to directly teach the Christian lifestyle, its substantive content must be such as to constitute an inseparable part of
daily Christian living.

Great attention must also be paid to structural content if a religion
lesson is to directly yield Christian living outcomes. Pedagogical procedure is of utmost importance in the facilitation of learning. Yet
pedagogical procedure is perhaps the area to which religious educationists and educators, notably those adhering to the theological approach to religious instruction, have accorded the least attention.[66]

Pedagogical procedure is what makes learning directly happen. As such, pedagogical procedure is necessarily directed to persons. To be sure, pedagogical procedure intrinsically concerns that which happens to persons. It sets up conditions of learning which may be religious and growth-producing, or which may be harmful to personal development and holistic Christian living.[67] If a religion lesson is to effectively teach the Christian lifestyle directly, then it must incorporate as fully as possible all four major variables involved in a pedagogical situation, namely the teacher, the learner, the subject-matter content, and the environment. Though the environment has been shown to be very powerful in directly producing a wide range of learnings including lifestyle behaviors, nonetheless religious educationists by and large have grossly neglected it, at best contenting themselves with a comment or two here and there.[68] To teach lifestyle directly and effectively, the environment should be architected in such a manner that its elements are oriented in a functional fashion,[69] namely thrusted toward the direct facilitation of lifestyle outcomes. The environment exerts a profound impact on the human being in all his dimensionalities, including psychomotor, cognition, and affect.[70] In this connection Neil Postman and Charles Weingartner integrate empirical research with philosophical theorizing in stating that "the most important impressions made on a human nervous system come from the character and structure of the environment within which the nervous system functions; the environment itself conveys the critical and dominant messages by controlling the perceptions and attitudes of those who participate in it. Dewey stressed that the role an individual is assigned in an environment—what he is permitted to do—is what the individual learns. In other words, the medium itself, i.e., the environment, is the message. "Message here means the perceptions you are allowed to build, the attitudes you are enticed to assume, the sensitivities you are encouraged to develop—all of the things you learn to see and feel and value. You learn them because your environment is organized in such a way that it permits or encourages or insists that you learn them."[71] John Dewey notes that lifestyle behaviors, like cognitive and affective behaviors, cannot be hammered in or plastered on to a person. Rather, Dewey states, the environment in which a person lives and learns directly leads that person to live one way rather than another, to feel one way rather than another, to think one way rather than another. The environment strengthens some behaviors and weakens others. Thus the environment gradually produces in an individual a certain system of conduct, a certain disposition of action.[72] In the specific zone of religious instruction, Maria Harris lends her support to the contention that the environment itself can educate if properly set up. Harris also endorses the view that a great deal of conscious and deliberative care must take place while structuring a pedagogical environment so that the environment can itself directly engage all phases of the learner's personal existence, especially the more profound religious dimensionalities.[73]

Throughout my professional career I have repeatedly asserted as a pedagogical dictum that anything which can be learned can be directly taught, and furthermore, anything which has been learned at one time or another has been directly taught at one time or another. The empirical research evidence on the teaching-learning process, regardless of the setting in which this process occurs, lends ample confirmation to my dictum.

The Importance of Lifestyle Content

Of all the substantive contents of religious instruction, surely lifestyle is the most important. Lifestyle is simultaneously a substantive content in its own right and the functional coordination of all the other substantive contents. It is a substantive content in its own right because it possesses its own distinctive structure and set of operations. It is the functional coordination of all the other substantive contents because it is in and through lifestyle that all the other substantive contents are actualized. There is a certain wisdom in the question which seems so superficial at first sight: "How do I know what I think, and how do I sense what I feel, until I do what I do?"

The supreme importance of lifestyle fundamentally lies in the fact that lifestyle is what a person really is. Interestingly enough, the contrary philosophical positions of being-ism and becoming-ism both agree with the foregoing statement, though each from its own basically distinctive vantage point. The being-ists hold that function necessarily follows being[74] in the sense that a person cannot act other than what he is. For their part, the becoming-ists typically reject metaphysical essences such as human nature or "being," asserting instead that a person's activities are in fact his very self.[75]

In the twentieth century, and especially in the second half of the twentieth century, the tremendous overarching importance of lifestyle in human existence has come to be explicitly recognized. Much of the stress on lifestyle can be traced to the prevailing zeitgeist of that century, a zeitgeist which, in Quentin Lauer's felicitous phrase, can be termed "the triumph of subjectivity."[76]

The emphasis on heightened subjectivity and individualistic lifestyle is especially pronounced in Existentialism, a philosophical movement which has exerted considerable influence on life, education, religion, and theology. For the Existentialist, the purpose of all life and education is personal authenticity, the here-and-now fulfillment of all that I am. A person is authentic only to the extent that he *is,* only to the extent that he actualizes his existence in lifestyle activities. A person first is; only in living out his personal existence authentically can he later define who he is.[77] In a large sense, the Existentialists treat the verb "to be" as transitive.[78] Thus Existentialists decry as obscene any attempt to separate cognition, affect, or psychomotor activities from the process of living. A person is, a person engages in the process of living, a person becomes authentic, only to the extent to which he makes free personal choices. If René Descartes could declare: "I think, therefore I am," the Existentialists can affirm: "I choose, therefore I am." Martin Buber, a leading religious Existentialist, puts it this way: "And if there were a devil it would not be one who decided against God, but one who, in eternity, came to no decision."[79] In Existentialism, choice and existence are not static but are perpetually in the process of becoming. This ongoing process of becoming is not somehow separate or distinct from the person's here-and-now existence, but rather is his lifestyle, is his series of free personal choices and acts of decision. A person becomes himself by living a lifestyle in one or another concrete existential situation, a situation which, though connected to other individuals and things, nonetheless is primarily personal and private.

The overall substantive content of religious instruction is religion. The essence of religion in itself is lifestyle. Though persons and groups in different eras and cultures emphasize one or another fundamental feature of religion, all agree that religion is first and foremost a matter of lifestyle. In a multivolume work on the history of comparative religion, Giuseppe Messina and Ugo Bianchi assert that religion as lived/felt/conceptualized in various eras and cultures has not been a cognitive-based one, that is to say a religion of the personalistically sterile rationalistic type. Nor has religion in various societies throughout the ages been an affectively-based one, that is to say a religion which is simply an expression of free-floating unrealistic sentiment. Rather, as evinced throughout the world during all the millenia of human existence, religion has consisted in a person's holistic encounter with a sacred reality or what is perceived to be a sacred reality. This holistic encounter has been of such a nature that the individual is thereby empowered to successfully mesh the temporal and the spiritual into a united overall way of life which the religionist can and should live. In all major religions throughout the history of the world, the cognitive, affective, and psychomotor domains are inserted into a comprehensive lifestyle. Ritual, cult, or liturgy have been classically regarded as especially focused and enriched forms of this lifestyle.[80] Another scholarly examination of comparative religion down through the ages concludes by noting that religion has always shown itself to be fundamentally concerned with lifestyle. This study asserts that religion has never been so much a matter of organization, not so much a set of cognitive doctrines, but instead the adherence to a certain pattern of lifestyle activities which were advocated and inspired by great religious personages.[81]

Comparative Religion. As I have shown elsewhere,[82] every universal religion accords primacy of place to lifestyle. Indeed, lifestyle is probably the most ecumenical feature of religion since each and every universal religion, regardless of its beliefs, places lifestyle at the center of its system.

Hinduism, the oldest of extant universal religions, attaches supreme importance to lifestyle. Hinduism is so lifestyle-oriented that it is at home with almost any cognitive religious doctrine, no matter how diverse. For Hinduism, lifestyle is directly tied in with selfless love, with emptying oneself of worldly attachments, and with coming purely into union with the Brahman.

Zen Buddhism is essentially a purposeful and controlled religious lifestyle. "Like all true teachers [Buddha] does not wish to impart an opinion, but to teach the way."[83] Zen is not a revelation of enlightenment (*satori*), but rather a way to enlightenment. The lifestyle of Zen is such as to help the individual existentially break through the inherently tangled web of his cognitive rationality so as to arrive at the personal intuitive experience of the seamless fabric of all reality.

Islam is so deeply meshed with personal lifestyle that very few individuals convert from it to other religions. In Arabic, Islam means surrender. A person whose lifestyle is deliberately geared toward surrender to God in Islam is a Muslim, an Arabic word which means a person who has surrendered himself to God. This surrender is total in that it takes place in every phase of the individual's personal and social life. That Islamic law (*shari'ah*) is lifestyle-grounded can be immediately appreciated by looking at the word itself. In Arabic, *shari'ah* means "the way leading to the watering place."

Judaism is fundamentally a religion of the *Torah,* which is to say it is basically a lifestyle-centered religion. For Judaism, all life is basically a convenant relationship with God if that life is to be considered a religious one. The *Torah* sets forth the spirit, goal, and specifications whereby the Jew is to live that kind of lifestyle which is faithful to this covenant relationship. Official, rabbinically-defined law is *halakhah,* whose etymological root means to go on or to follow a certain lifestyle. *Halakhah* is thus congruent with the lifestyle emphasis of the *Torah,* as, for example, in Exodus 18:20: "Teach them the statutes and the decisions; show them the way they must follow and the work they must do."

Christianity is first and foremost a lifestyle-centered religion. It is a religion of doing God's will in all areas of one's here-and-now life.[84] It is a religion of the cross; thus Christianity involves a life of sacrifice,[85] a life in which a person's lifestyle and not just his words are crucified with Jesus unto salvation.[86] It is a religion in which a person through his lifestyle participates, as appropriate, in the redemptive mission of Jesus[87] and in so doing works out his own salvation.[88] Christianity is the living relationship a person has with God[89] through the man Jesus who is of the Godhead; this intersubjective relationship suggests that grace is a lifestyle force and thus is expressed better in existential lifestyle terms than in predicamental cognitive terms.[90] Grace is the power which transforms a person's daily living, a fact which is especially pointed and manifest in the sacraments.[91]

The gospels clearly show the primacy which Jesus accorded to lifestyle content. Over and over again Jesus stressed the centrality of lifestyle content both in his own life and in the religion which he was establishing.

The principal function of Jesus' mission on earth belonged not to preaching the good news but to living a certain kind of lifestyle, namely that of doing the Father's will (Jn. 4:34). This lifestyle, this ceaseless working to accomplish the Father's will, formed the axis and the supreme criterion for all Jesus' decisions and actions (see, for example, Mk. 14:36). Since the Father's will is ordained toward the redemption and sanctification of fallen human beings, the lifestyle which Jesus adopts is that of the good shepherd who lays down his life for his sheep (Jn. 10:11–18).

If any person desires to adopt the religion Jesus advocates, he must first and foremost adopt a special lifestyle. "If anyone wishes to be my servant, he must follow my way" (Jn. 12:26), that is to say, adopt Jesus' lifestyle as far as possible. To adopt the lifestyle of Jesus means to renounce one's life for the sake of Jesus (Mt. 10:39). Such renunciation occurs primarily by orienting one's lifestyle in such a fashion as to do God's will. To do God's will one must lovingly keep the commandments (Jn. 14:15) and, in short, take up one's cross and follow Jesus (Mt. 16:24)—surely a matter, basically, of lifestyle. Jesus repeatedly indicated that anyone who does not take up the cross and adopt the lifestyle he proposed is neither worthy of him nor can be a true follower of his. The fundamental message of Jesus is this: Repent, change your lifestyle, live the good news which I am bringing you and indeed which I myself am. The sayings of Jesus basically deal with the centrality of lifestyle, as for example the beatitudes (Lk. 6:20–26). The beatitudes are all about lifestyle. Most parables have lifestyle as their core and thrust, as, for example, the parable of the prodigal son (Lk. 15:18–32), the wise and foolish virgins (Mt. 25:1–13), the good Samaritan (Lk. 10:3–37), the talents (Mt. 25:14–30), the wicked vinedressers (Mk. 12:1–12), Lazarus and the rich man (Lk. 16:19–31), the sower (Lk. 8:4–15), to name just a few.

The Ancient Church and the Catechumenate. Perhaps the principal reason why the writings, the attitudes, the thoughts, and most especially the practices of Christians in the apostolic and subapostolic periods are considered to be so crucially important is that these ancient Christians were in closer temporal contact with Jesus and with the original apostles than has been the case with Christians of other eras. Owing to their close temporal proximity to Jesus and to the original apostles, the first Christians were in a uniquely favored position to know and appreciate the genuine essence and true spirit of their new religion. In those early days, Christianity was known as "the Way,"[92] and the early Christians were called "the followers of the Way." Indeed, one writer asserts that before Christianity was known as Christianity or as anything else, it was known as "the Way."[93] "The

Way'' is obviously a term which indicates that the first Christians regarded their new religion as fundamentally a special lifestyle, a lifestyle to be followed in daily life.

Another especially clear evidence of the basic and all-encompassing lifestyle thrust of Christianity in the early church is that of the catechumenate.[94] In a historical account of the origins and development of the catechumenate in the ancient church, Michel Dujarier takes pains to categorically affirm that the catechumenate was essentially a preparation period for Baptism, a period which was deliberately structured to afford the catechumen both the time and the opportunity to effectively change his personal lifestyle in such a manner as to become congruent with the ideal Christian lifestyle. Only when the catechumen's lifestyle came into adequate alignment with the ideal Christian lifestyle would he be allowed to receive Baptism.[95] Dujarier's view is supported by Tertullian who regards the catechumenate as a lifestyle journey to Baptism. In Tertullian's view, the catechumenal journey consists primarily of learning, leading, and improving one's own Christian lifestyle positively by performing good deeds and negatively by eliminating evil behavior through the practice of penance, mortification, and suffering.[96] The early Fathers of the church typically[97] did not regard Baptism as itself bestowing a Christian lifestyle on the recipient; rather, by means of the catechumenate, the future recipient would first learn and then concretely demonstrate a lifestyle congruent with the ideal Christian lifestyle.[98]

The origins of the catechumenate can be traced back to the days of the original apostles. Paul mentions it briefly in one of his letters (Gal. 6:6). Justin Martyr (c. 114–165) highlights the basic lifestyle character of the catechumenate when he states that in the catechumenate it was customary to insert cognitive content into the larger lifestyle matrix of prayer and fasting. Indeed, the faithful prayed and fasted with the catechumens. The goal of all this, Justin declares, is that the catechumens learn to live the Christian lifestyle.[99]

The earliest forms of the catechumenate were nonecclesiastical. In other words, the origins and earliest development of the catechumenate lay principally in the domain of private initiative, with the teachers being predominantly lay persons rather than either clergy or laymen appointed or approved by the *ecclesiasticum*.[100] By the end of the second century, the *ecclesiasticum*, recognizing the tremendous importance of the catechumenate, brought this ancient mode of religious instruction under its control and put it into an organizational format. Jean Daniélou and Henri Marrou observe that the catechumenate was one of the very first ecclesial activities which the *ecclesiasticum* put under its direct control, a development of great significance when one recalls that during this time Christianity had no civil status and suffered persecution intermittantly.[101]

By the time the third century had rolled around, there was a more-or-less full-blown catechumenate under formal ecclesiastical control. The *Apostolic Tradition*[102] written by Hippolytus (c. 170 − c. 235) gives a reasonably detailed description of how the catechumenate operated.[103] According to the *Apostolic Tradition,* the catechumenate of that era was lifestyle-oriented through and through. Before a person was even allowed to enter the catechumenate, that individual had to present to ecclesiastical leaders one or more Christian acquaintances. The Christian acquaintance(s) vouched personally for the integrity of the applicant's lifestyle and for the sincerity of his motives for wishing to become a Christian. To back up this testimony with lifestyle deeds, the Christian acquaintance(s) served as spiritual guarantor(s) for the applicant.[104] Following the testimony of the Christian acquaintance(s), the ecclesiastical leaders carefully interrogated the applicant on his motives for wishing to become a Christian and on his present way of life—whether he was free or slave, married or single, and if married whether his way of life was generally compatible with the Christian view of marriage. If the applicant was in an occupation which clashed with leading a Christian lifestyle, then such an individual had to leave that occupation.

Generally the catechumenate lasted three years. However, because the catechumenate was lifestyle-directed and lifestyle-validated, the actual length of time that a learner spent in the catechumenate tended to vary, since some individuals acquired the desired lifestyle behaviors faster than others.[105]

Though the catechumenate did indeed contain a certain amount of cognitive material, nonetheless the purpose, context, and goal of the catechumenate was unquestionably that of lifestyle content. Thus Josef Jungmann states that the cognitive content taught during the catechumenate revolved around those books of the bible and those cognitive doctrines which manifest with special pointedness the basic principles of the Christian lifestyle.[106] Indeed, the cognitive content was taught in such a manner as (1) to intellectually elucidate the meaning of the Christian lifestyle which the catechumens were supposed to be learning and practicing, and (2) to be inserted as immediately and as relevantly as possible into their present lifestyle pattern so as to help bring that lifestyle pattern into greater compatibility with the ideal Christian lifestyle. Given the religious fervor characteristically present in early Christianity, the cognitive content in the catechumenate was probably admixed with a great deal of affectivity, as, for example, by spiritual exhortations, and the like. It should be emphasized that the cognitive content taught in the catechumenate was rather rudimentary as a general rule. Most of the early Christians, both catechumens and teachers alike, were illiterate and not at all intellectual in orientation. It would be false Hollywood-style romanticism to regard every catechumen as an incipient doctoral student and every religious educator as another Origen or Tertullian.

The nerve center, heart, and blood vessels of the catechumenate from top to bottom was lifestyle content. The structure and operation of the catechumenate clearly indicate that the early church regarded all nonlifestyle content, including cognitive doctrine, as ultimately useless in itself. The catechumen had to demonstrate by visible general activities and specific observable behaviors that he had learned that kind of lifestyle content regarded by the *ecclesiasticum* as directly Christian, imbued with Christianity, or at least compatible with the Christian way of life. The catechumenate was definitely a performance curriculum with respect to lifestyle. When, and only when, the catechumen had consistently demonstrated Christian lifestyle activities and behaviors over a long period of time could he take his "final examination," graduate from the catechumenate, and enter the period of immediate preparation for Baptism.[107] The "final examination" was an assessment of the activities and concrete behaviors which the catechumens had actually performed during their catechumenate. This "final examination," then, was not so much concerned with the cognitive content which the catechumens acquired[108] as it was concerned with, in the words of the *Apostolic Tradition,* "whether they lived a devout Christian life, whether they honored widows, visited the sick, and practiced all good works."[109]

When Christianity acquired civil legal status in the fourth century, and when huge numbers of people subsequently began to convert, it became increasingly difficult to retain the catechumenate in its pristine form. In the sixth century adult baptism became a rarity, and the catechumenate began to wane. In the Middle Ages, the catechumenate disappeared entirely, only to be revived in the early 1960s.[110]

Religion and Theology. Like the ancient church, the Christian churches of today typically affirm the superiority of lifestyle content over other kinds of content, including cognitive content. Thus the churches of the modern era are virtually unanimous in asserting that it is better to live a Christian lifestyle than merely to think about a Christian lifestyle. But when they attempt to make theology the norm for Christianity, these selfsame Christian churches directly violate their unequivocal assertion about the supremacy of lifestyle content over cognitive content. Religion is first and foremost lifestyle content with, of course, the other substantive contents admixed as well. Theology, on the other hand, is simply cognitive verbal content. On both the logical ground of consistency and the existential ground of wholeness, it is religion, not theology, which constitutes the only true and valid norm for Christianity. After all, Christianity is a religion having a theology, not a theology having a religion. Christian doctrine whole and entire is lived religion, and lived religion is heavily lifestyle in nature and operation. Cognitive doctrine forms only one aspect of Christian doctrine whole and entire. Theology is simply a cognitive interpretation of religion. Because it is a cognitive interpretation, theology is perforce tentative and admissible of error. Religion lived in good conscience is never tentative and never in personal error.

Historically speaking, the development of every single cognitive doctrine in the church has followed and not preceded ecclesial religious lifestyle. The supreme struggle of theology as a cognitive dimension of church doctrine is to remain faithful to the church's lived experience. The church in its lived experience has no need to conform to any theology; rather it is the task and the duty of theology to conform to the church's lived experience.[111] The church's ecclesial lifestyle, not theology, is normative. So often in the past, and in the present as well, theology has been somewhat removed from the church's lived experience, or even has gone counter to it. Small wonder, then, that one or another theology has grievously erred and in some cases has even led people away from true religious living. Jesus promised to be with the church in its lived experience for all time; he did not promise to be with its theology for all time.

Because the Christian religion is so lifestyle-soaked, no one particular type of theory is sufficient to explain it. Because theology constitutes only one particular type of theory, it can explain religion from only one vantage point. Theology views religion from one perspective only. Other kinds of theories look at religion from other perspectives, perspectives which offer substantially different but complementary insights into the nature and workings of the Christian religion. Such theories include psychology, sociology, education, aesthetics, politics, and the like.[112] To reduce the explanation of religion solely to one perspective, be this perspective theological theory or psychological theory or whatever, necessarily results in a distorted, narrow view of religion.

The Bible. In encountering the bible, one is repeatedly struck by the fact that it is a thoroughly lifestyle-oriented book. The bible is lifestyle-oriented in terms of what it states, in terms of what it advocates, and in terms of the eternally living form of its revelatory character. First and foremost, the bible is a book of religious lifestyle, religious experience, and religious instruction.

Over and over again the bible identifies itself with divinely approbated religious lifestyle. When making the point that the bible is at once living and geared to lifestyle, biblical scholars frequently cite Hebrews 4:12: "The word of God is alive and active. It cuts more sharply than a two-edged sword, piercing as far as the zone where life and spirit, joints and marrow, divide. It sifts every thought and every design of the heart." Commenting on the relevance of this passage, Luis Alonso Schökel states: "In the original Greek of this passage, the word 'alive' or 'living' is in the emphatic position as the first word of the sentence somewhat rhetorically as 'Living is the word of God and active.' It is living, as God is the living God, and its activity is the actualization of the power of God: it penetrates into the most intimate depths of a being, reaching that mysterious point of our vital and psychic principle which is touched and permeated by the Spirit. From within, it can judge and condemn because it forces man to take a position, to make a decision. . . . Let us look again at the four descriptive words used in the passage to characterize the word of God: alive, active, cutting, piercing."[113]

The letters of Paul the Apostle are replete with exhortations to his readers and listeners to adopt and improve on a Christian lifestyle. Anent this point, Kōshi Usami makes a careful analysis of the Greek words for walk (*peripatein*) and way (*hodos*) with respect to how both these words are central to the Letter to the Ephesians, with respect to how these two words are linguistically employed in this epistle, and with respect to how these two words as used in the epistle relate to their usage in the Greek of that time. As a result of his scholarly investigation, Usami concludes that the word walk (*peripatein*) as used in the Letter to the Ephesians definitely means a way of living, and that the verbal image of the way (*hodos*) constitutes a linguistic synthesis of several word groups related to a generalized pattern of living. Usami also shows that the verbal image of the way is a prominent feature of the Old Testament where it typically refers to a virtuous lifestyle or to an iniquitous lifestyle.[114]

In many of his letters, Paul highlights the theme of justification by faith. But as Joachim Jeremias points out, it is dangerous for us to attempt to reduce justification to an isolated act of God or to an isolated reception by the person of God's forgiveness. Rather, as Jeremias states, Paul views justification in a broadly lifestyle context. Like all God's totally gracious actions with humanity, justification occurs within the framework of a person's pattern of living, a pattern which includes the sacraments and good works and which is characterized by faith and hope and charity.[115]

The bible is past and present divine revelation. As past revelation, the bible is the historical account of the ways in which people of ancient times met the revealing God in their own experience.[116] As present revelation, the bible is the ongoing divine disclosure which takes place when a person meets in his own experience the aforementioned account of the ways in which people of bygone days met the revealing God in their own experience. Past biblical revelation occurred in the then-and-there lifestyle of the inspired writers of former millenia, while present biblical revelation occurs in the here-and-now lifestyle of persons today. It is past revelation living in present revelation which makes the scriptures, in the words of the Apostle Paul, "the saving power of God for everyone who has faith" (Rom. 1:16). It is past revelation living in present revelation which inbues the bible with "the power to effectively touch each person where that person is developmentally in his own immediate concrete existential situation."[117]

The thoroughgoing lifestyle character of the bible can be further appreciated when this inspired book is compared to the sacred writings of other major religions of the the ancient world.[118] God's actions as recounted in the bible take place in the full flush of personally lived experience and actual human history. God's actions are witnessed to by flesh-and-blood human beings living lives quite similar to the narrators of biblical history. The actions of the gods as recounted in the sacred writings of other religions are couched in mythic terms, terms which, though rich in meaning, nevertheless stand in sharp contrast to the tremendously human lifestyle terms in which the biblical narrative is framed. The geographical locus of divine action also differs markedly in the sacred writings of other major ancient religions as compared to the bible. In the sacred scriptures of other ancient religions, divine action takes place in some far-away territory, some never-seen land, the other side of the heavens or the recesses of the deep, some sacred and inaccessible domain belonging to the gods alone. In the bible, on the other hand, the geographical locus for divine action takes place on very familiar ground: the land of Egypt, the desert of Arabia, and especially in the valleys and hilltops and cities and villages of the ancient near East. To be sure, the inspired biblical writers link the sites of God's action with places well known to their audience at that time, namely the ancient sanctuaries of Bethel, Hebron, and the like; the cities of Jerusalem and Jericho, and so forth; the river Jordan, and the wadies and the wells, the groves, and the high places which are still an intimate part of the everyday life of the population of that area. In short, the action of God as recounted in the bible occurs in realistic concrete immediate lifestyle activities of actual historical human beings, and thus stand in contrast to the picture of the workings of the gods as delineated in many of the holy writings of other ancient religions.

The core message of virtually all the biblical figures who were aligned with God was basically the same, namely the reformation and improvement of people's religious lifestyle. Let us take the prophets of Israel as an illustration of this point. The fundamental message of the prophets, as Gerhard von Rad notes, was not that of presenting old or even new cognitive doctrine for the sake of developing fresh theological insights or of correcting some defective points in the already existing theology of that time. Rather, the basic message of the prophets was specifically targeted toward the societal lifestyle of Israel and toward the individual lifestyles of the Israelites at a certain time and in a certain situation.[119] A great deal of the relevance of the message of the Israelite prophets for today's world derives from the fact that our modern societal and individual lifestyles are just as disoriented from

God as were the societal and individual lifestyles which the prophets encountered in their day.

The lifestyle which Jesus lived and advocated is a holistic one.[120] He sharply underscored his own command that his followers adopt a holistic religious lifestyle by pointing to the Pharisees whose lifestyle was lopsided and hence not holistic. The lifestyle of the Pharisees was excoriated by Jesus as one consisting primarily of external show buttressed by cognitive doctrine and interpenetrated with cognitive interpretation of the law. Jesus stood squarely for a holistic religious lifestyle which includes not only a cognitive grasp of reality, but also proper underlying motives and attitudes, and conduct manifested in observable form.[121] Furthermore, the holistic lifestyle which Jesus advocated was highly personalistic in that it has as its axis the establishment and continuance of a personal relationship with him.[122]

The bible, then, is really the record of progressive and continuing revelation through and in and for the lifestyle of individuals and societies. This nuclear fact contains within it serious and far-reaching consequences for both biblical theology and for religious instruction.

Biblical revelation through and in and for lifestyle is a crucial fact for biblical theology[123] because it enables the bible to be approached as a living open book rather than a fossilized record. Otto Kaiser put it this way: "As long as the church held to the belief that revelation was a firmly delimited, eternally valid event which took place in the inspiration of a book, it could not direct its attention primarily towards clarifying the history of revelation, but only towards demonstrating its freedom from contradiction, perspicuity, and intelligibility to the ordinary man."[124] Biblical revelation through and in and for lifestyle is a fructifying fact for religious instruction because it indicates that faithful teaching of the bible for religious instruction purposes is optimally done through and in and for lifestyle.[125] To teach the bible biblically is to effect a synapse between the lifestyles recorded in the bible and the lifestyles of the here-and-now learners, and between the lifestyle which *is* the bible and the lifestyles of the here-and-now learners. To teach the bible biblically is to place the text and context of the sacred text into interactive existential relationship with the learners.[126] The métier of the bible is religious experience and lifestyle. It is precisely this existential métier which forms the ground common both to the bible in its authenticity and to the learners in their authenticity. If the bible is to be taught in a way which is fundamentally true to itself, namely a book which is soaked with lifestyle and religious experience, then it is incumbent upon the religious educator when teaching the bible to use that kind of substantive content and structural content which is holistically experiential and which revolves around lifestyle. Empirical studies have amply demonstrated that the bible cannot be successfully taught as experience and as lifestyle when the substantive content of such pedagogy is not primarily lifestyle and holistically experiential, as for example when teaching the bible from a totally cognitive perspective.[127] It is pedagogical folly to expect that people will learn to act biblically from just reading the bible or simply from reflecting cognitively on the bible. People learn to act biblically by doing the bible holistically in their own personal experience and lives.[128]

Religious educators should be particularly at home with the bible not simply because sacred scripture is a prime foundation of their personal Christian lives, but also because it is a religious instruction book.[129] Though theologians properly use it as a touchstone and as a mine for theologizing, the bible is not a book of theology. Rather, the bible is preeminently a religious instruction book. After all, sacred scripture simultaneously consists of God presently teaching every person who encounters it, and the history of how and when and where God taught his people in the past. That the bible is primarily a religious instruction book and not a theological treatise (or a political treatise or an economic treatise) is a fact recognized from the dawn of Christianity to the present day. Thus the Apostle Paul remarks: "Every inspired scripture has for its use teaching the truth and refuting error, or for reformation of manners and discipline in right living, so that every man who belongs to God may be efficient and equipped for good work of every kind" (2 Tim. 3:16–17). Augustine writes that the Spirit of God who spoke through the holy authors of the bible was unwilling to teach human beings those things which could not somehow be profitable to their salvation.[130] Thomas Aquinas holds the same view: "The Spirit did not wish to tell us through the authors whom he inspired any other truth than that which is profitable for our salvation."[131] In our own day, the esteemed biblical theologian R. A. F. McKenzie writes that though the bible contains material from which theology can be educed, nonetheless taken as a whole the bible is not a book of theology.[132]

If the bible is preeminently a religious instruction book rather than a theology book, and if the bible is taught in a manner fundamentally in keeping with its basic nature and purpose, then the bible should be taught primarily as religion rather than primarily as theology.[133] Religion is above all a lifestyle affair (as contrasted to theology which is above all a cognitive affair). Consequently, any authentic teaching of the bible which is to be in congruence with the essential spirit and goals of the bible must perforce be done in a decidedly lifestyle fashion for decidedly lifestyle objectives. Teaching the bible in and through and for lifestyle does not mean that biblical theology is thereby eliminated from inclusion. Instead, teaching the bible in and through and for lifestyle means that any biblical theology which might be included should serve primarily religious instruction ends and not primarily theological ends.[134]

Liturgy. There can be little doubt that the liturgy is a thoroughly lifestyle-oriented activity.[135] The liturgy is lifestyle-oriented in terms of how it is constructed, in terms of how it takes place,[136] and in terms of the goals toward which it is targeted.

Lifestyle serves as one of the most important meeting places for liturgy and bible. It is crucial to remember, as John McKenzie points out, that the bible is not the direct divine communication itself but rather a set of human responses to that divine communication.[137] Thus biblical revelation does not consist in the pure and unadmixed word of God given directly to us by God in unmediated fashion, but rather the responses of the inspired writers to the divine communication they received in their own lifestyle situations.[138] "The response is the only thing that falls within the area of phenomena. The divine communication is known only by the response except by those who receive the communication directly."[139] Biblical revelation, then, consists of the divine experience of a relatively small group of persons who, in inspired fashion, communicate their response to this divine experience to everyone else. One of the supreme functions of the liturgy is to broaden the base of the inspired writers' responses by placing the substantive content of these responses into a new social reality. The liturgy is so deliberatively structured that it commemorates, preserves, and communicates in a new experiential form the original responses of the inspired writers to the divine communication which they experienced. The liturgy was not created out of thin air, nor are authentic liturgical reforms made for capricious reasons. On the contrary, the liturgy is so structured that the responses of the inspired writers to the divine communication (which is biblical revelation itself) can be placed into a more three-dimensional and celebrational form, a form which is intended to produce in the lives of the participants of the liturgy that kind of deep personal religious response which is as congruent as possible with the responses made by the inspired writers. The original responses of the inspired writers took place in the situational context of their own personal lifestyle. The liturgy does not seek to replicate that lifestyle, but rather to bring into being that kind of situational lifestyle context in which the participants can existentially take part in a fresh way in the same basic realities which formed the core and spirit of the original responses to the divine communication which occurred in the lifestyles of the inspired writers.

The fact that the liturgy is a ritual partially explains why it possesses the power to regeneratively continue in a new three-dimensional form the basic verities found in the bible. Ritual is the prescribed form of words and actions in a ceremonial structure. Ritual is suffused with life and lifestyle because, among other things, ritual works to restore, reinforce, and redirect the personal identities of its participants and the corporate identity of its sponsor.[140] As ritual, therefore, liturgy has not only a preservational function[141] but also a prophetic function with respect to the individual participants and to the whole ecclesia. Thus as a form of worship as well as a form of religious instruction, the liturgy has always occupied a central and indispensable place in the life of the church.[142]

Liturgy is not just a reflection or outward manifestation of religion. Rather, liturgy is a vital and vitalizing dimension of religion, a deeply personalistic way of doing religion.[143] It would seem that some Christians do not regard liturgy as doing religion. Thus Gregory Dix contends that a disconcertingly large number of clergy and laity in both the Anglican and Roman Catholic communions regard the Mass as a liturgy which is said rather than done. Dix states that priests typically think of themselves as saying the Mass rather than doing the Mass and that the laity think of themselves as hearing the Mass rather than doing it.[144] I suspect that many Protestant clergy and laity regard their Sunday worship services as respectively preaching and hearing the word rather than as doing the word of God in celebrational form. Yet virtually every Christian religion holds that active, holistic, lifestyle participation by both the officiating cleric(s) and the laity is central to every genuine liturgical celebration.

Because the liturgy is lifestyle-oriented, it is necessarily rooted in human experience. There are major liturgies for the major lifestyle events in a person's life, such as birth, coming to physical manhood or womanhood, marriage, ordination, very severe illness, and death. There are minor liturgies for less significant but still consequential events in human life such as planting, harvesting, and the like.[145] In so many of its forms, the liturgy grows out of human lifestyle experiences and seeks to make these experiences as pointedly religious as possible.

The liturgy is not content to embrace human lifestyle experiences in themselves. The liturgy also seeks to encompass the two most fundamental contexts in which all lifestyle experiences occur, namely space and time. The liturgy generally occurs in that kind of space which is purposively structured to enhance the religious elements which the liturgy embodies. In a church, for example, architectural form and spatial juxtaposition of the sanctuary, the baptismal font, the altar of sacrifice, the altar of repose, pulpit, stained glass windows, statuary, pews, aisles, and so forth, are all deliberatively arranged so as to be optimally conducive of here-and-now holistic lifestyle enactment of the liturgy. The liturgy also structures time for holistic lifestyle activity.[146] Many of the Christian denominations have constructed a liturgical year whose seasons revolve around the life of Jesus—Advent, Christmastide, Epiphany time, Lent, Eastertide, Pentecost time, post-Pentecost time. In some Christian communions, each specific day within these liturgical seasons commemorates the life of some saint. In those Christian confessions in which monasticism has exerted influence, the liturgical day is divided into liturgical hours beginning with prime and terce, and ending with vespers and compline. The purpose of structuring time liturgically is to help Christians to reenact in their own temporal lifestyle the significant events in the history of salvation, from Adam to the present.

The liturgy is intentionally geared to facilitate a renaissance and a transformation in the lifestyles of both the individual participants and the ecclesia as a community.[147]

The liturgy helps facilitate a renaissance and a transformation in the lifestyle of the individual by offering the participant an especially enriched existential encounter with the living presence of Jesus.[148] This is quintessentially true when the liturgy is a eucharistic one. Most liturgiologists agree that the liturgy implies the holistic participation of the worshiper, that is, a participation which involves the entire range of the individual's behaviors, cognitive, affective, and psychomotor.

The liturgy is carefully structured, not simply to bring all the elements of the human personality holistically into play, but to bring these elements into play in such a fashion that they are at once integrated into and pitched toward the highest personal level possible.

The liturgy also helps facilitate a renaissance and transformation of the ecclesia as community. Each individual Christian participates in the liturgy both as a person and as a member of the ecclesial community. Consequently the liturgy typically has a corporate character in which the word "we" and not the word "I" predominates, and in which the participants stand or sit or walk or talk as a whole group.[149] Thus the liturgy enriches the lives of individual Christians, not only for the sake of their own personal sanctification, but also for the sake of helping to continue building up a God-filled ecclesial community,[150] a community which partakes in a privileged way in unfurling God's salvation to others.[151] Because it involves at such an intimate level the lifestyles of both individuals and the ecclesial community, the liturgy represents an ideal foundation upon which to build the reality of Christian community among the individual members of the local church.[152] To be sure, the Sunday liturgy is one of the few times in which most of the local ecclesia is gathered together in a common activity for a common purpose in an enriched communal religious lifestyle experience.

The liturgy is not only an act of worship; it is also fundamentally an act of religious instruction.[153] It is grossly incorrect to regard religious instruction as simply an accidental[154] or a tangential accompaniment of the liturgy. Religious instruction belongs to the essence of every kind of liturgy and to every part of the liturgy. The Mass, for example, is wholly a religious instruction act in both of its two major parts, in the liturgy of the word (bible readings and homily), and in the liturgy of the Word (the specifically eucharistic celebration of the Word made flesh).

The liturgy as a direct form of religious instruction was very much emphasized by Roman Catholic religious educationists in the 1950s and 1960s. A major rallying cry of that era, a rallying cry which should always remain central to the liturgy as religious instruction, was this: "The liturgy gives what it teaches."[155] What this rallying cry so beautifully and so succinctly expresses is that the liturgy itself not only concretely teaches about Jesus, and not only lets the learner existentially participate in the deepest mysteries of Jesus, but also directly brings about the attainment of religious outcomes.[156] If there is any setting in which the substantive content of religious instruction is so fully, so existentially, so actively, and so effectively present, it is the liturgy. If there is any setting in which the structural content of religious instruction is so marvelously architected, it is the liturgy. If there is any setting in which a true lifestyle participation in the essential mysteries and teachings of Jesus is concretely actualized, it is the liturgy.[157]

There is an ancient and venerable axiom in the church which states: *"Lex orandi, lex credendi."* The practice of praying determines the practice of believing. A major font for the development of cognitive church doctrine has been the prayer life of the church, especially the supreme ecclesial prayer that is the Divine Liturgy. Put into religious instruction terminology, the axiom *"Lex orandi, lex credendi"* means that a particularly effective and ecclesial way to teach a person cognitive doctrine is to place that individual in a lifestyle situation in which the ecclesia as ecclesia is praying.[158] The liturgy is a lifestyle context, and lifestyle contexts contain as well as generate cognitive and affective outcomes—not vice versa.

As I previously stated, the liturgy not only incorporates substantive content of the richest sort but also embodies structural content of the most effective type.[159] The liturgy is a structured learning situation par excellence, a situation in which all four major variables of the teaching-learning act are both prominent and interactive.[160] Unlike most religious instruction activities, liturgical celebration properly accords heavy emphasis on the environmental variable through its architecture, statues, paintings, candles, windows, vestments, and the like. The liturgy is experiential instruction in an especially gripping and inclusive form,[161] a form which places the learner in holistic lifestyle interaction with the ecclesia at its best.

A prominent feature of many liturgies is singing. As Joseph Gelineau remarks, "the Christian liturgy was born singing, and it has never ceased to sing."[162] Hymns contain a great deal of cognitive content in their lyrics.[163] In hymns, the cognitive lyrics are given an intentional affective cast. This is especially noticeable in Negro spirituals and in old-standby Protestant hymns like "Amazing Grace." The melody of hymns obviously abounds in affective content. Additionally, hymns share with all music an almost transcendental quality,[164] a quality which gives them a definite lifestyle temper. The church, and civil governments too, recognize the relation of music to lifestyle. Thus, for example, church events rich in lifestyle such as processions, typically are accompanied by moving hymns like *"Vexilla regis prodeunt"* to deepen the lifestyle involvement of the participants. Civil governments use songs for their own lifestyle goals such as marching songs for soldiers tramping into battle.

In its structure and enactment, the liturgy is religious lifestyle in an especially enriched and focused fashion. The liturgy as lifestyle cannot be adequately taught by providing cognitive content about the liturgy such as the meaning of the entrance prayer or the history of the greater doxology. Rather, the liturgy as lifestyle can only be adequately taught by doing the liturgy, by existentially and holistically participating in a liturgical event. Cognitive enlightenment and affective support can and should be added to this direct firsthand participation before, during, and/or after the liturgical participation as is pedagogically appropriate.

In both nature and purpose, the liturgy is essentially an act of worship and an act of religious instruction. Consequently, if the religious educator is to be true to the liturgy as liturgy, he must teach it primarily as religion rather than primarily as theology. The liturgy is done in, through, and for religious purposes. Theology can be brought in as appropriate to provide one important source of cognitive illumination for liturgical celebration. Religion is on center stage in the liturgy, and it should not be displaced by theology, musicology, or anything else.

Limitations of Lifestyle Content

Lifestyle comprises the all-inclusive shape and operational flow of the totality of a person's behavior. Lifestyle is the integrated living out in behavioral form of all the molar substantive contents. To teach religion (the overall substantive content of religious instruction) is essentially to teach operational religious lifestyle, that delicious and holistic functional integration of all the individual substantive contents. Therefore in and of itself, lifestyle has no limitations as a molar substantive content of religious instruction.[165]

THE FORM OF LIFESTYLE CONTENT

The form of lifestyle content is holistic living. With respect specifically to religion, the form of lifestyle content is holistic religious living.

Though historically, ontically, religiously, and ecumenically not the most satisfactory of terms, nonetheless the word spirituality has been frequently used to denote holistic religious living.[166] The holistic life-style character of spirituality is nicely encapsulated by one scholar who defines it as a word used "to describe those attitudes, beliefs, and practices which animate people's lives and help them reach out to-wards super-sensible realities."[167] As holistic religious living, spir-ituality should not be regarded as an exclusively Catholic or even an exclusively Christian matter. All religions, Christian and non-Chris-tian, have their spiritualities.[168]

A dominant strain running through the definitions and descriptions of Christian spirituality down through the centuries has been spir-ituality as a personally lived encounter with God in human experience. For example, a recurrent theme in spirituality as taught by Augustine of Hippo is the marked tendency to combine psychological ascent with divine ascent.[169] Summarizing major Christian views on spirituality from New Testament times to John of the Cross, Rowan Williams states that spirituality is presented in these writings as the existential response of a person to God's calling.[170] Reviewing various specific forms of spirituality proposed and lived in the history of the church (e.g., Ignatian spirituality, charismatic spirituality), Josef Sudbrack concludes that "concrete spiritualities can be grasped less as a [cogni-tive] doctrine than as personal existence."[171] Not a few of the finest modern theologians also view spirituality primarily from an existential and experiential perspective. Karl Rahner, for example, contends that at bottom Christian spirituality deals with the establishment and the living out of a personal relationship with Jesus Christ.[172] John Mac-quarrie places especially heavy emphasis on the experiential character and core of spirituality when he states that spirituality is a form of the practice of religion "which has to do with becoming a person in the fullest sense," that is to say, open to the human experience of tran-scendence in one's personal life.[173]

Religious Experience

Religious experience lies at the base of spirituality and pervades all of spirituality. To be sure, spirituality cannot be understood, felt, or lived apart from religious experience.

Religious experience can be active or passive or both. As passive, religious experience is that which is existentially undergone. Some passive religious experiences are intense while others are diffused. As active, religious experience involves an existential reaching out or initiating. Some active religious experiences are energetic and enthusiastic while others are prosaic and unexciting.

In order to be in a position to better understand religious experience, I am first going to deal separately with religion and then with experience.

Religion. As I observe toward the beginning of Chapter One, there is no full agreement in virtually any field on the exact meaning of the term religion.[174] Some writers appeal to etymology in order to arrive at a consensus on the meaning of the term religion. However, there is no agreement on the precise etymological locus of the word religion on the part either of Latinists or of etymologists of modern languages.[175]

My own definition of religion is as follows: religion is that form of lifestyle which expresses and enfleshes the lived relationship a person enjoys with a transpersonal being as a consequence of the actualized fusion in his self-system of that knowledge, belief, feeling, experience, and practice that are in one way or another connected with that which the individual perceives to be divine. This definition is holistic because it existentially involves and indeed integrates all domains of human existence. This definition is personalistic in that it regards religion as the activity of a person in relationship. This definition is experiential because it places religion squarely in the realm of human experience.

Religion is an experience which is profoundly and inextricably enmeshed in the human personality.[176] This powerful fact pertains both to the nuts-and-bolts physiological dimensions of the person such as taste and smell and pain, and to the more molar processes like cognition and affect and unconscious.[177] Because religion is so inextricably part-and-parcel of fundamental human functioning, it is only natural that the human being strives to experience his religion both in a personal manner, such as in prayer, and in a corporate manner, such as in the ecclesia. A person is an intersubjectivity; a person is a subjectivity living in and interacting with an historical-social environment. Hence, a person's religious experience must perforce occur both in his own isolated subjectivity and within the framework of historical-social forces like the church.[178] The basic nexus of religion in its personal form and in its societal form is the capability to receive and empower religious experience.[179]

There is a growing emphasis on religion as religious experience, that is to say an experience in which the whole person participates actively and passively. Spirituality is being more and more recognized as a path of personal experiencing rather than something pumped into the person as, for example, an injection of a dose of religion. Martin Buber states that when a person declares that he believes in God, he really means that he meets God in experience.[180] From the experiential view, religion is the existential bridge bringing together God, world, and self.[181] More and more Christians are appreciating the fact that "the unfolding of the self is the ontic ground of the unfolding of Christ."[182] Religion is a dynamism in personal experience, a dynamism which is at once the potentially most powerful engine and the potentially most holistic context available to the individual for optimum holistic growth as a human being.[183]

Experience. Religious experience is a type of experience, or perhaps more accurately, a way of experiencing. It is a truism that experience is one of the most enigmatic concepts in philosophy, one of the most controverted notions in theology, one of the most unsettled issues in social science, and one of the most abused principles in religious instruction.

Experience can be defined as the life of the self or the self in activity. Thus experience is very broad because it includes everything the life of the self involves; its range is as broad as the self in activity. To affirm that experience is the life of the self is to affirm that experience is where a living being "is present to itself precisely as self, an original center and source of free initiative."[184]

Of the many fundamental characteristics of experience, four are particularly worthy of mention in connection with religious experience. These four are holism, process, interaction, and certitude.

Experience is holistic in that it is the all-inclusive life of the self, and thus is wider than any one particular human function such as cognition, affect, or the like. Experience as holistic also indicates that no one basic human function actually works in isolation, but rather is operatively integrated to some degree at least with other basic human functions.[185]

Experience is processive in that it is the ongoing, dynamic living out of one's existence. As processive, experience has within itself the possibility and indeed the necessity for growth and transformation.

Experience is interactional in that it is the living encounter of self with environment.[186] Self cannot live solely by or with self. Self can only exist in dynamic engagement with reality which is nonself.[187]

Experience dynamically unites the subjective pole and the objective pole in human existence.[188] Thus experience as product and process includes both subject and object[189] on the psychological terms of the experiencing subject.[190]

Experience is certain because it takes place in the life of the self and hence is both immediate and subjectively sure. Since experience is "me," and since experience unites subject and object in the personally lived "me," it is automatically endowed with a special kind of supreme subjective certitude which constitutes irrefutable evidence.[191]

Experience constitutes human life in its most fundamental concrete manner of functioning. Thus, in the final analysis, experience is the only way in which reality, and with it truth and love and God, is available to human beings.[192] Religion is the human activity in which the individual encounters God in experience and lives this encounter in experience. Thus the God who the person encounters is not God in himself, but the God in personal experience.[193] While God is infinite in himself, our experience of him is finite. The quality, texture, and form of our experience of God is completely conditioned by the breadth and depth and shape of our general experience. The contours of our personal relationship with Jesus necessarily follow the contours of our manner of experiencing in general and the manner of our personal relationships with self and others in particular.[194]

As I state in my section on experience in *The Shape of Religious Instruction*[195] there is a growing trend among Christian theologians to regard experience as itself revelatory of God. In such a view, experience is where God is met in personal encounter.[196] To open oneself to encounter God in personal experience is more fraught with risk than just thinking about God.[197] But to open oneself to encounter God in personal experience is also much more rewarding.[198]

The power and comprehensiveness of a person's reservoir of past experience is such that it pervades, colors, and to a certain extent conditions every new activity in which the human being engages. This is true with scientific activity as well. The task of all science, be it theological science, physical science, or social science is to investigate phenomena as carefully and as nonsubjectively as possible and from such investigation set up criteria for these phenomena which are as free from the outside influence of subjective experience as possible. Experience in itself has no meaning; it just is. As Aristotle observed long ago, the task of science is to place each experience into that kind of universal framework where it can have both meaning which is personal and meaning which renders that experience useful to others. The work of social science as an empirical mode of investigation is to validate experience in terms of its own dimensionalities and in terms of laws and theories which can be legitimately derived from it. Social science never denies that an experience has taken place. What social science attempts to do is to ascertain what kind of experience it is, what gave rise to it, and what flows from it. Social science also tries to discover how the experience of one person fits in with the experience of other individuals. When many experiences, especially those occurring in a scientifically rich context,[199] admit of a similar meaning, laws and then theories can be constructed. In this way a person can gain confidence that the meaning he attaches to one or another of his own experiences is valid. In this way, too, a person can validly universalize, as allowed by the data, the meaning of his experience.

What I will write in the remainder of this chapter up to the major section on practical consequences should be interpreted from the perspective of religious living as basically religious experiencing. Thus, for example, active religious living in its most fundamental aspect is the endeavor of an individual to experience God in his life as fully as possible and to share or facilitate that experience in others. I mention this because all too often the term religious experience is reserved to the passive mode only, as for example, mysticism or some other deeply awared experience with God which is receptively undergone.

Active Religious Living

Holistic religious living involves the person in all phases of his energies ranging from the most vibrant to the most subdued, from the most outgoing to the most reserved. In a word, holistic religious living is both active and passive.[200]

Though a person's own religious lifestyle may tend more to the active than to the passive mode or vice versa, nonetheless a holistic approach suggests that there typically should be some passivity present in the active mode and some activity present in the passive mode.[201] If a person becomes totally active in his religious living, he thereby tends to thwart his holistic need to encounter himself in the aloneness of his being. If a person becomes totally passive in his religious living, he thereby tends to thwart his holistic need to encounter others in the socialness of his being. Holistic religious living suggests that while the active or the passive mode might predominate in a person's lifestyle pattern, nonetheless there should be a sweet oscillation between centering and decentering, between attachment and detachment, between involvement and letting go.[202]

What fundamentally unites the active and the passive modes of religious living is love.

Active religious living is that whose axis is reaching out or initiating. The person whose religious lifestyle is predominantly active contends that action or living is primary. In this view, action incarnates one's personhood so that an individual is what he does. Truth lies in action, not in conceptualization. Conceptualization is nothing more than an attempt to give cognitive meaning and cognitive order to action. Thus conceptualization is just part of the truth because conceptualization is just a way of looking at action; it is not action itself, and indeed is far removed from action. A person achieves self-fulfillment, personhood, and transcendence by and through action.

Holistic religious living suggests that all spirituality, active as well as passive, requires the involvement to an appropriate degree of all the major functions of the whole person, cognitive, affective, and psychomotor. Thus in active religious living, there should be a cognitive component, an affective component, and a psychomotor component— as well as a persistent passive undercurrent lest religious action degenerate into empty activity. The cognitive component, for example, can be fruitfully integrated into active religious living by interpenetrating one's actions as much as possible with intellectual considerations derived from religionology and from the particular sphere of action in which one is engaged. Religionology offers a fuller experiential base and a greater variety of perspectives than does theology. The theory of one's own particular sphere of activity is necessary for the individual to retain realism, balance, and a proper vision of the objectives appropriate to that particular sphere of activity.

Specialists in the theory and/or practice of Christian spirituality down through the centuries have recognized the risks and potential pitfalls involved in active religious living. The name often applied to falling prey to these pitfalls is "activism." To be sure, activism constitutes a grave threat to all persons involved in active religious living, including religious educators.

To assist persons in successfully skirting the risks of active religious living (and passive religious living as well), various lifestyle-oriented safeguards have been developed. One of the classic safeguards is known by the ancient term "discernment of spirits." The roots of this term lie in the New Testament (1 Cor. 12:10, 1 Jn. 4:1). The term was used by the early church Fathers, notably by John Cassianus (c. 360– c. 435) and John Climacus (579–649). Though spiritual writers have not always employed this term in exactly the same way, nonetheless there is general agreement that discernment of spirits refers to the critical process by which a person endeavors to ascertain whether his actions stem from God or the devil—or, in less particularistic theological terms, whether his actions are leading him toward personal sanctification or away from it. The process of discernment of spirits is lifestyle-oriented because it (1) evaluates the entire repertoire of a person's behaviors (2) within the context of that individual's overall lifestyle, and (3) seeks to directly enrich the overall lifestyle by inserting the results of the discernment process directly into the person's present and future pattern of religious living. Discernment of spirits, then, is rooted in the quality, texture, and direction of one's daily experiences.[203]

While the process of discernment of spirits was for centuries the exclusive province of theology, social science has begun to take an interest in this area. To be sure, the process of discernment of spirits, involving as it does empirical methodology in the investigation of human behavior, more properly belongs to the domain of social science than to the domain of theology.[204] To be sure, some more forward-looking theologians specializing in spirituality are coming to recognize this point. Thus Ernest Larkin, a theologian of spiritual living, states that theological categories lie outside the actual theory and practice of discernment, since the process of discernment "is not a speculative description of causes but a practical judgment and decision about life choices. This process is experiential and evaluative."[205]

It is important to note that from both the theological perspective and the social-scientific perspective, the process of discernment of spirits is characterized by performance objectives.[206] Theologically, discernment of spirits is based on and measured by the gospel statement: "By their fruits they shall be known" (Mt. 7:20).[207] Social-scientifically, discernment of spirits is based on empirical observation and assessment of a person's behavior.

In a large sense, the practice of examination of conscience is one concrete form through which the global process of discernment of spirits is operationalized. Examination of conscience in a religious context is the process of focusing on one or more specific behaviors occurring within a specified period of time in order to ascertain how the behavior fits in with the person's overall pattern of living and whether the behavior enhances or detracts from that individual's Christian lifestyle.[208] Like the process of discernment of spirits, the practice of examination of conscience can be performed privately or in a group setting. Furthermore, it can be done by oneself or with the help of a religious counselor or spiritual director or soul friend.[209]

A person can make an examination of conscience at any time, although many specialists in spirituality suggest that it be done once a day (either at evening prayers or at morning prayers). This daily examination of conscience can be fruitfully supplemented by a monthly and a yearly grand examination of conscience so as to place one's religious growth or decline in a larger framework.

Ignatius of Loyola has been especially influential in giving shape and precision to the practice of examination of conscience. In his classic work, *Spiritual Exercises*,[210] Ignatius states that there are two basic kinds of examination of conscience, namely the general examination and the particular examination. In a general examination, the person focuses upon all the behaviors in which he has engaged during the time frame under scrutiny. In the particular examination, the person focuses upon one special motif and assesses his behaviors in light of this motif. This motif can be positive such as a virtue to be cultivated. More often than not, this motif is negative, namely a defect to be corrected. In Ignatius' view, a particular examination tends to be more efficacious than a general examination since it enables the individual to carefully monitor his defects one by one and thus overcome them more easily—divide and conquer. Many specialists in spiritual living suggest that in the particular examination of conscience a person concentrate on his predominant fault (such as pride or vanity) since many of the person's religious failings are connected in one way or another with that individual's predominant fault.

The religious educator would do well to teach learners how to make the examination of conscience so that the quality of their religious living can be enriched and the direction of their religious living can be sharpened. However, the religious educator should realize that the examination of conscience, though an important pedagogical technique, is not as valuable as the evaluation made in a laboratory for

Christian living. The examination of conscience typically takes place after the day's events have taken place, while laboratory evaluation meshes appraisal with the here-and-now lifestyle activities and behaviors now occurring.

Passive Religious Living

Passive religious living is that whose axis is undergoing or receiving. The person whose religious lifestyle is predominantly passive contends that waiting docilely but attentively is primary. Mary of Bethany, not her sister Martha, is the model (Lk. 10:38–42). In this view, truth lies in resting or remaining in oneself so that one can be prepared to embrace whatever helpful reality might come along. A person achieves self-fulfillment through the in-gathering of one's forces.

Holistic religious living suggests that all spirituality, passive as well as active, requires the involvement to an appropriate degree of all the major functions of the whole person, cognitive, affective, and psychomotor. Passive religious living holistically considered does not consist of just inertly waiting, but rather waiting in an attentive, alert, and open mode. The name usually given to defective passive religious living, namely religious living characterized by inert waiting, is quietism.

In much of the religious, social-scientific, and theological literature, the term "religious experience" is used exclusively to mean passive religious experience in general and passive intense religious experience in particular. This identification of all religious experience with only one of its two major forms, namely the passive mode, is inaccurate and misleading. As I indicated earlier in this chapter, religious experience can be active as well as passive, just as the lifestyle pattern in which an experience occurs can be active or passive. This point should be borne in mind when, in the following pages, I deal with religious experience of the passive kind.

There are many gradations or stages of passive religious experience ranging from very simple forms of religious encounter all the way up to mysticism. Though many spiritual writers over the centuries have proffered their views on the progressive levels of religious experience, there is as yet no empirically verified taxonomy of the different stages of passive religious experience.[211]

Passive religious experience does not occur in a manner outside of the way in which a particular person experiences reality. Rather, passive religious experience occurs according to the mode of the individual engaged in this experience, according to the way he personally meets reality. The character of one's personality at once colors and qualifies the passive religious experience, and in turn is affected by the passive religious experience.[212] This empirical fact holds true even with intense passive religious experiences like the mystical encounter. As Augustin Léonard observes, even mysticism is not the direct inpouring by God, but always occurs according to the recipient's pattern of experiencing, according to the recipient's ongoing lifestyle.[213] Passive religious experience is potent over the long term to the extent to which it affects a person's lifestyle and to the extent to which it is functionally integrated into that lifestyle.

The fact that passive religious experience occurs within the developmental framework of the individual's own pattern of experiencing raises this difficulty: What is the specific character of a passive religious experience which enables it to be properly called a religious experience? What essentially sets off passive religious experience from other kinds of experience? The force and magnitude of this problem is brought into even bolder relief when one takes into account Paul Pruyser's well-supported position that while all of a person's psychological processes appear to participate in a passive religious experience, none of them is specific to religion.[214] My own answer to this difficulty is that the unique or distinguishable character of passive religious experience is that it represents a personal encounter, or at least a perceived personal encounter, in awareness, of the transcendent, the numinous, the divine.[215] One writer puts it well: "By transcendent reality [in this case] we do not simply mean a transcendent separate being. It may also be an enveloping reality to which the visible world belongs as part or aspect, but which is more than the visible world and thus transcends it. It would be conceived also as a higher state in which we are finally separated from the world and which is a state of the highest bliss. . . . The essence, then, of [passive] religious experience is that it is an experience of standing in a beneficial beatific relation to a 'transcendent,' whatever may be the way in which this transcendent is conceived and described in human words."[216]

The basis of the difficulty discussed in the previous paragraph has a happy side to it. Because passive religious experience occurs within the here-and-now existential mode of the person engaged in this experience, it is therefore at once natural to a human being and amenable to scientific empirical investigation. As natural to a human being, passive religious experience of every kind is properly regarded as native to a person's normal capabilities rather than as a bizarre, oddball, or psychologically diseased occurrence.[217] As amenable to empirical investigation, passive religious experience of every kind can be analyzed, examined, and explored in a wide variety of scientifically controlled and noncontrolled conditions without having to resort to investigative cop-outs such as, "It's an unfathomable mystery to the human mind."

The quality of a passive religious experience tends to grow progressively more holistically lifestyle in character as the level of this experience becomes deeper. Thus in mysticism, the deepest multi-tiered level[218] within passive religious experience, all human functions tend to harmoniously converge into an integrated holistic lifestyle activity. To be sure, self-reports by persons who had a mystical experience, especially those individuals who have had such an experience with relative frequency, such as the mystics, indicate that during the mystical experience the person is typically aware that all his human functions are integratively fulfilled and holistically completed.[219] Of interest to religious educators is the fact that most spiritual writers down through the centuries assert that the axis and the ground of holistic mystical experience is love. Based on self-reports of mystics and of persons who have undergone mystical experiences both spontaneously and in controlled laboratory situations, the holistic lifestyle activity which characterizes mystical experience includes a dramatically new and enriched form of consciousness. Such consciousness is essentially nonrational rather than rational.[220] This dramatically fresh state of consciousness, coupled with the fact that mystical experience is an inherently natural feature of the human condition, adds further plausibility to Richard Bucke's contention that mystical consciousness represents a new, third form of consciousness which may well constitute the next major evolutionary step in the ascent of the human race and thus be an awareness in which all persons will engage on a regular basis.[221] Bucke's view bears a certain consonance with that of Pierre Teilhard de Chardin.[222] Small wonder, then, that the mystical experience is regarded by some spiritual writers as a kind of foretaste, however dim and analogic, of the beatific encounter which a person will enjoy in heaven.[223]

A wide variety of different and often contrary theological opinions have been offered to explain the ultimate basis of passive religious experience. These widely divergent opinions range from the strong neo-Platonism of the early Church Fathers to the highly subjective theology of some of the mystics in the modern era. The principal difficulty in devising a satisfactory theological and philosophical explanation boils down to transcendism versus immanentism. Is God experienced directly (transcendence) or is he experienced only indirectly (immanence)? This enormous difficulty is brought to salience when we look at the problem from an ontological perspective. God is of a totally different ontological order than are human beings. God is unconditioned while we are conditioned, he is absolute while we are finite, he is wholly other while we are wholly here, and so forth. In a word, God is completely transcendent. But if God is completely transcendent, then experiential contact with him of a direct sort is obviously impossible.[224] Because theology forms a vital dimension in the foundations of religious instruction, it is only natural that religious educators have taken one or another position with respect to the transcendent or immanent explanation of passive religious experience.[225] Since social science is value-free with respect to its being based on one or another particular theological opinion, it is able to adequately explore the dynamics of passive religious experience regardless of whether transcendism or immanentism proves to be the ''correct'' theological stance. Social science is grounded in social-scientific facts and laws and theories, not in theological facts and laws and theories. Passive religious experience takes place empirically in a person's own concrete existential situation and so can be successfully investigated from a social-scientific perspective. To be sure, any worthwhile theological explanation of passive religious experience must not only take into account but must also to a certain extent be based on data derived from the social-scientific study of passive religious experience.[226]

One gets the impression that, with the exception of certain postconciliar authors and of specialists in mysticism, some Catholic theologians seem leery and indeed almost afraid of passive religious experience. The basis of this wariness and even fear appears to lie in the fact that passive religious experience is highly subjective and hence somehow falls outside the control of the *ecclesiasticum*.[227] These Catholic theologians seem to think that any emphasis on passive religious experience will inevitably result in Protestantism with the latter's stress on the primacy of subjective religious experience. Yet this Protestant emphasis, so essential for any religion which is vibrant and vital, is one of the very things which Catholicism most needs and ought to most treasure. The genuinely religious person tends to mesh the two wings found in most organized religions, the mystical and the institutional, the subjective and the objective.[228] Though subjective passive religious experience is the re-creative source of life and grace in the life of each individual Christian and in the life of the ecclesia, nonetheless "its truth and value cannot be adequately appraised apart from its connections with other truths and values."[229] No great mystic—the apogee of subjective passive religious experience—ever allowed his religious experience to become the sole basis of his religious lifestyle. The great mystics typically believed that the product and the process of their religious experience ought to be integrated with scripture, tradition, and the ecclesia. Though the great mystics always had their profound religious experiences alone, these individuals more often than not were keenly aware of their own personal place within the life of the ecclesia. Thus the great mystics tended to view their role as one which is of service to the whole church rather than for the benefit solely of themselves.[230] Therefore mystical experiences, and indeed all other subjective passive religious experiences, ought to have religious instruction consequences in that they exist not just for the personal sanctification of the person undergoing the experience, but also for the sanctificational education of others.[231]

It should never be forgotten that faith is a construct which was devised to give conceptual expression to certain kinds of behaviors, to certain kinds of experiences. In the act of faith, a person encounters and is existentially related to the revealing God. This encounter and existential relation occurs in experience.[232] Faith, the gift totally of God, occurs only in and through personal experience. Thus religious experience, active as well as passive, is faith's medium and métier, and in no way is alien or somehow opposed to faith.

In the final analysis, the axis of a person's Christianity is not one or even a series of his passive religious experiences. Rather, the axis of a person's Christianity consists of the holistic and integrative incarnation of his passive religious experience into his personal lifestyle, into his overall pattern of living.

Mysticism. One of the central features of religion is its mystical life. To be sure, a fundamental energizer and vital force of any truly living religion is the set of mystical experiences of its founder, a set which, in Christianity, is shared to an appropriate degree by the great mystics and by every other individual who has undergone a mystical experience. Thus Abraham Maslow can write that "it looks quite probable that the peak-experience may be the model of religious revelation or the religious illumination or conversion which has played so great a role in the history of religions."[233]

Though mystical experience is very important in personal and ecclesial religion, it has received scant attention in the field of religious instruction. A religious instruction book which deals with mystical experience in an extended fashion is rare. When mystical experience is treated in a religious instruction book, it typically is just mentioned in passing. For religious educationists and educators who are cognitivists, activists, or who like their religion cool and laid-back, mystical experience is more often than not an embarrassment, a triviality, or some sort of mental unbalance. David Arthur Bickimer—who, tellingly, espouses a social-science approach to religious instruction—is one of the very few contemporary religious educationists who specifically urges that a major focus of religious instruction should be on the facilitation of mystical and other intense forms of religious experience in learners.[234]

Mystical experience, like all forms of passive religious experience, is not poured in by God in a manner untouched by any terrestrial influence. Rather, mystical experience is always and everywhere conditioned by the cultural milieu in which the person lives as well as by the dynamics of that individual's here-and-now personality.

David Arthur Bickimer is not alone in his contention that intense religious experiences, including mystical experiences, are more common than some people believe.[235] Arguing against the theological position prevalent in the eighteenth and nineteenth centuries, Cuthbert Butler contends that mystical experiences are available to everyone and not just to the holy or to the theologically learned.[236] Testifying from his long experience as a religiously oriented psychotherapist and spiritual counselor to thousands of people, Morton Trippe Kelsey states that religious experiences, including an intense one like mysticism "do not belong just to the intelligent or the sophisticated. Quite the contrary, they are given to children and simple peasants, as well as to philosophers and theologians; they come to sinners bent on destruction as well as to pious folk who feel they need no special help. This encounter is the real leveler of mankind."[237] Social scientists have confirmed that many people, including a relatively high percentage of persons who would not be labeled holy or religious according to Christian ecclesiastical norms, have attained mystical experience.

Mysticism is a human experience which is not limited to any one religion; it is found in all major world religions.[238] The type of encounter a person has with God in mystical experience varies according to the religion of the individual. A religion, especially an organized religion, is, after all, a matter of culture as well as a matter of personal living. The difference in the texture of mystical experience is especially pronounced in Eastern as contrasted to Western religions.[239] In Hinduism, for example, persons report that in mystical experience they become united with the transcendent in such a manner that they lose their individuality and become one with Brahmin in absorption. In Western mainstream Christian mysticism, persons report that in mystical experience they become united with the transcendent in such a manner that their individuality becomes enhanced.

A person's mystical experience always takes place within the existential context of that individual's personality dynamics and lifestyle. Mystical experience is quintessentially holistic, and harmoniously involves all major human functions. In this vein Evelyn Underhill writes that mystical experience is not simply an activity of the mind and heart, but indeed a form of organic life. Mystical experience, declares Underhill, involves the organization of the whole self, conscious and unconscious, under the spur of the hunger of love. Mystical experience involves the remaking of the whole personality on high levels in the interests of the transcendental life. Underhill notes that the great mystics are emphatic in their commonly held view that "spiritual desires are useless unless they initiate this costly movement of the whole self toward the Real."[240] The holistic character of mystical experience extends to the psychomotor domain, not just in the way the whole body is deeply involved in the mystical experience,[241] but even in some cases, purportedly, in the appearance of unusual psychomotor phenomena such as stigmata, luminosity, the emission of fragrant odors from the body, and so forth.[242]

While many scholars more or less concur on the spirit of mysticism, there seems to be no single definition of mystical experience upon which all or even most scholars can agree. Indeed, William Ralph Inge found at least twenty-six different definitions of mystical experience.[243] Part of the difficulty in formulating a definition of mystical experience satisfactory to the scholarly community stems from the fact that mystical experience has been conceptualized differently in various historical eras. For example, the early Fathers of the church tended to view mystical experience in a more-or-less objective fashion, namely participation in the life of Jesus through being existentially grasped by the Lord especially as one encounters him in the bible. This encounter with Jesus in the scriptures does not come about through the cognitive study of the bible, but rather by living in conscious congruence with the scriptures and thus being existentially grasped by the Jesus of and in the bible. The early Church Fathers, then, tended to conceptualize mystical experience in a much broader fashion than do mystics and specialists in the spiritual life living in the modern era. Also, the early Church Fathers had little or no interest in the subjective psychological state of the person engaged in mystical experience. The transition to the modern emphasis on the psychological subjectivity of mystical experience began with Dionysius the Aeropagite around the beginning of the sixth century.[244] However, it was not really until the great mystics of the Middle Ages and the early modern period, culminating in Teresa of Avila, that mystical experience began to be regarded primarily from the standpoint of personal subjectivity.

There seem to be at least eight fundamental characteristics of mystical experience on which most scholars of spiritual living seem to agree.[245] *First,* mystical experience is one of personal passivity, a state in which the individual senses that what is transpiring is essentially something which is given to him. The person "feels as if his own will were in abeyance, as if he were grasped and held by a power not his own."[246] In mystical experience, the individual is aware that the experience is a profoundly subjective one; however the individual is also aware that this subjectivity consists in an altered state of being in which he is the passive recipient of some revelation or disclosure having supreme importance to him. *Second,* mystical experience is overpowering, one which overwhelms the individual, one which is enormously charged with the intensity of being—an intensity born of numinosity.[247] *Third,* regardless of its particular substantive content, mystical experience confers a powerful sense of psychological certitude on the person undergoing this encounter, an absolute conviction the experience constitutes a truly significant revelation of reality. Thus mystical experience is its own authority.[248] *Fourth,* in mystical experience a person is wholly caught up in what he perceives to be the basic oneness of all reality, an unforgettable sense of cosmic unity. *Fifth,* mystical experience involves an overwhelming awareness of presence, a sense of utter nearness of the divine, an intimacy with the holy.[249] *Sixth,* mystical experience brings with it a deeply awared sense of joy and exultation suffused with a feeling of well-being. *Seventh,* an awareness of simultaneity replaces the successive character of time, so that in mystical experience everything is now. *Eighth,* mystical experience is basically incommunicable, especially by words.

The eight characteristics of mystical experience listed above have been identified by scholars of religious living as a result of their analyses of the empirical self-reports given by persons who underwent mystical experiences, especially the great mystics. In order to offer greater clarity and precision to these and other purported characteristics of mystical experience, in order to discover possible unexplored features of mystical experience, and in order to subject a wide range of alleged characteristics of mystical experience to direct empirical test, some contemporary social scientists have begun to empirically examine in a more or less here-and-now fashion the features of intense religious experience, including the mystical encounter. Of especial interest to religious educators are two of these empirical studies, namely that conducted by Ralph Hood and that conducted by Robert Margolis.

Ralph Hood constructed his mysticism scale (M Scale)[250] from an initial pool of 108 items which he generated from the basic categories of mystical experience delineated in Walter Stace's classic book in the field.[251] Utilizing the structured question technique with his research subjects, Hood developed a 32-item scale of empirically reported mystical experience falling into eight core categories.[252] Because each of the Hood categories are stated in operational terms, they are especially useful to the religious educator who wishes to facilitate mystical experience.

The following are Hood's categories together with his operational definition of each. *Category #1*: Ego Quality. Refers to the experience of a loss of a sense of self while consciousness is nevertheless maintained. The loss of self is commonly experienced as an absorption into something greater than the mere empirical ego. *Category #2*: Unifying Quality. Refers to the experience of the multiplicity of objects of perception as nevertheless united. Everything is in fact perceived as "a One." *Category #3*: Inner Subjective Quality. Refers to the perception of an inner subjectivity to all things, even those usually experienced in purely material forms. *Category #4*: Temporal/Spatial Quality. Refers to the temporal and spatial parameters of the experience. Essentially both time and space are modified with the extreme being one of an experience that is both "timeless" and "spaceless." *Category #5*: Noetic Quality. Refers to the experience as a source of valid knowledge. Emphasis is on a nonrational, intuitive, insightful experience that is nevertheless recognized as not merely subjective. *Category #6*: Ineffability. Refers to the impossibility of expressing the experience in conventional language. The experience simply cannot be put into words due to the nature of the experience itself and not due to the linguistic capacity of the person having the experience. *Category #7*: Positive Affect. Refers to the positive affective quality of the experience. Typically the experience is of joy or of blissful happiness. *Category #8*: Religious Quality. Refers to the intrinsic sacredness of the experience. This includes feelings of mystery, awe, and reverence that may nevertheless be expressed independently of traditional language.

Whereas Hood's investigation uses Stace's core categories as the structural framework for his investigation of mystical experience, Robert Margolis' empirical investigation starts off completely from scratch.[253] The Margolis typology of religious experience was constructed on the basis of an analysis of the reports which persons who claimed to have undergone intense religious experience personally stated to Margolis.[254] Thus his categorization of intense religious experience was arrived at in an a posteriori and an empirical fashion rather than in an a priori and a speculative manner.

Margolis' four core factors of intense religious experience, together with major elements associated with each,[255] are as follows: *Factor #1*: Transcendental Experience. Similar to classical mystical experience described by most writers in the field. Involves coming into contact with a higher plane of reality than normal experience; this contact dramatically changes the way in which the person perceives himself and the world. Elements associated with transcendental experience are: security; increased feelings of relatedness to God or to the Universe; feelings of peace; a new reality (noetic quality); feelings of ecstasy or joy; feelings of unity or oneness; "out-of-the-body" experience. *Factor #2*: Vertigo Experience. Involves at least a temporary disorientation for the person. It is often triggered by music or drugs. "Out-of-the-body" sensations are common, and the individual feels as if he is losing control and often is initially frightened by the experience. Thus, like the first factor (transcendental experience), vertigo experience involves a significant alteration in the way an individual perceives himself and his work. Yet his reaction is often one of fear and loss of control rather than feelings of positive affect such as peace, ecstasy, and security. Elements associated with vertigo experience are: listening to music; drugs; "out-of-the-body" sensations; loss of control; initial negative reaction (fear); and visions or voices. *Factor #3*: Life Change Experience. In many cases involves descriptions of thoughts, feelings, or sensations that tend to be vague or difficult to specify. Thus there are many nonspecific changes in internal states both cognitively oriented and affectively oriented. In many ways, however, this experience seems to mark the beginning of a significant life change for the individual in that his thinking and his feeling about himself and/or his relationship to God are profoundly affected. Elements associated with life change experience are: nonspecific change in internal state (affect-oriented) such as "something came over me like a wave"; unity or oneness; talking to a friend; nonspecific change in internal state (cognitive-oriented) such as "I began to analyze my life very differently"; attending a church service. *Factor #4*: Visionary Experience. Often occurs during a "dream." This experience, although associated with a dream, is perceived as constituting a genuine contact with a divine presence. Elements associated with visonary experience are: experience of a divine presence; visions or voices; a dream; experience of love, experience of ecstasy or joy.[256]

Margolis asserts that the four factors in his typology share the characteristics of unity, ineffability, noetic quality, positive affect, and time/space distortions.[257]

Empirical investigations of intense religious experience like those conducted by Ralph Hood and Robert Margolis represent an important advance in gaining more valid data and more reliable insights into the deepest levels of religious living. By use of increasingly more sophisticated empirical methodology, social scientists will hopefully progress far beyond the crucial first steps pioneered by scholars like Hood and Margolis.[258]

Of pointed interest to religious educators is the question of whether or not intense religious experience, including mystical experience, can be directly facilitated. On the basis of empirically oriented self reports given by a wide variety of individuals coming from different cultures and eras, and also from a growing body of controlled empirical research, it seems reasonably certain that intense religious experience including the mystical state has been directly facilitated and can be directly facilitated in the future. Some of the procedures for direct facilitation of mystical experience have been discovered, while others have been developed. In his review of the pertinent literature, Wilhelm Pöll has found three main categories into which the direct facilitation of intense religious experience falls, namely situational stimuli, physical stimuli, and chemical stimuli. Situational stimuli are environmental factors which directly facilitate intense religious experience.[259] Physical stimuli are those which directly impinge upon or actually involve sensory functions of the human organism.[260] Physical stimuli in this category do not include drugs. Examples of physical stimuli include: certain kinds of musical and sensory rhythms, dances, some religious music; certain corporeal exercises like yoga, fasting and diet; sensory overload or deprivation; sexual intercourse; extreme fatigue, and so forth. Social scientists have devised experimental situations of divers kinds which, by use of physical stimuli, intense religious experience including the mystical state has been directly facilitated.[261] Chemical stimuli are those which involve the ingestion or application of drugs of one sort or another. These drugs include psilocybin, mescaline, peyote, and certain narcotics. The use of chemical substances to directly facilitate intense religious experience is not new; it was and still is used in primitive tribes for this purpose. Summing up the pertinent empirical research, Walter Houston Clark states that in certain persons under certain circumstances certain chemical stimuli tend to facilitate "profound religious experience largely of a mystical character."[262] It should be noted that chemical stimuli do not render defective the mystical experiences they induce. Thus Clark's review of the empirical research shows that when intense religious experience was facilitated in hardened criminals as a result of ingesting psilocybin, remarkable results were achieved, namely a transformation of their lives in a positive direction.[263] Furthermore, states Clark, "one of the striking observations made by those [clinicians] who have worked with psychedelics is that the therapeutic results seem enhanced when the experience is reported as religious."[264]

Many Christian theologians, including some who are normally regarded as progressive, erroneously downgrade the quality and the divine tonus of deliberately facilitated mystical experience regardless of whether this experience was achieved by situational stimuli, physical stimuli, or chemical stimuli. I suspect that this misguided disvaluation of directly facilitated mystical experience is a consequence of a residual though often unrecognized bias against flesh-and-blood, against human initiative, and against the social-science enterprise. Jean Mouroux, for example, claims that experimentally induced or otherwise empirically facilitated intense religious experience is not an authentic Christian encounter and is not in conformity with Roman Catholic tradition.[265] There is no real evidence to support Mouroux's view. Indeed, his perspective seems to squeeze God out of human initiative and eliminate any contact a person can make through his own activity with God. Mouroux seems to forget that God discloses himself in many ways and not just in the ways Mouroux prefers. The fact that intense religious experience can be facilitated in no way denies the fact that God always takes the initiative in disclosing himself. The key issue in this case, therefore, is not whether God takes the initiative but how he takes the initiative. God's vitalizing omnipresence and omnipower in all of creation suggests that when a human being is affected by created reality, God is thereby and therewith taking the revelatory initiative. Karl Rahner and Herbert Vorgrimler, for their part, endeavor to disvalue deliberately facilitated mystical experience by reducing this kind of intense religious encounter to magic. Thus they write: "Whereas magic seems to bring about the encounter [with God in mystical experience] through special means, mystical contemplation is always experienced as a gift."[266] This argument begs the question and ignores the issue. The fact of the matter is that in Christian theology, all reality is properly regarded as a gift of God. The key issue in mystical experience, therefore, is not whether the experience is a gift of God but how this gift is given and received. The use of human means to facilitate contact with the divine in no way detracts from the source or nature of the gift. Nor does the use of human means to facilitate mystical experience represent a doctrine of works which leaves God out of the picture. The use of human means to facilitate contact with God is an essential part of any religion (e.g., prayer); thus any attempt to apply the term magic to human means is not only false but in fact lies outside Christian tradition. Furthermore, some of the great Christian mystics and the overwhelming majority of Christian theologians specializing in spirituality down through the centuries distinguish two authentic types of Christian mystical experience, namely, acquired mystical experience which is achieved by some sort of human effort and infused mystical experience which occurs spontaneously. To be sure, Catholic theologians have usually claimed that infused mystical experience is superior to acquired mystical experience. The arguments these theologians have used to support this hierarchical ordering of mystical experience might well crumble when they are reviewed in the light of social-scientific findings. Relevant social-scientific findings, I suspect, will show that so-called infused mystical experiences might often (and maybe even always) be induced by situational and physical factors, and hence really do not constitute that kind of direct zap from God which many theologians would have us believe.

What can the religious educator do in order to directly facilitate intense religious experience, including mysticism, in learners?[267] In general, the religious educator should structure the pedagogical situation in such a manner as to exclude as far as possible those activities known to inhibit mystical experience and to include those activities known to facilitate mystical experience.

Foremost among the factors known to block intense religious experience is the cognitive process of ratiocination. Thus a religion lesson which has as an objective the facilitation of intense religious experience should exclude as far as possible all ratiocinatively oriented pedagogical practices such as lecture, case, action-reflection including the so-called "shared praxis,"[268] and the like. Indeed, some of the pedagogical activities designed to directly promote intense religious experience include instructional practices geared to remove cognitive blocks to peak awareness. Such practices as those proposed by Barry Weinhold and Lynn Elliott, often accord special attention to nonverbal and to psychomotor procedures in order to get away from the inherently cognitive thrust of verbal content.[269] Eastern religions have devised a number of pedagogical practices for effectively removing cognitive blocks which inhibit intense religious experience. Zen Buddhism, for example, uses the anti-ratiocinative pedagogical technique of the *kōan* and the psychomotor technique of *Zazen* to block the intrusion of ratiocinative cognition and thus help facilitate enlightenment (*satori*).[270] As Jean Houston observes, "of all the hard facts of science, I know of none more solid and fundamental than the fact that if you inhibit thought (and persevere) you come at length to a region of consciousness below or behind thought, and different from ordinary thought in its nature and character—a consciousness of quasi-universal quality, and a realization of an altogether vaster self than that to which we are accustomed."[271]

In structuring the pedagogical situation to directly facilitate intense religious experience such as mysticism, the religious educator would do well to accord heightened prominence to what are called "trigger stimuli," namely those variables which tend to touch off intense religious experience. Some trigger stimuli which have proven effective in this connection include exercises designed to bring one's unconscious functions into active play, significant nature experiences,[272] certain kinds of dance, selected types of music, and environments lush with extra-rich sensory stimuli. Some potentially effective trigger stimuli, that is, those stimuli which seem to hold significant promise but whose effectiveness is not yet empirically proven, include so-called "light shows" and biofeedback.

Mystical experience is a vital substantive content in religious instruction. Hence the pedagogically qualified religious educator should include mystical experience in the curriculum, as appropriate. What makes mystical experience so potentially urgent for learners is that intense religious experience culminating in the mystical encounter represents the high point in the human search for authenticity, self-fulfillment, and self-realization on this earth.[273] Mystical experience is at once a self-enhancement and a self-critique: a self-enhancement in that it brings our own human functions to a new kind of completion, and a self-critique in that it shows that there is something incomplete and defective in the way we normally function. To be sure, mystical experience constitutes a basic element—and I believe a vital criteriological element—in defining the religious self.[274] To neglect to educate the learner in the development of the mystical side of his nature is to do disservice to the learner and to provide him with a less than complete religious education.

Many Christians who work to save the world seek to do so by political action, economic reforms for social justice, and the like. But these and similar activities will remain barren husks and empty of genuine power if they are not interpenetrated with a fundamental change in consciousness. The zenith of such a fundamental change in consciousness is intense religious experience, especially mystical experience. When all is said and done, this is why mystical experience is so necessary for religion and so important for religious instruction.

Prayer

Prayer in its widest and truest sense is the union of a person with God. This union can be a psychomotor union, a cognitive union, an affective union, or a lifestyle union.

Psychomotor prayer is the union of a person with God through the body. One of the most ancient and most venerable of all psychomotor prayers is fasting. Another traditional form of psychomotor prayer is that of willingly enduring physical pain in and for Jesus. Such physical pain may come from a nonintentional source such as from a physical malady or it may be deliberately self-inflicted such as by wearing an uncomfortable garment like an irritating woolen shirt.

Cognitive prayer is the union of a person with God through intellectual processes. In cognitive prayer a person reflects on his relationship to God, explores some biblical teaching in terms of its relevance to himself and the world, assesses his progress in religious living, and so forth. Examples of cognitive prayer include ratiocinative meditation, and reflectively reciting formal prayers composed by holy persons of old or by ecclesiastical authorities.

Affective prayer is the union of a person with God through affective processes. In affective prayer a person expresses his love for God, pours himself forth in sentiments of adoration, desires to glorify God, and so forth. Examples of affective prayer include hymns sung with emotion and ardent utterances of love for God.

Lifestyle prayer is the union of a person with God in and through a concrete pattern of living. Lifestyle prayer may be passive or active. Passive lifestyle prayer is one in which a person's entire being is holistically and existentially joined to God in a basically receptive mode. In passive lifestyle prayer the person simply rests in God. An example of passive lifestyle prayer is the so-called prayer of simplicity[275] in which a person dwells as in an existential gaze upon God in any one or more of his attributes.[276] In active lifestyle prayer, the dynamisms and energies of a person's holistic behavioral repertoire are placed into that kind of mode in which they are rendered conducive to union with God. Examples of active lifestyle prayer are performing a spiritual or corporal act of mercy, and of performing the duties of one's occupation with zest and commitment in and for God.

Some theologians of the spiritual life correlate the various major forms of prayer with levels of religious living. Adolphe Tanquerey, for example, states that cognitive prayer is characteristic of the lowest level of religious living, namely the purgative way.[277] Affective prayer is characteristic of the middle level of religious living, namely the illuminative way. Lifestyle prayer, especially of the passive variety, is typical of the highest level of religious living, namely the unitive way.[278]

It would seem that Jesus regarded prayer as primarily a lifestyle activity since he enjoined us to pray always (Lk. 18:1). It is obviously impossible for a person to spend every minute of his life in psychomotor prayer, in cognitive prayer, or in affective prayer. The only way in which a person can follow Jesus' command to pray always is for his lifestyle to be a prayer. Lifestyle prayer, as the very term implies, is holistic prayer in which psychomotor, cognitive, and affective elements are present and active.[279]

A significant number of Christian scholars and specialists in the spiritual life forthrightly assert that prayer and lifestyle go hand in hand.[280] Adolphe Tanquerey maintains that in its fullest sense and most advanced level, prayer means that a person's lifestyle can best be described as a "habitual prayer," that is to say a lifestyle transformed into living in and with and for God, to be united with God in the totality of one's being and becoming.[281] Robert Faricy puts this same point in lovely language: "Prayer is remaining in the Lord, being united with him."[282] Summarizing his treatment of the biblical view of prayer, especially in the New Testament, the Protestant scholar Charles Smith states that "a lifelong and whole-person response to the divine reality, a posture of the will oriented toward the divine majesty, is the essence of prayer."[283]

When prayer is seen as a lifestyle activity, the conflict between prayer and action tends to evaporate.[284] Prayer can only conflict with action when it becomes solely a separate activity involving less than the person's whole lifestyle, as, for example, prayer of a cognitive meditation variety. When prayer becomes a lifestyle content, the possibilities of activism diminish and possibly even vanish.

The classic forms of prayer take on a quite different hue and valence depending on whether they become types of psychomotor prayer, cognitive prayer, affective prayer, or lifestyle prayer. Thus, for example, the prayer of adoration is significantly different depending on whether this prayer is performed by prostrating oneself in a holy place (psycho-motor prayer), by intellectually meditating on God's omnipotence and its relation to present existence (cognitive prayer), by expressing emotions of homage and feelings of abject creatureliness (affective prayer), or by living a pattern of life which is itself a continual act of veneration (lifestyle prayer). The same principle applies to the other classic forms of prayer, including the prayer of petition, the prayer of thanksgiving, the prayer of reparation, and the prayer of expiation.[285]

Almost all the research and treatises on prayer down through the centuries have been done by theologians. Although the best of these theologians did indeed incorporate empirical data into their speculations, still their research and treatises perforce proceed according to the speculative mode. Our understanding of the nature, dynamics, and results of prayer would be enormously increased if social-science research and theory were brought directly to bear on the act of praying. What is sorely needed, among other things, is more controlled social-science research to separate the relevant variables involved in prayer and to derive (or confirm) empirically valid categories of prayer. Prayer is a human activity and thus amenable to empirical investigation.[286]

Prayer should occupy a very prominent place in religious instruction. The substantive content of religious instruction is, after all, religion. Prayer in all its forms, especially in its lifestyle form, is one of the finest and purest ways in which religion is operationalized.

The religious educator would be amiss were he to regard prayer as inherently separate from or otherwise outside of the ecclesial function of cognitive Christian dogma. It must be emphasized that in religious instruction (as distinct from theological instruction), cognitive Christian dogma takes on a religious meaning when it is inserted into the context of prayer. This statement holds true for every cognitive Christian dogma from the loftiest to the lowliest. In this vein Gabriel Moran perceptively observes that the Christian creed, that collection of fundamental cognitive Christian dogmas, can be most fruitfully viewed as a prayer. A Christian creed, writes Moran, is a collection of key cognitive doctrinal statements which are assembled only in order to bring together the Christian community in the unity of its prayer of faith.[287] The separation of cognitive Christian dogma from its prayer context is done by theologians for the purpose of intellectual analysis and theological inspection. One basic error made by the *ecclesiasticum* down through the centuries has been to reify this artificial separation and to forget the dogma's original context. By cutting off dogma from its ecological and nuturing soil, the *ecclesiasticum* has been able to transmogrify dogma into a hound dog for sniffing out deviation and heresy, as well as a club to bludgeon would-be deviants into approved orthodoxy.

The religious educator should teach the learners how to pray psychomotorically, cognitively, affectively, and above all lifestylistically. The first three of these types of prayers should be interwoven into the lesson as pedagogically appropriate. But above all, the religious educator should teach the learners how to make their lifestyles a prayer. There are many pedagogical ways of accomplishing this objective. One can begin, for example, with a pedagogical procedure suggested indirectly by Damian Lundy.[288] In one sense, Lundy remarks, prayer is looking—looking in, looking back, looking forward, looking out. Thus to help learners to begin to make their lifestyles a prayer, the religious educator might wish to teach them to look in by contemplating their present personal experiences, to look back by recalling their past positive and negative personal experiences, to look forward by opening themselves to future personal experiences of significance, and to look out by exercising a loving concern for others. When these kinds of looking take place in a laboratory for Christian living, they can be bonded right here-and-now into lifestyle development.

Recognizing that it is impossible and often undesirable for persons to spend all their time in prolonged meditation, Ignatius of Loyola recommended a pedagogical procedure whereby persons could help make their lifestyle a prayer.[289] This pedagogical procedure is called the practice of the presence of God and, like Lundy's looking procedure, is very behaviorally oriented. The practice of the presence of God consists in the deliberate and as far as possible the constant seeking of God's presence in all things and then existentially uniting oneself with that presence. God's presence should be sought in everything a person sees, tastes, hears, understands, loves, lives—in short, in everything a person experiences.

Some religious educators see the role of prayer in the religion lesson as something which begins and ends the lesson. Other religious educators, somewhat more advanced with respect to the place of prayer in the religion lesson, see the ideal religion lesson as one which, impelled by its own dynamism, naturally erupts into a prayer at its conclusion.

Other religious educators, more advanced still, strive to teach in such a manner as to have the learners of their own accord make short cognitive and affective prayers at various times during the lesson. But the most advanced of all religious educators with respect to the place of prayer in the religion lesson are those who attempt to structure the pedagogical situation in such a fashion that the religion lesson is itself a lifestyle prayer.

Levels of Religious Living

Throughout the history of Christianity, the image of the journey of ascent has been repeatedly used to describe the process of religious living. This image seeks to portray religious living as the process in which a person grows into progressively closer union with God. A person helps to hasten this process by removing obstacles which tend to block such a union and by engaging in activities which tend to promote this union.

Specialists in Christian spirituality have traditionally identified love as the axis, criterion, and goal of the journey of a person's lifestyle ascent to God.[290] Thomas Aquinas endeavors to prove this point by noting that the perfection of any reality consists in the attainment of its ultimate end. God is the ultimate end or goal of every human person. Since it is love and only love which unites the person with God, it is love which constitutes the axis, criterion, and goal of the human being.[291] Of special interest to religious educators is the fact that Aquinas links the lifestyle ascent to God through love with empirical evidence. Thus he writes: "Bodily growth can be gauged by those observable effects which were not previously present. Similarly in spiritual growth, the different stages of love can be gauged by those observable effects which love produces in the person who possesses this virtue."[292] Aquinas was neither the first nor the last person to identify progress in the journey of religious ascent with identifiable empirical evidence.[293] There are also scriptural roots for this position, as, for example, in Matthew 7:20, Luke 9:23, 1 Corinthians 3:1-2, and Philippians 3:13-17.

In an attempt both to chart and to facilitate the journey of lifestyle ascent to God, Christian scholars have traditionally placed the levels of this ascent into hierarchical categories with each category typically linked to an identifiable set of empirically observable behaviors. The Apostle Paul speaks of two stages in the journey of ascent, namely religious childhood and religious adulthood (omitting the middle stage of religious adolescence). Using operational terms, Paul states that religious children are capable only of the milk of basic teachings and not the solid food fit for religious adults (1 Cor. 3:1–3, Heb. 5:12–14).[294] Other authors delineate a larger number of stages. John Climacus identifies thirty different degrees in the journey of ascent, placing them into three discrete series.

The number of stages proposed by writers on the spiritual life can usually be boiled down to three. Occupying the lowest stage are those who are in the early phases of the religious journey. In the middle stage are those whose religious journey is marked by a goodly degree of proficiency. At the highest stage are to be found the relatively few persons who have attained an exceptionally high degree of success in the religious ascent.

Most Catholic spiritual writers have traditionally adopted the famous three-stage division of the religious journey of ascent first developed by Dionysius the Areopagite around the beginning of the sixth century. Called the three ways, this hierarchical categorization had its original roots in the Greek mystery religions. Though Dionysius originally applied the three ways to stages of mystical union with God, subsequent writers on spiritual living broadened the three ways to include the totality of the religious journey.

The three ways of the religious journey of ascent to God developed by Dionysius and later adopted by most specialists in the spiritual life are, in ascending order, the purgative way, the illuminative way, and the unitive way. The purgative way is the stage in which beginners find themselves. The behaviors of persons in the purgative way center upon efforts to purify themselves of serious sin and to make the first positive steps in the ascent by endeavoring to consolidate themselves in God's grace. The illuminative way is the stage in which persons who are relatively proficient in religious living find themselves. The behaviors of persons in the illuminative way center around efforts to eliminate minor sins as far as possible and to become illumined as to union with God by performing progressively important and frequent acts of virtue as well as dying to self to a certain degree. The unitive way is the stage in which persons who are extremely advanced in religious living find themselves. These persons are relatively free from even minor sins. The behaviors of persons in the unitive way center around attaining increasingly deeper and more holistic union with God through the fulfillment in a very high degree of love and by opening themselves to intense passive religious experience.[295]

Interest in the three ways declined sharply in the thirty years following World War II. However, since the mid-1970s the hierarchical stage-description of the religious journey of ascent to God has been making a comeback. An important engine powering this comeback has been social science. The empirical research conducted by some developmental psychologists like Lawrence Kohlberg and James Fowler, to name just two, has yielded results which have some striking intersections with the classical three ways. Benedict Groeschel, a Christian social scientist, attempts to show the psychological basis for the three ways. He inserts the three ways into psychological theory and offers psychological characteristics of the orientations and the behaviors involved in each of these three ways. To be sure, one of the major contributions made by Groeschel is that he sees the entire religious journey of ascent to God from a social-scientific point of view. In a passage of great importance for religious educators he writes: "Perhaps the best description of the spiritual life is the sum total of responses which one makes to what is perceived as the inner call of God. However, the spiritual life is not locked up inside a person. It is a growing, coherent set of responses integrated into the complex behavior patterns of human life."[296] I am personally convinced that if we are to get a better and a more accurate picture of the real nature and operation of the religious ascent to God, whether this ascent be viewed as the three ways or in any other manner, we shall have to proceed social scientifically, namely to make social-scientific observations which yield empirical data which are then inserted systematically into laws and theory. If the church is truly serious about the religious journey, then it should do all in its power to encourage such research.

Some Lifestyle Patterns

The religion which the religious educator strives to facilitate in learners is not a disembodied one; rather it is embodied in a variety of lifestyle patterns. Hence, if the religious educator wishes to effectively teach religion, he must necessarily do so within the existential context of the learner's actual lifestyle pattern.

Because there is a host of basic lifestyle patterns, it is manifestly impossible to deal with all of them in this section. What I will do, therefore, is to briefly discuss two of the most important and most frequently lived basic lifestyle patterns. I will present both of these basic patterns in the form of a continuum, since people enflesh these lifestyle patterns on one or another point of a continuum.

One foundational principle should be kept in mind when dealing with a learner's lifestyle pattern, namely that religious living is essentially a personal affair. What is one individual's manner of serving God may not be another's.[297] All holiness occurs according to the mode of the person in that person's lifestyle. There is no objectively "best lifestyle pattern" for religious living because an actually lived lifestyle pattern is never objective—it is always subjective, always lived in the flesh-and-blood lifestyle of a human being. Hence it is impossible to state, for example, that the lifestyle pattern of community religious living is superior in itself than the lifestyle pattern of individual religious living, or that the lifestyle pattern of conservative religious living is better than the lifestyle pattern of liberal religious living. Each person must live religiously in a manner which is most congruent with his own personality. Critiques of conservative theology or liberation theology or the like are directed toward the adequacy and fruitfulness of these viewpoints themselves. Critiques of a person living a conservative or liberal lifestyle pattern are directed toward whether or not this particular conservative lifestyle or that particular liberal lifestyle is in fact enabling the person to come closer to God.

Individual-Community Lifestyle Pattern Continuum. The importance of both the individual religious lifestyle pattern and the community religious lifestyle pattern is affirmed over and over again in the history of Christianity.

The religious lifestyle of the desert Fathers was very much individually oriented. Thus Benedicta Ward writes that *hesychia,* which is stillness and quiet and tranquility, constitutes "the central consideration in the prayer of the desert Fathers. On the external level it signifies an individual living as a solitary; on a deeper level it is not merely separation from noise and from speaking with other people, but possession of interior quiet and peace."[298] Virtually all the great mystics in the Middle Ages and in the modern period underwent their intense religious experiences alone and not in a group. Contemporary specialists in spirituality tend to emphasize that the hubbub of today's world and its countless mass activities make it imperative for the Christian to turn inward to discover God and self. Testifying about his own life and in all probability about the lives of other kindred persons,

Douglas Steere writes: "Until I have been lured into the desert, until I have been brought in solitude to the very ground of my being, where I am beyond the grip of my surface self with all of its plans and distractions, I am not able to hear the divine whisper. . . . It is then I discover at the heart of things that my solitariness is transcended and I am not alone."[299] Thomas Merton constructs a strong case for the necessity of all workaday Christians, no matter how active, to build islands of solitude into their lives. Merton also argues persuasively for the eremetic life of religious hermits.[300] For fifteen years Merton wrote and worked and taught in every way he could to "insure that monks in the communal life, when they reached maturity, would bear fruit in the solitary life" as hermits. Merton finally gained approval from his abbot "to live as a hermit himself, and it was easy to see that he became not only more a monk, but also more human: closer to men, to all men, more universal." Merton believed that his desire to be a hermit was a call from God.[301]

Community life has also had a definite and valuable place in the history of Christianity. Indeed, the very notion of church or ecclesia suggests community. The liturgy is the official prayer of the church as a community of faith. To be sure, the liturgy is the church community as it is a community in prayer. Theologians are more and more interpreting the famous dictum "outside the church there is no salvation" to mean that salvation occurs in the ecclesia, in the community of the people of God, and by virtue of the people of God. The tradition of Western monasticism, founded by Benedict of Nursia and flourishing to this day, bears eloquent witness to the religious richness and fecundity of the cenobitic life. Modern authors, notably the so-called "political theologians" are arguing for the necessity of Christianity to be essentially a corporate, communal, political religion.

In my view, a person who lives an individual religious lifestyle should at times be involved in corporate endeavor, as appropriate. I also believe that a person who lives a corporate religious lifestyle should at times be highly individualistic in religious living, as appropriate. The great mystics considered themselves to be an intrinsic part of the ecclesia and important contributors in their own way to the life of the ecclesia. From out of their basic lifestyle posture of individualism, some great mystics like Teresa of Avila and Thomas Merton even engaged in direct active work of ecclesial and world reform. Many of the great Christian heroes whose lifestyles were definitely communal nevertheless assiduously cultivated their own privately oriented spiritual life. One only has to think of John Wesley, Thomas Aquinas, and Dorothy Day to appreciate this point.

Supremely exemplifying the position which I advocate in the previous paragraph is Jesus. Jesus founded a community of disciples and lived his public ministry in this communal milieu. He spent much of his time in groups of one sort or another. But Jesus was also a man of great individualism. He often went away to be alone, especially in deep personal moments involved in coming to grips with himself (as in the temptations) and with major events (as in Gethsemane). On the basis of what we read of him in the bible, it is impossible to state whether Jesus' lifestyle was primarily individual or primarily communal—which is precisely my point.

Conservative-Liberal Lifestyle Pattern Continuum. Though the terms conservative and liberal are often overworked and vague and trite, still they are useful to describe basically different general orientations in lifestyle.

A conservative religious lifestyle is typically one which seeks to preserve established Christian theories and practices. A conservative religious lifestyle is one which endeavors to faithfully follow the dictates and prescriptions of one or more duly constituted religious authorities such as the bible in Evangelical Protestantism and the magisterium in Roman Catholicism. This lifestyle orientation is typically on guard against any unwarranted intrusion of modern theories or practices which appear to deviate from and thus contaminate standard biblical or ecclesiastical teaching. The conservative religious lifestyle is nicely exemplified by Eugene Kevane, one of its staunchest supporters. Kevane cites with hearty approval the following papal statement about the Roman Catholic Church: "Orthodoxy is her first concern; the pastoral Magisterium her primary and providential function." Kevane sharply castigates contemporary Catholic religious instruction as being creedless and representing a naturalistic philosophy of the human person. Modern Catholic religious instruction, writes Kevane, is Modernism with a perverse contemporary twist.[302] To insure that a conservative religious lifestyle be taught in Catholic circles, Kevane urges that all religious instruction become catechetics, namely religious instruction inspired and controlled by the *ecclesiasticum*. Kevane further advocates that catechists be trained in special catechetical institutes which are under the direct control of the Vatican.

A liberal religious lifestyle is typically one which seeks to modernize and advance established Christian theories and practices. A liberal religious lifestyle is one which endeavors to examine all past Christian theories and practices to see if and how they make sense in the modern world. A liberal religious lifestyle plumbs Christianity to locate its finest possibilities and richest potentialities for fructifying the human person as person. It is wary of the *ecclesiasticum*. This lifestyle orientation is typically open to all new secular developments which can be incorporated into or meshed with Christianity in such a manner as to push Christianity into ever newer zones of fulfillment. Whereas the conservative religious lifestyle tends to stress fidelity and the letter of the law, the liberal religious lifestyle tends to emphasize authenticity and the spirit of the law.

Two of the most important new developments in liberal lifestyle orientation are those discussed by Lawrence Kohlberg and Andrew Greeley, both of whom are social scientists.

On the basis of extensive cross-cultural empirical research, Kohlberg discovered six stages of moral reasoning common to people all over the world. In general, the higher the degree of moral reasoning, the more the person has moved away from an orientation of self-interest and law-and-order, and conversely the more the person has moved toward an orientation of universal-interest and humanitarian spirit. Thus the highest of Kohlberg's six stages of moral reasoning is the "universal ethical-principle orientation." In this stage, writes Kohlberg, "right is defined by the decision of conscience in accord with self-chosen ethical principles appealing to logical comprehensiveness, universality, and consistency. These principles are abstract and ethical (the Golden Rule, the categorical imperative); they are not concrete moral rules like the Ten Commandments. At heart, these are universal principles of justice, of the reciprocity and equality of human rights, and of respect for the dignity of human beings as individual persons."[303] Kohlberg states that Stage 6 is, at bottom, a form of postconventional morality. (Postconventional morality is one which takes its shape and direction from universal principles derived from the use of autonomous conscience. Conventional morality is one which takes its shape and direction from existing cultural or institutional norms.) Kohlberg's research-based conclusions have powerful implications for religious instruction since they suggest that the more a person grows in moral consciousness, the more that individual will move away from the conventional morality promulgated by civil society and by the churches, and the more that individual will move toward a postconventional morality which he himself fashions.

As a result of some scattered empirical data plus an enlightened attempt to read the times, Andrew Greeley claims to have discovered the emergence of a new American Catholic liberal religious style which he calls communal Catholicism.[304] It seems to me that Greeley's zestfully thoughtful description of communal Catholic behaviors finds counterparts in similar liberal religious lifestyles present in other American Christian confessions. For this reason I am broadening Greeley's term to include what I shall call the communal Christian.

The communal Christian's primary loyalty is to the community of fellow religionists past and present rather than to the organized institutional church. Thus the communal Christian feels allegiance to and belongingness with the ecclesia and not with the *ecclesiasticum*. The communal Christian is committed to the worldview and to the religious (not ecclesiastical) tradition of his denomination; however he tends to interpret this worldview and tradition flexibly on the basis of how much they fulfill his personal and religious life. This does not mean that the communal Christian is selfish and makes himself the measure of all things. Rather it means that the communal Christian sees his denominational worldview and tradition as principally targeted toward helping him attain Christian perfection instead of being fixed and congealed entities into which he must somehow squeeze however unnaturally. The communal Christian does not regard ecclesiastical functionaries as authoritative sources or as indispensable guides in religious matters. Ecclesiastical functionaries may or may not be helpful in religious matters, but their dictates or suggestions are not binding in themselves. The communal Christian does not accept the official stances of the *ecclesiasticum* on social or economic or political matters just because these are the stances of the *ecclesiasticum*. The communal Christian seeks his own counsel, though he might wish to listen to what the *ecclesiasticum* has to say. The communal Christian is relatively indifferent to what the *ecclesiasticum* as an institution does or does not do. For example, the communal Catholic does not really care much about whether the *ecclesiasticum* takes this or that stand on a certain social issue, or whether this or that bishop assumes the leadership of a given diocese. The communal Christian is cool toward the *ecclesiasticum*; he is not angry at it because he is not really involved with it emotionally or otherwise. The communal Christian will tend to avoid seeking posts in the ecclesiastical apparatus or in any sector related to the institutional church such as a Christian college. The communal Christian is deeply committed to his denomination and to his religious heritage, viewing both as essentially independent from the denomination's *ecclesiasticum*. The communal Christian participates in the sacramental and liturgical activities of his denomination. The frequency of this participation is not determined by any commands or suggestions of the *ecclesiasticum,* but by the degree to which he believes that these activities will help him in his own religious living. The communal Christian is not looking for holy ministers of the sacraments and of liturgical activities, but for competent ministers. If a competent minister is also holy, this is an added plus. (The communal Christian regards these ministers primarily as facilitators of religious experience and sacramental life and not principally as members of the *ecclesiasticum*.) The communal Christian is deeply concerned with his own religious commitment and his own religious living, and is especially eager to see to it that his children learn to live a committed Christian life.[305]

Another liberal religious lifestyle pattern which has come into increasingly wide attention since the late 1960s is that inspired by political theology and/or by liberation theology.[306]

Though they are sometimes uncritically lumped together to mean the same thing, political theology and liberation theology are somewhat different. Political theology arose in the German-speaking portion of Europe roughly around the time that liberation theology was aborning in Latin America. Both political theology and liberation theology are quite radical and very left-wing as judged by standard theological and religious perceptions; however, political theology tends to be less radical and less left-wing than liberation theology. As Francis Fiorenza has noted, "in general the difference between political theology and liberation theology can be drawn fairly sharply."[307]

Political theology arose as a reaction to the effects both of the Christian liberal enlightenment and of the secularization of society as these two molar developments have found expression in theological and philosophical Existentialism, in theological and philosophical personalism, and in some aspects of transcendental theology. The primary axis of political theology is hermeneutical—specifically, to develop a substantially different hermeneutic between theory and "praxis."[308]

Political theology has two fundamental objectives, one negative and the other positive. Both objectives are as necessary as they are complementary. The negative objective is to deprivatize theology and religious living so that these two areas move away from their emphasis on the individual person and toward a stress on the group and society at large.[309] The positive objective is to prophetically confront church and society with the light and heat of eschatology. This light and heat of eschatology will enable the Christian to break through the bourgeois culture and middle-class structure in which the church is currently encased so that what will result is the empowerment of freedom and the realization of eschatology.[310] The Christian church, then, is authentic to eschatology when it acts as a collective force or institution of the critical liberty of the faith. Every truly eschatological theology must, therefore, become a political theology, that is a socio-critical theology.[311] The major political theologians such as Johannes Baptist Metz and Jürgen Moltmann tend to reject the notion that political, economic, or social action should flow directly from political theology or from religious faith. Moltmann rejects any immediate and direct politicization of eschatology.[312] In a famous statement which just about everyone seems to quote when mentioning political theology and political involvement, Dorothee Sölle writes that "there are no specifically Christian solutions to world problems."[313] Political theologians, notably Metz, contend that there is an autonomous area which serves as an intermediary between political theology and political/social/economic activity.[314]

Liberation theology arose as a reaction to the heavy-handed political oppression and gross socioeconomic injustice prevalent throughout much of the past and the present in Latin America. Liberation theology is a critique not only of oppression and injustice in the civil arena, but also of manifest and latent oppression in the church arena as well. Thus liberation theology sharply castigates all forms of political and ideological colonialism, the theories of economic and social developmentalism, existentially detached Christian liberalism, and that theology of social action and of the lay apostolate which was prevalent in the late nineteenth and most of the twentieth century. The primary axis of liberation theology is the endeavor to discover the applicability of the core message of the Christian faith to present society and culture. Liberation theology has the fundamental objective of revealing in all their immediacy and universality the twin bases of freedom and revolution which form the ever-fresh dynamic core of the Christian message, and then applying this message in "praxis" to the immediate and worldwide political, social, and economic scene.[315] Liberation theology sees freedom as both the central path of personal salvation and the primary focus of Jesus' mission on earth. In this perspective, the entire life of Jesus was directed toward the liberation of religion: thus Jesus liberated true religion from its oppression by Jewish cultural norms, Jewish theology, Jewish sensibilities, and the Jewish piety of his day.[316] In this connection Gustavo Gutiérrez, one of the most esteemed names in liberation theology, flatly remarks that the entire bible is first and foremost an account of salvation as a process of political liberation from political oppression. The most decisive event in the Old Testament, according to this view, was the Exodus from Egypt in which the Chosen People were liberated from political oppression. The work of Jesus was a continuation and indeed a perfecting of this Exodus liberation. The political liberation achieved in the Exodus event, together with its perpetuation throughout the remainder of the Old Testament, represents the self-creation of the human person, while the political liberation propounded and indeed enacted by Jesus in his ministry is itself the re-creation and the complete fulfillment of the human person.[317] The liberation effected by the Exodus event and most especially by Jesus was not confined to the so-called "spiritual" world, but rather embraced the whole of creation. The Kingdom of God, a central theme in the New Testament and therefore in the theorizing of liberation theologians, comprises all reality, physical as well as nonphysical, temporal as well as eternal.[318] Theologians of liberation tend to see the liberation process as involving two dimensions.[319] The first dimension consists in liberation from the bondage of self (or of one's present congealed consciousness), while the second dimension is liberation from the oppression of sociopolitical structures. What holds self in bondage is sin. What holds sociopolitical structures in bondage is estrangement or alienation on the one hand and oppressive political and ideological forces on the other hand.[320] Estrangement flows typically through the law.[321] Liberation is therefore in diametrical opposition to what some theologians call oppression, to what Paulo Freire labels domestication, and to what social scientists term socialization.[322] Liberation theologians tend to strongly affirm the notion that political, economic, and social action should flow directly from theology and religious faith. Indeed, Gustavo Gutiérrez[323] holds that faith norms and criteria, as decided by theology in dialectic with Christian communities in "praxis," have an immediate relationship with and direct role in bringing about here-and-now specific political actions.[324] For his part, Leonardo Boff forthrightly declares that the work of Jesus on earth "is eminently social and public in character. It touches upon the *structure* of society and religion in his day. . . . His praxis vis-à-vis religion, sacred laws, and tradition is truly liberative rather than reformist."[325] Christianity is essentially a religion of liberation, and authentic liberation can only be achieved through political, social, and economic action.[326]

Two important forms of liberation theology which have ramifications for the religious instruction enterprise are black theology and feminist theology.

Black theology arose as a reaction to the manifest political oppression and the brutal racial discrimination which black people have undeniably suffered in the United States since the days of slavery. The growth of black theology was greatly accelerated by the civil rights movement initially led by Martin Luther King, Jr. and subsequently animated by more radical black leaders such as Malcolm X, Eldridge Cleaver, Rap Brown, and the like. The primary axis of black theology is the attempt to discover the relevance of the core message of the Christian faith for black society today. Black theology has a dual fundamental objective: the liberation of black people from the political and socioeconomic oppression under which they currently labor, and the injection of the redemptive life-giving black experience into the moribund Christian churches and into the racist civil society. Like liberation theology of which it is a form, black theology affirms that liberation constitutes the essence of Jesus' mission. In this vein James Cone, a major black theologian, states that by becoming a slave himself (Phil. 2:7) Jesus thereby liberated the human race by opening up the full realities of human existence formerly closed to human beings. In a statement which encapsulates the cognitive basis and affective flavor of black theology, Cone states: "If the gospel is a gospel of liberation for the oppressed, then Jesus is where the oppressed are and continues his work of liberation there. Jesus is not safely confined in the first century. He is our contemporary, proclaiming release to the captives and rebelling against all who silently accept the structures of injustice. If he is not in the ghetto, if he is not where men are living on the brink of existence, but is, rather, in the easy life of the suburbs, then the gospel is a lie. The opposite, however, is the case. Christianity is not alien to [revolutionary political] Black Power; it is Black Power."[327] Black theology does not see itself as a provincial theology of liberation, one springing from the ghetto and remaining there. On the contrary, black theology sees itself as a major liberational and redemptive factor in the world and in the church. Both world and church are sorely in need of what the black experience has to offer, declare black theologians of liberation. Black theology seeks to equip the black churches as a highly potent force in directly bringing about political liberation.[328]

Feminist theology arose as a reaction to the personal, political, and socioeconomic oppression which some American women contend has been an intrinsic aspect of church and society since the beginning of time.[329] The growth of feminist theology by and large was an outgrowth ultimately of the black civil rights movement, penultimately of liberation theology, and immediately of the women's liberation movement (feminism) in civil society. The primary axis of feminist theology is the discovery of the essence of the Christian faith, an essence which feminist theologians maintain has been basely hidden and even severely distorted by unwarranted male cultural and political accretions. Feminist theologians see their movement as having a dual fundamental objective: the liberation of women from the civil and ecclesiastical oppression under which they believe they travail, and the injection of the redemptive and warmly caring female experience into what they regard as grossly male-chauvinist Christian churches and crassly sexist civil society.[330] Feminist theologians declare that the purportedly sinful male chauvinism in Christanity is not restricted to such palpable manifestations as a male-dominated clerical caste or offensively sexist liturgical language; indeed the allegedly rampant sexism of Christianity is noxiously present in the fundamental symbols and dogmas of the faith itself. Thus Mary Daly, a major feminist theologian, writes: "The [biblical and popular] symbol of the Father God, spawned in the human imagination and sustained as plausible by partriarchy, has in turn rendered service to this [sexist] type of society by making its mechanisms for the oppression of women appear right and fitting. If God in 'his' heaven is a father ruling 'his' people, then it is in the 'nature' of things and according to divine plan and the order of the universe that society be male-dominated. Within this context a mystification of roles take place: the husband dominating his wife represents

God 'himself.' The images and values of a given society have been projected into the realm of dogmas and 'Articles of Faith,' and these in turn justify the social structures which have given rise to them and which sustain their plausibility.''[331] Through direct political action, through consciousness-raising, and through mobilizing women everywhere, feminist theologians hope to throw off what they believe are the civil and ecclesiastical shackles which oppress women so that, thus liberated, women will be able to freely bring their own unique and precious gifts to bear on the redemptive and liberating mission of Jesus.

SOME PRACTICAL CONSEQUENCES

The acquisition of cognitive content requires that the teaching process move from the unknown to the known. The aquisition of affective content requires that the teaching process move from the unfelt to the felt. The acquisition of lifestyle content requires that the teaching process move from the unlived to the lived.

To teach lifestyle content is to teach holistically in such a manner that a person's experiences are holistically lived in the here-and-now concrete existential situation. Full-blooded, immediate, holistic experiencing thus constitutes the basic stuff of lifestyle content.

To be rendered eminently serviceable to instructional endeavor, experience must be put into that kind of form which enables it to be teachable. Two educational efforts in this regard are especially worthy of attention, namely the cone of experience developed by Edgar Dale and the taxonomy of experience constructed by Norman Steinaker and M. Robert Bell.

The cone of experience aims at classifying experience on the basis of specific levels of existential holism and personal immediacy. The cone of experience has as its axis the properties intrinsic to the experience itself. This model places learning experiences on a conical continuum from the base (the most concrete, direct, and immediate experiences) to the tip (the most abstract, most indirect, and most remote). The closer an experience is to the base of the cone, the more existentially holistic it is, and therefore the more pedagogically powerful it tends to be in itself. From the base upward, these experiences are: direct purposeful experiences (for example, participating in a march for peace); contrived experiences (for example, simulation games or role-playing); dramatized experiences (for example, acting out a particular part in a religious play); demonstrations (for example, a demonstration by the teacher of the use of certain liturgical altar vessels); field study trips (for example, an excursion to an ecumenical religious education center); exhibits (for example, ancient realia such as coins from the time of Jesus); television; motion pictures; still pictures, radio, and audiorecordings; visual symbols (for example, flat maps of the Holy Land, diagrams, charts, and chalkboards); and verbal symbols, namely words.[332]

The taxonomy of experience aims at classifying experience on the basis of general levels of holistic personal appropriation and existential involvement. The taxonomy of experience has as its axis the psychological degree to which the experience is being lived by the person. There are five major categories listed in the taxonomy of experience.

The first category in the experiential taxonomy is exposure. Exposure is defined in the taxonomy as consciousness of an experience. Consciousness involves two levels of exposure and a readiness for further experience. Major divisions of the whole exposure category include sensation, response, and readiness. The first two divisions are regarded as levels of exposure.

The second category in the experiential taxonomy is participation. Participation is defined in the taxonomy as the decision to become physically a part of an experience. Major divisions of participation are representation and modification. Both of these divisions are regarded as levels of participation.

The third category in the experiential taxonomy is identification. Identification is defined in the taxonomy as the coming together of the person and the object experienced in an affective and cognitive context. Major divisions of identification are reinforcement of a decision to identify with the experience, affective attachment to the experience, cognitive involvement with the experience, and sharing the experience with others. These divisions are regarded as temporal stages through which identification passes.

The fourth category in the experiential taxonomy is internalization. Internalization is defined in the taxonomy as the incorporation of the experience into one's lifestyle in such a way that the experience changes that lifestyle to some degree. Major divisions of internalization are expansion and intrinsicness. Both of these divisions are regarded as levels of internalization.

The fifth category in the experiential taxonomy is dissemination.

Dissemination is defined in the taxonomy as making the experience and its fruits available to others. Major divisions of dissemination are informational and homiletical. Both of these divisions are regarded as levels of dissemination.[333]

Instruction which takes place in an holistic existential mode is distinctly different from instruction which occurs in a cognitive mode.[334] This statement holds true for all cognitively-based teaching procedures such as lecture/telling, discussion, action-reflection, or whatever.

According to James Coleman, there are two major sets of differences between information assimilation learning and experiential learning. (Information assimilation learning is the cognitive type of learning which typically takes place in classrooms, Sunday sermons, bible discussion groups, theological reflection sessions, action-reflection activities, and the like.) These major sets of differences have to do with the steps in which the two processes take place and the basic characteristics of these two processes.[335] (It should be underscored that Coleman is comparing the information assimilation process and the experiential process in terms of the acquisition of cognitive content and not in terms of the acquisition of affective, psychomotor, or lifestyle content.)

According to Coleman's analysis, there are four steps involved in the information assimilation process. The first step is receiving information through the medium of a symbol, usually a verbal symbol. The second step is grasping and organizing information in such a way that the general principle of which it is an instance is understood. The third step is inferring some particular application from the general principle. The fourth and final step is moving from the purely cognitive- and symbol-processing sphere to the sphere of action.

The major steps of the experiential process proceed in an almost reverse sequence from the above. The first step is carrying out an action in a particular situation and holistically observing the effects of that action. The second step is understanding these effects as they occur in a particular situation so that if exactly the same set of circumstances would reappear, the person could anticipate what would follow from that action. The third step is understanding the general principle under which the particular instance falls. The fourth and final step is the application through action in a new circumstance within the range of generalization.

Underlying all the steps involved in the information assimilation process is the fact that the information is transmitted and received in a symbolic medium, typically words. In sharp contrast, underlying all the steps involved in the experiential process is the fact that the information is generated only through the series of steps themselves.

As Coleman sees it, the information assimilation process has four basic characteristics. First, it can enormously reduce the time and effort necessary to learn something new. This characteristic flows from the fact that the information assimilation process occurs in a symbolic medium, usually words. The information assimilation process is the cognitive crystallization in a symbolic medium of the experiences of others throughout time and cultures; thus it is the collection of distilled inferences derived from a broad range of experiences. Second, it depends very heavily upon a symbolic medium, usually words and other abstractions. Third, it necessarily uses artificial and extrinsic motivation.[336] Fourth, the information which is acquired is often forgotten rather quickly and easily, especially when it is gained apart from a sufficiently integrative structure.

The four basic properties of the experiential learning process stand out in sharp contrast to those of the information assimilation process. First, it is time-consuming, since it involves actions which have to be enacted with sufficient frequency in enough circumstances to permit the development of an adequate generalization from experience. Second, in its ideal form it does not use a symbolic medium, but only action together with observation of concrete events which follow the action.[337] There is no formidable barrier to cross from symbolic medium to action, only modifications of the action to fit the circumstances. Third, motivation is natural and intrinsic.[338] Fourth, the information which is acquired is often learned rather easily and retained rather long, especially as compared to the information gained in the information assimilation process.

From what I have written thus far in this section, it should be obvious that experiential instruction, especially when it is fully holistic and richly lifestyle in texture, is not a particular teaching method or a specific pedagogical technique. Rather, experiential instruction is a general style of teaching.[339] Style of teaching is the basic overall pattern or mode which serves as the indicator of the specific direction which the activities of the teaching-learning act will take.

While most people seem to agree that experience is indeed the best teacher of holistic lifestyle content, there is no guarantee that all experiences automatically provide high-level and useful learning. Experiences differ in quality, potency, immediacy, holistic character, lifestyle permeation, and so on. John Dewey expresses the principal curricular issue in experiential teaching when he observes that "the central problem of an education based on experience is to select the kind of present experiences that live fruitfully and creatively in subsequent experiences."[340] Experiences which are genuinely educational, then, are ones which have the capability of generating new and richer experiences, new and richer opportunities for learning. From a complementary vantage point, experiences which are the most educative are those which are personally significant. Significant experiences, as Carl Rogers reminds us, are experiences which cause a definite growth-producing effect on a person's life and lifestyle.[341] The educational significance of an experience is not primarily determined by its intrinsic power, even if its intrinsic power is overwhelming. Rather, the educational significance of an experience is determined primarily on the basis of whether or not it makes a difference in the person's cognitive, affective, and most especially lifestyle activities.[342] When arranging for the incorporation of significant experiences in the religion lesson, the religious educator should realize that significance is determined not only by the quality of the experience itself but also by how the learner understands, feels, and lives this experience in his own personal life.

It is probably safe to say that while religious educationists and educators pay lip service to experiential teaching of a holistic lifestyle character, most of them are in actual fact either lukewarm toward it or oppose it. This seems especially true of adminstrators of religious instruction activities in formal settings. In general, there seem to be at least nine major objections against lifestyle-oriented experiential religious instruction which these people voice at one time or another. Interestingly, these objections are directed primarily at religious instruction conducted in formal settings. For some strange reason, a goodly number of religious educationists and educators appear to believe that while lifestyle-oriented religious instruction is beneficial and even ideal in informal settings like the home or the senior citizens club, it is inappropriate and even detrimental in formal settings like a classroom. No wonder religious instruction in formal settings has been so ineffective when religious educationists and educators believe that in order to be successful it must be cut off from holistic lifestyle experiencing. (After all, both the research and everyday observation have shown that it is this very holistic lifestyle experiencing which makes religious instruction in informal settings so potent and so richly educative.)

The first objection raised against experiential teaching is that for many years it has been a muddled and confused concept in religious literature and parlance. In his review of some of the pertinent literature, William Bedford Williamson found that while experience was used by religious educationists in some instances to refer to empirical observation, in most instances it was used in one of three ways: as a term to describe a "new" instructional corrective to traditional pedagogical procedures, as a motivational slogan to create or maintain interest, or as a mystical or psychological event. Williamson goes on to note that Christian religious educationists have tended to use the term experience either analytically (meaning at best "Create interest in teaching"), or prescriptively (urging the adoption of the slogan "We learn from experience").[343] I readily concede that the terms experience and experiential teaching have indeed been muddled, confused, and abused in the field of religious instruction. But it is a venerable axiom of logic that abuse does not negate proper use. The reason why this term was confused and muddled and abused by religious educationists and educators seems to be that these persons failed to steep themselves in the nature and function of experiential teaching. One major cause for this failure appears to have been the fact that these persons apparently believed that the term experiential education was self-evident and therefore required no serious study, no theoretical anchorage, no empirical research, and no carefully orchestrated implementation. Another major cause for this failure seems to have been the fact that these persons tended to operate out of a theological conceptualization of experience rather than out of an educational one: the direct unmediated application of experience from one area of endeavor to a substantially different field inevitably produced confusion, a confusion all the more exacerbated by the fact that there were different theologies of experience.

The second objection raised against experiential teaching is that it has been previously tried in religious instruction and has failed miserably. In the 1960s and during much of the 1970s, all sorts of experientially based religious instruction programs were in vogue among the Christian denominations. These programs and instructional initiatives were eventually abandoned when many learners, religious educators, parents, and pastors complained that little or no solid learning was taking place. My response to this objection is that the so-called experiential religious instruction programs of the 1960s and 1970s were not really experiential instructional activities in the proper sense of this term. The programs and activities of the 1960s and 1970s were usually nothing more than social "happenings." As "happenings" these programs and activities were typically vague and amorphous, relatively bereft of careful pedagogical planning, seriously lacking in adequate teacher intentionality, woefully deficient in specified performance objectives, almost always lacking in assessment procedures, and in general devoid of objective criteria of any sort. Experiential instruction of the type I am advocating is diametrically opposed to the pedagogically discredited "happening" sort of activity.

The third objection directly or indirectly brought against experiential religious instruction is that it weakens the locus of pedagogical authority. If the axis of pedagogical activity lies in the experiences engaged in by the learner, then the traditional authority of the denominational *ecclesiasticum* both in itself and as represented in the approved subject-centered curriculum will be eroded.[344] My response to this objection is that experience-centered religious instruction does not weaken authority in and of itself, but only a certain kind of authority. Experience-centered religious instruction puts pedagogical authority right where it actually is and right where it ought to be, namely in the lived encounter of the learner with the other three major structural variables present in every religious instruction act, namely the teacher, the environment, and the subject matter. In actual practice, pedagogical authority always resides in this lived encounter, no matter how authoritatively based (or authoritarian) the curriculum might be. This is a well-established social scientific fact. Further, a major pedagogical goal for virtually all religious instruction programs other than those operated for the purpose of indoctrination or other heavy-handed forms of socialization is that each learner develop for himself the most fruitful way of walking righteously in God.

The fourth objection voiced against experiential religious instruction is that it does not adequately shield learners from mistakes, even when such mistakes are sinful acts. Religious instruction should lead to a deepening of grace and religious living, not to error and sin. My response to this objection is that vibrant religious instruction is a great human adventure, and not a set of rules for safety. Mistakes are inevitable in robust living; mistakes are absent only when a person's life is inhumanly narrow and asphyxiating. The ultimate measure of one's Christian life is not so much the infrequency of one's mistakes and sins but rather the depth of one's remorse for one's sins and the degree of one's positive acts of Christian love. A person often learns more from his mistakes and sins than from other sources. This is a well-known fact and to a great extent explains the basic reason why Catholic theologians recognize Augustine rather than Thomas Aquinas as the "Doctor of Grace." Religious educators should trust learners—trust them to learn and to grow.[345]

The fifth objection raised against experiential religious instruction is that it represents a retreat from solid cognitive content, especially from the dogmatic teachings of the church. When emphasis is placed on religious experiencing, cognitive content is squeezed out. My response to this objection is that experiential religious instruction of the holistic variety necessarily includes cognitive content. Because the cognitive content in experientially suffused religion teaching is meshed with here-and-now personal living, such content tends to be learned better and retained longer than cognitive content in a traditional subject matter centered curriculum. It should be noted that most of the cognitive content found in religious instruction curricula had its original source in personal and especially in ecclesial religious experience. When these previously lived experiences were abstracted into cognitive content, a great deal of their existential vitality and ecologically rooted intellectual force was lost. Only when a religious instruction curriculum has its axis in here-and-now lived experiencing can the original vitality and intelligibility of the pristine personal and ecclesial religious experiences be truly learned.[346] Far from being a retreat from cognitive content, experiential religious instruction is a forward march into full-blooded Christian living, a forward march which is capable of endowing otherwise barren cognitive content with vitality, vigor, and genuine meaning.

The sixth objection brought against experiential religious instruction is that it constitutes a new role for the religion teacher, a role for which the teacher is typically unprepared. Whereas in a subject matter centered curriculum the religion teacher functions typically as an information dispenser, discussion leader, or the like, a religion teacher in an experience-based curriculum operates as an active resource person, as an energizer, and above all as an individual who helps facilitate that kind of significant experience required by the existential exigencies of the learning task. My response to this objection is that far from being a drawback or worthwhile objection, the new role for the religion teacher necessitated by experiential religious instruction represents a major advance in potential pedagogical effectiveness. To be sure, experiential religious instruction requires a basically different form of preservice and inservice preparation from that which currently exists. There is nothing wrong with this; certainly it is the price which every professional in any field must pay in order to constantly improve the quality of services rendered. Personal inconvenience is not a valid argument against professional improvement. Personal convenience stands as one of the gravest threats to professional activity.

The seventh objection raised against experiential religious instruction is that it frequently demands changes in the design and implementation of pedagogical space. In experiential religious instruction there is no longer a front of the classroom, for example.[347] Classrooms will often have to be enlarged and in some cases totally redesigned. My response to this objection is similar to my answer to the previous objection. The price of progress is a change in old ways, in old designs, in old modes. Such a price was paid as long ago as the 1960s by alert public school educators who radically redesigned classroom space in accordance with such well-received educational proposals as the Trump Plan. The classroom is an environment and as such constitutes one of the four major structural variables in every teaching act. If the teaching act is to change basically, such as in the case of experiential religious instruction, then all four structural variables in the teaching act must necessarily undergo alteration, including the environment. Because it is a purposive environment characterized by certain contingencies of reinforcement, a religion classroom both encapsulates and promotes a certain culture, a certain set of behaviors.[348] This new culture, these new kinds of behaviors facilitated by a change in the classroom environment are important if experiential religious instruction is to flourish.

The eighth objection leveled against experiential religious instruction is that it is time consuming, especially as contrasted with the lecture technique, with the discussion technique, with any one of the forms of the action-reflection technique, and so forth. Because it is time consuming it is impractical—or so runs this objection. My response to this objection is that the amount of time necessitated by experiential religious instruction must be weighed against its potential benefits. A person can learn to repeat the Ten Commandments in a relatively short period of time. But it takes a long long time to learn to live the Ten Commandments. There is no shortcut to lifestyle outcomes. These outcomes perforce take time to acquire. If the religious educator wishes to teach learners to live religiously, then such a teacher must realize that this process requires a great deal of time and effort.

The ninth objection brought against experiential religious instruction is that this kind of teaching is not the proper function of the school or the classroom. Rather, this kind of religious instruction properly belongs to the whole congregation.[349] My response to this objection is threefold. First, this objection represents a wholly unwarranted exclusion of lifestyle content from religious instruction activities conducted in formal settings. Such a wholly unwarranted exclusion means that religious instruction is no longer instruction in religion since religion is necessarily a matter of lifestyle. Second, this objection assumes that church schools are not an integral and vital part of the church congregation. Such an assumption is clearly contrary to the fact—unless, of course, the church all-day school or Sunday School is operated outside of the ecclesial context of the congregation. Third, this objection is based in part on a naive and probably incorrect assumption that the church community independent of its school can successfully perform the major task of religious instruction, namely teach religious lifestyle content. As a general rule, most members of a church congregation are not very active or involved in church affairs and participate relatively little in ecclesial activities.

To assist religious educators working both in formal and informal settings to place their instructional activities on an experiential base, national, regional, and even local religious education offices would do well to compile a bank of experiential teaching-learning activities of empirically proven educational significance. These religious education offices would also do well to develop their own empirically validated experiential learning packages for the use of religious educators.[350] Of course the success of any bank of experiential teaching-learning activities and also of experiential learning packages ultimately depends on the degree to which the religious educator's pedagogical style is itself holistically experiential. If the religious educator's pedagogical style is not holistically experiential, then not even a rich bank of experiential teaching-learning activities or a large number of experiential learning packages can bring about genuine experiential teaching. Religious educators can improve the experiential cast of their teaching style in a teacher performance center.[351]

One of the most celebrated pedagogical techniques for teaching lifestyle content in a holistically experiential form is the project.[352] A project is an instructional activity involving some sort of interdisciplinary educative task concretely performed by the learner in such a manner that he holistically integrates various modes of human functioning and subject matter contents.[353]

The project technique has seven basic characteristics. *First,* it is holistic. It requires the active here-and-now integration of the learner's cognitive, affective, and psychomotor functions in such a manner that the learner will live the project's activities in his personal life.[354] *Second,* the axis of the project is primarily "learning by doing." In a project, the learner does not cognitively, abstractly, or passively study about a reality; rather, the learner holistically, concretely, and actively engages in a particular pedagogical activity. *Third,* the project is generated through lifestyle, proceeds in a lifestyle fashion, and results in lifestyle outcomes.[355] The learning activities involved in the completion of a project are modes of conduct in active living process.[356] *Fourth,* the project technique is interdisciplinary in that it involves a personal on-the-hoof integration of subject matter contents from different sciences, disciplines, fields, and areas of life. *Fifth,* the project is purposeful in that it is personally significant for the learner, generally educative for him, and geared to bringing about desirable changes in the learner's cognitive, affective, and psychomotor functions.[357] *Sixth,* the project revolves around a specific problem of personal relevance or social concern.[358] *Seventh,* the project consists of learning experiences which are intelligent outgrowths of the needs and major interests of the learner or group of learners.

In William Heard Kilpatrick's view, the project technique has as its unifying nucleus the purposeful activity itself. As it is true with pragmatic philosophers and act theorists, purpose resides in the person's actual existential involvement in the activity at hand. Kilpatrick proposes four types of projects built around concrete problem-solving situations. These four types are: (1) projects which carry out some idea or plan, e.g., writing and presenting a play; (2) projects which provide enjoyment of an aesthetic experience, e.g., composing and performing a short piece of music for use in next Sunday's liturgy;[359] (3) projects which directly aim at resolving some existing difficulty, e.g., examining racial discrimination in the community and actually implementing ways to ameliorate such discrimination; (4) projects which assist the learners in gaining specific knowledge or skills, e.g., writing a letter in Spanish to a Hispanic official in the National Council of Churches in order to learn Spanish.

The classic four steps by which a project is developed are choosing the project, planning the project, working on the project, and evaluating the project.[360]

The project technique is grounded in many basic pedagogical principles, including the following. The learner is first and foremost an active person who is organismically oriented toward the pursuit of his own goals. An instructional activity is optimally educative when it involves the interaction of the learner with other persons, things, ideas, and the like. The result of this dynamic interaction is a change both in the environment and in the learner. This very change brought about in and through the interactive experience is what constitutes learning.[361]

The project technique enjoys mixed empirical support. The classic experimental research study on the project was conducted by Ellsworth Collings in a rural school over a four year time span. As a result of the data, Collings concluded that the project technique produced superior lifestyle and cognitive outcomes as contrasted to traditional pedagogical techniques.[362] The Progressive Education Association's extensive critical evaluation of selected new pedagogical practices was favorable to the project technique.[363] On the other hand, Norman Wallen and Robert Travers' review of some research found that the project technique was not especially effective in either a pharmacological course or in a college botany course in terms of the acquisition of cognitive facts.[364]

The heyday of the project technique was in the 1920s and 1930s.[365] It declined in popularity in the 1940s and especially in the 1960s when the post-Sputnik era in American education witnessed a heavy emphasis on narrow disciplinary study. In the 1970s and 1980s the project technique made a comeback, especially in alternative instructional settings which were established either because traditional pedagogical techniques had failed or because learners wished a more personally relevant and more lifestyle-oriented way of learning.[366]

CONCLUSION

Lifestyle is the most important substantive content in religious instruction. To be sure, no religious instruction is truly *religious* instruction unless it is first and foremost a lifestyle affair.

Lifestyle content can be aquired only in an experiential fashion in which the learner is afforded the opportunity to live one or more patterns of lifestyle behavior. A person can gain lifestyle content only by living it as holistically and as fully as possible. This point surely is one of the central themes of the gospels.

NOTES

1. Robert Frost, *Kitty Hawk.*
2. This is basically the same definition which I initially offered some years ago in an article entitled "Behavioral Objectives in Religious Instruction," in *Living Light* IV (Winter, 1970), p. 13.
3. See, for example, the first few pages of Chapters Four and Five.
4. Commenting on this point, William Schutz states: "I feel that the deepest level of [human] change is in the body, the next deepest level is with the feelings, and the least so in the intellect. Put another way, if a body change is not accompanied by parallel changes in the feelings and thoughts, the change is still real, but there is the danger that the body will eventually return to its former condition because the original cause of the body aberration still exists. However, intellectual insight not accompanied by emotional and body changes is really not a true insight and will lead to minimal change if any at all. On the simple level, this is frequently seen in a group when a person working on a problem finally gets an insight but doesn't look happy. He still has tension in his body, tension that indicates he hasn't really uncovered the basic issue." William C. Schutz, *Here Comes Everybody* (New York: Harper & Row, 1971), pp. 174–175.
5. The word *appropriately* is very important here. Not all cognitive learnings, for example, require extensive amounts of psychomotor activities as accompaniments. Sigmund Freud could work out his theories while walking in the Vienna Woods, while Albert Einstein could formulate them in the quiet of his chambers. Notwithstanding, it is well to remember the psychomotor exertion depicted by Auguste Rodin in his celebrated sculpture "The Thinker."
6. As I write this last sentence, it is the afternoon of All Saints Day, 1983, a civil and religious holiday here in Rome where I am passing my sabbatical year. I spent the morning with my wife and two sons exploring the Colosseum with guidebooks in hand. Holistic functionalism suggests that because I devoted some hours walking through the Colosseum (appropriate psychomotor processes) and being emotionally charged with its beauty and grandeur (appropriate affective processes), I thereby acquired broader, deeper, and especially more significant cognitive learnings than had I simply pored over these cognitively rich guidebooks back home in Birmingham.
7. Carl R. Rogers, *Freedom to Learn* (Columbus, Ohio: Merrill, 1969), pp. 158–159.

8. I am not entirely pleased with my phraseology in the last nine sentences of this paragraph. I eventually decided on the phraseology which I do employ because it seems to be more pedagogically potent, despite its lack of total technical precision. The second part of the opening sentence of this paragraph describes the correct relationship between an abstraction and the concrete reality from which this abstraction is drawn, as, for example, between concept and act or between theory and practice.

9. On human compartmentalization, see Harold C. Lyon Jr., *Learning to Feel—Feeling to Learn* (Columbus, Ohio: Merrill, 1971), p. 116.

10. Schubert M. Ogden, "The Reality of God," in Ewert Cousins, editor, *Process Theology* (New York: Newman, 1971), p. 121. Ogden's statement implicitly assumes a certain psychophysiological stance. Groups taking a different psychophysiological stance assert that feelings and thoughts are products of brain cells and the central nervous system. In either case, however, the primacy of the body is asserted.

11. Two important qualifications have to be made. *First,* the rise of ultra-cognitivism in religious instruction was occasioned by many major factors, only one of which was the direct reaction mentioned in the text. With some religious educationists, a major factor was the admirable desire to make the field of religious instruction intellectually respectable. With others, such as Thomas Groome, a major factor in their espousal of an ultracognitivist approach has been the influence upon them of the almost unbelievably hypercognitivist stance of the philosophical social scientists associated with what is popularly known as the Frankfurt School of Critical Theory. *Second,* there were many important cognitivist and ultracognitivist views circulating during the hypermoralistic and the touchy-feely phases. Two examples drawn from the field of Roman Catholic religious instruction illustrate this last point. Gerard Sloyan was a powerful cognitivist voice in the 1950s and early 1960s decrying the asphyxiatingly narrow hypermoralistic position. Gabriel Moran, a brilliant though conceptually erratic cognitivist, has since the mid-1960s provided a series of trenchant critiques of both the hypermoralistic and the touchy-feely stances. As is typically the case with cognitivists as well as with ultracognitivists, neither Sloyan nor Moran accord a central place to the body or to psychomotor processes in the actual here-and-now work of religious instruction.

12. Whether the ultracognitivist position will be as short-lived as its holistic merit warrants is difficult to predict as of the time that the present volume is being written. I should note that there are some influential religious educationists who prefer a holistic Christian lifestyle to a skewed ultracognitivist one. John Westerhoff, the tractarian, is very much in the holistic camp, and some of the later writings of Maria Harris suggest that she strongly leans in this direction as well.

13. For Groome, the center, basis, and axis of all human activity, and therefore of lifestyle, is cognition. Apparently stung by previous criticism from many quarters that his views were totally lopsided in the cognitivist direction, Groome proceeded to deal with lifestyle and with affectivity in his book, *Christian Religious Education.* Though he does indeed offer some words in praise of lifestyle and affectivity in various spots throughout this volume, Groome never really swerves from his original ultracognitivist position. Thus, for example, he entitles the first chapter of the most important and most instructionally relevent section of his book as follows: "In Search of a 'Way of Knowing' for Christian Religious Education." In this chapter, Groome unambiguously argues for a

praxis *way of cognition* as the basis and the total process for *all* adequate religious instruction. His next chapter deals with a philosophical rationale of what he terms the praxis way of knowing. For Groome, affectivity (which is not even mentioned in his index) is at best reduced to a mode of knowledge ("the affective way of knowing," in Groome's terminology) or at worst to a kind of accompaniment to cognition whose purpose is to grease the wheels of cognitive activity in the intellectual dialectic. (In passing, I should note that in positing an "affective way of knowing," Groome is affirming an impossibility, namely the impossibility of one domain of human activity not only operating along the lines of a wholly different domain but also yielding results belonging to another wholly different domain. Affect, of course, is not knowing, nor a mode of knowing, nor an activity directly yielding cognitive results. Affect is a human activity which works through and yields a kind of awareness—affective awareness. Awareness is quite different from knowing. While it is incorrect to speak of affective knowledge, it is correct to speak of affective awareness, as any artist can readily testify. There is also psychomotor awareness—not psychomotor knowing—about which any athlete can testify.) Lifestyle, in Groome's view, is a kind of doing, a doing which can be directly generated by cognition. Such a direct production of lifestyle by cognition is, of course, an ontic and a psychological impossibility—unless, of course, Groome views all doing, including lifestyle, as cognition on the hoof. This well might be Groome's stance, though he never really comes to grips with this pivotal epistemological and instructional issue.

14. For a discussion of the integralist position, together with the cognitivist and the moralist positions, see James Michael Lee, *The Purpose of Catholic Schooling* (Dayton, Ohio: National Catholic Educational Association and Pflaum, 1968).

15. *"Tantum homo habet de scientia, quantum operatur."*

16. Thomas Aquinas, *De Veritate,* q. 10, a. 8.

17. Lawrence Kohlberg makes the same basic point with respect to moral judgment. Kohlberg is highly critical of social-scientific studies which attempt to assess virtuous behavior solely and exclusively in terms of overt activity. In Kohlberg's view, any true assessment of virtuous behavior must not only empirically examine overt behavior but also must include an empirical examination of that cognitive behavior which necessarily accompanies overt activity. For Kohlberg, cognitive behavior of the moral sort has its own distinct structure and axis of functioning. Virtuous behavior always of necessity includes cognitive behavior of the general and of the specifically moral kind, behavior which is integrated with overt performance. (Alas, Kohlberg the cognitivist gives relatively short shrift to the affective component of virtuous behavior.) For a fuller discussion of this point, see C. M. Beck and E. V. Sullivan, "Introduction," in C. M. Beck, B. S. Crittenden, and E. V. Sullivan, editors, *Moral Education: Interdisciplinary Approaches* (Toronto: University of Toronto Press, 1971), p. 15; James Michael Lee, "Christian Religious Education and Moral Development," in Brenda Munsey, editor, *Moral Development, Moral Education, and Kohlberg* (Birmingham, Ala.: Religious Education Press, 1980), pp. 337–343.

18. While Berard Marthaler probably affirms this point while hearing confessions, he forthrightly denies it with respect to the religious instruction process. See Berard L. Marthaler, "Review," in *National Catholic Reporter* VIII (November 19, 1971), p. 8.

19. From the specifically Christian perspective, the fulfillment of this pedagogical

enablement is transfiguration. In his New Testament account of the transfiguration of Jesus, Luke states that the three apostles saw Jesus "in his glory." I interpret this statement to mean that the hitherto less manifest areas of Jesus' personality now were radiantly observable, and the hitherto manifest areas of his personality were rendered even more manifest. The transfiguration of Jesus included the physical and the psychomotor. Luke tells us that the fashion of Jesus' face was altered.

20. By positing a dichotomy between what she labels "inner space" and "outer space," Mary Boys seems to suggest that religious educators would do well to target their efforts toward the deeper "inner space" of the learner rather than to the superficial "outer space." It is against such a bifurcation with its rejection of holism and humanity that educators like David Bickimer protest. Mary C. Boys, *Biblical Interpretation in Religious Education* (Birmingham, Ala.: Religious Education Press, 1980), pp. 231–244; David Arthur Bickimer, *Christ the Placenta* (Birmingham, Ala.: Religious Education Press, 1983).

21. The corpus of John Westerhoff's writings evince conceptual confusion and internal contradiction on this point. Though the basic thrust of all his tracts is clearly holistic, nonetheless in some of these tracts he sharply dichotomizes between "inner" and "outer" dimensions of reality and of the human person. Thus, for example, he at times conceptualizes faith as a kind of inner activity—and, possibly, a kind of inner substance. In this view, the task of Christians is to "act out the Christian faith" and to "prove the faith" through overt behaviors. Such statements, obviously, suggest a function or even a substantive entity called faith which is "in there" somewhere, a function or substantive entity independent of overt activity. An opinion of this kind suggests that the role of religious instruction is to pierce the "outer" person, get at the "inner" person, and bring the influence of that "inner" person directly to bear on the "outer" person. Because he is a tractarian, Westerhoff certainly is entitled to engage in conceptual confusion and internal contradiction. The problem with Westerhoff's conceptual confusion and internal contradictions on this and a host of other issues, therefore, lies not with Westerhoff but with that portion of his readership which treats him as a scholar rather than as the tractarian he has repeatedly affirmed he is. See, for example, John H. Westerhoff III, "A Socialization Model," in John H. Westerhoff III, editor, *A Colloquy on Christian Education* (Philadelphia: Pilgrim, 1972), p. 88; John H. Westerhoff, *Tomorrow's Church* (Waco, Tex: Word, 1976), p. 83

22. In Chapter Four, I review some of the empirical research on this issue.

23. I write "more-or-less" because the lifestyles of different persons integrate the larger domains and the smaller segments of human functioning in varying gradations. These varying gradations of functional integration are occasioned by a host of factors ranging from the degree to which an individual is a fully functioning person to the way the different zones of one's personality must necessarily be deployed to successfully complete a particular developmental task or a specific workaday task with which the individual is currently faced.

24. I use the term "greater or lesser" for the same reasons delineated in the previous footnote.

25. James Michael Lee, *The Flow of Religious Instruction* (Birmingham, Ala.: Religious Education Press, 1973), p. 297.

26. Michael Warren erroneously contends that my stress on behavioral modification

"simply emphasizes Lee's view of the content of religious instruction as external to the learner." I find several difficulties in Warren's statement, two of which are worth mentioning briefly. First, he seems to be implying that all content is internal. Actually, of course, content in itself is external until it becomes part of the learner's own self-system. If content were all internal, then objective standards (including the theological standards which Warren so highly prizes) would no longer exist; all content would be hopelessly relativized. The task of religious instruction is to enable the learner to so modify his own cognitive or affective or psychomotor behavior that the formerly external content becomes a working part of the learner's behavioral repertoire. Perhaps Warren's critique was historically influenced in part by a flabby and indeed a sham version of Existentialism then in vogue at the time he wrote his critique, a flabby and a sham Existentialism in which much of religious instruction then wallowed. Second, Warren cavalierly offers his critique in what apparently is an appalling ignorance of my many books and articles which appeared in print prior to his critique. Paradoxically, one of these books includes a slim volume which was published by a formal arm of the official Catholic *ecclesiasticum* in whose Washington offices he was working at the time of his critique. More paradoxical still, Warren seems not to have read carefully even the article of mine at which he directed much of his critique. If there is any major recurring theme running through all my books, articles, conferences, and the like, it is this: *homo integer*. Translated into the pedagogical realm, *homo integer* means that all the dimensions of the human being, as appropriate, should become actively involved in a personalistic manner in the learning task. Michael Warren, "All Contributions Cheerfully Accepted," in *Living Light* VII (Winter, 1970), p. 28.

27. This pedagogical process constitutes an important aspect of my overall position that teaching consists essentially of structuring the learning situation.

28. To appreciate more fully the point I am making here, see James Michael Lee, *The Shape of Religious Instruction* (Birmingham, Ala.: Religious Education Press, 1971), pp. 72–74.

29. A curriculum is a learning program or learning package. A curriculum can vary in structure from highly fluid to very tight. A curriculum can be enacted in an informal setting such as in a home or in a formal setting such as a classroom. Most parents, especially of very young children, frequently have a kind of highly fluid curriculum into which they place their offspring. It is erroneous to equate curriculum with a rigid course of study occurring only in schools.

30. B. F. Skinner, "Why We Need Teaching Machines," in *Harvard Educational Review*, XXXI (Fall, 1961), p. 389.

31. Carl R. Rogers, *Freedom to Learn*, p. 140.

32. In this connection, Jerome Bruner writes: "One hears often the distinction between 'doing' and 'understanding.' It is a distinction applied to the case, for example, of a student who presumably understands a mathematical idea but does not know how to use it in computation. While the distinction is probably a false one—since how can one know what a student understands save by seeing what he does—it points to an interesting difference in emphasis in teaching and learning." Bruner's statement takes on added weight, in the context of my discussion in the body of the text, when it is recalled that he is a cognitive psychologist. Jerome S. Bruner, *The Process of Education* (Cambridge, Mass.: Harvard University Press, 1960), p. 29.

33. Richard C. Anderson, "Educational Psychology," in Paul R. Farnsworth, Olga McNemar, and Quinn McNemar, editors, *Annual Review of Psychology,* volume XVIII (Palo Alto, Calif.: Annual Reviews, 1967), p. 143.
34. I am using examples drawn from the pedagogy of Jesus, not to validate performance-based learning, but rather to illustrate the obvious penchant for performance-based learning on the part of a person who is generally regarded as an outstanding religious educator. Pedagogical, social-scientific validation of the success of Jesus' teaching activities rests not upon the (exalted) nature of the person employing this pedagogy, but rather upon empirically proven data which demonstrate the degree of this success. Somewhat the same point about empirical observable verification is made by Jesus himself in Matthew 9:6. For a further discussion of this point, see James Michael Lee, "Religious Education and the Bible: A Religious Educationist's View," in Joseph S. Marino, editor, *Biblical Themes in Religious Education* (Birmingham, Ala.: Religious Education Press, 1983), pp. 38–47.
35. For a brief introduction to behavioral objectives, see James Michael Lee, *The Flow of Religious Instruction,* pp. 276–277. The classic treatment of behavioral objectives is Robert F. Mager, *Preparing Instructional Objectives* (Palo Alto, Calif.: Fearon, 1962). A helpful book which links behavioral objectives to the various taxonomies of human functioning (cognitive, affective, and psychomotor) is Robert J. Kibler, Larry L. Barker, and David T. Miles, *Behavioral Objectives and Instruction* (Boston: Allyn and Bacon, 1970).
36. I agree with Lawrence Kohlberg on this point. As I state elsewhere, "Kohlberg's fundamental position is that any adequate theory of the aim of education must be based on adequate psychological facts and explanations of [human] development. Conversely, no satisfactory theory of education can be erected primarily on forces, hypotheses, or institutions outside of or extrinsic to the developing person. This does not mean that the aim of education is devoid of extrinsic philosophies or ideologies. Rather, Kohlberg maintains that the way in which extrinsically derived aims are incorporated into educational activity in its processes or goals must be done in a manner consistent with and indeed based upon the learner's developmental self. Learners critically test the educational value of what they have learned by the criterion of how it has objectively furthered their own developmental process." James Michael Lee, "Christian Religious Education and Moral Development," p. 344.
37. Such a social-scientific form is proper to instruction. Conversely, this form is not proper to religion, philosophy, or theology.
38. On this point, see Margaret Ammons, "Objectives and Outcomes," in Robert L. Ebel, editor, *Encyclopedia of Educational Research,* 4th edition (New York: Macmillan, 1969), p. 911.
39. For a treatment of behavioral objectives as both humanistic and promotive of religious growth, see David Arthur Bickimer, *Christ the Placenta,* pp. 78–83.
40. Some religious educationists decry behavioral objectives. The arguments advanced by these individuals tend to be so scanty, so weak, and so tangential to the central issue that I can only wonder whether these religious educationists have ever carefully examined curricula framed in behavioral objectives—or even, I regret to say, read much (any?) of the literature on behavioral objectives. If these religious educationists would even cursorily examine their own lesson plans or scrutinize their own pedagogical behaviors as they teach (to say nothing of the examinations which they give), they would in all probability discover that

their own instructional practice is veritably chock-full of behavioral objectives.

41. The first sentence in this paragraph looks at the issue from the *learning* perspective, while the second sentence focuses on this issue from the *teaching* perspective. Both perspectives are complementary but separate, and should not be confounded with one another. On this point, see James Michael Lee, *The Flow of Religious Instruction*, pp. 39–55.

42. See, for example, James Michael Lee, *The Purpose of Catholic Schooling*, pp. 56–58.

43. One of the most celebrated and influential passages in all of John Dewey's writings is: "And education is not a mere means to a [moral] life. Education is such a life. To maintain capacity for such education is the essence of morals." John Dewey, *Democracy and Education* (New York: Macmillan, 1916), p. 417.

44. The corpus of both hard empirical investigations and of theoretical research is that transfer of learning constitutes the most important intermediate- and long-range outcome of teaching in formal and informal settings. For a review of some of the pertinent research on transfer of learning, together with its significance for religious instruction, see James Michael Lee, *The Flow of Religious Instruction*, pp. 141–147.

45. The term primary experience is used here in an instructional sense rather than in a depth-psychology sense. For an important and influential treatment of primary experience from an instructional viewpoint, see John L. Childs, *Education and Morals* (New York: Appleton-Century-Crofts, 1950), pp. 135–154.

46. Second-hand experiences are, at best, hand-me-down learning experiences.

47. I am inserting this parenthetical observation in view of the reductionist efforts of certain well-meaning Christian theologians in the 1970s and 1980s to transmogrify all reality to politics, force, and oppression/liberation.

48. It seems to me that all genuine liturgical reform must necessarily take into account the pedagogical fact that in addition to its sacramental nature, the liturgy has a central and indispensable pedagogical nature and function. This pedagogical nature and function are most fruitfully fulfilled when the liturgy is so structured that it constitutes the finest possible laboratory for Christian living.

49. John Dewey, *Democracy and Education*, p. 59.

50. "Manipulating the variables" is a social-scientific term which means working with and rearranging the fluid ingredients involved in a task in such a manner as to yield satisfactory analytic and/or synthetic results. Therefore, this term, as it is used here, has nothing to do with the way in which manipulation is conceptualized in other sciences, disciplines, or fields such as political science, literature, philosophy, or theology.

51. For a more detailed treatment of the mutual relation of theory and practice, see James Michael Lee, "The Authentic Source of Religious Instruction," in Norma H. Thompson, editor, *Religious Education and Theology* (Birmingham, Ala.: Religious Education Press, 1982), pp. 117–121.

52. One of these sources is definitely not Gabriel Moran. From out of the blue Moran gratuitously declares that an educational laboratory consists of nonintentional education and is thus the contrary of schooling. He states that schooling consists of intentional education. Moran's gratuitous and strange definition of laboratory is without lexical, historical, or logical foundation. As I shall shortly show in the body of the present book, an instructional laboratory represents one of the most important pedagogical advances made in modern times, an advance predicated on the hypothesis that intentional instruction can be rendered more effective by

transforming didactic teacher-talk pedagogy into one which revolves around concrete holistic here-and-now performance. See Gabriel Moran, *Education for Adulthood* (New York: Paulist, 1979), pp. 33–35, 105–129.

53. Benedictus, *Regula*, prol. 45. Timothy Fry and his associates note that for Benedict, the monastery is first and foremost a *schola*, namely a formal setting in which education takes place. The purpose of this *schola* is to enable persons to attain salvation through the active practice of spiritual living, especially asceticism and love. Timothy Fry et al, *The Rule of St. Benedict* (Collegeville, Minn.: Liturgical Press, 1981), p. 92.

54. Johann Heinrich Pestalozzi, *How Gertrude Teaches Her Children*, translated by Lucy E. Holland and Francis C. Turner, edited by Ebenezer Cook (London: Sonnenschein, 1894).

55. Friedrich Wilhelm August Froebel, *Gesammelte pädagogische Schriften*, Herausgeber Richard Lange (Berlin: Enslin, 1861 & 1862).

56. Maria Montessori, *The Montessori Method*, translated by Anne E. George (Cambridge, Mass.: Bentley, 1965).

57. John Dewey, *The School and Society* (Chicago: University of Chicago Press, 1900).

58. The word *necessarily* is a key here. Many kinds of laboratories in the natural sciences and in some sectors of the social sciences do indeed significantly reduce personal expression and suppress free human activity. Such cases, however, represent only one kind of laboratory. Many types of social laboratories such as a T group or a laboratory for Christian living are deliberatively built around the axis of optimum personal experience and free human activity.

59. Roger Lincoln Shinn, *The Educational Mission of Our Church* (Boston: United Church Press, 1962), p. 9.

60. Consequence in this connection may mean: (1) vertical in the sense of teaching in the convergent mode; (2) lateral in the sense of teaching in the divergent mode.

61. On this point, see James Michael Lee, *The Flow of Religious Instruction*, pp. 28–38; Harold William Burgess, "In Quest for the Connection: Toward a Synapse of Theory and Practice," in Marlene Mayr, editor, *Modern Masters of Religious Education* (Birmingham, Ala.: Religious Education Press, 1983), pp. 174–183.

62. For a brief treatment of the structured-learning-situation strategy, see James Michael Lee, "The *Teaching* of Religion," in James Michael Lee and Patrick C. Rooney, editors, *Toward a Future for Religious Education* (Dayton, Ohio: Pflaum, 1970), pp. 59–64.

63. Ferdinand Kopp, "Basic Principles of the Activity School," in Josef Goldbrunner, editor, *New Catechetical Methods*, translated by M. Veronica Riedl (Notre Dame, Ind.: University of Notre Dame Press, 1965), pp. 67–68.

64. James Michael Lee, "The Authentic Source of Religious Instruction," in Norma H. Thompson, editor, *Religious Education and Theology*, pp. 165–177.

65. This sentence also states the basic reason undergirding the second sentence in the previous paragraph.

66. This point is well documented and amply illustrated throughout Harold William Burgess, *An Invitation to Religious Education* (Birmingham, Ala.: Religious Education Press, 1975).

67. On this point, see Sara Little, *The Role of the Bible in Contemporary Christian Education* (Richmond, Va.: Knox, 1961), p. 145.

68. For a documentation, together with concrete examples of this point, see Harold William Burgess, *An Invitation to Religious Education*.

69. Wayne R. Rood, *The Art of Teaching Christianity* (Nashville, Tenn.: Abingdon, 1968), pp. 70–71.

70. For a review of some of the pertinent empirical research on this point, see James Michael Lee, *The Flow of Religious Instruction,* pp. 65–73.

71. Neil Postman and Charles Weingartner, *Teaching as a Subversive Activity* (New York: Delacorte, 1969), p. 17.

72. For Dewey, the word environment denotes not only the surroundings which encompass an individual, but also the specific continuity of the surroundings with a person's own active tendencies. John Dewey, *Democracy and Education,* p. 13.

73. Maria Harris, "The Aesthetic and Religious Education," in John R. McCall, editor, *Dimensions in Religious Education* (Havertown, Pa.: CIM, 1973), p. 143.

74. Hence the philosophical axiom: *"Actus sequitur esse."*

75. Hence the philosophical axiom: "I am what I do."

76. J. Quentin Lauer, *The Triumph of Subjectivity* (New York: Fordham University Press, 1958). This book deals with transcendental philosophical phenomenology with special attention to Edmund Husserl. Philosophical and psychological phenomenology in various forms both pure and diluted have exerted enormous impact in the modern world—in the direction of subjectivity.

77. Van Cleve Morris, "Existentialism and Education," in *Educational Theory* IV (October, 1954), pp. 248–250. For Existentialists a person's existence comes first. The living out of his existence determines his "essence."

78. When Jean-Paul Sartre, a leading Existentialist philosopher, italicizes the verb "to be" in his novels, it is to emphasize the transitive quality of the verb. He writes, for example, "I *am* that suffering," or again "I *am* that nothingness." As George Kneller remarks, in Existentialism there are no copula verbs, except as copulas express the very event of being. In order to understand the philosophical grounding for such statements and concepts, it is helpful to read Jean-Paul Sartre, *Being and Nothingness,* translated by Hazel E. Barnes (New York: Washington Square Press, 1966), pp. 89–128. George F. Kneller, *Existentialism and Education* (New York: Wiley, 1958), pp. 21–22.

79. Martin Buber, *I and Thou,* 2d edition, translated by Ronald Gregor Smith (New York: Scribner's, 1958), p. 52.

80. Giuseppe Messina and Ugo Bianchi, "La storia delle religioni nei suoi problemi e nei suoi metodi," di Giuseppe Castellani, editore, *Storia delle religione,* 5ta edizione, volume I (Torino, Italia: Pozzo-Salvati-Gros Monti, 1962), pp. 12–14.

81. G. Parrinder, "La place de la religion dans l'histoire de l'humanité," dans Conseil de L'Europe, *La religion dans les manuels scolaires d'histoire en Europe* (Strasbourg, France: Le Conseil, 1974), p. 66.

82. James Michael Lee, "Discipline in a Moral and Religious Key," in Kevin Walsh and Milly Cowles, *Developmental Discipline* (Birmingham, Ala.: Religious Education Press, 1982), pp. 156–179. In those pages I attempt to show that the way in which a person most effectively learns and lives a particular lifestyle is discipline. I define discipline as the purposeful learning and living of a lifestyle.

83. Martin Buber, *I and Thou,* p. 91.

84. Iris V. Cully, *Change, Conflict, and Self-Determination* (Philadelphia: Westminster, 1972), p. 107.

85. Because the Christian lifestyle demands sacrifice, the Christian lifestyle involves a measure of heroism. Saints are the ultimate Christian heroes. In a conversation

with his niece, Friedrich von Hügel remarked that if a person does not see sacrifice and renunciation and a right asceticism in the gospels, it is hard to know what that person sees in the gospels. Gwendolen Greene, "Introduction," in Friedrich von Hügel, *Letters from Baron Friedrich von Hügel to a Niece*, edited by Gwendolen Greene (London: Dent, 1928), pp. xix–xx.

86. In this vein John Westerhoff the tractarian states: "Remember, the heart of the gospel is not speaking; it is action. Paul makes that very clear when he points to the crucifixion as the heart of the gospel message. It is the action, not the words, of Christ which is a stumbling block (1 Cor. 1:23–24)."

87. James D. Smart, *The Teaching Ministry of the Church* (Philadelphia: Westminster, 1954), p. 87.

88. Karl Rahner, *The Christian Commitment*, translated by Cecily Hastings (New York: Sheed and Ward, 1963), p. 38.

89. Anent this point David Hunter writes: "It must be remembered always that the Church is not primarily in the business of disseminating information. What it disseminates is the Gospel, and the Gospel is always the Word. This Word, as man encounters it, is always the product of a relationship between God and man. Indeed, it is more than the product; it is the activity of God in all of history in the broadest sense." David R. Hunter, *Christian Education as Engagement* (New York: Seabury, 1963), p. 114.

90. E. Schillebeeckx, *Revelation and Theology*, volume II, translated by N. D. Smith (New York: Sheed and Ward, 1968), p. 127.

91. "We may also look for the secular equivalents of the sacraments. For what God is doing through the sacraments in an explicit fashion, he is doing in a more implicit manner through the words and gestures that are part of life itself. . . . The sacraments appointed by Christ reveal to us how God offers transformation to men through the ordinary events of their lives." Gregory Baum, *Man Becoming* (New York: Herder and Herder, 1970), p. 70.

92. G. Parrinder, "La place de la religion dans l'histoire de l'humanité," p. 66.

93. John A. T. Robinson, *The Difference in Being a Christian Today* (Philadelphia: Westminster, 1972), p. 24.

94. For a fine treatment of the catechumenate, see Michel Dujarier, *A History of the Catechumenate: The First Six Centuries*, translated by Edward L. Haasl (New York: Sadlier, 1979).

95. Michel Dujarier, "L'évolution de la pastorale catéchuménale aux six premiers siécles de l'église," dans *Maison Dieu* LXX (2ième trimestre, 1962), p. 50.

96. Tertullian, *De Poenitentia*, VI; Tertullian, *De Baptismo*, XX.

97. See, for example, Origen, *Homiliae in Lucam*, XXI.

98. Michel Dujarier, "L'évolution de la pastorale catéchuménale aux six premiers siécles de l'église," pp. 49–50.

99. Justin Martyr, *I Apologia*, LXI.

100. Karl Baus, *From the Apostolic Community to Constantine*, volume I of Hubert Jedin and John Dolan, editors, *History of the Church* (London: Burns and Oates, 1980), p. 276.

101. Jean Daniélou and Henri Marrou, *Nouvelle Histoire de L'Église*, tome I, *Des origines à Saint Grégoire le Grand* (Paris: Seuil, 1963), p. 191.

102. This document constitutes the most detailed and most complete extant source on the constitution and organization of the church, the confection of the sacraments, and the Roman liturgy in the second and early third centuries.

103. Hippolytus, *Apostolic Tradition*, XV–XIX.

104. Karl Baus, *From the Apostolic Community to Constantine*, p. 276. The concept and the reality of godparents did not exist at that time.

105. In a classic book on the historical origins of the baptismal liturgy, Alois Stenzel observes that there was no hard and fast rule in the ancient church (2nd and 3rd centuries), especially in the East, on the length of the catechumenate. Since it was lifestyle-oriented, the catechumenate had to last a goodly amount of time. However, the notion that three years constituted a hard-and-fixed duration of the catechumenate is a false stereotype—though it should be noted that the catechumenate generally (but not always) lasted three years. In short, the catechumenate took as long as was necessary for individual catechumens to acquire that kind of lifestyle compatible with Christianity, to give up incongruous professions if need be, and so forth. "Die stets wachsende Zahl der Taufbewerber genügte, um einen schulmässigen, d. h. planmässigen und gemeinsam erfolgten Unterricht angebracht erscheinen zu lassen. Die Norm für die Dauer des Kat. musste natürlich bei einer Sammelbildung relativ hoch ausfallen. Die Zahl von drei Jahren kehrt stereotyp wieder, auch dann noch, als sie durch die Unsitte, die Taufe möglichst weit hinauszuschieben, längst illusorisch geworden war. Es könnte ein Zeichen für die späte Redaktion der Cann. Hipp. sein, wenn sie auf diese Zeitangabe verzichten (cn.17) und dem Lehrer die Entscheidung überlassen. Dass man die Disposition immer für entscheidend gehalten hat und von da her die starre Zeitnorm auflockern konnte, ist schon bei Hippolyt vorgesehen (HKO 17, 1f.; Dix 28); nur eben: die Zugkräftigkeit dieser Vergünstigung liess nach. Sorgfalt in der Vermittlung des Glaubenswissens war durch die neben der Grosskirche sich auftuenden Sekten geboten. Aber das allein hätte wohl kaum drei Jahre verlangt. Dieser lange Zeitraum ist Beweis dafür, dass man das Hauptgewicht auf die sittliche Formung legte. Das hatte natürlich seinen Einfluss bereits auf die Zulassung." Alois Stenzel, *Die Taufe: eine genetische Erklärung der Taufliturgie* (Innsbruck: Rauch, 1958), p. 133.

106. Josef Jungmann, one of the great twentieth-century scholars of early church liturgy, bases his statement on the explicit testimony of both Origen and Athanasius. Josef Jungmann, "Catechumenate," in *New Catholic Encyclopedia,* volume 3 (New York: McGraw-Hill, 1967), p. 238.

107. The period of immediate preparation for Baptism was relatively short in duration, at least when compared to the catechumenate. It was a period of somewhat more liturgical and cognitive salience than the catechumenate. Some scholars contend that the period of immediate preparation for Baptism actually comprised the second stage of the catechumenate. Other scholars maintain that the period of immediate preparation for Baptism was distinct from, though organically related to, the catechumenate. At any rate, Jungmann states that in the East the persons in the immediate preparation stage for Baptism were called the enlightened ones, in Rome the chosen ones, and in the rest of the West the competent ones.

108. Josef Jungmann, "Catechumenate," p. 238.

109. Hippolytus, *Apostolic Tradition,* XX, translation mine.

110. Sacra Congregatio Rituum, "Decretum generale: Ordo Baptismi adultorum in varios grados distribuitur . . ." in *Acta Apostolicae Sedis* LIV (30 Maii, 1962), pp. 310–338.

111. This statement holds true even for Roman Catholicism. When the highest ecclesiastical magisterium declares a particular theological interpretation to be infallible church doctrine, this magisterium takes pains to point out that the theological

interpretation has, in fact, been an integral part of the ecclesia's lived experience for centuries; all the magisterium does in promulgating a cognitive doctrine is to frame the ecclesia's lived experience into cognitive theological form.

112. For a succinct but meaty treatment of some of the most influential theories of religion from the end of the nineteenth century onward, see Christoph Elsas, "Problemgeschichtliche Einleitung," in Christoph Elsas, Herausgeber, *Religion* (München: Kaiser, 1975), pp. 74–76.

113. Luis Alonso Schökel, *The Inspired Word*, translated by Francis Martin (New York: Herder and Herder, 1965), pp. 361–362.

114. Kōshi Usami, *Somatic Comprehension of Unity: The Church in Ephesus* (Rome: Biblical Institute Press, 1983), pp. 20–55.

115. Joachim Jeremias, *The Central Message of the New Testament* (London, SCM, 1965), pp. 51–70.

116. "En expliquant, d'une part, la condition actuelle de l'homme, d'autre part, le sens de l'oeuvre historique de Dieu, le livre inspiré introduit ainsi dans le tableau des origines le fait du péché humain qui, dès cette époque, interfère avec la volonté divine puis, de siècle en siècle, continue de dresser des obstacles devant le déroulement du dessein de Yahvé." P. Grelot, "Une synthèse d'histoire sacrée," dans Henri Cazelles, redacteur, *Introduction à la Bible,* tome II, 2ième edition (Paris: Desclée, 1973), p. 759.

117. James Michael Lee, "Religious Education and the Bible: A Religious Educationist's View," p. 1.

118. The points made in this paragraph appear in R. A. F. McKenzie, *Faith and History in the Old Testament* (Minneapolis, Minn.: University of Minnesota Press, 1963), p. 6.

119. Gerhard von Rad, *The Message of the Prophets,* translated by D. B. G. Stalker (London: SCM, 1965), pp. 100–101.

120. Though John Westerhoff is a theological tractarian and not by any means a biblical scholar, he seems to be correct to a certain extent when he states that the bible "makes no separation between mind and body, thinking and doing. They are one. The emphasis is always on what we are—that is, the union of what we know and what we do." John H. Westerhoff III, "Toward a Definition of Christian Education," in John H. Westerhoff III, editor, *A Colloquy on Christian Education,* p. 65. Westerhoff would do well to explore in some depth the epistemological and psychological ramifications of the above-quoted statement, especially with reference to his frequent unwarranted positing of discrete and organically disconnected realms of "inner" and "outer."

121. On this point, see Joachim Jeremias, *New Testament Theology,* volume I, translated by John Bowden (London: SCM, 1971), pp. 203–223.

122. This personalistic axis is especially pronounced in the Gospel according to John. Thus W. K. Grossouw states: "The spirituality of the fourth Gospel exists entirely in personal relationship to Christ and in 'having the Son'; for whoever has the Son has life, the only true life, the life which is 'eternal.'" W. K. Grossouw, "Christian Spirituality in John," in Michael J. Taylor, editor, *A Companion to John* (New York: Alba, 1977), p. 216.

123. Biblical theology is a vital tool for religious educators and hence should be accorded serious attention by every religion teacher.

124. Otto Kaiser, *Introduction to the Old Testament,* translated by John Sturdy (Oxford, England: Blackwell, 1975), p. 4.

125. For a further development of this point, see James Michael Lee, "Religious Education and the Bible: A Religious Educationist's View," pp. 24–33.

126. Thomas H. Groome, "Principles and Pedagogy in Bible Study," in *Religious Education* LXXVII (September–October, 1982), p. 505.

127. See notes 51 and 52 in Chapter Four.

128. In a pointed, though in some ways a slightly simplistic statement, Harvey Cox remarks: "The Bible is basically a drama and we are all in it. When the author appears onstage after the last scene, he will not ask whether you believed it or whether you analyzed it. He will ask whether you did it." Harvey Cox, "Letter," in *Time*, international edition (n. v., January 13, 1975), p. 28.

129. For a further development of the points discussed in this paragraph, see James Michael Lee, "Religious Education and the Bible: A Religious Educationist's View," pp. 3–8.

130. Aurelius Augustinus, *De Genesi ad Litteram Libri Duodecim*, 1, 9, 20.

131. Thomas Aquinas, *De Veritate*, q. 12, a. 2, *corpus*.

132. R. A. F. McKenzie, *Faith and History in the Old Testament*, pp. 5–6.

133. I am speaking here of *teaching the bible* (such as characterizes a religion lesson) rather than *teaching about the bible* (such as characterizes a theology lesson).

134. Some scholars like Walter Wink and Reginald Fuller charge that the historical-critical method of biblical interpretation employed by many modern biblical theologians is bankrupt because it excludes religion from its purview. In answering this charge, Raymond Brown concedes that some biblical scholars who employ the historical-critical method do indeed regard as unscientific any interest in what the sacred text meant religiously to the inspired writers. But Brown adds, and rightly I think, that it is time such prejudices be identified as regrettable accretions rather than as intrinsic principles of the historical-critical method. *Abusus non tollit usum*. Raymond E. Brown, *The Critical Meaning of the Bible* (New York: Paulist, 1981), pp. 24–25.

135. The word liturgy comes from the classical Greek word *leitourgia* which means a service done for the common welfare of the people. R. C. D. Jasper states that in the New Testament the word *leitourgia* is used to indicate an act of service or ministry. Josef Andreas Jungmann writes that no complete agreement has been reached on the definition of the liturgy because various liturgiologists and ecclesiastical functionaries have placed the major emphasis on different aspects of activities generally classed as liturgical, e.g., the outward forms of divine worship. For purposes of my treatment in this section, and indeed throughout all my writings, I am taking the word liturgy to mean the worship offered to God by the church itself, or more technically, in the words of Pius XII, the integral public worship of the mystical body of Christ, both head and members. R. C. D. Jasper, "Liturgies," in J. G. Davies, editor, *A Dictionary of Liturgy and Worship* (London: SCM, 1972), p. 222; Josef Andreas Jungmann, "Liturgy: I. Liturgies," in Karl Rahner et al., editors, *Sacramentum Mundi*, volume 3 (New York: Herder and Herder, 1969), pp. 320–321; Pius XII, "Mediator Dei" in *Acta Apostolicae Sedis* XXXIX (2 Decembris, 1947), pp. 521–604.

136. With respect to these two characteristics of the liturgy, namely construction and enactment, I think it is relatively safe to say that the more a denomination embraces a sacramental system, the more the liturgy tends to be characterized by lifestyle construction and enactment of the multidimensional kind.

137. Transcendists typically assert that this divine communication, like all divine

communication, takes place directly from God breaking into the human condition from a transcendent, wholly other world. Immanentists typically assert that this divine communication, like all divine communication, takes place indirectly, namely in mediated fashion through terrestrial realities of one sort or another. As Ian Knox correctly indicates, my position is an immanentist one. See Ian P. Knox, *Above or Within?: The Supernatural in Religious Education* (Birmingham, Ala.: Religious Education Press, 1977).

138. From a strictly theological perspective, the denial of this assertion is tantamount to the denial of the doctrine that the bible is simultaneously the work of God and the work of the inspired writer.

139. John L. McKenzie, *A Theology of the Old Testament* (Garden City, N.Y.: Doubleday, 1974), p. 64. McKenzie continues: "No demonstration is necessary to show that those who receive the communication are unable to share it; they are able only to declare their response. If one wishes to describe an encounter with a second person to a third person who does not know the second, he can describe it by the use of analogy; he has met persons. Unless the listener has met the gods, he has no analogy for a divine communication."

140. For an expansion of this important point, see James Michael Lee, "Discipline in a Moral and Religious Key," p. 189.

141. In this vein, Aidan Kavanagh writes that "if a culture has any root in the real order, it is to be found in the patterns of repetitive behavior by which a group of people conceives of and enacts those values which enable the group to survive its own particular context of stresses and threats that would destroy it." Aidan Kavanagh, "The Role of Ritual in Personal Development," in James D. Shaughnessy, *The Roots of Ritual* (Grand Rapids, Mich.: Eerdmans, 1973), p. 147.

142. I believe that John Westerhoff is only half right when he states: "Even when every other function of the church has been curtailed its worship has been kept alive." Analysis of the history of the church in every period clearly indicates that there were *two* functions which the church never curtailed, namely liturgy and religious instruction. John H. Westerhoff III, "A Socialization Model," pp. 84–85.

143. Victor Turner, "Religion in Current Cultural Anthropology," in Mircea Eliade and David Tracy, editors, *What is Religion?* (New York: Seabury, 1980), pp. 68–71.

144. Gregory Dix, *The Shape of the Liturgy,* 2d edition (Westminster, England: Dacre, 1945), pp. 12–15.

145. On this last mentioned point, see Christopher Kiesling, "Liturgical Pedagogics," in James Michael Lee and Patrick C. Rooney, editors, *Toward a Future for Religious Education* (Dayton, Ohio: Pflaum, 1970), p. 128.

146. On the intersection of liturgy and time, see I. H. Dalmais, "Le temps dans la liturgie," dans Irenée Henri Dalmais, Pierre Jounel, et Aimé Georges Martimort, *L'église en prière*, 2ième edition, tome IV de *La liturgie et le temps* (Paris: Desclée, 1983), pp. 13–19.

147. Odo Casel, *La mystère du culte dans le Christianisme,* traduction de J. Hild (Paris: Cerf, 1946), pp. 83–92.

148. On the liturgy as experiential encounter, see Morton Kelsey, *Encounter with God* (Minneapolis, Minn.: Bethany Fellowship, 1972), p. 221.

149. Josef Andreas Jungmann, "Liturgy: I. Liturgies," p. 321. To emphasize the corporate character of the liturgy, Jungmann states from a decidedly Roman

Catholic point of view: "The Church is only at worship, that is, we only have liturgy, when divine service is held by a legitimately assembled group of the faithful (from parish, religious order, or ecclesiastical institute), under the leadership of someone holding office in the Church. Here the Church becomes visible, here it is 'Event.' "

150. J. D. Crichton, *The Church's Worship* (London: Chapman, 1954), pp. 40–41.

151. J. G. Davies states that Israel's vocation was to be a holy people, a light unto the Gentiles. Israel's vocation was to enable the Chosen People to remain holy and/or to become holy. Temple liturgy is both the guarantee of the purity of Yahwism and the center to which the Gentiles are to come. "In marked contrast to this centripetal view of the liturgy in the Old Testament, the liturgy is regarded in the New Testament as centrifugal. The church's mission is to go out, to participate in the divine mission (Mt. 28:19; John 20:21; Acts 1:8)." J. G. Davies, "Mission and Worship," in J. G. Davies, editor, *A Dictionary of Liturgy and Worship,* p. 272.

152. For a treatment of the relation of liturgy and community, though from a somewhat different perspective than mine, see Godfrey Diekmann, *Come, Let Us Worship* (London: Darton, Longman, & Todd, 1962), pp. 172–175. See also John H. Westerhoff III, *Values for Tomorrow's Children* (Philadelphia: Pilgrim, 1970), p. 7.

153. Some liturgiologists overlook this very important point; so also do some religious educationists and some official ecclesiastical documents on religious instruction. Thus, for example, the *Directorium catechisticum generale,* the Roman Catholic directory for catechetics worldwide, expressly regards catechesis (religious instruction conducted under Roman Catholic ecclesiastical auspices) as adequately explaining the liturgy, as developing a proper attitude toward liturgy, and in promoting future participation in the liturgy. In other words, the *Directorium* regards liturgy as something outside of catechetics, something to which effective catechetics leads. The liturgy, in this view, is not a form of religious instruction; it is only a form of worship. Sacra Congregatio pro Clericis, *Directorium catechisticum generale* (Città del Vaticano: Libreria Editrice Vaticana, 1971), pp. 30–31 (#25). This basic formal separation of liturgy from catechesis is underscored on p. 26 (#17). See also Berard L. Marthaler, *Catechetics in Context* (Huntington, Ind.: Our Sunday Visitor, 1973), p. 58.

154. I am using the term accidental here in its precise Aristolean sense.

155. For an especially fine discussion of this point, see Johannes Hofinger, *The Art of Teaching Christian Doctrine,* 2d edition (Notre Dame, Ind.: University of Notre Dame Press, 1962), p. 35.

156. The degree to which the learner attains these outcomes is, of course, dependent upon the quality of the individual's participation in the liturgy.

157. My participation in, and my analysis of, the liturgy has from the outset exerted considerable impact on the way I view the religious instruction act, especially structural content. On this point, see James Michael Lee, "To Basically Change Fundamental Theory and Practice," in Marlene Mayr, editor, *Modern Masters of Religious Education,* p. 263.

158. Willis D. Nutting, "A Crash Program Needs Imagination," in J. T. Dillon, editor, *Catechetics Reconsidered* (Winona, Minn.: St. Mary's College Press, 1968), p. 51.

159. Hugh Wybrew states that it is usual in liturgical worship to make a sharp

distinction between rite and ceremonial as if the latter were a dispensable adornment of the former. In reality, Wybrew contends, the two are inseparable. The rite, states Wybrew, is the set of words which are to be performed, while ceremonial is the way in which the liturgy is performed. Hugh Wybrew, "Ceremonial," in Cheslyn Jones, Geoffrey Wainright, and Edward Yarnold, editors, *The Study of the Liturgy* (London: SPCK, 1978), p. 432.

160. For a discussion of the nature and interaction of the four major variables present in the teaching-learning act, see James Michael Lee, *The Flow of Religious Instruction*, pp. 230–268.

161. Randolph Crump Miller, *The Clue to Christian Education* (New York: Scribner's, 1950), p. 4.

162. Gelineau continues this thought as follows: "A good number of elements of present-day liturgy appeared on the scene only gradually—for example the feast of Christmas or church buildings. Others are met with only in a particular cultural area—the iconostasis, or stained glass windows. Singing, however, must be regarded as one of the fundamental constituents of Christian worship. This fits the fact that Christian worship is the public proclamation of the mirabilia Dei and of the good and joyful news, an act of thanksgiving, of praise, and blessing for the freedom won for us by the resurrection." J. Gelineau, "Music and Singing in the Liturgy," in Cheslyn Jones, Geoffrey Wainright, and Edward Yarnold, editors, *The Study of the Liturgy*, p. 432.

163. Sigmund Mowinckel points out that in Old Testament days, hymns offered the finest summary of what the Israelites thought Yahweh was, and hence showed that cultic system in an especially important light. Sigmund Mowinckel, *The Psalms in Israel's Worship*, volume I, translated by D. R. Ap-Thomas (Oxford, England: Basil Blackwell, 1962), pp. 97–105.

164. Joseph Gelineau puts it beautifully when he asks somewhat rhetorically: "Serace en vain que les hommes auront appelé divine la musique? et la mélodie fille de Dieu?" Joseph Gelineau, *Chant et musique dans le culte chrétien* (Paris: Fleurus, 1962), p. 15.

165. When in the other chapters of this book I deal with the limitation of one or another molar substantive content, I do so from the perspective of the full and complete actualization of that content in itself. I am treating the limitations of lifestyle content in the same way. Thus I am bypassing any limitations of each substantive content due to some defect or some lack of full actualization of that content.

166. Historically, the term spirituality has in various eras been applied to: (1) a supposedly more exalted form of religious lifestyle allegedly falling within the exclusive province of the clergy and religious; (2) the temporal property set aside for, or owned by, clergy and religious. Ontically, the term spirituality suggests the radical separation of spirit and body in personhood. Religiously, the term spirituality conveys as strong antiholistic and hence anti-incarnational bias, namely that the life of the spirit should be cultivated apart from or even over against the life of the body. Ecumenically, the term spirituality was frowned upon and even roundly denounced in some Protestant denominations, although in recent times the term has begun to gain favor among many Protestant groups, especially those charismatically inclined.

167. Gordon Wakefield, "Spirituality," in Alan Richardson and John Bowden, editors, *A New Dictionary of Christian Theology* (London: SCM, 1983), p. 549. Attitudes are affective, beliefs are cognitive, and practices are lifestyle.

168. Some religions do not use the term spirituality to refer to the holistic religious lifestyle which they advocate and practice. An especially fine scholarly treatment of the history of Christian spirituality is the three-volume work written by Louis Bouyer and his associates entitled *History of Christian Spirituality*. The first volume deals with the spirituality of the New Testament and the Fathers, the second volume with the spirituality of the Middle Ages, and the third volume with Orthodox spirituality, Protestant spirituality, and Anglican spirituality.

169. This is the view of the distinguished scholar Vernon Bourke. See Vernon J. Bourke, "Augustine of Hippo: The Approach of the Soul to God," in E. Rozanne Elder, editor, *The Spirituality of Western Christendom* (Kalamazoo, Mich.: Cistercian Publications, 1976), p. 11.

170. Rowan Williams, *The Wound of Knowledge: Christian Spirituality from the New Testament to John of the Cross* (London: Darton, Longman, & Todd, 1979), p. 2.

171. Josef Sudbrack, "Spirituality: I:D. Consequences," in Karl Rahner et al., editors, *Sacramentum Mundi*, volume 6 (New York: Herder and Herder, 1970), p. 151.

172. This concept of spirituality is also central to Evangelical Protestantism in North America. Karl Rahner, *Foundations of the Christian Faith*, translated by William V. Dych (New York: Seabury, 1978), pp. 305–311.

173. John Macquarrie, *Paths in Spirituality* (London, SCM, 1973), pp. 1–9, 39–40 (quote from p. 40).

174. The bases of some of these disagreements, especially in theology, seem silly and triumphalistic. An example of a silly basis is Dietrich Bonhoeffer's contention that religion is anti-Christian because it falsely posits a separate sector called religion (special worship, beliefs, practices, institutions) as opposed to the secular sector. Thus religion essentially appeals to a person's weaknesses; it thus demands that he lead a life walled off, or at least essentially distinct, from secular existence. What is needed, Bonhoeffer states, is a "religionless Christianity," one which is devoid of religion with its unwarranted bifurcation of reality into the sacred and profane. Bonhoeffer's argument is silly because he erroneously equates all religion with only one version of it, namely a transcendist, other-wordly, and in many ways a nineteenth-century view of religion. An example of a triumphalistic basis is Karl Barth's contention that religion is nothing more than a sham substitute for Christianity and represents humanity's pathetic efforts to construct a system which fundamentally pits the human being against God. For Barth, Christianity, which is the revelation of God, is above and outside all religion and thus is God's judgment condemning all religions as false. Barth's argument is triumphalistic on at least two counts: it is rooted in a highly constricted asphyxiating view of the form and breadth of God's revelation, and it is tragically blind to the deep and godlike spirituality of countless persons all over the globe, persons belonging to a wide variety of religious groups. See Benkt-Erik Benkston, *Christus und die Religion* (Stuttgart: Calwer, 1967), pp. 58–65. For another and particularly well-done explanation of Barth's view of religion, one which contrasts Barth with Paul Tillich, see Wolfhart Pannenberg, *Theology and the Philosophy of Science*, translated by Francis McDonagh (London: Darton, Longman, & Todd, 1976), pp. 316–322. Of interest is Pannenberg's contention that Barth's view on religion is to some degree a reaction against the liberal Protestant position that theology is the science of religion. In such a reactive stance, Barth pronounced that theology is the science of God and not of religion. Pannenberg points out that for Barth, revelation

interprets religion; religion does not interpret revelation. For Paul Tillich, religion is the name for the experience of divine revelation.

175. Everyone agrees that the modern word religion is derived from Latin. The dispute centers around which Latin word constitutes the true root of the modern word religion. Is the true root *relegere* or *religare*? Some scholars assert that the touchstone origin lies with Cicero's use of the word *relegere* in the sense of "to travel over again, to go on a journey again, to traverse again." Most other scholars assert that the touchstone origin lies with the word *religare*, meaning "to bind back, to fasten" as used by Augustine (and also by Lactantius). In *De natura deorum*, L. II, c. xxvii, n. 2, Cicero writes: "*Qui omnia quae ad cultum deorum pertinerent retractarent et tanquam relegerent, sunt dicti religiosi a relegendo, ut elegantes ex eligendo.*" There are numerous passages in *De vera religione* in which Augustine uses the word religion in the sense of *religare*; he does the same in *Retractiones* I. 13. For a good summary of this dispute, together with a goodly portion of technical etymological data, see E. Magnin, "Religion," dans A. Vacant, E. Mangenot, et É. Amann, redacteurs, *Dictionnaire de Théologie Catholique*, tome III, partie 2 (Paris: Letouzey et Ané, 1937), pp. 2182–2813; Charlton T. Lewis and Charles Short, *A Latin Dictionary*, revised edition (Oxford, England: Clarendon, 1969), pp. 1556–1557.

176. For an expanded discussion of this point with special reference to the personality at various developmental levels, see Academy of Religion and Mental Health, *Religion in the Developing Personality* (New York: New York University Press, 1960).

177. This is a prime thesis of a brilliant book which I regard as a classic in the field of religious psychology, namely Paul Pruyser, *A Dynamic Psychology of Religion* (New York: Harper & Row, 1968).

178. Hubert Halbfas, *Theory of Catechetics* (New York: Herder and Herder, 1971), pp. 19–20.

179. From a theological perspective Howard Grimes states: "The New Testament knows no distinction between the *organized* church and the *fellowship* which is basic to it." Howard Grimes, *Realms of Our Calling* (New York: Friendship, 1965), p. 26. This theme is a leitmotiv in the religious education writings of Howard Grimes. On this latter point, see Howard Grimes, "How I Became What I Am as a Religious Educator," in Marlene Mayr, editor, *Modern Masters of Religious Education*, pp. 135–159.

180. Martin Buber, *I and Thou*, 2d edition, p. 60.

181. On this point, from a psychotherapeutic perspective and a theological view respectively, see Morton Kelsey, *Encounter with God*, p. 231; Wayne R. Rood, *On Nurturing Christians* (Nashville, Tenn.: Abingdon, 1972), p. 75.

182. Josef Goldbrunner, *Realization*, translated by Paul C. Bailey and Elisabeth Reinecke (Notre Dame, Ind.: University of Notre Dame Press, 1966), p. 190.

183. Christopher H. Mooney, "Teilhard de Chardin and Christian Spirituality," in Ewert H. Cousins, editor, *Process Theology* (New York: Paulist, 1971), pp. 306–307.

184. Robert O. Johann, "Experience *and* Philosophy," in Irwin C. Lieb, editor, *Experience, Existence,* and *the Good* (Carbondale, Ill.: Southern Illinois Press, 1961), p. 27, italic deleted.

185. Thus, for example, cognitive activity does not occur in isolation. When a person thinks, his cognitive processes are accompanied to some degree by affective and psychomotor functions as well. The degree to which his affective and psycho-

motor functions are integrated with his cognitive processes in any given intellectual activity is determined by many factors including the nature of the task at hand, the degree of cognition he uses in dealing with the task at hand, his psychophysiological make-up, and so on.

186. "Although, to be sure, I cannot step outside my experience in order to survey [the world] as a whole, I am nevertheless present to myself as transcending any of the particular worldly engagements as well as the reflective efforts that go to make up that experience. This partial transcendence, therefore, provides the stable point of view to which I can return reflectively, to assess and formulate the structure and direction of any particular excursion. None of these excursions by itself, of course, is equal to the full richness of total experience. But, since each of them is only a particularization of the fundamental interrelation of self and world, it would seem necessary to contain the basic pattern of experience as a whole, a pattern whose details could be filled in by reflection on the endless variety of successive particular experiences." Robert O. Johann, "Experience and Philosophy," p. 36.

187. Philosophical and psychological developmentalists contend that the interactional character of experience creates an essentially new self. For developmentalism, a person *is* an interactive emergent, namely the consequence of the ongoing organism merged with the environment. On this point, with particular reference to religious instruction, see James Michael Lee, "Christian Religious Education and Moral Development," pp. 327–328, 343–347.

188. Thus Gabriel Moran points out that experience is relational with respect to two of the most fundamental polarities of human existence, namely subject and object. As a relational process, observes Moran, a person does not so much have experience as participates with other realities in experience. Gabriel Moran, *Design for Religion* (New York: Herder and Herder, 1970), pp. 64–65.

189. Friedrich von Hügel states that the data of a person's actual experience "are subject *and* object, each giving to and taking from the other; the two, and not the one only, are (somehow and to some co-relative extent) included within the single human consciousness." Friedrich von Hügel, *Essays and Addresses on the Philosophy of Religion,* volume 1 (London: Dent, 1921), p. 51.

190. Here is where the all-important function of perception comes into full play. The object in personal experience is not the object in itself but the object in subjective experience. This fact accounts for different cognitive interpretations and affective feelings on the part of various persons to one or another object in the environment.

191. Karl Lehmann, "Experience," in Karl Rahner et al., editors, *Sacramentum Mundi,* volume 2, p. 306.

192. On this latter point, see Gregory Baum, *Man Becoming,* p. 14.

193. It is in this sense that I mean such statements as the one which appears on page 17 of *The Shape of Religious Instruction,* namely that a person can encounter Jesus as Jesus is in Himself. Such an interpretation should be obvious, not only because the statement I just mentioned appears in a section of *The Shape* explicitly dealing with experience, but because it is the only interpretation allowed by my overall theory of human functioning found throughout the trilogy.

194. This last sentence is the conclusion of virtually every relevant empirical study in the field of the psychology of religion.

195. James Michael Lee, *The Shape of Religious Instruction,* p. 16.

196. Ramon Echarren, "Communicating the Faith in Present-day Society," in Alois

Müller, editor, *Catechetics for the Future* (New York: Herder and Herder, 1970), p. 14.

197. Morton Kelsey, *Encounter with God,* p. 129.

198. Maxi religious conversions, and mini ones too, are usually the result of opening oneself to God in holistic personal experience and being transformed to a greater or lesser degree in the process.

199. A scientifically rich context is one in which the conditions are controlled in such a manner that the independent-dependent variable(s) is/are isolated as far as possible.

200. A major theme in Pierre Teilhard de Chardin's magnificent treatise on the spiritual life is that authentic religious living necessarily involves the divinization of a person's activities and the divinization of that person's passivities. Pierre Teilhard de Chardin, *The Divine Milieu,* translated by Alick Dru et al. (New York: Harper & Row, 1960).

201. I state this as a general rule and not as an absolute one. Thus, for example, a few highly unusual persons can successfully engage in purely passive religious living such as that of a hermit. Still, even hermits often have an active dimension, not just when they receive visitors but in their apostolate. For example, when Thomas Merton was granted permission to live as a hermit, he still engaged actively in writing with a view toward helping others.

202. Christopher H. Mooney, "Teilhard de Chardin and Christian Spirituality," p. 309.

203. Edward Malatesta, "Introduction," in Jacques Guillet et al., *Discernment of Spirits,* translated by Innocentia Richards (Collegeville, Minn.: Liturgical Press, 1970), p. 9.

204. The difference between a social-scientific approach and a theological approach to the process of discernment of spirits is nicely illustrated by the following quotation from a Christian psychiatrist writing for spiritual directors: "Classically, discernment involves distinguishing among inclinations that may be of God, of the evil spirit, or of oneself. . . . I doubt that it helps to become overly preoccupied with arbitrary distinctions between what is 'of the self' and what is 'of God.' The real question, I think, is whether the 'self' aspects of an experience facilitate or hinder one's growth toward God, or whether they are consonant with or antagonistic toward God's will. To assume that something of the self must inherently be against God is to deny that aspect of ourselves that is made in God's image and to devalue our own intentionality towards God." Gerald G. May, *Care of Mind, Care of Spirit* (San Francisco, Calif.: Harper & Row, 1982), p. 34.

205. Larkin's next statement (not included in the quotation cited in the text) that the process of discernment is wisdom rather than science must be understood in the sense in which the terms wisdom and science are used in Aristotle, Thomas Aquinas, and John of St. Thomas. I use these terms in Chapter Four of this book much in the same way that Larkin does. Ernest E. Larkin, "Discernment of Spirits," in Gordon S. Wakefield, editor, *A Dictionary of Christian Spirituality* (London: SCM, 1983), p. 116.

206. Richard McBrien would do well to reflect on this point.

207. This point was made in Ernest E. Larkin, "Discernment of Spirits," p. 115.

208. Jésus Maria Granero, "Spirituality: III. Special Features. B. Examination of Conscience," in Karl Rahner et al., editors, *Sacramentum Mundi,* volume 6, p. 161.

209. A. Barruffo, "Discernment," dans Stefano De Fiores et Tullo Goffi, redacteurs, *Dictionnaire de la vie spirituelle*, traduction de François Vial (Paris: Cerf, 1983), pp. 271–279.

210. Ignatius of Loyola, *Spiritual Exercises*, translated by Lewis Delmage (New York: Wagner, 1968), #s 24–43 (pp. 17–24).

211. Theologians of the spiritual life have usually developed their descriptions of the different stages of religious experience on the basis of empirical self-reports given by persons at one or another level of passive religious experience (especially self-reports of mystical experiences) and on the basis of empirical observations by spiritual directors of persons under their pastoral care. While such self-reports and observations do indeed provide some empirical foundation for the classifications made by theologians of the spiritual life, nonetheless greater procedural rigor and more precise research design are needed in order to devise a truly adequate taxonomy of passive religious experience.

212. J. H. Walgrave, "Faith as a Fundamental Dimension of Religious Experience," in Thomas Mampra, editor, *Religious Experience: Its Unity and Diversity* (Bangalore, India: Dharmaram, 1981), p. 8.

213. Thus, Léonard states, "Christian mystical experience appears in the course of history clothed in diverse garb." A. Léonard, "Studies on the Phenomena of Mystical Experience," in (no editor listed), *Mystery and Mysticism* (London: Blackfriars, 1956), p. 80.

214. I regard this magnificent book as one of the most significant works on the psychology of religion written in the twentieth century. Paul W. Pruyser, *A Dynamic Psychology of Religion* (New York: Harper & Row, 1968).

215. Berard Marthaler seems to share this view. Berard L. Marthaler, *Catechetics in Context* (Huntington, Ind.: Our Sunday Visitor, 1973), pp. 149, 151.

216. I should add that the degree to which a person experientially stands in a beneficial beatific relation to a "transcendent" is what determines the level of that person's passive religious experience. J. H. Walgrave, "Faith as a Fundamental Dimension of Religious Experience," pp. 7–8.

217. In this connection Abraham Maslow writes that "mystery, ambiguity, illogic, contradiction, mystic and transcendent experiences may now be considered to lie well within the realm of nature. These phenomena need not drive us to postulate additional supernatural variables and determinants." Religionists, myself included, do indeed make such postulations; however, these postulations do not alter the *fact* of the experience but only *one explanatory sector* of this fact. Abraham H. Maslow, *Religions, Values, and Peak-Experiences* (New York: Penguin, 1964 and 1970), p. 45.

218. It would seem that there are different degrees within mystical experience. Thus mysticism is a multitiered state rather than a single-stage phenomenon.

219. Louis Gardet, *La Mystique* (Paris: Presses Universitaires de France, 1970), p. 5.

220. It is important to recall the distinction between nonrational and rational which I made in Chapter Four and pursued in Chapter Eight.

221. Richard N. Bucke, *Cosmic Consciousness* (New York: Dutton, 1901), pp. 61–82.

222. Pierre Teilhard de Chardin, *The Phenomenon of Man*, translated by Bernard Wall (New York: Harper & Row, 1959).

223. For existential, holistic, and lifestyle reasons, I prefer the term beatific encounter to the term beatific vision.

224. This statement holds true for the person in terrestrial existence. In the beatific

encounter, we are transported into an envelope of transcendence, as it were. How this takes place, and how we will directly experience God in a transcendent fashion (if our experience of him in heaven will indeed be of a transcendent variety) is currently a mystery since we have no reliable empirical data on which to come to an adequate solution. For a short, stimulating treatment of the problem of the passive religious experience of God on earth, see Jacques Servais, "Faire l'expérience de Dieu?" dans *Nouvelle Revue Théologique* CV (Mai-Juillet, 1983), pp. 410–415.

225. For a seminal treatment of transcendism and immanentism in twentieth-century American religious instruction, see Ian P. Knox, *Above or Within?: The Supernatural in Religious Education* (Birmingham, Ala.: Religious Education Press, 1976).

226. For a superb award-winning social-scientific account and explanation of passive religious experience, see André Godin, *Contemporary Psychology of Religious Experience,* translated by Mary Turton (Birmingham, Ala.: Religious Education Press, 1985).

227. This leeriness and near-fear seem to be especially prevalent among "official" theologians to the magisterium, Catholic encyclopedia writers, and other theologians whose lives and positions in one way or another depend on ecclesiastical favor. See, for example, M. B. Schepers, "Experience Theology," in *New Catholic Encyclopedia,* volume 5, p. 753; Karl Lehmann, "Experience," p. 309.

228. Abraham Maslow, *Religions, Values, and Peak-Experiences,* p. vii.

229. Peter A. Bertocci, "Psychological Interpretations of Religious Experience," in Merton P. Strommen, editor, *Research on Religious Development* (New York: Hawthorn, 1971), p. 27.

230. Evelyn Underhill, *The Essentials of Mysticism* (New York: Dutton, 1920), pp. 25–43.

231. Jean Daniélou, *Platonisme et théologie mystique,* 2ième edition (Paris: Aubier, 1953), pp. 309–314.

232. Thus the theology of faith properly investigates not only what is believed but also the personal experience in which the belief occurs.

233. Abraham Maslow, *Religions, Values, and Peak-Experiences,* p. 26.

234. David Arthur Bickimer, *Christ the Placenta.* When representatives of the publisher which issued Bickimer's book exhibited this volume at a sales booth at a major 1983 gathering of Catholic religious educators on the West Coast, they got all sorts of strange looks from the conventioneers except, of course, from mystically oriented individuals who were very excited about this volume. The publishers also received some odd correspondence from religious educators about this book, including an unsigned letter from the midwest, a letter which appears to have been written by a religionist or religious educator suffering from sexual problems.

235. *Ibid.,* p. 37.

236. Cuthbert Butler, *Western Mysticism,* 2d edition (New York: Harper, 1922), pp. lix–lxii. This volume is generally regarded as one of the finest books written on mystical experience.

237. Kelsey then continues, in a deliberately sad vein: "A great many [Christian] church people feel that such experience, without respect for intellectual, moral, or social boundaries, can have no value." Morton Kelsey, *Encounter with God,* p. 148.

238. William Johnston, *The Inner Eye of Love: Mysticism and Religion* (London: Collins Fount, 1978), p. 61.

239. For a helpful book clarifying many of the similarities and differences between Eastern and Western mysticism see Rudolph Otto, *Mysticism East and West,* translated by Bertha L. Bracey and Richenda C. Payne (New York: Macmillan, 1960). Otto uses the great Eastern mystical writer Āchārya Śankara and the great Western mystical author Meister Eckhart as his basis of comparison. Āchārya means master, as does Meister.

240. Evelyn Underhill, *Mysticism* (New York: Meridian, 1955), p. 90.

241. This intimate involvement of the psychomotor domain is depicted so well in Gian Lorenzo Bernini's classic sculpture "The Ecstasy of Saint Teresa" located in the Church of Santa Maria della Vittoria in Rome.

242. Many of these reports appear in biographies of the saints. It is the task of the scholar to effectively separate the actual from the hagiographic in such accounts. A step in the right direction with respect to the topic I am treating was taken in Herbert Thurston, *The Physical Phenomena of Mysticism* (London: Burns Oates, 1952).

243. William Ralph Inge, *Christian Mysticism* (London: Methuen, 1899), Appendix A. Because mystical experience is so intensely subjective, it readily lends itself to a variety of descriptions.

244. For a helpful treatment of mystical experience as viewed by Dionysius the Aeropagite, with special attention to the relationship of his ideas with the views on mysticism held by the early church Fathers, see Andrew Louth, *The Origins of the Christian Mystical Tradition* (Oxford, England: Clarendon, 1981), pp. 159–178. Dionysius writes of the soul passing beyond ordinary consciousness into a new state of consciousness, a state of darkness in which God dwells. This divine darkness, or "cloud of unknowing" (a term apparently coined by Dionysius) works to unify the soul in its passivity with God.

245. Even here, persons from different cultural milieux, notably East and West, tend to see each of these characteristics in not altogether the same light.

246. F. C. Happold, *Mysticism* (London: Penguin, 1964), p. 46.

247. Sarvepalli Radhakrishnan, *Religion in a Changing World* (London: Allen and Unwin, 1966), pp. 1–4, 106.

248. In this connection Peter Bertocci states that the personal value and the power of intense religious experience (its psychological certitude versus logical certitude) will always remain private and not coercive for those who have not enjoyed a profound religious encounter. Peter A. Bertocci, "Psychological Interpretations of Religious Experience," p. 8.

249. On the relationship between intense religious experience and intimacy, see Bernard Lee, "The Appetite of God," in Henry James Cargas and Bernard Lee, editors, *Religious Experience and Process Theology* (New York: Paulist, 1976), pp. 375–378.

250. Ralph W. Hood, Jr., "Construction and Preliminary Validation of a Measure of Reported Mystical Experience," in *Journal for the Scientific Study of Religion* XIV (March, 1975), pp. 29–41.

251. Walter T. Stace, *Mysticism and Philosophy* (Philadelphia: Lippincott, 1960). Stace's categories readily lend themselves to empirical social-scientific investigation because they are presumably cross-culturally ahistorical, and unbiased by religious ideology (Stace, pp. 38–40). Commenting specifically on this point, Hood states: "Now while this is, of course, too much to assume, Stace's concep-

tualizations appear to tend in that direction and have the proven value of empirical fruitfulness, at least as criteria for rating categories" devised and validated by several other empirical researchers (Hood, p. 39). Hood also notes that Stace's categories are based on two fundamental assumptions. "First, the mystical experience is itself a universal experience that is essentially identical in phenomenological terms despite wide variations in ideological interpretations of the experience. Second, the core categories of mysticism are not all definitionally essential to any particular individual mystical experience since there are always borderline cases forming what are 'family resemblances' based on fulfillment of only some of these core categories." (Hood, p. 30).

252. Each of Hood's basic categories contains four items (eight categories with four items apiece total the thirty-two). Each item is behaviorally stated either positively or negatively, e.g., "I have had an experience of . . . ," or "I never had an experience of . . . ."

253. Robert D. Margolis and Kirk W. Elifson, "A Typology of Religious Experience," in *Journal for the Scientific Study of Religion* XVIII (March, 1979), pp. 61–67.

254. Margolis recruited his forty-five research subjects in a large variety of ways, including notices in newspapers and as a result of contact with a large number of denominations ranging from traditional denominations to Eastern religious sects. All persons who volunteered for the study were screened by Margolis to ascertain whether their reported intense religious experiences did indeed represent some kind of intense religious experience broadly considered. Margolis interviewed the subjects to arrive at his data. For each of the religious experiences the subject reported, a standard set of five questions was used dealing with antecedent events, the experience itself, and ways in which the experience affected the subject's life. Although an attempt was made to confine the interviews to these five questions, Margolis frequently probed. When more than one experience was volunteered by the subject, the experimenter repeated the same set of questions for each reported experience. In all, the forty-five research subjects reported a total of sixty-nine intense religious experiences. Interviews were taped in an office setting and later transcribed. "A content analysis of the 69 reported experiences was performed to determine the primary characteristics of an [intense] religious experience. Categories were established by reading the experiences and listing the dominant themes of the experience. Following this, each experience was rated for the presence or absence of each theme, and the number of times each theme occurred. After the tabulation was completed, it was decided that any theme which occurred more than five or more times would be included in the typology. . . . As a result of later factor analysis, the typology was developed."

255. The elements associated with each factor are listed in descending order of frequency within that factor.

256. Although each of the four factors appears to be quite different, they all involve intense emotional experience and with the exception of Factor 2 have a positive affective tone.

257. On positive and negative affect in the four factors, see the previous note.

258. In a critique of Hood's M Scale, two sociologists express serious reservations about the value of the structured question procedure to adequately measure a mystical experience. These two social scientists contend that the structured question procedure might well be methodologically deficient and even inap-

propriate because each respondent's interpretation of the meaning of a mystical experience can admit of vast differences. Thus, these social scientists remark, "the researcher has no way of knowing from the responses to such structured questions whether a respondent has had a mystical experience, one of several types of psychic encounters, or a totally irrelevant experience that was, nonetheless, impressive for the respondent." This defect also occurs in the Margolis study. L. Eugene Thomas and Pamela E. Cooper, "The Mystical Experience: Can It be Measured by Structured Questions," paper presented at the annual meeting of the American Sociological Association, Chicago, September, 1977, pp. 14–15. For a revised version of this article, see L. Eugene Thomas and Pamela E. Cooper, "Measurement and Incidence of Mystical Experiences: An Exploratory Study," in *Journal for the Scientific Study of Religion* XVII (December, 1978), pp. 433–437.

259. Wilhelm Pöll, *Das Religiöse Erlebnis und seine Strukturen* (München: Kaiser, 1974). (Compare the Pöll classification with Arnold Ludwig's classification of altered states of consciousness. The Ludwig classification was treated in Chapter Eight.) Pöll writes as follows about this kind of stimulus: "Der situativ-konzentrativen Stimulierung ist es um die Herstellung einer seelischen Ruhelage in dem Sinne zu tun, dass man zeitweilig und soweit existentiell möglich, sich frei macht von vordringlichen Beanspruchungen durch die Umwelt und die eigene Leiblebendigkeit (Vitalität) und so ihnen gegenüber zu einem Verhältnis emotionaler Entspannung und Ausgeglichenheit gelangt. Es geht also um die aktuelle distanzierende Entflechtung aus dem Verklammertsein in die Geschäfte und Bedürfnisse, auf dass man um so mehr ohne Ablenkung und Einschränkung bis in die Tiefen des Unbewussten hinein für die Wirklichkeit von Transzendenz und im besonderen des Heiligkeitsbereiches offen sei." (p. 263).

260. Pöll defines physical stimuli—which he calls sensory-excitative stimuli—in this fashion: "Demgegenüber ist die sensitive Stimulierung auf eine tiefgreifende Erregung des Organismus bedacht und lässt darum auch die Benennung als exzitative Stimulierung zu. Sie setzt ein als intensive Reizung der Sinnesorgane, die bis zur Hervorrufung beträchtlicher Schmerzempfindungen gesteigert werden kann und auf jeden Fall in die Daseinslebendigkeit des Organismus, d. i. seine Vitalsphäre, stösst" (p. 265).

261. See, for example, Jean Houston and Robert E. L. Masters, "The Experimental Induction of Religious-Type Experiences," in John White, editor, *The Highest State of Consciousness* (Garden City, N.Y.: Doubleday Anchor, 1972), pp. 303–321.

262. Walter Houston Clark, "The Relationship between Drugs and Religious Experience," in *Catholic Psychological Record* VI (Fall, 1968), p. 147.

263. *Ibid.*, p. 152.

264. *Ibid.*, p. 149.

265. Jean Mouroux, "Religious Experience," in Karl Rahner et al., editors, *Sacramentum Mundi*, volume 5, p. 292.

266. Karl Rahner and Herbert Vorgrimler, *Theological Dictionary*, edited by Cornelius Ernst, translated by Richard Strachan (New York: Herder and Herder, 1965), p. 302.

267. Such facilitation should be undertaken only by religious educators possessing adequate theoretical background and practical pedagogical skill.

268. Shared praxis is a highly cognitive pedagogical practice invented by Thomas Groome. Shared praxis is an especially ratiocinative mode of action-reflection.

Whereas some action-reflection procedures include in the same pedagogical episode both the actual action together with ratiocinative reflection upon this action, Groome's shared praxis involves the ratiocinative reflection upon some activity which typically takes place outside the lesson itself.

269. See Barry Weinhold and Lynn C. Elliott, *Transpersonal Communication* (Englewood Cliffs, N.J.: Prentice-Hall, 1979), pp. 149–150.

270. For a brief discussion of *Zazen* and the *kōan,* see James Michael Lee, "Discipline in a Moral and Religious Key," pp. 160–162.

271. Jean Houston and Robert E. L. Masters, "The Experimental Induction of Religious-Type Experiences," p. 303.

272. See Ralph W. Hood, Jr., "Eliciting Mystical States of Consciousness with Semi-structured Nature Experiences," in *Journal for the Scientific Study of Religion* XVI (June, 1977), pp. 155–163.

273. This seminal point was made in William Johnston, *The Inner Eye of Love: Mysticism and Religion,* p. 61.

274. See Walter Houston Clark, "Mysticism as a Basic Concept in Defining the Religious Self," in André Godin, editor, *From Religious Experience to Religious Attitude* (Chicago: Loyola University Press, 1965), pp. 31–42.

275. One of the most famous proponents of the prayer of simplicity was Jacques Bossuet.

276. The prayer of simplicity can be regarded as a kind of first step in passive lifestyle prayer, with later steps all being geared to deepening and making more holistic and lifestyle character of this prayer. Thus this kind of prayer can be regarded as one beginning in a wide category of passive lifestyle prayer, namely the so-called passive prayer of union. The higher the level of the passive prayer of union, the more the person becomes intensely and holistically involved. Characteristic of all levels of prayer of union is the complete holistic involvement of all the person's sectors of human functioning so that the person tends not to be distracted by "outside" influences but passively bathes quite fully in the personal here-and-now existential encounter. See Jordan Aumann, *Spiritual Theology* (Huntington, Ind.: Our Sunday Visitor, 1980), pp. 340–354.

277. These famous three levels or ways of religious living will be briefly discussed in the following subsection of this chapter.

278. Adolphe Tanquerey, *The Spiritual Life,* 2d edition, translated by Herman Branderis (Tournai, Belgium: Desclée, 1932), pp. 321–324, 461–464, 637–642.

279. Holism suggests, of course, that in psychomotor prayer, cognitive and affective functions are present but do not predominate; that in cognitive prayer, psychomotor and affective elements are present but do not predominate; and that in affective prayer, psychomotor and cognitive elements are present but do not predominate. Holism also suggests that psychomotor prayer qua psychomotor prayer, cognitive prayer qua cognitive prayer, and affective prayer qua affective prayer can and ought to assume their proper and individual roles within a person's overall lifestyle prayer.

280. This statement holds true even when prayer is considered as a separate activity done in some specified manner as, for example, ratiocinative meditation. Writing of this kind of prayer (sometimes referred to as "formal prayer" in the theological literature), Friedrich von Hügel states that "the decisive preparation for prayer lies not in the prayer itself, but in the life prior to the prayer." In other words, "formal prayer" necessarily takes on the contours and coloration of one's own lifestyle. Thus, for example, if a person is flighty and frequently

distracted from the task at hand, then such an individual will probably exhibit this personality characteristic when "formally praying." Friedrich von Hügel, *The Life of Prayer* (New York: Dutton, 1929), p. 28.

281. Adolphe Tanquerey, *The Spiritual Life,* p. 243.

282. Faricy then continues by stating that "in one sense prayer is an end in itself with no purpose beyond itself, because God created us to be united with him, and beyond that union lies no further goal. But in another sense, prayer's purpose remains always outside prayer itself, ahead of it, because prayer is a process of leading toward an always fuller union with the Lord and a deeper remaining in him. Prayer, then, is a union that grows always closer and deeper." Robert Faricy, *Praying* (Dublin: Villa, 1979), pp. 36–37. Of note in this quotation is Faricy's placement of prayer in a distinctly process dimension, viewing prayer as a process content more than a product content.

283. C. W. F. Smith, "Prayer," in George Arthur Buttrick et al., editors, *The Interpreter's Dictionary of the Bible,* volume 3 (Nashville, Tenn.: Abingdon, 1962), p. 867.

284. On this point, see Charles A. Bernard, *La prière chrétienne* (Bruges, La Belgique: Desclée de Brouwer, 1967), pp. 291–298.

285. In classic Christian spirituality, the prayer of petition consists in requesting some favor from God. The prayer of adoration is that in which we respectfully and joyfully acknowledge God's supreme domination and our absolute dependence. The prayer of thanksgiving is the expression of our everlasting gratitude for God for everything we have received from him, great or small. The prayer of reparation is one in which we evince our great sorrow for having offended God, coupled with the assurance that we will try as hard as possible to discontinue offending God. The prayer of expiation is one in which we offer ourselves as victims in union with God to atone for our sins and for the sins of others, and thus join Jesus more closely in his own expiational activities.

286. One example of the benefits of social-science research and theory with respect to prayer is that advanced by Charles A. Curran, an experienced Christian psychotherapist who writes that "one might go a step further and talk about a therapeutic of prayer. Communication with the other, and all the conditions of faith, confidence, and love that we have described have, in counseling and psychotherapeutic experience, increasingly proved helpful. The same consequences might be proposed with even greater and more extensive results in man's communion and communication with God. This seems to be an ancient idea which in some measure has been lost. Augustine, we said, used the Greek word "*therapeia*" for his concept of grace. That is, he conceived of the relationship between God and man not simply as a gift from God to man, as the Latin word "*gratia*" would imply, but also as a cure, as a healing of man. In God was the final solace for man's restlessness, incompleteness, and inadequacy, and for the primitive condition of anxiety that seems to be intrinsic to humanity itself." Charles A. Curran, *Psychological Dynamics in Religious Living* (New York: Herder and Herder, 1971), pp. 137–138.

287. Gabriel Moran, *Theology of Revelation* (New York: Herder and Herder, 1966), p. 142.

288. Damian Lundy, "The Beginnings of Prayer," in *The Way* XXIII (October, 1983), pp. 276–283.

289. Ignatius of Loyola, *Letters,* translated by William J. Young (Chicago: Loyola University Press, 1959), p. 240. Though Ignatius offered this pedagogical prac-

tice to Jesuits living away from Rome, nevertheless this procedure is equally useful and applicable to persons in all sorts of lifeways and lifeworks.

290. Jordan Aumann, *Spiritual Theology,* pp. 102–121; Joseph de Guibert, *The Theology of the Spiritual Life,* translated by Paul Barrett (London: Sheed and Ward, 1954), p. 44.

291. Thomas Aquinas, *Summa Theologica,* II-II, q. 184, a. 1.

292. *Ibid.,* q. 24, a. 8, translation mine.

293. Joseph de Guibert, *The Theology of the Spiritual Life,* pp. 258–264.

294. I should observe that while the Letter to the Hebrews was traditionally attributed to the Apostle Paul, a great number of modern scripture scholars believe that this Letter was actually written by someone else. However, the Letter does clearly evince the influence of Paul's views.

295. Many of the better and most influential specialists in spiritual living have given tentative empirical descriptions of persons in each of the three ways. This is how Joseph de Guibert puts it: "In general, beginners are those . . . in whom the impediments to charity remain almost unchecked, who have not yet set themselves seriously to remove impediments, great and small, to charity which arise from character or other causes, who have not yet applied themselves to the exercise of the spiritual life and have neither practice nor experience therein. . . . Persons who belong to this stage include (a) innocent children who have not yet attempted to correct their natural defects and curb their evil inclinations and who are not formed in the spiritual life; (b) recently converted sinners, i.e., those who have lived long in sin and who now wish to lead a truly Christian life; (c) persons who have not made any progress and who have always been content to remain in the lowest stage of Christian perfection, not because they do not know better, like the simple souls of which we have just spoken, but because they are too indolent, or because they think that perfection is not for them and so do not trouble themselves about it; (d) persons who, because of an erroneous concept of perfection, have entered on a false way of spiritual life; (e) persons who have grown tepid."

Persons in the second stage are those who are ordinarily free from serious sin and who do not easily fall prey to temptation; however they may occasionally sin seriously, after which they soon repent. They are careful to avoid minor sins. "They know themselves well and are practiced in the principal exercises of the spiritual life, performing them conscientiously (i.e., liturgical prayer, mental prayer, examen of conscience, spiritual reading). They have a firm, penetrating, and personal knowledge and conviction of the fundamental truths of the spiritual life."

Persons in the third stage live "a deep and constant life of charity. The love of God and the desire to be with him and to do all things in and with and for him stand at the center and suffuse their lives." Joseph de Guilbert, *The Theology of the Spiritual Life,* pp. 258–291.

296. Benedict J. Groeschel, *Spiritual Passages* (New York: Crossroad, 1983), p. 4, italics deleted.

297. This principle has long been a cornerstone of my concept of religious education in all its forms. See, for example, James Michael Lee and Nathaniel J. Pallone, *Guidance and Counseling in Schools: Foundations and Processes* (New York: McGraw-Hill, 1966), p. 122.

298. Ward then continues: "Thus it is possible to use the term of many who do not live the hermit life. It means more specifically guarding the mind, constant remembrance of God, and the possession of inner prayer. Hesychasm is the

general term and hesychast is the noun used to describe the person seeking to follow this [inner and individualistic] way of prayer." Benedicta Ward, "Glossary," in *The Sayings of the Desert Fathers,* translated by Benedicta Ward (London: Mowbrays, 1975), p. xvi.

299. Douglas V. Steere, *Together in Solitude* (New York: Crossroad, 1982), p. 92.

300. Thomas Merton, *Contemplation in a World of Action* (London: Allen and Unwin, 1971), pp. 237–327.

301. Jean Leclercq, "Introduction," in *ibid.,* p. x.

302. Eugene Kevane, *Creed and Catechetics* (Westminster, Md.: Christian Classics, 1977), pp. 299, 253–259.

303. Lawrence Kohlberg, "Stages of Moral Development as a Basis for Moral Education," in Brenda Munsey, editor, *Moral Development, Moral Education, and Kohlberg,* pp. 92–93.

304. Actually, this kind of lifestyle has been lived for decades by a portion of European Catholics. However, American communal Catholicism is by no means a direct or indirect import from Europe, or even a fallout from the European experience.

305. Andrew M. Greeley, *The Communal Catholic* (New York: Seabury, 1976), pp. 1–17.

306. I am including the religious lifestyle patterns inspired by political theology and/or by liberation theology under the rubric of liberal as I am conceptualizing this term in this section of the present volume. It should be noted that political theologians and liberationist theologians usually consider themselves as postliberal in the sense that they believe that they are going beyond what they regard as the nice but fundamentally nonrevolutionary nostrums of pre-1960 liberal Christianity. Thus political theologians and the liberation theologians conceptualize liberal Christianity in the technical sense of a particular ideology and spirit (and in one sense even a kind of movement) which began in certain late-nineteenth-century European Protestant circles. I, on the other hand, am taking the term liberal in a much broader, nonspecific, and nontechnical sense.

307. Francis P. Fiorenza, "Political Theology and Liberation Theology: An Inquiry into their Fundamental Meaning," in Thomas M. McFadden, editor, *Liberation, Revolution, and Freedom* (New York: Seabury, 1975), p. 5. This is an especially clear and succinct presentation of the basic differences between political theology and liberation theology.

308. The term "praxis" has become a terribly muddled one in recent years. The word "praxis" in its various late-twentieth-century meanings comes from the common use of this word in the German language. (Karl Marx, as well as many of the most important neo-Marxist thinkers and Christian political theologians, have had German as their native language. The major Latin American theologians of liberation—quite a few of whom pursued their studies (and their travels) in Europe—encountered this word from their everyday contacts with villagers, with fellow international students, from the writings of Marx and the neo-Marxists, from lectures by political theologians, and later back home from the speeches of Soviet-inspired revolutionaries such as home-grown Communist Fidel Castro.) As it is typically and traditionally used in the German-speaking world, "praxis" is a Greek-imported German word meaning simply "practice." (Its secondary meaning in the German language is the office setting where a medical specialist conducts his professional practice.) Some political theologians use the term "praxis" in this sense. Many neo-Marxist philosophers, social scientists, and theologians use the term "praxis" in the same basic sense in

which Marx did, namely the dialectically interactive interpenetration of theory with practice in such a manner that the emancipatory potential inherent in practice is thereby released. A veritable full keyboard of neo-Marxists and persons heavily influenced by neo-Marxists have composed their definitional variations on this same theme, ranging from Jürgen Habermas, to Paulo Freire, to Thomas Groome. Liberation theologians and their supporters also offer a wide range of definitions of "praxis"; thus, for example, a certain Dan DiDomizio defines "praxis" as "that kind of life experience characterized by the active revolutionary struggle for human liberation." One could only wish, if even just for the sake of clarity to say nothing of intellectual respectability and theoretical fecundity, that these persons could arrive at some sort of agreement on a basic definition and core conceptualization of "praxis."

309. Johannes B. Metz, *Theology of the World,* translated by William Glen-Doepel (New York: Herder and Herder, 1969), pp. 107–118.
310. Johann Baptist Metz, *The Emergent Church: The Future of Christianity in a Postbourgeois World,* translated by Peter Mann (New York: Crossroad, 1981), pp. 1–81.
311. Johannes B. Metz, *Theology of the World,* pp. 107–118.
312. Jürgen Moltmann, "Hope and the Biomedical Future of Man," in Ewert Cousins, editor, *Hope and the Future of Man* (Philadelphia: Fortress, 1972), pp. 89–104.
313. Dorothee Sölle, *Political Theology,* translated by John Shelley (Philadelphia: Fortress, 1974), p. 59. Sölle is a leading political theologian.
314. Metz identifies this intermediary as political ethics. To my way of thinking, it would be more logical and more potent with respect to action for the proposed autonomous intermediary to be political science rather than political ethics. At any event, Metz contends that the intermediary be autonomous and not just a messenger boy bringing political theology to the political/social/economic arena.
315. For an easy-to-read essay which captures the affective texture and lifestyle interest of liberationalism while indirectly giving some of its cognitive fundaments, see T. Richard Shaull, "Grace: Power for Transformation," in Thomas M. McFadden, editor, *Liberation, Revolution, and Freedom,* pp. 76–87.
316. This point is made in Delwin Brown, *To Set at Liberty* (Maryknoll, N.Y.: Orbis, 1981), pp. 92–98.
317. Gustavo Gutiérrez, *A Theology of Liberation,* edited and translated by Caridad Inda and John Eagleson (Maryknoll, N.Y.: Orbis, 1973), pp. 155–160.
318. In this vein, Leonardo Boff, a major theologian of liberation, writes that one fact is clearly deducible from the New Testament, namely that "the kingdom of God, contrary to what many Christians think, does not signify something that is purely spiritual or outside this world. It is the totality of the material world, spiritual and human, that is now introduced into God's order." Leonardo Boff, *Jesus Christ Liberator,* translated by Patrick Hughes (Maryknoll, N.Y.: Orbis, 1979), p. 56.
319. The point I am making here is presented with skill and clarity in Peter C. Hodgson, *New Birth of Freedom: A Theology of Bondage and Liberation* (Philadelphia: Fortress, 1976), pp. 308–315. Hodgson is a North American theologian attempting to develop a theology of liberation arising from and therefore more suitable to the United States, Canada, and Europe.
320. One cannot help noticing the similarity between this position, even in its language, with that of Karl Marx.
321. These and other basic tenets of liberation theology have drawn fire from many

Christian quarters both orthodox and not so orthodox. For example, Andrew Greeley states that ''the quintessential slogan mouthed ad nauseam in enlightened Catholic circles is 'the third world.' Any cause, idea, movement, panacea that is fortunate enough to be identified with the third world is automatically assured of support. It is toward the third world that we tired old northern hemisphere types better look for virtue, wisdom, and expiation from our guilt as oppressors and victimizers. Never mind that much of what passes for third-world theology is a pathetic mixture of vulgar Marxism and quotations from conciliar documents and quite innocent of economic, sociological, or even empirical, data. . . . It is impossible to discuss the third world with those who throw at me the slogans 'exploitation,' 'oppression,' 'victimization.' Once these words are uttered the discussion is terminated; any attempt to raise questions about specific issues in specific countries or regions is ruled out of court. I suspect that many third world enthusiasts have very little idea of the economic, social, and political particularities of the different parts of the third world. Nor do they seem interested in acquiring knowledge about these particularities. It is not merely that their thought lacks sophistication and depth; they are not even aware of the necessity or the possibility of specification and depth as characteristic of thought. . . . The enthusiasm of the Catholic elites for [liberation theology], as Geno Baroni notes, is a sign that the [Catholic] elites are on the verge of cultural bankruptcy. . . . It may be that liberation theology has some pertinence in Latin America, though I doubt it. . . . In any case, the liberation theologians haven't liberated anybody, and they are not likely to do so.'' Andrew Greeley, *The Communal Catholic,* pp. 38–39, 40, 41, 109.

322. Socialization may be defined as a process by which a social group seeks to influence a person in such a manner that he will think, feel, and live according to the customs, norms, and meanings of that social group. Though the socialization process does indeed proceed interactively, nonetheless virtually all social scientists specializing in socialization view it as a form of social control—what Paulo Freire, from his philosophical vantage point, calls domestication. Socialization, then, is contrary to and thus opposed to liberation. Though this point should be obvious to everyone, it sometimes is not. John Westerhoff is a case in point. Throughout most of his estimable career as a theological tractarian writing principally on religious education, Westerhoff has advocated both socialization and liberation in his books and articles. At an annual convention of the Association of Professors and Researchers in Religious Education held in Toronto in the late 1970s, Westerhoff publicly announced that socialization and liberation are fundamentally the same process and hence in no way opposed or contrary to one another. While the boundaries allowed for factual inaccuracies and theoretical contradictions are practically without limit in the case of a tractarian, nonetheless Westerhoff's position on the similarity of socialization and liberation strains to burst through even these almost limitless boundaries. I do not know of a single reputable socialization theorist or researcher who would agree with Westerhoff's position. To be sure, the very definition of socialization which Westerhoff himself offers in his book *Generation to Generation* (p. 41) clearly indicates that socialization is in fact intrinsically opposite to liberation. To make matters worse, the few theorists whom Westerhoff does cite in his discussion of socialization in *Generation to Generation* all view socialization in such a way as to be diametrically opposed to liberation.

323. Gustavo Gutiérrez, *Theology of Liberation,* pp. 235–236.

324. Critics like Richard Neuhaus assert that, whether he realizes it or not, Gustavo

Gutiérrez ultimately equates the mission of the church with political revolutionary struggle. Richard J. Neuhaus, "Liberation Theology and the Captivities of Jesus," in *Worldview* XVI (June, 1973), p. 45.

325. Leonardo Boff, *Jesus Christ Liberator,* p. 283.

326. A passage from John McKenzie, the biblicist, might be instructive here about a central theme of Israelite belief which distinguishes it from other ancient religions. "As far as we know Mesopotamian, Canaanite, and Egyptian religions lived in an eternal present. When the political societies which were undergirded by these religions perished, the religions perished with them. The belief of Israel proved itself independent of the political societies of the monarchies of Israel and Judah. Further analysis discloses that this independence was at least implicitly an assertion that the concerns of Yahweh were larger than the concerns of Israel and Judah. It is more than the development of monotheism; it is an understanding that if the nations have no gods, then Yahweh is their god. His future does not depend on the future of the people who worshiped him." John L. McKenzie, *A Theology of the Old Testament,* p. 317.

327. James H. Cone, *Black Theology and Black Power* (New York: Seabury, 1969), pp. 35, 37, 38.

328. Olivia Pearl Stokes, "Black Theology: A Challenge to Religious Education," in Norma H. Thompson, editor, *Religious Education and Theology* (Birmingham, Ala.: Religious Education Press, 1982), pp. 98–99.

329. For a helpful book highlighting some of the many dimensions of women as viewed by female scholars who regard women as being oppressed in religion and theology, see Rosemary Radford Ruether, editor, *Religion and Sexism: Images of Women in the Jewish and Christian Traditions* (New York: Simon and Schuster, 1974).

330. In this vein Letty Russell writes: "Feminist theology has common roots with many types of so-called Third World liberation theologies. With male domination of the social structures, women have a growing consciousness of their own oppression. Some women have adopted the term Fourth World, referring to themselves as an oppressed world majority. . . . Like Third World liberation theology, feminist theology arises from an experience of oppression in society." Letty M. Russell, "Liberation Theology in a Feminist Perspective," in Thomas M. McFadden, editor, *Liberation, Revolution, and Freedom,* p. 89.

331. Mary Daly, *Beyond God the Father: Toward a Philosophy of Women's Liberation* (Boston: Beacon, 1973), p. 13.

332. Edgar Dale, *Audio-Visual Methods in Teaching,* 3rd edition (New York: Holt, Rinehart and Winston, 1969), p. 107.

333. Norman W. Steinaker and M. Robert Bell, *The Experiential Taxonomy* (New York: Academic Press, 1979), pp. 10–11. Steinaker and Bell note that "the categories in this taxonomy are stated in positive terms, even though . . . an experience can elicit either a positive or a negative reaction" (p. 11).

334. When I use the terms experience, experiential teaching, experiential learning, and the like, in this section, I almost always use them in a holistic lifestyle sense, namely holistic lifestyle experience, holistic lifestyle experiential teaching, and so on.

335. James C. Coleman, "Differences Between Experiential and Classroom Learning," in Morris T. Keeton et al., editors, *Experiential Learning* (San Francisco: Jossey-Bass, 1976), pp. 49–61.

336. Because the action comes at the end of the learning event rather than at the

beginning, there is no subjective incentive for learning until the connection between the information and the action becomes clear—which may not be until the third step in the sequence. Hence motivation must be extrinsically supplied in an attempt to remedy the gross deficiency in action.

337. Thus the experiential process is ineffective when the consequence of the action is separated in time or space from the action itself. When the consequence is perceptibly connected to action, then such experiential learning provides a direct guide to future action.

338. Since action occurs at the beginning of the sequence rather than at the end, the subjective need for learning exists from the outset.

339. In order to adequately understand the meaning and force of this statement, it is necessary to realize that I am writing it in the direct context of the taxonomy of the teaching act which I develop in *The Flow of Religious Instruction,* pp. 32–35.

340. John Dewey, *Experience and Education* (New York: Macmillan, 1938), p. 27. This sentence, and indeed the whole of *Experience and Education,* constitutes Dewey's sharp rebuke of those many progressive educators who equated experience with automatic learning, educators who never realized that the degree of learning in experiential teaching necessarily depends on the quality of the experience in which the learner engages.

341. Carl R. Rogers, *Freedom to Learn,* pp. 158–159.

342. Roger Lincoln Shinn, *The Educational Mission of Our Church* (Boston: United Church Press, 1962), pp. 18–19.

343. William Bedford Williamson, *Language and Concepts in Christian Education* (Philadelphia: Westminster, 1970), p. 145.

344. Gabriel Moran, *Design for Religion* (New York: Herder and Herder, 1970), pp. 24–25.

345. On this last point, see Carl R. Rogers, *Freedom to Learn,* pp. 95–97.

346. For a development of this point, see George Isaac Brown, *Human Teaching for Human Learning* (New York: Viking, 1971), pp. 15–16.

347. John Hendrix and Lela Hendrix, *Experiential Education: X-ED* (Nashville, Tenn.: Abingdon, 1975), pp. 16–19.

348. On this point, see B. F. Skinner, *Beyond Freedom and Dignity* (New York: Knopf, 1971), pp. 143, 191.

349. Thus Rachel Henderlite writes that "it seems clear that 'education into faith' is not the function of a school. It is rather a function of the whole congregation as the congregation is moved by the Holy Spirit. In my own judgment, the only way in which such faith as this can be elicited is through inclusion in a community of faith where the whole life of the community is shaped and governed by the community's commitment to its Lord." Rachel Henderlite, "Asking the Right Questions," in John H. Westerhoff III, editor, A *Colloquy on Christian Education,* p. 204.

350. Some instructional specialists have developed experiential learning packages for use in general education. Religious education offices might find these useful in devising their own packages. See, for example, Sivasailam Thiagarajan, *Experiential Learning Packages* (Englewood Cliffs, N.J.: Educational Technology Publications, 1980).

351. For a brief description of a teacher performance center, see James Michael Lee, *The Flow of Religious Instruction,* pp. 288–289.

352. The project technique has a long and venerable history, especially in instruction

taking place in informal settings and in those cases throughout the history of education in which pedagogical leaders attempted to model classroom practice on life as holistically lived outside the school setting. The twentieth-century use of the project technique owes its chief impetus to a highly influential article written by William Heard Kilpatrick entitled "The Project Method," in *Teachers College Record* XIX (September, 1918), pp. 319–335. For a brief but meaty history of the project and of learning by doing, see Thomas Woody, "Historical Sketch of Activism," in National Society for the Study of Education, *The Activity Movement*, Thirty-third Yearbook, Part II (Bloomington, Ill.: Public School Publishing, 1934), pp. 9–43.

353. If this definition seems somewhat vague it is because educators have never come to full agreement on precisely what defines the project. As G. Max Wingo remarks, no common definition of the project was ever developed. Indeed, the term project came to be used interchangeably with the activity movement and with learning by doing, thus further compounding the confusion. Boyd Bode's critical comment about the activity movement is thus applicable to the project technique, namely that it is comprehensive in scope, obscure in meaning, and lacking in precise definition. In my own survey of the literature on the project, I found that while educators have been typically vague on the definition of a project, nonetheless they usually have been in general agreement about what the project involves. G. Max Wingo, "Methods of Teaching," in Chester W. Harris, editor, *Encyclopedia of Educational Research*, 3rd edition (New York: Macmillan, 1960), p. 852; Boyd H. Bode, "Comments and Criticisms," in National Society for the Study of Education, *The Activity Movement*, pp. 78–81. This last-mentioned book is possibly the finest single printed resource on the project technique.

354. Thus James Hosic and Sara Chase observe that the project technique is primarily a way or practice of living. Indeed, Kilpatrick himself holds that ultimately the project is not just a pedagogical technique but a whole philosophy of life. James F. Hosic and Sara E. Chase, *Brief Guide to the Project Method* (Yonkers, N.Y.: World, 1924), p. 3; Samuel Tenenbaum, *William Heard Kilpatrick* (New York: Harper, 1951), p. 137.

355. Typically, advocates of the project technique believe that "the modification of conduct is a worthy end of education, at least, a more worthy end than that of information for its own sake. . . . Conduct is modified in proportion as the act is carried to completion." John Alford Stevenson, *The Project Method of Teaching* (New York: Macmillan, 1922), p. 13.

356. A. Gordon Melvin, *The Activity Program* (New York: Reynal & Hitchcock, 1936), p. 155.

357. For Kilpatrick, a purposeful activity enjoys the distinct pedagogical advantage of uniting cognition with lifestyle. Purpose resides in the learner, of course. Samuel Tenenbaum, *William Heard Kilpatrick*, p. 135.

358. It should be remembered that Kilpatrick is an adherent of John Dewey's philosophy. For Dewey, problem solving constitutes the basis, axis, and goal of all authentic education. In this connection James Hedegard writes that "in Dewey's system, the ideal learning situation is provided by a real problem to solve. In working toward the solution, the learner is provided with continual feedback. A problem which is involved and lengthy and which permits no feedback until the preferred solution is complete would not be a good learning task." James M. Hedegard, "An Overview of Historical Formulations," in Laurence Siegel,

editor, *Instruction: Some Contemporary Viewpoints* (San Francisco: Chandler, 1967), p. 12.

359. It should be noted that while the typology itself is Kilpatrick's, the specific illustrations are mine. Kilpatrick, for example, would hardly be interested in the composition and performance of liturgical music as a project activity.

360. For an extended discussion of this point, together with the philosophy undergirding these four steps, see M. Carter, "The Philosophy of the Project Method," unpublished doctoral dissertation, Fordham University, 1935.

361. Adelaide M. Ayer et al., "Description of Some Ways of Interpreting the Principle of Activity When Applying It to School Work," in National Society for the Study of Education, *The Activity Movement*, p. 66.

362. Collings used the equivalent group method of empirical research. Ellsworth Collings, *An Experiment with a Project Curriculum* (New York: Macmillan, 1923). Collings also found that the lifestyles of the parents in fourteen ordinary phases of conduct in the home also improved much more than was the case with parents whose children were taught in the traditional manner (pp. 340–341).

363. Progressive Education Association, Committee on Evaluation, *New Methods Versus Old in American Education* (New York: Bureau of Publications, Teachers College, Columbia University, 1941).

364. Norman E. Wallen and Robert M. W. Travers, "Analysis and Investigation of Teaching Methods," in N. L. Gage, editor, *Handbook of Research on Teaching* (Chicago, Rand McNally, 1963), p. 483.

365. The project technique also spread to other countries such as England. See G. Cowan, *Project Work in the Secondary School* (London: Longmans, Green, 1967), pp. 1–9.

366. See, for example, Gene Stanford and Albert Roark, "Schools without Walls," in Louis Rubin, editor, *Curriculum Handbook* (Boston: Allyn and Bacon, 1977), pp. 381–391.

CHAPTER TEN

TOWARD A REDIRECTION

"To catalogue everything, test everything, understand everything. What is above, higher than the air we breathe; what is below, deeper than light can penetrate. What is lost in sidereal space, and what the elements conceal. . . . The sun is rising ahead. . . . The past is left behind. . . . The only task worthy of our efforts is to construct the future." [1]
—Pierre Teilhard de Chardin.

Any genuine redirection in teaching the substantive content of religious instruction must necessarily revolve around two pivotal points, namely the nature of substantive content and the composition of substantive content.

The Nature of Substantive Content

The proper nature of the substantive content of religious instruction is religion—not religion in itself but religion as it exists in the religious instruction act. There can never be any fruitful redirection of the substantive content of religious instruction unless this basic fact is constantly followed.

Theology, church history, ethics, and the like, are not religion, and hence can never in themselves comprise the overall substantive content of religious instruction. However, theology, church history, ethics, or the like, can and in many cases ought to contribute, as appropriate, to the overall substantive content of religious instruction. Religion is a personal, existential, holistic, flesh-and-blood relationship which a person has with God and with all of creation in God. Theology is simply a scientific cognitive study of God and his workings in the world; church history is simply a scientific cognitive study of past events in the life of the ecclesia and the *ecclesiasticum*; ethics is simply the scientific cognitive study of moral principles of action. Therefore, to offer the learner primarily theology or church history or ethics instead of religion is to offer him a stone instead of bread (Mt. 7:9).

The supremely personal nature of religion enables this overall substantive content to be the locus in which two basically different kinds of truths may meet and even become functionally integrated. These two disparate kinds of truth are ontic truth and human truth. There is a whole set of truths which flow from the nature and operation of reality, and there is another whole set of different truths which flow from the nature and reality of a flesh-and-blood human being. A hierarchy of truths exists within each of these two basic sets. Depending upon the exigencies of a particular person's here-and-now concrete existential situation, some ontically rooted truths will have more force for him, while other ontically rooted truths will have less force even though the truths with less force occupy a higher place in the ontic hierarchy of truth.[2] From the standpoint of substantive content as well as structural content, therefore, the wisest pedagogical starting point is always to take the learner where that person is existentially and developmentally.

The eminently personal character of religion also enables this overall substantive content to serve as a locus for bringing together two otherwise disparate elements interpenetrating all human existence, namely, time and transcendence. Thomas Mampra beautifully expresses this crucial point: "Born and bred in time, but always transcending time in spirit, man creates time-bound and space-limited cultures and traditions, while aspiring for timelessness and transcendence. Religion as a human phenomenon is a meeting point of these two factors: time and transcendence. . . . The deeper one enters into the inner dimensions of one's own religion, the profounder becomes one's experience of time and transcendence. In his quest for transcendence, man discovers a greater degree of unity whereas in his existence conditioned by time and space, he encounters factors of diversity."[3]

Whether it is individual or social, the substantive content of religious instruction must always be preeminently personal, namely, conducted in a holistic manner and directed toward the fullest possible union with God.[4] When God is loved and lived in one's personal life, when God becomes fire in one's bones and breath in one's lungs, then such an individual is living religiously or at least is beginning to do so.

Probably the most effective way to successfully teach the overall substantive content of religious instruction is to structure the pedagogical situation in such a manner that the learners can live religiously. Central in the successful teaching of overall substantive content, then, is heavy emphasis on religious conduct, on holistic religious performance. Scripture does not state that Christian cognition is the desideratum for the religious person; rather, the bible unambiguously indicates that first and foremost the desideratum is holistic Christian living. Cognition is valuable in the Christian scheme of things to the extent to which it broadens and enriches everyday Christian living. Religion is a way of exercising one's humanity, of operationalizing one's own individual personhood in highly concrete, holistically performance terms. Religion is holistic human conduct—and this is what religious educators ought to be teaching when they teach the overall substantive content of religious instruction.[5]

The Composition of Substantive Content

The proper composition of the substantive content of religious instruction is multidimensional. There can never be any fruitful redirection of the substantive content of religious instruction unless this fundamental fact is always in evidence.

To assert that the substantive content of religious instruction is multidimensional is to assert that this substantive content is necessarily composed of many subcontents. In this third volume of my trilogy I have shown that there are eight major molar subcontents which, in concert, go to make up the substantive content of religious instruction.

Three major conclusions of intense practical importance flow from the fact that the substantive content of religious instruction is multidimensional.

The first of these major conclusions is that the substantive content of religious instruction is not adequately taught when one or more of its major molar subcontents is downplayed or minimized.[6] Religion necessarily involves the full range of all eight subcontents; all must achieve salience in the lesson, as appropriate, lest the "religion" which is taught be a lopsided, defective, or feeble one. Much of Christian religious instruction down through the centuries has failed because the multidimensionality of substantive content was ignored or suppressed—in other words, what was taught was not really total religion but only a few of its many dimensions. To be sure, religious educationists usually propose religion lessons which are three-dimensional at best (product content, verbal content, cognitive content), with the other major molar dimensions being grossly minimized or ignored. Affective content, nonverbal content, and unconscious content usually get very short shrift. Even those religion lessons which deliberatively incorporate process do so not so much as a substantive content but as a structural content. One of the most effective things a religion teacher can do in terms of greatly improving the religion lesson is to move the substantive content away from its present two- or three-dimensional reality into the full eight-dimensional range of authentic substantive content. Religion teachers will be delighted to discover that many of the dimensions of substantive content which they previously neglected will prove more pedagogically potent than those dimensions which had formerly occupied their sole instructional attention. This is especially true when the religious educator brings to salience the affective dimension and the lifestyle dimension of substantive content. In this connection, it is well to recall that Augustine himself tells us that prior to his conversion it was not so much Ambrose's cognitive teachings which held attraction for him but rather the fact that Ambrose treated him with kindness.[7]

The second major conclusion flowing from the important fact that substantive content is necessarily multidimensional is that the most effective substantive way of teaching religion is to teach it in an interdisciplinary fashion, namely in a manner which *itself* integrates all eight subcontents into a harmonious whole. If religion—and in our case religion as it exists in the religious instruction act—is indeed a dynamic living fusion of all eight subcontents, then obviously the most effective way to teach religion is to teach it in an inherently integrated interdisciplinary fashion. A curriculum or lesson built around Christian living, especially when performed in a laboratory for Christian living, is an especially powerful way to teach religion in a genuinely and robustly interdisciplinary fashion. Certainly religion can never be taught in an interdisciplinary manner by teaching just one of its components or subcomponents such as theology, and then, after this task is completed, attempt to tack on some other contents like affect or lifestyle.[8]

The third major practical conclusion flowing from the vital fact that substantive content is necessarily multidimensional is that the structural content to which it is joined in the here-and-now religious instruction act must also be multidimensional. There has to be a basic compatability between substantive content and structural content. Thus each of the eight molar subcontents of religious instruction, as well as each of the diverse subsubcontents present within each of the eight molar subcontents, should be joined to a different and appropriate type of structural content. Pedagogical failure will ensue from any attempt to simply use one or just a handful of pedagogical practices to teach the entire rainbow of substantive contents. In this connection, it should be remembered that one or another structural content is not simply the vehicle by which a given substantive content is shipped to the learner. Structural content is a full-fledged major pedagogical content in its own right, a content which, in dynamic interaction with the substantive content to which it is joined, go to make up as a single meshed unit the basic nature and form of the religious instruction act. Consequently, the task of the religious educator is not to choose the teaching procedure which he thinks is right for a previously chosen substantive content, but rather to find out which substantive content and which structural content are intrinsically apt and functionally appropriate for each other. (In the first of these two cases, the structural content is chosen solely with respect to its aptness and appropriateness to the previously chosen substantive content. In the second of these two cases, the structural content and the substantive content are chosen more or less together; furthermore, they are selected with respect to how each is reciprocally apt and appropriate to the other.) What is taught in the religion lesson is not substantive content, but the compound of substantive content and structural content.

Two Examples

To illustrate some of the points I am making in this very brief chapter, I will give two examples. The first example illustrates how the multidimensionality of substantive content is, as a general rule, wantonly ignored in modern religious instruction. The second example illustrates what can happen in religious instruction endeavor when the multidimensionality of substantive content is given its due.

In what is obviously a summation of both the thesis and the spirit of his book *Christian Religious Education,* Thomas Groome spends most of his last chapter drawing a parallel between the book's thesis and the biblical account of Jacob wrestling with an unnamed man (Gn. 32:23–31).[9] Though Groome hedges somewhat, he does assert among other things that this biblical narrative is "paradigmatic of the whole human quest to know God, the wrestling it requires, and the limits of our knowing." Groome's statement is certainly true—as far as it goes. The major flaw in Groome's statement encapsulates one of the major flaws in his book, namely the abject failure to incorporate into his theory the whole multidimensionality of substantive content (and also the concomitant failure to incorporate into his theory the necessary multidimensionality of structural content.) Groome regards Jacob's struggle as primarily one of knowing, a cognitive affair. From what Groome writes about Jacob's encounter, he also would admit of process content. In commenting on the religious instruction significance of Jacob's wrestling, Groome also brings in verbal content.[10]

An analysis of the biblical account of Jacob's wrestling with the unnamed man directly reveals and indirectly suggests that this struggle included the entire range of substantive content, and not the few which Groome would have us believe. (Jacob's struggle with the unnamed man was a religious instruction event. This point should not be forgotten.) A major product content of this pedagogical episode was that Jacob's hip was wrenched from its socket (v. 26), a content which remained with him. The struggling itself constituted a primary process content. Among the cognitive contents which the scripture states Jacob acquired was his intellectual understanding that his life was spared though he had encountered God (v. 31). The affective content which Jacob gained included a whole change in basic attitude and values (v. 29). The verbal content of this pedagogical event is nicely put in the account of the dialogue between Jacob and the unnamed man (vv. 27–30). Most of the struggle with the unnamed man obviously took place in the nonverbal mode, since wrestling is not a verbal activity. Though the biblical account does not directly indicate that the entire struggle took place in a dream or vision in the night, it is quite possible that it was the case; hence unconscious content played a major role in the dream or vision. Even if the instructional event occurred outside of a dream or vision context, Jacob's unconscious processes were perforce at work in the encounter as well as in his interpretation of this encounter. Lifestyle content, deeply admixed with psychomotor behavior, is paramount among all the contents which Jacob acquired in this pedagogical incident, as is evidenced by the fact that his holistic self was engaged in the struggle and that his name was changed from Jacob to Israel.[11]

Any religious instruction theory which is less than inclusive of all eight molar substantive contents is bound to fail sooner or later. This is one major reason why Thomas Groome's religious instruction theory will fail, just as all the rest of the less-than-fully multidimensional proposals made in religious instruction over the centuries have also failed.[12]

The second example I wish to briefly adduce illustrates what can happen in religious instruction endeavor when the multidimensionality of substantive content is given its due. This example is that of the journey to Emmaus (Lk. 24:13–36). The Emmaus event was primarily an instructional transaction whose performance objective appears to have been the existential recognition of Jesus by two of his followers. Viewed from the pedagogical perspective, the Emmaus journey shows what can happen in a religion lesson when the full multidimensional range of substantive content is not given adequate expression—even when the lesson is facilitated by a master teacher.

Throughout the trip to Emmaus, the religion lesson centered primarily on cognitive and verbal content. Using questioning and telling techniques primarily, Jesus provided the learners with a particularly rich diet of cognitive and verbal content. Despite all this, the learners failed to recognize Jesus. Then the range of substantive content suddenly broadened, and the texture of the structural content also changed markedly. As they sat down (or reclined) in a dining area, Jesus took bread, blessed it, broke it, and offered it to the disciples. With this pedagogical act, the eyes of his followers were opened and they recognized Jesus. What had happened pedagogically that the desired teaching outcome was finally attained after so many failures on the road? Jesus added a whole new range of molar substantive contents to the previously ineffective verbal and cognitive contents, and placed these new molar substantive contents into a new interactive structural framework. Especially salient among the new molar substantive contents were affective content, nonverbal content, and lifestyle content. Sitting down to eat is an activity surrounded by and permeated with affectivity.[13] Taking the bread, blessing it, and giving it to the learners is a nonverbal transaction. Finally, the whole event was quintessentially one of lifestyle content, an episode which existentially and holistically relived the supreme lifestyle moments of the Last Supper.

Giving substantive content its proper multidimensional due is not easy for the religious educator. It is far simpler for the religion teacher to treat substantive content as if it had only two or three dimensions. But effective religion teaching is not an easy task. To be sure, one of the principal reasons why successful religion teaching is difficult is that it necessarily involves the appropriate interaction in the instructional episode of the full range of substantive content.

A Final Note

Because it is necessarily flesh-and-blood (nature) and necessarily multidimensional (composition), religion should be enjoyable to teach and enjoyable to learn. Religion teaching becomes a chore and a bore when its substantive content is robbed of its intensely personal nature and of its interactive multidimensionality. If religious educators truly wish to vitalize their religion lessons, they should accord to substantive content its proper holistic humanness and its proper holistic multidimensionality. Often such a process requires considerable redirection in outlook as well as in effort. Such is the challenge and the promise of religious instruction endeavor.

NOTES

1. Pierre Teilhard de Chardin, *Album,* various translators (London: Collins, 1966), p. 127.
2. This point is made in Karl Rahner, "Hierarchie der Wahrheiten," in *Diakonia* XIII (November, 1982), pp. 376–382. I also make the same point in James Michael Lee, *Principles and Methods of Secondary Education* (New York: McGraw-Hill, 1963), pp. 179–180.
3. Thomas Mampra, "Preface," in Thomas Mampra, editor, *Religious Experience: Its Unity and Diversity* (Bangalore, India: Dharmaram, 1981), p. i.
4. Commenting specifically on the relevance of Pierre Teilhard de Chardin's theories to the work of religious instruction, Robert Faricy writes: "What catechetics has to learn from listening to and reflecting on the ideas of Teilhard de Chardin can be summarized in a sentence. Religious education must be directed toward a full and broad personal union with God in Christ, and through the world." Robert Faricy, *Christian Faith and Everyday Life* (Middlegreen, England: St. Paul, 1981), p. 79. Faricy is an advocate of Teilhard's thought. His otherwise fine book is marred by his belief (pp. 76–78) that process is basically different from content, despite the fact that a central and recurrent theme in Teilhard's writings is that process fundamentally is content, and an enormously important content at that.
5. Conduct is such that not only does it spring from motivation but also at times creates motivation—and even occasionally bypasses cognitive and/or affective motivation. Writing movingly but nonetheless scientifically about his personal ordeal in Nazi Konzentrationslägern, the distinguished psychotherapist Bruno Bettelheim states: "Experience with both [psycho] analyzed and un[psycho] analyzed persons in the [concentration] camps was convincing demonstration that when the chips were down, it was utterly unimportant why a person acted the way

he did; the only thing that counted was how he acted. . . . Only dimly at first, but with greater clarity, did I also come to see soon that how a man acts can alter what he is." Michael Novak has the following to say about the dynamic and formative interplay among cognition, perception, motivation, and action as these are mediated in concrete here-and-now experience: "When Paul Tillich was transplanted from Germany to the United States, the tenor of his thinking changed profoundly. When Reinhold Niebuhr moved from Yale to become a pastor in Detroit, and again after he had visited Germany and seen the rise of Hitler, the content of many of his concepts changed. Basic experiences often alter one's cognitive life. It does not follow that one's ordinary cognitive methods suffice to give a full account of these experiences." Bruno Bettelheim, *The Informed Heart* (Glencoe, Ill.: Free Press, 1960), p. 16; Michael Novak, "'Story' and Experience," in James B. Wiggins, editor, *Religion as Story* (New York: Harper & Row, 1975), p. 175.

6. It is impossible to eliminate completely any substantive subcontent such as unconscious content or nonverbal content since each of the eight molar subcontents are perforce present in every religion lesson.

7. "Et eum amare coepi primo quidem non tamquam doctorem veri, quod in ecclesia tua prorsus desperabam, sed tamquam hominem benignum in me." Aurelius Augustinus, *Confessiones,* V, 13, 23.

8. Daniel Tanner and Laurel Tanner contend that if Ralph Tyler's model had been accepted as a paradigm for the curriculum field "it is unlikely that the curricularists would have been so easily seduced by the doctrine of disciplinarity which reigned supreme in curriculum development through the 1960s. For, according to Tyler's model, one of the key sources of educational objectives is concerned with studies relevant to contemporary life—such as the investigation of problems relating to health, natural resources, citizenship, and so on. Such concerns were largely ignored by advocates of disciplinary doctrine. A second source, according to Tyler, is concerned with studies of the learners themselves—their nature and needs. As we have seen, proponents of the discipline-centered curriculum reforms tended to conceive of the child as a miniature version of the mature scholar on the forefront of his or her discipline. They ignored the basic work of Piaget and his predecessors who demonstrated how the child's thought processes are qualitatively different from that of the adult and how these processes undergo qualitiative stages of transformation." Daniel Tanner and Laurel N. Tanner, *Curriculum Development,* 2d edition (New York: Macmillan, 1980), pp. 69–70. In the third chapter of this comprehensive book there is an extensive treatment of the Tyler curriculum model. It would appear that Mary Boys' political views of the curriculum do not allow her to grasp the interdisciplinary thrust and humanistic texture of the Tyler model. See Mary C. Boys, *Biblical Interpretation in Religious Education* (Birmingham, Ala.: Religious Education Press, 1980), pp. 206–211.

9. Thomas H. Groome, *Christian Religious Education* (San Francisco: Harper & Row, 1980), pp. 277–278. I am using Groome's book as my example here because his volume is one of the relatively few well-conceptualized, genuinely scholarly, and truly theoretical treatises written in religious instruction since the end of World War II. In making my critique of the wanton disregard of the full multidimensionality of substantive content by religious educationists, I believe that it is proper that I direct my attention to a high-level book rather than to a low-level one.

10. Verbal content is paramount in Groome's theory of religious instruction. This fact

is pointedly exemplified in the dedication of his book. He dedicates his book to the memory of his parents "who together told me both Story and Vision." I strongly suspect that the lifestyle which his parents lived, together with their nonverbal and affective behavior (to say nothing of their unconscious communication), exerted far greater religious instruction impact on the future priest-professor than all the verbal and cognitive content which they offered.

11. A change of name in adulthood has pointed an all-encompassing lifestyle significance in the bible, as, for example, the change in name from Saul to Paul.

12. There are other important reasons why Groome's theory will fail. For example, he conceptualizes pedagogical procedure in an incredibly restricted fashion. Thus his theory, in its present form at least, admits of only one instructional practice, namely that of a variant of the action-reflection procedure which he labels "shared praxis." In effect, then, the range of Groome's structural content is unidimensional rather than multidimensional. Consequently, the best that can be said of Groome's theory with respect to structural content is that it is a theory simply of one single pedagogical procedure ("shared praxis"), rather than a theory dealing with the wide range of structural content.

13. This well-known fact helps to explain why bachelors like to take their ladyfriends to dinner and why businessmen often prefer to deal with prospective customers over a meal.

EPILOGUE TO THE TRILOGY

"Each greedy hand will strive to catch the flower
When none regards the stalk it grows upon.
Each creature seeks the fruit still to devour
But leaves the tree to fall or stand alone.
Yet this advice, fair creature, take of me,
Let none take fruit, unless he take the tree." [1]

—Anonymous Elizabethan Poet

The Content of Religious Instruction is the final volume of my trilogy on religious instruction. The second volume of the trilogy is *The Flow of Religious Instruction,* while the first volume is *The Shape of Religious Instruction.*

The trilogy both in its sum and in its parts does not deal with the entire range of intentional religious education. It deliberately excludes from its purview two of the three basic constituents of intentional religious education, namely religious counseling and the administration of religious education activities. The focus of the trilogy is squarely on the third of these three fundamental components of intentional religious education, namely religious instruction.

Religious instruction is a term which unequivocally means the *teaching* of religious wherever, whenever, and however this mode of teaching is enacted.

The zone of religious instruction properly includes such important concerns as the goals of religious instruction, the cultural milieu in which religious instruction takes place, the political forces which impact upon religious instruction, the theology and philosophy and history of religious instruction, and the like. Vital as these concerns might be, one fact stands out from and cuts through all of them, namely, that the here-and-now concrete teaching act is both the center and the axis of religious instruction activity. Everything else within the entire scope of intentional religious instruction flows from and flows into the here-and-now religious instruction act.

Any goal of religious instruction is existentially irrelevant to religious instruction until it is translated in operational fashion[2] into teachable substantive and structural contents. No one teaches goals; rather one teaches specific substantive and structural contents designed to yield the desired goal(s).

The cultural milieu in which religious instruction takes place is not important in itself as far as religious instruction is concerned. Its significance for religious instruction derives only from the extent to which it constitutes an environmental variable in overall content. Culture does not teach in and of itself. Culture only teaches in the manner and in the degree to which it dynamically and existentially interacts with the other variables present in the religious instruction act. If the cultural milieu did teach in and of itself, then everyone in a given culture would end up more or less identical—in short, cultural determinism.

The political forces which impact upon religious instruction are significant for religion teaching, not in themselves, but only to the extent to which they become part of the religious instruction act itself. An investigation of the political forces impinging upon the religious instruction act is of necessity directed toward an examination of the political context in which the religious instruction act occurs and toward an exploration of the political meaning of the religious instruction act. Such an investigation, therefore, yields the political significance of the religious instruction act and not the religious instruction significance of the religious instruction act.[3]

The theology and philosophy and history of religious instruction are nothing more than background resources for the religious instruction act. The theology of religious instruction, the philosophy of religious instruction, and the history of religious instruction are just what their names indicate—the theology *of*, the philosophy *of*, the history *of*. In other words, the theology of religious instruction, the philosophy of religious instruction, and the history of religious instruction are not religious instruction activity but rather are exterior scientific concerns *about* religious instruction. These background resources do not belong to the same ontic order as the religious instruction act itself, a fact which sharply limits but by no means eliminates their considerable significance for the religious instruction enterprise. It is also important to note that there is a basic difference between the theology and philosophy and history *of* religious instruction, on the one hand, and the role which theological and philosophical and historical *subject matter* may play in the pre-mediational composition of the substantive content of religious instruction, on the other hand. The theology and philosophy and history of religious instruction are external to the religious instruction act. The theology and philosophy and history of religious instruction exist not primarily for religious instruction use, but chiefly for theology or philosophy or history use. The theology and philosophy and history of religious instruction can help religious instruction from the outside by presenting their findings for possible use by the religious educator in reflecting on the theological or philosophical or historical meanings of the religious instruction act. In sharp contrast, theological or philosophical or historical subject matter as pre-mediated substantive contents are internal to the religious instruction act. In the religious instruction act, the subject matter of theology or philosophy or history become fused into what becomes the religious instruction act.[4]

Though it is at once the center and the axis of religious instruction, the teaching act has been woefully neglected throughout the entire history of religious education. A 1984 review of some of the pertinent literature strongly suggests that, with very rare exceptions, religious educationists have tended to assume the nature and function of the religious instruction act rather than scientifically study it or systematically improve it.[5]

Surely no on-target discourse about, or genuine improvement in religious instruction is possible when nearly every specialist in the field disregards the center and axis of the religious instruction act itself. Small wonder, then, that the field of religious instruction has wallowed in such a pathetically low state, a state which rendered it easy prey for every sort of amorphous and empirically unsupported pedagogical proposal. Indeed, one gets the impression that the more amorphous and empirically unsupported are these pedagogical proposals, the more blindly and the more enthusiastically will religious educationists and educators tend to embrace them. Reuel Howe's pedagogical "theory" of dialogue and Thomas Groome's pedagogical method of shared praxis nicely illustrate this point. Howe's dialogue "theory" which was all the rage in American religious instruction circles in the late 1950s and early 1960s is highly amorphous and vague.[6] Howe's "theory" is an engaging concoction of foggy statements and high-sounding rhetoric about the nature and function of the teaching process. Howe's "theory" never deals with the stuff of the religious instruction act—the actual data on the pedagogical transaction, the conditions under which the variables involved in the pedagogical dynamic are interrelated, or why the pedagogical act operates as it does—in other words, fact and law and theory respectively. Groome's method of shared praxis which was accepted with paradoxical uncriticalness[7] by quite a few religious educationists in the first part of the 1980s is empirically grounded in the skimpiest of data and is based on scientifically invalid facts.[8] The skimpy data which Groome adduces to support the generalizability of his instructional method come solely from a few religion courses which he himself has taught— data gathered not in a scientific manner but simply reported in anecdotal fashion. Still worse in terms of verification, his data are lacking in scientific validity since the assemblage, evaluation, and interpretation of these data were all done solely by the very person who himself was a central variable in the pedagogical method under investigation.[9]

The purpose and objective of my trilogy on religious instruction is to provide a solid theoretical foundation for the field of religious instruction. This theoretical foundation aims to be comprehensive and systematic. As such it integrates into a single multifaceted overarching theory the relevant facts and laws operating in the religious instruction act. Only in this way is it possible to put the field of religious instruction on that kind of solid footing so necessary to render the religious instruction act optimally fruitful and relatively immune to fads and gimmicks.

The trilogy as a whole and in each of its three major parts represents an attempt to put the teaching of religion on a firm and fruitful scientific basis.[10] In order to place the teaching of religion on a scientific footing, I have endeavored to gather the relevant empirical facts on the teaching-learning dynamic, offer scientific laws which specify and govern the relationship among these facts, and finally insert these facts and laws into a theoretical framework which will explain, predict, and verify teaching practice. In this manner I am striving to replace the pedagogical hunches and intuitions upon which most religious educators seem to base their teaching procedures with a formal scientific matrix, a matrix which is indispensable for effective religious instruction over the long haul.

I would have preferred to have written a genuinely in-depth set of books and to have conducted some sophisticated empirical research on specific topics of major importance to religious instruction. However such a task is not possible for any scholar unless there first exists a solid scientific and theoretical foundation for a particular discipline or field as a whole, a foundation which provides a meaningful and fruitful housing for his theoretical monographs and scientific research. Even a cursory glance at the history of religious instruction reveals that the field has been consistently bereft of this kind of foundation. Consequently I took it upon myself in this trilogy to establish such a scientific and theoretical foundation for religious instruction. Therefore the trilogy should not be considered as an advanced work, a work which explores topics with requisite depth and subtlety. Rather, the trilogy is a work for beginners in the field of religious instruction. It provides nothing more than a broad introduction to the field, namely the bases and the primary components of religious instruction activity. As an introductory work, the trilogy necessarily covers a vast amount of territory; hence its intent and strength lie in its breadth and not in its depth. In order for the trilogy to be as deep as I would have liked, it would have had to be expanded to at least thirty volumes.

Though the trilogy is a work of breadth rather than of depth, nonetheless I believe that it is still a work of scholarship. After all, mature scholarship is required, not only for an in-depth examination of a focused topic, but also for the establishment of a broad scientific and theoretical base for any given field. Unfortunately, mature scholarship has been a relatively rare commodity in the field of religious instruction.[11] With only a touch of facetiousness one can remark with some legitimacy that not a few religious educators (and educationists?) appear to derive their basic principles of religious instruction from bumper stickers and banners rather than from high-class scientific books and research treatises in the field.

The trilogy is best seen as a unitary work. Though each volume is indeed a separate treatise in itself, nonetheless each volume attains its true meaning and full comprehensibility when it is directly placed into the overall context of the trilogy as a whole.

The first volume of the trilogy, *The Shape of Religious Instruction,* establishes the rock-bottom foundation and rationale for the existence of religious instruction endeavor as a distinct enterprise in its own right, that is to say, as a separate field. The key chapter in this book, Chapter Seven, clearly demonstrates how and why religious instruction is a mode of social science and not a branch of theology. Chapters leading up to the crucial Chapter Seven delineate the role of religious instruction within the entire range of religious education, the major complementary focal points of religious instruction, the existential manner in which religion teaching is necessarily enacted, the character of religious instruction as a field rather than as a discipline, and the form and operation of both theology and social science. Chapter Eight enunciates the proper role which theology plays in religious instruction activity. Chapter Nine is a deliberate and necessary digression from the linear unfolding of the book's thesis in that it shows how the practice and the effectiveness of religion teaching is explained by terrestrial variables rather than by spooky, ethereal, and unfathomable forces. The last chapter sets forth a few important ways in which the book's message can be used to bring about a fruitful redirection of basic religious instruction theory and practice.

The final two volumes of the trilogy deal with the two major global contents of religious instruction, namely structural content and substantive content.

The second volume of the trilogy, *The Flow of Religious Instruction,* deals exclusively with structural content. Structural content is the teaching process. Structural content is not simply how a religious educator teaches, but also how the religious instruction act qua pedagogical act is itself something which is learned by learners. The key chapter in this book, Chapter Seven, points out inadequate pseudo-theories of teaching religion and then goes on to identify genuine and productive teaching theory. Chapters leading up to the crucial Chapter Seven delineate the range of structural content, the place of structural content within the basic goals of religious instruction, the foundational difference between teaching religion and teaching theology, a workable taxonomy of the teaching act, the distinct form and function of teaching theory as contrasted to learning theory, and some key empirical findings about the way in which learning occurs. Chapters Eight and Nine enunciate respectively the nature and the structure of the teaching process itself. The last chapter sets forth a few important ways in which the book's message can be used to successfully enhance the understanding and effectiveness of structural content in religious instruction endeavor.

The third volume of the trilogy, *The Content of Religious Instruction,* deals exclusively with the other of the two global contents of religious instruction, namely substantive content. The substantive content of religious instruction is lived religion in all its rich dimensionalities. The key chapter in this book, Chapter Nine, highlights the central role which lifestyle occupies both as the purest religious content in its own right and as the dynamically integrative meeting place of all the other major substantive contents. The first chapter delineates the character and scope of religion as the overall substantive content of religious instruction. The other seven chapters leading up to the crucial Chapter Nine set forth the distinct nature and principal forms of molar substantive contents: product content, process content, cognitive content, affective content, verbal content, nonverbal content, and unconscious content. The last chapter sets forth a few important ways in which the book's message can be used to successfully enhance the understanding and the multidimensionality of substantive content in religious instruction endeavor.

Earlier in this Epilogue I observed that the trilogy is a theoretical work. Let me now expand on this statement. The kind or order of theory which the trilogy represents is nothing less than that of macrotheory. A macrotheory is an overall and global form of theory into which are inserted theories and subtheories of lesser scope.[12] For example, theological theory is the macrotheory of theological science, just as physical-scientific theory is the macrotheory of chemistry. A macrotheory forms the matrix and foundation of theory in that it sets forth the parameters of one or another theory and explains in fundamental fashion why that theory works. To illustrate: Theological macrotheory delineates the theological boundaries and theological fundaments of one or another theory of the sacrament of penance and attempts to delineate in theological fashion why one or another of these theories adequately explains, predicts, and verifies the nature and operation of the sacrament.

The most important feature of the trilogy, a feature which permeates every volume and every chapter, is that it seeks to provide a fundamental macrotheory for the religious instruction act. Previously, the theoretical macrotheory underlying the religious instruction act was theological macrotheory. I state this despite the fact that theological macrotheory was seldom if ever elaborated in any kind of comprehensive, systematic fashion. The trilogy seeks to replace theological macrotheory with social science macrotheory. To this end I devote a great deal of space to presenting empirical and theoretical evidence which forcefully demonstrates that the nature, structure, operation, and effectiveness of the religious instruction act can be adequately handled only by social-scientific macrotheory.

A macrotheory is the most fundamental explanatory/predictive/verificational basis of any area of human endeavor. Though a book surely cannot be judged by its cover, nonetheless I have attempted to make the book covers of the trilogy as a whole suggest the essential fundamentality and all-inclusiveness of social-scientific macrotheory for the work of religious instruction. The cover of *The Shape* is red, *The Flow* yellow, and *The Content* blue—the primary colors of the spectrum. Just as all other colors are variations or combinations of these three basic colors, so are all religious instruction theories and laws and procedures derivations in one form or another of a foundational macrotheory. For this reason, too, I fully expect that everything I will write on the topic of religious instruction from now until the end of my career will be manifestly or latently contained in the trilogy. In this sense an understanding of the trilogy is essential to adequately grasp the grounding of whatever else I may write or teach in the future. This fact does not mean that I will cease to grow. Rather, it means that the contours and direction of this growth have been broadly charted by the trilogy.

As macrotheory, the social-science approach inherently seeks to explain, predict, and verify all theories and all pedagogical practices falling within its domain.[13]

Like lesser-order theories, macrotheory has two fundamental properties, namely, comprehensiveness and systematicness.

The social-science macrotheory of religious instruction is comprehensive in that it includes as far as possible the whole range of relevant concepts, facts, laws, and lesser-order theories which are in some way organically or operationally related to the religious instruction act. Consequently, the social-science macrotheory of religious instruction avoids identification with any particular form, setting, or procedure of actual here-and-now religious instruction endeavor. Only in this way can the social-science macrotheory adequately explain, predict, and verify every religious instruction act no matter its particular form, no matter its particular setting, no matter its particular procedure. Thus the social-science macrotheory necessarily avoids taking sides about which theological view is correct[14] or which denomination is the most authentically Christian.[15] The social-science macrotheory of religious instruction necessarily avoids any particularities with regard to the setting in which the teaching act takes place. The macrotheory is eminently applicable to all religious instructional settings both formal and informal. The social-science macrotheory avoids any particularity in terms of procedure. Hence it cannot be identified with any pedagogical strategy such as discovery, with any pedagogical method such as affective teaching, with any pedagogical technique such as role playing. The social-science macrotheory is capable of explaining, predicting, and verifying every kind of instructional procedure. Even more than this, the social-science macrotheory is not particularistic even with respect to any specific lower-order theory of teaching such as Lawrence Kohlberg's theory of moral instruction or Paulo Freire's theory of revolutionary praxis teaching. Because it is comprehensive, the social-science macrotheory applies to all particular teaching and learning theories, and indeed to all particular theories of religion including specific social-scientific theories of religion.[16] Consequently the social-science macrotheory in itself is value-free in terms of an inherent embrace or rejection of any particularity which in one way or another is constitutive or explanatory of the religious instruction act.

The social-science macrotheory of religious instruction is systematic in that it assembles the whole range of relevant concepts, facts, laws, and lesser-order theories in such a fashion that they form an organized whole. Systematicness denotes that any change in one part of the system necessarily has interactive impact upon the other parts of the system, and indeed upon the system itself. Every single pedagogical procedure is an integral part of a larger ecology rather than just an isolated phenomenon. To rip any part of a system out of the ecology of that system is ultimately to severely minimize both the near-term and the long-term effectiveness of the ripped-out part.

Systematicness also suggests that both the large picture and the small details are important—the large picture and the small details both of the macrotheory itself and the religious instruction practice from which this macrotheory is ultimately drawn. The big picture is very much influenced by the precision, arrangement, and interaction of the small details embodied in it. Conversely, the meaning, feeling, and existential thrust of the details are significantly affected by the big picture. A religious educator who just has the big picture with few details will be just as ineffective as the teacher who simply has the details but no big picture. Generality and specificity are both essential for effective religion teaching, and both are provided in abundance by an adequate macrotheory of religious instruction.

The social-science approach to religious instruction is just that, namely, a macrotheoretical *approach*. A macrotheoretical approach is not at all the same as a concrete act. The social-science approach to religious instruction, therefore, is not to be equated with one or more concrete religious instruction acts.[17] As an approach, the social-scientific macrotheory forms the intellectual matrix in which a particular concrete pedagogical practice is theoretically grounded. An approach is a way of looking at, entering into, and interpreting a concrete reality; it is not that concrete reality itself.

A fundamental and pervading thesis of the trilogy is that religious instruction is a mode of social science rather than a branch of theology. This thesis is not an a priori formulation. On the contrary, this thesis is the result of a careful examination of the crucial issue of which macrotheory is more appropriate and more helpful to the concrete religious instruction act.

Whereas theological macrotheory is utterly incapable of explaining why a religious instruction practice works or fails as a teaching act, social-science macrotheory possesses this explanatory power. Whereas theological macrotheory is utterly incapable of predicting which religious instruction practice will work in a future set of pedagogical circumstances, social-science macrotheory possesses this predictive power. Whereas theological macrotheory is utterly incapable of verifying whether a religious instruction practice works, social-science macrotheory possesses this verificational power. *Here, then, is the cardinal question, a question typically skirted or brushed under the rug by the advocates of the theological macrotheory: Which macrotheory adequately explains, predicts, and verifies religious instruction practice? All theorizing, all speculation, and all enactment of the religious instruction act necessarily begins with this question.*

It is no more imperialistic to assert that religious instruction is a mode of social science than it is to assert that chemistry is a form of physical science. Imperialism means the invasion and control of a reality not properly belonging to the imperialist. Legitimacy, on the other hand, means the possession and control of a reality properly belonging to the legitimate person or group. For example, it would be imperialistic for England to control native Germans in Bavaria for a long period of time, but it is legitimate for Bavarians to control the native Germans in Bavaria for a long period of time. A macrotheory is imperialistic when it inadequately explains, predicts, and verifies the phenomena with which it deals. Such inadequacy is prima facie evidence that the macrotheory is imperialistic, that is to say, has invaded a territory where it does not properly belong. Conversely, a macrotheory is legitimate when it adequately explains, predicts, and verifies the phenomena with which it deals. Such adequacy is prima facie evidence that the macrotheory is legitimate, that is to say, controls a territory where it properly belongs. The phenomena of the religious instruction act are adequately explained, predicted, and verified by social-science macrotheory. Hence this macrotheory is legitimate and not imperialistic.

The illegitimate imperialistic invasion of theological macrotheory into the domain of religious instruction has had at least two major deleterious results.

The first unfortunate result of theological imperialism is tied up with the wholesale bootlegging of social-science practices into the religious instruction act. Because theological macrotheory is utterly incapable of generating let alone dealing satisfactorily with religious instruction phenomena, pedagogical practices generated and interpreted by social-science macrotheory have to be bootlegged into the religious instruction act by persons who do not know the macrotheoretical ecology of these practices and hence are unable to explain, predict, or verify these practices. Hence these bootlegged pedagogical practices typically fail to achieve much of their potential effectiveness because they are cut off from their natural life-sustaining ecology, namely, social-science macrotheory.

The second deleterious result of theological imperialism has been the plethora of bizarre theological excuses manufactured to cover up the inability of theological macrotheory to adequately explain, predict, and verify the workings of the religious instruction act. These theological excuses are usually framed in pious, high-sounding rhetoric in order to hide the stark impotency of the theological macrotheory of religious instruction. The result is theobabble. For example, advocates of the theological macrotheory of religious instruction ethereally claim that teaching effectiveness is explained on the ground that "God is the teacher"; ineffectiveness is explained by God's free withholding of grace at that time. This so-called explanation ignores the issue— human beings do the religion teaching and therefore the role and interactive functioning of the human teacher must be explained.[18] Is the teacher a puppet, a mechanical intermediary? What does the religion teacher do when teaching? How do the variables in the here-and-now religious instruction dynamic interact with one another? These are only a few of the key questions which can be successfully resolved only by a macrotheory adequate for religious instruction. Theobabble will not resolve these key questions. Religious educationists and educators are in a real sense blasphemous when they employ important constructs like faith or biblical statements such as "the Spirit blows where he wills" as cover-ups for ignorance or as shields against the facts.

It is incorrect to assert that religious instruction possesses phenomena and operations so uniquely proper to itself that it therefore possesses its own distinctive macrotheory, a macrotheory neither theological nor social-scientific but instead religious instructional. The validity of such an assertion crumbles at even the most preliminary of analyses. If the assertion were valid, then why is it that social-scientific macrotheory can adequately explain, predict, and verify religious instruction phenomena and operations? No one has ever come forward, nor do I believe it is possible for anyone to come forward in the future, with even the smallest bit of evidence to support the proposition that the operational axis of the religious instruction act properly belongs to a category lying outside the generally agreed-upon molar sciences such as mathematics, philosophy, natural science, social science, theology, and the like. Let us take Thomas Groome as an example of the point I am making. In 1981 Groome grandly proclaimed that it was imperialistic to assert that religious instruction is a mode of theology, of social science, or of any other molar category of science.[19] In a book published the previous year, Groome flatly stated that religious teaching is essentially a political activity. He immediately followed this statement by defining political activity as "any deliberate and structured intervention in people's lives which attempts to influence how they live their lives in society."[20] I should emphasize that political activity is not autonomous with respect to an already-existing form of wider scientific category. To be sure, political activity is classified by virtually all specialists in that area of human endeavor as one type of social science. One would be hard pressed to find a political scientist who would assert that political activity falls outside the broader realm of social science or who would assert that political activity can be satisfactorily explained by a macrotheory other than social-scientific macrotheory. Indeed, Groome's definition of political activity as deliberate and structured intervention is precisely how educators, sociologists, and psychologists—social scientists all—describe the essential axis of their activity.

The fact that religious instruction is a mode of social science does not mean that theology is irrelevant or unimportant in the act of teaching religion. As I suggested earlier in this Epilogue, theology has two important roles to play in augmenting the effectiveness of religious instruction. First, theology has an internal role to play because theological subject matter often (though not always) comprises a constitutive element in the pre-mediated substantive content of religious instruction.[21] Second, theology has an external role to play because a theology *of* religious instruction[22] provides important and helpful information from a domain outside religious instruction on how religion teaching can be improved. A theology of religious instruction is necessarily targeted primarily to theology. However, theological science can hand over the fruits of its reflection to religious instruction so that, armed with this external information, religious instruction can if it chooses expand its horizons, deepen its perspectives, and correct those emphases which need correcting.[23]

Because theological imperialism has been rampant in religious instruction for so many centuries, religious educators tend to attribute to theology an absoluteness, a scope, and a foundation which it does not possess.

Theology is not absolute; it is quite tentative. All theories by their very nature are tentative, and theology is theoretical in nature. There have been and still are today a welter of different theologies, many of which contradict or deny one another. Even the "official" ecclesiastical theology of specific denominations has undergone change, often of a radical variety. For example, the theology of Thomas Aquinas was at first "officially" condemned by the Roman Catholic *ecclesiasticum,* only to be later resurrected as its "official" theology. Many of the Modernist theological tenets roundly condemned by Roman Catholic "official" ecclesiastical theology in the late nineteenth century became accepted staples of post-Vatican II "official" ecclesiastical Roman Catholic theology.

The scope of theology is limited to theological reflection on other nontheological realities. This means that theology is not a pastoral activity (such as religious instruction) but only an external cognitive reflection on pastoral activity. Paul Tillich puts the matter succinctly when he states: "Theology is neither preaching nor counseling; therefore the success of a theology when it is applied to preaching or to the care of souls is not necessarily a criterion of its truth."[24] In somewhat the same vein Edward Farley asserts that it is a grave mistake to identify theology with the transforming power of redemption, with ecclesial reality, with pastoral action, or the like.[25] In Farley's view, theology is always a process of cognitive appraisal and assessment, a process which seeks to understand pastoral activity or any other reality not from that reality's own perspective but from a theological vantage point.[26] It should be underscored that religious instruction itself, not theology, is prior and primary for religious instruction activity. Gustavo Gutiérrez, the liberation theologian, summarizes beautifully the point I am making in this paragraph: "Theology is reflection, a critical attitude. Theology *follows*: it is the second step. What Hegel used to say about philosophy can likewise be applied to theology: it rises only at sundown. Theology does not produce pastoral activity; rather it reflects upon it."[27]

The foundation of Christian theology is not God's unmediated word in the bible (special revelation), or God's unmediated outpouring in the activities of the world (general revelation). God's revelation in the bible and in creation is always and everywhere mediated by human beings; existentially it cannot be otherwise. One form of this mediation is theological science. Thus a theologian's personal experiences color and in some cases profoundly alter his theological reflection, a fact which would hardly be possible if theology were the unmediated understanding of God's revelation.[28] Let us look at the mediational character of theology from another perspective. A touchstone of, and a pervasive influence in theological mediation of God's revelation in the bible and in creation is philosophical science. Christian theological reflection more often than not is grounded in philosophical processes—and in Hellenistic philosophical processes at that. The form and structure of Christian theological reflection would be markedly different if it were grounded in Far Eastern philosophical processes. Additionally, theological reflection would be even more different and possibly more believable than it is today if it were consciously and overtly grounded in a mixture of philosophical processes, natural-scientific processes, and social-scientific processes.[29]

Social-scientific processes have, in fact, been situated more deeply in the very foundation of theological science than some advocates of the theological macrotheory of religious instruction might realize. For example, Benedict Groeschel observes that the theological interpretation of the classical stages of religious living is essentially grounded not in theology but in social science.[30] Indeed, quite a few social-science facts/laws/theories lie at the very foundation of theological science and not always on the other side of theology's border. Once theologians overtly and consciously realize this basic point, then the quality and even the method of theological investigation will be greatly enriched. Once religious educationists and educators become overtly and consciously aware of this basic point, they will possibly lose some of their unease and fear of social science. Theology has no legitimate right to be positivistic about social science.[31] Theological reflection and religious instruction both suffer when theology is made an idol[32]—and, conversely, when social science is made an idol.[33]

Once upon a time all reality was explained almost exclusively by theology. Then came the modern era and educated people discovered that reality can be explained by a host of other macrotheories such as those offered by social science, natural science, and the like.[34] Instead of eagerly embracing these new explanations of reality as valuable new avenues of discovering God's unbounded richness in creation, theologians and ecclesiastical officials imperiously tried to retain theology as the sole basic explanation of reality and the judge of all the other sciences—in short, theology as queen of the sciences. One of the many unfortunate results of this closed-minded theological imperialism was the unnatural split which developed between theology and the other sciences. Theology never really incorporated the other sciences or even accommodated to them at the foundational level. Theology was simply content to use selective nontheological findings as external crutches to buttress this or that theological notion, or at worst to cut itself off as completely as possible from what it castigated as Godless and antireligious science. Theology has yet to recover from this terrible mistake, a mistake it continues to make even in our own day.

If religion is to attain a leading place in the contemporary world, it will have to broaden its almost exclusive reliance on theology and come to realize that religious phenomena are best explained/predicted/verified by a conglomerate of sciences, including natural science and social science. In our day and age, natural science reigns supreme. The intellectual, theoretical, and practical leadership of our era lies in natural science. Religion will have to incorporate the insights and explanations of natural science into its foundational fabric if it is to grow in strength, in relevance, and above all in truth. Social science, for its part, is becoming more powerful with each passing decade. As the world becomes increasingly more oriented to personal fulfillment and to the building of a genuinely human community here on earth, social science will gradually replace natural science as the dominant force in the world. If religion is to be vital, it must broaden itself to include at its deepest foundation not only theology, but the other sciences as well. If it fails to accomplish this crucial task, it will end up as a fossil, an inert remnant of a bygone era.

Social science ought to be incorporated into the foundational fabric of religion on its own terms and not simply as a tool or as an apologetic for theology. Social science can help religion ripen when social science is used on its own terms with its own procedures. Conversely, social science can be of little assistance to religion when it is simply regarded as a "handmaid of theology," to employ the classic expression of theological imperialism.

Various activities differ with respect to the degree to which their basic foundation is theological, social scientific, literary, or the like. The thesis of this trilogy is that activities of religious education have social-scientific macrotheory as their primary and overarching foundation. All forms of intentional religious education—guidance and counseling, administration, and in our case religious instruction—are more fruitfully explained/predicted/verified by social science rather than by theology, literature, or any other kind of science.

Placing the social-science macrotheory at the foundation of religious instruction endeavor does not lessen God's influence in the religion teaching act. Rather, the social-science macrotheory endeavors to genuinely discern how God's influence actually does operate in the day-to-day activities of the world through which he remains creatively present. Religion teachers can make their lessons more open to God's influence when they recognize the pedagogical lines along which this influence travels. Knowledge of how a given reality operates is superior to unreal fantasies about how that reality is presumed to operate.

The mission of every Christian religious educator is clearly stated in the command which Jesus himself gave just before ascending into heaven, namely that of teaching religion to every person (Mt. 28:19). Religious educators are truly faithful to Jesus' command only to the extent to which their pedagogical practice is rooted in that kind of comprehensive and systematic macrotheory which can satisfactorily explain and predict and verify the religious instruction act.[35]

NOTES

1. Anonymous Elizabethean poet, *Beware Fair Maid.*
2. For a short treatment of operationalizing, see James Michael Lee, *The Shape of Religious Instruction* (Birmingham, Ala.: Religious Education Press, 1971), pp. 65–74.
3. Gabriel Moran seems to be one of the very few politically grounded contemporary religious educationists who understands this point. Moran clearly indicates that while he has some interest in the topic of the religious instruction act, his principal and overriding attention is directed toward the political implications of the religious instruction act as this act is embedded in specific institutional forms and in the overall political process. Political meaning, not religious instruction meaning *in se,* constitutes the thrust of the later Moran's writings. Those critics who take Moran to task for not offering general religious instruction explanations or for failing to proffer specific religious instruction suggestions are severely off the mark since Moran's work is not directed toward the religious instruction act in and of itself. Because the later Moran's speculative concerns flow from political analysis rather than from religious instructional analysis, he is at his weakest when he occasionally strays from his home turf and attempts to offer religious instruction meanings for the religious instruction act. This weakness, glaring at times, has been noted by some critics, myself included. See Gabriel Moran, "From Obstacle to Modest Contributor: Theology in Religious Education," in Norma H. Thompson, editor, *Religious Education and Theology* (Birmingham, Ala.: Religious Education Press, 1982), pp. 57–58.
4. On this seminal point, see James Michael Lee, "The Authentic Source of Religious Instruction," in Norma H. Thompson, editor, *Religious Education and Theology,* pp. 144–146, 165–172.
5. Mary C. Boys, "Teaching: The Heart of Religious Education," in *Religious Education* LXXIX (Spring, 1984), pp. 252–272. Much of the research reported in this generally fine Boys' article was actually done by Ann Louise Gilligan. Of interest to religious educators is that Boys lists herself at the end of this illuminating article as an associate professor of scripture. It is a sad but telling comment on the wanton neglect of the theory and practice of the pedagogical act on the part of the religious instruction community that one of the very few twentieth-century scholars genuinely interested in the anatomy of the religious instruction act holds faculty rank in scripture. One would expect that religious educationists whose faculty appointment is in religious education or in educational studies would be in the forefront with respect to scholarly investigation of the theory and practice of the religious instruction act.
6. Reuel Howe, *The Miracle of Dialogue* (Greenwich, Conn.: Seabury, 1953).
7. I write "paradoxical uncriticalness" because the critical use of rationality to dialectically unmask the surface of a reality so as to penetrate its essence is the axis of Groome's method of shared praxis.

8. Thomas H. Groome, *Christian Religious Education* (San Francisco: Harper & Row, 1980), especially pp. 207–232.

9. The scientific invalidity of the field data reported by Groome flows from, among other things, the ruinously confounding variable known in the social-scientific literature as experimenter bias, experimenter expectancy, and terms of this sort. See Fred N. Kerlinger, *Foundations of Behavioral Research*, 2d edition (New York: Holt, Rinehart and Winston, 1973), pp. 314–347; Robert Rosenthal, *Experimenter Effects in Behavioral Research*, 2d edition (New York: Irvington, 1980).

10. By scientific here is meant that kind of scholarly activity which collects systematic observations, builds laws, and develops theories. Scientific activity thus is far wider than the zone of the natural sciences. To be sure, theology is a science. There are other sciences as well, such as social science, mathematical science, and so forth.

11. Richard McBrien, a theologian, puts the matter succinctly when he writes: "Let it be said candidly and openly: religious education has a less than elevated reputation within the academic community at large and within the theological community in particular. . . . And until religious educators confront more sharply their own fundamental methodological questions, this reputation will stalk them as tenaciously as a shark in the wake of a slow-moving trawler." Richard P. McBrien, *Living Light* XIII (Summer, 1976), p. 170. McBrien is in a position to empathize with the plight of religious instruction's low level of scholarship. Until the mid-1960s, the theology department in most American church-related colleges and universities was regarded by the professors in other parts of these institutions as among the very weakest in terms of scholarship. Indeed, scholars in secular universities today more often than not have a low opinion of theological scholarship and indeed of the scholarly legitimacy of theology itself.

12. Macrotheory is different from metatheory. Metatheory is the theory of theory, a critical theoretical examination of the nature and structure of theory itself.

13. Explanation, prediction, and verification are the three essential functions performed by theory. On this point see James Michael Lee, "The Authentic Source of Religious Instruction," pp. 117–121.

14. Advocates of the theological macrotheory of religious instruction almost inevitably end up enmeshing this macrotheory in some particularity. Thus, for example, Françoise Darcy-Bérubé sharply takes me to task for not specifically and unequivocally advocating one or another theological position. What Darcy-Bérubé fails to understand is that social science has neither the competence nor the inclination to advocate one or another theological position as the best theological position. All social science can do with regard to a theological position is to point to the social-scientific dimensions or consequences of varying theological stances. Furthermore, Darcy-Bérubé does not seem to be able to grasp the basic point that by intrinsic necessity a social-scientific macrotheory cannot be equated with any one particularity, be that particularity a social-scientific particularity or a theological particularity. Françoise Darcy-Bérubé, "The Challenge Ahead of Us," in Padraic O'Hare, editor, *Foundations of Religious Education* (New York: Paulist, 1978), p. 118.

15. Again Françoise Darcy-Bérubé marvelously illustrates the truth of this point. Darcy-Bérubé's attempted identification of macrotheory with denominational particularity—an identification to which the theological macrotheory of religious instruction seems to be almost ineluctably drawn—destroys the applicability (comprehensiveness) of the theological macrotheory to those religious instruction

acts deployed by persons of different denominational affiliations, and thus destroys macrotheory in the process. Such a particularistic tendency frequently results in intolerant views. For example, Darcy-Bérubé, a person whose theological macrotheory of religious instruction is highly particularistic, denounces the religious pedagogy used by Billy Graham in his crusades as "opposed to the Christian view of man" (p. 118). She also insists that religion as lifestyle can be authentically Christian only when it is in conformity with the theological view of the "correct" religious lifestyle (presumably the one to which she herself subscribes). In this vein she explicitly states that the Jehovah's Witnesses fail to meet her particularistic theological criteria with respect to the "correct" religious lifestyle and therefore have defective religious instruction practices (p. 119). *Ibid.*

16. While the social-science macrotheory of religious instruction does not of itself take sides with respect to one or another particular social-scientific theory of teaching or of religion, nonetheless this macrotheory possesses the capacity to properly assess the adequacy and fruitfulness of these theories for the religious instruction act. See Robert A. Segal, "Assessing Social-Scientific Theories of Religion," in *Bulletin of the Council on the Study of Religion* XIII (June, 1982), pp. 69–72.

17. Thus, for example, the social-science approach is value-free while every concrete religious instruction act is necessarily value-laden. Unfortunately, certain people in the field of religious instruction do not seem to understand this elemental point.

18. Theobabble of the sort I am mentioning here tends to be rejected by almost all theologians except those adhering to Occasionalism in one form or another.

19. Groome made this oral assertion at the 1981 annual meeting of the Association of Professors and Researchers in Religious Education. With less force and with more subjective nuancing, Gabriel Moran adopted the same stance in Gabriel Moran, "From Obstacle to Modest Contributor: Theology in Religious Education," p. 58.

20. Thomas H. Groome, *Christian Religious Education*, p. 15.

21. For a discussion of the religious instruction act as an operational and an ontic mediation of structural content and substantive content, see James Michael Lee, *The Flow of Religious Instruction*, pp. 17–19, 21–22, 29–31, 300–301; James Michael Lee, "The Authentic Source of Religious Instruction," pp. 165–174.

22. As I pointed out earlier, there is a tremendous difference between equating theology with religious instruction and asserting that there is a theology of religious instruction.

23. Philosophy of education performs a similar external role with respect to religious instruction. But a philosophy of religious instruction can no more be equated with religious instruction itself than can a theology of religious instruction be equated with religious instruction itself. Many religious educationists tend to ignore this important point. Jim Wilhoit is one example. Wilhoit fails to understand that metaphysical issues bearing upon religious instruction endeavor are not directly religious instruction issues but rather issues which, though impinging upon religious instruction activity, nonetheless remain outside it. Not until such issues are translated into religious instruction modes can they be rendered teachable and learnable, that is to say, religious instruction-able. Once these external metaphysical issues are translated into teachable/learnable realities, they are *eis ipsis* empirical and so can be empirically tested. Wilhoit's failure to realize this basic distinction between religious instruction, on the one hand, and the philosophy/theology of religious instruction, on the other hand, leads him into all sorts of

follow-up errors. One such error is his assertion that the religious educator's own personal worldview forms the necessary theoretical matrix for devising optimum pedagogical practice. In making this assertion, Wilhoit sinks inextricably into a hopeless relativism and ultimately destroys the possibility of a macrotheory which is legitimately generalizable to all religion teachers in all conditions and in all settings. Unsupported slogans such as the one declaring that my social-science approach provides social science but not religion reinforce my contention that it is difficult for Christian religious educators to embrace comprehensive theory and eschew particularism. In my view, Wilhoit's basic errors do not as a whole vitiate the laudability of his attempt to interface social-science theory with religious instruction. See Jim Wilhoit, "The Impact of the Social Sciences on Religious Education," in *Religious Education* LXXIX (Summer, 1984), pp. 367–375.

24. Paul Tillich, *Systematic Theology,* volume 1 (Chicago: University of Chicago Press, 1951), p. 4.
25. Edward Farley, *Theologia* (Philadelphia: Fortress, 1983), pp. 185–195.
26. Edward Farley, *Theological Reflection: An Anatomy of Theological Method* (Philadelphia: Fortress, 1982), pp. xv–xvi.
27. Gustavo Gutiérrez, *A Theology of Liberation,* translated by Caridad Inda and John Eagleson (Maryknoll, N.Y.: Orbis, 1973), p. 11.
28. Reinhold Niebuhr, for example, stated that his pastorate of thirteen years in urban Detroit gave him empirical data which determined the course of his theologizing more than any books he read. See Heinrich-Constantin Rohrbach, *Theologians of Our Time* (Notre Dame, Ind.: University of Notre Dame Press, 1964), p. 79.
29. On this point, see Charles R. Meyer, *Religious Belief in a Scientific Age* (Chicago: Thomas More Press, 1983).
30. Groeschel goes on to state that though the social-scientific foundation of the classic theological stages of religious living was soon accommodated to the Christian experience by Augustine, Gregory of Nyssa, and other Fathers and Doctors of the church, nonetheless the foundation remained substantially a social-scientific one. Benedict J. Groeschel, *Spiritual Passages* (New York: Crossroad, 1983), p. 194.
31. For a brief description of theological positivism, see James Michael Lee, "The Authentic Source of Religious Instruction," pp. 146–147.
32. In his treatment of idolatry in theology and in social science, David Bakan uses Paul Tillich's notion of idolotry, namely substituting an immediate concern for an ultimate concern. Idolatry is generalized by Bakan to mean the worship of the means toward the fulfillment of the impulse as the actual fulfillment of the impulse itself. David Bakan, *The Duality of Human Existence: An Essay on Psychology and Religion* (Chicago: Rand McNally, 1966), pp. 5–9.
33. Though the possibility of social science becoming an idol for religious instruction is extremely remote, nonetheless a certain strain in psychology, sociology, anthropology, political science, and other social sciences has unfortunately idolized social science.
34. It would be grossly inaccurate to construe this statement as an expression of Comtean positivism. Auguste Comte holds that in the final stage in the development of human thought, theology is completely jettisoned as a superstitious and hence unscientific way of explaining/predicting/verifying human phenomena. My statement, on the contrary, still maintains the legitimacy and usefulness of theology as a macrotheory, as appropriate. However, my statement also encapsulates

my contention that theology must share primacy of macrotheoretical place in explaining/predicting/verifying human endeavor, including religious activity.

35. There is no teaching without corresponding learning. Hence Jesus' command implies the effective facilitation of learning. Since Jesus always encouraged his followers to do things as well as possible (Mt. 5:48), it follows that his religious educators should be as pedagogically effective as possible.

INDEX OF NAMES

INDEX OF SUBJECTS